THE ARTHUR OF THE IBERIANS

ARTHURIAN LITERATURE IN THE MIDDLE AGES

VIII

THE ARTHUR OF THE IBERIANS

THE ARTHURIAN LEGEND IN THE SPANISH
AND PORTUGUESE WORLDS

edited by

David Hook

UNIVERSITY OF WALES PRESS
2015

© The Vinaver Trust, 2015

All rights reserved. No part of this book may be reproduced in any material form (including photocopying or storing it in any medium by electronic means and whether or not transiently or incidentally to some other use of this publication) without the written permission of the copyright owner except in accordance with the provisions of the Copyright, Designs and Patents Act 1988. Applications for the copyright owner's written permission to reproduce any part of this publication should be addressed to The University of Wales Press, 10 Columbus Walk, Brigantine Place, Cardiff, CF10 4UP.

www.uwp.co.uk

British Library Cataloguing-in-Publication Data.
A catalogue record for this book is available from the British Library.

ISBN 978-1-78316-241-3
e-ISBN 978-1-78316-242-0

The right of the Contributors to be identified separately as authors of this work has been asserted by them in accordance with sections 77, 78 and 79 of the Copyright, Designs and Patents Act 1988.

Typeset by Mark Heslington Ltd, Scarborough, North Yorkshire
Printed by CPI Antony Rowe, Chippenham, Wiltshire

PUBLISHED IN COOPERATION WITH

THE VINAVER TRUST

The Vinaver Trust was established by the British Branch of the International Arthurian Society to commemorate a greatly respected colleague and a distinguished scholar

Eugène Vinaver

the editor of Malory's Morte Darthur. *The Trust aims to advance study of Arthurian literature in all languages by planning and encouraging research projects in the field, and by aiding publication of the resultant studies.*

ARTHURIAN LITERATURE IN THE MIDDLE AGES

Series Editor

Ad Putter

I   *The Arthur of the Welsh*, Edited by Rachel Bromwich, A. O. H. Jarman and Brynley F. Roberts (University of Wales Press, 1991)

II   *The Arthur of the English*, Edited by W. R. J. Barron (University of Wales Press, 1999)

III *The Arthur of the Germans*, Edited by W. H. Jackson and S. A. Ranawake (University of Wales Press, 2000)

IV   *The Arthur of the French*, Edited by Glyn S. Burgess and Karen Pratt (University of Wales Press, 2006)

V   *The Arthur of the North*, Edited by Marianne E. Kalinke (University of Wales Press, 2011)

VI   *The Arthur of Medieval Latin Literature*, Edited by Siân Echard (University of Wales Press, 2011)

VII *The Arthur of the Italians*, Edited by Gloria Allaire and F. Regina Psaki (University of Wales Press, 2014)

VIII *The Arthur of the Iberians*, edited by David Hook (University of Wales Press, 2015)

CONTENTS

	Preface *Ad Putter*	ix
	List of Contributors	xi
	List of Abbreviations	xiii
	Introduction	1
I	Arthurian Material in Iberia *Paloma Gracia*	11
II	The Surviving Peninsular Arthurian Witnesses: A Description and an Analysis *José Manuel Lucía Megías*	33
III	Arthurian Literature in Portugal *Santiago Gutiérrez García*	58
IV	The *Matière de Bretagne* in Galicia from the XIIth to the XVth Century *Pilar Lorenzo Gradín*	118
V	The *Matière de Bretagne* in the Corona de Aragón *Lourdes Soriano Robles*	162
VI	The Matter of Britain in Spanish Society and Literature from Cluny to Cervantes *Carlos Alvar*	187
VII	The *Post-Vulgate* Cycle in the Iberian Peninsula *Paloma Gracia*	271
VIII	The Hispanic Versions of the *Lancelot en prose*: *Lanzarote del Lago* and *Lançalot* *Antonio Contreras*	289
IX	The Iberian *Tristan* Texts of the Middle Ages and Renaissance *María Luzdivina Cuesta Torre*	309

X	*Amadís de Gaula* Rafael Ramos	364
XI	Arthur Goes Global: Arthurian Material in Hispanic and Portuguese America and Asia David Hook	382
XII	The Contemporary Return of the Matter of Britain to Iberian Letters (XIXth to XXIst Centuries) Juan Miguel Zarandona	408
	Bibliography	446
	Index of Manuscripts	511
	Index	513

PREFACE

This book forms part of the ongoing series Arthurian Literature in the Middle Ages. The purpose of the series is to provide a comprehensive and reliable survey of Arthurian writings in all their cultural and generic variety. For many years, the single-volume *Arthur in the Middle Ages: A Collaborative History* (ed. R. S. Loomis, Oxford, 1959) served the needs of students and scholars of Arthurian literature admirably, but it has now been overtaken by advances in scholarship and by changes in critical perspectives and methodologies. The Vinaver Trust recognized the need for a fresh and up-to-date survey, and decided that several volumes were required to do justice to the distinctive contributions made to Arthurian literature by the various cultures of medieval Europe.

The series is mainly aimed at undergraduate and postgraduate students and at scholars working in the fields covered by each of the volumes. The series has, however, also been designed to be accessible to general readers and to students and scholars from different fields who want to learn what forms Arthurian narratives took in languages and literatures that they may not know, and how those narratives influenced the cultures that they do know. Within these parameters the editors have had control over the shape and content of their individual volumes.

Ad Putter, University of Bristol
(General Editor)

THE CONTRIBUTORS

Carlos Alvar (Université de Genève)

Antonio Contreras (Institut d'Estudis Medievals, Universidad Autónoma de Barcelona)

María Luzdivina Cuesta Torre (Departamento de Filología Hispánica y Clásica, and Instituto de Estudios Medievales, Universidad de León)

Paloma Gracia (Universidad de Granada)

Santiago Gutiérrez García (Universidade de Santiago de Compostela)

David Hook (University of Oxford)

Pilar Lorenzo Gradín (Universidade de Santiago de Compostela)

José Manuel Lucía Megías (Universidad Complutense de Madrid)

Rafael Ramos (Universitat de Girona)

Lourdes Soriano Robles (Institut de Recerca en Cultures Medievals, Universitat de Barcelona)

Juan Miguel Zarandona (Universidad de Valladolid)

ABBREVIATIONS

ABA	*Anais das Bibliotecas e Arquivos*
ACCP	*Arquivos do Centro Cultural Português*
ADMYTE	Archivo Digital de Manuscritos y Textos Españoles
AEM	*Anuario de Estudios Medievales*
AES	Asociación Española de Semiótica
AHLM	Asociación Hispánica de Literatura Medieval
AHN	Archivo Histórico Nacional, Madrid
ALMA	*Arthurian Literature in the Middle Ages*
ANTT	Arquivo Nacional da Torre do Tombo
AR	*Archivum Romanicum*
ASEAN	Association of South-East Asian Nations
BBC	*Butlletí de la Biblioteca de Catalunya*
BBIAS	*Bibliographical Bulletin of the International Arthurian Society*
BETA	Bibliografía española de textos antiguos
BF	*Boletim de Filologia* (Lisbon unless stated to be Rio de Janeiro)
BGL	*Boletín Galego de Literatura*
BHi	*Bulletin Hispanique*
BHS	*Bulletin of Hispanic Studies*
BITAGAP	Bibliografía de textos antigos galegos e portugueses
BITECA	Bibliografia de textos antics catalans, valencians i balears
BNE	Biblioteca Nacional de España, Madrid
BNF	Bibliothèque Nationale de France, Paris
BNM	see BNE
BOOCT	Bibliography of Old Catalan Texts
BOOST	Bibliography of Old Spanish Texts
BRABLB	*Boletín de la Real Academia de Buenas Letras de Barcelona (Butlletí de la Reial Acadèmia de Bones Lletres de Barcelona)*
BRAE	*Boletín de la Real Academia Española*
BSCC	*Boletín de la Sociedad Castellonense de Cultura*
CCM	*Cahiers de Civilisation Médiévale*
CEC	Centro de Estudios Cervantinos
CEHM	*Cahiers d'Études Hispaniques Médiévales*
CLHM	*Cahiers de Linguistique Hispanique Médiévale*
CuN	*Cultura Neolatina*

CSIC	Consejo Superior de Investigaciones Científicas
EL	*Estudos Linguísticos*
FCE	Fondo de Cultura Económica
HR	*Hispanic Review*
HRJ	*Hispanic Research Journal*
JHP	*Journal of Hispanic Philology*
JHR	*Journal of Hispanic Research*
KRQ	*Kentucky Romance Quarterly*
LC	*La corónica*
LPGP	Brea López, Mercedes (ed.), 1996. *Lírica profana galego-portuguesa*
MPh	*Modern Philology*
MR	*Marche Romane*
NBAE	Nueva Biblioteca de Autores Españoles
NLW	National Library of Wales/Llyfrgell Genedlaethol Cymru, Aberystwyth
NRFH	*Nueva revista de filología hispánica*
ÖNB	Österreichisches Nationalbibliothek, Vienna
PMHRS	Papers of the Medieval Hispanic Research Seminar
PMLA	*Publications of the Modern Language Association of America*
PPU	Promociones y Publicaciones Universitarias
PUF	Presses Universitaires de France
RAE	Real Academia Española
RBC	Research Bibliographies & Checklists
RFE	*Revista de Filología Española*
RFLLL	*Revista da Faculdade de Letras, Línguas e Literaturas*
RFR	*Revista de Filología Románica*
RGF	*Revista Galega de Filoloxía*
RH	*Revue Hispanique*
RL	*Revista Lusitana*
RLC	*Revue de Littérature Comparée*
RLM	*Revista de Literatura Medieval*
RLP	*Revista de Língua Portuguesa*
Ro	*Romania*
RPh	*Romance Philology*
RPM	*Revista de Poética Medieval*
RR	*Romanic Review*
SATF	Société des Anciens Textes Français
SBPS	*Santa Barbara Portuguese Studies*
SEMYR	Sociedad de Estudios Medievales y Renacentistas
SMV	*Studi Mediolatini e Volgari*
UAM	Universidad Autónoma Metropolitana, Mexico City
UNAM	Universidad Autónoma, Madrid

UNCSRLL	University of North Carolina Studies in Romance Languages and Literature
UNED	Universidad Nacional de Educación a Distancia
UWP	University of Wales Press
VR	*Vox Romanica*
ZFSL	*Zeitschrift für Französische Sprache und Literatur*
ZrP	*Zeitschrift für romanische Philologie*

INTRODUCTION

David Hook

To edit a large-scale collaborative survey of the current state of knowledge of the presence of the Arthurian legends in Iberia is to be reminded forcefully not only of the problems associated with the definition of those terms, but also of the provisional nature of much of that knowledge, and of the rapidity of its continuing development in several important respects. To deal with these matters in turn: firstly, by 'Iberian' is meant simply the languages and cultures of the Iberian Peninsula in which manifestations of Arthurian themes are known, that is to say, the medieval Romance languages and dialects of Iberia and the polities and territories associated with them, their later overseas territorial acquisitions around the Atlantic, the Indian Ocean and the Pacific, and post-medieval Arthuriana in Iberoromance languages and in modern Basque. The question of what constitutes 'Arthuriana' is, of course, open to varied interpretations, as readers of previous volumes in this series will be aware; in the Iberian context this team of scholars has taken it to embrace not only works of creative literature (whether translated and rewritten from foreign sources, or wholly original) but also those of historiography and genealogy where material appears in them that involves elements drawn from the corpus of legends closely or loosely associated with King Arthur and the human characters and other beings, or the locations and events, related to the world of Camelot, Tintagel, Logres, the Round Table, and the quest for the Grail. Our survey has deliberately included coverage of texts with only passing reference to or merely possible reminiscences of material from the Arthurian legends, and texts generally inspired by the latter, as well as texts primarily focused on that material, on the grounds that such allusive familiarity and such imitation and adaptation are important indicators of the extent and depth of its penetration into and impact on the Iberian world, and furnish evidence of its evolution and mutation over space and time. Similar reasoning underlies the inclusion here of the incidence of Arthurian personal names, which appear in Iberia in the first half of the XIIth century as an exotic import, and gradually become part of the general Iberian anthroponymic stock, finally spreading across the world. It is obvious that the inspiration here, as for other Iberian Arthuriana, comes from outside the physical boundaries of the Peninsula. Where identifiable and possible Arthurian themes appear in art within the boundaries of our area, these are also recorded as part of the panorama of evidence; and it is of interest to note that one of these involves an apparent, though not certain, penetration of the Muslim cultural world by Arthurian material found in painted decoration in the Alhambra at Granada.

Within this general brief, authors have had autonomy in deciding the precise content and approach of their individual chapters.

Speculation whether this broad definition of the subject results primarily from the relatively small number of Arthurian literary texts in Iberian languages should be resisted; there is growing evidence that there were more texts, and more copies of those texts, in circulation in medieval Iberia than has been traditionally thought to be the case. This leads to my second point, the evolving knowledge of Peninsular Arthuriana. First and foremost, the textual basis itself of Arthurian studies in Iberia has developed (and is continuing to develop) in important ways since the best-known, and at the time authoritative, general surveys were published (e.g., Entwistle 1925; Lida de Malkiel 1959). These developments are a result of significant discoveries in libraries and archives, so that the appearance of previously unknown material in the form of binding fragments and reused manuscript leaves on the one hand, and the reappearance of material temporarily mislaid in the past on the other, perhaps goes some way to compensating for the occasional obscurity surrounding some material seen and described by earlier scholars but not at present accessible or even known still to survive. Such cases are not confined to minor provincial archives; important discoveries have been made even in major and well-explored libraries, such as the further illuminated Tristán fragments found in the Biblioteca Nacional de España, Madrid, by two scholars on our team, Carlos Alvar and José Manuel Lucía Megías; or the other, independent, translation into Portuguese of the story of Joseph of Arimathea, found in the San Tirso fragment at Porto, which is causing a major reconsideration of the transmission of the story and of the relationships of the previously-known text. Whilst an important mislaid textual witness has been retrieved in the Archivo Histórico Nacional in Madrid, another remains at present untraced in an archive at Cervera, and the fate of some material formerly in private hands is currently obscure. Such issues are discussed at the appropriate points in this volume.

In addition, modifications to our understanding of Arthurian material in Iberia have of course arisen from the ordinary processes of scholarly reassessment of known and accessible texts. As an example, the *Estoria del noble Vespasiano* (printed in Spain and Portugal in the 1490s), formerly accepted as part of Peninsular Arthurian literature (grudgingly by a sceptical Entwistle, but unquestioningly in some Portuguese Arthurian scholarship until quite recently), is no longer regarded as having any significant active connection with this material in Iberia. Its at best marginal relevance to Peninsular Arthurian studies is that it preserves a variant text of the *Destruction de Jerusalem* or *Vengeance Nostre Seigneur* tradition that had obviously been pressed into service at some point to provide what would today be called a prequel for Joseph of Arimathea's wanderings, and had been expanded by an adaptation of Evalach's dream from the 'Long Version' of the *Estoire del Saint Graal* which was deployed to explain the Incarnation to the emperor Vespasian. However, the language in which and the date at which these modifications had been introduced is uncertain; this form of the text is known in Italian, Catalan, Castilian Spanish and Portuguese, but all these Peninsular texts may derive ultimately from a so far unidentified French version. At some point early in its transmission this modified version of the text was obviously intended for inclusion in a cyclical manuscript that was to incorporate the Grail story, and an allusion to the material that was to follow later in the narrative in that copy survives in Catalan witnesses to Version II of the text. This function had, however, been lost by the time this version was separately printed and copied independently in Castilian and Portuguese during the last decade of the XVth century (Hook 1986; 1992; 2000: 120–2), and the relevant sentence was modified as a result.

Moreover, the inclusion of the burgeoning modern Arthurian material in Iberian languages means the scope of the field of study is also greatly expanded chronologically and in terms of literary genres. The treatment of post-Renaissance Arthuriana has, of course, been part of some previous accounts, as Harvey Sharrer's study of its presence in XVIIIth-century Portuguese chapbooks notably reminds us (1978, 1984b); but in the general surveys it has not been covered on the scale and in the systematic manner in which it is examined in our final chapter, by Juan Zarandona, which includes a wide-ranging catalogue of the different literary works in various genres in which he has identified Arthurian elements. It is also the case that the geographical scope of the material covered in this volume is considerable, because of the historical process of the Iberian expansion overseas, which preceded that from most other European language areas. Arthurian material was, for instance, taken to Spanish America a century before the first English settlement reached North America; indeed, the first Spaniard bearing an Arthurian personal name (Tristán) sailed on the second voyage of Columbus in 1493.

Finally, the preparation of this volume has underlined the extent to which the discovery of Arthurian references in other texts is often a matter of serendipity. Alan Deyermond was not specifically looking for Arthurian material when he noted that the conception of Arthur was used to explain the doctrine of the Transubstantiation in a Castilian sermon (Deyermond 1984); likewise a reference in XVIth-century historiography and later texts to a Visigothic queen as a descendant of King Arthur, independently examined by me (Hook 2004) and by Lourdes Soriano (in the present volume), came to my attention while examining an XVIIIth-century antiquarian manuscript in the course of other studies. Similarly, my initial realisation that much remained to be discovered about early Arthurian names in the Peninsula arose as a result of reading documentary collections for a study on legal language in medieval Spanish epic texts. With both names, and isolated literary allusions, a valuable service to the progress of our knowledge would be made by recording all such discoveries whether or not one is working consciously on Arthurian material. It is a great pity that the current bureaucratization of scholarship and the application to it of crassly inappropriate evaluation criteria risk (alongside their other more significantly pernicious consequences) leading to the creeping elimination of that useful genre, the 'brief note' section of academic journals.

An inevitable concomitant of the scholarly assessment of the textual corpus (and the sheer volume and diversity of secondary writing on this material is such as to render the established accounts by Entwistle, María Rosa Lida de Malkiel and others outdated and incomplete in terms of coverage, and limited in terms of diversity of perspective) is a marked scholarly disagreement on many questions. The controversies exemplified in the present volume over the interpretation of a number of enigmatic Galician-Portuguese lyric references, or over the significance and implications of Arthurian personal names found in XIIth-century documents, are good examples of the ways in which scholarly debate has progressed; and, if a degree of consensus is sometimes reached on some matters previously contentious, other questions have taken their place as subjects for continuing argument, to which this volume contributes. The chapters by Carlos Alvar, Santiago Gutiérrez and Pilar Lorenzo Gradín show clearly the range of interpretations possible for some obscurely allusive passages, and the problems involved in reaching evidence-based conclusions on such material and in relating it to precise historical and political contexts where this is necessary for its elucidation. Similar is the problem of the interpretation of artistic production in non-textual forms such as sculpture, in which Arthurian themes may or may not be represented. A case in point is the column at Santiago de Compostela which has been variously interpreted as depicting Tristan or Ulysses (see the comments of Carlos Alvar, Santiago Gutiérrez, and Pilar Lorenzo Gradín here). Even in such apparently simple matters as the date of a medieval legal document, further consideration and fresh evidence may lead to its redating; thus a document from Sahagún mentioning an individual named Merlin, thought by its first editor, Staaff, to date from 1171 and cited as such by me in 1991, has since been redated by Fernández Flórez (1994) to the second half of the XIIIth century (Hook 1996: 142, no. 4), with far-reaching implications for the interpretation of the significance of the name. This is now to be considered much later than previously believed and is therefore almost certainly not the earliest occurrence of the name in Iberia.[1]

For the controversy over the interpretation of the significance of the use of personal names of Arthurian type in medieval and later Iberia, but particularly over those dating from the XIIth century, some modern parallels may assist us. According to a press report (*The Guardian*, 25 June 2013, Part 2, p. 3), 146 female babies born in the United States of America during the year 2012 received the forename 'Khaleesi', inspired by a title (rather than a name) signifying female royal status in a popular fantasy television romance, *Game of Thrones*, based on the fictions by George R. R. Martin. The newspaper reported that this represented an increase of 450 per cent since 2011; the names of other characters in the series have also been given to newborn children. A subsequent article written in *The Guardian* by a former prime minister of Australia, Julia Gillard, not only attests her own interest in the fantasy but seeks to explain its fascination in terms of its relation to socially relevant themes of political power, and of human behaviour, ethics, and relationships.[2] In a different sphere, the Khaleesi Hair Studio in the county town of Dorset, Dorchester, was registered as a company in September 2013, its name no doubt intended to evoke an association with glamour and style. Thus is a sudden vogue for a contemporary fictitious narrative and for a name drawn from its fantasy world documented in our own century; in this case we are close enough to the phenomenon chronologically to give this anthroponymic innovation a definite *terminus a quo*, to study it with meaningful statistical information, and to attempt to explain its motivation with first-hand testimony from its followers.[3] For the vogue for Arthurian names in medieval Spain, in contrast, we lack the immediacy of this background information, and are, of course, dependent upon the chance survival of written historical records of various kinds, largely administrative documents. Arthurian names from these sources are generally located in material not commonly read by literary scholars.[4] The point is that in the period of their earliest appearance in documents in the Peninsula, Arthurian names are as completely alien to the established onomastic resources and patterns encountered in these contemporary documents as are Khaleesi and Tonibler in the USA and Kosovo respectively; they constitute, in onomastic terms, an exotic import, whether inspired by the characters in literary texts or by admired real-life individuals already called after these figures. It must also be borne in mind that a belief in the historical reality of the Arthurian court was probably quite widespread in Iberia, though it would be necessary to distinguish between genuine acceptance of its historicity and politically opportune lip-service to and exploitation of this. By way of illustration, we may note the fact that on the occasion of the marriage of Mary Tudor with Philip II of Spain at Winchester Cathedral in 1554, some members of the Spanish court present at the ceremonies also took time out to visit the Round Table preserved in that town, which Henry VIII had previously exhibited to the Holy Roman Emperor Charles V in a calculated political exploitation of the legends. The accounts of the 1554 visit left by members of the Spanish royal retinue then furnished material for a further crop of derivative Arthurian references in Spanish historical texts into the XVIIth century.[5] It should be noted, in passing, that Winchester, with its alleged Arthurian connections, was probably not fresh news to the Spanish crown in 1554; these had already been exploited as part of the legitimation of the new Tudor dynasty by Mary's grandfather, Henry VII, whose son Prince Arthur was born there (he was, of course, married to Catherine of Aragon before his death and the latter's marriage to Henry VIII).

That the Arthurian heroes were indeed a subject of discussion in Iberia and its various territories beyond the geographical bounds of the Peninsula is indicated by occasional pieces of evidence; one telling case is examined here by Lourdes Soriano. Another similarly revealing instance is found in a letter written on 6 July, probably in 1396, from a herald to a member of the Aragonese royal house. In this, the writer (who had just travelled from Palermo to Barcelona and thence to Pedralbes for an audience with the king, thereby reminding us of the important Aragonese presence in Italian-language areas, a fact of some significance for questions of textual transmission) reports that Lancelot and Tristan have been ousted as topics of conversation by the dashing local chivalry present at current festivities.[6] It is, of course, unfortunately the case that such eloquent evidence of the social discussion of Arthurian fictions is all too rarely encountered, but this oral dimension must have been a significant factor in the popularity of the legends.

The Aragonese connection with regions of Italy that underlies this document reminds us also that Iberia was a complicated geopolitical space during the period in which the Arthurian legends were spreading and entering the period of perhaps their greatest vogue before our own age. Such unitary concepts of 'Spain' as may have existed remained mental constructs rather than political realities for the entire period between the end of Visigothic rule in the second decade of the VIIIth century and the *de facto* unification of the kingdoms in the fifteenth (with the marriage of Fernando and Isabel bringing together the Castilian and Aragonese domains) and XVIth century (with the annexation in 1512 of southern Navarre, and, from 1580 to 1640, the brief reincorporation of Portugal into the Spanish crown). During the centuries after the collapse of the Visigothic rule, a progressively diminishing portion of the land surface of the Peninsula was under Muslim control (though even there the penetration of Arthurian elements cannot be totally excluded, as is recorded in this volume), but north of the frontier between Islam and Christendom the growing area under the control of the various northern rulers was a dramatically shifting patchwork of polities which eventually coalesced into the major kingdoms of Portugal, León, its frontier offshoot (and eventual dominant partner) Castile, Navarre, and Aragon-Catalonia. The generally southward progress of the process traditionally referred to as the 'Reconquest' was not completed until 1492, when the Muslim kingdom of Granada ceased to exist as a politically independent unit, and was incorporated into Castilian-ruled Andalucia. By this time, of course, Portuguese maritime endeavours, followed later by Castile, had already developed the Atlantic navigation that led to contact with the Americas and a colonial penetration of Africa and coastal Asia until Iberian influence, and with it elements of the Arthurian tradition, had become truly global. Relevant historical information is given where appropriate in the chapters of this volume to add necessary detail to this overview; for fuller background information on the history of the period, various convenient English-language accounts are available (Barton 2004; Hillgarth 1976–8; MacKay 1977; O'Callaghan 1975), which contain ample bibliographies for further reading.

The political and linguistic patchwork of medieval Iberia finds an echo today in the current democratic Spanish Constitution's recognition both of autonomous regions within the kingdom of Spain, and of the Romance languages of Galician, Catalan and Castilian. The remaining Iberian regional language, Basque, is represented in this volume by some works of modern Arthurian fiction, catalogued in the chapter by Juan

Zarandona. The organisation of our book deliberately reflects the linguistic reality of the Peninsula, with separate chapters devoted to Arthurian material from Portugal, Galicia, the Aragonese and Catalan-speaking territories, and Castilian Spanish. This approach has, of course, some disadvantages as well as obvious benefits, but the authors of the various chapters have paid due attention to the many connections and contacts between these areas and languages, which are perhaps most clearly exemplified by the early case of King Alfonso X of Castile's poetic compositions in Galician-Portuguese. To ensure that these vital links and overlaps are fully expressed, moreover, other chapters deal thematically with topics that cross these linguistic and political boundaries, such as the texts of the *Post-Vulgate* cycle (studied as a group by Paloma Gracia), or the Arthurian revival (examined by Juan Zarandona). On a more prosaic level, the regional languages affect, too, bibliographical citation, with authors' names occurring sometimes in Castilian forms, sometimes in Catalan (as in the case of Antoni Rubió i Lluch/Antonio Rubió y Lluch); adoption of the form used at the time of publication has been sought, but occasionally a reprint silently regionalises the form of a name from that used on the original title page. Place names are similarly affected (Lérida/Lleida, etc.). The problem is not likely to cause confusion given the cross-referencing in the index and bibliography, but it needs to be noted; it is addressed in the bibliography by use of brackets for the necessary additional information, a solution also adopted to overcome the problem caused by variable practice among Spanish authors and publishers in giving only paternal, or both paternal and maternal, surnames. Thus works by, for example, Pere Bohigas Balaguer and Pedro Bohigas are in fact by the same scholar, as are those by Diego Catalán and Diego Catalán Menéndez-Pidal. With one eye on library catalogues and another on title pages, therefore, the entries in the bibliography and the index attempt to ensure that authorial entities are not multiplied beyond necessity.

There are also questions of preferred terminology in which our volume, respecting multiple viewpoints on unresolved matters, reflects current scholarly debate and differing usage rather than imposing a single norm. Such is the use by different contributors of the two distinct terms '*Post-Vulgate* cycle' and '*Pseudo-Robert de Boron* cycle' to refer to the same group of texts. If the equivalence of these labels is held in mind throughout, no confusion should be caused for the reader by this dual designation; to assist in this process, such terms are cross-referenced in the index. Naturally the reader should also be alert to the provisional nature of many of the conclusions advanced in any study of this kind of material, in which so many gaps in lines of transmission affect the textual basis, and so many questions of interpretation of both textual content and contextual evidence remain matters of scholarly contention. Where uncertainty exists, and where multiple interpretations are possible, the contributions in our volume reflect this situation rather than seeking to achieve a meaningless unanimity through avoiding the underlying controversies. If the result is occasional mutual contradiction between one chapter and another, the reader may be confident that this would also be the experience of attending an academic debate on the point in question and that it merely reflects the current state of the known evidence. To assist appreciation of the Iberian material, from major texts to passing poetic allusions, in its own terms and not merely as an adjunct to the reconstruction of lost French texts, the volume opens with two chapters which set out the nature of the material and which provide a clear orientation in this complex field. An overview of the presence of major Arthurian texts in Iberian languages, and their European relationships, is given by Paloma Gracia; and José Manuel Lucía Megías supplies a detailed account of the manuscript and printed witnesses of these texts, and discusses the problem of the interpretation of the physical evidence provided by manuscript texts and their context. The remaining chapters present the material in two distinct approaches, as outlined above. Three chapters deal with the Arthurian material in the principal Romance languages of the Peninsula other than Castilian. The western language group is covered by Santiago Gutiérrez's study of the material in Portuguese and that of Pilar Lorenzo Gradín dealing with the closely related Galician area. The Aragonese and Catalan material from the east of the Peninsula is examined by Lourdes Soriano. The central chapter of the volume, by Carlos Alvar, takes an overview of the entire Iberian situation and, as well as dealing with knowledge of Arthurian material in Castilian sources and its impact on Spanish society and culture, examines also the presence of this material in works not themselves principally concerned with Arthurian matters. His analysis of the impact of the Arthurian legends on Cervantes deals with one of the most internationally significant literary outcomes of the Peninsular Arthurian vogue. The next four chapters deal separately with the medieval literary texts considered by the editor to have had the greatest significance for Spanish literature and Europe in terms of their impact (or that of their heroes). These are the *Post-Vulgate* cycle considered as a whole, studied by Paloma Gracia; the Tristán texts, examined by Luzdivina Cuesta; the Lancelot texts, dealt with by Antonio Contreras; and *Amadís de Gaula* and its offspring, covered by Rafael Ramos. In this combination of analysis by language area and treatment by topic, our volume aspires to transcend the limitations of a single perspective on or approach to the material; it is our hope that the resulting multiple approaches will enhance readers' appreciation of the texts and the associated evidence, and all their complexities. The final two chapters deal with aspects of the extension of Arthurian material beyond the bounds of medieval Iberia, both geographically and chronologically, with the editor's examination of the spread of Arthurian texts and names during the Iberian exploration and settlement around the Atlantic and Pacific Oceans, and with Juan Zarandona's study of the productive resurgence of Arthurian material in the Iberian languages in the nineteenth and twentieth centuries, in which he includes a section on modern Latin American Arthuriana.[7]

Acknowledgements

I am grateful to the contributors for their enthusiastic participation in this long-running project, and for their patience. The same virtuous quality has characterised the General Editor, Ad Putter, and the commissioning editor at the University of Wales Press, Sarah Lewis. Clarity and promptness have characterised the correspondence of the UWP editorial division under Dafydd Jones and that of our indefatigable and eagle-eyed copy editor, Henry Maas. Many other debts of gratitude have been incurred along the way since the founding General Editor, W. R. J. Barron, first invited me to edit this volume, at the suggestion of Ian Michael. The Faculty of Medieval and Modern Languages of the University of Oxford generously gave me the status of Faculty Research Fellow from 2011; among my Oxford colleagues I take this opportunity of thanking in particular Edwin Williamson, Juan Carlos Conde, Xon de Ros and Jonathan Thacker, of the Sub-Faculty of Spanish, for their role in this and for their scholarly collegiality, with the hope that the completion of this book provides some justification for their confidence. Bibliographical information was kindly provided by John Edwards at Oxford, and Jorge Ferreira of the Arquivo Distrital do Porto. Helpful suggestions and constructive comments were offered by the anonymous peer reviewer for the publisher, to whom contributors and editor alike owe our thanks. All who are engaged in research depend heavily upon our academic librarians, and it is a pleasure to record my thanks to Emer Stubbs at Bristol, and to Joanne Edwards and Helen Buchanan at the Taylorian. We also depend fundamentally upon the work of previous scholars, and in Peninsular Arthurian studies the bibliography of this volume indicates precisely the extent and duration of this dependence; were it customary for an edited scholarly volume to contain a dedication, an obvious dedicatee for this one would be Harvey L. Sharrer. The translation of the chapters of the present book from Spanish, with the exception of that by Juan Zarandona who wrote his contribution in English, is the work of the editor; the contributors have approved the resulting texts of their chapters and I wish to thank them all for their cooperation and tolerance in the rather lengthy checking and revision process involved in producing these (relatively) literal English versions. They are not, therefore, responsible for such stylistic infelicities as readers may perceive in the work, which result from the fact that my primary concern has been to reflect accurately the contributors' meaning rather than to create a literary masterpiece. Finally, Susan Hook has cheerfully tolerated so much piled and revised paper around the house for so long that this must represent a special form of Arthurian heroism fully worthy of a more eloquent tribute of thanks than these few words can claim to be: *diolch o'r galon i ti*.

Notes

[1] Another form of misdating is, alas, the common misprint; such a case occurred with my reference to Juan de Mariana (1536–1624), where an unfortunate mistyping not spotted at proof stage has produced through the resulting transposition either chronological chaos or a miraculously extended lifespan for the Jesuit historian (Hook 2004: 65). Naturally I take full editorial responsibility for any similar remaining lapses of proof-reading in the present volume.

[2] Julia Gillard, 'Game of thrones and seats of power', *The Guardian*, 8 April 2014: 5.

[3] The same may be said of the appearance of the form 'Tonibler' and related names in Kosovo since Nato intervention in the conflict there in 1999, though in this case the alien inspiration was an actual foreign politician admired in that region because of a specific and time-limited involvement there (see Julian Borger, 'Blair's Boys', *Guardian Weekend*, 20 June 2014: 18–27). Returning to *Game of Thrones*, during filming of further episodes at Osuna in Andalusia in 2014, Ashifa Kassam reported that a 'Khaleesi Salad' was developed in local cuisine in order to cater for cast and crew (*The Guardian*, 3 November 2014).

[4] For example, records of the parish of the Virgen de las Angustias at Ayamonte (Huelva) record two cases of Ginebra, in 1539 and 1540 (Hook 2002: 120), although it is of course uncertain whether these women were so named after the adulterous Arthurian queen, Boccaccio's virtuous heroine (*Decameron*, II:9), or some similarly named individual locally.

[5] For these episodes, see Martin Biddle (2000: 22, 285, 333, and 484–6), who gives full bibliographical references. I am grateful to Dr John Edwards for his kind assistance on this matter.

[6] Casula 1977: 126–9, no. 107; from Caja 7, carta 1051: 'ara dien que no ha mes gent ell mon ni cavales sino aquells qui aqui son stats, car no.s parla mes de Lançalot ni de Tristany mes que parlen d.aquells qui aqui son stats' (orthography and punctuation as in the edition cited). The document is filed in the Archive among others dated only by day and month together with a batch dated 1396; that it was written in this year seems a reasonable, if inevitably provisional, conclusion.

[7] In all quotations throughout the volume, orthography and internal references are those of the edition cited. Matter omitted by chapter authors is marked by bracketed ellipses […].

I

ARTHURIAN MATERIAL IN IBERIA

Paloma Gracia

The reception of Arthurian material in Iberia was truly important: it was both early and very extensive, since many of the major texts were known and translated.[1] It also penetrated deeply into Peninsular culture, even into life itself, and was continuous and enduring; it remained vigorous throughout the entire Middle Ages and well into the XVIth century, when the early presses of Toledo and Seville published the *Demanda del Santo Grial* at least twice (1515, 1535), and some years later even than this, between 1540 and 1544, the Portuguese codex of the *Livro de Josep Abaramatia* was copied.

The introduction of Arthurian material into the Peninsula poses problems for scholarship that are difficult to resolve. It must have taken place at different times, for different reasons, and by different routes. The penetration of Arthurian themes into Catalunya was an entirely natural process.[2] The geographical proximity of Catalunya and Provence, and the former's links with Provenzal culture (so intimate that the Catalan troubadours, who were both numerous and important, composed their poems in Provenzal), meant that the Principality easily accepted these themes from the north of France. The early (but erroneous) attribution by critics of the *ensenhamen* of Guerau de Cabrera to the Catalan troubadour Guerau III led to their dating to 1160 this earliest witness to the penetration of Arthurian material into the Peninsula. However, the date of this composition, in which Guerau addresses his jongleur Cabra to reproach him on the poverty of his literary repertoire and, in reciting to him the long list of themes that should form part of it, includes various Arthurian names, has been reassigned to a later date by Cingolani (1992–3b). This scholar, in attributing the *ensenhamen* to Guerau III's grandson Guerau IV, places it between 1196 and 1198, and not in Catalunya but in Provence.

The fact that some Provenzal troubadours allude to Arthurian themes at an early date does not necessarily indicate the presence of these works in the area; it is more plausible to think that knowledge of the material may have been due, rather, to journeys and personal contacts with authors from the north of France. The French narratives would not have spread to the south until around 1180; first, the *chansons de geste* would have circulated, and then the Arthurian romances, known from the end of the XIIth century in Provence, whence they would have spread into Catalunya.[3] Besides, the simplicity of the troubadours' allusions to the Arthurian world makes it difficult to decide on the nature of the works to which they are referring, so that many of these references could arise from their merely reflecting a fashion, from the echo of a knowledge acquired by hearsay.

If everything leads us to believe that Catalunya did not know the work of Chrétien de Troyes, it is a very different situation in the case of the first of the prose Arthurian cycles, the *Vulgate*. We have witnesses for the Catalan translation of two sections of the cycle: the *Lancelot en prose* (known in Catalunya as *Lançalot*), and the *Queste del Saint Graal*, entitled in its Catalan version *Stòria del Sant Grasal*.

The witnesses are scanty. Of the *Lancelot en prose* there are known only two Catalan fragments: the first of them is preserved on two folios in a Catalan script, dated to the middle of the XIVth century, in the private library of Francesc Cruzate of Mataró;[4] these relate the enchantment of Lancelot in the Forêt perdue, which corresponds to the text edited by Sommer (1908–16: V, 121–4), although it is far from being a literal translation. The second is copied on a single folio preserved in the Arxiu Parroquial of Campos, Mallorca, and also dates from the XIVth century: it relates the combat between Lancelot and Caradoc, although it ends shortly before the knight kills the giant and liberates Gauvain; the text corresponds to that edited by Sommer (1908–16: IV, 134–6).[5] Bohigas (1962) observed that both copies displayed some affinities in the use of certain letter forms and the presence of archaisms, which led him to suggest the possibility that they contain sections of the same translation; this, because of the freedom with which the French original had been translated, would be different from the Catalan translation of the branch corresponding to the *Queste del Saint Graal* (known as the *Stòria del Sant Grasal*), which is much more literal. As far as concerns the dating of the Catalan translation of the *Lancelot en prose*, and despite the fact that before February 1362 there is no evidence of the existence of an explicitly Catalan *Lançalot*, Bohigas suggested the possibility that the dating of the translation should be pushed back to the end of the XIIIth century; he proposed 1339 as the latest date possible, because this was the year in which King Pere III ordered payment of the amount owing for a copy of the *Lancelot*, which this scholar presumed would have been produced in Catalan. It must be noted, however, that the arguments of Bohigas both regarding the date of the translation of the *Lançalot*, and its relation with the *Stòria del Sant Grasal*, are extremely weak.

The *Stòria del Sant Grasal* is preserved in a codex of the Biblioteca Ambrosiana in Milan, I.79. sup., containing 130 folios.[6] Its colophon offers a date (16 May 1380) and a personal name, G. Rexach. Rexach could have been both the copyist and the translator; such is the opinion of Miguel Adroher (2005–6), who has pointed out the affinity between the *Stòria del Sant Grasal* and the *Queste del Saint Graal* copied in MS fr. 343 of the BNF, and has underlined the wealth of Catalan innovations, especially those directed at replacing the original Cistercian tone with a spirituality of Franciscan inspiration.

No Catalan translation is preserved of the *Mort le roi Artu*; however, an author called Mosen Gras recreated the work closely, condensing some of its episodes, which cover approximately a fifth of the original. The *Tragèdia de Lançalot* emphasises the sentimental values of the *Mort le roi Artu*, transforming selected sections with the object of emphasising the amorous tragedy.[7] Mosen Gras dedicated the *Tragèdia de Lançalot* to Joan de Torrelles, Count of Iscla, who took part in various military campaigns in the service of Alfonso the Magnanimous, king of Aragon; the work is preserved in an incunable, probably printed in 1496, of which a copy is in the Biblioteca de Catalunya.

Of the Catalan version of the *Tristan en prose* or *Tristany de Leonis* there are preserved only brief fragments.[8] The first of these occupies folios 32r–35v of the *Codex Miscel·lani* (or MS 1 of the Arxiu de les Set Claus) and is copied in a script of the second half of the XIVth century; its text corresponds to paragraphs 56–7 and 71a of the analysis by Löseth (1891).[9] The *Codex Miscel·lani* is a factitious codex, now preserved in the Arxiu Històric Nacional de Andorra la Vella; it consists of 153 folios and eight endleaves, and contains numerous texts of diverse content, dated between the XIIIth and XIVth century. The compilation could have been the work of the notary Miquel Ribot d'Aixirivall, who was active at the end of the XVth century or the beginning of the XVIth. The second fragment is copied on four folios in the Arxiu Històric Comarcal de Cervera (B-343), although its present whereabouts are uncertain;[10] the script is of the end of the XIVth century and corresponds to paragraphs 20–2 of the analysis by Löseth. A final fragment, corresponding to Löseth's paragraphs 22–7 and 34–8 has recently been discovered; it is currently deposited in the Biblioteca de Catalunya, Barcelona, where it awaits cataloguing (Santanach i Suñol 2010).

There is something that attracts attention in these Catalan translations of the prose Arthurian cycles, and this is the contrast between the paucity of the surviving witnesses and the number of copies, relatively high, that enriched Catalan libraries: references are numerous, and come from the Principado, Mallorca, and Valencia;[11] not from Aragon, where Cingolani (1990–1: 114–15) comments that the inventories scarcely register books, and that the few books that do appear are generally related to the professional interests of their owners. Inventories, letters and wills drawn up between the beginning of the XIVth century and the end of the XVth have left us precious information. Comparison with what happens in the Castilian-speaking area is inevitable; the discreet presence of Arthurian texts in libraries has left a panorama far richer in references. This abundance of Catalan references to Arthurian books suggests that this type of literature must have aroused considerable interest, especially in the royal house, which displayed an enormous enthusiasm for the material and in which there was a traffic of books being bought, translations ordered, books being given, or being loaned. From the royal house there would have radiated outwards the taste for Arthurian literature, which would have extended to nobles and merchants, whose libraries contained Arthurian works, in Catalan and in French alike. The impression arises that an enthusiasm more concentrated upon specific titles and dates results, in Catalunya, in a smaller number of extant copies, with greater numbers in Castile, where the interest seems to become more pronounced as the XVth century advances, and which leaves more manuscript witnesses and a good number of printed editions.

The Catalan references to 'Lancelots', 'Tristans', and 'Books of the Holy Grail' are significant (Cingolani 1990–1), although it is certain that they refer to a smaller number of copies; some are referring to codices that were changing hands. Cingolani collects at least eighteen references to the presence of codices of the *Lancelot en prose* or the *Lançalot*, without its being possible to determine if this is the original in French or the Catalan adaptation. Many involve registers from the royal house: Jaume II (1291–1327) possessed at least two copies of the work, which he presented to princes Ramon Berenguer and Pere, on 6 August 1319 and 10 December 1321 respectively. Pere III (1336–87) paid for the copying of a *Lancelot* on 8 September 1339 and again on 17 April 1346.[12] Between these dates, on 19 November 1342, he ordered the return to the monastery of Sigena of a copy of a *Livro del Sant Graal* that had been stolen from it. Joan I (1387–96) had a *Lançalot* bound in 1374 and five years later received as a loan a manuscript of the French version. Cingolani (1990–1) brings together thirteen references to 'Books of the Holy Grail', with varying titles, and twenty-one references to 'Tristans', two involving King Joan I, who seems to have promoted the translation into Catalan of the Arthurian originals.[13]

As far as historiography is concerned, and by contrast with what occurred in Castile, the *Historia regum Britanniae* seems to have had little resonance in Catalunya. It is possible that the conception of Arthur narrated by Geoffrey (in the original version, or in one of its French recreations) may have inspired the legend of the conception of King Jaume I narrated in the *Cròniques* of Ramon Muntaner and Bernat Desclot (Delpech 1993; Montoliu 1925). Leaving aside this questionable influence, the presence of the *Historia regum Britanniae* is in practice limited to the partial Catalan translation contained in MS esp. 13 of the BNF, dated to the beginning of the XIVth century, and extremely literal. The presence in this MS of the Catalan version of Geoffrey's work could be linked to the *Histoire ancienne jusqu'à César* copied into the greater part of it; the reason is that one of the witnesses of the French universal history offered a translation of the *Historia regum Britanniae*, so that, since the *Histoire* had already incorporated within its French tradition an adaptation of the work of Geoffrey, it is plausible that the model of the Catalan version may also have contained a translation of the Latin work (Simó 2007; 2008).

Very different was what occurred in the centre, or rather (to include Salamanca and León) the centre and west of the Peninsula. Here, the Arthurian legends were known at an early date, to such an extent that they seem to have arrived in a state previous to the works of Chrétien de Troyes, and earlier even than the work of Geoffrey of Monmouth. A good part of the Iberian Peninsula seems to have known the Arthurian material in its varied and earliest forms, and to have shown itself receptive to this material from a date earlier than the completion of the *Historia regum Britanniae*. The proof of this is the existence of individuals baptised with Arthurian names, who are documented from

1136. The first is Martín Galván, who is followed, in chronological order, by Artus (1151), Galas (1156), Guillem Artus (1167), Martin Merlim (1186), Merlinus (1190) and many others. The names Galaz, Galván and Merlin were not unusual in the Peninsula during the Middle Ages; they appear in all kinds of medieval documents, even as family names. What is most surprising is the early date of their appearance; the first known Galas occurs in a document of 12 April 1156, in which princess Sancha donates one of her properties to the order of St John of Jerusalem, that is to say, at a date earlier than *Li contes del Graal*. These names are recorded in documents with precise dates, which come mainly from the area of Burgos and León; they are alien to the contemporary Peninsular onomastic tradition, for which reason they could result from an oral diffusion of Arthurian material, in versions that do not survive and that would obviously have been different from the reworkings created by literary culture at later dates. They were, however, sufficiently well known for Peninsular couples to want their children to bear the names of their heroes (Hook 1990–1, 1991; 1992–3a; 1996).

In contrast to Catalunya, where the reception of the Arthurian literature is linked to the enthusiasm of its kings and princes for the prose Arthurian cycles, and is therefore the result of a fashion, the centre and west of the Peninsula gave an early acceptance to the works of Geoffrey of Monmouth and Wace, the interest in which was aroused by the political dimension of the material. This fact was accompanied by an important presence of this material in historiography, the history of England being that narrated by Geoffrey and Wace.

The *Historia regum Britanniae* was repeatedly used in annals and chronicles; its exploitation is attested by the *Crónicas navarras* (1186) and the *Anales Toledanos Primeros* (1219). The reason for this early presence of the Arthurian legend in Peninsular historiography is unknown: the marriage of Eleanor, daughter of Henry II of England, and Alfonso VIII could have favoured it. However, the extent of the queen's role is uncertain and would surely be limited to encouragement of the diffusion of the material in Castile.[14] Eleanor could also have had something to do with the interest displayed by her grandson, Alfonso X, in the text of Geoffrey (Kasten 1970); but the inclusion of the *Historia regum Britanniae* in the *General estoria* could have been suggested, in addition, by another influence: that of French historiography. This is merely a hypothesis, but since Alfonso relied heavily on the *Histoire ancienne jusqu'à César* as a source for his *General estoria*, and since a version of the French work, such as that preserved in MS fr. 17177 of the Bibliothèque Nationale de France (BNF), contains a translation of a substantial part of the *Historia regum Britanniae*, the possibility exists that the manuscript used by Alfonso X could have contained this translation, and could have inspired the incorporation of the Arthurian material. The *Estoria de las Bretannas* is dispersed among the different sections of the *General estoria* in an unequal distribution: it begins with the story of Brutus, at the end of Part II and ends in Part V, when the compilation relates the events of the time of Julius

Caesar. The various points at which the *General estoria* adds material derived from the *Historia regum Britanniae* are dictated by the biblical references contained in Geoffrey's text. The interpolation is accomplished with care, avoiding incoherence and redundancy, and is in harmony with the Alfonsine project in terms of both what is wrought in structural complexity, and what relates to its ideological aims (Simó 2008).

Possibly related to the *Histoire ancienne jusqu'à César*, but through the Catalan version of this already mentioned, is Fernández de Heredia's incorporation into his *Grant Cronica d'Espanya* of an Aragonese translation of part of the *Historia regum Britanniae*. However, as the Middle Ages advanced, it seems that the influence of the *Historia regum Britanniae* as a source for Peninsular historiography waned; and despite the fact that many Castilian and Portuguese texts narrated the history of Brutus, these accounts do not derive from Geoffrey's original text but either from the *Roman de Brut* or from the adaptations of the *Historia* that had already been made into varieties of Iberoromance (Catalán 1962: 357–408). This the case with the *Livro das linhagens* of Pedro, Count of Barcelos, the *Crónica de 1404*, the *Libro de las generaciones*, the *Sumas de la historia troyana*, and the *Victorial* of Gutierre Díaz de Games.[15]

El segundo y tercero libro de don Lançarote de Lago is the title that MS 9611 of the Biblioteca Nacional de España, Madrid (BNM) gave to the Castilian adaptation of the *Lancelot propre*.[16] The MS has 355 folios, and dates from the XVIth century; but it is a copy of an earlier one, which, as the *explicit* informs us, was continued by a *Libro de don Tristán*, the copying of which was completed on 24 October 1414.[17] The model of this *Lançarote* would have been a version of the *Vulgate* close to the one copied in MS fr. 751 of the BNF and, although the Madrid MS contains approximately half the *Lancelot propre*, it may be presumed that the translation would have covered the whole of the original.[18] As far as the area where it was made, Sharrer (1981) has indicated the possibility that it was produced not in Castile, but in the north-west of the Peninsula, in a linguistic mix combining characteristically western, Galician-Portuguese, and Leonese features. This version of the *Lançarote* is not a literal translation: omissions are frequent, which affect significant characters and episodes, but do not compromise the overall coherence of the work. The fundamental innovation affects the ending, since the final section (fols 352*v*–355*r*) derives from the *Post-Vulgate*, which has been explained (Bogdanow 1999a; Bohigas 1924) by the need to offer a transition between the third book of *Lançarote* and the *Libro de don Tristán*, which must have been copied immediately after it.[19]

Other sections of the *Vulgate* could also have been translated into Castilian; it is reasonable to consider that the passage from the *Queste del Saint Graal* from this cycle, which is interpolated in chapters 379–91 of the *Demanda del Santo Grial* (Bogdanow 1983, 1986–7), replacing the original *Post-Vulgate* version, must have come from a pre-existing, complete Castilian translation of the *Vulgate Queste del Saint Graal*. There are more hazy indications, such as the references made by some

Arthurian and non-Arthurian works to titles from the *matière de Bretagne*, of doubtful identification, and the very existence of which may be questioned: Deyermond (1997) studied certain references to supposed works, cited under the titles *Merlín* and *Libro de Galaz*, and which could have involved respectively a *Merlin* and a *Queste del Saint Graal* from the *Vulgate* cycle.

The *Post-Vulgate* cycle enjoyed greater success in Castile: it was translated in its entirety and was copied and printed on several occasions. Its study presents problems that are difficult to resolve, on top of the questions raised by the cycle in its original language. Firstly, the problem of the language of translation, since the Portuguese and Castilian versions are intimately related and derive from a first common translation, but we do not know whether the French text was translated first into Castilian and thence into Portuguese, or vice versa. Secondly, such is the wealth of Castilian versions, and so significant are the innovations and divergences among them, that it is still impossible to trace a clear evolution from the translation, which was surely a literal one, to the XVth-century versions, bearing in mind the complexity indicated by the fact that these differences extend to the very structure, which in some cases is cyclical and in others is not.

We have only a single manuscript of the Castilian version, in which were copied three segments deriving from the *Post-Vulgate*, which are interspersed with various treatises of a religious nature; it is, therefore, a kind of partial testimony to a cyclical version, since it is to be presumed that its model would have contained the whole of the trilogy. The manuscript is now MS 1877 of the Biblioteca Universitaria de Salamanca (formerly MS 2-G-5 of the Biblioteca del Palacio Real, Madrid); it consists of 308 folios, was copied and/or compiled by Petrus Ortiz (Bogdanow 1991–2001: I, 210–16), and edited by Pietsch (1924–5). It contains sections of each of the parts of the cycle, entitled *Libro de Josep Abarimatía, Libro* (according to two lists of contents; or, according to the heading of the text itself and adopted by modern critics, *Estoria*) *de Merlín,* and *Lançarote* (the title given by the copyist to the section corresponding to the *Mort Artu*). It is difficult to determine what modifications Petrus Ortiz may have made to his model. Collation of his version and the French original reveals that the latter was abbreviated, but it is difficult to determine whether the abbreviation was the work of Petrus or not, since his model probably already presented a version both abbreviated and divided by chapter headings. What is entirely probable is that some modifications, summaries, and commentaries are to be attributed to him, undertaken in order to incorporate these Arthurian materials into his compilation.

The most extensive Arthurian section of MS 1877 is that of *Josep,* which begins with the imprisonment of Joseph of Arimathea and ends with the narration of some events associated with King Evolat, in Sarraz; this occupies folios 252*r*–282*r*, and its content corresponds to pp. 12–48 of Sommer's edition (1908–16: I). The *Estoria de Merlín* is copied on folios 282*v*–296*r*, and corresponds to the narrative content of pp. 1–33 of the edition of Gaston Paris and Jacob Ulrich (1886: I); it begins with the council of demons at which the decision is made concerning the conception of Merlin, and ends when the seer asks Blaisen to write the history of the Grail, this being the last episode in which Petrus introduces additions of any significance (Gracia 2007; 2011). *Lançarote* is the adaptation of a brief section of the *Mort Artu*. It occupies folios 298v–300v of the MS and corresponds to sections 630–54 of the Portuguese *Demanda*, chapters 394–417 of the *Demanda* in Castilian; its abrupt beginning and end suggest that the segment is incomplete.

There are, however, important printed witnesses: the *Baladro del sabio Merlín con sus profecías* was published in Burgos in 1498, and *La Demanda del Santo Grial con los maravillosos fechos de Lançarote y de Galaz su hijo*, a title which brings together, as its first and second books, those derived from *Merlin*, followed by its *Suite*, and by the *Queste del Saint Graal* from the *Post-Vulgate* cycle.[20] The *Demanda del Santo Grial* was printed on at least three occasions; but of the presumed edition of Seville, 1500 (known only from a reference to it by the bibliographer Nicolás Antonio in his *Bibliotheca Hispana Nova*, published in 1672), no copy survives, and of that of Toledo 1515 we have only the second book. Only the edition of Seville (1535) is complete and offers both books: a *Baladro* and a *Demanda* as such, among which, under the title 'Aquí comiençan las profecías del sabio Merlín, profeta digníssimo', is inserted a sizeable collection of prophecies relating to events in Castilian politics, of which the latest dates from 1467. It is probable that the editions of 1515 and 1535 derive, independently, from this presumed Seville edition of 1500, from which they would have deviated little, to judge by the similarity between the corresponding *Demandas*, which offer basically the same text.

A different situation is that of the *Baladros* of 1498 and 1535. Both derive from a common ancestor to which they owe many of their principal characteristics; however, there is a gulf between the incunable of 1498, in which the biography of Merlin is given as an independent story, beginning with his birth and ending with his death, and the very different approach in the 1535 edition, in which the life of the seer serves as a prelude to the adventure of the Grail. The 1498 version contains original prologues and an epilogue, also new; equally innovatory is the rewriting of the part that tells of the origin of Merlin, which greatly amplifies the version in its ancestor and strives to elevate its quality. From the point of view of the intention of the work, the most important feature of the incunable is the omission of the story of the Caballero de las Dos Espadas and that of an appreciable part of the elements and references involving the Grail, because, no doubt, this version lacked the *Demanda* as a continuation; the result is that, with Merlin's links to the Grail thus diluted, the religious dimension of the seer is diminished in the incunable, and his role is distorted. Nonetheless, the *Baladros* of 1498 and 1535 share the greater part of the work, in versions that are textually very close; both include the same sections that are not encountered in the surviving French versions. These are the prophecies derived from the *Historia regum Britanniae*, and the episodes of Merlin's dream, Ebrón el Follón and Bandemagus, as well as the profound revision of the ending; there is also the incorporation of the *Estoria de dos amadores* and the episode that narrates the delivery of Merlin to the devils and the death of the prophet, as he utters that rending shriek, or *baladro*, which gives the work its title.

The second book of the printed editions of 1515 and 1535 (the *Demanda del Santo Grial*) also presents important innovations in relation to the *Post-Vulgate Queste-Mort Artu*. Such are the suppression of certain passages that disapprove of the conduct of Arthur's men, or that constitute a condemnation of traditional chivalry, and that seem to have been omitted with the aim of accommodating the work to late medieval Spanish society. The most important change is the end of the work, in which the Castilian author substituted the *Post-Vulgate* version for the *Vulgate*, in the so-called 'Variant Version' (Bogdanow 1983, 1986–7); Arthur does not kill Mordred, so that XVIth-century Castile absolved the king of such a crime.

Various Castilian *Tristans* are preserved in manuscript and print, bearing witness to a tradition which put down deep roots in the Iberian Peninsula. They are radically innovating and differ greatly from the *Tristan en prose*; although they contain episodes of their own, they display some points in common with the Italian and Catalan versions, which seem to belong to the same family and from which they could even be descended. To explain these affinities, two main hypotheses have been formulated. One is that the French model of the Catalan-Aragonese-Castilian and Italian group would have been an anomalous *Tristan en prose*, very different from the surviving specimens, and circulating only in Italy and in the east and centre of the Iberian Peninsula; the other is that the Catalan-Aragonese-Castilian group would have descended from an Italian original, now lost. Notwithstanding this, and although it has been debated profoundly and at length, the problem of the Iberian *Tristans* is far from being resolved.[21]

There are two surviving manuscript witnesses. The first, known as the *Cuento de Tristán de Leonís,* is MS Vat. Lat. 6428 in the Vatican Library, with 131 folios, although it is incomplete; this copy is, linguistically, in Castilian-Aragonese, and dates from the end of the XIVth century or the beginning of the XVth.[22] The second is an illuminated manuscript of the XVth century, of which sixty fragments survive, divided between MS 20262/19 and MS 22644 of the BNM.[23] This offers a version close to that transmitted by the Catalan witnesses, although it differs from the *Cuento de Tristán de Leonís*, and would have been the model for the printed tradition.

The first edition of *Tristán de Leonís* dates from 1501, from the press of Juan de Burgos at Valladolid;[24] and from this edition would have been taken the later ones, printed in 1511, 1525 and 1528 (and the lost editions of 1520 and 1533), all printed at Seville (Cuesta Torre 1993b, 1994a, 1997d; see also her chapter in the present volume). The printed text follows a model very similar to that transmitted in MSS 20262/19 and 22644, the arrangement of the episodes in which it respects, but in relation to which it abbreviates or amplifies some passages. The most important innovation is the modification of the end of the work (Seidenspinner-Núñez 1981–2), since the printed text abandons the solution of the *Tristan en prose* that its model probably offered, and replaces it with another modified to accommodate the spirit of the sentimental romance, which was most influential at this time. Another important transformation is the replacement of the plainer style of the manuscript with a more rhetorically elaborate one, which is also in keeping with the sentimental romance. These modifications have been attributed to the printer Juan de Burgos (Sharrer 1988a).

In 1534, a version was printed in Seville entitled *Tristán de Leonís y el rey don Tristán de Leonís el joven, su hijo*.[25] This offers as its principal innovation the inclusion of an extensive second book devoted to the children of Tristan and Iseult; its adventures take place mostly in Spain. The first book corresponds to the original *Tristán de Leonís*, the text of which is reproduced in its main outlines, although its style is simplified and new episodes are incorporated, in addition to the necessary additions describing the conception of the children. The style of the second book is characteristically Renaissance and reflects the world and political thought of the period of Charles V. The biography of the emperor seems to be reflected in that of Tristan the Younger, the parallels being so important that the work could have been conceived as an instrument of propaganda in his favour (Cuesta Torre 1996, and in the present volume, Gimber 1996).

Tristán de Leonís inspired two anonymous letters: the *Carta enviada por Hiseo la Brunda a Tristán de Leonís*, which is the one sent by Iseult to Tristan lamenting his marriage to Iseult aux blanches mains, and an innovating *Respuesta de Tristán* containing his apologies. The letters were composed at the end of the XVth century, and are preserved in the miscellaneous MS 22021 of the BNM, fols. 8v–10v. Although they are clearly linked to an episode from *Tristán*, these letters do not appear to have belonged to any version of the *Tristan en prose*, but seem to have been created independently under the inspiration, and within the conventions, of sentimental fiction, the genre which dominated the Spain of the Catholic Monarchs, and which was devoted to analysing amorous emotion. Their attribution to any author is questionable, but two of the principal writers of sentimental romance have been suggested as possible authors: firstly Juan Rodríguez del Padrón (Sharrer 1981–2), and later Juan de Flores.[26]

In the field of rewriting, there were Castilian authors who, although far from the texts of the Arthurian works, were inspired by these to recreate their themes and motifs in works of a completely different form and spirit. Lancelot and Tristan were the protagonists of some traditional ballads (*'romances'*), brief epic-lyric poems composed from the end of the XIVth century and throughout the XVth, anonymous, and circulating orally, which ended up being collected and incorporated into the great XVIth-century poetic collections, the *Cancioneros* ('songbooks'). The ballads 'Herido está don Tristán', 'Tres hijuelos había el rey', 'Lanzarote y el orgulloso' and 'Lanzarote y el ciervo de pie blanco' can be related only vaguely with the *Lancelot* or the *Tristan en prose*; they are likely to have been composed from vague recollection of *romans* read or heard (Milá y Fontanals 1874), but their lyricism and fleetingness, combined with an extraordinarily tragic and fatal spirit, is captivating. 'Herido está don Tristán' is the ballad which has attracted most attention from scholars.[27] It relates the death of Tristan, caused by the lance-thrust dealt by King Mark, and coincides with the ending of *Tristán de Leonís*, particularly tragic; in some of its versions, the ballad links the end of the lovers to the birth of a lily which leaves any woman who eats it pregnant (Kurtz 1986–7; Pelegrín 1975). 'Lanzarote y el ciervo de pie blanco' takes up the very moment at which Lancelot, who is pursuing a white stag, enters into dialogue with a hermit and the latter attempts to restrain him, warning him of the danger he is courting, and cursing a woman, who seems to be the cause of the adventure and the death of other knights.[28]

The Arthurian material penetrated into the west of the Peninsula with ease, along the natural route offered to it by the Camino de Santiago.[29] In fact, the few possible early traces left by Arthurian material in Peninsular architecture are found in Galicia: an historiated column from the old north entrance to the cathedral of Santiago de Compostela, dated to the first decade of the XIIth century, can be related, albeit vaguely, to a scene from *Tristan* (Moralejo Álvarez 1985); also, the tympanum of the monastery of Santa María de Penamaior, in the province of Lugo, dating from the first half of the XIIIth century, seems to represent the protagonist of *Le Chevalier au Lion* (Sánchez Ameijeiras 2003).[30]

The pilgrimages turned Santiago de Compostela into a centre for the reception of French literature, and they explain the role played by the city of Astorga in the development of Peninsular Arthurian material, as well as the Leonese and western linguistic characteristics that are sprinkled throughout the Castilian derivatives of the *Post-Vulgate* cycle, including the codex of *Lanzarote del Lago* preserved at Madrid. South of Galicia, political and mercantile relations between Portugal and England would have facilitated the penetration of the material, especially during the reign of Afonso III. This king's exile in France, and his marriage to Matilda, Countess of Boulogne, would have favoured the penetration of Arthurian texts into Portugal; it is even possible that Afonso III, on returning from exile, could have taken to Lisbon manuscript copies of some French texts. Whilst Castile is linked to Catalunya so far as concerns the derivatives of the *Tristan en prose*, in relation to the other manifestations of Arthurian material Catalunya evolves independently and on the margins of the Peninsular developments, but Castile is intimately related to Galicia and Portugal. The productions of these three territories are so closely interwoven (Lorenzo Vázquez 2002) that it is difficult to indicate the direction of the influence, which shifts from one generation to another and from one moment to another. For the great prose cycles, it seems that the direction of influence runs from the west towards the centre of the Peninsula, but in the case of historiography it is initially in the opposite direction, since the Castilian chronicles are the earliest to accept the *Historia regum Britanniae*; at later dates, however, the direction of the influence shifts and the situation appears, rather, to be more mixed.

The Galician-Portuguese troubadours make quite plain, in the mid-XIIIth century, the success of the Arthurian legends in the west of the Peninsula (Sharrer 1988b). Most of the allusions are concentrated in the works of Martin Soares and Gonçal'Eanes do Vinhal, whose respective references to 'Don Caralhote' in the *cantiga* by Martin Soares 'Hunha donzela jaz aqui' and to the 'cantares de Cornoalha' in the *cantiga* 'Maestre, todolus vossos cantares' have been discussed at length by scholars (D'Heur 1973–4, 1976; Alvar 1993). Although the compositions coincide chronologically with the reign of Afonso III of Portugal, who has been credited with an important role in the introduction of the *Post-Vulgate* cycle into the Peninsula, both troubadours were linked to the court of Alfonso X of Castile, whose interest in the material is evident in the partial incorporation of the *Historia regum Britanniae* in his *General estoria* and in the references to Arthurian material in his poetic output: in his *Cantigas de Santa Maria* composed in Galician-Portuguese, to which must be added the possible reference to Lancelot's cart in the profane *cantiga* 'Vi un coteife de mui gran granhon' (Lorenzo Gradín 2008a).

No witnesses of the *Vulgate* cycle are preserved in the Galician or Portuguese languages; but the manuscripts of the *Post-Vulgate* are extremely important, since they preserve, wholly or in part, each of its three branches. Of the first part of the cycle, the *Livro de Josep Abaramatia*, two witnesses are known, which give a version very close to the one which must have served as a model: the first (Dias 2003–6) consists of a single bifolium, retrieved from the binding of a notarial volume, in the Arquivo Distrital do Porto, which has been dated to the end of the XIIIth century, which would make it the earliest known Arthurian manuscript from the Iberian Peninsula. The second witness is the XVIth-century manuscript in the Torre do Tombo, MS 643, at Lisbon.[31] From the section corresponding to the *Suite du Merlin* there are preserved two fragments of a Portuguese version found in MS 2434 of the Biblioteca de Catalunya, from the XIVth century.[32] The Portuguese *Queste* and *Mort Artu*, or *Demanda do Santo Graal*, is found complete in the XVth-century MS 2594 of the Österreichische Nationalbibliothek in Vienna (ÖNB).[33]

The Peninsular descendants of the *Post-Vulgate* cycle are intimately related and it is clear that the *Demanda* in Portuguese and its Castilian counterpart both derive from a common ancestor. The cycle seems to have been translated from French on but a single occasion in the Peninsula, and it is from that initial translation that all the known witnesses descend. Although, however, the name of the translator is known – Joam Vivas, who appears in the *Josep* in Portuguese and in the Castilian *Demanda* – there is no certainty about the language into which the French original was translated. Scholars have debated this question at length, relying in some cases on the examination of the Arthurian sections of the Salamanca manuscript, in others on the collation of the

Portuguese and Castilian texts of the *Demanda*. The debate began at the end of the XIXth century, though the most important works were published in the mid-1920s: in 1924–5 Pietsch changed the view that he had expressed in his previous works, and defended the priority of the Castilian text, like Entwistle, who believed that the first translation had been made into Castilian, under the patronage of King Sancho IV, around 1291. The Portuguese thesis, however, is the one that has attracted the most solid, the most numerous, and the most recent expressions of support; it has been upheld by Lapa (1929–30), Pickford (1961), Bogdanow (who firmly defended the priority of the Portuguese in 1974–5 and 1975, although she would later be more cautious), and Megale (2001). From the identification of Joam Vivas as a Portuguese cleric, a member of a rich Lisbon family, with access to the court of Afonso III, Castro (1983) formulated the hypothesis that the king could have known the cycle during his residence in France and could have taken a copy to Portugal in 1245.

There survive two leaves of the Galician version of the *Tristan en prose*, which date from the end of the XIVth century, at the Archivo Histórico Nacional, Madrid (Códices Leg. Carp. 1501 B, n. 7; see the accounts by Lucía Megías and Lorenzo Gradín in this volume). They relate the episode of the 'Chevalier a la Cotte mal taillee', corresponding to paragraphs 91–3 of the analysis by Löseth (1891). The manuscript seems to be a copy of another fuller one, also in Galician or in Portuguese, which would have contained the translation of a French original textually close to MS 2542 of the ÖNB at Vienna, in a version that must have had a different origin from the Catalan and Castilian *Tristans*, since it contains episodes not found in the latter.[34]

The most important and poetically beautiful recreation of Arthurian material in Galician-Portuguese consists of five anonymous lyric poems, the so-called *Lais de Bretanha*, the composition of which is placed at the end of the XIIIth century or the beginning of the XIVth. The *Lais* are preserved in the *Cancioneiro da Biblioteca Nacional de Lisboa*, and in Vatican Library Cod. Vat. Lat. 7182, and the copy is preceded by rubrics that declare or clarify the Arthurian content of the compositions.[35] Their composition is linked to the lyric *lais* of the *Tristan en prose*, although their relationship with the French model varies from one to another. 'O Marot aja mal-grado' and 'Ledas sejamos ogemais!' include references to characters or passages from Arthurian legend; the remaining three, 'Amor des que m'a vos cheguei', 'Don Amor, eu cant'e choro', and 'Mui gran temp'á, par Deus, que eu non vi' are recreations of pieces contained in the *Tristan en prose*. (See the chapters by Santiago Gutiérrez García and Pilar Lorenzo Gradín in the present volume.) More difficult to relate to specific Arthurian texts, and of uncertain dating, are the traditional Portuguese ballads that contain allusions or motifs related to Tristan; their identification is difficult because in some the names have been altered and in others themes appropriate to Arthurian material have been mingled with Carolingian motifs (Braga 1914; Martins 1979a).

The historiography from the Peninsular west took up the history of Britain derived from the *Historia regum Britanniae* in three main works: the *Livro de Linhagens*, the

Crónica de 1404, and, to a more limited extent, the *Crónica Geral de 1344*. The *Livro de Linhagens* and the *Crónica Geral de 1344* are attributed to Pedro de Portugal, Count of Barcelos (1289–1354), a bastard son of King Dinis of Portugal. Both the *Livro de Linhagens* (a private compilation of noble genealogies) and the *Crónica de 1404* incorporate a narrative of the history of the kings of Britain from the first, Brutus, to the last, Cadwallader, derived from the *Liber regum*. However, the version used would not have been the original *Liber regum*, composed in Navarre around 1200 and in the vernacular, but a version entitled *Libro de las generaciones*, which incorporated a summary of the history of the kings of Britain, and the principal source of which would have been the *Brut* of Wace, completed with information derived from the *Post-Vulgate* cycle.[36]

Leaving aside, however, the details of the translations and adaptations of the Arthurian texts in the three main Peninsular romance languages, what is certain is that their influence was much more extensive than these reveal. Castile enjoyed an ample tradition of prophecies attributed to Merlin, linked at the same time with those derived from the *Post-Vulgate* and with the historiography, which circulated as a collection and were incorporated in various works. The prophetic collection attributed to Merlin constitutes an amalgam of materials whose origins, dates, and purposes are diverse; from this arise the difficulties that they pose, whether in terms of understanding the events to which they allude, or of the problems in reading and editing them. The fullest collection preserved is the one inserted in the first and second books of the *Demanda del Santo Grial* printed in Seville (1535) under the heading 'Aquí comiençan las profecías del sabio Merlín, profeta digníssimo'. There are various nuclei to be distinguished in this collection:[37] the so-called *Visión de Alfonso en la ciudad de Sevilla*, according to which an angel reveals to King Alfonso X that the curse he has uttered will cause the loss of his lineage to the fourth generation, and of which there is a Catalan version; the *Profecías que revela Merlín a Maestre Antonio*, which begin with the loss of Spain to the Moors by King Roderick; and the *Profecías de Merlín cerca de la ciudad de Londres*, which allude to Alfonso X, Alfonso XI, Pedro I and Enrique II and which extend as far as the year 1377. This final nucleus of the collection was translated into Catalan and is preserved in MS 271 of the Biblioteca de Catalunya, copied at the beginning of the XVth century. It offers a text of the prophecies superior to the one of the Seville *Demanda del Santo Grial*, more correct, and containing elements that the Castilian version printed in 1535 has lost.[38] Prophecies attributed to Merlin and related to this tradition or collection were the model for those contained in the *Poema de Alfonso XI*, the *Crónica del rey don Pedro*, and the *Cancionero de Baena*.

Still in the field of literature, it is necessary to point out the important traces left by the Arthurian texts in the creation of original narrative. In the Peninsula the Arthurian material as such led on to the fiction of knighthood, in the Castilian romances of chivalry, among which there stands out the earliest and most important of them:

Amadís de Gaula.[39] The origins of *Amadís* are obscure, since the early version, which has been dated between the XIIIth and XIVth century, does not survive and we have only a rewritten version of the end of the XVth century, the work of Garci Rodríguez de Montalvo, who must have fundamentally modified the first version of the work. It is particularly significant that the ending of the first *Amadís*, which was lugubrious and was probably inspired by the *Post-Vulgate* cycle (Lida de Malkiel 1952–3), was replaced. The biography of the protagonist, although it is set in a newly created court with fresh characters, is essentially constructed on Arthurian models, from which it differs in the central consideration that matrimonial love has replaced the adulterous love of its models. There are few passages for which it is possible to indicate a specific source or a direct derivation; nonetheless, the imitation extends throughout the work from start to finish, revealing an author who knew Arthurian literature intimately; the best parallel is Cervantes later in *Don Quijote* in relation to the romances of chivalry. The author of the original *Amadís* was an assiduous reader of the great cycles of the *Vulgate*, the *Post-Vulgate*, and the *Tristan en prose*, under the inspiration of which he composed an original work which adapted themes, motifs, episodes and adventures, fluently manipulating the technique of interlace narrative (see the chapter by Rafael Ramos in this volume).

We know this first version of *Amadís* imperfectly, since its characteristics are just glimpsed through the late rewriting by Montalvo. As his work progressed, the revision by Montalvo seems to have become more extensive and far-reaching; with it, the Arthurian model of the first version acquired a new dimension. Hundreds of years had passed since historical chivalry and courtly love had given meaning to the Arthurian romances; in this society of the late Middle Ages the motifs and archetypal themes seem to have been reduced to literary clichés, as stereotyped as an ideal world. This clinging to the past when the external reality that had inspired the romance had undergone deep change deprived the elements of Arthurian origin of their meaning, relegating them to the status of decorative details. Proving oneself through adventures had been reduced to a courtly diversion and now served to provide pleasure or laughter. These elements now constituted a kind of elaboration on a literary theme that permeated the life being narrated, like an emblem of a better past (Gracia 2002).

The romance of chivalry is superseded in the Catalan sphere, where, late in the XVth century, was written the first modern novel, also chivalric: *Tirant lo Blanc*, whose author Joanot Martorell based himself on the old Arthurian tradition, but produced a contrafactum of the model (Alemany Ferrer 1995). In *Tirant*, the Arthurian element does not predominate in as subtle a way as in *Amadís de Gaula*, but is much more obvious much of the time, and, in fact, echoes of the *Lancelot en prose* and the *Mort le roi Artu* have been noted in the work.[40]

This material is concentrated in a curious and controversial episode of *Tirant*, which is set in Constantinople, where during the course of a festival Morgana arrives in search of Arthur. The Arthurian-French element here is mixed with what was already deeply rooted Peninsular material marked by its own innovatory characteristics, since the source of the episode is *La Faula*, a narrative composed about 1375 by the Mallorcan Guillem de Torroella, in a Catalanised Provenzal.[41] This relates his journey, on the back of a whale, to a marvellous island, where he is received by Morgana, and he recounts the conversation that he had with Arthur on the circumstances in which the latter had recuperated from his wounds.

Relations between chivalric and Arthurian literature had become, by the end of the Middle Ages, a game of mirrors, since French Arthurian literature continued to serve as a source of inspiration, but was now combined with the Peninsular recreations. Inspired by *La Faula*, Joanot Martorell created an extraordinary episode of the marvellous in the context of a realist work. It is, however, one whose function and nature are not clear: the didactic and moral intention of the passage has been emphasised (Brummer 1962; Wolfzettel 1994), as has its markedly theatrical character, since it seems a piece of drama, related to courtly spectacle and festival, an 'entremés' or interlude performed in Constantinople (Hauf i Valls 1990a; Riquer 1990, 1992).[42] *Tirant* displays yet another instance of this interrelation between foreign Arthurian material and its Iberian equivalent, even more delicate, when the mature and married empress of Constantinople sings to Hipòlit, her young, besotted knight, the 'romanç' of Tristan: a specimen of a genre so characteristically Peninsular as is the *romance* or ballad, which is none other than 'Herido está don Tristán' (Riquer 1953). Literature is here introduced into literature itself, interfering with the reality that it narrates; the characters attend a theatrical performance in which the protagonist is Arthur, and the empress sings a ballad about Tristan.

The innovating genres born in Castile late in the XVth century show the productivity of Arthurian material, still vigorous enough to affect native literary production. The direction of influence was oscillating: from the Arthurian to the home-grown, from the home-grown to the Arthurian. Arthurian motifs are incorporated into a work as singular, and of such literary quality, as *Celestina* by Fernando de Rojas, the first known edition of which was printed in Burgos in 1499, but which was composed some years earlier than this. The work is concerned with the destructive effects of love and the corruption of servants, one of whom is called Tristán; courtly love is condemned and the work is dominated by the sexuality of the licentious Celestina and the prostitutes who ply their trade under her tutelage. The parallels between *Celestina* and *Cligès* have been amply emphasized by critics.[43] The latter have not, on the other hand, paid attention to the reverse phenomenon, that is, the incorporation of Celestinesque elements in the *Baladro del sabio Merlín* printed in 1498, also at Burgos. The woman who in the *Post-Vulgate Suite du Merlin* collaborates with the devil to corrupt the girl who will be Merlin's mother has become, in the *Baladro*, an old woman who, like Celestina, inveigles herself into the house of the sisters through a ruse and corrupts the younger of them; the narration underlines the complicity between old woman and maiden, and their dialogues greatly augment such elements of the Arthurian antecedent as could involve the obscene and concern prostitution, reflecting the universe of *Celestina* (Gracia 2013a).

This web of reciprocal influence is displayed with particular depth in the most innovating genre in Castile at the end of the Middle Ages: the sentimental romance, devoted to reflection on amorous passion and its consequences, which are always tragic. Juan Rodríguez del Padrón initiated the genre with *Siervo libre de amor*, composed around 1439. The romance includes a brief story, the 'Estoria de dos amadores', which tells of the retreat of the lovers Ardanlier and Liesa in a palace excavated from the rock, and which constitutes the most significant testimony of this web of influence. Juan Rodríguez del Padrón would have been inspired by the story in the *Post-Vulgate Suite du Merlin* of Anasten, son of King Assen, which Merlin relates to Niviene shortly before she imprisons him, and which also has the motif of the withdrawal of the lovers to an underground palace. But, in turn, the 'Estoria de dos amadores' would have inspired the changes introduced by the *Baladro del sabio Merlín* in the episode of Merlin and Niviene, modifying the redaction of the original *Suite* to bring it into line with the 'Estoria' (Lida de Malkiel 1954). That is, the direction of influences would have run firstly from the Arthurian to the sentimental romance, later going into reverse and running from the sentimental fiction to the Peninsular Arthurian material. The Arthurian material served as nourishment to the sentimental romance, which, in turn, offered original elements to the Peninsular recreations of Arthurian material. Thus the romance *Grimalte y Gradissa*, by Juan de Flores, coincides in a significant way with *Tristán de Leonís*, printed in 1501 (Waley 1961; Deyermond 1986), exemplifying this 'cross fertilisation' between the sentimental and the Arthurian of which Sharrer spoke (1984a).

This thematic proximity caused the sentimental and chivalric romances to become tinged easily with Arthurian elements; in the case of the sentimental fiction, the cause was the predominance of courtly love, and in the case of the chivalric fiction it was adventure. A passage from the *Estoire del Saint Graal* served as a source for a dream-vision in the *Historia del noble Vespasiano* in Castilian, and thence for the Portuguese *Estoria do muy nobre Vespesiano*, in its narration of the legend of the destruction of Jerusalem by Vespasian (Hook 1986). The *Cárcel de amor* by Diego de San Pedro shows affinities with the *Mort Artu*; the probable source of this would have been the *Post-Vulgate* version (Deyermond 1986). It is obvious that the influence of Arthurian material affects many of the works composed in the three principal Peninsular Romance languages, some of which are more interesting for their inherent quality, others for the extent of the material. Among the former there stands out the *Libro de las bienandanzas e fortunas* written at the end of the XVth century by Lope García de Salazar; the book is a strange historiographic compendium which covers history from the creation and the flood to the formation of Castile and the history of Vizcaya and other lordships in the north of the Peninsula. Lope García de Salazar used a good number of Arthurian texts as sources: adaptations which go back in the last analysis to the *Historia regum Britanniae* or the great cycles, the *Tristan en prose* and above all the *Post-Vulgate*, all three branches of which he knew, but whose ending he modified by incorporating a passage on the survival of Arthur in the island of Brasil, to which the king had been taken by Morgana (Sharrer 1971, 1979a). Other works are significant not because of the extent of the Arthurian influence, which is slight, but because of their literary quality and because of their importance in the history of Peninsular literature. It is interesting to note that, besides the significant works already mentioned because the impact of Arthurian material on them is notable or obvious, other major works incorporated elements of Arthurian origin: the *Llibre de l'orde de cavalleria* by Ramon Llull, which may be connected in certain passages with the *Lancelot en prose* or with the *Queste del Saint Graal* of the *Vulgate* (Soler i Llopart 1989); and *Curial e Güelfa*, which traces the amorous itineraries of its protagonists in a manner similar to those of the *Lancelot en prose* or the *Mort Artu* (Butinyà i Jiménez 1987–8). In a more doubtful and marginal way, the *Libro de buen amor* (Crawford 1925) and the *Libro de Alexandre* (Michael 1967) contain motifs related to this material.

Reference was made at the beginning of this chapter to the fact that the reception of Arthurian material in the Peninsula was of long duration and ran so deep that it even influenced life. It has been argued that the reading of Arthurian material by Isabel la Católica could have influenced the queen's conduct and policy (Michael 1989); but let us conclude, as an illustration of the impact of Arthurian material on Peninsular life, with the two phenomena which open and close, in chronological terms, this panoramic survey of its influence. The earliest testimony of its effect, that of the baptism of children with Arthurian names, reveals a powerful impact that is personified in the existence of an individual called Martín Galván, already adult by 1136 (Hook 1991). About three hundred years later this same society converts literature into a way of life; it is not now a matter of children whose names evoke the legendary heroes, but of individuals who model their lives on the life stories they read in Arthurian works. The natural direction from history to literature that had made knighthood into the ideological basis of the verse of Chrétien de Troyes is inverted at the end of the Middle Ages, when it is life that is constructed on the basis of literary models and Spanish knights errant wander around the Iberian Peninsula and head abroad in search of adventures, while other foreigners came to Spain with the same motives, as is demonstrated by documented chivalric vows, passages of arms, and challenges to duels (Riquer 1967).

Even the great festivals of kings and princes echoed these themes; such was the case of the festival that took place in Binche, in 1549, arranged by Maria of Hungary for the emperor Charles V on the occasion of the journey of his son Philip to Flanders. The description of one of the entertainments – the adventure of the 'Dark Castle' (*castillo tenebroso*) presents affinities with certain literary works, such as the *Demanda del Santo Grial* and the *Baladro*, which are mingled with the more obvious influence of *Amadís*. Essentially, in this part of the festivities, the men essayed a series of adventures which marked out the knight chosen to liberate his captured and enchanted companions from the castle; it was a kind of game that was contested following the model of the characteristically Arthurian adventures, marked by a succession of tests in which there were not lacking magic swords that only the destined knight could attain. The Arthurian and chivalresque element is intimately linked to life, since far from constituting a mere adornment, this was all full of political significance and was associated with the accession of Charles V to the throne of the Low Countries (Devoto 1975).

In short, the Iberian Peninsula reveals early echoes of legendary material transmitted orally, and later witnessed a widespread diffusion, the greatest in the Romance-speaking countries, of the work of Geoffrey of Monmouth and of the different versions of the Arthurian material produced in the XIIIth century. This material endured, thanks to translations and recreations of varying character and depth, the incidence of which increased as the Middle Ages progressed, until they came to embrace multiple literary forms. It permeated vernacular literary composition, was interwoven into home-grown genres, and ended up serving as a model for life itself during the transition to the Renaissance.

Notes

[1] The classic general studies of Entwistle (1925) and Lida de Malkiel (1959) have become obsolete in various respects; however, the importance of Entwistle's book means that it is essential to take it into account in any fresh study that is undertaken. As regards bibliography, that of Sharrer (1977) is much more than a critical bibliography, since as well as its assessment of studies on Peninsular material published up to that date, it contains a description of each of the witnesses; the organisation by Sharrer of the Iberian Arthurian texts continues to dominate to the present works published on this material. Miller (2006) has described carefully the state of scholarship on the principal themes in a very useful critical work. Mérida Jiménez (2010) records the principal publications. (The present study forms part of the work undertaken in the Research Project FF12009–13556 (DGCYT 2009), financed by the Ministry of Economy and Competitiveness of Spain and FEDER).

[2] There are various general studies on the diffusion of the Arthurian material in Catalunya, by Bohigas (1961), Riquer (1997), Lucía Megías (2005c), and Soriano Robles (2010; see also the latter's chapter in the present volume).

[3] The troubadour references to Arthurian themes were minutely analysed by Pirot (1972) and Cluzel (1954–6), who studied those contained in the *sirventes* by Guerau de Cabrera, although both authors, starting from an early dating of this work to 1160, indicated early versions of lost Arthurian works as sources for the allusions, which are rendered unnecessary by the later dating proposed by Cingolani (1992–3b).

[4] Bohigas (1962) includes an edition of the fragment, as well as its study.

[5] This was revealed in 1903, in a brief article signed by Rubió y Lluch (1903), which included a transcription signed by Matheu Obrador.

[6] This was edited by Crescini and Todesco (1917), who had published an article on the work in 1913–14. See the works in which Martines (1994, 1995a) indicates that the *Stòria del Sant Grasal* is characterised by reinforcing the allegorical elements with religious significance and by intensifying the symbolic value of the quest for the Grail, which the Catalan text expresses in a more direct form than does the *Queste del Saint Graal*; see also Brummer (1989).

[7] Edited and studied by Riquer (1984).

[8] Santanach i Suñol (in press) has prepared a critical edition of these fragments; on the Iberian *Tristán* texts, see Ros Domingo (2001), who underlines the importance of the Catalan texts; and Cuesta Torre in the present volume.

[9] The text was edited by Aramon y Serra (1969) and the codex has been studied in an exemplary work by Santanach i Suñol (2003).

[10] BITECA (manid 2175) notes that, in November 2005, the folios had disappeared, although the Archive stated that they could have been merely mis-shelved. Fortunately we have the edition of Duràn i Sanpere (1917) of this *Tristany* which was, or is, in Cervera.

[11] For example, in the anthology produced by Madurell i Marimon (1974) of archival documents that contain information on the possession of books in Catalunya, of a total of 147 inventories, approximately 10 per cent record Arthurian manuscripts, which gives an impression that one in every ten owners of books had an Arthurian manuscript; the proportion is fairly high considering that the majority of these references involve a very small number of titles. The best-represented title is the *Conquesta del Sant Grasal* (which refers to the Catalan version of the *Queste del Saint Graal* or *Stòria del Sant Grasal*), and there are also various cases of a *Tristany*, but those of *Lancelot* are few and there is a single *Merlin*. Most of these must have been copies in Catalan.

[12] Pere III also had a tapestry on the 'istoria Militum Mensa Rotunda' and another on the 'istoria del rey Artús', which the inventories describe (Riquer 1989). See also, on the Arthurian manuscripts and the literary enthusiasms of the royal house, Riquer (1994), and the classic study of Pagès (1936).

[13] According to Cingolani (1992–3b), the Arthurian cycles in prose would have spread in stages in Catalunya: firstly, during the reigns of Jaume II, Alfons III and Pere III, the works would have been read in the original language. Later, they would have been translated into Catalan, through the intervention of Joan I; and only from the XVth century would they have truly influenced vernacular literary production.

[14] For Entwistle (1922, 1925), Leonor would have contributed decisively to the penetration of Arthurian material into the Iberian Peninsula; not so for Deyermond (1984), for whom her role would have been limited to favouring the diffusion in Castile of the work of Geoffrey of Monmouth, which was already known in Navarre.

[15] See Cardim (1923) and Paredes Núñez (1993) for the sources of the *Livro das Linhagens*, and Barrick (1961) and Beltrán Llavador (1994) for those of the *Victorial*.

[16] Edited by Contreras Martín and Sharrer (2006), Bogdanow (1999a) has offered the details of the correspondences between *Lançarote* and the *Lancelot propre* in the edition by Sommer (1908–16); while the second book (fols 1–277*r*) corresponds to volumes III, 429.29–IV, 71.37, and IV, 72.9–431.24, book III (fols 278*r*–350*v*) corresponds to vols IV, 341.25–358.15, V, 67.15–138.24, and V, 147.37–193.25.

[17] As stated by its *explicit*, which the XVIth-century copyist reproduced: 'Aqui se acava el segundo y tercero libro de don Lançarote de Lago y ase de comenzar el Libro de don Tristan, y acabose en miercoles, veinte y cuatro dias de octubre, año del nasçimiento de Nuestro Salvador Jhesu Christo de mill e quatroçientos y catorze años' (f. 355*v*).

[18] Deyermond (1997) has suggested that this 'libro de pliego entero, de mano, en papel, de rromançe, que es la *Ystoria de Lançarote*, con unas coberturas de cuero blanco' that formed part of the library of Queen Isabel la Católica, according to the inventory of 1503 (Ruiz García 2004), would have contained a complete version of the *Lancelot propre*. Deyermond also alludes to an edition of 1528, the existence of which, as he notes, has never been corroborated.

[19] The links between *Lançarote* and the *Post-Vulgate Suite du Merlin* and the *Tristan en prose* constitute an important aspect of the problem of the Peninsular evolution of the Arthurian cycles in prose; the question was addressed by Bohigas years ago (1924, 1925b). Additionally, Miranda (2004) has taken into account these links in expressing his own particular view of the configuration of these cycles, specifically in proposing that the *Post-Vulgate* which spread through the Iberian Peninsula included a *Lancelot* and a *Tristan*, which should be added to the trilogy reconstructed by Bogdanow (1966).

[20] The most important edition of the *Baladro* of 1498 is that of Bohigas (1957–62), while that of Hernández (1999), contains, alongside the transcription and some studies, a facsimile reproduction of the incunable. The Toledo (1515) *Demanda* has not been published, although the Seville (1535) edition has been, the two books of which were published by Bonilla y San Martín (1907). The most important general studies on these printed editions continue to be those of Bohigas (1925a) and Bogdanow (1966, 1991–2001). On some of the principal innovations, see Michon (1996), Lendo Fuentes (2003) and Gracia (2012).

[21] On this question see Cuesta Torre (1993c), Ros Domingo (2001), Alvar (2001), Soriano Robles (2003a), and Beltrán (1996). The Italian thesis was formulated by Northup (1912, 1913–14), but has been taken up again on various occasions, in high-quality studies such as that by Heijkant (1989); see also Iragui (1996).

[22] There are editions by Northup (1928) and Corfis (1985).

[23] MS 20262/19 was edited by Bonilla y San Martín (1904); the fifty-nine fragments of MS 22644 were published by Alvar and Lucía Megías (1999).

[24] Edited by Cuesta Torre (1999a) and Bonilla y San Martín (1912).

[25] Edited by Cuesta Torre (1997e).

[26] The attribution is by Gómez Redondo (1988); the article has a careful edition of the letters.

[27] The best edition is by Di Stefano (1988); see Cuesta Torre (1997c) on the problems presented by the ballad.

[28] See Chicote (2001). The Lancelot ballads were edited by Catalán (1970).

[29] For a general study, see Gutiérrez García and Lorenzo Gradín (2001) and also Castro (2001).

[30] Possible representations of Arthurian subjects, related to the legends of Tristan and Lancelot, have also been identified in the south of the Peninsula, in the paintings that decorate the Sala de Justicia at the Alhambra in Granada. The paintings were created in the reign of Muhammad V, in the mid-XIVth century (Dodds 1979; Robinson 2008).

[31] Edited by Carter (1967); see also Castro (1976–9) and Bogdanow (1960b).

[32] This involves three folios that were part of the binding of two incunables, corresponding to chapters 380–1 and 494–6 of the edition of Roussineau (1996). It was described by Soberanas (1979), who edited the text and studied it in detail; there is another edition in Lorenzo Gradín and Souto Cabo (2001: 197–200).

[33] The *Demanda do Santo Graal* has been published on various occasions. The most interesting editions are those of Magne (1955–70), which gives a facsimile reproduction of the manuscript as well as its transcription, and Piel (1988), which was completed by Freire Nunes. Freire Nunes (1995a) in turn published an edition, and also the most important study on the work (1999a).

[34] Revealed by Serrano y Sanz (1928). Pensado Tomé (1962) published a detailed study and a careful edition, which included a facsimile reproduction of the folios and a palaeographic transcription as well as the critical edition; Lorenzo Gradín and Souto Cabo (2001: 73–103) offer a palaeographic and critical edition, and a general study. The best works are those of Michon (1991), who compares the Galician version with the French manuscripts, Castro (1998) on language and date of the MS, and Soriano Robles (2006) on the textual filiation of the fragment; also that of Cuesta Torre (1993c) to place the Galician *Tristan* in the overall context of the Peninsular derivatives of the *Tristan en prose*.

[35] Michaëlis de Vasconcelos (1904) edited and studied the *Lais* preserved in Lisbon, relating them to the lyric *lais* contained in the *Tristan en prose*; and Pellegrini (1928) transcribed the version in the Vatican codex. See also for general studies Ferrari (1993), Gutiérrez García and Lorenzo Gradín (2001: 95–109, 191–5), which includes an edition of the five poems.

[36] This was well studied by Catalán (1962), especially in the section on 'El *Libro de las Generaciones* y la historiografía portuguesa del siglo XIV', pp. 357–411, where he collates in detail the sections relating to the history of the kings of Britain in the *Libro de las generaciones*, the *Livro de Linhagens* and the *Crónica de 1404*, and studies the use made by the *Livro de Linhagens* and the *Crónica de 1404* of the *Libro de las generaciones*, as well as the use that this latter in turn made of the *Roman de Brut* of Wace.

As regards the innovations of the *Crónica de 1404*, it seems that the author used a copy of the *Post-Vulgate* cycle that contained all three of its parts (an *Estoire del Saint Graal*, a *Merlin* followed by a *Suite*, and a *Queste del Saint Graal* and *Mort Artu*), which he designated with the title *Estoria del Sancto Grayal*.

[37] See Catalán Menéndez-Pidal (1953: 60–70), Bohigas (1941), Gimeno Casalduero (1975: 103–41) and Tarré (1943).

[38] The text from MS 271 was edited by Bohigas (1928–9); see also his article (1920–2).

[39] The classic, fundamental study is that of Williams (1909); for a general overview, see Avalle-Arce (1990) and Cacho Blecua (1987–8), and, for specific motifs and episodes, see Michels (1935), Gili Gaya (1947), Riquer (1980) and Gracia (1995, 1999).

[40] Butinyà i Jiménez (1990), Ramos (1995) and Badia (1993c).

[41] *La Faula* has been studied by, among many other scholars, Riquer (2005), Badia (1989), Martínez Pérez (1994) and Hauf i Valls (2000).

[42] See also on this episode Alemany Ferrer (2005a, 2005b), and Beltrán Llavador (1983).

[43] This is the case with Cantalapiedra (1990), Lida de Malkiel (1962), Gerli (1983), McGrady (1986), Riquer (1957). Hook (1993) studies the use of the name 'Tristán' for the character of the young servant.

II

THE SURVIVING PENINSULAR ARTHURIAN WITNESSES: A DESCRIPTION AND AN ANALYSIS

José Manuel Lucía Megías

1. Some Data on the Medieval Diffusion of Arthurian Witnesses in the Iberian Peninsula

Documentary references for the survival and diffusion of manuscripts of Arthurian material in medieval Castile are few. As Isabel Beceiro has observed (2007: 247), this paucity of information is explained by three causes: firstly, the lack of book-lists from post mortem inventories or gifts around the time of death until the 1430s, which means that we have few documentary sources for approaching the manuscripts that royalty and nobility must have possessed and read before the XVth century; secondly, the fact that all the important documents are from the regions of Castile, León and Extremadura, or from royal sources, which means that we do not have documentation from the area in which most of the Arthurian personal names have been discovered, the Atlantic and Cantabrian fringe; and finally, the fact that all the inventories and gifts involve great lords and ladies.

These factors and limitations do not permit us to draw the true map of the diffusion of Arthurian manuscripts in the courts and in the libraries of Castile, which must have been much more abundant than is recorded in the documentation; this is limited to a handful of manuscripts owned by various nobles during the XVth century. These include Doña Aldonza de Mendoza, wife of the Duke of Arjona and sister-in-law of the Marqués de Santillana, who died in 1435, and who owned three copies of *Amadís de Gaula* and two of *Tristán*;[1] the third Count of Benavente, Don Alonso Pimentel y Enríquez, who had a Bible to which had been added a fragment of the *Baladro del sabio Merlín*;[2] and the *Demanda del santo Grial* owned by the first Count of Haro, Pedro Fernández de Velasco, according to his inventory of 1455 (Lawrance 1984). Nor must we forget the Arthurian manuscripts owned by Queen Isabel I (Ruiz 2004): *Terçera parte de la Demanda del Santo Grial*, the *Ystoria de Lançarote* and a *Merlin* that 'habla de Josepe Avarimartin'.[3] In 1473, Catalina Núñez de Toledo, who was from a family ennobled by Juan II and Enrique IV, bequeathed to the convent of the Visitación in Madrid a *José de Arimatea*. (Cátedra and Rodríguez Velasco 2000: 65–6).

This scarcity of documentary references, and the associated chronological limitation, contrast markedly with the results obtained from the same kind of analysis for the Catalan area. Stefano Maria Cingolani (1990–1) has examined the data from inventories, wills and letters from the beginning of the XIVth century (the reign of Jaume II) to the end of the XVth, and has identified up to sixty references to possession or acquisition of Arthurian texts (see Appendix II.1). Taken together, kings and the higher nobility stand out as habitual owners, although there are some cases of merchants, widows of constables, pharmacists, physicians, churchmen and even a royal inspector of weights and measures, 'pesador de peso real', who had, in their libraries or in their houses, manuscripts of texts relating to Arthurian material or to Tristan. Equally, as also occurs in France, it is *Tristan* (with forty references) and the texts of the *Vulgate* cycle that enjoyed the greatest diffusion.

In turn, among the data retrieved by María Rosario Ferrer Gimeno (2011) from Valencian inventories, we find three references to Arthurian material quite distant from the noble libraries, since the owners are a merchant, a clergyman, and the widow of a baker (see Appendix II.1).

These data enable us to visualise a Peninsular Middle Ages in which the adventures of the knights of the Round Table, in addition to their oral diffusion, enjoyed a notable presence in written form. This presence is not, however, matched by the witnesses that currently survive and those about the existence of which we know.

2. The Surviving or Known Hispanic Arthurian Witnesses

More than 500 manuscripts and fragments of Arthurian texts are known in French, from the XIIth century for texts in verse (from MS French d. 16 of the Bodleian Library, Oxford, which has transmitted Thomas's *Tristan*, and MS 942 of the Bibliothèque Municipale de Tours, which preserves the *Cliges* of Chrétien de Troyes), and the XIIIth century for the prosifications (the oldest being the beginning of the *Vulgate* cycle preserved in MS 255 of the Bibliothèque Municipale of Rennes) (Middleton 2006). More than 500 witnesses, which cannot be more than half of those which must have been circulating during the Middle Ages, without forgetting that more than 70 per cent of the known witnesses transmit just two works: the *Vulgate* cycle, and the prose *Tristan*.

When these statistics for the survival of Arthurian witnesses in French are borne in mind, the state of affairs in the Iberian Peninsula is, by contrast, depressing, since of the hundreds of manuscripts that must have been copied and circulated in Iberia in Castilian, Catalan, Galician-Portuguese and Portuguese during the Middle Ages, we have evidence of only eighteen manuscripts, some of them currently of unknown whereabouts. To these we must add nine printed witnesses. Moreover, the manuscript witnesses are known thanks to some fragments that have survived, and not always in good condition or complete. The fragmentary character of most of the Hispanic Arthurian manuscript material permits us, however, to nurture the hope of further discoveries, like the three made in recent years. These are some Galician-Portuguese fragments of the *Estoria del santo Grial* from the cycle of Pseudo-Robert de Boron (in 2003–6; no. 7 below), almost sixty fragments of an illuminated manuscript in Castilian of *Tristán de Leonís* (2008; no. 22b below), and, recently, a new Catalan fragment of *Tristany* (2010; no. 19 below). On the other side of the coin must be mentioned a witness, known and published some time ago, but now of unknown whereabouts, which remains as a challenge to researchers: a Catalan fragment of the *Vulgate* cycle *Lancelot* (no. 1). To this must be added a fragment in Catalan of the *Storia del Santo Grasal* of the *Vulgate* cycle, which is cited in bibliographies on the basis of a reference by Bohigas (no. 4).

2.1 Witnesses of the *Vulgate* (1215–30) and *Pseudo-Robert de Boron* (1230–40) Cycles[4]

The translations into Portuguese, Galician-Portuguese, Castilian and Catalan of the *Vulgate* cycle and that of *Pseudo-Robert de Boron* are preserved in sixteen witnesses, of which twelve are manuscripts, some of them consisting of just a few folios.

2.1.1. *The Vulgate Cycle*

Few witnesses survive of the final three parts of the cycle, which must have been much better known in the Peninsula than the surviving translations suggest.

2.1.1.a. *Lancelot*

Two manuscript witnesses of *Lancelot* survive.

[1] Private Library of Sr. Francesc Cruzate, of Mataró (whereabouts of the folios currently unknown)
Language: Catalan.
Description: *c.*1340–60. Two fols (original foliation lxxxv–lxxxvj), paper, two columns.
Reused as covers for a XVIth-century account book from Barbastro. Severely cropped outer margin, partially affecting the text.
Edition and study: Bohigas (1962 [1967]), with a partial reproduction of fol. 86.
Bibliography: Sharrer (1977): Aa1; Philobiblon: BITECA, Manid 1175; Mérida (2010): 292.

[2] Arxiu Parroquial de Campos, Mallorca (shelfmark unknown)
Language: Catalan.
Description: *c.*1380–1400. One folio (original foliation: clxxxvij), on vellum. Reused as covers for a more modern book in the same Archive.
Edition and Study: Rubió y Lluch (1903) and Obrador (1903), with a facsimile reproduction of part of one of the folios.

Bibliography: Sharrer (1977): Aa2; Philobiblon: BITECA, Manid 1174; Belenguer (2008); Mérida (2011): 292.

2.1.1.b. *Quête*
Of the *Quête* a single witness survives; the present location of another cited by various scholars remains unknown.

[3] *La Storia del Sant Grasal*. Biblioteca Ambrosiana, Milan: MS I.79 Sup.
Language: Catalan.
Description: Copy dated 18 May 1380, produced by an inhabitant of Mallorca ('Aqast lebre és d'en G. Rexach, lo qual l'a escrit hi acabat dimecras a XVI yorns de mayg de l'any M CCC LXXX', Gimeno Blay 2007: 336). It consists of II + 1–132 + VI folios, on paper, in two columns. Up to fol. 20 initial letters are in blue. Fols 11*v*, 12*r*, 132*v*, 133*r*, 135*v* and 137*r* are blank. The text of *La Storia del Sant Grasal* occupies as far as fol. 130*v*; on fols 131*r*–132*v* has been copied an anonymous *Vita, miracoli e morte di S. Bernardo*, and on the remaining folios a *Vita di Santa Margherita*. The manuscript belonged to the scholar Gian Vicenzo Pinelli, whose library was purchased by the Ambrosiana in 1609.
Editions: Crescini and Todesco (1917), with a facsimile of the first and final folios; Martines (1993).
Bibliography: Sharrer (1977): Ab1; Philobiblon: BITECA, Manid 1240; Mérida (2010): 293.
Studies: Martines (1995b, 1995c, 1996, 2002); Adroher (2005–6).

[4] Unpublished Catalan Manuscript in Mallorca
Sharrer (1977: Ab2): 'Dr. Bohigas informs me of the existence of a fragment of the Catalan *Queste* in a private library in Majorca which he intends to edit. No other information is available.'

2.1.1.c. *Morte d'Artur*
A fragment of 9 printed pages of an incunable is the only known witness of the *Morte d'Artur*.

[5] *Tragedia ordenade per mossen Gras la qual es part de la gran obra dels actes del famos caualler Lançalot del Lac*. Barcelona: Diego de Gumiel, *c*.1496 (according to Haebler 1917: n. 303–5) or Barcelona: Juan Valdés, *c*.1497–8 (according to Cátedra 1986: 80–2). A single fragmentary copy of this incunable is known: Biblioteca de Catalunya, Barcelona, 10-V-39.
Language: Catalan.
Description: 9 leaves, printed in black letter type, survive from an original sixteen.
Edition and Study: Riquer (1984).

Bibliography: Sharrer (1977): Ac1; Philobiblon: BITECA, Manid 1578; Mérida (2010): 293-4.

2.1.2. *The Pseudo-Robert de Boron Cycle*
2.1.2.a
Of the *Estoire del Saint Graal* there survive three witnesses in Portuguese, in Galician-Portuguese, and in Castilian.

[6] *Liuro de Josep Abarimatia intetulado a primeira parte da Demanda do Santo Grial* Archivo Nacional da Torre do Tombo, Lisbon, MS 643
Language: Portuguese.
Description: A copy of about 1543 produced by the copyist Manuel Álvares, from an original dated 1314, as indicated in the colophon. 316 folios (4 + 311 + 1) on paper, in cursive script. It belonged to Teotonio de Bragança, bishop, and founder of the Carthusian house of Scala Coeli in Évora (1598); until the XIXth century it was in the library of that institution. It was acquired around 1834.
Editions: Carter (1967); Castro (1984); Miranda (1988); facsimile edition in the Biblioteca Digital of the Torre do Tombo (http://digitarq.dgarq.gov.pt/details?id=4248673).
Bibliography: Sharrer (1977): Ae3; Philobiblon: BITAGAP, Manid 1140; Mérida (2010): 294.
Studies: Castro (1979, 1998b, 2001, 2002b, 2003-6, 2007, 2008-9); Gutiérrez and Lorenzo (2001); Bogdanow (2003, 2006); Harney (2003); Pio (2007); Neto (2012).

[7] Arquivo Distrital do Porto: PT/ADPRT/NOT/CNSTS01/001/0012 (shelfmark: I/18/2 - 2.12)
Language: Galician-Portuguese.
Description: One folio, vellum, beginning of the XVth century (according to Dias, 2003-6) or the XIVth century (according to Nascimento 2008); it was reused as binding for a notarial manuscript of 1632.
Edition: Dias (2003-6).
Bibliography: Philobiblon: BITAGAP, Manid 3747; Mérida (2010: 294-5).
Studies: Dias (2003-6); Nascimento (2008); Ailenii (2009).

[8] Biblioteca Universitaria de Salamanca: MS 1877 (fols 252*r*-82*r*)
Language: Castilian.
Description: codex of the XVth century; 302 fols (220 × 150 mm), paper; black ink with red capitals. Formerly in the Royal Library (Biblioteca de Palacio), Madrid (*olim* MS 2-G-5).
Editions: Pietsch (1924-5: 1-54); García de Lucas (1998); Lucía Megías (2001a: 460-4).

Bibliography: Sharrer (1977), Ae1; Philobiblon: BETA, Manid 2528; Mérida (2010: 295).

2.1.2.b. *Merlin*
Merlin survives in two manuscript witnesses.

[9] *Suite de Merlin*: Biblioteca de Catalunya: MS 2434
Language: Galician-Portuguese.
Description: First half of the XVth century, three folios, vellum, written in two columns. The old foliation lxvij (half), cxxxij and cxxiij has been preserved; reused as reinforcement in the binding of an incunable edition of the *Chronicon* of Archbishop Antonino Pierozzi, printed in 1491 (Inc. 43–4).
Editions: Soberanas (1979); Lorenzo Gradín and Souto Cabo (2001: 161–72).
Bibliography: Philobiblon: BITAGAP, Manid 1604; Mérida (2010: 296).
Study: Ailenii (2011).

[10] Biblioteca Universitaria de Salamanca: MS 1877 (fols 282*v*–96*r*)
Language: Castilian.
Description: see no. 8 above.
Editions: Pietsch (1924–5: 55–81); García de Lucas (1998); Lucía Megías (2001a: 443–8).
Bibliography: Sharrer (1977), Ae1; Philobiblon: BETA, Manid 2528; Mérida (2010: 296).
Study: Gracia (2007).

2.1.2.c. *Quête* and *Mort Artu*
Two notably different witnesses survive of the *Quête* and *Mort Artu*:

[11] *A historia dos cavalleiros da mesa redonda e da Demanda do Santo Graal*: Österreichische Nationalbibliothek, Vienna: Lat. Ser. Vetus 2594 (*olim* Historia profana 532)
Language: Portuguese.
Description: codex copied *c*. 1425–50; 208 folios, vellum, in two columns. It belonged to Pedro de Navarra y de la Cueva, Marqués de Cábrega, and was purchased for the library in 1671.
Editions: Magne (1944; 1955–71); Buescu (1968); Piel and Freire Nunes (1988); Megale (1988); Freire Nunes (1995a, 2005).
Bibliography: Sharrer (1977), Ae6; Philobiblon: BITAGAP, Manid 1149; Mérida (2010: 296).
Studies: Megale (1991, 2005).

[12] Biblioteca Universitaria de Salamanca, MS 1877 (fols 298v–300v)
Language: Castilian.
Description: See no. [8] above].
Editions: Pietsch (1924–5: 85–9); García de Lucas (1998); Lucía Megías (2001a: 457–9).
Bibliography: Sharrer (1977), Ae1; Philobiblon: BETA, Manid 2528; Mérida (2010: 297–8).

2.1.2.d. *Second Version (Castilian) of the* Pseudo-Robert de Boron *Cycle*
Of this second Castilian manuscript version, now lost, which would have included the *Merlin* and the *Suite*, as well as the *Quête* and the *Mort Artu*, there is evidence only in the form of the following printed editions.

[13] *Baladro del sabio Merlín con sus profecías* (Burgos: Juan de Burgos, 1498)
Known copy: Oviedo, Biblioteca Universitaria: R-33215.
Language: Castilian.
Description: 106 fols, paper. With woodcuts.
Editions: García Morales (1956–60); Bohigas (1957–82); Fuente del Pilar (1988); Hernández González (1999); Lucía Megías (2001a: 429–37).
Bibliography: Sharrer (1977), Ae4; Philobiblon: BETA: Manid 1196; Mérida (2010: 298–9).
Studies: Morros (1988); Cátedra and Rodríguez Velasco (2000); Gracia (2013b).

[14] *La demanda del Sancto Grial* (Toledo: Juan de Villaquirán, 1515)
Known copy: British Library, London: G.10241 (fols 97r–194v) Bound with the first part of no. [15] below.
Language: Castilian.
Description: 194 folios: xcvij–cxciiij; paper, two columns, Gothic type. The first 96 folios of this edition are lacking.
Editions: {1} Partial: Sommer (1907: 545–90); Lucía Megías (2001a: 437–43). {2} Complete: Trujillo (2004).
Bibliography: Sharrer (1977): Ae7; Philobiblon: BETA, Manid 4155; Mérida (2010: 299).
Studies: Gracia (1998).

[15] *Baladro del sabio Merlín con sus profecías + La Demanda del Sancto Grial* (Sevilla: Juan Varela de Salamanca?, 1535)
Known copies: Biblioteca Nacional de España, Madrid: R-3870 (fols. 1r–96r);[5] Universidad Complutense, Madrid: BH FLL Res.244 (lacking the first 9 leaves);[6] Bibliothèque Nationale de France, Paris : Rés. M.Y^2.22); British Library, London: G.10241 (only Part I: fols 1–96v), bound with the copy of no.[14] above; National

Library of Scotland, Edinburgh: G23.a.1a; University of Illinois at Urbana-Champaign, X862D39, Od1535; Newberry Library, Chicago, Case YA 14.21.
Language: Castilian.
Description: 4 (flyleaves) + 202 fols: [1] + ij-xcj + xcvij + xcvij^{bis}–cxciiij + [8: indexes] + 4 (flyleaves), paper, two columns in Gothic type.
Edition: Bonilla (1907).
Bibliography: Sharrer (1977): Ae5, Ae8; Philobiblon: BETA, Manid 4157; Mérida (2010: 298–300).
Studies: Miranda (2004); Gracia (2010b).

2.1.3. *Parallel Version of the* Lancelot *and the* Pseudo-Robert de Boron[7]
[16] *El segundo y tercero libro de don Lançarote de Lago:* BNM, MS 9611
Language: Castilian.
Description: XVIth-century copy from an original of 1414. 355 folios, on paper (lacking folios 6, 280 [278], and 281 [279]).
Editions: {1}. Partial: Klob (1902), fol. 150, 310*v*–11*r*; Bonilla y San Martín (1913), fols 119*r*–21*v*, 261*r*–6*v*, 281*r*–5*r*; Bohigas (1924), fols 351*v*–5*v*; Lucía Megías (2011: 448–57). {2}. Complete: Sharrer and Contreras (2006).
Bibliography: Sharrer (1977: Aa3); Philobiblon: BETA, Manid 117; Mérida (2010: 292–3).
Studies: Bohigas (1924, 1925a, 1925b); Lucía Megías (1994); Contreras (1997, 2000, 2002d, 2005d, 2006a); Chicote (2001); Correia (2010, 2012).

2.2 Surviving Witnesses for the *Tristan en prose*
The existence of six manuscript witnesses for *Tristán de Leonís* is known, besides a successful printed edition of 1501 which saw at least four reprintings during the first decades of the XVIth century from the presses of several different Seville printers.

[17] Arxiu de les Set Claus de Andorra: MS 1 (fols 32*r*–35*v*)
Language: Catalan.
Description: Four fols, second half of the XIVth century or beginning of the XVth, with modern foliation (32*r*–35*v*) and old foliation (xxxiij–xxxvi), in a factitious codex entitled *I llibre de privilegis*; paper, cursive script, two columns.
Editions: Aramon i Serra (1969).
Bibliography: Sharrer (1977): Ad1; Philobiblon: BITECA, Manid 2416; Mérida (2010: 300).
Study: Santanach i Suñol (2003).

[18] Arxiu Històric Comarcal, Cervera. Shelfmark B-343 (but currently of unknown whereabouts)
Language: Catalan.

Description: Four fols of the late XIVth century; paper, which formed part of the binding of a more modern manuscript.
Editions: Duràn i Sanpere (1917).
Bibliography: Sharrer (1977), Ad2; Philobiblon: BITECA, Manid 2175; Mérida (2010: 300).
Studies: Soriano (1999b); Ros Domingo (2001).

[19] Biblioteca de Catalunya, Barcelona: MS 8999/1
Language: Catalan.
Description: Two folios, XVth century. Donated to the Biblioteca de Catalunya on 18 July 2008 by Eulàlia Durán. They contain two separate sections of the work.
Bibliography: Philobiblon: BITECA, Manid 2175; Mérida (2010: 300).
Study: Santanach i Suñol (2010).

[20] Archivo Histórico Nacional, Madrid:[8] Códices Leg. Carp. 1501 B, n. 7
Language: Galician-Portuguese.
Description: 2 fols, last third of the XIVth century. Found in the binding of the will of the Marqués de Santillana, in the Archivo Histórico Nacional, with the shelfmark Leg. Carp. 1501 B, n. 7 (*olim* leg. 1267, no. 10$_2$; leg. 1762, num. 8$_7$), made in Guadalajara in 1551.
Editions: Serrano y Sanz (1928); Pensado Tomé (1962); Lorenzo Gradín and Souto Cabo (2001: 73–103).
Bibliography: Sharrer (1977): Ad3; Philobiblon: BITAGAP, Manid 1483; Mérida (2010: 301).
Studies: Soriano (1999a); Lorenzo Gradín and Díaz Martínez (2004); Ailenii (2010).

[21] *Cuento de Tristán de Leonís:* Biblioteca Apostolica Vaticana, MS Vat. Lat. 6428
Language: Castilian (Aragonese).
Description: 131 folios, lacking the first five; written in two columns; paper. The text is marked by numerous duplications.
Editions: Northup (1928); Corfis (1985); Lucía Megías (2001a: 473–9).
Bibliography: Sharrer (1977): Ad5; Philobiblon: BETA, Manid 1304; Mérida (2010: 301).

[22] Biblioteca Nacional de España, Madrid: [a] MS 20262$_{19}$ (Bonilla Fragment) and [b] MS 22644$_{1-51}$ (Alvar-Lucía Fragments)
Language: Castilian.

[22a]
Description: One folio, paper. Reused as wrapper for some notebooks of Agustín Durán, which contained his notes on the *Diablo Cojuelo* of Vélez de Guevara.

Edition: Bonilla y San Martín (1904).
Bibliography: Sharrer (1977): Ad4; Philobiblon: BETA, Manid 1462; Mérida (2010: 302).

[22b]
Description: Fifty-nine fragments from the same XVth century MS, with 20 miniatures (on fragments 6r, 8v, 9v, 11v, 14r, 17v, 18v, 20v, 39r, 39v). These were retrieved from the original binding of MS 12915 of the Biblioteca Nacional de España, in which there still remain traces of some miniatures.
Edition: Alvar-Lucía (1999).
Bibliography: Philobiblon: BETA, Manid 4507; Mérida (2010: 302).
Studies: Lucía Megías (1998b, 2001b, 2005a, 2008); Alvar (2001).

[23] *Libro del esforçado cavallero don Tristán de Leonís* (Valladolid: Juan de Burgos, 1501)
Language: Castilian.
Known copies: British Library, London, C.20.d.24.
Description: 94 folios (a–l$_8$ m$_6$). Lacks title page and fols 1–2 (supplied in MS with a titlepage and list of chapters) and 73. Paper, two columns, printed in Gothic type.
Editions: Bonilla y San Martín (1912); Cuesta Torre (1999a); Lucía Megías (2001a: 479–86).
Bibliography: Sharrer (1977): Ad7; Philobiblon: BETA, Manid 4153; Martín Abad (2001: no. 1491, p. 497); Mérida (2010: 303).
Studies: Eisele (1981); Cuesta (1993b; 2002).

[24] *Libro del esforçado cavallero don Tristán de Leonís* (Sevilla: Jacobo Cromberger, 1511)
Language: Castilian.
Known copy: Library of Congress, Washington, DC: PQ 6437.T8 1511 (Rosenwald Collection no. 1273).
Bibliography: Martín Abad (2001: no. 1492, p. 497); Mérida (2010: 303).

[25] *Libro del esforçado cavallero don Tristán de Leonís* (Seville: Juan Varela de Salamanca, 1520, 16 June)
Language: Castilian.
Known copies: No surviving copy known. The edition is recorded in the *Regestrum* of Ferdinand Columbus (Fernando Colón), no. 4008, a copy acquired on 12 November 1524 in Valladolid at a cost of 68 maravedís.
Bibliography: Martín Abad (2001: no. 1493, p. 497); Mérida (2010: 303).

[26] *Libro del esforçado cavallero don Tristán de Leonís* (Seville: Juan Varela de Salamanca, 1525, 24 July)

Language: Castilian.
Known copies: Bibliothèque Mazarine, Paris (370) and Biblioteca Nazionale, Turin (Ris. 24-11).
Bibliography: Mérida (2010: 303).

[27] *Libro del esforçado cauallero don Tristán de Leonís y de sus grandes fechos en armas* (Seville: Juan Cromberger, 1528, 4 November)
Language: Castilian.
Known copies: Biblioteca Nacional de España (R-8.522); British Library, London (G.10259); Pierpont Morgan Library, New York (E-22.48E).
Bibliography: Philobiblon: BETA, Manid 4158 (Mérida (2010: 303).
This printed text gave rise to two original creations in the XVIth century: the *Carta de Iseo y respuesta de Tristán* (Biblioteca Nacional de España, MS 22021, fols 8v–12v), inserted into a codex containing various works of sentimental fiction by Diego de San Pedro (partially edited by Sharrer, 1981–2, and in full by Gómez Redondo, 1987); and a new romance of chivalry that narrates the adventures of *Tristán de Leonís el joven*, printed at Seville in 1534, edited by Cuesta Torre (1997e).

3. Towards a Typology of the Arthurian Witnesses: the Triumph of the Common Chivalric Codex

Barely a score of manuscript witnesses have transmitted the surviving part of the traditions and adaptations of the material relating to Arthur and Tristan that must have been produced in the Iberian Peninsula during the Middle Ages. Of these, only five are complete codices; the rest are fragments that have survived, in the majority of cases, through being reused as part of the bindings of other works during the XVIth and XVIIth centuries, or have survived as part of factitious manuscripts. Both the complete manuscripts and the information that we can extract from the roughly seventy-seven folios surviving as fragments allow us to formulate a typology concerning the codicological model that dominated the diffusion of Arthurian material in written form in Spain in the XIVth and XVth centuries, which we can describe as the 'common chivalric manuscript'.

Elisa Ruiz (1998) established the following typology for XVth-century Castilian manuscripts: (1) courtly manuscripts, whether these be 'pure' or 'Gothicising' humanistic, devotional or pseudo-courtly; (2) ecclesiastical; and (3) common, among which there may be distinguished recreational books, instructional books (known also as desk books, study books, or professional books), and personalised books.

As may be imagined, the courtly books are the most costly copies, created to be enjoyed by the eyes and hands of royalty and nobility. These have been preserved on the shelves of the most prestigious and best-endowed libraries; they are luxury objects which have circulated little, but have remained in the possession of their owners, and after them their heirs. In the Hispanic context, we have just one courtly chivalric manuscript: MS Esp. 36 of the Bibliothèque Nationale de France, which contains the *Libro del cavallero Cifar*, and which dates from the final third of the XVth century; it was commissioned by King Enrique IV of Castile. The codex, of 100 folios with vellum for the first leaf and paper for the remainder, measures 400 × 260 mm, and contains 262 miniatures. Among these there stand out those produced in the studio of Juan Carrión, one of the most prestigious of medieval Castile, who was active in Ávila and Segovia from around 1440 until the 1470s. Besides the *Cifar* manuscript (and numerous oil paintings and altarpieces), in his workshop were illuminated the initials of the *Historia romana* of Orosius, now preserved in Cambridge, Fitzwilliam Museum, and most notably the *Libro de la monteria* by Alfonso XI (Royal Library, Madrid, MS 2105), with the arms of Enrique IV of Castile, from which there survive six miniatures of the original iconographic programme which must have consisted of fourteen.

This sole representative of the 'courtly chivalric codex', produced at the court of Enrique IV of Castile, appears in 1526 in the inventory of the manuscripts belonging to Margaret of Austria, the younger sister of Philip the Fair: 'Item ung aultre grant [livre] à deux cloans d'argent, qui ce nomme Cavaliers Syfer en Espaignol', from the library of Charles de Croy, which she had acquired in 1511. From the library of Margaret it passed to that of her niece, Maria of Hungary, sister of the emperor Charles V, as may be seen in the inventory of 1565: 'Aultre grand livre nommé Cavalier Syfar en espaignol ave[c] deux cloans d'argent'. From then on, it is cited consecutively in the inventories of the library of the Dukes of Burgundy in 1577 and 1614–17, as follows: 'Le Cavalier Sifar en espaignol, couvert de cuir, escript à la main en papier, illuminé' (MS Fr. 5675, fol. 93v, no. 636). In 1796 it was transferred from Brussels to Paris together with a large number of manuscripts from the Burgundian library, and passed directly into the holdings of the Bibliothèque Française, where it has remained ever since (Lucía Megías 1996a).

Whilst in XVth-century France there triumphed the courtly chivalric codex, transformed into a luxury product rather than serving as the transmitter of a specific text with its specific adventures and teachings, to meet the expectations of the ever more flourishing bibliophile market (Middleton 2006: 49), in the Iberian Peninsula the model of the common chivalric manuscript developed. This falls within the category of 'recreational books' that make up the greater part of the holdings of the libraries of the XVth century, and which is characterised by the range and heterogeneity of both its consumers and its content. The category of 'recreational books' is made up of works whose content satisfied a wide section of the population, from a readership of little learning to the most demanding reader. It involved a literature conceived as a means of amusement, that is to say, that swathe of works which was classed in Italy as 'libri volgari'. The most characteristic features of such copies, containing texts in the vernacular, were their modest material format and their archaising appearance. The product was manufactured frequently by copyists whose professional work was in administration; some were put together by individuals for their own use. Hence most of the resulting manuscripts have as a common denominator the fact that they are written in cursive Gothic script (Ruiz 1998: 418).

When we consider the surviving single-text chivalric codices (including the XVIth-century copies following medieval models), as well as the loose folios that have come down to us, we see that in the great majority of cases we find the same characteristics (Appendix II.2). They are produced on paper (or on low-grade vellum), they are of middling size (around 280 mm in height), and with a wide variety of types of gatherings; all of these characteristics suggest production not with the object of satisfying a patron by the preparation of a 'livre de luxe', but quite the reverse: to offer a product for rapid consumption aimed at a wide spectrum of purchasers, whence the low quality of the writing platform and the scanty care taken over the presentation of the volumes. It is necessary only to compare the workmanship and the external characteristics of the manuscript of the *Libro del cavallero Cifar* preserved at the Bibliothèque Nationale de France with that in the Biblioteca Nacional de España (MS 11309), from the beginning of the XVth century, which provides a good example of the 'common chivalric codex', with its 195 paper folios, measuring around 290 × 210 mm, without any ornamentation whatsoever. To this type of codicological product (which must have enjoyed a certain success in the embryonic publishing industry of the late Middle Ages) could also be assigned the codices which spread the original chivalric works composed in Castilian and Catalan during the Middle Ages: *Amadís de Gaula* (Bancroft Library, Berkeley, California: BANC MS UCB 115), *Curial e Güelfa* (BNM, MS 9750), and *Tirant lo Blanc* (l'Arxiu de la Diputació de València, fons de la Duquesa d'Almodovar, e.4.1, caixa 15).

One of the characteristics that has been singled out for these 'common' books is the absence of any kind of decoration; the initial letters have scanty filigrees, and there is a complete absence of miniatures. In the context of the Hispanic witnesses, we have one exceptional case: the Castilian codex of *Tristán* (MSS 20262_{19} and 22644_{1-51} of the Biblioteca Nacional de España), which attests the existence of a subtype of the common chivalric codex, namely, its illuminated variant. Its miniatures, however, are characterised not by occupying a specific space in the body of the folio, but by being located in the lower margin or in the blank spaces at the end of a chapter, produced with a simple sketch, with a little colour. This is a model of production that we find in Arthurian codicological traditions separate from the French model, such as the Italian, as may be seen in the late XIVth- or early XVth-century codex that contains the French *Compilation* of Rustichello da Pisa (BNF, MS fr 1463) (Cigni 1992). What is surprising, from our present perspective, is that this illuminated variant of the common chivalric codex should have suffered the same fate as the great majority of the Peninsular Arthurian witnesses: to be sold by weight for reuse in bindings of the period.

In a manner parallel to the codicological model of the common chivalric codex, the Arthurian works – understood not as a textual unit but as a source of other textual models – also enjoyed a certain diffusion in medieval Castile. Thus we encounter such material in Book II of the *General Estoria* of Alfonso X in relation to the *Historia regum Britanniae* of Geoffrey of Monmouth ('Estoria de Bretaña en latín') and in the *Libro de las generaciones*, which uses as a textual source the *Roman de Brut* of Wace (Catalán 1962), and which, in its turn, became the source for other works (*Livro das linhagens* of Don Pedro Count of Barcelos, the *Crónica de 1344*, and the *Crónica de 1404*), which modified some of the Arthurian information on the basis of material obtained from the *Pseudo-Robert de Boron* cycle. But beyond the multiple echoes (more or less quoted textually) which can be found in a good proportion of medieval Hispanic literature (which is only to be expected if we bear in mind its oral and written diffusion beyond that which the surviving witnesses attest), it is now important to rescue these cases of 'textual fragments' of Arthurian material inserted in longer works, which can even modify their textual nature. The example of the *Bienandanzas e fortunas* of Lope García de Salazar can be a good counterpoint to assist us to understand and characterise the manuscript preserved at the Biblioteca Universitaria in Salamanca, which documents a particular form of the diffusion of Arthurian material, very distant from that represented in the model of the common chivalric codex analysed above.

Among the witnesses recorded by Sharrer (1977) for the Hispanic diffusion of the *Pseudo-Robert de Boron* cycle, we find the following entry, which was not included in the list given earlier in this chapter:

[Ae2] Castilian fragments in Lope García de Salazar's *Libro de las bienandanzas e fortunas* (compiled between 1471 and 1476), in MS copy (dated 1492 by the scribe Cristóbal de Mieres), Madrid, Real Academia de la Historia, 9–10–2/2100 (*olim* 12–10–6-17), fols 183*r*–189*r* (also in Madrid, Biblioteca Nacional, MS 1634 (*olim* G-4), a 16th-cent. copy of the Mieres text).

As Sharrer noted, rather than being a copy of a specific witness, what Lope García de Salazar did was to use the Arthurian texts of the *Pseudo-Robert de Boron* cycle as the main source when he came to relate in his work the history of Great Britain, beginning his account with the foundation of the kingdom by Brutus, the arrival in England of Joseph of Arimathea with the Holy Grail, and the birth of Merlin, and ending it with the reign of King Arthur. In this way, this historian's approach was that he 'condenses and summarizes the three branches of the *Roman du Graal* as part of his history of England' (Sharrer 1977: 36). The text can now be read in modern editions by Marín Sánchez (1999) and Villacorta (2000).

The textual exploitation of Geoffrey of Monmouth by Salazar turns these stories into 'historical sources', which, as such, he can adapt to his ideological interests (in the same way as would have happened, for example, in the Alfonsine scriptorium). This reuse can give us the key to understanding the appearance of three Castilian extracts from the *Pseudo-Robert de Boron* in a wisdom anthology such as that

preserved in Salamanca's Biblioteca Universitaria, MS 1877, which, according to the index that appears at the end, originally must have been composed of the following works:

> En este libro son conpilados onze tratados. [1] ¶ El primero se llama libro del arra del anima. De como se rrazona el cuerpo con el anima e el anima con el cuerpo. E aun es llamado dialogo. [2] ¶ El segundo de la vida de Sant Macario e de Sergio e Alchino. En como fueron ver su santa vida a una cueva cerca el parayso terrenal. [3] ¶ El tercero de la vida de Berlan e del infante Josafa. [4] ¶ El quatro tratado de las vidas de los sanctos padres. [5] ¶ El quinto es de Frey Johan de Rocaçisa. [6] ¶ El sesto de Josep de Abarimatia, e el qual es llamado del Sancto Grial, que es la escodilla en que comió Nuestro Señor Jesu Cristo el jueves de la çena con sus discipulos, en la qual escodilla cogió Josep la sangre del nuestro salvador Jesu Cristo. [7] ¶ El VII. tratado es llamado libro de Merlin. [8] ¶ El VIII. el libro de Tungano. [9] ¶ El IX. de los articulos e sancta fe de los cristianos. [10] ¶ El X fabla de Lançarote e del rrey Artus e su mugier.

The codex has been reordered and some of the folios have been lost (at both beginning and end), so that in its present state the contents are as follows:

ff. 1–94*v*: Libro de las leyes
ff. 95–213*r*: Barlaam e Josaphat
ff. 213*v*–237*v*: Vida de los Sanctos padres
ff. 237*v*–251: Libro que compuso Frey Juan de Rrocacisa
ff. 252*r*–282*r*: El libro de Josep Abarimatia
ff. 282*v*–296*r*: La Estoria de Merlin
ff. 296–298*r*: Libro de los articulos e fe de los cristianos
ff. 298*v*–300*v*: Libro de Lançarote.

We are not faced with a miscellaneous or factitious codex, in which there have been inserted loose folios from a single-text codex that transmitted a complete translation of the *Pseudo-Robert de Boron* cycle, but rather with the use of extracts from the Arthurian stories (from the Holy Grail to the birth of Merlin, ending with a series of adventures from *Lancelot*, in which there is emphasis on the confrontation between families as the origin of the downfall of the kingdom), within a compilation marked by a clear orientation towards religious and wisdom texts. In this way, the Arthurian extracts in the Salamanca manuscript document a different mode of reading and interpretation of the Arthurian material, as an example of the teachings on which the compilation lays emphasis, and they cannot be interpreted as elements independent of the rest of the texts and extracts with which they share a codicological unity (that is to say, a unity of transmission and of reading).

The two fragments of the Catalan *Tristany de Leonis* have been preserved in miscellaneous codices, of a notarial character. The four folios which are, presumably, still preserved in the Arxiu Comarcal at Cervera, and which Duràn i Sanpere studied in 1917 (no. 18 above), recount the beginning of the possible Catalan translation, which corresponds to the

dolorosa naixença de Tristany al temps de morir la seva mare la reina Elisabella. y el rescat, per intervenció de Merlí, del rei Meliadux, encantat per la donzella de la torre perillosa, i de l'infant Tristany, perdut en la forest, Aixa com el segón matrimoni del rei i l'intent d'emmetzinament de Tristany comès per sa madrastra. (Duràn 1917: 284–5)

On their position in the miscellaneous manuscript we have no information other than the words with which Duràn began his work (1917: 284): he states that while sorting some documents of notarial origin in the Arxiu Municipal de Cervera, he was surprised to encounter some folios containing a literary work in Catalan prose, and that his surprise was increased by the realisation that this was a fragment, no less interesting for being brief, of the Catalan version of *Tristany de Leonis*. He notes that it would be difficult to determine how this precious sample of ancient Catalan literature could have come to form part of a quire ('plec') of notarial documents, inventories, and contracts of different dates and completely unconnected ('deslligats') with one another. Now, the two folios currently preserved at the Biblioteca de Catalunya (no. 19 above) were found in Duran's working notes, so that they could equally well have formed part of some other factitious codex upon which he had been working.

Of the other four folios preserved at the Arxiu Històric Nacional of Andorra, of the other Catalan translation of *Tristan en prose*, we have much more information thanks to the exhaustive study by Santanach i Suñol (2003). The codex, which belonged to the Arxiu de les Set Claus (where Aramon i Serra knew it; no. 17 above), contains, as in the previous case, a considerable number of texts and documents of extremely heterogeneous character and varied origins, which, as one might expect, is composed to a great extent of legal documents and juridical documents referring to the valleys of Andorra: privileges (with a complete copy of the *pariatge* of 1270, a partial copy, and a translation into Catalan), claims, agreements, etc. (Santanach i Suñol 2003: 418), together with a series of texts of scientific and medical content, some works of spirituality, an incomplete treatise on the administration of the sacraments, and finally some literary texts, giving a total of thirty-five different texts. Among the latter are the *Tristany de Leonis* and an incomplete version of the *Doctrina puerill* of Ramon Llull, which should more properly be classed under the heading of doctrinal rather than literary works. Where could this miscellaneous codex have come from? Was it formed, casually and fortuitously, from fragments and loose folios found at the Archive, as seemed to be the case with the *Tristan* fragments from Cervera, or did it have some practical purpose? Until a few years ago the former of these two hypotheses was favoured, and the formation of the manuscript was placed at the end of the XVIIth century when the Consell General de les Valls d'Andorra began a policy of transcription and conservation of the privileges and legal documents that had been granted by the previous Councillors; but Santanach i Suñol has formulated a new hypothesis on the nature of the codex and its date. According to this, we would not be dealing with what might be termed an administrative juxtaposition (for a purely archival function) of a series of documents encountered by chance, but with a collection of very precise documentation for the work of a notary, Miquel Ribot d'Aixirivall, who practised in the valleys of Andorra during the last third of the XVth century and the first years of the XVIth. Four of the documents preserved in this miscellaneous codex are copied, with identical errors, in his *Llibre de la terra d'Andorra*, compiled between 1486 and 1497, which is kept in the Arxiu de les Set Claus (MS 12), and in the copy of the folios of the *Doctrina pueril* there is a series of marginal annotations made by the notary himself.[9] This perspective seems to me to be more in keeping with the methods of work of the period than the view, always negative, always random, given of miscellaneous codices as a mere mixed bag where everything is jumbled together with neither reason nor logic. From this new codicological perspective, what significance should be attached to the inclusion of four folios (those numbered 33–6 from a complete codex, now lost) of *Tristany de Leonis* in this compilation of a notary's working collection? Were they included because they were from a literary work (which seems less than logical in the context of its transmission), or because of their contents? In the Andorra fragment there are related the doubts and regrets of Tristan when he has married 'madona Isolda de les Blanxes Mans' but cannot forget 'Isolda la Bronda'; the arrival of the news of the marriage at the court of King Arthur and King Mark; the rage and sadness of Isolda, who sends her faithful servant Brangina to King 'Coel de la Petita Bretanya' with a letter for her lover, which leads him to take the decision to abandon his wife to return to the arms of his mistress, a journey that he undertakes with Gedis, his brother-in-law, with whom he arrives at the Gasta Forest in the 'regisme de Longres', where he learns of the disappearance of King Arthur in the Forest five months previously, from a hermit who shelters them on their first night.

A marginal note on fol. 33*r* of the codex, in small and irregular writing, dated by Santanach to the XVIth century, may give us the key to the reason for the preservation of this fragment of *Tristany*: 'Car si en matrimonis d'i demanave egalldat en nosaltres se trobaria [?] ayxi de persones com en etat ho [...] d'onors y d[a]cors tals sa des ... quan sens demostransa de ninguna tamor [?] la .i. a l'altr[a].' Were these folios of the Catalan *Tristany*, taken from a complete codex of the work (now lost), preserved as an 'authority' on a legal case involving matrimony, on a notarial question, rather than as a sample of a medieval chivalric text? If this hypothesis (a rather bold one, certainly) should somehow modify the 'textual nature' of the Andorra fragment of *Tristany*, this nuancing would not affect in the least the actual textual form which has been transmitted, since it has not been incorporated within another textual unit (as certainly happens in the Salamanca codex), but is instead preserved among the working papers of a notary, in a manuscript codex in which he brought together diverse materials for his professional purposes, and which could be classed as a 'codicological compilation'.

4. The Paucity of the Hispanic Witnesses of Arthurian Material: Some Hypotheses

With the data set out above, we are in a position to advance some hypotheses on the various causes that may permit us to explain the paucity of surviving Hispanic manuscript witnesses for the material relating to Arthur and to Tristan. These range from general factors (the need for paper and vellum in the expanding publishing industry, and the removal of works of entertainment from the great noble libraries of the period) to some more precise ones, such as the triumph, in publishing terms, of the Castilian romances of chivalry among contemporary readers, with the resulting marginalisation of manuscript transmission during the first half of the XVIth century.

The growing number of scholars devoting themselves to the study of the surviving manuscript fragments, in their majority from bindings of the XVIth and XVIIth centuries, has led to our beginning to understand that the high proportion of Arthurian fragments in relation to the scanty number of surviving complete codices is in fact a constant feature of the transmission of texts in Iberia. From the notarial protocols of the Archivo Histórico Provincial of León, for example, there have been retrieved 543 folios representing 300 manuscripts, while in Catalunya there survive around 2,600 manuscripts dating from before the advent of printing, while about 7,000 fragments have been recorded, representing some 3,000 different manuscripts (Alturo i Perucho 1999: 16; Mundó 1980). In the BITAGAP section of the Philobiblon database, more than 130 Galician-Portuguese fragments have been recorded. In a letter from the Aragonese historian Jerónimo de Zurita to the Archbishop of Tarragona, Antoni Agustí, later than 1579–80, announcing that he has bequeathed his books to the Carthusian house of Aula Dei, the writer explains how he had obtained many of them:

> [libros que le habían] costado buen dinero y trabajo, en cuarenta años que han pasado que los voy recogiendo y escapando del poder de impresores y libreros, que andan comprando pergamino para despedazallo; y aún estos dias han venido a mis manos algunos de poder de libreros, que los avían condenado para esto, que son de estimación, y acuden a mí por lo que más vale que a lo que ellos cuesta, tomándolos a peso del pergamino o papel. (cited from Soberanas 1979: 176)

Paper has always been considered to be one of the weakest aspects of the Spanish publishing industry: paper of quality required for printing (almost entirely imported from Italy, with the resulting higher price), and paper of low quality for use in binding or printed products of low price and rapid consumption (bulls, indulgences, images, chapbooks ...). For these reasons, medieval manuscripts (including illuminated ones of the common category) could become a source of income when reading and keeping them had ceased to be a primary concern.

Such 'instrumental fragments' could form part of the bindings (nos 9, 18, 20, 22) or serve as the covers with which later documents or printed editions were protected, thereby being turned into mere paper or parchment with a new function (nos 1, 2, 7, 20). In the first case, the medieval folios of *Amadís de Gaula* were found, and in the second, the leaves of *Tirant lo Blanc* recently discovered at the Arxiu de la Diputació, Valencia, mentioned above.

This economic reality would be combined with two other tendencies, especially in the first half of the XVIth century, which would favour the removal of many of the manuscript chivalric volumes from the libraries in which they had been housed until then. Firstly, the success of the printed romances of chivalry, which would become one of the staples of the burgeoning Hispanic publishing industry (Lucía Megías 2000; 2008), would lead to many of the common chivalric manuscript codices being replaced by printed editions, with more legible Gothic type, and, in the eyes of some, of more modern manufacture. For this reason, it is not surprising that we encounter early printed editions (1498 and 1501) of the Arthurian texts of the *Pseudo-Robert de Boron* cycle and of *Tristán*, which enjoyed considerable publishing success, particularly in the case of the latter. To this factor, which we may class as an aesthetic consideration, there was added another, as the Counter-Reformation gave impetus to methods of control over what was published and what was kept in the noble libraries of Spain: there was an increasing tendency to remove the literature of entertainment from these collections. The case of the library of the Marqués de Astorga, Don Alonso Osorio, may serve as a good example of the 'chivalric scrutiny' to which many contemporary noble libraries were subjected. On 25 July 1573 there was completed the 'Memoria de los libros que don Alonso, mi señor, tiene hoy día de la fecha d'esta memoria', which gives a total of 707 entries (Cátedra, 2002: 242–397). Among these we encounter twenty-seven printed romances of chivalry (including the copy of the *Demanda* printed in Seville in 1535 now found in the National Library of Scotland), as well as a 'Lançarote, escrito de mano'. Twenty years later, on the death of the Marqués, a notarial inventory of his property was drawn up, completed on 3 January 1593. In this second inventory there are 1,203 entries, but no trace is found of any of the printed romances of chivalry, nor of the manuscript chivalric codex listed previously. How many of the medieval chivalric codices that still survived in libraries at this time disappeared during those years, the existence of some of which is known to us now merely because they were sold to printers and booksellers for the reuse of their paper and their parchment?

The second half of the XVIth century is also the time of a return to the manuscript as the means of diffusion of romances of chivalry, given the difficulty of printing the expensive folio editions of these books. There are the years of the manuscript romances of chivalry (Lucía Megías 2004), the years of the diffusion in handwritten manuscripts of unpublished texts, and of copying some medieval codices, as the cases of *Lanzarote del Lago* (no. 16) and the Portuguese *Josep de Abaramatia* (no. 6) make clear.

The triumph of the common chivalric codex as the principal mode of diffusion of material relating to Arthur and Tristan in the Iberian Peninsula, the triumph of the Castilian romances of chivalry as the dominant genre published in the XVIth and XVIIth centuries, the blossoming demand among paper merchants and booksellers for the materials, paper and parchment, of which medieval manuscripts were made, and the spread of ever greater control of possession of works of entertainment in the libraries of the nobility, combined to favour the disappearance of the vast majority of the medieval codices that had spread the stories of the adventures of the knights of the Round Table. The fact that many of these were used to reinforce bindings during this period, or as the covers of documents, has enabled the survival, albeit as fragments or sometimes merely as one or two leaves, of many of the single-text codices that delighted hundreds of readers (and listeners) of the period.

The systematic study of miscellaneous and factitious codices in Peninsular libraries and the work of analysing original bindings dating from the XVIth and XVIIth centuries will lead to further discoveries over the coming years; and, as has been underlined by the fragment of the French *Lancelot* found in the Biblioteca Universitaria at Coimbra (Miranda 2011), used as reinforcement in the binding of a legal text of 1546, these surprises will not be restricted to material in Castilian, Catalan, Galician-Portuguese, and Portuguese.

Appendix II.1

Documentation of Arthurian Witnesses in Inventories, Wills, and Letters of the Catalan Middle Ages (Cingolani 1990–1: 75–90; Ferrer 2001)

1. *Vulgate – Profecies de Merli*

   [1] 1383 (24/XI): Joan I requested from his archive the *Merli* that he owned
   [2] 1408 (3/XI): Pere de Queralt possessed a copy
   [3] 1408 (8, 16, 25/II): Raymon de Mur purchased the *Merlin* that had belonged to Joana de Foix
   [4] 1410: Martí I owned a copy of *Profacies de Merli* in French (surely the same copy as [1])
   [5] 1459 (15/V): Francesc Sunyer owned a *Merli* on paper

2. *Vulgate - Lançalot*

   [6] 1319 (6/VIII): Jaume II gives the infante Ramon Berenguer a *Liber de Lançalot*
   [7] 1321 (10/XII): Jaume II gives the infante Pere a *Lansalot*
   [8] 1334 (1/X): Bernat de Castell owned a 'Lancelot en paper' (he also owned a *Tristan*, no. 42)
   [9] 1339 (8/IX): Pere III paid for a *Lancelot*
   [10] 1346 (17/IV): Pere III paid for a copy of *Lancelot*
   [11] 1362 (17/11): Pere III asked if the *Lançalot* in Catalan that he had requested had been sent to Valencia
   [12] 1374 (?/III): Joan I had a *Lançalot* bound
   [13] 1379 (20/VI): Joan I received a *Lançalot* in French on loan from Francesc de Perellós

[14] 1408 (3/XI): Pere de Queralt owned a *Lencolot* in French, on vellum

[15] 1408 (8, 16, 25/II): Johanni de Sagonia purchases a *Lançalot* in French that had belonged to Joana de Foix

[16] 1418 (19/XI): Jaume Salvador, merchant, sold to the merchant Ramon Canyelles the *Istoria de Lançolot*, in Catalan

[17] 1422 (24/XII) and 1423 (3/II): Berenguer de Copons, Lord of Llor, owned a *Lançalot del Lach*, in French

[18] 1430: Pere Becet owned a *Lanselot* on paper

[19] 1441: *Lancelot del Lach* on paper

[20] 1448: Caterina, widow of the Alguacil Guillem Dezcoll owned a *Lançolot del Lac* on paper

[21] 1466: Joan de Muntreial, merchant, owned a *Lançolot*

[22] 1466 (9/VI): Francesch Camelles, knight, owned a *Lansalot*, on paper

[23] 1488 (21/V): Bertran Ramon, noble, owned a *Lansalot del Lach* in French, on vellum

3. *Vulgate – Queste du Saint Graal*

[24] 1342 (19/XI): Pere III returned to the Monastery of Sigena a *Livro del Sant Graal* that had been stolen

[25] 1400 (8/IV): Joan Sicart, merchant, owned a *Conquesta del Sant Grasal*

[26] 1405 (23/III): Antonia, the widow of Rainer de Ventura, gave to Caterina, wife of Berenguer de Ribes, a box in which there was a *Conquesta del Sant Gresall* on paper, in large format

[27] 1415 (20/XII): A *Sent Greal* was sold by Alamany de Ispania to Arnaut Cupia

[28] 1418 (19/XI): Jaume Salvador, merchant, sold to Ramon Canyelles, merchant, an *Istoria de la Conquesta del Sant Greal* copied by Domingo Folco

[29] 1422 (24/XII) –1423 (2/II): Berenguer de Copons, lord of Llor, owned a copy of the *Libre del Sant Graal* in Catalan on paper

[30] 1423 (29/XII): Guillem de Cabanyelles, merchant, owned a copy of the *Conquesta del sant Gresal* in Catalan on paper

[31] 1437 (5/VIII): Nicolau Quint, merchant, owned a *Sant Greal* in Catalan on paper

[32] 1455: Carles d'Arago, prince of Viana, owned a *Del sent Greal*, in French

[33] 1459 (15/V): Francesc Sunyer owned a *Sant Gresal*, in Catalan, on paper

[34] 1469: Jaume Rovirola, pharmacist, possessed a copy of the *Sant Grazal*, in Catalan

[35] 1484: Juan Despujol, Benifice-holder, owned a *Sanct Gresl*

[36] XVth century: March Roch, physician, owned *Les histories del Sant Gresals*

4. *Vulgate – Mort Artu*

[37] 1349 (28/VII): Pere III ordered in Rosellon a *Tavla retunda* and paid for it in Perpignan on 14/IX/1356

[38] 1410 (but 23/VII/1448): Bernat de Tous, castellan of Tous, owned a *Destrucció de la taula redona*, on paper
[39] 1422 (14/X): Na Tomasa, mother-in-law of Albert de Montergull, owned a *Romanç de la taula redona*, on paper

5. *Roman de Tristany en prosa*
[40] 1315 (17/V): Jaume II gave to the infante Pere a *Librum de Tristany*
[41] 1331 (2/XII): Joan de Mitjavila, merchant, owned a *Romanç de Tristany*
[42] 1334 (1/IX): Bernat de Castell owned a *Tristany*
[43] 1338 (11/X): Bernat de Gualbes owned a *Romansium de Tristany*, in French
[44] 1377: Guillem d'Oms, Benefice-holder, owned a *Liber de Tristany*, on paper
[45] 1383 (17/X): Joan I owned a *Tristan*
[46] 1383 (18/X): Violant requested from Joan I an illustrated *Tristany*
[47] 1392 (11/I): Ramon de Nostranye, rector of S. Miguel de Companet, owned a *Tristany*, on paper
[48] 1396: Bernart de Torrents owned a *Tristany* on paper
[49] 1396: Antonio Camello, painter, owned a *Libre de Tristany*, on paper
[50] 1403 (3/X): Pere Fuster, 'scriptor compotorum universitatis', owned a *Tristany* on paper
[51] 1408 (3/XI): Pere Queralt owned a *Tristany*
[52] 1408 (3/XI): Pere Queralt owned a *Tristany e de Palamedes*
[53] 1410 (but 23/VII/1448): Bernat de Tous, lord of the castle of Tous, owned an *Istories de Tristany*, on paper
[54] 1422 (14/X): Na Tomasa, mother-in-law of Albert de Montergull, owned a *Livre de Tristany*, on paper
[55] 1424 (19/X): Francesc Marques owned a *Tristany*, on paper
[56] 1433 (4/IX): Antoni Solovent, merchant, owned a *Tristany*
[57] 1437 (31/I): Bernat Isern, royal weights and measures inspector, owned a *Tristany de Leonís*, on paper
[58] 1455: Carles d'Aragó, prince of Viana, owned a *Tristany de Leonís*
[59] 1466 (8/III): Juan de Junyent, merchant, owned a *Tristany*, on paper
[60] 1467 (20/VII): Gabriel Gual owned a *Tristany*, on paper

6. References in Valencian documents
[61] 1416: Pere Cardona, merchant, owned a *Tristany* ('Item, altre libre vermell, de paper, vell, apel·lat Tristany')
[62] 1436: Berenguer Vidal, clergyman, owned a *Conquesta del Sant Greal* ('Item, un libre en paper, vell, ab cubertes de fust, appel·lat: Conquesta del Sant Greal')
[63] 1464: Violant Arguilagues, widow of Vicent Arguilages, baker, owned a *Merlin* ('Item, altre libre en paper ab cubertes de perguami [sic] appel·lat: Lo somni de Merli')

Appendix II.2: Table of the Iberian Manuscript Witnesses for the Matter of Britain

N°	title	date	lang.	folios	material	format	cols	script[1]	Illumination
UNITARY CODICES									
1.	*Storia del Sant Grasal-Vulgata* (Milan)	1380 (18 May)	Catalan	132	Paper	272 x 201	2	–	Initial letters (up to f. 20)
2.	*Liuro de Joseph Abaramatia-Pseudo Robert de Boron* (Torre do Tombo, Lisbon)	s. XVI (exemplar: 1313–14)	Portuguese	316	Paper	250 x 190	2	Cursive	NO
3.	*Demanda do Santo Graal-Pseudo Robert de Boron* (Vienna)	s. XV	Portuguese	208	Vellum	300 x 220	2	Libraria	NO
4.	*Lanzarote del Lago-Vulgata* (BNE)	s. XVI (exemplar: s. XV)	Castilian	355	Paper	290 x 200	2	–	NO
5.	*Cuento de Tristán de Leonís* (Vatican)	1390–1410	Castilian	131	Paper	–	2	–	NO
FRAGMENTS OF UNITARY CODICES									
6.	*Lançelot-Vulgata* (Mataró)	s. XIV	Catalan	2	Paper	302 x 205	2	Cursive	Initial letters
7.	*Lançelot-Vulgata* (Mallorca)	s. XIV	Catalan	1	Vellum	290 x 200	2	Cursive	NO
8.	*Quêtel Vulgata* (Mallorca)	s. XV	Catalan	–	–	–	–	–	–
9.	*Liuro de Josep Abaramatia-Pseudo Robert de Boron* (Porto)	s. XIV (or s. XV)	Gal-port.	1	Vellum	277 x 202	2	Libraria	Initial letters
10.	*Suite de Merlin-Pseudo Robert de Boron* (Biblioteca de Catalunya)	s. XIV	Gal-port.	3	Vellum	295 x 137	2	Cursive	NO

11.	*Livro de Tristan* (Archivo Histórico Nacional, Madrid)	s. XIV	Gal.port.	2	Vellum	245 x 195	2	Cursive	Initial letters
12.	*Tristany* (Cervera)	s. XIV	Catalan	4	Paper	225 x 115	1	–	NO
13.	*Tristany* (Andorra)	s. XIV/XV	Catalan	4	Paper	290 x 210	2	Cursive	Initial letters
14.	*Tristany* (Biblioteca de Catalunya)	s. XV	Catalan	2	Paper	300 x 222	1	Cursive	NO
15.	*Tristán de Leonís* (BNE)	s. XV	Castilian	59 + 1	Paper	215 x 70	2	Cursive	Miniatures (20 survive)
TEXTUAL FRAGMENTS									
16. i	*Fragmentos artúricos-Pseudo Robert de Boron* (Salamanca)	s. XV	Castilian	47 (from a total of 302 folios)	Paper	220 x 150	1	Libraria	NO
OTHER CHIVALRIC MANUSCRIPTS (CASTILLIAN AND CATALAN)									
	Libro del caballero Cifar (BNF)	s. XV	Castilian	192	Paper	400 x 260	2		Miniatures (262)
	Libro del caballero Zifar (BNE)	s. XV	Castilian	195	Paper	290 x 210	2		NO
	Curial e Güelfa (BNE)	s. XV	Catalan	228	Paper	294 x 220	1		NO
	Amadís de Gaula (Bancroft)	s. XV	Castilian	4	Paper		2		NO
	Tirant lo Blanc (Valencia)	s. XV	Catalan	2	Paper	310 x 225	2		NO

[1] In all cases, a form of Gothic script is involved; the distinction made is between the formal *Libraria* styles and the less formal *Cursiva* styles.

Notes

[1] Archivo Histórico Nacional, Madrid: Osuna, Legajo 1837, no. 5 (Beceiro 2007: 248). In the first of the known Castilian inventories, that drawn up on 18 November 1430, immediately after the death of Don Alfonso Tenorio (who had become Adelantado of Cazorla, grandson of the archbishop of Toledo Don Pedro Tenorio), mention is made of his modest library, consisting of 24 books (Beceiro 2007: 348–60). Besides various books of jurisprudence appropriate to his profession and some religious works, there stands out the presence of a manuscript of *La Gran Conquista de Ultramar* ('Otro libro escripto en papel toledano a colunas que es la Conquista de Vltramar, las coberturas de papel, el cuero bermejo viejo labrado') and another of *Amadís de Gaula* ('otro libro escripto en papel, toledano el qual es de Amadis las coberturas de papel el cuero prieto labradas').

[2] 'La briuia complida en romançe con vn poco del libro de Merlin en papel çebti mayor con tablas de madero cubiertas de cuero colorado' (Beceiro 2007: 463).

[3] 'Otro libro de pliego entero, de mano, en rromançe, que es la terçera parte de la Demanda del Santo Grial, las cubiertas de cuero blanco' (Ruiz 2004: C1 154, p. 432.); 'Otro libro de pliego entero, de mano, en papel, de rromançe, que es la Ystoria de Lançarote, con unas coberturas de cuero blanco' (a lost manuscript) (Ruiz 2004: C1 195, p. 449); and 'Otro libro de pliego entero, de mano, escripto en rromançe, que se dize de Merlin, con coberturas de papel en cuero blancas, y habla de Josepe Avarimartin' (Ruiz 2004: C1 51, p. 464.)

[4] On the preference for this terminology rather than the more commonly-used 'Post-Vulgate', see Miranda 1998 and 2011, and Laranjinha 2010.

[5] Digitalised in the 'Biblioteca Digital Hispanica': *http://www.bne.es/es/Catalogos/BibliotecaDigital/*.

[6] Digitalised in the Biblioteca Dioscorides de la Universidad Complutense de Madrid: *http://www.ucm.es/BUCM/atencion/24063.php*, and thence in Europeana: *http://www.europeana.eu/*.

[7] On this point I follow the conclusions reached by Miranda (2012) and Correia (2012).

[8] I am grateful to Professor Juan Carlos Miranda for informing me of the rediscovery of this important Arthurian witness.

[9] Santanach's final conclusion, which it is interesting to take into account (Santanach i Suñol 2003: 422–3), is that it is a persuasive idea that Miquel Ribot was the compiler of the documents included in the manuscript at the Arxiu de les Set Claus, and that he could have restricted himself to collecting together only the texts that he knew he was going to copy and read; but that it is worth recalling that the texts are scattered throughout the volume and that it does not appear that they had ever been bound together before being incorporated into the *Còdex miscel·lani*. Santanach suggests that alternatively Ribot could equally well have used a volume put together by someone else before it came into his hands; but that in either case the fact that a single individual consulted various texts which now form part of the *Còdex* before the end of the XVth century makes it unlikely that, if they were not previously bound together, they had still not dispersed two centuries later.

III

ARTHURIAN LITERATURE IN PORTUGAL

Santiago Gutiérrez García

The Diffusion of Arthurian Literature in the West of the Peninsula

Although the study of the Matter of Britain in Portugal may have its own particular features, the process of its diffusion exhibits, in general terms, similar characteristics to those encountered in other areas of the Iberian Peninsula. These arise principally from the existence of a scanty textual tradition, which Nascimento (2008: 130) characterises as 'escassa e não pouco problemática' and which hardly reflects the true extent of the penetration that must have been achieved by the Arthurian stories in the kingdom of Portugal during the Middle Ages. To this must be added the fact that the most complete witnesses of this textual corpus, the *José de Arimateia* and the *Demanda do Santo Graal*, are preserved in late copies, from the XVIth and XVth century respectively. For these reasons it is necessary to resort to other types of sources of information, such as the study of personal names and indirect references, which, in addition to offering a far more ample perspective, precede by at least half a century the first allusions to Arthurian stories in Portugal. Such is the case, for example, with personal names, since while the earliest date that has been advanced for an Arthurian text in Portuguese is in the mid-XIIIth century, the first Arthurian name encountered in Portugal, Merlim, is found in a document of 1190 from Coimbra (Hook 1996: 140–1), with the next earliest being the appearance of Galvam in a document dated to 1208 (Sharrer 1986: 518; Hook 1996: 141).

It is precisely the personal names that reveal Portugal and Galicia to have been areas permeated by an intense Arthurian influence, greater even than that observed in other areas of Iberia such as Castile. In the case of Portugal, Beceiro Pita (2007) observes an earlier diffusion of Arthurian names there in comparison to the centre of the Peninsula, as well as their greater diffusion among the various levels of the nobility, so that, whilst in Castile we do not encounter any real popularisation of Arthurian names until the final part of the XVth century, in the territory of Portugal this had already occurred in the XIVth century. Moreover, Portugal would have served as intermediary between north-west Europe and other areas of Iberia in the propagation of Arthurian names, which spread from this kingdom through Portuguese lineages. These had adopted the fashion of incorporating this type of name among their members and exported this custom when they spread beyond their own area and settled in Castile or married into Castilian families. Amongst others, there are Ginebra

Ribeiro, who married the Galician Nuño Freire de Andrade in the mid-XIVth century; Ginebra de Acuña, wife of another Galician, Gómez Pérez das Mariñas;[1] the Portuguese Silvas, who settled in the Salamanca area during the XVth century and took with them the name 'Tristán'; perhaps the Tristáns of Extremadura, based on the frontier of Badajoz; and, finally, the Castilian lineages of the Dazas and the Niños, who adopted the name Tristán through the influence of Portuguese women, Doña Maria de Silva and Doña Beatriz de Portugal respectively. Perhaps the presence of Arthurian names in the south and the centre of Galicia, reflected in the contemporary documentation from Ourense and the valley of the River Sil (Beceiro Pita 2007: 276–8), may also arise from such Portuguese influence.

The study of cultural influences through onomastic evidence is affected, at all events, by certain factors. The scarcity or the uncertainty of some of the data which it offers limit, for example, any attempt to establish the routes of penetration of the Matter of Britain into Portugal and into the Peninsula as a whole. On this question, the tracing of personal names scarcely casts any further light beyond the information obtained from the analysis of the literary texts, and is focused principally on emphasising the variety of relations which are established among the different territories. For this reason, obscurity still cloaks the routes taken by the Arthurian stories towards their assimilation in the Iberian Peninsula. For similar reasons, scholars suggest a number of possible explanations, a sign that none of these is by itself sufficiently convincing. Hutchinson (1984, 1988), for example, recapitulates the relations between England and Portugal until the end of the Middle Ages as a way of reaffirming the close relations between the two kingdoms and underlining the historical circumstances in which the English could have transmitted these narratives to the west of the Peninsula: the support given by England to D. Afonso I Henriques and his successors; the presence of crusaders from Britain at the conquest of Lisbon, Alcácer do Sal and Silves; the international alliances, such as those established during the Hundred Years War, which brought Portugal to England's side against its adversary Castile, which supported France; episodes related to this military confrontation, such as English aid to Portugal during the war against Castile in 1383–5 and the expedition of John of Gaunt (1386–7); royal marriages, with special attention to that in 1387 which united D. João I and Philippa of Lancaster, daughter of John of Gaunt and sister of Henry IV of England; and, finally, the commercial relations and the arrival in Portuguese harbours, such as Caminha, Vila do Conde, Porto and Lisbon, of English ships. Conde de Lindquist (2006), in turn, has widened the perspective to the Peninsula as a whole and suggests as possible routes the Viking incursions, the alliances with the Plantagenet and Angevin monarchies, pilgrimages along the Road to Santiago, and the Norman and Aragonese influences in Portugal. From the specific point of view of the study of personal names, Beceiro Pita (2007: 266–75) maintains that the greater familiarity with Arthurian onomastics encountered in the regions along the Cantabrian and Atlantic coasts of the Peninsula, especially Portugal, Galicia, and the Basque

Country, would be caused by maritime communication between the ports of those coasts and those of north and western Europe. She adds that it would also be necessary, however, to take into consideration the Road to Santiago, the wars and political events in which Castile, Portugal, England, Brittany and France were involved, and also the greater affinity between feudal structures among the western nobility and the model of vassalage relations and structures reflected in the Arthurian romances. As will be appreciated, many of these arguments are excessively general, since in some cases they involve historical events with no direct link to any precise literary data, and, in other cases, like the marriages between the Spanish and English royal houses, they relate to specific individuals who are not otherwise documented as being involved in the circulation of these works.

One of the latter group of suggestions focuses on the figure of the Portuguese infante Fernando Sanches, son of King D. Sancho II, who was married in 1212 to Joanne of Flanders, Countess of Flanders and Hainaut, to whom Manessier dedicated his *Continuation* of the *Perceval* of Chrétien de Troyes. The link between the Portuguese monarchy and the house of Flanders went back further, since Joanne's mother, Teresa Matilde, was the daughter of D. Afonso I Henriques, while her father, Philip of Alsace, was the dedicatee of Chrétien's *Perceval* (Miranda 1996: 98). All told, the thesis that has gained the widest acceptance among critics associates the diffusion of Arthurian literature in Portugal with the figure of D. Afonso III 'o Bolonhês'. Although it had been formulated by other scholars throughout the XXth century (Michaëlis 1904: II, 512), the author who has contributed the most solid arguments in its favour is Castro (1983). Following him, others have taken up his conclusions, reinforcing the idea that the Arthurian material must have entered Portugal when D. Afonso, Count of Boulogne, returned to the kingdom (Dias 2003–6: 6). This monarch had lived in France between 1229 and 1245, where he had held the title of Count of Boulogne. His participation in French cultural life is attested by the dedication addressed to him by Moniot d'Arras in one of his *chansons*, *Plus aim ke je ne soloie* (Dyggve 1938: 47–56). The vitality of the court of Boulogne and the circles in which his wife Matilde moved is reflected in the inclusion of Philippe Hurepel, the latter's first husband and a bastard son of Philippe II Auguste of France, as a character in the *Roman de la Violette* by Gerbert de Montreuil. On his return to Portugal, it is supposed that D. Afonso would have taken with him a version of the *Post-Vulgate* cycle (1230–40), the completion of which would have taken place a few years earlier, and he himself would have encouraged its translation into Portuguese during the third quarter of the XIIIth century, according to the hypothesis formulated by Michaëlis (1904: II, 512) and taken up by, among others, Lapa (1982a: 315) and Castro (1983, 1988b: 201–2). This is supported by the allusions contained in the Portuguese *José de Arimateia* and the Castilian *Demanda del Santo Grial* to a certain Joam Vivas, who is said to have translated these texts from French.[2] Now Castro (1983: 91–7) documents a Portuguese friar by that name, who belonged to the Order of Santiago, in the mid-XIIIth century. The individual in question owned properties in Lisbon, was related to the monastery of Chelas on the outskirts of that city, and would have been in contact with court circles since he had received one of his properties as a donation from D. Sancho II. However, the role assigned to Afonso III in the propagation of Arthurian material in the Iberian Peninsula is based, once again, not on direct evidence, but on mere conjectures derived from circumstances such as his involvement in literary patronage, his sojourn in France, or the coincidence of dates assigned by critics, not always with definitive arguments, to the first translations of Arthurian texts into Portuguese, or, with greater reliability, to the first indirect Arthurian allusions, such as those contained in the Galician-Portuguese lyric. The documentary weakness of this thesis has been recognised by one of its strongest supporters, who admits that acceptance of it needs to be subject to necessary reservations and to an eventual transition from the possible to the probable (Castro 1988b: 202; 2001: 203).

Leaving aside the dating of the earliest translations since there is no concrete information, the allusions in troubadour lyrics would constitute, as suggested above, another fact on which to base the central role of Afonso o Bolonhês in the diffusion of the Matter of Britain (see the chapter by Pilar Lorenzo in this volume). This is because these allusions are documented from the middle of the XIIIth century, that is to say, approximately after Afonso's return to Portugal. Several of them, however, and specifically the earliest, do not need to be explained in terms of the involvement of the Portuguese monarch. To go no further, Martin Soarez's allusion to a 'Don Caralhote', in *Ũa donzela jaz preto d'aqui* (B1369, V977), does not refer to an episode in the *Post-Vulgate*, but would be a parody of the imprisonment of Lanzarote at the hands of Morgana in the *Lancelot-Graal* (Gutiérrez García 1998).[3] Moreover, although Martin Soarez was a Portuguese troubadour, there is no reason to suppose that the literary information that he uses in his satire could have been obtained only in his native land, since he had frequent contacts with authors at the Castilian court and was even exiled in Castile, at least between 1245 and 1247, as a supporter of D. Sancho II.

Something similar occurs in the case of Gonçal'Eanes do Vinhal, a contemporary of Martin Soarez, who mentions some 'cantares de Cornoalha' in his *Maestre, todo 'lus vossos cantares* (V1007). Although of Portuguese origin, after the coronation of D. Afonso III he settled in Castile, where he spent almost his entire career as a poet. In reality, the first troubadour allusion to the *Post-Vulgate* is found in *Don Gonçalo, pois queredes ir daqui pera Sevilha* by Alfonso X of Castile (B466), in which it is possible that a comparison is made between the target of the composition, Eanes do Vinhal himself, with Baalain, the Knight of the Two Swords in the *Suite du Merlin* (Gutiérrez García 2000–1). Other appearances of Arthurian material in the poetic production of Alfonso X are even more difficult to relate to a specific source. One such case is the miracle from the *Cantigas de Santa María*, no. 108 (*Como Santa Maria fez que nacesse o fillo do judeu o rostro atras, como llo Merlin rogara*), which hints at the existence of a brief narrative, later collected in the *Prophecies de Merlin* attributed to

Richard of Ireland (1276); another is the reference to Arthur as responsible for the resettlement of the town of Dover, contained in *Cantiga* no. 35 (*Esta é como Santa Maria fez queimar a lãa aos mercadores que offereram algo a sua omage, e llo tomaran depois*).

The information outlined above indicates, therefore, a range of different channels by which the Arthurian material entered the Iberian Peninsula, together with a multiplicity of sources and traditions. Whilst all of this does not rule out the possibility that Afonso o Bolonhês may have introduced the *Post-Vulgate* to the Iberian Peninsula, it certainly undermines the importance that literary scholarship, particularly Portuguese literary scholarship, has accorded to him in the Iberian diffusion of this literary cycle. Furthermore, Trujillo (2009: 423) also questions why D. Afonso III should be related to the introduction of the *Post-Vulgate* and not, for example, with that of the *Vulgate*, a cycle which, around 1245, was better known and more accessible than the very recent work of Pseudo-Boron. In the light of the above-mentioned *cantiga* by Martin Soarez, for example, Sharrer (1994: 176, 178) proposes to include the *Vulgate* among the texts that Afonso o Bolonhês would have brought from France, at the same time as recognising that there must have been multiple routes by which the Matter of Britain entered the Hispanic territories. For this scholar there existed two major foci of diffusion, which developed independently of each other, each with its own textual traditions, and which ended up coming together in the centre of the Peninsula. In the west, the *Lancelot-Graal*, *Tristan en prose*, and the *Post-Vulgate* would have reached Galicia and Portugal, while in the east, in Aragon and Cataluña, the first two would have been circulating, but not the *Pseudo-Boron* cycle. In turn, Castile knew the *Vulgate* and the *Post-Vulgate* from western versions, while the *Tristan* would have been known from a Catalan or Aragonese translation (see also Castro 2000: 151).[4]

This explanation of the process of entry of Arthurian material into the Hispanic world and its assimilation there relies, to a great extent, on the surviving texts, which, as stated above, provide only evidence which is deceptive (because it is merely partial) concerning what must have been a much more complex reality. It also depends on the dates that are assigned to the first Iberian versions. Specifically, Sharrer (1994: 178) supposes a Portuguese translation of the *Lancelot* in the mid-XIIIth century, at a date placed between the return of Afonso III and the *cantiga* of Martin Soarez. The latter text would attest not only the circulation of the *Lancelot propre*, but also an Iberian adaptation that would make possible the phonetic play on the similarity between 'Lanzarote' and 'Caralhote'. We insist, however, that nothing obliges us to suppose that Martin Soarez must have known this work in the Portuguese court, with which he would have had only restricted contact precisely in the first years of the reign of Afonso III. Besides, other troubadour allusions would derail the thesis outlined by Sharrer for the diffusion of the literary texts, but from the opposite viewpoint: that is to say, by questioning whether Castile would have known of the cycles of the *Vulgate* and the *Post-Vulgate* through the western realms. This is hinted at by the allusion, already mentioned, to the Knight of the Two Swords by Alfonso X, which would demonstrate an early knowledge of the *Pseudo-Boron* cycle in the centre of the Peninsula. And without leaving the poetic production of Alfonso X, there is the allusion he makes to Lancelot, through the motif of the degrading cart, in *Vi un coteife de mui gran granhon* (B479, V62), which indicates the diffusion of the *Lancelot propre* (Lorenzo Gradín 2008a) or even of a version derived from the *Chevalier de la Charrette* of Chrétien de Troyes (Gutiérrez García 2007b).[5]

As has been observed above, however, the difficulties involved in reconstructing the Hispanic diffusion of Arthurian literature are intensified when the geographical criterion is combined with its chronological equivalent and we move to consideration of when the French texts were translated into the Peninsular languages. The dating offered by Sharrer for the earliest version of a possible western *Lanzarote*, in the mid-XIIIth century, is aligned with other proposals which have tended to place thereabouts the first Iberian translations. Nunes (1908: 226), for example, noticed the proximity between the language of the *José de Arimateia* of MS 643 in the Arquivo Nacional da Torre do Tombo (TT) and that of the troubadours, an observation that has been repeated down to the present (Castro 2001: 203). For his part, Lapa (1982a, 1982b) put back to the second half of the XIIIth century the first Portuguese version of the *Demanda do Santo Graal*, while Dias (2003–06: 198) proposed the final years of that century as the time at which the *José de Arimateia* of MS PT/ADPRT/NOT/CNSTS01/001/0012 (shelfmark: I/18/2 - 2.12) of the Arquivo Distrital do Porto (ST) was produced. All this would fit in with the well-known thesis that brought together in a single phase the diffusion of these French texts and their translation into Portuguese, under the inspiration of D. Afonso III. However, doubts have been expressed about the simultaneity that is claimed for both these processes (Trujillo 2009: 423), with attention being drawn to the fact that in order to bring about the linguistic transfer involved there would need to be both a demand for this by a readership and conditions for assimilation sufficiently developed to carry out the rewriting of the texts. With regard to the first condition, it is not clear that, contrary to the assertion of Castro (1983: 97), the necessary difference existed within the court circle of D. Afonso III. This milieu was so thoroughly imbued with French culture and with so good a knowledge of the *langue d'oïl* that any transfer from one language to the other would have been unnecessary in order to permit comprehension and enjoyment of the Arthurian romances. Despite the fact that the date of its arrival in Portugal remains uncertain, MS A19 of the Biblioteca Geral da Universidade, Coimbra, which contains two fragments of the *Vulgate Lancelot*, could attest this diffusion in the Peninsula of Arthurian texts in French (see Correia and Miranda 2009–11; Miranda 2013). For the second condition to be fulfilled, it would be necessary to suppose a longer lapse of time since the arrival of these texts, or, otherwise, a longer period of coexistence with the texts of the Matter of Britain than that which is being assumed for the prose cycles. In this sense, Gómez Redondo (1999:

1545) considers the first half of the XIVth century the moment at which the assimilation of the French chivalresque narratives is sufficiently developed to permit their rewriting in the various Hispanic languages and, next, for them to coexist with the first vernacular narrative efforts, such as the *Libro del caballero Zifar* or *Amadís de Gaula*. Around these same dates would, finally, be placed the fragments of the Portuguese *Merlim* (Soberanas 1979), or, now in the second half of the XIVth century, those of the Galician *Tristán* (López-Martínez Morás 1999; Lorenzo Gradín and Souto Cabo 2001; Pensado 1962). A similar proposal had been advanced by Lida de Malkiel (1959: 406–7), who emphasised the slowness of the process of assimilation of the Arthurian narratives, in parallel with the lateness of their achieving a widespread diffusion, outside court circles. And, from another perspective, Rossi (1979: 50–60) called into question the translation of the Portuguese *Demanda* in the second half of the XIIIth century, in the light of the maturity of this translation when compared to others produced during the XIVth century, which would therefore, in theory, be later, but which are in fact less polished. In support of his reservations, he points out that many of the archaisms used by Lapa to establish his very early dating for the text survive in other works of much later date, even of the XIVth and XVth centuries, such as the *Horto do Esposo* or the Galician *Miragres de Santiago*.

Alongside the documentary indications, and without denying the validity of conclusions drawn by scholars from this source, it cannot be denied that the tendency to advance the date of the translation of the first Portuguese texts to make it coincide with the reign of D. Afonso III has often been affected by extra-literary considerations. It is certainly tempting to associate the figure of this sovereign with the diffusion of the *Post-Vulgate*, since there are preserved in Portuguese the three sections into which this cycle is divided – the *Livro de José de Arimateia*, *Merlim* and the *Demanda do Santo Graal* – and that knowledge of the *Pseudo-Boron* appears in Portugal during the period in which troubadour production flowered. For these reasons, it is logical to suppose not only the circulation of the entire cycle in Portugal, but also its solid implantation, brought about by its early arrival and a rapid familiarization with its texts. Notwithstanding this, the association of the translations with Afonso III also implied the resolution of the dispute over the indebtedness of one of the Peninsular literatures to another, of whether Portuguese and Galician depended on Castilian or vice versa. At times, in fact, this hypothesis has gone to the extreme of suggesting that the translations could have been produced on French soil and would, therefore, have been available only to the Portuguese monarch.[6] Fundamentally, then, there underlay all this an impetus to reassert identity involving literary systems in a state of conflict, through the process of subjecting to a symbolic dependence that literature which had relied not on French versions, but on another intermediary Peninsular version. At all events, for this to be feasible, it was necessary to suppose that all the known Iberian texts derived from a common archetype, a hypothesis which had one fact in its favour: namely, the mention, both in the Portuguese *José de Arimateia* and in the Castilian

Demandas, of the Joam Vivas alluded to above. The latter, because of his ubiquity, was considered to be the individual responsible for the Peninsular reworking of the entire *Pseudo-Boron* cycle (Castro 1983: 91–2; 2000: 154).[7] We have seen, however, that this assumption of a single Iberian archetype has become increasingly difficult to maintain in the light of the analysis of fresh texts, such as the ST manuscript of the *José de Arimateia* already cited, which obliges us at least to consider that two versions of this work were circulating in Portugal from an early date (Dias 2003–6: 54).

The question of priority, however, does not seem to have been definitively resolved, even though its most vehement iterations may appear to be disputes belonging to the past. Rather, some of its presuppositions and conclusions have transcended the field of Arthurian literature, in the strict sense, and have extended to other chivalresque narratives. Without going any further, the pretension to a Portuguese origin for *Amadís de Gaula* still remains alive, despite the fact that it is accepted today by scarcely anyone except scholars of that nationality.[8] Or there is the interest aroused in the mid-XXth century by *Palmeirim de Inglaterra*, which was driven by nothing other than the desire of each nation to prove that its version was the original, and which declined once the Portuguese origin of the work had been demonstrated (Finazzi-Agrò 1978: 36–7; Vargas Díaz-Toledo 2012b: 148–9). The arguments adduced, as we shall shortly see, have also changed as the years have passed, seeking greater support in data that are capable of being assessed empirically, or, in their absence, in coherently argued hypotheses. All this is far, in any case, from theories which, decades ago, were based on the juxtaposition of concepts such as literature, ethnicity or national character. All the same, the continuity of logic that links them all is encapsulated in Castro's observation (2000: 153–4) in the same line as Lapa's research into the priority of the Portuguese texts over those in Castilian. According to Castro, if Lapa had had at his disposal the historical facts that are known today on the identity of Joam Vivas, the supposed translator of the *Post-Vulgate* contemporary with Afonso III, he would not have needed to defend the priority of the Portuguese versions by using anthropological theories.

For Castro himself (2000: 149), the nationalist impetus that guided Lapa does not undermine either his arguments or the validity of his conclusions. Like so many other scholars who have dealt with the Matter of Britain in the Peninsula, what interested Lapa, rather than the texts themselves, were the origins of the Iberian chivalresque narratives and, given their dependence on the French models, the arrival of Arthurian literature in the Peninsula, how, when, and by which routes it arrived and which Iberian language was the first to produce versions in the local vernacular. For him, Portuguese priority was based on philological data, such as errors of copying in the Castilian versions where the Portuguese texts were correct, or the linguistic analysis of the surviving texts. For him, both the *José de Arimateia* and the *Demanda do Santo Graal* appeared to be very close in this respect to the language of the Galician-Portuguese troubadours, and he even detected in these works archaisms that the latter did not use. But at the same time, for Lapa this proof of antiquity was almost to be expected, since, because of the Celtic substratum in Galicia and Portugal, the Arthurian stories became acclimatised in those lands before other regions of the Peninsula thanks to an affinity of ethnicity and temperament, while this same factor was the decisive element in the rejection of the stories by Castilians (Lapa 1970c: 222–7).

Similar arguments, based on the identification of ethnicity, language, and literature, had been common in earlier research. Michaëlis herself (1904: II, 505–6), likewise a defender of Portuguese priority and of the entry of the Matter of Britain into Iberia through the west of the Peninsula, had considered philological enquiry with ethnic arguments, although she recognised its limited persuasiveness. Thomas (1952: 21), too, whilst conceding that the Arthurian stories had entered Spain through Cataluña, considered that through the Road to Santiago these had encountered a similar natural opening in Galicia and Portugal. Their acclimatisation in those lands was favoured by the existence of an established school of lyric poetry, but also by what he referred to as an exalted spirit of consanguinity because of the legacy of early Celtic inhabitants. Even when, among Spanish critics, the dependency of the Castilian texts was accepted, appeal had been made to the reflection in literature of questions of national temperament and Volksgeist. Thus, Milá y Fontanals (1874 [1959]: 27, 472) explained that the lateness of Castile in comparison to Portugal was caused by the greater degree of realism in its literature and its national character, which rejected the gallantry and fantasies of the Arthurian material and which accepted these narratives only at the cost of reducing these elements. As the XXth century advanced, however, other authors followed the proposed priority of Portuguese, although basing their conclusions ever more firmly on more scientific arguments. At the level of philology, for example, a more exacting methodology has been applied above all in linguistic and philological analysis of the texts. This has been the route followed by various authors, favourably disposed to the thesis of Portuguese priority, among them Menéndez Pelayo (2008: I, 268), Klob (1902), Nunes (1908), Lapa (1982a, 1982b), Pickford (1961) and, more recently, Bogdanow (1985–87; 1990; 1991–2001: I; 2003), Castro (1983, 2000, 2002a), Miranda (1996, 1998a), Megale (2001) and Pio (2004, 2007). At the same time, within this shared methodology, some of these scholars have offered individual explanations which sometimes include doubts and hesitations concerning the routes of entry into the Peninsula followed by the Matter of Britain. Sommer (1907), for example, was one of those authors who did not favour Castilian or Leonese as the language of the first Iberian translation. Others, such as Pietsch and Bogdanow, as we will see below, modified their conclusions as a result of subsequent research.

The opposite position, that is to say, Castilian priority, has also had its standard-bearers, like Baist (1897, 1907), whose participation in the polemics was not always burdened by scientific criteria. Other defenders of this position have approached the question through the analysis of the texts, but in not a few cases Castilian priority has had to be reconciled with the presence of an obviously western linguistic substratum in these. This is the case with Bohigas Balaguer (1925a: 81–94; 1933: 183–4), who at first maintained Castilian priority, but who, faced with the evidence adduced by Lapa, accepted the Portuguese origin of the Castilian *Demanda del santo Grial* and, although he resisted doing the same with the *José de Arimatea*, adopted a more cautious attitude when it came to defending the priority of the Castilian version. In the light of the evidence produced by the linguistic analyses, it is no accident that Entwistle (1942), one of the most steadfast defenders of the thesis of Castilian priority, should base his study on the cultural context in which the texts were composed and on the contexts of literary reception and circulation, rather than on this kind of approach.

The key, then, has been in conceding that this linguistic stratum arose either from a Galician or Portuguese antecedent, which would have involved acceptance of Portuguese priority over Castilian, or in attributing it to a dialectal influence from Leonese or even Galician-Leonese. In this latter case, such a language could be considered as a westernised Castilian, a solution that would preserve Castilian priority. The difficulties involved in establishing clearly a position based on the language are exemplified in the study carried out by Pietsch on the Arthurian texts contained in MS 1877 of the Biblioteca Universitaria, Salamanca. This scholar began by defending the Portuguese origin of the texts, because of the linguistic traits he believed he had found in them. Nonetheless, when years later he returned to his analysis to produce the critical edition of these texts, he ended up favouring a Castilian original which, thanks to successive copyists, had become impregnated by Leonese forms during the century between the translation and the surviving witnesses (Pietsch 1913–14; 1915–16; 1924–5). His edition was the target of severe criticism, because of the application of questionable criteria for restoring the text (caused, in any case, by an excess of linguistic zeal) (Gracia 2009: 191), but also because of the implications that his proposal entailed for the diffusion of Peninsular Arthurian material. It is to this second aspect that some of the objections of Castro (1988a) are related; the latter denied the existence of a hybrid language such as that defended by Pietsch, on which the latter based his thesis of Castilian priority. Bogdanow (1960b, 1966, 1974–5, 1975) also upheld the Leonese thesis, albeit not without doubts. Subsequently, through the analysis of the Iberian versions of the *Demanda* in relation to the French texts, she discovered passages in which the Castilian text misinterpreted readings that were correct in the Portuguese text, but also others (albeit fewer) in which the Castilian version was closer to the French texts. She finally concluded that the Iberian archetype would have been a lost text produced in Galician-Portuguese. Other authors, such as Lida de Malkiel (1959), Steiner (1966–7), Lapesa (1980) and García de Lucas (1997) have insisted, though with certain differences in their conclusions, either on the existence of a Leonese-western substratum in the Castilian texts, or on the importance of the centre-west region (and its dialectal variants) for the diffusion of the Arthurian narratives in the centre of the Peninsula, even questioning the Portuguese substratum in some texts, such as those included in MS 1877 at Salamanca, as do Darbord and García de Lucas (2008).

The problems posed in attempting to offer a definitive solution on this question lie as much in the fragmentary character of the surviving textual tradition as in the linguistic interpenetration visible in the centre-west region of the Peninsula during a significant part of the Middle Ages. Thus, for example, Mariño (1998: 152–76) has studied a series of documents and works produced in this region between the XIIIth and XVth centuries, in which there can be observed a mix of Portuguese, Galician, Leonese and Castilian features. This indicates that although during these years the various Ibero-Romance dialectal varieties were gradually developing their distinctive characteristics, until well into the XVth century the idea persisted that they all formed part of a single linguistic and cultural continuum (Fernández-Ordóñez 2006: 1794). That is to say, that in the period when the Arthurian texts were copied awareness of linguistic hybridisation as we now conceive it was very slight and was outweighed by diversity within a single linguistic area. Even assuming that the Arthurian texts being analysed were not from this geographical area, and were not composed during this period, the foregoing observations certainly give at least an idea of how complicated it can sometimes be to determine the precise provenance of certain western characteristics present in texts dating from as late as the XVth century.

If the question of which Hispanic language saw the first translation on the Arthurian texts has proved controversial, the same is certainly true of the attempt to determine which texts circulated in the Peninsula, and, in the context we are considering, which of them did so in the western zone. The complex panorama that may be discerned through the surviving texts, the uncertainties surrounding their precise sources and the routes of their diffusion, as well as the relations that exist among them, makes it ill-advised to limit analysis to a specific kingdom or a single linguistic area. The Arthurian allusions contained in the Galician-Portuguese lyric furnish a good example of this (see the chapter by Pilar Lorenzo in this volume). Because they are so laconic, they tell us nothing about which specific text inspired each of them (and in some cases not even which work), nor when, nor how, it was known to the poet who used it. Moreover, because of the continual mobility of authors among the different courts of the troubadour world, it is extremely difficult to establish the precise place in which to locate the source of literary information that could explain the allusion. To go no further, this is the case with the allusions made by Martin Soarez and Eanes do Vinhal, mentioned above, because of their periods of residence at the Castilian court, and it also applies to the allusion by Fernand'Esquio to the Besta Ladrador in *Disse hum infante ante sa companha* (B1607, V1140), since this troubadour, who originated from the north of Galicia, perhaps resided at the court of the Counts of Traba but also at that of D. Denis I of Portugal. Likewise, it is illusory to suppose that a *cantiga* composed at one court would not have circulated rapidly, soon becoming known in others. By such means are explained numerous cases of lyric intertextuality which do not always imply any personal contact between the poets. In such circumstances, the most advisable course would be to assume that the Arthurian works known at one court were also known in others (referring here not to the specific versions contained in particular manuscripts, but to the works conceived as a supratextual reality), if only because the Galician-Portuguese troubadour milieu appears to us as a literary and cultural continuum to which other contemporary artistic production would not have been alien, obviously including in this the fictional Arthurian universe, which was spreading throughout the entire medieval west so vigorously. Thus it will not have escaped notice that two of the great prose cycles of the XIIIth century, the *Lancelot-Graal* and the *Post-Vulgate*, have left identifiable traces in authors both from Castile (Alfonso X) and Portugal (Martin Soarez, for the first cycle and Estevan da Guarda for the second).[9] Something similar, moreover, is suggested by the tradition linked to the historiographic texts. The accounts of the reign of Arthur contained in the *Livro de linhagens* of Don Pedro de Barcelos and the *Crónica de 1344* certainly go back to the *Historia regum Britanniae* of Geoffrey of Monmouth and the *Roman de Brut* of Robert Wace, but they do so through the different versions of the extremely popular *Liber regum*, a work composed in the north-centre of the Peninsula towards the end of the XIIth century or the beginning of the XIIIth. It is this same influence that can be detected in other historiographic works, such as the *Crónica de 1404* or the *Libro de las fortunas y bienandanzas* of Lope García de Salazar. In other words, yet again there would have existed an incessant transfer from one Hispanic kingdom to another, so that the study of each of the surviving Arthurian texts, in Portuguese, Galician, Castilian or Catalan, must not lose sight of the overall Iberian cultural context.

The textual instability of medieval literary works has complicated the task of identifying some of the great cycles composed in France in the XIIIth century and reworked in subsequent centuries. The classic study of Pickford (1959) on the evolution of the prose Arthurian *roman* gives a complete view of the openness of the medieval text and of how at times the boundaries between works disappear. In addition, the studies that Bogdanow produced on the *Post-Vulgate* cycle and *Pseudo-Robert de Boron*, which she called the *Roman du Graal*, reflect the problems that are sometimes involved even in the very identification of a work. Accordingly, as was hinted above, these difficulties extend to the description of the prose Arthurian cycles that circulated in the Peninsula, and this question is further complicated because the surviving Hispanic textual witnesses are so fragmentary. Leaving aside the Galician *Tristán*, the textual tradition of which is independent of the other Iberian texts of the *Tristan en prose*, the controversy in the western Iberian zone which occupies us here is focused on the relationship between the surviving Portuguese witnesses and the *Vulgate* and *Post-Vulgate* cycles, and even whether there may have been circulating some other different compilation alongside these.

Since Gaston Paris edited the *Suite du Merlin* from the Huth Manuscript (1886), it was known that there existed a cycle independent of the *Lancelot-Graal*, although its characteristics remained uncertain. For Paris (1887), it comprised a trilogy prior to the *Vulgate*, but later authors, such as Wechssler (1895, 1898) and Brugger (1906–10), gave it a more complicated structure, although they continued to support the earlier date of the cycle. Wechssler, who called it the *Pseudo-Robert de Boron* cycle, hypothesised three redactions of it. The first, which does not survive, reproduced the organisation of the *Lancelot-Graal* in six branches, while the other two consisted of partial versions of this one. Sommer (1907, 1908), on the other hand, reaffirmed the existence of a trilogy; but, basing himself on intertextual references scattered throughout the different sections of the cycle, rejected the theory of three successive redactions. Finally Bogdanow identified the *Post-Vulgate* as a narrative with three sections: the *Estoire del Saint Graal*, the *Merlin* followed by a *Suite du Merlin*, and the *Queste del Saint Graal*, completed by a summary version of the *Mort Artu* (Bogdanow 1959; 1966: 40–59; 1999a: 443; 2006). The difficulties in identifying the cycle described are centred on two aspects. On the one hand, there is the fragmentary transmission of the cycle as a whole (Bogdanow (1966: 171) refers to it as *disjecta membra*), with lengthy sections of the narrative lost, above all in the central part, and with other sections which survive only in versions translated into other languages and sometimes at late dates, as is the case with the Iberian texts. On the other, the narrative has a complex intertextual relationship with the other contemporary prose cycles, since not only does it represent a modification of the *Lancelot-Graal*, but it also incorporates elements from the *Tristan en prose*. Subsequent discoveries, like the fragments of the *Post-Vulgate* from the Archivio di Stato in Bologna and the Biblioteca Comunale at Imola, have shown the complexity of the intertextual relationship of the *Post-Vulgate* with the other prose Arthurian cycles, a situation which had indeed been revealed previously in the study by Pickford (1959) already cited.

This extreme complexity in the configuration of the prose cycles seems to be reflected in the surviving Portuguese witnesses and, from a wider perspective, in the rest of the Iberian texts. This affects not only the difficulty of establishing the specific sources or the textual branches from which the Iberian texts descend, but also the doubts that have arisen concerning to which narrative complex these texts belonged and what its structural design was; to such an extent that there has even been a suggestion that a very full *summa* was circulating in Iberia. This, which has been denoted the *Lancelot-Tristan* cycle (Miranda 1996: 94), would have brought together the *Estoire del Saint Graal*, the *Merlin* with the *Suite du Merlin*, the *Lancelot*, the *Folie Lancelot*, the *Tristan en prose* and the *Queste del Saint Graal*, with a final summary of the *Mort Artu* (Laranjinha 2010a; Miranda 1998a). This compilation would have arisen as a modification of an earlier cycle, composed around 1220, of which there formed part the *Estoire del Saint Graal*, the *Merlin*, the *Lancelot propre* and the *Queste del Saint Graal*, followed by a brief version of the *Mort Artu*. That is to say, the earlier cycle had undergone a remodelling, producing a later cycle conceived, not as Bogdanow maintained in the case of the *Post-Vulgate*, as an abbreviation of the earlier one, but as an amplification, in the manner of a definitive *summa*. One of the key elements in this hypothesis would be constituted by MS 9611 of the Biblioteca Nacional, Madrid, which contains a long section of the *Lancelot propre* in Castilian. In this, points of contact with the *Suite du Merlin* have been detected, but also perhaps it was combined with a section of the *Tristan en prose* thereby forming a fuller narrative (Bogdanow 1999a: 448).[10]

Before accepting this type of proposal as valid, it is necessary to ask oneself to what extent it would be correct to consider these cycles as stable entities, especially since their length, their intertextual relationships, and the conditions in which literature circulated between the XIIIth and XIVth centuries, with the rise of miscellany manuscripts (Rico 1997), would have favoured the partial transmission of these vast narrative assemblages. In other words, the high degree of instability from which they would have suffered, and the continual process of rewriting that they would have undergone, would lead frequently to their dismemberment into their separate parts or their fusion with others deriving from other narrative assemblages. The compilations of Rustichello da Pisa (*c*.1272) or Michael Gonnot (*c*.1470) are specimens of the extent to which a new story could be constructed on the basis of a collection of isolated episodes conveniently arranged with a narrative thread. It is not necessary to embrace such extreme proposals in order to admit the frequency of cases of textual contamination among late medieval witnesses of the prose Arthurian cycles or the fusion of various of these to accommodate them within new rewritings of the existing cycles. This would explain, without needing to go any further, the proliferation of variant versions of the Arthurian texts, not a few of them now lost, and the problems involved in identifying the specific sources of the Iberian witnesses. It would also, moreover, illuminate the peculiar features of the Castilian *Lanzarote*, without any need to resort to a vast assemblage of texts, such as has been proposed. This means that it would perhaps be more prudent to continue to postulate the affinity of the Portuguese texts to the known *Post-Vulgate* cycle, albeit very probably to a reworked version of it, rather than to some new cycle. It is precisely the Portuguese texts that help to demonstrate that there circulated in the Peninsular realms at least two versions of this cycle. This is what would be shown by the two surviving manuscripts of the *José de Arimateia*, from Lisbon (TT) and Porto (ST), but also by the *Merlim* of the Biblioteca de Catalunya, which would correspond to a redaction closer to the French original than are the Castilian *Baladros*.

The *Livro de José de Arimateia*

The *Livro de José de Arimateia* is preserved in two manuscript witnesses. MS 643 of the Arquivo Nacional da Torre do Tombo in Lisbon dates to the XVIth century and consists of 316 folios (250 × 190 mm), written in round cursive Gothic script in a single column. MS 1/18/2-Cx2 of the collection designated NO-CNSTS 1/1 Liv. 12 in the Arquivo Distrital do Porto, of the late XIIIth century or the beginning of the XIVth, consists of a bifolium (277 × 202 mm), written in two columns in a cursive Gothic script. The first of these two (here designated by the siglum MS TT), therefore, is a late copy, and is equipped with a prologue in which the circumstances in which it was transcribed are set out clearly. According to this preliminary note, it was copied by Manuel Álvares, *corregidor* of the island of São Miguel in the Azores, from an earlier version, which, he declares, came from Riba d'Âncora, where he found it when his father was serving as *corregidor* in the region of Entre Douro e Minho. Manuel Álvares himself states that this version was contained in an illuminated manuscript and attributes to this book a date at least two centuries earlier.[11] On the basis of the data offered by this introduction, with particular attention to the dedication to D. João III and to the period during which Manuel Álvares was *corregidor*, Entwistle (1942: 120) places the copy between 1521 and 1557, during the reign of that monarch. Notwithstanding, he hazarded that either this copy, or the version on which it was based, would have circulated at the beginning of the XVIth century among the poets of the *Cancioneiro Geral* of Garcia de Resende (1516), since José de Arimateia is mentioned by one of them, called Pêro de Moura.[12] Subsequently, Martins (1952) tightened the dating, limiting it to the period between 1552 and 1557 when he assumed that Manuel Álvares had exercised his office of *corregidor*.

Castro (1976–9: 179–81), by contrast, notes that Manuel Álvares arrived in the Azores in December 1552, not as *corregidor* but accompanying the new magistrate, Manuel da Câmara, and in the capacity of collector of taxes. In his nomination some weight had been attached to the fact that he had been the governor of the islands of São Miguel and Santa Maria and that he therefore knew the islands. In reality, Álvares took up office on 24 May 1540, and, whilst it is not known when he relinquished his post, since the term of office of a *corregidor* was roughly three years, this is likely to have occurred in 1543. In fact, he is documented again in Lisbon in 1546. These dates, which advance by a decade Martins's proposed dating, fit better with another piece of information offered in the prologue, in which the University of Coimbra is mentioned as 'principiada e acabada'. By this expression it must be understood that this institution had become fully functional, with the constitution of its organs of governance and the installation of the schools in the monastery of Santa Cruz. This had occurred between 1537 and 1538, in other words slightly before the allusion by Manuel Álvares (Castro 1976–9: 176–7). Everything points, then, to the period between the end of 1539 and 1543, with a greater likelihood for the latter date, as the point at which the *José de Arimateia* of the Torre do Tombo MS 643 was copied. Castro (1991: 180), at all events, offers another piece of information to take into account: since the drying agent used during the copying consisted of sand from the Tagus and the area around Sines, it may be thought that the work was carried out in Lisbon, which would prompt us to think of the years in which no activity at all by Álvares in São Miguel is documented.[13]

The codicological characteristics of the manuscript and its copying process have been studied by Castro (1984) and Nascimento (1984). Although Manuel Álvares asserts that he himself had copied the text, from folio 16 he had the collaboration of another nine copyists, under his supervision. This explains the calligraphic diversity visible in the manuscript. The copyists worked independently, after the original codex had been dismembered and its quires had been distributed. Once the reproduction had been completed, Álvares brought the nine quires together and numbered their folios. The new manuscript is not, however, a mere copy of its exemplar, which is now lost. Álvares confesses that, whilst he respected the original structure of the narrative, he modernised such linguistic features as he considered to be archaic, a factor which affects modern attempts to date the original text.

As is stated in the prologue, Manuel Álvares offered his copy to D. João III and indeed the manuscript remained in the royal library until the end of the XVIth century. It then became the property of D. Teotónio de Bragança, archbishop of Évora from 1576 to 1602, and after his death it was deposited in the library of the Charterhouse of that city. When in 1834 the religious orders were suppressed in Portugal, the manuscript was transferred to the Arquivo Nacional at the Torre do Tombo in Lisbon, where it remains today. The first scholar to become interested in the manuscript, around 1846, was Francisco Adolfo de Varnhagen, whose account was used by later scholars such as Reinhardstöttner, Wechssler and Michaëlis, as the basis for their references to the work, though without consulting this. The first transcription, albeit a partial one, was made by Klob (1902: 170–1), who was also the first since Varnhagen to examine the codex directly. After this one, other partial editions follow in sequence, by Nunes (1906: 52–62; 1908), Bohigas Balaguer (1925a: 105–10, 113–17), De Brito (1943), Neto (1948: 244–8), Martins (1952: 289–98), Neto (1956: 51–4, 177–81), Roberts (1956: 46–49) and Castro (1984). The first palaeographic edition of MS TT was published by Carter (1967), while a critical edition has appeared only very recently (Ailenii, Laranjinha, Correia and Miranda 2013).

In the final years of the XXth century there appeared a second witness for the *José de Arimateia*, which complemented the information until that point derived solely from MS TT. This new exemplar had served as covers for a manuscript codex of the notary João da Costa, of Santo Tirso, and formed part of the cartulary holdings of Santo Tirso and Penafiel preserved at the Arquivo Distrital do Porto (whence its designation here by the siglum MS ST). It was discovered in 1992 by Nuno Guina Garcia, while undertaking a codicological project during his studies at the University of Coimbra, but its correct identification and study are the work of Dias (2003–6). Although the fragment is seriously eroded by use, this scholar identified the text as corresponding to chapters 57, 58, 61, 62 and 63 of MS TT. Linguistic and palaeographic analysis permitted her to date it to the end of the XIIIth century or the beginning of the XIVth, though Nascimento (2008: 139) inclines towards the second of these possibilities. Its greater antiquity compared to the version in MS TT made necessary a reconsideration of the relations between the Portuguese witnesses of the work and the French texts, but also of the routes of the transmission in Portugal of the *Estoire del Saint Graal* and, clearly, of Arthurian literature in general throughout the Peninsula. Until then, research into the date of redaction of *José de Arimateia* took as its starting point the information given both in the prologue of MS TT, in which Manuel Álvares dated the codex found by him to two hundred years earlier, and in the colophon. According to the latter:

> Este liuro [m]andou fazer João samches mestre | esco lla dastorga no quimto ano que o est[u]do de | coimbra foy feito e no tempo do papa clemente | que destroio aordem del temple e fez O concilio | geral Em viana e posho emtredito Em castela | e neste ano se finou a Rainha doua Costamça | em são fagumdo Ecasou o y m famte dom felipe | com a filha de dom afomso ano de 13lij Anos. (Carter 1967: 119, 379)

Some scholars have doubted the information thus obtained, questioning whether this version of *José de Arimateia* was copied in 1314. The first was Varnhagen (1879: 167), and after him Klob (1902: 172), Rossi (1979: 59–63), and even Lapa (1982a: 321). Others, such as Castro (1976–9, 1983, 1984), Dias (2003–6) and Nascimento (2008), have accepted the veracity of the passage and have developed their hypotheses attempting to unite the figures of Joam Vivas, translator of the text, and João Sanches, instigator of the version that would later be copied by Manuel Álvares. Castro (1984: 92–4) supposed that the original version of the book, in Portuguese, was taken to Astorga to be transcribed there at the behest of João Sanches and once the task was completed it was returned to Portugal. However, the existence of MS ST has made it necessary to reformulate this proposal. Dias, for example, states that at the end of the XIIIth century there were circulating in Portugal two versions of *José de Arimateia*. One of them, translated by Joam Vivas, would be represented by MS ST and would represent a witness extremely close to the original in the transmission of the *Estoire del Saint Graal*. That in MS TT, on the other hand, exhibits traces of a mixed version, and therefore would not descend from the translation by Vivas. Nascimento, for his part, believes the transfer of the manuscript to be unnecessary. He identifies João Sanches (or Juan Sánchez) among the *magistri scholarum* of Astorga, having acceded to this position in 1301 in succession to a certain Alfonso Martínez. And he supposes that, because of his position, he would have been linked to the cathedral chapter of Coimbra, which would locate him in that Portuguese city and not in Astorga; he perhaps even had contact with the Portuguese royal house, as may be deduced from the allusion made in the colophon to Doña Constança, daughter of D. Denis and wife of Fernando IV of Castile. The *magister scholarum* would have known the *José de Arimateia* in Coimbra, and it was there that he would have ordered it to be copied. Now Nascimento dates the script of MS ST to the first years of the XIVth century, thus approaching the date offered by the colophon of the Lisbon manuscript. For this reason he believes it possible that the book, after being disbound in order to be transcribed, was not reassembled. From one of those loose quires there would have survived the bifolium which today we know as MS ST. However, the textual analysis carried out by Ailenii (2009) corroborates the idea of Dias that both witnesses are independent of each other and that MS ST is not a redaction intermediate between the lost original of the Portuguese translation and the XVIth-century version represented by MS TT.

The discovery of MS ST, however, has redefined (as indicated above) the position occupied by the Portuguese texts at the heart of the textual tradition of the *Estoire del Saint Graal*. In her pioneering studies on the *Post-Vulgate* cycle, Bogdanow (1960b; 1966: 158–9) observed, on the one hand, that the *Pseudo-Boron* reproduced with minimal alterations the *Vulgate Estoire del Saint Graal*, a fidelity that is reflected in *José de Arimateia*, which contains scarcely any episodes that do not find an equivalent in the *Vulgate* version. On the other, she noted that the almost sixty witnesses of the *Estoire* can be grouped into three redactions: the short, long, and mixed. The difference between the first two lay, basically, in that when compared to the long, the short version omitted certain descriptive passages and began with a shorter prologue, while the mixed redaction alternated between the readings of the other two. The same scholar concluded that the *José de Arimateia* of MS TT was close to the witnesses of this third, mixed, version, especially to MS 2427 of the Bibliothèque Municipale de Rennes (R). Such a coincidence could have one of only two causes: either both manuscripts shared contamination by a common ancestor, or because of their mixed content they represented the archetype from which the witnesses of the other two textual families descended (Bogdanow 1960b: 347).

In responding on to this question, Castro (1988b: 201–3), who had not yet incorporated the Porto fragment into his analysis, took as his starting point the early dating of the mixed manuscripts, among them R, which is dated to the first half of the XIIIth century (Stones 1977), but also the estimated date at which the Portuguese translation would have been carried out, only slightly later. This leads him to conclude that in so short a period there would have been no opportunity for the formation of two textual families of the *Estoire del Saint Graal* and for both to come together again in the mixed version, for which reason this last would have been earlier than the other two. Moreover, the comparison of R and TT demonstrates that the French manuscript exhibits many defective readings, at times unique to it. From this he concludes that R does not occupy a position intermediate between the Portuguese version and its French ancestor, but that both share a French ancestor, from which there would have arisen the textual family to which R belongs as does the ancestor of the Iberian translations (O), and of which *José de Arimateia* formed part. Subsequent analyses have opened the possibility that MS TT may also be related to the first French edition of the *Estoire*, printed in Paris in 1516 (Pio 2004, 2007).

José de Arimateia opens with a brief account of the circumstances of its composition. There it is stated that God appeared in dreams to a monk, to whom he gave a book he had written in Latin. In this book were related the mysteries of the faith and the story of the Holy Grail. Over the following days, the monk experienced various miracles, until God appeared to him again and ordered him to make a copy of the book, the contents of which are set out thereafter. The story begins with the arrival of Joseph of Arimathea in Jerusalem, after the death of Christ, to take charge of his crucified body. Joseph keeps as a relic the Grail, which is the bowl from which Christ ate during the Last Supper, which has been filled with the blood of the Crucified Christ. The Jews imprison Joseph, and God prevents his dying from starvation thanks to the nourishment with which the Grail furnishes him. He remains in prison until he is released by Vespasian, who, suffering from leprosy, had been cured by the sudarium of Veronica. Joseph is baptised by St Philip, and a voice orders him to construct an Ark to safeguard the Grail, and to leave Jerusalem. He departs with his family and a group of the faithful, and arrives at the city of Sarras, in which he begins to preach the Christian faith and in which he and his son Josefes, ordained bishop by order of God, hold theological debates with Evalac, the pagan monarch of the place, and his priests. Evalac is at war with King Tolomer of Egypt and before going into battle Josefes gives him a white shield with a red cross on it, which will protect him if he becomes a Christian. During the battle, seeing himself in danger of being killed, Evalac implores the protection of God, and a White Knight appears, assisting him and his brother-in-law Sarafes. Evalac and Sarafes are converted and adopt the names, respectively, of Mordaim, and Nascião, and Joseph and Josefes convert Sarras to Christianity. During the conversions and baptisms, an angel wounds Josefes in the thigh with a lance. Later, Nascião is struck blind, for having approached the Ark in an attempt to see the marvels of the Grail. Another angel again wounds Josefes in the same spot, and both he and Nascião are cured with the blood which flows from the wound suffered by Josefes.

Mordaim is taken to an island, which is the dwelling place of the pirate Focaries. There he is visited by a boatman sent by God, who comforts him, but he is also tempted by emissaries from the devil. Meanwhile, reacting to the king's disappearance, a knight from Sarras called Calafer imprisons Nascião and his sister Queen Sargocinta. An angel releases Nascião and transports him to the Insola Tornante, the history and properties of which are described. As a reprisal for the liberation of Nascião, Calafer orders the imprisonment of Celidones, Nascião's son, but nine heavenly hands drag him through the air and Calafer dies. Salomão's ship reaches the Insola Tornante, and its history and the symbolism of the objects it carries are explained: the bed of Salomão, the beams cut from the wood of the Tree of Life, planted by Eve; the sword of David, with its sheath and straps. All of this was arranged by the wife of Salomão to prepare for the future arrival of Galaaz, descendant of David and Salomão himself. To the place to which Celidones had been taken there comes King Label, who attempts to convert the child; but Celidones explains some symbolic dreams the king has had, and after explaining the mystery of the faith to him, succeeds in converting him and has him baptised by a nearby hermit. The next day Label dies, and his men, in revenge, put Celidones out to sea to drift together with a lion, which miraculously does not harm him. During his voyage, Celidones passes Salomão's ship; a few days later he rejoins his father, and together they abandon the Insola Tornante. They reach an island inhabited by a giant, who attacks Nascião. The latter defends himself with the sword of David, which breaks. Later it will be repaired by Mordaim, whom they also encounter out at sea. A heavenly voice warns them to abandon the ship of Salomão, and Nascião is wounded because he unsheathed the sword of David, which was not destined for him.

Next there are related the adventures of the messengers sent by Sargocinta in search of Mordaim; this includes the story of Hipocras, whose tomb they find on an island. The messengers pick up, far out at sea, the daughter of King Melião of Babel, who will later become the wife of Celidones, and finally they encounter Mordaim and Nascião, with whom they return to their land. Before they disembark, there appears St Ermoines, travelling across the waters, who cures Nascião of his wound and orders Celidones to embark alone in another boat and go off in search of adventure. But once in his own land, Nascião misses Celidones and Joseph, and, in response to his prayers, God orders him to put out to sea. There he embarks on the ship of Salomão and has a dream about the descendants of his line, over the nine generations which reach as far as Galaaz.

For their part, Joseph and Josefes have abandoned Sarraz to preach the faith of Christ. On arriving at the sea, God helps them to cross, sailing on the shirt of Josefes, but only those who have remained chaste during the journey can accompany them. Thus they reach Great Britain, the land God has promised to them. The sinners have to seek other transport, because they would sink, and they are collected by Nascião in the ship of Salomão. So they meet Joseph again, in Great Britain, and shortly after they are joined by Celidones, whom they encounter in a castle of the island. Joseph and Josefes begin to evangelise the country, to preach, to work miracles and to combat the pagans who do not accept the new faith. Mordaim remains blind for attempting to see the miracles of the Holy Grail, but God grants his prayer to live until he sees Galaaz, on whose coming he will regain his sight. Celidones marries the daughter of King Melião and Mordaim gives them as a dowry the kingdom of Norgales. From them will be born a son, Nascião, who will be the king of the kingdom of Foraiã. After the wedding Mordaim retires to a hermitage and Nascião stays in the city of Galeforte, caring for Sargacinta and the shield of the red cross.

It is also explained that the empty seat at the table of the Grail recalls that occupied by the traitor Judas at the table of the Last Supper and an account is given of the punishment received by Mois, one of the companions of Josefes, when he attempted to sit in it. Another of the companions of Josefes, called Bron, had twelve sons. The youngest, called Elaim o Groso, makes a vow to remain a virgin and serve the Holy Grail; for this reason Josefes names him as his successor. Two of his brothers are Sador, the ancestor of Tristan, and Perom. During the evangelising journeys of Josefes, the Grail nourishes those who accompany him, but only those of them who are without sin. Normally it provides the food that each one desires, but on one occasion it succeeds in feeding a multitude with a single fish. Since Elaim is the one who provides the faithful with fish, he receives the name of the Rico Pescador. Other miracles follow through the mediation of Josefes, such as the resuscitation of a pagan knight and the cure of his brother, or the crossing of a river by walking on the water. But there is also revealed the sinful nature of some members of the company, such as Simeu and Canam, who conspire to kill their relatives. One of them, Perom, does not succeed in recovering from the poisoned wound inflicted on him by Simeu, and will be cured only in the kingdom of Orcauz, where the drifting boat arrives. There he marries the daughter of the king, and from his lineage will descend King Lot of Orcania, brother-in-law of King Arthur.

After fifteen years travelling around Great Britain and Ireland, Josefes returns to Galeforte, where his family and Nascião had settled. His mother has died and his brother Galat has become the best knight of the country. He receives the kingdom of Gales and marries the daughter of the king of the Lomgas Ynsolas. Both will be ancestors of Yvão, a knight of the Round Table. Joseph dies a short time later, and Josefes himself predicts his own end. Before dying, he paints a cross in his own blood on the white shield and predicts that it can be borne only by Galaaz. Then he cedes the custody of the Grail to Elaim, and dies. Elaim and other members of the family depart to preach, and reach the Terra Foreyra. Its king, Galymfres, is cured of leprosy, converts, adopting the name of Arfasão, and proposes to Elaim that they build a castle in Orberique, where the Grail shall be safeguarded. His daughter marries Josues, brother of Elaim. A dense story describes the generations that follow, which link Elaim and Josue with Lanzarote and Galaaz. The work ends with indications concerning the structure of the cycle of which *José de Arimateia* forms part and with a reference to João Sanches and how he ordered it to be written.

These last observations turn out to be fundamental when it comes to interpreting the work, since the elements that comprise it can be understood only as parts making up a greater whole, consisting of two further sections. These were centred, as the narrator explains, upon Merlin and the Grail (one supposes that this means the quest for it), and would have been separated to facilitate handling the text.[14] In accordance with this, a good proportion of the characters and episodes that occupy these pages are conceived as the precursors of others, to reappear in other sections of the same cycle or whose significance will be fully realised in those later sections. Of this, there are many examples of various kinds throughout the text. Sometimes it is a question of characters who are ancestors of Arthurian knights, such as Perom, Sador, Orcauz and Galat, mentioned already. On other occasions, they are markers or marvels, which will be encountered or resolved by those knights, like the inextinguishable fire that consumes Mois, which will be quenched only with the arrival of Galaaz (Carter 1967: 106, 342–3); the grave of Simeu, which likewise will be opened by the son of Lanzarote (Carter 1967: 113, 365); the bed of the Paço Avemturoso, in which nobody will be able to sleep until Galvão has done so (Carter 1967: 116, 371), and so on. Premonitory dreams also act as antecedents, the symbolism of which relates to future events. Such an unfolding has a function of creating narrative cohesion, understandable given the enormous dimensions of a cyclical narrative, such as the *Post-Vulgate*. From this assemblage there stand out two elements: the white shield that Mordaim receives in his battle against Tolomer, which will be the one carried by Galaaz in the *Demanda do Santo Graal*, and the ship of Salomão, symbol of the Church, and the objects that it contains, among them the sword of David or 'da Estranha Cinta', which will also play a central role in the later quest for the Holy Grail.

All this corresponds to the compositional poetics of a cyclical narrative, which does not construct its characters by endowing them with psychological depth, but structurally; that is to say, by justifying their deeds through other previous deeds that serve as antecedents (Bogdanow 2003: 48). In accordance with this principle, *José de Arimateia* takes on the role of the foundational narrative, of the origin of chivalresque civilisation, in which is contained the how, the why and the when of the essentials of Arthurian knighthood. That is to say, the ideological foundations of this are already contained in these early times that begin with the death of Christ. In this sense, the episode of the conversion of Mordaim and Nascião is fundamental: they represent, respectively, the monarchy and knighthood. Correia (2005) observes in this a division of powers, according to which knighthood reserves for itself the role of the defence of the kingdom, symbolised in the shield of Mordaim (a defensive weapon), since thanks to this shield he is rescued, during the battle against Tolomer, by a warrior angel. This angel, in turn, provides an axe (an offensive weapon) to Nascião. In Galaaz, the descendant of Nascião and himself a knight and the king of Sarras, both functions are united, but always under the sign of religion. Sometimes, however, the limits between the two are crossed and conflict arises. This occurs, for example, when Nascião unsheathes and breaks the sword of David, a sign of royalty destined for Galaaz. The weapon will be repaired only by Mordaim, that is to say by a king, while Nascião is punished for his action. But despite their mutual dependence, chivalry seems to occupy a place morally superior to royalty, since it will be closer to divine favour than the latter is. For this reason, Nascião converts to Christianity before Mordaim does (Miranda 1993: 160; 1998b: 96).

Equally, the lineage of the guardians of the Grail descends directly from Nascião, through his son Celidones, and only indirectly from Mordaim, maternal uncle of Celidones, even if at the end of the work the Grail ends up in the guardianship of a king, Arfasão, who built the castle of Orberique. But both institutions, monarchy and knighthood, can be understood only in terms of Christianity, whence their dependence upon the Church, the third institution whose foundation is related in *José de Arimateia*. It is represented by Josefes, its first bishop, who has been nominated by God. Since his office proceeds directly from the deity, from it there will derive the legitimacy of the other two:[15] that of royalty, because God charges Josefes with the task of ordaining future bishops and priests, and also with anointing kings;[16] that of knighthood, because this in turn emanates from royalty. Galaaz brings together in himself all three, not only because of his relationship with Nascião, Mordaim and Josefes, but because it is for him that the three objects that symbolise the three institutions are destined. These are the white shield, representing knighthood; the sword, representing royalty, and the Grail, the emblem of the priesthood (Miranda 1998b: 103).

Together with the configuration of the key institutions for the medieval world, *José de Arimateia* is a foundational narrative also from a spiritual perspective. The epic of José and his descendents reproduces the scheme of revelation and exodus in the case of the people of Israel. For this reason, the episodes of biblical inspiration are not surprising in the work; such are the miraculous multiplication of food, bread, and fish, in which Josefes and Elaim play a leading role (Carter 1967: 94, 293–4; 104, 330–2), the crossing of the sea to Great Britain on the shirt of Josefes (Carter 1967: 91, 286–9), or the crossing of the river walking upon the water (Carter 1967: 106, 338–40), which recall the crossing of the Red Sea by the Israelites, as well as the Gospel passage in which Christ walks on the waters of the Sea of Galilee. The idea of the chosen people is transferred to the sacred lineage of the guardians of the Grail, a relic that is kept in an Ark, as an image of the Ark of the Covenant in the Old Testament. Moreover, the intense zeal for evangelisation and conversion that these first Christians carry out aligns them with the task of Christianisation carried out by the Apostles, in such a way that their pilgrimage to Great Britain, the western limit of the known world, can be compared to the apostolic dispersion in the New Testament, while the conquest of the island is inspired by that of Palestine by the Israelites under the command of Joshua. The influence of the apocryphal gospels, in turn, is palpable in the opening chapters, centred upon the wanderings of Joseph of Arimathea in Jerusalem, and on the story of Vespasian, suffering from leprosy and miraculously cured by the intervention of God.

The conversion of the pagan peoples is based on a programme of preaching of Christian dogma, especially three points: the Resurrection of Christ, the Immaculate Conception of the Virgin, and the mystery of the Holy Trinity. The programme of propagation of the faith is accompanied by the idea of conversion, so much in force since the spiritual renovation of the XIIth century, which will apply not only to pagans, but also to Christians themselves. The work, in this respect, has to be placed in relation to the other sections of the *Post-Vulgate*, in particular to the *Demanda do Santo Graal* and its promotion of Christian knighthood, despite the fact that the latter work dilutes with knightly adventures the mystic element that characterised the *Queste del Saint Graal* in the *Vulgate* version. *José de Arimateia* displays intransigence towards characters who sin or who do not act according to the divine designs, for which they are frequently chastised with physical punishments. Nascião and Mordaim are blinded for wanting to see the mysteries of the Grail (Carter 1967: 102, 321–4), Nascião is wounded for unsheathing the sword of David, and Josefes for paying less attention to the conversion of the pagans than to the punishment of those who resisted. In all these cases, in which those affected are characters who are viewed positively, the punishment has a purifying effect, which marks the process of spiritual perfection through penitence. But in those other cases of characters who are viewed negatively, such as Mois and Simeu, to the purgative element is added an exemplary purpose, whence the fact that their expiation is revealed to the community of Christians headed by José. At all events, sometimes certain passages are suppressed which could have made the behaviour of one or other of these sinners more worthy of censure. This is what occurs with King Label, who according to the *Estoire del Saint Graal* had decapitated his sister, after attempting to rape her, and had thrown her body into the sea. The Portuguese version omits this crime, to make the salvation of the character more coherent; he is converted but does not pay for so atrocious a sin (Gonçalves 2001: 96).

José de Arimateia, on the other hand, retains the allegorical tone which mixes an imagery that is at times apocalyptic with mystic interpretations appropriate to Christian exegesis. The ship of Salomão, already mentioned, and the sacred objects that it houses relate to this allegorical dimension, but so do the priestly vestments of Josefes (Chambel 2011; Martins 1983c), the dreams (both those related to matters of lineage and those which are purely religious),[17] visions (like that of the stag guarded by four lions, which walk on the water: Carter 1967: 106, 23–38);[18] and even the wanderings of some characters, such as the story of King Label, whose shipwreck symbolises the life of the sinner (Gonçalves 2001). The space of *José de Arimateia* has a symbolic component, too, dominated by the idea of journey and wandering. In the geography of the work there abound islands with sheer cliffs, lost in the middle of the sea, among which the protagonists sail in unmanned boats. This space, which, as Martins reminds us (1975a: 107), switches between one world and another, represents the site of solitude and temptation, as against inhabited spaces, with castles and cities inhabited by pagans, which represent the site of evangelisation (Chase 2003: 66). Like space, time assumes a transcendent dimension, based also on the symbolism of allegorical constructions, which eliminates earthly measurements and which, like the ship of Salomão, permits movement from past to present, and, thanks to prophecies, to the future. The time of the story is converted to the time of the Church and of Salvation, eschatological and apocalyptic in character, which culminates in Galaaz. Thanks to the latter's perfection, his advent, so frequently prophesied, will involve the end of time and its conquest by eternity (Neves 2001).

Woman occupies an ambiguous position, in accordance with the duality which medieval thought established between Eve, the cause of the fall of humankind, and Mary, who redeemed it. The female characters in general take on a secondary role, in part because the work possesses a tone close to that of hagiography, but also because of the importance that lineage structures based on patrilineal transmission assume (Laranjinha 2011a). It is no accident, then, that the descendants of Bron, from among whom will emerge Elaim, the successor of Josefes, should be twelve males. Moura (2002) observes that the treatment of women in *José de Arimateia*, even though marked by medieval misogynist topoi, is not excessively severe, and moreover develops as the story progresses. Thus, women from the remote past receive a more negative treatment, while there is praise of those who are situated in the present or the future. It is certain that the first women find virtue in their role as wives, such as Eliap, the wife of Joseph of Arimathea, Fragantina, the wife of Nascião, or Sargacinta, the wife of Mordaim. However, the last-named was a Christian many years before the conversion of her husband, which shows that women can serve divine intentions better than men. Another example of this and of the ambivalent role of female characters is embodied by the wife of Salomão, who is unfaithful to her husband, but who takes the initiative in constructing the ship intended for Galaaz. Also the story of Hipocras introduces the topos of the deceitful woman, in an episode that recalls the genre of the exemplum, while those other sections nearest to hagiography show woman as the vehicle for diabolical temptation. Here should be placed the woman who tempts Mordaim during his stay on the island of the pirate Focaries. All in all, the great sinners, who defy God and receive exemplary punishment, are men: Mois, Simeu, various pagan leaders opposed to conversion ...

From the entire network of intertextual references which endow *José de Arimateia* with semantic density, there stands out the obviously limited importance attached to the figure of King Arthur, compared to the dominant role fulfilled by Galaaz, in whom there culminates the chosen lineage of the guardians of the Grail. The reign of Arthur, according to this, is above all the period in which there will be made manifest the marvels of the Grail, a relic which, with the characters associated with it, constitutes the thematic nucleus of the cycle. It is for this reason that, as Bogdanow points out (2003: 50), the *Pseudo-Boron* cycle describes itself as the *Haute Escriture del Saint Graal* or *Contes del Saint Graal*. Precisely because of the central place that it occupies in the structure of the cycle, the variations noticeable in the description of the Holy Grail attract attention. At the beginning of *José de Arimateia*, it is described as a dish, and in fact, as Chase observes (2003: 69), it is not identified with the chalices which Josefes will use shortly afterwards during the first mass celebrated in Sarras. Later, however, it is described as 'santo vaso', the holy vessel (Carter 1967: 35, 104; 104, 329; 104, 330; 104, 331; 116, 371 etc.). The confusion, already present in the French texts, could be caused by an attempt to reconcile the tradition drawn from Robert de Boron with the innovations introduced by the *Vulgate*, in which the Grail is linked to the mystery of the Eucharist.

The Fragments of the *Livro de Merlim*

The central section of the *Post-Vulgate* is represented in Portuguese by two brief fragments, which reproduce passages from the *Suite du Merlin*. These are vellum folios that Amadeu-J. Soberanas discovered in the Biblioteca de Catalunya in Barcelona

(MS 2434, or 'Ba'), and which he revealed in an article published in 1979. The first consists of half a folio, 295 ×137 mm, numbered lxvij. The second forms the central bifolium of a quire, measuring 425 × 293 mm, and corresponds to folios cxxij and cxxiij. Both fragments, which would have belonged to the same codex, are written in two columns, with a writing block of 230 × 70 mm, in cursive Gothic script, datable to the first half of the XIVth century. When they were discovered, the fragments formed the covers of the two first volumes of the third incunable edition of the *Chronicon* of Antonino Pierozzi published in Basel by Nicholas Kesler in 1491. It is not known when the codex to which they belonged was dismembered and they were reused as covers. Soberanas describes the language of the text as Galician-Portuguese and, although because of its brevity he recognises that these conclusions cannot be regarded as definitive, certain features (the graphs *lh* and *nh*, preference for the diphthong *ui* and the verbal form *ouujr*, distinction between voiced and voiceless sibilants etc.) incline him to consider it to be Portuguese. From the chronological perspective, the presence of some archaisms, such as the adverb *chus* (< Latin plus) would confirm the antiquity of the text. The fragments have been edited twice: the version offered by Soberanas, which appeared in the article revealing their existence, and the edition by Lorenzo Gradín and Souto Cabo (2001).

The first of the fragments deals with the run-up to the death of Merlin, when, accompanied by the Lady of the Lake, he comes to the mausoleum in which she will imprison him. The surviving text, which corresponds to chapters 380–2 of the *Suite du Merlin* in the edition by Roussineau (1996: 330–1), coincides almost completely with the story of prince Anasten. He falls in love with the daughter of a poor knight, but his father, King Assen, opposes the relationship. Fearing the vengeance of the king, Anasten seeks refuge in the depths of a wood, where he orders a chamber to be excavated from the rock. Hidden there they lead a happy life, and, when they die, they are buried in this very chamber, which thus becomes their tomb. The second, longer, fragment reproduces chapters 493–6 of Roussineau's edition (1966: 455–60). It begins with the combats between Galvam and Marot, who have lost their reason and who have to be separated by Yvã. A lady explains to them that their sudden enmity is caused by an enchantment cast by a lady, whose love they rejected. Because of the wounds they have inflicted on each other, Galvam and Marot are obliged to spend several days convalescing in an abbey. Once they have recovered, they continue their journey together and come across a high and inaccessible rock, on the summit of which there are twelve ladies. Marot explains that the latter possess the gift of prophecy, and that the oldest of them is an enchantress who is hostile to Merlin who, in reprisal, shut them up on the summit of the rock until they die. The text ends at the moment at which the knights begin to converse with the ladies.

One of the interesting aspects of the Portuguese fragments lies in the fact that none of the surviving witnesses of the *Suite du Merlin* contains both these passages. Soberanas (1979: 178–87) analyses the first Portuguese text, comparing it with the versions of the *Baladro del sabio Merlin* published in Burgos (1498) and Seville (1535), British Library MS Add. 38117 (the Huth Manuscript, or 'H'), and Cambridge University Library MS Add. 7071 (MS 'C'). He does not carry out such a collation for the second fragment, on the other hand, because it is found only in Bibliothèque Nationale de France MS fr. 112, a late witness of XVth-century date which has undergone a thorough process of amplification. The conclusions that he extracts from his textual analysis, nonetheless, permit him to conclude that the Portuguese manuscript derives from an independent source, which is closer to C than to H. It must be taken into account that, according to Bogdanow (1960a: 198) the Cambridge MS would represent a second redaction of the *Suite du Merlin*, while H and the Castilian *Baladros* reflect a third state of the text.[19]

The distance between MS Ba and the rest of the Peninsular witnesses is particularly striking and entails no less interesting conclusions. In the *Baladros* (Burgos, 38: 171–2; Seville, 325–30: 147–9) the story of Anasten is amplified and has a different ending.[20] Assen orders a search for the lovers and finds their refuge in the wood. Taking advantage of the absence of his son, out hunting, he kills the lady. On his return, Anasten finds his lover dead and kills himself. Assen, repenting of his crime, fulfils the final wish of his son, of being buried there next to his lover. The edition of 1498 has even more details, such as the epitaph of the tomb of the lovers, in which there has been identified the influence of the *Historia de dos amadores* of Juan Rodríguez del Padrón (Lida de Malkiel 1959; Sharrer 1984a), which must be due to the intervention of its publisher, Juan de Burgos. But beyond modifications of this nature, the printed editions of Burgos and Seville are not only closer to one another in this episode than in other passages, but their shared readings separate them from the French texts (Gracia 2007: 241). In addition, the divergences between the Portuguese text and the two Castilian witnesses perhaps suggest the existence of two different redactions of the *Suite du Merlin* in the Peninsula. Furthermore, if the theory of a single common archetype from which all the Iberian texts descend is upheld, it would then be necessary to suppose that the amplification of the Castilian versions took place not in France but in Spain. The tragic ending presented by the printed editions of Burgos and Seville, related to the tastes of XVth-century sentimental fiction, seems to point towards the second of these hypotheses. Now before drawing hasty conclusions, the analysis of these modifications, which falls outside the subject of this chapter, must take into account also the fact that the amplifications continue during the scene of the death of Merlin and affect a whole series of chapters in which Bandemagus, the knight who witnesses the seer's end, travels along the route that goes from Arthur's court to the tomb in the wood. Gracia (2007: 234, 238), in this respect, contemplates the possibility that such amplifications were in fact the work of a Spanish adapter, but expresses caution when it comes to accepting the hypothesis of a single Peninsular archetype. The same prudence, it should be said in passing, is shown by Soberanas (1979: 178) in proposing the opposite hypothesis, that is to say, that the added episodes which feature Bandemagus may be of French origin. In a recent article Gracia (2013b) firmly defends this possibility. Whatever the situation, the existence of MS ST of *José de Arimateia*, another similarly early text, opens the possibility that the later versions of the XVth and XVIth century, among which the *Baladros* are counted, may give a very partial view of what actually constituted the diffusion of Arthurian material in the Peninsula.

The second of the Portuguese fragments reproduces the episode which in the French version is known as the Roche aux Pucelles, the Rock of the Ladies, and which has a certain tradition in the texts of the Matter of Britain (Lorenzo Gradín and Souto Cabo 2001: 184–93). Independently of the faery origins of the motif of the ladies who inhabit an inaccessible or protected space, which could be related equally with the supernatural islands of Celtic tradition such as Avalon, as with the Castellum Puellarum of the *Historia regum Britanniae* of Geoffrey of Monmouth, the reinterpretation of the motif carried out in the *Suite du Merlin* shows the immediate influence of *Meraugis de Portlesguez*, a verse narrative written by Raoul de Houdenc (*c*.1210). In this work there already appear the inaccessible mountain, the group of ladies and their association with prophecy and with Merlin. The knightly protagonist arrives at this place so that the seer can reveal to him the place in which he will be able to find Gawain. However, the most striking thing about this *roman* is that the rock receives the name *esplumeor Merlin* or 'moulting cage of Merlin', the enigmatic refuge to which, according to the *Perceval en prose* (*c*.1200), the prophet had retired after the destruction of the Arthurian kingdom. Pseudo-Boron took up a secondary episode of *Meraugis de Portlesguez* and gave it a structural function at the heart of the *Post-Vulgate*, in accordance with the compositional logic of the prose cycles. This it achieved, on the one hand, by explaining what Raoul de Houdenc had left in the shadows of mystery, that is to say, the identity of the twelve ladies and how they had come to be on top of the mountain; and on the other, by involving various characters and the associated narrative complexes, thanks to the motif of the enchantment. The prophecies of Merlin, in turn, permitted him to relate this passage with the prophecies on the destruction of the kingdom of Logres (Bogdanow 1966: 185–8).

But the episode of the Roche aux Pucelles, as elaborated in the *Post-Vulgate*, is also related with other cyclical texts of the XIIIth century. Thus, the madness of Galvam and Marot, which precedes their arrival at the mountain, was already encountered in the episode of the Pillar of the Dolorous Mountain, found in the Second Continuation of the *Perceval* of Chrétien de Troyes (Roach and Ivy 1971: lines 31421–32027).[21] According to this *roman*, the pillar in question had been enchanted by Merlin, so that it would produce madness in all knights who tied their horses to it, except for the best knight in the kingdom. Additionally, the idea of the vengeance of Merlin, linked to an enchanted place and a group of ladies, appears in the *Livre d'Artus*, in the version of the *Suite-Vulgate* reproduced in BNF MS fr. 337 (of the end of the XIIIth century). There it is related that Merlin established the marvels of an enchanted place, called the

Isle Tournoyant, to take revenge upon a noble who wished to kill him. Moreover, he transported thither the noble's daughter, who would remain prisoner in that place until the best knights in the world came there and put an end to the spells (Sommer 1908–16: VII [1913]: 301–2). The relationship of this story with the Portuguese fragment is not limited to a single similarity concerning the vengeance of Merlin after having been threatened with death. The motif of the Insola Tornante appeared previously in the *Estoire del Saint Graal,* both in its *Vulgate* version and in the *Post-Vulgate,* and therefore reappears in *José de Arimateia* (Carter 1967: 69, 199–202). In this work, the marvels of the island are not attributed to Merlin, but are of natural origin (according to the theory of the Four Elements, it involved a floating island, drifting across the sea, which had become caught in a magnetic field) but also with a supernatural origin, because on it Nascião comes across the ship of Salomão.

The *Demanda do Santo Graal*

The final section of the *Post-Vulgate* consists of a *Queste del Saint Graal,* which is distinguished from that of the *Lancelot-Graal* because, amongst other features, it incorporated elements of the *Tristan en prose* and ended with a summary version of the *Mort Artu.* In Portuguese, there is preserved a witness of this work, the *Demanda do Santo Graal* contained in Österreichische Nationalbibliothek MS 2594. It is a codex consisting of 202 folios measuring 297 × 222 mm, four of which are paper and the remainder vellum. The text occupies 193 folios and is arranged in two columns, which vary from 25 to 47 lines. In its production at least five separate hands were involved, using a *bâtarde* script of the XVth century. The majority of chapters open with a rubric, but there are sections of the text in which the space reserved for the rubric remained blank, while sometimes the copyist transcribes in the margin rubrics that should have been incorporated into the text block (Bogdanow 1991–2001, I: 208–10).

As stated, the manuscript of the *Demanda* dates from the XVth century; from the linguistic analysis of the text, Michaëlis de Vasconcelos (1908: 6) concluded that the copy was made in the period of D. Duarte I (1433–8), a thesis later taken up by Lapa (1982a: 312; 1982b: 346–7). Later scholars reaffirmed this chronology, pointing out that D. Duarte had in his library a *livro de Galaaz,* together with copies of a *livro de Tristão* and another of *Merlim* (Megale 2005: 137). Notwithstanding, the relationship between this monarch and the Vienna ÖNB MS lacks any more solid evidence, and has even been denied by Castro (2001: 196), who considers that the Vienna ÖNB manuscript is later than the death of D. Duarte. The surviving manuscript is a copy of another one, which would not have been the original text either. Its late character, as in the case of MS TT of *José de Arimateia,* affects the linguistic analysis of the text, through the resulting process of modernisation to which it was subjected, but has not prevented the identification of features of much earlier date, which Klob (1902: 198–202) put at the beginning of the XIVth century and which Braga and Michaëlis (1897) placed in the second half of the XIIIth century. Michaëlis (1908: 6) even ventured to suggest that the first state of the language of the *Demanda* was of the reign of Alfonso X, although she postponed her definitive conclusions to a future study which she never published. Lapa (1982a: 312–15) supported this chronology, underlining the resemblance between certain expressions used in the text with those encountered in the language of the troubadours, together with linguistic features that likewise belong to this period.[22] This scholar even suggested a possible linguistic influence of the northern region of Trás-os-Montes, which would have related it to the neighbouring areas of Astorga and the possible involvement of Joam Sanches in the copying of *José de Arimateia*.[23] But he also noted, as had Nunes (1908), Braga and Michaëlis (1897: 213) and Bell (1922: 64, 71), the French substratum, which revealed the origins of the original text and which would explain the presence of expressions such as *sergente, onta, a meu ciente, malmenar* etc. It was mentioned above how the early chronology proposed by Lapa was called into question by Rossi (1979: 50–60), since some of the examples on which Lapa based his hypothesis are found in later texts from the XIVth and XVth centuries.

The first identifiable owner of the MS was Pedro de Navarra y de la Cueva, Marquis of Cábrega. The volume arrived in Vienna in 1670 or 1671, when the library of the Marquis was acquired by what would later become the Österreichische Nationalbibliothek. There it was given the shelfmark N. 348, which is written on one of the front endpapers. In the XIXth century it was renumbered and bound in calf with the imperial arms and the title *A Historia dos Cavaleiros da Mesa Redonda e da Demanda do Santo Graal* (Bogdanow 1991–3: I, 208–9). From the first half of that century the codex has aroused the growing interest of scholars.[24] The first attempt at identification was made by Mone (1838: 551), who transcribed the *incipit* thinking that it was a copy of *Lancelot*. Years later it was mentioned by Wolf and Hofmann (1856a: I, lxxxiv–lxxxv) and Varnhagen (1872: 20–4). In 1887 Paris identified it as the final section of the *Pseudo-Boron* trilogy, whose central part, *Merlin*, he had published the year before. Its position in this cycle was later reaffirmed by Braga and Michaëlis de Vasconcelos (1897: 215), who also dated its original redaction. From then on work began in order to relate the *Demanda* with the various witnesses of the French prose cycles. Thus, Pauphilet (1907) related the Vienna manuscript to the version offered by BNF MS fr. 343, while Sommer (1907) collated them also with BNF MSS fr. 112 and 340 and with the Castilian versions. The analyses of the Portuguese work, then, were integrated into the discussions which for years attempted to resolve the characterisation of the *Post-Vulgate* as a cycle independent of and different from the *Lancelot-Graal*.

The first partial edition, of the first seventy-two folios, was published by Reinhardstöttner in 1887; his work was complemented by Sommer (1907), who brought out various sections that Reinhardstöttner had left unpublished. At the turn of the century, both Wechssler (1895, 1898) and Klob proposed to edit the entire text. However, this task was never accomplished, and only Klob succeeded in publishing several passages (Klob 1900–1; 1902: 198–201). Later anthologies were based on these early transcriptions, such as Nunes (1906: 81–2), who followed Klob in his *Crestomatia*, and Roberts (1956: 49–52), who reproduced and emended texts transcribed by Reinhardstöttner. In 1927 Magne began the publication of extracts from the work in the *Revista de Lingua Portuguesa*, but his final instalment was interrupted two years later, when he had already established the text of fols 1–56a, together with the final section, with the narrative of the *Mort Artu* (Magne 1927, 1928, 1929). The complete edition, which was delayed until 1944, was the subject of numerous criticisms, among other reasons because of excessive editorial interventions, the modernisation of spelling, and certain editorial decisions.[25] As a reply, this scholar offered a second edition, with numerous emendations of his first version, and in which the critical text was accompanied by the facsimile edition and a glossary. The work was published as a whole between 1955 and 1970. For his part, Piel had begun to work on an edition in the same year in which Magne's first instalment appeared. It was to be published by the University of Coimbra Press, but in 1934 this was closed by the Portuguese authorities, when a considerable part of the text had already been printed (27 quires of 16 pages, totalling 432 pages). After this contretemps, Piel abandoned the project and the work he had carried out was deposited in the Imprensa Nacional de Lisboa, where it was rediscovered in 1987. Freire Nunes revised the work of the German scholar and completed the edition, which appeared in 1988 (Castro 1988b: 195–6; Freire Nunes 1999a: 60–1). Later, Castro (2003–6) found new preparatory materials for the edition by Piel, which he used to propose some alternative readings to Freire Nunes, and to call, as Bogdanow had (1985–7), for an interpretative critical edition that would take into account the French witnesses in the reconstruction of the Portuguese text. In her edition of the *Post-Vulgate Queste del Saint Graal*, Bogdanow also used parts of the Portuguese *Demanda* for those passages in which the French text did not survive. Finally, 2005 saw the publication of a second edition of Piel and Freire Nunes (1988), which takes into account a number of readings contained in the unpublished work of Piel which Castro brought to light.

The Portuguese *Demanda do Santo Graal* constitutes the most complete surviving exemplar of the *Post-Vulgate Queste del Saint Graal*, whence the importance that this work has for knowledge of the cycle in question. Its study obliges us to take into account the complex web of textual relations that the Vienna ÖNB manuscript establishes with the other versions of the *Queste*, such as the French witnesses, all of them incomplete, and the printed editions in Castilian of Toledo (1515) and Seville (1535). But it is also necessary to pay attention to those indicators that link the *Demanda* with other prose cycles, such as the *Vulgate* and the *Tristan en prose*. The analysis carried out by Bogdanow (1966) of this group of texts led her to suppose that the Portuguese *Demanda* derived from a second redaction of the *Post-Vulgate*, which in turn would have shared a common source (the first redaction) with the reworking of the *Queste* that was integrated into the second version of the *Tristan en prose*. The divergences from this latter version are caused by the fidelity which the *Tristan* exhibits in some passages in relation to the *Vulgate* redaction of the *Queste del Saint Graal*, which Pseudo-Boron reinterprets or modifies, or to the amplifications in which the latter indulges, and to the referrals to other parts of the cycle, with which he attempted to give cohesion to his narrative. Precisely for this reason, the Portuguese *Demanda* represents a more faithful version of what the original *Post-Vulgate Queste* must have been, compared to the *Queste* included in the *Tristan en prose*. The latter was conceived as an adaptation to form part of this cycle, for which reason it eliminated all those elements that in the first version sought the cohesion of the story at the heart of the *Post-Vulgate* cycle (Bogdanow 1991–2001: I, 44, 60–97; Freire Nunes 1999a: 84).

The analysis of the Iberian redactions of the *Queste del Saint Graal* of Pseudo-Boron has been conditioned, as was suggested above, by the dispute about the priority of some Iberian texts over others. Its conclusions began with the hypothesis that all of these versions derived from a single text, crafted in the Peninsula, and are based on the general closeness between the Portuguese and the Castilian versions. Bogdanow (1975), who recognised the interdependence of the Hispanic witnesses, grouped them together in a single branch of the textual tradition. They all derive from a single original, which shares a common ancestor with BNF MS fr. 116 and which exhibits a more distant relationship, by way of a hyparchetype, which she designates as z^1, with the textual family represented by BNF MSS fr. 112 and 343. The comparison of the Portuguese manuscript with the Spanish printed editions reveals that the latter are less faithful to the French original and contain more errors of copying and misinterpretations. Since the surviving Iberian exemplars are late, it is not always clear whether these errors are the responsibility of the Castilian translator or later copyists. However, some of the erroneous readings in the printed editions could be explained on the basis of an original text in Portuguese, while the opposite possibility (that is, Portuguese passages in which an error results from misinterpretation of a Castilian text) is documented on a single occasion, which, moreover, Castro (2002a) dismisses on the basis of linguistic and palaeographic criteria.[26] For this reason, Bogdanow is inclined to accept a first translation into Portuguese, from which the remaining Peninsular witnesses would have descended.

Despite the difficulty of establishing the origin of the divergences among the Portuguese and Castilian versions, for the reason stated, scholars have attempted to treat these systematically, seeking to establish on the basis of them some principle of composition. The greater brevity of the Castilian *Demandas* is caused, in the main, by a greater number of omissions in comparison to the Portuguese text. Bohigas (1925a: 56–65) identified the most important modifications: the advice given by a hermit to the Arthurian knights before they set out on the Grail quest; the explanation of the symbolism of the shield of Galaaz; the symbolism of the ship of Salomão; the scene of the conversion of Lanzarote; and the explanation in spiritual terms of certain adventures. Conversely, the passages which appear in the Castilian versions but are not reproduced in the Portuguese contain the death of Yvan de las Blancas Manos, the failed attempts of Arthur to construct a tower, which Charlemagne would build, and the encounter of Galaaz and Count Bedoin. Both *Demandas*, moreover, part company in the ending of the Grail quest, with the last scenes in Corberic, and the transition to the *Mort Artu*, until Agravaín discovers the relationship between Lanzarote and Ginebra. The comparison between the Castilian printed editions and the Portuguese manuscript reveals that the former are less interested in the symbolism and the spiritual dimension of the story and the marvellous elements, and are on the contrary attracted to the combats and the profane and courtly adventures. Their tastes are close to those of the nascent genre of the romances of chivalry, which were flowering at the time of their publication, at the beginning of the XVIth century. The Portuguese *Demanda*, for its part, maintains not only these spiritual aspects scorned by its Castilian counterparts, but also those others that sought to integrate the work in the macrotextual complex of the *Post-Vulgate*. Put another way, the Castilian *Demandas* have undertaken the ideological and editorial modernisation of the content, while the Portuguese maintains an awareness of the cyclical cohesion of the original texts (Freire Nunes 1999a: 85–91; Hall 1982; Trujillo 2004: 97–136; 2009: 421–33; 2013).

Alongside these specific discrepancies, the storyline of the Portuguese *Demanda* follows very closely that found in the Castilian redaction.[27] It begins with the investiture of Galaaz as a knight and his arrival at Camelot on the feast of Pentecost. This very day, amid a series of marvels, the Holy Grail appears and the knights of King Arthur, incited by Gawain, set off in search of the relic. The story then concentrates on the parallel adventures that the principal knights encounter, with special attention paid to those belonging to the rival clans of King Bam and King Lot. Throughout the quest, many of the participants die. Arthur's kingdom, weakened by this, suffers an invasion by Mars of Cornualha, allied to the Saxons. Arthur is besieged in Camelot and is saved from defeat only by the assistance of Galaaz. Finally, Lanzarote's son reaches Corberic, cures King Peleam and together with another eleven knights contemplates the Holy Grail. After Galaaz has witnessed, alone, the mysteries of the Grail, he departs accompanied by Boorz and Perceval to the city of Sarraz. There Galaaz dies, after being declared king, and the Holy Cup ascends to Heaven. Perceval retires to a hermitage, but Boorz returns to Camelot, where the disputes between Lanzarote and the sons of Lot are growing. Arthur discovers, through the fault of the latter, the relationship between Ginebra and Lanzarote, and the latter has to flee from Camelot. During the war between Arthur and Lanzarote, at the gates of Gaunes, Morderet takes possession of the kingdom of Logres and forces the king to return in haste. After the battle of Salesberes and the disappearance of Arthur, Lanzarote and his lineage disembark in Britain and rout the sons of Morderet. Then Lanzarote becomes a hermit and dies a short time later. Faced with the power vacuum affecting the kingdom, Mars invades Logres again, desecrates the tomb of Lanzarote, and destroys Camelot and the Round Table. The work ends with the death of Mars at the hands of Paulas, a knight of the lineage of King Bam.

It is usually asserted that, in its adaptation of the *Queste del Saint Graal*, the *Post-Vulgate* devalued the theological and spiritual element offered by the *Vulgate*. Pseudo-Boron, in effect, diluted the mystical experience of Galahad in the complex of adventures in which the knights of the Round Table took part. According to Bogdanow (1966: 221), his aim was to offer a story not only about the chosen knight, but about the *roiaume aventureux* of Logres as a whole. The reasons for this modification are, clearly, ideological, since the new cycle does not have the same motivations that led to the composition of the *Lancelot-Graal*. But these would also be of a type related to composition, since, as is shown by the numerous metapoetic reflections that are scattered throughout his work, Pseudo-Boron sought the harmonious composition of a cycle, in which each section of the narrative would have a balanced length and each fact would have its explanation. The multiplication of adventures responds, then, to the overall poetics of the prose cycles, which in this case are attempting to track the 150 knights who set off on the quest for the Grail, or at least the most distinguished of them. The colophon constituted by the *Mort Artu*, incorporated at the end of the *Queste*, abounds in this vision, for which reason it adds a series of earthly events, alien to the spiritual enterprise in which Galahad was the protagonist.

Observations of this nature apply also to the Portuguese *Demanda*, which is, of course, a version of the *Post-Vulgate Queste*. In it, the end of the kingdom of Logres will be caused by the internecine struggles between the opposed lineages of Bam and Lot, and by the invasion by Mars of Cornualha. That is to say, after Galaaz's epiphany, Logres falls because of political decline and moral decay of the knightly universe, presided over by a weakened Arthur incapable of controlling these destructive forces. Thus, the quest for the Grail begins not at the initiative of the king, but as that of a negative character like Galvam, who wishes to contemplate the Holy Cup without the veil which had shrouded its appearance at Camelot.[28] Similarly, Arthur is impotent when it comes to suppressing the internal disputes and confronting the first invasion by Mars. His character, besides being weak, is tarnished by some blameworthy actions, as is shown by the story of Artur o Pequeno, his bastard son. The similarity between this and the story of the conception of Meraugis by Mars brings Arthur close to the pervasively negative character of the king of Cornualha (Laranjinha 2007–8: 14).

However, it must not be forgotten that the nucleus of the story remains the quest for the Holy Grail, in the same way as its protagonist is Galaaz. The loss of certain theological elaborations, which characterised the *Vulgate Queste*, does not diminish, for example, the importance given to Christian virtues in the *Demanda* as a guide to the behaviour of the knights, or condemnations of profane chivalry. Lanzarote's son treasures virtues of a varied nature, in the same way that in him there comes together the triple dimension of the knightly, the royal and the sacerdotal. For this reason, some of his characteristics relate to an element of sanctity, while others exalt his knightly valour. These virtues – virginity, humility, restraint in the use of arms, sense of justice, clemency, practice of communion, confession, and penitence – stand out for their intrinsic value but also for their opposition to the defects in the knighthood of Logres (Miranda 1998b: 104–5). For this reason, Galaaz serves as a double counterpoint, to Lanzarote and to Galvam, both of them representatives of traditional knighthood, which because of its adherence to earthly values fails in the quest for the Grail (Zierer 2012a: 37).[29] Each embodies, however, different attitudes. Compared to Lanzarote, who repents of his lust and in part redeems himself, Galvam recognises his sins, but is incapable of contrition. The knights receive a retribution in proportion to the moral condition of their conduct and all those who exhibit some defect end up paying with death and condemnation. This idea of proportional recompense applies even to those knights who, like Galaaz, Perceval and Boorz, aspire to perfection. Among these there is established a gradation of access to the Grail and the contemplation of its mysteries. And after these three chosen ones, another nine knights, virtuous but to a lesser extent, contemplate the Grail in the Paaço Aventuroso of Corberic, thus creating an imitation of the Twelve Apostles and the rite of the Last Supper. The rest constitute earthly knighthood, the lowest step in this hierarchy, which is condemned to destruction.

The most censured sin, as was the case in the *Vulgate*, continues to be lust. A hermit explains the quest of the Holy Grail as the separation of the good knights from the bad, identifying the latter with the lustful (Piel and Freire Nunes 2005: 166, 132). In consequence, the trio of knights of the Grail is arranged according to their distance from this sin: Boorz, chaste but not a virgin, occupies the lowest place, after Perceval, a virgin and virtuous, but open to temptations, and Galaaz, inaccessible in his perfection. Even a pagan knight, such as Palomades, receives a more benevolent treatment than his antagonist, Tristan, who, although Christian, is lustful. Palomades is converted and achieves the contemplation of the Grail in Corberic, at the time when he is the protagonist of a quest parallel to that for the Grail: that of the Bestia Ladrador, in which the other knights fail because they conceive it as just another chivalric adventure and do not recognise its redemptive element. Tristan, for his part, is not only excluded from the quest for the Grail, but appears in a dream to Lanzarote, among the fires of Hell, suffering alongside Iseo and Guinevere.[30] Lust is interpreted as the route of entry for the remaining vices and as the beginning of perdition, which leads to eternal condemnation and precipitates a chain of sins (Gracia 1993: 206; Zierer 2012b: 41). Thus, just before the quest begins, a knight of the court dies, punished by God, since he had raped his sister and mother and killed both, as well as his brother and father (Piel and Freire Nunes 2005: 9, 24–5; 33, 41). Tanas, the grandfather of Artur o Pequeno, attempts to rape his daughter-in-law, kills her and follows this by killing his son and daughter and abandoning his grandson in a wood (Piel and Freire Nunes 2005: 362, 273–4). In addition, Mars causes Ladiana to be killed, so that it will not be revealed that he has had a son by her, called Meraugis (Piel and Freire Nunes 2005: 278, 224–5). In various of these stories, lust is associated not only with killings and suicides, but also with incest. But this aspect extends to other parts of the *Post-Vulgate*, as is shown by the incestuous conception of Mordered, which goes back to the *Suite du Merlin*, and the consequences of which affect the denouement of the cycle. The almost obsessive insistence with which Pseudo-Boron repeats this narrative scheme shows his horror at such crimes, but also reveals his wish to indoctrinate.[31] One of the most abominable examples that is narrated explains the origin of the Bestia Ladrador, the fruit of the curse that the son of Hipomenes utters against his sister before dying. She had accused him of having raped her, when in reality he had rejected her incestuous urgings, for which reason he was executed. The Bestia embodies the association of sin with monstrosity and reveals the latter to reflect both the struggle between Good and Evil and the moral degradation of knightly society (Siqueira 2012: 91–2).

After lust, other sins come to rule the universe of courtly chivalry. Leonel, for example, is seized by anger towards his brother and in his frenzy kills Calogrenante and a lady (Piel and Freire Nunes 2005: 177–80, 142–5); Erec sins by an excess of pride and places his honour before the life of his sister, whom he finds himself obliged to kill in order to maintain a *don contraignant* (Piel and Freire Nunes 2005: 293–6, 233–6);[32] the hate and envy of Galvam and his brothers towards the lineage of King Bam precipitates the destruction of the kingdom and is one of the central motifs of the final section of the *Demanda*; and Galvam himself, the most degraded knight of the kingdom, is accused of perjury and disloyalty by Erec (Piel and Freire Nunes 2005: 342, 260) and acts as a coward, traitor, and murderer without pity towards other companions of the Round Table. But an example like that of Erec, cited above, or those of Calogrenante, Bagdemagu, Meraugis and so many other knights, who all fulfil the requirements of the knightly code, discover that it is this which drives them towards perdition and which through its contradictions condemns the entire kingdom to impiety and destruction. This tragic destiny often works through chance and through paradoxical situations, such as that which leads so many companions of the Round Table to kill one another because they have exchanged arms and do not recognise one another during the combat. The supreme paradox of Arthur in the *Suite du Merlin*, that during the festivals at his coronation he engenders the person who will cause his death, enshrines this atmosphere of fate, of *mescheance*, which Bogdanow (1966: 216) recognises as one of the central themes of the entire cycle.

It is, therefore, possible that the *Demanda* may reduce the theological sophistication of the *Vulgate Queste*, but it reveals itself to be just as preoccupied as, or more so than, the latter with sins and with the punishments that sinners merit. And the Portuguese version accentuates this rigour in comparison with, for example, the French texts, as has been shown by Van Coolput-Storms (1999) in his analysis of the episode of the castle of Bruto (Piel and Freire Nunes 2005: 108–20, 90–8). The God of *Pseudo-Boron* is not the merciful God of the *Lancelot-Graal*, but one who shows himself to be justice-dispensing and implacable, and who punishes above all through fire: the knight who dies at the beginning catches fire while leaning out of a window (Piel and Freire Nunes 2005: 9, 24–5); the lady who obliges Erec to kill his sister is consumed in a burning cloud (Piel and Freire Nunes 2005: 297, 236–7); the enchanter of King Pelles burns after the devils carry him through the air (Piel and Freire Nunes 2005: 391, 297); Castelo Felom is burned by Galaaz, Estor and Meraugis (Piel and Freire Nunes 2005: 510, 378); a storm of hail and lightning destroys the fortress where Perceval's sister dies (Piel and Freire Nunes 2005: 445, 332); and various sinners appear in dreams and visions, purging their sins among the flames, such as Guinevere, crowned with a burning crown of thorns, Tristam, Iseo and Ivam o Bastardo (Piel and Freire Nunes 2005: 202, 161–2; 207, 166–7). Also Simeu burns in his tomb, awaiting the extinguishing of the flame which tortures him on the arrival of Galaaz so that he can die (Piel and Freire Nunes 2005: 465–7, 344–6). The sin of the last-named character was related in *José de Arimateia*, and his punishment, also by fire, is similar to that of Mois, who in that work occupied the forbidden seat at the Grail table. Both reveal the continuity which, also in this aspect of sins and faults, exists in the various sections of the *Post-Vulgate*. In these the purifying value of flame is considered, as is the redemptive character of penitence, but also the progressive conversion of Purgatory into Hell, which Le Goff has pointed out (1996: 46).

This infernalisation of faults and their associated penalties is linked to the rigour with which those who show themselves opposed to the Christian faith are treated. Although the *Demanda* lacks the evangelical vocation observed in *José de Arimateia*, the pagans opposed to Christianity pay with their lives for their recalcitrant attitude or their criminal behaviour. It happens in this way at Castelo Felom and the castle of Count Arnalt. Galaaz massacres the inhabitants of the latter location, and a hermit calms his scruples with these words: 'Nosso Senhor vos gradece muito quanto i havedes feito. E sabede que vos nom enviou acá por al senom pera matá-los, ca nom som cristãos, senom os peores homens do mundo' (Piel and Freire Nunes 2005: 430, 324). The numerous manifestations of Evil include also the practice of necromancy, here clearly associated with the devil, just as Merlin, its best-known representative, was in the *Suite*. Morgan, for example, appears in a dream to Lanzarote 'mui fea e mui espantosa', dressed in a wolf skin and surrounded by devils (Piel and Freire Nunes 2005: 202, 161). And the enchanter at the court of Pelles, already mentioned, confesses how he sold his soul to the devil. For this reason, he loses his powers in the presence of Galaaz, before being dragged off by devils.

But the exemplary dimension of the *Demanda* is not only revealed through the display of negative models. Galaaz, despite being a figure stylised through his perfection, is proposed as an example of Christian knighthood, in which the ascetic way culminates in the mystic experience of the contemplation of the Grail and its mysteries. The son of Lanzarote is a messianic figure, whose arrival was already announced in *José de Arimateia* and whose activity assumes a redemptive dimension. Some of his actions are tinged with an aura of sanctity, such as his miracle-working powers, which at times make him a Christ-figure. The serge with which he girds his body cures a lady affected by leprosy who puts it on (Piel and Freire Nunes 2005: 407–8, 307–9); he releases a 'mad woman' who in reality was possessed by the devil (Piel and Freire Nunes 2005: 401, 303–4); he cures a paralysed man (Piel and Freire Nunes 2005: 624, 456–7); he is immune to the poison of Mares (Piel and Freire Nunes 2005: 484–6, 359–60); he inhibits the powers of the magician of King Pelles (389, 295–6); he is liberated from prison in Castelo Felom by God, who demolishes the tower in which he is imprisoned (Piel and Freire Nunes 2005: 509, 377–8); and he himself, on his arrival, liberates Simeu from the fire in which he was burning (Piel and Freire Nunes 2005: 465–7, 344–6). On occasions he is referred to as 'santa cousa' (Piel and Freire Nunes 2005: 58, 59; 401, 303) and Simeu himself recognises his holiness: 'Ta santidade e ta verdadeira vida me livrou de gram coita.' It is precisely the freeing of Simeu and Mois that will be classed as miracles (Piel and Freire Nunes 2005: 582, 430). His pre-eminent position in the assembly of the twelve knights of Corberic who attend the mass of the Grail, inspired by the Last Supper, likewise underlines the Christological component in his mission. However, his identification with Christ is counterbalanced by the similarity of some of his actions with those that are related not in the Gospels but in the Acts of the Apostles, and by his designation as 'sergente de Jhesu Cristo' by Simeu (Piel and Freire Nunes 2005: 467, 345) and the heavenly knight who gives him the white shield (Piel and Freire Nunes 2005: 49, 53), and even by the label of 'servo de Jhesu Cristo' (Piel and Freire Nunes 2005: 58, 59). From this perspective, he would be an agent of Christ, rather than the knightly incarnation of the latter (Faria 2006a; Miranda 1998b: 70–1). Besides, Galaaz is not the only character with saintly conduct and redemptive features. The sacrifice of the sister of Perceval follows an identical model, because she offers her blood and with it she sacrifices her life to cure a woman with leprosy, that is to say, a sinner (Piel and Freire Nunes 2005: 437–44, 327–32).[33] The *Demanda*, without freeing itself from misogynist prejudices of the Middle Ages, dilutes the negative vision of woman through its redemptive female characters, like the one cited, or those who are victims of the violence unleashed by the masculine world of the knights. On the one hand, the daughter of Hipomenes provokes the death of her brother, and Guinevere precipitates with her lust the perdition of Lancelot and the entire kingdom; but, on the other, the mother of Artur o Pequeno suffers the double abuse of being violated by Arthur and killed by her father, while Erec's sister is an innocent victim, who appears in dreams to her brother in the form of a sacrificial lamb (Piel and Freire Nunes 2005: 292, 233).

All this doctrinal content, which is transmitted through a symbolic mode of expression, affects the meaning of certain events or elements in the story, such as animals (Chambel 2000; De Medeiros 2002). Some of these elements, like the ship of

Salomão, the white stag kept by four lions, and the shield of Galaaz, were already present in *José de Arimateia* and their reappearance contributes once again to the semantic cohesion of the cycle. Likewise there stand out the dreams and visions, which are usually of a heavenly nature and which serve to admonish the characters. Their structural function affects both the reading of the work on a spiritual plane and its function as a lineage narrative. To these is joined its allegorical-exegetical dimension, since its interpretation often requires the active involvement of readers (Contreras 2005e, 2010). This last aspect would emphasise a possible reading of the work as an exemplary narrative, in which there are shown a series of modes of behaviour counterposed, negative and positive, which would be offered as a model to the knightly society of late medieval Portugal.

The Five Galician-Portuguese *Lais de Bretanha*

In the corpus of the secular lyric in Galician-Portuguese there exists a group of five anonymous *cantigas*, with the shared characteristic that their poetic content refers to the fictional Arthurian universe. However, unlike other *cantigas*, which have specific allusions to characters or motifs from this literary material, the so-called *Lais de Bretanha* are compositions belonging to the French prose cycles, translated into Galician-Portuguese. That is to say, they are brief Arthurian fragments which were included in the compilations of troubadour lyrics. These poems are copied on fols 10r–11r of MS Cod. 10991 of the Biblioteca Nacional, Lisbon (*Cancioneiro* B), and on fols 276r–278v of codex Lat. 7182 of the Biblioteca Apostolica Vaticana (L), in both cases following the same order: *Amor, des que m'a vos cheguei* (B1, L1), *O Marot aja mal-grado* (B2, L2), *Mui gran temp'á, par deus, que eu non vi* (B3, L3), *Don Amor, eu cant'e choro* (B4, L4) and *Ledas sejamos ogemais!* (B5, L5). Their separate study in the context of Galician-Portuguese lyric is justified not only by their Arthurian filiation, but also because they are placed in the mouths of characters extracted from that narrative tradition, to whom their authorship is also attributed. This last characteristic, moreover, like the circumstances of their composition, made it necessary to provide notes to explain the texts (Michaëlis 1904: II, 480). Thus, that of Lai 1 informs us that it was composed by Elis o Baço, Duke of Sansoña, who had fallen in love with Iseo when he went to Britain to fight Tristan and thereby avenge the death of his father.[34] Lai 3 is preceded in B by the indication 'Don Tristan, o Namorado, fez [e]sta cantiga' (Lagares 2000: 108), while L and the *Tavola Colocciana* (C) attribute it to 'Don Tristan'.[35] Of Lai 5 it is stated that it was the work of a group of ladies, who dedicated it to Lanzarote during his sojourn in the Insoa da Lidiça;[36] while the ladies responsible for no. 2 addressed it to Marot, who sent to a prison in Ireland all the ladies whom he captured. He behaved in this manner in vengeance for the death of his father, who had died taking care of a lady.[37]

Another of the particular features of the *Lais de Bretanha* within the troubadour corpus arises from its anomalous location in B. In fact, the five *cantigas* were copied on the first folios of the codex, at the head of the lyric corpus and outside the criteria of classification (by genre, author, and chronology) according to which this collection was organised. Their anomalous location is confirmed by the indications in the *Tavola Colocciana*, in which the *Lais* also occupy positions 1–5. This indicates that, in effect, these texts were incorporated into the great Galician-Portuguese poetic collections in a late phase when the rest of the *cantigas* had already been classified and transcribed.

It remains to establish who was the author of the *Lais*, who introduced them into the troubadour corpus, and in which cultural milieu they were composed and incorporated. Michaëlis de Vasconcelos (1904: II, 479) linked this process with the figure of the Count of Barcelos, Don Pedro, a hypothesis which has not been disproved by subsequent scholars (Ferrari 1993: 377). In the first place, scholars have recognised the work of compiling *cancioneiros* carried out by this individual, to whom is attributed the preparation of a codex of *cantigas*, which would have been the archetype of the surviving *cancioneiros* B and V. Secondly, this author and patron of troubadours maintained a court with an appreciable cultural activity, which includes the collection and composition of lyric texts, but also historiographic and narrative works. The allusion to the shriek of Merlin in a *cantiga* by Estevan da Guarda (*Com'avẽeo a Merlin de morrer*, B1324/V930), a troubadour from his court circle, and the presence of brief stories about the reign of Arthur in two of the works compiled there, the *Livro de linhagens* and the *Crónica geral de 1344*, would suggest that perhaps the count possessed a solid knowledge of the Arthurian material. However, and as we will see below, from the information given by Don Pedro in these two works it is impossible to deduce that he had a special familiarity with Arthurian literature, but that, rather, his knowledge was of the Hispanic chronicles and the succinct narrative with which this historiographic tradition furnished him, and the prose romance cycles, already known by other troubadours. And as far as concerns the allusion to Merlin by Estevan da Guarda in particular, it is neither innovatory nor surprising, since the circulation of Arthurian texts among the troubadours is documented continuously from the mid-XIIIth century. Even the allusion to another motif from the *Post-Vulgate* cycle, the Bestia Ladrador, which is brought into one of his *cantigas* by Fernand'Esquio (B1607/V1140), an author somewhat earlier than Estevan da Guarda, should perhaps be located at the court of D. Denis, which this troubadour would have frequented. In this respect, Bautista (2013) recognises that, although D. Pedro could have made use of the prose cycles in his works, he did so in order to obtain a limited amount of secondary information from them (the wound caused to Gawain by Lancelot, Morderet's death from a lance-thrust etc.), and with a purely utilitarian purpose, from an historiographic perspective. Bautista goes so far as to suggest a negative view of Arthurian literature on the part of D. Pedro. Therefore, one may conclude that the Count of Barcelos was indeed aware of Arthurian literature, but nothing permits us to suppose that, apart from the attribution of the *Lais*, he was more devoted to or more familiar with it than other contemporary Iberian authors. His connection with these five poetic texts would be better based on his role in the process of compilation of *cancioneiros* and on the late incorporation of these poems, but not on any exceptional interest in the Matter of Britain.

At all events, we must not confuse the date at which the *Lais* were composed with the quite different date at which they were incorporated into the troubadour poetic corpus. The first of these can only be assigned a very imprecise date, because of lack of information. The references to episodes in the French prose cycles barely do more than place us in the second half of the XIIIth century, like the allusions to the genre of the *bailada*, which became fashionable in the Galician-Portuguese lyric around those years (Brea 1998). But attempts to link the *Lais* to specific troubadours are mere supposition, without any support from convincing evidence. Thus, as possible authors various candidates have been proposed, from the preferred Count D. Pedro, to, more indiscriminately, troubadours who happen to indicate awareness of Arthurian literature in their poetic production, such as Don Denis, Estevan da Guarda, Fernand'Esquio, Gonçal'Eanes do Vinhal, Johan Garcia de Guilhade, Martin Soarez or even D. Pedro de Aragón, who visited Portugal in 1297 (Michaëlis 1904: II, 384) and to whom Fernán Rodríguez Redondo attributes the composition of some *lais*.[38] Be this as it may, the relative stylistic homogeneity of the *Lais de Bretanha* permits us to supposes that at least in their Galician-Portuguese version they are all from a single pen (Ferrari 1993: 377).

Another of the subjects that has attracted the most attention from critics is the identification of the sources of the five *Lais*. It did not take long for these to be located in passages from the French prose cycles, thus confirming that the Galician-Portuguese texts were translated from originals from north of the Pyrenees. However, this identification unveils a complex panorama with various problems, which in addition reveal the varied provenance of this little corpus of *cantigas*. Lai 1 was inspired by *Amors, de vostre acointement* (or the *Lai de Hélys*), found in the long version of the *Tristan en prose* (Löseth 1891 [1974]: 399; Ménard 1987–97: VI, 316); Lai 3 is also based on another lyric text from this *roman*, *Lonc tans a que il ne vit cele* (Löseth 1891 [1974]: 404; Ménard 1987–97: VI, 368); and the origin of Lai 4 is identical, since it was inspired by the *Lai du plour* or *D'amours vient mon chant et mon plour* (Löseth 1891 [1974]: 538; Ménard 1987–97: IX, 170–1). The location of these texts within the *Tristan en prose* reveals a certain closeness among them, especially with regard to nos. 1 and 3, which derive from almost consecutive chapters of this *roman*.[39] The three are found in the section of the *Post-Vulgate Queste del Saint Graal* that was incorporated into the second redaction of *Tristan*, which could indicate either that only the *lais* from this section of the story have survived, or that the compiler did not use the entire work, but merely this section.

At all events, the Galician-Portuguese *Lais* are not a faithful translation of their French equivalents. The eight monorhymed quatrains of *Amors, de vostre acointement* are converted in *Amor, des que m'a vos cheguei* into ten quatrains rhyming in abba, plus a coda of three lines in which the word 'Amen!' is repeated nine times. The invocation of Love in the French text alternates, in the Galician-Portuguese, with references to the beloved lady and with threats which the speaker addresses to Love himself in the event that the lady should reject him. The amplification is even greater in the case of *Mui gran temp'á, par Deus, que eu non vi* in comparison with *Lonc tans a que il ne vit cele*. In this case, the French stanza of nine lines, with a rhyme-scheme of ababbabbb is converted into three stanzas of seven lines, rhyming abbacca. The theme, in which Tristan accuses himself of having been disloyal to Iseo, through his long absence, is developed in the Iberian version with motifs appropriate to the Galician-Portuguese lyric, such as the *sanha* of the lady, the lover's fear of appearing before her, and the *coita*. By contrast, *D'amours vient mon chant et mon plour*, which contains fourteen lines rhyming ababbaabbaaabb, is reduced in the Peninsular *Lai* to three quatrains rhyming in abab. The bulk of these modifications has been explained as part of a process of adaptation of the French *lais* to Galician-Portuguese stylistic models. The homogeneity of the Hispanic troubadour corpus justifies this approach, since in it such processes of stylistic levelling during the adaptation of motifs and genres from foreign sources are not unusual, such as in the case of the *alba* and the *chanson de toile*. However, it is appropriate to take into account that the amplifications in Lai 1, and to a lesser extent in Lai 3, even though they incorporate stylistic features characteristic of the poetic language of Galician-Portuguese, remain close to the prose text which in *Tristan* precedes or follows the *lais*. This means that these amplifications would have been implemented when the lyric texts and the narrative which framed them were still directly related (Gutiérrez García 2007a).

Separate treatment of Lais 2 and 5 is appropriate since they have no known French sources. Their narrative references, moreover, do not involve the *Tristan en prose*, but separate episodes in the *Post-Vulgate*, a cycle which, unlike the previous one, does not contain lyric inserts. Lai 2 is inspired by a scene in the *Suite du Merlin*, in which a group of ladies defaces the shield of Morholt, while exclaiming 'Diex doinst honte a chelui que te sout porter, car il nous a mainte honte porcachie!' (Roussineau 1996: II, 422). Yvain, one of the knights who contemplates the scene, comments that this hatred is caused by the many insults perpetrated by Morholt against the ladies of this land and that the resentment was mutual. The origin of the enmity, however, remains unexplained.[40] Lai 5 is inspired by a similar scene reproduced in the *Folie Lancelot*. Here, a group of ladies from the Isle de Joie dances around Lancelot's shield, while expressing their joy that the best knight in the world lives among them. The scene is also reproduced in the *Lancelot propre* in the *Vulgate*, but, as Sharrer observes (1994: 179–80),[41] only in the version in the *Folie Lancelot* do the ladies pronounce the phrase which, as in the case of Lai 2, would have inspired the composition of a lyric poem:

'Voirement est ce ly escus au meilleur chevalier du monde' (Bogdanow 1965: 70).[42] It is most probable, then, that the author of the *Lais* developed the two lyric texts on the basis of the implied elements suggested to him by both scenes in the prose narrative, leaving open the possibility that these two lyric poems could have been incorporated into a narrative frame. The information available to us is insufficient to allow us to determine whether their composition was in French or directly in Galician-Portuguese. However, and although linguistic analysis of the five *Lais*, for example, does not reveal any significant presence of Gallicisms, it is no less certain that the work of *amplificatio* involved in the compositions of nos. 2 and 5 recalls the poetic process of the French prose cycles.

It is obvious that the relations between these two compositions and the *Pseudo-Boron* cycle conceal some further complications, since the rubric accompanying Lai 2 explains the motive of the hatred that Morholt felt for the ladies, which is not mentioned in the *Suite du Merlin*. As we have mentioned above, this is caused by the fact that his father had died while guarding one of them, and this is why Morholt kept them locked up in a prison in Ireland. This detail is not given in the surviving French versions of the *Suite du Merlin*, but is found in the Castilian text of the *Baladro del sabio Merlín*, in which it is clarified that in addition Morholt's father had lost two of his brothers for the same reason (Burgos, 28, 121; Seville, 255, 98–9). This detail would relate the source of the *Lais* to this late version of the *Post-Vulgate* (Entwistle 1942: 61–2), but also, at least indirectly, to *Guiron le Courtois*. In this work, this is attributed not to Morholt but to Brehus sans Pitié, in the same way that in the passage of the *Baladros* alluded to above, when this practice of Morholt's was explained, he was compared, for his cruelty, to Brehus. Consequently, the influence of this character on Morholt would be parallel to that which *Guiron* may have exercised on the source of the *Lais* and on the *Baladros* (Gutiérrez García 2001).

The heterogeneity of the five *Lais de Bretanha* obliges us to consider the formation of this small group of Arthurian *cantigas*. One might imagine a first phase, in which the three pieces derived from the *Tristan en prose* formed an initial anthology, of three texts only, not solely because their originals were found in this *roman*, but because in it they occupy passages that are relatively closely grouped within it. This would lead us to consider that the compiler who collected them was working with a section of the *Tristan*, corresponding to the section involving the quest for the Holy Grail. Later, the remaining two would have been translated, on the basis of allusions in the *Post-Vulgate*, and would have been added to the previous three. However, it is also possible that all five came from a miscellaneous codex, which itself brought together episodes from different Arthurian cycles in prose. In this context, Soriano Robles (2003b) calls attention to possible candidates such as BNF MS fr. 12599, which brings together the three *lais* about Tristan that inspired the Iberian texts, plus the narrative context which inspired Lai 5; to BNF MS fr. 112, which despite its late date (1470) adds the material preceding the context of Lai 2; or even ÖNB MS 2452 in Vienna, because of the close similarity which its version of the *Tristan en prose* displays with the fragment of the Galician *Tristan*. Although none of these offers a definitive reply to the questions raised by the Peninsular *Lais*, it is interesting to note that they all exemplify the tendency to group in a single volume the requisite passages from both cycles. On this point, finally, it would be appropriate to note, if only as a suggestion, that the sequence of the three Galician-Portuguese *Lais* from the *Tristan* reproduces that of the prose narrative from which they are derived. It is, moreover, necessary to take into account that Lai 2 was at the outset the one which opened the group of five *cantigas*. This is confirmed by the allusion made in one of the rubrics concerning this *Lai*, finally transcribed as the second in the sequence, 'é a p*rime*ira [cantiga] q*ue* achamos q*ue* foi feita'. In accordance with the narrative of the prose cycles, the episode of Morholt's shield precedes the stay by Lancelot on the Isle de Joie and the quest for the Grail. Thus four of the five *lais*, as may be seen, appear to have been classified in accordance with the narrative logic of the prose *romans*. Only Lai 5 would be out of place, since, from the episode to which it relates, it should be in second place. This latter possibility, finally, should not be discounted either, in view of the instability which on this point is exhibited by the other *Lai* from the *Post-Vulgate*.[43]

Perhaps because of their position on the boundary between the troubadour tradition and the Matter of Britain, perhaps because of the excessive attention paid to the question of their sources, the five *Lais de Bretanha* have not been the subject of attempts at a critical edition until very recently. The first edition available was the diplomatic edition of Molteni (1880: 7–8), which formed part of the edition of the *Cancionero de la Biblioteca Nacional de Lisboa*. At the beginning of the XXth century, Michaëlis (1904: I, 629–36) presented an interpretative edition, but her work, as well as taking into account only the text of B, offered questionable readings and textual solutions. Later Nunes (1906) included the compositions among the troubadour *cantigas* he selected for his *Crestomatia arcaica*, while Pellegrini (1928) published another palaeographic edition, this time based on the texts from L, although they were collated with those of B. As a result, in 1993 Ferrari (377) still lamented that this little poetic corpus lacked a usable critical edition. No doubt as a result of this complaint, recent scholars have attempted to make good this deficiency, such as Megale (2002a), who based readings on B because it was considered closer to the original redaction, and Amaral (2006), who, however, based his reading of L on Pellegrini's transcription and not on consultation of the original text.

The *Livro de linhagens* of D. Pedro de Barcelos and the *Crónica geral de Espanha de 1344*

If the involvement of the Count of Barcelos in the composition of the *Lais de Bretanha* is mere supposition, it is certainly more evident in the account of the reign of King

Arthur included in the *Livro de linhagens*. The prologue of this guide to the nobility informs us that in fact its composition was due to the son of D. Denis, D. Pedro de Barcelos.[44] That some critics have called this into question[45] is due to their not having considered medieval ideas concerning the concept of authorship, which did not always involve the direct action of the author on the text. As occurs in the celebrated case of Alfonso X of Castile, authorship was at times restricted to a task of coordination, correction and supervision (Díez de Revenga 1985). Nothing, then, contradicts the redaction of the *Livro de linhagens* under the auspices of D. Pedro, nor even that his pen could have intervened on occasion in its redaction. Notwithstanding, Cintra (1951a [1984–90]: I, clix–clxii, clxxx–cxc; 1951b; 1956–7) demonstrated that the *Livro* was composed at the wish of the Count, among other reasons because of the relationship that he established between passages in this and the *Crónica geral de 1344*, which is also attributed to him.

The *Livro de linhagens* constitutes the most distinguished Portuguese example of a genre which had become popular in Europe in the XIIIth century. The first known Portuguese example is the so-called *Livro velho*, dating perhaps to the last third of the XIIIth century. It formed part of the holdings of the Arquivo Real, but disappeared, possibly at some point in the XVIth century, so that its content is known only thanks to late copies. An identical fate befell the *Livro do Deão*, which was part of the same codex. This second peerage was drawn up between 1337 and 1349 and constitutes one of the fundamental sources of the *Livro de linhagens* of the Count of Barcelos, to the point that at times it has been considered to be a first version of D. Pedro's peerage. It is supposed that the latter was written between 1340 and 1344, although it underwent various reworkings throughout the XIVth century. As Mattoso (1980) accepts, the exact evolution of the work has been a problem until the present, among other reasons because some of the historical events that it recounts otherwise remained unknown. In the present state of studies, at least two reworkings are recognised. The first occurred in 1360–5 and must have been carried out at the order of Gonçalo Gonçalves Pereira, who was prior of the Order of the Hospitallers and archbishop of Braga. With it the content of the original version was brought up to date, adding genealogical data which that version had not contemplated and reordering the original material, dividing the text into paragraphs. The second reworking, more literary in tone, was carried out in 1380–3 and added various stories, especially in Titulo XXI, designed to exalt the figure of Álvaro Gonçalves Pereira, son of Gonçalo Gonçalves Pereira and prior of Crato.

Because of the great popularity of the *Livro de linhagens*, more than fifty manuscript witnesses are preserved, which go right up to the XIXth century. The oldest of the surviving MSS is the fragmentary manuscript of the Biblioteca do Palácio da Ajuda, of the XIVth century, which perhaps served as the exemplar for the work of the second reviser (Mattoso 1980: 12–35). Its thirty-nine folios reproduce titles XXI (incomplete) and XXII–XXXV (with gaps in XXX), and were bound with the *Cancioneiro da Ajuda*, forming a factitious volume. During the late Middle Ages and the early modern period, the *nobiliario* of D. Pedro was copied on numerous occasions, while the first printed edition was published by Juan Bautista Labaña in 1640 (Mattoso 1980: 9–29). Despite this popularity, until recent times there were no reliable editions and even today there is no edition produced according to strictly philological criteria. In 1856 Herculano published in *Portugaliae Monumenta Historica* an edition which also included the *Livro velho* and the *Livro do Deão*, based on the manuscript of Ajuda and on the version preserved in the Arquivo Nacional da Torre do Tombo in Lisbon. The result, unsatisfactory because of its numerous errors of transcription, made another edition necessary, which Mattoso published in the same collection in 1980. The editor confessed that his textual approach had paid more attention to historical criteria than philological ones (Mattoso 1980: 8). The editions mentioned have been complemented by that of the Ajuda manuscript published by Brocardo (2006). The latter is not presented as a definitive edition and limits itself to offering a readable text, without any pretensions to fulfil the linguistic demands of a critical edition.

As in the case of other European peerages, which take on the characteristics of chronicles or annals (Mattoso 1981a: 46), that of the Count of Barcelos inserts the genealogy of the Portuguese nobility in a wider frame of reference. For this reason his *nobiliario* sums up in its chapters the monarchs of Israel from the Bible, or further on, inserts the history of the Trojan lineage from its founder Dardanus. This story connects, through Aeneas and Brutus, with the British dynasty and continues until its extinction with the death of King Cauadres and the fall of Britain into Saxon hands. The reign of Arthur constitutes its culminating phase, whence the fact that it receives special attention, which includes his ancestors. And so it is related how Urtigar took possession of the throne after he assassinated King Constant. The brothers of Constant, Aurelius Canbrosius and Uterpamdragom, kill Urtigar, recover the crown, and rule successively in Britain. Next there is related the war between Uterpamdragom and the Count of Cornwall because of the latter's wife, called Ygerna, and the assistance that Merlin gives the monarch in this conflict and in the birth of Arthur. Once king, Arthur confronts Luçius Liber, emperor of Rome, whom he routs, but his nephew Mordech seizes the kingdom. The war between Arthur and Mordech is decided at the battle of Camblet, in which Mordech dies and Arthur is taken, grievously wounded, to Islavalom, from whence he has still not returned.

A passage very similar to that analysed, although shorter, reappears in the *Crónica Geral de Espanha de 1344*. The original redaction of this work has been lost, so that in Portuguese only a reworking of *c*.1400 survives. But the person responsible for this reworking eliminated all the materials that seemed inappropriate for the history of the Hispanic kingdoms, among them the summary of the history of the kings of Britain. As a result, the first version of the *Crónica* survives only in its Castilian translation, while the Arthurian passages are reproduced in a single witness, MS 2656 of the Biblioteca Universitaria de Salamanca (M). The conclusions drawn from the analysis of the *Livro de linhagens*, with reference to the sources and the textual filiation of the

Arthurian narrative, are in good measure applicable to the version of this reproduced in the *Crónica geral*. However, everything seems to indicate that the redaction contained in the chronicle was not directly derived from that given in the *nobiliario*, but that D. Pedro extracted both from a common source and adapted them to the demands of two works conceived with different purposes.

Entwistle (1942: 33–40) compared the narrative thread of this story as given in the *Livro de linhagens* and the *Crónica de 1404*, and noticed that both correspond, in their general outlines, with that of the historiographic tradition that begins with the *Historia regum Britanniae* of Geoffrey of Monmouth. The same scholar noted also that certain details of both Peninsular works (some aspects, for example, of the battle between Arthur and Mordred) which diverged from the *Historia*, were close, on the other hand, to the *Morte d'Arthur* of Thomas Malory and the *Morte Arthur*, an English poem of *c.*1400, which was Malory's inspiration. That is to say, it was a question of details that went back to the Arthurian romances of the XIIIth century. For this reason he proposed that the source of this group of texts would have been what Sommer designated the *Suite de Lancelot*, which included the section of the *Mort Artu* of the Arthurian *Vulgate*. According to Entwistle, the account by the Count of Barcelos would have been based on a version of this textual complex, already translated into Castilian (see also Catalán and de Andrés 1971: lvii–lviii). For his part, Cardim (1923 [1929]) believed that he had found the main source of D. Pedro not in Geoffrey of Monmouth, but in the *Polychronicon* of Ranoulf Higden (XIVth century) and in the *Roman de Brut* of Robert Wace (*c.*1155).

However, Serrano y Sanz (1919–21) had already pointed out that D. Pedro had used an historiographic account, known as the *Liber regum* or *Cronicón Villarense*, composed in Navarre around 1200. Given its diffusion, throughout the XIIIth century various adaptations of this work were made. The *Liber regum toletanus* (*c.*1220), the oldest, and the *Libro de las generaciones* (*c.*1256–70) were based on the first version of the text. In contrast, the *Libro de las generaciones II* and the version of the *Liber regum* associated with the Galician *Crónica de Castilla*, incomplete and somewhat later works, did not follow the earliest version of the text (Catalán and de Andres 1971: li–lxii). Cintra (1950a) studied the relation between titles I–VI of the *Livro de linhagens* and the *Liber regum*, identifying the version on which D. Pedro had based himself. However, he did not locate the version from which title II, which contains the Arthurian narrative, derived. It was Catalán (1962: 365) who specified, following the proposals of Serrano y Sanz and those of Cintra, that the count of Barcelos had found in the *Libro de las generaciones* the summary of the British kings. After comparing them with the *Anales navarro-aragoneses* (pre-1196) and the *Anales Toledanos I* (pre-1219), this scholar concluded that this story already formed part of the first redaction of the *Liber regum* (Catalán and de Andres 1971: lx).

Now, it is possible that D. Pedro may have had at his disposal more than one version of the *Liber regum*, difficult to distinguish from each other because of the mixture of materials they contained, and that even that this redaction was in reality a historiographic compilation produced above all on the basis of the *Liber regum toletanus*, which for its summary of the British kings had resorted to a fragmentary version of the *Libro de las generaciones* (Bautista 2010: 19–21). The most probable situation is that this compilation had been produced in Galicia and from there came to the hands of D. Pedro. According to Catalán (1992), this hypothesis is based on various factors. One of them is the affinity between various Peninsular historiographic works, composed between the end of the XIIIth century and the beginning of the XVth, among them the *Livro de linhagens*, the *Crónica de 1344*, the *Crónica de 1404* and the Galician translation of the *Crónica de Castilla*. But it is also necessary to take into account the Galician, not Portuguese, characteristics of the latter work, such as the allusions to Mondoñedo contained in one of its witnesses, BNE MS 8817. Catalán (1992: 196; 1997: 343) maintains that Mondoñedo had played a central role in the diffusion of this historiographic model throughout the north-western Peninsula, thanks to the relations between its cathedral and the see of Braga. However, Bautista (2010: 36–40) questions the Mondoñedo origins of the compilation used by Pedro de Barcelos and suggests that the latter would have been produced in Santiago de Compostela, in the time of Fernando IV of Castile (1295–1312).

Arthurian Literature in Portugal between the XVIth and XVIIIth centuries: The Portuguese Romances of Chivalry

As occurs in other literary traditions, so too in the case of Portugal the Matter of Britain retained its vitality well beyond the conventional end of the Middle Ages. At the start of this study, the question was posed of the extent to which the medieval witnesses that survive reflect faithfully the impact that the Arthurian narratives had had during the medieval period in the Iberian Peninsula. A similar question needs to be posed when we turn to the survival of these stories during the modern period. If the panorama of the Iberian literatures is compared, for example, with that of France, we observe a far more limited and precarious persistence, both in terms of the variety of Arthurian works involved and in terms of the number of editions that these had during the XVIth century. It would appear that the decline in the Matter of Britain was particularly rapid and marked in Hispanic territories, since printed editions of these works are limited to *Tristán de Leonís* and two stories from the *Post-Vulgate*, namely the *Baladro del sabio Merlin* and the *Demanda del Santo Grial*, which reach only as far as 1535 with the appearance of the Seville edition of the latter. In Portugal we do not even know of any printed editions of Arthurian texts. This leads Castro (1988a: 1123–4) to consider that Portuguese Arthurian literature had very shallow roots, being limited to isolated copies that were excluded from the great currents of literary circulation and never even made the leap into print. However, the Middle Ages teach us that the transmission of literary works is subject to the effects of chance and that very often the number of surviving copies is insufficient to explain the cultural life of a period. Castro (1998: 136) is right when he asserts that each individual book has its own separate destiny.

Over and above the vicissitudes suffered by these texts, the fate of Arthurian literature ran in parallel, to a great extent, with that of chivalry, since it was at one and the same time a reflection of this and a model for it. And, contrary to the idea that knighthood was a superseded institution and in decline by 1500, Keen (2005: 238) maintains that in those years it was still capable of a final burst of splendour. Although its social function had changed, the chivalric spirit survived to inspire the modes of behaviour of the European nobility and to provide many of its identifying features. Among these were feasts and tournaments, which recreated episodes from the Arthurian narratives, and the literary tastes of the aristocracy. The capacity of the Matter of Britain to embody the chivalric values of ethics, confraternity and prowess flowered even in apparently secondary matters, which reveal, however, how deep was the extent of assimilation of Arthurian mythology in the Iberian Peninsula and especially in Portugal. Thus, in the second half of the XIVth century, Nun'Álvares Pereira, Condestabre of Portugal in the reign of D. João I (1385–1433), took as the model for his conduct Galaaz, especially in his decision to remain a virgin. The *Crónica do Condestabre* (Calado 1991: 4, 8) tells us that Nun'Álvares was a reader of the Arthurian romances and that in them he understood that the heroism of Galaaz arose from his virginity, whence his resistance to his marriage with Leonor Alvim, whom he finally wed. This and other traits of chivalric heroism and holiness of the Condestabre reappear in the *Crónica de D. João I* of Fernão Lopes, who likewise records the desire for Arthurian emulation of Nun'Álvares (Baquero Moreno 1990: I, 34, 69). In this same work, however, we encounter another indication of the importance of the Arthurian novels for the ideology of the Portuguese nobility of that period. After the failed attempt to capture the Extremaduran town of Coria, King D. João I lamented that his army did not contain any of the knights of the Round Table: 'Grão mimgoa nos fizerão ojeste dia aquy os cavaleiros da Tavola Redomda, ca çertamente se elles aquy forão nos tomaramos este logar' (Baquero Moreno 1990: II, 75, 197–8). One of his men, Mem Rodrigues de Vasconcelos, replied in irritation, comparing himself and his companions to Galahad, Tristan, Lanzarote and Keu, but lamenting in his turn that it was not King Arthur who was leading them. Very different would be the king's opinion concerning the members of the Corps of Lovers, the army corps which, under the command of the same Mem Rodrigues, contributed to the Portuguese victory at Aljubarrota (1385) and the name of which was inspired by chivalric and Arthurian stories.

For his part, D. Afonso V (1438–81), grandson of D. João I, during his visit to France, for a diplomatic interview with Louis XI (Vicente 2011), visited the French city of Vierzon.[46] There he took an interest in the manuscript of 'hum muy rico e antygo livro da Estoria de Lançarote e Tristam' held at the abbey of Saint-Benoît. The chronicler who relates this journey, Rui de Pina, not only records that the locality in question corresponded with the Arthurian Ageosa Guarda (Joyeuese Garde), but that this story was 'por ventura mais verdadeira do que cá se magina' (Pina 1977: 191, 109). Let these examples serve to dismiss the idea that in the final years of the Middle Ages Arthurian chivalry was an outmoded model in Portugal.

The absence of Arthurian texts in the Portugal of the XVIth century should not be interpreted, then, as indicative of a marginalisation of this kind of narrative and of the ideology that inspired it. Rather, other factors in literary evolution should be taken into account to explain this absence. One would be the blossoming of Castilian romances of chivalry, following the model established by Garci Rodríguez de Montalvo's *Amadís de Gaula* (1508). In Spain one can observe, for example, an attempt to recover the Arthurian romances between the end of the XVth century and the beginning of the XVIth, not only because there persisted a reading public for which these works were suited, but also perhaps because the flowering of the romance of chivalry inspired editors to publish printed editions of the by then thoroughly familiar Arthurian narratives (Frontón 1989: 41). The relative success of this effort is shown in the reprints of the two works from the *Post-Vulgate*, the above-mentioned *Baladro del sabio Merlín* and the *Demanda del santo Grial*;[47] and above all the eight known editions of *Tristán de Leonís*.[48] This flowering, however, is rapidly exhausted and scarcely outlasts the first third of the XVIth century. The reason would be the definitive displacement of the old Arthurian stories by the new ones arising in the wake of *Amadís*.[49]

The genre inaugurated by *Amadís de Gaula* should not be presented as a rupture in relation to a previous stylistic model, the Arthurian narrative, but as developing and transcending, and thereby renewing, chivalresque narrative. The so-called 'sons of Amadís', that is to say, the chivalric romances of the XVIth–XVIIIth centuries are not, essentially, anything other than the grandsons of Arthur, and examples of Neo-Arthurianism (Trujillo 2011: 419), the innovations brought by which arise from the model of the Matter of Britain, still very much alive in the work of Montalvo. Now, the comparison between the panorama of printing in Spain and that in Portugal reveals an unequal evolution, both in the number of editions and in their chronological distribution. If in Portugal many fewer romances of chivalry are printed than in Castile, this may be due not to a less profound implantation of Arthurian literature in that kingdom but to the lesser development there of the printing industry. This may also be the reason why the blossoming of chivalric printed editions does not occur in Portuguese territory until the years between 1581 and 1605, while in Castile it reaches its peak at mid-century, with 1558 as the highest point (Vargas Díaz-Toledo 2012a: 41, 53). It is, therefore, viable to consider that the Portuguese reading market was fed, to a great extent, not only by manuscript copies, but also by books written in Spanish and produced in Spain. The more so because the fluidity in the relations between the literatures of both kingdoms favoured allophony and often rendered the work of translation unnecessary.

The Arthurian stamp on Portuguese romances of chivalry can be seen in different ways (see Vargas Díaz-Toledo 2013). The most diffuse affects the assimilation of narrative structures and motifs, taken directly from the Arthurian cycles, or else indirectly through *Amadís* and the first Castilian chivalric romances. This is why the key events in the lives of many of their characters (knights, ladies, magicians) recall in some way those who inhabit the pages of the Arthurian romances, with Arthur held up as the model of the just monarch, Lanzarote or Tristan as those of the champions and faithful lovers, and Merlin and Morgana as those of the enchanters. The conception of adventures as initiation tests, a succession of which marks out the development of the chivalric character, also fits within this generic influence, alongside the code of conduct of the characters, the conception of war as a series of individual combats, the symbolic geography (woods, roads, castles) among other components of the narrative. Alongside this level of influence, however, which in some way is visible in many of the Renaissance romances of chivalry, there exist more specific references to the fictional Arthurian universe, which reveal the ideological continuity which authors and readers of this period established between the Arthurian world and the new chivalric heroes.[50] This continuity takes the form, in the Portuguese texts, of the dependence on Arthurian knighthood manifested by some of the knights (and the ideological universe that they represent), of which they wish to be the descendants.

Such is the case, for example, in the anonymous *Crónica do imperador Maximiliano* (mid-XVIth century), one of the characters in which is a king of England, Artur by name. His ancestor of the same name was the mythical British monarch, who had lived two hundred years earlier. The similarities between both figures involve the physical aspect, but also their personalities and their powers, since, just like his ancestor, the Artur of the *Crónica* is considered to be a just and excellent sovereign, and also a great conqueror (Palma-Ferreira 1983: 25, 303). Although at the outset he is represented as a negative character, the enemy of King Venceslau of Hungary, Artur later becomes his ally against the Saxons, until he becomes the most powerful and feared monarch in the world. Among his warrior enterprises there stands out this struggle against the Saxons, who instead of invading, as they previously did, the isle of Britain, now threaten, like the Turks of the XVIth century, Hungary and all Central Europe. The association of the *Crónica* with the Arthurian universe, considered as a myth-producing reference for chivalry, reappears in the motif of the Arco da Memória of Bruto, who is considered to be the 'primeiro governador de Inglaterra', and in the allusion to the marvels of Balduque o Voador, the magician-king Bladud of the *Historia regum Britanniae* (Wright 1996: 30, 18) and the *Roman de Brut* (Arnold 1938–40: 90–1, lines 1627–56).

The link between the chivalry and monarchy of Portugal and the Arthurian past is even more strongly expressed in the *Memorial das proezas da Segunda Távola*

Redonda by Jorge Ferreira de Vasconcelos, which Entwistle (1942: 191) considered, perhaps with some exaggeration, to be the last landmark 'of the life of the Arthurian myths in the Peninsula'. The first surviving edition was published in Coimbra in 1567, but it is very probable that in 1554, also in Coimbra, there had appeared a fuller version, now lost, which would have been entitled *Livro primeiro da primeira parte dos Triunfos de Sagramor, rey de Inglaterra e França, em que se tratam os maravilhosos feitos dos cavaleiros da Segunda Távola Redonda*. The work opens with a brief account of the origin of chivalry, which is identified with the foundation of the Order of the Round Table. After this there is described the war between Arthur and Mordred, which destroyed the kingdom of Logres, the choice of Sagramor as the successor of Arthur, and the renewal, during his reign, of the chivalric life. The new characters, belonging to the next generations after that of the knights of Arthur, have an avowed debt to the ideological frame of reference of the Arthurian *romans*. As Subirats (1982, 1986) has shown, these references mould the image of the ideal knight proposed by Vasconcelos, except that the latter, fully aware that the mythical universe of the Round Table constituted a model that was already outdated in Renaissance Portugal, opts to create a second Table, which combined ideological continuity and an awareness of cultural distance (Finazzi-Agrò 1978: 48). At times, the more or less explicit presence of the Arthurian substratum, together with this awareness of cultural distance, gives rise to intertextual games that are not without irony. The wise Merlindia, for example, is inspired by the name of Merlin, but her femininity reveals the influence of the model of the female enchanter which is introduced by Urganda in *Amadís*. But more than this, Vasconcelos blurs the boundaries between fiction and reality, thereby linking the Arthurian universe to the Portuguese monarchy. In the prophecies that Merlindia utters in the presence of Sagramor and his court, the future knights are in reality Portuguese nobles of the XVIth century. Equally, the final section of the story centres upon the tournament celebrated in Xabregas, near Lisbon, in 1522, in which Prince D. João, son of D. João III, was knighted, and in which Da. Juana de Austria, the daughter of Carlos I of Spain, who had just arrived in Portugal to marry the king, was welcomed. It is for this reason that the chivalric adventures of the first part are able to be interpreted as a reflection of those that would later occur in the kingdom of Portugal (Lucía Megías 2001c: 395).

In contrast to the choice made by Montalvo, who placed Amadís as a predecessor of Arthur's Britain, the Portuguese authors locate their stories centuries later than the reign of Arthur. This allows them to establish, as in the case of *Palmeirim de Inglaterra* by Francisco de Moraes (*c*.1541), a contrast between ancient chivalry, represented by the Arthurian heroes and those of the *Amadís* cycle, and the new chivalry, embodied in Palmeirim and the other knights of the Portuguese romances (Marín Pina 2007b). This also, however, justifies the ideological debt of the Portuguese monarchy in relation to Arthurian chivalry, since in not a few works, above all from the first half of the XVIth century, there is a desire to link both institutions, with the former as the heir to the latter. The apology for the Portuguese monarchy through its identification with the roots of chivalry is found not only in the *Memorial* by Vasconcelos. The *Crónica do imperador Clarimundo* goes deeply into this venture into dynastic propaganda, at the same time as it seeks a greater connection with the Greek world while still maintaining a chivalric model in which it is identified with its Arthurian roots (Brandenberger 2008: 56). For this reason, it makes its protagonist at one and the same time a descendant of the Trojan Aeneas (though Arthur, through Brutus, also claimed a Trojan origin) and an ancestor of Afonso I Henriques, the first king of Portugal. It is no accident that its author, João de Barros, was the keeper of the wardrobe to D. João III, to whom he dedicated his romance. Various narrative resources are devoted to this end, such as prophecies, digressions, and traits that favour the identification of Clarimundo with D. João III. Vasconcelos' *Memorial*, for its part, aspired to being a *speculum principis*, addressed and dedicated to the future King, D. Sebastião I, at that time still a prince, as previously the *Triunfos de Sagramor* had been dedicated to Prince D. João.[51] And, finally, let us not forget that *Palmeirim de Inglaterra*, whilst it relates to a different aesthetic model, less propagandistic and more related to Rodriguez de Montalvo's *Amadís* (Vargas Diaz-Toledo 2007: 1102), is placed within this chivalric effervescence overseen by the court of D. João III, the monarch to whom moreover Manuel Álvares dedicated his copy of *José de Arimateia*. In fact, Francisco de Moraes formed part of the embassy that this sovereign sent to France in 1541, under the command of Francisco de Noronha, Count of Linhares. All of it reveals the involvement of the Portuguese monarchs in the promotion of chivalric mythology and in particular of Arthurian narrative.

But reference to the Arthurian world does not always relate to an explicit desire to link its prestige to that of the Avis dynasty, since there are also allusions which are not underlain by political connotations. Some of these are contained in *Palmeirim*, in which the character of Rosiram de la Brunda is linked to the history of Tristan and Iseo. It is said of Rosiram that she was descended from the daughter whom Iseo and King Mares conceived on their wedding night, even if there were those who believed that the father of this child, also called Iseo, had been Tristam de Leonís (I, 24, 149). In this same work, the mythologisation of Arthurian knighthood and its continuity in England was revealed in the Torre das Façanhas, which was built in the city of London. In it were kept the arms of the most distinguished knights there had ever been and among these were those of Lanzarote, Morlot o Grande, and other members of the Round Table (I, 40, 271). Other analogies with the Arthurian world could be extracted from some episodes of *Palmeirim*, such as the Torre de Dramusiando, for which a possible inspiration has been sought in the Val des Faux Amants of the *Lancelot propre* (Correia 2012b). However, and on top of possible textual parallels, the relation between the two passages arises from the ample diffusion, noted above, of certain motifs of Arthurian origin which are inherited by the Renaissance romances of chivalry.

Equally devoid of political significance would be those other allusions present in late works, composed after the rout of Alcazarquivir (1578), with the disappearance of the chivalric spirit embodied in D. Sebastião and with the ascent of Philip II to the Portuguese throne (Lucía Megías 2001c: 397). At this time, romances of chivalry were read principally for pleasure and were aimed above all at a female readership. Among these works are the fourth part of the *Crónica do imperador Beliandro*, written between 1685 and the beginning of the XVIIIth century (Diaz Vargas-Toledo 2012a: 144). In it, the sage Falarina possesses a magic mirror, capable of revealing amorous infidelities, whose manufacture is attributed to Merlin. The latter, in the form of a skeleton, occupies an octagonal house to which Belindo, one of the protagonists, goes. There he hears the seer pronounce a series of prophecies on the future glories of Portugal, with which the *Crónica* does not seek political justification so much as a new appropriation of the chivalric spirit through a literary game. Merlin reappears in the anonymous *Historia do principe Belidor Anfibio e da princeza chamada Corsina*, from the early XVIIIth century. In this case, the protagonist enters the Alcácer Impenetrável (the impenetrable fortress), located in the Vale dos Encantos, in which he encounters various characters whom he has to free from a spell cast by the Arthurian magician.

The reasons for this prolonged survival of Arthurian and chivalric material are complex and, although on occasion these may relate to causes specific to Portugal, such as its involvement in the overseas and African conquests and colonisation (Olival 2012: 210), they often find a more adequate explanation when placed in the context of the European transition from the late Middle Ages to early modern Europe. Now, from the literary point of view, attention is drawn to the inclination Portuguese writers felt towards the Arthurian-English chivalric model. This does not mean that there are not examples of eastern and Mediterranean orientation among the Portuguese romances of chivalry, nor that there is no role in them for the Greek Empire and the court of Constantinople. To give only some examples, the importance of that city as the symbolic centre of romances of chivalry, studied by Stegagno-Picchio (1966),[52] is maintained in the cycle of the *Palmeirims*; in the same way in which Clarisol de Bretanha must demonstrate his heroism by confronting the great warriors of antiquity and some Graeco-Roman deities, such as Mars or the Furies; or finally the fact that one of the manuscript romances of chivalry of the second half of the XVIth century, which also involved the Byzantine Empire, adopted the name of *Argonáutica da cavalaria* with all its connotations. The Arthurian inheritance, then, is observed in the recurrence with which successive authors continue to consider Britain or England as the place of origin of chivalry. Without going any further, we may note that allusions to the Arthurian world, sometimes precise ones, continue to be made, even in those works of Graeco-Byzantine orientation or an exotic one; and also how various Portuguese chivalric heroes adopt as an epithet one of those two toponyms: Palmeirim de Inglaterra, Duardos de Bretanha, Clarisol de Bretanha. Far from being merely anecdotal, this tendency coincides with the vision offered by these books, of England as the homeland of chivalry and tournaments. The belief that the English knights descended directly from those of the Round Table is formulated explicitly in the *Argonáutica da cavalaria*, for example, but is also transmitted by stories in other genres, such as the episode of the tournament of the Doze de Inglaterra, narrated by Luis de Camoens in *Os Lusíadas* (Hutchinson 2007). Here, twelve Portuguese champions go to Great Britain at the invitation of John of Gaunt, to defend the honour of twelve English ladies who had been unable to find champions among their compatriots. The success of the Portuguese serves to reinforce the links between the chivalric elites of both kingdoms, but also to suggest that the Portuguese have inherited the English role in the sphere of courtly chivalry and to present the period of D. João I as a myth-generating point for Portuguese chivalry.

The apparent conservatism of this idea could be caused by political reasons, understandable if one bears in mind the involvement of the crown in the composition of the first romances of chivalry. Among these political factors could be included the country's lesser involvement, when compared with Spain, in Mediterranean affairs, the membership of Portuguese monarchs (from the reign of João I onwards) of the Order of the Garter, of English origin (Olival 2012: 208), and the successive alliances of Portugal and England throughout the XIVth and XVth centuries. Equally, purely literary reasons must also have been no less influential. It must not be forgotten that the renewal of chivalric literature in the XVIth century has one of its points of origin in Castile and in *Amadís de Gaula* one of its founding landmarks. Portugal occupies, in relation to that centre, a peripheral place, so that innovations not only arrive later, but moreover do not always imply the marginalisation of the older material. Thus, despite the fact that the first romances of the 1500s already incorporate elements found in Montalvo's work, its model does not triumph conclusively until *Palmeirim de Inglaterra* by Moraes. And, equally, the stylistic change led by Feliciano de Silva in Spain, more oriented towards entertainment and gratuitous marvels, is not consolidated in Portugal until the final quarter of the XVIth century (Vargas Diaz-Toledo 2007: 1103–4). The vitality shown by the diffusion of the manuscript romances of chivalry in Portugal also contrasts, by its duration, with the chronology that could be established for Spanish literature, In the latter, this genre could be considered residual after 1600, but in Portugal, at the same date, we see the composition of the *Crónica do Imperador Beliandro*, whose success is attested by the forty surviving manuscripts. The *Crónica de D. Duardos*, by Gonçalo Coutinho, although written somewhat earlier, at the end of the XVIth century, survives in fifteen manuscripts, many of them from the XVIIth century (Vargas Diaz-Toledo 2010: 222; 2012a: 178–9). The cultivation of these narratives continues, moreover, into the XVIIIth century, as is shown by the *Historia do principe Belidor Anfibio*. Whether this is considered to constitute backwardness in reception or merely conservatism in an aesthetic and ideological model, the survival of the chivalric spirit in Portugal helps to keep alive Arthurian literature and its descendants until well into the XVIIIth century, long after the Middle Ages and the society that saw its birth.

Notes

[1] The father of Ginebra de Acuña was Martim Vasques da Cunha (or Martín Vázquez de Acuña), conde de Valencia de Don Juan, who lived 1357–1417). He was a Portuguese noble at the court of D. João I, who took part in the battle of Aljubarrota and was exiled to Castile at the end of the XIVth century because of a conflict with the Crown (Romero Portilla 2002). This individual is the protagonist of one of the best-known passages in the *Crónica de D. João I* by Fernão Lopes, when the Portuguese monarch laments having had to raise the siege of Coria because he did not have in his army the knights of the Round Table. Mem Rodrigues de Vasconcelos replied, comparing his companions with equivalent Arthurian champions; Martin Vasques was compared to Dom Galaaz (see below, p. 106).

[2] 'por yso diz ha estoryaa que nenhũ homem podera saber as aventuras do greall amte comvem trespasalas muyto mas an osa estorea que por abocade Jhesu cristo foy na terra en viada nom metera em Joam vivas hũ pomto de falsydade' (Carter 1967: 70, 204); 'ouue nome sargoçimta por amor da molher del Rey mordaym e foy depois muy boa dona e muy samta cousa e foy molher de çilidones asym como joão biuas volo deuysara nes ta estorea e por esta linhajem a tirou de framçes e a tresladou Ruber de bur bom de latim ẽ que a primeiro e[s]tpreveo aquele yrmitão a que noso senhor mostrou' (Carter 1967: 87, 273–4); 'ni yo Joannes Biuas, no vos dire ende mas de lo que vos el dize, ca so frayle, e no quiero mentir' (Bonilla y San Martín 1907: 52, 181).

[3] The interpretation by D'Heur (1973–4) is likewise based on the *Vulgate* cycle, but on the imprisonment of Galván in the castle of the giant Caradoc. The Galician-Portuguese lyric corpus is preserved in a number of manuscripts, designated by various sigla. In this chapter the following MSS are mentioned: Cancioneiro de la Biblioteca Nacional de Lisboa (B), Cancionero de la Biblioteca Apostólica Vaticana (V), Cod. Lat. 7182 of the Biblioteca Apostólica Vaticana (L) and the Tavola Colocciana, or index of troubadours in Cod. Lat. 3217 of the Biblioteca Apostólica Vaticana (C). These sigla are accompanied here by a number indicating the position occupied by the cantigas in each manuscript.

[4] The western provenance of the Castilian *Lanzarote* is based on the linguistic analysis of MS 9611 of the Biblioteca Nacional, Madrid, in which there are observed linguistic traits that Sharrer (1981) identifies as Galician-Portuguese or Leonese.

[5] However, because of the fame of Tristan as a model lover, it cannot be deduced from the allusion to him by Alfonso X himself in *Ben sabia eu, mia senhor* (B468) that there is any association with the *Tristan en prose*.

[6] Such is, for example, the hypothesis of Lapa (1982a: 315–16), in view of the Gallicisms found in the Portuguese text of the *Demanda do Santo Graal*.

[7] Entwistle (1942: 162), on the other hand, as defender of the priority of the Castilian versions over the Portuguese, considered Juan Vivas to be the Castilian translator of the *Post-Vulgate* trilogy.

[8] On the disputes over the existence of an early *Amadís* in Portuguese and the fragility of their hypotheses, see, among others, Cacho Blecua (1987–8: I, 57–67) and Rossi (1979: 68–76).

[9] Furthermore, the possibility that in the Peninsula there circulated some version contaminated with episodes from both cycles would complicate even more any analysis. See, for example, the influence of the *Post-Vulgate* presented by the Castilian *Lanzarote del Lago* in BNM MS 9611 (Bogdanow 1999a).

[10] The relation of the Castilian *Lanzarote* with the *Post-Vulgate* would be reinforced by the references that the former makes to a *Livro de Galaaz*. Behind this title there has been identified an Iberian version of the *Queste del Saint Graal* from the *Post-Vulgate*, similar, then, to the text of the Portuguese *Demanda* (Correia 2010d).

[11] 'Oqual eu achey | en Riba Damcora em poder Dehũa velha Demuy antiga idade | no tempo que meu paay Corregedor De vossa corte seruia v. a. De Corregedor | Dantre Douro 2 minho. O qual liuro segundo por elle parece he | sprito em pergaminho 2 iluminado Eacaise De dozentos annõs | que foi sprito' (Carter 1967: 76).

[12] 'O gram felisteo chamorro, / Joam de Melo, copeiro, / que nos montes é parceiro / de Marin Pirez Bigorro, / Senhor, des que se degola / co barril na montaria, /copa-se com carminhola / do comprido Mestr'Escola / ou Josep Barimatia' (Dias 1990–2003: I, 302). Entwistle (1942: 120) does not mention the author of the verses in question, Pêro de Moura, who added them to a poem Álvaro Barreto had sent to D. Afonso V. Dias, on the other hand, does (2003–6: 4).

[13] As far as concerns the time at which Sebastião Álvares, father of Manuel Álvares, supposedly found the manuscript which served as his textual source, Castro (1976–9: 183) limits it to the years 1527 and 1536, during which his period of office as governor of Entre Douro e Minho is located.

[14] 'agora se cala a estorea de todas estas linãges que de çelidones sairão e torna Aos Outros Ramos que se chama estorea demerlim que Comvem por toda ma neyra Jumtar Com a estorea do greal por que he dos Ramos e lhe pertemç[e] E saibão todos A queles que esta Estorea Ouuyrem que esta Estorea Era jumtada Com A demerlim na qual he Comemça me mto da mesa Redomda E A naçem ça de ar tur E com em ça m em to das aventuras mas por noso liuro uom *[illegible]* ser muy grã de Repartimo lo Cada hũu Em sua parte por que cada hũu por sy serão milhores de trazer' (Carter 1967: 119, 379).

[15] God reminds Josefes of it thus: 'por esto quero eu que tu Reçebas da minha mao a mais allta ordem que homem mortal posa aver nem Reçeber' (Carter 1967: 39, 112).

[16] 'E tambem faras bispo Em cada çidade omde o meu nome for Reçebido per tua pregaçon e sagra los as e vmgilos as e outro sy faras Aos Reis que per ty Ouuerem fee' (Carter 1967: 43, 121).

[17] The religious and genealogical components are usually mixed, because of the sacred character of the lineage of the custodians of the Grail. Thus, in the dream of Evalach, in which a lamb and a wolf appear, symbols of Christ and the devil, it is related to his prompt conversion; but the subsequent appearance of Celidones anticipates the beginning of the lineage from which Galaaz will be descended. The dreams of King Label and Duke Gaanor, by contrast, refer only to the salvation of the soul through conversion (Martins 1975a: 112–17).

[18] The symbolism of animals has been studied by Chambel (2000).

[19] The redaction closest to the original corresponds to the MS in the Archivio di Stato, Siena, which, however, does not reproduce any of the passages from the Portuguese fragments (Micha 1957; Bogdanow 1966: 25, 228–41, 272).

[20] Faced with the general tendency to abbreviation in relation to the French sources, exhibited by the *Baladros* and the *Merlin* of MS 1877 of the Biblioteca Universitaria, Salamanca (Gracia 2007: 237).

[21] The Short Version of the Second Continuation of *Perceval* is dated to the beginning of the XIIIth century, while the Long Version would have been composed shortly after.

[22] Some of the expressions and words indicated by Lapa are: *a rem do mundo que eu mais amava, non nos en chal, mal trager, en mal ponto, enxeco, enmentar, dar grado, fazer enfinta, endõado*, the use of *senhor* and *entendedor* with both masculine and feminine etc. Other notable traits are the adverb *chus*, which was archaic even for the troubadours in the second half of the XIIIth century, the preterite *dei* (< Lat. DEDIT) and certain forms of the third person of this tense, such as *feri-o, pedi-lhe, saysse, sai-lhe* and *sumisse*.

[23] Thus, for example, the graph -*ss*- for the ending -*ossa*, and in other forms that opt for -*s*- (*fremossa, nessa, oussedes, perigossa, coussa*).

[24] On the editorial vicissitudes of the manuscript, see Freire Nunes (1999a: 58–61) and Megale (1986–7).

[25] See, for example, the commentaries of David (1945), Lapa (1982c) and Piel (1945).

[26] The key of the passage would be in the translation of the French verb *avés trouva*, which the Castilian editions of Toledo (1515) and Seville (1535) translate correctly as *falledes*, and which the Vienna manuscript renders as *fallades*. For Castro (2002a) a form of the verb *achar* is not necessary,

since *fallar*, with the meaning of 'to find', is documented in the XIIIth and XIVth centuries, when the Portuguese translation would have been made. For it to be preserved in the successive copies of the *Demanda* in Portuguese the vacillations of the system of graphs for the lateral and palatal lateral phonemes would have been a contributory factor, as would confusion in spelling with the verb *falar*.

[27] This obviates the need for a detailed summary of the work, so we will limit ourselves to some brief indications of its plot. On the Castilian version, see the chapters by Gracia and Lucía Megías in this volume.

[28] 'prometo ora a Deus e a toda cavalaria que, de manhãã, se me Deus quiser atender, entrarei na demanda do Santo Graal [...] que ja mais nom tornarei aa corte, por cousa que avenha *ante que* milhor e mais a meu prazer veja o que ora ví' (Piel and Freire Nunes 2005: 26, 36).

[29] The relation between the failure of both knights and their respective sins appears in Piel and Freire Nunes 2005: 161, 129; 207–8, 166–9; 516, 382.

[30] The punishment for her lust and that of Tristan and Iseo, as a mirror of his own conduct, appears to Lanzarote in a dream (Piel and Freire Nunes 2005: 207, 166–7).

[31] Gracia (1993: 202–6) enumerates up to six stories of this type in the *Demanda*, at the same time as underlining its Oedipal content and its association with the motif of the heroic birth.

[32] The rigidity of Erec contrasts with the more flexible attitude of Galaaz. The perfect knight is disposed to satisfy the sexual demands of a lady, who threatened to kill herself if he did not accede to her requests. The sacrifice of Galaaz, who places the life of a sinner before his own honour, does not actually come about, because the lady dies before her desire has been satisfied (Laranjinha 2010b: 1099–1102).

[33] A similar episode is found along the exempla in the *Horto do Esposo* (Freire Nunes 2007: iii, I, 39–40), an allegorical-doctrinal narrative of the end of the XIVth century or the beginning of the XVth, which has led to suggestions of an Arthurian influence on this work. This is what Maler supposed (1956: II, 27–8) and it is accepted by Pereira (2007: lxxiv), who considers that in the monastery of Alcobaça, where the *Horto do Esposo* had been compiled, there would have been a copy of the *Demanda*. See, at all events, the comparative analysis of Madureira (2002), who highlights the similarity of both episodes and the use of a common tradition, but also the by no means negligible distance separating them.

[34] 'Este lais fez Elis o Baço que foi Duc de Sansonha, quando pas[s]ou aa Gran Bretanha, que ora chaman Ingraterra. E pas[s]ou lá no tempo de Rei Artur pera se combater con Tristan porque lhe maatara o padre en ũa batalha. E andando ũu dia en sa busca, foi pela Joiosa Guarda u era a Rainha Iseu de Cornolaha; e viu-a tan fremosa que adur lhe poderia home no mundo achar par, e namorou-se enton dela; e fez por ela este laix. Este lais posemos aca porque era o melhor que foi fe[i]to' (Lagares 2000: 106).

[35] The *Tavola Colocciana* is an index of authors and *cantigas*, which follows the order of the *cancioneiros* of the Biblioteca Nacional de Lisboa and the Biblioteca Apostolica Vaticana. It was drawn up by the Italian humanist Angelo Colocci, who likewise ordered the copying of both *cancioneiros*, and is reproduced on fols 300–7 of MS Lat 3217 of the Biblioteca Apostolica Vaticana.

[36] 'Este laix fezeron donzelas a Don [L]ançaroth quan[d]o estava na Insoa da Lidiça, quand'o Rainha Genevra achou con a filha de Rei Peles e lhi defendeo que non paresces[s]e ant'ela' (Lagares 2000: 109).

[37] The rubric of f. 4v explains that 'Esta cantiga é a primeira que achamos que foi feita, e fezeron-na quatro donzelas en tempo de Rei Artur a Maraot d'Irlanda por la [...] tornada en lenguagen palavra per palavra' (Lagares 2000: 105). That of f. 10rv completes the information given by the former: 'Esta cantiga fezeron quatro donzelas a Maroot d'Irlanda, en tempo de Rei Artur, porque Maroot filhava todalas donzelas que achava en guarda dos cavaleiros, se as podia conquerer deles, e enviava-as pera Irlanda pera seeren sempre en servidon da terra. E esto fazia el porque fora morto seu padre por razon dũa donzela que levava en guarda' (Lagares 2000: 107).

[38] The attribution of these *lais* is found in *Don Pedro este cunhado del-Rei* (B1614, V1147), in which it is said that 'Mui ledo seend', u cantara seus lais' (line 13), but also that the Infante 'chegou ora aqui d'Aragon' (line 2). From this it may be deduced that he had spent little time in Portugal and, on the other hand, that he had composed these *lais* before his journey. From so succinct an allusion it cannot even be deduced which characteristics these pieces had, and whether or not these were poems inspired by Arthurian material or lyric *lais*, without any link to this literary tradition.

[39] The *Lai de Hélys* is placed at the start of the Grail quest. A year has not yet passed since the knights of Logres have left in search of the relic, when Tristan arrives at a fountain, at which he hears an enamoured knight complaining. The latter turns out to be Hélys, son of Helyant, Duke of Cornwall, who is in love with Iseo and who, between his amorous laments, sings the *lai* that begins *Amors, de vostre acointement*. After fighting over the love of Iseo, both knights make peace and, accompanied by Palamedes and Dinadan, continue their journey together and lodge at the castle of a relative of Baudemagu. The next morning, on the march again, Tristan sings *Lonc tans a que il ne vit cele*, since the spring weather and the birdsong remind him of Iseo. The *Lai du plour* is located shortly after Marc invades Logres and takes Iseo away with him. One day Tristan lodges at the castle of Brehus sans Pitié and there he hears a lady sing a *lai*. At the request of Tristan, the lady next sings *Li soleux luist et clers et biaus*, which Tristan composed for his beloved, and he replies with the *Lai du plour*, which he had composed while traversing the forest of Hautone.

[40] 'il het si morteument les demoiseles de cest pais qu'il lour fait toutes les hontes et toutes les laideurs qu'il puet. Et pour les hontes qu'il lor fait le heent elles si morteument que elles il vaurroient avoir trait le cuer del ventre' (Roussineau 1996: ii, 422).

[41] Already Entwistle (1942: 59) had identified the passage that inspired the refrain of the Galician-Portuguese *Lai*, although he restricted himself to locating in it in the *Lancelot du Lac*.

[42] Sharrer (1988b: 565) suggested two possible sources of inspiration for Lai no. 2: the episode of the Roche aux Pucelles in the *Suite du Merlin*, and the *Lai Voir distant* from the *Tristan en prose*. In the first case, the influence seems rather doubtful, since the ladies of the Roche aux Pucelles are seers, lack any satirical intent and do not take part in a dancing scene. In the second case, the influence would be limited to the coincidence of satirical tone in both pieces.

[43] In the numbering given by Colocci to the *Lais*, at all events, it seems that at first the number 4 had been assigned to *Ledas sejamos ogemais!* (Cancionero B 1982: 30, f. 10vb). This is indicated by the number that accompanies this *cantiga*, in which can be detected a 4 with a 5 overwritten on it. Whether this constituted a copyist's error, rapidly corrected, or constitutes a vestige of an old order of the *lais*, this corrected numeral would indicate, at the very least, that in fact the vacillations within this little corpus can be extended to the two poems linked to the *Post-Vulgate*.

[44] 'Porêm eu comde dom Predro filho do muy nobre rrey dom Denis ouue de catar por gram traballo por muitas terras escripturas que fallauam dos linhageens. E veemdo as escripturas com grande estudo e em como fallauam doutros gramdes feitos compuge este liuro' (Mattoso 1980: 230).

[45] This question has been studied by Ferreira (2011), Mattoso (1981a: 34–50; 2009a), Saraiva (1971) and Veiga (1942).

[46] The chronicle of Rui de Pina does not give the name of this settlement, but, echoing a local legend, identifies it with the Joyeuse Garde – Ageosa Garda – that is to say, with the castle of Lancelot. See, on the correct identification, Denis (1934: 299–302).

[47] Two editions of the *Baladro* survive: Burgos (1498) and Sevilla (1535), and there are a further two of the *Demanda*, Toledo (1515) and Seville (1535). However, it is known that in Seville there appeared another edition (1500), now lost, of both sections of the *Post-Vulgate* (Gracia 1996: 15).

[48] The first printed edition of *Tristán de Leonís* dates from 1501. After this, reprints follow one another: 1511, pre-1520, 1520, 1525, 1528, 1533, 1534. It is believed that there could have been another two printings, earlier than 1511, with which we would have ten editions in little more than thirty years (V. Beltran 1996; Cuesta Torre 1993b).

[49] The influence of the romances of chivalry is reflected also in the 1534 edition of *Tristán de Leonís*. In this, there are inserted the adventures of the children of Tristan and Iseo, in the tastes of the new fashion. The lack of continuity in this model indicates the difficulty of renewing Arthurian material, even in a story, like this one, with a marked sentimental content (Cuesta Torre 1997a).

[50] See on this the comments of Trujillo (2011: 424), in accordance with the testimony of three Spanish authors, Pero López de Ayala, Cervantes and Luis Vives.

[51] The interpretation of the work as a didactic manual of amorous matters has been raised by Pereira (2000).

[52] This author identifies two stylistic models in the romances of chivalry, according to whether their setting is Britain and France or Constantinople and the orient. The former adopt a more rigid vision of chivalric orthodoxy, display less geographical scope, and take Arthur as a monarchic symbol. The latter are inclined towards a Byzantine and oriental ambience, open to foreign societies such as the Arabs and Slavs, and are focused on Constantine as an ideal monarch. However, the boundaries between the two types, the first more conservative than the second, are not rigid and there is no shortage of stories which, like *Tirant lo Blanc* and *Amadís de Gaula*, moved between both worlds (Stegagno-Picchio 1966: 117–23).

IV

THE *MATIÈRE DE BRETAGNE* IN GALICIA FROM THE XIIth TO THE XVth CENTURY

Pilar Lorenzo Gradín

1. Introduction

Except during the brief reign of García (1065–73), Galicia experienced and contributed to, in alternating sequence, the destinies of the two kingdoms of León and Castile during a good part of the XIth and XIIth centuries, until both crowns were finally united in 1230 under Fernando III. The County of Galicia played a most important role in the cultural history of the Middle Ages in the Iberian Peninsula from the discovery, in the time of Alfonso II (c.813), of the remains of the apostle St James at Santiago de Compostela. The constant flow of pilgrims to the far west of Iberia increased to a surprising degree from the end of the XIth century. This constant movement of travellers led to a large swathe of the territories of León and Castile becoming immersed much more deeply in the great European cultural developments. The success of the Road to Santiago was exploited by one of the most outstanding figures in the history of Galicia, Archbishop Diego Gelmírez (c.1070–1140†). After winning the friendship of Raymond of Burgundy, Count of Galicia and Portugal, and obtaining the prebends from the Holy See, which awarded him the archiepiscopal pallium in 1103, he would make Santiago into one of the three great pilgrim destinations of Christendom. Under his authority, Compostela became the principal centre of cultural exchange with Europe in the Iberian Peninsula.

In this chain of events, one must also underline the essential role played by Galicia after the death of Alfonso VI, who, following the death of his son Sancho in the battle of Uclés (1108), left no male heir to the crown. The second marriage of his daughter Urraca with Alfonso I of Aragon in 1109 caused a rift at the heart of the Castilian and Leonese nobility, with one faction preferring that the throne should be occupied by Alfonso Raimúndez, the son of the queen and the deceased count Raymond of Burgundy. Once the crown had passed to Urraca and Alfonso of Aragon (1109), royal power was weakened by confrontation on three fronts. Firstly, the Galician nobility, represented by the Count of Traba Pedro Froilaz and Diego Gelmírez himself, who were at that time responsible for the upbringing of Urraca's son, whom they proclaimed king at Compostela in 1111; secondly, the Castilian and Leonese nobility, aggrieved by the monopoly the Aragonese aristocracy had obtained over their lands with the advent of the new Aragonese king; and thirdly, the higher levels of the Church hierarchy, headed by Pope Paschal II and Bernard, archbishop of Toledo, who, faced with the adverse situation which had come about, declared Urraca's marriage to the Aragonese monarch null and void for reasons of consanguinity. On the death of the queen (1126), Alfonso 'el Batallador' lost his legal claims to the crown of León and Castile, which passed irrevocably into the hands of Alfonso Raimúndez, who succeeded to the throne as Alfonso VII. The new king was crowned in León Cathedral in the presence of Diego Gelmírez and the most distinguished members of the Castilian and Leonese nobility on 10 March 1126. On his death in 1157, Galicia continued its distinctive course, linked to León with Fernando II and Alfonso IX, and was involved in the various conflicts that brought this kingdom into confrontation with Portugal and with Castile. The definitive union of the Castilian and Leonese crowns with Fernando III, noted above, opened a new period which was dominated in a specific way by the impetus this monarch gave to the process of the Reconquest in Andalucia.

The events which marked the first half of the XIIth century, specifically the childhood upbringing of the emperor Alfonso VII in the powerful Galician house of the Traba clan, as well as the development of the Road to Santiago under the protection of the monarchs of León, became the determining factors that led to the emergence of Galician – called above all for geopolitical reasons Galician-Portuguese – as the language of lyric poetry from at least the end of the XIIth century to the mid-1300s (Tavani 1980b: 9–24; Brea 1994: 41–56; Souto Cabo 2012). The use of a single language with minimal variants in the entire poetic production of the centre and west of the Peninsula explains the inclusion in this chapter of *cantigas* by troubadours who originated not only from Galicia, but also from various regions of Castile and Portugal. The fortunes of the apostle's tomb and the cultural consequences arising therefrom, linked to social and political factors noted above, and the crucial role played by the Galician nobility in the adaptation of the 'chant courtois' in western Iberia (Oliveira 1993; Souto Cabo 2012), are the justifications for dedicating a separate chapter to Galicia in this book.

The routes of penetration of the Arthurian narratives into the kingdoms of Castile and Portugal were varied in character (Entwistle 1942; Lida de Malkiel 1959: 406–18; Freire Nunes 1999a: 8–35).[1] In this literary import process, however, scholars have emphasised three essential factors: (1) the cultural role played by the 'Camino de Santiago' and its associated ferment; (2) the matrimonial politics practised by the monarchs of Portugal, Castile and León, involving members of the French and English aristocracy;[2] and (3) the long residence (*c.*1229–45) of the future Portuguese King Afonso III 'o Bolonhês' at the Capetian court of his aunt Blanche of Castile (Ventura 2006: 44–72). Connected to these direct influences are the frontier contacts that constantly arose between Portugal, Galicia and Castile throughout the Middle Ages. Thus, relations between representatives of the ecclesiastical and seigneurial territories on both sides of these frontiers would surpass merely economic and political interests in such a way that cultural exchanges also accompanied these. As is well known, the

Galician nobility (above all those of the southern borderlands) and those of the north of Portugal often sealed their alliances through matrimonial links. Also to be taken into account is the exodus of Portuguese nobles to the Castilian court during times of political upheaval (as occurred, for example, during the civil war which brought Sancho II into conflict with Afonso III, or with the conflict that began with the crisis of 1319–24 between Don Denis and his heir, Prince Afonso). To these factors it would be appropriate to add crusades (both those within the Iberian Peninsula and those undertaken to the Holy Land), which led to armies originating from different geographical areas and cultures sharing a journey, adversities and also entertainment during relatively long periods.

In this varied and complex chain of transmission of the Arthurian tradition to the Peninsular west, we must also consider the intermediary role of the Occitan troubadours. From at least Marcabru (fl. *c*.1130–49) onwards, the *matière de Bretagne* (and especially the legend of Tristan and Iseut) had been incorporated into the themes of the *grand chant courtois* to become part of a far-reaching polemic (Roncaglia 1958; Haidu 1968; Meneghetti 1984: 139–46; Rossi 1992). The long sojourn of this Gascon troubadour at the court of Alfonso VII between 1134 and 1143 marks the beginning of direct contacts between Castilian and Leonese aristocratic circles and the Provenzal lyric (Milà i Fontanals 1966; Alvar 1977). From the decade of the 1140s, visits by Occitan poets to the courts of Castile and León occur constantly, and this situation must also have facilitated access to models from the Arthurian world known by these Provenzal poets themselves. Among these contacts, a special significance attaches to the figures of Guerau Cabrera (*c*.1130–98) and Guillem de Berguedà (1138–92). As will be remembered, Cabrera alludes in his famous *ensenhamen Cabra, juglar* (Cingolani 1992–3b) to various characters from the Arthurian stories (Erec, Gauvain, Tristan ...) while Guillem de Berguedà reveals a knowledge of a version of the *Tristan* in verse (Riquer 1971: I, 177). Both authors were associated with Galicia through the kinship links which their families had with the important house of Traba which, as noted above, wielded a significant influence on the crown of Castile-León from the time of Alfonso VII (Pallares and Portela 1983; López Sangil 2005; Souto Cabo 2012).

When scholars consider the diffusion of the *matière de Bretagne* in Castile and Galicia, they find that, from the beginning of the XXth century, the question upon which a large proportion of critical discussion centred was that of the language in which the first translation of the Arthurian *Vulgate* and *Post-Vulgate* cycles was written: Portuguese, Castilian, Leonese ...?[3] If the facts are analysed with the necessary detachment, it cannot be denied that the period of residence by the Count of Boulogne in the north of France must have been crucial for direct knowledge of the literature which was in vogue at that time in the lands of the *langue d'oïl*, in which the reworking of the *Post-Vulgate* had appeared (having been completed a few years before the return of Prince Afonso to Portugal in 1245: Bogdanow 1966). The circumstances of the life of Afonso III make him the ideal agent for the adaptation of the latest Arthurian prose *romans* into the literary traditions of the west of the Peninsula. As will be seen below, we have only indirect evidence of the circulation of the *Vulgate* in the second half of the XIIIth century, but of the *Pseudo-Robert de Boron* we have the three Portuguese witnesses which comprise the French cycle and which reveal its rapid acclimatisation in Portuguese territory (on which see the chapter by Santiago Gutiérrez García in this volume). To the copies previously known to scholars there was added in 2002 the discovery of a vellum bifolium in the Arquivo Distrital do Porto (Dias 2003–5; Ailenii 2009), which contains a fragment of the *José de Arimateia* from the end of the XIIIth century or the beginnning of the XIVth. The importance of this discovery is not merely a matter of its date, but also of its textual relationships, since it derives from a French source different from that used in the late copy found in the Torre do Tombo at Lisbon (MS 643). If this is the case, there would have been circulating in Portugal two versions of the *Estoire del Saint Graal* derived from different manuscripts, which would underline the success of this literary inspiration emanating from a court thoroughly imbued with French tastes.

The hypothesis of a Portuguese original from which the late Castilian copies would derive is supported particularly by the famous *autonominatio* that a certain Joam Vivas introduces into the *Livro de José de Arimateia* in Portuguese (1543) and in the printed editions of Toledo (1515) and Seville (1535) of the Castilian *Demanda del Santo Grial*. In this intricate process of textual transmission, Ivo Castro (1983) identified Joan Vivas with a cleric of the Order of Santiago, who worked in the service of Afonso III 'o Bolonhês' and who, in 1263, authorised a donation to the nunnery of Chelas (Coimbra). According to the argument of the Portuguese scholar, the translation of the *Post-Vulgate* cycle would have been undertaken initially in Portugal in the learned circles of Afonso III. Of this first, lost, version a copy would have been made in Astorga, signed by João Sanches, whose name is recorded in the famous colophon of the Portuguese *José d'Arimateia*.[4] This work, preserved in its entirety in a late copy made in 1543, would have derived from this version and not from the early original. This hypothesis is plausible, well founded, and, obviously, seems to be the most economical for explaining the diffusion of the cycle of the *Roman du Graal* in Castile, a diffusion which would have been facilitated by the linguistic similarity between the two neighbouring languages. The process of translation into Castilian would thus have been more rapid and must have been accomplished in a relatively short time, as is shown by the fragment of the *Merlín* from the beginning of the XIVth century (Pietsch 1924–5: I, 20–1). Moreover, the case for the priority of Portuguese in the adaptation of the *summa* of the *Post-Vulgate* would be reinforced by the Lusisms scattered throughout the Castilian *Demanda*. As a consequence, the intervention of King Afonso III is shown to be crucial for the knowledge and diffusion of the *Post-Vulgate* trilogy (and probably for that of its immediate predecessors) in the literary circles of the Crown of Castile. With this point clarified, it must be stated, however, that as both the texts themselves and the study of personal names show, Arthurian literature arrived in Castilian territory in successive or parallel waves, which involve the existence of other routes of circulation leading from Aragon, France or Italy.

The historiographic tradition of the *Fuero de Navarra* (c.1205), the *Liber regum* (or *Chronicon Villarense*, whose first version is earlier than 1211), the *Anales Toledanos Primeros* (c.1217) and, above all, the *General Estoria* (c.1270–80) of Alfonso X (specifically, parts II to IV), is inspired, directly or indirectly, by the *Historia regum Britanniae* of Geoffrey of Monmouth. These texts reveal that, from the beginning of the XIIIth century, the work of the Welsh cleric was well known in Peninsular intellectual circles (Gómez Redondo 1998: I, 98ff.). However, it is very probable that, as is shown by personal names and artistic sources, the knowledge of the *fabulae Arturis* appeared in Portuguese and Castilian territories from the beginning of the XIIth century, that is to say, chronologically earlier than, or in tandem with, the appearance of that foundational text of Arthurian narrative. At least, this is what is to be concluded from a charter of donation, drawn up around 1118–38, in the north of Portugal (specifically, in the locality of Faõies, situated near the city of Chaves, towards the frontier with the Galician province of Ourense). In this document there appear two sons of the noble Odório Guedaz (of the family of the Guedões) and Aragunta Gomez, whose Christian names are Rolam and Galvam (Mattoso 1985b: 100–1).[5] As David Hook pointed out in his studies (Hook 1990–1, 1992–3a, 1996), personal names do not prove the direct influence of specific literary texts, but, even when they are few in number, they certainly do reveal the penetration into courtly circles of a recent aesthetic fashion inspired by foreign literary genres. Despite this caveat, the data derived from personal names show that the new paradigms spread through various sectors of the nobility from the middle of the XIIth century. From the middle of the following century, there is evident a growing frequency in the use of Arthurian names, which reached its peak in the final decades of the XIVth century and during the whole of the XVth. Thus, from 1151, and especially from the early 1200s, there appear ever more frequently in the documentation from the kingdoms of León, Castile, and Portugal names such as Artus (1151, 1167, 1200, 1203, 1206, 1217), Galvan (1136–39?/1156?, 1178, 1182, 1193, 1195, 1204, 1208, 1262 ...), which is certainly the most commonly attested, and Merlin (1186, 1190 ...). From the final quarter of the XIVth century until the end of the XVth, the most successful name is, as in France, Tristan (Beceiro Pita 1993). To the references already known and catalogued by scholars, I add here, because of its rarity in the area under consideration, the existence of a squire named Perceval ('Porsival'), who appears as a witness in a Galician document of 1438 from the monastery of Santa Maria de Montederramo (Ourense).[6]

The data provided by the sources examined by scholars indicate that, as in other areas of western Europe (Pastoureau 1990: 112–25), Arthurian personal names enjoyed a certain favour among members of the middle and lower nobility. By contrast, the aristocracy and upper nobility rarely adopted names derived from the Arthurian narratives. The fashion was concentrated above all in female offspring and bastard sons; this situation was probably brought about by the importance, for the nobility, of patrilinear identification for reasons of property inheritance.

The circulation of the *matière de Bretagne* in Galicia at an early date could also derive support from the arts, if, as Serafín Moralejo originally suggested (1985), one of the sculptures which until the XVIIIth century adorned one of the twisted columns of the old Porta Francigena (completed in the first years of the XIIth century) of the cathedral at Santiago de Compostela represents Tristán in his boat, after having been wounded by Morholt of Ireland.[7]

2. The *Matière de Bretagne* and Troubadour Lyric: General Allusions

In the Galician-Portuguese lyric tradition there stands out on the conceptual level a series of texts that depart from the conventional aesthetic content of the troubadour canon, and enrich this with new contributions drawn from various sources. Specifically, from around 1250, one of the literary seams that opened new possibilities for the traditional thematic repertoire of troubadour production was that of the *matière de Bretagne*.[8] The greater part of the allusions that appear in the *cantigas* are endowed with a far-reaching significance because, as will be evident from the pages that follow, they attest both the variety of texts used by the troubadours and the circulation of copies of which no trace survives today in either Castile or Portugal. In addition, it is also appropriate to stress that contact with the prose Arthurian cycles determined the adaptation and cultivation of the *lai lyrique*. The surviving manuscript tradition has preserved only five examples of this genre, which illustrate another form of the flowering of the *fabulae Arturis*, since they involve poems which, from their rhetorical and stylistic characteristics, were extracted (and translated) from the relevant prose works to stand as independent poetic creations (Pellegrini 1959; Gutiérrez García 2007a; Lorenzo Gradín 2013; to underline this point, see the examination of the *lais de Bretanha* by Santiago Gutiérrez García in the present volume).

The generic references to the Arthurian stories introduced into their *cantigas* by the troubadours give, because of their very imprecision, a very insubstantial chronology, which allows us only to place them in the second half of the XIIIth century. Gonçal'Eanes do Vinhal, a Portuguese noble who took part in various campaigns of the Reconquest of Andalucía and who was linked in a particular manner to the figure of Alfonso X (Viñez Sánchez 2004: 11–97), was one of the first poetic voices to incorporate into his output a reference to the world of Arthurian fiction. The troubadour directed a satirical *cantiga* against an unskilled performer who compensated for his own ineptitude by pillaging the poems that others composed:

> Maestre, todo'lus vossos cantares
> ja que filhan sempre d'unha razon
> e outrossy ar filhan a mi son,
> e non seguydes outros milhares
> senon aquestes de Cornoalha,
> mays este[s] seguydes ben, sen falha;
> e non vi trobador per tantos logares.
>
> D'amor e d'escarnh'en todas razões
> os seguides sempre, ben provado
> eu o sey que avedes filhado,
> ca se ar seguissedes outros sões
> non trobariades peyor por én,
> pero seguydes vós os nossos mui ben
> e ja ogan'y fezestes tenções
>
> en razon d'un escarnho que filhastes
> e non[o] metestes ascondudo [...]
> (Gonçal'Eanes: *LPGP* 60, 5, l. 1–16)

The reproach does not consider the legitimate variant of the *cantiga de seguir*, that is to say, a poem which has recourse to the various grades of metrical imitation accepted by the tradition itself and collected in one of the passages of the *Poética fragmentaria* that precedes *Cancioneiro* B (Cardoso 1977; Tavani 1980b: 136–8; Canettieri and Pulsoni 1995).[9] The troubadour attacks, in this instance, the poor skills of his victim, whose deficiencies lead him to plagiarise the content and music alike (*razon* and *son*) of other people's poems.

The generic character conferred by the designation 'cantares de Cornoalha' in this text (line 5) prevents us from establishing precisely the subject matter and the genre of the pieces to which the allusion refers. Jean-Marie d'Heur suggested that it could involve *lais* (D'Heur 1976: 185–94); specifically, one would have to consider lyric *lais*, in view of the fact that Gonçal'Eanes specifies that they are *cantares* accompanied by music. In any case, as can be seen from the second stanza of the text, the troubadour distinguishes these compositions from *cantigas de amor*, *cantigas d'escarnio*, and from the *tensós*, which seems to indicate that they had some special feature which differentiated them from the genres which make up the greater part of the Galician-Portuguese repertoire. The key to the distinctive nature of these pieces lies in the toponym 'Cornoalha', which can refer to two different geographical regions, both linked to Arthurian fiction: Cornualles in England (Cornwall), and Cornuailles in Brittany. Beyond question, it is the south-western kingdom of England that plays the most important role in the spatial configuration of a great proportion of the Arthurian narratives. Although from the work of Geoffrey of Monmouth it was famous as the location of the castle of Tintagel (the place of Arthur's conception) and because the tragic battle of Camlann took place in that area, its fame was established first and foremost by its having been the location of the court of King Mark. This last detail meant that this geographical area was identified with the love affair of Tristan and

Iseut. Hence, one may hypothesise that the compositions which were appropriated by the *maestre* censured by Gonçal'Eanes were probably associated with some episode from the legends of Tristan (Sharrer 1989: 563). At all events, the generic character of the reference does not prevent us from ruling out (as happens with the Arthurian *lais*, and specifically with some of the *lais de Bretanha* that opened the old Colocci-Brancuti *cancioneiro*, such as those devoted to Morholt and Lanzarote: Gutiérrez García and Lorenzo Gradín 2001: 93–108; Gutiérrez García 2007a) the possibility that the texts in question received this label because, rather than Tristan, they had other characters and episodes of the Arthurian cycle as their inspiration.

The image, simultaneously mythic and literary, of Tristan is present in two *cantigas de amor* of Alfonso X and Don Denis in order to establish a correlation with perfect love (Alvar 2013b). In this context, it is appropriate to underline the fact that the Galician-Portuguese lyric renounces the dialectic that had been created in the intellectual circles of the north and south of France by the *fin'amor* of Tristan and Iseut (Roncaglia 1958; Haidu 1968; Meneghetti 1984: 139–46). In the Hispanic troubadours, the legend of Tristan appears stripped of all this polemic burden; the references to the problematic philtre and the fatal character of the passion that leads to death are omitted, to recover purely the fossilised image of the perfect lover. It could be said that the adherence to the model is shown to be 'superficial', as a cultural echo that limits itself to continuing the process of allusion carried out by troubadours and trouvères of the stature of Bernart de Ventadorn, Folquet de Romans, Peire Cardenal, Blondel de Nesle or Raoul de Soissons (Toury 2001: 273–95). Consequently the ideological dispute that the love of Tristan had aroused in certain cultural circles north of the Pyrenees is absent from the lyric tradition of the Iberian troubadours.

In the *cantigas* of the Castilian king and his grandson the exemplum of the hero from Cornwall serves only as a mark of culture that permits both texts to be inscribed within a continuum marked by the *auctoritas* of the lyric models in Provenzal and French. Thus, Don Denis seems to wish to reinforce these links in a particular manner by endowing the lover of Iseut with the designation of *amador*, as Bernart de Ventadorn had done in *Tant ai mo cor ple de joia* (*Plus trac pena d'amor / de Tristan l'amador / que.n sofri manhta dolor / por Izeut la blonda*, Ferrari 1984: 52; Rossi 1992). As a consequence, both monarchs take up the nexus Tristan = *amador* and have recourse to the fictional character to intensify their amorous sufferings. In the process of creation, and taking into account the unique character offered by the allusions in the corpus transmitted to us, it seems no accident that Don Denis should have taken up the figure of Tristan from the Alfonsine cancionero. With this allusion, the celebrated Portuguese troubadour inscribed his production in a clearly defined aristocratic chain of transmission and established a dialogue with Alfonso el Sabio to renew the codified *cantiga de amor*. Whilst in Alfonso X's text there exists a syntony between the sentiments of the lady and those of the troubadour (in this case, the exemplum serves to favour the hyperbole of the sadness, *coita*, caused by separation of the lovers), in the poem by the Portuguese king the passion of the Arthurian hero is used as an argumentative strategy by the lover to obtain pity from the intransigent lady. In either case, in both texts, Tristan is set up as representative of the authentic character of courtly love, so that his figure becomes (as in Bernart de Ventadorn, Peire Cardenal or Raoul de Soissons, all mentioned above) a privileged element of comparison that permits the true nature of masculine sentiment to be proved:

> E, pois que o Deus assi quis,
> que seu sõo tan alongado
> de vós, mui ben seede fis
> que nunca eu sen cuidado
> en viverei, ca ja Paris
> d'amor non foi tan coitado
> nen Tristan;
> nunca sofreron tal afan,
> nen [ter]an
> quantos son nen seeran.
>
> Que farei eu pois que non vir
> o mui bon parecer vosso?
> Ca o mal que vos foi ferir
> aquele x'este o nosso,
> e por ende per ren partir
> de vós muit'amar non posso
> nen farei,
> ante ben sei ca morrerei
> se non ei
> vós, que sempre i amei.
> (Alfonso X, ed. Paredes 2001, xii, lines 11–30)
>
> Senhor, fremosa e de mui loução
> coraçom, e querede vos doer
> de mi, pecador, que vos sei querer
> melhor ca mi; pero sõo certão
> *que mi queredes peior d'outro rem*
> *pero, senhor, quero-vos eu tal bem*
> [...]
> Qual maior poss'; e o mui namorado
> Tristam sei bem que nom amou Iseu
> quant'eu vos amo, esto certo sei eu;
> e con tod'esto sei, mao pecado,
> *que mi queredes peior d'outro rem*
> *pero, senhor, quero-vos eu tal bem*
> (Don Denis: *LPGP* 25, 113, lines 1–6, 13–18)

The imprecise nature of the exempla cited does not allow us to specify the narrative model which underlies them, although it is appropriate to record that, as has been suggested elsewhere (Gutiérrez García and Lorenzo Gradín 2001: 95–109; Gutiérrez García 2007a; Lorenzo Gradín 2013), the *lais de Bretanha* that begin *Cancioneiro* B (and in particular *Amor, des que m'a vos cheguei, LPGP* 157, 5; *Don Amor eu cant'e choro, LPGP* 157, 18; and *Mui gran temp'á, par Deus, que eu non vi, LPGP* 157, 32) show the impact that had been attained in Galicia and Portugal by what is known as the long version of the French *Tristan en prose*.[10] As will be seen in the following pages, the only direct testimony of the diffusion of this narrative cycle in the west of the Peninsula is the Galician fragment of the *Livro de Tristan*, which, although datable towards the final quarter of the XIVth century, shows evidence that it was a copy of an earlier version (Castro 1998; Lorenzo Gradín and Díaz Martínez 2004), which was already circulating in the west of the Peninsula towards the end of the XIIIth century.

3. The *Cantigas de Santa Maria* and Arthurian Fiction

In the adaptation of the Arthurian stories in the kingdom of Castile there stands out Alfonso X's *cantiga, Como Santa Maria fez que nacesse o fillo do judeu o rostro atrás, como llo Merlin rogara* (Mettmann 1988: II, no. 108). The entire miracle is structured around a story of which Merlin is the protagonist. It is related that the latter is the offspring of the devil, a point which, as is well known, had been introduced by Geoffrey of Monmouth in the *Historia regum Britanniae* (Faral 1993: III, ch. 106).

The action of the *cantiga* is set in Scotland. A Jewish *alfaquí* (that is to say, a learned man or doctor in religious matters) denies the Incarnation of Christ in the presence of the British seer. To prove the falsity of this affirmation, Merlin prays to Mary that the child expected by the Jew's wife should be born with his face looking backwards. Thus it comes about, and although the father wishes to kill the newborn baby, Merlin protects him and takes advantage of the miracle so that, with the passage of time, the young man is restored as an irrefutable proof of the virginity of Mary. Faced with such an occurrence, the Jews convert to Christianity:

> E o praz'uviou chegar
> que a judea pariu;
> mais ben se podo sinar
> quen aquel seu fillo viu,
> ca atal o gẽerar
> fez Deus como llo pediu
> Marlin con felonia.
> *Dereit'é de ss'end'achar*
> *[mal quen fillar perfia*
> *contra Santa Maria].*
>
> Que o rostro lle tornar
> fez Deus o deant'atras,
> como lle fora rogar
> o fillo de Sathanas
> por en vergonna deitar
> a seu padre Cayphas,

> que ant'o non criya.
> *Dereit'é de ss'end'achar* [...]
> (Alfonso X, ed. Mettmann 1988: II, no. 108, lines 62–77)

A very similar story is contained in *Les Prophécies de Merlin*, a prose work compiled in Italy between 1272 and 1279 by a cleric, probably of Venetian origin, who conceals his identity under the fictitious name of Richard of Ireland (Paton 1927: II, 328–45). The anonymous author reveals his preoccupation with the political situation in Italy and the Holy Land, and to this end makes use of the political prophecies of the Arthurian seer to apply them to the reality that surrounds him. Influenced by the ideology of Joachim of Fiore, the cleric included in his work miscellaneous material on Merlin, from which he mingled the political prophecies with another type of stories of a literary nature in which the British seer is the protagonist (Paton 1927: II, 229–300; Zumthor 2000: 104–7). There is a series of evident similarities between the brief Italian narration and the Alfonsine *cantiga*: the action takes place in Scotland; the dispute with the enchanter about the Incarnation of Christ involves a Jew who is 'le plus saige' of his community; and, finally, the sin of the heretic has as its consequence the birth of a child 'qui la bouche avoit derriere' (Paton 1927: I, 492). However, the text of Pseudo-Richard of Ireland does not specify that the punishment imposed on the Jew is the result of a prayer by Merlin to the Virgin, nor does it offer the detail of the final conversion of the Jews.

Whilst the date proposed for the composition of the Italian compilation overlaps with the writing of the *Cantigas de Santa Maria* (set at *c.*1270–82: Mettmann, ed. 1986: I, 21–4; 1987), it is not very likely that *Les Prophecies* are the direct source of the text by Alfonso X. The *cantiga* which concerns us is contained in the second phase that has been identified in the configuration of this Marian compilation (in other words, the phase corresponding to MS T, Biblioteca de El Escorial, T.I.1), the production of which is placed between *c.*1274 and 1277. This situation has led critics to postulate a common origin for the story in both works, which would have reached Castile and the *Marca Trevisana* by Venice independently (Sharrer 1989: 564). This hypothesis could be reinforced by the very arrangement of the north Italian work, which is presented as the aggregation of various narrative units which could previously have circulated independently. Since it has been impossible to determine whether the story of Merlin is the creation of the Venetian author or is dependent upon an unknown French source, it is impossible to establish the route of transmission followed by the text to reach Castile. In any case, it is important to indicate that the *cantiga* of Alfonso X rises above the generality of material concerning Merlin and opens it into another dimension of a religious and exemplary nature.

Two more generic allusions to the Arthurian tradition are found in *CSM* 35. The text relates how a dean of Lyon takes with him some relics of the Virgin and embarks with them on a ship full of merchants heading to England to buy wool. During the crossing, the ship is attacked by corsairs. The captain suggests placing themselves under the protection of the relics of Mary, to whom the merchants offer valuable goods in exchange for coming out of the attack alive. But once the danger has passed, greed makes them withdraw their offerings. On their return to France, God punishes the insult they have given to his mother, causing a thunderbolt to hit the ship, which burns all the merchandise they had acquired. The merchants realise their sin, and, in repentance, return together with the French dean to offer their gifts to Saint Mary:

> Disso maestre Bernaldo: 'Esto mui gran dereit'é
> de vos nembrar das relicas da Virgen que con Deus ssé,
> a que fezestes gran torto guardando mal vossa fe.'
> E non quis en mais do terço, que fezo loco coller.
> *O que a Santa Maria der algo ou prometer,*
> *dereit'é que ss'en mal ache se llo pois quiser tolher.*
> (Alfonso X, ed. Mettmann, 1986: I, no. 35, lines 130–4)

The first reference to the Arthurian material is found in line 41 of the text proper, in which it is specified that the destination of the ship is 'Bretanna, a que pobrou rei Brutus'. This information, although it was incorporated into the historiographic tradition previous to the *Historia* of Geoffrey of Monmouth, probably reached King Alfonso through the Welsh Latin chronicle, which, it will be recalled, was extensively used in the Alfonsine court for the composition of the chronicles. It is well known that Brutus, great-grandson of Aeneas, after being expelled from Italy, went to Greece and was visited in a dream by the goddess Diana. She indicated to him that he should steer his ships beyond Gaul, where there is found an island on which he would build a 'second Troy'. In fact the hero, after various adventures, reached the coast of the kingdom which, in his honour, received the name Britain.

The second reference to Arthurian literature is found in line 92 of the *cantiga*, in which the narrator indicates that, after the disappearance of the pirate galleys, the crew of the ship protected by the Virgin catch sight of Dovra, 'a que pobrou rey Artur'. Whilst Wace erroneously identified the original Dorobellum of the *Historia* of Geoffrey with the locality of Douvres/Dovre (Dover), what is certain is that none of the known texts associates the foundation of this city with the British king.[11] Although in the *Merlin* and the *Mort Artu* of the *Vulgate* Cycle, Arthur chooses this port for his journeys to the continent (and moreover the latter work specifies that it is where Gawain died), at no time do the *romans* mention the detail given by Alfonso X in his text. We cannot rule out the possibility that the Castilian king associated Arthur and Dover through a lapse of memory or even by necessities of composition. In this context, we must note that the second hemistich of the line in question is a parallel with line 41 (Alvar 2010a: 229) and demands a rhyme in *-ur*, an uncommon solution in the Galician-Portuguese corpus, which, therefore, did not offer many personal names that match the required rhyme.

The dependence of the Marian *cantigas* on the Arthurian literary universe is clear in one of the passages in *cantiga* 419. The miracle narrated here revolves around the death and Assumption of Mary. All the apostles gather at the burial of the Mother of God, except Thomas. Once she is buried, her body is taken up to heaven by St Michael and other angels. At this moment, Thomas sees the miracle and begs the Virgin for a proof of what has happened. She gives him a ribbon, which the apostle shows to his companions, after having been reproached for not having been present at the burial:

> Santo Thomas chorando respondeu-lles adur:
> 'Dized'u a metestes; mais sei eu que nenllur
> achar nona podedes quant'o Breton Artur,
> ca eu a vi na nuve sobir, e me chamou.
> *Des quando Deus sa madre aos çeos levou,*
> *de nos levar consigo carreira nos mostrou.*
>
> E por que me creades esta çinta me quis
> dar, e de seu feito sejades todos fis;
> que eu vi o seu corpo mui mais branco ca lis
> ir sobindo aos çeos, e mui poc'y tardou.'
> *Des quando Deus sa Madre aos çeos levou*
> *de nos levar consigo carreira nos mostrou.*
> (Alfonso X, ed. Mettmann, 1989: III, no. 419, lines 130–41)

In this case the traditional incredulity of the apostle is transferred to his companions. To confer greater expressive force to his words, Thomas establishes in his account an analogy between the disappearance of Mary's body and that of Arthur. The public is faced with the evocation of the well-known motif of the *espoir breton*, that is to say, the belief that the celebrated monarch, wounded after the final combat with Mordred at the battle of Camlann, had not died but had been taken to the isle of Avalon to be cured of his wounds (Faral 1993 [1929]: II, 299–308). The finding of the Virgin's body in her grave would be as impossible as the discovery of the remains of Arthur. As is known, the king's disappearance was firmly established with the work of Geoffrey of Monmouth;[12] and by the adaptation of the *Historia regum Britanniae* by Wace in the *Roman de Brut* (1155):

> Arthur, si la geste ne ment,
> fud el cors nafrez mortelment;
> en Avalon se fist porter
> pur ses plaies mediciner.
> Encor i est, Bretun l'atendent,
> si cum li dient e entendent;
> de la vendra, encor puet vivre.
> Maistre Wace, ki fist cest livre,
> Ne volt plus dire de sa fin
> qu'en dist li prophetes Merlin;
> Merlin dist d'Arthur, si ot dreit,
> que sa mort dutuse sereit.
> Li prophetes dist verité;
> tut tens en ad l'um puis duté,
> et dutera, ço crei, tus dis,
> se il est morz u il est viz.
> (*Roman de Brut*, ed. Arnold, 1940: II, lines 13275–90)

Whilst the prose cycles re-elaborate the final episode of the life of the British king and whilst the *Vulgate Mort Artu* and the *Queste dou Saint Graal* of Pseudo-Robert de Boron renounce the king's fantastic return and narrate his death, Alfonso X departs from this part of the tradition, and by contrast with Wace does not submit the fabled version to any critical judgement either. For Alfonso's purpose, the Assumption of the Virgin is not open to discussion; it is a tenet of faith that presents no problems. For this reason, the celebrated Castilian troubadour king assigns priority to the authority of the historiographic sources that he has at his disposal (Gómez Redondo 1998: I, 730, 744, and *passim*), among which, as has been stated, the tradition of Geoffrey of Monmouth's work occupied an essential position. Therefore, irrespective of the veracity of the return of Arthur, the reference is employed because it invokes an historical memory that is incorporated into the *cantiga* because of the truth associated with the chronicle.

4. From Chrétien de Troyes to the Prose Cycles

The traces left by Arthurian literature in the work of Galician-Portuguese troubadours can be followed not only through the personal names used in the *cantigas*, but also sometimes through certain words or turns of phrase that seem to conceal intertextual references to the *romans* of the Arthurian universe. This *modus operandi* is what may lie behind the following *cantiga de escarnio* of Alfonso X (Gutiérrez García 2007b; Lorenzo Gradín 2008a):

> Vi un coteife de mui gran granhon,
> con seu porponto, mais non d'algodon,
> e con sas calças velhas de branqueta.
> E dix-eu logo: – Poi-las guerras son
> *ai, que coteife pera a carreta!*
> [...]
> Vi un coteife mal guisa'e vil,
> con seu porponto todo de pavil
> e o cordon d'ouro tal por joeta.
> E dix'eu: – Pois se vai o aguazil,
> *ai, que coteife pera a carreta!*
> (Alfonso X, ed. Paredes, 2001: no. xxv)

Expert scholarship (Ballesteros Beretta 1984: 362–71; Paredes Núñez 1992; Lanciani and Tavani 1995: 109–11) has placed the composition of this text between 1264 and 1265, associated with the events arising from the rebellion of King Aben Alhamar of Granada. The target of the satire is a *coteife*, that is to say, one of those 'villein knights', *caballeros villanos*, who entered the lowest rank of the nobility not by hereditary transmission of lineage but for services provided during the military campaigns in Al-Andalus (Fossier 1988: 235–7; Mattoso 1988: I, 229–32; Flori 1998: 111–14). This second-class knighthood, unique in the whole of western Europe, was composed principally of peasants who had succeeded in amassing sufficient income to possess a horse. At first sight, the author criticises the external appearance of one of these *coteifes*, who presents a lamentable physical aspect and whose military equipment is antiquated and defective. In accordance with these facts, Rodrigues Lapa (1970a: 11) interpreted the refrain of the text as reinforcing the ridiculous portrait of this warrior, whose only use during fighting would be that appropriate to a carter. Although the historical and literary sources do not attach negative connotations to those charged with driving carts and wagons, both documentation and iconography show that this was an activity appropriate to the social estate of the *laboratores*. In this line of interpretation, the troubadour would relegate the protagonist of the satire to a more plebeian and less committed activity than that of bearing arms. However, the presence of the 'cordon d'ouro' and the 'alguazil' in the final verse of the text raises certain doubts about the interpretation given to the *cantiga* so far. The *alguazil* was the functionary charged with exercising justice in the name of the king, above all among the peasantry (Juárez Blanquer and Rubio Flores (eds), 1991: *Partida* II, ix, 20). Among his areas of authority was the supervision of prisoners condemned for having committed robbery, taken part in fights, or having wounded or killed someone. According to the gravity of the offence committed, the penalties for the condemned could run from light sanctions to death on the gallows. Given this, it is not clear what could be the role of the *alguazil* faced with a man who, instead of appearing like a real knight, has more of the bearing of a carter. It seems evident that, if the troubadour laments that the officer of justice was departing, it was because the *coteife* he had before his eyes had the appearance of a delinquent whom it would be appropriate to detain. In this context, the suspicious gold chain displayed by the protagonist contrasts with the miserable clothing he is wearing and, perhaps, stands out as proof of his status as an evildoer inclined to robbery. Therefore, the final lines of the text would give the key to the interpretation of it: the lamentable outward appearance of the villein knight would correspond to his dubious moral status. In fact the historical sources (Arias Bonet (ed.), 1975: *Partida* I, xxviii, 6) reveal the presence of men who went to the military campaigns not to increase their honour and glory but merely to participate in the reward of booty, or even to take advantage of the troubled situation and rob valuable objects from their fellow soldiers (Delumeau 1989: 296–304).

In the light of the concluding lines of the text, its hermeneutics are shown to be more coherent; but what is the role of the cart in the discursive strategy of the poem? In my view, the word was introduced by Alfonso as a literary allusion which permitted the privileged audience of the text to establish a rich network of associations with other literary products that circulated in courtly circles. In this case, the cart would evoke to this audience the celebrated passage in *Li Chevaliers de la charrette* of Chrétien de Troyes.[13] In this, it will be recalled, Lancelot, after a moment of doubt provoked by Reason, climbs into the degrading cart driven by the dwarf, because of his love for Guinevere. Chrétien defines the uses of such a means of transport in some very revealing lines:

> De ce servoit charrette lores
> Dont li pilori servent ores,
> Et en chascune boene vile
> Ou or en a plus de trois mille,
> N'en avoit a cel tans que une,
> Et cele estoit a ces comune,
> Ausi con li pilori sont.
> A ces qui murte et larron sont,
> Et a ces qui sont chanp cheü,
> Et as larrons qui ont eü
> Autrui avoir par larrecin
> Ou tolu par force an chemin:
> Qui a forfet estoit repris
> S'estoit sor la charrete mis
> Et menez par totes les rues;
> S'avoit totes enors perdues,
> Ne puis n'estoit a cort oïz,
> Ne enorez ne conjoïz.
> (Chrétien de Troyes, *Charrette*, ed. Roques, 1978: lines 321–49)

As can be observed, the cart, as well as being destined for murderers and those defeated in judicial duels, is, as Chrétien himself insists on two separate occasions (lines 328, 330–3), the vehicle destined for thieves, which is what the Alfonsine *coteife* appears to be.

The heirs of Chrétien de Troyes, and in particular the anonymous author of the *Lancelot propre* of the Vulgate cycle (*c*.1215–30), take up the episode again, although the original functions assigned to the cart are greatly compressed in the prose *roman* (Gutiérrez García 2007b):

> A cel tens estoit tel costume que qui voloit home destruire ou honir en totes terres, si le faisoit on avant monter en charete, ne des lors en avant ne fust escotés en cort, ains avoit perdues totes lois [...] Mesire Gauvain chevalche aprés la charete tant qu'il commence a avesprir. Et lors vienent a un chastel et si tost com il entrent, si commencent totes les gens Lancelot a huer et le mesaament et arochent et demandent al nain qu'il a meffet. (*Lancelot en prose*, ed. Micha 1978: II, xxxvi, 24–5)

In a later passage, the cart, driven by a dwarf and pulled by a horse whose ears and tail have been cropped, arrives at Arthur's court with a knight on the feast of Pentecost. The knight can leave the cart only if someone offers to take his place. At mealtime, nobody wishes to sit beside him, except Gauvain, who remembers the scorn suffered by Lancelot for riding in such a vile conveyance. The unknown knight leaves the court and, shortly afterwards, the cart reappears before the king and his knights, bearing the Lady of the Lake. She reproaches Arthur because nobody in his court would take the place in the cart of the knight who had arrived in it previously. What is more, she doubts whether any of those present would have the courage to replace her in it. At this moment, Gauvain climbs aboard the cart. The Lady of the Lake criticises the king for lack of courtesy and reveals that the knight who had previously been in the dishonourable vehicle had done this 'por l'amor de Lancelot qui por cele dame i monta et fist de que tu n'oissaises enprendre por li qui ta feme est, et por lui devroient estre charetés honorés a tos jors mes' (*Lancelot en prose*, ed. Micha 1978: II, xl, 21).

When the Lady departs, Arthur realises the identity of the knight whom they had not helped on the previous occasion: it is Bohort, the cousin of Lancelot. To make up for the lack of consideration all had shown for one of the best representatives of chivalry, the king himself, Guinevere and the rest of the knights at court go in search of the Lady of the Lake. On the way, they see Gauvain in the cart and one after another they begin to climb onto it to make up for their earlier omission:

> Et li roi vet avec, si ont trové en mi la vile mon seigneur Gauvain ou li nains le menoit encore en la charete. Et la roine saut sus et il descent et li rois i monte lez la roine, ne onques ne remist chevaliers en l'ostel le roi qui n'i monstast: ne des lors en avant, tant com li rois vesqui, ne fu nus hom dampnés mis en charete, ains avoit en chescune vile un viel roncin sans coe et sans oreilles, si i montoit k'en cels que l'en voloit honir et si les menoit l'en par totes les rues. (*Lancelot en prose*, ed. Micha 1978: II, xl, 23)

The rewriting and reinterpretation of the episode of the humiliation of Lancelot, the loss of the original significance of the cart, and the substitution of the punishment imposed on the condemned, indicate that the central work of the *Lancelot en prose* was not the textual reference that inspired the secular *cantiga* of Alfonso X. It is certain that, in contrast to what occurs in the case of the prose cycles, there is no direct proof of the diffusion of the *romans* of Chrétien de Troyes in Castile and Portugal, but this does not mean that they could not have circulated among the cultural elites. Here, it is worth recalling the importance that must have been attached to the aristocratic relationships to which reference was made earlier in this study, since in parallel with these there could have circulated literary and cultural exchanges from other areas of Europe. It must not be forgotten that medieval civilisation formed a network in which kings and nobles participated as patrons of the arts and letters, as well as the clergy, writers and *juglares*. This heterogeneous cultural world was known and experienced by different routes, direct or indirect, as the phenomenon of intertextuality itself demonstrates. In this context, the cart referred to by Alfonso would be a specific intellectual marker of the secular production of the Castilian monarch, who thereby would have established for part of his audience a network of connections favoured by the presence of a word unique in the Galician-Portuguese lyric (*carreta*), which refers to the emblematic passage of the first European *roman* devoted to Lancelot.

Knowledge of the production of Chrétien de Troyes could find a piece of supporting evidence in art, if, as suggested by Sánchez Ameijeiras in one of her studies (2003), the relief in the tympanum of the Cistercian monastery of Santa Maria de Penamaior (Lugo) represents Yvain and the grateful lion, that is to say, the two principal protagonists of the *Chevalier au lion* by Chrétien (*c.*1177–81). In this case, the iconography of the relief would reflect two central moments of the narrative: on the left is placed, near the marvellous fountain, the figure of Yvain, who is shown as armed with his lance and leading the empty mount of Keu; on the right, there is a seated lion with a curious tail, which would evoke the celebrated episode in which the protagonist saves the animal from the jaws of a serpent. Although the character of Yvain is taken up again in the prose cycles, since the relief from Lugo has been dated about 1225, it would be appropriate only to consider a possible influence of the *Lancelot propre* from the *Vulgate* cycle (*c*.1215–30). However, in this work there is no mention of the famous episode from Chrétien which explains the epithet attached to the protagonist, for which the narrator provides a wholly new explanation (West 1978: 309–10; Alvar 1991: 410–13): when Lionel, cousin of Lancelot, kills the lion which had appeared at court, he presents its skin to Yvain as a proof of recognition so that he can line his shield with it, since Yvain had presented him with a similar weapon on the eve of Pentecost:

> Alors que Melians vint a cort, começoit ja a avesprir et celui jor avoit esté Lionials chevaliers et le jor meesmes s'estoit il combatus au lion coroné de Libe [...] Si l'ocist Lionals par grant proesce, si com li contes que de lui est le devise, et celui jor otroia il la pel del lion a mon seignor Yvain a porter a son escu, por ce que mesire Yvain li avoit doné son escu a porter la veille de la Pentecoste et li avoit fere tot fres, et li escus estoit esquartelés de quatre colors d'or et d'azur et d'argent et de sinople. (*Lancelot en prose*, ed. Micha 1978: I, 245, xviii.3)

The prose text is quite distant from what had been narrated by Chrétien. In this context, the imagery of the Galician tympanum (in which there is no sign of the crowned lion of the *Lancelot en prose*) would refer us to the story related by Chrétien, and therefore its testimony would constitute a proof of the knowledge of at least one part of the production of the French writer in one of the locations on the Road to Santiago.

Alfonso X himself could again have had recourse to the Arthurian *romans* in the following *cantiga de escarnio*:

> Don Gonçalo, pois queredes ir d'aqui pera Sevilha,
> por veerdes voss'amigo, e[u] non o tenh'a maravilha:
> contar-vos-ei as jornadas légoa [e] légoa, milh[a] e milha.
> [...]
> E pois que vossa fazenda teedes ben alumeada
> e queredes ben amiga fremosa e ben talhada,
> non façades dela capa, ca non é cousa guisada.
>
> E pois que sodes aposto e fremoso cavaleiro,
> g[u]ardade-vos de seerdes escatimoso ponteiro,
> ca dizen que baralhastes con [Don] Joan Co[e]lheiro.
> [...]
> E non me tenhades por mal, se en vossas armas tango:
> que foi das duas [e]spadas que andavan en ũu mango?
> ca vos oí eu dizer: – Con estas pato ei e frango.
>
> E ar vos oí-vos eu dizer que a quen quer que chagassen
> con esta vossa espada, que nunca se trabalhassen
> jamais de o guareceren, se o ben non o agulhasen.

> E por esto [vos] chamamos nós 'o das duas espadas',
> por que sempre as tragedes agudas e amoadas,
> con que fendedes as penas, dando grandes espadadas.
>
>   (Alfonso X, ed. Paredes 2001: I, VII, VIII, X, XI, XII)

In the view of some scholars (Lapa 1970a: 65; Alvar 1984; Víñez 1994; Paredes 2001: 122), the origin of this composition could have been two satirical *cantigas* that the troubadour Gonçal'Eanes do Vinhal had put in the mouth of Jeanne de Ponthieu (*Amigas, eu oí dizer*, LPGP 60,3, and *Sei eu, donas, que deitad'é d'aquí*, LPGP 60,16). In both texts, the widow of Fernando III (†30 May 1252) asks the Castilian monarch for pardon for her lover, the rebel prince Don Enrique. The discord between Alfonso and Enrique 'el Senador' was unleashed around 1248 by the possessions granted to both brothers in Andalucian territory after the fall of Seville. The situation worsened in 1255, the year in which Enrique rebelled in Andalucía against his brother with the support of various nobles. The disputes were resolved definitively in that year with the rout of the prince and his expulsion from Castile (Ballesteros Beretta 1984: 104–38; González Jiménez 2004: 137–54). From our point of view, the placing of the two *cantigas* by Eanes do Vinhal in the section devoted to *escarnio e maldizer* in the Italian apographs B and V indicates that, rather than being a sign of mediation in the conflict by the Portuguese troubadour (Lapa 1970a: 66), they are a literary game that takes as their pretext a specific political situation. Alfonso X could have appreciated the ludic dimension of the poems of his vassal and, taking them literally, composed the joke with which we are concerned in order to attack Don Gonçalo for having an ambiguous and equivocal attitude in the struggle which pitted the king against his brother. If the suggested historical context is correct, then it would permit the Alfonsine *cantiga* to be dated a little after 1255. Even so, we would like to point out that the text still contains many obscure points, which require more detailed study in order to uncover its true meaning, but this lies beyond the scope of this chapter. In any case the place of the *cantiga* in the manuscript tradition (in a section that brings together the poetic writings of Alfonso before his coronation in 1252: see Oliveira 2010), alongside the references made by Alfonso to a meeting between Gonçal'Eanes and Johan Soarez Coelho (a vassal of the Portuguese *infante* Fernando de Serpa, brother of the Count of Boulogne, and of King Sancho II), suggest that a better date for the *escarnio* would be *c*.1248, since Coelho himself returned to Portugal at the end of that same year (Mattoso 1985a: 425–6). The *cantiga* appears to criticise the pretexts that Gonçal'Eanes gives to the prince for his journey to Seville. It seems to suggest that the Portuguese uses his enigmatic lover as a excuse for his trip (*e queredes ben amiga fremosa e ben talhada / non façades dela capa*), when in fact he flees to Seville to have a personal encounter with Johan Soarez Coelho (perhaps due to some sort of a settling of scores or because of purely political interests?). It should be noted that Vinhal and Coelho served in opposing parties during the Portuguese civil war from 1245 to 1247. As a result, while Don Gonçalo remained loyal to the legitimate King Sancho II, Coelho took the side of the usurper of the crown, Afonso III. Since the Castilian king and his family had protected Sancho II – who, after his defeat in the conflict, exiled himself to Castile, dying there on 4 January 1248 – it would not be strange if prince Alfonso incited Eanes do Vinhal to wound Coelho without any consideration (with him he could not be 'escatimoso ponteiro'). Is there, behind these verses, some kind of ironic critique of Don Gonçalo's apparent fear of fighting against his adversary? A question to which at present there is no satisfactory answer, since we lack firm evidence that would enable the Alfonsine *cantiga* to be linked to a specific situation, thereby enabling us to appreciate the true scope of the satire. Also worthy of note for our purposes here is the fact that, in the final part of his discourse, Alfonso X labels Goncal'Eanes with the periphrasis 'o das duas espadas', 'he of the two swords', which must have been sufficiently familiar in cultured circles to establish the necessary correspondences with the target of the satire. The possible literary reference hidden in the epithet could refer to four characters of the *matière de Bretagne*: namely, Palamedes, Samaliel, Balain and Meriadeuc (Gutiérrez and Lorenzo Gradín 2001: 73–9).

Whilst the last-named is the principal protagonist of the anonymous verse *roman* entitled *Li Chevalier aus Deus Espees* (Trachsler 1997: 119–21),[14] composed before 1250, and for the diffusion of which in the Iberian Peninsula there is no evidence, its influence on Alfonso X can probably be discounted. By contrast, the remaining named characters are present in romances that circulated through the centre and west of the Iberian Peninsula.

As far as concerns Samaliel and Palamedes, they appear, among other texts, in the *Queste dou Sant Graal* of the *Post-Vulgate* cycle (ed. Freire Nunes 2005: 394–401), and in the *Tristan en prose* (ed. Curtis 1963: I, 159–64; ed. Ménard 1997: IX, 211–35), while Balain is a character in the *Suite Merlin* of Pseudo-Robert de Boron (ed. Roussineau 1996: I, 67–195).

Samaliel receives the epithet of the 'Knight of the Two Swords' because he wears the sword of his father, Prince Froles, killed by Arthur, and also the one that Galahad girds on him on dubbing him knight. Both the narrator and the seneschal Keu clarify the role of any knight who carries two swords, as the corresponding passages of the *Queste* and *Tristan en prose* attest:

> Ao serẽao lhi avẽo que chegou a ũa casa u Keia o Moordomo albergava. E quando Keia lhi viu duas espadas maravilhou-se ca nom era de custume entom de nem ũũ cavaleiro trager II espadas em no reino de Logres se nom fosse por promote-lo ou por jurâ-lo. E se algũũ fosse tam honrado que trouxesse II espadas de custume nom podesse recear II cavaleiros que a batalha o chamassem. (Freire Nunes, *Demanda* 2005: §538, 394)

> Au soir li avint que aventure l'aporta en une maison u Kex li senescaus estoit hebergiés. Et quant il vit que Samaliel portoit .II. espees, il se merveilla que ce pooit estre, car dont n'estoit il pas coustume que nus cevaliers portast .II. espees, s'il nel portast pour veu ou pour serement. Et se aucuns portast .II. espees acoustumeement, il ne pooit refuser .II. chevaliers ne ne devoit, en quelque lieu qui l'apelaissent de bataille et de mellee [...] Nus cevaliers, fait il, ne doit porter .II. espees s'il n'est trop boins cevaliers, car .II. cevaliers le pueent asaillir en tous lex ensamble, et sans blasme. Mais ce ne porroit on faire d'un autre. (*Tristan en prose*, ed. Ménard 1997: IX. §103, 227–8)

Therefore, two swords are carried only by those *milites* who are distinguished for their prowess and their bravery in combat. Samaliel proves his valour by vanquishing the seneschal in the joust, and later by defeating Girflet and Gaheriés. The presentation of this character in the *Tristan en prose* is always positive, since, when the moment comes to avenge himself on the king for the death of his father, he desists from his mission and, as a proof of his forgiveness, one day when he encounters Arthur asleep in the forest of Camelot he takes the king's sword, leaving him his father's weapon. When the king awakes, he appreciates the courtesy of the young man and decides to wear for ever the sword that he had left him. The motivation for Samaliel's epithet and his role in the narration offer few parallels with the career of Gonçal'Eanes in Castile and with the episodes censured in his *cantigas*, for which reason it is, a priori, not very probable that his two swords were the model that inspired the passages in the Alfonsine *cantiga*.

As far as Palamedes is concerned, he appears in the first part of the *Tristan en prose* in the tournament convoked by the Doncella de las Landas, who will take as her husband the victor in this contest. The pagan knight participates in the tournament with two swords, since he is disposed to fight with two adversaries at the same time. As Gauvain makes clear to the king of Ireland, in a situation in which he were to be vanquished by any adversary who was not among the members of the Round Table, he would not be able to bear arms for a year. As could be foreseen, the courage and energy of this character determine his final victory in the contest and make him worthy of the hand of the Lady, which the protagonist rejects (Löseth 1974 [1891]: §§29–30, 21–2):

> Li chevaliers chevauchoit mout bel [...]; et sachiez qu'il portoit deus espees. Et tot maintenant que messires Gauvens li vit d'ax aprochier, il dit au roi: 'Sire, vez ci venir un mout boen chevalier.' 'Coment le savez vos?' dit li rois. 'Sire, fait il, je le sai par la costume del reaume de Logres, et je la vos dirai. Jamés n'i sera chevalier si hardi qui ost porter deus espees s'il n'est tel cevalier de son cors qu'il ne refusast en nule maniere l'encontre de deus chevaliers. Par ce conoist l'en les chevaliers parfaiz, car de la grant hautesce de lor cuer et del grant hardement que il ont portent il deus espees, por ce qu'il soient coneu d'entre les mauvés et les coarz [...] 'Sire, fait il, la costume dou torniement sai je bien, et ce ne refusase je mie, se je marier me poisse.' (*Tristan en prose*, ed. Curtis 1963, I: §§322–6, 161–3)

Of the characters mentioned, the one who plays the most ambiguous role is, beyond doubt, Balain le Sauvage. As the *Post-Vulgate Suite Merlin* recounts, he introduces himself at the court of Arthur when he unbuckles (like Meriadeuc) the sword from the enchanted belt of a lady sent to Carduel by the Lady of Avalon. Until then, this trial had not been passed by either the king or any other knight of Logres (ed. Roussineau 1996: I, 69), However, this lady herself announces to Balain that the weapon he has won will be the cause of his ill fortune, for with it he will slay the man whom he most loves in the world. The same day, the young man cuts off the head of a lady because he believes that she had poisoned his brother; Arthur immediately expels him from the court. In order to regain the king's favour, Balain fights with and captures King Rion, who was seeking an oath of vassalage from Arthur. This action wins him the king's pardon, but new misfortunes await the protagonist. When he sets out in search of the invisible knight who kills his enemies by treachery (Garlan), he enters the Grail castle, where he wounds, with a lance that must not be touched, the brother of the unknown knight, who turns out to be King Pellehan. The castle begins to collapse and Merlin informs Balain that he has delivered the Dolorous Stroke, which causes the desolation of the land of Listenois. A short time afterwards, Balain – who carried a shield that is not his own – fights on an island against an unknown knight who finally turns out to be his brother Balaan. Although at the end of the combat both warriors recognise each other, the wounds that they have inflicted on one another cause their deaths. Merlin carves on the stone of the tomb which houses the bodies of the two brothers the tragic blow of the 'Knight of the Two Swords', 'qui fiste de la Lanche Venceresse le Cop Dolereux par coi li roiaumes de Listinois est tornés a dolour et a essil' (*Post-Vulgate Suite*, ed. Roussineau 1996: I, 193).

The misfortunes that surround Balain pose many doubts about his possible literary use by Alfonso X. The swords of Gonçal'Eanes do not seem to have delivered any 'Dolorous Stroke', nor is there any sign in the *cantiga* that permits us to divine that they have caused any unfortunate deaths or the ruin of a kingdom; rather, on the contrary, the effectiveness of the blows struck by the Portuguese noble is indicated; with his spirit and energy he is capable even of cutting through rocks.

Consequently, and with the necessary caveats, the character who seems to lie behind the epithet 'O das duas espadas' could be Palamedes. If the use of the epithet derives from the compilation of the *Post-Vulgate* or from the *Tristan en prose*, it would be a proof that would confirm the circulation of the cycles in question in Castile at the threshold of the second half of the XIIIth century. At all events, it is appropriate to state that the information given by the Alfonsine text is very vague, since the antonomasia applied to the Portuguese troubadour refers only to his courage and skill in the use of the sword. He, like the protagonists of the Arthurian tales mentioned, had won honour and fame at a foreign court (Castile) because of his unquestionable mastery of the art of war. As a matter of fact, Gonçal'Eanes abandoned Portugal around 1240 to take part in the Andalucian expeditions in the ranks of King Fernando III. His valuable contributions to the conquests of Murcia (1243) and Seville (1248) made him one of the beneficiaries of the famous Repartimientos (Viñez 2004: 17–38). The privileged position that this Portuguese noble reached in the kingdom of Castile culminated in 1257 with the concession of the lordship of Aguilar de la Frontera (Córdoba) to him by Alfonso X.

The two texts that follow provide more precise information on the spread and knowledge of the Arthurian prose cycles in literary circles of the Peninsular west. The first is a *cantiga de escarnio* of the Portuguese Martin Soarez (*c*.1200–62):

        Ũa donzela jaz [preto d'] aqui,
        que foi ogan'ũa dona servir
        e non lhi soube da terra sair:

> e a dona cavalgou e colheu [i]
> Don Caralhote nas mãos: e ten,
> pois-lo á preso, ca está mui ben.
> e non quer d'el[e] as mãos abrir.
> [...]
> A bõa dona, molher mui leal,
> pois que Caralhote ouv'en seu poder.
> mui ben soube o que d'el[e] fazer:
> e meteu-o logu'en un cárcer atal,
> u muitos presos jouveron assaz;
> e nunca i, tan fort'e preso jaz,
> [quer] que en saia, meios de morrer.
> (Martin Soarez: *LPGP* 97, 44, I–III).

The female protagonist of the lines quoted decides to avenge herself upon a runaway Caralhote whom she locks firmly in her peculiar 'prison', previously frequented by innumerable prisoners.[15] The principal key to the text revolves around the personal name 'Don Caralhote', which Elsa and José Pedro Machado in their edition of B (Machado 1954: VI, 104) indicated was modelled on Lanzarote, although D'Heur (1973–4) followed this trail and specified that the *cantiga* was based on an episode from the *Vulgate* cycle *Lancelot*, of which Gauvain and the giant Caradoc are the protagonists. The section in question relates how the giant had taken Arthur's nephew prisoner in the castle of the Douloureuse Tour because he considered him guilty of the killing of his brother Gadras li Noir. The grievous prison of Gauvain (who is helped only by a lady in the service of Caradoc) is prolonged until Lancelot comes to that place and kills Caradoc. Beginning from this episode in the *Vulgate* Cycle, D'Heur suggested that the name Caralhote was the result of a crux between the names Caradoc and Lanzarote. Whilst the link between the 'Chevalier de la charrette' and the protagonist of the *cantiga* is beyond question, more doubts attach to his relation with Caradoc and with the part of the story that this character occupies. Thus, the prison of Gauvain has no erotic connotations, since the person who guards him is the mother of the giant herself, and the lady who comes to his aid does not pursue an amorous relationship with him. Taking these considerations into account, we have suggested that another episode from the *Lancelot en prose* is the model for the parody penned by Martin Soarez (Gutiérrez García and Lorenzo Gradín 2001: 58–65). If the suffix *–ote* derives from the adaptation of the ending of the name Lanzarote, it is logical to think of some episode of which the latter was the main protagonist of the *roman*. Between the passage of Gawain's imprisonment already mentioned and that of his eventual liberation, the narrative, according to the principle of *entrelacement*, tells how Lancelot breaks the spells of Morgana in the 'Val sans Retour' only to be kidnapped later by the fairy. The spells in that place, known also as the 'Val aus Faus Amans' (because all those who have ever been unfaithful to their ladies are trapped there), had been woven by the fairy after having been betrayed by a man whom she had loved. After overcoming the trials of that fairy place, Lanzarote falls in the trap prepared by Morgana, who kidnaps the hero after placing in his hand a ring which causes him to fall asleep:

> Al termine que les aventures furent commenciees avint chose que ele avoit un chevalier amé molt [...] Mais il amoit une damoisele plus de li [...]. Un jor avint que entre le chevalier et la damoisele qu'il amoit furent assamblé en cel val, kar c'estoit un des plus deleitables lieus del monde. Endementriers qu'il furent iluec, si furent encusé à Morgain qui molt s'en faisoit prendre garde [...] Lors [Morgue] espandi par tot le val son enchantement en tel maniere que jamais chevaliers n'i entrast qui en issist [...]; ne Morgue ne cuidoit mie que nus chevaliers poïst estre qui en alcune chose n'eust faussé vers amors; et por ce le volt ele issi establir qu'ele voloit son ami avoir *en sa prison* tos jors mes [...] Celui jor que li dux descendi el val avoit ja *tant de chevaliers laiens en prison qu'il estoient par conte deus cent et cinquante trois* [...] Quant Morgue et sa compaignie en ot Lancelot mené en la forest [...] si le fis avaler en un lieu parfont et noir, ki molt estoit bien tailliés a estre *chartre* ennuiose. Quant Lancelot i fu avalés, si li furent les mains liees et le pie tot en dormant; et lors fu li anials ostés que Morgue li avoit mis el doi, por tenir endormi [...] et si se veint a lui Morgue et l'apele par son non, si li dist: 'Lancelos, or vos ai je en *ma prison*, or vos covendra il fere une partie de mon talent.' (*Lancelot en prose*, ed. Micha 1978–83: I, xxii 2–4, xxvi 1–7; my italics)

The narrator specifies in a later passage that Morgana's vengeance is not only for what happened in the Valley, but is also occasioned by Guinevere's having separated her from her lover Guiamor de Tarmelide. Moreover, the fairy is aggrieved by the *fin' amor* between Lancelot and the queen. This kidnapping, which is the first of three suffered by the hero in the narrative, is explained in the final abduction prepared by Morgana:

> A mienuit vint Morque laienz conme cele qui toutes les nuiz i venoit, si tost com il estoit endormiz, car ele l'amoit tant conme fame pooit plus amer home pour la grant biauté de lui, si est moult dolante qu'il ne la volit amer, car ele nel tenoit mie *en prison* por haine, mes vaintre le cuidoit par anui, si l'an avoit maintes foiz proié: mais il ne l'an voloit oïr. (*Lancelot en prose*, ed. Micha 1978–83: V, lxxxvi, 21; my italics)

As can be seen, the parallels between the passages cited and the *cantiga* by Martin Soarez are numerous. The troubadour fills his verses with the emblematic values represented by Lancelot in the episodes from the *Lancelot propre*: Caralhote is, like the hero of the Arthurian court, victim of a kidnapping, but he is not the perfect and loyal lover, any more than the female protagonist of the text, whose lustfulness is made plain. Caralhote's imprisonment evokes, clearly, both that suffered by the lovers in the 'Val sans Retour' and that of Guinevere's lover himself. The author uses the technique which the fragmentary *Poetica* of *Cancioneiro B* designates 'palavras cubertas'.[16] In this case, the author employs the metaphor of imprisonment and gaol to refer, respectively, to the sexual act and to the *pars pudenda* of the woman (Marcenaro 2010: 112–18). Similar expressions are found in the Latin tradition, in which, from an early date, there are documented various terms characterised by the semanteme 'enclosed place' (*fornix, lupanar, caverna, casa* ...) to designate both the brothel and the female sexual organ (Montero Cartelle 1991: 97–102; Uría Varela 1997: 344–6, 443–7).

It is difficult to specify where Martin Soarez acquired his knowledge of the *Vulgate Lancelot* cycle, since access to the Arthurian compilation could have been obtained in Castile or in Portugal. As will be recalled, in 1247 the troubadour left his native land to accompany King Sancho II in his exile in Castile. He remained at the court of Alfonso X for nearly fifteen years (*c*.1260), after which he returned to Portuguese territory (Oliveira 1994: 387–8). If we grant precedence to Afonso III in the adaptation of the cycles of the *Vulgate* and *Post-Vulgate* in Portugal, it is evident that the exile of the troubadour makes it impossible that he should have known those texts in 1247, but this does not imply that he could not have had access to them subsequently. Soarez's stay in Castile does not entail cultural isolation from his home country, since contacts between the two kingdoms were fluid, as is shown, among other facts, by the journeys of Portuguese troubadours to the neighbouring royal court above all throughout the second half of the XIIIth century. Moreover, the text does not offer any data which would permit us to eliminate entirely its having been written after the troubadour's return to his own land. In any case, in all this process of literary accommodation what is relevant is that, although nowadays there survive no Galician, Portuguese and Castilian witnesesses of the *Vulgate* datable to the XIIIth century, the *cantiga* of Martin Soarez shows that the cycle was known in the centre and west of the Peninsula from about 1250–60. This fact would corroborate the hypothesis that defends the descent of the Castilian *Lançarote* of the XVIth century (BNM MS 9611) but which, according to its colophon, is a copy of an earlier witness fom 1414,[17] from a lost Portuguese exemplar that, as certain archaisms and linguistic features of the text show, was already circulating in the centre and west of Iberia from at least the end of the XIIIth century (Lida de Malkiel 1959: 40; Alvar 1983: 1–12; Sharrer 1994: 175–90).

In the final generation of Galician-Portuguese troubadours is situated the poetic activity of Fernand'Esquio who, by the references that he makes in one of his texts to the localities of Santiago and Lugo (*LPGP* 38, 6), belonged to a family of the lower Galician nobility linked to the monastery of San Martin de Jubia in A Coruña (Oliveira 1994: 336). His cantiga *Disse un infante ante sa companha* also proves his familiarity with the prose cycles of the *matière de Bretagne* (Corral Díaz 1999). This protagonist of the text laments not having obtained the horse which a noble had promised him during the campaigns against the Muslims ('na fronteira'). For this reason the gift offered but never received by the vassal is assimilated to a fabulous literary animal, the celebrated 'Besta Ladrador' of the Arthurian fictions:

>Dis[s]e hum infante ante sa companha
>que me daria besta na fronteyra:
>e non será ja murzela, nen veyra,
>nen branca, nen vermelha, nen castanha;
>pois amarela nen parda non for,
>a pran será a besta ladrador
>que lh'adurán do reino de Bretanha.
>
>Atal besta como m'el á mandada
>non foy home que lhe vis[s]e as semelhas:
>non ten rostro, nen olhos, nen orelhas,
>nen he gorda, nen magra, nen delgada,
>nen he ferrada, nen é por ferrar,

nen foy home que a vis[s]e enfrear,
nen come erva, nen palha, nen cevada.
(Fernand'Esquio, *LPGP* 38, 3bis lines 1–14)

As will be recalled, the mysterious animal appears for the first time in the *Perlesvaus* in prose (*c.*1212) and subsequently is taken up again in the *IV Continuation-Perceval* by Gerbert de Montreuil (*c.*1225–30).[18] In the first-mentioned text (ed. Nitze and Jenkins 1972: I, lines 5985–6005), the protagonist sees emerging from a wood a beast as white as snow, bigger than a hare and smaller than a fox, with emerald-green eyes, which is given no respite by the twelve dogs it is carrying in its belly. Despite Perlesvaus's attempt to assist it, a knight tells him that he should leave it to go. The animal stops in front of a red cross, the offspring emerge from its belly and tear it apart. The knight and the lady who were present together with the protagonist collect the blood and flesh of the creature in golden receptacles. A little later two priests come to that place; one kisses the cross, while the other beats it with rods. Days later, Perlesvaus reaches the house of his uncle, the Hermit King, who gives him the allegorical meaning of the extraordinary episode he has experienced: the Beste is Christ, while the twelve dogs who tear it apart represent the Jews of the Old Testament, responsible for the crucifixion of the Saviour.

The *Continuation* of Montreuil adapts the episode from the *Perlesvaus* with slight modifications (Nitze 1936: 409–18; Muir 1957: 24–32; Bozóky 1974: 127–48). Perceval reaches a plain where he sees two hermits in front of a cross; one beats it, while the other venerates it on his knees. Suddenly, there arrives an animal driven wild by the barking of the pups it carries in its belly. The hero pursues it, until the creature splits in two, its offspring devour it, and finally kill each other:

> Perchevaus toz s'en merveille
> Que de demander est refrains.
> Car la beste, qui tote est prains,
> S'en va par devant lui fuiant.
> [...]
> Après cele beste s'en va
> Tote ior tant qu'il l'a atainte
> Car de corre fu si atainte
> Et tant l'ont si faon grevee
> Qu'en deus est partie et sevree:
> Et si faon fors de li salent
> Qui la deveurent et assalent:
> Sa char ont dusqu'as os mengié,
> Et tantost sont tot erragié,
> Et tant se sont esvertué
> Que tot se sont entretué.
> (*IV Continuation Perceval*, ed. Williams 1922: I, lines 8380–8406)

Further on, as happens in the *Perlesvaus*, the Hermit King (Elyas Anais) reveals for Perceval the transcendental significance of the Beast and its pups (ed. Williams 1922:

I, lines 8586–8758): the beast is now a symbol of the Church and its pups represent the faithful who do not respect the celebration of the Eucharist. The pups which kill one another are men who abandon the teaching of the Church to devote themselves to earthly goods. Therefore, in the two works discussed, the enigmatic animal takes on an allegorical character and offers a positive religious *senefiance*. Moreover, it is worth noting that in both it is referred to only with the noun 'beste'.

A similar animal is found in the opening pages of *L'Estoire del Saint Graal* in the *Vulgate* Cycle (dated, it will be recalled, *c*.1215–30). In this case, the *beste*, which, for the first time in the tradition, receives the qualifier *diverse*, guides the author of the work to the place where can be found the book which Christ himself had given and which has been mysteriously lost. Once again, the animal has a positive nature and the author picks up and amplifies the hybrid description given by the author of the *Perlesvaus*:

> Si regardat devant moi & vi une crois sor la rive de la fontaine. Et desos cele crois si gisoit cele beste que la vois m'avoit dite, & quant ele me vit si se leva & m'esgarda moult longement & iou lui. Mais com plus l'esgardoie & iou plus m'esmerveilloie de lui. Car ele estoit diverse seur toutes autres bestes. Car ele estoit blanche comme noif [negie] & avoit teste & col de berbis, si avoit pie de chien & quisses & estoient noir comme carbon. & si avoit le pis & le crepon & le cors de goupil & kueue de lyon. (*Vulgate Estoire*, ed. Sommer 1909: I, 8–9)

However, in the *Suite-Merlin* of the *Post-Vulgate* (*c*.1230–40) and in the *Tristan en prose*, the meaning of the *beste* changes and it is loaded with evil connotations.[19] In the *Suite* of Pseudo-Robert de Boron the narrative begins with the incestuous conception of Mordred, engendered by Arthur with his sister, the Queen of Orcanie. After this malign event, the king has a nightmare in which he sees a dragon and other monsters that destroy his kingdom. After a hard fight, Arthur succeeds in killing the dragon, but emerges from the confrontation fatally wounded. When he awakes, the king goes out to hunt with his household, from which, in keeping with a frequent narrative schema, he draws away to pursue a stag. Arthur stops beside a fountain, at which there arrives the monster, to which attention is called by the barking proceeding from its insides:

> il escoute et ot un grans glas de chiens qui faisoient aussi grand noisen que se il fuissent .xxx. ou .xl., et venoient viers lui, che li samble si cuide que che soient si levrier, si lieve la teste et commence a regarder cele part dont il les ot venir. Et ne demoura gaires que il vit venir une beste moult grans ki estoit la plus diverse qui onques fust veue de sa figure, qui tant estoit estraingne de cors et de faiture, et non mie tant defors comme dedens son cors. (*Suite Post-Vulgate*, ed. Roussineau 1996: I, § 5, pp. 3–4)

A little later, Merlin, appearing in the form of a fourteen-year-old boy, tells the king of his sin of incest; subsequently the magician transforms himself into an old man to tell Arthur that the adventure of the Beste is destined for Perceval, the descendant of King Pellinor. This knight, whom Arthur had not previously recognised, pursues the monster. The narrator relates that he will die on calling for help because he has been wounded, and his illegitimate son Tor, the result of his raping a shepherdess, does not come to his assistance, because he thinks that it is a joke.

The fantastic animal is, therefore, linked in the *Post-Vulgate Merlin* to the king's incest; the violence of the pups against their mother evokes the horrendous tragedy that will cause the treachery of Mordred against his progenitor and in all of Logres (Laranjinha 2010a: 131–40). Hence the conclusion of the marvellous adventure is destined for a virgin knight ('qu'il istera de sa mere virges et en terre enterra vierges. Ceste viertu avra li chevaliers qui ceste beste te dira l'aventure', *Suite*, ed. Roussineau 1996: I, 14), who will make up by his virtue for the evils caused by lust. In any case, the detail which interests us here is that both the narrator and the characters (Arthur, and Pellinor himself, described as 'Li Chevaliers a la Diverse Beste') refer to the animal using the qualifiers *diverse* or *mierveilleuse beste*. In our view, this detail is fundamental and indicates that the source of Fernand'Esquio is not this work, which prompts us to explore other directions.

The first cyclical *roman* to employ the word *glattissant*, equivalent to the 'ladrador' of the *cantiga* by Esquio, is the *Tristan en prose*, in which this designation appears in both the Short Version (V. I) and the Long Version (or *Vulgate*, V. II), dated later than 1240:

> L'appellation 'beste glatissant', la plus descriptive, celle qui a été retenue par la tradition critique, est attestée à partir du *TP*, aux alentours des années 1235–40 [...]. La bête n'est plus présentée comme une femelle gravide portant *véritablement* des petits qui aboient dans son ventre [...] Dans le *TP* comme dans le *Perceforest*, les 'brachets' ou les 'chiens' servent de termes imageants. Le cri n'est plus celui des petits *dans* le ventre de la bête, c'est celui de la bête elle-même. (Dubost 1991: 504)

In this work the monster appears linked to a new character from the Arthurian universe: the pagan Palamedes who, together with Lancelot and Tristan, is considered in the first part of the romance (Löseth 1974: §1–183) to be one of the best knights in the world. Palamades is specifically known by the epithet of 'Le Chevalier a la beste glatissant' (Curtis 1976: II, §636, 216).

In the long version of the *Tristan en prose* the animal appears on various occasions, among which, clearly, there stands out the episode in which the hero (who is, with his lover, protected by Lancelot in the Joieuse Garde) goes out hunting one day. Tristan comes to a fountain and hears the noise caused by the proximity of the strange animal. At this moment, there appears the figure of Brehus sans Pitié, who arrives shortly before the beast. Tristan and Brehus both see the beast, which drinks rapidly in order to continue without delay its endless course. Then Palamedes appears, 'ki avoit reconmenchie la cace de la Beste Glatissant' (ed. Ménard, 1992: V, §11, 80). From this moment, Brehus fights the knight who is pursuing the beast, because he considers that he has an equal right to take part in that strange *queste*. In mid-fight, Brehus tells his adversary that Mark has been imprisoned by Arthur and that Iseut is with Tristan in Logres (and not, as Palamedes believed, in Cornuailles). It is then that the pagan knight, who is permanently in love with the queen, renounces the pursuit of the enigmatic beast: 'Il est mestiers que je voie, s'il estre puet, la flour et la biauté du monde [...]. Des ore mais vous laisse je la queste de la Beste Glatissant, car en autre queste me metrai orendroit' (*Tristan en prose*, ed. Ménard 1991: V, 83–4).

After alluding to the release of Tristan from a castle in Norgalles by Palamedes, the narrator proceeds to the description of this hybrid beast:

> L'estoire dist que la Beste Glatissant avoit teste de serpent et le col avoit ele d'une beste que on apeloit dolce en son langage; et le cors avoit ele d'une beste qu'on apeloit lupart; et les piés avoit ele d'une beste que on apeloit cerf; et les quisses et la queue avoit ele d'une beste que on apele lyon. Et quant ele aloit, il issoit de son ventre un si tres grant glatissement comme si ele eüst dedens li jusques a .xx. brakés. (*Tristan en prose*, ed. Ménard 1993: VI, 389)

From the moment when the Saracen knight renounces his peculiar adventure, the *Tristan en prose* abandons the *Beste glatissant*. However, its presence acquires an essential function in the *Queste* of the *Post-Vulgate* cycle, in which, in contrast to the *Tristan en prose*, the relationship between Palamedes and the beast is stressed, while the love of Iseut is relegated to a secondary position. At the outset, the animal is pursued by Ivain and Girflet, until they meet an elderly knight who welcomes them into his home and tells them that in the past he used to frequent Arthur's court; it is Esclabor li Mesconneus. One day when he was pursuing the beast with eleven of his sons, one of them wounded the animal in a leg and it uttered a terrifying shriek which caused them all to faint (ed. Freire Nunes 2005: 101–3). When Esclabor awoke, all his sons were dead, save the one who had remained at home with his mother: this was Palamedes, who from then on had been pursuing the monster tirelessly. During one of his encounters with the knights of Arthur he fights with Galaaz, who spares his life on condition that he becomes his vassal and converts to Christianity (ed. Freire Nunes 2005: 420–2). After embracing the new religion, the knight goes to Camelot and occupies a seat at the Round Table. In subsequent passages, Galaaz, Perceval and Palamedes himself encounter the beast near a lake and, finally, 'Le Chevalier a la Beste', purified by abandoning his paganism, concludes his *queste* by fatally wounding the animal. It utters a deafening bellow and is devoured by the flames that make the waters of the lake boil, so that from this moment on it is known as the 'Lac de la Beste'. The noise is not now that of the whelps, but that of the monster itself, whose cry (or *baladro*) is now caused by the deadly wound caused to it by Palamedes (ed. Freire Nunes 2005: 431–3).

The author of the final work in the *Pseudo-Robert de Boron* cycle presents, therefore, innovations compared with the *Tristan en prose*, which provide conclusions to open questions and give a greater coherence to the aventure of the *Beste Glatissant*. Among these there stand out the revelation of the diabolical conception of the monster, which is the fault of King Pelles in the final part of the text. The daughter of King Hipomenes, enamoured of her brother Galaaz, who refuses time and again to commit incest, is seduced by the devil, who appears in a fountain in the guise of a handsome youth, and begets a son with her. It is then that the maiden, annoyed by the constant rejection she receives from her brother, accuses him of rape. This calumny causes Hipomenes to condemn the young man to an atrocious death, suggested by his daughter: the exemplary knight will be given to a pack of hungry dogs. Before dying, the young man says the following words to his sister:

> Tu me fazes sofrer vergonha sem mericimento mas Aquele me vingará que prende as grandes vinganças das grandes deslealdades do mundo. E aa nacença do que tu trages parecerá que nom foi de mim, ca nunca de homem nem de molher saiu tam maravilhosa cousa como de ti sairá; que o diaboo o fez e diaboo sairá em semelhança da besta mais desassemelhada que nunca homem viu. E porque a cães me fazes dar haverá em aquela besta dentro em si cães que sempre ladraram em remembrança e referimento dos cães a que tu me fazes dar. E aquela besta fará muito dano em homens bõõs e ja mais nom quedará de fazer mal atá que o bõõ cavaleiro que haverá nome Galaaz como eu, seerá em essa caça. Per aquel e per viinda morrerá o dooroso fruito que de ti sairá. (*Demanda*, ed. Freire Nunes 2005: 451)

The facts set out here indicate that the Galician troubadour could have obtained the inspiration for the composition of his text equally from either the *Tristan en prose* or from the *Post-Vulgate* cycle *Queste*, works in which the beast is identified by the peculiar sound that emerges from its belly (*glatissant*). We do not believe that the variety of colours the author uses in the first stanza of the *cantiga* for purposes of amplification are a significant and decisive factor in establishing the direct influence of one text in preference to others. This feature could result from the troubadour's own imagination, since, as in the final stanza of the text, his aim is to emphasise the qualities that the promised horse does not have (which, obviously, it does not have because it does not exist). The hybrid character of the monster, from which its varied colouring derives, is used to stress the trick perpetrated by the noble, since his promise of the horse, which has never reached the faithful vassal, is as illusory as the fictitious animal of the Arthurian *romans*.

There is concrete proof of the circulation in the west of the Peninsula of the two cycles referred to, and besides the epithet *Besta ladrador* permits us to suppose that the troubadour had access to copies of these already translated from French. Specifically, the Galician fragment of the *Tristan en prose* that survives (ed. Lorenzo Gradín and Souto Cabo 2001: 71–103) transmits a small part of the adventures of Lanzarote, who pursues Brun le Noir, who is known as the 'Valet a la Cote Mautailliee' (Löseth 1974: §91–3; Curtis 1988: 17–35). Brun and the lady who accompanies him to the Destrois de Sorelois (the well-known Demoisele Mesdisanz) one day reach a valley in which, after hearing a pack of forty dogs, they see the terrible *Beste* appear before their eyes. One of the squires accompanying them tells the lady the name of the animal and that of its pursuer: 'Demoisele, or sachiez que après ceste beste vient uns des mieudres chevaliers dou monde que l'en apele Palamedes. Il a ja ceste beste chaciee longuement, ne prendre ne la puet' (*Tristan en prose*, ed. Curtis 1976: II, §664, 237).

Although because of its fragmentary state the Galician text does not contain the passage reproduced here, it is reasonable to assume that, before its dismemberment, it would have contained it (Michon 1991: 262). In the case of Fernand'Esquio, and taking into account his probable Galician identity, it is tempting to give more weight to a possible influence of the *Tristan en prose* than to the *Post-Vulgate Demanda*, especially since the *Tristan* fragment is known to display a series of linguistic features that place it in the Galician area (Castro 1998: 135–49; ed. Lorenzo Gradín and Souto Cabo 2001: 27–55). However, given that the fundamental peculiarity that the *cantiga* reflects, namely the epithet *Besta ladrador*, is present in both works, there is no irrefutable proof that tilts the scales in favour of a specific text. It would, therefore, be risky to rule out influence of the *Pseudo-Robert de Boron Queste* on the Galician troubadour. As has been noted above, the majority of critics are unanimous in conceding priority to the Portuguese translation of the *Queste* over the Castilian versions, for which reason scholars have suggested that the *Demanda* was already circulating in Portugal in the second half of the XIIIth century. As is known, the Portuguese translation of this work influenced, in turn, the surviving Castilian texts, which display linguistic traces of the Portuguese model used in the translation (Pickford 1961: 211–16; Lapa 1982a: 303–40; Castro 1983: 81–98). Taking into account the constant relations between Galicia and Portugal throughout the entire XIIIth century and the first half of the XIVth, there are, therefore, no conclusive reasons to rule out Esquio's having had the *Post-Vulgate Queste* in mind for the *Besta ladrador* of his satire.

To complete this survey of the traces of the Matter of Britain in Galician-Portuguese lyric, it is appropriate to refer to a satirical *cantiga* of one of the latest of the troubadours: the Portuguese Estevan da Guarda (1299–1362), who was in the service of Don Denis and his son, Don Pedro, Count of Barcelos. This poet composes an *escarnio* which turns to the fatal love of the magician Merlin, playfully inverting the end of the British seer, and applies his cries to the risible death of a certain Martin Vasquez. This individual had already been the object of jokes by the troubadour in two other *cantigas* (*LPGP* 30,18 and 30,22) for his manifest incompetence in astrological matters:

> Com'avẽeo a Merlin de morrer
> por seu gran saber, que el foi mostrar
> a tal molher, que o soub'enganar,
> per essa guisa se foi cofonder
> Martin Vasquez, per quanto lh'eu oí
> que o ten mort'ũa molher assi,
> a que mostrou por seu mal seu saber.
> [...]
> E, o que lh'é mais grave de teer,
> per aquelo que lh'el foi ensinar,
> con que sabe que o pod'ensarrar
> en tal logar u conven d'atender
> tal morte de qual morreu Merlin,
> u dará vozes, fazendo sa fin,
> ca non pod'el tal mort'estraecer.
> (Estevan da Guarda: *LPGP* 30, 7, I–III)

As will be recalled, the imprisonment of the magician is found for the first time in the *Lancelot propre* in a passage narrating how the seer fell in love with the Lady of the Lake and taught her all his knowledge (Zumthor 1943: 132–8; Gutiérrez García 1999: 152–4). The episode was given a superficial reworking in the *Vulgate Suite*, which relates how Viviana tricks the seer with a magic pillow so as to prevent him from consummating his love:

> Mais tant savoit ele de ses afaires quant ele savoit qu'il avoit volente de iesir od lui, ele avoit enchante & coniure .j. orellier qu'ele li metoit entre ses bras & lors s'endormoit Merlins [...] bien i parut car tant s'abandouna & tant li aprist de son sens unes fois & autres que il s'en pot tenir por fol al dararain. Si sejourna avoec lui lonc tans & tos iors li enqueroit ele de sen sens & de sa maistrie si l'en aprist moult & ele metoit tout en escrit quan qu'il disoit comme ch'ele qui bien estoit endoctrinee de clergie, si retenoit asses plus legierement ce que Merlins disoit. (*Suite Vulgate*, ed. Sommer 1979: II, 421)

Subsequently, and under the pretext of never being separated from him, Viviana begs Merlin to show her the spells for imprisoning someone. The magician knows that this will be tried out on him, but, because of his love, he agrees to the request of his superior pupil. One day as both are walking through the forest of Broceliande, the Lady imprisons him in an invisible tower, in which she visits him often to make his imprisonment more pleasant:

> et tant qu'il vindrent a un iour qu'il aloient main a main devisant pour euls deduire parmi la forest Broceliande. Si trouverent un buisson bel & vert & haut d'une aube espine qui estoit tous cargies de fleurs. Si s'assistrent en l'ombre. Et Merlins mist son chief el giron a la damoisele & elle le commencha a trastonner tant qu'il s'en dormi [...] & le tint illuec qu'il s'esvilla. *Et il regarda entour lui & li fu*[st] *avis qu'il fust en la plus bele tour del monde* [...] Et lors dis a la damoisele: 'Dame deceu m'aves se vous ne demoures avec moi quar nus n'en a pooir fors vous de ceste tour desfair.' Et elle li dist: 'Biaus dous amis, iou y serai souvent & mi tendres entre vos bras & iou vous. Si feres des oremais tous a vostre plaisir' [...] *ne onques puis Merlins n'en issi de cele foreteresce ou s'amie l'avoit mis*, mais elle en issoit & entroit quant ele voloit. Si se taist li contes chi endroit de Merlin & de s'amie & parole del roy Artu. (*Suite Vulgate*, ed. Sommer 1979: II, 427; my italics)

The imprisonment of the seer is given a significant twist in the *Suite-Merlin* of the *Post-Vulgate* cycle, in which the fairy hates her lover because he is descended from the devil, a point which, as is well known, goes back to Geoffrey of Monmouth. Since the Lady fears losing her virginity, she seeks the prophet's death astutely:

> Et Merlins amoit tant la Damoisele du Lac qu'il en moroit, ne il ne li osoit requerre que elle fesist pour lui pour chou qu'il savoit bien que elle estoit encore pucelle [...] Il lui avoit apris des enchantements tant que elle ne savoit gaires mains de lui. Elle connissoit bien qu'il ne baoit fors a son pucelage, si l'en haoit trop mortelment et pourcachoit de canques elle pooit sa mort. Et elle avoit ja descouvert a un sien cousin chevalier qui avoec li aloit que elle feroit morir Merlin si tost que elle en verroit son point [...]. Ensi dist de Merlin la Damoisiele del Lac par maintes fois, car elle le contrehaoit trou pour chou qu'il estoit fiex dou dyable. (*Suite Post-Vulgate*, ed. Roussineau 1996: II, 329–30)

As happened in the previous narratives, the Lady imprisons the magician, but this time in a tomb in which he will end his days: this is the sepulchre of Anasten and his lady, situated in the 'Forest Perilleuse' of Darnantes. Shortly after the tragic event, Bandemagus passes by the place and hears the lament of Merlin, but can do nothing to release him from his captivity. The seer ends his days in that tragic *locus Amoris* and, before dying, utters his celebrated and deafening *brait*:

> il ne fu puis nus qui Merlin oïst parler, se ne fu Bandemagus, qui i vint iiii jours aprés chou que Merlins i avoit esté mis. [...]. Et lors li dist Merlins: 'Bandemagus, ne te travaille a ceste lame lever, car tu ne hom ne la levera devant que celle meismes la lieve *qui chi m'a enserré*, ne nule forche ne nul engien n'i averoit i mestier, car *je sui si fort enserrés* et par paroles et par conjuremens que nus ne m'en porroit oster fors cele meesmes qui m'i mist. [...] Et sachies que li brais dont maistre Helies fait son livre fu li daerrains brais qui Merlins gieta en la fosse ou il estoit del grant duel qu'il ot quant il aperchut toutes voies que il estoit livrés a mort par engien de feme et que sens de feme a la sien sens contrebatu. *Et del brait* dont je vous parole fu la vois oïe par tout le roiaume de Logres si grans et si lons coume il estoit, et en avinrent moult de merveilles, si coume li branke le devise mot a mot. Mais en cest livre n'en parlerons nous pas pour chou qu'il le devise la, ains vous conterai chou qui nous apartient. (*Post-Vulgate Suite*, ed. Roussineau 1996: II, 336–37; my italics)

The details given in the passage cited here are those which enable us to suggest the *Post-Vulgate Suite* as the model for the *cantiga* by Estevan da Guarda, since in earlier *romans* the imprisonment of Merlin is never associated with his death, nor is reference made to his terrifying cry. The imitation of the model is obvious, as are the departures from the source text which are introduced. Thus Martin Vasquez, unlike the British seer, goes to and returns from the spot where the woman to whom he has taught his particular 'arts' is found. The power of enclosure ('ensarrar en tal logar') has an erotic significance in the *cantiga* and refers, just like the 'prison' of Martin Soarez, to the female sexual organ. The prophet's fatal love and his cry are, therefore, subjected to a semantic inversion, which causes the process of rewriting the tragic nature of the fictional episode to slip towards obscenity. The 'death' and 'dying' of the weakened protagonist of the *cantiga de escarnio* continue the erotic meaning that these words already had in Latin (Adams 1982: 128–31; Montero Cartelle 1991: 61–4). Equally, the noun 'lugar' was employed, from archaic Latin (*loci-loca*), as a euphemism for the male and female genitals (Adams 1982: 128; Montero Cartelle 1991: 61–3; Uría Varela 1997: 344–5). To these facts must be added the use of 'ensarrar' as a *verbum venereum*. Estevan da Guarda used, then, a prestigious literary model which was circulating in Portuguese court circles to play with the audience's horizon of expectations, since, after establishing the appropriate associations with the underlying text, they would burst out laughing on realising the parodic distortion involved. Good fortune has confirmed the existence of a Portuguese translation of the *Suite* of Pseudo-Robert de Boron at the beginning of the XIVth century, that is to say, at the time when this troubadour was active. This is the celebrated fragment of the *Livro de Merlin* preserved in the Biblioteca de Catalunya, MS 2434 (see Gutiérrez García, in this volume), which transmits the episode immediately preceding the one that is inverted in the *cantiga*, that is to say, the story of King Assen and his son Anasten (Soberanas 1979; ed. Lorenzo Gradín and Souto Cabo 2001: 147–94).

The majority of the texts seen thus far employ the models derived from the *matière de Bretagne* as a weapon for parodic inversion. The troubadours invert the contents of those *contes* that Jean Bodel defined in the prologue to his *Chanson des Saisnes* (*c*.1200), 'si vain et plaisant' (Brasseur 1989: I, line 9), and make them fit a new context, which demands from the audience two simultaneous processes: the evocation of the text being referred to, and the dialectical relationship established with the newly created poetic product. This interrelation would amuse the audience when it perceived the distance separating the Arthurian narrative from the realist poetry of *escarnio e maldizer*.

5. Arthurian Times and Historiography

In all the historiographic texts produced in Galicia, the presence of information derived from the *matière de Bretagne* is noted only in the *Crónica de 1404*.[20] The ample chronological span covered by the work (from the creation of the world to the reign of Enrique III of Castile) allows it to interweave within its framework a mixture of historical and literary sources, among which there stands out, in the present context, the *Historia regum Britanniae* which, as will be seen, leaves its traces in the chronicle indirectly.

The textual transmission of the *Crónica* tells us as much about the origins and ideology of its anonymous author as it does about the diverse materials which had an influence on its composition. This range of sources does not result, however, from the direct consultation of their texts, but from the influence of the immediate models on which the text is based. Among these, the chronicles compiled at the instigation of Alfonso X occupy first place, in particular the famous 'versión crítica' of the *Estoria de España* (*c*.1282–4), as well as the translation of the *Crónica Xeral* and the *Crónica de Castela*, which was copied into the text in its entirety (Catalán 1997: 165–79; Lorenzo Vázquez 2000: 387). The Galician origin of the compiler is detectable in various interpolations into the text, among which there stand out several references to Galicia and the apostle St James, as well as the ostentatious elimination of the passage from the *Chronica* of Isidore of Seville on the Galician origin of the heretic Priscillian (Pérez Pascual 1990: I, 138; Lorenzo Vázquez, 1993: 185; 2000: 389). Various local details incorporated by the chronicler have allowed Diego Catalán to suggest as the probable place of composition of the text the cathedral of Mondoñedo (Lugo), a centre with which other Galician historiographic texts are associated, such as the translations of the amplified 1289 version of the *Estoria de España* and the text of the *Crónica de Castilla* itself (Catalán 1997: 229–40).

Of the three manuscripts that transmit the *Crónica de 1404* only that preserved in the Hispanic Society of America in New York (MS B2278, known also as the Vindel manuscript), written on paper and produced about the middle of the XVth century, is a complete exemplar, which, in addition, provides on its final leaf the date of completion of the work:[21]

> Et rregnou seu filho, el rrey don Anrrique; et anda o seu rregno en quatorze ānos quando esta estoria foy acabada, ēna era da encarnaçom mill et quatroçentos et quatro ānos. Ffinito libro sit laus gloria Cristo. Quis scripsit scribat et semper cum Domino vivat. (Pérez Pascual 1990: 534)

The other two witnesses in which the text is preserved are MS M62 of the Biblioteca Menéndez Pelayo at Santander, dated to the beginning of the XVth century and written on vellum, which has various areas of damage and is a fragmentary text, since it transmits only the section from Count Fernán González to the conquest of Valencia by El Cid; and MS X-i-8 of the library of the monastery of El Escorial, dated around 1450, which covers the section from the beginning of the world to the history of El Cid and the flight of the son of the Moroccan King Abubacar from Valencia.

Whilst the work was originally written in Galician, later copyists have attempted to translate it into Castilian, with varying success. Thus, the Escorial MS translates the text literally, and therefore, as well as being marked by omissions, has numerous errors, Galician forms, and incorrect interpretations of the original. The New York manuscript, consisting of 363 folios, gives a translation into Castilian for only the first fifty-eight of these; its rendering is also rather careless, with many errors of translation, among which there stand out the Galician forms and Castilian ultracorrections that are scattered throughout the text.

In the tradition of the *Estoria de España* and the *General Estoria* of Alfonso X, the chronicler worked on a grand historiographic project, covering everything from the mythical beginnings of the world to the history of his own time (the period of Enrique III of Trastámara, 1333–79). The work follows closely the Alfonsine models, and, in keeping with these, Peninsular history is inserted into the universal scheme. The text is divided into four parts: (i) from Genesis to the arrival of the Goths in the Iberian Peninsula; (ii) the period from the Goths to King Ramiro I; (iii) the longest section, from Ramiro I to the death of Fernando III; and finally (iv) the work encompasses the events that stretch from the accession of Alfonso X to the throne until the time of Enrique III.

In the first part, the author uses the Bible as the fundamental basis of his historiography, and, under the aegis of the sacred text, there are inserted into the chronological periodisation other facts and time sequences (the history of the Gentiles), as Alfonso X has done, following the path trodden by Eusebius of Caesarea and Jerome in the *Canones chronici* (Gómez Redondo 1998: I, 694–7). The concept of embracing the six ages of man dictates that there should be woven into the text a diversity of sources (Ovid, Dares and Dictys, Flavius Josephus, the *Roman de Thèbes*, the *Pharsalia*, the *Historias de proeliis* ...), which are, however, derived from the models immediately underlying the text and not from the direct consultation of these ultimate sources. Compared with the other historiographic works produced in the Alfonsine scriptorium, the Galician text presents a simple organisation, from which any moral commentary or reflection of a personal character is absent.

The alternation between the biblical account and the pagan narratives causes the Chronicle to collect in its initial section various episodes from the history of Britain (MS B2278, fols 19*v*–26*r*). In this instance, the narration goes back to the end of the Trojan War, which facilitates its connection to the beginnings of the British dynasty in the time of Brutus. The story continues with the various kings who succeeded to the throne of Great Britain until it ends with the fall of the Britons to the Saxons in the time of Cadwallader (Cadvaladro). The Arthurian episodes most worthy of attention are as follows: the conception of Arthur during the night at Tintagel, the king's war with the Romans, the battle of Camlann between Arthur and Mordred, and, finally, the famous journey of the wounded king to the Isle of Avalon (Catalán and de Andrés 1971: 279–84).

Although the ultimate sources of the events narrated are the *Historia regum Britanniae* of Geoffrey of Monmouth and the *Roman de Brut* of Wace, it is certain that the Galician author obtained these 'ready-translated' from a version of the so-called *Liber regum* or *Cronicon Villarense* from Navarre, the first redaction of which dates from the beginning of the XIIIth century. A second reworking of this text (*c*.1220), the so-called Toledan version (Martin 1992: 103–5), was used by Archbishop Rodrigo Jiménez de Rada in his famous *De rebus Hispaniae* (*c*.1243–6). However, the information given in the Galician text is derived from the third redaction of the *Liber regum* (*c*.1260–70; Catalán and de Andrés 1971: 213–337; Bautista 2010: 33–40), which amplifies enormously the first version of the work and offers, for Arthurian times, much of the information also recorded in the *Nobiliário* (*c*.1340–4) and the *Crónica Geral de Espanha* (1344) of Don Pedro de Barcelos. It must be noted, however, that the adherence to the central outline of the Navarrese source by the Galician chronicler was quite independent of its use in the Portuguese texts (Catalán 1962: 310–408).

As regards the episodes that interest us here, it should be noted that the passage dealing with the nocturnal events at Tintagel is notably reduced, and that the magical intervention of Merlin (who, of course, has used his magic arts to transform the appearance of Uther into that of Igerna's husband the Duke of Cornubia) is eliminated from it:

Et quando lo rrey sopo que el duque era ansi ydo, ayunto luego su hueste e çierco el duque en aquel castiello. E envio luego por Merlin e, con su ayuda, tanto fiez que fue muerto el duque. Et el rrrey tomo Yguerna por mugier e ovo della un fijo, a que dixeron Artur. Este fue el buen rrey Artur de que todos fablan, que fue tan buen rrey commo podedes ver por su libro, se lo leyerdes. (*Crónica 1404*: Catalán and de Andrés 1971: 280)

This detail, together with others present in the text, has enabled Diego Catalán to determine that the model followed by the Galician author was the third redaction of the *Crónica Villarense* mentioned already, which survives with the title of the *Libro de las generaciones*. This version is transmitted in a XVth-century copy produced by Martín de Larraya (Catalán 1962: 370–83). This work, rather than using the *Historia* of Geoffrey of Monmouth, closely follows the *Brut* of Wace for Arthurian times. The use of the reworking by Larraya in the Galician work is obvious in certain chapters, among which there stands out the episode of the serpent that will unleash the final battle between Arthur and Mordred. The king's nephew offers to negotiate, and both contenders meet on the plains at Salesbieres, while the armies of the two sides wait for the order to engage in combat:[22]

> E desçendieron del monte a un llano que dezian Salabres. Mas ellos estando en esta fabla salio una grand serpiente del monte. Et quando la vio rrey Artur, metio mano a la espada e enpeço de yr en pus della, e Mordarechq otrosi tambien. Et as sus gentes, que estavan açierca, quando esto viron, pensaron que el uno queria ferir al otro, que ellos non vian la serpiente que ellos vian. Et enton las azes fueron ferir unas con otras, e fue la batalla muy grand, e morieron ay de una parte e de la otra los mas. (*Crónica 1404*: Catalán and de Andrés 1971: 283)

The third version of the *Liber regum* was known in Galicia, as shown by the *Crónica de Castela* (*c*.1295–1312), in the initial section of which is incorporated a brief passage from the Navarrese chronicle (Lorenzo Vázquez 1975: I, xli–xlii).

As well as the reworking of the *Libro de las generaciones*, in the Galician text we may note the insertion of materials derived from other sources, such as those of the French *Post-Vulgate* cycle, from which, in all probability, was derived the fictitious information given about the end of Arthur. The king is taken from the battlefield by the few knights who have survived the massacre:

> Et rrey Artur ovo el canpo por si, e fue ferido por tres lançadas. Et fiezosse levar a sus cavalleros pocos que con el ficaran vivos por tal se podria guarescier. Et d'aqui endelant non sabemos del se es vivo se muerto, nin Merlin non dixo del mas nin yo non se mas del; pero los bretones dizen que aun el es vivo. Et a rrayña, su mugier, vio que avia fecho grand mal et fiezse monja en Corberque, en una mongia, et a poco tiempo morio. (*Crónica 1404*: Catalán and de Andrés 1971: 283–4)

The intervention of the knights who are loyal to their king in the final episode is not from the Navarrese chronicle and seems to suggest knowledge of the *Demanda*, a text which, as will be recalled, relates how Lucan and Girflet come to the king's aid after the fatal combat (Freire Nunes 2005: 489). However, as can be seen in the passage cited, the Galician author does not narrate the death of Arthur in accordance with the final work of the *Post-Vulgate* cycle, but follows faithfully the information given in the *Libro de las Generaciones*. Therefore, although the chronicler maintains the genealogical structure of the Navarrese work, at times he acts according to personal criteria in compiling his text, which leads sometimes to the incorporation into the narrative thread of information taken from other literary texts that were circulating in cultured circles.

Thus, the Galician author refers to other sources from the Arthurian cycle when he indicates, for example, that whoever wishes to know more of the prophecies of Merlin should consult the *Libro del Valadro Merlin* (Catalán and de Andrés 1971: 278), or when he says that the details of the transfer of the Grail to Britain by Joseph of Arimathea are collected in the *Libro del Sancto Grayal* (Catalán and de Andrés 1971:

265). These references indicate that the chronicler knew, at the very least, the translation of the *Pseudo-Robert de Boron* cycle which, in accordance with the French source, comprised the trilogy formed by the *Estoire del Saint Graal*, the *Merlin* (whose *Suite* ended with the famous *Baladro*) and the *Queste* (Catalán 1962: 393–401). These allusions show that the author did not content himself with the substantial material offered by the chronicles and tried to complete it at times with brief passages derived from other books that were in fashion in noble circles.

6. The Translations of the Prose Cycles: The *Livro de Tristan*

In 1928 Manuel Serrano y Sanz found in the Archivo Histórico Nacional, Madrid, specifically in the Archive of the Dukes of Osuna, two Galician fragments on vellum of a *Livro de Tristan*. The folios had been preserved by being reused as binding of a notarial copy of the will of the Marquis of Santillana, produced in 1551. Serrano identified the text erroneously as a translation of the Vulgate cycle *Lancelot* (Serrano y Sanz 1928: 307–14). This mistake was caused by the fact that the majority of the surviving chapters of the fragment are devoted to Lanzarote, as well as by an erroneous interpretation of the abbreviation used by the copyist for the name of Tristan (*T'r*), which gave rise to the existence of an unknown knight called 'Don Ter'.

In 1962, José Luis Pensado produced a practically definitive edition of the text, and correctly linked it to the tradition of the French *Tristan en prose* (Pensado 1962). For decades, these vellum leaves (which reproduce a small part of the particular version of *Tristan* that was circulating in the west of the Iberian Peninsula) were believed to have been lost, but they had merely been mis-shelved in the Archivo Histórico Nacional at Madrid, where they were located by the Portuguese scholar Pedro Pinto towards the end of 2009 (BITAGAP manid 1483). The fragments have now been renumbered in the Archivo with the shelfmark Códices, Leg. Carp. 1501B, n. 7, and have been digitalised, thereby greatly facilitating research.

This Galician witness, dating from the second half of the XIVth century (Ailenii 2013a, 2013b), contains the announcement by Glingain to Iseo that Tristan is still alive, and continues with part of the adventures of Lanzarote on the way to the Destrois de Sorelois. The text does not contain a coherent narrative sequence because at least two intermediate folios are missing, which would fill in the narrative gap in the story. The contents are divided into thirteen chapters rubricated in red ink, so that text and paratext are clearly distinguished in the manuscript.

The context of the initial part of the fragment relates to the episode in which Iseut writes a letter of consolation to Kaherdin (the brother of Iseut aux Blanches Mains), who had fallen in love with the queen. By pure chance, Tristan reads the missive, withdraws, overcome by jealousy, to the depths of the wood of Morrois, and goes mad. One day news of his death reaches the court. His lover sinks into grief and despair, until, as the Galician text begins by relating, Guinglain notifies the queen that the death of Tristan is a false rumour.

The greater part of the Galician version reproduces part of the adventures of Lanzarote in search of Brunor li Noir, to whom Keu, because of his appearance when he arrived at Arthur's court, had given the sobriquet 'Caballero de la Cota Mal Tallada'. One day, when Arthur is going out to hunt, Brunor wins the favour of the court by overcoming a lion which had broken its chain, stupefying all present including the ten knights (among them the king's famous seneschal) who were in the room and who had fled in a cowardly fashion from the fierce beast. As the *Tristan en prose* relates, there later came to Arthur's court a lady with a shield which had been given to her by a dying knight. This was Ditis l'Amoureux, who, before dying, had asked the young lady to go to Arthur's court to propose to the distinguished knights gathered there that they should complete the adventure of the shield. Ditis wished to liberate Sorelois from the oppression to which it had been subjected by the sons of the giant Ceron, but he had failed in his endeavour on being wounded by one of his enemies. The lady places the adventure before the court, but nobody wants to undertake it. Only Brunor, who has just been knighted, decides to accept the challenge. The lady leaves Camelot enraged that Arthur has permitted this novice knight to undertake an enterprise of such importance. Brunor catches up with the lady, who reproaches him continually for his youth and his inexperience (whence her nickname the 'Demoiselle Mesdisant').

The Galician fragment next relates the adventures of Lanzarote who, following the route taken by the Caballero de la Cota Mal Tallada, finds Brandelis and Keu, who do not recognise him. Lanzarote fights and overcomes Neroneus de l'Isle, who was guarding one of the bridges leading to Sorelois. As the last part of the Galician text to be preserved relates, the next day Lanzarote separates from his companions and arrives at the Castle of Uter, in which, as he had already been informed by Neroneus, the following custom was in force:

> Car bien sachiés que tout li cevalier errant ki de la maison le roi Artu sont et ki vienent cele part i sont aresté et retenu et mis en prison, ce m'est avis; et autresi retienent il les damoiseles conmunaument qu'il truevent en conduit de cevalier, qui que il soit. (Ménard, ed. 1987: I, §23, 86)

Lanzarote arrives at the castle, where Brunor and the Demoiselle Mesdisant have been taken prisoner. After relating Lanzarote's victory over six knights, the Galician translation breaks off at the moment in which the hero is about to begin fighting the lord of the fortress (Uter). Before going out to the field, Uter is sure of his victory on learning that his adversary is wounded and fatigued:

> davalle força que o cavaleiro con que se avia a combater que perdera muito doo sangui, ca se non podia combater con VI cavaleiros que non fosse cansado, e non poderia durar contra el que era folgado. (ed. Lorenzo Gradín and Souto Cabo 2001: §xii, 103)

As is well known, this episode ends, in the French *Tristan en prose*, with the victory of Lanzarote, who liberates all the prisoners in the castle and continues his journey towards Sorelois without revealing his name. In later passages, the narrative tells how the Caballero de la Cota Mal Tallada fails in the adventure of the Destrois, which will be brought to a satisfactory end by Lanzarote himself (Löseth 1974 [1891]: §92–3; Ménard, ed., 1987: §71, §1–74). Since Löseth's study (1891), scholars have established that from about 1235 on, two new versions of the *Tristan en prose* were developed, influenced by an early text, now lost (*c.*1215–30): these are the texts labelled V. I and V. II, dated later than 1240 since both are influenced by the Arthurian *Post-Vulgate* cycle (Baumgartner 1975: 30–97; 2000; 2006; Roussineau 1998). The second version, transmitted in a large number of manuscripts and considered to constitute the 'vulgate' of this *roman*, is the one from which the Galician fragment derives.

The direct source of the Peninsular text has not been precisely identified. This is caused, to a great extent, by the large number of manuscripts that contain the episodes narrated in the version with which we are concerned: twenty-four of the eighty-two that contain the work, distributed among various European libraries (in Paris, London, Edinburgh, Vienna, Aberystwyth, Rome etc.). The partial *collatio* undertaken thus far by scholars (Michon 1991: 259–68; Soriano 1999a; Lorenzo Gradín and Díaz Martínez 2004: 371–96) has shown that, whilst the text has many readings in common with what Renée Curtis calls the 'd' family,[23] to which belongs MS 2542 of the ÖNB, Vienna, designated MS 'A' (*c.*1300) – considered one of the most representative and faithful of the *Vulgate* version of this *roman* (ed. Ménard, 1990, I: 10–7) – the absence of important passages in relation to the French exemplar, and, above all, the great number of unique readings in MS A reveal that this is not the direct source of the Peninsular adaptation. Equally, the unique readings of the Galician text itself show likewise that it does not derive from other manuscripts that make up this and other families of the French work.

The majority of the divergences that the Galician *Tristan* presents in relation to the MSS with which it has been collated consist of omissions or simplifications in syntax or semantics (summaries, paraphrases, change from direct speech to reported speech and vice versa, omissions of phrases, and suchlike), in the case of which it is impossible to specify whether such variants were produced during the process of translation or, on the other hand, were already present in the source used by the adapter. More significant are, however, certain errors associated with the process of copying, such as omissions and repetitions caused by homoeoteleuton (or leap from like to like) and by duplication, which may cause incoherence in the narrative sequence, or give rise to a careless text. A good example of this is provided by the duplication reproduced here, for the better understanding of which the French text of A is quoted, for comparison only, after the passage concerned:

Todo aquel dia pensara Lançarote en Don Tristan, que non pensou en al. Aa noite lle avẽo que seu camĩo o levou a casa do home bõo, u a[n]te daquela noite jouvera o *da Saia Mal Tallada e a Donzela Maldisente; ali soube as novas dele. En outro dia mañãa, quando quis cavalgar*, dissolhe seu os[pe]de e rogoo ben como rogara *ao da Saia Mal Talladada e a Donzela Maldisente, e ali soubo el novas deles. En outro dia mañaa, quando quis cavalgar*, dissolle seu ospede e rogoo ben, assi como rogara o da Saia Mal Tallada. E Lançarote disso que en seu fillo non meteria mão [...] (ed. Lorenzo Gradin and Souto Cabo 2001: §II, 89–90; my italics)

[Tout celui jor pensa Lanselos a monseigneur Tristan k'il ne pensa mie granment a autre cose. Au soir li avint en tel maniere que ses chemins l'aporta droitement chiés le preudome u chil a la Cote Mautaillie avoit le soir devant geü entre lui et la Damoiselle Mesdisant. Laiens aprist il nouveles de la Damoisele Mesdisant et de celui a la Cote Mautaillie, car le preudom meïsmes li dist k'il avoient laiens dormi le soir devant. A l'endemain, auques matin, Lanselos se lieve et apareille. Et quant il se dut de laiens partir entre lui et ses escuiers, tout autretel proiiere com li preudom avoit faite le jour devant a celui a la Cote Mautaille pour son fil fist il a Lancelot. Et Lancelos li dist k'il ne toucheroit a son fil ...] (*Tristan en prose*, ed. Ménard, 1987: I, 63).

The textual differences present in the repeated elements of the Galician version are minimal ('ali' versus 'e ali'; 'soube as novas dele' versus 'soubo el novas deles') and, therefore, could have been produced either in the act of translation or in the production of a new copy. Although there exists, a priori, the possibility that a translator (like a copyist) could commit a visual error or even repeat a passage already translated after having interrupted his work for an interval, it is difficult to believe that he would not have noticed such an accident and would have failed to correct it. A translator (like an author) keeps control of the text, since he is working with sequences of a certain length which oblige him to revise (more than once) the work undertaken. In the case with which we are concerned, the repetition is not a matter of simply one word or a brief phrase, but has a certain length and occurs in close proximity in the text. This circumstance leads us to believe that the translator must still have been carrying in his memory the segment just copied, and in this case he would have realised that he was translating again into Galician a passage already translated, and would have deleted it. Taking into account these factors, addition by repetition finds a more convincing explanation if we think in terms of the existence of a copyist who was not very skilled, who had before his eyes a model written in his own language and who, was, therefore, more indifferent to the text and more passive in his attitude. Accidental errors like that examined here bring into question whether the fragment is from an author's (or translator's) manuscript, and allow us to postulate the existence of a Galician or Portuguese text, now lost, from which the fragment examined here derived (Michon 1991; Castro 1998; Lorenzo Gradín and Díaz Martínez 2004: 387–91). This factor, together with the presence of linguistic archaisms (such as the unstressed possessives *sou* and *sa*, which practically disappear from Galician documents in the second half of the XIIIth century, to be replaced respectively by *seu* and *sua*) (Castro 1998; Lorenzo Gradín and Souto Cabo, eds, 2001: 47–9), allow us to date the presumed source of the fragment to around the final years of the XIIIth century and the beginning of XIVth.

The Galician translation bears witness to the circulation in the western zone of the Iberian Peninsula of a variant redaction of V. II of the *Tristan en prose* at a date not very distant from the composition of the *Vulgate* version of the cycle in France. At the same time, the fragment reflects its singularity within the Hispanic traditions, since, as is well known, the rest of the known versions (Castilian and Catalan), including the fifty-nine manuscript fragments of the Biblioteca Nacional, Madrid, published and studied by Carlos Alvar and José Manuel Lucía (1999), come from a different textual source from that attested by the Galician text (Cuesta Torre 1994a: 27–47; Beltrán 1996; Alvar 2001).[24]

Notes

[1] For recent bibliography of the Hispanic literary witnesses to the *matière de Bretagne*, see Sharrer 1977, 1996a, 1996b, and Mérida Jiménez 2010. For the diffusion of Arthurian narrative in the western zone of the Iberian Peninsula, see the chapter by Santiago Gutiérrez García in this volume.

[2] Without any claim to comprehensiveness, the reader is reminded of the following connections: in 1170, Alfonso VIII of Castile married Leonor, daughter of Henry II Plantagenet and Eleanor of Aquitaine, at whose court Wace had composed his famous *Roman du Brut* (1155); in 1211, the marriage of Fernando of Portugal and Countess Jeanne of Flanders – daughter of Philippe of Alsace, to whom, as is well known, Chrétien de Troyes dedicated his *Perceval* – took place; the latter had commissioned Manessier to compose the *Troisième Continuation* of *Perceval* (*c*.1214–27); in 1254 the future King Edward I of England married princess Leonor of Castile, sister of Alfonso X; and, to close this rapid survey, it is appropriate to note the marriage of Beatriz de Guzmán, natural daughter of Alfonso X, to Afonso III of Portugal in May 1258.

[3] For further information and a detailed bibliography, see Castro 1983: 81–4.

[4] The content of this famous colophon is as follows: 'Este livrou mandou fazer João Sanches, mestre escolla d'Astorga, no quinto ano que o estudo de Coimbra foy feito e no tempo do Papa Clemente que destroio a Ordem do Temple e fez o Concilio Geral em Viana e pos ho emtredito em Castela e neste ano se finou a Rainha Dona Costamca em São Fagundo e casou o Ymfante Dom Felipe com a filha de Dom Afomso. Ano de 13lii anos' (Carter 1967: 379).

[5] The document reads thus: 'In nomine Patris et Filii et Spiritus Sancti, amen. Ego famula Dei Aragunti Gomice una cum filiis vel filiabus meis Marina, Urraca, Petro, Menendo, Maior, *Rolam*, *Galvam*, Flamua, Gomice, cartulam testamenti facimus pro remedio anime domni Odarii Guedazi Deo et Sancte Marie Bracarensis ecclesie et domno Pelagio Bracarensi archiepiscopo successoribusque vestris et clericis ibi comorantibus villa Faiones integra exceptis illa parte de Menendo Guedazi et de Elduara Valasquici' (Da Costa 1978: II, 144, doc. 404; my italics).

[6] The name appears in the list of witnesses present at the concession of a charter by the abbot of Montederramo to some residents of the village of Burgo de Caldelas (8 August 1438): 'Testigos que a esto foron presentes. Alvaro Vasques de Valdiorres et Johan Ares et *Porsival*, escudeiros, moradores en terra de Caldelas, et frey Diego de [Meira] et Frey Alvaro et frey Gonçalvo, monjes do dito mosteiro [...]' (Doc. 1577: 1954–5; my italics). I am grateful to Prof. Ramon Lorenzo for giving me a copy of this important reference in advance of the publication of his study of the documentary collection from this Galician monastery.

[7] In this context, it is appropriate to point out that that recently an alternative interpretation of the helicoidal element in this column has been suggested. According to Francisco Prado-Vilar, the iconography of the column could refer to a 'Christological' Ulysses, sailing safely and peacefully on his return journey to Ithaca. In this case, the image would relate to the other three scenes that make up the column, which, in this new interpretation, would represent the episodes of the lure of the Sirens, the monster Scylla, and the hero blocking with wax the ears of one of his companions. In this case, for this scholar 'la columna de Ulises de la *Porta Francigena* representa el *nostos* del héroe griego como un paralelo itinerario físico y

espiritual del peregrino a modo de espejo moral que habría de advertir al viajero de los peligros del camino – las tentaciones de la carne, las herejías, el desfallecimiento – y, a la vez, ofrecer seguridad en su feliz resolución' (Prado-Vilar 2010: 266–7).

[8] Unless indicated otherwise, the *cantigas* are quoted from Brea, ed., 1996, with the siglum *LPGP*.

[9] The paragraph of the *Arte de trobar* that precedes old *cancioneiro* Colocci-Brancuti is as follows: 'Outra maneira há i en que trobam do<u>s homens a que chamam 'seguir', e chamam-lhe assi porque convem de seguir cada um outra cantiga a som ou en p<alav>ras ou en todo' (ed. Tavani 1999, tit. III, cap. Nono, p. 44).

[10] For the existence of two main versions of the *Tristan en prose* (V. I and V. II) the study carried out long ago by Löseth remains essential (1891). As is well known, it was after this that E. Baumgartner assigned to both a date later than *c*.1240, since both are influenced by the Arthurian *Post-Vulgate* cycle (Baumgartner 1975: 17–98). In addition, this French scholar identified the existence of mixed versions (which use V. I and V. II) and isolated versions of later dates (V. III and V. IV). For the postulated V. I and the probable non-existence of an early prose *roman* from which the rest of the written tradition would have derived, see the latest considerations by Cigni 2012.

[11] Caesar arrives at this port with the aim of conquering Britain in the time of Cassivellaunus (Arnold 1938: I, lines 4553, 4572, 4576 etc.). Similarly, it is the place at which Vespasian intended to arrive in the time of Arviragus (ibid., lines 5110–14). However, the *General Estoria* uses the work of Geoffrey for these passages, and in its Part V the author correctly translates the Latin form into the Castilian 'Dorobello' (Sánchez-Prieto Borja 2009: II, V, x, 406).

[12] The famous passage in Geoffrey's chronicle is as follows: 'Sed et inclytus ille rex Arturus letaliter vulneratus est, qui, illinc ad sananda vulnera sua in insulam Avallonis evectus, Constantino, cognato suo et filio Cadoris, ducis Cornubiae, diadema Britanniae concessit, anno ab Incarnatione Domini DXLII' (Faral 1993: III, 278).

[13] On the functions of the cart and its role in the *roman* of Chrétien, see above all Rychner 1968 and Shirt 1973.

[14] It is worth noting that the influence of this *roman* is obvious in certain passages of the *Suite-Merlin* of the *Post-Vulgate* cycle, and, specifically, in the use of the motif of the two swords (Micha 1959: 380). As will be seen, the *Pseudo-Robert de Boron* trilogy was well known in the centre and west of the Peninsula, so that, rather than *Li Chevalier aus Deux Espées*, it would be more probable that this work was one of the possible sources of inspiration for the epithet used by Alfonso X in his *cantiga*.

[15] The burlesque name of the lover is formed from the noun *caralho* which, in both Galician and Portuguese, is used colloquially to refer to the male sexual organ. See Montero Cartelle 1996.

[16] The well-known passage from the *Arte de trobar* is as follows: 'Cantigas d'escarneo som aquelas que os trobadores fazen querendo dizer mal d'alguen en elas, e dizen-lho por *palavras cubertas* que hajan dous entendimentos, pera lhe-lo non entenderen [...] ligeiramente: e estas palavras chaman os clerigos "hequivocatio"' (Tavani 1999: 42; my italics).

[17] The colophon passage is as follows: 'Aqui se acava el segundo y tercero libro de don Lançarote de Lago y á se de comenzar el *Libro de don Tristán*, y acabóse en miércoles veinte y cuatro días de octubre año del nascimiento de Nuestro Salvador Jesucristo de mill e cuatrocientos y catorze años' (Contreras Martín and Sharrer, eds, 2006: 386).

[18] Nitze pointed out that the immediate antecedent of the monster would be the passage of the *Gesta regum Anglorum* (*c,*1120–5) of William of Malmesbury, in which King Edgar sees a *canis femina*, whose appearance is given a religious explanation in the work (Nitze 1936).

[19] It is not easy to date the *Post-Vulgate Suite*, in relation to the original *Tristan en prose*, since it does not appear to be indebted to either V. I or V. II of the latter work, both of which, it will be recalled, interpolate episodes from the *Suite* (ed. Roussineau 1996: I, xl; 1998).

[20] It is appropriate to point out that there is an incomplete Galician version of the *General Estoria* of Alfonso X. dated *c*.1330, which translates in their entirety only the first six books and half of the seventh out of the twenty-nine which make up the first part of the Alfonsine compilation (Sánchez-Prieto Borja

2009). The Galician *Xeral Estoria* ends, therefore, at the 'third age', and specifically with the episode that relates the struggle of Jacob with the angel. Thus the Galician text does not contain the episodes relevant to the history of Britain which, it will be recalled, begin in the second part of the six which comprise the enormous Castilian chronicle (Lorenzo Vázquez 2000: 380–3).

[21] The *Crónica* has been edited by Pérez Pascual in his unpublished doctoral thesis (1990). For textual quotations, I have used this unpublished edition and the passages cited in Catalán and de Andrés (1971: 215–337). I am grateful to Prof. Pérez Pascual for kindly granting access to his study and the accompanying edition of the text.

[22] The anecdote is also found in the English poem, *Le Morte Arthur* (*c*.1400), and in *La Morte Darthur* of Thomas Malory. It has not been possible, at present, to establish the common source which inspired both the Navarrese chronicle and the English authors (Catalán 1962: 386–90).

[23] This scholar grouped the manuscripts into six families (*a, b, c, d, e, f*). Despite the usefulness of, and the effort involved in, her work, Philippe Menard has commented as follows: 'Dans l'état présent des recherches, il nous paraît tout à fait prématuré de prétendre distinguer diverses familles de mss. assurées dans l'immense masse de copies du *Tristan*. Les divers groupements dégagés par Mlle Curtis ne nous convainquent pas toujours. Dresser un stemma nous semble une entreprise parfaitement arbitraire' (Ménard, ed, 1987: I, 25).

[24] This chapter forms part of the research undertaken in Research Project FF12011–25899, supported by the 'Dirección General de Investigación' of the Ministerio de Economía y Competitividad of Spain.

V

THE *MATIÈRE DE BRETAGNE* IN THE CORONA DE ARAGÓN

Lourdes Soriano Robles

1. The Reception of Arthurian Material in the Crown of Aragón (XIIth–XIIIth centuries)

The penetration and the earliest diffusion of the *matière de Bretagne* in the Corona de Aragón are known only sketchily and conjecturally. Since the earliest surviving literary witnesses are late (in the case of Catalan material, dating from the XIVth century), researchers have been obliged to resort to other types of source to discover when the Arthurian legends began to spread through the Iberian Peninsula. Specifically, scholars have unearthed notarial documents in which they have discovered personal names of Arthurian origin (Hook 1991, 1996) and, in inventories of the property of deceased persons, the titles of Arthurian works (Cingolani 1990–1; Soriano 2010); they have also studied artistic representations (Olivar 1986; Llompart 1986); and, above all, they have identified allusions to characters and themes from these legends in literary and historiographic texts, which have proved to be the most abundant source of information to date (Entwistle 1975; Lida de Malkiel 1959; Bohigas 1961; Riquer 1964 [1984]: II, 193–221; Riquer 1997).[1]

The first literary allusions are found in troubadour texts that have been dated to the second half of the XIIth century, that is to say, nearly contemporary with the creation of the first *romans* in northern France. The first known reference to a character from the *matière de Bretagne* in Occitan lyric verse, Arthur, is the work of the troubadour Marcabrú as early as 1137.[2] In the case of the Catalan troubadours, however, the first known allusion does not appear until half a century later, in the poem 'Sirventes ab razon bona', dated between 1187 and 1190, by Guillem de Berguedà, in which reference is made to Tristan. The same character reappears in another of his poems, 'Un sirventes ai en cor a bastir' (*c*.1190) (Espadaler 2014: 25–8). In a third composition, 'Lai on hom mellur'e reve' (*c*.1190), he alludes for the first time to the motif of the 'hope of the Britons', although in a rather vague fashion and without linking it specifically to the name of Arthur.[3]

Stefano M. Cingolani (1990–1: 42–6) advises the exercise of caution in the case of such allusions, since they can be of dubious or untrustworthy value as evidence for establishing a probable date for the circulation of Arthurian works or legends in Catalunya, if account is taken of the fact that sometimes the troubadour could have known them during a stay in France, where he could even have composed the poems in which such references are encountered. Nor is it inappropriate to recall that this literary baggage could have arrived through the compositions of the Occitan troubadours who were welcomed and protected at the courts of the Aragonese monarchs in the XIIth and XIIIth centuries. As has been pointed out on more than one occasion, various factors including the geographical (the proximity of Catalunya and the Midi of France), the linguistic (the affinity between Catalan and Occitan) and the socio-political (feudal relations and matrimonial politics among the aristocratic families on both sides of the Pyrenees), favoured their continued presence at the courts of the Crown of Aragon, like those of Alfons I, 'aquel que trobet' (1164–96), or Jaume II (1291–1327) (Riquer 1996). We must, then, bear in mind, as Bohigas once noted (1982: 278), that in order to understand the diffusion of the *matière de Bretagne*, the Catalan literary production of this period must be studied in the context of Occitan literature.

Guillem de Berguedà, as we saw above, refers to Tristan in his sirventeses and to King Arthur in his love poem; but in both sirventeses 'Tristan' is merely the *senhal* or alias that designates the Occitan troubadour Bertran de Born (ed. Riquer 1971: I, 154–62; II, 180–1, 190–1), while the reference to Arthur as the hope of the Britons had also been used previously by the seigneur of Hautefort in the *planh* composed on the death of Geoffrey of Brittany, 'A totz dic qe ja mais no voil' (1186) (ed. Gouiran 1987: 299–309): 'S'Artus, lo segner de Cardoil / Cui Breton atendon e mai, / Agues poder qe tornes sai, / Breton i aurian perdut / E Nostre Segner gazagnat' (lines 33–7).[4]

After Guillem de Berguedà, in chronological sequence, the next allusions to Arthur and Tristan are found in the 'Ensenhamen a Cabra joglar' (1196–8) of Guerau IV de Cabrera, a composition that was long considered to be the first testimony for the knowledge and diffusion of the *matière de Bretagne* in Catalunya. In the course of its more than 200 lines, the troubadour viscount rehearses the literary repertoire that the ignorant jongleur Cabra should know in order properly to fulfil the needs of his trade, among which there stand out, in quantitative terms, allusions to epic and to works on Classical themes. References to characters from Arthurian fiction, however, are few (Arthur, line 58; Erec, lines 73–5; Tristan, Iseut, lines 185–6; Gauvain, lines 187–8) and, when due consideration is given to them, actually involve names that are cited repeatedly in the poetry of the troubadours (Gutiérrez García 2003b: 105–6, 108–9; Gaunt and Harvey 2006: 531). This makes one suspect that knowledge of the Arthurian theme on the part of Guerau IV was rather superficial: the viscount could have had access to it, as Cingolani has pointed out (1992–3b: 195, 199–200), during his stay in Arles in 1194, coinciding with the diffusion of the Arthurian narratives in *langue d'oïl* through the French Midi, where he could even have composed the *ensenhamen*.

From this perspective, neither the composition by Guerau de Cabrera nor those of Guillem de Berguedà can be used as evidence to prove the diffusion of the *matière de Bretagne* in Catalunya during the XIIth century. Neither can the poems of the later

Catalan troubadours who evoke Arthurian characters, in a topical and repetitive fashion, during the second half of the XIIIth century.

In fact, among the characters from the *matière de Bretagne* cited, the repertoire used is limited and there are barely half a dozen to whom reference is made: Guillem Ramón de Gironella (1260–85) alludes in his composition 'Gen m'apareill' to Erec and Enide; Cerverí de Girona (1259–85), a troubadour in whose compositions there are more references to the *matière de Bretagne*, cites Tristan (up to five times), Iseut, Gauvain, Lancelot, Perceval, Yvain and Arthur. Finally, in the *coblas* that the occasional troubadour King Pere el Gran exchanged with Peire Salvatge, from his participation in the cycle of sirventeses of 1285, he alludes to Arthur. In all the poems of Cerverí de Girona, as a case in point, Tristan is used as a reference exemplifying the amorous suffering of the troubadour, while the character of Arthur is newly employed, both by Cerverí de Girona and by King Pere el Gran, for his messianic dimension, as the 'hope of the Britons'.[5] Allusions, therefore, are unfailingly commonplace, without our being able to postulate a direct knowledge of the texts, especially those by an unusual author. This is even more the case if we take into account the fact that troubadours such as Cerverí de Girona travelled outside the Crown of Aragon (Cingolani 1990–1: 44).

This court poet in the service of Jaume I is the last of the Catalan troubadours to refer to Arthurian characters. It is not until the end of the XIVth century that they are found again in the poetry of one of the poets in whose works the weight of the troubadour tradition is most appreciable: Andreu Febrer (1375/80–1437/44). However, he and other poets who in the course of the XIVth and XVth centuries allude in their compositions to Arthurian characters do it in the same manner as the troubadours: as models to whom to compare oneself in amorous conflicts. In this way there will be formulated the famous 'galleries of lovers', in which there are enumerated literary characters and pairs of famous lovers with exceptional love stories who will be invoked as authorities. French narrative and in particular the *matière de Bretagne* will bring a vast array of characters and themes, which can be seen growing throughout the XIVth and XVth centuries with new names obtained from the Italian authors of the Trecento, and, later, with some names derived from Castilian and from Catalan literature (Riquer 1995: 153–6; Espadaler 2014: 28–32).[6]

It is, therefore, difficult to demonstrate on the basis of these secondary references that the *matière de Bretagne* circulated in Catalunya during the XIIth–XIIIth centuries, and that, in the case of the Catalan troubadours, knowledge of it was actually acquired in this region itself. Besides, when these references are taken as a whole, we agree with De Caluwé that neither in the poetry of the Catalan troubadours nor in that of their Occitan counterparts can there be found any original development that enriches the motif, the plot or the character cited. That is to say, neither group contributes to the development of Arthurian literature, for this finds its expression instead in another language, the *langue d'oïl* (De Caluwé 1981: 362).

Whilst in the French Midi and in the Corona de Aragón knowledge of the *matière de Bretagne* seems limited, and restricted to the troubadour milieu, in the north of France at this time the works of Chrétien de Troyes and those relating to Tristan had been for some years in the process of amplification and prosification, thereby initiating the great *summae* of Arthurian material known as the *Vulgate* with its five branches and the *Tristan en prose* (1215–40). These works achieved an extraordinary diffusion throughout Europe, and the higher nobility of the Crown of Aragon too was receptive to the Arthurian *romans*. The latter were now presented in another textual form in the course of the XIIIth century, in which the characters who had been protagonists in various works were brought together within the bounds of a single court ruled over by the magnificent figure of Arthur, which would become the model, albeit a literary one, of the ideal court, in which the best knights rivalled one another in matters of love and chivalry. Tristan would join the Round Table and his participation in the collective enterprise would underline the chivalric dimension of the character, a fact that would not pass unnoticed by the Catalan writers who, from the middle of the XIIIth century, cite Tristan alongside other knights (Espadaler 2014: 32–8).

The first signs of the influence of the Arthurian *roman* in prose go back to the time of Jaume I (1213–76), whose reign, like those of his ancestors, is a good demonstration of the relationship between Crown and culture in its most varied fields (Claramunt 1996: 358). Just as the cultivation of poetry relied on the monarch's patronage, so too did that of historiography, in which the king himself was a practitioner in its promotion, with the composition of the *Llibre dels fets*, a chronicle in which he relates (through the use of the plural of majesty) the deeds in which he participated during his reign. This, together with the other three chronicles, Desclot, Muntaner and Pere el Cerimoniós, known as the four great chronicles, came to constitute, as Serra Desfilis (2002: 21–3) notes, a kind of secular gospels of the monarchy, in which the deeds of the kings during one of the most important episodes for the history of the Crown of Aragón are recorded, and as *specula* for princes and nobles. Although in these texts the Catalan royalty did not endeavour to trace their origins back to legendary ancestors (the mythical Brutus or Arthur of the English monarchs), it certainly can be observed how the historical memory of the monarch and his dynasty is mixed with mythical and legendary elements, and a heavy dose of providentialism, foreshadowed in the chronicle of Jaume I and developed in those of Desclot (composed between 1283 and 1288) and Muntaner (composed half a century later, between 1326 and 1328).

In chapter 5 of the *Llibre dels fets*, Jaume I relates his conception and birth, and how these came about practically through divine volition because of the aversion his father, Pere el Catòlic, felt towards his wife Maria de Montpellier (ed. Soldevila 2007: 52–4). However, whilst the circumstances of the conception occurred in a natural manner according to the brief account in the chronicle, they acquire legendary and messianic proportions under the pen of the chroniclers Bernat Desclot and Ramon Muntaner, marked by reminiscences of the conception of Arthur or Galahad. First M. de Montoliu

(1925) and later F. Soldevila (1957) noted the similarities of the episode in the chronicles of Desclot and Muntaner with Arthurian fiction. While Montoliu concentrated on the conception of Arthur and the substitution of Uther Pendragon for the Duke of Tintagel in Igerna's bed, as related by Geoffrey of Monmouth in his *Historia regum Britanniae*, Soldevila attempted to reconstruct, on the basis of assonances detected in the chronicle of Muntaner, an epic poem on the birth of Jaume I, which would have been composed probably in Montpellier, and that the chronicler would later have prosified. Years later Bohigas (1982: 280) pointed out much closer points of contact between the narration of the conception of Jaume I and that of Galahad in the *Lancelot en prose*, and recently J. Pujol (2002) has confirmed, with textual evidence, the dependence of the episode of Desclot on the Arthurian *roman* of the *Vulgate*. According to Elliott (1984: 35–6), this treatment given to the episode by the chronicler, converting it into a variant of the folkloric motif of the substitute sweetheart, was politically necessary to reinforce the legitimacy of the future King Jaume I with the aim of putting an end to the pretensions of his rivals to the throne; in these circumstances, the birth of an heir of unquestionable legitimacy must have seemed miraculous. The account, moreover, wrapped a mystic aura around the conception and birth of Jaume I, which associates him with that of other great heroes of legend such as Arthur, Galahad or Charlemagne.

Muntaner knew the *Vulgate Lancelot*, but was also familiar with the *Tristan en prose*, as is shown by the stylistic relationship between both texts (Izquierdo 2003) and the enumeration of Arthurian knights that he gives in chapters 51 and 134.[7] Among these he alludes to Palamedes, Brunor le Noir (the Cavaller de la Cota Mal Tallada) and Lamorat de Gales, who are found only in the vast prose narratives of Tristan (Riquer 1964 [1984]: I, 466). Clearly, he does not forget Arthur either, whose feasts are eclipsed by those celebrated by King Pere.[8] Moreover, the chronicler also knew the Occitan *roman* of *Jaufré*, to which he refers on two occasions. In chapters 116 and 148, and employing a formula that is very similar on each occasion, he informs the reader that the narration of the deeds of prowess carried out by the Catalan and Aragonese knights who participated in the conquest of Calabria, were it written, would occupy more folios than the deeds of Jaufré.[9]

The *novas de Jaufré*, which belongs in the mainstream of the postclassical verse *roman* (Gutiérrez García 2007–8: 504), was written by an author (or authors) whose identity is still unknown, and is dedicated, as the initial lines tell us, to a king of Aragón 'Paire de Pretz e fil de Don'. The study of this designation, which is also used by Cerverí de Girona in his *Maldit-Bendit*, like that of the non-fictional digressions in the work, and the study of the sources underlying *Jaufré*, lead us to state with some confidence that the king of Aragón who is praised in the dedication is none other than Jaume I and that this chivalric *roman* was composed between 1272 and 1276 (Espadaler 1997, 1999–2000, 2002).[10]

The work is set in the British context of the court of King Arthur, to which the knight who is its protagonist belongs, and it relates the amorous adventures of the latter with Brunissén and the knightly challenges he faces with Taulat de Rogimon. The work stands out for the lyricism of the passages of sentimental tone in it, and for its humorous and parodic treatment of episodes inspired by the Arthurian narrative of Chrétien de Troyes. *Jaufré* had some diffusion and impact: on the one hand, it survives in eight witnesses (among them a *membrum disiectum* in the Arxiu Històric de Barcelona, MS B-109) with a textual transmission almost inseparable from that of troubadour lyric and that brings us close to the interpretation given to this work by medieval readers (Lee 2003); on the other hand, and beside the references to the character by Muntaner (see above), the verses of *Jaufré* resound in *La Vesió* of Bernat de So (Espadaler 1997: 201) and his adventures are represented in the pictorial series that decorates the walls of the Moorish room at the royal palace of the Aljafería of Zaragoza from the times of Pere el Cerimoniós (Español 2001: 18–19, 60).[11]

If literature associated the birth of Jaume I irreversibly with Arthurian fiction, likewise at his death in 1276 the troubadour Mathieu de Quercy dedicated to him a heartfelt *planh* ('Tant suy marritz que no·m puesc alegrar') in which he compared the grief for the loss of the Catalan monarch with that suffered by the Britons at the disappearance of Arthur: 'Ay! Aragos, Cataluenha e Serdanha / e Lerida, venetz ab mi doler, / quar ben devetz aitant de dol aver / cum per Artus agron silh de Bretanha' (Riquer 1983: III, CVIII, 1542, lines 30–3).[12]

The final signs of the influence of the *matière de Bretagne* in works of the XIIIth century come from the pen of Ramon Llull, author of an enormous oeuvre of a doctrinal and penitential character, who also allowed himself to be seduced by Arthurian themes in his youth and surely during his sojourn at court. The prologue of the *Llibre de l'orde de cavalleria* (1274–6), which was later to be plagiarised by Joanot Martorell in *Tirant lo Blanc*, is composed on the basis of the motif of the wise knight-hermit who instructs the young future knight, which Chrétien de Troyes also used in *Li Contes del Graal*. Llull, who knew this tradition, employs it in his treatise by way of a *captatio benevolentiae* and tells us of the arrival of a young squire, en route to the royal court at which he is due to be dubbed a knight, at the hermitage in which an elderly knight lives as a recluse. The latter, after devoting years of his life to wars and tournaments, now devotes himself to penitence and contemplation. The squire begs the old man to explain what the order of chivalry is, and the veteran hands him a book, the *Libre de l'orde de cavaylaria*, which occupies the seven chapters of which the work consists, and which the young man reads and proposes to take to court so that it may be useful to everyone who also wants to honour knighthood (Riquer 1984: I, 246–53; Soler 1989).

Written some years later, *Blaquerna* (*c*.1283) is referred to by Llull on various occasions significantly as 'lo *romanç* d'Evast e Blaquerna', a title which reveals the author's intention to incorporate that work within that chivalric narrative genre as well as wanting to express a complex of teachings and moral and mystical experiences (Riquer 1984: I, 277–8). In it, Llull again uses the same chivalric pattern as was used in the *Llibre de l'orde de cavalleria*, and sets in motion the hermit Blaquerna, as a knight errant, through the forest where he successively meets all manner of people whom he 'combats' verbally instead of with arms, instructing them successfully (Bohigas 1982: 282–4; Riquer 1984: I, 277–80; Soler and Santanach 2009: 29–30). Alongside this narrative frame, the influence of Arthurian literature has been perceived, and in particular that of the *Queste del Saint Graal*, especially in book II (chs 47, 50–1, 64). Here, in the wood Blaquerna meets characters (knights and ladies) in situations typical of the Arthurian romance: the superstitious knight who is taught doctrine by the Christian; the proud knight who kidnaps the lady, carrying her off from the castle of her widowed mother; the enamoured knight who loves the most beautiful lady in the world and is ready to fight anyone who denies the truth of this.

2. The Circulation and Translation of Arthurian Works. The first indigenous creations (XIVth century)

The XIVth century is the period of greatest diffusion of the Arthurian material, during which archival documentation shows that copies of the *romans* in French began to circulate, translations into Catalan were made and the first native works inspired by the Arthurian fictions in *langue d'oil* were composed.

During the first half of the century, the reception and circulation of Arthurian literature seems to be restricted still to a single milieu, namely, the court. The first information we have of the circulation of copies of prose *romans* goes back to the reign of Jaume II (1291–1327), after his marriage to Blanche d'Anjou (Cingolani 1992–3: 492). Chancery documentation from his reign unearthed by Rubió y Lluch (1908–21) reflects the interest of the monarch – a refined and cultured king, a lover of music and a great patron of Gothic style (Claramunt 1996: 364) – in books, though not in those of entertaining literature. Through the documents we see how he disposed of the Arthurian works in his possession, passing them on to his children: a *Lancelot* to the Infant Ramon Berenguer in 1319 and a *Tristan en prose* and another *Lancelot* to the Infant Pere in 1315 and 1321, respectively (Rubió y Lluch 1908–21: II, 33–5, doc. xl; Madurell 1974: 23, doc. 1; Cingolani 1990–1: 79). It seems that both works were the most popular during this period, since other members of the nobility are also recorded as possessing copies (Soriano 2010).

The period corresponding to the reign of Pere IV of Aragon (1336–87, Pere el Cerimoniós) would, however, turn out to be the phase in which there are evident both a more lively interest in Arthurian fiction and a greater activity in producing such material. King Pere was one of the monarchs who was most concerned with all fields of culture throughout his lengthy reign, exercising a patronage and an encouragement of learning comparable with those of Alfonso X el Sabio (Claramunt 1996: 368). He was, moreover, a restless bibliophile, a voracious reader and an excellent connoisseur of French literature and of Arthurian narrative in particular. The chancery registers of his reign show a special interest in the Arthurian *Vulgate*: he bought a copy of *Meliadux* in 1339 (Rubió y Lluch 1908–21: I, 117, doc. 201), commanded payment to be made for two copies of *Lancelot* that he had ordered, the first in 1339 and the second in 1346 (Rubió y Lluch 1908–21: I, 119, doc. 105, and I, 135, doc. 137), and also for the *Mort Artu* in 1349 (Rubió y Lluch 1908–21: I, 146, doc. 144). He also asked insistently, and demanded, that there be sent to him a *Lancelot* in Catalan that his son the Infant Joan had been reading (Rubió y Lluch 1908–21: I, 201, docs 204–5); and enjoined that there should be returned to the monastery of Sigena, which enjoyed royal protection, a copy of the *Queste* that had been stolen from it (Rubió y Lluch 1908–21: II, 69, doc. 68). This fascination with Arthurian matters went beyond the mere possession of books since, as mentioned above, a pictorial series on Jaufré decorated King Pere's rooms in the Aljafería. The collecting enthusiasm of the king was open, moreover, to other artistic representations, in particular to a new fashion imported from France, that of tapestries. This was an enthusiasm that he shared with his third wife, Leonor of Sicily. Thus, the monarch also had the rooms decorated with narrative tapestries or 'draps de ras istoriats' (which owe their name to the city of Arras, where they originated), of which it is believed that he had eventually collected about thirty, some of them woven with scenes of King Arthur or the knights of the Round Table. In 1356 Queen Leonor was presented with the bill for the purchase of various French tapestries with narrative scenes, among them one with the 'istoria militum Mense rotunde', the story of the knights of the Round Table, and according to an invoice signed in 1368 the king had bought in Paris, through Pericó Desplà, an extensive French tapestry which represented the 'istoria del rey Artus' (Olivar 1986: 11–34).

One of the king's principal passions was history (Claramunt 1996: 368–9; Espadaler 2001: 916–20), and he himself contributed, as his ancestor Jaume I had done, to the composition of the *Crònica reyal* of his reign. The ambitious historiographic project of the king, as may be traced through his correspondence, led him to request, on the one hand, chronicles of the monarchs of France, the Crown of Castile, Navarre, Sicily, Portugal and even of places further afield, those of the kings of Hungary, Dacia, Norway etc.; and, on the other, to order the copying of manuscripts with the idea of assembling a library which he intended to house at Poblet, to promote their translation into Aragonese, and to promote the composition of the *Compendi historial* that he commissioned from Jaume Domènech, a project continued by Fray Antoni Ginebreda on the death of the former. Among his correspondents there stands out one figure, that of Juan Fernández de Heredia, Castellan of Amposta and Grand Master of the Order of St John of Jerusalem, with whom the monarch shared his passion for history and from whom he requested a copy of the historical compendia and works that the Master was compiling in Aragonese.

MS esp. 13 of the Bibliothèque Nationale de France, Paris, relates to this model of historical compendium supported through the royal scriptorium. It is a copy dated 1410–30 of a compilation of historiographic texts, on fols 83*v*–97*v* of which there survives a fragment of the only translation into Catalan of the *Historia regum Britanniae* of Geoffrey of Monmouth (Bohigas 1985: 123–32, 180–203). This, far from being transmitted here as an independent and complete unit, has become part of a textual compilation (Lucía Megías 2005c: 231–5) made up of historiographic works. The textual character of the translation is thereby modified, and in this way the work of the Welsh monk ceases to be part of a fabulous pseudo-chronicle of England to become a chapter in something that is intended to be a serious history of the world, from the moment at which the author inserts it alongside other texts such as the *Compendi historial* of Gauchier de Denain, the *Crónica d'Espanya* of Rodrigo Jiménez de Rada, and the *Genealogia dels reis d'Aragó* of Jaume Domènech, to mention only some of the titles included in the volume.

As in the majority of the Catalan translations of these Arthurian texts, the translator is unknown, as is the date of translation of the *Historia regum Britanniae*; however, Bohigas (1985: 179) dates it before 1385 thanks to a curious detail that cannot be ignored. On comparing the Catalan version with the surviving Castilian adaptations, the Catalan scholar noted that the only one of them which has a close relationship (a correspondence he considers to be literal and complete in many passages) is that which Fernández de Heredia includes in some chapters of the *Grant Crónica d'Espanya* found in BNM MS 10133, the copying of which was completed in the first days of 1385. From this it follows that the Catalan text, which was the source of Heredia's version, must be earlier than that year.

From the final quarter of the XIVth century there also dates the only witness for the Catalan translation of the *Profecies de Merlí*, copied in MS 271 of the Biblioteca de Catalunya, Barcelona, and earlier than the surviving Castilian texts. In contrast to the remaining Arthurian texts translated into Catalan, which derive from French originals, in this case the anonymous translation was taken from the Castilian reworking which was later published at the end of the *Baladro del Sabio Merlín* printed in Seville in 1535 (Bohigas 1928–32: 261–70). It includes only the prophecies that Merlin uttered while washing his hands and face in a fountain, near the city of London, since Merlin wanted to know various things that would happen in different parts of the world, in particular in the Peninsular kingdoms until the year 1377. Specifically, there are references to Alfonso X and his descendants down to the extinction of this dynasty with the death of Pedro I el Cruel and the advent of the Trastámaras as the ruling dynasty of Castile. Like the translation of the *Historia regum Britanniae*, the *Profecies* are transmitted as part of a miscellany manuscript, composed of religious works, canon law and papal correspondence, a fact that implies a textual transmission of a different kind and which distances the *Profecies* from the context of chivalric fiction to transform them into part of a miscellaneous compilation in an unrelated genre (Lucía Megías 2005c: 231–5).

Joan I inherited from his father, Pere el Cerimoniós, his enthusiasm for and love of well-made books, in addition to a library which, even though it was not very important, increased its holdings as time progressed (Riquer 1989: 115). His marriage to Violant de Bar (r. 1380–96) contributed particularly to the diffusion of French language and culture at court, as Violant became a bridge between the culture of the Crown of Aragon and that of France, giving entrée not only to Cassical authors but also to the latest French literary novelties in the literature of entertainment. This monarch was a Francophile who, as he himself affirmed, 'nos nos delitam molt en llegir e axí pròpiament en francès, com en nostra lengua materna' (Rubió y Lluch 1908–21: II, 233), and the French language was so established at his court that, on his death, his sister-in-law María de Luna wrote in a letter to the king of England that 'havie muller francesa et era tot francès'. This fact explains why some Arthurian works had not passed through the filter of translation, as, for example, was the case with *Meliadux*, a work of which he owned a copy in French (Rubió y Lluch 1908–21: I, 314, doc. cccxliv); we must suppose that this work had a relatively small circulation, restricted to the royal circle, and in its original language.[13]

Although no trace has remained of the presence of *Meliadux* in the Crown of Aragon, there are today in Catalan and Spanish libraries witnesses of French manuscripts of the *Vulgate* which attest to the circulation and possession of these works in their original language during the late Middle Ages. There stand out in the first place fragments of a *Lancelot en prose* deposited in the Arxiu Comarcal de la Cerdanya in Puigcerdà (Fons Martí i Terrada, without a shelfmark) which, together with those from the Deulofeu i Fatjó collection (also in Puigcerdà), formed part of a codex copied between 1310 and 1320, written in Italy (Delcorno Branca 1998a: 22, reproduced in Riquer 1984: II, 196). There is also preserved in the library at Montserrat a *membrum disiectum* from the XIIIth century (shelfmark 1042-VIII), the text of which is still to be identified, and in which there can be read 'la gent le roi artu' (Olivar 1977: 320). It is also appropriate to add the copy of the *Roman de Lancelot du Lac* held in the BN Madrid (MS 485), which had belonged to Gaspar Galcerán de Gurrea y Aragón, Conde de Guimerà, and which surely came from Catalunya (Entwistle 1975: 97–8); and MS P-II-22 of the Real Biblioteca del Monasterio de El Escorial, which belonged to the library of Gaspar de Guzmán, Conde-Duque de Olivares (Soriano 2013).[14]

Joan I, while he was still Infant, encouraged the translation of works into Catalan around the decade 1360–70, among which were included the principal French *romans* of the *matière de Bretagne*: the *Vulgate Lancelot* and the *Tristan en prose* (Badia 1991: 36; Pujol 2006: 632; Cingolani 1990–1: 83).[15] Only the *Queste del Saint Graal* was translated into Catalan outside the court circle, and this is, moreover, the only translation with a signed and dated colophon: G. Reixach, Wednesday 16 May 1380, according to the Julian calendar (Adroher 2005: 86–7).

Of this translation activity there were preserved, until the last century, a few fragmentary witnesses, some of which have still not been rediscovered today: three fragments of the *Tristan en prose* belonging to three manuscripts of the work, divided among Cervera, Andorra and Barcelona (Sharrer 1977: 25–6; Santanach i Suñol 2010); and two of the *Vulgate Lancelot*, also from different manuscripts, in Palma de Mallorca and Mataró, at present of unknown location (Sharrer 1977: 17–18; see also the chapters by Lucía Megías and Contreras in the present work). Finally, a manuscript that transmits the *Queste del Saint Graal*, now preserved in Milan, is the only translation that has come down to us in a complete state (Sharrer 1977: 20).

Another indication of the extensive circulation of these works in the court is the criticism levelled against them by authors such as Antoni Canals and Bernat Metge, in whose opinion they were otiose works. Canals, for example, in the Catalan translation he made of the *Carta de Sant Bernat a la seva germana* (*De modo bene vivendi*) between 1396 and 1410 (*a quo/ad quem*) and that he dedicated to Galceran de Sentmenat, chamberlain of King Martí I, advises against the reading of this type of entertaining literature since in it the Christian will not find the salvation of his soul:

> Aci pot entendre vostra devocio que hom deu legir libres aprovats no pas libres vans axi com les faules de Lançalot e de Tristany nil romans de la guineu ni libres provocatius a cobeiança axi com libres de amors libres de art de amar Ovidi *de vetula* ni libres qui son inutils axi com de faules e de rondales mes libres devots libres de la fe crestiana hon sta nostra salvacio. (ed. Bofarull 1857: 420)

Bernat Metge, in Book III of *Lo somni* (the composition of which was completed in 1399), when he tackles the question of the intellectual formation of women, criticises the peevish attitude shown by the latter, and writes:

> De vanitat han així plen lo cap, que impossible és que t'ho pogués dir; emperò diré't ço que me'n recorda. Elles entenen ésser en gran felicitat haver molt delicadament e lloçania, e saber parlar diverses llenguatges, recordar moltes cançons e noves rimades, al·legar dits de trobadors e les *Epístoles* d'Ovidi, recitar les històries de Lancelot, de Tristany, del rei Artús e de quants amorosos són estats tro a llur temps. (ed. Badia 2003a: 139)

Martí I l'Humà (1396–1410), the brother and successor of Joan I, continued the cultural policy of his predecessors. A man with a solid Classical and literary formation, among his books there is also the occasional title belonging to Arthurian literature, such as *Meliadux* in French, which he must surely have inherited from his father or brother, as well as a *Profecies de Merlí* (Soriano 2010). A deeply religious individual, he gathered together a veritable treasure trove of relics, among which one in particular stands out (and also one for which the knights of the Round Table had undertaken their adventures years before): the Holy Grail. In 1399 he obtained, through the intermediacy of Pope Benedict XIII, from the monks of San Juan de la Peña the holy chalice which they kept in the monastery, a goblet identified in the Middle Ages as the chalice of the Last Supper, as was also the Grail. Once he had obtained it, the relic was deposited in the Palace Chapel at the Aljafería of Zaragoza, and, later, in Barcelona, until Alfons el Magnànim presented it to Valencia Cathedral in 1424, where it is today preserved as 'the Holy Grail' (Beltrán Llavador 2006a: 124; see also Alvar in the present volume).

If up to this point we have seen that the chivalric fictions were received and circulated in a clearly defined cultural and social milieu, in the court or in aristocratic circles, towards the end of the XIVth century they crossed the threshold of the court to take their place in the libraries of another kind of readers who were beginning to demand copies of Arthurian works and who emerged from other social strata which had become wealthy: honourable citizens (lawyers and doctors), professionals (notaries, apothecaries, barber-surgeons), and skilled craftsmen (especially prosperous ones: tailors, furriers and silversmiths) (Soriano 2010), or the merchant class, one of the best-studied from the perspectives of culture and the history of the book. From the end of the XIVth century, there is a record of the presence of copies of works of history, romances of chivalry and other works of entertainment in the libraries of merchants since books were, to an ever greater extent, considered to be one of the manifestations of a particular social status and to confer social prestige on their possessor.[16] The merchant sought to ennoble himself through culture, for which reason, together with the books that permitted him to carry out his work, there began to appear frequently in his library works that up to this point had circulated among the higher classes. In this way, and like any medieval man, the merchant resorted to religious readings, and in some cases allowed himself to be seduced by the nascent humanistic culture but, above all, also found pleasure and recreation in the romances of chivalry because reading a romance signified sharing the universal culture of the aristocratic class (Aurell i Cardona 1996: 140–73; cf. Tavani 1980a: 36–7).

Little by little, Arthurian literature was filtering through every level of society; and popular literature also betrays evidence of its influence. Two public announcements survive, from the end of the XIVth century and the beginning of the XVth, published on the occasion of the festival of San Bartolomé de Igualada, in which there persists the tradition of Morgane as an enchantress and the port of Tintagel as a place of imprisonment. In the first, dated 19 August 1394, Bernat Vallés, by order of the Batlles (Mayors), published an announcement that the 'young pilgrim enchanted by the fairy Morgana' would attend the vigil of San Bartolomé after having been delivered from his imprisonment by the intervention of the saint when, on his way back from the Holy Land, the fairy Morgana kept him imprisoned by enchantment in a place called the Valley of False Trickery. In the second announcement 'by the Irish knight who undertakes great deeds of prowess to disenchant his lady', on 20 August 1404, it was explained that an Irish knight would attend the vigil at the chapel of St Bartholomew for the love of a lady who was held by enchantment in the port of Tintagel, because through penitence and the vigil he wished to obtain the grace of heaven on behalf of his unfortunate beloved. These brief edicts of an edifying character were addressed not to a specific elite but to a wide public of citizens with the intention of attracting them to the vigils of the festivals dedicated to the saints (Bohigas 1982: 287; texts in Segura, ed., 1907–8: II, 167–9).

In the same way, in the oral tradition of Mallorca, Morgana also lives on, particularly in two *rondalles* (stories), 'La Fada Morgana' and 'Na Joana i la fada Mariana' (a popular deformation of the same name), which Antoni M. Alcover had the opportunity to hear in Mallorca and collected in his *Aplec de rondaies mallorquines d'en Jordi d'es Racó* (Vidal Alcover 1980). Leaving aside the variations in storyline that they present, both texts tell the same tale: a young woman, called Joana, is proclaimed to be wiser than the Fairy Queen Morgana; the latter then subjects her to a test from which Joana emerges victorious thanks to the aid of the son of the queen, whom she ends up marrying.

Thus, by the end of the XIVth century, as we have seen, the prose *roman* had become sufficiently established among readers to give rise to the appearance of the first indigenous works inspired by the *matière de Bretagne* and which borrow from the French romances their characters, settings, and plots. Nonetheless, and in contrast with the French textual model, the creation of these new texts would be conditioned by the weight of the Occitan-Catalan stylistic tradition that preceded it, and they would therefore be composed in the form of *novas rimadas* (Cingolani 1992–3a: 493). These works, which date from the last third of the XIVth century, are the anonymous *Blandín de Cornualla*, and *La Faula* by Guillem de Torroella.

Blandín de Cornualla is preserved in the Biblioteca Nazionale Universitaria of Turin in a unique late copy produced in Italy during the XVIth century. However, the text must have been composed between 1375 and 1400, as can be concluded from the study of the arms and armour (Asperti 1986). The question of Catalan authorship is still not resolved, although some scholars favour a Catalan as its anonymous creator (Van der Horst 1974): an author whom they link to an Avignonese working environment, having regard to the importance of the papal court and its contacts with Italy, which would explain the manuscript's itinerary.[17]

The work, in its 2,386 lines, relates the adventures of two young knights who are friends, Blandín de Cornualla and Guiot Ardit de Miramar, who swear loyalty to each other and undertake together a journey in search of adventures:

> En nom de Dieu començarai
> un bell dictat et retrairai
> d'amors et de cavalleria,
> et d'una franca companyia
> que van fer dos cavaliers,
> de Cornualla bons guerriers,
> que vòlgron per lo món anar
> e llur aventura cercar.
>   (ed. Pacheco 1983: 27, lines 1–8)

It ends with their union with the ladies Brianda and Yrlanda in a finale that represents the triumph of the *recreantisse* so criticised by Chrétien de Troyes in his *Erec et Enide*:

> E Blandín de Cornivalla,
> e Guillot, se Dieu me valla,
> van remanir am lors mullers,
> e féron com bons cavallers.
> E d'aquí non vòlgron partir,
> ni vòlgron plus guerra seguir,
> mas que féron com bona gent,
> e Dieus lor donet prou de ben.
>   (ed. Pacheco 1983: 79, lines 2381–94)

The absence of the element of the marvellous in favour of realism in descriptions, the presence of para-folkloric themes (consider, for example, the adventure of the disenchantment of Brianda, constructed on the basis of the story of the Sleeping Beauty),[18] and the parody of Arthurian commonplaces characterise the romance, making it, in this sense, indebted to *Jaufré* (De Caluwé 1978). In fact, the search for 'adventure' and the place name 'de Cornualla' that serves as a guarantee of authenticity, are really the only link between this work and Arthurian fiction.

By contrast, in *La Faula* one can begin to observe some specific traits which individualise this text within the range of native works on Arthurian themes and which distance it, consequently, from works such as *Jaufré* and *Blandín de Cornualla*. In the first place, the narrative is written in a heavily Catalanised Occitan with insertions in French, a deliberate bilingualism that highlights the author's linguistic knowledge, at the same time as it reveals the skill of Torroella in versifying in French, a language in which three of his characters speak: Arthur, Morgane and the serpent (Gudayol 1990). On the other hand, there stands out the use of the first person, which gives the story an autobiographical character, in the style of a confession or confidential dialogue with the reader (Pacheco 1983: 99–102).

The work was composed by the Mallorcan Guillem de Torroella, before 1374, when he was still young ('Guillems ay noms de Torroella; / mos payres era cavallers, / mas eu soy enquer escuders / car no ay l'orde recebut.' ed. Vicent Santamaria 2011: 309, lines 818–21). *La Faula* is considered to be an interesting document on the evolution of the British legends of King Arthur and an essential element for knowledge of their diffusion in Catalunya (Riquer 1984: II, 206–20) because from it the individual sources used by Torroella can be identified, some more obvious than others, and all related to Arthurian fiction, although they are never explicitly named by the author. On the one hand, there are the narrative *lais*, from which there came the marvellous elements that appear throughout the work (Ors 1986), and on the other is the Sicilian legend of Arthur (the 'Mediterranean Arthur'; Lee 2006). This last explains the otherworld retirement of the king, in this case at Mount Etna, after having been killed by his nephew Mordred at the battle of Salesbières, and which in French fiction gave rise to the myth of the 'British expectation' as narrated in the *Mort Artu*. This distinctive Mediterranean variant was already recorded by Gervaise of Tilbury in his *Otia imperialia* compiled around the year 1211 (Graf 1892–3: I, 304–5; Bresc 1987), in which he explains that, as the Sicilian people relate, a servant of the bishop of Catania, pursuing over the foothills and flanks of Etna a loose palfrey that had escaped from him, came upon a valley where a magnificent palace stood. There he found King Arthur prostrate upon a bed, recovering from his wounds, which gape anew each year; upon learning of the reason for the young man's arrival, the king ordered that the palfrey be restored to him so that he could return it to the bishop, and then related to him how he was wounded years before fighting against his nephew Mordred and Childeric at the battle of Salesbières.

Despite the similarity of the two texts, *La Faula* was not composed from the story in Gervaise of Tilbury, but rather Torroella must have known the legend through some lost text or through the oral traditions of Sicily (Entwistle 1975: 189; Riquer 1984: II, 218, cf. Lee 2006: 109–10) or, as seems more probable, from a specific work, *Floriant et Florete*, a French *roman* written about 1250 which is thought to be the most direct source of *La Faula*. In this romance we are told how Floriant, son of King Elyadus of Sicily, is kidnapped while a child by Morgane, who keeps him in the castle of Mongibel (that is, Etna). Floriant grows up and the fairy wishes to become his lover, and one day when the young man leaves Palermo in pursuit of a stag (which we later learn has been sent by Morgane), he enters a marvellous palace in which he finds her seated on a bed. They speak, among other things, of King Arthur, who is still ruling in Britain, She explains to him, in particular, that once the monarch has been mortally wounded, she will take charge of conveying him there.

The Sicilian legend, however, in its manifestation in the French romance, is constructed around Morgane, not King Arthur. In the same way that Floriant is attracted by her with a lure, likewise Torroella departs one morning from the port of Sóller and, travelling on a whale, is guided by a parrot to the resting place of Arthur in Sicily, where the king is living in seclusion with his sister Morgane (Riquer 1991). On his arrival at the island, the first creature which Guillem encounters is a serpent which, speaking in beautiful French, informs him that he is 'en l'isl'Enxentea, / hon repayre Morgan la fea / e mesire lo roy Artus' (ed. Vicent Santamaria 2011: 302, lines 179–81). The serpent disappears and Guillem falls asleep. The next day, he sees a palfrey approaching, richly saddled in the French fashion, and on the ivory saddlebows are carvings in relief:

> ab mant'estoria d'amors:
> de Floris e de Blanquaflor;
> d'Isolda la Bronda e de Tristany
> – qui per amor s'ameron tan –,
> de Tisbe e de Piramus,
> de Serena e d'Allidus,
> de Paris: ab qual gent conques
> Elena, que dins Troya mes!
>   (ed. Vicent Santamaria 2011: 303, lines 235–42)

In the long and detailed description of the accoutrements of the palfrey, which occupies some seventy lines, Guillem explains that it also has one hundred harness bells that reproduce 'un lays de Tristany / que molt es plasent per ausir' (ed. Vicent Santamaria 2011: 303, lines 286–7). Guillem mounts the palfrey to see where it will take him, desirous of hearing news of King Arthur ('que del bon rey Artus pogues / saber algun novell certa', ed. Vicent Santamaria 2011: 303, lines 304–5). He arrives then at a laurel tree from whose branches there hang some gloves which must belong, Guillem imagines, to the owner of the palfrey. He then sees two small dogs which accompany him to the palace (and which, as Espadaler 1986: 141 reminds us, have some reminiscences of the partridge-hunting dog which leads Blandín and Guiot into adventure). Guillem understands that his destiny is governed by the will of the palfrey and when he dismounts, there appears before him a lady, Morgana, who informs him that

>	tu est venus d'oltra la mar
>	per avoir si tres gran ventura,
>	c'unque, si tant com terra dura,
>	n'avient onne aysi beylla,
>	estranye, ni si novella,
>	ne si complida de tots bens.
>		(ed. Vicent Santamaria 2011: 306, lines 494–9)

In line 504 the first part of the text ends, at which point Torroella puts us in touch with the marvellous and gives us the keys to reading correctly not only the meaning of the fantastic journey but also the whole of the poem (Espadaler 1986: 140–1).

The second part begins when Guillem enters the palace with Morgana. The decoration impresses Guillem, in particular the paintings which depict the best Arthurian knights, from Tristan, followed by Lancelot, to Yvain (lines 558–98). Once in the presence of Arthur, Guillem can contemplate him while Morgana passes a ring before his eyes so that he can see him through some silver grilles. The king has a surprisingly young appearance (thirty years or so, Torroella states, when the chronicles tell us that his reign lasted for some eighty years), and Guillem has to be sure if the person in whose presence he is: 'ets vos, senyer, lo rey Artus, / aycell qui atendon li breto?' (ed. Vicent Santamaria 2011: 310, lines 922–3). The king's reply constitutes a summary of the *Mort Artu* in its general outline, a work which Torroella knew at first hand, and possibly through a Catalan translation (Butinyà 1990). But the king, from behind the grille, is absorbed in contemplating his sword. The narrator then explains to us that he is flanked by two women dressed in mourning: one is Love and the other Valour, who were formerly queens, but are now widowed and orphaned, whence the black garments they are wearing. The king addresses his sword in French and laments the loss of the values of chivalry (ed. Vicent Santamaria 2011: 308, lines 758–85).

The narrative scheme of the work, however, makes plain that the key point of all the story is precisely the speech of King Arthur; as Morgana says to Guillem, his arrival there was not fortuitous, 'car por noant ne'stes venus' (ed. Vicent Santamaria 2011: 308, line 733). Guillem has been chosen so that, once he returns to Mallorca, he shall explain to the world what he has seen and convey the message of King Arthur, which gives rise to the literary mission laid upon him (Badia 1991).

At all events, the key moment of the narrative occurs when Guillem asks Arthur the reason for his sadness (ed. Vicent Santamaria 2011: 312, lines 1110–15). Arthur asks Guillem to look at his sword, in which can be seen the 'mala felonia' that has come into the world. Guillem then inspects the sword and sees that on one side of the blade there are some men with blindfolded eyes, who are happy and content ('jolis e beau', line 1165), while on the other he can see men with their hands and feet tied, like unhappy wretches uttering great lamentations. The king then explains to Guillem, who has not understood the message, what its meaning is (ed. Vicent Santamaria 2011: 312, lines 1162–83): those with their eyes blindfolded 'sont les riches roys' (line 1163) who scorn honour and valour and, if they are content, it is because avarice, that repugnant vice, has ensured that they are laden with possessions, but bereft of merit and valour. Those who are tied hand and foot are those who value valour but, through incapacity or poverty, cannot impose their valour and firmness on the world.

Of the explanation by Arthur, and in particular of line 1163, there are two different readings which lead to two different interpretations: 'rics reis' for Espadaler (1986: 144), but 'rics indignes' for Badia (ed. 2003b: 149–52). While for some we are faced with a moralising discourse (Badia 1991, 2003b), for others it would contain a monarchical and political statement (Espadaler 1986, 1999).[19] Bohigas and Vidal Alcover (1984: ix) already noted the possibility of a political ulterior motive relating to the successor of the last king of the royal house of Mallorca, the Infant Jaume IV of Mallorca (1337–75). In this case the work could be alluding to the unfortunate prince, to his return and to the restoration of the royal dynasty of Mallorca. Going more deeply into this question, Espadaler believes that the words of Arthur, criticising the blindness and avarice of the kings, could not have passed unnoticed by any Mallorcan who received this message around 1370, since the memory of the loss of the throne by the native dynasty at the battle of Llucmajor (1349) was still alive. The victory of Pere el Cerimoniós meant the annexation of the kingdom of Mallorca to the Crown of Aragon. The last legitimate king of Mallorca, Jaume III, having disappeared in the middle of the century, in Mallorca during the last quarter of the century a king was, above all, that figure who was no longer present, and the 'Britons', named thus scornfully, who supported Jaume IV, still hoped that the pretender to the throne would return from his imprisonment in the Castell Nou in Barcelona (Toldrà 1992–3: 475–6). The evident parallels between *La Faula* and the Arthurian myth could demonstrate that we are not faced with an innocent, artistic work, but with an unequivocally political text that makes use of Arthurian fiction to transmit a particular message (Espadaler 1986: 144; 1999: 16).

Badia, and also Toldrà (1992–3), on the other hand, indicate the inconsistency of this reading, basing themselves on the lack of originality of the ideas developed in the brief Arthurian excursus, and the more so since there are no explicit facts to support this messianic reading involving the return of a lost king. Behind the message of Torroella, Badia sees a *locus classicus* of moralisation of power and fortune, related to the discourse on the decadence of chivalric values and the remedies that will have to be applied. In this way, the work of Torroella would have to be included within moralising literature and placed in the tradition of Catalan writing in the XIVth and XVth century that treats the same topics (Badia 1993b: 98; 2003b: 23–5).

La Faula had an immediate and important literary impact. Not only are four manuscripts of it preserved, the majority of them fragments transmitted in *cancioneros* (a fact which attests to a specific textual transmission which must be aligned with that of *Jaufré*), but also its traces are detectable in the narrative structure of the *Cobles de la divisió del regne de Mallorques* by Anselm Turmeda, written in 1398, in the *Llibre de Fortuna e Prudència* of Bernat Metge, written in 1381, and in chapters 189–202 of *Tirant lo Blanc* by Joanot Martorell, which we will discuss below (Arretxe and Vich 1993; Badia 1993b).

3. The Influence of the Prose Romans on the Catalan Romances of Chivalry and on the Historiography of the Late XVth Century

The prose *roman*, as we have seen so far, was introduced and diffused in its original language during the reigns of Jaume II and Pere el Cerimoniós, was translated into Catalan thanks to the direct or indirect encouragement of Infant Joan I, and inspired the first native products such as *La Faula* of Torroella and the anonymous *Blandín de Cornualla*. Once we reach the XVth century, the use of Arthurian materials culminates in the two Catalan romances of chivalry par excellence: the anonymous *Curial e Güelfa* (written during the 1450s or 1460s) and *Tirant lo Blanc* by Joanot Martorell (begun in 1460, published in 1490), at the same time as its popularity seems to have become exhausted after the appearance of the *Tragèdia de Lançalot* of Mossèn Gras.

Both these romances appear at an historically significant moment for Catalan literature. The accession to the throne of the Castilian Trastámara dynasty, after the death without issue of Martí I l'Humà, apparently did not affect the relationship between the world of culture and royal power, and, whilst one can observe a growing independence of literature thanks to the spread of knowledge and the erosion of the formerly closed boundaries between traditional cultural sectors, the court continued to be the place where literature was consumed and, moreover, the place where the literary fashions to follow were established (Badia 1993a; Turró 2001: 104).

For Alfons V el Magnànim, too, literature and art formed part of a genuine programme of political propaganda by the monarchy, and in this sense the king sought, through iconography, to legitimise firstly his government, and secondly his own person as the monarch endowed with all the qualities necessary to carry out the highest enterprises (García Marsilla 1996–7: 39–40; 2001: 21–4; Beltrán Llavador 2006b: 122–6). Through images he succeeded in causing a much more direct and noticeable impact on society, and the king knew better than anyone how to exploit their potential by incorporating, for example, chivalric emblems derived from Arthurian literature in the creation of his personal image. In his devices the symbol that appears with the greatest frequency, of Arthurian origin and not lacking a subliminal messianic royal message, is that of the 'Siti Perillós', represented by a high-backed armchair in flames, sometimes surrounded by various texts in Latin or in Catalan. The symbol, an imitation of the empty seat at the Round Table destined to be occupied only by the knight of perfect virtue who will find the Holy Grail, when applied to the life of the king, could be interpreted as the throne of Naples, which he alone was destined to occupy. Implicitly, through this symbol it would be necessary to associate him with Galahad himself. The first use of the device is documented in 1426, and from then on its use is constant on the monarch's campaign tent, on the ceramics of the royal palaces at Valencia and Naples, on royal galleys, on the garments of the members of his personal guard, on the king's clothing, and on the most diverse utensils for daily use.

It was not, however, simply the 'Siti Perillós' that Alfons V el Magnànim used; he also employed other Arthurian motifs in the scenery of jousts and tournaments to show off his military prowess which also had the same propaganda intention. Thus, for example, for the decorations he ordered to be constructed for the ludic spectacle he had organised in Valencia in 1426, he commanded the construction of a 'gran castell de fusta appellat de la Fada Morgana en lo qual havia V torres', in which the king and three of his high officers would defend themselves against the assault of their rivals (García Marsilla 1996: 37–9; 2001: 27–8).

Like Alfons V, other men of the XVth century organised feats of arms, jousts and tournaments inspired by the French romances of chivalry (Riquer 1967: 68–9). While these knights, at the height of the XVth century, relied upon literature to give free rein to their chivalric amusements, at the same time literature was filled by historical characters from a remote or recent past who were depicted as carrying out fictitious actions with a high degree of verisimilitude, linked in some fashion to their original historical deeds, as is the case in *Curial e Güelfa* (Varvaro 2001: 162; Beltrán Llavador 2010: 448–9). In this sense, particular significance attaches to the presence of Boucicaut and other French knights like Guillaume du Chastel alongside the by now classic Lancelot, Tristan, Gauvain or Brunor in this chivalric romance, whose anonymous author, through the assimilation of Classical culture and its coexistence with sources from the romance tradition (among them the Arthurian *roman*) sets out to offer an ethical and literary message related to certain intellectual preoccupations that he shared with his readers (Cingolani 1994: 147–50, 158–9; Pujol 2002: 35).

Nonetheless, this coexistence can be called into question if we bear in mind that for the anonymous author Arthurian literature as entertainment remains in second place, and precedence is given to new models derived from the rediscovery of the Latin classics from the pens of men of 'reverenda lletradura' such as Dante, Boccaccio and Petrarch. According to Badia and Torró, it is no accident, then, that the linguistic note made by the anonymous author makes use of the past when he indicates that out of respect for tradition (and for the Catalan translators of *Lancelot* and the *Tristan en prose*) he will use the Gallicism 'errar':

> En aquest llibre se fa menció de cavallers errants, jatsia que és mal dit 'errants', car deu hom dir 'caminants'. 'Erre' és vocable francès, e vol dir 'camí', e 'errar' vol dir 'caminar'. Emperò jo vull seguir la manera d'aquells catalans qui traslladaren los llibres de Tristany e de Lançalot, e tornaren-los de llengua francesa en llengua catalana, e totstemps digueren 'cavallers errants', car aquest vocable 'errants', que vol dir 'caminants', null temps lo volgueren mudar, ans lo lleixaren així, no sé la raó per què. E així diré jo 'errar' per 'caminar', seguint la costuma dels antics, jatsia que parlaré impropi e seré algun poc digne de reprensió. (ed. Badia and Torró 2011: 65–8, 218)[20]

At the same time, it is in these episodes of knight errantry of Curial that this protagonist shows himself most critical and belligerent with the most cruel and violent aspect of Arthurian knighthood, that is to say, those elements which cause chivalry to depart from its most noble, courtly and festive aims (Badia and Torró 2010). In this sense, we could compare the attitude of Curial to that of Dinadan in the *Tristan en prose*.

Joanot Martorell, on the other hand, as a good knight, delights in each and every aspect of chivalry in *Tirant lo Blanc*: the festive, the cruel, the bellicose (with a crusade included), because his intention is to present a hero capable of recovering the lost prestige of knighthood. For this reason, he turns his gaze, among other sources, towards the Arthurian *Vulgate* in a series of chapters that have a markedly doctrinal and exemplary tone, in which the author evokes the mythical past of chivalry, since it is not insignificant that Tirant is Breton and belongs to the lineage of Uther Pendragon, the father of King Arthur (Sales Dasí 1991). It is well known that the basic sources of the first part of *Tirant* (chs 1–39) are *Guy de Warwick* and the *Llibre de l'orde de cavalleria* of Ramon Llull which had already been combined in *Guillem de Varoic*, the first version of these introductory episodes, which Martorell later expanded and revised in converting them into the opening of his romance, returning frequently to the original sources and adding other texts which nuance the meaning of the initial discourse, among them *Lancelot du Lac* (Riquer 1990: 95–7, 257–71; Badia 1993b; Ramos 1995; Pujol 2002: 39–49).

The presence of the Arthurian tradition is, however, more obvious with the inclusion of *La Faula* of Torroella, which Martorell used deliberately in chapters 189–202 of *Tirant*. These episodes, known as the 'entremès del rei Artús', describe the feasts which the emperor of Constantinople organises to receive the Muslim ambassadors of the Sultan of Cairo, during the course of which the performance of this interlude takes place. This must be related to the mimes and performances typical of the XVth century and documented in the context of the courtly theatre of the royal household (Hauf 1990a). After lunch, there come before the emperor four ladies, Honor, Castedat, Sperança and Bellea, informing him that there has arrived at court a ship bearing Morgana, who has been fruitlessly seeking the famous King Arthur for four years. The emperor, followed by all his knights, heads for the harbour, and goes aboard the mysterious ship where he encounters Morgana dressed completely in mourning. He explains to her that he has in his power a knight of great presence, whose name he does not know, who has a remarkable sword, Escalibor, and who is accompanied by an aged knight called Fe-Sens-Pietat (Breus sans Pitié). Morgana accompanies the emperor to meet the knight and is led to a room in which the latter is in a cage with silver bars, absorbed in contemplating his sword. Morgana at once recognises her brother, but he does not know her, and Arthur begins an elaborate dissertation on the decadence of the present time, replying to questions posed to him without taking his eyes off his sword. Freed from the cage by the emperor, he continues his discourse, focusing on questions of chivalry, and, when the emperor removes his sword, Arthur neither sees nor knows anyone until Morgana passes a small ruby before his eyes and he recovers consciousness. The festivities continue until, after dinner, all head back to the ship, and take leave of Morgana, Arthur and the ladies. All are amazed at what they had seen, which appears to have been done entirely by enchantment. Thus Martorell turns King Arthur into a kind of oracle capable of replying to every question put to him as if he were an authentic source of knowledge of chivalry (Riquer 1990: 150–6; Hauf 1990a; Badia 1993b; Alemany 2005b).

In other places Martorell alludes at length to Arthurian characters (Bohort, Galahad, Gauvain, Lancelot, Perceval and Tristan), whom he turns into examples of classic chivalry which must be recovered and taken as an example, giving pre-eminence among them to Lancelot (Sabaté and Soriano 2000: 1583–4).

One of the last exploitations of Arthurian fiction is produced during the second half of the XVth century when Mossèn Gras composed the brief *Tragèdia de Lançalot* which has reached us through a single damaged copy of an incunable. It is a reading and rewriting of the first chapters of the *Mort Artu* from the French *Vulgate* in the same classicising and sentimental mode as *Curial e Güelfa*. Gras condenses the French text, passing over the chivalric action and concentrating in particular on the emotional conflict between Lanzarote and Ginebra, in an attempt to give a Renaissance garb to motifs drawn from the Arthurian tradition (Riquer 1984: 34; Pujol 2002: 35).

One of the latest cases we can detect of the presence of Arthurian material in the texts of the Middle Ages is found, again, in historiography, and specifically in the *Cròniques d'Espanya* of the royal archivist and treasurer Pere Miquel Carbonell, a work begun in 1495 and completed in 1513, although it would not be published until 1547. Although Carbonell defends in his prologue the veracity, rigour and exhaustiveness of his compilation and of his duty as chronicler, since he has found in other historical works that great error has been committed by not verifying the materials with the result that there have been included 'molts errors, rondalles e coses increhibles [...] per defectes de no haver hagut o fundament dels predits auctors aprovats de les gestes dels quals han scrit, o per culpa dels transcriptors' (ed. Alcoberro 1997: I, 171–2), his objective is somewhat undermined by the insertion of a long excursus on King Arthur in the section dedicated to the Gothic kings and in particular in his account of Theodoric. Carbonell, as other chroniclers before him had done (Soriano 2007), does not wish to fail to recapitulate what has been written about the king and therefore devotes to him a little more than two pages, relating in summary fashion his warlike deeds and his successes just as Geoffrey of Monmouth tells them, even if Carbonell's actual source is unknown.[21]

In the XVIth century, the references in Catalunya to the *matière de Bretagne*, its characters, and its plots begin to decline in frequency, as happens in the rest of the Peninsula. The characters to whom reference was formerly made as exemplars of good knighthood or as lovers tend to be replaced by other examples, under the influence of humanism. Symptomatic of this situation is the fact that the list of knights recorded by Muntaner in chapter 51 (Rotlan, Oliver, Tristany, Llancelot, Galeàs, Parceval, Palamides, Borus, Escors de Mares, Morat de Gaunes) is drastically reduced in the edition of his *Crònica* that was printed in 1558: there remain only Roland and Oliver, and the list is now headed by Alexander.

Notes

[1] It is impossible to list here every study devoted, to a greater or lesser extent, to examining the reception of the *matière de Bretagne* in Catalunya and to analysing each and every one of the texts which mention its characters and motifs. For this, the reader should refer to the magnificent recent repertoire of Rafael M. Mérida Jiménez (2010); and to the studies of Antonio Contreras Martín (for the Lancelot material) and María Luzdivina Cuesta Torre (for the Tristan texts) in the present volume. I am extremely grateful to Glòria Sabaté for her patient reading of this study and her wise suggestions.

[2] It should be remembered that this reference dates from the year after Geoffrey of Monmouth completed the composition of his *Historia regum Britanniae* (c.1135/36). This is not the place to examine how knowledge of the *matière de Bretagne* reached the troubadours so rapidly and at so early a date; for this see Aurell (2007: 210–50).

[3] 'que no·l fassa semblar breto' (Riquer 1971: II, XXVIII line 38).

[4] De Caluwé (1981: 362) accurately notes that the troubadours, irrespective of their region of origin, were well aware of, and mentioned, Arthurian characters but 'à l'exception de la légende de Tristan et Iseut, ces sujets les ont manifestement peu impressionnés. Ils ne les évoquent en fait que dans des citations laconiques, au sein d'oeuvres qui son manifestement destinées à plaire aux souverains anglais ou catalans, ou alors ils s'en moquent.'

[5] 'E plass'a Dieu que·l plus dreyturiers vensa / qu'ieu ja nulh temps per bocelh de breto / no layssarai lo senhal de basto', lines 52–4 (Riquer 1975: III, CXII-337, 1597). The meaning of the expression 'bocelh de breto' seems to be far from being defined, although there is a consensus that it is to be related to the motif of the 'hope of the Britons'.

[6] The recent article by Espadaler (2014: 32–9) analyses the allusions to the *matière de Bretagne* made by these XIVth- and XVth-century poets. Here I record only the galleries of characters encountered in the two great XVth-century Catalan romances of chivalry. The anonymous author of *Curial e Güelfa* lists, in the feasts dreamed by Güelfa in Book III, the following: 'Aquí vírets Tisbes e Píramus fer-se meravellosa festa, Flors e Blancaflor, Tristany e Isolda, Lançalot e Genebra, Frondino e Brisona, Amadís e Oriana, Fedra ab Hipòlit, Aquil·les tot sol menaçant son fill Pirro, Tròiol e Briseida, París e Viana e molts altres, del quals, per no ésser llong, me callaré' (ed. Badia and Torró 2011: 516). In *Tirant lo Blanc*, Joanot Martorell also includes one of these 'galleries', depicted on the walls of one of the rooms in the palace of the emperor of Constantinople: 'E lo capità pres del braç a la emperadriu e entraren en una cambra molt ben emparamentada e tota a l'entorn storiada de les següents amors. De Floris e de Blanchesflors, de Tisbe e de Píramus, de Eneas e de Dido, de Tristany e de Isolda, e de la reyna Ginebra e de Lançalot, e de molts altres que totes llurs amors de molt subtil e artificial pintura eren divisades' (chs 117–18, ed. Hauf 2008: 469, 473 and 475–6 n. 1). Further on, in ch. 189, Martorell makes use of them again in the production of the *entremès del rei Artús*; in this case, with the exception of the first two pairs (Ginebra-Lançalot, Tristany-Isolda), the others are taken from Ovidian texts (ed. Hauf 2008: 790, 802 n. 29).

[7] In both cases what Muntaner is trying to do is to enhance the figure of Pere I el Gran, and therefore the French knights are cited, yet again, as a point of comparison. We read in chapter 51: 'E en aquell puig se faïen tots dies tan grans fets d'armes, que no era en comptar. E qui volia veure ardiment e bondat de senyor, vós la pògrets veure en aquell lloc, que, con lo torneig era mesclat e lo senyor rei coneixia que els crestians n'havien lo pijor, ell brocava enmig de la pressa e feria entre ells. Mas no us cuidets que anc Rotlan ne Oliver ne Tristany, Llancelot ne Galeàs ne Parceval ne Palamides ne Borus ne Escors de Marès ne el Morat de Gaunes ne neguns altres poguessen fer tots dies ço que el rei En Pere faïa; e aprés d'ell tots los rics hòmens, cavallers, almogàvers e hòmens de mar qui lla eren' (ed. Soldevila 2011: 101). In chapter 134: 'E tot açò esdevenia per la gran amor que havien al senyor rei e per ço que li veïen fer de ses mans. Que ço que el rei faïas no era obra de cavaller, mas obra de Déu pròpriament; que Galeàs ne Tristany ne Llançalot ne Galvany ne Boors ne Palamides ne Perceval lo Galois ne el Cavaller ab la Cota mal tallada ne Estor de Mares ne el Morant de Gaunes, con tots ensems fossen ajustats ab tan poca gent con lo senyor rei d'Aragon era, no pogren tant fer en un jorn contra quatre-cents cavallers tan bons con aquells ere, qui eren la flor del rei de França, con féu lo senyor rei d'Aragó e aquells qui ab ell eren aquella hora' (ed. Soldevila 2011: 242–3). King Arthur is also a point of comparison as the ideal monarch around whom there come together the best knights, as in chapter 66: 'D'altra part, que sabia lo cor del rei En Pere, que era lo mellor cavaller del món e que menava ab si sos bons cavallers de sa terra, que anc lo rei Artús no hac a la Taula Redona' (ed. Soldevila 2011: 116).

[8] Chapter 161: 'E aquí feu-se la pus bella festa e el pus bell fet d'armes que anc en torneig se faés, del rei Artús a ençà' (ed. Soldevila 2011: 277).

[9] A comparison also made with the extremely lengthy *Lancelot du Lac* in ch. 128 (Riquer 1984: I, 464; ed. Soldevila 2011: 230). The references to *Jaufré* are as follows: ch. 116: 'Que tantes de cavalleries e de fets d'armes s'hi faïen en los llocs que prenien, que en neguna història del món no oïres de majors meravelles que les gents qui eren ab lo senyor infant e l'almirall faïen; que cent, entre rics hòmens e cavallers, de catalans e d'aragoneses, havia en aquella cort, que de cascun d'ells, de llurs proeses e cavalleries, pogra hom fer major romanç que no és aquell de Jaufré.' (ed. Soldevila 2011: 208); ch. 148: 'que de cascun [...] pogra hom fer, de llurs proees e cavalleries e de tots fets d'armes, major llibre que no és lo Llibre de Jaufré' (ed. Soldevila 2011: 261).

[10] For the controversy on the dating of *Jaufré* and its authorship, see the references to the different positions and proposals indicated in the bibliography cited. See also Gaunt and Harvey 2006: 534–41.

[11] This is attested by a document from the king's chancery dated in Barcelona on 23 February 1352, in which the monarch orders the execution of works in that room: 'Queremos e us mandamos que de la cambra morisca de la Aliafaria en las paredes de la qual es pintada la Istoria de Jaufre, fagades arrancar todas las losas de piedra marmol, e feyt la enrajolar o trespolar en manera que sea exuta e bien seca quando nos seremos alla' (Rubio y Lluch 1908–21: I, 159–60, doc. CLX).

[12] Almost two centuries later, Jaume Roig, in his *Spill o Llibre de les dones* (*c*.1460) would give a misogynist reading of the legend of the conception of Jaume I as a further example of the malice of women (lines 2317–46) (Carré 2007: 164).

[13] The only writer to refer to her is the Franciscan Francesc Eiximenis, who frequented this court in the capacity of a spiritual counsellor, when he cited her in his *Dotzè del Crestià* (chs 894–5) with the intention of moral exemplarity; however, the allusion is a second-hand one (Hauf 1990b: 10–12). This Minorite Friar also supported, at times, the censure of readings such as the *Tristan en prose* (Riquer 1997: 54). Ramón de Perellós, a diplomat in the service of Joan I, is the author of the *Viatge al Purgatori de Sant Patrici*, in which we encounter an allusion to Gauvain and to the Chevalier à la Cote Mal Taillée that is a little disconcerting. On his journey back from Ireland, explains Perellós, on reaching the Island of Britain and heading for London, in the port of 'Daureont, hon vi lo cap de Galuany, car aqui mori, he ayssimeteys la cota mal tallada car ayssi se appelaue aquel cauailler que la portaua.' Elsewhere he alludes to the 'ylla de Armant, que fo del rey de cent caualles en lo temps del rey Artus' (ed. Miquel y Planas 1914: 172, 141 respectively).

[14] In the case of Catalunya and in accordance with the information produced by the documentary sources, there was no reader, whether belonging to the royal houseold or to lower social strata, who owned a complete set of the entire *Vulgate* cycle, in contrast to (as Cingolani points out) what was happening in the great seigneurial libraries of northern Italy, for example, that of the Este of Ferrara, the Gonzaga of Mantua, or the Visconti-Sforza of Milan in Pavia. On these libraries see Daniela Delcorno Branca (1998a:14–15). I am greatly indebted to Carme González Graell for informing me of the new Puigcerdà fragments which she is currently editing. and for granting me access to them.

[15] Whilst scholars are not unanimous in establishing a precise chronology for the translations from French to Catalan, the one considered here is that proposed by Cingolani based on the study of the indirect references found in documentary sources (chancery registers and *post mortem* inventories). Compare also Pujol, for whom a complete *Queste del Graal* and fragments of *Lancelot* and *Tristan* (Sharrer 1977: 17–18, 20, 25–6), translated probably during the first half of the century, are the surviving remnants (Pujol 2006: 632); see the chapters by Lucía Megías, Contreras and Cuesta in the present volume.

[16] It should be borne in mind, as Aurell notes (1996: 167) that we are still far from the introduction of printing, so that the reproduction and collection of copies was for a privileged few.

[17] Cingolani (1995) gives an assessment of the form and style of *Blandín* and a comparison with other Romance-language texts, among which there stands out *Rainaldo e Lesengrino*, a brief poem from northern Italy with which *Blandín* shows a great similarity in formal and technical terms (irregular metre, with strong caesura, assonanting rhyme, the use of formulae, lines and entire passages repeated), and a textual tradition and physical production characteristics that are almost identical. *Rainaldo* is a 'popular' poem, whose formal characteristics should be attributed to the deficient technical capacity of its author, probably a jongleur, and the need for oral recitation. In this sense the term 'popular' would define a type of text and reception that is not from the 'high' context of courtly or upper bourgeois literature, but that refers, rather, to a type of 'low' reception, directed to a public of lower status. This type of audience would explain the formal characteristics of *Blandín*, which have not been understood by critics focusing on another type of diffusion of the text by including it within the category of Arthurian narrative, and linking it, consequently, to the type of diffusion associated with that category.

[18] Contemporarily, there develops the anonymous *Frare-de-Goig i Sor-de-Plaer*, *noves rimades*, which has many points of contact with the Neo-Arthurian *roman Perceforest* (Riquer 1984: II, 256).

[19] The different positions, which are summarised here in their general outlines, have been examined in detail by S. Vicent Santamaria (2005, 2007, 2008 and 2011 ed.).

[20] 'In this book mention is made of "knights errant", although "errant" is used wrongly, because one should say "travelling" : "erre" is a French word, and means "way" and "errer" means to "travel". But I intend to follow the usage of those Catalans who translated books about Tristan and Lancelot and turned them from the French into Catalan language. They always said "knights errant;" for they were never willing to alter this word "errant", meaning "travelling", and so they left it, for what reason I cannot tell. So I shall say "errant" for "travelling" also, following the old usage, although I shall be speaking incorrectly and be rather deserving of reproach' (ed. Waley 1982: 69–70).

[21] In another later chronicle, the *Història general de Catalunya* compiled by Antoni Viladamor in the second half of the XVIth century, we encounter a brief reference to Arthur. Here, when Vilamor deals with King Reccared, he explains how the latter was married to Queen Badda, of whom it seems that few details were collected by historians with the exception of 'Garivay que diu era filla del rey Artur de Inglaterra' (ed. Miralles 2007: 690). The reference, therefore, is a second-hand one, from Garibay. On Badda in post-medieval Spanish and Portuguese historiography, see also Hook 2004.

VI

THE MATTER OF BRITAIN IN SPANISH SOCIETY AND LITERATURE FROM CLUNY TO CERVANTES

Carlos Alvar

Originating in France, the Order of Cluny established itself in the Iberian Peninsula from the end of the XIth century. The rulers of the four Christian kingdoms of that era (León, Castile, Navarre and Aragon) not only favoured the recently arrived monks in founding new monasteries, but also procured their rise to the highest positions at the head of the hierarchy of the Hispanic Church; the Visigothic tradition was ruptured by the massive influx of French monks, and was replaced by a new model. Likewise, the culture inherited from the Visigoths – some of them as eminent as Isidore of Seville – was replaced: the 'Visigothic' script, more difficult to read than the Carolingian, was replaced; Charlemagne became the liberating hero for Christians against the Arab invaders and, naturally, it would be the French emperor who opened the road that facilitated pilgrimage to Santiago de Compostela. The great efforts and achievements of Charlemagne would serve to justify the presence of so many French monks, the imposition of new liturgical models and the rejection of the autochthonous religiosity and culture, with the resulting relegation of clergy trained in the Peninsular kingdoms.

During the XIIth century, the monarchs supported all the changes and underlined the 'Europeanisation' of their territories through marriage with foreign princesses and the presence of successive waves of crusaders, who experienced very uneven fortunes in the Peninsular wars against the Muslims. The Hispanic political situation in the XIIth century was an extremely troubled one, with kingdoms uniting, territories separating, independence and conquests; the kingdom of Castile imposed itself little by little over the others, despite the divisions provoked by Alfonso VII (1126–57), which again separated Castile and León-Galicia, and also resulted in the independence of Portugal. Aragon and Navarre also separated, on the death of Alfonso I (1104–34), after half a century in union. Castile and León did not reunite once more until 1230, with Fernando III (1217–52), this time definitively. Aragon, Navarre, and Castile-León were only united in any sense from the period of the Catholic Monarchs (1469). The County of Barcelona constituted, with the kingdom of Aragon, the Crown of Aragon (under Alfonso II, from 1164); the Crown expanded its dominion over various Pyrenean counties, the County of Provence, and the territories conquered from the Muslims or elsewhere in the Mediterranean (Mallorca, Valencia, Sicily, Corsica, Sardinia and Naples). The marriage of the

Catholic Monarchs brought about the union of the kingdoms of Castile-León and those that formed the Crown of Aragon.

This turbulent political scene in the XIIth century demanded alliances with rulers who could intervene in the conflicts were it necessary to do so. Alfonso VII of Leon and Castile was the son of Raymond of Burgundy, and the father-in-law of Louis VII of France through the marriage of his daughter Constanza (1152); Alfonso VIII of Castile married Eleanor who was the daughter of Henry II of England (1170), and married his own daughter Blanca to Louis VIII of France. Ramon Berenguer III, count of Barcelona, had married Dulce of Provence in 1112. This matrimonial policy was maintained throughout the XIIIth century.

This brief historical note is necessary in order to understand on the one hand the various routes by which European influence penetrated Iberia, and on the other the cultural independence – associated with political independence – of the various Peninsular kingdoms: Aragon looked towards the south of France; Castile was attracted by the domains of Aquitaine and disputed them with England; Portugal sought alliances with the Military Orders, with England and with Burgundy. The symbols of Peninsular spirituality, moreover, became the Road to Santiago and the presence of French monks of the Order of Cluny.

I. The Earliest Witnesses

1. Visual Arts

It is not surprising that from a very early date there should begin to appear traces of the presence of Arthurian themes in the Iberian Peninsula. As in Italy, moreover, the earliest evidence is provided by iconographic representations in churches, although in contrast to the Italian examples the identification of Arthurian characters arises from interpretations by modern scholars since in the Hispanic cases the names of the characters represented are not specified. Hence, there exists some uncertainty about the issue.

To the first decade of the XIIth century belongs the relief on the shaft of a column from the Puerta Francigena (the destroyed north portal) of the cathedral of Santiago de Compostela. In it can be made out a knight in a boat, covered with his shield; he is recumbent, asleep or – more surely – badly wounded after combat, to judge by the position of his head, and his unsheathed sword; at his feet there is an animal which could be either a dog or a horse. There is a nick in the blade of the sword. Another two scenes represented there are more difficult to identify, since they represent a wounded knight and a lady, and a warrior who is defending his horse against an attack by birds of prey.

There is a parallel between the scene depicted and the episode in the story of Tristan in which there is related the voyage that brings the protagonist to Ireland after the combat with Morholt (Moralejo 1985: 58). The deterioration of the relief and the early date of its execution are not an insuperable obstacle to considering that it illustrates a scene from this legend, half a century before the surviving texts and a decade earlier than the famous archivolt of Modena. Among other possible identifications of the individual depicted, however, it has been suggested that it could be a representation of Ulysses (Prado-Vilar 2010). The problem is examined in more detail in the chapter by Pilar Lorenzo in this volume.

Another relief, also in Galicia, seems to represent the *Chevalier au lion* of Chrétien de Troyes. On a tympanum from the Cistercian monastery of Santa Maria de Penamaior (Lugo), from the first half of the XIIIth century, Rocío Sánchez Ameijeiras (2003) has identified as Yvain the figure on the left, a knight who advances with his lance couched, followed by a riderless horse beneath a tree, a clear indication that this is a knight who has been victorious in combat, and who has unseated his opponent (who would be the seneschal Keu); the lion to the right is essential to the identification of the knight, since both elements are associated in the story by Chrétien. The circle at the centre, the square beneath it, and the tree with the birds would represent schematically the fountain, the pillar on which the water falls, and the tree which provides shade; the lion on the right, facing in the same direction as the knight, shows the association of both in the same enterprise. This representation relates to a tradition that was widely diffused thanks to the Cistercian monks, who identified in the most distinguished knights of the Round Table the exemplarity demanded from the *milites Christi*.

In the inscription on the tympanum is the text DIDACUS P | ERA MCC:IV:I, in other words, 'P. Didacus, era 1204', equivalent to the year AD 1166, and which must refer to the year of the foundation of the church, not to that of the carving of the tympanum, which is considerably later, since it must be placed around the year 1225 in which the house acquired the status of an abbey after decades of decline. The protection of King Alfonso IX of León and of the powerful Traba clan was central to the new development of the monastery.

To these scanty pieces of information must be added those obtained from the milieu of King Pedro IV 'el ceremonioso' of Aragon (1336–87), which do not survive today: mural paintings with the 'estoria de Jaufré' which were in the palace of the Aljafería at Zaragoza (documented in 1352); the tapestry with 'las historias de los caballeros de la Tabla Redonda' bought by Queen Leonor of Sicily, wife of the Aragonese king, for her daughters in 1356 in the south of France; the tapestry with the story of King Arthur bought in Paris by Pedro IV for his wife in 1368; and the trappings, used for the entry of Pope Martin V into Valencia in 1402, in which there figured Tristan and Isolde among other famous lovers (Sánchez Ameijeiras 2003: 297–8; Loomis and Loomis 1938: 26–7; Soriano in the present volume).

Dodds (1979) has also interpreted as Arthurian the subjects of the paintings in one of the false vaults of the Hall of the Kings or of Justice at the Alhambra of Granada.

The existence of seven different scenes can be distinguished there, separated by huntsmen. Six of the scenes can be related directly to western art, and specifically to the French tradition: the sequence involves an adaptation of the episode of the encounter of Tristan and Isolde near the fountain, which is mingled with the iconography of the Fountain of Love. Further on a wild man has captured a lady, and is attacked by a Christian knight; the lady holds a chained lion, a possible reminiscence of the episode of the 'Bridge of the Sword' in which Lancelot has to confront the animal after successfully overcoming the test. Next comes a couple playing chess, while a knight fights against a lion, in what could be scenes derived from the legend of Tristan and that of Lancelot. The ensemble thus seems to mix different motifs, without there being a single story or any narrative continuity among them, thus making it obvious that on the part of the artist there was an absence of any interest in, or a failure to understand, the model being followed. The similarity of the images with the figures that adorn French ivory caskets of the first half of the XIVth century is evident; in these, frequently, the same episodes as are illustrated at the Alhambra are represented. The contiguity of the scenes on the ivory caskets would no doubt have contributed to the confusion of the artist, who was unaware of the text which underlay the iconography. The painter was a Muslim and followed the techniques of the Mudejars who were working under the orders of Pedro I in Castile. The artist, then, must have fulfilled a commission of Mohamed V between 1350 and 1375, when the Nasrid ruler was preoccupied with maintaining his political prestige among Muslims, and also with the Christians: his palace, recently renovated, contained the same kind of mural paintings as the palaces of the western aristocracy, as Ibn Jaldun indicated. The superiority of the Arabs was obvious from the seventh scene, in which an Arab mortally wounds a Christian in combat, perhaps in a joust.

In fact, there are ivory caskets of French origin from the first half of the XIVth century, such as that preserved in the Louvre (Objets d'art, OA 10957–60), which presents all these motifs together, without any need to have recourse to the story of Lancelot. Thus, on the front panel there is a lady between wild men; a knight who is protecting the lady from her two attackers; under the lock of the casket there is a lion; then, the knight takes the lady and leaves her at the entrance to a castle or a walled city. The rear panel shows a character (Love) among the branches of a tree, who wounds Iseo (wearing a crown) and Tristan with his arrows; next there is a falconry scene; then the representation of the episode of the meeting between the two lovers at a fountain, and, finally, the game of chess. On the left-hand side of the casket some knights return to the castle after a day's hunting, and carry the head of the white stag. On the right-hand side, there is a falconry scene.

The origin and purpose of these pictures in so alien a location in relation to the western tradition as the Arab palace of the Alhambra are now clear. They were executed in the mid-XIVth century, at the moment of the greatest success and diffusion of Arthurian literature in the Iberian Peninsula. It must not, however, be forgotten that, as stated above, these identifications are based on interpretations by scholars, and that courtly scenes are frequently encountered in caskets of this period. Hence the different view of those who consider that the scenes in the Alhambra could relate to the story of Flores and Blancaflor, as well known in the XIVth century as the legend of Tristan, and, like the latter, also depicted widely on ivory luxury objects of French origin such as mirror-backs, caskets, and suchlike.

As far as illumination is concerned, the outstanding discovery is the recent find of fifty-nine fragments of a Castilian *Tristán* of the beginning of the XVth century, encountered in 1999 by the present writer and José Manuel Lucía Megías (BNE MS 22644; Alvar and Lucía 1999: 9–135); these fragments are to be added to those already in existence, and increase the surviving fragments of the same manuscript (MS 20262/19, described by Bonilla y San Martín 1904: 25–8), but also add twenty-five miniatures to the scanty repertoire of medieval Hispanic illumination. In these images are depicted the most distinguished knights of the world of Tristan, and at times they are identified by their respective names.

Among the possessions of Queen Isabel I of Castile there is mentioned a tapestry with Arthur and Galahad (Sánchez Cantón 1950: 112, 114, 146), but nothing is known about it; it may possibly have been manufactured in workshops in France or the Low Countries, like so many other works of art from the Catholic Queen's collection.

2. Onomastics

Personal names provide more indications of knowledge of Arthurian characters. It is clear that this involves a type of information that must be treated with extreme caution, since at best it merely attests the existence of a fashion, which is not necessarily of indigenous origin, since frequently the model followed could have arrived from other countries. The presence of individuals of French origin in the north of the Iberian Peninsula from the end of the XIth century was favoured by the establishment there of the Order of Cluny and by the abundant fiscal exemptions and incentives of every kind granted by the monarchs, which facilitated its establishment along the Road to Santiago and in the principal urban nuclei of Christian Spain (Défourneaux 1949; Lapesa 1980: 199–203).

It is no easy matter, then, to know if the personal names represent a superficial or a profound knowledge of Arthurian material in Hispanic territory; if they relate to foreign fashions and belong to immigrants from beyond the Pyrenees; or if they identify subjects of the Peninsular kingdoms who were baptised by French clergy, or whose parents took as their inspiration a Cluniac monk who had this name. Moreover, sometimes inherited patronymics may be involved, or various occurrences of a particular name refer to the same individual. These are legitimate doubts which allow us only to accept the existence of these names and the early familiarity with the relevant Arthurian characters, but the names do not in any way constitute a solid base for accepting knowledge of Arthurian literature in Christian Spain. Their historical existence is, however, beyond question, and the number of cases serves to show the development of a fashion that would become ever stronger thanks to the artistic and literary material.

David Hook (1991, 1993, 1996) has established a list of forty-three individuals earlier than the year 1300 who have Arthurian names; to this list the present writer has been able to add some further cases (Alvar 2013a). The evidence begins with a Leonese document of 1136/39 with Martinus Galuan, an individual who reappears in documents between 1156 and 1159. An Artús is encountered in 1151 in the area of Tavèrnoles (Alt Urgell); the document is dated by the fifteenth year of the reign of King Louis of France, which is to say either 1122 or 1151, according to which King Louis is involved. Then there appear Galas (1156), Merlin (1171?, although an alternative XIIIth-century date has subsequently been suggested for this document), and Merlim (1186); but there is no occurrence of any other name from the cycle, or instances of them are very rare: there is no trace of Yvain (which may have been assimilated into 'Juan' in the documents), nor (before 1300) of Perceval, Boores or Tristan, to list only the most distinguished knights of the Arthurian court. There is one Lanzarote, a member of the household of King Sancho IV, and this is also the name of one of the falcons of the infante Don Juan Manuel (who had another called Galván). Galicia, Portugal and León, on the one hand, and the Pyrenean region, from Navarre to Lérida, on the other, are the regions in which Arthurian personal names appear to have taken root, with a clear preference for the name 'Galvan'.

Table V.1: Early Arthurian Names

Date	Name	Place	Notes
1136/39?	Martinus Galuan	León	
1151	Artus	Tavèrnoles (Alt Urgell)	
1154–67?	Artus	Tavèrnoles (Alt Urgell)	
1156	Galas	Arenas (Castilla-León)	
1167	Guillem Artus	Tavèrnoles (Alt Urgell)	
1171?/s.XIII?	Merlin	Sahagún	
1178	Ciprianus Galuan	Antimio de Arriba (León)	
1178	Galvan	Medina del Campo	
1182	Galuan	Burgos	
1186	Martinus Merlim	Portugal	
1190	Merlinus	Portugal	
1193	Dominicus Galuan	Ranera	
1195	Galuan	Cabañeros	
1200	Arturus	Salamanca	
1203	Artus	Alagón-Veruela	

1204	Galuan	Roncesvalles	
1204	Galuan	Sahagún	
1205	Sancho Galuan	León	
1206	Artux	Burgos	
1208	Galvam	Portugal	
1210	Martinus Galuan	Carrizo (León)	
1211	Artux	Burgos	
1212	Sancius Galvan	Villaverde de Sandoval (León)	2 documents
1216	Juan Galvan	León; Santiago de Compostela, 1231.	
1217	Artus	Palencia	
1218	Enebra	Plasencia	
1220	Galuan de Carrione	Palencia	
1220	Galuan	Salamanca; 1227, 1230	3 documents
1223	Martin Galvan	Santillana del Mar	5 documents
1237	Pelayo Galvan	León, 1237, 1245	3 documents
1238	Pedro Galvánez	Nuez-Moreruela (León)	
1243	La Galvana	S. Pedro de Eslonza	
s.XIII, 2nd half	Merlín	Sahagún	
1251	Artus	Cerbillón (Huesca)	
1253	Ruy Galvan	San Pedro de Montes (León)	
1257	Johan Galvan	Ponferrada (León)	
1260?	Galuanya	Murcia	
1260?	Johan Artus	Murcia	2 documents
1260	Johan Galuan	León	
1262	Galuan de Niuela	Burgos, 1302, 1313	3 documents
1264	Ruy Galvan/Roderici Galuani	Salamanca 1265, 1270, 1298	4 documents
1264	Maria Galvánez de Astorga	Villa Garcia	
1264	Miguel Galuan	Villa García	
1269	Galuan	Audanzas	
1280	Pedro Galvan	S. Miguel de Fontalin	
1294	Sancha Galvan	Salamanca	
1295	Guillen Galvan	Aragón	
before 1295	Lançarote García Pérez	Castile	
1300	Galvan	Olite (Navarre)	

Their proximity to the route to Santiago and to the Cistercian monasteries could explain the geographical distribution of the names; the instances from Murcia are not important in this context, because they occur in the *Repartimientos*, that is to say, the registers of land grants made to individuals who had arrived there with the armies of Alfonso X at the conquest of the city from the Muslims and who were allotted properties; they would, then, have most probably come from Castile and León. From the XIVth century onwards the incidence of forenames or surnames of Arthurian origin increases. In Galicia, the name of Ginebra is repeatedly used in the family of Las Mariñas, since Teresa Ginebra Acuña Téllez Girón (born *c.*1395 to Martín Vázquez de Acuña, Conde de Valencia de Don Juan, a noble of Portuguese origin known in that kingdom as 'Dom Galaaz') was the mother of Teresa de Haro, wife of Gómez Pérez, lord of Las Mariñas; the grand-daughter of Ginebra de Acuña was Ginebra de Haro; Ginebra de Toro was probably the illegitimate daughter of Archbishop Fonseca (a lineage frequently allied to that of Las Mariñas). The name Ginebra endured among the lower and middle ranks of the Galician nobility, until at least during the the second half of the XVIth century, and it must be remembered that it was chosen by Valle Inclán for the protagonist of *Voces de gesta*, located in a past that was simultaneously real and legendary (Beceiro Pita 2007: 277 n. 96).

It is well known that the legend of Tristan and Iseo had a life quite independent of that of the Arthurian material; the early arrival in the Peninsula of the text of *Tristán de Leonís* and the rapid popularity that it achieved explains the frequency with which the name of the protagonist appears throughout the XVth century, a situation reinforced by the presence of some members of the Portuguese nobility, such as the Silvas, as refugees in the kingdom of Castile after the battle of Aljubarrota (1385): among the members of this family there were various individuals bearing the name 'Tristan'. The name is common both as a baptismal name and as a surname, as Hook established (Hook 1993: 70–5) and as may be seen from the two sections of Table V.2.

Table V.2: 'Tristán' as forename and byname or surname

Date	Personal Name	Place	Documents
c. 1350	Tristán Valdés		
c.1450–75	Tristán, son of Alvaro López	Pontevedra	
c. 1350	Tristán Valdés		
c. 1350	Tristán Valdés		
c. 1350	Tristán Valdés		
1475–85	Tristán de Leguizamo (Leguizamón)-Tristán Díaz de 'Laquiza'	Bilbao	4
1475–93	Tristán Daza-Tristán de Aza	Bilbao	2
1476	Tristán de Salazar		

1477	Tristán de Silva		
1478	Tristán de Arauso	Écija	
1479	Tristán Barma		
1480–96	Tristán de Espinosa	Cospedosa	
1482	Tristán Francés, *regidor*	Pontevedra	
1483	Tristán	Rabe (Medina del Campo)	
1484–8	Tristán de Medina		
1484	Tristán de las Casas	Osuna	
1485–99	Tristan Holguín-Tristán Holguin	Medellín	2
1485–7	Tristán de Villareal-Tristán de Villaherrael		2
1485	Tristán Vázquez	Bayona de Miño	
1485	Tristán de Silva	Córdoba?	
1486	Tristán Redondo	Cuenca	
1488	Tristán de Machileón	Valle de Arana	
1489–92	Tristán de Guevara	Tormantos	
1489–95	Tristán de Molina	Castillo de Garcimuñoz	
1489–90	Tristán de Valdés	Carreño (Asturias)	
1489–95	Tristán de Quesada	Seville	
1490–6	Tristán del Castillo-Tristán de Castillejo	Villanueva de Barcarrota-Candemuñó	6
1490	Tristán Ortiz	Sevilla	
1490	Tristán Cruzado	Almansa	
1490	Tristán de Silva		
1490–3	Tristán de Silva	Madrid	
1490	Tristán de Cepeda	Zamora	
1492	Tristán de Écija	Gómara	
1492	Tristán de Vallos	Alcaraz	
1492	Tristán de Arajo-Tristán de Araujo	Orense	2
1493	Tristán de Zúñiga	Palencia	
1493	Tristán Bogado- Tristán Govado	Portugal	
1494	Tristán de Silva	Ciudad Rodrigo	
1494–5	Tristán de Sandoval	Sotillo	
1494	Tristán de Merlo	Córdoba	

1494	Tristán de Gante		
1494	Tristán de Abrojo	Galicia	
1494	Tristán de Agramonte	Alcalá de Henares	
1494	Tristán de Çaballos	Camargo (Santander)	
1494–5	Tristán de Arcilla-Tristán de Arcila	Aranda	2
1494?–9	Tristán de Sahagún	Burgos	
1496	Tristán de Domesain	San Juan Pie de Puerto	
1497	Tristán de Azcue		
1498	Tristán de Molina		
1498	Tristán de la Peña	Guadarrama y Colmenar Viejo	
1498–9	Tristán de Quevedo	Jaén	
1499	Tristán de Ballesteros	Alcaraz	
1499	Tristán de Avendaño-Tristán de Aredaño-Tristán de Avedaño	Cuenca	
1499	Tristán Holguin		
1505	Tristán de León		
1505	Tristán		
1513	Tristán [Cavallero]?	Ciudad Real?	
1518	Tristán Enríquez, *notary*	Chantada (Lugo)	

Table of Surname Occurrence

1476	Catalina Tristán		
1477	Francisco Tristán		
1477	Juan de Tristán		
1484	Gonzalo Tristán		
1485–98	Juan Tristán	Seville	
1487–9	Martín Tristán		
1487–92	Francisco Tristán	Seville	
1489	Pedro Tristán	Camas	
1489	Lope Martínez de Tristánez	Mena	
1489	Juan Tristán	Utrera	
1490	Juan Tristán	Sanlúcar	
1490	Juan Tristán	Lebrija?	
1491	Juan Tristán	Medina del Campo	
1492	Gonzalo Tristán	Sevilla	
1493–9	Luis Tristán	Écija	
1495	Pero Tristán	Miruelo-Cudeyo?	

1497	Juan Tristán	Écija	
1498–9	Pedro Tristán, Juan Tristán		
1509	Diego Tristán	Granada	
1511–12	Rodrigo Tristán		
1513	Francisco Tristán	Toledo	

The presence of names of Arthurian origin in Galicia has been studied by Pardo de Guevara (2012: 86–94), and, in more detailed aspects, by Usero González (1986) and Dopico Blanco (2007). Pardo de Guevara emphasises two fundamental reasons in order to explain the relative frequency with which the Galician nobility gave the names of the knights of the Round Table to its offspring: on the one hand, the relations with Portugal from the death of Pedro I (1365), especially on the part of legitimist families opposed to the Trastámaras and supportive of English pretensions; and on the other, commercial relations between England and the Atlantic ports of Galicia. To these reasons one must add the decline of the old families which had supported King Pedro, which fell into disfavour after his fratricidal assassination at Montiel and which sought in the prestige of the Arthurian names an antiquity that would whitewash the more recent members of the family in the period of the Catholic Monarchs.

Half-a-dozen personal names are documented in Galician areas in the XVth and early XVIth century:

1. Ginebra
   Ginebra de Ribeiro, wife of Nuño Freire de Andrade, almost certainly of Portuguese origin.
   Cited above.
   Ginebra das Mariñas, *c.*1450–75, discussed above.
   Ginebra de Haro, married in 1508, from the family of the last-mentioned.
   Ginebra, daughter of Ares de Noguerol, who received a dowry in 1490, married the *regidor* of Betanzos, Ruy Domínguez de Vilouzás, and made her last will and testament in 1531.
   Ginebra, daughter of Juan de Noguerol, who inherited in 1508.
   Ginebra de Toro, possibly the natural daughter of Archbishop Fonseca, mentioned above.
   Ginebra de Deza, who married Gómez Moure, a merchant of Orense, in 1514.
   Ginebra de Araujo, who lived in the first half of the XVIth century and was married to Vasco de Romay, lord of the Coto de Quadro.
2. Lanzarote
   Lanzarote Mariño, documented at the end of the XVth century, lord of the Sierra and royal confectioner of Juan II.

'Lanzarote' is a name that appears in the Lago family in the region of Cedeira (Coruña) from the last third of the XVth century, when Lanzarote de Lago de Obaño 'O Vello' must have been born; he died in 1531. He was the son of Juan de Lago (d. 1510) and Leonor Rodríguez de Lago. He was a squire and in 1514 he married Isabel Gómez. His grandson Lanzarote de Lago e Andrade bore the same name; he was a captain, and the lord of the estate of Barallobre and a *regidor* of Pontedeume. He died before 1591.

3. Lionel

Lionel de Montaos, mentioned in the will of his father, Pedro Vermúdez de Montaos, in 1445.

Lionel de Limia, first Viscount of Vilanova de Cerveira, born before 1423 and died in 1495.

Lionel García, in Graña de Brión (Ferrol), who seems to have been a relative of Lanzarote de Lago de Obaño.

Lionel de Andrade, who lived in the second half of the XVth century. in Cerceda (Lugo).

Leondres López, documented in the area of the monastery of Meira in 1496, and dead before 1512.

4. Tristán

The name is documented in the lineage of the Cru y Montenegro family, in Pontevedra, from the middle of the XVth century; such is the case of Tristán, son of Alvaro López (Montenegro?), a merchant and ship-owner who met a violent death in 1479 but who was already of adult age in 1444. His second grandson bore the same name in the first half of the XVIth century.

Tristán de Tumiraos, a nobleman, is documented in Cedeira.

Tristán Francés was *regidor* of Pontevedra in 1482.

Tristán Enríquez was a notary in Chantada (Lugo) in 1518.

5. Iseo

An 'Isén' López is documented at the end of the XVth century, and another Isén de Lago in the XVIth century, both of them in the Eume area.

Iseo González Taboada, wife of Juan de Gayoso Noguerol, who drew up her will in 1529. She was the sister of Galaor Taboada, lord of Orbán, and a descendant of hers was Iseo de Taboada, daughter of Pedro Pardo de Trebolle, in the XVIth century.

Iseo Núñez de Berbetoros is documented in 1543.

In addition to these names, there is a Broos or Brooz (Bores) in Chanteiro, a Galván Díaz de Robles in Cedeira and a Héctor de Andrade in the same region at the end of the XVth century, which confirms the interest in Arthurian characters aroused in the lower nobility of the area, perhaps through the pretensions of the Lago family, in whose ancient coat of arms there was a tower over water and, protecting it, a lady with long hair, with a sword, who was no doubt identified with the Lady of the Lake (Dopico Blanco 2007: 1994).

It may be added that a bastard son of King Carlos III of Navarre and María Miguel de Esparza was called Lancelot (1386–1420); he rose to become vicar-general and apostolic administrator of the diocese of Pamplona, and patriarch of Alexandria. He is buried in Pamplona cathedral. The form of the name (Lancelot) reveals a clear borrowing from French, which is not surprising since Carlos III, born in France in 1361, was Count of Evreux (1387–1404) and Duke of Nemours (1404–25).

II. Literary References

Until the beginning of the XIIIth century there was no literature written in a Romance language in the Iberian Peninsula, with the exception of the *kharyas* or *jarchas* (short poems of two or three lines which formed the ending of compositions written in Arabic or Hebrew, and which have been dated to the middle of the XIIth century). It would, therefore, be futile to seek literary evidence containing references to the Matter of Britain.

From approximately 1200, there appear epic texts in Castilian (the *Poema del Cid*) and an abundant courtly poetry in Galician-Portuguese, in part following Provenzal models (*cantigas de amor* and *cantigas de escarnho*), and, in part, deriving from oral tradition (*cantigas de amigo*), which exhibits certain affinities with the Mozarabic *jarchas* and with the Castilian *villancicos* of two centuries later. In the Crown of Aragon, Catalan-speaking poets wrote in Provenzal, and, in this context, are usually studied among the troubadours of the south of France (Gaunt and Harvey 2006: 528–45).

In the *Libro de Alexandre*, which translates and reworks Gautier de Châtillon's *Alexandreis*, neither of the copyists of the two surviving manuscripts (Paris and Madrid) transmits the name of King Arthur as it appeared in the Latin original ('Arthuro Britones'). One of those copying the Castilian texts produced 'Cuemos preçian mucho por Artes los bretones' (Madrid, st. 1798a) while the other (Paris) wrote 'Commo se paresçian muchõ por orgullosos los bretones'. Both lines are incorrect, and it must be thought that the original of the Castilian version would have contained the name of King Arthur, like the Latin source text: 'Cuémo se precian mucho por Artús los bretones' (Lida 1945: 48; Hook 1996: 136), and that the copyists of this first translation, who understood neither the name of the king nor the sentence as a whole, blundered while carrying out their task. Were this the case, we would be faced with an early literary reference, although it would have little value as evidence for the diffusion of the Matter of Britain: for one thing, the date of the *Libro de Alexandre* is a matter of controversy, though it can be placed in the first third of the

XIIIth century (Alvar 1996; Casas Rigall 2007: 18–30); for another, it must not be forgotten that we are dealing with a translation, and, as such, the original witness belongs to another cultural domain.

The author of the *Libro de Alexandre* must have been a contemporary of Diego García de Campos, a canon of Toledo cathedral and a cleric of undoubted culture which he acquired during his theological education at the University of Paris, who went on to become the chancellor of Castile under Alfonso VIII. Diego García was the author of an allegorical and moral treatise, *Planeta* (1218), divided into seven books, like the spheres of the universe, whence the work's title. In the prologue, the author waxes lyrical in his praise of the book's dedicatee, Archbishop Rodrigo Jiménez de Rada of Toledo, whom he considers a great reader 'ad recreationem quam ad instructionem' of every kind of work, among which are encountered 'arturi secundum rabanum' and 'ricardi secundum merlinum'. David Hook has raised questions about the authorship of the work concerning Arthur and about the hypothetical production by Merlin, since there is no other information on these questions. In any case, both Diego García and Jiménez de Rada knew the Matter of Britain, perhaps from the same texts as provided the information in the *Liber regum*, as is discussed below, since it must not be forgotten that the *Planeta* was composed in the following year and possibly in the same city where the reference to the battle of Camlann was recorded in the *Anales Toledanos I*. Elsewhere in the same prologue, Diego García alludes to Charlemagne as the emblematic figure of the French while Arthur fulfils the same role for the British: 'Nec francorum Carolo nec Arturo Britanniae fidem servant' (Hook 1996: 137).

1. Poetry in Galician-Portuguese

The Galician-Portuguese language area, in common with the rest of western Europe, did not fail to succumb to the attractions of the Matter of Britain. Martin Soares (between 1230 and 1270), Joam Gracia de Guilhade, Gonçal'Eanes do Vinhal, Alfonso X of Castile (in four cantigas), D. Denis of Portugal, Estevam da Guarda and Fernand'Esquio allude in their verse to situations or characters related to Arthurian literature (Sharrer 1988b; Alvar 1991). Together with all these allusions there are the five 'lais de Bretanha', attributed to Tristan, which open the Cancioneiro da Biblioteca Nacional (Lisbon), and which coincide with Vatican Library MS Vat. Lat. 7182; these naturally present very different problems from those posed by the short allusions contained in the *cantigas* previously mentioned. Detailed discussion of the texts is given in the chapters by Pilar Lorenzo and Santiago Gutiérrez in the present volume; it suffices here to record the extent of the allusions and references to themes and characters of the Matter of Britain in the Galician-Portuguese literature in Table V.3.

It should be noted that there are problems of interpetation concerning the significance and sources of certain personal and geographical names (e.g., Caralhote, Cornaualla); these are examined by Lorenzo in Chapter IV. Some of the issues,

Table V.3: The Matter of Britain in Galician-Portuguese Lryic Poetry

Author	Date/Composition	Character/Theme/Name
Martin Soares	1230–70. Ũa donzela jaz	Caralhote
Martin Soares	1230–70. Joan Fernandes, que mal vos talharon	Cort mantel?
Alfonso X	1270–82. Cantigas Santa María, 35	Arturo, Dover, Bruto, Bretaña
Alfonso X	1270–82. Cantigas Santa María, 41	Breton, Artur
Alfonso X	1270–82. Cantigas Santa María, 108	Merlín, Caifás
Alfonso X	before 1284. Ben sabia eu	Tristán
Gonçal'Eanes do Vinhal	before 1285. Maestre, todo'lus vossos cantares	Cantares de Cornoalha
Fernand'Esquio	beginning of XIVth century. Disse hum infante	Besta Ladrador; Bretanha
Estevam da Guarda	c.1314. Com'avẽeo a Merlin	Merlín
D. Denis	before 1325. Senhor fremosa	Tristán, Iseo

however, may be illustrated usefully here by reference to a *cantiga* by Martin Soares (whose literary activity is located between 1230 and 1270): *Joan Fernandes, que mal vos talharon* is a satire in which mockery is directed at the quality of the tailoring in the tunic belonging to the victim of the satire, which has been made too short for him, in such a way as to emphasise his physical deficiencies. Without doubt, the mockery is part of that abundant group of compositions devoted to the clothing or physique of their target; this is the superficial aspect, or, if one prefers, the literal interpretation. Frequently, however, the *cantigas* hide another level of interpretation; the composition of Martin Soares may stand as an example of this, in which there is a literal reading, and an obscene one. The invective that occupies us here repeats the verb 'talhar' or a derivative of it on eight occasions, and there are five occurrences of the adjective 'corta' (reinforced at the end of the text by 'cortés'). It seems unnecessary to underline the burlesque weight attached to the idea of the 'saya mal talhada' or 'saya corta'.

It is also frequent in the satirical poetry that the final line and even the final word of the composition may contain the key to the interpretation of the mockery; our *cantiga* concludes with the adjectives 'cortes e cansado', unrelated to the mockery that has been constructed. It is possible that 'cortes' has been dragged in by analogy with 'corta', and that in this sense it would have little humorous effect; but the term acquires greater significance if it is interpreted as antiphrasis. From what other Galician-Portuguese poets say of Joan Fernández (such as Joan Soárez Coelho, Martin Soares and Roi Gómez de Briteiros), he must have been a convert from Islam to Christianity; his position in the court (one imagines) would not have been what he thought he deserved.

As regards marriage, it is well known that it constitutes one of the foci of attention in all satirical or burlesque poetry. In the case of Joan Fernández, who was married, his companions are alluding to the fickleness of his wife with a Muslim. Thus, there are witnesses that the victim of the *escarnio* by Martin Soares was 'mal talhado' as Afonso Eanes do Coton observes to him, that possibly he was held in little esteem at court, and that he was 'mal casado'. The mockery is transparent and increased with the inadequate clothing. It is not necessary to seek further explanations. However, another *cantiga*, discussed by Pilar Lorenzo, in which Martin Soares seems to allude to Caradós and Lanzarote in the name Don Caralhote justifies our seeking a deeper meaning hidden below that badly cut tunic.

At the end of the XIIth century or the beginning of the XIIIth a composition appeared in French, halfway between the *fabliau* and the *lai*, that dealt with the proof of conjugal fidelity, according to folkloric models that were widely distributed; the *lai* in question received the title of *Le mantel mautaillié* or *Lai du cort mantel*, and presented some situations analogous to those of the *Lai du cor* by Robert Bicket. The cloak was a good fit only for the lady who had been faithful to her husband; in the entire court there was only one woman who was capable of wearing it (or of drinking from the horn without spilling the wine), to the resulting shock of King Arthur and his entourage. The fortunate husband who had not been tricked was called, fortuitously, Caradós: the printer Caxton refers to 'Cradocks Mantel' in his edition of Thomas Malory's *Le Morte Darthur* (1485; ed. Vinaver 1977: xiv). In any case, it is necessary to indicate that two different persons are involved: one is the treacherous lord of the Dolorous Tower who imprisons and tortures Galvan, and the other is the knight who appears in the stories of the 'Manto mal cortado', who in turn should not be confused with the 'Doncel de la cota mal cortada'.

The Catalan noble Ramon de Perellós recounts in his *Viatge al Purgatori de Sant Patrici*, towards 1398, that on his return from his long and extraordinary journey he passed through 'Daureont' (Dover), where he saw the head of Galvan and the 'cota mal tallada'. It is well known that the *Viatge* is to a great extent a version of the *Tractatus de Purgatorio Sancti Patricii*, a Latin text of around 1189, by a Cistercian monk from Saltrey, which enjoyed an extraordinary popularity, to judge by the thirty-odd manuscripts that contain the text, and which had already been translated into Catalan in 1320 by Fray Ramon Ros de Tárrega. On the basis of the *Tractatus*, Ramon de Perellós amplifies and adds the details that he considers appropriate, often derived from his own experience.

The death of Galvan in Dover relates to the final part of the *Vulgate*, *La mort le roi Artu*, although his body was sent for burial at Camelot. The veneration of Galvan's skull at Dover seems obviously to be a local tradition, possibly later than the *Vulgate*, since other Arthurian works in which the episode is related do not refer to this port, but to 'Rutupi Portus' (Geoffrey of Monmouth) and 'Romenel' (Wace). Moreover, a local tradition was the display of the 'cota mal cortada'; it must not be forgotten that the author of this narration asserts that the 'manto' (or the 'cota') was deposited in an abbey in Wales, where ladies and maidens could try it on. Perellós could have known both traditions in the English port, or they could have reached him through some literary text. (See also Soriano in the present volume.)

Martin Soares puts his mockery into effect by repeating continually the most significant terms ('talhar', 'corta'), in accordance with the technique of *annominatio*. The key to its interpretation – and therefore the success of the mockery – must have been based on the parallel which would have been established between the situations related in the *Mantel mautaillié* and the 'cota mal talhada' of Johan Fernandes. I believe that the hypothesis is obvious: around 1243 Martin Soares – and other members of his circle, for otherwise the mockery would have lacked meaning – could have known a version of this *lai*, in which the name of Caradós would also have been given. It must be borne in mind that the motif of the cloak, the coat, the horn, or the shield that serve to prove chastity is very frequent in Arthurian literature and was used, among others, by Raoul de Houdenc in the *Vengeance Reguidel*, by the author of the *First Continuation of Perceval*, and by the Prose *Tristan*; but to restrict the scope of this survey, it would be necessary to think of a text similar to the *Livres de Caradoc*, included in the *First Continuation of Li Contes del Grial* of Chrétien de Troyes.

The interpretation of some obscure allusions to episodes and characters from Arthurian texts (such as those in the *cantigas* by Martin Soares, *Joan Fernandes, que mal vos talharon* and *Ũa donzela jaz*), which were clearly intended to be within the understanding of members of the circle of the Galician-Portuguese poets who composed the works containing these references, leads us to conclude that the Matter of Britain spread through the various Galician-Portuguese areas by means of short texts, sometimes related to the surviving prose narrations, but on other occasions unrelated to them. My hypothesis draws support from the existence in French of *lais* and *fabliaux* and brief narratives, and makes it necessary for us to reconsider the diffusion and reception of the best-known Arthurian texts.

2. Romances of Chivalry

On the death of Sancho IV of Castile (1295), the heir to the throne, his son Fernando, was scarcely ten years of age, so that the widowed queen, María de Molina, had to assume the regency, and in order to govern sought the support of the Church, following the same policy as the deceased king. The premature death of Fernando IV (1312) at the age of 26, and the almost immediate death of Queen Constanza (1313), obliged the Queen Mother to assume the regency once more, in the face of the hostility of a section of the nobility. The fact that the heir, Alfonso, born in 1311 was so young presaged a gloomy future of uncertainty: the king's minority would last at least fifteen years; the Queen Regent, who was already approaching fifty, would probably not survive to see the coronation of her grandson. The nobility sought above all its own advantage, without any kind of scruples. It was in this context that the Matter of

Britain spread through León and Castile, thanks to the support of the Church, which saw in the courtly model of the *Post-Vulgate* an example to pacify the rebellious stirrings of the Castilian and Leonese nobility and to provide it with some models of behaviour subordinated to religious and chivalric ideals. It was a model in which the knights who triumph are those who live within severe and narrow monkish norms, as authentic Christian knights, loyal to their king and disposed at all times to defend widowed ladies and orphan children against the snares of the powerful and the danger posed by the strongest. The satisfaction with which this literature was received in the Castile of the first years of the XIVth century, during which María de Molina was beset on all sides, comes as no surprise.

It is no coincidence that the first surviving translations of Arthurian texts should belong to the first years of the XIVth century, and this period should witness the birth of fiction in Castilian in which authors followed the model of the Matter of Britain. This is the case with the *Libro del cavallero Zifar* and the first version of *Amadís de Gaula*.

2.1 *Libro del cavallero Zifar*

The *Libro del cavaller Zifar* is the first original chivalric narrative in Castilian, a rich fusion of the most varied literary traditions: governance of princes, chivalric narrative, lives of saints, wisdom literature, sermons etc. The composition of the prologue can be dated to a few years after the Jubilee, towards 1303 or 1304, while the *Libro* itself could date from between 1301 and 1303, with a *terminus ad quem* in any case of 1343.

The authorship of the *Libro* is unclear. The presence of Ferrant Martínez as a character in the prologue has led some scholars to consider that the archdeacon of Madrid (who died in 1309) was the author of the narrative, and that the milieu in which he carried out his work was Toledo cathedral. There is, however, nothing to corroborate this hypothesis. On the other hand, if a late date (subsequent to 1321) is considered for the composition, then Ferrant Martínez would be merely a character in the prologue. A reading of the *Libro* suggests that the author may possibly have been a cleric linked to Toledo cathedral, who had good relations with the royal court, and who was well educated, knowledgeable about Arabic culture, but anti-Semitic; such a profile is frequently encountered in other authors of the period.

Although it is asserted in the prologue that the *Libro* was translated from 'Chaldean' to Latin and from Latin to Castilian, such words enshrine a literary topos rather than reflecting reality. The mixture of traditions, moreover, complicates any search along such lines: similarities have been found between a story of Indian origins ('The King who lost everything') and *Zifar*, a narrative that was enriched by the legend of St Eustace, with the *Flores de filosofia* (which are incorporated almost entirely in the 'Castigos del rey de Menton' section), and with other oriental stories; but alongside the many motifs of oriental origin there are other episodes with clearly Arthurian roots, such as that of the 'Islas Dotadas'. All of this taken together imparts a distinctive character to the work as a whole.

Indeed, the storyline of the *Libro* is derived from folklore and from the life of St Eustace, a Roman general (called Plácidas before his conversion to Christianity) who suffered every kind of vicissitude, including separation from and reunion with his family, until he underwent martyrdom on the orders of the emperor Hadrian, although the *Libro* sets the action in India (no doubt because of the origins of the story which provided its basis). The development of this narrative, which combined the characteristics of the Byzantine romance, with separations and final recognitions, predominates in the first part of the work, and then gives way to deeper didactic concerns, expressed in the form of advice to the king of Mentón (Zifar) to his son Roboán. The final part of the *Libro* is devoted principally to Roboán and his companions in arms, who undergo the most varied of adventures, until Zifar's son becomes king of Tigrida. The work as a whole is adorned with twenty-five exempla, miracles and facetiae and around sixty proverbs, which abound particularly in the mouth of Ribaldo, a rustic servant of Zifar, who has this characteristic in common with Sancho in *Don Quixote*. The possible influence of an early version of *Tristán* on the work has been studied by Cuesta Torre (1994a: 219–21).

The fusion of such varied materials, together with the frequent didactic digressions, lead to the narrative thread's being lost repeatedly, in such a way that it is not easy to understand the intentions of the author. Notwithstanding this, there is general acceptance of the undoubted unity of the work, constructed around the central idea that God rewards those who follow his will. The *Libro* takes this idea as its starting point, as if it were the *thema* of a sermon, and proceeds to develop it through the use of numerous rhetorical resources, among which there stand out *interpretatio*, *digressio* and parallel and symmetrical constructions, which even affect the very mode of composition of the work, giving it a structure which has as its culminating point the moment at which Zifar becomes king of Mentón and the advice that he gives to his son. Here can be placed the dividing line between the past (El Caballero de Dios) and the future (Roboán). Such a division highlights the importance attached to didacticism in the work, which becomes a governance of princes as Zifar teaches his son Roboán and the author teaches the reader. In this world of teaching there is a marked tendency to highlight daily necessities and the dangers that beset the knight, far from the idealism of the chivalric narratives, but this does not mean that the element of the marvellous is lacking. Everything combines to make the *Libro* a most unusual work.

On two occasions the author of the *Cavallero Zifar* recalls episodes related to the Matter of Britain. The first of these is a brief allusion by the Caballero Amigo to the fight between the 'Gato Paul' and King Arthur (Wagner 1929: 215), referring here to the adventure of the Chat de Losane recounted in the *Vulgate Merlin* (Sommer 1908: 441–2). It is surprising that this episode should be remembered also by Lope García de Salazar in his *Libro de las bienandanzas e fortunas* (*c.*1475), discussed below.

More important is the use of the Matter of Britain in the episode of the Islas Dotadas. This may be summarised as follows. Roboán asks the emperor of Tigrida why he never laughs; so that he may understand the reason adequately, the emperor takes Roboán to the beach and orders him to board a small boat. Scarcely has he done so when the boat puts out to sea. Should Roboán succeed in the adventure, he will achieve the highest state possible; should the opposite apply, he will return in a year's time. A few days later the boat reaches an island; Roboán disembarks, follows a long tunnel, and at the far end finds ladies and kings who are awaiting him so that he can marry Nobleza, the empress of the Islas Dotadas, daughter of the Lady of Parescer and Don Yván, the son of King Orián (Urién) and nephew of King Arthur. Nobleza was married to another man, who lost her through his lack of sense, but if Roboán is intelligent and loves her loyally, he will be the greatest emperor in the world.

Hardly has he arrived at the city than an archbishop marries him to Nobleza, and immediately there begin the lavish feasts for the wedding. Almost a year after the marriage, the Devil leads Roboán, while out hunting, to meet a most beautiful woman, who informs him that Nobleza has the best hunting dog of all and will give it to him if he asks for it; and thus it happens. Some time later, the encounter is repeated, and this time the lady tells him that Nobleza has the best of hawks, which she will give to her husband if he asks for it. Again Nobleza gives her husband the animal for which he asks, although seeing him surprised she warns him that if he leaves her he will lose her for ever. A few weeks later, Roboán again meets the beautiful lady, and she tells him that Nobleza has the fastest horse in the world. Roboán hesitates for two days and two nights, and finally asks Nobleza for the horse. She agrees to give it to him, though she tells him that she will delay handing it over for three days, since her maidens have to complete the embroidery on a banner that they are making. At the end of the allotted time, she presents Roboán with the horse and the banner, and he rides out to hunt, but Nobleza reproaches him for what he is doing, since she knows that the horse will take him away from her for ever and will thus end their happiness, at the very moment when she is pregnant and expecting his child. The banner will, however, aid him to emerge successful from any situation, however difficult it may be. Roboán then attempts to dismount, but he pricks the animal with his spur and it gallops away with its rider and carries him to the beach on which he had disembarked a year previously. The boat carries him back to Tigrida again, after he has lost everything that he had achieved in the Islas Dotadas. The emperor then appears, who asks him if he will ever be able to laugh again. Roboán at once understands that the emperor was the previous husband of Nobleza, and had also failed in the adventure. On their way back to the palace, the emperor and Roboán meet the beautiful lady by a fountain; she mocks them, and makes all kinds of grimaces at them. Faced with this, both begin to laugh, since they finally realise that each has someone who can share the grief of the failure they have experienced.

All the elements of this adventure indicate an origin in the Matter of Britain: the voyage in a boat without a helmsman, the island, the tunnel, the immense wealth at the other end; the surprisingly sudden marriage with Nobleza, the taboo and the resulting transgression; the loss of everything that has been attained, the return to the place of origin ... (Wagner 1903: 44–57; Entwistle 1925: 71–5; Schreiner 1981; Carrasco 2010). And, as if this were not enough, Nobleza is the daughter of Don Yván, the son of King Urién, and one of the ladies in her entourage is a reader:

> The lady had the book of the story of Don Yván, and began to read from it; and the lady read very well and in a very accomplished way, and very measured, in such a way that the prince understood very well everything that she read and took great pleasure and great delight in it, for certainly there is no man who hears the story of Don Yván who does not receive great pleasure from it because of the very good words that are in it. And every man who wishes to have delight and pleasure and to have good habits should read the book of the story of Don Yván. (Wagner 1929: 459).

> La donzella llevava el libro de la estoria de don Yván e començó de leer en el. E la donzella leyé muy bien e muy apuestamente e muy ordenamente, de guissa que entendié el infante muy bien todo lo que ella leyé e tomava en ello muy grande plazer e grand solaz, ca ciertamente non ha omne que oya la estoria de don Yván que non resciba ende muy grand plazer, por las palabras muy buenas que en él dizié. Et todo omne que quisiera aver solaz e plazer et aver buenas costumbres debe leer el libro de la estoria de Don Yván.

As is related by the ladies who accompany Roboán as soon as he lands on the Islas Dotadas, the mother of Nobleza was 'la señora del Parescer, que fue a salvar e guardar del peligro muy grande a don Yván, fijo del rey Orián, segund se cuenta en la su estoria, cuando don Yván dixo a la reina Ginebra que él avié por señora una dueña mas fermosa que ella' (Wagner 1929: 458). These words could serve to orient us with regard to the origin of the episode, since they seem to refer to the adventures of Lanval in the *lai* of that name by Marie de France, or to those of Graelent, in the anonymous *lai* that bears the name of its protagonist. The impossibility of finding a text closer to the story in the *Cavallero Zifar* is perhaps due to the loss of such a work, since it is clear that a large part of the motifs and themes of the Matter of Britain were spread through *lais* and oral tradition, but not by this alone: tapestries, paintings, and other forms of sumptuary arts carried the themes from one land to another. The insistent reference to Yvain is also striking; his story seems to have been depicted around 1225 on the tympanum of the Cistercian monastery of Santa Maria de Penamaior (Lugo), as noted above.

2.2 *Amadís de Gaula*

The prologue to the Zaragoza edition of *Amadís de Gaula* produced by Jorge Coci in 1508 concludes by stating that the work was corrected and emended by Garci Rodríguez de Montalvo, on the basis of ancient originals, and that he had carried out his work by removing many superfluous words and changing others into a more elegant style with reference to chivalry and its deeds. There is no doubt about the existence of an earlier text, a fact which is corroborated by four manuscript folios from the beginning of the XVth century which have come down to us. It is logical, moreover, that Montalvo, the *regidor* of Medina del Campo, should have wished to modernise the work, since not only had the language evolved and developed an elegance of style for speaking of knights, but also fashions had changed profoundly in Castile as the XVth century had progressed.

Almost fifty years before the surviving text of the manuscript folios was written the poet Pero Ferrús (... 1369–79 ...) provides clear testimony that *Amadís* was not unknown:

> Amadís el muy fermoso
> las lluvias y las ventiscas
> nunca las falló ariscas
> por ser leal e famoso:
> sus proesas fallaredes
> en tres libros e diredes
> que le Dios dé santo poso.

The printed version of Garci Rodríguez de Montalvo has four books, plus a fifth devoted to the *Sergas de Esplandián*. It is clear that in the period between the time of Pero Ferrús and that of the first edition (1508) there have been added to the work both a book and a continuation. Moreover, the final line of the verse clearly indicates beyond question that the protagonist died, which does not occur in the Zaragoza edition. I also add that, as the *Sergas* attest, written by Montalvo himself, Amadís died at the hands of his own son Esplandián, who was unaware of the identity of his adversary, and his wife Oriana committed suicide.

The indirect references take us back to the beginning of the XIVth century or to the reign of Sancho IV (Avalle-Arce 1990: 101), in such a way that our hero could be a contemporary of the *Cavallero Zifar* or the *Conde Lucanor*, or even earlier. Thus, for example, in Logroño in 1294 there is a possible documentary reference to an 'Espladian' (*sic*), which may reflect the existence of the literary character.

It is obvious that the linguistic and social changes experienced between the moment of the composition of this first *Amadís* and the beginning of the XVIth century (or the final years of the XVth) must have been numerous and very profound. Among these changes the arrival of the Trastámaran dynasty in power and the reign of Isabel la Católica would not have been the least significant, these being the phases that correspond with different versions of the work with which we are concerned.

The focus of interest here is the first 200 years of the life of *Amadís*, since although no further copies of the work have survived from the era before the Zaragoza edition other than the early XVth-century manuscript leaves, the abundant allusions and references made by other writers or poets of previous periods, together with the subtlety of modern critics, allow us to intuit with a fair prospect of accuracy the contents of the work. In addition, twenty-seven references scattered over 200 years assist us to reconstruct the avatars of the knight and to establish, thanks to this reconstruction, these modifications, all of them the fruit of social changes which appeared in Castile from the end of the XIIIth century to the first years of the XVIth; *Amadís de Gaula* can definitively serve, thanks to its rich textual history both direct and indirect, to trace the history of *mentalités* in Castile during this lengthy period (Gómez Redondo 1999: 1542).

One can conjecture that the first *Amadís* shared a didactic and moralizing spirit characteristic of the Arthurian romances, whilst it must have presented a clear inclination towards the religious and military values central to 'molinismo', that is, the ethics and conduct imposed by the regent María de Molina, and which were, definitively, the impetus behind the acclimatisation in Castilian territory of the texts referring to King Arthur and the knights of the Round Table. This did not involve simply any type of texts, but rather those most closely and directly linked to the Lateran Reforms of 1214, the *Vulgate* and the *Post-Vulgate*, in which Lancelot and Tristan were encountered for the first time. It is not by chance that the heroes of the Grail quest were to participate, albeit in a marginal way, in the world of Amadís.

In this sense, it is appropriate to recall that the Arthurian texts linked to the Fourth Lateran Council strive to Christianise the adventures of the knights of the Round Table in the light of the teachings of the Cistercians: frequent confession, when faced with the danger of death or before taking communion; virtually daily communion; the presence of saintly hermits prepared to administer the necessary sacraments so that knights should never be separated from the grace of God; the myth of the Grail converted into the mystery of the Transubstantiation, and, finally, the punishment received by the Arthurian world because of the adultery of Lancelot and Guinevere, with the consequent destruction of the kingdom provoked by the confrontation of Arthur and Lancelot, the death of Galván, the confrontation of Arthur and his son Mordred, the death of the latter at the hands of his father... All the sins are punished, and in that world the only hope that is left is that of Boores, Perceval and Galaz, the three knights who contemplate the Grail thanks to their Christian virtues, which distance them from the way of life of the knights errant.

And in fact Amadís would become a model of conduct for nobles, as is attested by Juan García de Castrogeriz in his gloss to the *De regimine principum* of Egidio Colonna, before 1325:

> Et allí fabla mucho Vegecio de las penas que davan a los malos cavalleros, ca algunos son tan gloriosos que non fazen fuerça sinon del paresçer, et semejan cavalleros et non lo son, ca sus cavallerías cuentan entre las mugeres, de los cuales dize el poeta Enico [= the comedy *Eunuchus*] que éstos cuentan maravillas de Amadís et de Tristán et del Cavallero Syfar, et cuentan de faziendas de Marte et las de Archiles, et pónense entre los buenos, maguera ellos son astrosos. (Guardiola 1988: 339)

But the situation had changed by the end of the XIVth century, when the chancellor Pedro López de Ayala laments in the stanzas of his *Rimado de palacio* that he had wasted time hearing 'libros de devaneos, de mentiras provadas, | Amadís e Lançalote, e burlas escantadas' (st. 163; López de Ayala, ed. Orduna 1987). The knight who had previously served as a model is now blamed for causing time to be wasted; a shift in appreciation caused, no doubt, by the change of mentality over the course of the century. Ayala was a serious man, for which reason the court and the courtly model were scorned by him, since those who should have occupied themselves with maintaining values allowed themselves to be swayed by comfort and luxury; from that perspective, Amadís became a character worthy of censure, since nobody follows his model, or, to put it another way, the old Chancellor seems to be aware of the changes produced under the society of the Trastámaras. For him, as for other members of the nobility, chivalric adventures, feats of arms, must have recalled perhaps too closely the turbulence which had occurred throughout the century, and which came to a head with the death of King Pedro at the hands of his brother Enrique at Montiel. This was a world which had produced nothing but dramatic situations like the Hundred Years War (begun in 1337), the presence of the Papacy in Avignon, or the military disaster of Aljubarrota, all of which he had personally experienced at first hand.

The *Cancionero de Baena*, earlier than 1425, contains various references to Amadís which allow us to appreciate the reception of the work or at least enable us to understand what it presents as the most outstanding aspect of the personality of the knight: his capacity for love now acquires a new dimension. It is not unusual to find lists of famous lovers at the heart of extensive compositions.

The firmness of the sentiments of Amadís is now an example worthy of imitation, and therefore the allusions to him are repeated insistently: the book consists of three parts; its protagonist goes to Germany where he spends four years and where he possibly suffers from the inclement weather and the hardships of the savage life, according to the verses by Pedro Ferrús mentioned above, who also adds some words which raise considerations concerning the death of Amadís.

Given the importance which at this time was accorded to some aspects of Classical literature, specifically the stories of Troy, and taking into account the alterations undergone by the endings of some texts known in versions in Latin and other languages, it is very probable that Amadís died at the hands of his son Esplandián, just as Ulysses died at the hands of his son Telegonus in the *Telegonia*; the inevitable consequence was the suicide of their respective wives, Penelope and Oriana. What is more, it is very probable that Oriana threw herself from a window thereby putting an end to her life, as Melibea would later do in *Celestina*, perhaps following the bad example she had taken from Oriana. The latter must by then have been a well-known literary heroine, whose prestige would have gone well beyond the literary texts themselves; the love of this famous couple had become a model worthy of imitation.

Leaving aside conjectures and resemblances, what is certain is that in the XVth century, at least until the end of the reign of Enrique IV, Castile again became the scene of civil wars and continual confrontations. From the long reign of Juan II (1405–54) and during the twenty years in which Enrique IV reigned (1454–74), one revolt or disturbance, one confrontation or conspiracy, followed another. This continued into the first years of the rule of the Catholic Monarchs. Neither the crisis of values nor the despair visible in the writers of the period, such as Fernán Pérez de Guzmán, or Jorge Manrique a quarter of a century later, should surprise us.

The situation changed from the end of the Castilian war of succession in 1479. The accession of the Catholic Monarchs constitutes, as is well known, a recovery of a system of values based essentially on royal authority and on unity (legislative, territorial, religious). As a result, religion and loyalty occupied a privileged position in the new system.

Nobody now spoke of the decadence of society; perspectives changed radically, to such an extent that in the course of a very few years chroniclers were praising the valour and prudence of the contemporary nobility. There rapidly spread a providentialist idea of the monarchy, which had arrived to save Spain from an immediate and dishonourable end, had the previous situation continued; it is no surprise that Esplandián, son of Amadís and a clear emulator of the Arthurian Galaz, should now displace his father, since in the new value system it is the son who embodies the ideals of the period.

Garci Rodríguez de Montalvo was a faithful servant of the Catholic Monarchs and as such exerted himself to put together a new version of the book of *Amadís*, maintaining the essential characteristics, well known to the public, but adapting the whole to a design more in keeping with the current ideology. Thus is explained the addition of the *Sergas de Esplandián*, which would lead him to change the existing ending: Amadís could not now die at the hands of his son:

> Pasó esta cruel y dura batalla, así como habéis oído, entre Amadís y su hijo, por causa de la cual algunos dijeron que en ella Amadís de aquellas heridas muriera, y otros que del primer encuentro de la lanza, que las espaldas le pasó, Y sabido por Oriana, se despeñó de una ventana abajo. Mas no fue así. Pero la muerte que de Amadís le sobrevino no fue otra, sino que quedando en olvido sus grandes hechos, casi como so la tierra, florecieron los del hijo con tanta fama, con tanta gloria, que a la altura de las nubes parecían tocar.

To understand the changes of mentality in a more exact way it is necessary to seek Garci Rodríguez de Montalvo in the first person, that is to say, to have recourse to the texts in which he explains the work that he has carried out. In this sense great importance attaches to the words he wrote in the prologue to the work, addressed to the Catholic Monarchs (who are, be it noted, still alive), whom he compares with the heroes of antiquity, celebrated by historians who in their chronicles underline the valour of the deeds they accomplished. Those wise chroniclers would not have hesitated to devote their efforts to the great deeds of Isabel and Fernando (Cacho Blecua 1987–8: 220–1).

But the *regidor*'s words go well beyond this when he indicates that there are not only on the one hand those who narrate the truth and on the other those who related things that mingle reality and exaggeration, but also those who invent everything, 'historias fengidas en que se hallan las cosas admirables fuera de la orden de natura, que más por nombre de patrañas que de crónicas con mucha razón deven ser tenidas y llamadas' (Cacho Blecua 1987–8: 223). And so, he announces that, not daring to rectify the wise chroniclers, he has devoted his mind to correcting the three books of *Amadís*, and to translating and emending Book IV with the *Sergas de Esplandián*, which appeared in a stone tomb near Constantinople, and was brought to Castile by a Hungarian merchant. In this way, young knights and their elders will find in them what is suited to each one of them.

That is to say, Montalvo is fully aware that there are real histories and feigned histories, on the one hand, and that on the other the reworking that he is carrying out is aimed at a diverse public, consisting of both younger and older readers. This consideration of the readership is a clear revelation of the interest of the narrator in transmitting his message and in ensuring that it reached the circles to which it was directed. The content of this message was not at variance from the ideology established by the monarchs whom he exalts and praises at the start of his prologue comparing them to the most representative figures of Classical antiquity, at the same time as he converts himself into an historian comparable to Sallust or Livy.

Nor must it be forgotten that the reference to Constantinople merely revives a memory painful for the West: the fall of the city to the Turks in 1453. The knights errant must abandon their Arthurian individualism to unite their forces and attack the enemies of the faith. It is an idea that appears and reappears with emphasis in the writers of the period of the Catholic Monarchs and to which Montalvo himself was not insensitive. Esplandián has a mission to accomplish beyond the jousts and combats, of little importance, of the earlier heroes.

Montalvo has reworked some earlier materials, consisting of three books, or perhaps four, to which he has added the story of Esplandián; this, then, would be the moment at which he begins to conceive the development of the narration of the adventures of the son of Amadís when our *regidor* takes up the narrative again, recording the extraordinary circumstances of the discovery of an unknown book:

> Pues luego no ternemos por estraño haver pareçido en cabo de tantos años este libro que oculto y encerrado se halló en aquella muy antigua sepultura que el prólogo primero de los tres libros de Amadís se recuenta; en el cual se haze mención de aquel cathólico y virtuoso príncipe Esplandián, su hijo, en quien estos dos nombres muy bien empleados fueron, como las más de cerimunia preciados, y por tales quiso ser dellos intitulado, desechando todos los otros que, ahunque más altos parescan, son más a lo temporal que a lo divinal conformes, pues que, la vida fallesciendo, ellos en uno con ella falleçen. (Cacho Blecua 1987–8: II, 1302)

It should be noted that the two adjectives (catholic and virtuous) so appreciated by Esplandián, who rejects any other titles, are attributes very different from those accorded to the knights in the preceding pages, including his own father, and that are nonetheless very characteristic of the period: it is sufficient to recall that Pope Alexander VI conceded to Fernando and Isabel the title of Catholic Monarchs in 1494. The son of Amadís is comparable in this sense to the Monarchs. Montalvo has not written these words by accident, forgetting completely the ancestors of the new hero since they are no use to him now. Esplandián, like Galaz, the son of Lancelot, is a Christian knight, fundamentally religious; for this reason he could not have killed his father, as was read in the earlier versions, and thus is born a new ending for the work.

Esplandián is imbued with a spirit completely different from that which motivated the deeds of Amadís. Montalvo emphasises this much in producing a portrait of the son of Amadís laden with religious virtues, at the same time as he establishes the premises for a providentialism very characteristic of the period of the Catholic Monarchs. But what calls our attention is that the accumulation of virtues that makes Esplandián into a Christian knight also brings him indubitably close to the figure of Galaz. Nonetheless, Montalvo scorns the narrative model established by the Arthurian stories, and attempts to distance himself from them, whence the fact that the personality of Esplandián acquires a particular brilliance.

Equally, significance also attaches to the actions carried out by Esplandián after he has become emperor; we are faced with a series of recommendations that seem rather to be a manual of education of princes.

In fact, in contrast with the Arthurian tradition that acquired a new lease of life in the 'Trastámaran' version of *Amadís*, the new system of values does not accept the death of the protagonists nor of the other characters who, like King Lisuarte, had previously died. The repentance of sinners and their recognition of their sins can be turned into a weapon as powerful and convincing as death itself.

Nor must it be forgotten that one of the characteristics of the reign of Isabel was the search for and establishment of order and peace in the various social contexts, for which reason we may accept without difficulty that King Lisuarte's repentance merely re-establishes a situation in accordance with the new tendencies emanating from the monarchy. Naturally, the virtuous Esplandián will be the one responsible for putting an end to the previous disorder, which was a consequence, to some extent, of the not very practical activities of his own father.

In this process of 'moral rearmament' undertaken by Montalvo, the struggle with the Endriago on the Insula del Diablo is especially significant. The Endriago is a hybrid monster, conceived from the incestuous relationship between the giant Bandaguido and his daughter Bandaguida. The latter, to put into effect her sinful and immoral intentions, did not hesitate to put an end to her own mother. The result was this monstrous being which, while suckling, caused through its poison the death of every wet-nurse who attempted to breast-feed it. Then, when just one year old, it killed its parents and almost all the inhabitants of the Insula del Diablo.

Amadís confronts it with his thoughts fixed on Oriana, in accordance with the presuppositions of chivalry: love should give him the strength to conquer, and the mere fact of thought being focused on his beloved should suffice for his fatigue to disappear. To love is equivalent to being invigorated. However, these resources are of little avail to Amadís, and the Endriago is about to finish off the best of knights, until the latter's luck changes when he ceases to think of Oriana and remembers God and the Virgin. This confrontation went further than mere worldly chivalry:

> No tardó mucho que vieron salir de entre las peñas el Endriago muy más bravo y fuerte que lo nunca fue, de lo cual fue causa que, como los diablos viessen que este cavallero ponía más esperança en su amiga Oriana que en Dios, tuvieron lugar de entrar más fuertemente en él y le fazer más sañudo, diziendo ellos: d'éste le scapamos, no ay en el mundo otro que tan osado ni fuerte tan fuerte sea que tal cosa ose acometer. (Cacho Blecua 1989: 1141)

Thinking about God gave victory to Amadís; on the point of dying, the Endriago vomits forth a demon who flees making an enormous noise. Earthly knighthood has been replaced by heavenly chivalry and in this transformation, in accordance with the times, Amadís does not play much of a part. In the Peña de la Doncella Encantadora the process is consummated, with the best knight in the world unable to finish the adventure reserved for his son. The words uttered to Amadís by Grasandor leave no room for doubt: 'Dexemos esto para aquel donzel que comiença a subir donde vós descendís' ('Let us leave this for that youth who is beginning to ascend as you descend'; Cacho Blecua 1989: 1708).

As Cuesta Torre indicates (1997a: 57ff.), neither the *Cavallero Zifar* nor *Amadís* forms part, strictly speaking, of the Arthurian cycle; she points out that neither King Arthur and his court, nor Tristan and Iseo, have any role other than appearing as a prophecy in *Amadís* (Book I, chapter X), while Arthur and Ivain are merely the subject of allusions in *Cavallero Zifar*. These works must, however, be credited with having successfully adapted the Arthurian tradition to the Hispanic context, maintaining the spirit of the model thanks to their wise use of motifs and topics, such as that of the isolated lady in the midst of danger posed by woods and open spaces; that of the determined woman, who does not wait for the knight to seduce her, but who herself takes the amorous initiative and seeks sexual consummation; the motif of the *don contraignant*; the vessel which sails without a helmsman; and so forth. And naturally, great tourneys, combats and feats of arms, not to mention the investitures of knights, amorous relations, kidnappings, rescues, wounds sustained in combat and their cure, the presence of animals and monsters, giants and dwarfs, wet-nurse, miracles, prophecies, premonitory and prophetic dreams, supernatural or inexplicable events, varied fantasies, tricks, disguises, and talismans of all kinds (Giménez 1973). Perhaps it may be easier to indicate that the Hispanic texts introduce the idea of crusade (found in the Franco-Italian epic, in Pulci, Boiardo and Ariosto), and the identification of love and marriage, the social ascent of the knight who is ignorant of his identity as the son of the king, and moralisation, which is present in almost all the Hispanic representatives of the genre. Incest and adultery vanish, and in those instances in which reference is made to them, it will always be as a sin punished with the most terrible penalties. Times have changed and the religious symbolism of the Arthurian *Vulgate* and its successors is left far distant. What attracts is action and adventure in itself, and sons bring to a conclusion the adventures which their fathers were unable to complete, a feature which will give rise to immense and extended family cycles, headed by Amadís and Palmerín; but Tristán will also have his own son, Tristán el Joven, which will cause obvious changes to the tradition.

Nobody now doubts that *Amadís* and *Tristán* are related (Cuesta Torre 2008b: 147–73), nor that the *Cavallero Zifar* was inspired by Arthurian material (Wagner 1903). Since, however, the *Cavallero Zifar* did not have much literary influence, it is *Amadís* that became the model followed by the romances of chivalry; and in general terms the features absent from the model are also lacking from its imitations and successors. Despite the existence of translations and editions of the most important Arthurian texts (*Baladro del sabio Merlín*, *Demanda del santo Grial* and *Tristán de Leonís*), the Hispanic romances of chivalry are not much disposed to have recourse to the characters of the Matter of Britain, and when they do, they use them as mere references, almost irrelevant; at least, this is attested by a random examination carried out of a score of books published or written during the XVIth century:

Table V.4: The Matter of Britain in Spanish Romances of Chivalry

Date	Title	Author	Character(s) cited
c.1305	Libro del Cavallero Zifar	Anon.	Artur, Ginebra, Yván, Orián, Libro de la historia de Yván, Gato Paul
1508	Amadís de Gaula	Garci Rodríguez de Montalvo	Artús I, 1; Artur I, 4; Morlote I, 10; Grial, Josefo, José Abarimatia IV, 128; Lançarote, Tristán, Iseo, Mares, Galeote, Brunes, Balaín, Segurades, Bravor, Uterpandragón IV, 129
1512	Primaleón	Francisco Vázquez	
1516	Floriseo	Fernando Bernal	Tabla Redonda II, 15
1517	Arderique	Anon.	Artús, Morderec, Salbrí, Morgaina I, 1; Galván, Héctor I, 17
1518	Clarián de Landanís I	Gabriel Velázquez de Castillo	Lanzarote and Ginebra, Tristán and Iseo CXXVIII
1519	Claribalte	Gonzalo Fernández de Oviedo	
1522	Clarián de Landanís II	Alvaro de Castro	José Abarimatea XI
1525	Lisuarte de Grecia	Feliciano de Silva	
1526	Polindo	Anon.	Tristán and Iseo XXXVII
1530	Florindo	Fernando Basurto	
1530	Amadís de Grecia	Feliciano de Silva	

1532	*Florisel de Niquea III*	Feliciano de Silva	Artur LXXXVIII
1532	*Florambel de Lucea*	Francisco de Enciso Zárate	Artús, Escaliber; Gilflet, Morgaina, III, 7ff.; *Demanda del Santo Grial* III, 12
1533	*Platir*	Fco. Enciso Zárate?	
1542	*Baldo*	Anon.	Artús III; Tabla Redonda III; Merlín XXV; Tristán XXV
1547	*Palmerín de Ingalaterra I*	Francisco de Moraes	Lançarote del Lago, Tábola Redonda, Morlot el Grande XL; Tristán and Iseo XXIV
1549	*Félix Magno I y II*	Anon.	Artús I
1556	*Felixmarte de Hircania*	Melchor de Ortega	
1576	*Febo Troyano*	Esteban Corbera	
1580	*Espejo de Príncipes II*	Pedro de la Sierra	Merlín II, 24; VI, 21
1599	*Flor de caballerías*	Francisco Barahona	Artús I,15; II, 1 Tabla Redonda II, 1
1602	*Policisne de Boecia*	Juan de Silva y de Toledo	

It is significant that almost half of these books do not allude to any character from the Matter of Britain. It is also important that overall there are barely fifty allusions, and that a single text contains almost a quarter of the references, namely, *Amadís de Gaula*. The work of Garci Rodríguez de Montalvo and the *Cavallero Zifar* are the works that display the greatest variety of Arthurian references, alongside some other cases, such as Francisco de Enciso Zárate, who, in his *Florambel de Lucea* (1532), seems to have read the *Demanda del Santo Grial*. The abundant presence of King Arthur (20 per cent of the cases), followed by Tristan and Iseo (10 per cent each), and to a lesser extent Lancelot and Guinevere, all goes to show that in general this is a matter of fossilised names, of recurrent examples of pairs of lovers, belonging to a world which is identified by reference to its king. It is, moreover, striking that Feliciano de Silva, the author of three romances of chivalry, son of Tristán de Silva, cites barely a pair of names in his works.

There are few references to the world of Arthur in a genre that derives directly or indirectly from the French texts; and these few references do not have all the same significance, since in some cases they involve mere names, with no further ramifications, while in others the traces of the Arthurian tradition are clear. A couple of brief examples will suffice to make the point.

El libro del esforçado cavallero Arderique was published in a single edition in Valencia in 1517, although it is possible that it already existed in 1477. Its author and origin are unknown, but it has been thought that it could have reached Castile from a translation into Catalan of a French original; none of this is, however, certain, for no texts of it are known other than the three surviving copies of the first edition printed in Castilian (Molloy Carpenter 2000: ix). In this shadowy situation, the allusions to Arthurian material are not particularly illuminating. A notable element is the account of the end of the reign of Arthur at the beginning of the work: the confrontation between the king and Morderec, who has attempted to usurp his throne during the absence of Arthur, who has gone to Rome to be named emperor. After the battle of Salbrí (Salisbury), in which the traitor dies, Arthur retires to the shore of the sea, accompanied by three knights; he embarks on a ship belonging to his sister, the fairy Morgaina, and disappears. Everyone in the kingdom remains in expectation of the return of the king.

Thus the starting point of *Arderique* is the ending of the *Mort Artu*. Throughout the narrative there appear other characters, like Galván, brother of Brunor and Héctor, who could be Arthurian, but nothing seems to confirm such an origin, so that it is necessary to consider this an instance of names of whose origin the author is not aware. Such ignorance should not surprise us, since the anonymous author seems to have read nothing more than the final folios of the story of the knights of the Round Table.

Francisco Enciso de Zárate, secretary to Pedro Alvarez de Osorio, fourth Marqués de Astorga, published the *Corónica del invencible cavallero Florambel de Lucea* in Valladolid in 1532 (Aguilar Perdomo 2009). It was not the only romance of chivalry by this author, since he may also have written *Platir*, which appeared the following year. The interest of the Marqués de Astorga in this kind of literature, which is obvious from his library (Cátedra 2002), contributed, no doubt, to his secretary's composition of parts I, II and III of *Florambel*, and possibly *Platir*, as mentioned.

One adventure, that of the 'Arbol Saludable' (III, 7ff.), results from Arthur's desire to know if the knights of England are now better or worse than when he reigned. Beside the tree there are seated on golden thrones a very handsome man with a crown, and an elderly lady; from their attire it is obvious that they are of high rank. The protagonist of the book, Florambel, defeats the two knights who were guarding the Arbol Saludable, but is badly wounded. The lady cures him with a fruit from the tree; they then descend inside the tree to some richly adorned rooms. When they prepare to eat, Florambel and his friend Lidiarte become aware that the young man with the crown is King Arthur and the lady is Morgaina, who recounts to them how she saved her brother after the battle with the sons of the traitor Morderec. Finally, the fairy Morgaina gives the sword Escaliber, which belonged to her brother, to Florambel, 'y quien quisiere saber las virtudes d'esta espada y por cuál aventura el rey Artur la ganó, lea el libro de *La búsqueda del santo grial* y allí lo fallará' (III, 12).

In the second half of the XVIth century there were published nineteen different romances of chivalry, in a total of eighty-one editions. The *Espejo de príncipes y caballeros* (1555), with seventeen editions, accounts for nearly 20 per cent of the total; in second place comes the story of *Reinaldos de Montalbán*, with ten impressions; third place is shared by *Amadís de Gaula* (1508), *Lepolemo* or *Caballero de la Cruz* (1521) and *Belianís de Grecia* (1545), with seven editions each. Then come *Palmerín de Oliva* (1551), with five reprints, and various continuations of *Amadís de Gaula*: *Lisuarte de Grecia* (1514, Book VII of *Amadís* by Feliciano de Silva), *Amadís de Grecia* (1530, Book IX, parts III and IV); all of them, like *Primaleón* (1512, Book III of *Palmerín*) were reprinted up to four times. Not a single title related to the Matter of Britain succeeded in appearing after 1550; not a single work was reprinted or reworked in the second half of the XVIth century.

3. Sentimental Fiction and Love Letters

From the middle of the XVth century, until 1548, there appeared a series of romances in which episodes of arms, combats and deeds of prowess occupy second place or are absent completely.

The basis of these 'sentimental fictions' is found not in France, but in Italy, and their greatest inspiration is from the *Elegia di madonna Fiammetta* by Boccaccio and the *Historia de duobus amantibus* by Eneas Silvio Piccolomini. Although chivalric narratives continue to serve as the background, the ambience in which they flourish (and in which some of the authors of these romances had a deserved prestige) is none other than that of the court itself in which *cancionero* poetry was the obligatory adornment of every gentleman with any sense of self-worth. Thus, the fusion of these three factors (Italian amorous narrative, chivalric narrative and *cancionero* poetry) would fashion the 'sentimental' sub-genre, which is represented by a score of texts between 1450, the year in which was published the *Siervo libre de amor* by Juan Rodríguez del Padrón (*c*.1390–1450), and 1548, with the appearance of Juan de Segura's *Proceso de cartas de amores*.

Throughout the century during which this class of fiction endured, a series of characteristics tends to remain unaltered. Autobiographical presentations are frequent (though they do not always appear), derived from lyric, and especially from the *Heroides* of Ovid and from *Fiammetta*; but in contrast with what occurs in those works, the first-person voice in the Castilian texts is always that of a man. In imitation of the *Heroides* and the *Historia de duobus amantibus*, letters occupy an important place in the development of the action, since this is the mode not only for expressing the deepest feelings, but also of attaining love and death. Generally, the plot is the result of two parallel love stories, which usually separate irredeemably the unfortunate protagonist from the lady whom he loves (and who does not return his affection), which gives rise to abundant debates on love and its multiple characteristics and consequences. The inclusion of these texts contained in the letters, and of speeches and conversations, and other testimonies transmitted in direct speech, reflects the same preoccupations that some historians and chroniclers had shown, and which are then inherited by the authors of romances of chivalry; this is, beyond question, a stylistic trait borrowed from Latin authors and it attests the arrival of humanism in fictional narrative.

If the techniques are linked to historiography, the Matter of Britain appears to have provided more than a few elements for the expression of the emotional vicissitudes of the protagonists of this genre. Indeed, the dominant scholarly opinion emphasises the presence of characteristics derived from the Arthurian tradition, which are elaborated by the authors of sentimental fiction and 're-exported' to the romances of chivalry, in a circular journey of mutual influence (Sharrer 1984a).

The presence of the Arthurian tradition in sentimental fiction is found at three levels: the same motifs, specific textual reminiscences and the construction of the characters, including in some cases their very names (Blay 1998: 261).

In the *Siervo libre de amor* (1450) by Juan Rodríguez del Padrón there is an episode in which the traces of Arthurian influence are easily recognisable: this is the 'Estoria de dos amadores', which displays notable similarities with Gottfried von Strassburg's *Tristan* and with other texts associated with this story, which reappears in the 'Casa de la sabia Doncella' in the prose *Tristan* and in the Aragonese *Cuento de Tristán de Leonís* at the beginning of the XVth century. In Castilian literature it is represented in the *Baladro del sabio Merlín*, a reworking of the *Suite Merlin*, which would be printed years later at Burgos in 1498 but which no doubt circulated in manuscript before then (Bonilla y San Martín 1907: 147b n. 1; Lida de Malkiel 1959: 417). Rodríguez del Padrón may possibly have enriched the text contained in the *Suite Merlin* or in its lost XVth-century Castilian version, adding to it elements of the tragic history of Doña Inés de Castro (murdered in 1355), an event which had greatly moved contemporaries and which was long remembered in the Iberian Peninsula (Alonso 1999). This new composition would be recovered when the *Baladro* was printed, so that in this case there was produced the first crux between an Arthurian text and a sentimental narrative; the outcome of the story would be tragic, with the murder of the lady and the suicide of the knight (Sharrer 1984a).

The intertextual play between the two genres is a frequent feature and the loans from one to the other, both within and outside the same genre, are also abundant, so that it is not always easy to determine the origin and the route of transmission of some features, just as it is equally difficult to establish the relative chronology of these borrowings. It is possible that some lost version of *Tristan* may have influenced Rodríguez del Padrón and that the success of his *Siervo libre de amor* may have given rise to imitations of detailed points in new editions or reworkings of *Tristán*.

In the meantime, however, other authors of sentimental fictions read the story (whether a lost version or not) of the lovers from Cornwall and the slim book of Rodríguez del Padrón, giving space in their works for these new versions and adding to the anonymous Tristan material even more material: such is the case of the letters in BNE MS 22021, which are sometimes attributed to Rodríguez del Padrón and at other times to Juan de Flores, who was the author, in the final quarter of the XVth century, of two highly popular sentimental romances: *Grisel y Mirabella* and *Grimalte y Gradissa*.

Grimalte y Gradissa stands out for its use of letters as a means of expression of the deepest thoughts of the lovers, an aspect which would have a special significance and which will be discussed below. Not only must the letters be mentioned, however, for the same applies to the important contributions from *Grimalte y Gradissa* that seem to have been incorporated in the version of *Tristán* printed in 1501: moralisations, stylistic elaboration, letters, all of which features would extend, a few years later in 1508, to *Amadís de Gaula* as reworked by Garci Rodríguez de Montalvo (Waley 1961).

The presence of wild men in sentimental fiction (Siervo in the romance whose title includes his name; Pámphilo in *Grimalte*, etc.) seems to find a correlation in the madness of Tristán and other lovers such as Lanzarote who withdraw from the world because they believe that their sentiments are not reciprocated, or to purge some sin against Love; but the allegorical value of the character should not be underestimated, as a representation, more or less carnivalesque, of some passions (Deyermond 1964 [1993: 17–42]).

Firmer ground is encountered in *Grisel* by Juan de Flores, which speaks of the 'law of Scotland', by which lovers should be punished according to the degree of culpability that each of them had in the relationship: the more guilty would die at the stake and the other would be exiled. Such a norm is found in the *Cárcel de Amor* of Diego de San Pedro and in Arthurian texts, such as the *Prose Merlin*, the *Prose Tristan*, and the *Post-Vulgate Roman du Graal* (Matulka 1931).

There may also be Arthurian roots underlying a long episode in the *Cárcel de Amor* of San Pedro: Persio, who is jealous of the loves of Leriano and Laureola and accuses them to the king. Leriano defends the honour of his lady, but she is condemned to death; Leriano rescues her, attacking the gaol; he kills Persio; then the warlike lover retreats to his castle at Susa, where he is besieged by the king, until finally the truth is known about the false accusation of Persio. Deyermond (1986 [1993]: 52) has indicated the structural parallel, the presence of repeated narrative motifs and the coincidence of numerous details of this episode and the account of the combats in the *Mort Artu* from the moment at which Agravain and Mordret accuse Lanzarote and Ginebra of holding an illicit relationship. The essential differences that are found between the episode in the *Cárcel de amor* and that at the end of Prose *Lanzarote* (or rather, of the *Post-Vulgate*) are caused by the status of the lovers in both texts, since in one the queen is married and, therefore, the love is adulterous, while in the sentimental fiction the lovers are unmarried, pure and chaste. Deyermond himself takes even further the relationship of Diego de San Pedro with Arthurian literature in emphasising the equivalences between names of persons and places in the *Cárcel de Amor* and in various works of the Matter of Britain:

Laureola	Laurette au Blanc Chief, Laurette de Brebaz	*Meraugis de Portlesguez*
Leriano	Leriador	*Estoire de Merlin*
Galio	Galehot	*Mort Artu*
Persio	Persides le Bloi	Prose *Tristan* (and other texts)
Suria	Surie	*Estoire de Merlin, Estoire du Graal*

In *Triste deleitación* (1458–67), the protagonist finds himself suddenly in a world identifiable with the Other World, in which game abounds, in great quantity, in huge and beautiful meadows. This has led some scholars to propose that it involves an eschatological motif drawn from the Arthurian or Breton tradition; but a reading of the text leads one to think rather of Ovid, Virgil, Dante and Boccaccio, authors cited by the enigmatic 'F.A.D.C.' who wrote the work.

3.1 *Carta de Iseo* and *Respuesta de Tristán*

One of the most striking characteristics of the Peninsular sentimental fiction is the presence of letters with amorous content. By resorting to these, the authors are merely incorporating into their romances elements found in reality, at the same time as providing readers with new models for their amorous relationships *in absentia*. This should not be seen as a novelty; since at least in the literary tradition the practice of correspondence had already been recommended to lovers by the *Ars amandi* of Ovid, and the same author provided abundant examples in his *Heroides*. It is no surprise that authors steeped in a profound familiarity with the Classical world, like the French writers Guillaume de Machaut, Jean Froissart, Christine de Pisan and Charles d'Orléans, should have had recourse to the use of letters in some of their works on amorous themes. Others, like Peter Abelard in the XIIth century, had also left evidence of the vicissitudes of their relationship in a series of letters that were translated from Latin to French and which acquired great diffusion. The fashion for correspondence included in narrative works had been imposing itself throughout the XIVth century in France and was not long in reaching the Iberian Peninsula.

Thus, the *Siervo libre de amor* of Rodríguez del Padron (1450) is presented as if it were a letter addressed by the author to Gonzalo de Medina. It is possible that Rodríguez del Padrón was merely imitating Eneas Silvio Piccolomini, who had constructed the amorous plot of his *Historia de duobus amantibus* (1444) around the exchange of ten letters between Eurialo and Lucrecia. Similarly, Rodríguez del Padrón himself, in translating Ovid's *Heroides* (*Bursario*), provides abundant examples for the later development of epistolary literature not necessarily linked to sentimental fiction; and, even more, he increased the Ovidian stock by adding three letters of his own confection (*Carta de Madreselva a Mauseol*, *de Troilo a Briseida* and the reply *de Briseida a Troilo*). In this way, a fundamental tradition in the genre was established.

The epistolary mode for one thing, the vogue for sentimental fiction for another, and finally the power of attraction exercised on the public by the love affair of Tristan and Isolde had as their result the creation of a *Carta* from the queen of Cornwall to the knight and the consequent *Respuesta* of the latter.

Gómez Redondo (1988) has studied in detail the *Carta enviada por Hiseo la Brunda a Tristán de Leonís quexándose* and the *Respuesta de Tristán desculpándose* (BNE MS 22021). In a section separated from a codex divided into four parts (BNE MS 22018, 22019, 22020 and 22021), which contained various works by Juan de Flores, there are several letters: those that interest us here occupy fols 8*v*–12*v*. They appear to belong to the beginning of the XVth century and indicate a reading of a version of *Tristán*. The two letters are anonymous, which has caused some hesitation over the attribution of their authorship. According to Gwara (1997: 80–1) and Sharrer (1981–2), they were written by Juan de Flores. For his part, Gómez Redondo (1988) considers that they could be the work of Juan Rodríguez del Padrón, taking into account the similarities which they present with the exchange of letters between Troilo and Briseida.

The letters allude to three characters: Hiseo de las Blancas Manos, Bragel and King Mares; they have, moreover, Hiseo la Brunda and Tristán de Leonís as interlocutors. The first letter expresses the complaints of Iseo la Rubia because Tristán has married Iseo de las Blancas Manos (Löseth 1891: §§60, 71); Tristán, in his reply, refutes each of the reproaches directed against him by his lover.

In reality, the Tristan material is merely a pretext for the elaboration of a love letter: the world of Arthurian or British chivalry is fused with that of sentimental fiction; but in addition there is an absolute mimesis with daily reality, since in the XVth century there abounded love letters, real or fictitious, as models for the drafting of letters that should reflect more or less exactly the sentiments of the knights and ladies of the court.

The two letters exchanged between Iseo and Tristan presuppose a reading of a medieval version of the story of the two lovers, as stated above. They are not the result of a partial copy of the text, nor are they a fragment of one, since the various Peninsular versions of Tristan contain nothing similar: none of the Catalan *Tristany* of Andorra, the *Cuento de Tristán de Leonís*, and the printed edition of 1501 (*Libro del esforçado caballero Don Tristán de Leonís*, reprinted with some variants in 1528) presents the complaints of Iseo in the terms in which the *Carta* does, despite the fact that in all these versions there is included a letter written at the moment at which the queen of Cornwall discovers that Tristan has married, and demands that he return to her presence.

We should accept that this text is an exercise that takes as its basis an amorous relationship well known to the public, on this basis of which the anonymous author constructs a letter following Ovidian models.

4. *Cancionero* Poetry

From the final years of the XIIIth century onwards there had emerged in the Iberian Peninsula important alterations in literary genres which, definitively, reflect changes in aesthetics, and the appearance of a new literary sensibility, to which new politicial and socio-cultural circumstances could not be unrelated. The Provenzal lyric disappears and the presence of troubadours in Peninsular courts ceases; shortly after the death of King D. Denis of Portgual (1279–1325) poetic production in Galician-Portuguese begins to be collected together, and after an obscure period (between 1360 and 1375) there began to write the earliest poets included in the first collection of poetry in Castilian, the *Cancionero de Baena*.

At the end of the XIIIth century or the beginning of the XIVth an important event occurs: the translation into Castilian and Portuguese of some Arthurian texts, and the acclimatisation of the narrative techniques of the French prose romance through the first romances in Castilian, the *Libro del Cavallero Zifar* and the first version of *Amadís de Gaula*. The translation of the stories of Tristan and of the *Post-Vulgate* cycle would be, from the first moment of their translation, a source of new references, of allusions among poets and writers in general, and would give rise to an increase in the use of Arthurian forms among personal names.

Tristán is cited by the archpriest of Hita in the *Libro de buen amor* around 1330:

> ca nunca tan leal fue Blancaflor a Flores
> ni es agora Tristán con todos sus amores. (1703ab)

The two lines of the archpriest are of even greater importance since they seem to allude to versions of French works that are now lost. It would even be possible to conclude that 'the vogue for Tristan was more recent in Spain than that of Flores and Blancaflor' (Corominas 1973: 626, st. 1703b).

In any case, the adverb 'agora' brings the story of *Tristán* into the present, or, to put it another way, refers to very recent innovations; it would not be surprising were the archpriest to be remembering a translation or a version that is now lost. Let us recall that a very few years before the archpriest wrote the *Libro de buen amor*, King D. Denis of Portugal also associated Flores and Blancaflor with Tristan as examples of lovers.

This is possibly the first allusion in Castilian to the narrative of the deeds of the Cornish knight; the prestige of Tristan, and the story of his ill-fated loves, would increase as the XIVth century progressed and during the XVth century. It is he who monopolises almost all the interest of the poets, who identified themselves with King Mark's nephew because of the firmness of his feelings, while their own beloved was comparable only with Queen Iseo in her beauty.

The poetry of the XIVth century, however, whether in Castilian or in Portuguese, is barely known from 1350 onwards; the situation begins to change when Juan Alfonso de Baena includes among the oldest poets of his collection some who can be placed in the final quarter of the XIVth century.

After Baena, many authors brought together similar compilations, giving a total of around 200 different manuscript *cancioneros*, containing in all something more than 800 authors and 7,000 works, datable between 1360 and 1564, the year in which there was published the first *cancionero* composed entirely of XVIth-century works. Through the literary techniques used and their aesthetic parameters, the poets of the *cancioneros* are the inheritors of the Galician-Portuguese poetry and the remote descendants of the Provenzal troubadours. The Matter of Britain is distributed unevenly in these poetic collections, as Cuesta Torre (1999b) has shown.

The *Cancionero de Baena* was completed around 1430, but its earliest texts go back to 1360. In fifteen compositions there are allusions to the following characters: Guinevere and Iseo, Galaz, Lanzarote, Tristan, Merlin, King Arthur, King Ban de Magunz, King Ban de Benoic and Joseph of Arimathea, besides a reference to the *Demanda del Santo Grial*. Alfonso Alvarez de Villasandino is the poet who has the most frequent recourse to Arthurian references, since he does this in five poems that can be dated to 1398–1405, although he cites only three characters: Iseo, Merlin and Ban de Magunz. For the number of references Pero Ferruz is the most notable poet, since he alludes to Ginebra and Iseo, Galaz, Lanzarote, Tristan and Arthur in a composition of 1407. Francisco Imperial (1406 and 1412), who was of Genoese descent, proud of his extensive literary knowledge, and had a good knowledge of Dante, also makes a show of having read works of the Matter of Britain.

The *Cancionero de Palacio*, between 1437 and 1443, is more committed than that of Baena to innovatory poetry. It contains a single composition, by Juan de Dueñas (around 1426–45) with Arthurian references, since it mentions Tristan and Iseo, and the Insula del Ploro.

The *Cancionero de San Román*, composed in 1454, is a continuation of, and is complementary to, the *Cancionero de Baena*. In six poems in this collection – works by Juan Alfonso de Baena, Lope de Estúñiga, Juan de Dueñas, Francisco Imperial – there are allusions to Palomades, Galaz, Lanzarote, Tristan, Merlin, Ginebra, Iseo and the Round Table. Baena himself cites Camelot as if it were a person; Baena, Juan de Dueñas, around 1426–45, and an anonymous author of 1445 all speak of the prophecies of the seer Merlin.

The *Cancionero de Estúñiga*, around 1462, composed in an Aragonese milieu, contains a single *canción* with references to 'Bruna' and 'Lançalota'.

The remaining *cancioneros* barely contain a single allusion each to Arthurian material. In the *Cancionero de Herberay*, c.1465, from a Navarrese background, there is an allusion to Merlin and to Mares, although the latter could equally refer to the god of war, Mars. In the *Cancionero de Barrantes*, c.1490, there is also a reference to Merlin; and in the XVIIIth-century copies of the *cancioneros* of *Pero Guillén* and *Martínez de Burgos* there are a pair of texts in each, in which there are, respectively, references to Galaz, Ginebra, Iseo la Brunda, Lanzarote, Tristan and Merlin, and to Merlin, the Holy Grail, Lanzarote del Lago and Tristan.

The printed *cancioneros* are no richer in Arthurian references, The *Cancionero General* of Hernando del Castillo (Valencia: Cristóbal Koffman, 1511) and its corrected and expanded second edition (Valencia: Jorge Costilla, 1514) include a couple of compositions containing the names of Ginebra, Iseo, Lanzarote, Tristan, Balan and Merlin. Merlin, finally, reappears in the *Cancionero de obras de burlas* (Valencia: Juan Viñao, 1519).

Table V.5 presents all the references, with indications of the date in the cases where this is known or may be conjectured, with the identification number from Dutton's repertoire (1991) and the reference of the oldest *cancionero* to contain the poem in question in which the Arthurian name is found. In many cases the same composition can be found repeated in various *cancioneros*, sometimes at a considerable chronological remove from one another. It is obvious that in these cases only the first appearance is relevant to our present purposes: repetition of a text may be for technical reasons associated with the production of a *cancionero*, or the popularity of the poet or the poem in question; for example, the work by Fernán Pérez de Guzmán cited here is found in five manuscript *cancioneros* and in as many printed ones.

Table V.5: The Matter of Britain in *Cancionero* verse

Author	Incipit/Date/Dutton ID no.	Cancionero	Characters
Pedro Ferruz	*Jamás non avré cuidado.* XIVth century. ID1431	Baena	Ginebra, Iseo, Lanzarote
Pedro Ferruz	*Los que tanto profazades.* Pre- 1407. ID1436	Baena	Artur, Galás, Lanzarote, Tristán
Alvarez Villasandino	*Amigos ya veo acercarse la fin* 1398–1405. ID1237	Baena	Merlín
Alvarez Villasandino	*Perlado que afana.* 1405. ID1264	Baena	Ban de Magunz
Francisco Imperial	*En dos setecientos e mas dos e tres.* 1405. ID0532	Baena	Ginebra, Iseo, Galaz, Lanzarote, Tristán
Fray Migir *or* Pedro de Valcárcel	*Al grand padre santo.* 1406. ID0542	Baena	Galaz, Lanzarote, Tristán
Nicolás	*Maestro señor.* c.1410. ID1610	Baena	José Abarimatia
Francisco Imperial	*Muchos poetas.* Pre-1412. ID1383	Baena	Ban, Tristán
Francisco Imperial	*Ante la muy alta corte.* ID0539	Baena	Galaz, Lanzarote, Tristán
Juan de Guzmán	*Invención dilecta.* Pre-1416. ID1527	Baena	Ban, Tristán

Alvarez Villasandino	*Muy poderoso varón.* Pre-1427. ID1349	Baena	Merlín
Alvarez Villasandino	*Ocho letras.* ID1289	Baena	Iseo
Alvarez Villasandino	*A nuestro señor el rey de Castilla.* ID 1339	Baena	Merlín
Pérez de Guzmán	*Tú, hombre que estás.* ID0197	Baena	Ginebra, Iseo
Diego Martínez de Medina *or* Fernán Sánchez Calavera	*Non quiero nin amo.* ID1457	Baena	Merlín
Juan Alfonso de Baena	*Para rey tan excelente.* 1432. ID0285	S. Román (Baena)	Lanzarote, Galaz, Tristán, Merlín, Camelot
Suero de Ribera	*A vos linda loaré.* Pre-1440 ID2456.	Palacio	Ginebra, Camalote, Lançarote
Anon.	*Suelto es el grant.* 1445. ID0519	S. Román	Merlín
Juan de Dueñas	*Vi, señora, una carta* Pre-1445. ID2606	Palacio	Iseo, Tristán
Juan de Dueñas	*El sol claro la luna escuresca* Pre-1445. ID0479	S. Román	Profecías de Merlín
Lope de Estúñiga	*Dezir sobre la cerca de Atiença.* 1446. ID0353	S. Román	Mesa Redonda
Juan de Tapia	*Siendo enemiga.* 1432–60? ID0568	Estúñiga	Bruna, Lançalota
Fernando de la Torre	*Capítulo XIXº de unos naipes por coplas.* Pre-1465. ID0594: *Manificencia y virtud*	Fernando de la Torre	Dama del Lago, Lançarote
Hugo de Urriés	*A vos los muy.* Pre-1465. ID2190.	Herberay	Mares?
Anon.	*En Avila por la A.* ID2304	Herberay	Merlín
Comendador Román	*Don poeta desflorado.* ID3015	P. Guillén	Merlín
Juan Barba	*Manda el alto poderoso.* ID2993	P. Guillén	Galás, Ginebra, Iseo, La Brunda, Lanzarote, Tristán
Jerónimo de Pinar	*Tome Vuestra Magestad.* 1498. ID6637, *Juego trobado de naipes*	General 1511	Tristán

Hernán Mejía	*Porfiáis damas que diga.* Pre-1511. ID6097	General 1511	Balán, Ginebra, Iseo, Lanz, Tristán
Anon.	*Si os valga.* ID6781	General 1511	Merlín

The majority of the references are found in compositions of the first half of the XVth century; to be more precise, in the *Cancionero de Baena*, which has its roots in the final quarter of the XIVth century. And, to a great extent, it is a matter of references which do not reveal a direct knowledge of Arthurian literature.

The most popular of the characters from the court of Arthur among the *Cancionero* poets is, beyond doubt, Merlin (cited on ten occasions), whose prestige was reinforced by the abundance of prophecies attributed to him during the XVth century (Tarré 1943; Guadalajara 1996) and also by the possible diffusion of the *Baladro del sabio Merlín*, the first printed edition of which was produced in Burgos in 1498. He is matched closely by Tristán (ten citations) and Iseo (seven cases), based, no doubt, on the success of the various versions of their love story which were circulating in Castile since shortly before 1330, as the archpriest of Hita in the *Libro de buen amor* attests. Lanzarote (eight instances), Guinevere and Galaz (six citations each) occupy the next positions in this popularity chart, making obvious the diffusion of the first Castilian versions of *La demanda del santo Grial*. The remaining characters, including King Arthur, are scarcely mentioned at all, while other notable heroes of the king's retinue are unknown to the poets; among them, Galván becomes the great loser, perhaps because he was too well known from everyday nomenclature and for being the constant companion of Gaiferos.

5. Balladry and Chapbooks

The earliest Spanish balladry (the *romances*, making up collectively the *romancero*) appear in the XIVth century, at the same time as the epic poetry disappears and the prose romance imitating Arthurian models begins to develop. The *romances* are narrative poems that are generally short, of an epic or lyric character, and are equivalent in some aspects to the English ballads. They are usually extremely concise and dramatic, without any kind of digression. Some of these *romances* went on to swell the pages of the *cancioneros* and others remained alive in the oral tradition until the present, appreciated during the XVth and XVIth centuries for their simplicity of expression and their music, so that they rapidly penetrated all social groups and achieved an enormous diffusion. The descendants of the Jews expelled from Spain in 1492 still sing today some of those old *romances*, which they have preserved in their oral heritage.

Some *romances* took as their theme contemporary historical events; others seem to derive from fragmentation of epic poems; some have a lyric character and there are others inspired by chronicles or by literature that was in vogue, and, particularly, by Carolingian and Arthurian stories. This last group is known as the *romances novelescos*, and is based principally on material referring to Roland, Charlemagne, the Twelve Peers and other heroes of the 'royal cycle', including Durandarte: the last-named, from originally being Roland's sword, is converted with the passage of time into yet another French champion.

The Matter of Britain provides hardly any themes or characters to the *romancero*. It is difficult to situate the *romance* of the death of Tristan in the known tradition, although logic could suggest that it should be included among the texts that predate the first printed version of the loves of Tristan and Iseo (Valladolid: Juan de Burgos, 1501), since it is cited before 1498 in the *Juego de naipes trovado* of Jerónimo de Pinar, dedicated to Isabel the Catholic (González Cuenca 2004: III, 179ff.; Menéndez Pidal 1968: II, 46ff.):

> Y el romance que aquí os dan
> es aquel que havéis oido
> mucho triste y dolorido:
> 'Mal se quexa don Tristán' (lines 405–8)

It is also highly possible that Joanot Martorell, who began *Tirant lo Blanc* between 1455 and 1460, was alluding to a very similar lyric composition when he wrote that 'La senyora, per fer-li plaer, canta un romanç ab baixa veu de Tristan i com se planyia de la llançada del rei Marc.' The remainder of this romance could not have been much different from that published by Di Stefano (1993: 225–6):

> Mal se quexa don Tristán que la muerte le aquexaba;
> preguntando por Iseo, de los sus ojos lloraba:
> '¿Qué es de tí, la mi señora? ¡Mala sea la tu tardada!,
> que si mis ojos te viessen, sanaría esta mi llaga.'
> Era él este planto haciendo, y la reina que llegava:
> '¡Quien os hirió, mi señor, herida tenga de rabia!'
> 'Hiriáme el rey mi tío de esta cruel lançada.
> Hirióme desde una torre, que de cerca no osava.'
> Juntóse boca con boca, allí se salió el alma.

The *romance* enjoyed great popularity, and was printed in at least thirteen collections of *romances* or in chapbooks or broadsides (*pliegos sueltos*) between 1516 and 1581, in four different versions, of thirty-two and twenty-eight octosyllabic lines and two versions of eighteen lines, as Di Stefano has established (1988: 271–303). The differences between the two branches can be seen from the version cited above, which possibly existed by the middle of the XVth century, and the one which was most widely diffused throughout the XVIth century:

> Ferido está don Tristán de una muy mala lançada;
> diérasela el rey su tío por celos que d'él catava;
> el fierro tiene en el cuerpo, de fuera le tembla el asta.
> Valo a ver la reina Iseo por la su desdicha mala.
> Júntanse boca con boca cuanto una missa rezada.
> Llora el uno, llora el otro, la cama bañan en agua,
> Allí nace un arboledo que açucena se llamava:

> cualquier mujer que la come luego se siente preñada
> comiérala reina Iseo por la su desdicha mala.

Despite the differences existing between the two branches and the four versions, the transmission of all the witnesses of the *Romance de la muerte de Tristán* is characterised by its aesthetic conservatism: it involves chapbooks which frequently include the gloss by Alonso de Salaya from Cantabria (Rodríguez-Moñino 1997: nos. 509, 658, 882, 883, 883.5), an author immersed in the *cancionero* tradition and therefore untouched by the Petrarchan poetic innovations that had been brought in by Boscán and Garcilaso de la Vega years before. Moreover the chapbooks in which the different versions of this *romance* are collected seem to have been grouped according to a clearly defined criterion: to give examples of thwarted love and tragic love. Without a doubt, this was the perception that readers and listeners of the *romance* had, and this was the very aim which had led Jerónimo Pinar to include it in his *Juego de naipes*, a game for a court society in which not all ladies could consider themselves fortunate in their loves (Di Stefano 1988).

Two *romances* with Arthurian content have Lanzarote as their protagonist. These are *Tres hijuelos avía el rey* and *Nunca fuera cavallero*. Another romance, *Cavalga doña Ginebra*, relates an adventure involving the queen. *Tres hijuelos avía el rey* enjoyed some popularity in the XVth century, to judge by the fact that Jerónimo Pinar used one of its lines in the *Juego de naipes*, when he recommends that one of the ladies should sing with great pleasure 'Dígasme tú, el hermitaño', although it may be that the version sung by the ladies of the court of Isabel the Catholic was that which replaced the question about the white stag with a question about love, more in accordance with the amusement of the court (González Cuenca 2004: III, 196–7). The *romance*, as it is transmitted in the single witness of the *Cancionero de romances* (Antwerp 1550), has the characteristics of an adventure from the Matter of Britain:

> Tres hijuelos avía el rey, tres hijuelos que no más.
> Por enojo que uvo d'ellos todos maldito los ha:
> el uno se tornó ciervo, el otro se tornó can,
> el otro se tornó moro, passó las aguas del mar.
> Andávase Lanzarote entre las damas holgando;
> grandes bozes dio la una: 'Cavallero, estad parado.
> Si fuesse la mi ventura, cumplido fuesse mi hado.
> Que yo casasse con vos y vos comigo de grado,
> y me diéssedes en arras aquel ciervo del pie blanco.'
> –'Dároslo he yo, mi señora, de coraçón y de grado
> si supiesse yo las tierras donde el ciervo era criado.'
> Ya cavalga Lançarote, ya cavalga y va su vía;
> delante de sí llevava los sabuesos por la traílla.
> Llegado avía a una hermita donde un hermitaño avía.
> –'Dios te salve, el hombre bueno'. – 'Buena sea tu venida.
> Caçador me parescéis en los sabuesos que traía.'
> 'Esse ciervo del pie blanco, ¿donde haze su manida?' –
> –'Quedáisos aquí, mi hijo, hasta que sea de día;

> contaros he lo que ví y todo lo que sabía.
> Por aquí passó esta noche dos horas antes del día;
> siete leones con él y una leona parida.
> Siete condes dexa muertos y mucha cavallería.
> Siempre Dios te guarde, hijo, por doquier que fuer tu ida,
> que quien acá te embió no te quería dar la vida.
> ¡Ay dueña de Quintañones, de mal fuego seas ardida!,
> que tan buen cavallero por tí ha perdido la vida.'
> (Di Stefano 1993: 223–4)

The assonances permit the division of the *romance* into three different series (*-á, a-o; í-a*), which raises the suspicion that we are faced with a juxtaposition of several texts. The first of these refers to the metamorphosis of the three sons of the king into a stag, a dog and a Moor; it is a frequent theme in folktales. Next, and abruptly, Lancelot appears as the protagonist of an episode which has no relation to the preceding lines: the setting has changed, the characters have changed, and the subject has changed; now we find ourselves in a courtly ambience in which a lady asks the knight to marry her and to give her as a present the stag with the white foot. The third text, with another change of assonance, presents Lanzarote who, while out on a day's hunting, arrives at a hermitage and asks the hermit about the stag – thematically, there may be some continuity with the preceding section. The hermit gives lodging to Lancelot and allows him to share in a vision; 'seven lions and a lioness which has just whelped' would be symbolically equivalent to the seven counts and the many knights who have fallen victim in the hunt for the white-footed stag. The *romance* known to us today ends with a curse directed against a woman called Quintañones, who could be the same one who asked Lancelot to marry her in the second section, but could equally be a different lady, if the independence of each of these texts is accepted (Entwistle 1925: 208).

In Jerónimo Pinar's *Juego de naipes* it is not clear which version of the *romance* was involved, but there is no doubt about the text being followed by Elio Antonio de Nebrija. On speaking of metrics in his *Gramática de la lengua castellana* (Salamanca 1492), he gives as an example of the technique of assonance three lines of 16 syllables of 'that *romance antiguo*':

> Digas tú el hermitaño que hazes la vida santa
> aquel ciervo del pie blanco dónde haze su morada.
> – Por aquí passó esta noche una ora antes del alva.

And, some pages further on, on referring to syllable-count and to rhythm, he again takes as an example 'this *romance antiguo*':

> Digas tú el ermitano que hazes la santa vida
> Aquel ciervo del pie blanco dónde haze su manida.

Nebrija, in 1492, knew two different versions of a part of the third segment of the *romance*: one, with assonance in *á-a* and the other with assonance in *í-a*. But little more can be deduced from the humanist's brief quotation. In any case, the *romance* was the subject of a *contrafactum* in the *Cancionero musical de Palacio* (1505) and in the *Cancionero general* of Hernando del Castillo (1511), but neither of those adaptations maintains the relation with Queen Guinevere's knight. Nor is it maintained in the gloss contained in the *Comedia Thebayda* (Valencia 1521, cena IX), but all the texts, whether direct or indirect quotations, copies or reworkings and glosses, attest the popularity of the *romance* even before its publication in Antwerp in 1550. And the *contrafacta* continued, even more understandably, after the publication of the *Cancionero de romances* there, as is the case in the *Cancionero llamado Flor de enamorados* (Barcelona 1562).

There is no doubt that the fact that the starting point 'Dígasme tú, el ermitaño' becomes the basis for the quotations and reworkings gives reason to suppose that it had an independent life; but as Diego Catalán (1970: 82–100) has indicated, it is very probable that at least the first and third parts were a unit from the outset, since in this way the human identity of the white stag would have been established beyond any doubt. He notes that the disconnection of the various motifs that constitute the ballad contributes powerfully to the creation of the supernatural ambience of mystery in which the action develops and which culminates in the enigmatic words of the hermit (Catalán 1970: 92–3).

Be this as it may, the Arthurian resonances of the whole are beyond debate; and a further two works, one French (*Lai de Tyrolet*) and the other Dutch (*Roman van Lancelot*) seem to have a relationship with our text, albeit that the relationship is merely thematic and is not one involving details. It is probable that other texts existed, different from those that survive and older than them; these hypothetical texts could have served as a source for both of the Spanish *romances*, and also for the other works that are linked to them thematically (Entwistle 1925: 203–9).

Nunca fue cavallero is not attested in the XVth century, for which reason it could be a later recreation, but it was widely diffused in the XVIth century and its opening lines later acquired fame thanks to their presence in *Don Quixote*. The text is preserved in a XVIth-century manuscript (BNE MS 1317) and in a couple of *pliegos sueltos* (Rodríguez-Moñino 1997: nos. 353, 711), one of them at least earlier than 1540; in addition, it was published in the *Tercera parte de la Silva de varios Romances* (Zaragoza, 1551), and was the subject of a gloss written by Martín de la Membrilla. The musician Luis de Milán cites it in *El cortesano* (1561). The most complete version (that of the manuscript in the BNE, published by Di Stefano 1993: 224–5) seems to refer to the episode of the death of Meleagant, which is found in *Le chevalier de la charrette* by Chrétien de Troyes and in the prose versions of the story of Lancelot:

> Nunca fuera cavallero de damas tan bien servido
> Como fuera Lançarote quando de Bretaña vino:
> donzellas curavan d'él y dueñas de su rocino;
> esa dueña Quintañona, esa le escanciava el bino,
> la linda reina Ginebra se lo acostava consigo.
> Estando al mejor sabor, que sueño no avía dormido,

> la reina toda turbada movido le ha un partido:
> – 'Lançarote, Lançarote, si antes fuérades venido,
> no dixera el Orgulloso las palabras que abía dicho:
> que mataría al rey Artús y aun a todos sus sobrinos
> que a pesar de vos, señor, él dormiría conmigo.'
> Lançarote que lo oyó gran pesar ha recebido.
> Lleno de muy gran enojo sus armas avía pedido;
> Armóse de todas ellas, de la reina se ha partido.
> Va buscar al Orgulloso, hallólo baxo de un pino;
> conbátense de las lanças, a las hachas han venido:
> ya desmaya el Orgulloso, ya cae en tierra tendido,
> cortádole ha la cabeça, sin hazer ningún partido.
> Tornóse para la reina, de quien fue bien recebido.

The reworking of the episode adds the character of the 'Dueña Quintañona', equivalent to the 'Dueña de Quintañones' of the *romance* of the hermit, and which seems to be a Castilian version of the Dama de Malohaut, the beautiful young woman who falls in love with Lanzarote for the deeds that he accomplishes, whom she takes prisoner to attain his love and whom she finally releases. The Dama de Malohaut ended up as a friend and confidante of Queen Guinevere and became the friend of Galahot thanks to the intervention of the queen herself (Alvar 2004: 117–18).

The *romance* of *Tres hijuelos avía el rey* echoes the falling in love of the Dueña Quintañona and her efforts to win the love of the knight. *Nunca fuera cavallero* places the lady in the entourage of Queen Guinevere, as her closest serving-lady. Both *romances* could refer, then, to different episodes from the story of Lancelot, as Entwistle pointed out long ago (1925: 198–209). The passage of time meant that the term 'dueña', originally a term of respect applied to widowed ladies of high standing, evolved into a synonym for a lecherous old go-between (Marianella 1979), which gives a comic twist exploited by Francisco de Quevedo (in his *Sueño de la Muerte*), while the joke by Cervantes (*Don Quixote*, I, 49), is directed more at the age of the 'dueña' and her activity as a cupbearer, but both cases are based on this *romance*.

Queen Guinevere reappears in another *romance* published for the first time in the middle of the XVIth century, *Cavalga doña Ginebra* (*Cancionero manuscrito de Pedro del Pozo*, 1547, and printed at Zaragoza, 1551). The denouement of both versions is very different, since the manuscript version has a moralising character, 'el diablo es sutil y a entrambos engañaría', while the printed version is more uninhibited:

> Cavalga doña Ginebra, y de Córdova la rica
> con trezientos cavalleros que van en su compañía;
> el tiempo haze tempestuoso, el cielo se escurescía.
> Con la niebla que haze, escura, a todos perdido havía,
> sino fuera a su sobrino, que de riendas la traía.
> Como no viera a ninguno, d'esta suerte le dezía:
> – Toquedes vos, mi sobrino, vuestra dorada vozina,
> porque lo oyessen los míos, qu'estavan en la montiña.
> – De tocalla, mi señora, de tocar, si tocaría,

> mas el frío haze grande, las manos se me elarían,
> y ellos están tan lexos, que nada aprovecharía.
> – Meteldas vos, mi sobrino, so faldas de mi camisa.
> – Esso tal no haré, señora, que haría descortesía,
> porque vengo yo muy frío y a vuestra merced elaría.
> – D'esso no curéis, señor, que yo me lo sufriría,
> qu'en callentar tales manos cualquier cosa se çufría.
> El, de que vio el aparejo, las sus manos le metía;
> pellizcara le en el muslo y ella reido se havía.
> Apearon se en un valle que allí cerca parescía,
> solos estavan los dos, no tienen más compañía.
> Como veen el aparejo, mucho holgado se havían.
> (Catalán 1970: 85–6; Di Stefano 1993: 158–9)

It would be useless to try to find an inspiration for this *romance* in a specific episode of Arthurian literature. The only 'nephew' (*sobrino*) who has or attempts to have a sexual relationship with the queen would be Mordret at the end of *La mort Artu*; but there is not the slightest willing concession on the part of Guinevere, who is the victim of the violence of Arthur's nephew. This *romance* has a humorous tone, and the joke is constructed around a topic already present in the *Aeneid* and which reappears in a host of texts of every kind, and in which lyric and narrative motifs are combined to cover the erotic insinuations, as J. M. Pedrosa has pointed out (2012). The *romance* of Guinevere and her nephew presents undoubted similarities with that of *Por los bosques de Cartago*, in which Dido and Aeneas find themselves in a similar situation, which was published in the *Cancionero de romances* of 1550 and in Timoneda's *Rosa de amores* of 1573.

Two *romances* take up the figure of Galván, but as in the case of Queen Guinevere in the previous *romance*, this knight now has no connection with the nephew of King Arthur since his activity is centred in the French court, in the circle of Roland and Gaiferos. These ballads are *Estávase la condessa* and *Vámonos, dixo, mi tío*. Both *romances* constitute a single narrative unit, since the second continues with some words spoken by Gaiferos which are introduced by a *verbum dicendi* at the end of the first *romance*. Thus, *Estávase la condessa* sketches the plot and *Vámonos, dixo, mi tío* gives the dénouement, with the return and revenge of Gaiferos. In both romances Count Galván is a cowardly traitor who ill-treats his pious wife the countess, mother of Gaiferos, and is beheaded by her son.

The degradation of the figure of Gauvain began in the *Queste del Saint Graal* with his tendency to frivolity and womanising, and in the *Tristan en prose* Arthur's nephew no longer enjoys the prestige that he had in the verse *roman*, since he is considered to be envious, treacherous and cowardly (Yllera 1991). In the *romances* referred to here, however, only the name is left, and it is impossible to link the character to the Matter of Britain or the world of Arthur.

6. Historiography

6.1 Liber regum *and* Anales Toledanos Primeros

The first historiographic references to King Arthur in the Iberian Peninsula are found in the *Anales navarro-aragoneses* (1196; ed. Ubieto Arteta 1989: 40), which are transmitted together with the *Liber regum*, where we read that 'Era D.LXXX. aynos fizo la bataylla el rey Artus con Modret en Quibleno.' A few years later the *Anales Toledanos Primeros* (1214) pick up the same statement (ed. Flórez, 1767: XXIII, 381): 'Lidio el rey Zitus con Modret su sobrino en Camblenc. Era DLXXX.' In both cases the report is dated in accordance with the Hispanic era, which corresponds to the year AD 542. The detail that Mordret was the nephew of Arthur indicates that the Toledo text used a slightly fuller version than that followed by the Navarrese manuscript. Furthermore, it is noteworthy that the date corresponds clearly to that given by Geoffrey of Monmouth for this event, after referring to the wounds suffered by the king and how he went to the isle of Avalon 'ad sananda vulnera sua'; leaving as his successor Constantine, 'diadema Britanniae concessit, anno ab incarnatione Domini DXLII' (Faral 1993: III, 278). However, the prolix style of Geoffrey has little relation with the bald note transmitted in the Hispanic texts; to find the name of the protagonists in the battle and the place where it occurred, it is necessary to read several pages of his text, and to deduce what had happened amidst the enumeration of the combatants and strategic or military manoeuvres. It is, moreover, surprising that our texts do not take any other information from the brilliant description by Geoffrey. In contrast with the *Historia regum Britanniae*, the *Annales Cambriae* are much more stark: '537. Gueith Camlann in qua Arthur et Medraut corruerunt' (ed. Faral 1993: III, 44–50).

To understand the sudden interest of the two Hispanic kingdoms in events in England it is necessary to remember that relations between Castile and the Plantagenets towards the end of the XIIth century were institutionalised with the marriage of Eleanor, daughter of Henry II of England, to Alfonso VIII of Castile (1170). The role taken by the young queen is recorded vividly thanks to the poems of some of the Provenzal troubadours who visited her court, such as Guillem de Berguedà (*Un sirventes ai en cor*), who declared himself both in public and in private to be her vassal, and Raimon Vidal de Besalú, who gives a vivid picture of the life of the court in his famous *Castia-gilos* (Alvar 1977: 135–8).

Conflicts between Castile and Navarre towards the end of the XIIth century were frequent and Henry II of England (1133–89) repeatedly intervened to re-establish peace or to relieve the tensions that existed; so it happened in 1170 and 1176. It must be remembered that the king of England was also the Duke of Aquitaine, a territory bordering the kingdom of Navarre, and which became part of the dowry of Eleanor when she married Alfonso VIII, in addition to Gascony, which promptly became an enduring *casus belli* between Castile and England. It is important to recall that Richard Coeur de Lion was married to Berenguela, daughter of Sancho VI of Navarre (1191), and that the wife of Alfonso VIII of Castile, Eleanor, was Richard's sister: these family relationships explain the continual intervention of the king of England in Castilian and Navarrese affairs towards the end of the XIIth century.

It would not be unusual if the *Historia regum Britanniae* or some vernacular text derived from it, more intelligible for the laity (such as Wace's *Roman du Brut*), should have reached Pamplona on the occasion of the marriage of Berenguela and Richard; nor would it be surprising if another copy had reached Castile in similar circumstances; but there were other motives and other embassies, so that there was no lack of opportunities for this. It could even be that a single copy went from one court to the other, or that the information recorded in one text was reused a few years later in another.

What is certain is that the *Liber regum* (with the *Anales navarro-aragoneses*) added to the *Fuero* (or lawcode) of Navarre (1196) reports the final combat of Arthur and his nephew Mordret, and that a few years later the *Anales Toledanos Primeros* (completed before 1217) repeat the same information, with the stark style characteristic of these works of historiography, as we have seen. The political and family relationships between the kingdoms of Castile and Navarre would have facilitated, no doubt, the knowledge of this final battle between nephew and uncle. It would be more difficult, if not impossible, to know whether this knowledge came through the work of Geoffrey of Monmouth or through some other more miscellaneous historiographic work.

Towards the year 1200, there was written in Navarre the vernacular *Liber regum* (or *Cronicón Villarense*, from its oldest copy), which was to have an extraordinary diffusion in the Iberian Peninsula and which was reworked and updated on various occasions throughout the XIIIth and XIVth centuries. Its author, perhaps a monk of the monastery of Fitero, established the line of descent from Adam to Christ, and those of the emperors of Persia, Greece and Rome, of the Visigothic kings, those of Asturias, and of the judges, counts and kings of Castile, the kings of Navarre, Aragon and France, and that of El Cid. In its first version, the *Liber regum* (between 1196 and 1209) and the *Anales navarro-aragoneses* (1196) soon came to form a unit with the *Fueros de Sobrarbe y de Navarra* (Catalán and de Andrés 1970: LIII ff.) These must have arrived together in Toledo at the beginning of the XIIIth century; the archbishop of that diocese was Rodrigo Jiménez de Rada (born *c*.1170), who was archbishop from 1210 to 1247 and was the author of an extensive historiographic work known as the *De rebus Hispaniae* or the *Historia Gothorum*.

Jiménez de Rada was born in Navarre, of Navarrese paternal descent while his mother was of Castilian origin. He was educated in Bologna and Paris and was rapidly made a counsellor of Sancho VII of Navarre, which did not prevent his enjoying the confidence of the kings of Castile, Alfonso VIII and Fernando III. His journeys between the two kingdoms were continuous, and, no doubt, he could have been the link necessary for transmitting incipient Navarrese historiography to Toledo.

In any case, the *Liber regum*, compiled between 1196 and 1209 as we have seen, was used by the *Anales Toledanos I* (*c*.1214), and towards 1220 a new version of the text was produced, which in turn would be exploited by Archbishop Rodrigo in his *De rebus Hispaniae* (completed in 1243), as established by Diego Catalán (Catalán and de Andrés 1970: LVI). The 1220 version in turn gave rise to an interpolated version.

Towards 1260, and before 1270, the *Liber regum* was reworked in Navarre, using for this a manuscript that contained the Navarrese version of around 1200; the new text was copied among others by Martín de Larraya in the XVth century, who gave it the title of *Libro de las generaciones*. The Navarrese reworking of the third quarter of the XIIIth century introduced a genealogy of the kings of Troy and Britain, based on Wace's *Roman du Brut* for everything relating to the journey of the Trojan hero to the islands, and to his descendants in Britain. On reaching the battle of Camlann, the reworking of the *Liber regum* departs from Wace and introduces an episode which is found only in *Le Mort Arthur*, an English stanzaic poem of around 1400, for which it is necessary to assume a source common to both texts, earlier than 1260.

Like Jiménez de Rada, Alfonso X had recourse to the *Liber regum* in compiling the *Estoria de España* (before 1270); the text followed by the Castilian king was possibly the interpolated version arising from the reworking of 1220.

Don Pedro, Count of Barcelos, also used the *Liber regum* (in its Navarrese reworking of 1260), incorporating it bodily into his *Livro das linhagens* (1343); he also used it in a less systematic way in the *Crónica de 1344*. Other Galician-Portuguese chronicle texts also took advantage of the great success of the *Liber regum* in reworkings that are not always easy to identify. Thus, for example, in 1404 a chronicle was compiled in Galician-Portuguese that follows the steps of the *Crónica de 1344* of Pedro de Barcelos, although it seeks to amplify certain pieces of information relating to the genealogy of the kings of Britain on the basis of a text that contained an abbreviated version of Wace's *Roman de Brut* different from that used by the author responsible for reworking the *Liber regum* in 1260.

Entwistle believed that the origin of the information contained in the *Libro das linhagens* and the *Crónica de 1344* by Don Pedro should be sought in a summary in a Romance language of the *Historia regum Britanniae* of Geoffrey of Monmouth (1925: 38–47); and the same origin would underlie the information on King Arthur and his ancestors found in the *Crónica de 1404*, although the Count of Barcelos and the later chronicler would have used the material at their disposal in different ways. Catalán (1962: 370–401) has shown that Wace's *Roman de Brut* (1155) was the essential basis of all of them, possibly thanks to a version produced in Navarre before 1260.

The chronicler of 1404 wrote when Joam Bivas had already translated into Portuguese or Castilian the *Post-Vulgate* (1313), so that part of his information is obtained from the *Livro de Josep Abarimatea*, from the *Demanda del Sancto Grial* and from the *Baladro del sabio Merlín*.

6.2 *The* Grande e General Estoria *of Alfonso X*

Alfonso X, king of Castile (1252–84), had already used the *Liber regum* in compiling the *Estoria de España*, so that he knew at least the information relating to the battle of Camlann. But in addition the historians in the royal circle did not hesitate to undertake a history with a wide scope which, definitively, merely elaborated the previous tradition. Nothing is known of the date at which the *General Estoria* was begun; its composition interrupted for some time the work on the *Estoria de España* or *Crónica General* and it took advantage in part of materials already assembled for the latter, but it is probable that the two historiographic projects developed simultaneously for a time and even that the *Estoria de España* made use of materials compiled for use in the *General Estoria*. It is believed that the writing of the latter was already under way in 1272 and that the work lasted until the king's death in 1284.

The general plan was extremely ambitious: to produce a universal history, from the creation of the world to the time of King Alfonso. To carry out this plan, the team of historians divided the history of the world into 'ages', following the model of Isidore of Seville: the first age extended from Genesis and the creation of the world until Noah; the second age lasted until Abraham; this is the point at which a great deal of material contained in the *Metamorphoses* and *Heroides* of Ovid was incorporated, as well as the story of Thebes (taken from the French *Roman de Thèbes*), the labours of Hercules and the destruction of Troy (taken from Dares the Phrygian). The third age ran from Abraham to David; in this part were included the wanderings of Ulysses and the history of the kings of Britain (according to information from Geoffrey of Monmouth); and finally the life and work of King Solomon and other material from the Old Testament. Next came the fourth age, with the empires of Babylon, Persia, Egypt, Greece and Rome, with particular attention paid to the deeds of Alexander the Great (following the *Alexandreis* of Gautier de Châtillon). The fifth age is the subject of the rest of the *General Estoria*, since the work remained incomplete and did not get as far as beginning the narrative of the sixth age, which should have covered the period from the birth of the Virgin Mary to the reign of Fernando III or even that of Alfonso X himself. In the fifth age there are retold the history of the Maccabees, together with a translation of Lucan's *Pharsalia* and the history of Rome until the birth of Christ.

This brief summary suffices to enable one to understand the undertaking of the *General Estoria*, which is converted in this way into a compendium of universal history in which there is accommodated every kind of subject matter, from geography to religious beliefs, from everyday life to astronomy, education, zoology, medicine and justice.

We do not known when the *Historia regum Britanniae* of Geoffrey of Monmouth reached the royal scriptorium, but it is certain that Alfonso X's collaborators made use of it from part II to part V of the *General Estoria*, elaborating the materials in accordance with the habitual practices of the historiographic team: that is to say, that the complete work ('estoria complida') was divided into various chronological units ('estorias departidas'), which were then inserted into the work in the place corresponding chronologically to them. In this way, there was translated and incorporated into the *General Estoria* a third of the *Historia regum Britanniae*, according to the following scheme:

> Part II: (1 Kings: 60–80). In accordance with the 'estoria de las Bretañas', this covers from the birth of Brutus to the combat with the giant Gormagoc and the foundation of the new Troy.
> Part III: Among the contemporaries of the successors of Solomon is found King Eubrauco and his son Brutuo Verdescudo, who ruled in Britain (ch. I), and Leír and Rud Hubras (ch. XII); next are included the reigns of King Blandud and his son Leír (chs LX–LXIV).
> Part IV. The Alfonsine historians considered as contemporaries of the Persian Xerxes Rivallo, Dumvallio and others, because they lacked specific chronological indications (Xerxes, ch. XVII), until the invasion of France by Belinnio and Brennio (ch. XXV).
> Part V (text II, 'Mandate of Julius Caesar'). After the complete version of the *Pharsalia* of Lucan, the *General Estoria* narrates the deeds of Caesar, including the relations of the latter with Casibelano (chs IX–XIV).

Nowhere does the *General Estoria* cite Geoffrey of Monmouth by name, which leads one to think that the Alfonsine historians had an exemplar that lacked the introductory folios, possibly related to the family represented by the manuscripts of Harlech, Leiden and Paris, which they subjected to numerous amplifications to adapt the text to the work's public (Kasten 1970: 109).

Unfortunately, King Alfonso's collaborators did not progress beyond the birth of Mary, so that their use of the work of Geoffrey of Monmouth stopped at the beginning of the Roman conquest, far from the deeds of Arthur and his knights. We do not know if the compilers of the *General Estoria* had a complete translation into Spanish of the *Historia regum Britanniae*, at least in draft, or if they were translating Geoffrey's work into Castilian as they reached in its chronological order each successive section which it was necessary to tackle.

Definitely everything seems to indicate that Hispanic historiography knew at least two different traditions concerning the Matter of Britain: that represented by Wace's *Roman de Brut* on the one hand, and that derived from the *Historia regum Britanniae* on the other. In both cases, the versions were faithful renderings and were circulated during the second half of the XIIIth century, between 1260 and 1284. The Navarrese reference from the end of the XIIth century and the Toledan one from the beginning of the next century are so skeletal that it is difficult to know whence they came, but it is very probable that the first redaction of the *Liber regum* knew the narratives contained in the *Roman de Brut*.

6.3 *Leomarte,* Sumas de historia troyana, *and Lope García de Salazar,* Libro de las bienandanzas

Alfonso X's *General Estoria* succeeded in integrating into its content materials derived from the most varied sources, given the universalist nature of that work. The presence of the *Historia regum Britanniae* in the chapters devoted to the climax and consequences of the Trojan War is fully justified, since Brutus was one of the heroes who succeeded in escaping from Ilion and, after a long voyage, establishing himself in the west of Europe, founding the kingdom of Britain. The prestige of the *General Estoria* and its author are fundamental for understanding the diffusion of the text in circles close to the court and among historians; from the final quarter of the XIIIth century the stamp of Alfonsine historiography can easily be appreciated in every kingdom of the Iberian Peninsula, and, with greater reason, in writers who deal with the events that followed the end of the Trojan War. So it is that the *Historia regum Britanniae* leaves traces at second hand in authors such as Leomarte and Lope García de Salazar. And consequently the limitations of the work of the Castilian monarch are also inherited by his imitators: no doubt the chronological barrier is the most important, since Alfonso X did not go beyond the birth of Mary, and therefore did not get as far as dealing with the immediate predecessors of King Arthur. Nor, in consequence, does either Leomarte or Lope García de Salazar do so.

Absolutely nothing is known about Leomarte, the hypothetical or fictitious author of the *Sumas de historia troyana*; his work is assigned, with some doubt, to the first half of the XIVth century (Rey 1932). In accordance with the parameters of the *General Estoria* of Alfonso X, the *Sumas* relate the origins of Troy and the war which led to its destruction; then they turn to the Matter of Rome: the story of Aeneas and that of Brutus (chs ccxv–ccxxxvii); finally there are included various 'fablas' and 'estorias' such as the fable of Procne and the story of Oedipus (Gómez Redondo 1999: 1640). The rich content of this work goes beyond the four main thematic strands: there are numerous details, secondary narrations, relevant explanations and moralisations that give a particular colour to the text, so that some of its heroes, such as Brutus, become examples of knights errant in search of their own destiny.

The case of Lope García de Salazar is quite different. Born in Vizcaya in 1399, he took part in the continual strife among clans and factions that occurred in the north of the Peninsula during the reigns of Juan II and Enrique IV of Castile. Fashioned in this continuous warfare as a true 'lord of the blade and the gallows', he was exiled, hated by his kin and finally locked in his own house for a period of five years, before being poisoned in 1476. In 1454 he wrote a *Crónica de Vizcaya*, but his most important work was the *Libro de las bienandanzas e fortunas*, compiled as a way of passing the time during his imprisonment between 1471 and 1475, although its stated objective was to bring together all the events that had occurred since the creation of the world, down to those in which he had himself participated. All this was grouped into twenty-five books which go from the most general (the whole world) to the most specific

(Europe, the Iberian Peninsula and finally Vizcaya, to which he devotes the last six books). To produce such a long work, García de Salazar relied on the *Crónica de 1344* and the Alfonsine histories, as well as other less remote ones, such as the *Crónica de Alfonso XI*, and those of *Pedro I*, *Enrique II*, and *Juan I*, by Pero López de Ayala (Villacorta 2000: xvi–xxxiv). It is obvious that the sources used varied according to the subject being covered, and, in the absence of information from his books, García de Salazar did not hesitate to have recourse to oral traditions, whether in relation to epic poetry or the customs and beliefs of his country, which makes him an author of great interest for the information that he transmits.

As far as concerns the legendary history of Britain, which constitutes Book XI, the debt to the *Historia regum Britanniae* of Geoffrey of Monmouth is obvious, as has been pointed out by Sharrer, but with the caveat that García de Salazar knew the work at second hand, through a lost version of the *Sumas de historia troyana* of Leomarte, which had in turn summarised the version included in the *General Estoria* of Alfonso X (Sharrer 1979a: 13–21). García de Salazar reduces descriptions and explanations to their essential elements, but adds various commentaries, arising from his own experience or from sources that are difficult to establish. Brutus and the Greek inheritance on the one hand and King Arthur on the other constitute the twin pillars on which is constructed the version of the Matter of Britain included in the *Libro de las bienandanzas e fortunas*. However, everything seems to indicate that the Biscayan author used, in addition to the historiographic material cited, a strange version of the *Post-Vulgate*, which does not correspond with the known texts in some episodes.

García de Salazar begins his Arthurian narrative by briefly summarising the *Josep Abarimatia* (or *Estoire del Saint Graal*), although he modifies some details in accordance with information which could derive from *La Vengeance Nostre Seigneur*, a text which was translated into Spanish and Portuguese with the titles of *Estoria del noble Vespasiano* and *Estoria do muy nobre Vespasiano*, probably from a French prose version which in turn had included material deriving from the *Estoire del Saint Graal* (Hook 1986, 2000). García de Salazar follows closely the *Post-Vulgate Merlin* in his summary, but in the continuation (*Suite*) he resorts to some details belonging to the *Vulgate*: the combat with the monstrous cat (el Gato de Lausana), the defeat by Duke Flores, unless the episode was reworked on the basis of the allusion contained in the *Libro del cavallero Zifar*. The Biscayan historian also alters the end of King Arthur, in narrating that after the battle against Mordred the badly wounded king embarked for the Isle of Brasil, which Morgana had enchanted in such a way that it cannot be found. Besides these peculiarities, García de Salazar's *Libro* contains others that are much more difficult to trace to any origin, which lead one to consider a crux between various texts, without excluding some version of a prose *Tristán*. It is clear that the identification of these texts is impossible or extremely problematic. In addition, the author also knew very well the tradition of the prophecies of Merlin, since he includes one taken from the *Crónica de Pedro I* of Pero López de Ayala.

García de Salazar very obviously knew a mixture of Arthurian texts which is not itself always clear in detail, but which perhaps may have been already combined in the original or which may have been mingled by our author, without his necessarily being clear at every moment about what he was doing; the impulse towards concision was more powerful for him than the coherence of the text he was writing, and everything was treated as though it involved events that really occurred, and not as a literary fiction (Sharrer 1979a).

6.4 *Gutierre Díaz de Games,* El Victorial

Lope García de Salazar devoted the last six books of his *Bienandanzas e fortunas* to narrating the history of the most distinguished families of Vizcaya, not forgetting, obviously, his own. So what had begun as a universal history ended up as a local chronicle, of so restricted a scope that the events related involve a very small group and a very small area. García de Salazar thereby comes near to a new model of historiography, represented by the private chronicles or 'chivalresque biographies' (Beltrán 1996: 64), in which the central figure is not the king but an important figure. Some heroes, such as El Cid or Fernán González, had been the subject of personal chronicles, so it should be no surprise that other nobles should aspire to the same distinction; and they did not have to look too far, since the *Liber regum* and its reworking as the *Libro de las generaciones*, widely used during the XIVth and XVth centuries, ended with the genealogy of the Cid and an account of his deeds.

Among the chivalresque biographies there stands out, by reason of the quality of its author and the variety of adventures that he recounts, *El Victorial*, a work in which Gutierre Díaz de Games (*c*.1378?–post 1443) relates the deeds 'of arms and love' carried out by his lord, Pero Niño, Count of Buelna, between 1404 and 1410, although the chronicle is later (*c*.1435), and also has even later additions.

In it there are recounted the childhood and adolescence of the protagonist, his naval campaigns in the Mediterranean and the Atlantic, his presence in the English Channel to assist the French, and his continual harrying of the English. On his return to the Iberian Peninsula, Pero Niño would take part in the war against Granada (1407), would secretly marry Beatriz de Portugal and would play an active part in the busy political life of the kingdom. All this is embellished with advice (including reference to the prophecies of Merlin), descriptions of palace festivities and of tournaments, like those of Valladolid in 1428. This chivalric biography is skilfully elaborated with a mixture of historical deeds and folkloric and literary elements which endow the protagonist with a heroic significance (such as his victory over a giant, or the confrontation with a wild animal). Pero Niño follows the footsteps of genuine knights errant, but without losing sight of points of reference such as Alexander the Great or Julius Caesar. Hence, it is no surprise to encounter Brutus as the protagonist of a story that begins in accordance with Wace's *Roman de Brut*, and fills chapters 54 to 61, with the sole aim of explaining why the English are different from all other Christians.

Taking as his basis 'la *Corónica de los Reyes de Yngalaterra*', Díaz de Games relates who Brutus was, recites his genealogy and recounts how he accidentally killed his father and left the country to head west. From that moment on, the author tells how Menelaus had two children, Nestor and Dorotea, and begins a tale that has nothing to do with the *Roman de Brut* nor with the *Historia regum Britanniae*, nor any other text of the Matter of Britain known to us, in such a way that it would be no surprise if it had all emerged from the imagination of Díaz de Games. Nestor attempts to disinherit his sister Dorotea with the assistance of Brutus, but a letter from Dorotea makes him change his mind. Letters and conversations lead to the marriage of Brutus and Dorotea. Then the Trojan assembles a sizeable armada and heads off in search of adventures; grief leads Dorotea to write another letter to her husband, who in the meantime has reached Galicia and thence proceeds to England. Dorotea has to confront the Africans, whom she defeats by 'the arts of mathematics and necromancy'. Finally Brutus and Dorotea are reunited in Anglia, where they live happily for many years, eventually leaving a son as king and returning to Greece themselves. The author then turns to the circumstances of the outbreak of the war between France and England, which is still continuing at the time when he was writing.

Rafael Beltrán points out that the story of Brutus and Dorotea is modelled on the love affair of Dido and Aeneas, although it has a happy ending, and the same model underlies the letter sent to Brutus by Dorotea when the former departs, after having married her. The two letters exchanged by the young lovers could derive from that sent to Pandraso by Brutus, which is found in Geoffrey of Monmouth. And the conversations that lead up to the marriage have their origin in the discussions among the Trojans on the advantages that would arise from a marriage between Brutus and Inojenis, daughter of Pandraso. Brutus' arrival in Galicia coincides with the episode of Corineus in the *Historia regum Britanniae*, taken up also in the *Sumas de historia troyana* of Leomarte (Beltrán 1996: 122–5).

7. *La Celestina*

La Celestina has come down to us in two very different versions, attributed to the *converso* lawyer and graduate of the University of Salamanca, Fernando de Rojas (*c*.1470–1541). The first of these, known as the *Comedia de Calisto y Melibea* (Burgos, 1499?), has sixteen acts and bears no author's name (the opening pages of the only known copy are lost). It must have been an immediate success, since new editions were not long in appearing (Toledo, 1500; Seville, 1501), in which the text is preceded by a letter from the author 'to a friend of his' ('a un amigo suyo') and the name of the author, Fernando de Rojas. In this, the author states that he has confined himself to continuing a story that he had found in an unfinished state (attributed by some to Juan de Mena and by others to Rodrigo de Cota).

There is convincing evidence to indicate that in 1502 there appeared new editions of the work, in which it was entitled *Tragicomedia de Calisto y Melibea* or *Libro de*

Calixto y Melibea y de la puta vieja Celestina. In a new prologue, the author, alert to the views of his public, relates that he had been obliged to make some changes, such as prolonging the protagonist's love affair by a month, which had led to the addition of five new acts. Besides this, he had retouched some passages in the existing sixteen acts, and gave a marked moralising and didactic tone to the whole.

Among the characters is a servant of Calisto called Tristán or Tristanico, whose diminutive reveals his youth and his status as a servant. There is no relation between the name and the character, nor with the personality of the lover of Iseo. In the case of Calisto's servant, his role has some features of that of the theatrical fool (or 'gracioso'), both for his comments that serve to orient the reader in the action and serve the purpose of stage directions, and for his vision of the environment in which he exists, which is frequently tinged with humorous aspects or provokes amusement. Like so many other XVIth-century servants, his moral status is not so distant from that of roguery, with ethical principles that are easily undermined. The *Tragicomedia* does not alter the character traits that Tristán had in the first version of the work, although he does acquire a certain additional importance by becoming the servant who is closest to Calisto and is the indirect cause of the latter's death (Hook 1993). In any case, the name is not now associated with the nephew of King Mark of Cornwall, but does underline the abundance of 'Tristans' in the urban society of Castile from the mid-XVth century which we have already noted.

8. The Tradition of the 'Profecías de Merlín'

Alfonso X's *Cantiga de Santa María* no. 108 tells of Merlin's action against a Jew who did not wish to believe in the virginity of the Mother of God; Merlin's arguments were useless in the face of the contumacy of the learned '*alfaquí* of Scotland'. Powerless, the protector of Arthur could only invoke the Virgin Mary to perform a miracle that would make manifest the Jew's error: that the child born from the pregnancy of the latter's wife should be born with its face backwards. All happened as Merlin, 'o filho de Sathanas', had requested, and Merlin himself prevented the Jew from killing his son. This is not a prophecy, but it makes it plain that in the second half of the XIIIth century the supernatural power of Merlin was well known in the kingdom of Castile, as was perhaps his diabolical origin.

The existence of prophecies in the literary tradition and above all in historiography is an enduring one, with roots in the Bible, in the Apocalypse, in some cases, and in Classical works (Virgil, for example) in others. The activity of Joachim of Fiore (1135–1202) and his followers contributed to strengthening the apocalyptic tendency of prophecies in western Europe. A different and much older origin is found in the prophecies of Merlin included by Geoffrey of Monmouth in the *Historia regum Britanniae*, which were not long delayed in spreading across the continent. However, it would be Maistre Richard d'Irlande who would give the definitive impetus to the subgroup of Merlin's *Prophecies*, enriching them with the apocalyptic tradition in some cases, and giving them a political content.

Richard d'Irlande is the pseudonym of a Venetian who wrote in French between 1272 and 1279. *Les prophésies de Merlin*, a long series of prophecies that Merlin had dictated to 'Maistre Antoine', bishop of Wales, and other scribes. The influence of the Joachimite or spiritual Franciscans is evident throughout the text, which is designed to spread propaganda on behalf of the Guelphs, mingled with moral and religious teaching (Burgess and Pratt 2006: 352–7; Tarre 1943: 147ff.).

The work of Richard of Ireland was an immediate and widespread success among visionaries from the XIIIth century on, especially in France, Italy and Spain, among other reasons because the prophecies attributed to Merlin alluded to different kingdoms and places in these countries, thus facilitating the inclusion of new material which was always accurate since it was added *post factum*: the attribution to Merlin was necessary to lend antiquity to the prophecy, and, with the antiquity, prophetic force.

In 1348 Rodrigo Yañez composed the *Poema de Alfonso XI* in which he recounted the deeds of the Castilian king (1311–50), in an exercise in panegyric that completed the *Crónica* (by Ferrán Sánchez de Valladolid, interrupted in 1344) and the *Gran Crónica* (commissioned by his son Enrique II from Juan Núñez de Villazán in 1376) about the same monarch. This interest in writing and rewriting the historical events is motivated not only by the celebration of great victories, but also by the need for justification of the 'grave contradictions which the king had been obliged to accept since 1325' and in order to provide an explanation of his royalist ideology (Gómez Redondo 2002: 278–84; 1999: 1260–84). Alfonso XI had been orphaned shortly after his birth and the regency was entrusted to his mother Constanza de Portugal; but she died in 1313 and the new regent was his grandmother María de Molina. The king's minority was to be a long one, and the dangers which beset him would be numerous, thanks to the ever more powerful nobility and the menace of Islam. The rigour with which he dealt with his political opponents should be no surprise; he did not hesitate to execute one of his tutors, Juan de Haro, known as Juan el Tuerto, 'the one-eyed'.

In the *Poema de Alfonso XI* Rodrigo Yáñez exalts the victories of El Salado (1340) and of the conquest of Algeciras (1344), successes which removed the threats overhanging the kingdom, and the public relationship of the monarch with María de Guzmán, by whom he had ten bastard children (from 1330 onwards), among whom was Enrique, lord of Trastámara (1333–79). The latter would impose a new ruling dynasty after his fratricidal assassination of his half-brother Pedro I at Montiel (1369).

Rodrigo Yáñez alludes on two occasions to prophecies of Merlin as a means of justifying events which could not have occurred in any other way, since they had already been announced from time immemorial, and through which implicitly divine intentions were being accomplished. The first of these involved the assassination of Don Juan el Tuerto in the city of Toro (1326):

> En aquesto otorgaron,
> el buen rey dio sentencia,
> a don Joan luego mataron

>   que fue señor de Valencia.
>   En Toro complió su fin
>   e derramó la su gente.
>   Aquesto dixo Melrin,
>   el profeta de Oriente.
>   Dixo: 'El león d'España
>   de sangre fará camino,
>   matará el lobo de la montaña
>   dentro en la fuente del vino.'
>   Non lo quiso más declarar
>   Melrin, el de gran saber;
>   yo lo quiero apaladinar
>   cómo lo puedan entender:
>   El león de España
>   fue el buen rey ciertamente;
>   el lobo de la montaña
>   fue don Joan, el su pariente,
>   e el rey cuando era niño
>   mató a don Joan el Tuerto;
>   Toro es la fuente del vino
>   A do don Juan fue muerto. (stanzas 241–6)

The attribution of prophecies to Merlin must have been a commonplace of the genre in the mid-XIVth century. That the seer was not associated with the Arthurian character is proved by the fact that he is considered to be from the orient, like so many other sages who appear in the gnomic and wisdom literature of the Middle Ages. An obscure quatrain is explained and interpreted ('apaladinada') by the author, who evidently knows the keys of his own metaphorical construction.

The triumph of the battle of El Salado (1340), which gave the definitive supremacy to the Castilians over the Banu Merim, is the second occasion on which it is announced that the victory had been prophesied, like the adventures reserved for the most distinguished knights of the court of King Arthur:

>   Mal desonrado salio
>   de Tarifa el moro marín;
>   en aquel día Dios complió
>   una profecía de Merlín.
>   Merlín fabló d'España
>   e dixo esta profecía
>   estando en la Bretaña
>   a un maestro que í avía.
>   Don Antón era llamado
>   este maestro que vos digo,
>   sabidor e letrado,
>   de don Merlín mucho amigo. (stanzas 1810–12)

The prophecy occupies twenty-two stanzas and the author devotes a further eight to its explanation, after which he expresses his pride in the work he has carried out:

> La profecia conté
> e torné en dezir llano
> yo, Rodrigo Yáñez la noté
> en linguaje castellano.
>   Copras de muy bien fablar,
> segunt dixo Merlín;
> agora quiero contar
> del rey Benamarín. (stanzas 1844–5)

In this instance, there is no doubt about the origin: Merlin's interlocutor is called Antón, equivalent to the 'maistre Antoine' of Richard of Ireland. Nor is there any room for doubt over the prophet's country: Britain. The political content of the prophecy is elaborated, after the model of the *Prophécies*, on the basis of symbolic animals: crowned lion (king of Castile and León), sleeping lion (king of Portugal), porcupine, lord of the great sword (the Banu Merim ruler), wild beasts and dogfish (aged and infant Moors), dragon (king of Granada)...

The objective of this prophecy is to exalt an episode of the Reconquest: the recuperation of the territories in pagan hands is the habitual theme of the prophecies that are produced in the Iberian Peninsula during the Middle Ages, since it is no accident that it is one part of the rationale for the historical destiny and the political thought of the Christian monarchs of Spain. In the specific case of the Salado prophecy, a recurrent theme, the Reconquest, is linked with a most fashionable tradition of western Europe at this time, the attribution of a prophecy to Merlin.

Pero López de Ayala (1332–1406) served Pedro I and subsequently Enrique II, Juan I and Enrique III; he was the first historian of the Trastámaran dynasty, to which he was linked for forty years, during which he compiled three chronicles that broke with the Alfonsine tradition in their parameters (*Crónica del rey don Pedro y del rey don Enrique su hermano hijos del rey don Alfonso onceno*; *Crónica del rey Juan I*; *Crónica del rey don Enrique III*).

Speaking of the events that occurred during the twentieth year of the reign of Pedro I, López de Ayala introduces a letter 'that the sage moor of Granada called Benahatin sent to King Don Pedro when he knew that he was going to relieve Toledo, which it is said was found in the chests of the chamber of King Don Pedro after he was killed at Montiel' (XX, iii). In it, the Moor, a counsellor of the king of Granada, replies to a request from the king of Castile in which he asked him to interpret 'a prophetic saying, which you say was found among the books and prophecies that you say Merlin made'. The Moor Benahatin copies in his letter the text of the prophecy that had been sent to him by Pedro I:

> En las partidas de occidente entre los montes e la mar nascerá una ave negra, comedora, e robadora, e tal que todos los panares del mundo querría acoger en sí, e todo el oro del mundo querrá poner en su estómago; e después gormarlo há, e tornará atrás, e non perescerá luego por esta dolencia. E dice más caérsele han las alas, e secársele han las plumas al sol, e andará de puerta en puerta, e ninguno la querrá acoger, e encerrarse ha en selva, e morirá y dos veces, una al mundo, e otra ante Dios, e desta guisa acabará.

López de Ayala devotes the rest of the chapter (six printed pages) to explaining the prophecy, which, obviously, alludes to Pedro I himself and to his death. The brevity of the prophecy contrasts with the space devoted by the chronicler to its interpretation by the Moor Benahatin.

It seems evident that Benahatin is none other than Ibn al-Jatib de Loja, a wise counsellor of King Mohamed V of Granada at a time at which political, diplomatic, and cultural relations between Pedro I and the Nasrid monarch were especially close. It is at this time that there were undertaken the paintings, identified as possibly on the theme of Tristan, at the Alhambra.

It could be that López de Ayala had recourse to the figure of the famous Ibn al-Jatib to introduce an apocryphal letter. However, the fact that there is preserved in BNF ms esp 216, a codex of the early XVth century with a copy of this letter different from that used by López de Ayala, and of another earlier one sent by the same Benhatin himself to Pedro I, leads to the suspicion that the letters had a real existence and that the Castilian king wrote to the wise Muslim counsellor to obtain a response to his worries about certain prophecies attributed to Merlin. According to J. L. Moure (1983), a Jewish translator would have translated into Romance the Arabic text later used by López de Ayala in his *Crónica*. These conclusions do not invalidate the existence of the prophecies in the time of Pedro I, nor the fact that the name of Merlin may be nothing other than a hook on which to hang a politically partisan message: the justification of the assassination of Pedro I and 'the exaltation of the political programme with which Enrique II established himself in Castile'. All this constructed on a metaphor that is found in one of the homilies of Gregory the Great: the eagle that loses its feathers and wings symbolises the Roman Empire, which would soon come to its destruction (Gimeno Casalduero 1971: 84).

The sage Ibn al-Jatib did not write the first part of the letter, which involves the prophecies, but restricted himself to interpreting the text that may have emerged from circles favourable to King Pedro's half-brother Enrique. López de Ayala did not invent the letters, but adapted them slightly to the *Crónica* that he had begun to compile at the request of Enrique II, around 1379, ten years after the violent death of Pedro I (Gómez Redondo 1999: 1785ff.).

Towards 1435 Gutierre Díaz de Games wrote *El Victorial*, the chivalric biography of Pero Niño, discussed above. Among the historical material that serves as the outline for the narration of the singular life of its subject, the author mixes elements drawn from the most diverse origins, or from his own imagination, as seems to be the case of the story of Brutus and Dorotea examined above.

We are told that when he was barely ten years old 'at the orders of the king Pero Niño was sent to a tutor' to instruct him as befitted a good courtly knight, capable of being constantly at the prince's side (chapter 19). This silence about the name of the tutor and the very content of the chapter leave no room for doubt that this is all an invention of the author, or an adaptation of pre-existing materials, or perhaps a blend of the two. The biographical thread is here stretched to the limit, among other reasons because the biography of heroes should say virtually nothing of their childhood except for a brief reference to their moral and intellectual formation, as in the case of Alexander the Great. And in fact the entire chapter is constructed from a mixture of the *Libro de los buenos proverbios* by Hunayn ibn Ishaq (known in Castilian since the middle of the XIIIth century), Christian virtues, and hagiographies, producing an authentic mirror of princes. In the final section of the chapter, less condensed than the preceding sections, the tutor recommends to his pupil that he should not believe those who predict what is to happen, and even less if it involves great successes, and continues to advise the young man that

> Guardadvos: non creades falsas profezías ni ayades fiuzia en ellas, ansí como son las de Merlín e otras. Que verdad os digo que estas cosas fueron engeniadas e sacadas por sotiles honbres e cavilosos para privar e alcançar con los reyes e grandes señores, e ganar dellos, e tenerlos a su voluntad en aquellas vanas fiuzias, en tanto que ellos fazen de sus provechos.
>
> E si paras mientes, como viene rey nuevo, luego fazen Merlín nuevo. Dizen que aquel rey á de pasar la mar e destruir toda la morisma, e ganar la casa santa, e á de ser enperador [...]
>
> Merlín fue un buen honbre e muy sabio. No fuye fijo del diablo, como algunos dizen [...] Mas Merlín, con la grand sabiduría que aprendió, quiso saber más de lo que le cunplía, e fue engañado por el diablo, e mostróle muchas cosas que dixese, e algunas dellas salieron verdad. [...] Ansí, en aquella parte de Angliaterra dixo algunas cosas que fallaron en ellas algo que fue verdad, mas en otras muchas fallesció. E algunos que agora algunas cosas quieren dezir, conpónenlas e dizen que las fabló Merlín. (Díaz de Games 1997: 325–6)

The tutor, or the author, is well informed about the figure of Merlin and his origins. He also knows the habitual themes of the Hispanic prophecies: finish off Islam, reconquer the Holy Land, obtain the title of emperor (among the Peninsular kings). It is more difficult to ascertain the identity of the 'new king' about whom the prophecies are made; possibly it is concerned with prophecies renewed at the death of Enrique III and after the accession of Juan II when he was barely a year old (1406): there is no allusion to the legitimacy of the dynasty that had been on the throne since 1369, nor to the crisis besetting the kingdom, but only to the Reconquest, in the oldest Hispanic tradition.

This is the atmosphere in which the poets of the *Cancionero de Baena* and their successors were working, and in which there appeared new prophetic texts, such as a *Vision de Alfonso X*.

Alfonso Alvarez de Villasandino composed in 1398 a *dezir* motivated by the appointment of Pedro Fernández de Frías, cardinal of Spain, to the rank of Condestable (*Amigos, ya veo acercarse la fin*; *Baena* 97):

> Verdat me paresce que dixo Merlín,
> en unas figuras que puso entricadas,
> que por cruel fuego serían soterradas
> las alas e plumas del gran serafín.
>
> La más parte tiene con el puercoespín
> e tiene avaricia consigo grand vando;

> ya los inorantes andan disputando
> las glosas e testos de Santo Agostín
> e los aldeanos fablan buen latín [...] (lines 5–13)

If the allusion to the wings and feathers refers us to the prophecy included in the *Crónica* of López de Ayala, a few years earlier than Alvarez de Villasandino's text, the reference to the porcupine takes us back to Rodrigo Yáñez and his *Poema de Alfonso XI*, when he brings together the prophecies on the battle of the Salado (1340), an idea that is reinforced in line 25, where the Banu Merim are recalled ('Non fazen mención de Benamarin').

Alvarez de Villasandino himself addressed some verses to the king of Castile, Juan II, before 1417 since the Schism was still in progress (*Salga el león que estaba encogido*: *Baena* 199), which conclude with a finale in which there are found the names of two great prophets, Merlin and Johannes de Rupescissa:

> Del fuerte leon suso contenido
> dize el Merlín, concuerda fray Juan,
> que entre los que fueron e son e serán
> en España reyes será ennoblecido. (lines 73–6)

When Alvarez de Villasandino wrote these verses the king was still a minor, but this does not prevent (quite the contrary) the poet from resorting to the prophetic model of Merlin and lauding the glorious future awaiting the young monarch. Our poet even recalls the prophecies of Merlin in another *dezir* addressed to the king (*Muy poderoso varón*: *Baena* 209):

> [...] pues Merlin
> propuso muy secretado
> un dicho ya declarado:
> Qu'el tomado
> es tornado
> tomador e grant dalfín,
> espantable palacín. (lines 46–52)

Alvarez de Villasandino is not the only poet of the *Cancionero* who alludes to the prophecies of Merlin. Juan Alfonso de Baena, the eponymous compiler of the collection, sent to Juan II a long *dezir* in 1432, in which he recommends some measures to remedy the discord with the Infantes de Aragon (*Para un rey excelente*: *Baena* +586, pp. 739 ff.):

> Cessaran carros, carretas
> de andar por los caminos,
> cessarán a los mesquinos
> los males d'estas saetas,
> cessarán muchos profetas
> de Merlín e Rocacisa,
> cessarán por esta guisa
> atabales e trompetas. (lines 1691–8)

The *Visión de Alfonso X* is preserved in a manuscript in the BNE (MS 431), of the end of the XIVth century, and, in Catalan translation, in a codex of the Biblioteca de Catalunya (MS 271), slightly later, in which there are grouped other prophecies of Merlin in Catalan and in Latin. The *Visión* is included, complete, in the collection of the *Profecías de Merlín* that is printed for the first time in the edition of the *Baladro del Sabio Merlín y Demanda del Santo Grial* (Sevilla 1535).

In the *Visión* it is narrated that on Saturday 12 April 1284 an angel appeared to Alfonso X in Seville and announced to him that because of his pride in stating that if he had created the world he would have made a better job of it than the Creator had, he had been condemned to suffer the rebellion of his son Sancho against him. This sentence was communicated to an Augustinian friar from Molina, who related the matter to his prior and the latter told the infante Don Manuel. For his part, the rebel Don Sancho also would suffer punishment for his rebellion: the confirmation of the king's curse, which the latter had uttered against him and his descendants to the fourth generation. The extinction of the dynasty would lead to the arrival of a new king, just and honourable, who would bring peace. The Virgin Mary had interceded with her Son because of the many prayers that King Alfonso had devoted to her, and had been vouchsafed the knowledge that the king would die one month later, 'after thirty days had passed' (Bohigas 1941).

The political motivation of the *Visión* is obvious; it was issued in support of the new Trastámaran dynasty and must, therefore, be later than 1369. In the Catalan text the year 1377 appears as the final limit of the prophecies of Merlin, but this date is pushed to 1467 in the version in the *Baladro*, in what may merely be a chronological updating. Alfonso X died on 4 April 1284, so that 12 April could not have been the date of the vision attributed to him, and clearly the chronology of the death one month later is not correct either. Equally, 12 April did not fall on a Saturday that year (neither did 4 April) but 12 April 1377 certainly did, in what may be considered a significant coincidence.

The beginning of the *Visión* recalls closely that of other well-known eschatological experiences, such as the *Disputa del alma y el cuerpo* (*Revelación de un ermitaño*) and the *Visión de Filiberto* of 1382.

With regard to the curse directed by Alfonso X against his son Sancho, it is well known because of the *Libro de las armas* or *Libro de las tres razones* of don Juan Manuel, nephew of the Castilian monarch and cousin of the prince. Don Juan Manuel relates that when Sancho IV was on his deathbed (1294), he had an interview with him; the king informed him how his grandfather Fernando III had not bestowed his blessing upon Alfonso X, and how the latter had not wished to bless his own son, so that Sancho himself could not give to Don Juan Manuel something that he did not himself have. From this arises the 'curse' which is collected in the text under consideration, far from the intention with which Juan Manuel had used it; and from this too there appears the name of Manuel in the story that precedes the *Visión*, and possibly also the reference to Molina, the lordship of one of Alfonso's uncles, cited also in the text that could have served as the basis for the frame in which the *Visión de Alfonso X* is set. If my hypothesis is sound, this text appeared in the circle of the Trastámaras, not from that of Juan Manuel, and it would possibly be necessary to situate it in the final years of the reign of Enrique II (died 1379), which is when the survivor of the fratricidal encounter at Montiel redoubled his efforts to justify the legitimacy of the new dynasty, commissioning his chronicle from López de Ayala.

But by then the prophecies attributed to Merlin had become a common resort for members of the court, to judge by those collected in the *Poema de Alfonso XI* or the *Crónica* of López de Ayala. And not there alone; in 1377, infante Fray Pedro de Aragón, a Franciscan, uncle of King Pedro I of Castile and a famous visionary (c.1304–80), wrote an exposition of the *Cedrus alta Libani* in which he cites the most celebrated 'prophets' of the time: Merlin, Joachim of Fiore, and Johannes de Rupescissa, but also comments on some prophecies applied to Enrique II of Castile, analogous to those that would later appear in the 1535 edition of the *Baladro del sabio Merlín* (Bohigas 1941: 380).

The codex which contains the Catalan translation of the *Visión de Alfonso X* (Biblioteca de Catalunya MS 271) includes also another text translated from Castilian to Catalan (Bohigas 1928–32: 261) and which relates how the wise prophet, while at Arthur's court near London, made known to the king the things that would occur in various parts of the world, among them Spain, until the year 1377. The prophecies are clear as far as the reign of Enrique II and then they become more obscure and difficult or impossible to decipher: after the 'great lion' (Alfonso XI) there comes the 'pollino lujurioso, asno de maldad' (Pedro I), who will be defeated by the puppy or 'pollino leon perezoso' (Enrique II). Following the Joachimite model, the prophecy concludes with the conquest of the Holy Land and with peace.

Both the *Visión de Alfonso X* and the prophecy of *Merlín en Londres* reappear together with other prophecies between the end of the *Baladro del sabio Merlín* and the beginning of the *Demanda del Santo Grial* in the volume printed in Seville in 1535 (Bonilla y San Martín 1907: 155–62). In effect, under the title *Aqui comiençan las Profecias del sabio Merlin, profeta dignissimo* there are included in this edition, but not in the Seville incunable of 1498, four batches of the prophecies of Merlin, all of them related to events in the history of Castile. After a preface in which Merlin is presented in the palace of King Arthur, there is another preface in which Merlin is washing his hands near the city of London; thereafter there is copied the *Visión de Alfonso X*; where this group ends there is a reference to Master Antonio with the prophecies Merlin dictates to him; the group is interrupted to introduce another group related to the London prophecies. Finally, there are included other prophecies which seem to be related to Fernando the Catholic (Bohigas 1941: 386–7).

The collection of prophecies found at the end of the *Baladro* can be presented in the following schematic form:

1. Merlin at the palace   pp. 155a–155b, l. 36   preamble
2. Merlin at London   pp. 155b, l. 37–155b, l.48   preamble
3.1 Vision of Alfonso X   pp. 156a, l. 7–157a, l. 14
4.1 Maestre Antonio   pp. 157a, l. 15–158a, l. 37
5.1 Merlin at London   pp. 158a, l. 38–159b, l. 35
6.1 Fernando the Catholic up to the end of the text (p. 162)

It is not difficult to find in the prophecies in the *Baladro* a blend of earlier texts, which had enjoyed an independent existence of their own from the time of the *Poema de Alfonso XI* (1348); texts in which can be seen the traces of Geoffrey of Monmouth, Richard d'Irlande, Joachim of Fiore and John of Rupescissa. Nor are there lacking echoes of Rodrigo Yañez, Pero López de Ayala, or of Alfonso Alvarez de Villasandino and Juan Alfonso de Baena. The prophetic genre has a traditional character, passing from one author to another; or perhaps all of them made use of common sources, leaves on which some of the prophecies were copied singly. The advent of the House of Trastámara made use of millenarian and apocalyptic prophecies for its own advantage, to justify the killing of the king and to legitimise the new dynasty. It must not, however, be imagined that the 'prophecies of Merlin' in Castilian or in Catalan were an exception; on the contrary, they must be considered within a much richer panorama that extends from the XIVth century and reaches at least as far as the Council of Trent, which in 1557 prohibited in its *Index* the *Merlini Angli libri obscurarum praedictionum*.

9. The Nine Worthies

The Marqués de Santillana records, in his *Proemio e Carta al Condestable de Portugal* (1449) that

> Entre nosotros usóse primeramente el metro en asaz formas; asi como el *Libro de Alexandre*, *Los votos del pavon* y aun el *Libro del Arcipreste de Hita*; e aun d'esta guisa escrivió Pero López de Ayala, el Viejo, un libro que fizo de las *maneras del palacio* e llamaron los *Rimos*. (López Estrada 1984: 58)

The brief paragraph cited is of interest here because of its reference to a lost work, *Los votos del pavón*. From the allusion by Santillana, who includes the work among others of the *mester de clerecía*, it must have been written in *cuaderna vía* (quatrains of fourteen-syllable lines with consonantal monorhyme). The book of the same title in French by Jacques de Longuyon (*Voeux du paon*) was, no doubt, the basis of the Castilian version, which could have adapted not only the metrical form of the original (laisses of monorhymed Alexandrines) but also its content, frequently considered as an extension of the deeds of Alexander the Great; the use of the *cuaderna vía* would, therefore, have been a natural solution. Jacques de Longuyon dedicated his work to Thibaud, bishop of Liège, who died in 1312. Throughout the XIVth century, copy followed copy in French (there are more than thirty surviving manuscripts); then came the translations, almost all of them from the beginning of the XVth century, into Dutch, Scots, Middle English, Middle German, among others.

The wide diffusion of the work of Jacques de Longuyon assured, in turn, the success of some of the episodes contained in the work. Thus, of the vows made on the peacock that was to be eaten, the reference to the Nine Worthies, the most valiant knights of all time (Joshua, David and Judas Maccabaeus among biblical characters; Hector, Alexander the Great and Julius Caesar from among the pagans; and Arthur, Charlemagne and Godfrey of Bouillon among the moderns; see Cropp 2002). The nobility of western Europe did not take long to adopt the names of the Worthies and to represent these heroes in their palaces and castles.

It is hard to tell when *Los votos del pavón* was translated into Castilian. In the mid-XIVth century there was at the Aragonese court a tapestry with the *Istoria Novem Militum* and a few years later, in 1356, Pedro IV named the Nine in a letter addressed to the treasurer of Gerona cathedral (Bautista 2009: 11).

The known indirect witnesses lead us to think that from the last quarter of the XIVth century there was known the custom of making vows during some significant celebration: thus it occurred at the feast for the coronation of Sibila de Fortià, wife of Pedro IV of Aragón (1381), and a few years later, in the *Crónica carolingia* written in Castile between 1388 and 1390, the pledges were made over a roast peacock, which would then be eaten before they were undertaken (Bautista 2009: 4–8). Other witnesses are rather later: in *El Victorial* (1431–6) there appears a scene similar to that in the *Crónica carolingia*, which perhaps refers to some real events that occurred a quarter of a century earlier (Beltrán 1997: 378–9; Bautista 2009: 9). Contemporary with *El Victorial* must be the *dezir* written by Juan Alfonso de Baena to King Juan II (c.1432), in which in a similar fashion to the chivalresque biography of Don Pero Niño he alters the list of heroes, omitting King Arthur, although he does admit Lancelot, Galahad, Tristan and 'Camalote' to the list of famous and valiant figures.

Thus in Castile Arthur disappears from the roll-call of the Nine Worthies for reasons that are not at all clear. It can be supposed that the absence of the name of the British king from the Castilian list of the Worthies may be caused by his absence from the text that served as the source for the rest, as Bautista indicates (2009: 15); even so, it is impossible to know which text this was, and what motivated its author's omission of King Arthur, with Charles Martel sometimes being incorporated in his place. Had times changed and with this the perception of the Matter of Britain, or is it a reflection of an anti-English attitude? Were this so, why then are other knights of the Round Table retained, along with some Castilian heroes such as Amadís?

10. Libraries

The Castilian nobility had begun to be interested in letters towards the end of the XIVth century; at the same time, the possession of books, the formation of libraries, became not only a sign of distinction but a display of power in addition (Lawrance 1985).

The inventories of libraries of the lay nobility are not numerous, and they are generally poor in terms of references to texts of the Matter of Britain. We can cite scarcely half a dozen XVth-century libraries containing books about King Arthur and his knights (Faulhaber 1987; Beceiro Pita 1983, 1993; Beceiro Pita and Franco Silva 1986):

- Aldonza de Mendoza, granddaughter of King Enrique II, Duchess of Arjona, half-sister of Iñigo López de Mendoza, Marquis of Santillana, d. 1435: 3 copies of *Amadís de Gaula*, 2 copies of *Tristán*, *Historia del rey Canamor y de Turián su fijo*.
- Alonso Pimentel y Enríquez, third Count of Benavente, inventory of c.1447: *Baladro del sabio Merlín*
- Pedro Fernández de Velasco, first Count of Haro, inventory of 1455: *Demanda del Sancto Grial*
- Isabel I, queen of Castile: *Historia de Lanzarote*, *José de Arimatea* (or *Historia del Santo Grial*) and *Baladro de Merlín*, *Demanda del Santo Grial*.

The fact that the Marquis of Santillana, who had a good knowledge of French and Italian literature in the first half of the XVth century, did not have any Arthurian text in his library (Schiff 1905) is noteworthy; nor, apparently, did his nephew Fernán Pérez de Guzmán, who died in 1463 (Vaquero 2003). At the end of the XVth century, the great libraries did not possess copies of works linked to the Matter of Britain, a feature replicated in those of the first half of the XVIth century and one that contrasts with the relative publishing success enjoyed by these works in the same period. The criticism of moralists and serious writers was sufficient for nobles, whose libraries were formed at the suggestion of members of various religious orders, to refrain from acquiring copies of stories considered to be not very edifying. At least, this is the impression created by the *Epístola* sent by Bishop Alonso de Cartagena between 1430 and 1454 to the first Count of Haro, Pedro Fernández de Velasco, in which he considers that veracity, or at least verisimilitude, should be the basis of all writing; he says, however, that there are some works that present themselves as histories, but that not only did none of the events related in them actually occur, but also could never have occurred 'sicuti Tristani ac Lanceloti Amadisive ingentia volumina'; and therefore such writings 'etsi nocive nimium non sint, infructuose tamen et nullius utilitatis esse videntur' (Lawrance 1979: 54). Notwithstanding, there was a copy of the *Demanda del santo Grial* in the Library of the Count of Haro.

Attacks on romances of chivalry (among them those that related to the Matter of Britain) increased with the advent of humanism and during the Renaissance, in accordance with the Aristotelian conception of narrative: almost a hundred criticisms of romances of chivalry in general suffice to give an idea of the warnings of the moralists and the literary preceptors against the Matter of Britain and its Hispanic continuations. Lack of utility, non-existent or scant verisimilitude, authorial ignorance and literary incompetence are sufficient reasons to exile these works – Arthurian or not – from the republic of letters (Sarmati 1996). Special mention is deserved by the rich library of Isabel la Católica, among whose volumes there was a complete cycle of the *Vulgate* or the *Post-Vulgate* (Ruiz García 2004: 449, 464, 432). The same books, although only partial, are found in the library of the University of Salamanca (MS 1877) and were published by Pietsch (1924–5; see also Sharrer 1977: 33–5).

In the XVIth century, Queen Juana of Castile (1479–1555), daughter of the Catholic Monarchs, did not have among her books any containing the adventures of King Arthur and the knights of the Round Table. The empress Isabel of Portugal (1503–39), wife of Charles V, had only a printed *Demanda del Santo Grial* (perhaps in the edition of 1535). The library of the emperor Charles V himself, of which the inventory was drawn up in 1558, contained nothing relating to the Matter of Britain, despite the known liking of the ruler for romances of chivalry, and especially for *Le Chevalier delibéré*, of Olivier de la Marche. María of Austria (1505–58), queen of Hungary and sister of Charles V, who spent the final years of her life in Spain, had a copy of the *Perceforest* in French, in the edition of 1528. Finally, King Philip II (1527–98) did not admit any text related to the matter of Britain in his rich library (Gonzalo 2005).

Since monarchs and aristocrats do not seem to have had any special interest in the deeds of the knights of the Round Table, it is no surprise that the libraries of the nobility in general did not have any space for this group of texts either. The inventory of the Casa del Sol, drawn up in 1623, has given us information about one of the most important libraries of its age, that of Diego Sarmiento de Acuña, Count of Gondomar (d. 1626); among its more than 6,000 printed volumes and 731 manuscripts there is barely anything Arthurian: a copy of the *Demanda del Santo Grial* (Seville 1535) and another of *Le preux chevalier Artus de Bretaigne* (Paris 1536), and this despite the interest felt by Gondomar for romances of chivalry (Lucía Megías 2007: 151–87).

Despite, however, the scanty information provided to us by inventories of libraries, it is obvious that further copies did circulate (always of the same titles) during the XVth and XVIth centuries, although clearly in retreat before the advance of the Hispanic romances of chivalry, headed by *Amadís de Gaula* (Díez Borque 2010). Thus, in 1473, Catalina Núñez de Toledo gave to a convent of Franciscan nuns 'el libro que se llama Josep Abarimatea, estoriado e escripto en papel, con unas coberturas coloradas, con unos bollones de laton e unos textillos colorados', valued at 3,000 maravedis. A few years later, an anonymous inventory of 1494–1506 of a library at Cuenca with nearly 300 books includes a *Libro del esforzado cavallero don Tristán de Leonís*, which is surely that printed at Valladolid in 1501 (Albert and Fernández Vega 2003: 40–1).

No doubt the examination of further inventories and library catalogues would probably reveal further copies, but there is no question that these would always be of

the same titles and in the same proportions. The resulting panorama is neither particularly rich, nor varied.

11. Other Grails

In the mid-XVth century, Pero Tafur, a gentleman of Seville, recounts in his *Andanças e viajes* that Jerusalem was conquered by Pisans, Venetians and Genoese. On dividing the treasures of the city, they divided them into three parts:

> en la una pusieron el Santo Grial, que es de una esmeralda, en la otra pusieron dos columnas, en las cuales dizen que se veíe cada uno el mal que le tratavan e lo que queríe él, en la otra pusieron todo el tesoro, E dizen que echaron suertes e cupo el Santo Vaso a Génova, do agora está, el cual yo vi, e las columnas con Jerusalén a los pisanos, las cuales truxeron a Pisa, e el tesoro a Veneja, e desto dixen que es toda su riqueza. (Pérez Priego 2006: 375)

The information is extremely sparse, and the silence leads us to believe that our noble traveller was ignorant of any relationship between the Grail, Joseph of Arimathea and the story of King Arthur, because were the opposite to be the case it would be easy for some statement to have arisen about the presence of the chalice in Genoa, and about the object itself, since the emerald of which it is made is more closely related to the 'lapis exulis' of Wolfram von Eschenbach than to the goblet of the *Vulgate* tradition. It is clear that our traveller has picked up information provided in the *Legenda aurea* of Jacobus de Voragine, where there is recounted a similar episode, since the Genoese had acquired the object after the conquest of Caesarea (1101). For his part, the Italian Dominican had surely been inspired by the *Historia rerum in partibus transmarinis gestarum* of William of Tyre (d. 1186); the episode of the conquest of Caesarea by the Genoese and the discovery of the object in a temple built by Herod in honour of Augustus Caesar is translated into Castilian in the *Gran Conquista de Ultramar*, towards the end of the XIIIth century, when the Matter of Britain was already known in the Peninsula:

> E en el templo hallaron un vaso verde de piedra, assi como una pila, tamana como un tajador, que era clara e muy hermosa. E los ginoveses creyeron que era esmeralda (e aún lo piensan oy día), e tomáronlo en precio de muy gran haver en su parte de la ganancia de la villa; e leváronla a su tierra e pusiéronla en la iglesia, e aún agora está aí. E el primero día de Cuaresma meten en ella ceniza, e de allí la ponen a los hombres. E muéstranla assí como por las reliquias; ca ellos dizen que es una esmeralda. (ed. Cooper 1979: II, 570–1)

Towards 1535, Micael de Carvajal from Extremadura composed one of the first theatrical works in Castilian, the *Tragedia Josephina*, inspired by the story of Joseph and Pharaoh's wife, with some Celestinesque tendencies, a work which enjoyed an extraordinary popularity throughout the whole XVIth century, with at least four editions between 1535 and 1546. It was prohibited by the Inquisition in 1559, and remembered still forty years after that, when in 1599 permission was sought for it to be performed. In the *Tragedia Josephina*, the herald or 'presentador' defends the author's work and his many efforts to amuse the public, since to achieve this

ha trastornado Amadís con la demanda del sancto Grial de pe a pa, por remembrar oy algo que sin perjuizio fuesse: y no halla sino casos atroces de muertes, armas, campos, revueltas, peleas, golpes, espadadas tan estrañas que por ventura en la tal representación el corrimiento passado agora sea correncia. (Gillet 1932: 6–7)

In other words, Micael de Carvajal did not find sufficient material in *Amadís* and in the *Demanda del Santo Grial* to write a didactic and moralising play, and for that reason had to resort to scripture. The censure of the romances of chivalry is explicit, and it must be supposed that the works cited would be known and appreciated by the public as pleasing entertainment.

In any case, by the mid-XVIth century the expression 'la demanda del santo Grial' had become a proverb, since Pedro Vallés records it in his *Libro de refranes* (1549). It must be presumed that the meaning of the phrase would be something like 'the search for something impossible', but later collectors of sayings such as Sebastián de Covarrubias (*Tesoro de la lengua castellana o española*, 1611) and Gonzalo Correas (*Vocabulario de refranes y frases proverbiales*, 1627) do not include this saying, clearly showing that it was no longer current by then, no doubt because its point of reference, the Holy Grail, was no longer part of the collective imaginary in the second half of the XVIth century. Thus Covarrubias speaks of the Grail in the following terms:

Grial. Nombre de lugar y apellido, Grial, cierto adorno y vestidura de las reinas en Castilla y Francia. El catino que tienen los ginoveses de esmeralda en su tesoro, dice Palmerino que antiguamente le llamaron los castellanos el santo Grial, en el *Vocabulario de metales*.

Covarrubias is not mistaken in his reference, since Juan Lorenzo Palmireno, in the 'séptimo abecedario' of his *Vocabulario del Humanista*, published in Valencia in 1569, writes:

En el reino de Granada es la ciudad de Almería, llamada por algunos Gran Puerto; aquí fue obispo Sant Indalecio, discípulo de Santiago Apóstol. Siendo de moros, la conquistó el rey don Alonso de Castilla, llamado Emperador: ayudóle el conde de Barcelona, y gran armada de ginoveses. Acabada la batalla, hallaron gran riqueza: el rey tomó la ciudad para sí, y hizo dos partes del despojo: la una fue un plato de esmeralda, y la otra parte de lo demás dio que escogiessen. Entonces los ginoveses tomaron el plato; los de Barcelona, las otras joyas. Y así le tiene hoy la Señoria de Génova en gran estima. Dizen que en este plato cenó Nuestro Redemptor Jesu Christo el jueves de la Cena, y que por desdichas y guerras de christianos vino a poder de moros, hasta el tiempo que he dicho. Es este plato de esmeralda tan grande, que cabrá en él un cabrito entero. Es de seis puntas y tan fino, que si se partiesse en piecas como la uña, valdrían un millón de oro; pues, cuánto más valdrá siendo una sola pieça. El es, en fin, joya singular y única en el mundo. Los castellanos antiguos le llaman el Santo Grial; Musa Brasavolo en su libro *Examine simplicium* le llama 'Paropsyden Domini'. (75)

The reference is to the Ferrarese scholar Antonio Muso Brassavola, who lived during the first half of the XVIth century and published his *Examen omnium simplicium medicamentorum, quorum in officinis usus est*, in Lyon, 1537.

Everything seems to indicate that in humanist circles there was a clear tendency to distance oneself from the Arthurian legends when speaking of the Vessel of the Last

Supper. It also seems evident that the ultimate source from which these accounts all derive is, directly or indirectly, the *Historia* of William of Tyre, which no doubt held more authority for them than did the Arthurian romances or even Geoffrey of Monmouth. But despite all this, it is surprising that not one of these humanists should have established any relationship between the two groups of texts, especially at a time when the Arthurian fictions were enjoying great popularity. It is also surprising that Caffaro da Caschifellone (*c*.1080–*c*.1164), who fought at the capture of Caesarea and gave a detailed narration of the deeds of the Genoese during the First Crusade, with the conquest of Tortosa and Almería, should not have spoken of the emerald goblet in his *Liber de liberatione civitatum Orientis*. The allusion by Palmireno to its discovery in Almería finds an explanation if we bear in mind that Caffaro himself and other Genoese knights took part in the conquest of Almería as well as that of Caesarea. It is also significant, moreover, that the existence of this important relic begins to gain prominence from the early years of the XIVth century, when Cardinal Lucca Fieschi obtained it as a pledge for a loan that he made to the city of Genoa, which would not recover the relic until 1327. This was the period when the whole of Europe was amusing itself with 'round tables' in imitation of the court of King Arthur, and only a few years before Edward III created the Order of the Round Table (1345), a predecessor of the Order of the Garter.

The existence of another Grail is also attested in the kingdom of Aragon, in 1399 in the monastery of San Juan de la Peña. Martin I asked for the Holy Goblet and fray Bernardo delivered it to him so that it would be kept in the palace of the Aljafería in Zaragoza; from there it was taken to the royal chapel in the palace at Barcelona, where it was found at the death of King Martin, according to an inventory of 1410. Some years later, in 1424 Alfonso V ordered that it should be taken to the royal palace at Valencia, whence it would be taken in 1437 to the cathedral in the same city, where it is still housed. According to the legend, two days before his martyrdom, St Lawrence sent the goblet of the Last Supper from Rome to Huesca in the year 258 so that it should not fall into the hands of the emperor Valerian; it was Bishop St Indalecio who was charged with carrying out this delicate mission (note the coincidence with some of the information transmitted by Palmireno). After passing through various monasteries, the Grail would have gone to the cathedral at Jaca, recently constructed by Ramiro I (d. 1063); thence it would go to the monastery of San Juan de la Peña, on the occasion of the first mass celebrated in the Roman rite, restored thanks to the Cluniac reform (1071). These are assertions that are difficult or impossible to verify. The certain fact is that the Holy Grail venerated in Valencia – from the same century when it was venerated at Genoa – is made of three sections of different dates: the cup is of red stone (chalcedony, carnelian, sardonyx or agate), forming a hemisphere, with a small base-ring. All this is original and of eastern production, from a Hellenistic or Roman workshop, datable to the first or second century BC. The foot is another inverted goblet, of the same type of stone, although of lower quality; it has an Arabic inscription in cufic script and is possibly linked to al-Mansur, towards the end of the Xth century. The stem is of gold, and adorned with pearls and precious stones worked according to a style customary in the XII–XIVth centuries; it has two handles. The overall construction of the piece could be the work of a Gothic goldsmith of the end of the XIIIth or first half of the XIVth century, with Mozarabic and Mudejar influence, but essentially Carolingian in style. The Grail had assumed its present form by 1410, when it is listed in the inventory of King Martin I.

Covarrubias adds in his brief definition, moreover, that the Grail is a place name and a personal name. It has not been possible to locate any present-day settlement of that name, nor any name 'Grial' or 'Graal', but towards 1571 Fray Luis de León dedicated his Ode XI (*Recoge ya en el seno*) to the *licenciado* Juan de Grial, the learned editor of the works of Isidore of Seville (1599) and the secretary of Pedro Portocarrero, bishop of Calahorra (1589). It is possible that Covarrubias had in mind the dedication by the learned Augustinian, or that he had personal acquaintance with the dedicatee, who could have adopted this name as a religious name.

12. Cervantes and Lope de Vega

The criticism of the most orthodox followers of Aristotle against the romances of chivalry and, definitively, against the narratives of the Matter of Britain, for being useless and unrealistic texts, had an effect on the diffusion of the adventures of the knights of the Round Table in Spain. However, it is not understood why the adventures of Amadís de Gaula and the many other heroes of his line should have endured, but not a single title corresponding to the Matter of Britain succeeded in appearing after 1550.

Notwithstanding, any reader of *Don Quixote* (1605 and 1615) will recall easily the presence of ballads of Tristan and the figure of Merlin in the cave of Montesinos or the allusions to King Arthur of Britain, which serve the protagonist of the novel by Cervantes as an argument on the truth of the stories of knighthood:

> Si es mentira [la historia de Amadís] tambien lo debe ser que no hubo Héctor, ni Aquiles, ni la guerra de Troya, ni los doce Pares de Francia, ni el rey Artús de Inglaterra, que anda hasta ahora convertido en cuervo y le esperan en su reino por momentos. Y también se atreverán a decir que es mentirosa la historia de Guarino Mezquino y la demanda del Santo Grial, y que son apócrifos los amores de don Tristán y la reina Iseo, como los de Ginebra y Lanzarote.

It is surprising to recall that when Cervantes wrote these words, there had been no new editions of the deeds of the knights of the Round Table for more than half a century: after 1535 we know of no new printing of the *Historia de Tristán* or the *Demanda del Santo Grial*, while from the same year onwards the learned Merlin had not reappeared in print.

Cervantes had a good knowledge of some elements of the Matter of Britain: the detailed allusions to specific characters, as we have just seen, and the presence of Merlin in the episode of the Cave of Montesinos are sufficient witness to prove that the deeds of Arthur's knights were not completely unknown to him; but we would seek in vain evidence of deeper knowledge:

–¿No han vuestras mercedes leido – respondió don Quijote – los anales e historias de Ingalaterra, donde se tratran las famosas fazañas del rey Arturo, que continuamente en nuestro romance castellano llamamos el rey Artús, de quien es tradición antigua y común en todo aquel reino de la Gran Bretaña que este rey no murió, sino que, por arte de encantamiento, se convirtió en cuervo, y que, andando los tiempos, ha de volver a reinar y a cobrar su reino y cetro; a cuya causa no se probará que desde aquel tiempo a éste haya ningún inglés muerto cuervo alguno? Pues en tiempo deste buen rey fue instituida aquella famosa orden de caballería de los caballeros de la Tabla Redonda, y pasaron, sin faltar un punto, los amores que allí se cuentan de don Lanzarote del Lago con la reina Ginebra, siendo medianera dellos y sabidora aquella tan honrada dueña Quintañona, de donde nació aquel tan sabido romance, y tan decantado en nuestra España, de: 'Nunca fuera caballero / de damas tan bien servido / como fuera Lanzarote / cuando de Bretaña vino'; con aquel progreso tan dulce y tan suave de sus amorosos y fuertes fechos. (I: xiii)

It is not known where the idea that King Arthur had returned transformed into a crow came from, to which allusion is made by Cervantes and other authors of his period on various occasions (but see Biddle 2000: 486–7, note 6). As regards the Lady Quintañona, it is clear that this is a borrowing from the ballad *Nunca fuera cavallero de damas tan bien servido*, discussed above.

Besides references to characters from the Matter of Britain, the *Quixote* inherited a series of resources, episodes and narrative elements which have their remote origins in the versions of the various texts of the *Vulgate* and the *Post-Vulgate* which had appeared in Castile at the end of the XVth century and in the first years of the XVIth. It must, however, be noted that some of these materials could have reached Cervantes indirectly through *Amadís de Gaula* or other chivalresque texts.

In the first place, the concept of 'adventure' as the *raison d'être* for knight errantry, which seeks to improve the world through risk. On any impulse, knights find their strength through love, an idea which justifies any action and which motivates them to undertake the most extraordinary adventures. Life in search of adventures is a life full of dangers and it is the supreme virtue of knightly courage, where love and valour are proved: from Erec to Don Quixote, all knights are motivated by an idealised image of their lady; not to act thus implies incurring the grave vice of *recréantise*, a mixture of neglect, cowardice, dereliction, lack of interest in the lady, in other words, a definitive lack of love. To recognise the superiority of the victor's lady is not only an act of deference or respect; it is, above all, the acceptance of defeat in love and in arms. It is no accident that an equivalence is established between loving and superiority; he who loves the most deeply is the best, and love is nothing other than the result of the contemplation of the supreme beauty. Clearly, however, one could not love simply any woman: the social condition of the lady marks out the quality of the knight; the best of knights could love only the best of women; and thus, Lancelot of the Lake fixed his affections on Queen Guinevere, wife of King Arthur; Tristan, on Iseo, also a queen, wife of King Mark [...] and Don Quixote, on Dulcinea del Toboso. The parody is obvious, but it does not invalidate the underlying assumptions, on the contrary it reinforces them and thereby underlines the depths of the Ingenious Gentleman's madness.

Love is the necessary impulse for undertaking the adventures which will change the destiny of the knight through the most varied dangers. But the knight errant must encounter these adventures in which he demonstrates how much he loves, and in consequence his great valour. The court of King Arthur is the space of order, of harmony, threatened constantly by the forces of evil, represented generally by magicians and enchanters, although also by devils and vices. The knight who goes out in search of adventures goes to fight against the threats to that order and will have to confront evil and irrational enchantments, that is to say, the world of marvels, which arise, invariably in the wild setting of the forest. Each disaster for Don Quixote is the result of the intervention of these perfidious enchanters who fear the power and the glory of the bold knight, for which reason they do not permit him to achieve the longed-for triumphs in the adventures reserved for him. Don Quixote moves in another age, when the world was still inhabited by the malign forces disposed to disrupt the balance and harmony of good; the magicians and wizards would busy themselves causing all manner of havoc, in accordance with a tradition initiated in the XIIth century and surviving unaltered in the romances of chivalry.

By undertaking a particular adventure, the knight is merely fulfilling the divine intention and, for that reason, sometimes the 'adventure' represents the will of God and is synonymous with divine providence. And that is how Quixote interprets matters, in his mad subjectivity.

Adventure and love are two terms that are indissolubly wedded to the life of the knight errant. The literary tradition adds to this grouping the idea of 'marvels', but a long process of rationalisation and the slow imposition of religion has pushed aside everything that is inexplicable, since a Christian society can only be the work of God and respond to his designs. The marvellous is transformed into the miraculous, which is the realm of God and his saints.

Each adventure is a narrative unit complete in itself, with its autonomous identity: characters, places and action differ from one adventure to another, with the sole unifying thread of the protagonists, and sometimes the heroes are merely witnesses of what happens to others, who relate their own wanderings, generally at court in the presence of a scribe who notes faithfully all that occurs so as to leave a record of it for posterity, giving rise in this way to the (fictitious) chronicles of the various knights. So Blaise records the deeds of Merlin, and Blioberis does the same for others at the court of King Arthur. The move to the feigned history is inevitable: the learned Xarton busies himself with the deeds of Lepolemo, the Knight of the Cross; and, naturally, Cide Hamete Benengeli does the same for those of Don Quixote.

Don Quixote departs from his village in La Mancha three times, according to Cide Hamete Benengeli; two of these are in the first part of the novel, while the third sally occupies practically all the continuation of 1615. On this journey the most varied adventures and events follow one another with dizzying speed; on his long itinerary the road is the thread which unites the episodes. But alongside this guiding thread there are other elements which weave the story of this singular tapestry: on the one hand, the castle of the Dukes, which is a centre where adventures and events are generated, equivalent to the inn run by Juan Palomeque in part I. On the other, we encounter the protagonist and his squire who ride through roads and paths, visit settlements and uninhabited countryside, traverse woods and forests, fight or take their repose in meadows and on river banks, who reach the heights of the stars and plumb the depths of chasms. One may suspect that many of these places, inhabited or not, hide a symbolic significance, the keys to the interpretation of which already had a long tradition by the time of Cervantes. Don Quixote, in his chivalric madness, is fully aware of what is hidden behind each bend in the road, and knows that a cave is something more than an appearance, or that a boat at the bank of a river has a reason for being there and a function in the narrative of his adventures, since he is not only a reader of romances of chivalry, but also the instigator of the narrative that his chronicler will have to write, and is thinking at all times about how his history will be written (Alvar 2009: 95–120).

The wood is the place of purification or perfection before a new phase of life begins. In this sense, its character as a place of initiation is beyond question. After failure in love, or because of defeat in combat or in quest and adventure, knights take refuge in the wood and live a life of privations and suffering, of asceticism, which will permit them to occupy the place they merit. It is, definitively, a previous stage to various states; and one of the possible goals is the Other World, and the wood becomes in a very special way the prelude to the Other World, which can be reached only after going through the wood and crossing its rivers.

Both symbolic aspects, the place of initiation and the prelude to the Other World, are intimately linked and are very difficult to separate. As is obvious, in the chivalric texts the symbolism is not always maintained, or it is mingled with less profound and more everyday visions which contribute to the creation of an atmosphere at one and the same time magical and real.

Don Quixote enters woods on various occasions. At the insistence of Sancho, he takes refuge in one while his squire goes to El Toboso to seek news of Dulcinea. This is the moment of the closest approach of the knight to the lady of his vigils (II, x).

But beyond question the wood acquires its greatest literary dimension in chapters XXXIV and XXXV of part II, in which it is retold how the method for disenchanting Dulcinea is discovered. As is habitual in Cervantes, reality and fiction are mixed: the duke and duchess arrange a hunting party in which our two protagonists will take part. During the hunt a boar will be pursued; afterwards, they will go to eat in some marquees set up in the middle of the woods, where there will be great quantities of all types of foods, and then, when night is falling, there will be a great racket with the noise of battle, and there will pass before them a postillion dressed as the Devil, followed by a procession of four carts with the sages Lirgandeo, Alquife, Arcalaus and Merlin. It is another practical joke, but the performance matches the apparitions that are found in woods in the Arthurian romances and the romances of chivalry.

There are also many meadows of different kinds in the *Quixote*, according to the literary tradition to which belongs the episode in which we meet this term, since to a great extent the descriptions are inheritors of a tradition, which Cervantes frequently mocks. Thus, the bucolic meadows are green, peaceful places which invite us to love, to rest. In contrast with the bucolic tradition, chivalric meadows are places appropriate to experiencing the most varied adventures: Dulcinea appears in a meadow and then departs on her hack (II, x); the wedding feast of Camacho takes place in a meadow (II, xix), and finally they meet the duke and duchess in a meadow (II, xxx). Without doubt, however, the outstanding case is the meadow in which Don Quixote awakes after descending to the cave of Montesinos (II, xxiii), in which he will again see Dulcinea. The meadow, like the wood, is a place for unforeseeable adventures, but also for public meetings, and in the chivalric tradition public meetings give rise to demonstrations of valour and skill in which the relevant knight always distinguishes himself. But alongside this there exists reality, which serves as a point of reference, with its municipal meadows (II, x).

In the Matter of Britain, the sea is not one of the principal settings. If truth be told, it is a space of transit, merely transitional, which has the role in the narrative economy of the genre as an occasional connection between adventures and characters. The mariner is, for this reason, an infrequent character in the Arthurian romance and his milieu, the sea, is a strange space, feared because it is unknown and even inaccessible: one travels rapidly in crossing it, but on the other hand the crossing is experienced as a dangerous adventure. Thus, when Meraugis and Galván escape in the boat from the Isla sin Nombre, they do not dare to head out to sea, but sail along the coast until they come to a favourable country.

Frequently the sea known to the Arthurian knights forms scarcely a stretch of water which surrounds a marvellous place, near the mainland, a city, a castle, a magical island: the Isla de Oro, the Isla sin Nombre, etc. In similar terms, the Grail Castle is situated, in one of the versions of the story of *Perceval*, in a sea-girt location reached by an avenue covered by the interlinked branches of cypresses, pines and laurels that grow on either side, at the same time as a raging sea and a tempest shake the trees. It also has a similar meaning in the Tristan legend. This type of sea journey could be related with the motif of a voyage to the Other World, or *imrama*, in Celtic literature. To the same source may be assigned various boats, customarily without a crew, which cross the sea in Arthurian romance, which also expresses the transitional meaning of this space as well as having a symbolic significance that clearly hints at death and the world of eschatology: the ship of Solomon, that which takes to Carlion the corpse of Raguidel, that of the dying Arthur heading to Avalon, or that in which Tristan, wounded by the poisoned arrow of Morholt, is carried before the winds to Ireland.

Then there are the Nao de la Gran Serpiente in *Amadís de Gaula* or the boat enchanted by Alquife which conveys Lisuarte de Grecia in the novel by Feliciano de Silva, and the vessels that sail in the *Espejo de príncipes y cavalleros* of Diego Ortúñez de Calahorra, so close to that which Don Quijote finds on the banks of the River Ebro (Sales Dasí 1999a).

Don Quixote reaches the sea at Barcelona (II, lxi–lxv), without any maritime adventure ensuing, nor even a sea-crossing since our knight does not take part in the skirmish between the galleys and the ship carrying Ana Felix, nor does he intervene in the rescue of Don Gaspar Gregorio, much to his irritation since he intended to go to Barbary to rescue him (II, lxiv). However, the beach at Barcelona is transformed into a symbolic space since it is there that he is defeated and to some extent one could say that the knight Don Quixote comes to his end by the shores of the sea, as if to anticipate the journey to the Other World in the Arthurian texts.

Rivers have the same narrative function as the sea in the Arthurian narratives and in numerous romances of chivalry; they are the tenuous thread which separates the real world from the imagined Other World, and in any case rivers always announce an extraordinary adventure; to attain it, it is necessary to cross the river as if this were a rite of passage.

Don Quixote, like so many Arthurian knights, finds a boat without oars when he reaches the banks of the Ebro, with nobody on board, tied to a tree on the bank:

> Miró Don Quijote a todas partes, y no vio persona alguna; y luego, sin más ni más, se apeó de Rocinante y mandó a Sancho que lo mesmo hiciese del rucio, y que a entrambas bestias las atase muy bien, juntas, al tronco de un álamo o sauce que allí estaba. Preguntóle Sancho la causa de aquel súbito apeamiento y de aquel ligamiento. Respondió don Quijote:
>
> –Has de saber, Sancho, que este barco que aquí está, derechamente y sin poder ser otra cosa en contrario, me está llamando y convidando a que entre en él, y vaya en él a dar socorro a algún caballero, o a otra necesitada y principal persona, que debe de estar puesta en alguna grande cuita, porque éste es estilo de los libros de las historias caballerescas y de los encantadores que en ellas se entremeten y platican: cuando algún caballero está puesto en algún trabajo, que no puede ser librado dél sino por la mano de otro caballero, puesto que estén distantes el uno del otro dos o tres mil leguas, y aun más, o le arrebatan en una nube o le deparan un barco donde se entre, y en menos de un abrir y cerrar de ojos le llevan, o por los aires, o por la mar, donde quieren y adonde es menester su ayuda; así que, ¡oh Sancho!, este barco está puesto aquí para el mesmo efecto; y esto es tan verdad como es ahora de día; y antes que éste se pase, ata juntos al rucio y a Rocinante, y a la mano de Dios, que nos guíe, que no dejaré de embarcarme si me lo pidiesen frailes descalzos.

As a good reader of romances of chivalry, Don Quixote is convinced of the destiny that his voyage will present to him; briefly, he expects to sail out to the boundless sea and cover an enormous distance, until he has passed the equinoctial line. But the chivalric tradition knew that the equinox established the separation between two worlds, since the Other World is situated in the Antipodes, an uninhabited kingdom, the kingdom of the pygmies or of the dead.

Among the episodes of the third journey is found Don Quixote's descent into the Cave of Montesinos, which turns out to be so surprising because of the events that occur there that the narrator finds it necessary to make some comment (II, xxiv). However, the cave, as well as what happens in it, would seem normal to readers of the romances of chivalry, accustomed to these occurrences in the activities of their heroes.

In fact, as J. M. Cacho Blecua (1992) has established, the presence of caves in chivalric narratives acquires an ambiguous charater, in which are mingled the delightful and the sinister, the marvellous and the fearsome. It is normal, then, for writers – and also for readers – to want to underline the extraordinary significance of the cave through a series of signs that serve to guide a reading: the pursuit of unusual animals (white stags, boars ...), the location of the cave in the middle of a thick wood, its distance from any settlement, and, therefore, from the world of norms and laws.

The cave is outside the guidelines that regulate daily life, and from this come the signs that announce the entrance to an extraordinary domain. All that occurs inside the grotto will be subject to its own logic, which does not coincide in any way with that of the world outside. Definitively, it is necessary to think that on entering the caves of the romances of chivalry one crosses the line that separates the world of the living and the Other World; an Other World that can be conceived as a paradise or as a hell. A place in which there abound all kinds of riches and foods, and in which there are not lacking valiant knights from previous ages and beautiful ladies with a life of their own (this is the case of the English *Sir Orfeo*, 1370, or of the kingdom of Herla in the *Nugis curialium* of Walter Map, *c*.1183, and so many other texts). The remote tradition of the Matter of Britain survives still, transformed and enhanced, in *Clarian de Landanís* (I, cxxviii), in *Polindo* (xv), or in *Olivante de Laura* (prologo, I). But caves are presented, not infrequently, as infernal places, recalling at times the dwelling of Pluto, as it is described in narratives relating to Orpheus (*Lidamarte*, xxxii).

The caves that lead to the Other World are those that constitute the centre of the journey of initiation, an extraordinary test which only chosen heroes can complete; on entering the cave these knights can obtain material riches, but there is no lack of cases in which the descent to the depths brings them knowledge of the most varied subjects; these are the moments of greatest importance, reserved for only a few heroes.

Don Quixote descends to the cave of Montesinos (II, xxii–xxiv) after having prepared himself for the 'peligrosa y nueva aventura', fully aware of a literary tradition that sank its roots into folklore. It is a journey of initiation, as A. Redondo indicates (1981), in which there appear all the elements that characterise the journey to the Other World, and for this reason Sancho alludes to 'hell' and speaks of 'descent to the other world' (II, xxiii). In this context, the deep sleep of our knight merely accords with the character of his adventure, as well as giving to Cervantes the possibility of rescuing, with some element of verisimilitude, a barely believable situation.

The riches of the place, the presence of Montesinos and Durandarte, who died in a remote past and who are nonetheless still fully alive, leave no room for doubt that our hero has reached the Other World. This is why nobody eats and time runs in a different way, which obliges Don Quixote to request food when he returns to the surface and raises serious doubts about his story, because of the protagonist's perception of time, believing that he has been below ground for three days, and that of his companions, who calculate that scarcely an hour has passed.

The parodic and burlesque tone with which the entire episode is endowed by Cervantes is not an obstacle to appreciating the force it has as an initiation. The final success will be the revelation of the enchantment of Dulcinea and that she can be disenchanted. On his return, Don Quixote awakes anew to life (Redondo 1981; Canavaggio 1992).

There remains one more episode which is also significant, and which beyond doubt must be read as a counterpoint to the adventure of the 'enchanted barque' that the protagonist finds on the banks of the Ebro: this is the scene on the beach at Barcelona, in which the Knight of the White Moon routs Don Quixote. By the shores of the sea his adventures end and the civilian life of Alonso Quijano recommences; this is the ending that is appropriate to a hero of his standing, as had happened to so many others after the battle of Salesbieres. The protagonist's removal from all knightly activity is forced on him by his defeat, and by wounds both physical and spiritual; but it will not be a definitive departure, for he can return to deeds of arms after a year has passed. The echo of the end of King Arthur and of the hope of the Britons for his return leaves no room for doubt.

Cervantes has been an attentive reader of the books of the Matter of Britain that he had at his disposal; this is what we conclude from the presence of adventures, the concept of love, and its chivalric consequences, the narrative geography (woods, meadows, river, sea), some scenes and episodes (the boar hunt, the enchanted barque, the Other World, the defeat by the shores of the sea, and the possibility of the protagonist's return). Cervantes surpasses his models through the use he makes of irony, humour, parody and the mixture of personal experience and immediate reality with the inheritance that reached him, directly or indirectly, through Arthurian literature.

There is a contrast between the Arthurian knowledge of Cervantes and that of other XVIth- and XVIIth-century authors; the latter are very parsimonious with references to characters or situations derived from the Matter of Britain. It can be affirmed that Cervantes recreates the ambience of XIIth- or XIIIth-century chivalry, or that he reworks it in accordance with an ideal model that is located in the XVth century: in reality, it would be difficult to establish the chronological moment chosen by Don Quixote as the Golden Age of chivalry, but there is no doubt that this recreation is coherent in the protagonist's mind and that for it to be so, Cervantes has made use of the literary materials at his disposal.

Don Quixote is, however, an atypical case among the romances of chivalry and in Spanish literature of its time. One would look in vain for any other text with so many Arthurian connotations, as we have seen already in discussing the romances of chivalry and the sentimental romances. Nor does the theatre make use of the Matter of

Britain. The extraordinary development of the *comedia* that appears in the XVIIth century is centred, essentially, on historical and religious themes, on contemporary matters or those derived from a small number of literary texts among which the Arthurian narratives do not feature. This is no surprise, since it was many decades since Castilian versions of the stories of Lancelot and Tristan had been reprinted; scarcely a couple of relevant texts survived in the *romancero*.

Lope de Vega may stand as an example since he is the author of an enormous number of plays, perhaps around a thousand, and since he had recourse to all kinds of material. He never once refers to Lancelot, Galahad, Perceval or Joseph of Arimathea; according to the census by Morley and Tyler (1961), among the hundreds of thousands of lines of verse by Lope de Vega, there appear only one reference to Galván and Merlin, two references to Arthur and Guinevere, and a score to Tristan (one of them the well-known servant in *El perro del hortelano*). The absence of Iseo leads one to believe that in most cases Lope is not referring to the nephew of King Mark. It seems as though, given his excellent knowledge of the theatrical arts, Lope de Vega does not seek interference from other genres, that could distract the audience; or perhaps these were simply names that no longer carried any meaning for inhabitants of Spain in the XVIIth century.

As far as the theatrical works of Cervantes are concerned, the Sacristan in *Los baños de Argel* takes the name Tristán, a native of Mollorido, and a musician by profession (lines 725ff.). In this choice of name for the Sacristan various factors converge: for one thing, the name itself seems to be a paronomasia constructed from the phonological similarity of the ending of two designations (Sa*cristán*-Tris*tán*); secondly, the profession of musician reveals a knowledge of the Arthurian character, although the Sacristan adds that he is a 'divine musician' because he rings the bells. Finally, it seems clear that 'Tristán' had become a name for servants and comic characters (*graciosos*), from the period of *La Celestina* onwards.

Chronological Appendix

c.1110	Relief possibly depicting Tristán, Santiago de Compostela cathedral.
1136	Martinus Galvan, name documented at León.
1151	Artus, name documented at Alt Urgell, Lérida.
1156	Galas, name documented in Castile-León.
1171?/XIIIth century	Merlin, name documented at Sahagún, León.
1196	*Anales navarro-aragoneses* (with *Liber regum 1*), at Pamplona.
1217	*Anales Toledanos I.*
1218	Diego García, *Planeta*.
1218	Enebra, name documented at Plasencia, Extremadura.

c.1220	*Liber regum 2* compiled in Navarra.
c.1225	Relief possibly depicting Yvain at a monastery in Lugo (Galicia).
pre-1230	*Libro de Alexandre.*
c.1260–70	*Liber regum 3* compiled in Navarra.
c.1250–1314	Allusions found in Galician-Portuguese poetry.
1272–84	Alfonso X, *General Estoria.*
pre-1295	Lançarote, name documented in Castilla.
c.1300	The Grail of Valencia cathedral.
c.1300	*Amadís de Gaula 1.*
c.1305	*Libro del cavallero Zifar.*
1313	*Livro de Josep Abarimatia*, Portuguese version.
1325–6	Lançarote and Galván, names of falcons mentioned by D. Juan Manuel.
c.1330	Translation of *Tristán*? Reference in the *Libro de buen amor.*
1343	Portuguese *Livro das Linhagens.*
1344	Castilian versión of the *Crónica del Conde don Pedro de Portugal.*
1348	Rodrigo Yáñez, *Poema Alfonso XI*, with prophecies of Merlin.
1300–50	Leomarte, *Sumas de historia troyana.*
1356	Nine Worthies cited in Aragón.
1350–75	Paintings possibly of Tristán at La Alhambra, Granada.
c.1370	Castilian *Visión de Alfonso X*, with prophecies of Merlin.
1377	Catalan translation of the *Visión de Alfonso X.*
c.1379	Pero López de Ayala, *Crónicas,* with prophecies of Merlin.
c.1380	Catalan *Lançalot.*
1380	Catalan *Estoria del saint Grasal.*
1360–1430	*Cancionero de Baena*, with references to various Arthurian characters.
1398–1405	Alfonso Alvarez de Villasandino, poet of the *Cancionero de Baena.*
end XIVth century	Catalan *Lançalot.*
end XIVth century	Galician-Portuguese *Lançarote.*
1404	Castilian *Crónica* including material from the *Liber regum.*
1407	Pero Ferruz, poet of the *Cancionero de Baena.*
1406–12	Francisco Imperial, poet of the *Cancionero de Baena.*
1414	Original of the Castilian *Lanzarote del Lago* copied in BNE, MS 9611.
beg. XVth century	Miniatures of Tristán in the fragments of the BNE, Madrid.
beg. XVth century	*Cartas de Iseo y Tristán.*

beg. XVth century	*Cuento de Tristán de Leonís*, Castilian-Aragonese version in Vatican MS.
beg. XVth century	*Amadís de Gaula 2*, fragmentary version known from surviving folio.
*c.*1432	Juan Alfonso de Baena, *Dezir a Juan II*.
*c.*1435	Gutierre Díaz de Games, *Victorial*.
1400–38	*Demanda do Santo Grial*, Portuguese version.
1438	Alfonso Martínez de Toledo alludes in *Arcipreste de Talavera* to Tristán de Leonís and Lançarote de Lago.
*c.*1437–43	*Cancionero de Palacio*.
*c.*1445	Rodríguez del Padrón, *Siervo libre de amor*.
*c.*1454	*Cancionero de San Román*, with references to several Arthurian characters.
pre-1460	*Romance de Tristán*, cited by Joanot Martorell, in *Tirant lo Blanc*.
1470	*Libro de José Abarimatia*, *Estoria de Merlín* and *Lançarote*, fragments of Biblioteca Universitaria de Salamanca, MS 1877.
1475	Tristán, name documented at Bilbao.
1475–1500	Juan de Flores, sentimental romances.
*c.*1485	Diego de San Pedro, *Cárcel de amor*, published at Seville (1492).
*c.*1490	*Cancionero de Barrantes*.
1496	*Tragèdia de Lançalot*, Catalan incunable.
pre-1498	Ballads (*romances*) of Tristán and Lanzarote.
1498	*Baladro del sabio Merlín*, published at Burgos by Juan de Burgos.
1498	Jerónimo Pinar, *Juego de naipes* with allusion to Tristán and Lanzarote.
1499?	First edition of *La Celestina*, with a character named Tristán.
1501	*Libro de Tristán de Leonís*, published at Valladolid by Juan de Burgos.
1508	*Amadís de Gaula*, reworking by Rodríguez de Montalvo, printed at Zaragoza.
1511	*Cancionero General* by Hernando del Castillo, printed at Valencia.
1515	*Demanda del santo Grial*, printed at Toledo by Juan de Villaquirán.
1516	*Floriseo*, by Fernando Bernal, printed at Valencia by Diego Gumiel.
1517	*Arderique*, anonymous, printed at Valencia by Juan de Viñao.

1528	*Libro de Tristán de Leonís,* published at Seville by Juan Cromberger.
1534	*Corónica de Tristán de Leonís*, printed at Seville by Domenico de Robertis.
1535	*Demanda del santo Grial* y *Baladro del sabio Merlín*, Seville edition.
pre-1540	*Romance* 'Nunca fuera cavallero'.
pre-1547	*Romance* 'Cavalga doña Ginebra'.
XVIth century	Romances of chivalry.

VII

THE *POST-VULGATE* CYCLE IN THE IBERIAN PENINSULA

Paloma Gracia

Between 1235 and 1240 the cycle known as the *Post-Vulgate Roman du Graal*, or simply as the *Post-Vulgate (P-V)*, was composed.[1] This compilation brought together sections derived from the work of Robert de Boron, the *Vulgate* and the *Tristan en prose*, in a rewriting the extent of which varied from one section to another. This cycle told of the origins of the Grail, in a version close to the *Estoire del Saint Graal*, continued with the histories of Merlin and of Arthur, according to the prosification of the *Merlin* of Robert de Boron and a *Suite du Merlin* very different from the *Vulgate* version, and concluded with the end of the Grail adventure and the destruction of Logres, in a profound remodelling of the *Queste del Saint Graal* and the *Mort le roi Artu*, known as the *Post-Vulgate Queste-Mort Artu*.

No manuscript survives that includes the whole of the *P-V*, which is the main problem with this cycle; the surviving manuscripts are incomplete and, on occasion, involve folios that include copies of other compilations, or loose fragments. The Iberian versions corroborate the existence of the *P-V*, since some of their manuscript and printed witnesses cover one or more of its branches; they give an idea of the configuration of the original cycle, since they preserve, when taken together as a whole, the greater part of the *P-V* and therefore facilitate its reconstruction.

The history of critical scholarship on the *P-V* begins with the identification of its sections in manuscripts traditionally considered to belong to the *Vulgate*, especially the Huth Manuscript (now in the British Library, MS Add. 38117), which includes the prosified *Merlin* of Robert de Boron and continues with the innovating *Suite du Merlin*. In the prologue to their edition, Gaston Paris and Jacob Ulrich (1886) advanced the hypothesis that the manuscript formed part of a trilogy earlier than the *Vulgate*, the last section of which would have been a *Queste* and *Mort Artu*, preserved in the *Demanda do Santo Graal*. Although the hypothesis was the subject of argument and the idea of the priority of the *P-V* over the *Vulgate* was soon rejected, while new theories were formed regarding the number of branches that it embraced and the different reworkings to which it had been subjected, the work of Paris and Ulrich made possible a slow and progressive identification of the parts that constitute the cycle, scattered in copies of other compilations. In broad outline, works on the *P-V* have concentrated upon the establishment of its structure, the identification of fragments in various manuscripts, and its relations with the *Vulgate* and the *Tristan en prose*. Beyond any doubt, the greatest progress in knowledge of the *P-V* is that represented by the publications of Fanni Bogdanow, beginning with her *The Romance of the Grail* (1966), which offered a reconstruction of the storyline of the cycle, the analysis of its sections and its sources, and the study of its significance.

Leaving to one side the Iberian reworkings, the reconstruction is based on a series of manuscripts in French:

1. *Suite du Merlin*, the Cambridge MS (Cambridge University Library Additional MS 7071) and the Huth manuscript (now BL Add. 38117), both incomplete. MS 112 of the BNF contains two sections: the end of the *Suite* is preserved in Book II, the narration of which continues in Book III in a relation that can also be read in MS 12599 of the BNF; both sections were published by H. Oskar Sommer (1913) and by Fanni Bogdanow (1965) under the titles *Die Abenteuer Gawains, Ywains und Le Morholts* and the *Folie Lancelot* respectively.
2. The most significant segments of the *Post-Vulgate Queste-Mort Artu* are preserved in three manuscripts of the BNF: MSS 112 (Book IV) and 340 for the *Queste*, and MS 343 for the *Mort Artu* (Bogdanow 1991–2001: I, 98–207). Brief fragments have been discovered in recent decades by Monica Longobardi (1987a) and Fanni Bogdanow (1976, 1985, 1991), in libraries at Bologna, Geneva (Bodmer 105) and Oxford (Bodleian Library, Rawlinson D 874); passages identified in some manuscripts of the second version of the *Tristan en prose* are also to be taken into account.

According to the author of the *P-V*, who adopted the name of Robert de Boron and thus acknowledged the debt he bore to his predecessor, the cycle would be formed by three branches of equal length (which do not coincide with those which scholars distinguish in studying it, since, according to the structure outlined by the author, the first of these originally covered everything up to a point quite far advanced into the story of Merlin). To reconstruct the structure and content of the cycle is, however, a difficult task, not only because of the fragmentation of its manuscript tradition, but also because of mismatches in the storyline of the surviving parts.

The main outline of the story can, though, be summarised as follows. The *P-V* begins with the account of the origins of the Grail, that is to say, with a version of the *Estoire del Saint Graal*, of the *Vulgate* cycle, which is followed by the prosification of the *Merlin* of Robert de Boron and the *Suite du Merlin*, which is interrupted in the early years of the reign of Arthur. Its continuation is less certain: it lacks a section equivalent to the *Lancelot propre*, but it is almost certain that the original cycle also lacked such a section, and, in fact, this omission would have been one of its most notable innovations in relation to the *Vulgate*. The absence of the story that should have linked the *Suite* and the *Queste* is a different matter: there is a chronological gap between the two sections, since the narrative of the *Suite* ends when Galaad and

Perceval are still not yet born; missing, therefore, is a section which would have explained the significance of the protagonists in the quest for the Grail and would function as a prelude to the *Queste* and the *Mort Artu*. Of this section, which is difficult to reconstruct, there have been identified only a few segments in BNF MSS 112 and 12599: that published as the *Folie Lancelot*, which links with that known as *Die Abenteuer*. The allusions to episodes narrated in the *Suite* or the development of those narrated in the *Queste* make it certain that these segments belong to the *P-V* cycle, which is connected in particular to the *Agravain* and the first version of the *Tristan en prose* in this section. Fragments preserved in Italian libraries also bear witness, although very fragmentary witness, to this part of the *P-V*.

The final part of the cycle, known as the *Post-Vulgate Queste-Mort Artu*, is a rewriting of the *Queste del Saint Graal* and the *Mort le roi Artu*, in which both the story and, above all, the spirit of the *Vulgate* have undergone a profound transformation. The original version has been preserved only partially: a long section of the part relating to the *Queste* has been identified in BNF MS 343, to which must be added the fragments in BNF MS 112 (Book IV) and in certain manuscripts of the *Tristan en prose*. As regards the *Mort Artu*, there are only two short episodes in BNF MS 340, but its contents can be established with the help of the Portuguese and Castilian versions, the *Demanda do Santo Graal* and the *Demanda del Santo Grial* respectively.

According to Fanni Bogdanow, the *P-V* translated in the Iberian Peninsula was composed, like the French original, of an *Estoire del saint Graal*, a *Merlin* continued by a version of the *Suite*, and a *Queste del saint Graal* and *Mort Artu*. Witnesses survive in both Portuguese and Spanish. In Portuguese, there are manuscripts of each of the three branches: the first part of the cycle or *Livro de Josep Abaramatia* is preserved in a XVIth-century MS at Lisbon (Torre do Tombo, 643); the section corresponding to the *Suite du Merlin* is preserved in MS 2434 of the Biblioteca de Catalunya, from the XIVth century, while the final part is copied entirely in MS 2594 of the Österreichische Nationalbibliothek, Vienna, from the XVth century.

Of the Castilian version, we have only one manuscript: MS 1877 of the Biblioteca Universitaria de Salamanca (formerly MS 2-G-5 of the Biblioteca del Palacio Real, Madrid), compiled in 1469–70 by Petrus Ortiz. It contains sections of each of the parts of the cycle: the *Libro de Josep Abarimatía*, *Libro* (or *Estoria*) *de Merlín* and *Lançarote* (the name given by the copyist to the section corresponding to the *Mort Artu*). There are, however, important printed witnesses: the oldest is the *Baladro del sabio Merlín con sus profecías*, printed in Burgos in 1498. The two last parts of the cycle were published together, although divided into two books, under the title of *Demanda del Santo Grial con los maravillosos fechos de Lanzarote y de Galaz su hijo*; of the Toledo edition of 1515 only the second book is preserved, that is, the *Demanda del Santo Grial*; the Seville edition (1535) is the only one that contains a *Baladro*, followed by a *Demanda*, as the first and second books. These two editions of

1515 and 1535 seem to have derived independently from an edition published in Seville in 1500, now lost.

The *P-V* Rewritten in the Iberian Peninsula and the Perception and Survival of its Cyclical Nature

If the French cycle itself presents certain obscure areas, there is much more obscurity concerning the Spanish versions, in relation to which even the most fundamental questions raise doubts. The language and date of the earliest Peninsular translation have been debated at length, and there is even disagreement over the very content of the French manuscript from which the translation was made. According to Fanni Bogdanow, the *P-V* translated in the Iberian Peninsula was composed, like the original cycle, of an *Estoire del Saint Graal*, the *Merlin* and *Suite du Merlin*, and a *Queste del Saint Graal* and *Mort Artu*. Against this view, Miranda (1994, 2004), basing himself on the final chapters of the *Lançarote del Lago* and considering the possibility that a *Tristan en prose* may have made up part of the cycle, has proposed a Peninsular *P-V* of five branches, that is, with the addition of a *Lancelot* and a *Tristan*; although, however, it is obvious that there were links between the three great cycles, as is made clear in the BNM *Lançarote del Lago* manuscript, the hypothesis is open to question. Fanni Bogdanow (1999a) indicated the link that exists between the last section of the *Lançarote del Lago* and the *P-V*, where an extract of the section preceding the *Folie Lancelot* concluded the third book, functioning as a transition to a *Libro de don Tristan* which was copied immediately following; but this does not necessarily mean that *Lançarote* and *Tristan* would have constituted branches of the Peninsular *P-V*, and merely shows the ease with which the different branches of the cycle could combine with contiguous materials, as well as separating from these. The registers of the library in the inventory of Isabel la Católica, dating from 1503, reveal that the queen owned three Arthurian volumes: a *Demanda del Santo Grial*, a *Merlin* and a *Lançarote*; the fact that these copies were in identical bindings and were of the same size suggests that they belonged to the same collection (Cátedra and Rodríguez Velasco 1999: 46).[2] The idea of a collection leads one to consider that the various Arthurian narratives were perceived as forming a single universe, which would have made it easy to copy the different Arthurian materials as a unit (Gracia 2010a).

The Iberian *P-V* maintained its three branches for a long period, although it is certain that copies of the complete trilogy coexisted with copies of two of its parts or of a single element; it is a separate question whether its three branches were copied as a whole, which could have been accomplished only with difficulty, especially the *Merlin* branch, which tended gradually to lose the narrative beyond the disappearance of the seer. Both indirect and direct testimony reveals the existence of these cyclical copies. A manuscript of the trilogy would have been used by the author of the *Crónica de 1404* to complete a history of the kings of England, derived from the *Brut* of Wace, although through a Peninsular intermediary. The author refers to this *P-V* as *Estoria del Sancto Grayal et de rrey Artur*; it extended from the *Estoire del Saint Graal* to the *Mort Artu*, and he used it as a secondary source. From it he obtained some elements derived from the *Merlin*, the long interpolation on Josephas or Seiephas (Josephus), son of Joseph de Baramatia (Joseph d'Arimathie), and some information on the facts surrounding the end of King Arthur. The origin of this cyclical *P-V* is shared between Galicia and Castile, since the author of the *Crónica de 1404* was Galician by origin, but resided in Castile, at least in 1390. The three Arthurian sections of MS 1877 of the Biblioteca Universitaria de Salamanca are Castilian, though with western elements; each of these sections is derived from the three branches of the trilogy, and their final version dates from 1470. This cyclical *P-V* could have been the source of Lope García Salazar, who would have been composing his *Libro de las Bienandanzas e Fortunas* shortly after the Salamanca codex was created, adapting some fragments of the cycle which he would have known in its three branches, although it is difficult to determine whether or not they were collected in a single volume.

The cyclical character of the *P-V* could also, in some way, have survived even in the case of codices that were not cyclical but which, although they contained only a single branch, state that what had been copied therein constituted part of a trilogy. This is what seems to be indicated by that register of the inventory of the library of Isabel la Católica, which states that she possessed 'otro pliego entero, de mano, en rromançe, que es la terçera parte de la *Demanda del Santo Grial*': the reference could be specifying that the copy concerned contained the third part or book of the *Demanda*, that is to say, a *Demanda* properly designated as such, perceived as a branch of a cycle. Something similar could have happened in the Portuguese sphere, which lacks witnesses that bring together more than one branch; nonetheless, the perception that the parts copied individually made up a cycle could have persisted. This is suggested by the title of MS 643 of the archive of the Torre do Tombo at Lisbon: *Livro de Josep Abaramatia intetulado a primeira parte da Demanda do Santo Grial*; in specifying that this was the first part, the rubric is declaring that the book belonged to a cycle, of which it constituted one branch. The colophon of the Lisbon codex adds other revealing elements: the author declares, in what is a Portuguese innovation, that he has not included the story of Merlin so that his book is not too big. Since, however, this commentary arises from the expansion of some words from the *explicit* of the *Estoire del Saint Graal* which served to introduce the *Estoire de Merlin*, it is difficult to know at what point in the Portuguese evolution of the *P-V* these two branches would have been separated.[3]

In the field of printed editions, the problem becomes, if it be possible, even more thorny. Although the 1498 *Baladro* contains only the Merlin branch, it is difficult to know if its model contained any other section or part of one, since it is possible that one of its prologues may have been partially inspired by a *Libro de Josep Abarimatía*.

The nature of the model followed by the incunable is uncertain, just as uncertainty attaches to the model from which there ultimately derives the sequence of printed editions of 1515 and 1535, supposedly initiated by the lost edition of 1500, from which both of these could have derived. Although the only surviving copy of the 1515 edition has lost its first book, the cyclical character of this print is obvious, as is that of the edition of 1535, which presents a *Baladro* followed by a *Demanda* as the first and second books, and which alludes to the juxtaposition of texts that it publishes as the *Historia del Santo Grial* or *Libro del Santo Grial*; however, the distinctively curious feature of its composition could arise from its discovering the possibility of reuniting branches previously copied independently, rather than demonstrating the continuity of the cyclical model. What the XVth-century printed editions do reveal, in having brought together under the label of first and second books the Castilian derivatives of the *Merlin* and the *Suite* (as far as the seer's death) and of the *Queste* and the *Mort Artu*, is that the materials published were perceived as parts of a greater whole.

MS 1877 of the Biblioteca Universitaria, Salamanca (formerly MS 2-G-5 of the Biblioteca de Palacio, Madrid)

In 1954, the government of General Franco decreed that what is now MS 1877 of the University Library at Salamanca, together with around 500 other codices that had been taken into the Royal Library at the Palacio de Oriente in Madrid a century and a half previously, should be returned to Salamanca, whence they had been removed on the occasion of the closure of the Colegios Mayores of the University. This codex combines the interest of being the only one to group together segments derived from all three branches of the *P-V* with that of having been one of the most important witnesses in the history of the modern scholarly reconstruction of the trilogy.

The manuscript was the focus of the studies of Karl Pietsch, which were as early as they were profuse, and with whose name it will always be linked. Pietsch began his series of studies devoted to the codex in 1913–14, with a learned article on the Arthurian sections of the manuscript. In this, he formulated the hypothesis of the existence in Spain of a trilogy composed by the *Libro de Josep Abarimatía*, the *Estoria de Merlín* and the *Demanda del Santo Grial*. On the language of the translation, he drew attention to the presence of distinctive Portuguese features in the Arthurian sections of the manuscript, but remained doubtful whether the presence of these forms was the consequence of their arising from a Portuguese translation or from the Leonese origin of the translator. The idea was repeated in his studies of 1915–16, 1920–1 and 1925; the most important was undoubtedly his *Spanish Grail Fragments*, published in 1924–5, in the first volume of which Pietsch edited the Arthurian sections of the former MS 2-G-5. In the introductory study, he underlined the presence, in the Portuguese *Josep* and in the Castilian *Demanda* (and moreover in a similar context in each case), of the name by which the compiler refers to himself: Juan Vivas (Joam Vives/Joannes Bivas). This Pietsch considered to guarantee that both works formed separate parts of a cycle. Since, moreover, the Castilian and Portuguese cycles were related, he posed the problem of the language in which the translation was produced, which he resolved by relying on Gottfried Baist, following whose defence of the priority of the Castilian *Josep* over the Portuguese (Baist 1907) Pietsch upheld the priority of Castilian in the whole of the cycle, a question to which we will return below.

Despite the early date of the publications of Pietsch, the Arthurian segments of the codex still present many uncertainties, and the only certainty is that later scholars have devoted few studies to them. Pietsch devoted the greater part of his publications to the language of these sections, so that this is the aspect that has been most intensively studied; however, the edition he produced of these texts is of questionable value (Castro 1988a; Gracia 2009, 2011). The criteria he used to establish the text are dubious, and his editorial intervention is so extensive that the edition must be used with caution, with the additional inconvenience that no other edition has been published.

The manuscript (Bogdanow 1991–2001: I, 210–16) consists of 308 folios, including the endleaves, and gives the name of its creator, Petrus Ortiz, as well as two dates, 1469 and 1470, the second of which corresponds to the year in which Petrus had revised the volume. It contains three different lists of chapters: one listing eight treatises, which is what corresponds to the present state of the codex, while the others, covering more treatises, relate to some previous arrangements, which had subsequently been reduced for some reason of which we remain ignorant.[4]

The three Arthurian sections of the manuscript are copied interspersed with various religious treatises and saints' lives. They display, taken together and in keeping with other Peninsular derivatives of the *P-V*, a tendency to abbreviate the text of their models and to divide the narrative into sections by introducing numerous chapter headings. Despite this, and despite the fact that the model has been greatly abbreviated, Petrus adds at some points a terse explanation of a religious nature which reveals his desire to make plain the moral lesson conveyed by the text. The three sections are in keeping with the content of the whole codex, but while the *Josep* and the *Estoria de Merlín* are complete and even offer a partial summary of events that are not narrated, the *Lançarote* poses some questions, since it opens and closes abruptly and is extremely short.

The *Josep* occupies fols 252r–282r and its contents correspond with pp. 12–48 of the edition by Sommer (1908–16: I). Of the three Arthurian sections of the codex, it is the longest, and occupies fifty-two pages of the edition by Pietsch (3–54). There are sixty-six chapter headings, although the chapters are, in general, extremely short. The narration covers matters from the imprisonment of Joseph Abarimatia, accompanied by the dish which contained the blood of Christ, and ends at Sarraz, when King Evolat, who has been extensively catechised, promises to Josafas that he will embrace Christianity, before routing his enemy, the king of Egypt, Tolomer.

The *Estoria de Merlín* is copied on fols 282v–296r, pp. 57–81 of the edition by Pietsch, and corresponds to the narrative content of pp. 1–33 of the edition of Gaston Paris and Jacob Ulrich (1886: I). Divided by twenty-six chapter headings, it begins with the council of Devils that decides upon the conception of Merlin, and ends when the seer asks Blaisen to write the history of the Grail, as well as his past and future story. It is in this last episode that Petrus introduces the most important innovations, adding to the story conveyed by his model two summaries of the argument, which he continues, supplementing it in some ways (Gracia 2007). These additions are revealing: the first of them because the errors found in it show that Petrus knew little of the Arthurian world, and the second because it narrates succinctly the episode of the 'Bestia Labrador' (a 'Beste Glatissant' mutated from 'ladrador' to 'labradora'), which seems to have been what he found the most interesting in the stories of Merlin and Arthur.

Lançarote is the title used for the section that corresponds to the *Mortu Artu*, which is extremely short and in which the sentences derived from the model are interspersed with brief summaries of those which are omitted. It occupies fols 298v–300v of the codex, pp. 85–9 of the Pietsch edition, and corresponds to §§630–54 of the Portuguese *Demanda*, chapters 394–417 of the Castilian *Demanda*.[5] It begins abruptly, when Arthur is informed of the relationship between Lanzarote and Ginebra. The lovers are exposed, because of which Arthur condemns Guinevere to be burned at the stake; but she is liberated by Lancelot, who sends a maiden to the king as an ambassador. The passage also closes abruptly on relating that it was Galván who first replied to the maiden. Since this is the final treatise contained in the codex, it is possible that the fragmentary state of this text is caused by the accidental loss of material; however, it can be deduced from the list of thirteen treatises of the emended version that the length of *Lançarote* in the previous version was approximately the same as the present extent.

The Iberian *Post-Vulgate Estoire del Saint Graal*

There are surviving witnesses in Castilian and in Portuguese; while in Castilian there is only the relevant section of the Salamanca codex,[6] there are two separate witnesses of the Portuguese translation. The older of the two consists of a single bifolium, retrieved from the binding of a notarial volume, preserved in the Arquivo Distrital do Porto (PT/ADPRT/NOT/CNSTS01/001/0012; shelfmark: I/18/2 - 2.12), which has been dated to the end of the XIIIth century; this is, therefore, the earliest textual witness for Arthurian material in Iberia, and the only one which, like its French model, has no chapter headings and no divisions in the text. Its discovery is a highly significant development (Dias 2003–6) and has given rise to essential studies of fundamental importance.[7]

As regards the second witness, the *Livro de Josep Abaramatia intetulado a primeira parte da Demanda do Santo Grial*, it gives a complete version of the work. Given its proximity to the *Vulgate Estoire del Saint Graal*, and given that there is no clear witness for the first branch of the original French trilogy, the Portuguese adaptation gives us an idea that the latter opened with a version of the *Estoire*, modified only to the extent necessary to allow it to open the new cycle. The manuscript is preserved in the Torre do Tombo, Lisbon, as MS 643. It contains 311 folios and is dedicated to King João III; it was copied by various copyists in the service of Manuel Álvares, who seem to have respected some of the linguistic archaisms of the codex that they were copying.

Like its French model, a prologue, in which the author explains how he obtained the book that he is copying, leads into a narrative that begins seven years before the Crucifixion of Christ. It relates the conversion of Evelac, king of Sarraz, the transfer of the Grail to Great Britain and the evangelisation of this land, ending with the marvels associated with the death and tomb of King Lancelot, the grandfather of the knight of the same name, which would not cease until the arrival of Galahad and Lancelot. Since the *Libro de Josep Abarimatía* of the Salamanca codex does not contain the prologue preceding the history of Joseph, the narrative in the Portuguese version goes hand in hand with the Castilian from the Portuguese chapter XV to its chapter L, where the Castilian text finishes.

The text in the *Livro de Josep Abarimatía* is extremely close to the *Estoire del Saint Graal* in the codex preserved as Rennes, Bibliothèque Municipale, MS 255, which alternates between the long and short versions of the work (Bogdanow 1960b; Castro 1988b). A collation of the *Josep Abaramatia* and the Rennes codex reveals small but significant differences, among which there stand out the changes introduced in certain references to future episodes, the purpose of which is to link this part of the story to the innovating *Suite du Merlin* and the *Post-Vulgate Queste-Mort Artu* which followed it. Thus, the sword stroke which in the *Estoire* begins the adventures of the kingdom of Logres is replaced by a lance-thrust, since the author has in mind Balain's Dolorous Stroke; these innovations may be attributed, in principle, to that lost French model, although this is an area of some uncertainty.

For the history of the Iberian *P-V*, particular importance attaches to three personal names that appear in the Lisbon codex. The first is that of the *corregidor* Manuel Álvares, who introduces the Portuguese adaptation of the *Estoire* explaining that the codex being copied was an illuminated manuscript 200 years old; the information that he gives on the circumstances of this copying operation have enabled its date to be fixed as between 1540 and 1544 (Castro 1976–9; Nascimento 1984). The second of the names is that of Joam Vivas, who appears twice in the text; both instances are comments in the first-person singular, in which Joam Vivas names himself in a way that seems appropriate to the author. However, the role played by this Joam Vivas, whose name is repeated in the Castilian *Demanda*, is doubtful; he could have been the translator, but other explanations are possible. The point is important, not only because it is an element linking the Portuguese and Castilian adaptations of the cycle, but also because the nature of the role played by this Joam Vivas is important in the question of the priority of Portuguese or Spanish in the Peninsular translation of the cycle, the scope of which changes if he is considered to be the Iberian translator. The colophon of the codex is of particular interest; it introduces the third of the personal names mentioned, that of João Samches:

> Este livro mamdou fazer João Samches, mestre escolla d'Astorga no quimto ano que o Estudo de Coimbra foy feito e no tempo do papa Clemente que destroio a Ordem del Temple e fez o comçilio geral em Viana e pôs ho emtredito em Castela e neste ano se finou a Rainha Dona Costamça em São Fagumdo e casou o Ymfamte Dom Felipe com a filha de Dom Afonso ano de 13lij [> 1309] anos.[8]

In relation to the date '13lij' and despite the fact that the colophon tells us that this is the date AD, it is expressed according to the Era Hispanica, and is scarcely legible since it has been overwritten; converted to the modern calendar, it refers to the year 1314, which is therefore the *terminus ad quem* for the Iberian translation of the *Post-Vulgate*. In the context of the discovery of the two-leaf fragment in Porto, Aires A. Nascimento (2008) has studied this colophon, pointing out that the final elements of the date as initially written – '13lij' – were later modified to give the date of '1309'. As far as concerns the historical events to which reference is made, these are associated with King D. Dinis, although the Spanish element is important. Nascimento emphasises the allusion to the creation of the *Studium generale* in Coimbra, which would have caused the original '13lij' to be modified to '1309'; the accuracy of the events mentioned, which he studies minutely, leads him to an extensive discussion of João Samches, or Juan Sánchez, who would have ordered the production of the previous codex and who holds the university post of 'maestro de escuelas' in Astorga and for whom Nascimento hypothesises a presence in Coimbra, where João Samches would have made efforts to obtain a copy of the *Josep Abaramatia*.

The Iberian *Merlin* and *Post-Vulgate Suite du Merlin*

Parts of the *Merlin* and *Suite du Merlin* from the Iberian *P-V* survive in Spanish and in Portuguese. We have only one witness for the Portuguese version: three vellum folios that formed part of the binding of two incunables, and which make up the present MS 2434 of the Biblioteca de Catalunya.

These folios were discovered by Amadeu-J. Soberanas (1979), who established the importance of the find and published an article including an edition and a meticulous study of the leaves; there is now also an edition by Pilar Lorenzo Gradín and José Antonio Souto Cabo (2001).[9] These leaves were copied, it seems, in the first half of the XIVth century, and their language reveals features that lead to the conclusion that they originated from south of the River Miño; they correspond to chs 380–1 and 493–6 of the edition by Roussineau (1996). The first fragment, half of fol. LXVII, contains the story of prince Anasten, which is also narrated in the Huth manuscript (BL Add 38117), MS Add 7071 of Cambridge University Library, and the printed editions of the *Baladro* of 1498 and of Seville, while the second fragment, fols CXXII and CXXIII, contains the episode of the 'Roche aux Pucelles' found only in MS 112 of the

BNF. The comparison of the known versions reveals that the Portuguese text is closer to the French versions than are the *Baladro* editions, since it contains essential elements, such as the name of the prince and his father, that are omitted in the *Baladro* texts. With regard to the position of the Portuguese fragments in relation to the known witnesses for this section of the cycle, and with the necessary caveats, Soberanas maintained that they are closer to the text of the Cambridge manuscript than to the Huth codex.

Besides the *Estoria de Merlin*, contained in MS 1877 of the Biblioteca Universitaria de Salamanca, we have two 'Merlins' in Castilian, which cover the sections of the *Merlin* and *Post-Vulgate Suite du Merlin* up until the disappearance of the seer. These witnesses are the two printed editions: the *Baladro del sabio Merlín con sus profecías*, printed by Juan de Burgos (Burgos, 1498),[10] and the 'Baladro' published as the first book of the *Demanda del Santo Grial con los maravillosos fechos de Lançarote y de Galaz su hijo* (Seville, 1535), which is followed by the *Demanda* in the true sense of that title.[11] There would have been two other printed 'Baladros': one, certainly, that would have preceded the second book of the *Demanda* printed by Juan de Villaquirán at Toledo in 1515, and another, dubious, one which would have formed part of the supposed edition of 1500, also from Seville. That is to say, there is a possibility that in 1500 there was published in Seville an edition juxtaposing the 'Baladro' and the *Demanda*, in the same formation, as first and second books of the *Demanda del Santo Grial*, in other words, with the same configuration as the Toledo edition of 1515, even though the latter's first book is not preserved in the only known copy. The 1498 incunable is represented by a single witness, in the Biblioteca Universitaria at Oviedo.[12] The single known copy of the Toledo edition of 1515 is incomplete, since it contains only the second book (in other words, the *Demanda* as such); this is in the British Library (G.10241), bound with the first book of the Seville edition of 1535. To the London copy of the 1535 edition must be added five complete copies of that Seville edition: Chicago, Newberry Library (Case YA14.21), University of Illinois at Urbana-Champaign Library (X862D39 Od1535), Paris, BNF (Rés. m. Y^2 22), National Library of Scotland, Edinburgh (Sign. G.23.a.1a), and BNE, Madrid (R/3870).[13]

The three 'Merlins' that are known are intimately related to one another. The *Baladros* derive from a common ancestor, which would have shared, in turn, an ancestor with the *Estoria de Merlín* of the Salamanca codex. As is well known, the *Baladro del sabio Merlín con sus profecías* published in Burgos and this first book of the Seville edition derive from a common ancestor which contained the majority of the features that separate the Castilian *Merlins* from the *Merlin* and *Post-Vulgate Suite du Merlin* from which all ultimately derive. The *Baladro* texts have in common the systematic abbreviation to which the French original was subjected, partially compensated for by the rewriting, found in the incunable, of the story of the conception and birth of the seer, and by the expansion of the recreation of the episodes associated with the death of Merlin. Both printed editions share all the sections not found in the surviving French versions, that is to say, the prophecies derived from the *Historia regum Britanniae*, the episodes of Merlin's dream, Ebrón el Follón and Bandemagus, as also the rewriting of the seer's end with the incorporation of the *Estoria de dos amadores*, Merlin's delivery to the Devils and his death uttering the terrible cry that gives the work its title. Two omissions have, in textual terms, a separative significance: the omission of the story of the Chevalier as Deux Espees from the incunable, and the suppression, in the Seville edition, of one part of the story of the 'Dueña', named Diana in the Burgos incunable, which is abruptly interrupted, likewise omitting the narrative of the journey of the Lady of the Lake and Merlin to the court, which continues in the incunable. The additions also increase the distinction between the two editions: the collection of prophecies, relating to contemporary political events in Castile although they are attributed to Merlin, which is added in the Seville edition after the *Baladro*, as against the prologues and the epilogue incorporated into the Burgos incunable.

The comparison of the printed editions and their French models shows that the Seville edition is the closest to the French redactions, from which the incunable is distanced not only by the addition and suppression of material but above all because there is a deliberate intention to elaborate upon, and improve upon, its ancestor, which is not found in the Seville edition. From many points of view, the incunable offers a version superior to that of the Seville edition, since in elaborating upon its ancestor in its own style, on occasion it achieves a rhetorically elegant prose, and contains fewer errors; there is a conscious pursuit of style, and its author was guided by a literary ambition which is revealed in the care that is taken over expression, and which is not found in the author of the Seville printed edition. While the latter presents an adaptation adhering to an ancestor which goes back to the original Castilian translation, just lightly modernising its language, the Burgos incunable explains and attempts to improve upon its source; notwithstanding this, the character of this version is not consistently maintained, but rather varies from one section to another and extends from a fundamental rewriting of the beginning of the work to a light reworking for much of its length, while at times its retouching of its model is even more superficial than that of the Seville edition.

Another feature that distinguishes between the two printed texts is the fact that the Seville edition includes the second and third parts of the trilogy. In the version given by the incunable, some of the allusions to the Grail have been omitted, as well as the important episode of the Chevalier as Deux Espees, which seems to have been deliberately suppressed because it is an obvious introduction to the section relating to the Grail which the incunable does not contain. It is clear that the absence of a book equivalent to the *Demanda del Santo Grial* has important consequences for the spirit of the narrative: detaching the section about Merlin from the cycle of which it forms a part means robbing the Arthurian universe of the Grail, leaving it without a conclusion or, to put it another way, giving it an ending, that of the delivery of the seer to the Devils and his death accompanied by a disturbing cry, which betrays the spirit of the original trilogy.

The Iberian *Post-Vulgate Queste – Mort Artu*
The Iberian witnesses for the third branch of the *P-V* are particularly interesting, since they permit the reconstruction of what must have been the French original of the cycle. Both manuscript and printed witnesses survive; MS 2594 of the ÖNB of Vienna preserves the Portuguese version, to which must be added MS 1877 of the Biblioteca Universitaria of Salamanca, discussed above, which gives a brief selection from the Castilian branch; and the Castilian printed editions, likewise already mentioned, of 1515 and 1535.[14] The Portuguese and Castilian versions are related, since the four witnesses derive from the original Iberian translation of the cycle, and the three Castilian witnesses are, in turn, related. From the Castilian translation of the trilogy there would have split off the branch represented in the Salamanca manuscript, while the printed editions, which differ in little except for the changes in the size of the type and the slight linguistic modernisation found in the edition of 1535 when compared with that of 1515, are collateral descendants of a common ancestor, which is currently identified as the lost edition of Seville 1500.

The Vienna manuscript dates from the XVth century, has 199 folios, and lacks a title, since that of *A historia dos cavalleriros da Mesa Redonda e da Demanda do Santo Graal*, which identifies the work, is found only on the spine of the binding.[15] At least six copyists were involved in producing this copy, which exhibits various lacunae. As regards its language, it exhibits both archaisms going back to the XIIIth century and modern forms from the period in which it was copied (Megale 2001).

The Portuguese and Castilian *Demandas* derive from a single translation. Their comparison makes it plain that both suppressed some passages. This tendency to omit is more marked in the Castilian version, which must have suppressed deliberately many of the elements of a doctrinal nature, particularly the symbolic episodes; however, the main characteristic of a good part of the omissions and additions in the Castilian text is its carelessness (Bohigas 1925a: 56–67). The principal difference between the two is, notwithstanding this, that the Castilian printed editions substitute for a considerable part of the ending of the *P-V* version an adaptation of the *Vulgate Queste del Saint Graal*, in the so-called 'Variant Version' (Bogdanow 1983, 1986–7), which notably amplifies the original redaction. The interpolation extends from the arrival of the three chosen knights at Corbenic to the death of Galahad (chs 373–91), a point at which the *Demanda del Santo Grial* picks up again the *P-V* version and coincides with the Portuguese *Demanda*, opening the section devoted to the *Mort Artu*.

The Problem of the Language of the First Iberian Translation

No absolute certainty exists concerning the Peninsular language into which the French original of the *P-V* cycle was translated, which leaves in obscurity some fundamental questions concerning when, where and in what circumstances the cycle was translated. Scholars have debated this matter at length, basing their arguments on the study of the fragments of the codex preserved in the Biblioteca Universitaria at Salamanca, or on the comparison of the Portuguese and the Castilian texts of the *Demanda*.

The relationship between the Castilian and the Portuguese *Demandas* has been a long-established topic of debate. What was discussed, since both were translations from a French original and since both were related to each other, was whether the French original had been translated into Portuguese and from this Portuguese version the Castilian had been produced, or whether the language of the first translation had been Castilian, from which the Portuguese version had derived.

Nineteenth-century critics approached this problem from a perspective that lacked philological rigour. The majority of critics of that period did not consider the issue to be a problem, and most favoured the priority of the Portuguese text, although arguments used were weak. In favour of Portuguese priority were Milá y Fontanals (1874: 380–5) and Menéndez y Pelayo (1905–15: I, 171), basing themselves on the principle of the natural syntony between the west of the Peninsula and Arthurian themes and the area's natural inclination to lyricism in contrast with the epic mindset of Castile, an argument to which Carolina Michaëlis (1900–1) added the historical relationship between the royal houses of Portugal and France. Otto Klob (1900–1) also supported the Portuguese hypothesis, arguing that the *Demanda do Santo Graal* is a direct translation from a French original; he devoted only a single sentence to the question, but that was in small capitals: the assertion was as definitive ('Que existiu em Portugal na primeira metade do seculo XIV o cyclo do Graal inteiro, traduzido directamente do original frances', p. 333) as it was devoid of supporting arguments, since Klob restricted himself to calling for the comparison of the Portuguese and Castilian versions. Some voices were raised in opposition, although with poor arguments; Gottfried Baist (1897) asserted that the literary capacity of Portugal was limited to lyric and not narrative, and upheld the Castilian origin of the *Livro de Josep Abaramatia* (1907).

In 1913–14 Karl Pietsch published the first academic article on the Arthurian sections of the former MS 2-G-5 of the Biblioteca de Palacio, now at Salamanca. He drew attention to the presence of specifically Portuguese features in the Castilian witnesses, although he had doubts over the origin of these. The idea was repeated in other contexts, finally metamorphosing into his *Spanish Grail Fragments* (1924–5), in which he revealed himself to be fully convinced of the priority of the *Libro de Josep Abarimatía* over the Portuguese version, and of the priority of Castilian for the whole of the cycle. The importance of the language of the first Iberian translation became a matter of the highest priority in the discussion. The firm defence of the priority of the Castilian text would be extensively questioned by scholars, rapidly finding both supporters and detractors, which would lead to a hardening of positions.

A significant endorsement of the Castilian hypothesis came in 1925 with the publication of William J. Entwistle's important *The Arthurian Legend in the Literatures of the Spanish Peninsula*, in which he maintained that the translation had been made into Castilian by Fray Juan Bivas in the reign of Sancho IV, towards 1291. In the same year, Pedro Bohigas published his doctoral thesis on *Los textos españoles y gallego-portugueses de la 'Demanda del Santo Grial'*, heavily influenced by the ideas of Karl Pietsch. Essentially, Bohigas compared the Castilian *Demanda* with the Portuguese version and the French original, which was, inappropriately, the *Queste del Saint Graal* of the *Vulgate* cycle. He maintained that all the surviving witnesses – the former MS 2-G-5, the *Libro de Josep Abarimatía*, the *Baladro* of Burgos and that of Seville, the Castilian and Portuguese *Demandas* – derived from a single version, whose archetype must have been close to the MS now at Salamanca. In so far as the language of the first translation was concerned, Bohigas followed Pietsch with a barely critical spirit which would soon change.

The Portuguese response came swiftly, in 1930, in a work by Rodrigues Lapa (1929–30), who reviewed the arguments advanced by Pietsch. He could not understand why Pietsch had come down in favour of Castilian priority if he recognised that the copyists had been concerned to Castilianise the texts and since he had even proposed corrections to the Castilian version making use of readings from the Portuguese. There is, clearly, a negative commentary, attributing Pietsch's pro-Castilian position to the influence of his former teacher Gottfried Baist: 'Que teria influído nele? A amizade e os conselhos de G. Baist, seu antigo mestre, tão intransigentemente hostil às coisas portuguesas?' (1929–30: 307). Nor could he understand why Bohigas had considered the hypothesis of Castilian priority to be solid when he asserted that some readings of the Spanish texts were best explained in terms of a Galician-Portuguese original. Lapa considered that the impression given by the examples adduced by Pietsch was clearly that of a translator from the Leonese zone who had translated a Portuguese original, since there were specifically Portuguese forms in the text. To defend the priority of the Portuguese, he collated the texts in Portuguese, French and Castilian, line by line, attempting to explain certain erroneous readings of the Castilian *Demanda* as misunderstandings of the Portuguese *Demanda* which would have been its source: an exhaustive analysis, but with the limitations of its period, since it was based on an incomplete edition, in the case of the Portuguese *Demanda*, or an inappropriate one, in the case of the French text and even the Castilian one.

Be that as it may, the analysis was found convincing, since three years later a brief review of Rodrigues Lapa's work by Pedro Bohigas was published by *RFE* (1933). Although in a roundabout manner, with many clarifications, and insisting extensively on the scant conviction with which he had previously supported the priority of the

Castilian, Bohigas recognised that some of the phrases from the *Demanda del Santo Grial* examined by Lapa were explicable only in terms of a Portuguese original. However, the question was far from being resolved, is still not resolved today and will no doubt be the subject of many more studies.

Despite the arguments advanced by Rodrigues Lapa, R. J. Steiner favoured the hypothesis of a mixed language (1966–7), with a Castilian basis but with a strong Leonese and Portuguese influence; but most distinguished scholars supported the Portuguese thesis. Firstly, Cedric Edward Pickford (1961) reproached Lapa for not taking into account the French original. Pickford supported Portuguese priority from the basis of a study in which he compared the personal names as they appear in MS fr. 112 BNF and the forms they have in the *Demandas*, and, although he recognised that onomastics alone cannot prove the priority of the Portuguese version, for him it certainly did demonstrate that this one had been the first to have been translated, in a faithful rendering, even a literal one. Subsequently Fanni Bogdanow (1974–5, 1975) tenaciously defended the Portuguese thesis, starting from an argument similar to those of Lapa since she bases herself on the interpretation given by the *Demandas* to the passages that contain a single French expression, 'plus chiers tenus' (MS fr 112 BNF). This is translated erroneously by the Castilian *Demanda*, but accurately in the Portuguese. With the passage of time, although Bogdanow continued to support the Portuguese thesis, she did not do this so assertively.

The extensive debate on the question of the priority of the Portuguese *Demanda* has had its continuators: Ivo Castro (1983) maintained that the language of the Peninsular translation of the *P-V* was Portuguese, starting from the hypothesis that King Afonso III would have taken the manuscript to Portugal on his return from France. What is certain is that this is not a more decisive argument than those phrases that reveal the language of the original which a poor translator had been incapable of understanding, which are brought up by supporters and detractors to prove one or the other thesis. Castro's is a plausible hypothesis: a point in history involving someone who could easily have had a copy of the cycle made, and which coincides with the documented history of an individual whose identity could coincide easily with that of the translator.

To complete this critical panorama, it is worth adding that Castro (1988a) has defended the convenience of considering the Arthurian sections of the former MS 2-G-5 as Castilian; also Bogdanow (1991–2001: I, 477–81), who previously defended the Portuguese thesis energetically, has affirmed, after undertaking an important comparative analysis of the different versions which tends towards the Portuguese side, that it is difficult to envisage the question's ever being resolved definitively.

A final remarkable study was published in 2001, which Heitor Megale devoted to the systematic collation of the *Post-Vulgate Queste-Mort Artu* and the Castilian and Portuguese *Demandas*: first of the chapter headings and later of three passages. The collation is meticulous and, although the collation of the headings offers no revealing information, that of the three selected episodes certainly does, since the Portuguese version is revealed as being closer to the French original. From this greater affinity Megale concludes that the Portuguese *Demanda* has priority. However, a greater affinity is not a decisive element in the question of priority: the XVIth-century printed editions offer a more developed version in relation to their model (Gracia 2010a), and it is to be expected that this model would also have displayed the same tendency in relation to its respective antecedents and so on progressively until reaching the Castilian translation of the cycle, which would be closer to the French version than are the printed editions. Conclusive arguments would be those based on the identification of elements that reveal that the translation has been made from another Peninsular language and not directly from French, and no fresh evidence has been adduced for this since the last elements that Bogdanow adduced in the 1970s; in fact the reverse, since some of these have been questioned (Castro 2002a). Hence, at least in my opinion, the problem has not been resolved, but in my view continues in the same state as it was then: with very few options in favour of the hypothesis of a Castilian priority, some more for that of a mixed language, and more still for the Portuguese, in favour of the last of which the greater part of the arguments point, without their yet being conclusive.

Notes

[1] This study forms part of the work undertaken in the Research Project FF12009–13556 (DGCYT 2009), financed by the Ministry of Economic Affairs and Competitiveness of Spain and FEDER.

[2] 'Otro libro de pliego entero, de mano, en rromançe, que es la terçera parte de la *Demanda del Santo Grial*, las cubiertas de cuero blanco. Otro libro de pliego entero, de mano, escripto en rromançe, que se dize de *Merlin*, con coberturas de papel de cuero blancas, y habla de Joseph Avarimatin. Otro libro de pliego entero, de mano, en papel, de rromançe, que es la *Ystoria de Lançarote*, con unas coberturas de cuero blanco' (Ruiz García 2004: 432, 449, 464).

[3] 'Si se test ore a itant li contes de totes les lingniees Celydoine qui de lui oissirent et retorne a une autre branche que l'en apele *L'Estoire de Merlin*, que il covient ajoster a fine force avec *L'Estoire del Graal*, por ce que branche en est et i apartient', *Estoria del saint Graal*, ed. Ponceau (1997: II, 577). Fanni Bogdanow (1966: 160) transcribes the passage, marking in italics the part added by the Portuguese translator: 'E agora se cala a estorea de todas estas linagens que de Celidones sairão e torna aos outros ramos que chama Estorea de Merlim, que comvem por toda maneyra jumtar com a Estorea do Greal, porque he dos ramos e lhe pertemçe, *e saibão todos aqueles que esta estorea ouvyrem que esta estorea era jumtada com a de Merlim, na qual he comemçamemto da Mesa Redomda e a naçemça de Artur e comemçamemto das aventuras, mas por nosó livro nom ser muy gramde repartimolo cada huũ em sua parte, porque cada huũ por sy serão milhores de trazer. Aquy se acaba este livro [...]*' (311*rv*).

[4] See also, on the manuscript, Valero Moreno (2010b) and Pietsch (1920–1).

[5] See Bogdanow 1991–2001: I, 214–16.

[6] An illuminated copy of *Josep Abarimatía* of high price was in Madrid in 1473, forming part of the library of the convent of the Visitación of the Order of Clares, the inventory of which records: 'Otro libro que se llama de *Josep Abarimatea*, estoriado e escripto en papel, con unas coberturas coloradas, con unos bollones de laton e unos texillos colorados, que vale tres mill maravedís' (Cátedra 1999: 23). It is interesting that the *Josep Abarimatía* was one of the seven volumes chosen by Doña Catalina Núñez de Toledo, patroness of the convent, and perhaps also by the nuns or their spiritual mentors, to fulfil the function of

the essential library with which it was endowed. Since these were titles selected for reading by the nuns, some of which were bought expressly for them, this would be the Castilian *Josep Abarimatía*.

[7] For a meticulous collation of the fragment with the *Livro de Josep Abaramatia* preserved at the Torre do Tombo and with the *Estoire del Saint Graal*, in the editions of Sommer (1908–16) and Ponceau (1997), see the works by Aida Fernanda Dias (2003–6) and Simona Ailenii (2009).

[8] I reproduce the transcription by Nascimento (2008: 131). The palaeographic edition by Carter (1967), very careful but difficult to read, is still the only complete edition of *Josep Abaramatia*; this passage is transcribed on pp. 39 and 379. Ivo Castro has repeatedly announced his intention to publish an edition, the characteristics of which he has described on various occasions (2002b, 2007).

[9] This more recent edition, coordinated by Pilar Lorenzo Gradín and José António Souto Cabo (2001), includes a palaeographic transcription and a reliable study of the fragments.

[10] According to Harvey L. Sharrer (1988a), many of the innovations of the *Baladro* printed in Burgos are due to the intervention of the printer.

[11] Any study of the *Baladros* must take into account the fundamental volume on the *P-V* by Fanni Bogdanow (1966), which contains valuable information on the position which these printed editions occupy in the cycle as a whole, as well as specific study (pp. 25–39); in this context, her article (1960a) and that of Bienvenido Morros (1988) are also worth consulting. The divergences of the *Baladros* in relation to the *Merlin* and *Post-Vulgate Suite du Merlin* were indicated by Pedro Bohigas (1925a: 40–52; 1957–62: III, 164–79), whose detailed examination included consideration in each case of its possible relationship with the French model; however, the question of the supposed innovations raises significant doubts. No specific study has been has been published for most of them; proper analysis has been given only to some aspects relating to the innovatory final episode, among which there stand out that of Bogdanow (1962), which put an end to the belief that a *Conte du Brait* had served as source for the episode of the death of Merlin, and that of Meneghetti (1987), on the sources of the *Estoria de dos amadores*; I have myself devoted a work to the prophecies derived from the *Historia regum Britanniae* (Gracia 2012). Noteworthy panoramic studies are those of Lendo Fuentes (2003) and Michon (1996).

[12] There are two usable editions: the classic one by Bohigas (1957–62), containing a description of the incunable (I, 9–10), and the transcription by María Isabel Hernández, included in *El baladro del sabio Merlín con sus profecías* (1999: 3–185), which, together with a group of studies, accompanies the facsimile reproduction of the incunable published as a separate volume.

[13] The printed edition can be read only in the inadequate edition by Bonilla y San Martín (1907). See Bogdanow (1991–2001: I, 220–4) for an analysis of the various known copies; the Madrid copy has been digitalised and forms part of the open access Biblioteca Digital Hispánica (*http://bibliotecadigitalhispanica.bne.es*).

[14] The 1535 *Demanda* was published, together with the *Baladro*, by Bonilla y San Martín (1907), and has been translated into French by Vincent Serverat and Philippe Walter (Vivas 2006); the 1515 edition is still unpublished.

[15] The *Demanda do santo Graal* was edited by Augusto Magne, first in 1944, in a version from which he eliminated those passages which seemed to him to be immoral, and, secondly, in 1955 and 1970, accompanied by the facsimile reproduction of the manuscript and its transcription. Both editions were criticised by Lapa (1948) and by Megale (1986–7 [1990]). The incomplete edition by Joseph Maria Piel (1988) was completed by Irene Freire Nunes, who also published on the text herself (1995a, 1999ab).

VIII

THE HISPANIC VERSIONS OF THE *LANCELOT EN PROSE: LANZAROTE DEL LAGO* AND *LANÇALOT*

Antonio Contreras Martín

In the Iberian Peninsula, the *Lancelot en prose* of the *Vulgate* cycle (Sommer 1909–12; Micha 1978–82, 1987; Kennedy 1986, 2006) was known and moreover achieved both success and diffusion, whether in its original language or in the form of translations, variant versions, adaptations or compilations (Soriano Robles 2013). Despite this, only two textual witnesses have survived to the present: a partial version, *Lanzarote del Lago* (Bohigas Balaguer 1924; Contreras Martín and Sharrer 2006), in the Castilian-Leonese territories, and some fragments of *Lançalot* in those of the Catalan linguistic zone (Rubió y Lluch 1903; Bohigas Balaguer 1962).[1]

1. The Manuscripts

Lanzarote del Lago is preserved in a XVIth-century manuscript (BNE MS 9611). This was copied from a codex dated 1414, according to its *explicit*; but this in turn was without doubt a copy of an earlier version.[2] The surviving MS is written on ivory-coloured paper, and 352 folios, measuring 284 × 198 mm, written in legal and rounded legal scripts of the XVIth century, remain from the original nucleus of the manuscript. Detailed palaeographic study reveals that four different hands were involved in the copying process (Contreras Martín and Sharrer 2006: xii–xiv; Contreras Martín 2006a: 67–71; 2010: 93–6).[3]

Lançalot is represented by fragments belonging to two different manuscripts (Bohigas Balaguer 1962: 101), probably of vellum, which survived because they had been reused as bookbindings, in other words, because of their purely practical use (Lucía Megías 2005c: 247–53; Soriano Robles 2010: 1702). The first fragment was discovered by the diocesan archivist and canon of Palma cathedral, Monsignor Matheu Rotger, at the beginning of the twentieth century in the Parish Archive of Campos (Mallorca), and has been dated to the last quarter of the XIVth century (*c*.1380–1400). Its present location is unknown, and we have only the transcription produced by Matheu Obrador and published by Antonio Rubió y Lluch (Rubió y Lluch 1903). It is a single leaf measuring 400 × 200 mm, written in two columns of forty-two lines each, in a formata Gothic script, and numbered 'Clxxxvij', which reveals it to have been part of an extensive manuscript volume.[4]

The second fragment of *Lançalot* had come to form part of an XVIth-century account book from Barbastro (Aragon); it dates from the middle of the XIVth century (*c.*1340–60). It was part of the private collection of Francesc Cruzate (Mataró, Barcelona), but its present whereabouts are not known.[5] This fragment consists of two leaves measuring 302 × 205 mm, written in two columns in a formata Gothic script, and foliated LXXXV–LXXXVI, which confirms that they formed part of a longer manuscript book. The inner columns measure 240 × 90 mm and are complete, while the outer columns have been cropped on the outer margin and now measure 240 × 70 mm. Each chapter begins with an initial letter, in a sequence alternating in blue and red, with simple calligraphic ornament. The leaves are stained with damp, which renders their decipherment difficult (Bohigas Balaguer 1962).[6]

2. The Dating and Sources of *Lanzarote del Lago* and *Lançalot*

The first version of *Lanzarote del Lago* should be dated to the middle of the XIVth century, on the basis of the analysis of its chivalric vocabulary and its heraldry (Contreras Martín 2003, 2007a), rather than to the first quarter of the XIVth century as proposed by Entwistle (Entwistle 1925: 212) or to the mid-XIIIth century as maintained by Sharrer (Sharrer 1994: 177). For Entwistle, the *Lanzarote del Lago* would have been translated around the same dates as '*Merlín y Demanda* and *Tristán*'. Sharrer, for his part (Sharrer 1996b: 178), suggests that, as he had previously mooted (Sharrer 1981, 1991, 1996a), the work would have been introduced, like the *Post-Vulgate* cycle, by Afonso III of Portugal (1248–79), in whose reign it would have been translated, and that this could explain the presence of various linguistic traits associated with the western Peninsular varieties (Leonese, Gallego or Portuguese). Sharrer's proposal has, however, been used by Miranda (2004: 57) to assert that *Lanzarote del Lago* would have derived from a version in Gallego-Portuguese, and this is also maintained by Correia (2010a: 72).[7] Now, analysis of the corpus of linguistic features which could be identified as Leonese, Gallego or Portuguese shows it to be extremely scanty, and it could be explained not only on the basis of an original written in one of those linguistic modes, but also as resulting from the involvement of copyists of northwestern origin who introduced these features, or as the result of its having been copied in that region (Contreras Martín 2012a).

According to the conjecture advanced by Miranda (Miranda 1988a: 246; 1988b: 191), there would have been a *Lancelot* which would have differed both from the *Lancelot en prose* (cycle version) and from *Lancelot do Lac* (non-cycle version) (Kennedy 1980), and which would have formed part of a supposed cycle different from the *Vulgate* and the *Post-Vulgate*. Following this, and after comparing *Lanzarote del Lago* and one part of the fragments of *Lançalot* with various manuscripts that contain common readings and differ partly from the 'canonical' versions, and observing resemblances between the French and the Hispanic texts, Isabel Correia (Correia 2010a, 2010b) has recently suggested the possible existence of a different *Lancelot* (Correia 2010a: 72) which would have been the version that served as the source of the Hispanic texts.

However, exhaustive analysis of *Lanzarote del Lago* and its comparison with firstly the published French versions (Sommer 1909–12; Micha 1978–82; Kennedy 1980), and secondly, following Sharrer's suggestion (Sharrer 1977), with MS 751 of the BNF which contains a different version, reveals that it is the latter with which the Castilian text has the closest similarities, especially because there are some exclusive readings on which only these two agree. From this it follows that one could suggest that the source of the Castilian text must have been a version related to a text that belonged to the same textual family (Contreras Martín 2002a).[8]

Be this as it may, the datings proposed in the attempt to determine the point at which the Castilian version was produced take fully into account the fact that the *Lancelot en prose* or *Lanzarote del Lago* had a considerable influence on the composition of *Amadís de Gaula*, the original version of which could date back as far as the first years of the XIVth century (Entwistle 1925: 211) or even the final years of the XIIIth century (Avalle-Arce 1990: 99; Gómez Redondo 1998–2007: II, 1461).[9]

The fragments of *Lançalot*, however, although scanty, demonstrate the existence of this text by the mid-XIVth century, that is to say, during the reign of Pedro IV of Aragon (Entwistle 1925: 92–4; Contreras Martín 2002d, 2004, 2007d). Confirmation of this is provided by two letters dating from 1362, written respectively on 17 February and 16 March that year, in which the king orders Pere Palau to send him 'a Catalan *Lançalot*' belonging to his heir, Prince Joan, who had previously been reading it in Barcelona (Rubió y Lluch 2000: I, CCIV, CCV, 201–2). For his part, Bohigas Balaguer (Bohigas Balaguer 1962: 4) ventured to propose that the first translation into Catalan could have been made at some date before 1339, and could even go back to the end of the XIIIth century. So far, however, no document has been discovered that could confirm this suggestion.

As has been indicated, analysis of the Cruzate fragment by Isabel Correia (Correia 2010b: 580–1) has led her to propose as its source a different *Lancelot*, which would have presented a distinct ideological and spiritual model with which the fragment concurred. Despite this, the exhaustive comparison of the Catalan fragments with the published French texts (Sommer 1909–12; Micha 1978–82; Kennedy 1980) and with BNF MS 751 provides absolutely no support for these assertions. If, moreover, the social and cultural context in which the work must have been translated is taken into account, which was the apogee of the reign of Pedro el Ceremonioso (Riquer 1989), such an 'ideological and spiritual model' would contradict the concept of chivalry and monarchy propounded by the king, and this renders the idea untenable (Contreras Martín 2002a, 2007d).

3. *Lanzarote del Lago* in Castile and Portugal, and *Lançalot* in the Crown of Aragon

The presence of the *Lancelot en prose* in the Iberian Peninsula is beyond question, although references to it are few (Alvar 1983; Sharrer 1988b, 1996a,b; Chicote 2001), in contrast to the situation with other works of the Matière de Bretagne. Ignoring the possible allusions to episodes from the *Lancelot* contained in a *cantiga* by the troubadour Martin Soares ('Hunha donzela jaz aquí'; 1230–70) and in another by King Alfonso X 'the Learned' ('Vi un coteife de mui gran granhon'), as well as that in a Lai de Bretanha ('Ledas sejamos ogemais!'; end of the XIIIth century), the oldest testimony so far discovered that permits us to speak of an assimilation and even of some circulation of the *Lancelot en prose* in Castile and Portugal is the use of the personal name 'Lanzarote' by one of the fifteen gentlemen of the chamber of King Sancho IV in 1293–4, 'Lançarote Garcia Perez' (Gaibrois de Ballesteros 1922: LXXIII). The use of this name by an adult individual allows us to conclude that, at least in the final quarter of the XIIIth century, the story of Lancelot was already known (Alvar 2013a).

In the XIVth century, we encounter references to *Lançarote* or *Lanzarote*.[10] Thus, in the *Libro de la caza* (c.1327) of Don Juan Manuel (1982: 558) a falcon is given this name, which can be taken as indicative of some diffusion of Arthurian material; and towards the end of the century, in the *Rimado de Palacio*, the chancellor Pero López de Ayala alludes to having 'heard' '*Lançalote*' during his youth (López de Ayala 1987: stanza 163). It appears that the ballads (*romances*) 'Lanzarote y el ciervo de pie blanco' and 'Lanzarote y el Orgulloso', included in the *Cancionero de 1550*, also date from the XIVth century (Díez-Mas 1994: 252–4, 255–6).

It is in the XVth century that we encounter allusions and documentation which attest that *Lanzarote* had become widely known (Cuesta Torre 1999b). Among literary references are, for example, those by some poets of the *Cancionero de Baena* who mention Lanzarote alongside other Arthurian characters and subjects (Dutton and González Cuenca 1993). Fray Migir, who seems to be the earliest of the poets included in the *Cancionero*, mentions Lanzarote in his *Dezir a la muerte de Enrique III* (stanza 13, lines 98–104). He is also named by Pedro Ferrús in his *Dezir de Pedro Ferruz a Pero López de Ayala* (stanza 305, lines 50–6) and also in his *Cantiga de Pero Ferruz para su amiga* (stanza 301, lines 33–7), which also contains the name of his lover, 'Ginebra' (Guinevere). In addition, Micer Francisco Imperial alludes, in his *Dezires al nacimiento de Juan II*, to the episode of the Dolorous Guard from the *Lancelot en prose* (stanza 226, lines 249–56 and 187–92). There are also references to Lanzarote in Suero de Ribera's *Canción LXVI* (lines 13–20) in the *Cancionero de Palacio* (Álvarez Pellitero 1993); in the *Corbacho* by Alfonso Martínez de Toledo (1998: 285); and to his infancy together with the Lady of the Lake in Fernando de la Torre's *De vnos naypes por coplas que fizo Mossen Fernando a la señora Condessa de Castañeda* (lines 39–40; Díez Garretas 1983). Similarly, it should be noted that Queen

Isabel I 'the Catholic' apparently had in her library a copy of the '*Historia de Lanzarote*' (*Inventario de los bienes muebles existentes en el Tesoro del Alcázar de Segovia, al cargo de Rodrigo de Tordesillas, hecho por el secretario Gaspar de Gricio por mandato de Isabel la Católica* (Segovia, November 1503) (Ruiz García 2004: 304).

Finally, we must record that Miguel de Cervantes, in *Don Quijote de la Mancha* (1605), would take up anew the opening lines of the ballad 'Lanzarote y el Orgulloso' ('Nunca fuera caballero de damas tan bien servido / como fuera Lanzarote cuando de Bretaña vino / doncellas curaban d'él y dueñas de su rocino'; Díaz-Mas 1994: 255, lines 1–3), reworking them so that the nobleman from La Mancha becomes the protagonist: 'Nunca fuera caballero / de damas tan bien servido / como fuera don Quijote / cuando de su aldea vino: / doncellas curaban dél; / princesas, del su rocino' (Cervantes 2004: I, 57).

In the territories of the Crown of Aragon, leaving aside the allusion to Lanzarote contained in the *Ensenhamen* of Guerau de Cabrera ('Ni d'Arselot la contençón'; Milá y Fontanals 1889: 284, line 207), composed between 1150 and 1165 (Riquer 1965: 665) or at the beginning of the XIIIth century (Cingolani 1992–3b),[11] the *Lancelot en prose* or *Lançalot* were in circulation, as is shown by documents that have been discovered which allow us to speak of the existence of twenty-two copies of the work, nine of them in French (together with another nine more doubtful cases) and eight in Catalan (with one additional less certain case) (Soriano Robles 2010: 1706). The oldest testimony that can be interpreted as indicating the assimilation and even the circulation of the *Lancelot en prose* in the territories of the Crown of Aragon is the mention of a *Lancelot* bequeathed by Jaume II to his son Ramón Berenguer on 6 August 1319 (Rubió y Lluch 2000: II, XLIX, 47–8), from which the chaplain Domènec Gil d'Arenós made a copy between 1336 and 1339, paid for by Pedro el Ceremonioso (8 September 1339) (Rubió y Lluch 2000: I, CV, 119–20). Another copy was made by Jaume Capcir, chaplain of the church of San Juan in Perpignan (France), also commissioned by the king (17 April 1346) (Rubió y Lluch 2000: I, CXXVII, 135–6). The first mention of a *Lançalot* dates from 1362, in the letters sent by Pedro IV of Aragon to Pere Palau on 17 February and 16 March, as already mentioned (Rubió y Lluch 2000: I, CCIV, CCV, 201–2).

Similarly, the inclusion in *La Questa del Sant Grasal* (1380) of an allusion to an episode of enormous symbolic importance in the *Lancelot en prose*, the handing of the sword to Lancelot by Guinevere, after his investiture as a knight by King Arthur, makes it obvious that the translator was familiar with that work:

> Lavos antra devant la ragina Ginebra lanemich qui no estave verament confesade pues que ela fo maridade, en aytant que elat ragarda volantera aytant con tu astiguist an son hostal lo yorn que tu davias eser caveler per so romasesas per que tu fist lo sagrement e per la falonia qal Rey nach hoblida de seyirte lespase e puyxs tan anvia le regina altre que tu lin avias anviade per .j. caveler. (f. 62*va*)

His knowledge of it could have been acquired directly by having access to a copy of the work in Catalan or in French, or indirectly through hearing it read aloud (Contreras Martín 2002d: 589–90).

The widespread circulation of *Lançalot* can be appreciated from the important role given to Lanzarote in the 'Tractat sobre l'art de la guerra' (chs 213–337) in Francesc Eiximenis's *Dotzè del Crestià* (1385–6), which is in effect a manual on the education of princes, in which he is credited with a collection of rules and general counsels preceding the section on the art of war and chivalry (chs 215–16) (Contreras Martín 2012c).

At the end of the XVth century we encounter references to *Lançalot* in the romance *Curial e Güelfa*, which mentions translations ('Empero jo vull seguir la manera d'aquells catalans qui traslladaren los llibres de Tristany e de Lançalot, e tornare-los de llengua francesa en llengua catalana'; Badia and Torró 2011: 218); and in Joanot Martorell's *Tirant lo Blanch* (1490), which alludes on several occasions to the hero and moreover mentions the representation of Lanzarote and Ginebra in art ('e de la reyna Ginebra e de Lançalot llurs amors de molt subtil e artificial pintura eren divisades'; Martorell 2005: I, 473).

4. *Lanzarote del Lago* and *Lançalot*: Structure and Composition

The compiler of *Lanzarote del Lago* worked under the influence of a principle of cyclical composition, a technique which is known from the XIIIth century onwards, in various language areas, and the object of which is initially to group together and rework Arthurian texts, later to weld works into branches or cycles, and finally to fuse genres together (Contreras Martín and Sharrer 2006: XI–XII).

The surviving text of *Lanzarote del Lago* narrates the events which occupy Book II and part of Book III of the *Lancelot en prose*, the 'Livres de Galehaut' and 'Livres de Agrevain' (Contreras Martín and Sharrer 2006: 3–283b, 283b–383a). These are:

1. After defeating the Saxons and conquering their Castillo de la Roca, Arthur returns to Britain, and Lanzarote and Galahot abandon the court for a brief sojourn in Sorelois, with ominous dreams and forebodings (1a–9b);
2. The episode of the False Guinevere and the love of Guinevere and Lancelot, in other words, Arthur and the boar hunt (9b–68b);
3. During the search for Galván, a prisoner of Caradós de la Dolorosa Torre, various adventures befall a number of knights (Sagremor is wounded, Lanzarote frees Trahán el Alegre, Lanzarote is captured by Morgana), which culminate in the liberation of Galván by Lanzarote (68b–112a);
4. Various companions undertake a search for Lanzarote, during which Galahot dies (112a–125b);

5. The episode of the cart, with the challenge of Meleagant, the capture of the queen, the journey of Galván and Lanzarote to Gorre, Lanzarote's visit to the tombs of Galaad and Symeu, the night of passion between Lanzarote and the queen and the accusation by Meleagant, Lancelot's victory and the freeing of the prisoners from Gorre (125b–167b);
6. Galván begins the search for Lanzarote: Lanzarote as the prisoner of Meleagant, the convocation of the tournament of Pomeglai, Lanzarote's attendance at the tournament, and his conduct at the queen's orders leading to his victory, the harsher imprisonment of Lanzarote, the challenge by Meleagant; Lanzarote's return to the court, the defeat of Meleagant and his death (167b–179a);
7. The beginning of various adventures centred upon the quest of Lanzarote (the confusion of Grifón del Mal Paso, the poisoning and cure of Lanzarote, imprisonment at and flight from the Castillo de la Carreta, the stay at the castle of Corbenic and the conception of Galaz, Lanzarote in the Bosque Perdido breaks the enchantment of the Danza Mágica and wins at the Magic Chess, the imprisonment at the castle of the nephews of the Duke of Karlés, the tournament at Camelot and the victory and proclamation of Lanzarote) and on that of Galván (the freeing of Saigremor from the prison of Mathamás, Galván at the castle of Corbenic); and the development of various adventures involving as their protagonists Héctor de Mares (the liberation of Dodinel, his capture by Terriquam), the Duke of Clarence, Boores de Gaunes (the adventure in the castle of Glocedún), or Yvaín (the adventure of Maldito el Jayán) (179a–381b);
8. The decision to renew the quest of Lionel, Héctor de Mares, Agravaín, Guerrehet, and Mordred (381b–2a);
9. The encounter of Lanzarote and Ginebra and the latter's lament at being the cause of the failure of the adventures of the Holy Grail; and Lanzarote's undertaking of the search for Tristán, with the journey to the Isla de Merlín and to the Isla Profunda (382a–386b).

The narrative corresponds faithfully to the French original, in both its Long Version (Micha 1978–82: LXXIa, 29; I–LXVIII, LXXV–LXXX, LXXXII–LXXXV; Sommer 1909–12: III, 429–30; IV, 3–182, 195–358; V, 67–138, 147–93; Kennedy 1980: I, 573–606) and its Short Version (Micha 1978–82: I-XXXIII, XXXV–XXXIX, XLII, LVI–LXI; Sommer 1909–12: IV, 365–89), although some sections have been suppressed. These omissions, however, do not affect either the argument of the work or its narrative structure, which remains entirely coherent, since either they involve adventures recounting secondary events or their protagonists are not among the principal characters: Mordret (Micha 1978–82: LXIX, 1–23; Sommer 1909–12: IV, 358–62), Agravaín (Micha 1978–82: LXX, 1–18; Sommer 1909–12: V, 3–9), Gueherret (Micha 1978–82: LXXI, 1–69; Sommer 1909–12: V, 9–35), Gueheriet and his brothers (Micha

1978–82: LXXII, 1–64; Sommer 1909–12: V, 35–8), the court of Arthur, Boores and Lionel (Micha 1978–82: LXXIII, 1–11; Sommer 1909–12: V, 59–61), and Arthur and Guinevere (Micha 1978–82: LXXIV, 1–10; Sommer 1909–12: V, 61–3). In addition, some original episodes have been added on the final folios (fols 349*r*–352*v*; Contreras Martín and Sharrer 2006: 383a–386b), in which there is a mixing of sources that is not encountered in the rest of the work. Here material is incorporated that belongs to the other two cycles that make up the Matière de Bretagne, the *Tristan en prose* and the *Post-Vulgate* (Bohigas Balaguer 1925; Bogdanow 1999a; Contreras Martín 2005d): 'Doncella Decapitada' – *Tristán* in BNE MS 22644 (Alvar and Lucía Megías 1999: fragments 10–13), *Cuento de Tristán de Leonís* (Northup 1928: XXI–XXII) and the 1501 edition of *Tristán de Leonís* (Cuesta Torre 1999b: XLV); the Isla de Merlín and the Golpe Doloroso – *La Suite du Roman de Merlin* (Roussineau 1996: II, 240, 195) and the *Baladro del Sabio Merlín* (1535: ch. CCC); the Isla de Merlín and the combat between Galván and Lanzarote – *Mort Artu* (*Roman du Graal*) and *Baladro del Sabio Merlín* (1535: ch. CCC); and the Isla de Merlín and Merlín's Bed – *La Suite du Roman de Merlin* (Roussineau 1996: I, 239, 193–4).

4.1 *Lanzarote del Lago*: **the Art of the Romance and Other Questions**
Lanzarote del Lago, like its French sources, is conceived as a perfectly articulated and interwoven work in which each of the elements of which it is composed occupies a significant place in its configuration. This principle is applicable not only to the part which depends on the French source, but also extends to the original section, which is constructed in an identical manner. The elements which constitute the *Lanzarote del Lago* permit us to observe, on the one hand, the way in which the compiler handles them skilfully and coherently, and, on the other, the relationship which is established with the literary tradition of Castile. These elements are the compiler's literary terminology, the elements comprising the narrative art, the investiture of knights, arms and armour, and heraldry.

4.1.1. Literary Terminology
Medieval literary terminology is ambiguous and imprecise (Contreras Martín 2006a: 72–6). *Lanzarote del Lago* uses the terms 'cuento', 'historia' and 'libro' with different meanings. The word 'cuento' ('conte', in the *Lancelot en prose*), which is polysemic and is characterised by its ambiguity, is used here with a double meaning. The first meaning is employed to refer to a written source whose origin is the oral account given by the knights on returning from their adventures, which the clerks then write down (379a–b); the second is that employed to allude to the narration which is under way or to the narrative process from which the most relevant material is being selected and emphasised (217a). In this way, through 'cuento', with its double meaning, the narratorial 'I' is eliminated and 'cuento' is transformed into the authorized source.

Like 'cuento', the word 'historia' is polysemic, in the same way as are 'historie' and 'estoire' in medieval French literature, and is used either to designate in general any story or else in a specific manner to refer to the narration of real events belonging to the past. In the work, 'historia' ('conte', in the *Lancelot en prose*) is used both to refer either to the narrative which is being related or to the narrative process itself (93a), and to refer to the written source, the result of the oral account given by the knights (381a). Additionally, 'historia' is used with the sense of 'account' ('estoire' in the *Lancelot en prose*), as in the case in citing the title of a work: 'la *Historia del Sancto Greal* nos lo testimonia', and 'la gran *Historia del Sancto Greal* lo devisa cumplidamente' (332a and 331b), and as an account of events with pretended historical authenticity (331b).

The term 'libro' is also used to refer to a work or to its title, as in 'en el *Libro de don Galas*' (381b), that is, the *Demanda del Santo Grial*; or to indicate the sections into which a work is divided (283b); or to refer to the material on which it is written (25b).

The wide range of meaning of these terms is entirely consistent with the long-standing use made of them in medieval Castilian literature, which was to continue in *Amadís de Gaula* (Zaragoza, 1508), the *Sergas de Esplandián* by Garci Rodríguez de Montalvo (Seville, 1510) and *Tristán de Leonís* (Valladolid, 1501).

4.1.2. The Art of the Romance
The component elements of the art of the romance, in other words, the techniques used by the author to construct his literary universe, are narrative structure, focalisation and mode, the chronology of the work, and Arthurian geography.

4.1.2.1. Narrative Structure
The complex narrative structure of *Lanzarote del Lago* is based on the use of formulas and formulaic expressions, on the technique of interlace narrative, on the combination of motifs both paradigmatically and syntagmatically inseparable, and on the use of 'specular encounters'.

Formulas and formulaic expressions (Contreras Martín 2002a: 244–9, 294–333) which are related to the practices of oral performance and to the delivery of literary works, and their possible reading aloud, serve to allude to events narrated previously or subsequently in the work. The use of such formulas serves to project into the present the truth of the past ('e oiredes': 4b).

Likewise, through such formulas the recipients of the text are made to share in knowledge of its events, so that they are transformed into a witness to the truth of what has been narrated and will be narrated, and are themselves identified, ultimately, with the narrator of the text. This brings us back once more to the techniques of oral performance. In the same way, it should be noted that the dialogue between author and recipient is shown also in the use of devices of direct appeal through verb forms in the second person plural ('E sabed que aquel anillo hera el que la reina le diera', 99b), in the use of descriptions bringing events into the present ('Entonces se començó el torneo e viérades muchas feridas de lanças e de espadas', 376a), and in the use of first-person plural verbal forms through which the act of communication is brought into the present in such a way that author and recipient share the same space and time ('y por esto lo savemos oy', 380b). These are techniques with a long tradition of use in Castilian literature, since some of them are already documented in the early XIIIth-century epic poem, the *Cantar de Mio Cid*, and they are still live literary resources in *Tristán de Leonís* and *Amadís de Gaula* in the early XVIth century.

Two particular formulas or formulaic expressions, firstly 'Mas agora dexa el cuento' or 'Mas agora dexa la istoria' and secondly 'Agora dize el cuento' or 'E dice la istoria', plunge us straight into the very weave of the narration and into the technique of interlace (Contreras Martín 2005b: 10–12). Both formulas are used to indicate the end of one narrative sequence or the end of a chapter and the beginning of another. They are either integrated into the text, or form part of chapter headings.[12]

Equally, it should be noted that the essential importance of these formulas as a resource contributing in a fundamental way to the articulation of the narration was clear to the compiler of the work. This is obvious from his use of them firstly to interweave the adventures of Héctor de Mares with those of Yvaín (294b), after suppressing part of the French text, and then later those of Yvaín with those of Galván (345a–b), after omitting the adventures of Boores, and, finally, on adding the adventures of Tristán to those of Lanzarote (383a).

The interlace technique, in my view, consists of interrupting and returning later to an episode involving the same character, and so on successively with others. In this way, a dense narration is achieved in which various narrative threads are kept alive simultaneously and are interwoven in a multifaceted single whole. In the light of this definition, then, it is necessary to distinguish between pure interlace, impure interlace or false interlace, retrospection, chain of consequences, narrative suspense, and quest (Contreras Martín, 2005b: 12–24).

Interlace as such is found only in the alternating interruption and resumption of the adventures of Saigremor (245b–253a) in sequence with those of Dodinel el Salvaje (253a–255a) and those of the latter with those of Grifón del Mal Paso (255a–257a). In so far as concerns false or impure interlace, one must distinguish three groups: (a) those cases in which the characters' adventures are developed without any subsequent continuation, despite the existence of a boundary chapter which seems to interrupt them, examples of which are the adventures of Galescaín, Duke of Clarence, which are left in suspense by the narration of the origin and history of the Valle sin Retorno (92b–94b, 92b–93b), the adventures of Lanzarote del Lago (125a–168b, 217a–236a, 296a–306b, 316b–341a, 346a–381b), the adventures of Galván, who is accompanied by Héctor de Mares (277a–290b, 277a–283b); (b) those in which situations already begun are continued in one or more chapters, exemplified by the adventures of Saigremor, which are interlaced with events already related (240b–253b, 78b–80a), and the presentation of Meleagant at the court of Arthur to fight against Lanzarote, and the combat and the death of the challenger (173b–176b, 176b–179b); and (c) those in which the actions of various characters are developed simultaneously (the quest of Lanzarote, 260a–296a; the quest of Galván, 68b–112a).

Retrospection is another mode of articulating the narration. It originates in the frequent breaks and interruptions, and is applied to adventures that could appear to be irrelevant and that could therefore be replaced by others or suppressed without affecting the story, although in reality they fulfil a quite specific role in the development of the character who is their principal focus. Examples are the adventure of the knight who decapitates the maiden and upon whom Lanzarote imposes the penance of presenting himself at various courts (354a–356a, 360a–362a); the tournament organised by King Narbaduc, the prize of which is the award of a falcon and a sparrowhawk, in which Galván and Héctor de Mares fight (276a–281b); the adventures of Héctor in the castle of Marigart (290a–294b); the combats undertaken by Yvaín to recover the horse of one lady and the sparrowhawk of another (294b–296a).

A chain of consequences occurs when an incident that could be viewed, in itself, as minor or irrelevant leads to a series of adventures which develops, despite a succession of interruptions, as the narrative progresses. An example is the presentation of the arms of Grifón del Mal Paso to Lanzarote, which, when the latter reciprocates by giving his to Grifón, leads to the belief that Lanzarote is dead, which in turn unleashes the quest to find him, thus bringing about his confrontation with his companions when he fights alongside the sons of the Duke of Karlés, from whom he obtains the freedom of the brothers of Galván (224b–225a, 255b–257b, 260a–296a, 311b–314a). Another case is the death of Meleagant, which leads to Lanzarote fighting against Argodrás el Rubio to save Meleagant's sister from death (178a–180a, 229b–233b); while a third is the tournament of the king of Brangoire and the vows uttered, which lead to the combat between Boores and Lanzarote and his defeat while attempting to capture Ginebra, and to the need for Patridés del Cerco de Oro to fight against Lanzarote in order to fulfil his vow, which in turn, after his defeat, causes him to present himself before Bandemagus to inform him of the death of his son (207a–211b, 240b–243a, 233b–235a, 240a).

Narrative suspense is a procedure that consists of the conscious interruption of the narrative thread in order to pick it up again later in the same chapter or in a following chapter. Cases include the moment at which Yvaín is about to free a lady tied to a tree by her hair, when he is suddenly obliged to postpone this in order to confront a succession of knights (78a–79a); the occasion when, despite the risk of death facing Meleagant's sister for having assisted Lanzarote, the latter first escorts the body of his companion Galahot to the Dolorous Guard to bury him (217a–218b, 218b–221a); and the situation in which Lanzarote is freed by the daughter of the Duke of Rocedón in exchange for his preventing her wedding, and returns later to put her suitor to flight (318a–319b, 358a–359a). Others are encountered when Lanzarote is detained by the enchantment of the dance in the Valle sin Retorno, and subsequently breaks the enchantment (340b–341a, 346a–349a); and when the attitude of Yvaín brings about the freedom of Maldito el Jayán, whom Boores subsequently routs (341a–345a). There are also the adventures of the Duke of Karlés and the events in his nephew's castle (311a–314a, 350b–354a); and the case of the lady who cures Lanzarote when he drinks poisoned water from a fountain, who in turn is saved by him when she is threatened with rape by some vassals of a cousin of Claudás de la Tierra Deserta, and who finally, at the behest of the queen, clarifies the relationship between herself and Lanzarote (301a–311b, 333b–335b, 369b–370b).

The quest is another of the devices by which the narrative is articulated and structured, since it is through it that there arises the need for the knights to undertake actions and journeys, thereby to find themselves, since the wandering life is synonymous with the ideal of knight errantry. In the work we encounter six major quests and six minor ones. As far as concerns the six major quests, three are preserved in their entirety; these are the search for Galván undertaken by Lanzarote, Yvaín and Galescaín, Duke of Clarence, to liberate him from his kidnapper Caradós de la Dolorosa Torre (68a–112a); the search for Lanzarote, held prisoner by Morgana, undertaken by Galahot, Lionel, Galván and Yvaín (112a–124a); and the search for Ginebra, kidnapped by Meleagant, carried out by Lanzarote and Galván (124a–180a). One is retained partially, namely the search for Lanzarote undertaken by ten knights, although the exploits of only four are narrated (Aglován, Galván, Héctor de Mares and Yvaín), who are joined by others (Keu, Saigremor and Dodinel, 260a–381b); one survives in embryonic form (the search begun by Lanzarote, Boores, Galván and Gueheriet to find Lionel, Héctor de Mares, Agravaín, Gueherret and Mordred, 381b–382a); and one is wholly original (the search for Tristán made by Lanzarote, 384b–386b). The six minor quests have all been retained more or less intact. These are: the search undertaken by Lionel to find Lanzarote (80a–81b); that begun by Boores with the encouragement of Lanzarote, for whom he searches, the end of which is not preserved (188a–239b); the search for Boores by the lady of Honguefort, to obtain his forgiveness (199b–200a, 215b–217a, 238b–239b); that for the Caballero de la Caja who is rescued by Lanzarote (73a–75b); the search for Dodinel undertaken by Saigremor (245a, 252b–255a, 259a–260a); and the search for Lionel by Lanzarote (314ab, 316b–341a, 346a–362a).

The quest is a mechanism which, as is the case also with the combination and repetition of motifs and episodes, permits the amplification and prolongation of the narrative. The compiler, aware of the value of the quest as a driving element in the narration, makes use of it to interweave the exploits of Lanzarote, who up to this point has been the indisputable protagonist of the work, with that concerned with the adventures of Tristán, which has not been preserved. Hence he launches Lanzarote on the quest for Tristán to give him his unconditional support.

The combination and repetition of motifs and episodes is employed to extend the narration by means of 'amplificatio' according to the precepts of medieval handbooks of rhetoric or *artes poeticae* (Contreras Martín 2002c). The work makes use of a group of allomorphemes (each of the terms employed to refer to the same motif), which are combined with one another as the text progresses and can appear in groups of greater or lesser complexity referred to as allosemantemes (each of the possible variant combinations of a signified, in other words a grouping of allomorphemes), which serve to express a series of topoi or motifs through which reference is made to concepts such as 'imprisonment', 'liberation', 'wound', 'concealment or enchantment'. These combinations and their use create a dense network of relationships and a delicate equilibrium within the fabric of the story. The compiler displays his awareness of their effectiveness in narration when he puts them to use in creating the original episode of the Isla de Merlín (385ab).

The 'specular encounter' is another of the mechanisms employed in articulating the narrative (Contreras Martín 2005c). It is produced when a character encounters an interlocutor, who can take various forms, and represents merely variations on a single motif ('revelation'), functioning as a mirror in which there are revealed to the character facts or facets which are unknown or obscure to him, whether relating to the past by analepsis or to the future by prolepsis, and which are intended to contribute to constructing his biography. There are four 'specular encounters', of which the final one is original: in the Santo Cementerio, the protagonist finds the tombs of Galaad, son of Joseph of Arimathea, and of Symeu, representing past and future (143b–144ab,145ab); the tomb of Galahot and his burial in the Dolorous Guard, again past and future (218ab); in the Bosque Peligroso, he undoes the enchantments of the Danza Mágica, the past (346ab); and in the Isla Perdida the future, the Golpe Doloroso, is announced (384b–385a). The compiler's introduction of this device into the original part underlines his understanding of the important role that it plays in the elaboration of the biography of Lanzarote del Lago, and with it the events of the hero's youth are interwoven with those of his maturity, old age and death, related in the *Mort Artu* and the *Demanda del Sancto Grial*.

Because of their productive potential, all these mechanisms employed in configuring the narrative structure are subsequently used extensively in the composition of other Castilian chivalric romances, such as the *Libro del cavallero Zifar* and *Amadís de Gaula*, which are greatly indebted to the tradition of Arthurian fiction represented by *Lanzarote del Lago* and *Tristán de Leonís*.

4.1.2.2. Focalization and Modality

The narrator hides behind another narrative authority which is referred to as 'cuento' or 'historia'. Additionally, the presence of a recipient, whether this be a listener or a reader, to whom the narrator addresses himself directly – by employing formulas and formulaic expressions constructed around the verb 'to hear' (oir), by using resources of direct invocation through second-person plural verbal forms, and by using the first person plural – implies the existence of an 'I', latent when the text is read privately (although it must not be forgotten that in a majority of cases even private reading was performed aloud) or overt when it is read before an audience, a fact which brings us back to the practices that are characteristic of orality and oral performance. This is an 'I' that transforms the narrator into a guarantor of the truth and authenticity of the events related, and endows them with credibility.

In the work, the 'I' is used in an implicit fashion, since the Spanish verb form (here in the first person singular) does not require the explicit use of the personal subject pronoun (e.g., 'ansí puestas, como vos digo', 208b, 'as [I] am telling you'). Even after having recourse to the authority of 'cuento', the narrator adds his own testimony, converting himself into the guarantor of the information ('Dize el cuento que ellos estando comiendo, así como vos digo', 224a, 'The story tells how, while they were eating, as [I] am telling you ...').

In addition, his implicit presence is observed through the characters, since the latter speak of themselves or of others, in direct speech, reported speech, or a combination of both, which leads us into the field of modality. The dominant mode is direct speech, resulting from the alteration of style in relation to the French versions and from the addition of new material. This tendency is also encountered in the final folios.

Moreover, when to the dominance of direct speech is added the frequency of the combination of different modes, we can appreciate that the compiler has ventured to underline the role of dialogue and sequences combining dialogue and narrative, thereby rendering the narrative more fluent. However, this process of transformation, in so far as modality is concerned, is consistent with the ideas governing the construction of textual grammar followed in medieval Castilian prose in general, just as is the case with its French equivalent (Contreras Martín 2009).

4.1.2.3. The Chronology of the Work

The concept of time in *Lanzarote del Lago*, as in the *Lancelot en prose*, is complex, and all the devices employed to develop it are governed by the concern for creating coherence in the narration, and, as a result, in the cycle (Contreras Martín, 2002a: 391–482; 2006: 76–7). For the configuration of time in *Lanzarote del Lago*, as in the rest of the Vulgate cycle (of which there is currently no known Castilian representative), two concepts of time coexist, which set us in the context of the mythic and the historical, namely, circular time and linear time. In *Lanzarote del Lago* and in the rest of the cycle, ideas of past, present and future converge throughout the work, thanks to analepsis and prolepsis, and in this way yesterday, today and tomorrow form an indissoluble unity in the organisation of the Arthurian world and in the construction of the biographies of its characters. The tendency to seek the origins of the characters and of the facts that clarify and explain their past and future leads us to the sphere of the mythic, in which time is conceived in circular form and nothing and nobody can escape it. This circularity finds a representation in the figure of Fortune, whose wheel, a microcosm of the universe, spins tirelessly. On the other hand, the life of the characters in this world, with a genesis and an apocalypse (the birth and extinction of the Arthurian world), runs in accordance with a chronology ruled by the concept of linearity in existence, which transfers us to the sphere of the historical and the real.

Given that *Lanzarote del Lago*, like the *Lancelot en prose*, is conceived as the biography of Lanzarote and those of the other knights of the Arthurian world, we are given a detailed dating of the events in the life of the hero and in those of his companions. The object of this dating is none other than that of reinforcing the pretensions of the romance to the status of a chronicle, for which it was necessary to endow the narrative of the events with realism and verisimilitude in the interests of the 'veritas' characteristic of historical narrations. In *Lanzarote del Lago*, the sequence of time is established by means of a series of temporal markers that tend to create this sense of realism and verisimilitude by setting out, in a more or less detailed way, the actions and wanderings of the characters as they move through the Arthurian world. Thus, specific times are established for the beginning, development, and conclusion of an action ('quinze días antes de Natal', 9b), the duration of a period is marked out ('desde Natal fasta Pentecoste', 13a), feast days are noted ('Santa María de la Candelaria', 16a), as are the months ('nobienbre', 8b), days of the week ('lunes de las ochauas de Pentecoste', 49a), times of day ('Aquella noche', 8b) and the liturgical hours ('a hora de prima', 132a; 'ora de terçia', 39b; 'ora de nona', 86b; 'a las vísperas', 68b). Later chivalric narrative, such as *Amadís de Gaula*, will display an identical tendency to create and recreate the time frame within which its characters exist.

4.1.2.4. Arthurian Geography

Geography is one of the defining elements of the Arthurian world, since it is through this that there is constructed the space, whether real or fictitious, in which the adventures of the characters take place (Contreras Martín 2005a). In *Lanzarote del Lago*, as in the French sources the *Lancelot en prose* and *La Suite du Roman de Merlin*, although the origins of Lancelot go back to Judaea, geography is limited to the confines of France and Britain, with all the possible political and dynastic implications that this carries with it. This permits us to understand how the Arthurian imaginary is articulated. Its place names refer to kingdoms, regions and islands ('Logres', 11a; 'Extrañas Insulas', 24b), to cities and towns ('Carlión', 3a), castles, palaces, monasteries, hermitages and chapels ('Orgullosa Guarda', 7a; 'Monasterio Real', 338b; 'Hermita Gastada', 348a), woods and valleys ('Floresta de Camalot', 263a; 'Valle de los Falsos Amadores', 93b), rivers, lakes and fountains ('Lago del Diablo', 11a), fords, passes, bridges, crosses and roads ('Puente de la Espada', 148a; 'Cruz del Jayán', 363b).

4.1.2.5. The Investiture of a Knight

The entry of young aspirants into the world of knighthood is marked by a ceremony laden with profound symbolic value: the investiture. *Lanzarote del Lago*, unfortunately, preserves only the briefest description of the investiture, in mid-combat, of a young man, who is assisting Lanzarote ('E entonces ciñóle la espada e diole una palmada que Dios le hiciese ome bueno por el su placer', 150b). This is an act of investiture conditioned by the context of combat and the haste which this involves, in which there are two identifiable stages: girding on the young man's sword, and giving him a slap on the cheek. This involves a type of investiture documented in both historical and literary sources, but one which could raise doubts over the meaning of the term 'palmada'. On investigation, it is clear that the work uses the word with the meaning 'blow on the cheek', a usage which is encountered from the middle of the XIVth century, for which reason it seems acceptable to conclude that the Castilian version could not have been produced before 1350, since it would then have used the established and current term 'pescozada' rather than the neologism 'palmada' which carried with it the risk of not being understood by readers (Contreras Martín 2003).

4.1.2.6. Arms and Armour: Weaponry Offensive and Defensive

In *Lanzarote del Lago*, as in the French sources, combats fulfil a fundamental function and occupy an appreciable part of the work, to such an extent that the terms relating to arms and armour, which are an excellent tool for dating and one which contributes to our knowledge of the history and evolution of weaponry in the kingdom of Castile and León, enable us to observe how the compiler worked and assist in clarifying the date of the translation or composition of the text (Contreras Martín 2002b; 2006: 78–80; Contreras Martín and Jiménez Mola 1997). Most of these terms are those which appear in the works which constitute the three great cycles of French Arthurian romance (*Vulgate*, *Post-Vulgate*, and *Tristan en prose*), although words are also used that are documented later than the redaction of these cycles, as a result of the evolution of weaponry and armour. Cases include 'brafoneras' (1240–50), 'bacinete' (1295), 'gorguera' (1295), 'canilleras' (1338), 'quijotes' (1330–40), 'visal' (1414–35) and 'empuñadura' (1495). Their use (except for that of 'empuñadura') demonstrates the existence of some semantic hesitancy; this may indicate a situation of initial diffusion of these terms, which would explain why their meaning is not fixed, whence the vacilation; or a lack of understanding on the part of the compiler, explicable either because neologisms were involved or because he did not know the exact meaning of the French original; or the involvement of a copyist who could have used terms frequently employed in his own time, but which had been adopted by the language at a date subsequent to that of the translation of the text.

4.1.2.7. Heraldry

Heraldry is a fundamental element in the construction of the knightly identity, which clearly shows the relationship of mutual dependence and influence that was established between reality and literature, as is demonstrated by the fact that the heraldry of fiction intruded into real life and vice versa. This is exemplified perfectly in the case of Arthurian heraldry, the influence of which led to its being adopted or adapted by historical individuals. In the Arthurian romance heraldry appears both extensively and circumstantially. As happened with characters belonging to Classical and Carolingian material, a personal and distinctive heraldry was attributed to many characters from the Arthurian world. In some cases this led to a single character being assigned different coats of arms, as is shown by the blazoned shields described in the romances or those collected in the armorials that were drawn up.

In *Lanzarote del Lago*, the shields that are emblazoned conform to those described in the source, *Lancelot en prose* (Contreras Martín 1999, 2007a). One of these merits special attention: the shield of Yvaín ('el campo de plata e un león vermejo en medio d'él', 74b), since it allows us to place the work in a chronological span that leads us to the middle of the XIVth century. The term 'vermejo' faithfully reflects the French 'sinople', which in French heraldry until the mid-XIVth century was used to designate red, and is, therefore, a synonym of 'gules'. However, from the second half of that century it was used to denote 'green', a semantic change that does not extend to the Spanish kingdoms until the middle of the XVth century. The work, as a result, must have been translated before 'sinople' came to denote 'green', a development which would have made it unthinkable for the compiler to translate the French word as 'vermejo' (Contreras Martín 2003: 262; 2007c: 71).

4.2 The Catalan *Lançalot*

Bohigas Balaguer (1962: 3) observed, on analysing both the Catalan fragments, that they display some linguistic traits in common. This led him to assert that although they belong to different manuscripts, they were derived from the same earlier translation. It would, however, be necessary to carry out a detailed linguistic study of both fragments, which has not thus far been undertaken, and to compare these with usage contemporary with these texts, in order to establish the extent to which these are identical or distinct.

In contrast to the case of *Lanzarote del Lago*, the fragments of *Lançalot* do not allow us to carry out a complete analysis, because in the first place they belong to different manuscripts, and secondly because of their brevity and incomplete state. The Campos fragment contains the description of the combat between Lanzarote del Lago and Caradós de la Dolorosa Torre (Sommer 1909–12: IV, 134–7; Micha 1978–82: V, XXVIII, 1–16; III, XXVIII, 1–16), and the Cruzate fragment relates the adventures of Lanzarote del Lago in the Bosque Perdido, where the protagonist undoes the enchantment of the Danza Mágica and succeeds in the test of the Ajedrez Mágico (Sommer 1909–12: V, 149–150; Micha 1978–82: IV, LXXXIII, 1–13).

Now, comparison of *Lançalot* with the French versions (Sommer 1909–12; Micha 1978–82; BNF MS 751) enables us to observe that there is a high level of fidelity to these, although modifications have been introduced that are consistent with contemporary circumstances. Thus, the number indicating the value of the Magic Chess is retained ('mil', 186), but the monetary unit is altered ('marcs', for 'livres') in the Cruzate fragment; and there are modifications in the sphere of modality, since two cases of direct speech are added together with another case of the combination of modes, one in the Campos fragment ('Lansalot lo segui corren, criden i disen: ¡A, maluat e fello, e cuydes aysi finar la batalla! No faras pas, ans coue que le menem e fi', 23), and another in the Cruzate fragment ('"Et aysi, sèyer", dix lo prohom a Lansalot, "féu aqueyl clergue aquesta bayla en aquest lloc, aysí com vós avets vist per forsa d'encantament e sí roman"', 187), lacking in the original. This could relate to the tendency to enhance the role of dialogues and dialogued narrative sequences identifiable in the articulation of contemporary medieval narrative.

5. *Lanzarote del Lago*, *Lançalot*, and the Configuration of the Chivalric Imaginary

Arthurian narrative, in relating the biographies of its male and female characters, proposes possible ways of dealing with the courtly labyrinth of chivalry as the latter was defined and redefined from its initial formative phase to the XVIth century, which have as their purpose the attempt to provide answers to possibilities confronting the men and women of the time (Ruiz-Domènec 1993). *Lanzarote del Lago* and *Lançalot* are presented as manuals which offer models of conduct, in which there are partially narrated some of these biographies, constructed from the whole of the works of the *Vulgate* cycle and also the *Post-Vulgate* and the *Tristan en prose*. The narrative web of the work is articulated essentially through five characters (Lanzarote, Ginebra, Artús, Galahot and Boores), who form a sophisticated web of relations and offer models or examples which enable understanding.

The amorous relationship between Lanzarote and Ginebra could be interpreted on two levels (Contreras Martín 2000). Thus, Lanzarote, presented as the best knight in the world, a young royal heir, who displays an unconditional submission to and a devout veneration of a lady, Ginebra, a queen approaching maturity and at the peak of her splendour, as masterfully illustrated by the episode of the cart (Contreras Martín 1995, 2002d, 2013c) and that of the Magic Chess (Contreras Martín 2007b, 2013c), could be understood, on the one hand, as the unquestioning acceptance on the part of the aristocracy of the ideals and principles of monarchy upon which the dynastic state was being constructed, expressed through the image of the queen; and, on the other, as a representation of a knightly model, the courtly model, ruled by a principle of love which is reproachable, adulterous love, since it places in jeopardy the stability of the kingdom and therefore of the crown. It also prevents the full realisation of knighthood, as manifested in the greatest of adventures, the quest of the Holy Grail, though Lanzarote is still the person who will engender the individual who will achieve this: Galaz.

Arthur shows himself to be unpredictable and changeable, a behaviour absolutely reprehensible in royal authority. A monarch who first behaves as such since he saves his people, by hunting a terrible boar, but who later declines to confront an identical danger and abandons his kingly responsibility (Contreras Martín 2000, 2012b). A king, moreover, who, swayed by evil counsellors and by passion, rejects his legitimate wife, leaves his kingdom, and lives an adulterous life with the Falsa Ginebra, which provokes disorder in his realms. A monarch who dangerously delegates his roles to others, as in the rescue of Ginebra, kidnapped by Meleagant. A king who stays at his court, sunk in lethargy.

Galahot shows himself to be an excellent knight, and a good king, who, however, is incapable of controlling his feelings towards Lanzarote, which places his relationship in a confused and ambiguous situation, a dangerous one, which can lead to consideration of a feeling far deeper than the friendship which leads him to his death (Correia 2009). This conduct is inappropriate and execrable among knights, and even more so in a sovereign.

Boores, identifiable as the double of his beloved cousin Lanzarote with whom he is confused, is a knight of irreproachable conduct, surpassed in arms only by the latter. He is a knight loyal to his lineage and respectful of royalty, as befits the son of a king.

Notes

[1] For references to the texts I use Contreras Martín and Sharrer 2006, Rubió y Lluch 1903, and Bohigas Balaguer 1962.

[2] In the manuscript there is an interesting series of annotations which permit us to observe a case of the reception of the work (Lucía Megías 1994).

[3] See *http://sunsite.berkeley.edu/Philobiblon/BETA/1400.html*.

[4] See *http://sunsite.berkeley.edu/Philobiblon/BITECA/1174.html*.

[5] It appears that information concerning the whereabouts of the leaves has not been available for a considerable time.

[6] See *http://sunsite.berkeley.edu/Philobiblon/BITECA/1175.html*.

[7] In speaking of a *Lancelot* in Gallego-Portuguese, it does not seem to have been taken into account that the language used in Gallego-Portuguese poetry is a conventional literary variety that does not reflect the dialectal reality of the language, since when in the second half of the XIIIth century writing in Romance begins, among the texts produced north or south of the River Miño – in the Galician or the Portuguese zone respectively – there would already have existed linguistic differences which would in certain cases have been simply the manifestation of dialectal differences and in other cases should be interpreted as the result of the fact that the copyists were working within different traditions of writing, which were consolidated in the XIVth and XVth centuries (Mariño Paz 1998: 107).

[8] In reply (7 March 2006) to my enquiry about the language of BNF MS 751, the purpose of which was to discover the possible area in which the manuscript was copied, Dr Elspeth Kennedy very kindly informed me that in her opinion it did not display very many dialectal features, but that it did contain some features characteristic of the north of France (Wallonia, Artois, Picardy): 'nr' for 'ndr' (*tanres, devanres*); 'r' or 'rr' for 'dr' (*voras, vorroies*); 'ie' for 'iee' in the feminine past participle (*correcie* for *correciee, ansangnie* for *ansangiee*); 'i' for 'e' before a palatalized 'n' (= 'gn') (*grignors, signeur*); 'i' for 'e' before 'ch' (*picheors, pichie*); and 'ss' for 's' (*dissoit, contredissoit*). I note that this is the zone from which Afonso III of Portugal came (Boulogne), for which reason one could consider that a manuscript of the same family as this one could have been taken to the Iberian Peninsula. It becomes essential, then, to undertake a detailed study of the dialectal characteristics of this manuscript as also of all others considered to be related to it and which display differences from the 'canonical' versions, in order to be able to evaluate their relationships and consider them as possible sources.

[9] It is also necessary to mention the fact that Hook (1992–3b) has documented the use of 'Espladian' (*sic*), very similar to the name of the son of Amadís de Gaula, possibly as a patronymic ('Migael d'Espladian'), in 1294. For a discussion of problems in the interpretation of this evidence, and for the likely date of *Amadís*, see Rafael Ramos in this volume.

[10] Its diffusion reaches as far as the kingdom of Granada, since from the third quarter of the XIVth century there date the paintings produced by a mudéjar artist in the Sala de Justicia of the Alhambra on the orders of Muhammad V, which allude to the episode of the Puente de la Espada and that of Ajedrez Mágico from the *Lancelot en prose* (Dodds 1979).

[11] Given the date of composition of the work, with the allusion to the 'contención de Lanzarote', an allusion could be being made either to knowledge of a story of Lanzarote of a certain length and elaboration, such as *Le chevalier a la Charrete* of Chrétien de Troyes, or perhaps to narrative compositions transmitted orally, which related one or several episodes from the life of the knight, as proposed by Carlos Alvar for the Gallego-Portuguese area (Alvar 1993).

[12] The fact that the formula ('Mas agora dexa el cuento' or 'Mas agora dexa la istoria') is employed as a chapter heading from the first surviving leaf onwards and that, from f. 249*v* onwards, on almost every occasion on which it is used this duplicates or triplicates the formula contained in the text itself, leads one to think that this translation is an intermediate point between the French original, in which these formulae are integrated into the narrative, and a version destined for printing, where the chapter headings, as is the case with the rest of those that appear in the translation, are employed to indicate the end of a narrative sequence or the end of a chapter and the beginning of a new one, as, for example, in *Amadís de Gaula* (1508) by Garci Rodríguez de Montalvo, or in *Tristán de Leonís* (1501).

IX

THE IBERIAN *TRISTAN* TEXTS OF THE MIDDLE AGES AND RENAISSANCE

María Luzdivina Cuesta Torre

The legend of Tristan and Iseult is represented in medieval Castilian literature by some allusions in poems and prose works; by three versions of a ballad (Spanish *romance*) of epic-lyric character devoted to the death of Tristan and known by its first line ('Ferido está don Tristán'); by MS 22021 of the Biblioteca Nacional de España, Madrid, which contains two letters created in the style of the genre of the sentimental romance from the basis of an episode in the story of the two lovers (which are analysed in the chapter by Carlos Alvar); and by four prose romances, all anonymous, of which two are preserved in manuscript and two are known only from printed editions, and all of which are studied in the present chapter.[1] These are as follows:

1. *Códice de Tristán* of the BNE: MS BNE 20262–19, edited by Bonilla (1904: 25–8; 1912: 318–20), Menéndez Pidal (2nd edn 1971: I, 350); and MS BNE 22644, on vellum and paper, in Castilian, dated to the beginning of the XVth century by Alvar and Lucía (1999: 11), and edited by them.
2. *Cuento de Tristán* (Vatican MS Vat. Lat. 6428), edited in modern times by Northup (1928) and by Corfis (1985, 1994, 2013), dating from the late XIVth or early XVth century, on paper, in Castilian and Castilian-Aragonese (Sharrer 1977: 29).
3. *Tristán* or *Tristán de Leonís* (entitled *Libro del esforçado cauallero don Tristán de Leonís y de sus grandes fechos en armas*), with its *editio princeps* printed at Valladolid by Juan de Burgos in 1501. Other editions were printed at Seville by the Crombergers in 1511 and 1528 (and in 1533 according to Gallardo 1863: no. 1240, and Escudero y Perosso 1894: no. 336), and by Juan Varela in 1525 (and probably in 1520, according to Escudero y Perosso 1894: no. 215). A further three editions have been suspected: two earlier than 1511, and one from the Cromberger printing house before 1520, of which only a few folios survive (Cuesta 1997d). Study of the woodcuts carried out by Cacho Blecua (2004–5) demonstrates the existence of an edition of *Tristán* from the Cromberger press between 1501 and 1507, which supports Cuesta's hypothesis (1997d). Among the modern editions of this work the most important are those by Bonilla of the edition of 1528 (ed. 1907: 339–457) and that of 1501 (ed. 1912) and, for the latter text, Cuesta (1999a). A summary of the plot and

catalogue of the characters, together with a brief introduction to essential bibliography, are found in Cuesta (1998c).

4. *Tristán el Joven* (entitled *Corónica nuevamente enmendada y añadida del buen cavallero don Tristán de Leonís y del rey don Tristán de Leonís el Joven, su hijo*), printed at Seville by Domenico de Robertis in 1534, with a modern edition by Cuesta (1997e). There is a reading guide with a detailed summary of the plot (Cuesta 1999c).

A fuller description of all these witnesses can be found in the chapter by Lucía Megías in the present volume.

The four texts involved here must be considered to constitute different works because of the significant variations that they present in certain episodes, in style, and in intention. The two works preserved only in manuscript are incomplete to a differing degree because of textual losses during manuscript transmission. In the case of the *Cuento de Tristán*, the loss of folios affects the beginning of the narration and also a long final section which covers nearly half the work, on the assumption that its extent was similar to that of the Castilian *Tristán* printed in 1501. The manuscript records the story of Tristan from when his tutor Gorvanao advises him to leave the kingdom of Leonís until the point at which Queen Iseo accompanies Tristán to the tournament at Camelot and both receive a visit in their tent from King Arthur and Lancelot. In the case of the *Códice de Tristán*, the loss affects numerous folios scattered throughout the work, and partially the surviving folios, the margins of which have been trimmed (ed. Alvar and Lucía 1999: 10). The content of the fragments recounts the section from the tournament in Scotland at which the Caballero de las Dos Espadas, Palomades, is defeated, up to the war to avenge the death of Tristán and Iseo, the return of Quedín to Little Britain, and the death of Iseo de las Blancas Manos. It is almost certain that none of the manuscripts represents the first version of the legend of Tristán in Castilian in the form of a romance, since allusions are found in other literary works before these dates (see the chapter by Carlos Alvar in the present volume). However, these allusions are so brief or conventional that they do not permit any conclusions to be drawn concerning any features of any earlier version.

At the beginning of the XVIth century a new version was printed, known by the short-title *Tristán de Leonís*, based on a manuscript similar to the *Códice de Tristán* in content, but to which a new stylistic and ideological model has been applied, mingling with the familiar epistolary elements derived from chivalric literature related to Troy (Marín Pina 2004–5) and from the genre of sentimental romance which flourished during those years (Cuesta 1999a: introduction, especially pp. xxiii–xxvii).

The last of the editions of *Tristán de Leonís*, which was published in 1534, was completed with some chapters interpolated into the episode of the lovers' sojourn on the Isla del Gigante, which tell of the birth of the children of Tristán and Iseo, who are given the names of their parents, and the arrangements for their upbringing, as well as other adventures involving new characters. This made possible the addition, after the romance was completed, of a second part which was printed together with the first, devoted to narrating the adventures of these descendants, and following the patterns and conventions of the romances of chivalry which dominated Castilian fiction at this time. This edition of 1534 must be considered a different work, as is reflected in its title, which combined the two components, the old and the new, of which the narrative consists, bringing together with the copulative conjunction the names of the protagonists: *Corónica del buen cavallero don Tristán de Leonís y del rey don Tristán de Leonís el Joven, su hijo*. The anonymous author distinguishes between the 'ancient matter' which he took from earlier editions almost unaltered, except in the chapters that precede his interventions, and the new material that he incorporates. Although the work was not printed again in Spanish, it was translated into Italian: *Le opere magnanime de i due Tristani, cavalieri della Tavola Ritonda* (Venice: Michele Tremezino, 1555), in two octavo volumes.

MS BNE 22021 that contains the *Carta de Iseo y respuesta de Tristán* is an original work of the end of the XVth or beginning of the XVIth century that is inspired by the letter that Queen Iseo sends to Tristán on learning of his marriage to Iseo de las Blancas Manos, princess of Little Britain; see the chapter by Alvar in the present volume, and studies by Cuesta (1994a: 237–9), Sharrer (1981–2; 1984a: 155–7), Gómez Redondo (1987) and Gwara (1997: 80, 97–9). Since Iseo's letter is completely reworked, preserving merely the theme and the tone, and Tristán's reply does not figure in any of the prose romances about him, it is not possible to establish a clear relation between this witness and any specific Peninsular version of the legend of Tristán; but logic leads us to suppose that its anonymous author knew the episode from which he drew his inspiration through either *Tristán de Leonís* or the manuscript version which was in circulation prior to the printing of that work, and of which we have only the fragmentary witness of the *Códice de Tristán*.

Equally, the *Romance de Tristán* offers few precise data to enable us to identify the text known by its author, although the few facts that it does convey (the mortal wound dealt to Tristán by his uncle with a lance-thrust from a high place) coincide with what appears in *Tristán de Leonís* (Seidenspinner-Núñez 1981–2; Cuesta 1997c) and, probably, with what must have been contained in the *Códice de Tristán*, for which reason, taking into account the dates of its diffusion, we must conclude that it was the latter that gave rise to this ballad (Cuesta 2009b).[2]

The Castilian *Tristán* texts transmit two different versions of the story, although with a selection of episodes and content apparently identical in fundamental aspects. Since they are preserved in incomplete manuscript witnesses of different length, it is not always possible to compare them directly with each other or with other European witnesses. This difficulty can be remedied in part by supplying from the printed edition of *Tristán de Leonís* the text missing in the manuscript fragments. Essentially, the storyline is as follows.

The story begins with the establishment of the tribute paid by Cornwall to Ireland, the birth of Tristán, his stepmother's attempts to poison him, his journey with his tutor Gorvalán to the kingdom of Feremondo of Gaula, in whose court he rejects the love of Princess Belisenda (who finally commits suicide) and his establishment in Cornwall as an anonymous young nobleman. The hero's youth ends with the arrival in Cornwall of Morlot of Irlanda to collect the tribute, an event which provokes the knighting of Tristán by his uncle King Mares so that he can confront Morlot. Tristán mortally wounds Morlot, but receives in return a poisoned wound which does not heal, so he embarks in a drifting boat to seek his salvation. And so he arrives in Ireland, where Iseo, niece of Morlot, cures him and feels drawn to him. The protagonist distinguishes himself in a tournament, but when his identity is discovered he is exiled because of the death of Morlot. Back in Cornwall again, Tristán vies with King Mares for the love of the Lady of the Lago del Espina, and for this reason his uncle sends him to Ireland to ask for the hand of Iseo, with the secret purpose of having him killed by the Irish. Tristán saves the king of Ireland in a judicial duel at the court of King Arthur, and in reward the Irish ruler concedes Iseo's hand to him, for himself or for his uncle. The queen of Ireland hands to the lady Brangel the love philtre which the bride and groom must drink on their wedding night, but Tristán and Iseo drink it during the voyage. A storm drives them to the Isla del Gigante, where Tristán fights with the lord of the island and kills him, but later surrenders, out of gallantry, to the latter's son, the generous half-giant Galeote. In Cornwall again, Brangel replaces Iseo on her wedding night so that the king shall not notice the loss of her virginity. The lovers meet in secret, but Iseo is afraid that Brangel may denounce them and orders her to be killed, though she later repents. The knight Palomades takes the lady to the court again and as a reward receives the right to carry off Queen Iseo. Tristán rescues her. Other adventures follow, such as that of the horn which denounces adulterous women, which places the lovers at risk; they are finally found out and condemned, but succeed in escaping to the forest, where they live happily at the 'Home of the Wise Woman' until Mares seizes Iseo there while Tristán is absent hunting. Because of his poisoned wound, Tristán seeks a cure in Little Britain, where he helps the king to victory in a war, and receives as a reward the hand of his daughter Iseo de las Blancas Manos. However, he does not decide to consummate his marriage, and, when he receives a letter of reproach from Queen Iseo he decides to return to her. On the journey he is accompanied by Gorvalán and Quedín, the brother of his wife Iseo. They linger in the Floresta Peligrosa, where Tristán saves Arthur from death at the hands of the Doncella del Arte, and they have various adventures. Once in Cornwall, King Mares pretends to pardon Tristán, but organises a joust so that he may be killed by another knight. Tristán either overcomes, or obtains by courtesy the surrender of, the best knights of the Round Table, including Lancelot. One day the queen begs him that they should flee together to the kingdom of Arthur. And so they arrive, after some adventures, at Lancelot's castle, where they dine with him and Queen Guinevere, and lodge there afterwards. Tristán goes to a tournament organised by Arthur, accompanied by Iseo, and during the journey other knights join them, among whom there are the gracious Dinadán and Palomades. The latter attempts to violate the queen by trickery, but is discovered and has to flee. Tristan and Iseo remain at the court of Arthur until King Mares arrives there to demand justice. On Dinadán's advice, the lovers make both kings believe that their relationship is chaste and they return to Cornwall with Mares, although Tristán soon comes back. He stays at the court of Arthur, participating in the adventures that arise there, such as that of the Ancient Knight or the reception of Galahad to the Round Table and the beginning of the quest for the Grail. Finally he decides to return to Cornwall, and after six months there, having fallen asleep in the queen's bed, King Mares, alerted by Aldaret, wounds him from a garret with a poisoned lance. His death is a prolonged one, and Tristán has time to say goodbye to his friends, the king and Iseo, and to send his arms to the court of Arthur. Tristán dies first and the queen's heart breaks afterwards. Both are buried with great honour. The *Códice de Tristán* adds the story of the war of vengeance undertaken by the knights of the Round Table, Quedín and Gorvalán, and the death of Iseo de las Blancas Manos. *Tristán de Leonís* replaces this ending with a description of the beauty of the three princesses who died for the love of Tristán, among whom Queen Iseo was the most outstanding.

The Castilian Texts in their Iberian Context

To place them in the panorama of medieval literary production in the Iberian Peninsula, the Castilian *Tristán* texts are complemented by various manuscript texts preserved in extremely fragmentary form: namely, a single Galician-Portuguese fragment and three Catalan fragments. These are as follows:

5. The Galician-Portuguese *Livro de Tristán* (Madrid: Archivo Histórico Nacional, Legajo 1762, no. 87), dating from the last third of the XIVth century, is a fragment of two vellum leaves, written in two columns and with coloured initials, from the archive of the Dukes of Osuna. It was edited by Serrano y Sanz (1928: 307–14), who also gave a codicological description of it; and also, in the more careful form of a palaeographic and critical edition together with an introductory study and other annexes, by Pensado Tomé (1962). The text contains episodes that do not figure in any of the Castilian texts nor in the Catalan manuscripts (Cuesta 1994a: 233, 239–46). The account of its textual relationships has been revised subsequently by Michon (1991: 259–68), López Martínez-Morás and Pérez Barcala in the introductory study to the edition of the *Livro de Tristán* (Lorenzo and Souto 2001: 73–84, 87–103), Lorenzo and Díaz Martínez (2004: 371–96) and Soriano (2006). The manuscript was rediscovered in 2012 after

being mislaid for twenty years; in the bibliography by Mérida (2010: 301) it is still listed as lost.
6. The *Tristany* of the manuscript of the Ayuntamiento of Cervera (MS B-343 of the Arxiu Comarcal de Segarra), currently lost: four folios dating from the end of the XIVth century in Catalan. The text was edited by Duràn (1917).
7. The *Tristany* of MS 1 of the Arxiu de les Set Claus, Andorra: four folios in Catalan dating from the second half of the XIVth century, first reported by Bohigas in his review of Northup's edition (1929), but edited much later by Aramon (1969: 323–37). The miscellaneous codex in which they are contained has been described by Santanach (2003: 434–5).
8. The *Tristany* of Biblioteca de Catalunya MS 8.999/1, consisting of two bifolia, which preserve two fragments of a single codex in Catalan, and contain two non-consecutive sections of the narrative. The bifolia were donated to the Biblioteca de Catalunya in July 2008 by Eulàlia Duràn together with the papers of her father (the editor of the Cervera *Tristany*), which included an incomplete draft of the transcription of the text, for which reason it is possible that they may have been found in the archive at Cervera. Santanach, who reported their existence (2010), has announced that he is preparing an edition.[3]

Following the publication of the article by Lida de Malkiel in *ALMA* (1959 and reprints), the Iberian texts relating to *Tristán* suffered a long period of critical neglect. In recent years some works have appeared on the Iberian *Tristán* material as a whole, arising from doctoral theses on the subject: in 1994 the present author published part of her 1993 thesis, and Ros Domingo (2001) advances beyond his thesis of 1995. The doctoral theses of Iragui (1995) and Soriano (2000) are unpublished at the time of writing. The remaining treatments of the Peninsular *Tristan* texts have a partial perspective in so far as they refer to a single text, as is the case of Soriano (2006) on the Galician-Portuguese fragment, or to specific aspects of the material, as with Campos García Rojas's work on geography and the development of the hero in the Castilian printed editions (2002). Subsequently, various articles have appeared which give overall accounts of the current state of knowledge on the Iberian *Tristan* texts: Alvar (2001, reprinted 2010; and on the Peninsular Matter of Britain material in general, 2008), Beltrán (1996), Capra (2003), Faccon (1996), Lucía Megías (1998b), Gómez Redondo (1999: II, 1505–40) and Orazi (2006: 130–42). Nonetheless, at present all these studies require revision since the discovery of new texts can alter, to a greater or a lesser extent, the existing view of the relations among the various texts.

The Castilian Texts in the Medieval European Tradition

The Iberian *Tristan* texts arise within a lengthy and extensive literary tradition: extensive because of the number of versions, lengthy by virtue of its antiquity, which goes back to the XIIth century in its written form, but which has its roots in Celtic oral literature (Cuesta 1991, 1994b). The legend of Tristan was taken up by the authors of the *roman courtois* in French, German and other languages (Icelandic, Danish ...), remembered by the troubadours in their compositions and finally decanted into an extensive romance in prose, intimately connected to the Arthurian *Vulgate* and the *Roman du Graal* or *Post-Vulgate*: the *Roman de Tristán en prose*.[4] In this form it circulated in the Iberian, Italian, English, German and Slavonic domains.

The French prose work dates from before 1240, although it was remodelled on successive occasions, undergoing various alterations and giving rise to an enormous quantity and confusing tangle of manuscripts relating to different versions. Soriano (2006: 112–29) brings together in her list more than ninety manuscripts.

Baumgartner (1975: 50–2) considers that none of the extant texts preserves the original version, and reasserts the traditional division of the manuscripts into two great families, agreeing in this with Vinaver (1959 and reprints: 339–47) and Löseth (1891, rept 1974), who carried out an exhaustive analysis of the manuscripts of the work known at that time, which is still indispensable today. The divisions are:

–The so-called first version, or the short version, represented by MSS fr. 756 and 757 of the Bibliothèque Nationale de France, Paris (BNF), more faithful to the original, and labelled V.I. by Baumgartner, since he considered it earlier than the long version;
–The so-called second version, or long version (V.II), of which there exist thirty-nine manuscripts, which sometimes develops the text of the original, and at others abbreviates it. This version V.II is, for Ménard (1987: 9–18), the principal text of the work, and because it is the most widely-diffused is generally referred to as the 'Vulgate' of the *Tristan en prose*. Among the manuscripts that contain the full text are, for example, BNF MSS fr. 335–6 (*olim* 6970 and 6957), and MS 2542 of the Österreichische Nationalbibliothek, Vienna (ÖNB), which was used as the base manuscript in the edition by Ménard.

Both versions follow the same text of *Tristan*, but divergences begin from paragraph 183 of the analysis by Löseth (MS BNF fr. 757, which has been edited as representative of V.I, begins with paragraph 184), and both are, in any case, later than 1240, since they add interpolations from the Arthurian cycle of Pseudo-Robert de Boron and particularly from the *Queste* (Baumgartner 1975: 53–62). Some episodes of V.I lacking from V.II belong, according to Baumgartner's theory, to the original form of the romance, while according to the theory of Curtis they were incorporated later into V.I (that is to say, V.I would exhibit some more modern traits). Leonardi (1997: 217) considers Baumgartner's theory more probable.

Baumgartner studies separately a series of texts, created later than those belonging to V.I and V.II, characterised by being either mixed versions of these two with a section interpolated from the *Lancelot en prose* (texts which he classes as belonging to a version III, represented by MSS BNF fr. 97 and 100–1), or else amplified versions which combined these three versions with long interpolations from various sources well into the XIVth century (V.IV, represented by BNF MS fr. 99). He likewise treats separately some manuscripts which contain unique texts, with their own particular characteristics. Among the latter there stands out BNF MS 103, derived from V.IV, but which incorporates material from the XIIth-century poems, which makes it appear, wrongly, to be a very ancient representative of the work (Baumgartner 1975: 86–7).

But as Punzi points out (2005: 152–4), in reviewing the French manuscript tradition, it must be borne in mind that the surviving manuscripts represent four different types of products: those which present a complete version; those containing only one part (which shows that the manuscript tradition circulated in multi-volume copies), the first of which ends at paragraph 171 of the analysis by Löseth; those which select a particularly significant episode; and those which are the work of a compiler who intervenes to reconstitute and rejuvenate the text. This complicates enormously the process of comparing manuscripts and renders it more difficult to establish clear conclusions.

Compared with the *Tristan en prose*, the Castilian adaptations display features associated with V.I, and are characterised by maintaining a biographical structure, suppressing the account of the remote ancestors of Tristan. Regarding the final episode recounting the vengeance for the death of Tristan, which appears in very few manuscripts of the *Tristan en prose*, the discovery of the fifty-nine fragments of the *Códice de Tristán* edited by Alvar and Lucía has allowed us to correct the assumption that the Castilian *Tristan* texts lacked this material. Although it is absent from the later printed *Tristán* texts, it certainly was present in the *Códice de Tristán*, and could have been in the lost section of the *Cuento de Tristán* and the Catalan fragments. *Tristán el Joven* offers a reworking of the same theme, which could indicate that its author knew a version of the work in which this material was present (Cuesta 2009c). Nor do the Castilian texts contain the journey of Mark to Logres and his adventures (and misadventures) there, which do figure in V.II and did so in a reduced form in V.I, the 'short version' of the *Tristan en prose*. This indicates that its source could be either an abbreviated version of V.I, or a text which predated the addition of this material to the *Tristan en prose*.

If the Castilian *Tristan* texts are compared with the analysis of the *Tristan en prose* by Löseth (1891, rpt 1974), the following correspondences emerge:

–*Cuento de Tristán*: 24–44, 47, 49, 48, 45–6, 51–6, ?59, 71a–75a, passages without any equivalent in Löseth (Adventure of the *Paso de Tintayol*, adventure of the Horn, journey to the Joyosa Garda), 344, 355–354 (narrative inverted), arrival of Brangen (Brangel in the printed editions) at the Joyosa Garda, 376, 378 and 380 (Northup 1928: 17–18). Like the *Cuento*, the Catalan manuscript of Andorra and

the Castilian printed editions of the XVIth century take up only the beginning of Löseth's paragraph 57, a somewhat modified part of 59, and the end of 60.
—*Códice de Tristán*, MS 20262–19, edited by Bonilla (1904: 622).
—*Códice de Tristán*, MS 22644: 30–1, 41–4, 74a, adventure of the horn, 380 (conversation between Arthur and the lovers in their tent after a tournament) and proclamation of the tournament of Vercepó and agreement between the lovers and King Mares through the intervention of Arthur and the astuteness of Dinadán, 251, 252a, 196, 200, 202–3, 623, 108, 205–6, 621–2, 626, 547–50, distant parallels with 574–613 corresponding to the episode of vengeance, and the death of Iseo de las Blancas Manos.
—*Tristán de Leonís* (and therefore also that part of *Tristán el Joven* that reproduces it): 19–44, 47–9, 51–8, 60, 63, 71a, 72a, 73a, 74a, 75a, 363–5, 122, 376, 380, 251, 252a, 196, 200, 202–3, 623, 108, 205–6, 621–4, 445, 509, 392a, 395, 448, 626, 546–50 (Bonilla 1912: p. li).
—*Tristán el Joven* adds an original episode on the theme of vengeance for the deaths of the lovers, which has remote parallels with 574–613.
—The Galician-Portuguese *Livro de Tristan*: 68, 73, 75–93.
—The Cervera Catalan MS: 20–2.
—The Andorra Catalan MS: 56–7, 59–60, and 71a.
—The Biblioteca de Catalunya Catalan MS: 22–7 and 34–8.

It must be remembered that in Löseth's analysis paragraphs 1–619 belong to the *Tristan en prose*, but 620–43 summarise the *Compilation* or *Roman de Roi Artus*, written around 1272 in French by the Italian Rustichello da Pisa at the behest of Edward I of England while he was present at Acre together with his Queen Eleanor of Castile, in the context of the Eighth Crusade (Cigni 1994: 9). It would not be at all strange, then, if subsequently Eleanor possessed, and passed to her Spanish family (the royal house of Castile), a copy of the work of Rustichello. So, MS 20262–19 of the *Códice*, which recounts the adventures of the Ancient Knight, corresponds to the *Compilation*; it is the only work which relates this episode apart from the medieval Greek poem (dated between the end of the XIIIth century and the second quarter of the XVth) found only in the copy in Vatican Library MS Vat. Graec. 1822 (fols 200–5), of Cypriot origin (ed. Bonilla 1912: 301 n. 1; Cigni 1994: 367 col. c), the *Tristan Veneto* (which is here following the *Compilation*) and *Tristán de Leonís* and *Tristán el Joven*. The Ancient Knight is also the protagonist in four of the mural paintings at the castle of San Floret in Alvernia, built at the end of the XIIIth century, related to the adventures recounted by Rustichello (Cigni 1994: 368).

Faced with the complexity of the transmission of the *Tristan en prose*, in the case of the Castilian versions it is at present impossible to establish which specific manuscripts were used by the translators. None of the known French or Italian manuscripts could be the source of the Castilian *Tristán* texts. Nor is it possible to discount the possibility that the translators could in some cases have become co-authors of the texts, modifying these at will. The Castilian versions are different from one another; coincide closely with the brief Catalan fragments; are markedly original when compared to the various French versions edited by Curtis (1963, 1976, 1985 rpt 1985–6) (which contain the beginning of the work) and by Ménard (1987–97 for V.II, and 1997–2007 for V.I), or summarised by Löseth (1891 rpt 1974); and exhibit occasional points of similarity with the Italian versions, whilst on other occasions they diverge from them. In some episodes, they apparently coincide with the English version of Malory, according to Rumble (1969: 122–44) and Kennedy (1970: 6–10); Sharrer (1979b) takes up this theory, but dissent from it is expressed by Iragui (thesis 1995: 269–74) and Soriano (2001: 319 n. 2, and 1999b), with the latter pointing out that Malory's version is a form of Version II, while the Castilian texts follow V.I.

This textual panorama proves the existence of an idiosyncratic or anomalous version of the *Tristan en prose*, closer to V.I than to V.II, the definition, dating and characteristics of which have, however, been the subject of much debate and doubt, but the essential character of which would be its biographical emphasis and, consequently, the absence of a good part of the episodes in which Tristan does not appear (that is to say, it gives the appearance of an abbreviation or reduction of V.I). This specific, idiosyncratic version, sometimes called 'condensed', 'abbreviated', 'reduced' or 'anomalous',[5] the existence of which is beyond doubt, has been proposed as the common origin of the so-called Hispano-Italian family; this is a peripheral (Cuesta 1993a: 246–52; 1993c) or southern (Iragui 1996) grouping to which some (but not all) the Italian and Iberian *Tristan* texts belong.

In the light of the information obtained from the Italian texts, this special version (Y, in the designation of Entwistle and Ros Domingo, R in that of Delcorno Branca) apparently transmits, however, only a section of the first part of the *Tristan en prose*, corresponding to paragraphs 19–75a of the analysis by Löseth. Since the *Compilation* of Rustichello influenced some of the Italian texts, there is a problem in seeking to establish whether the agreement between these and the Castilian texts in the second part of the work is due to both traditions sharing this source, as Bonilla held (ed. 1912: xliv–lxi), or whether the material from the *Compilation* reached the Castilian texts through its prior incorporation into a *Tristan* 'X' in French, as Entwistle thought (1925 rpt 1975: 102–29, especially 118–20), or in Italian (Northup 1912: 216).

The source of the Hispano-Italian family is characterised by its lacking two important sections of the *Tristan en prose*: the long prologue relating to the history of the ancestors of Tristan and the adventures of the 'Pays du Servage' and the 'Valet à la Cote mal taillée' and the 'Demoiselle Mesdisant' (paragraphs 1–18 and 59–71 of Löseth).

While the existence of this distinctive version is not in question, the argument over the language of the redaction of it which reached the Iberian Peninsula has been intense. The first to defend the Italian origin of the Castilian versions then known was

Northup (1912: 194–222; 1913: 259–65; at greater length, 1928: 1–78). His various arguments are, according to Sharrer (1979b: 39), based on incomplete knowledge of the transmission of the French work from Löseth's analysis of the texts in what was then the British Museum Library and the BNF, besides his ignorance of the existence of the Catalan manuscript of Cervera published by Duràn i Sempere in 1917. Nor, obviously, could he take into account the Iberian and Italian *Tristan* texts published or discovered subsequently, a problem which also affects the work of Bohigas (1929: 284–9), who assumed a Catalan intermediary between the Italian version and the Castilian. The theory of an Italian origin was opposed by Bonilla (1912: xliv–lxi) and Entwistle (1925, rpt 1975: 102–9, esp. 118–20) who, still without knowing of the existence of the Galician-Portuguese fragment, defended the descent of the Iberian and Italian texts from an anomalous *Tristan en prose* with different characteristics. For Bonilla, this latter was linked to the *Compilation* of Rustichello, and for Entwistle it would have been its source. Alonso (1947: 189–204, esp. 201) did not believe in the existence of Italianisms in the Castilian texts and maintained that some expressions considered to be such by Northup (for example, *Joyosa, Guiosa* or Giosa, from the French *Joyeuse*) were already found in other earlier Castilian texts and could be explained equally on the basis of Gallicism. For her part, Scudieri Ruggieri (1966: 238–46) proposed, with little success, an Aragonese adaptation of the French *Tristan* as the source of the Castilian and Italian texts. Delcorno Branca (1980: 229) proposed the existence of a French *Tristan* of V.I which met with special favour in Italy and Iberia. More recently, this position has been defended by the present author (1993a: 198–263; 1993c: 65–75; 1994a: 233–71), who excludes from this Hispano-Italian group the Galician-Portuguese fragment (a position on which all the later studies agree), and hypothesises the existence of an early text of V.I of the *Tristan en prose*, that would have been preserved in the zone of Provençal influence from the period in which these first versions appeared, and circulated in the peripheral region of Iberia and Italy, while in the meantime in the north of France ever more elaborate and amplified manuscripts continued to appear. Together with the *Compilation*, this anomalous *Tristan* would have influenced the Italian, Castilian and Catalan *Tristan* texts.

In support of this possibility there may now be cited a fragment of a text of V.I of the French *Tristan en prose*, copied on the blank leaves of a XIIIth-century manuscript containing various Latin works on astronomical and mathematical subjects, the marginal notes in which make use of a Castilian containing Catalanisms (Leonardi 1996: 9–24). The possibility is also favoured by the opinion of Heijkant, who confirms the earlier view of Parodi, according to which the Italian *Tristano Riccardiano* represents an early redaction of the work (Punzi 2005: 159). The same theory is supported by Soriano (1999b, 2001; 2003a; unpublished thesis 2000: 116–18, 172–212), and Alvar (2001: 73; 2008: 36), although they add the hypothesis that this anomalous *Tristan en prose* would have been copied in Italy. Ros Domingo (2001:

258), in a work that is an expansion of his doctoral thesis of 1995, separates the Italian family from its Iberian relatives at the level of the anomalous version of the French *Tristan en prose* and assigns to the Iberian branch a Gallo-Romance source with occasional Germanic traits, which would have contained all the features which differentiate the Iberian texts from the Italian ones. However, Iragui (1996: 39–54), summarising his doctoral thesis of 1995 and without knowing of either the publications of Cuesta on the Iberian *Tristan* texts or (naturally) of the later work of Delcorno Branca (1998a, b) on the Italian texts, takes up anew the theory of Northup to defend as the common source of the Hispano-Italian family, which may be termed the southern European or (in the terminology of some scholars) 'Meridional' version (M), a lost manuscript which was at one and the same time the source of the M family, consisting of the French manuscripts copied in Italy in a Genoese scriptorium around 1300, and of a lost manuscript of this family, already in Italian, which would have reached the Iberian Peninsula.[6] Iragui's principal contributions consist of identifying the Italian texts that belong to this family (Iragui 1996: 39–40) and the division into two volumes of the manuscript of the hypothetical archetype of the M family.[7] The second of these volumes would not have influenced the surviving Italian texts (hence the absence of any distinction in his work between those of V.I and those of V.II, since there is no clear difference between these in the passages of the first part), but is preserved partially in MS BNF 760 (the adventures associated with the journey to the tournament at Louveserp and the end of the story) and BNF 1463 (an extract from the *Compilation* and the end of the story). The theory of the transmission of the story in two volumes is based on the fact that MSS fr. 760 and 1463 (the latter containing the oldest manuscript fragment of the *Compilation*) contain only this second part and give no sign of having a deficient beginning, from which he concludes that they were conceived as the second volume of a pair (Iragui 1996: 51). This second volume of the work would have begun after Löseth's paragraph 75a, with the return of Tristan to Cornwall after his marriage to Iseo de las Blancas Manos and his rescue of Arthur. Hence the adventures of the Ancient Knight would have featured in this second volume which does not survive in the Italian descendants, like the adventure of the Paso de Tintoíl, an episode found exclusively in the Castilian texts. However, it is difficult to believe in the dependence of the Castilian and Catalan texts on one written in Italian when there appear in the Castilian texts episodes and details that are not found in the surviving texts written in Italian dialects. It seems, rather, that the second part of what Iragui calls the M Family, or its source, circulated hardly at all in Italy but did circulate in the Iberian Peninsula.

Subsequently, Alvar (2001: 73) and Soriano (2001: 332) pointed towards what Curtis identified as the α family of the *Tristan en prose*, which coincides in part with that designated the M Family by Iragui (1996: 41–2), to which belong the incomplete manuscripts National Library of Wales, Aberystwyth, MS 446E (denoted W) and M (Modena), as being the most probable as the source of the Hispano-Italian version, in combination with the work of Rustichello. Both they and Ros Domingo (2001, ch. II) base themselves on the research of Delcorno Branca (1998b: 49–79) into French manuscripts of Italian origin of the end of the XIIIth century and the beginning of the XIVth produced at a scriptorium in Genoa in which there worked Pisan prisoners taken at the battle of Meloria (1284), and among the products of which there were found MSS W, M and BNF fr. 1463 which contains the *Compilation* of Rustichello.

Heijkant (2004: 388–9) points out some curious similarities within the Hispano-Italian group: all the texts of this group lack the episode of the repeated encounter of Lamorat and Gauvain (Löseth's paragraph 72a), and in all of them the martyrdom of Joseph of Arimathea on the Isla del Gigante is recounted. An important difference between the Iberian texts and the Italian ones is found in the negative and criminal character given to Palomades in the former.

Some passages in which the similarities between Italian and Spanish texts are particularly important have attracted special attention in recent years, and it is necessary to point out that not all of these are in the first part of the work. To some extent this casts doubt upon the theory of Heijkant (2004: 385) that Northup and Parodi were correct to argue that the anomalous *Tristan* contained only the first part of the work up to Löseth's paragraph 75a (an assertion brought into question also by the presence of the adventures on the way to the tournament of Louveserp in MS BNF fr 760 noted by Iragui), and that this second section, probably in another volume, left no trace in Italy. These passages are five, as follows:

1. Tristan's stepmother's attempts at poisoning, studied by Soriano (2001). In both *Tristán de Leonís* and the Cervera MS, and presumably also in the Catalan and Castilian MSS in which the episode does not now survive, her first and second attempts to poison Tristan occur in inverse order to their appearances in the French and Italian *Tristan* texts. Soriano (2001) compares the first attempted poisoning in the Hispanic texts with the version of the second poisoning in the Italian *Tristano Riccardiano* and in another Italian text, the *Zibaldone da Canal*, a mercantile manuscript from Venice dated around 1290–1300, which contains a brief fragment of the *Tristan en prose* concerned with the infancy of the hero, the language of which betrays an original source in French. Only in the *Zibaldone*, *Tristán de Leonís*, and in the Catalan fragment of Cervera is there the added element of the involvement of an animal (a dog in the Catalan and the Castilian), which dies from drinking the poisoned wine (Soriano 2001: 328). As far as concerns his stepmother's third attempt to poison Tristan, after the funeral of King Meliadux, it is found in *Tristán de Leonís*, though it is not preserved in the extant part of the Castilian manuscripts, which begin with later episodes, while the Catalan MS from Cervera is cut short before this. It is necessary to observe that this passage is at the beginning of the work, and that the third attempted poisoning features in the *Tristano Riccardiano*. On the one hand, the inversion of

the order shows the unity of the Iberian versions compared to the French and Italian witnesses, and, on the other, the third attempt at poisoning and the presence of the animal prove the existence of connections between some of the Castilian *Tristán* texts and some of their Italian counterparts.

The discovery of the Catalan MS in the Biblioteca de Catalunya allows us to appreciate now that in this fragmentary witness there are also three poisonings; that their order is the same as in *Tristán de Leonís* and in the Catalan MS of Cervera; and that, just as in these, in the first attempt one of the king's dogs is involved. Also, the *Panciatichiano* (ed. Allaire 2002: 138–40) presents the third attempt at poisoning.

2. The genealogy and adventures of the Ancient Knight, studied by Cuesta (2008b). The adventures surrounding this character which are included in the *Códice de Tristán* and *Tristán de Leonís* (and therefore also in the first part of *Tristán el Joven*) are not found in the French *Tristan en prose*, but are present in the *Compilation* of Rustichello da Pisa and in the *Tristano Veneto* (the character is mentioned in *Palomèdes* and in the *Tavola Ritonda* (ed. Heijkant 1997: 433, 452), but in these works he takes part in very different episodes. One of the adventures of this knight and his genealogy are summarised in Rodríguez de Montalvo's *Amadís de Gaula*, which demonstrates its popularity in the Castilian context. The episode could have been found also in the *Cuento de Tristán* in the Vatican MS and perhaps in the Catalan *Tristan* texts, but their fragmentary state prevents our proving that this was the case. The *Compilation* and the *Tristano Veneto*, the manuscript of which here copies the *Compilation* (*Tristano Veneto*, ed. Donatello, 1994: 19–24), differ from *Tristán de Leonís* in some details of the Ancient Knight's genealogy and in adding his joust with Lancelot and with all the vassal kings of Arthur. Here, the similarities between the *Tristano Veneto* and *Tristán de Leonís* are no doubt caused by the influence of the *Compilation*. The *Tavola Ritonda* also takes up material from the *Compilation*, although it does not do so in this specific episode.

3. The mortal wound of Tristan (Cuesta 2009b: 510). The episode belongs to the lost section of the Castilian manuscripts. *Tristán de Leonís* shows itself to be significantly independent of other versions of the episode and it is not possible to establish anything more than a remote association with the Italian family, which is very interesting nonetheless since it occurs in the final part of the work. It is interesting, moreover, that the feature that associates it with the Italian texts (the weapon used is a lance, instead of a sword) is absent from the *Compilation* of Rustichello, so that it must have reached both the Italian texts (*Tristano Panciatichiano*, *Tristano Veneto*, *Tavola Ritonda*, and the *cantare* entitled *La morte di Tristano*) and *Tristán de Leonís* and the *Romance de Tristán* by way of another intermediary text. Moreover, the *Tavola Ritonda* – a *summa* of the Arthurian cycle written in Tuscan dialect and dated to the second

quarter of the XIVth century that brings together the adventures of Lancelot and those of Tristan, preferring the latter as an exemplar of chivalry – together with the *cantare* agrees with *Tristán de Leonís* and the *Romance de Tristán* in showing King Mark/Mares wounding the protagonist from outside the room, while the *Tavola* is even closer since it includes a supernatural premonition of the fatal wound. However, these coincidences between two texts so distant in other respects seem to be the result of independent elaboration of elements present in a common source.

4. The death of the lovers and the description of their tomb (Cuesta 2010, 2014a). For the present author, the text of *Tristán de Leonís* is aligned with that of the *Tavola Ritonda* by the fact that the lovers' deaths are not simultaneous; by the circumstances of them, avoiding any hint of murder or suicide; and by the incorporation of religious elements such as the final confession and prayer. However, differences in expression and intention could not be greater, since while the *Tavola* attempts to glorify the protagonists' love, the Castilian text focuses on prompting a moralising reading of the episode, presenting a Tristan who turns his eyes towards God and eternity. This moralisation agrees with the apparent fear of offending God exhibited by the author in the epilogue of the 1501 edition, which differs in this respect from the epilogue of *Oliveros de Castilla*, which he plagiarises. Although the religious elements could be owed to additions carried out independently by the authors of *Tristán de Leonís* and the *Tavola Ritonda*, these could have been inspired by some references of this type present in a common source. Contreras (2010) indicates the elements typical of the ritual for the death of kings which are visible in the Castilian episode, giving it a more realist aspect.

Heijkant (2004: 389) indicates various correspondences between one of the Italian *Tristan* texts and *Tristán de Leonís* in the episode of the death of the lovers: Iseo sings; the lovers are lying down when surprised; the doctors cannot cure Tristan; Iseo is led by the knights close to the dying man and faints twice; Tristan dies in a Christian manner in the presence of an archbishop; Iseo does not die because of Tristan's embrace; her beauty is explicitly mentioned. The majority of the similarities are in the *Tavola Ritonda*, although Iseo's singing and the reference to her beauty are found in the *Panciatichiano*.

5. The war of vengeance for the death of Tristan and the punishment of Mares/Mark and Aldaret/Andret (Alvar 2001: 57–75, especially p. 73; Soriano 2003a: 203–17; Cuesta 2009a; 2009c). The episode, absent from the majority of the manuscripts of the *Tristan en prose*, is taken up with significant differences in the *Códice de Tristán*, *Tristán el Joven* (in both, Quedin and Gorvalan take part in the war of vengeance, with their host, and Lancelot with other knights of the Round Table; King Mares is pardoned; and Aldaret is punished), in MS BNF 24400 of the *Tristan en prose* (Dinadan undertakes the task of raising the people of Leonís

against their king alone; the war is unleashed, directed by Dinadan and Dinas; and Mark is pardoned: Löseth 1891 rpt 1974: 405–22), in the *Tavola Ritonda* (the war is undertaken by the combined armies of King Amoroldo de Irlanda, King Governal of Leonís and King Arthur; Andret dies at the orders of King Mark who is captured and dies of obesity fed by Lanzarote and Amoroldo), and in the *Tristano Veneto* and the *Cantare della Vendetta di Tristano* (in which the principal role is assumed by Lancelot, and Mark dies in the battle; in the *Cantare* Andret also dies in the battle at the beginning of the war). It is my view that, as far as concerns the episode of the vengeance, it does not seem that the proximity of the Castilian text to the *Tristano Veneto* or the *Cantare* is any greater than that which it has to the *Tavola Ritonda*, against what Alvar and Soriano had supposed. I consider that a good part of the content of the episode of vengeance is hinted at in previous passages in the work which are indeed found in the *Tristan en prose*, so that they could have been developed in a specific manuscript, the common source of the Italian and Castilian versions, and amplified in different ways by each of the latter.

A closer proximity between the *Cuento de Tristán*, *Tristán de Leonís*, and the *Tavola Ritonda* is also encountered during the sojourn of the lovers at the Joyeuse Garde (Alegre Guardia, Giosa Guardia): in both texts the residence there of Lancelot and Guinevere is mentioned, which ends in the reconciliation of Guinevere with Arthur.

The fact that in different episodes the Castilian *Tristan* texts coincide more closely with different extant Italian texts indicates, beyond doubt, that they do not derive from any one of them. It also seems very doubtful to suppose that they derive from another lost text in Italian which would have included all the similarities that are scattered through the surviving Italian texts, which are not encountered solely in the first part of the work. Besides, as Punzi recalls (2005: 160), French was not a foreign language in Italy at that time, but was the language of culture, so that a codex produced in Italy would not necessarily have to be one in Italian. The theory proposed by the present author, of the existence of an anomalous text of V.I of the French *Tristan en prose*, circulating in Italy and Spain and copied in Italy, seems to Soriano (1999b: 424) the best-suited also to the reality represented by the Catalan fragments, and Santanach (2010: 26) inclines towards that possibility. In the MS from which the Iberian texts (other than the Galician-Portuguese) originate, or perhaps only in the branch that would give rise to the *Códice de Tristán* and *Tristán de Leonís*, the work of Rustichello would already have been juxtaposed with the anomalous *Tristan* thus producing some of the traits shared with the *Tristano Veneto*.

Studies relating to the readership and possession of *Tristan* texts in the Peninsula, although there are still not enough of them (Cingolani 1990–1; Ferrer Gimeno 2011; Ramos 2006), have begun to shed some light upon this matter. Cingolani finds references to eight copies of *Tristan* texts in Catalan inventories of the XIVth and

XVth century, which reveals its popularity among the bourgeoisie; Ferrer Gimeno (2011) studies the libraries of Valencia between 1416 and 1474, finding a single copy among the possessions of a merchant who had an extremely active commercial relationship with Italy; Ramos (2006: 93) finds a *Libre de Tristany* in the inventory of a merchant drawn up in 1458 in the notarial office at Sant Feliu de Guixols. Soriano (1999b: 423–4) considers the Italian *Tristan* texts that could have circulated in the Peninsula but about which we have no information, while there are documentary references to more than twenty *Tristan* texts in French, and the testimony of *Curial y Güelfa* (1982: 120) speaks of the Catalans who translated the books of Tristan and Lancelot, from French.

In order to reach more precise conclusions about the origin of the extant Castilian and Catalan texts and also in order to know if the anomalous redaction of paragraphs 19–75a of Löseth continued further and reached as far as some episodes of the second part of the work, it is still necessary to collate the Iberian texts with the French MSS of the V.I family, copied in Italy, possibly at the Pisan-Genoese scriptorium. This workshop had specialised in copying and decorating Arthurian texts, and it seems that in it there were produced eight copies of the *Tristan en prose* towards the end of the XIIIth century (Delcorno Branca 1980: 211–29; Bertolucci Pizzorusso 2003). It is also necessary to undertake a similar collation with the third, fifth and sixth parts of the *Tristano Panciatichiano*, a text which was not published until 2002 (ed. Allaire); it follows, in its third part, a redaction similar to that of the *Riccardiano*, while for the rest of the text it uses BNF MS fr. 757, belonging to V.I, but not to the α family of Curtis or the Pisan-Genoese MS group (ed. Allaire 2002: 6–7).

Even more urgent, however, is a new examination of the question of the relationships among the Hispanic texts themselves, and between these and the Italian and French witnesses. This study should take into account, on the one hand, the French and Italian texts not studied by Cuesta, Soriano, Iragui and Ros Domingo in their general studies of the Iberian *Tristan* texts because at the time in question there were no easily accessible editions of these, and, on the other, the new Iberian witnesses discovered after those theories were formulated. The discovery of new fragments of the *Códice de Tristán* published in 1999 came later than the studies of the present author (1993a, 1993b, 1994a), and Iragui (1995, 1996); although Ros Domingo (2001: 16 n.5) cites the edition by Alvar and Lucía Megías, he does not take the text into account in his analysis, probably because he learned of this publication when his work was already completed. The later studies which do take the *Códice* into account for a comparative analysis involving other European witnesses relate to specific episodes, as has been seen. As long as the Catalan fragments recently discovered and reported by Santanach i Suñol (2003: 434–5), who describes and studies them (2010: 21–38), remain unpublished, they cannot be compared with the remaining witnesses except in the most general way. It is essential to have, first and foremost, a reliable palaeographic transcription of the *Tristany* of the Biblioteca de Catalunya.

In any case, the existing studies show that the Castilian and Catalan *Tristan* texts form a sub-family in relation to the Italian texts, in so far as they contain episodes found only in this group, readings unique to this group, and the same sequence of episodes when compared to the remaining texts.

Fig. IX.1: Relations of the Italian *Tristan* Texts and Those of the Iberian Peninsula

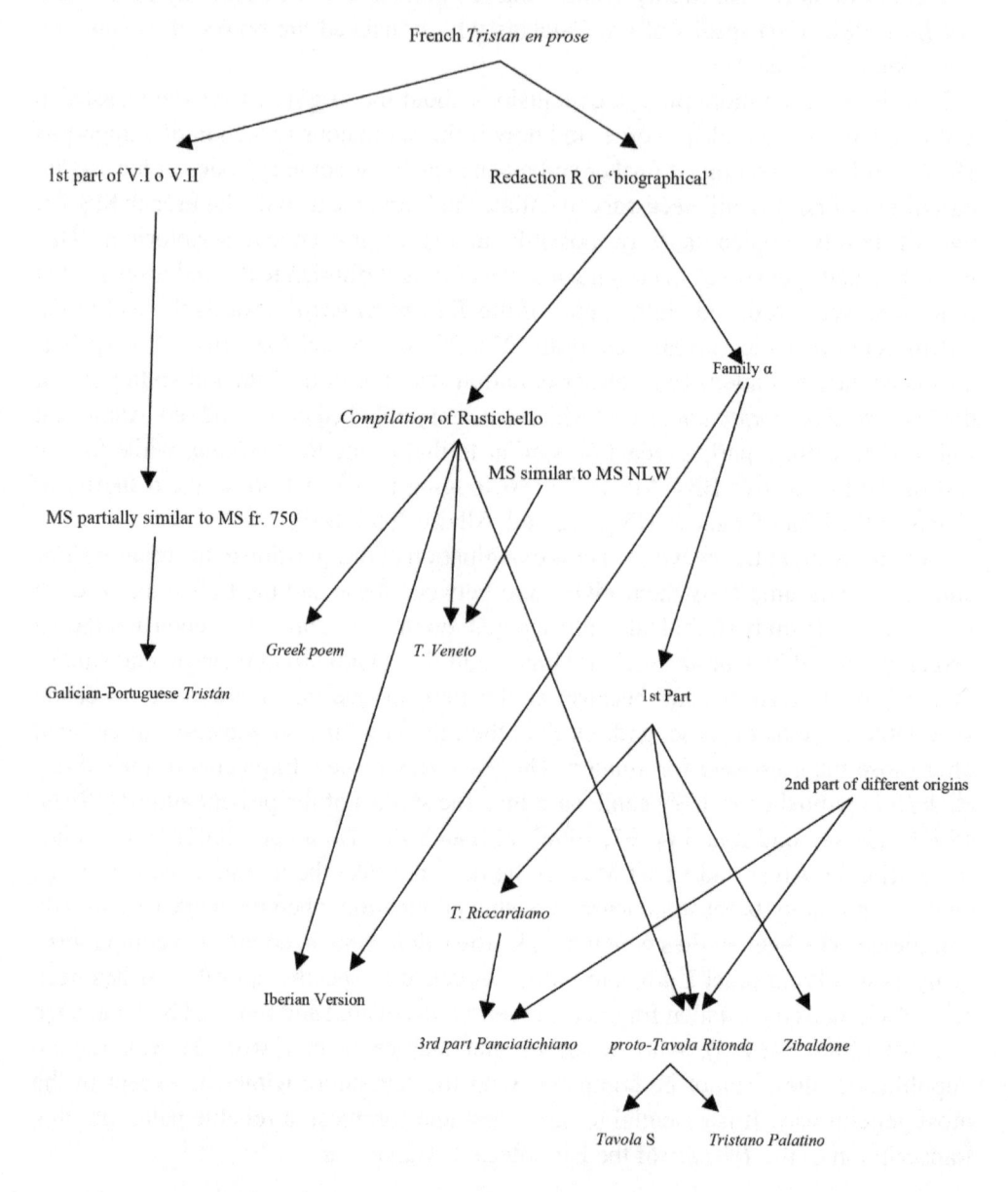

Relations among the MSS from the Iberian Peninsula

As far as concerns the relationships among the Iberian texts themselves, it may be observed that whilst the extant Catalan texts, albeit very fragmentary, coincide to a great extent with the Castilian texts, as will be seen below, the rather longer Galician-Portuguese fragment follows fairly closely a version similar to that offered by the French *Tristan en prose* of BNF MS fr 750 (Soriano 2006: 62). It cannot, however, be determined whether it belongs to V.I or V.II since it preserves passages belonging to the first part of the work, but using a source which does not coincide with any of the French manuscripts, according to Michon (1991: 266). This source in any case cannot have been the biographical or anomalous version, since it contains episodes and characters not found in the Catalan and Castilian *Tristan* texts, both manuscript and printed, and it is clearly separated from the other witnesses from the Iberian Peninsula (Cuesta 1993a: 226–34; 1993b: 91; 1994a: 239–45, 264; Soriano 2006 especially 51; Iragui 1995: 164–67; Ros Domingo 2001: 259–71). It can be stated, therefore, that there existed two lines of textual transmission of the legend of Tristan in the Peninsula: the Galician-Portuguese line, and that involving the remaining manuscripts. This latter textual family can be described as the central-eastern Iberian version because of its geographical location within the Peninsula. Given the fragmentary character of its manuscript texts, the basic traits of this version can be known from the printed *Tristán de Leonís*, once the original features which distinguish this particular edition are excluded.

The existence of these two independent lines renders obsolete, as far as the *Tristan* texts are concerned, the idea of Portuguese priority in the penetration of material relating to this hero into the Peninsula as maintained by Castro (1983). Independently of the date of the arrival of the theme in Galician-Portuguese literature, there was another route of entry for the Castilian and Catalan texts (Cuesta 1994a: 28–31). On the question of this priority, more information can be found in the chapter by Alvar in the present volume. In any case, as Conde de Lindquist reminds us (2006), the possible routes and dates of penetration of Arthurian literature into both regions should be seen as more varied and extensive, including the pilgrimage to Santiago de Compostela and relations with the world of the north.

It is necessary to revise Entwistle's proposal on relations between the Plantagenets and the Castilian Crown (1925 rpt 1975: 29–63) in so far as concerns the arrival in Castile of a particular version of *Tristan*, emphasising the role that could have been played by Edward I of England in the diffusion of the anomalous *Tristan*. This king was the patron of the production of the *Compilation* of Rustichello; was in Italy at a date close to the creation of the Pisan–Genoese workshop; was married to Eleanor (1254), the sister of Alfonso X of Castile, who makes the first references to Tristan by a Castilian author (albeit in poems written in Galician-Portuguese). Edward I visited Burgos in 1254, and received a return visit to London in 1255 from the future King

Sancho IV of Castile, nephew of Eleanor; and moreover the *Tavola* mentions as an authoritative source a book obtained by Piero, Count of Savoy (1203–68) perhaps during a journey to England, and which is 'now' in the possession of the Pisan Gaddo dei Lanfranchi (on whose identification see the 'Introduzione' by Heijkant to the edition of the *Tavola Ritonda*, 1997: 7–8).

As far as concerns the dating of the extant Iberian texts, they are all placed in the second half of the XIVth century, with the exception of the *Códice*, the script of which places it in the XVth century.

The Two Branches of the Central-Eastern Iberian *Tristan*

It is difficult to establish the relationships among the texts of the central-eastern Iberian family given the fragmentary nature of all the manuscripts, particularly those of the Catalan *Tristan* texts. The criteria for distinguishing subgroups must be based on their proximity in linguistic expression, in the order of the episodes, and in minor details of the plot. The present author (1993a: 210–26; 1993b: 83–93; 1994a: 58–9, 138–45) had proposed the separation of the *Cuento de Tristán* from the branch represented by the sole fragment of the *Códice* then known, the Catalan fragments of Cervera and Andorra, and *Tristán de Leonís*, considering that the *Cuento de Tristán* showed itself more independent in its manner of expressing fundamentally similar ideas; that in the brief section it preserves the Cervera manuscript cannot be contrasted with the *Cuento*, but reveals itself rather close to *Tristán de Leonís*; and that the Andorra fragment agrees with *Tristán de Leonís* against the *Cuento*.

Following the discovery of the new fragments of the *Códice de Tristán*, my own studies (1999a: xvi–xix) and those of Rubio Pacho (2001) have independently defended the existence of two branches among the Castilian *Tristan* texts, with the *Cuento* on one side, and on the other the *Códice* and *Tristán de Leonís*, together with the Andorra MS and probably that of Cervera.

Alvar (2001: 74; rpt 2010: 248, 255), in attempting to represent a greater proximity between the *Tristan* from Cervera and the *Códice de Tristán*, excludes from this group in his stemma the Andorra *Tristany*, which he considers to be an independent version within this Catalan-Castilian branch which he designates the 'Hispanic branch'. However, the fragmentary nature of the texts prevents a direct comparison, so that it is necessary to use *Tristán de Leonís* as an intermediary between the Cervera text and the Castilian *Códice*, and also to compare the two Catalan fragments. For this reason the difference becomes purely hypothetical.

Ros Domingo (2001: 258), who does not use the *Códice* for his argument nor include it in his scheme, does not separate the *Cuento* clearly from the Andorra and Cervera Catalan witnesses, nor from the fragments of the *Códice* known at that point (including the one published by Bonilla), but accepts that the *Cuento* uses the

Gallo-Romance source as well as its principal source in Catalan, derived from the former, which he believes they share. He indicates (2001: 163–85) specific passages in which the readings of the Andorra fragment correspond to those of *Tristán de Leonís*, others in which they coincide with the *Cuento*, and yet others in which they do not correspond to any of the Hispanic witnesses. This leads him to propose a stemma in which the Andorra and Cervera fragments and *Tristán de Leonís* descend separately from a single ancestor; the latter could also have influenced the *Cuento*, which would have derived directly from the source of this ancestor.

With regard to the Catalan fragments in the Biblioteca de Catalunya, the only study at present is that of Santanach (2010), who presents a schema of transmission rather different from that of Cuesta and Alvar. Although he divides the Catalan and Castilian witnesses into two branches, he groups in a single family the Catalan fragment of Andorra and the *Códice de Tristán*, from which the Castilian editions of the XVIth century derive, and he places in another family the *Cuento de Tristán* and a lost manuscript which would be the source of the two Catalan fragments in the Biblioteca de Catalunya and the Cervera fragment (Santanach 2010: 36). For this he relies on coincidences between the *Cuento* and the new Catalan manuscript in relation to the order of the episodes narrated and the development of the action (Santanach 2010: 34). That is to say, the Catalan and Castilian manuscripts are not grouped according to their languages, although, as Santanach indicates, the almost complete lack of passages common to all three Catalan witnesses makes the comparison extremely difficult, limiting it to the ending of the Cervera manuscript and the beginning of that of the Biblioteca de Catalunya. It is this brief parallel fragment that allows him to suppose that at this point the *Cuento* would not have presented a version distinct from that of the remaining witnesses in Catalan and Castilian (including the printed editions), indicating that this lack of distinguishing characteristics does not allow the Cervera fragment to be located clearly in either family, so that it may belong to either of them. For Santanach, the branch consisting of the *Códice*, *Tristán de Leonís* and the Andorra manuscript is characterised by presenting more conservative solutions compared to the branch represented by the manuscripts of the Biblioteca de Catalunya and Cervera and the *Cuento de Tristán*, which is much more innovatory (Santanach 2010: 35). Santanach's work constitutes a first approach to the problem and contrasts the Catalan fragments with *Tristán de Leonís*, since he cannot do it directly with the *Códice de Tristán* because no section common to all is preserved, assuming that it offers the same version. But the studies of Cuesta show that the printed text does not always follow the reading offered by the *Códice*. Some differences between the *Tristany* of the Biblioteca de Catalunya and the *Cuento*, on the one hand, and *Tristán de Leonís*, on the other, in the passages where no other witnesses exist, could indicate the existence of interventions by the person responsible for reworking the Castilian printed text, representing readings common to the entire manuscript tradition that were changed in the printed version. This would give the misleading impression of similarity between the Catalan manuscript and the *Cuento*. It is necessary, therefore, to examine the coincidences among the different witnesses, taking into account also the readings of the Italian manuscripts of the Hispano-Italian group.

On the question of the language of the archetype of the central-eastern Iberian branch, the priority of Catalan has been defended by Bohigas (1929: 284–9), Iragui (thesis 1995/6: 275–80), Soriano (1999b: 420) and Ros Domingo (2001: 249–58), with arguments drawn mainly from the study of the language, while Northup (1912: 219) asserted that he had found no traces of Catalanisms in any of the Castilian texts (though he was unable to see the Catalan manuscripts). Cuesta (1993b: 88) indicates that the differences between the *Cuento* and *Tristán de Leonís* indicate the use of a common source in a language other than Castilian, which obliged the translators to adapt the text instead of merely copying it, or are indicative of a high degree of originality and innovation on their part. Alvar (2008: 36) envisages two translations of an anomalous *Tristan* in French originating in an Italian scriptorium: one in Castilian-Aragonese and the other in Catalan or Castilian. Santanach (2010: 36) believes that the common origin of the Catalan and Castilian manuscripts could be a manuscript in either of these two Peninsular languages or in Aragonese, since the evidence is not conclusive. The linguistic studies carried out to date compare the Andorra MS with *Tristán de Leonís*, concluding that this Catalan manuscript has readings closer to the French manuscripts than does the Castilian version, but it remains necessary to carry out a comparison with the MS *Códice de Tristán* since the printed text has been modernised in various respects and some of its quirks may not have been present in its source.

Scudieri Ruggieri for her part believes that the French *Tristan en prose* was altered in an Aragonese translation, which would later have served as the source for the Castilian and Italian texts. Her argument is based on the word 'ploto', which she considers to be a misreading in Castilian of the Aragonese 'ploro' ('weeping', Castilian 'llanto': Scudieri Ruggieri 1966: 241; Cuesta 2008b: 153–4, 167). After the discovery of the fragments of MS 22644 it can be seen that the typographical error was introduced in the printed edition of 1501, from which it was later transmitted to the successive editions of *Tristán de Leonís* and to *Tristán el Joven*, since the *Códice de Tristán* contains the form Castillo del Ploro (ed. Alvar and Lucía 1999: 86).

Characteristics of the Central-Eastern Iberian Version

In the *Cuento de Tristán* (chs 130–41) and in the Castilian printed editions (chs 49–58) there is a series of adventures unique to this tradition, in other words, which are absent from the different versions of the *Tristan en prose* and the Italian *Tristan* texts, and which demonstrate the dependence of the texts of the central-eastern version on a common source. These are: the adventure of the Paso de Tintoíl, found only in the

Fig. 2: *Stemma* of the MSS from the central and eastern Iberian Peninsula

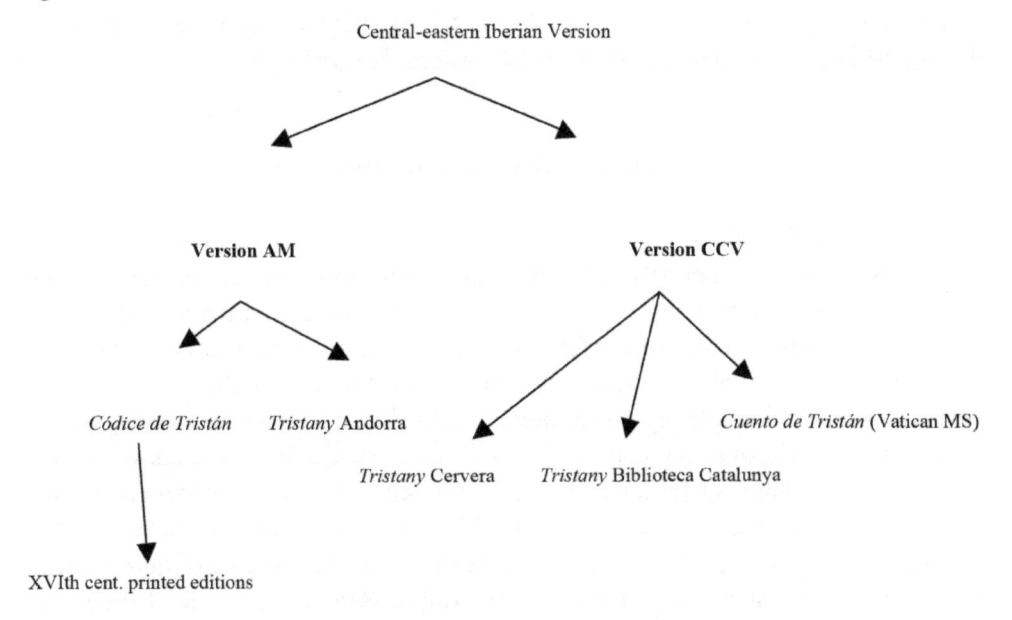

Central-eastern Iberian Version

Version AM **Version CCV**

Códice de Tristán   *Tristany* Andorra   *Cuento de Tristán* (Vatican MS)

Tristany Cervera   *Tristany* Biblioteca Catalunya

XVIth cent. printed editions

Cuento de Tristán and *Tristán de Leonís*, and a different development of the episodes of the lovers' flight from the court of Mares, the adventure of the horn and the journey up to their arrival at the Joyosa Guarda. Parts of these episodes are found in the fragments of the *Códice de Tristán* (from the flight from the court to the adventure of the horn, fragment 12 of MS 22644), but probably were present in their entirety as is the case in the *Cuento de Tristán* and *Tristán de Leonís*.

Another characteristic of this version is the amplification of the adventures in which Palomades is involved, and the negative and criminal character adopted by this individual in the episodes related in chapters 60 and 62–3 of *Tristán de Leonís* (the *Códice de Tristán* includes in fragment 15*r* a reference to Palomades that allows us to deduce that it too contained these episodes). Equally, the *Códice de Tristán* (fragment 19*r*) and *Tristán de Leonís* (ch. 65) are the only texts (since the fragment of the *Cuento de Tristán* ends before this point, although it presumably would have contained the episode) that relate the trick used by the lovers at the suggestion of Dinadan to obtain King Mares's pardon. This was inspired by the episode of the interposed sword that appears in the XIIth-century poems by Eilhard (in High German), Béroul (French), and in general in all the verse tradition.

In addition, it has already been seen that the adventures of the Ancient Knight, narrated in the *Compilation*, are unique to that text, in which it is stated that Rustichello copied the adventure from a book taken to Italy by Edward I of England on his way to the Crusade, which was supposedly his source (Rustichello, ed. F. Cigni 1994: 233, col. a), and that of the works based on him. All these episodes were probably found in the lost part of the *Cuento de Tristán* and in the lost sections of the Catalan manuscripts that now survive only as fragments; that is to say, they would have constituted a distinguishing characteristic of the Central-Eastern Iberian family.

The Castilian Manuscripts

The *Cuento de Tristán*

This work is known from MS Vat. Lat. 6428, dating from the end of the XIVth or beginning of the XVth century, which consists of 131 folios written in two columns but with some errors in the present folio sequence. Five folios are lacking at the beginning and it is impossible to know how many are missing at the end. For a full description, see the chapter by Lucía Megías in this volume. The narrative begins with the journey of Tristan to the court of King Framont de Gaulas and ends when King Arthur and Lancelot visit Tristan and Iseo in their tent during a tournament on the outskirts of Camelot, shortly after the lovers' flight from the court of Mares and their arrival in the Joyosa Guarda. It is a composite manuscript consisting of quires written by five different hands, of which one (D) exhibits Aragonese dialectal traits, also present to a lesser extent in other hands, which has led some scholars to speak of this manuscript as containing the Castilian-Aragonese *Tristán*. Copyists A, B and C seem to have operated in turn, relieving one another; D and E seem to have been preparing a separate copy of the text, since some passages are duplicated. The extensive surviving fragment contains fifty-four repeated pages, and Northup (Introduction 1928: 3) gives credence to the conclusion that this situation could involve different copies from a single exemplar erroneously combined in a single manuscript. Since the MS is preserved in the Vatican Library, it may be supposed that it came from the library of the Anti-Pope Benedict XIII, Pedro de Luna, which would link it, too, to an Aragonese context, since the Luna family originated in that kingdom.

The most detailed analysis of the *Cuento de Tristán* is still that by Northup in the introduction to his edition. Corfis, who has edited the text more than once (1985; *Cuento de Tristán de Leonís*, ADMYTE 0, 1994), offers brief details, which can be supplemented from the review by Sharrer (1977: 29). A new edition by Corfis was published in 2013, accompanied by a brief introductory study and numerous notes, relating particularly to variants. For the most part, critical interest has centred on the definition of its relation to *Tristán de Leonís* and on cataloguing the characteristics which distinguish it from the latter, an aspect of study begun by Northup (ed. 1928: 25–76). Gómez Redondo (1999: II, 1505–27) has taken an interest in the work's structure and in the ideology with which it is imbued, as well as in the stylistic aspects that distinguish it from the *Códice* and the printed Castilian version.

The characteristic which best defines the nature of the *Cuento de Tristán* is the tendency to a humorous and realistic presentation of events, indicated by Hall (1974:

187–9; 1983: 76–85), Rubio Pacho (1996), and the present writer (1999a: xvii), although these scholars differ over the interpretation of this feature. Before the discovery of the fifty-nine new fragments of the *Códice de Tristán*, Hall considered that *Tristán de Leonís*, like *Tablante* and the *Demanda*, reflects the favourable attitude towards chivalry of aristocratic society at the end of the XVth century and the beginning of the XVIth, and in consequence suppresses or modifies some comic scenes and realist details of the *Cuento de Tristán* to avoid anything that could give an unfavourable impression of the knight. This would involve supposing that the printed text derived from the *Cuento*, which, as has been seen, is not the case. I have previously pointed out (1999: xvii) that in one of the examples adduced by Hall, that of Quedin's complaint at not encountering adventures, a modification in favour of a chivalric ideology cannot be attributed to the author of *Tristán de Leonís* (ch. 42) since the Catalan MS from Andorra, dating from the second half of the XIVth century, agrees with *Tristán de Leonís* on this point. Furthermore, in other passages in which it is possible to compare the *Cuento* with the *Códice* it can be seen that the modification in favour of greater courtesy, and the consequent loss of a humour that degrades the protagonists, was either already present in the XVth-century *Códice de Tristán*, from which it passed to the printed editions, or was simply always a feature of the central-eastern Iberian line of textual transmission. It was therefore the author of the *Cuento* who decided to alter this trait, or who was following a different tradition. In favour of this hypothesis I have adduced the attitude of Tristan to Iseo de las Blancas Manos on abandoning her: the Andorra MS and the printed editions show us a hero who sympathises with his young wife, but is incapable of failing to obey the summons from Iseo la Rubia. The *Cuento de Tristán*, in contrast, presents Tristan as happy and even smiling on hearing the excuses with which Brangel deceives the princess. In this instance there is a realist attitude in all the texts, but it is pointing in a different direction, underlining in the first grouping the queen's foresight and in the *Cuento* the impulsive and crazy attitude of Iseo. Rubio Pacho (1996: 123–31) believes that the *Cuento* represents a decadent and critical vision of knighthood predating the exaltation of chivalry in the XVIth century. Even were this so, rather than being a characteristic of the age, since it is found neither in the Andorra text nor in the *Códice de Tristán*, it could involve a vision of the theme peculiar to the author. Santanach (2010) indicates that the Biblioteca de Catalunya MS coincides with the *Cuento*. Moreover, it can be added that realism is not exclusive to the *Cuento de Tristán*: the *Códice* (ed. Alvar and Lucía 1999: 87) and *Tristán de Leonís* (ch. 26) mention that Gorvalán gives a contraceptive potion to Brangel when she replaces Iseo on her wedding night, a detail not found in the *Cuento* (ed. Northup 1928: 123). In the flight from the court of Mares, an episode unique to the Castilian texts, in the *Códice* (Alvar and Lucía 1999: 101) and *Tristán de Leonís* (ch. 53) the lovers take the magic ring of the king and money or possessions. In the *Cuento* they take nothing and the queen regrets having taken nothing but her own clothes (Northup 1928: 249; Corfis 2013: 161–2).

Comparison of the *Cuento de Tristán* with the *Códice de Tristán* and, where this is impossible because of the fragmentary character of the manuscripts, with *Tristán de Leonís*, allows the present writer (1999a: xviii) to state that the storyline is the same, although with important variations in expression and in style, and even in the order, selection, and the content of some episodes. In general terms, they differ in the names of characters, in the length of passages, in dialogue, in the use of direct and indirect speech and in matters of detail, as well as in style, since the language is more modern and the style more polished and rhetorical in the *Códice de Tristán* and *Tristán de Leonís* than in the *Cuento de Tristán*.

It is the belief of the present author (1999a: xvii) that the distance between the *Cuento de Tristán* and the remaining Castilian texts increases in the final extant chapters of the manuscript, a feature that is corroborated indirectly by the recently discovered Catalan manuscript of the Biblioteca de Catalunya, which agrees with the Catalan text from Cervera and with the *Cuento de Tristán* in the only section common to all three, which is the beginning of the work. This leads one to suspect that perhaps these differences became greater in the lost section. In the final extant folios of the *Cuento* the dialogues are very different from those in the *Códice*, and the printed editions shorten the material. Gornayo accompanies Tristan and Iseo on their journey to Camelot and has a decisive influence on the arrival of Brangel at the Joyosa Guarda; the tournament at Camelot, which lasts for three days, is described in detail, day by day, indicating the changes in the colour of Tristan's arms; in the second tournament at Camelot, at which Tristan arrives accompanied by Iseo, and is visited in his tent by Arthur and Lancelot on the second day, it is Arthur who finds the tent. Precisely at this point the manuscript is interrupted, without there being any possibility of learning the details of the conversation between King Arthur and Queen Iseo, which are very significant in the *Códice* and in the Castilian printed editions, since Arthur reproaches Iseo with having abandoned her husband and complains of the evil committed by Queen Guinevere with Lancelot.

In the *Cuento de Tristán*, the names of the secondary characters are written differently from their forms in the remaining Castilian witnesses (including the names of relatively important individuals, such as Brangen, Gorvanayo, Goidís and Dinadani, and place names such as the Joyosa Guarda); at other times they have been completely altered, or have been confused with another character, as is the case with Brunor, who is replaced on one occasion by Brioberis and on another by Bravor, and with the husband of the Lady of the Espina, who receives various names in the *Cuento*, none of which coincides with what is given in the printed editions (Cuesta 1994a: 45–7; 1999a: xviii).

Some of the differences presented by the *Cuento de Tristán* in comparison with the *Códice de Tristán* allow us to appreciate more clearly the originality of the former in the depiction of the characters. The role of Gornayo (Gorvalan) is more important in the *Cuento*, and Queen Iseo is more determined, independent and extreme in her reactions. For example, an episode with an entirely different focus in each of the two versions, and which moreover does not appear in the French *Tristan en prose* or in the Italian versions, is the adventure of the Paso del Cuerno (ch. 53 of *Tristán de Leonís*). While in the *Cuento* the queen insists that Tristan must blow the horn and threatens, when faced with his refusal, to sound it herself, even causing Tristan to grow somewhat angry (ed. Northup 1928: 249), in the *Códice* and the printed versions she begs her lover not to sound it, for fear lest he receive some wound. In the same way, Rubio Pacho (2000, 2002) has underlined the negative character given by love and female characters in the *Cuento de Tristán*, which accentuates the misogynist tendencies of the *Tristan en prose*, which are attenuated in *Tristán de Leonís*, although, in my view (2008a: 168–71), there is also an ambivalent evaluation of love in this work. Ros Domingo (2001: 283–404) also underlines the negative representation of love, characterised as 'mad', and of the character of Tristan, as well as the moralising and Christian perspective of the narrator; and adds as a distinguishing feature of the work his vision of it as lacking in humour and sex. This view is, in my judgement, based on an erroneous understanding of the episodes in which Dinadani is the protagonist, whose misogynistic statements and criticisms of Tristan Ros Domingo takes seriously instead of perceiving their comic content. Dinadani behaves less courteously in the *Cuento* (Cuesta 1999a: xvi; Rubio Pacho 2000: 1572–3), but this results in a more humorous dimension of this character. His invectives are so exaggerated that they have to be taken as part of a burlesque conversation. In contrast to *Tristán de Leonís*, the *Cuento* is characterised by presenting more elements of violence, especially verbal violence; the hero's challenge to his uncle the king to the death as he flees from the court and settles in the Paso de Tintayol, the explicit mention of a possible suicide in Iseo's letter, the expression 'puta falsa' applied to Iseo by Dinadani (Rubio Pacho 2000: 1571–3).

Rubio Pacho (2001) maintains that the episode of the love philtre that unleashes the love of the two protagonists is less complex and presents its own moral connotations in the manuscript of the *Cuento de Tristán*. As regards the episode of the rescue of Arthur, the *Cuento* devotes more attention to the description of the combats. The different variants reveal, in his judgement, an organic character to the texts which renders risky their interpretation as simple translations or corrupt versions of an original, since they reflect very significant information and can enable us to understand the later development of Spanish chivalric fiction.

Iseo's letter in the *Cuento de Tristán* has been compared with the version offered by the Catalan fragment from Andorra (Cuesta 1993a: 214–17; 1993b; 1994a: 137–45). The striking proximity of some phrases proves beyond question the existence of a common archetype, since although the Castilian version is fuller than the Catalan, there is nothing there that can be attributed to *amplificatio*. In the case of the letter that Belisenda sends to Tristan, the text in the *Cuento* approaches in its content, but not in its expression, those of the *Tristan en prose* and the *Tristano*

Riccardiano, but displays some originality. The letters were from the first moment the extracts preferred by reworkers and translators of the romance to exercise their creative talents, as is shown by the fact that they have been replaced by others in *Tristán de Leonís* and the fact that MS 22021 of the BNE contains a 'Carta de Iseo y Respuesta de Tristán'. which are original creations. The similarity between the letter of Iseo in the *Cuento* and in the Andorra MS shows that the *Cuento* can offer trails leading to how the central-eastern Iberian version may have looked in those passages in which no other manuscript witness has been preserved and *Tristán de Leonís* shows signs of reworking.

Santanach (2010: 35) identifies innovation as characteristic of the *Cuento* and the MS of the Biblioteca de Catalunya, compared to the more conservative solutions given in the Andorra manuscript and *Tristán de Leonís*. These latter have a greater number of coincidences with the Italian tradition represented by the *Tristano Riccardiano*. It is an urgent task to compare in detail the MS of the Biblioteca de Catalunya with the Castilian and Italian manuscripts, in order to establish whether the features which distinguish the *Cuento de Tristán* arise from freedom and originality in translation on the part of its author, who separates it from the common trunk, or whether they result from the existence of a distinct textual tradition. The comparison of the *Cuento* with *Tristán de Leonís*, although it can offer some clues, can turn out to be misleading since the printed text is the object of a wide-ranging ideological and stylistic reworking, as will be seen below. In general, with the exception of the sections reworked in the printed text, the differences between *Tristán de Leonís* and the *Cuento de Tristán* that were pointed out by Northup (ed. 1928: 25–76) are found also when the *Cuento* is compared with the *Códice*.

In conclusion, the *Cuento de Tristán* coincides with the text of the *Códice* and the XVIth-century printed editions in so far as concerns the storyline, with a few exceptions, but its style is much more primitive, more ingenuous, less rhetorical. Normally, the same ideas are expressed in a very different way in these texts, and verbal coincidences are few. Furthermore, there are important variations in the content that affect the characterisation of the characters, more violent in the *Cuento*, and less courtly, who are sometimes presented with negative features. As regards the ideology transmitted by the text, it tends to offer a realist and critical look at the practice of the knightly ideal, which leads to an ironic and humorous interpretation of some episodes.

The *Códice de Tristán*

The *Códice de Tristán* (the identification and ordering of the fragments of which have required laborious work by its editors) adds to the interest of the text itself that of the miniatures that illustrate the story, which show that it was prepared for a reader of high social rank. Together with the Paris manuscript of the *Libro del caballero Zifar*, it constitutes one of the few medieval Castilian manuscripts in which there are preserved miniatures that are not devoted to the field of religious iconography.

Alvar and Lucía (1999: 9–12), in their description of the manuscript, differ from the view of Bonilla (1912: 318) on the dating of the text, which they consider to be of the XVth century. It is the work of a single hand; the writing block measures 215 × 70 mm. The fragments were preserved in the binding of another work. This manuscript was never used by printers, since it lacks the distinctive marks found in those used for this purpose. The fragments are now preserved as two manuscripts of the BNE, nos. 20262/19 and 22644, the second of which, consisting of fifty-nine fragments, some of which preserve the original foliation, represents the recently discovered material that was not available to scholars until the publication of the edition by Alvar and Lucía.

The following episodes of the *Códice de Tristán* are preserved, which differ greatly in length, and some of which have significant internal *lacunae*:

1. From the organisation of the first tournament in Scotland to Tristan's departure to fight in the second tournament, provided with arms that belonged to Morlot (corresponding to chs 11–12 of *Tristán de Leonís*).
2. From the end of the combat with Galeote to the wedding night of Mares and Iseo, the seizure of Iseo by Palomades, and her discovery by Gorvalan (chs 25–30 of *Tristán de Leonís*).
3. From the freeing of Arthur from the power of the Doncella del Arte until Tristan takes leave of Arthur (chs 45–6).
4. From the flight of Tristan and Iseo from the court of Mares until they fall asleep in the castle of the knight who guards the passage of the Horn Bridge (ch. 53).
5. From the end of the second tournament at Camelot and Arthur and Lancelot's visit to Tristan and Iseo in their tent until Dinadan arrives at the Joyosa Guarda (chs 58–9).
6. From the combat of Lancelot and Tristan at the tournament of Vecepon, the stay of King Mares at Arthur's court and the pardon of the lovers to the admission of Tristan as a knight of the Round Table, the arrival of the Ancient Knight at court, and his intervention in the combat in favour of the widowed lady and her daughter (chs 63–71 and 73–4).
7. From the end of the fight between Tristan and Galaz to Tristan's return to Tintoíl (chs 78–9).
8. From the mortal wound of Tristan until the latter asks for confession and takes communion (chapters 871–83).
9. The war of the Knights of the Round Table against Mares, the punishment of Aldaret, and the death of Iseo de las Blancas Manos (not corresponding to the printed text).

My comparison of the *Códice* and *Tristán de Leonís* (1999a: xix–xxiii) confirms my earlier impressions based on MS 20262/19 of the *Códice* (Cuesta 1993b: 86–9): in general, and with the exception of specific episodes that have been totally altered in

Tristán de Leonís (for example, the letters) and which are examined below, the differences between both texts consist essentially of orthographic and morphological differences, lexical variants and changes affecting syntax, suppression and amplification and small changes of content, in addition to the use in various passages of *Tristán de Leonís* of a rhetorical tone akin to that of sentimental fiction. Some of the chapter headings of the *Códice* coincide word for word with those of the printed editions (for example, fols 19*r* and 27*r* of the *Códice* and chs 65 and 70 of *Tristán de Leonís*), although, going by what survives, the manuscript must have had almost twice as many chapters as the printed text. The exemplar followed by *Tristán de Leonís* must have been another copy, since lost, of the *Códice de Tristán*, corrected and altered to a varying extent, according to the section involved, by whoever prepared the text for the press. The similarity between the texts in some places is so close that it permits us to reconstruct the damaged section of the manuscript. Unfortunately it is not possible to compare the *Códice de Tristán* with either the Catalan manuscript of Andorra (which contains the section from the wedding night of Tristan and Iseo de las Blancas Manos to the beginning of the combat between Tristan and Lamarad in the Gasta Floresta) nor with that of Cervera (which contains the freeing of Meliadux from the power of the enchantress and the first attempt at poisoning made by Tristan's stepmother), nor yet with the recently discovered manuscript of the Biblioteca de Catalunya, since they do not contain any common episode.

Only three passages of the *Códice* do not find any corresponding part in the text of *Tristán de Leonís*: part of fragment 10 referring to the episode in which King Arthur beheads the Doncella del Arte who had held him captive, and fragments 37 and 38 which tell of the war of vengeance for the death of the protagonist, undertaken by his friends, and the death of Iseo de las Blancas Manos. These passages have been suppressed for ideological reasons by the author-reworker of *Tristán de Leonís*, and because of this may offer further evidence on the characteristics of the version in the *Códice*. The passage involving fragment 10 allows comparison also with the *Cuento de Tristán*, which is not the case with fragments 37 and 38. This is very interesting, since it permits us to appreciate the great difference between the *Códice* and the *Cuento* in the expression of ideas, the order of events, and in part of the content. This passage in the *Cuento* was already compared with *Tristán de Leonís* by Rubio Pacho (2001: 69–72), who notes less attention to the description of combat than in the Aragonese version. In terms of ideology, the *Códice*, like the *Cuento*, depicts Tristán's disapproving attitude towards Arthur's action in decapitating the Doncella del Arte, even if the reproach is articulated openly and explicitly in the *Cuento* – 'ca no pertenesçia a vos de matar mujer ninguna' (ed. Northup 1928: 219; ed. Corfis 2013: 136) – in which the king justifies his action with a single sentence ('esto conuenia de fazer, ca en otra manera non era onbre seguro della'), while in the *Códice de Tristán* the protagonist adopts a much more courteous attitude, expressing only 'maravilla' at the king's action, and Arthur articulates a long paragraph explaining everything that has happened (ed. Alvar and Lucía 1999: 99). This explanation is also lacking from Malory's *Mort Arthur*, where it is the Lady of the Lake who orders him to behead the enchantress (Kennedy 1970: 8), but it is found in the French *Tristan en prose*. In contrast to both manuscripts, *Tristán de Leonís* suppresses both Tristan's astonishment and the king's explanation, and the death of the Doncella del Arte passes without comment. The *Códice* offers an intermediate solution, in relation to the *Cuento* and the printed versions, in so far as concerns respect for royal authority and courtly behaviour. The comparison of the three texts at this point allows us to appreciate the surprising partial coincidence between the content of the *Cuento* and that of the printed version that is not encountered in fragment 10 of the *Códice*. In the *Cuento*, the king takes the horse of a dead enemy and begins to fight; the Doncella Aventurera warns Tristán of the escape of the Doncella del Arte, and Tristán captures her and takes her to the king before continuing his fight with the enemy, while Arthur punishes the Doncella. In *Tristán de Leonís*, Tristán is warned by the king of the flight of the Doncella del Arte, captures her and hands her over to the king's justice; she is beheaded; devils carry off the Doncella and her castle is burnt; afterwards Tristán hands his own horse to the king. In the *Códice*, in which the beginning of the episode does not survive, Tristán asks the king to ride on his horse while he takes another: it is then that Tristán hands the Doncella del Arte to the king for punishment, Arthur beheads her, devils take away her soul, and her castle burns. In other words, the *Códice* differs in that it does not contain the warning about the flight of the Doncella, which would indicate yet again that the printed version derives from a different, although very similar, manuscript, while the *Cuento* is distinguished by lacking Tristan's display of courtesy in offering his horse to the king, and the divine punishment of the Doncella. Both additions support the theory of a less courtly behaviour on the part of the characters of the *Cuento*. The divine punishment, moreover, contributes to reinforcing Arthur's justification for having killed the Doncella, thereby diminishing any unease produced by this episode's failure to conform with the courtly ideology. Moreover, both manuscripts are distinguished from the printed text in the order of occurrence of the handing over of the horse and the death of the Doncella, although this alteration could be explained by a search for a more logical sequence of events.

Fragments 37 and 38 have received attention from critics because they refer to the episode of the vengeance for Tristan's death which is narrated, although with important differences, in some of the Italian *Tristan* texts (as stated above). Its presence in the *Códice* shows that this episode formed part of the Hispano-Italian *Tristán*, and leads us to suppose that it would have figured in the lost part of the remaining central-eastern Iberian manuscripts. Its absence from the printed *Tristán de Leonís* must be explained as an intentional modification motivated by the ideological orientation of this text, more respectful towards the authority of the king.

Gómez Redondo (1999: II, 1539–40) notes the importance of the use of irony and of narrative formulae, the presence of colloquial traits characteristic of orality, and the emotive language as distinguishing features of the style of the manuscript in contrast to the printed version.

In the *Códice de Tristán*, some characters who take part in one episode have different names, although these are phonologically similar to those which they have in the printed texts (for example, the kings and knights who attend the investiture of Tristan as a knight of the Round Table, and the arrival of the Ancient Knight). Special interest and importance attaches to the fact that the *Códice* gives as an epithet to Queen Iseo the nickname 'Brunda' (ed. Alvar and Lucía 1999: 86), which differs from that of 'Baça' given to her in the *Cuento*. It was, therefore, the version known from the *Códice* and not that from the *Cuento* that was familiar to the *cancionero* poets who refer to Iseo as 'Brunda' (for example, Juan Barba, or perhaps, if Juan de Tapia is referring to the same character, 'Bruna': Cuesta 1999b: 86–7, 90–1 'Personajes arturicos'), and that is also reproduced by Rodríguez de Montalvo in his *Amadís* (ed. Cacho Blecua 1999: 1678).

Apart from the studies carried out on the miniatures and especially on the relationship of these to the text which they illustrate (Lucía Megías 2001b, 2005a) and on the resemblances of the *Códice* to other textual witnesses of the Hispano-Italian family of *Tristan* texts, there have been no studies examining structural, formal aspects of the text, or of its content. The manuscript *Tristán* texts still offer a wide scope for literary research and a better knowledge of them, especially of their meaning, would provide much information about the evolution of Castilian fictional narrative in the final centuries of the Middle Ages and about the various ideological orientations that guided its authors.

The Renaissance *Tristán de Leonís*

In 1501 the printer Juan de Burgos brought out in Valladolid the first edition of *Tristán de Leonís*. The book was not a novelty in the strict sense, since the plot of the work and the names of its protagonists were already famous among potential readers by the beginning of the XVth century, as is revealed by *cancionero* poetry (Cuesta 1999b), or references to Tristán and Lanzarote in the *Arcipreste de Talavera* (1438), and, slightly later, the mention of King Hoel of Little Britain, his daughter Iseo de las Blancas Manos and her brother Cardoin (the 'Quedín' of *Tristán de Leonís*) in the *Libro de las bienandanzas e fortunas* of Lope García de Salazar (1471–6, ed. Marín Sánchez 2000 in CORDE, para. 221 *s.v.* Cardoin), or even, at the end of the century, the reference to the firmness and loyalty of Tristán in the *Libro de las veynte cartas e quistiones* of Fernando de la Torre (ed. Díez Garretas 1983: 133). The work offered an adaptation of the version that is known from the BNE manuscript of the *Códice de Tristán* and which was probably also a reworking dating from the beginning of the XVth century of what had been circulating in Castile from the first third of the XIVth century, as is attested by the allusion to the loves of Tristán in the *Libro de buen amor* (stanza 1703) and to Tristán, in the company of Amadís and Zifar, in the *Glosa al regimiento de príncipes* of Juan García de Castrogeriz (earlier than 1350). Nor was it the first time that this plot, in its general lines, had been printed: the French *Tristan* had been printed in Paris in 1489. Although, moreover, this was the first time that it had been printed in Castilian, Juan de Burgos had previously ventured into the publication of another work of Castilian Arthurian material, the *Baladro del sabio Merlín* (1498), and other works of chivalric fiction, such as the *Cronica troyana* (1490).

The *Tristán* printed in 1501 met with a notable success, to the extent that there were at least another seven editions printed in Seville. The Cromberger printing house produced, on paper with a hand-and-star watermark, editions in 1511, 1528 and surely the now-lost edition of 1533, as well as another, X, of which some loose leaves are preserved in the Pierpont Morgan Library, New York, discovered inside a copy of the edition of 1528 by Cuesta (1997d), the woodcuts and header of which coincide with those of the 1511 edition, although the distribution of abbreviations in the text does not; the text must have been printed before 1520, since it seems to have been the base text for the first edition printed at Seville by Juan Varela de Salamanca. Varela's Seville press produced the 1520 edition, currently of unknown whereabouts, and that of 1525. Finally, the Seville press of Domenico de Robertis printed *Tristán el Joven* in 1534, which includes as its first part a *Tristán de Leonís* marked by the peculiarity of inserting several chapters on Galeote and on the life of the lovers on the Isle of Ploto, and adds also an extensive second part with the adventures of the offspring of Tristan and Iseo who were both on that island.

All the surviving editions descend from the 1501 edition, although through another intermediary (edition B), some of the errors of which are transmitted to all the later editions, though each of them adds its own erroneous readings and occasionally a deliberate variant. In the case of the 1534 edition, the addition of new material means that it should be considered to be a different work. Besides these, the present author (1997d) has postulated the existence of another edition before 1511, Y, the source of the Cromberger editions. B or Y would be the pre-1507 Cromberger edition whose existence Cacho Blecua (2004–5) believes to be certain, basing himself on the use of the woodcuts from *Tristán* in the 1507 edition of *Oliveros*.

Tristán de Leonís in Images: the Woodcuts

As Cátedra emphasises (2007: 22), one should not minimise the importance that the existence of earlier woodcuts may have had in this period in the printing of particular works. Specifically, the *Tristán de Leonís* printed by Juan de Burgos has a wealth of illustration, since it contains eighty-two woodcuts distributed over eighty-three chapters, and of these twenty-five are used just once (Cacho Blecua 2010: 7).

Cacho Blecua (2004–5, 2007) analyses the relationships of non-textual dependence in the woodcuts added to the editions of *Tristán*, *Oliveros*, *Amadís*, and the *Coronación* of Juan de Mena, taking as his starting point the lapses in the link between text and image. In this way, he is able to establish which of the works making use of a particular

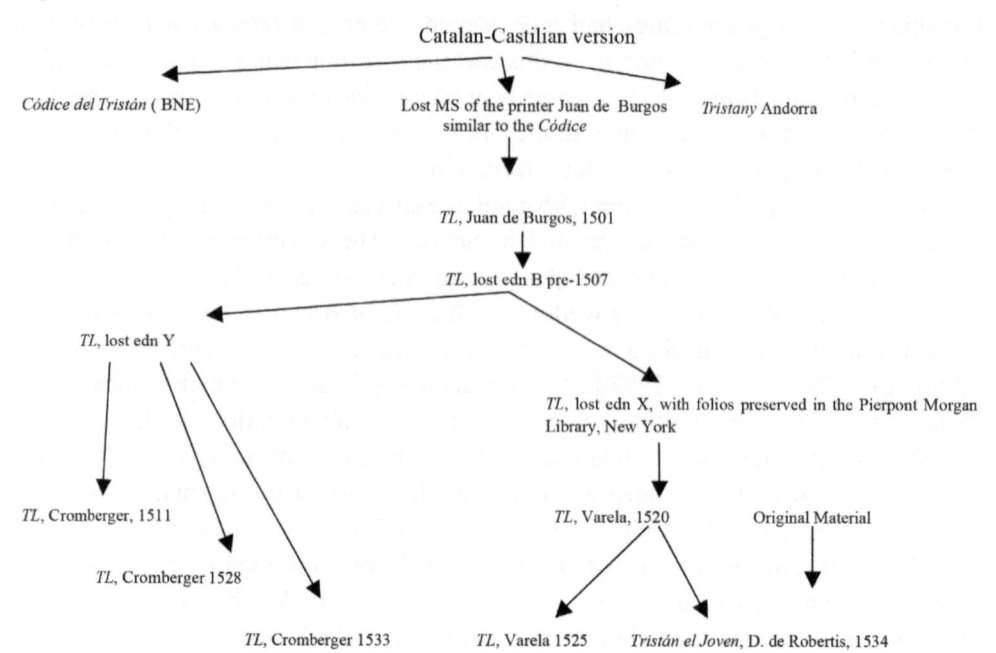

Fig. IX.3: *Stemma* of the Printed Editions of *Tristán de Leonís*.

```
                        Catalan-Castilian version
              ←―――――――――――――┼―――――――――――――→
   Códice del Tristán (BNE)   Lost MS of the printer Juan de Burgos   Tristany Andorra
                              similar to the Códice
                                      ↓
                              TL, Juan de Burgos, 1501
                                      ↓
                              TL, lost edn B pre-1507
              ←―――――――――――――――――――――――――→
   TL, lost edn Y
        ↓                             TL, lost edn X, with folios preserved in the Pierpont Morgan
        ↓                             Library, New York
   TL, Cromberger, 1511              TL, Varela, 1520        Original Material
        ↓                                   ↓                       ↓
   TL, Cromberger 1528
        ↓
   TL, Cromberger 1533    TL, Varela 1525   Tristán el Joven, D. de Robertis, 1534
```

woodcut is the one for which it was created. This permits him to be precise about the dating, and to corroborate the hypothesis of the existence of lost editions, earlier than those which are now extant, of romances of chivalry issued by the press of Jacobo Cromberger. The numerous images shared by *Tristán* and *Oliveros* imply the reuse of some blocks originally intended to illustrate an edition of *Tristán de Leonís*, which must necessarily predate the *Oliveros* printed in 1507 in the same Seville workshop. One-third of the engravings in *Amadís de Gaula* go back to a graphic model issued by the Cromberger printing house, and must be from a lost *Tristán de Leonís* which would have been published between 1503 and 1507. Some of the woodcuts of *Amadís* went on to appear in *La Coronación* by Juan de Mena. The shared images suggest that these books were aimed at a similar public, accustomed to using texts enriched by illustrations, which was probably drawn from the aristocratic strata.

The 1501 Edition by Juan de Burgos

The text of the 1501 edition consists of ninety-four folios measuring 184 × 260 mm and one title page. It is printed in black-letter type in two columns of forty-three lines. At the start of each chapter there is a small woodcut, normally alluding to the subject of the chapter; there are eighty of these, but many of the woodcuts are repeated on various occasions. The chapters are not numbered but they do have headings. The text begins on f. 3, with an ornamented capital, but without woodcuts. The colophon conveys the date and place of printing and the name of the printer; there follow, on the final leaf (94r), a statement by the translator or reviser (in reality a farewell or epilogue) and a woodcut. A single copy is known, in the British Library (C.20.d.24), which previously belonged to the library of Heredia; the first three folios have been refashioned (the title page and the two containing the 'Tabla'), and folio 73 is missing, which must have been lost before the Tabla was reconstituted, since the title of chapter lxviii is not given in it. On the title page there appears only the title of the work. The 'Tabla' occupies both sides of fols 1–2 and could have replaced 'una carta que embio maestre Guillaume de Namur a mosen Juan de Beraforte, que estava preso por mandado del rey Duarte', mentioned in the contents of the editions of 1511, 1525 and 1528, but which does not appear in them because its place is occupied by the 'Prohemio'. Neither the 'Carta' nor the 'Prohemio' figure in the surviving text of the London copy of the 1501 edition. The contents lists perhaps allude to a letter which must have appeared in one of the earlier editions of the work (the colophons of the editions of 1511, 1525 and 1528 emphasis that they have added tablas lacking in the earlier editions, which indicates a recognition that there were various editions before 1511). The 'Carta de Guillaume de Namur' or the 'Prohemio', or perhaps both, could have been at the front of the edition of 1501 on the first, lost, folios.

Tristán de Leonís (1501) Compared with its Medieval Source

The modifications carried out by the author of *Tristán de Leonís* in relation to his medieval source relate to various intentions. In the Renaissance work, specific passages are suppressed that were found in the *Códice de Tristán*, with the aim of shortening and reducing the text. In some cases, the cut may be caused by the corruption or loss of that part of the manuscript being used as an exemplar by the printer: the explanation of the award of seats at the Round Table, which the printer sums up with a brevity formula, corresponds to a point at which the text of the *Códice* is corrupt. But in general the motive for the omissions is ideological, or perhaps commercial, seeking to satisfy the expectations of a public to which the work was directed. Such are the war against King Mares for the death of Tristán, the punishment of Aldaret, and the return of Quedín to Little Britain on the death of Iseo de las Blancas Manos when she learns of the death of her spouse. These must all necessarily have been present in the printer's source, since in the epilogue it is stated that there were three women who lost their lives for the love of the hero, while in the work there are recounted only the deaths of Belisenda and Queen Iseo la Brunda. The author wished to transform the ending to come closer to the model of sentimental fiction, a genre triumphant at the time of the publication of the first edition, and also to avoid narrating a confrontation between the monarch and the knights. As has been seen, the elimination of the explanation given by Arthur to Tristán about his capture and enchantment by the Donzella del Arte and on the reason why he has killed her seems to relate to the same purpose of avoiding questions about royal authority.

In other cases there appears the opposite process, *amplificatio*: in a very rhetorical style, typical of sentimental fiction, dialogues and monologues are introduced in particularly dramatic passages. A good example is the lamentation of Iseo on seeing her dying lover: while the *Códice de Tristán* dwells on the description of the queen's gestures of grief, the printed texts add verbal laments to accompany these. Dissatisfied with the amplification carried out, the author even offers an explanation which justifies, with brevity *topoi*, the fact that more detail is not given of these words. Besides increasing the dramatic quality, some amplifications serve the function of offering a more religious depiction of the characters, as will be seen below.

Not all the modifications, however, involve especially dramatic passages, nor are they all due to the desire to use a more refined and rhetorical language or to impart a more religious tone to the work. Other amplifications seem simply to increase the verisimilitude or the realism of the setting. Thus it is with the account of the first tournament in Scotland: when King Languines goes to take part in favour of the king of Scotland, the preparations he undertakes to go to the tournament are narrated, calling together all his knights and amassing arms, horses, food and fodder; further on there is a paragraph added about how all came together and prepared for the tourney, laying out the place where this was to take place and erecting the tents, the vantage points and stands, and the barriers (at the end of chapter 11). The reworking of the manuscript by the 'author' of *Tristán de Leonís* extends throughout the entire text.

Special consideration must be given to all the amplifications carried out in the text through plagiarism of various works produced in the workshop of Juan de Burgos, which has led critics to suppose that there existed a close relationship between the author and the version given by *Tristán de Leonís* and the printer. For Sharrer (1984: 147–57; 1988a: 361–9), the person responsible for the plagiarisms was the printer himself, Juan de Burgos. These textual appropriations seem to have as their objective the setting of the work in the context of the fictional literature that was produced in the workshop in question, thereby facilitating its acceptance by the same kind of public as already enjoyed those other works.

Plagiarism of Sentimental Fiction and of Trojan Themes

Some cases of plagiarism had attracted the attention of Bonilla (1912: 387–8) in his edition of *Tristán de Leonís*; others were subsequently pointed out by Lida, Waley, Sharrer, and Marín Pina. The *proemio* is derived from *Oliveros de Castilla y Artús de Algarve*, printed by Fadrique de Basilea in 1499; the epilogue reworks that of the *Baladro del sabio Merlín*, printed by Juan de Burgos in 1498; the letters and the final description of the beauty of Iseo come from the *Crónica troyana* printed by the latter printer in 1490; but the most extensive contribution is that from *Grimalte y Gradissa* by Juan de Flores, a work from which there have been taken speeches, Iseo's prayer and the description of the lovers' tomb in chapters 82 and 83, besides the few verses that adorn the romance.

Bonilla also drew attention to the similarities between the scene in *Oliveros* in which the queen expires on seeing her dead husband, and the death of Tristan and Iseo. In this case, it is probably imitation in the other direction. In view of the fame enjoyed since the XIIth century all over Europe by the legend of the lovers and their tragic death; given that there already existed a ballad, known at the court of the Catholic Monarchs, '*Herido está don Tristán*', in which this well-known scene was reproduced and it is related how both expired while they were locked in a kiss; and since there exists a Castilian manuscript of *Tristán* from the XVth century which shows the current circulation of the material relating to Tristan at that time, it seems logical to suppose that Juan de Burgos, already having in his possession the manuscript for the proposed edition of *Tristán*, should have emphasised the similarities in the corresponding passage of his edition of *Oliveros*.

With regard to the portrait of Iseo with which the romance finishes, Entwistle (1925 rpt 1975: 117–20) pointed out that Brunetto Latini, a guest of Alfonso X around 1260, attributed to Tristan a rhetorical description of Iseo in his *Li Livres dou Tresor* and believed it possible that this description might have existed in a lost *Tristan* text. Gardner (1930 rpt 1975: 40) suggests that the passage came directly from the author of the *Tresor*. For Lida (1966: 134–48) the portrait of Iseo was added later after the main text was completed, as is shown by its late linguistic features, under the influence of the sentimental romance. These hypotheses were rendered obsolete with the discovery of the medieval manuscript which was involved in the transmission of the text of Guido de Colonna to the *Cronica troyana* of Juan de Burgos. Gilman (1978: 326–7, n.136), followed by Sharrer (1988a: 369), believes that the portrait of Helen of Troy in the *Historia Destructionis Troiae*, of which there exists a manuscript of the anonymous Castilian translation of the end of the XIVth century, was the source of the first edition of the *Crónica troyana* in 1490, printed by Juan de Burgos, and that from this work it passed to *Tristán de Leonís* and to the portrait of Melibea in Act I of *La Celestina*. In the same line of argument are the studies of Marín Pina (2004–5) in relation to the plagiarised letters from the Trojan work and those of Galle-Cejudo (2005) on the portrait of Iseo and its classical precedents.

Although Sharrer (1984a: 147–57) believed that the confluence of the Arthurian romance and sentimental fiction explains the differences that distinguish Iseo's letter in the *Cuento* from that in the printed edition, the discovery of the model of the letters in *Tristán de Leonís* as being the *Crónica troyana* printed by Juan de Burgos in 1490 places these modifications in a wider context than that of the adaptation of the model of sentimental fiction. Marín Pina has identified passages derived from the letters of Daymira to Hercules, Medea to Jason and Elisa Dido to Eneas in the letter of Iseo. The same occurs with the letter Belisenda sends to Tristan announcing her suicide: the *Cuento* and the printed editions do not coincide in a single line. That in *Tristán de*

Leonís is patently more rhetorical and much longer (Waley 1961: 10). The manuscript of the Biblioteca de Catalunya discovered recently contains Belisenda's letter, but a dampstain prevents our verifying whether it offers the same version as the *Cuento de Tristán*. Marín Pina also indicates the sections of the *Crónica troyana* that inspired Belisenda's letter in the printed edition.

For their part, following the path opened by Lida de Malkiel (1959, 1966), the relations existing between the printed *Tristán* and Juan de Flores's *Grimalte y Gradissa* have been underlined by Waley (1961: 1–14; 1972: xxv–xxvii), Seidenspinner-Núñez (1981–2), Sharrer (1984a), Parrilla (1988: xxxix–xl), and Gwara (1997: 78–9). As has been seen, the text of 1501 adds material taken from this work. Lida de Malkiel (1959: 406–18; 1966: 134–48) was the first to indicate two cases of borrowings, which she believed were attributable to the printer. These are two stanzas of incidental poetry, composed, according to Flores, by Alonso de Córdoba, and some of the language used by this Córdoba in the description of the tomb of Fiameta, which is reapplied to the tomb of Tristán and Iseo. The same view is held by Sharrer (1984a, 1988a). Waley extended the study of the relations between *Grimalte y Gradissa* and the 1501 *Tristán*, attributing the points of similarity to Juan de Flores and concluding that in the latter work there are seven passages taken from the former. Two of these are unaltered (the tomb of Tristan and Iseo, which replicates that of Fiameta, and the verses placed in the mouth of Melianes, which reproduce the final verses of *Grimalte*), and the remaining cases are carefully modified to suit their new context (1972: xxv). Gwara believes that the plagiarism of *Grimalte y Gradissa* in the 1501 *Tristán* and in another romance of chivalry, *Clarián de Landanís*, were not the work of Juan de Flores himself (1997: 77–9), to whom he does, however, attribute, from stylistic analysis, the *Carta de Iseo y respuesta de Tristán* in MS 22021 of the BNM (1997: 80, 97–9). This attribution was suggested previously by Sharrer (1981–2; 1984a: 155–7).

The influence of the sentimental romance must have been decisive at the moment of deciding on the ending of the work in the printed texts: the Castilian version of the XVth century ended with the narration of the death of Iseo de las Blancas Manos and the war of vengeance for the death of Tristan, with the punishment of Aldaret and King Mares' plea for forgiveness. But these episodes involved a diminution of dramatic tension: for any reader of sentimental romances, the perfect ending must be the death of the lovers. The death of the wife of the protagonist must not obscure that of Iseo la Brunda, who dies at the same time as her lover. The requited, but illicit, love of Tristan and Iseo should not compete in the mind of the reader with the innocent love of the scorned spouse of the knight. In this way the moral lesson of the text was intensified: an example of the negative consequences of 'loco amor', emphasised by Dinadán in other passages of the work, combined with the exaltation of the lovers, pardoned by God at their death.

In these intrusions of sentimental fiction into *Tristán* two factors were undoubtedly of considerable influence: firstly, they shared a favourite theme of that fiction, that of the tragic love that leads the lovers to their death, an almost conventional ending of many sentimental narratives; and secondly, letters expressing love and its opposite were one of the essential elements of that genre. The adulterous nature of the protagonists' love, with the obligatory tragic end announced by Dinadán and of which the lovers themselves were aware (on more than one occasion Tristan attempts to 'partirse del mal de la reina'), relates *Tristán de Leonís* to the genre of sentimental fiction (Cuesta 1999a: Introduction, pp. xxxi–xxxii). As is the case with such works, the plot is closed, love is the destroyer of social order (the nephew strikes at the honour of his uncle, the knight at that of his king) and of the life of those who suffer from it, whom it plunges into madness and shame (Iseo does not dare, at first, to flee with Tristan because in every court they would be considered 'falsos', traitors), and whom it subjects to persecution by envious courtiers (Aldaret and his lady) and the jealous husband (Mares). For Ros Domingo (2001: 283–404), it is precisely this contamination by sentimental fiction, together with the rewriting of the story of Tristan to focus on its protagonist and on the central theme of love, that distinguishes *Tristán de Leonís* from other Ibero-Romance versions.

The tragic outcome, with the death of the protagonists, gave the romance an adequate moral lesson against disorderly love, which would have gratified moralists, while the theme of love rendered impossible by social conventions would have pleased readers of sentimental fiction. The work thus had everything required to satisfy the reading public of the early XVIth century, and so to maintain the success already established during two centuries of its previous existence in medieval Spanish literature. These possibilities for commercial success must have weighed heavily in the mind of the first printer of the work, who also took care, as will be seen below, to include religious elements that suppressed the more subversive aspects of the story of the lovers.

The Reworker of 1501

Juan de Burgos began his work as a printer in Burgos in 1489. There he remained until 1499, publishing around twenty books, among them the *Baladro del sabio Merlín con sus profecias* and the *Doze trabajos de Ercules* of Enrique de Villena. In 1500 he temporarily abandoned Burgos to set up shop in Valladolid, where the previous year the presses of Petrus Giraldi and Michael de Planes had ceased operating. Some of the texts that he published in this period could have been inherited from other printers. In Valladolid, in 1501, he published *Tristán de Leonís* and the *Historia de los nobles cavalleros Oliveros de Castilla y Artús de Algarbe*. In 1502 he returned to Burgos. His last dated work was printed in October of that year. In May 1503 the printer Andrés de Burgos was working there, who seems to have used the typographic material and presses of Juan de Burgos (Norton 1966: 62–3). As a printer, Juan de Burgos reveals himself to be extremely interested in works of fiction and does not restrict his role simply to reproducing in print the manuscripts that came to his hands. The work of adaptation carried out in the case of *Tristán* also occurred, for example, in his edition of the *Crónica troyana* and in the *Baladro*. In the latter, as in *Tristán*, the influence of sentimental fiction can be detected, and also, again as in the case of *Tristán*, there are incorporated some verses taken from *Grimalte* and attributed to Alonso de Córdoba. As far as concerns the *Crónica troyana*, Juan de Burgos produced a new book that would triumph over the previously-known versions and become the canonical text for Renaissance reference. He used two sources for his version, the *Sumas* of Leomarte in a XVth-century version, and the medieval translation of the work of Guido de Colonna. In the prologue to his edition, he reveals that he had intended to divide it into four parts and mentions the chapters that would have corresponded to each, but he did not in the end put this arrangement into effect. The *Crónica troyana* permits us to see how Juan de Burgos conceived the work of the printer: the boundary between his work and that of a rewriter is imperceptible. Everything seems to indicate that it was Juan de Burgos himself, or someone who worked assiduously for him and systematically adapted the manuscripts that he was going to publish from his press, who was the author of the final reworking undergone by the Castilian *Tristán*.

Cátedra and Velasco raise another interesting possibility (2000: 79–94). Some of the works printed at the workshop of Juan de Burgos were found in manuscripts owned by the Comendador Cristobal de Santisteban (who was still alive in 1534). The printer's publications could have been commissions in which the involvement of Santisteban was not limited to the mere loan of material from his library. Cátedra and Velasco highlight the literary knowledge and stylistic skill involved, which seem to go beyond the capacity of a mere printer, and which reveal the borrowings inserted into various works from his press (2000: 91–2), abilities which Cristobal de Santisteban certainly had. They emphasise the latter's relationship with various publishers and his interest in the publication of texts, revealed in his obtaining privileges to print.

The Ideology of *Tristán de Leonís*

The most important modifications carried out in the 1501 *Tristán de Leonís* in relation to the *Códice de Tristán* are concentrated in the final episodes, and this can be related to the new ideology that the author of the work is attempting to impose on the material he is adapting. The plagiarisms and final modifications seem, in fact, to be intended not only to bring the work closer to the triumphant genre of sentimental fiction and to the successful *Amadís de Gaula*, but above all to attenuate, through an increase in the religious content, the moral conflict that could be posed by the exaltation of adulterous love for readers of the work at the beginning of the XVIth century (Cuesta 2008a: 169–75; 2014a). The new religious elements, absent from the *Códice de Tristán*, increase, throughout chapter 83, the pathos, the religious sentiment, and the devotion of the protagonists, Tristán and Iseo, by the following devices: by the vigil and prayer of Iseo, by several pleas to God and the Virgin made by Tristán in his lament for his imminent death, by his plea for forgiveness to all present, and by his final prayer.

The entire episode in which Iseo spends the night in a vigil praying for the salvation of her lover was created for *Tristán de Leonís*. The queen's prayer revolves around two ideas that are rhetorically amplified: (1) she begs God to spare Tristan's life, since the blame for his sins should fall upon her; and (2) if this is not possible, she prays that God permit her to die with him, so that this should be a clear case of divine justice. Both themes are well developed and arise from Iseo's complete ignorance of the effects of the love potion. The passage seems to be a moralising commentary on the romance. All in all, the prayer is well suited to the perspective of the enamoured queen. The desire to keep their love secret, expressed as a sign of repentance and an intention to reform, is in accordance with this character's attitude throughout the text. At the end of Iseo's prayer, there is included a passage taken from Juan de Flores's sentimental romance *Grimalte y Gradissa*, which the rewriter places in the mouth of Governal, who attempts to console the queen.

At the end of the night, Iseo's anguished prayer is followed by Tristán's confession and lament, his testamentary arrangements, and his farewell to those present, in which he begs for their forgiveness. Tristan's prayer, his confession, and his plea for forgiveness addressed to all those present are also found in the *Tavola Ritonda*, although in a different sequence and language, and must have appeared also after Tristan's plea for confession, absolution and communion which are preserved at the end of f. 36v of the medieval Castilian *Códice*. Some religious elements, therefore, must already have been found in the common source of the Hispano-Italian family of *Tristan* texts.

However, the detailed analysis of the final chapters of the work, contrasting them with the versions found in V.II or the *Vulgate* of the French *Tristan en prose*, that in BNF MS fr. 757 (representing V.I of the *Tristan en prose*), and from Italy the *Compilation* of Rustichello da Pisa, the *Tristano Veneto* (of the late XIIIth century), the *Tristano Panciatichiano* (XIVth century), and the *Tavola Ritonda* (in Tuscan dialect of the second quarter of the XIVth century), as well as the *Cantari di Tristano* (second half of the XIVth century), leads me to postulate a closer relationship between the Castilian text and that of the *Tavola*, while the coincidences between the remaining Italian representatives of the Tristan legend and *Tristán de Leonís* can, it seems, be explained on the basis of a common source not very different from V.I of the French *Tristan* (Cuesta 2014a).

In short, the religious sentiment imposed on the characters throughout this chapter must be attributed principally to the rewriter and not to his source. It is this religious sentiment with which he imbues Tristán that renders impossible the attitude of defiance in the face of death that this character adopted in the other versions. In *Tristán de Leonís* there is some nuancing of the hero's invitation to death to come whenever it wishes to do so, through the inclusion immediately afterwards of a prayer. It is not enough for the Tristán of the Castilian printed version to have his lover in his arms in order for him to die happy denying any importance to death: it is necessary for him to address himself to God and to think more of his soul than of his sweetheart. The rewriter does not fail to include, after Tristán's lament for his impending death, his testamentary arrangements, so that the hero dies after arranging his spiritual and earthly affairs.

The work of the rewriter is centred upon this episode in converting the deaths of Tristán and Iseo into Christian deaths, through three devices: the depiction of Tristán as a devout Christian; the elimination of his killing of Iseo, turning the latter's death into a natural one from grief rather than its being caused by the excessively tight embrace of her lover; and the suggestion of God's forgiveness of the lovers, making into a reality the plea of Iseo in her prayer to be allowed to die at the same time as Tristán.

The author's final prayer in the epilogue of the 1501 edition, which is suppressed in later editions, is intended to attest to readers his faith and devotion, which could have been brought under suspicion for having related this story of adulterous loves, just as Tristán's prayer in his last moments of life bears witness to his repentance and his Christian death. The significance of the religious elements incorporated into the epilogue is even greater since this epilogue is in other respects a calque of the one found in the *Baladro del sabio Merlín* printed in 1498, also by Juan de Burgos. The author of the epilogue (probably the same person who carried out all the rewriting or remodelling of the *Códice de Tristán*) considered it convenient to add to *Tristán* some religious elements that did not appear in the epilogue to the *Baladro*.

This recantation with which the 1501 edition ends perhaps reflects the fear of the reaction of readers at a specific point in time at which the glory of loving was overshadowed by the sin of loving, and at which the glorification of adulterous love was not permissible (Cuesta 2008a: 169–76), still less when it affected the monarchy; the war of succession which brought Isabel into confrontation with Juana la Beltraneja was not so long past, and the latter was accused of not being the daughter of Enrique IV but was claimed to be the result of adultery between Queen Juana and Beltrán de la Cueva. While the *Tavola Ritonda* modifies the ending of the French *Tristan en prose* to exalt the love of the protagonists and presents no conflict between their sinful love and its glorification, the author of the Castilian text avoids exalting the adulterous love of Tristán and Iseo, as he will later do in describing their tomb (Cuesta 2010), and attempts to concentrate the reader's interest on the lovers' repentance, undermining the content of the story passed to him by legendary tradition. The originality of the Spanish *Tristán* printed in 1501, reprinted so frequently during the XVIth century, has an extremely clear ideological orientation, caused either by the religious beliefs of the rewriter if he is sincere in these final manifestations, or else by his desire to avoid the reproaches of his readership. It would appear that he was successful in this, since of all the Arthurian works published in this period in Castilian, *Tristán* is the one which enjoyed by far the greatest number of editions, while *Lanzarote* (ed. Sharrer and Contreras 2006), another work with royal and adulterous love, remained unprinted.

Tristán de Leonís and the Romances of Chivalry

The work carried out by the rewriter of *Tristán de Leonís* succeeded, as its editorial success shows, in aligning the work closely with the Renaissance readership, among whom it would be received throughout the first third of the XVIth century as one more of the representatives of a newly fashionable genre: that of the romances of chivalry.

Precisely the same combination of knightly adventures (challenges, personal combat, jousts and tournaments, feats of arms, single and group combat) and amorous matters that had provided so many readers for *Tristán* would become typical of the most successful genre among the XVIth-century public, which, however, avoided adulterous love between the protagonists (Cuesta 1999a: xxvii–xxxiii). The successive editions of *Tristán de Leonís* contributed to the formation of the characteristics of the new genre, as did other medieval works on chivalric themes, whether Arthurian or not, that were printed in the first years of the XVIth century (Cátedra 2000: 17–8), although the enormous influence of *Amadís de Gaula* predominates over the rest. The sheer number of editions of *Amadís* and *Tristán de Leonís* in the first third of the century implies the existence of a readership among which were found also the writers of romances of chivalry, who absorbed from reading these works the features of the genre within which they themselves wished to create their own works: biographical structure, the *topos* of the pretended translation (Cirlot 1993; Marín Pina 1994), the exposure of the newborn hero (Gracia 1991), the imposition of a name related to the circumstances of his birth, to which is added the name of his country (Marín Pina 1990), amorous pursuit by women whom he does not love (a *topos* so common in the romances of chivalry that Don Quixote cannot but believe that Maritornes and Altisidora are attempting to undermine his fidelity to Dulcinea (Marín Pina 1998: 876–9), just as the evil lady and Morgana offer their love to Tristan), travelling ladies (Marín Pina 2007a, 2010), the imprudent granting of an unspecified boon and the rescue of the beloved who has been kidnapped (Tristán rescues the Dueña del Lago de la Espina and later Iseo), investiture as a knight by a king who is a near relation, generally the father, as occurs with Galaz and Amadís (an uncle, in the case of Tristán), the Ancient Knight (Lucía and Sales 2007)...

Magic and the supernatural, so characteristic of the Arthurian material and of the romances of chivalry (Cuesta 2014b) are represented in *Tristán* by Merlin, Morgana and the Holy Grail. Merlin, the model of so many enchanters both male and female in chivalric literature (Cuesta 2007) plays an active role in the opening chapters of

Tristán de Leonís: in the birth of the hero, in the revelation of the latter, and in his rescue. Moreover, he utters prophecies concerning his destiny, which places him among the three best knights in the world. Although he later disappears, occasional mentions of him, such as that made to the 'Padrón de Merlín', keep him in the reader's mind. In the text we also find ladies who know spells capable of causing loss of memory or freedom, such as those who enchant King Meliadux and King Arthur; magical objects sent by an anonymous woman, an identity behind which there hides Morgana, such as the enchanted horn which reveals adulterous women, and the broken shield which will become whole when the two sweethearts depicted on it become lovers; dwarfs with prophetic capabilities, such as those who are found at the courts of King Feremondo of Gaula and King Mares of Cornualla; the magic potion, an amorous drink which unleashes the love of the protagonists; premonitory dreams which foretell disasters, such as those of Tristan before being wounded by the young archer, those of Iseo de las Blancas Manos before losing her husband, or those of Iseo la Brunda before Tristan dies; the ring that makes its owner invincible and invisible; the ability of Morgana to guess the identity of who the unknown knight is ...

Another *topos* of the romance of chivalry taken from the Arthurian romance (but not only from this source) is the presentation of the fiction as history (Eisenberg 1982; Fogelquist 1982). If the account of the deeds of Arthur is supposed to be the work of the monk Blaise, to whom Merlin himself dictates his life story (Alvar 1991: 42–3), the deeds of Tristán, related by himself, are going to be preserved in the *Libro de Aventuras* of the Round Table. These are the predecessors of the wise magician whom Don Quixote will imagine to be the historian of his adventures.

The motifs of the island and the proud and idolatrous giant, frequent in the romances of chivalry of the XVIth century (Cuesta 2001), are represented in *Tristán* by the island of Ploto and the giant Bravor. The fabulous monsters are present in the work in the episode of the Bestia Ladradora. The squire who accompanies the knightly protagonist in the romances of chivalry is present in the character of Gorvalán (Urbina 1991: 27–34).

A particularly notable characteristic of *Tristán de Leonís* is humour. This feature of the work is probably one of those which it retains from its source, since there are also humorous touches in the surviving Castilian and Catalan manuscripts, as has been seen. Nor is humour lacking in the Renaissance romances of chivalry (Daniels 1992), in which this element must not be attributed solely to the influence of the humanistic comedy or Italian chivalric literature (Sales 1996: 152 n. 43): humour is already present in the Arthurian narratives and in *Amadís*. It is sufficient to recall the episode of Gandalín in the tower of Arcaláus, which must surely have influenced that of Sancho Panza and the fulling hammers: both squires suffer physiological reactions because of fear. *Tristán* is full of comic details: the story of bleeding noses with which the Dueña del Lago del Espina attempts to cover up her adultery; the scene in which King Mares threatens the lady's dwarf; the inelegant situation of Tristán on being rejected by the Lady of the Lake to whose rescue he has ridden; the fright of Palomades on meeting Brangel and believing her to be a ghost; Palomades' erotic dream, from which he is reluctant to be awoken by Gorvalán; the practical jokes of Lamarad at the expense of the cowardly knights of Cornwall; the episode of the enchanted horn; King Mares's fall when he attempts to capture his nephew; the disillusionment of Quedín at not encountering any adventures; the punishment of the bravado of Queas; the discussion between Queens Iseo and Ginebra about the attractiveness of Tristán; the reproaches made by Arthur to Iseo, complaining about Ginebra's infidelity to him; the affair of the helmet, thanks to which Dinadán learns to fly, because the knights who defeat him unhorse him in order to take his horse (a joke that reappears in *Florisel de Niquea*, IV, II, 12: Daniels 1992: 39–40); the comic insults of Dinadán to Tristán and Iseo; the jokes on the need to hold oneself well in the saddle during the tournament of Vercepó; Dinadán's observations on the misfortunes that follow upon love; the trickery practised on King Mares on believing that the lovers are sleeping separated by a sword...

The courtly ambience that surrounds the knightly world, the description of which constitutes one of the factors in the success of the romances of chivalry, was already accurately picked up in the Arthurian romance: the games of chess, the tents erected by the shores of the sea, the lofty vantage points whence ladies and kings contemplate jousts and tournaments, the music of the harp, the parades in the course of which the people have the chance to admire and compare the beauty of knights, ladies and maidens, the petitions to the king or to the heroes by supplicant knights and ladies, the messengers who arrive at court with news of other characters, the assembly of the whole court around the king [...] All this forms part of the framework in which the adventures of the protagonists develop.

Many of the *topoi* of Arthurian material passed to the romances of chivalry through *Amadís* and the *Tristán* texts; the latter, together with *Lanzarote*, had already influenced *Amadís* (Cuesta 2008b). The successive editions of *Tristán de Leonís* would, for publishers and readers, be incorporated within the publishing phenomenon of the romances of chivalry whose characteristics have been studied by Lucía (1998a): folio format, printed in two columns in black-letter type with decorated initials, and a title page with the title and a woodcut of an armed knight. The length of the text, although shorter than that of other romances of chivalry, was not, at all events, anomalous: hence the fact that the work did not adopt the quarto format of the brief chivalric narrative.

Tristán is not the only Arthurian work to be printed and read as one among other romances of chivalry in the XVIth century: Roubaud (2001) believes that at bottom there lies a desire to enhance, through contrast, the new fictions on the basis of the old, which the former would eclipse using similar mechanisms and devices. This attitude surely underlies the characteristics presented by the 1534 continuation, *Tristán el Joven*.

Tristán el Joven (1534)

Description

This work, published in Seville in 1534 by Domenico de Robertis and translated into Italian in 1555, with some modifications that impart a more clearly Renaissance character to it (Gimber 2004), is an adaptation and continuation of *Tristán de Leonís*, and occupies 207 folios printed in two columns, in black-letter type, which is (as we have seen) the customary format of Renaissance romances of chivalry, the genre to which it belongs. Three copies are currently known (Lucía Megías 2005b). The text is divided into two parts.

The first book of *Tristán el Joven* brings together the material that appeared in *Tristán de Leonís*, to which the 1534 author refers as 'materia antigua', but with the addition of new chapters in the central section, and with the suppression of a few passages. The original material created by the anonymous author of the 1534 text consists of the Prologue, in which he justifies the need for a continuation of *Tristán de Leonís*, an extensive interpolation spanning chapters XXVII to LXI of Book I (fols 20*ra*–50*va*), and the entire Book II, in which there are narrated the adventures of the two children of Tristán and Iseo, who bear the same names as their parents, up to their marriages. Furthermore, at the heart of the material taken from earlier editions of *Tristán de Leonís*, other minor modifications are carried out.

The thirty-five new chapters introduced in Book I give the first book a length similar to that of Book II. In them is narrated the story of the love affair of Ricarda, sister of Galeote, with the King of the Hundred Knights, the adventures of Galeote and Micer Antonio until the death of the former, and the stay of Tristán and Iseo on the Isla del Ploto, where the birth of their children occurs.

As regards the second part, which is the completely original creation of the anonymous author of 1534, it is much longer than the 'materia antigua' derived from *Tristán de Leonís*. Its first chapters tell of the war of vengeance for the murder of Tristán, the accession to the throne of Cornualla and Leonís of Tristán el Joven, still a child, the chivalric and amorous adventures of his uncles Palante and Plácido, the first loves of Tristán el Joven with Queen Trinea and the scenes of court life in which the beautiful princess Iseo is the central character. The central part of the work consists of the chapters devoted to the journey of Tristán el Joven to the court of Arthur to be armed knight by the king himself, his knightly adventures in defence of justice and against pagan giants, and his expedition to assist Queen Trinea in her war against the Idumeans, which he undertakes incognito, as well as the marriage of the young squires of the protagonist. The final chapters are devoted to relating how Tristán el Joven travels to Spain after having dreamed that there he will meet love, how he falls in love with the infanta María and succeeds in rescuing her from the Moorish knight who had kidnapped her, subsequently agreeing to marry her at the same time as her brother King Juan marries Princess Iseo. The weddings are celebrated in Leonís, and the work ends with the return of King Juan and Iseo to Spain, where both will reign.

The first studies of the work were by Eisele (1980), who set out the changes she had observed in relation to previous editions (1981), and Seidenspinner-Núñez (1987–8). Subsequently I (1989) edited the text, with an introduction, as a dissertation (*memoria de licenciatura*, which was the basis of my 1997 edition), at the same time as Gil de Gates presented her doctoral thesis, still unpublished. Until 1995, the date of Ros Domingo's doctoral thesis, in which the work occupies almost one hundred pages, the principal interest in the text had been on the part of the present writer, save for an article by Gil de Gates (1995; also 1997). Subsequently, the list of researchers working on the text was augmented by Gimber (1996 and 2004), Ros Domingo (2001: 283–404), a development of his earlier study, and above all Campos García Rojas, who has published numerous studies on it (Eisenberg and Marín Pina 2000: 435–9).

The Author

Although *Tristán el Joven* appeared as an anonymous work, a study of mine (2002a: 328–44, developing my 1993 thesis and 1997 edition) proposed as author a descendant of Garci Franco and María de Saravia who would have had some connection by family or patronage with the Manrique clan. Although it is not possible to identify a specific individual as the author with any certainty, it is my belief that he could be a great-grandson of Garci Franco, chaplain of Carlos I and brother of María de Guzmán, who married Francisco Vargas Manrique. This suggestion is based on several factors. Firstly, on the references to Peninsular geography in the text as the locations of important episodes: Fuerteventura and Burgos, of which the bishops were Pablo de Santa María and his son Alonso de Cartagena, who wrote in 1436 some *Allegationes* defending the rights of the Castilian Crown to the Canary Islands. Secondly, on important fictional characters in the work who can be identified with historical families or individuals, as indicated by the 'equals' sign: Silvera = Diego de Silva, who fought and became a prisoner on Gran Canaria (Perdomo 1942); el Franco = Garci Franco, a member of the Council of the Catholic Monarchs, married to María de Saravia, niece of Alonso de Cartagena; Pedro de Lara = Pedro Manrique, who claimed to be descended from the Siete Infantes de Lara and who obtained from Isabel I (in return for his renunciation of the corregidorship of Vizcaya) an indemnity which guaranteed to the Oñaz clan and its supporters their retention of all their property. Thirdly, on episodes in the romance which can be related to contemporary historical events: confrontations in the enduring Basque Country feud between the Oñaz faction and that of the Gamboa clan and their supporters, the succession of Carlos I to the throne, the matrimonial policy of the Catholic Monarchs and Carlos I. From this argument, another aspect of the work emerges: the projection of reality into fiction and the author's ambition to carry out the reverse process, the projection of fiction onto the reality of his time, an aspect that can be seen equally in the social, political, and moral ideology conveyed.

An Anti-Arthurian *Tristán*

For this author, the Arthurian world is merely a pretext and the story of Tristan simply a basis on which to construct his fiction about a character and a story well known to his readership. He is interested in the contemporary world, and makes use of the romance to attempt to imbue his public with his ideology.

Both the present writer (1993a: 464–6; 1997e: 55–9; 2002a: 308–9) and Ros Domingo (2001: 371–95) emphasise in published work the intense labour of deconstructing the Arthurian world undertaken by the XVIth-century author. It is clear that he wishes to propose as a model an alternative world to that described in the Arthurian texts, and for this purpose he makes use of two techniques. On the one hand, he progressively diminishes, as the story advances, the roles of the principal figures taken from *Tristán de Leonís*, and changes the nature of their character to the extent that they become totally different individuals, who share only their name with their Arthurian counterparts (this is what occurs, for example, with Gorvalán and Brangel). On the other hand, he mercilessly degrades such Arthurian characters as he uses in single episodes, attributing defects to them and ridiculing them. The most notable case is the transformation of Queen Ginebra, who is described as an elderly, lustful woman, who forgets her love for Lanzarote on seeing the handsome and youthful Tristan, pursues him insistently, and is rejected by him. In his design of the character of Ginebra the author could have had in mind the evolution that the image of the queen had undergone in the *romancero viejo*, as pointed out by Piñero (2005).

As regards the protagonist himself, Seidenspinner-Núñez (1987–8) has already pointed out that, as occurs with other sons of famous medieval chivalric heroes, Tristán el Joven completely replaces Tristán de Leonís as an exemplary model, an aspect which is reflected symbolically in the work by the award to the son of the father's seat at the Round Table (29). Compared with his father's knightly heroism, the son displays a prosaic, and at times comically prudent, behaviour (30–1). This arises from the fact that the chivalric ideal maintained by the author does not now correspond to a medieval heroic ideal, but to a Renaissance one imbued with a Christian spirit.

Since the author attempts, in his work, to supersede the Arthurian model, in many passages his starting point lies in the reworking of the themes he found in the previous editions of *Tristán*. The theme of suicide, which was related to the theme of passionate love, serves, in the continuation, to highlight the blindness and pride of those who will accept neither Christianity nor defeat (Campos García Rojas 2003). Tristan's journeys in search of healing of the damage from his wounds are turned, in *Tristán el Joven*, into a journey by the queen of Egypt who has been magically poisoned and who can obtain health only from the hands of the protagonist (Campos García Rojas 2009–10); in other words, where the father seeks healing on the journey, the son dispenses it to those who come to seek him. And while the father journeyed to obtain the hand of Iseo on behalf of King Mares, the son travels in order to obtain the hand of the sweetheart who is destined for him; what had been adulterous love in the older story becomes matrimonial love in the continuation (Cuesta 1990).

The Episode of Vengeance: Relations with the Medieval *Tristán* texts
To conclude this section on the relations between the text and previous *Tristán* texts, it is necessary to recall that the second book of *Tristán el Joven* begins with a series of chapters devoted to the vengeance against King Mares de Cornualla for the murder of Tristán and Iseo. The presence of this episode in the work, as well as some specific details of it, lead me (2009c) to maintain that the author of the 1534 work knew a text similar to that of the *Códice de Tristán*, which would presuppose a widespread and sustained circulation of the latter at that time, since *Tristán de Leonís* does not include this episode. The author, following the same procedures as elsewhere in the work, diminishes the role of the characters drawn from *Tristán* to increase that of the new characters whom he has created, for which reason the episode appears greatly altered. Nor, moreover, does the *Códice* survive complete, so that this suggestion, like the reconstruction of the partially legible episode in the *Códice*, must remain a mere hypothesis.

Genre and Style
Gil de Gates (thesis 1989: 288) considers *Tristán el Joven* to be a fruit of the medieval tradition, though she later modifies her statement and characterises the work as representative of a period of transition. In my belief (2002a), however, it is fully Renaissance both in style, since the author adheres to the ideas of Valdés on written language, and in the ideals that it reflects: it criticises secret marriage, valid during the Middle Ages (as recognised by Alfonso X), and offers a social and political model appropriate to ruling an empire, with the resulting power of the crown over the nobility. The genre within which *Tristán el Joven* is inscribed is not that of the medieval Arthurian chivalric romance, but that of the romances of chivalry, which around 1534 was already enjoying enormous success and vitality. The very concept of producing a continuation follows one of the unwritten rules of this genre: the romance of chivalry always left open the possibility of a continuation in which the leading role was played by the son of the protagonist. The 1534 author perceived the lack of a continuation of *Tristán de Leonís* with a second part narrating the adventures of his son as an anomaly and a defect, as he declares in his prologue (commented on by Soriano 2005), and to remedy this deficiency he decides to write it himself, although to do so he has to modify the 'historia antigua'.

The inclusion of the work in the genre of the romances of chivalry is evident not only in its physical presentation, with the characteristics which distinguish the publication conventions of that genre, and in the imitation of episodes from the most successful works, especially from *Amadís* and *Palmerín de Olivia* (Cuesta 1997a, 1997b, 1998), but, above all, in its use of the same range of *topoi*, with its incorporation of all the elements, settings, episodes and characters typical of that type of work: combats with pagan giants, a wise enchantress, proud knights, feats of arms, challenges, wars, love affairs, magical objects, islands... Some *topoi*, however, are drawn not from this genre, but from folklore: for example, the game of chess has a very important role in the episode of the Isla del Ploto, in the conception and birth of Tristán el Joven and his sister the infanta Iseo (Campos García Rojas 2000), and the theme of hunting, which sets off various narrative threads since it constitutes a journey or a displacement through the various scenarios in which the narrative is set, which themselves are possessed of a certain symbolism (Campos García Rojas 2001a).

The new chapters introduced in the interpolation in the first part, and all those of the second part, strike a discordant note relative to the inherited material, moreover, in matters of style (since they follow the Renaissance model), in their descriptive realism, and in the important role of humour and parody (Cuesta 2002a: 317–23). The author combines the rhetoric of courtly discourse placed in the mouths of the characters at solemn moments, with the frequent presence of the colloquial character of the spoken language both courtly and popular, through dialogue. In the dialogue, the mention of the speaker is sometimes suppressed when it is clear who is speaking, which imparts much greater liveliness to the narration. At other times, sentences with numerous verbs are what gives an almost visual vivacity to the scene. The use of the diminutive is notable, as is that of comparison and realistic, colloquial dialogue and the use of humour and ironic parody to introduce, in a veiled manner, his criticism of those who do not follow the mode of life and social relations that he is presenting as a model. Even a comic character, Miliana, is used didactically by the author when he makes it known that the infanta Iseo did not consent to people mocking her and asked that she be respected because of her advanced old age (Gil de Gates 1995). Gil de Gates (1997) perceives in the work a type of intimate humour that integrates members of the group within the social 'I', and another type of humour with the function of differentiating and with an outward gaze that stigmatises the Other by converting it into a comic character. These two types of humour are placed at the service of the author's ideological intentions. Humour and imitation are combined in one banqueting scene that Gimber (1996b) compares with other similar episodes in the *Cuento de Tristán*, *Tristán de Leonís* and *La Celestina*.

Humour and realism are united to offer, at times, passages in which parodic verisimilitude predominates (Cuesta 1997b). The author has no difficulty in depicting knights who sleep, eat, and go to confession before dying, as Cervantes would demand years later. This is not the only coincidence, fortuitous or not, with *Don Quijote*: a humour which recalls that of Cervantes fills a dialogue between boatmen (ch. CLXXX) and another between knights and shepherds (ch. CCIII), as well as many other episodes of the book. There also appear in the 1534 *Tristán* such *topoi* as leaving the horse's reins loose so that it can choose the road to follow (chapter CCIII), and that of faithful servants of knights 'cuando no se catan les vienen las mercedes muy crecidas' (chapter CXX). If, as Martins supposes (1983a: 33–44) on the basis of affinities between the characters of Dinadán and Sancho Panza, Cervantes knew *Tristán*, it is very probable that he should have known this edition, the closest to him chronologically, and the one in which humour based on realist parody is an extremely important factor.

Space and the Development of the Hero
Two bodies of material so different in style and ideology were, of necessity, difficult to amalgamate, and the unity of the work suffers as a result. One of the devices that assist the author in creating structural links between the old material and the new created by him is spaces and journeys, studied by Campos García Rojas. From the perspective of folk motifs (also strongly associated with symbolism) he has examined the 'feminine crossing', which when associated also with a space involving water confers interesting meanings not only on episodes and their narrative development, but also on the very construction of female characters such as Florisdelfa and Queen Tulia (2009–10). As far as concerns the motif of the journey, he indicates its relationship with the search for healing, and how this constitutes a trigger for the knight to leave his homeland not for any chivalric adventure, but for survival, so that he enters into encounters with the supernatural or with the elements which enable him to overcome his sickness (2009–10). The episode of Tristán's journey at random after being mortally wounded by Morlot first and then later by the young archer, is the inspiration in the second part of the work for the journey of Queen Tulia in search of a cure.

As far as concerns space, Campos García Rojas analyses the different elements of geography and their symbolic significance in so far as they constitute scenarios for the development of the hero. Islands, the Mediterranean Sea (2002a), the forest, Egypt (1997b), cities, castles, lakes and rivers, mountains, are specific and differentiated spaces, the symbolism attached to which from ancient times endows with particular significance and meaning the actions that occur in them (2000, 2002a, 2002b).

Social, Moral and Political Ideology: Marital Love and Imperial Policy
The author offers an ideology that fits well with Renaissance humanism, but that collides both with that diffused by the Arthurian romance and with some aspects of that espoused in the romances of chivalry. Specifically, this disharmony is noticed above all in the author's favourable attitude to marital love, in his rejection of magic, which he reluctantly accepts by presenting it only as the magic of entertainment (illusionism, an automaton, a speaking bird, journeys on a cloud), or as the work of the devil (the lady Florisdelfa). The character Florisdelfa is a good example of the author's negative attitude to magic practised by the female characters who constitute a threat to the protagonists, and of his condemnation of women who transgress the norms established for their gender (Campos García Rojas 1997a).

As far as love is concerned, *Tristán el Joven* is very different from the work of which it purports to be a continuation. The previous editions of *Tristán* presented love as a destructive force that inevitably unleashed tragedy, and conceived it as always being linked to adultery, while the 1534 text presents the amorous sentiment as a structural element in society, which leads to happiness and which is channelled through marriage (Cuesta 1990). For Ros Domingo (2001: 283–404) the distinctive feature of the *Tristán* printed in 1534 is the protagonist's transformation into a husband, sovereign, father and Christian, and the absence of conflict between love and society throughout Book II.

Another aspect of interest to the author is contemporary politics. *Tristán el Joven* is at one and the same time a reflection of and propaganda for the figure of Carlos I (better known outside Spain as the emperor Charles V) and perhaps also a proposal for a programme of government and a criticism of a model of behaviour (Eisele 1980; Cuesta 1996): the ruler must be a good Christian, visit the different parts of his kingdoms, unify his territories and achieve peace and understanding among the inhabitants of his different possessions, have counsellors among his relatives but not favourites, bestow in each kingdom posts on natives of that land, and promote among his relatives marriages of political importance. This interest in politics and the historical reality of his time is shared with other romances of chivalry from the period of the Catholic Monarchs and the first years of the reign of Carlos I (Marín Pina 1995). Many romances of chivalry disguised the reality of their time under an idealist style and technique (Cuesta 2002b). For his part, Campos García Rojas (2001b) perceives in addition a political interest on the author's part, which is related to the exemplary model of the Catholic Monarchs: in the episode of the Isla del Ploto in *Tristán el Joven* are reflected the political ideas of their reign as far as concerns the construction of a legacy. Moreover, spaces are strongly associated with the ideological requirements of the XVIth-century romances of chivalry; thus, events that unfold in the Mediterranean are frequently aimed at the conversion of the infidel or the destruction of the pagans, that is to say, to the messianic ideal of military and spiritual conquest that predominated at that moment (Campos García Rojas 2002a).

It is usually said that for the Arthurian romance adventure is a quest in which the very identity of the knight errant is at stake. In *Tristán el Joven* the motive of the adventure is different: it shares with other romances of chivalry the desire to entertain by relating the surprising events which befall its protagonist and which are simply an opportunity for him to display his courage, his skill, and his courtly qualities. But these adventures are narrated as a function of the ideology of their author. Thus, for example, the adventures serve the purpose of allowing the protagonists and his friends to put into practice the virtues that define the ideal knight, showing what is the correct behaviour. By contrast, the enemies of Tristan are characterised by their pride, vanity, discourtesy, cruelty, paganism, injustice [...] The adventures prove the negative consequences that these defects entail for their possessors, and reveal their well-deserved punishment.

The author of the 1534 text has wanted to make use of a story well known to his public, which had a long literary tradition behind it, and which belonged to the Matter of Britain, in order to:

1. criticise and, as far as possible, parody the Arthurian world and that of the contemporary romance of chivalry: to this end he uses the technique of pastiche and imitates episodes of other romances of chivalry (Cuesta 1997b);
2. present a political model, at whose apex of power is located the king, maintaining both rights and obligations, supervising the process of justice and the well-being of his subjects, surrounded by wise and loyal counsellors, delegating his power to reliable persons and being the mirror of all virtues; the author also wished to create certain parallels between the romance and reality, recording recent events that had occurred in the history of the Spanish monarchy (Cuesta 1996); and
3. propose a social model; the family appears as the basic structural element of this society, and, from this point of view, love, marriage and children take on a special significance (Cuesta 1990).

The world of the romance is idyllic and utopian in so far as it depicts a perfect society, without internal problems and whose coherence and virtues permit it to overcome all external obstacles. It is organised around a court of model personages, whom it describes in various situations, thereby making them always give the correct response. This social model is not proposed in an abstract manner, but fits perfectly within the situation being experienced by Spain at the time in question, during the reign of the emperor Charles V. The storyline shows much greater interest in reflecting the feelings of the characters, and, above all, for the 'social' relations than for the mere narration of adventures. Much importance is attached to clothes, to courtly speech, to the rituals of courtesy. The author, who makes part of his story take place in Spain, reveals himself to be a realist, and is particularly skilled in depicting family scenes, full of tenderness.

In short, the author takes advantage of the success of the romances of chivalry to diffuse and inculcate his own ideology among his readers, who, he hoped, would be numerous; for this reason he selected the most accepted genre and a very famous work, with a well-known story, and an ideology quite contrary to his own as far as the function of marriage was concerned. Naturally, there would be no point in attempting to attract to his ideology those who already shared it. In the political aspect, moreover, perhaps the implicit ideology was aimed at the emperor himself, or might even be propaganda for the policy of the latter (it must not be forgotten that it was translated into Italian in 1555 and that on 25 October of that very year the emperor abdicated; it would have been greatly to the latter's advantage to count on the good will of the Italian population towards him and his family), since although there are some veiled criticisms, in all other matters his behaviour and life correspond more or less exactly to the model proposed (Cuesta 1996). What Gil de Gates (1989: 76) considers to be a lack of adjustment of the work to the chivalric genre, caused by the author's inexperience, could well be the effect of his astuteness, in seeking to persuade his ideological opponents and the emperor himself (a known devotee of romances of chivalry) of his case.

Unfortunately for the author and the printer who took the risk of this venture, the successful Spanish fiction of the second third of the XVIth century followed other paths: adventure and entertainment were what appealed, not moralisation and ideological indoctrination. The effort made by the author to transform the medieval Arthurian material into chivalric Renaissance fiction produced a result that would fail to satisfy the devotees of either of these two types of reading matter.

The Impact of the Tristan Romances on Spanish Literature

Although this aspect is discussed by Alvar in his chapter, it is worth reflecting briefly on the place occupied by the romances concerning Tristan in Spanish literature from the XIVth century onwards. The references in the *Libro de buen amor*, the *Glosa al regimiento de principes* of Castrogeriz, and the poets of the *cancioneros* reveal knowledge of one version or another of the medieval romances by authors of the XIVth and XVth centuries. The possible influence of these texts on the *Libro del cauallero Zifar* cannot be ruled out, despite the doubts expressed by Lucía Megías (1996), and their influence on *Amadís* is certain (Cuesta 2008b). *Don Quijote* also offers some curious parallels (Cuesta 1997b). The very fact of the publication of *Tristán* among the first works of fiction to be taken up by printers reflects an interest on the part of the public which motivated them to ignore possible criticisms, since the work of rewriting the final passages and the colophon of the 1501 *Tristán* reveals clearly that the adapter feared that his work could be labelled immoral.

As regards the first third of the XVIth century, the number of editions invites us to reflect on the enormous diffusion that the printed *Tristán* must have had, since it is comparable with the number of editions achieved by *Amadís de Gaula*, the first and most famous of the romances of chivalry, at the same time. The existence of a continuation and a translation into Italian equally leads us to conclude that it was a success in publishing terms.

It is, however, curious that there are no reprintings later than 1534, a fact that should perhaps be attributed to a poor reaction to the continuation published in that year. The reading public does not seem to have been satisfied by the modifications carried out on the medieval material by the author of *Tristán el Joven*. Other Arthurian texts also cease to be printed about the same time, reflecting perhaps the public taste for new storylines and a rejection of the Arthurian material in favour of other fictional genres, especially the romances of chivalry.[8]

Notes

[1] The present study forms part of project number FFI2009–11483, supported by the Ministerio de Ciencia e Innovación, Spain.

[2] For the ballad, see Entwistle 1925: 111, 199; Surles 1984–5; Kurtz 1986–7; Di Stefano 1988: 203–9; Cuesta 1997: 133–9; 1998a; Beltrán and Vega 2004; Carlos Alvar in the present volume.

[3] I am grateful to Dr Lourdes Soriano for having informed me at that time of the publication of the article in which Santanach announced the discovery, and for providing me with a photographic copy of the manuscript.

[4] On the various aspects of this work, Baumgartner (2006: 325–41) gives a survey of the current situation.

[5] I prefer to avoid the description 'abbreviated', 'reduced' or 'summarised' because it implies a judgement about the precedence of V.I over this version, a question on which scholars still disagree. For Iragui the condensed version is later, and could justifiably be described thus. For other scholars, it could reflect a textual state of the text earlier than V.I and V.II.

[6] BL Harley 4389, Biblioteca Estense, Modena, ALPHA T.3.11 (*olim* 59), NLW, Aberystwyth, 446-E, Biblioteca Marciana, Venice, fr. XXIII (*olim* 234), BNF, f. fr. 760 and BNF, f. fr. 1463.

[7] *Tristano Riccardiano* and the part of the *Panciatichiano* derived from this, *Tavola Ritonda* and fragments of *Zibaldone da Canal*, excluding the *Tristano Veneto*, whose occasional points of similarity would be caused by its use of the *Compilation* of Rustichello.

[8] See also Cuesta Torre 2014a (Addenda to Bibliography, p. 466 below).

X

AMADÍS DE GAULA

Rafael Ramos

Amadís de Gaula is, without doubt, the most original and important representative of the Arthurian tradition in medieval Castilian literature. Superior to those works that are merely translations, this imitation of the adventures of Lancelot and Tristan succeeded in producing a masterly combination of the chivalric, amorous and fantastic adventures its author found in the French texts, to create an original story which nonetheless fitted into the established tradition in a completely new fashion. A brief summary of its storyline will amply demonstrate the point.

Immediately after his birth, Amadís, fruit of the illicit love of King Perión of Gaula and Princess Elisena, is thrown into the sea in a casket. A Scottish knight, Gandalés, comes across him far out at sea, and brings him up under the name of the Doncel del Mar, together with his own son Gandalín. An extraordinary enchantress, Urganda la Desconocida, predicts the great deeds of the unknown lad. One day there arrives at the Scottish court Lisuarte, king of Great Britain, accompanied by his daughter Oriana. Since the latter stays there a good while, it is arranged that the Doncel del Mar should place himself at her service. Each immediately falls in love with the other, although he is aged only twelve and she is just ten. Unaware, however, that his love is returned, the Doncel del Mar despairs because of the social gulf that separates them: she is the daughter of a king while he does not even know who his parents are.

Perión de Gaula, who has now married Elisena, comes to the Scottish court seeking assistance because the king of Ireland has invaded his territory. Oriana arranges that he should knight his son, whom he does not recognise, and that Amadís should go to Gaula to assist him, accompanied by his cousin Agrajes and by Gandalín. After defeating the king of Ireland in a duel the Doncel del Mar brings the war to an end; and thanks to the ring which was left with him when he was abandoned in the casket, he is recognised by his parents, who have in the meantime had another two children, Galaor and Melicia. Amadís, the heir to the throne, soon leaves Gaula and heads for Great Britain, where Oriana is awaiting him and where the best knights in the world are gathering. On the way, he arms his brother Galaor knight, without recognising him, and he also meets his benefactress, the enchantress Urganda la Desconocida. After a secret meeting with his beloved, he presents himself at the court of Lisuarte and places himself at the service of the queen. A few days later, he leaves in search of Galaor and encounters the dwarf Ardián, who accepts him as his master. He also confronts the evil magician Arcaláus the Enchanter, who will thenceforth be his principal enemy, and promises his assistance to Briolanja, whose uncle has usurped the kingdom of Sobradisa. On his return, he confronts an unknown knight who, it transpires, is Galaor; but Gandalín stops the fight and beheads the cousin of Arcaláus, who had engineered the entire situation so that the two brothers would kill each other. Galaor then enters the service of King Lisuarte.

The king convokes his court in London. Among those who attend is Barsinán de Sansueña, a secret ally of Arcaláus. They seize Lisuarte and Oriana, but the latter are liberated by Galaor and Amadís respectively. Upon their return, the two lovers make their vows to one another in secret, and give free rein to their passion. In London at last the knights who are loyal to Lisuarte subjugate Barsinán.

Once the session of the court is completed, Amadís, Galaor and Agrajes depart for Sobradisa to come to the aid of Briolanja. Confused by some ill-advised remarks of Ardián, Oriana believes that Amadís is in love with that young queen. Amadís and Agrajes rout the usurpers, and they are soon joined by Galaor, who has encountered another son of Perión de Gaula, Florestán. On the way back, these four knights visit the enchantments of the Ínsula Firme. On overcoming these amorous temptations, Amadís stays behind as the ruler of this extraordinary land, but then receives a letter from Oriana in which she repudiates him. He immediately leaves his companions and, under the pseudonym of Beltenebrós, withdraws to a solitary islet, the Peña Pobre, where he has the company of a hermit. Everyone seeks Amadís, particularly Oriana, who, on learning that he has overcome the tests of love at the Ínsula Firme, realises that her suspicions have been without foundation. Finally, one of her ladies discovers him, hands him a letter from Oriana and takes him to Great Britain, to the Castle of Miraflores, where the two sweethearts meet once more. Together they overcome the magical love tests set by the squire Macandón, thereby reinforcing their commitment to each other. Amadís, still hidden by the name Beltenebrós, frees Leonoreta, Oriana's sister, confronts Arcalaús once more, and takes part in the battle between King Lisuarte and Ciladán of Ireland, where he finally reveals himself to everyone. Urganda arrives at court, and foretells the future enmity between Amadís and the king.

Amadís and his relatives become ever more influential in Great Britain. This provokes the envy of some courtiers, who begin to sway Lisuarte against him. Amadís and his party leave Great Britain and depart for the Ínsula Firme, but Galaor remains with the king. Oriana discovers that she is pregnant, and secretly gives birth to a son, Esplandián, who is carried off by a lioness and brought up by the hermit Nasciano. Unaware of these developments, Amadís undertakes a long journey in search of adventure, under the pseudonyms of the Caballero del Enano and the Caballero de la Verde Espada. In this way he comes to the court of the king of Bohemia, where he aids King Tafinor against the Romans; to the islands of the Aegean, where he routs the diabolical Endriago; and to Constantinople. In the meanwhile, Lisuarte has received Esplandián at his court, without knowing that he is his grandson, and he is appointed in the service of Oriana, who soon discovers his true identity. Surprisingly, Lisuarte grants Oriana's hand in marriage to Patín, emperor of Rome. Amadís, now known as the Caballero Griego, returns to Great Britain just in time to learn of these plans and to organise a fleet which routs that of the Romans, in which they were carrying Oriana. Following a successful outcome to the battle, and the revelation of the identities of those concerned, all head for the Insola Firme.

The seizure of Oriana, however, provokes war between Great Britain and the Insola Firme; each side summons allies to its assistance. With so many kingdoms at hostilities with each other, Arcalaús persuades King Arábigo and other enemies of Amadís to attack and rout the Christian kings. After various battles between the supporters of Amadís and those of Lisuarte, Nasciano succeeds in making peace between them by revealing that Esplandián is the son of Amadís and Oriana, who had been secretly married. The forces of King Arábigo then attack those of King Lisuarte and rout them, but the army of Amadís comes up to aid him and together they defeat the invaders and capture King Arábigo, Arcalaús and the other enemy leaders. Finally, Lisuarte proclaims Amadís and Oriana the heirs to the throne of Great Britain.

This, in a very summary manner, outlines the plot of *Amadís de Gaula*, which is considered today to be the first great work of fiction in Spanish literature. However, the vicissitudes of its transmission and survival have led to various doubts on this matter. The language in which it was originally written, and its date of composition, have been debated at length; in current scholarship, however, the polemics over the origins of *Amadís* seem completely superseded. All surviving versions, both manuscript and printed, are in Castilian, with no indication of any other language underlying this. The earliest references to the work, and its earliest appearances in inventories of libraries, are also found in Castile. Finally, it is in the circles associated with the young Alfonso XI, king of Castile, that the gestation of the work makes most sense. All this automatically invalidates the speculations that accrued over several centuries, in which origins variously in French, Provenzal, Catalan, Galician, Arabic, or Hebrew have been suggested for the work. Only the Portuguese hypothesis deserves a detailed commentary, because it was the earliest, the most insistently repeated, and the only one in which a specific individual was suggested as the author.

The suggestion can be seen in 1464, when the historian Gomes Eanes de Zurara contrasted the work of true chroniclers with that of other writers more given to fictions 'such as are the earliest deeds of England, which was called Great Britain, and so the book of Amadis, though this was composed at the whim of a man who was called Vasco Lobeira, in the time of King Fernando, and everything in the said book is imagined by the author' (Brocardo 1997: 454). Although the reign of Fernando I of Portugal (1367–83) was later than the earliest Castilian references to *Amadís* (see below), and although a careful reading of the passage shows that Vasco Lobeira may have been, at most, the recipient of a copy or a version of the text (Riquer 1987: 30–1), and not the creator of the original, the hypothesis of his authorship was repeated time and again during the centuries that followed. Although Zurara's chronicle was not printed until 1792, there are known at least eleven manuscript copies of it, dating from the XVIth to the XVIIIth century, so that it is highly probable that it was the direct source of the later statements such as those of the humanists João de Barros, António Ferreira and Antonio Agustín, all of whom were well known for their voracious reading of medieval chronicles. In turn, from the statements by the latter two of them, printed towards the end of the XVIth century, there clearly derive those by scholars and bibliographers of the XVIIth and XVIIIth centuries, such as Manuel de Faria e Sousa, Nicolás Antonio, and Diogo Barbosa Machado, among others. As scholarship on the history of literature developed during the XIXth century, however, a Castilian origin for the work was becoming ever more firmly established.

Yet at the end of the XIXth century the hypothesis of a Portuguese origin received fresh support. From the *Cancioneiro de la Biblioteca Nacional de Lisboa* there emerged the cantiga 'Señor genta | mi tormenta' by João Lobeira, which seemed to have been rewritten as part of the poem 'Leonoreta | fin roseta' that appears in Amadís. Once more a Portuguese author named Lobeira seemed a possibility. The name 'Vasco' could have been an error or that of a descendant who might have continued the work of an ancestor. The basis of this whole hypothesis, however, has gradually been eroded. In the first place, the fact that João Lobeira was the author of a cantiga partly paraphrased in *Amadís* does not in any way imply that he was also the author of the latter work. Secondly, given its formal characteristics, it is clear that the composition of this Portuguese poem should not be dated to the period traditionally assigned to this poet (the second half of the XIIIth century), but to the era and to the court of Alfonso XI of Castile (V. Beltrán 1991). The latest efforts to sustain the hypothesis of a Portuguese origin for *Amadís* have, when all is said and done, been fruitless (Lapa 1970b), and are currently viewed as merely the final relics of a dated polemic. It is not impossible that there may have been early translations or adaptations into Portuguese, attributable to Vasco Lobeira or indeed to somebody else, but it is now beyond any doubt whatsoever that the work was of Castilian origin.[1]

Contrary to what may now seem to be the case, this polemic on the origins of the text, which lasted for several centuries, was not completely lacking in any basis, at least at the time when it initially became an issue. With medieval Castilian fictional writing then either unknown or poorly studied, *Amadís de Gaula* seemed an extraordinary work in the wider panorama of that literary tradition.[2] With a modern perspective, however, and when the work is set alongside the *Gran conquista de Ultramar* and the various *Crónicas troyanas*, alongside the translations of Arthurian texts and the stories of miracles and the fantastic in the *Antología castellana de relatos medievales* (MS h-I-13 of El Escorial Library), or alongside the *Libro del caballero Zifar* or the *Crónica sarracina* of Pedro de Corral, it is no longer considered to be a discordant element but is instead viewed as the most accomplished of all the known manifestations of medieval Castilian fiction.

It is not known for certain when *Amadís de Gaula* was composed. For some scholars, it was written between 1284 and 1295, although the arguments for this are weak and are based on simple conjecture (Avalle-Arce 1990: 99–100; 1991: I, 39–41).[3] It seems more appropriate to bring the date forward to the second quarter of the XIVth century (Entwistle 1925: 219; Lida de Malkiel 1952–3; V. Beltrán 1991; Gómez Redondo 1998–2007: II, 1545; Ramos 2003; Beceiro Pita 2007: 281; Rodríguez Velasco 2010: 137–8, 176). It seems, in fact, more convincing to place its appearance later than that of the translation of the principal Arthurian works in the first years of the XIVth century. Moreover, *Amadís de Gaula* makes proper sense only in the context of the social and political reforms introduced in the first years of the reign of Alfonso XI, between 1330 and 1340 approximately, in which the knightly class played an especially noteworthy role, so that it is easy to understand that in these specific circles there should have appeared literary works in which the figure of the knight in the service of the king was enhanced to the detriment of the great feudal lords who opposed him. Given this, particular importance attaches to its chronological coincidence with the new dating now suggested for the *Libro del caballero Zifar*, and for the earliest known references to the work and its characters: those contained in the *Libro de buen amor* of Juan Ruiz, dated to 1343, in the *Glosa castellana al Regimiento de príncipes de Egidio Romano* drawn up by Juan García de Castrojeriz around 1350, and in a passage in the *Rimado de palacio* of Pedro López de Ayala, datable to shortly after 1378 (but in which the author is referring to events of his youth, around

1345–50).⁴ *Amadís* must, as a result, have been composed some years earlier. It would make no sense for so popular a text, so frequently mentioned in later centuries even before it was printed (Riquer 1987: 11–25), to have been in existence for very long without allusion being made to it.⁵ The same date is indicated by the analysis of the lexicon of the work, since its most archaic forms can be dated to the middle of the XIVth century (Domingo del Campo 1984), and the study of the arms and armour used, which places it in the same period (Riquer 1987: 55–187). Whatever the case, however, by 1372 it was a book sufficiently famous throughout the entire Peninsula for Don Juan, Duke of Gerona, heir to the neighbouring kingdom of Aragón, to have a dog with that name (Riquer 1987: 14).

Despite this, we know the text of *Amadís de Gaula* almost exclusively from its printed editions dating from the XVIth century. Of its lengthy medieval wanderings there have survived barely four fragments (University of California, Berkeley, The Bancroft Library, MS 115), dated around 1420 (Rodríguez-Moñino, Lapesa and Millares Carlo 1956). The complete text has come down to us only from the version reworked and put through the press by Garci Rodríguez de Montalvo towards the end of the XVth century.⁶ The problems, however, do not end here. The earliest surviving printed edition of that reworking appeared in Zaragoza in 1508; but the first impression of the work must have appeared earlier than that, perhaps in Seville in 1496, and before that first surviving edition of 1508 there must have been at least another two, now lost (Ramos 1994). The stemma of its earliest printed transmission would have been as follows:

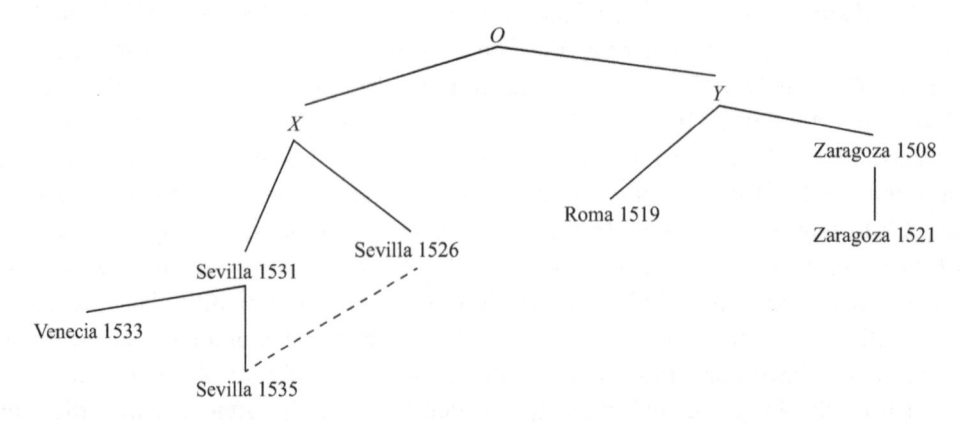

```
                          O
                         / \
                        /   \
                       X     Y
                      /|\   / \
                     / | \ /   Zaragoza 1508
                    /  |  Roma 1519   |
                   /   Sevilla 1526   Zaragoza 1521
         Sevilla 1531
        /    |
Venecia 1533 |
             Sevilla 1535
```

The editions of Zaragoza 1508 and Rome 1519 derive from a dreadful hyparchetype, with homoeoteleuta, *lectiones faciliores* and corrupt readings, although lexically it is in general very conservative. The first impressions from Seville, on the other hand, are generally faithful to a more correct hyparchetype (perhaps the edition of Seville 1511 mentioned in the inventory of the books of Fernando Columbus?), although they do introduce numerous lexical modernisations. Moreover, while the edition of Seville 1531 follows this hyparchetype rigorously and introduces only a few reasonable emendations, that of Seville 1526 delights in altering various aspects of its exemplar. The edition of Venice 1533 derives from that of Seville 1531, but its corrector, Francisco Delicado, carried out a fundamental revision of the text. The edition of Seville 1535 derives almost entirely from its predecessor, Seville 1531, but takes some of its sheets from the edition of Seville 1526, from which we can conclude that in the print workshop in question compositors worked using unbound copies as their exemplars.[7]

From what may be deduced as a result of collating the printed text with the manuscript fragments, it seems that Montalvo abbreviated the original text slightly and lightly modernised its lexicon. This is an assertion that must be made with some caution, given the brevity of the fragments.[8] On the other hand, he added numerous digressions of a moral, religious and political character, especially in praise of the Catholic Monarchs. In addition, he introduced some episodes scattered throughout the work which have no purpose other than that of linking *Amadís* with the continuation that he wrote himself, *Las Sergas de Esplandián*. Finally, it seems that he also suppressed those aspects that seemed to him to be the most licentious in the work that had come down to him. As he himself explained in the prologue, his labour consisted of going through 'correcting three books of *Amadís*, which were extremely corrupt because of the deficiencies of poor copyists and compositors, and copying and emending the fourth book with the *Sergas de Esplandián* his son, of which there is no record until now of its having been seen by anybody' (ed. Cacho Blecua 1987–8: I, 224). Indeed, various medieval authors (Pero Ferrús, Diego de Valera or whoever really wrote the *Molino de Amor*) referred to *Amadís* as a work composed in three books, so that this new distribution in four books and a continuation, the fifth, must be attributed to Montalvo. In general, everything suggests that, as he proceeded with his reworking of the medieval story, his interventions and modifications grew ever greater.

Among the elements clearly added in his reworking there stand out, for example, the episode of the Peña de la Doncella Encantadora, and those which lead to the appearance of the giant Balán, which extend over a good part of the fourth book, and which link directly with the initial episodes of the fifth. Also apparently his work are the great final weddings, in which almost all the protagonists are paired up, and through which peace is confirmed among the former combatants.

Without a doubt, the most important of his critical alterations is the change that the ending of the original text underwent. A good number of medieval allusions (Pero Ferrús, Fernán Pérez de Guzmán, *Curial e Guelfa*, *El Molino de Amor*, among others) in fact make it clear that the original *Amadís de Gaula* ended with a tragedy in which the young Esplandián killed his father, without recognising him, and that, when made aware of this news, Oriana commited suicide by throwing herself from a high window (Lida de Malkiel 1952–3). This was the traditional manner of ending a medieval chivalric fiction: the death of the protagonists, inherited from the Arthurian texts and the stories of the Trojan cycle. In the printed version, however, Esplandián merely wounds his father, who rapidly recovers. Nonetheless, Montalvo could not suppress so important a detail as the death of the principal characters, which must have been fixed in the memory of several generations of readers, so he resorted to a subterfuge:

> As you have heard, there took place this cruel and hard combat between Amadís and his son, because of which some claimed that in it Amadís died of those wounds, and others that it was from the first lance-thrust, which pierced him through to the back; and when Oriana learned of this, she hurled herself from a window. But it was not so, for that great master Helisabad, cured him of his wounds ... But the death that overtook Amadís was none other than, with his great deeds falling into oblivion as if buried beneath the earth, those of his son flourished with such fame and with such glory that they seemed to reach to the clouds. (trans. from the edn by Sainz de la Maza 2003: 253–4)

Alongside the substantial suppression of the earlier ending, there seem to be other modifications of quite varied type. Aldeva and Corisanda, who are the lovers respectively of Galaor and Florestán and who have a certain prominence in the first books, disappear from the story while they are heading for the court of King Lisuarte. The character of Galaor is transformed from being a knight who behaves licentiously towards as many women as he meets, into being the perfect husband for Briolanja. Urganda also undergoes a profound transformation. In her first appearances she comes over as an amorously inclined, changeable and cruel fairy being, who changes her appearance at will, seeks assistance from knights and distributes magical objects generously; but from the second book she always appears as an elderly woman of venerable aspect, travels on board her fantastic Serpent Ship and practically limits herself to giving linguistically cryptic prophecies of the future of the characters. Everything appears to indicate that Montalvo eliminated or minimised the most sensual elements, and those that departed furthest from religious orthodoxy, that he encountered in the original version.

Contrary to what might seem to be the case, remodelling of this kind was very common in medieval works, and the printed text of *Amadís* itself gives an excellent example of it. This is the well-known episode of Briolanja, in which the young queen solicits the amorous favours of the protagonist. In one version, that favoured by Montalvo, the protagonist rejects her offer, remaining faithful to his beloved. In the version of Prince Afonso of Portugal, on the other hand, Amadís ends up by acceding to her desires.[9] Moreover, each of these two versions contains its own specific variants. Thus Amadís, obliged by a 'don contraignant', was locked in a tower from which he could not be released until he had left Briolanja pregnant. When he did not agree to do so, he fell into a melancholy and was at the point of death, to such an extent that Oriana ordered him to please the young queen, and in fact he engendered a pair of twins with her.[10] In the other variant, however, it was Briolanja herself who took pity on the suffering of Amadís, and so freed him from his obligation. Of a single event, then, there survived two (or four) different versions.[11] In fact, the possibility has been suggested that in the lengthy period between the first composition of *Amadís* and the publication of the version by Garci Rodríguez de Montalvo, there may have been two or more reworkings of the story, perhaps with the addition of new episodes in each of them, so that the book would have been periodically refreshed in accordance with the tastes of its readers.[12]

Be this as it may, with its printed version *Amadís* acquired a form that we can regard as definitive, in which it was read across the whole of Europe throughout the XVIth and XVIIth centuries, and the person responsible for this undeniably successful version was Garci Rodríguez de Montalvo. Moreover, it was Montalvo himself who coined, in his prologue, a label to designate this type of stories for pure entertainment, divorced completely from reality and whose reading was intended only to entertain and to put forward good models of conduct for its readers: 'historias fingidas'.[13] Thus was born the first designation for prose fiction in the history of Spanish letters, the effectiveness of which was in no way diminished by the fact that in order to produce it Montalvo had recourse to the literary models that appeared to him to be closest in their style and most noble in their moral stance: namely, those offered to him by history (Fogelquist 1982). Of course, this designation came to enjoy a certain repute, since it would be used by, amongst others, Pedro Gracia Dei (early XVIth century), Alfonso de Valdés (1529), Gonzalo Fernández de Oviedo (*c*.1535–52), Antonio de Torquemada (1553), Damasio de Frías (*c*.1580) and Miguel de Cervantes (1616). The *Diccionario de autoridades* of the Real Academia Española (1734) even took up the term in order to define the word 'novela': 'historia fingida y rexida de los casos que comúnmente suceden o son verisímiles'.

Several different literary traditions come together in *Amadís*. The most important, naturally, is the Arthurian tradition, but the historiographic tradition and that of Troy are also weighty influences. Historiography provides the basic model of composition – logically and inevitably at that time – through which to develop an account in prose: the existence of an ancient original which is being copied faithfully, the deliberate omission of details that are not significant for the development of the argument, the various interpretations of the same phenomenon, and suchlike. The Troy legends, for their part, provide the work with a set of names of pseudo-Classical type (Apolidón, Arquisil, Fileno, Salustanquidio etc.), with some episodes involving the marvellous, like those of the Insola Firme or the Peña de la Doncella Encantadora (Gracia 1995; Suárez Pallasá 2006–8) and, as has been stated, with its tragic finale. Alongside these must not be forgotten another tradition that underlies the entire work, the lexicon of lyric poetry, which it directly reuses. The use in an amorous sense of words such as 'wound', 'service', 'captivity', 'care', 'death' and 'torment' makes sense only if one takes into account their metaphorical use by medieval poets.

Of all the traditions into which *Amadís* links, however, it is indubitably the Arthurian tradition that is the most significant.[14] This is not simply a question of the facts that the narrative involves relating chivalric adventures, guided by love and honour; that at every step we meet dwarfs and giants, monstrous beings, magicians and extraordinary marvels, enchanted castles and woods, hermits who reveal the meaning of dreams and attend to the spiritual needs of ladies and knights; nor even of the existence of a prophetic paraphernalia in common (Mérida Jiménez 2001). The Arthurian influence affects, naturally, every detail of the creation of this work. The entire geography of *Amadís* adheres to it, since its episodes take place mostly in England, Scotland, Norgales, Gaule, Leonnois, the Waste Land and in cities such as London, Bristoya (Bristol), Glocestre (Gloucester), Guncestre (Winchester) and Vindilisora (Windsor). Likewise, a good proportion of the names of characters seem to be calques of Arthurian forms: Nasciano, Ardán, Balais, Grasandor, Garín, Celinde, Esclavor, Sorelois, Nicorán...

The internal chronology of the work also adheres quite openly to the Arthurian tradition, so that the world of Arthur appears constantly as a background against which that of *Amadís* achieves its full significance. Whilst the adventures of the latter take place at an unspecified juncture 'not many years after the passion of our Redeemer and Saviour Jesus Christ' (ed. Cacho Blecua 1987–8: I, 227), the reader is soon advised that everything occurs before 'the advent of the most virtuous King Arthur, who was the best king of those who reigned there' (I, 243), and that King Lisuarte 'was the best king who ever was there, and who best maintained chivalry in proper form until the reign of King Arthur, who surpassed all previous kings in virtue, even though many kings reigned between the two of them' (I, 269). Besides these allusions, there are many other more indirect ones, such as the reference to a sword which ought to be 'thrown into some lake from which it can never be recovered' (I, 859), where the nod towards Excalibur must have been obvious to medieval readers. Similarly, there are explicit references to some of the great adventures of that emblematic era of chivalry, such as the arrival of the Holy Grail in England, the confrontation between Arthur and Flollo, the combats of Tristan with Morholt of Ireland and Bravor le Brun, the challenge by the Ancient Knight to the knights of Camelot, and the friendship between Lancelot and Galehaut (I, 243, 329–30; II, 1654–5, 1678–9). All these serve as counterpoint to the events related in *Amadís*, since either they are related to these, as prefigurations, or they are carried out by descendants of characters from this work.[15]

The broad outlines of the plot of *Amadís* are also fashioned according to Arthurian models, basically from the stories of Tristan and Lancelot in their prose versions. It is no accident that in the text there is a specific reference to 'el *Libro de don Tristán y de Lançarote*' (II, 1678) as a work known to all readers of *Amadís*. It certainly seems, moreover, that the Peninsular tradition regarded both works are forming part of a single cycle.[16] Some examples will make these points clear for both cases.

Like Lancelot, Amadís comes from Gaula, in French Brittany (*Amadís*, ch. 1; *Lancelot*, ch. 1a.1), and, like him, he displays signs of his courage and loyalty from infancy, which brings upon him a reprimand from his tutor (*Amadís*, ch. 2; *Lancelot*, ch. 9a.17). False news of the death of both characters reaches the royal court (*Amadís*, ch. 20; *Lancelot*, ch. 56.6). Both characters conquer their own lordships, the Ínsula

Firme and the Joyeuse Garde (*Amadís*, ch. 44; *Lancelot*, ch. 24a). They also suffer the unjustified jealousy of their lovers, and retreat to inaccessible places (*Amadís*, ch. 48; *Lancelot*, ch. 105.36). The shields of both are found by friends (Don Guilán el Cuidador; Galehaut), which brings upon the latter problems with other knights who recognise those heraldic arms (*Amadís*, chs 48–50; *Lancelot*, ch. 30.8–9). As time passes, Amadís and Lancelot retire to their strongholds or those of their allies with their lovers, where they protect them and where the ladies themselves insist on the importance, more than ever, of preserving the secrecy of their love (*Amadís*, chs 83 and 93; *Lancelot*, ch. 9.1–3; *La Mort le roi Artu*, ch. 96).

Many other details are derived from the story of Tristán. The starting point of the narrative, for example, is similar in both cases: 'Après la passion Nostre Seignor Jesu Crist [...] Joseph d'Abarematie [...] vint puis en la Grant Bretaigne' (ed. Curtis 1963–5: I, 40). It also seems that we should seek here the origin of the law of the kingdom of Gaula that punished immoral women, which lasted down to the time of King Arthur (*Amadís*, ch. 1; Löseth 1891: §§17–18), and which leads to the abandonment of Amadís in the casket. The character of Gandalín, foster-brother of the protagonist, son of the knight who rears him, and his squire and his confidant in matters of love, seems to have been modelled on the character of Governal, to such an extent that while the latter ends up marrying Brangaine, the lady of Iseult, Gandalín finally marries the Donzella de Dinamarca, the maid of Oriana (*Sergas*, ch. 140; Löseth 1891: §282g–h). The kidnapping of Oriana by Arcalaús, aided by a 'don contraignant' that Lisuarte cannot avoid, seems to have been inspired by the kidnap of Iseult by Palamedes (*Amadís*, ch. 34; Löseth 1891: §43).

In both cases, naturally, parallels could easily be multiplied. Even in multiple minor details, the influence of these Arthurian models is obvious, as the following examples show: the battle-cry of Lisuarte, 'Clarencia!', is identical to that of Arthur (*Amadís*: II, 1015; ed. Micha 1978–83: II, 47; VIII, 468, 481); the ruse by which one knight is able to make off with another's steed, tricking him with the supposed properties of a fountain (*Amadís*: I, 465; ed. Micha: VIII, 318–19); shields like those of Don Bruneo de Bonamar and Lancelot (*Amadís*: II, 1250, 1455; ed. Micha: VI, 233); the extraordinary swords which shatter at the first blow, leaving their bearers defenceless (*Amadís*: I, 563; ed. Sommer 1909: 161), or those made from the bones of extraordinary serpents (*Amadís*: I, 796–7; ed. Sommer: 121–2); or the vows uttered by knights at court, swearing solemnly to protect all women and ladies who come to them seeking succour (*Amadís*: I, 544–6; ed. Sommer: 320–1). Equally, both chivalric universes share a similar vision regarding everything that involves love and its power over knights. Thus it is that the latter can ride along utterly absorbed in their own thoughts of their lovers until struck by a branch, which returns them abruptly to the real world (*Amadís*: I, 685; ed. Micha: VII, 287). And the vision of these very lovers can distract them in mid-combat, bringing them to the brink of defeat (*Amadís*: I, 373; ed. Micha: II, 64–5). This influence is also manifest in the gradual emergence in the story of a loftier, more spiritual concept of knighthood (personified respectively in Galahad, the son of Lancelot, and in Esplandián, the son of Amadís); and in the intervention of the armies of Rome at the end of the story.

Some of the principal characters also seem to be directly inspired by the Arthurian tradition. Amadís, as has been stated, was formed with the models of Lancelot and Tristan in mind; the amorously inclined Galaor was based on Gawain, Lisuarte on Arthur; Arcalaús the Enchanter, in turn, seems modelled on the vengeful Morgana, while Urganda la Desconocida combines in equal measure some characteristics of Merlin and others of the Lady of the Lake.

It is, however, obvious that, in parallel with this imitation, there exists a desire to excel over, or rather to correct, the tradition being imitated, eliminating everything that seems open to criticism in moral terms. For this reason, Oriana, the lover of Amadís, is the daughter of the king, not his wife; and is kidnapped from the court together with the Donzella de Dinamarca, 'so that it may be more honourable and honest' (*Amadís*: I, 560); and the amorous union of the two protagonists occurs only after both agree on a secret marriage ('Yo haré lo que queréis, y vos hazed como, aunque aquí yerro y pecado parezca, no lo sea ante Dios', *Amadís*: I, 573), an institution that remained in practice until the Council of Trent. Perhaps for this reason, although the protagonists in both stories share an encounter through a window grille, in the first case Lancelot rips it off, giving free rein to his desires with Guinevere, while Amadís contents himself with kissing Oriana's hands through the bars (*Amadís*, ch. 14; Lancelot, ch. 39.36–8). It is clear that the Castilian story did not view adulterous relationships with approval. Only Don Guilán el Cuidador has a secret relationship with Brandalisa, the wife of the Duke of Bristoya (a cruel noble who is, opportunely, eliminated by the knights of Lisuarte), but at the end of the work he marries her. Moreover, the first adventure of the protagonist himself as soon as he has been knighted consists of coming to the aid of a knight who has been tricked by his wife.

In this vein, it is significant that both Amadís and Lancelot enter the service of the queen, not that of the king. While Lancelot, however, communicates his desire to Guinevere alone ('Dame', fait il, 'se vous plaisoit, jeure tendroie, en quel que lieu que jou a laisse, a vostre chevalier', ed. Micha 1978–83: VII, 285), leaving in suspense the question of whom he should serve in reality, the identification of Amadís as a knight of Brisena and her ladies is declared openly to the entire court ('queremos que él sea de nosotras para lo que oviéremos menester', 'we wish him to be our [knight] for whatever we may need', *Amadís*: I, 391), so that, when he severs his bonds with Lisuarte, nobody can perceive the slightest hint of treason. Quite the opposite, for his brother Galaor, a knight of the king, remains in Lisuarte's service and confronts the allies of his brother and his father. This same episode reveals another salient difference from the Arthurian models, since while Lancelot, his family members and his allies relinquish their allegiance to Arthur as a result of the love between Lancelot and Guinevere, Amadís and his household are brought into opposition to Lisuarte because of the advice of the latter's evil counsellors (*Amadís*, ch. 62; *La Mort le roi Artu*, ch. 91). In this way, in *Amadís* the confrontation among the knights is simply a political question, completely unconnected with the destructive power of love.

Be this as it may, it is also undeniable that the prose Arthurian works inspired the stylistic patterns within which *Amadís* was composed. Its long and complex storyline, broken into numerous episodes of which different knights are the protagonists (an aspect which prolongs and delays the linear development of the narration), is clearly derived from that tradition. Although to us this may seem to be a hindrance to the enjoyment of the book, in reality it was a wholly conscious strategy which this work imitated to perfection. Reading works of this kind was essentially a social amusement, which involved a number of people and took many days (Ramos 2003). A knight or lady read the work aloud and a fresh reader took over when the previous one tired. Hence such expressions as 'La historia dize que ...', or 'Agora cuenta la istoria que ...' (*Amadís*, II, 1338, 1561), which relate to this peculiar transmission, halfway between the oral and the written. If anyone among those who were following the story missed one or several reading sessions, upon their return they would have had no problem in following the thread of the story, which would not, in broad terms, have advanced very much. And, in such circumstances, the more important changes of direction or the resuscitation of previous narrative threads were adequately signposted within the text itself: 'Como ya se dixo ante desto en la primera parte ...', 'Como se vos ha dicho en el libro primero' (*Amadís*, I, 676, 743). Equally, techniques such as interlace, which permits alternation among the adventures of its many characters (Cacho Blecua 1986), the various appeals to the readers (Porta 1992), or the games of perspective that we find in this story (one incident may be narrated in different ways or from different points of view), had already appeared repeatedly in these models. Also the letters and poems that are scattered through the work seem to have been inspired by the similar elements found in the *Tristan en prose*.

Alongside all these imitations, however, it is also evident that many of the episodes introduced by Montalvo, as well as the *Sergas de Esplandián*, involve a reformulation, a surpassing (but without any desire for elimination or rejection) of the old Arthurian models. The fruitless adventures of knights such as Tristan and Lancelot are replaced by those of Galaz, just as the deeds of Amadís and his men are followed by those of Esplandián, which have a much more spiritual dimension (Van Beysterveldt 1982, subtly nuanced by Rodríguez Velasco 1991). The new knighthood represented by this character and, above all, the adventures which appear in the continuation of *Amadís*, carry these ideals to their highest expression, which is the struggle against the enemies of God (a theme scarcely sketched in *Amadís*), in such a way that gradually worldly chivalry based on love and earthly battles, ever more criticised and scorned, is abandoned in favour of the fight for Christendom. Equally, the love elements in these episodes (Esplandián and Leonorina, Talanque and Calafir, Maneli and Liota ...) are extremely chaste.

Effectively, in the appearance of the first edition of *Amadís de Gaula* (and the *Sergas de Esplandián*) there played a decisive role, in equal measure, the late XVth-century vogue for printing works of chivalry, which affected the whole of Europe (Goodman 1992; Ménard 1997), and the ideals of a crusade in Africa which were gestating at the court of the Catholic Monarchs, particularly after the conquest of Granada (Ramos 1994; Sales Dasí 1995; Marín Pina 1996). In the context of this last point, it is understandable that Montalvo, who lived in that very circle, should have promoted in his works those ideals of a chivalry fundamentally dedicated to defending Christendom, to the detriment of the merely courtly form of chivalry, and, above all, to that of wars among Christian rulers. This shift of chivalric interest is produced very gradually in *Amadís* (and can be attributed almost entirely to the alterations that Montalvo as editor introduced into the medieval text), but is obvious above all in the *Sergas de Esplandián*, a work that is completely his own original creation, in which the protagonist leads a coalition of Christian princes to the aid of Constantinople against the Turks.

Despite this conscientious ideological ballast, it is undeniable that, after its appearance in print, *Amadís* became the most famous of the romances of chivalry. Its previous success was known from the many references to it during the XIVth and XVth centuries, and its influence was evident in works such as the *Crónica sarracina* of Pedro de Corral (Pelayo, secret child of Favila and Luz, is abandoned in a casket by his mother), in the *Siervo libre de amor* by Juan Rodríguez del Padrón (Ardanlier, obeying his lover Liessa, agrees to the amorous demands of Yrena), or in the Spanish version of the *Tristan en prose* (in which it is feared that, after the death of Tristan, Iseult will hurl herself from the height of a tower; see Avalle-Arce 1990: 125). What followed, however, surpassed anything that could have been imagined (Le Gentil 1966; Cacho Blecua 2002). Between 1508 and 1586 it was published on at least eighteen occasions. To its own specific success must be added, moreover, that of its entire family, beginning with the *Sergas de Esplandián*, the fifth book of the series, and continuing down to the twelfth, *Silves de la Selva*, giving a total of more than forty editions (Eisenberg and Marín Pina 2000). Such fabulous success was confirmed, in addition, by the appearance of other chivalric cycles which are servile imitations of the saga of Amadís, as is the case with the Palmerín cycle and that of Clarián. With some justification, it could be said that the entire genre of romances of chivalry, which captivated Spanish readers throughout the XVIth century, was based on the repetition of motifs and stereotypes that had already appeared in *Amadís de Gaula* (Ferrario de Orduna 1992; Gil-Albarellos 1999). Only in the second half of the century, as the material became exhausted, did significant variations from this model become noticeable. Its influence was obvious also in the spectrum of reader expectations which affected the reception in Spain of many texts that existed before *Amadís* reached print, such as *Tirant lo Blanc*, the *Libro del caballero Zifar* or some Italian chivalresque *romanzi* (Gómez-Montero 1992; Ramos 1997; and Cacho Blecua 1999, taking into account Infantes 1988–9).

This success extended throughout all levels of Spanish society, from simple witches and soldiers, who called their dogs 'Amadís', to King Philip II, who delighted in disguising himself as a knight from the *Amadís* story and recreating its adventures (Chevalier 1968; Eisenberg 1973; Marín Pina 1991). It soon became an unavoidably necessary point of reference to describe any extraordinary or marvellous event, to such an extent that the conquistadors of America had recourse to this work upon encountering something beyond what their European imaginations could conceive. In the words of Bernal Díaz del Castillo:

> Y otro día por la mañana llegamos a la calzada ancha y vamos camino de Estapalapa. Y desque vimos tantas cibdades y villas pobladas en el agua, y en tierra firme otras grandes poblazones, y aquella calzada tan derecha y por nivel cómo iba a México, nos quedamos admirados, y decíamos que parescía a las cosas de encantamiento que cuentan en el libro de *Amadís*, por las grandes torres y cúes y edificios que tenían dentro en el agua, y todos de calicanto. Y aun algunos de nuestros soldados decían que si aquello que vían si era entre sueños. Y no es de maravillar que yo lo escriba aquí desta manera, porque hay mucho que ponderar en ello, que no sé como lo cuente; ¡ver cosas nunca oídas, ni aun soñadas, como veíamos! (Díaz, ed. Serés 2011: ch. LXXXVII, p. 308)

Even strikingly unusual features of the natural landscape of the New World could be observed through the filter of recollections of *Amadís*, as this account of crossing rapids in Mexico by Francisco López de Gómara records:

> Era aquel paso una losa o peña llana, lisa, y larga cuanto el río ancho, con más de veinte grietas por do caía el agua sin cubrilla, cosa que parece fábula o encantamiento como los de *Amadís de Gaula*, pero es certísima. Otros lo cuentan por milagro, mas ello es obra de la natura, que dejó aquellas pasaderas para el agua, o la misma agua con su continuo curso comió la peña de aquella manera. (López de Gómara, ed. Gurría Lacroix, 1979, p. 342)

Whilst the writer seems to incline towards an explanation based on natural processes of erosion by the river, he duly records alternative opinions of a miraculous origin or of an enchantment such as those narrated in *Amadís*.

At the same time as Spanish society in general was captivated by this work, adaptations of it began to appear in the *romancero* (García de Enterría 1990) and in the theatre, as in the *Tragicomedia de Amadís de Gaula* by Gil Vicente (1533), Andrés Rey de Artieda's *Amadís* and the *comedia* of the same title that was performed before Ana de Austria in 1570 (Ferrer Valls 1991: 28–34). Faced with this avalanche of readers, criticism of the work and the whole genre of romances of chivalry redoubled (Sarmati 1996), even if a few voices were raised, timidly, in defence of the models of behaviour that were presented beneath its surface fantasy (Baranda 1990–1). The most outstanding example of the influence of the work is undoubtedly *Don Quijote* by Miguel de Cervantes, in which the author deplores all the romances of chivalry, although he recognised the excellence of this one as 'the best of all the books ever composed in this genre' (Rico 2004: I, 84), and had his character imitate various specific episodes from it (Morros 2004).

The success of *Amadís* was not, however, confined to the Iberian Peninsula. There soon came translations into Hebrew (*c*.1540), French (1540–3, with fourteen further editions down to 1577), Italian (1546, with sixteen further editions to 1624), German (1569–71, with three further editions to 1617), Dutch (1574–98, with reprints down to 1625) and English (1590–1618). In every one of these new traditions, the Castilian text acquired fresh energy and inspired fresh works (O'Connor 1970; Weddige 1975; Simonin 1984; Bognolo 2003; Neri 2008; Flood 2013). Alongside the translations of the work and its continutations, there appeared new titles to add to the family of *Amadís*, such as *Flores de Grèce* (1552) and *Il secondo libro delle prodezze di Splandiano* (1564), as well as adaptations, such as Bernardo Tasso's *Amadigi* (1560), which brought the old Castilian story of chivalry to the field of the verse *romanzi* (Foti 1990). Selected extracts from *Amadís* and its continuations (*Trésors de l'Amadis*) became a manual of polite behaviour for courtiers in France, Germany and England that was reprinted time and again between 1559 and 1624 (Place 1954; Benhaim 2000).

Reading these translations, or, in many cases, the original Castilian text, allowed authors such as Pierre de Ronsard, Michel de Montaigne, Pierre de Brantôme, René Descartes, Ludovico Ariosto, Baldassare Castiglione, Pietro Bembo, Torquato Tasso, Philip Sidney, Edmund Spenser, Lady Mary Wroth, Ben Jonson, Thomas Dekker, Francis Beaumont, John Donne, John Milton and many others, to know and appreciate the work during the course of the XVIth century and a good part of the XVIIth. And clear though it is that these echoes were gradually fading, it is equally clear that at the end of the XVIIIth century, thanks to new versions that were produced at the dawn of Romanticism by the Comte de Tressan (1779), Robert Southey (1803) or the poetic rendering by Auguste-François Creuze de Lesser (1813), it came to be appreciated afresh by authors of the stature of Johann Wolfgang von Goethe, John Keats and Walter Scott.

Literature alone turned out to be inadequate to reflect the full magnitude of its impact, so that its influence spread also into other art forms, the most important of these being, in this context, the opera. Louis XIV personally commissioned the poet Philippe Quinault and the composer Jean-Baptiste Lully to produce an opera on *Amadis de Gaule*. The work was performed at the Académie Royale de Musique on 15 February 1684, was printed several times (1685, 1687, 1689, 1695 ...), and translated into Dutch by Thomas Arendsz in 1687. It even had sequels, among which there stand out several parodic versions, an incontestable indication of the theme's vitality: *La naissance d'Amadis*, by Jean-François Regnard and Charles Rivière Dufresny (1694); *Arlequin Amadis*, by Jean-Antoine Romagnesi and Pierre-François Biancolelli ('Dominique'), in 1731; the puppet version *Polichinelle Amadis*, by Denis Carolet (1732), among others. Such was its success that it remained in the repertoire of the principal companies until the middle of the XVIIIth century, and, when its popularity began to decline, Pierre-Montain Berton and Jean-Benjamin de La Borde produced a fundamental revision of it. During this period other authors had already mined this vein of inspiration, such as George Frideric Handel, who, with a biligual libretto by

John James Heidegger and Nicola Francesco Haym, composed *Amadis of Gaul. An Opera* (1715, with a mid-century Dutch adaptation by Kornelis Elzevier), or Johann Christian Bach, with a libretto by Alphonese-Marie-Denis de Vismes de Saint-Alphonse based on the earlier version by Quinault (1779). Although these three works took considerable liberties with the original story (for example, Handel's work is, in reality, an adaptation of the opera *Amadis de Grèce* by André Cardinal Destouches with a libretto by Antoine Houdar de La Motte, published in 1699), they are a solid proof of the success enjoyed by the story across Europe for a period of several centuries. Other musicians remained interested in the story well after the eighteenth-century vogue for it. Such is the case of Antoine-Chrysostome-Quatremère de Quincy, author of the opera *Le héros gaulois ou Amadis et Oriane*, now lost, but performed at the Académie Impériale de Musique on 11 February 1808; Jules Massenet, who composed his opera *Amadis* in 1895 (first performed in 1922) with a libretto by Jules Claretie; Tomas Bretón, who composed his symphonic poem *Amadís de Gaula* in 1882; and Robert Le Grand, author of the overture *Amadis et Oriane*. In the same area, it is necessary to mention various ballets based on these operas at various dates. The most interesting is possibly *Amadis des Gaules ou le Damoisel de la mer*, with choreography by François-Alexis Blache and music by Hippolite Sonnet. This had its first performance in Bordeaux in 1831, and we have information concerning subsequent performances in St Petersburg in 1833 and in Barcelona in 1847. Such was the success of the performance that it inspired the immediate publication there of an edition of Montalvo's *Amadís* (Barcelona, 1847–8).

Notes

[1] On a possible Portuguese manuscript, which would ultimately descend from the Castilian editions, see Infantes (1999).

[2] Until recently, it was still possible to refer to these works as 'the lost genre of medieval Spanish literature' (Deyermond 1975).

[3] To a great extent, this early dating was due to an erroneous identification, around 1318, of the *Ars Amandi* of Ovid, confused by this researcher with *Amadís* several years previously (Avalle-Arce 1982 and 1984, here with the specific reading 'Amadís'). See the objections advanced by Riquer (1987: 9–11). In discussing an early dating, it is also necessary to record that in 1294 there is a documentary reference to a 'Migael d'Espladian' in Logroño (Hook 1992–3b). In the absence of a detailed examination of the document in question, however, this may not be particularly important. Since the form seems to be a surname, it would be necessary for it to have been in use in the previous generation for a forename to have become a surname, and to allow for some years previous to this for *Amadís* to have become sufficiently successful for the name of a character to be given to a newborn child. This would imply that the composition of *Amadís* was earlier than that of the works of Alfonso el Sabio, which would be unimaginable.

[4] Juan Ruiz, *Libro de buen amor*, ed. Blecua (1992: 983c; but in the light of Blecua 2001); *Glosa castellana al Regimiento de príncipes*, ed. Beneyto Pérez (1947: III, 361); on the meaning of this allusion, see Guardiola 1988); Pero López de Ayala, *Rimado de Palacio*, ed. Orduna (1987: 163c).

[5] To the twenty allusions earlier than the first surviving printed edition that Riquer notes can be added many more: Rodrigo de Arana in the first quarter of the XVth century; Juan Alfonso de Baena before 1440 (Dutton and González Cuenca 1993: 668, 695); Alonso de Cartagena around 1440 (Lawrance 1979: 54); Juan de Dueñas, twice, around 1440–50 (Presotto 1997: 59, 78); Fernando de la Torre, around 1460 (Díez Garretas 1983: 132); Diego de Valera[?], between 1440 and 1470 (Blecua 2005); Juan Barba in 1464 (Cátedra 1989: 338); Pedro de Cartagena in the third quarter of the XVth century (González Cuenca 2004: II, 135); the *Cancionero de Toledo del Marqués de Santillana*, towards 1470 (Pérez López 1990); Juan de Flores, between 1470 and 1485 (Gargano 1981: 146); and others. The personal names used by the aristocracy also reflect the success of the work; in the early years of the XVth century there are references to a Florestán de Leguizamón, a knight from Vizcaya (Avalle-Arce 1990: 33–4), a lady called Briolanja Gonçalves and a courtier called Amadís, both Portuguese (Sharrer 1990–1); in 1464 and 1465 in Barcelona there are documentary references to another courtier called Amadís, possibly also Portuguese (Martínez Ferrando 1953–4: I, 189; II: 99); in 1475 we find Amadís Fernandes and in 1481 there is a lady called 'Briullanja' Alvares, both Portuguese too (Estorninho et al., 1978: p. 298, no. 2624; and p. 536, no. 2860, respectively). In 1496, a Briolanja Muñoz was the beneficiary of a royal grant of some properties in Huelva previously confiscated from two persons convicted of heresy (AGS, Registro del Sello de Corte, leg. 149610.5). Yet other cases may be added of Galaor, Florestán, Olinda and Oriana between the XIVth and XVth centuries in Castile (Beceiro Pita 2007: 284). Another Florestán occurs at Saldaña in a document of 1493 (AGS, Registro del Sello de Corte, leg. 149308.205), and a friar of this name was the prior of the convent of San Agustín at Valladolid in 1495 (AGS, Registro del Sello de Corte, leg. 149506.30). As far as the inventories of medieval libraries are concerned, the text is mentioned in 1430 among the books owned by Alfonso Tenorio, and in 1435 among those of Aldonza de Mendoza (Beceiro Pita 2007: 247–8).

[6] On the biography of this person, see Alonso Cortés (1933), Avalle-Arce (1990: 137–42), Blanco (1998), and, above all, Sales Dasí (1999b). Some scholars (Van Beysterveldt 1982: 76–7; Sholod 1982; Little 2002) insist on attributing a *converso* origin to him, although to the present no solid evidence has been produced to support this: on the contrary, the known documentation refers to him consistently as 'nobleman'.

[7] On the problems of transmission of the printed *Amadís*, see also the studies of Suárez Pallasá (1995), Ramos (1999, 2000, 2002) and Cacho Blecua (2007, 2010).

[8] See the exemplary analysis by Montaner (2008).

[9] There is no consensus on the identity of this Prince. The supporters of an early dating consider that it would be Alfonso of Burgundy (1263–1312), who resided in Castile in his final years (Cacho Blecua 1979: 459–61; Avalle-Arce 1990: 163). For others, it would be Alfonso de Avis (1475–91), married to a daughter of the Catholic Monarchs (Place 1956). It would also be necessary to consider other Alfonsos, princes of Portugal, over the course of the XIVth and XVth centuries.

[10] In the *Lancelot en prose*, the principal model of *Amadís* (see below), the protagonist is pursued amorously by the sister of Carmadan. As his refusal would incur his death, Queen Guinevere sends him a message in which she authorises him to fulfil the desire of the lady, thus saving his life (ed. Micha 1978–83: IV, 154–5).

[11] Ed. Cacho Blecua (1987–8: I, 612–13, 644).

[12] This is the hypothesis of Place (1956), reconsidered by Cacho Blecua (1979: 346–65) and Gómez Redondo (1998–2007: II, 1547–50), and conveniently nuanced by Gracia (1999). The musings of Avalle-Arce (1990) seem excessively bold.

[13] Ed. Cacho Blecua (1987–8: I, 223). His distinction between real history, possible history and fiction seems to derive from Isidore of Seville: 'Nam historiae sunt res verae quae factae sunt; argumentum sunt quae etsi facta non sunt, fieri tamen possunt; fabulae vero sunt quae nec factae sunt nec fieri possunt, quia contra naturam sunt' (*Etymologiarum*, I, xliv, 5). On the medieval survival of this tripartite division, see Valero Moreno (2010a).

[14] See principally the studies of Williams (1909), Avalle-Arce (1990), Gracia (1991, 1992), Suárez Pallasá (2006, although I do not accept all his conclusions) and Cuesta Torre (2008b). In general terms, in

the paragraphs that follow I accept the greater part of their suggestions and add some further points of my own.

[15] An example of the former is the combat between Amadís and Abiés of Ireland, which prefigures that of Tristan with Morholt: 'Miémbrate, Rey, que te dixo una donzella que, cuando cobrasses tu pérdida, perdería el señorío de Irlanda su flor, y cata si dixo verdad, que cobraste este fijo que perdido tenías y murió aquel esforçado rey Abiés, que la flor de Irlanda era. Y ahún más te digo, que la nunca cobrará por señor que aí haya hasta que venga el buen hermano de la señora, que hará venir soberviosamente por fuerça de armas parias de otra tierra, y éste morirá por mano de aquel que será muerto por la cosa del mundo que él más amará.' An example of the latter is what happens in the case of a descendant of Darioleta and Bravor, since 'dellos descendió aquel valiente y esforçado don Segurades, primo cormano del cavallero anciano que a la corte del rey Artur vino [...] y sin lança derribó a todos los cavalleros de gran nombradía que a la sazón en la corte se hallaron' (ed. Cacho Blecua 1987–8: I, 329–30; II, 1677).

[16] Cf. 'Aquí se acava el segundo y tercero libro de don Lançarote de Lago y á se de comenzar el *Libro de don Tristán*' (ed. Contreras Martín and Sharrer 2006: 386).

XI

ARTHUR GOES GLOBAL: ARTHURIAN MATERIAL IN HISPANIC AMERICA AND ASIA

David Hook

An important aspect of the worldwide diffusion of Arthurian material that results directly from its presence in the Iberian Peninsula is the spread of both knowledge and texts of Arthurian legends and their derivatives such as the *Amadís* cycle, as well as the personal names associated with them, to the various overseas territories settled by Spain and Portugal from the late Middle Ages onwards. The sources of information for this earliest phase of the global expansion of Arthuriana include both literary texts and contemporary administrative documents; sometimes the latter may be the only record of the presence of the former in a particular location at a specific date.[1] The literary texts that provide our evidence here fall into two categories: firstly, the surviving accounts of the period of the early explorations and conquests that mention Arthurian legends or material related to them while describing events and situations in the New World, Africa and Asia; and secondly, those copies of Arthurian romances and related texts which were themselves taken to the Americas and beyond, even if in some cases their transport thither is known only from lists of books preserved among the administrative records. The other classes of administrative documents most relevant to us are those recording the transoceanic migration of individuals bearing Arthurian names and of their relatives. Whilst the texts themselves have naturally attracted more attention from literary scholars, the evidence of such personal names must also be taken into account as part of the wider picture of the spread of Arthurian material beyond the shores of Europe, in which the late medieval Ibero-Romance expansion across the Atlantic and Indian Oceans and into the Pacific preceded that from other European language areas.

The first southward explorations along the west coast of Africa by Portugal in the time of Prince Henry 'the Navigator' bring the earliest cases of Arthurian names, with Zurara recording the roles of his captain Nunho Tristão and of the *escudeiro* Lançarote in successive voyages as far as Guinea in the 1440s.[2] An early and immediately visible consequence of the Arthurian vogue in the Peninsula is the naming or renaming of places overseas with forms embodying personal names of Arthurian type. One such is the island of Tristão off the coast of Guinea, recalling these voyages of Nunho Tristão; another is the better-known island group of Tristan da Cunha in the Atlantic, first recorded by the Portuguese Tristão da Cunha, after whom it is named. The island of Lanzarote in the Canaries, however, is a case that illustrates the complexities of such connections; though it bears a name of Hispanic Arthurian type, it has nothing to do with the Portuguese Lançarote who set out for Guinea, but is in fact the result of the earlier arrival there of the XIVth-century Genoese Lancelotto Malocello, rather than of a navigator of Peninsular origin. Whether so named after an individual explorer or called after a character or location in a book, such geographical designations constitute a clear reminder of the influence of the Arthurian legends during the period of overseas exploration and expansion by late medieval and early modern European navigators.

The Portuguese expeditions led, over the century following Prince Henry, to individuals bearing names of Arthurian type reaching as far as Abyssinia with the mission of Duarte Galvão in 1515 to establish diplomatic contact with the local Christian ruler whom the Portuguese optimistically identified at that time with the legendary 'Prester John'; to their dotting the coasts of the Indian Ocean to India and beyond; and finally to their reaching China with the journey there by Leonel de Sousa between 1552 and 1555.[3] A single journey by an individual is interesting from the point of view of plotting the global spread of Arthurian names, but no doubt had negligible, if indeed any, impact on local anthroponymic patterns, apart from occasional imposition of such a name as a European-style place name; the impact of prolonged residence, though, is a different matter in this respect. Probably more significant in onomastic history, therefore, are the Portuguese colonial officials and other individuals resident in the east who bore Arthurian names, from the highest ranks of governors and captains, down to a servant named Galaaz de Mata who is recorded at Cochim in January 1548. The remarks that follow deal mainly with the first half of the XVIth century, and are based largely on persons mentioned in the first four *Décadas* of the chronicle of Portuguese expansion in Asia by João de Barros, or in the administrative documents in the Torre do Tombo archives; but there were surely many more.[4] Inevitably, given the long-standing vogue for Arthurian names in Portugal itself, such names appear at overseas Portuguese possessions and outposts during the XVIth century and beyond without this fact necessarily indicating current interest in Arthurian material as opposed to the use of names from the by then established stock. Since what follows is not an organised and statistically meaningful sample, it is offered solely as an illustration; but (ignoring for the present the question of parental names) it is interesting to note that of forty-one identifiably different individuals of all social ranks located in these sources who had forenames of Arthurian type, there are twenty-one cases of Tristão (including Tristão da Cunha, nominated as viceroy in 1504 but who did not take up his office and was replaced in the following year), eight of Leonel or Lionel, four of Galas or Galaz, three of Lançarote, three of Lisuarte (a character from the *Amadís* story), one of Galaor (also from *Amadís*), and one of Galvão. Rarely can anything be discovered about the specific circumstances in which these individuals acquired their names, but sometimes a culturally significant fact is indeed accidentally revealed by the records that makes a particular case more important than others. When, for example, we learn from an account of fighting at

Goa that Galas Viegas and Galvão Viegas were brothers it seems a reasonable conclusion that in their case a deliberate choice had been exercised in naming two siblings after two fictional knights; such sibling evidence is particularly important, as will have been noted from the case discussed earlier in this volume by Pilar Lorenzo Gradín, in which two brothers were called after Gawain and Roland in northern Portugal at some date between 1118 and 1138. Diogo do Couto's reference to the Viegas brothers relates to events in India in 1535–6, and since Galvão Viegas is described by the chronicler as 'Alcayde Mor' of Goa he would probably have been born at least three decades earlier than that, and probably more.[5] On other occasions, the information gleaned is negative: thus, when Galaor da Framça was mentioned in dispatches sent from Safim (Morocco) on 8 July 1541 for his heroic performance in battle, having been wounded twice in the thigh by a lance and having had his horse killed, what may seem to us an obvious opportunity for an Arthurian reference was not taken up by Rodrigo de Castro in his report to King João III, and he instead used a time-worn but clearly still effective Classical parallel to extol the valour of the Portuguese combatants, 'porque nom ouve n[en]hum deles que nom fizese mais valentias do que dizem que fez Eitor em seu tempo'.[6] The reference here is most probably to the celebrated Trojan warrior conventionally used as an exemplar of heroism in such rhetorical comparisons, rather than to his more rarely deployed namesake Sir Hector from the Matter of Britain. One is reminded of the questions raised by the comments of Carlos Alvar and Lourdes Soriano in the present volume concerning the decline of interest in the Arthurian legends in Iberia in the XVIth century. Soriano's illustration of this by the changes in names listed in successive versions of Muntaner's chronicle, with a clear-out of many Arthurian characters in the 1558 edition, is a telling example.

Similarly distant from the seemingly deliberate choice of Arthurian baptismal names in the case of the Viegas siblings is the situation when two brothers of noble indigenous stock from Macaçar were baptised at Ternate in the Moluccas in 1536 with the names António Galvão and Miguel Galvão; the choice of these names, however, was evidently inspired not so much directly by Arthurian legends as by the name of the godfather of the former, the Portuguese commander there, António Galvão, who had replaced the tyrannical Tristão de Taíde (or de Ataide) in the post in that year, and who seems immediately upon his arrival there late in 1536 to have begun busily cultivating local elites, as well as providing for military responses, in an attempt to restore the Portuguese position.[7] António Galvão himself provides a classic case of an Arthurian name that, whatever the circumstances of its initial adoption, has become a transmissible surname, for he was the son of Duarte Galvão and grandson of Rui Galvão. He was also the author of the *Tratado dos descobrimentos*, first printed in 1563, in which the history of Spanish and Portuguese explorations is recorded. The *Tratado* incidentally reveals that António Galvão was himself obviously aware, at some level, of Arthurian material; it is interesting that he should trouble to record in his opening historical overview, alongside Greek, Roman, Gothic and other episodes of conquest and exploration, and the expansion of Islam, the detail that among other events around the year 474 'E Merlim em Inglaterra foi neste tempo' (Galvão 1944: 108). The relevance of this information to the ostensible subject matter is not immediately apparent; insufficient detail is given for us to determine whether this note was simply reproduced from a chronologically organised source, or whether it reflects something more than dependence upon such an annalistic tradition.

As with the Portuguese situation, so in the case of the Spanish overseas expansion the transient presence of Iberian voyagers at specific locations in their explorations (even if these were then or later renamed after them) is less significant in Arthurian studies than are the anthroponymic consequences of permanent settlement. Just as in the Portuguese cases, Spanish Arthurian names migrated with their bearers who settled in the New World (a century before the earliest English settlements were founded in North America in the decades after 1600), with the result that forms such as 'Galván' (Gawain) are in use to the present time as surnames both in Latin America and among Hispanic communities and persons of Hispanic ancestry in the United States. This process of name transfer and its consequences may perhaps be seen at its furthest social reach when in a document dating from 1543 there appears an indigenous male from Guatemala named 'Leonís', and when in 1562 we encounter an Amerindian woman who seems to have acquired the name of 'Iseo'; these cases are discussed in detail below.

The first individual bearing such a distinctive Arthurian name who is known to have ventured to the New World was the 'grumete' (cabin boy) Tristán who accompanied the second expedition of Christopher Columbus in 1493.[8] In at least two other respects besides its chronological priority his case is symbolically important: firstly because 'Tristán' is among the most popular Arthurian personal names to be found in late medieval and early modern Spain; and secondly because his lowly status is a salutary reminder that the social distribution of such names was by no means confined, as has sometimes been too easily supposed, to the upper levels of contemporary society (as indeed the case of the literary character of the servant Tristán in the Spanish classic *Celestina*, dating from the 1490s, also makes plain).[9] This early case of the cabin boy was followed by those of other similarly named individuals among the tens of thousands of migrants whose details are systematically recorded for Arthurian scholarship as an unintended consequence of the bureaucratic processes through which would-be emigrants from Spain to the Americas had to pass, in the interests of ensuring that no persons of Muslim or Jewish background settled across the Atlantic.[10] The records of these procedures in the Archivo General de Indias in Seville provide extensive lists of the names and origins of emigrants, in a system similar to that used in contemporary baptismal registers, and so often give details of their parentage as well as their dates of registration for emigration and their intended destinations, and sometimes even of their social status or occupation. A useful result of this is that two, and sometimes three, generations of family names are frequently recorded. During the first six decades of the XVIth century, there are several dozen cases of Arthurian names in the registers, whether borne by the actual emigrants or by their parents, or in some cases both. Although the emigrant names are of more immediately obvious relevance to the transfer of Arthurian material to the New World, the parental cases are also potentially important here, as we shall see. The establishment of a settled population making use of Arthurian names as part of its basic anthroponymic stock is obviously a much more significant phenomenon than the passage to or through a region of a single individual bearing such a name, though it is the latter who figure more largely on the map and in the accounts of the discoveries and conquests.

The pattern of Arthurian-type names transferred to Spanish America does not appear to differ much from that established for the medieval Iberian Peninsula by recent studies, at least in the key respects that the names of Arthurian origin constitute only a tiny proportion of the general corpus of personal names in current use, and that within this statistically minute subset certain of the names associated with the legends are more frequently encountered than are others.[11] Thus, documented occurrences of forms of 'Arthur' are rare both in the Peninsula at all dates and among the emigrants; the only case encountered among the latter in the period 1509–60 is in fact that of an individual of German origin, Tierre Artus (son of Maestro Juan Alemán and Elisabet), a native of Cologne, who embarked from Seville for the River Plate on 2 August 1535 (Bermúdez Plata, 1940–80: II, no. 1995; Boyd-Bowman 1964–8: II, no. 12882). Similarly, 'Merlin', very rare in the Peninsula as a personal name at all times, does not appear at all in the emigrant registers of the first six decades of the century, first showing up only in 1562 when Pedro Merlín from Salvatierra, son of Andrés Merlín and Ana González, registered on 12 April to emigrate to Peru to serve as Procurator of the Audiencia of Quito (Bermúdez Plata 1940–80: IV: 3607). 'Galván' and 'Tristán', on the other hand, are as numerically dominant among the early Arthurian names transferred to the New World as they are among those of the Peninsula itself. A few other names, known earlier in medieval Iberia from relatively infrequent occurrences, also crossed the Atlantic: 'Iseo' and 'Galaz' are two such. There are also names drawn from the Arthurian-inspired fictions of the *Amadís* cycle, with 'Esplandián' and 'Briolanja' both represented among the names going to the Americas; the case of the epithetic 'Agrajes' applied by Bernal Díaz to the boastful Pedro de Ircio, which derives from the same source, is discussed below. Restricting this survey to the decades of settlement up to 1560, the individuals bearing Arthurian and related names who appear in the lists of emigrants to America are as follows, in chronological order of their registration.[12]

1512
Diego Galván, son of Juan Galván and María de Espinosa of Burgos (20 August 1512; Bermúdez Plata 1940–80: I: 654; Boyd-Bowman 1964–8: I: 691).
Diego Galván, son of Juan Galván and Marina la Galvana of Madrigal (8 October 1512; Bermúdez Plata 1940–80: I: 799; Boyd-Bowman 1964–8: I: 1602).

Diego Galván, son of Francisco Pérez Galván, and María Galvana of Madrigal (12 October 1512; Bermúdez Plata 1940–80: I: 820; Boyd-Bowman 1964–8: I: 1603).[13]

1513

Iseo Hernández, emigrating with her sister Margarita González, of Lepe (30 September 1513; Bermúdez Plata 1940–80: I: 1594; Boyd-Bowman 1964–8: I: 1790).

Leonís [Tello Muñoz] (12 November 1513; Bermúdez Plata 1940–80: I: 1637; Boyd 1964–8: I: 3646).[14]

1517

Iseo de Valaris (2 March 1517; Bermúdez Plata 1940–80: I: 2382).[15]

Francisca Tristán (19 May 1517; Bermúdez Plata 1940–80: I: 2520).

1528

Diego Tristán, son of Juan Tristán and Juana Ramírez of Seville (5 March 1528; Bermúdez Plata 1940–80: I: 3600).

1534

Tristán Llorente, of Valladolid, emigrant to Cartagena together with his brother Pedro Llorente (17 June 1534; Bermúdez Plata 1940–80: I: 4627; Boyd-Bowman 1964–8: II: 12149).

María de Lanzarote, wife of Juan Bravo, emigrant to Cartagena (22 June 1534; Bermúdez Plata 1940–80: I: 4664).

Galaz de Medrano, emigrant to Peru (25 September 1534; Bermúdez Plata 1940–80: I: 4770; possibly to be identified with Boyd-Bowman 1964–8: II: 74, an 'hidalgo' ['nobleman'], though the latter has a different date and destination, 1535 to the River Plate, and was killed in 1536).

Tristán López, emigrant to Peru (6 October 1534; Bermúdez Plata 1940–80: I: 4837).

1535

Martín Galbán, of Zahara, emigrant to Nueva España (13 February 1535; Bermúdez Plata 1940–80: II: 45; Boyd-Bowman 1964–8: II: 3501).

Francisco de Leonís, emigrant to Cartagena, son of Leonís González, of Llerena (22 March 1535; Bermúdez Plata 1940–80: II: 297; Boyd-Bowman 1964–8: II: 1417).

Rodrigo Galván, emigrant to Cartagena, son of Francisco Martín and Catalina Galván of Villanueva del Fresno (24 March 1535; Bermúdez Plata 1940–80: II: 349; Boyd-Bowman 1964–8: II: 2052).

Tristán Enriquez, emigrant to Veragua (3 April 1535; Bermúdez Plata 1940–80: II: 540; Boyd-Bowman 1964–8: II: 1075).

Leonís de Villanueva, emigrant to Veragua (13 April 1535; Bermúdez Plata 1940–80: II: 767; Boyd-Bowman 1964–8: II: 3597).

Luis Tristán, son of Francisco Tristán of Valencia (23 July 1535; Bermúdez Plata 1940–80: II: 1526; Boyd-Bowman 1964–8: II: 11589).

Roque Galván, emigrant to the River Plate, son of Hernand Pérez de Galván and Catalina Martín of Villanueva del Fresno (28 July 1535; Bermúdez Plata 1940–80: II: 1718; Boyd-Bowman 1964–8: II: 2053).

1537

Tristán de Gustamante (= Bustamante?), emigrant to Peru (8 January 1537; Bermúdez Plata 1940–80: II: 3363; Boyd-Bowman 1964–8: II: 7824).

1538

Juan Galbán, emigrant to Florida, son of Francisco Galván and María Esteban of Valverde (23 February 1538; Bermúdez Plata 1940–80: II: 4333; Boyd-Bowman 1964–8: II: 1932).

'Leonos' [=Leonís] de Temiño, of Seville, emigrant to Florida (1 March 1538; Bermúdez Plata 1940–80: II: 4492; Boyd-Bowman 1964–8: II: 10234).

Tristán de Lozano, emigrant to Florida, son of Tristán Lozano and Doña María, of Marchena (8 March 1538; Bermúdez Plata 1940–80: II: 4587; Boyd-Bowman 1964–8: II: 8559).

Leonís de Figueredo, emigrant to Tierra Firme (9 October 1538; Bermúdez Plata 1940–80: II: 5266; Boyd-Bowman 1964–8: II: 9202).

1539

Juan Tristán, emigrant to Nueva España, son of Juan Tristán, 'Escribano de la Justicia', and Juana Rodríguez, of Seville (15 July, Bermúdez Plata 1940–80: III: 526; Boyd-Bowman 1964–8: II: 10275).

1542

Cristóbal Galván, emigrant to Tierra Firme, son of Diego Galván and María González, of Plasencia (5 September 1542; Bermúdez Plata 1940–80: III: 1717).

1555

Gaspar Tristán, son of Diego Tristán and Catalina Ortiz, of Valladolid (1555; Bermúdez Plata 1940–80: III: 2707).

Francisco Tristán, emigrant to Peru, son of Alonso Díaz Tristán and Leonor Hernández, of Seville, serving as factor of Alonso de Illescas (1555; Bermúdez Plata 1940–80: III: 2819).

1557

Martín Galván, of Villanueva del Fresno, emigrant to Nueva España with his wife Marina Gómez (1557; Bermúdez Plata 1940–80: III: 3706).

1559

Francisco Galaz, from Salvatierra de Tormes, emigrant to Nueva España, son of Alonso Galaz and Inés Martínez (22 March 1559; Bermúdez Plata 1940–80: III: 4177). Another entry for 28 May 1561 relates to the same individual, reminding us of the risk of duplication in the catalogues because of people returning to Spain and re-emigrating after an interval (Bermúdez Plata 1940–80: IV: 1483).

Iseo Centurión, emigrant with her husband Pedro Bermúdez of Seville and their son Alonso Muñoz (29 November 1559; Bermúdez Plata 1940–80: III: 4436).

1560

Juan Galaz, from Medina del Campo, unmarried son of Juan García Galaz and Juana Fernández de Bustillo, emigrant to Peru as servant to Diego López de Zúñiga y Velasco, Count of Nieva, Viceroy of Peru (7 March 1560; Bermúdez Plata 1940–80: IV: 517).

Some of these emigrants were clearly old enough to marry (Martín Galván, for example, in 1557, or Iseo Centurión in 1559); there is no specific clue as to the age of others, since the designation 'soltero' (single) attached to some of them in the registers is no guide, but their adult status unless otherwise specified seems to be a safe assumption. The chronological distribution of the names of these emigrants over the first six decades of the XVIth century may be seen from table XI.1, in which no distinction is made between their occurrence as forename or byname/surname. The numerical dominance of 'Galván' and 'Tristán' is quite clear. It should be remembered that data for the first ten years (subsumed in the first column) are much less complete than those for subsequent decades, but the overall pattern of relative frequency of the names is nonetheless clear.

Table XI.1: Distribution of Arthurian-type Names by twenty-year periods, 1501–60

Name	1501–20	1521–40	1541–60	Total
Galaz	-	1	2	3
Galván	3	4	2	9
Iseo	2	-	1	3
Lanzarote	-	1	-	1
Leonís	1	4	-	5
Tristán	1	8	2	11
Total	7	18	7	32

In addition to these, Boyd-Bowman records as transatlantic emigrants during these decades five further individuals with Arthurian names who are seemingly not registered in the *Catálogo de pasajeros a Indias* but for whose early presence in the Americas there is other documentary or textual evidence. In Mexico around 1531 was Alonso Rodríguez Lanzarote, son of Lanzarote Terreros, from Villanueva del Fresno (Boyd-Bowman 1964–8: II: 2058); an emigrant to the River Plate in 1535 was Tristán de Vallartes (Boyd-Bowman 1964–8: II: 4385); Juan Galaz emigrated to Lima in 1537 (Boyd-Bowman 1964–8: II: 3436); present in Mexico City in 1537 was Don Tristán de Luna y Arellano (Boyd-Bowman 1964–8: II: 10523); and as a *conquistador* in Guatemala we find Diego Tristán (Boyd-Bowman 1964–8: II: 10274) who had emigrated to Mexico around 1528 and returned there after 1539 (the year in which his brother Juan Tristán emigrated to Mexico, as recorded above).

Also to be taken into account here are those emigrants whose own names are not Arthurian, and who are not, therefore, listed above, but whose parents bore Arthurian names. These migrants will have taken with them to the Americas at the very least a lifelong familiarity with these names, and possibly a general awareness, if not a more specific knowledge, of their ultimate source as being from the Arthurian legends, although the extent of such awareness will naturally have varied since many of the names had been in use in Iberia for several centuries. In the case of the parental names, just as with those of the emigrants themselves, it is necessary to distinguish between the recently acquired forenames and the patronymics or transmissible surnames which will have been acquired one or more generations previously. The great vogue for 'Tristán' and 'Iseo/Yseo', for example, resulting from diffusion of the Tristram and Isolde story, is well attested in both the forenames and the patronymics or surnames of these parents of emigrants, in the latter case probably extending, therefore, over at least the two previous generations. A good example of this phenomenon of multi-generational transmission is Juan García Galaz (the father of the Juan Galaz whom we have seen above as an emigrant in 1560), within whose family this Spanish form of 'Galahad' had probably been passed down for three generations since it is best interpreted as a surname, rather than an epithetic byname, of the father of the Peru-bound migrant. Similar comments could be made concerning Hernán Pérez de Galván, father of Roque Galván who emigrated in 1535. There are over three dozen relevant parental names in the registers up to 1560; those not already cited as parents of migrants who themselves bore Arthurian names are as follows.

    Yseo de Saldaña (Bermúdez Plata 1940–80: I: 579), of Jerez de la Frontera, mother of the emigrant Antón de Rojas (14 June 1512).
    Tristán de Celada (Bermúdez Plata 1940–80: I: 1957), of Dueñas, father of the emigrant Alonso de Dueñas (9 July 1515).
    Tristán García (Bermúdez Plata 1940–80: I: 2138), of Huelva, father of the emigrant García Hernández (2 July 1516).

Pedro de Tristán (Bermúdez Plata 1940–80: I: 3245), of Talavera de la Reina, father of the emigrant Pedro de Talavera ([29] June 1527).
Iseo Álvarez (Bermúdez Plata 1940–80: I: 4350), mother of Antonio de Losada, emigrant to Nueva España (28 April 1534).
Isabel Galván (Bermúdez Plata 1940–80: I: 4526), mother of Sebastián Gutiérrez, emigrant on 13 June 1534 to Cartagena.
Rodrigo Tristán (Bermúdez Plata 1940–80: I: 4573), father of Juan de la Fuente, emigrant to Cartagena on 13 June 1534.
Tristán de Avellanedo (Bermúdez Plata 1940–80: II: 26), father of Diego de Avellanedo, of Seville, emigrant to Cuba or Santo Domingo (7 February 1535).
Leonor Galbán (Bermúdez Plata 1940–80: II: 70), mother of Juan Esteban, of Jerez de la Frontera, emigrant to Veragua (18 February 1535).
Ginebra Cuaresma (Bermúdez Plata 1940–80: II: 332), of Oviedo, mother of Antonio Bocarro, emigrant to Veragua (22 March 1535), and of Luis Álvarez, emigrant to Veragua (Bermúdez Plata 1940–80: II: 339; 24 March 1535).[16]
Iseo Rivera (Bermúdez Plata 1940–80: II: 400), of Seville, mother of Juan Ramos, emigrant to Nueva España (31 March 1535).
Tristán de Camargo (Bermúdez Plata 1940–80: II: 477), of Burgos, father of Gregorio de Camargo, emigrant to Veragua (2 April 1535).
Tristán de Valderas (Bermúdez Plata 1940–80: II: 652), of Fuente del Sabuco, father of Diego de Valderas, emigrant to Cartagena (7 April 1535).
Tristán García (Bermúdez Plata 1940–80: II: 652), of Huévar, Seville, father of Diego Gutiérrez (23 July 1535); the entry is unfinished and struck out, so presumably the would-be emigrant did not complete the procedures.
Tristán Ortiz (Bermúdez Plata 1940–80: II: 2085), of Salamanca, father of Cristóbal Bernal, emigrant to the River Plate (4 August 1535).
Martín Galbán (Bermúdez Plata 1940–80: II: 3380), of Villanueva del Fresno, husband of Ana López, father of Juan Topino, emigrant to Nueva España (8 January 1537).
Iseo de Belmana (Bermúdez Plata 1940–80: II: 4670), of Seville, mother of the emigrant Andrés de Laredo (12 March 1538).[17]
Tristán de Merlo (Bermúdez Plata 1940–80: III: 246), of Córdoba, father of Ana Saavedra, emigrant to Santo Domingo (21 April 1539).
Ginebra de Ordaz (Bermúdez Plata 1940–80: III: 1360), mother of Alonso de Torres, of León, emigrant to Nueva España (10 March 1540).
Yseo de Cañizares (Bermúdez Plata 1940–80: III: 2709), mother of Gabriel de Encinas, emigrant to Peru (1555).
Iseo Manuel (Bermúdez Plata 1940–80: III: 3339), mother of Juan de Baltierra, emigrant to Peru (1556).[18]
Francisca Galván (Bermúdez Plata 1940–80: III: 3755), of Valladolid, mother of Mateo de Segovia, emigrant to Tierra Firme and Peru (1557).

Tristán Ortiz (Bermúdez Plata 1940–80: III: 4213), father of Jerónimo León of Santo Domingo de la Calzada, emigrant to Venezuela (30 March 1559).

Consideration of the names of other members of the family of an emigrant in this way, where information concerning them is available, can offer other significant evidence, even if it is negative evidence. When Tristán Llorente registered for emigration to Cartagena (Bermúdez Plata 1940–80: I: 4627) on 17 June 1534, he was accompanied by his brother Pedro Llorente; in this instance, we can see that not all the siblings in this family were given Arthurian forenames. The same is true of Iseo Hernández who emigrated with her sister Margarita González in 1513. Similarly, in that same year, Leonís, emigrating with his parents Juan Tello and Juana Muñoz, and other family members, was the only sibling to have an Arthurian name; his brothers were Martín Muñoz and Francisco Tello. In 1517 Iseo de Valaris formed part of a family group together with her sisters, Ana Velázquez and Isabel Dávila. In each of these cases, therefore, only one of the two or three siblings recorded bore an Arthurian-type forename. In another category, members of the seemingly complex Galván clan of Villanueva del Fresno in Extremadura (a region of persistently high emigration for centuries) appear in various capacities in three separate emigrant registrations in 1535–7 and a fourth in 1557; their Arthurian names, by then transmissible family surnames, must date from a generation or more previous to that of the emigrants themselves. Since the same village also provided the emigrant Alonso Rodríguez Lanzarote, recorded by Boyd-Bowman in Mexico in 1531, there seems to have been a particular local penchant for Arthurian names at some point in the past. The chronological distribution of these parental names of Arthurian type can be seen from table XI.2; it will be noted that the dominance of 'Tristán' remains unchallenged, but that in the generations previous to the migrants themselves 'Iseo' is slightly better represented than is 'Galván' (6:4) whilst 'Ginebra', not recorded among the migrants, also appears twice. Absent entirely are Galaz, Lanzarote, and Leonís.

Table XI.2: Parental Names of Arthurian Type by twenty-year periods, 1501–60

Name	1501–20	1521–40	1541–60	Total
Galván	-	3	1	4
Ginebra	-	2	-	2
Iseo	1	3	2	6
Tristán	2	8	1	11
Total	3	16	4	23

To each of these lists of emigrants and their parents must be added some names from the anthroponymic repertoire of the Arthurian-inspired *Amadís* cycle, such as Briolanja Hernández (Bermúdez Plata 1940–80: II: 686; Boyd-Bowman 1964–8: II, 849), an emigrant to Veragua on 9 April 1535, who was the wife of Alonso González of Badajoz and the daughter of Hernando Rodríguez and Catalina Pérez; Esplandián de la Cerda (Bermúdez Plata 1940–80: II: 114; Boyd-Bowman 1964–8: II: 811 [not '8111' as indexed]), who emigrated to Veragua on 8 March 1535, son of Diego Núñez and Doña María de la Cerda of Badajoz (a lady whose honorific probably indicates some appreciable social status); and, in the category of parents of emigrants, Florestán de Fuentes (Bermúdez Plata 1940–80: II: 4712), husband of Elvira González, both residents of Cazorla, whose son Juan Romero emigrated to Florida on 15 March 1538. In 1555, Galeor Mosquera of Consuegra, son of Alonso de Mosquera and Ana Díaz, emigrated to Peru (Bermúdez Plata 1940–80: III: 3098); his name is that of the character Galaor, which was presumably unfamiliar to the register clerk who recorded it, whence the misspelling.

The case of Juan Romero reminds us, as do those of Juan Galbán, Leonís de Temiño and Tristán Lozano, all of whom also registered for Florida in the same year, that the Hispanic settlement of the Americas from the XVIth century onwards reached north far beyond the present US–Mexican border into what is now the territory of the United States. If they all completed their intended voyages successfully and reached their destinations, our emigrants, whose own points of origin in the Iberian Peninsula extended from Asturias to Andalucia, took Arthurian names (or at the very least knowledge of them) to destinations spread from the River Plate to Florida and from the Gulf of Mexico to Peru before the end of the fourth decade of the XVIth century. The earliest bearers of names derived from the Arthurian legends to reach North America were thus Spanish migrants. The geographical distribution of the names across the Americas may be seen in table XI.3, in which the migrants bearing Arthurian names are followed in the second numerical column by those in whose cases at least one parent bore an Arthurian name. Migrant destinations (the first column) are ranked in descending order of the number of migrants, since it is the presence of the latter on the ground that will have constituted a more important and immediate source of local awareness of Arthuriana; but the existence of migrants with non-Arthurian names whose parents had Arthurian names needs to be noted as a potential source of further onomastic diffusion, since in the Spanish family name system such parental names remained a live resource for use by subsequent generations. The table excludes names from the *Amadís* cycle. A case of dual registration of a 'parental name only' migrant for both Tierra Firme and Peru is also ignored in this table, since it is impossible to discern the actual intended destination. It must be borne in mind, of course, that we do not know how many of the intending emigrants actually arrived and settled at their originally-expressed destinations. Records for which the relevant migrant destination is either unrecorded or uncertain (which account for eleven of the migrants and six cases of the twenty-three parental names listed above) are ignored here; the incomplete, deleted register entry concerning Tristán García in 1535 is also omitted from the table. Despite such problem cases, the tabulated data is useful to show the extent of the geographical spread of the early Transatlantic movement of Arthurian names.

Table XI.3: Transatlantic Destinations of Migrants with Arthurian-type Names to 1560

Destination	Emigrant Names	Parental Names	Total
Peru	5	2	7
Nueva España	4	4	8
Cartagena	4	3	7
Tierra Firme	2	-	2
Florida	3	-	3
Veragua	2	3	5
River Plate area	1	1	2
Sto Domingo/Cuba	-	2	2
Venezuela	-	1	1
Total	21	16	37

Besides the emigrant registers at Seville on which these tables are based, there are, as we have seen from the additional Arthurian names found in Boyd-Bowman's catalogue of migrants, other sources for the Hispanic population of Spanish America during the first century of the European settlement. One such is the correspondence sent home by settlers and officials, in which we encounter, predictably, 'Galván' and 'Tristán'. Overall, the indications of social scale among the bearers of Arthurian names in the Americas are as varied as are those in the Peninsula: alongside Columbus's cabin boy in 1493 we may place no less a person than the Crown Treasurer of Tierra Firme in 1580, one Tristán de Silva Campofrío, who is mentioned in a private letter as a trustworthy third party to whom correspondence could be sent to await collection by the addressee.[19] Also highly placed was Don Tristán de Luna y Arellano, who had a distinguished career in the service of the Crown in the Americas. Trade is represented by Transatlantic migrants serving as factors for Peninsular merchants, such as Francisco Tristán who was acting in Peru on behalf of Alonso de Illescas in 1555. We may also contrast here the obviously comfortable state of the emigrant Alonso Galván in Mexico City in 1593 with the evident poverty of his stay-at-home cousin Juan Galván back in Spain at Medina Sidonia, to whom Alonso wrote on 23 January that year, reproaching him for failing to respond to previous invitations to better his lot by joining the writer in the New World, and warning Juan that no further remittances would be sent back to Spain in future to help to alleviate his situation unless he fell into line.[20]

Also similar to the problems encountered in dealing with the corpus of the medieval Peninsular Arthurian personal names are those posed by their American successors in so far as the interpretation of their significance is concerned. Since the Arthurian name forms appear to be alien to early Peninsular patterns of personal names, their emergence in Iberian documentation of the XIIth century suggests that they are likely to be a result of the growing international diffusion of the Arthurian legends, though many questions remain over individual cases concerning the general issue of whether the knowledge of the names was directly or indirectly caused by the legends.[21] In general, the probable modes of the incorporation of a Peninsular Arthurian name over successive generations of a family may be envisaged as involving: (a) initial epithetic or byname use for a child or an adult (after all, the derided Pedro de Ircio was an adult when nicknamed 'Agrajes' by his fellow *conquistadores* in Mexico, as we shall see), or (b) birth-naming of an infant, both directly inspired by knowledge of the legends (by whatever means and in whatever form); (c) naming an infant not after an Arthurian character but after an older relative or perhaps a socially admired or a well-known individual outside the family who was already endowed with a name of Arthurian type; and (d) use of an established name of this type merely because it sounded exotic or attractive. The eventual result of all these processes is (e), a forename of Arthurian origin becoming first a patronymic (whether suffixed as such or not) and finally (f) a transmissible surname. Only in (a) and (b) would there be a direct and immediate influence of the Arthurian legends; but naturally this inspiration by a read or heard text may occur at any date in the history of a family. Both (a–b) and (c) are processes familiar to us today, of course, with the naming of children among some social groups not only in imitation of however briefly admired figures from fields such as sport or some other branch of celebrity culture, but also sometimes after imaginary characters from film or fiction, while (d) is commonplace.[22] Where, then, we encounter an individual in the documentation of the Americas who has an Arthurian name as a patronymic or as a transmissible surname, this gives no evidence of the current direct influence of Arthurian legends, since the name would have entered the family concerned one or more generations earlier. Where, however, a person documented in XVIth-century Spanish America bears as a forename a name found in the legendary stock, as in the forename shared by both Columbus's cabin boy and the Crown Treasurer as well as many others, the possibility of direct literary inspiration in the naming of this individual must be recognised alongside those of family tradition or social imitation. This is particularly true of cases in which the forename concerned is a purely literary creation completely alien to the onomastic system and resources of the Iberian Peninsula before the first appearance of the character concerned, such as Amadís, Briolanja, Florestán and similar names from the *Amadís* cycle. At the opposite end of this scale of probabilities may be placed cases like that of the cousins Alonso Galván and Juan Galván in 1593; since both have different forenames, here we are likely to be dealing with an Arthurian name which, whatever the history of its initial adoption in this family, was by that date serving simply as an inherited and transmissible surname.[23]

Finally, an intriguing and culturally revealing, if numerically tiny, category of individuals not previously discussed is represented by those members of the indigenous population of the Americas who acquired Arthurian names introduced by their conquerors. Two documented cases of this process demand attention. The earlier is that of Leonís, 'a free Indian, native of the province of Guatemala', who had been brought to Spain and whose mistreatment was the subject of a royal order dated 12 October 1543 to the officials of the Casa de Contratación in Seville, commanding them to summon Gonzalo Ortiz and compel him to pay five *reales* a month to Leonís, whom he had been treating as a slave, to enable the latter to return to the Indies (Archivo General de Indias, Indiferente, 1963, Legajo 8, fols 273–4). Unfortunately there is no information on how, where or when Leonís acquired his Arthurian name. The other case involves 'an Indian woman', apparently called Iseo, 'a native of Peru', whose unmarried daughter Magdalena was registered by the emigration authorities in Seville on 21 February 1562 (Bermúdez Plata 1940–80: IV: 2067). We do know a little more of this curious case, in which the daughter of an Amerindian woman was herself registering to go from Spain to Spanish America, thanks to the survival of an earlier document dealing with the family concerned, which is that of the migrant Antonio de Losada. The latter (encountered in the list of parental names above as the son of Iseo Álvarez) had left Spain for Nueva España in 1534, but had obviously proceeded thence to Quito in Peru before 1554. In that year, in Spain his mother, Iseo Álvarez (who was by then widowed), petitioned for, and obtained, permission from the Consejo de Indias for her son's family (which included a daughter aged about seven or eight whom he had conceived with an indigenous woman) to travel to Spain to facilitate their religious instruction.[24] Presumably by 1562 Magdalena's indoctrination was deemed to be satisfactory since she was registering to return to the Americas. In this instance it seems most likely that the adoption of the name 'Iseo' by the indigenous woman was for family, rather than any other, reasons, and may be attributed to the influence, whether direct or indirect, of Iseo Álvarez. These two very different cases have in common the interesting fact that they clearly involve neither the simple imposition of a slave-owner's name on a slave nor the common situation of the baptism of an indigenous convert with the name of a Christian saint or that of a godparent, but beyond that there is insufficient information to draw any firm conclusions. Other similar cases of the penetration of Arthurian names into indigenous strata of society in Iberian America may perhaps remain, particularly in the archives of that region, to be brought to the attention of Arthurian scholarship; only with exceptionally fortunate documentary survivals, however, can we hope to learn anything of the specific circumstances in which any such individuals acquired these names.

Turning from the spread of personal names to the question of the movement overseas of Arthurian texts, it is well known that some among the earliest Spanish *conquistadores* took with them in their memories and imaginations the fictional worlds of their Arthurian and chivalresque readings, to such an extent that when one of them came to record his experiences of the New World this fictional material affected first his perception and then his manner of recording those experiences. Not only does Bernal Díaz del Castillo acknowledge that readers of his own relation of the conquest of Mexico may find its content similar in some respects to that of *Amadís de Gaula* and other such works of chivalresque fiction because of its sheer accumulation of battles and fighting; but, as Rafael Ramos reminds us in his chapter in this volume, he also states that he and other companions approaching Tenochtitlán with Hernán Cortés, on seeing the causeways and buildings of the capital of the Aztec empire, recalled the fantastic and magical worlds of which they had read, so that he faced a dilemma in deciding how to express these shared experiences without wearying the reader:[25]

> Y otro día por la mañana llegamos a la calzada ancha y vamos camino de Estapalapa. Y desque vimos tantas cibdades y villas pobladas en el agua, y en tierra firme otras grandes poblazones, y aquella calzada tan derecha y por nivel cómo iba a México, nos quedamos admirados, y decíamos que parescía a las cosas de encantamiento que cuentan en el libro de *Amadís*, por las grandes torres y cúes y edificios que tenían dentro en el agua, y todos de calicanto. Y aun algunos de nuestros soldados decían que si aquello que vían si era entre sueños. Y no es de maravillar que yo lo escriba aquí desta manera, porque hay mucho que ponderar en ello, que no sé como lo cuente; ¡ver cosas nunca oídas, ni aun soñadas, como veíamos! (Díaz del Castillo 2011: 308, ch. LXXXVII)

To this case may be added another in which a literary apology for this dependence emerges:

> Tornemos a nuestra batalla, que matamos muchos mexicanos y se prendieron cuatro personas principales. Bien tengo entendido que los curiosos letores se hartarán de ver cada día tantos combates, y no se puede menos hacer, porque noventa y tres días que estuvimos sobre esta tan fuerte y gran cibdad, cada día y de noche teníamos guerra y combates. Por esta causa los hemos de recitar muchas veces cómo y cuándo y de qué manera pasaban, y no los pongo por capítulos de lo que cada día hacíamos porque me paresció que era gran prolijidad y era cosa de nunca acabar, y parecería a los libros de *Amadís* o caballerías. (Díaz del Castillo 2011: 635–6, ch. CLI)

In this instance, at least, the genre of the romances of chivalry is tinged with negativity as a comparator, a model to be avoided as likely to detract from the credibility or readability of the author's account. The influence of this literary background may be seen also, perhaps, in the imposition of certain types of place names and topographical descriptors on the local landscape by the *conquistadores*. Whilst some such are understandably descriptive ('Isla Blanca' from its white sand, 'Isla Verde' from its lush vegetation), others recall the imaginary toponymy of chivalric romances. California (Díaz del Castillo 2011: 984–5, ch. CC), it has been convincingly suggested, may have been named after the occurrence of this name in the fourth book of *Amadís* in Garci Rodríguez de Montalvo's text, *Las sergas de Esplandián*. Stylistic influences of *Amadís* are noticeable throughout Bernal Díaz's account. The textual hinterland of this author was clearly an intense influence on him; he also brings the Roman destruction of Jerusalem from his reading of the *Libro de la destruición de Jerusalén* into his account of the slaughter at Tenochtitlán. The active presence of *Amadís de Gaula* in the imaginations of Bernal Díaz and his companions may be assessed by his report of their use of the name 'Agrajes', a character from *Amadís*, as an ironic epithet for a boastful but relatively ineffective soldier in Mexico

(Díaz del Castillo 2011: 1015, ch. CCV): 'Y pasó un Pedro de Ircio; era ardid de corazón y era algo de mediana estatura, y hablaba mucho que haría y acontescería por su persona, e no era para nada, y llamábamosle que era otro Agrajes sin obras, en el hablar; fue capitán en el real de Sandoval.' The point is reiterated elsewhere (p. 1088, ch. CCVIII): 'e a esta causa le llamábamos Agrajes sin obras, y sin hacer cosas que de contar sean murió en México'. Similar factors appear to lie behind the epithet given to a soldier from Seville named Tarifa, who was nicknamed 'de las Manos Blancas': 'púsosele aquel nombre porque no era para la guerra ni para cosas de trabajo, sino hablar de cosas pasadas' (p. 1032, ch. CCV). The epithet has a somewhat literary resonance about it, recalling 'Iseut aux blanches mains' (compare also Iseo de Belmana, encountered above in 1538), as well as the legendarily attractive hands of an early Count of Castile, Garci Fernández, protagonist of the story of *La Condesa traidora*. It may be noted that hints of effeminacy or some other sexual overtones are attached to the figure of the count in this legend.

Bernal Díaz was not, of course, alone in reflecting the influence of *Amadís* in his descriptions of the New World. As Rafael Ramos points out elsewhere in this volume in the case of Francisco López de Gómara's account, even some geological features recalled for some Spaniards the enchanted world of this fiction. The interpretation and literary representation of the New World through such an Arthurian and chivalresque fictional filter (whether by adoption of its modes, or overt rejection of them: as seen above, both processes exist in Bernal Díaz) is only one aspect of the encounter between the American reality and these imagined literary worlds, but it is a significant feature of the earliest decades of the conquest. The presence of Arthurian and related material in Spanish accounts of the Americas is not, however, simply a question of testimony such as that of a relatively unsophisticated reader like Bernal Díaz in reacting to the sights of the unfamiliar material world encountered across the Atlantic. At a more abstract intellectual level, for example, in discussing the myth of Quetzalcóatl in the prologue to Book VIII of his *Historia general de las cosas de Nueva España*, Fray Bernardino de Sahagún evidently considered that the concept of a former ruler from a golden past who had departed from the land but would one day return, according to the common expectation, was satisfactorily illustrated by drawing a parallel with King Arthur:[26]

> En esa ciudad reinó muchos años un rey llamado Quetzalcóatl, gran nigromántico e inventor de la nigromancia, y la dejó a sus descendientes y hoy día la usan. Fué extremado en las virtudes morales. Está el negocio de este rey entre estos naturales, como el del rey Arthus entre los ingleses.

Sahagún proceeds to account for the cautious welcome initially given to Cortés and his men in terms of indigenous expectations of the return of Quetzalcóatl, but notes wryly that the character of the expedition of the *conquistadores* turned out to be utterly different from the hopes of the inhabitants. The learned friar's assumption that his readers would readily understand the parallel is instructive; it is clear that dimensions of the Arthurian legends other than the mere narrative accumulation of combat and marvels were, he believed, appreciated sufficiently to make the comparison a viable one in this early exercise in comparative mythology. The reference is, however, insufficiently specific to permit identification of any precise source for it.

A similar comment could be made in the case of Fray Bartolomé de las Casas, the noted apologist for indigenous rights in the Americas. In the version of his account of Amerindian society and beliefs published by Edmundo O'Gorman as the *Apologética historia sumaria*, Las Casas draws numerous parallels between practices in the New World and those of biblical and Graeco-Roman Classical societies. In discussing idolatry and moral aberrations (Book III, ch. LXXXVI) he dwells upon sacred prostitution and other similar practices in the ancient world, and attributes some of these activities to diabolical intervention. Here, he goes beyond the biblical and Classical to bring in an apposite Arthurian parallel:[27]

> Y es aquí de considerar, tornando al propósito que traemos, que aunque aquestos sacerdotes usaban desta falacia y con ella engañaban al pueblo, los demonios, empero, algunas veces, por emplear su malicia inficionando las ánimas y los cuerpos de los hombres o mujeres, y no porque a ellos, en cuanto de sí es, rescibiesen dello contentamiento, porque no se deleitaban sino en apartar los hombres de Dios, mediante las operaciones de los que llamamos duen o duendes, solían usar mal de aquellas doncellas que se presentaban en los templos, de donde salían ellas preñadas, y nacer dellas hombres, como se dice de la madre de Merlín (e de estas tales se cree haber salido los gigantes), como dice Marco Varrón y Sant Agustín lo consiente, libro 15, capítulo 23 de La ciudad de Dios, y Sancto Tomás no menos lo afirma, de la manera que pueden hacer otras muchas cosas, permitiéndoselo Dios [...] (Las Casas 1967: I, 447)

It is frequently the case that 'se dice' introduces material drawn from common oral tradition, but this is not the only possible meaning of the phrase; the other authorities cited here are resolutely bookish, and it must be considered at least possible that the reference to Merlin's diabolical conception offered here as a parallel comes from a similar written or printed source, which Las Casas does not trouble to specify; though it is noticeable that he does not relate the Arthurian allusion to any specific source in the way in which St Augustine's work is very precisely cited.[28] The material relating to this in the Salamanca manuscript of the *Estoria de Merlin* shows the early presence of this episode in Iberia, though this particular witness is unlikely to have been his direct source; one of the later printed editions of the *Baladro del sabio Merlín*, in which this episode is set out at length in chapters I–II, climaxing with Merlin's conception, seems more probable for this role. Whilst acceptance of the diabolical conception of Merlin is also attributed to other authorities already cited in the *Baladro* itself, so that the possibility that Las Casas may have relied on some other work such as these cannot be entirely excluded, the existence of relatively recent printed editions of the *Baladro* is a persuasive factor. The relevant passage in the *Baladro* is as follows, in the edition by Bohigas:[29]

> E el diablo [...] yogo con ella, e engendró un hijo así dormiendo. Algunos quisieron dezir que a diablo no fué dado tal poder [...] comoquiera que el Vicencio, en un tratado que compiló de ystoria, en el libro vicésimo, a capítulos XXX, recuenta que fué este Merlín engendrado por el diablo [...] e

asímesmo el arçobispo Antonio de Florencia, en la segunda parte, en el título XI, a capítulo II, dize lo mesmo ser Merlín engendrado por el diablo.

It is striking that an ecclesiastical author should see fit to include an Arthurian allusion in a serious treatise, but this is by no means unprecedented; in discussing the quite extraordinary use of the episode of the conception of Arthur made by a XVth-century Castilian sermon-writer in order to illustrate the doctrine of the transubstantiation, Alan Deyermond draws attention to other cases in which Arthurian material had been exploited in similar contexts (Deyermond 1984: 52–4). The legends were obviously credited with either sufficient historical authority, or just with a wide enough currency and familiarity, to serve in some quarters as points of reference and comparison for a variety of concepts in fields quite remote from chivalry and adventure. One is reminded of the manuscript compilation discussed by José Manuel Lucía Megías elsewhere in this volume, in which Arthurian material may have served primarily to furnish a legally oriented precedent in marital matters.

The continued presence of Arthurian and related literature among the books read in the Americas is a different matter; as will be seen, there is documentary evidence of this throughout the XVIth century while this material was in vogue back in Europe. Much later, what may be thought, perhaps, to be an emblematic instance of the cultural extension of Arthuriana into the Hispanic American and Asian worlds comes when in the XIXth and XXth centuries we find the Spanish prose romance *Tablante de Ricamonte* (a title first printed in the early 1500s and then frequently reprinted in the reduced form of a chapbook in Spain down to the nineteenth century) used as the source for a metrical romance in the Tagalog language of the Philippines which was printed there as a popular chapbook in several successive editions. To this we shall return.

Alongside such isolated textual references as those discussed above, important evidence of the spread of Arthurian material across the Hispanic world is furnished by the presence of Arthurian titles among books taken to the Americas. Often where the books do not survive, there are records regarding their export to America from the Peninsula.[30] Given the paranoid religious attitudes that could emerge on either side in the period of the Reformation and the Catholic Counter-Reformation, it is neither a surprise that measures were enacted for the strict control (in theory, at least) of the titles exported to America during the XVIth century, nor a wonder that lists of these books were kept (sometimes, at least, and in varying detail) by the inquisitorial bureaucracy attempting to oversee the purity of faith and ideas in the Americas by weeding out theologically undesirable texts before cargoes were embarked or in advance of their being unloaded on arrival at the port of destination. In these lists, the presence of various works of sub-Arthurian chivalresque fiction suggests that whatever moral qualms may have been felt by some eminent Catholic figures about reading such material, in practice there was no strictly theological objection to its content and its export was therefore tacitly condoned, at least for use among Hispanic settlers but not the indigenous converts, about whose ability to distinguish fact from fiction there seems to have been concern. It is significant here that the original royal prohibition of 1531 on the transfer of fictional texts to Mexico evidently needed reiteration in 1536 and again in 1543 (Leonard 1992: 81–3). The repetition of legislation at such frequent intervals may well be an indication that its enforcement and observance was falling short of what was expected by its original proponents.

The testimony of cargo manifests and of booksellers' inventories and orders is a reliable indication of what was in fact finding its way across the Atlantic, as are the brief records of on-board inspections of books on arrival in port in the New World. Among the numerous (and often unspecified) books of chivalry ('caballerías') recorded in the latter, *Amadís* was found on board the ship *La Candelaria* in 1575 (Leonard 1992: 177; Fernández del Castillo 1914: 510). There are also references to copies of *Amadís de Gaula* and other romances of chivalry inspected on the *Santiago*, a vessel in the fleet commanded by Don Antonio de Manrique in 1576 (Leonard 1992: 161; Fernández del Castillo 1914: 372); to 'los cuatro de Amadis' on the *Santa Catalina* in 1579 (Fernández del Castillo 1914: 381); to 'Amadis de Gaula' on the *Nuestra Señora de Guadalupe* in the same year (Fernández del Castillo 1914: 381); to 'Amadís' on the *San Cristóbal* in 1580 (Fernández del Castillo 1914: 387); and on the *San Bartolomé* in the fleet of Juan de Guzmán in 1585 (Leonard 1992: 161). *Amadís de Gaula* shows up again on the *Santa María la Rosa* in 1599 (Fernández del Castillo 1914: 439), and on *La Concepción* in 1600 (Fernández del Castillo 1914: 444). There is no indication in the documents that any of these books was confiscated. From Peru, the Lima bookseller Juan Jiménez del Río (who seems previously to have been at least temporarily resident in Panama, reminding us, like the case of Antonio de Losada above, that the original destination of an emigrant did not necessarily remain their lifelong place of residence)[31] ordered the same title in 1583 in a list of books to be purchased on his behalf by Francisco de la Hoz when the latter returned to Spain (Leonard 1992: 355, item 84; discussion on pp. 218–25): '6 quatro de amadis que son seys cuerpos y cada quarto de amadis es un cuerpo encuadernados en pergamino'. Whether the required half-dozen vellum-bound copies of the 'Four Books of Amadis' ever in fact arrived in Lima is uncertain, but the order is itself sufficient to demonstrate that as late as 1583 a bookseller there considered that the title would still be marketable among his customers. The evidence of the inspections suggests that he was unlikely to have been disappointed. Even an Italian translation of *Amadís* crossed the Atlantic; it is recorded, together with various other Italian titles, among the books of the treasurer of Nueva Castilla (Peru), Antonio Dávalos, at Lima in 1582: 'Amadís de Bernardo Taso de toscano, 340 mrs' (Hampe Martínez 1996: 245, no. 25). The edition is identified by Hampe Martínez (1996: 122) as Bernardo Tasso's *L'Amadigi* (Venice: Fabio and Agostino Zoppini, 1581). Whether all the ninety-seven books listed in this inventory were actually intended for the treasurer's own use became a matter of contention with other branches of the Spanish bureaucracy, but this related to their taxable status rather than to any problem with their contents.

Other books of the *Amadís* cycle appear as separate titles in some lists of cargoes leaving the River Guadalquivir for the voyage to the Americas, but are variously obscured in the chaotic spelling of the documents. 'Vn Sergaz desplan dian' on the *San Gabriel* on 24 December 1591 (Torre Revello 1940: Appendix, p. xxxv, doc. 27) is of course *Las sergas de Esplandian*. The same title, valued at 4 reales, appears in a list dated 7 January 1594, alongside *Los quatro libros de Amadís*, valued at 8 reales (Torre Revello 1940: Appendix, p. xliii, document 30). The same valuation of 8 reales was placed in this document on a book which is probably the most important Arthurian work so far located in these records, and which represents the first documented transfer to the New World of a copy of *La demanda del Santo Grial*, here bound in two volumes (Torre Revello 1940: xliv, document 30). The text had been printed at Toledo by Juan de Villaquirán in 1515 (Norton 1978: no. 1112); another edition which could be abbreviated to this title was published in 1535. The title is given in the transcription by Torre Revello as 'La demanda delSanto gual en dos cuerpos', but whether the error is that of the modern editor (it would be a simple palaeographic confusion) or the XVIth-century clerk, the title intended here is quite distinctive and easily identifiable, even if the precise edition is not (though the two sections of the 1535 edition seem likely). This reference does not appear to have been noted by Leonard in his survey in *Books of the Brave*; its importance is that it attests the transmission to the Americas of a major work of a mainstream Arthurian theme rather than that of one of their later derivatives such as *Amadís* and its imitators.

Another form of evidence for the diffusion of Arthurian material, perhaps the ultimate manifestation of its success in cultural penetration, is its appearance in indigenous languages of the Iberian overseas territories. In the Philippines, the presence in the Tagalog language of versions of the story of *Tablante de Ricamonte* (a text recorded by Leonard 1992: 108, as being exported to America), a derivative of the Occitan *Jaufré*, is a modern reminder of something that may well have occurred elsewhere in other languages at earlier dates, in oral rather than printed form. For *Tablante*, the evidence from the Philippines takes the form of nineteenth- and twentieth-century cheap printed editions of a versified romance, a genre known locally as the *corrido*, entitled in one copy (in the University of Michigan Library) *Dinaanang Buhay ni Tablante de Ricamonte sampu ng mag-asawang si Jofre at ni Bruinesen sa kaharian ng Camalor na nasasakupan ng haring si Artos at reyna Ginebra* (Manila: Limbagan at Aklatan ni P. Sayo, 1926).[32] This may be translated as 'Life experienced by Tablante de Ricamonte and by the couple Jofre and Bruniesen in the kingdom of Camelot which is ruled by King Arthur and Queen Guinevere'. An earlier edition is in the Edward E. Ayer Manuscript Collection at the Newberry Library because it is accompanied by a handwritten Spanish translation; the printed chapbook source text here is assigned tentatively to Manila and provisionally dated between 1854 and 1873.

Another 1902 Manila edition with sixty-eight pages is cited by Damiana L. Eugenio (1987: 33) and by Charlotte Huet (2006).[33] An English summary of the plot of the Tagalog text is given by Dean S. Fansler (1916).[34] Eugenio also summarises the plot of the story in the 1902 chapbook version, and argues that its contents constitute a conflation of material taken from two separate Spanish sources, namely the *Chronica de los muy notables caualleros Tablante de Ricamonte, y de Jofre, hijo del conde Ason* (printed in 1513, 1519, 1526, 1558 and 1564), and a chapbook version entitled *Historia de los valientes caballeros Tablante de Ricamonte y Jofre Donason*.[35] Five editions of this title, two undated and the others of 1837, 1848 and 1879, are recorded by the Catálogo Colectivo del Patrimonio Bibliográfico Español; another of 1845 is catalogued in the Ticknor collection at Boston.[36] Eugenio analyses in detail the contribution of each of these two sources to the Tagalog text, finding that the latter basically narrates 'faithfully' nine of the main episodes offered by its Spanish models, and concludes that a factor in some omissions and changes made by the anonymous author probably relates to a 'meticulous concern for propriety in feminine behaviour' and 'local notions of propriety and chivalry' (1987: 39). The *Tablante* story is also reportedly known in another language of the archipelago, Bicol (Eugenio 1987: xix). The date at which the Tagalog text of *Tablante* was created has not been established; it survives in nothing earlier than the relatively modern printed editions mentioned above. The printed text of the *Tablante* story is in quatrains of twelve-syllable lines, a metrical form standard in the *corrido* genre.

Thematically, the Hispanic fictional material used in the *corrido* tradition in general clearly arose from the introduction to the Philippines, at some unknown date after the Spanish conquest from the mid-1560s, of chivalric romances and chapbook retellings of Carolingian, Arthurian and other narratives. *Corrido* material originating in medieval Spanish heroic traditions includes the stories of the *Siete Infantes de Lara* and *Bernardo del Carpio*.[37] Although printing was introduced to the Philippines in 1593 (Eugenio 1987: xvi), the earliest printed chapbook copy of a *corrido* cited by Fansler dates from 1815. The genre did not impress some nineteenth-century commentators; in 1878 the Augustinian friar Father Toribio Minguella, for example, expressed an extremely negative view of both its content and its literary quality (cited by Eugenio 1987: xiii). While Fansler referred to it as 'the mental pabulum of the ordinary native', more recent scholarship takes a more benign view of this versified expression of imported narrative themes, brought to the archipelago during the Spanish expansion across the oceans. Its combination of poetics, music and the kind of narrative motifs that have an obvious international appeal and frequently figure in traditional stories was a sufficiently successful development to have enjoyed a well-attested existence in oral transmission, alongside its printed manifestations, into the twentieth century. Few, if any, better examples of the impact of Arthurian-related subject matter on the popular cultures of regions so remote from the areas where the medieval European texts of the legends originated could be cited.

In the Portuguese-speaking world, too, the survival of medieval narrative themes in the compact form of chapbook editions in later centuries is solidly documented. An Arthurian manifestation of this, with the hero recast in the mould of Don Quixote (for example, his adventures are motivated by reading romances of chivalry), is the subject of the *Historia notavel, em que se trata da vida, e valerosas obras do animoso cavalleiro andante Lançarote do Lago* by António da Silva, 'mestre de gramatica', printed by Pedro Ferreira at Lisbon in 1746, which has been studied by Harvey L. Sharrer.[38] The chapbook format preserved in this way some part of the reading matter of medieval Europe for a readership largely composed of poorer economic groups and of juvenile readers. The social and literary phenomenon of the survival of medieval stories and characters into the XXIst century in the current vogue for neo-Arthurian fictional creation, studied in this volume by Juan Zarandona, extends also to the *literatura de cordel* of north-east Brazil. These popular chapbooks, documented in that remote region from the XIXth century onwards, contain (like their equivalents in the Philippines, Portugal and Spain) narratives intended for popular consumption; the Brazilian production of the XIXth century included various verse works on Carolingian and other well-known medieval themes.[39] Although it is not uncommon for some of this material to be loosely classed as 'Arthurian', the presence of specifically Arthurian material among the recorded titles of these traditionally ephemeral editions appears to be little documented, however, until the past decade. For Jerusa Pires Ferreira, who gives the clearest account of this problem, whilst reworkings of chivalresque motifs and themes are well attested in these popular verse works, identifiably Arthurian material is extremely uncommon; she notes that it is difficult to relate the elements that there are to particular textual sources.[40] Whilst monsters, serpents, dragons and giants appear widely as adversaries (as they do in most chivalric literature), specifically Arthurian names are generally lacking. Jerusa Pires Ferreira finds only a single reference to a prophecy of Merlin in one chapbook story of *Joana d'Arc a heroína da França* (by Delarme Monteiro Silva, undated), and a further allusion to Arthur himself in the story of the *Príncipe que veio ao mundo sem ter nascido* (by João Martins de Athayde, printed in 1950).[41] Her cautious position on the question is sensible: a generally chivalresque context and a dependence on narrative motifs common to the genre of chivalresque romance and indeed to much popular narrative do not really justify the broad description of this sub-category within the XIXth- and XXth-century *literatura de cordel* as 'Arthurian' without further qualification.[42] By this late date, so much chivalresque material had been in circulation for so long that intermediary texts, themselves perhaps inspired only indirectly by Arthurian works, are probably more credible as immediate sources and influences.

One must add, however, that more recent years have seen the direct appearance of clearly Arthurian-inspired material in chapbook format in Brazil, such as Fernando Vilela's *Lampião & Lancelote* (2006), which brings this Arthurian character forward in time to encounter the Brazilian bandit gang leader and folk-hero Lampião (the nickname of Virgulino Ferreira da Silva, 1897–1938); and of Cicero Pedro de Assis's *Rei Artur e os cavaleiros da Tavola Redonda* (2011). Publishers of such modified and reinvigorated *cordel* literature have found a market well beyond the social groups in the north-east of Brazil for which this traditionally modest format originally catered (e.g., Causo 2008; Luciano [2011]) as Arthurian material becomes part of modern fantasy literature. In the rapidly changing world of modern Brazil, the Internet is now a productive source of information on this latest phase in the centuries-long process of modifying and recreating Arthurian material for a changing readership in an evolving society.[43]

Notes

[1] The presence of a copy of an early edition of an Arthurian text in a modern Latin American library is, naturally, not necessarily evidence of its early arrival in the New World. Thus the copy of a 1539 Seville edition of *Amadís de Gaula* in the Fondo Rufino José Cuervo (no. 3196) of the Biblioteca Nacional de Colombia, Bogotá, was acquired by the library only in 1941 by Cuervo's bequest. Prior to the latter's ownership, it had been in the private library of Ricardo Heredia until its sale in 1891; Heredia in his turn had acquired it from the dispersal of the collection of Vicente Salvá, in whose catalogue published in 1872 it was no. 1509. There is no evidence of any Latin American provenance for this copy, therefore, prior to its acquisition by Cuervo (Cabarcas Antequera 1992: 9–12). Similar considerations are relevant to the copy of the 1533 Venice edition of *Amadís* in the Biblioteca 'Jorge M. Furt' at Los Talas, Luján, Argentina, which was acquired from the antiquarian bookseller Rothstein on 28 October 1949 (Germán Orduna and Lília E. F. de Orduna 1991: no. XVII, pp. 27–30, and p. [vi]).

[2] Zurara, ed. Dias Dinis (1949), II: pp. 74 (Nunho Tristão is ordered south), 98 (Lançarote requests permission to sail to Guinea), and *passim*.

[3] For Duarte Galvão, see João de Barros, *Asia*, ed. Cidade and Múrias (1945–6), III, pp. 12, 30–3 (Dec. III, book I, chs i and iv); for Leonel de Sousa see *Torre do Tombo*, ed. A. da Silva Rego (1960–70), I, no. 581, pp. 909–15 with the text of his report from Cochim to the Infante Dom Luis, dated 15 January 1556.

[4] For Galaaz de Mata see *Torre do Tombo* (1960–70), VIII, p. 523, no. 4437 (January 1548).

[5] For Galvão Viegas, see Barros, *Asia* (1945–6: IV, 415; Dec. IV, book VII, ch. xii); the information concerning his brother Galas Viegas is provided by Diogo de Couto (1736: 280, Decada IV, livro X, capitulo V). I have used the copy of the latter in the library of Queen's College, Oxford (27.D.15), thanks to the kind assistance of Amanda Saville.

[6] *Torre do Tombo* (1960–70), I, no. 469, pp. 770–5, at pp. 772–3, 775. On the rhetorical canon involved, see Bautista (2009), Cropp (2002) and the comments of Carlos Alvar and Lourdes Soriano in the present volume.

[7] Barros, *Ásia* (1945–6: IV, 562; Dec. IV, book IX, ch. xxi).

[8] Boyd-Bowman (1964–8): I: no. 2232.

[9] Hook (1993: 53–84), based on incidence of the name in documents from the Registro General del Sello, Simancas.

[10] A painstaking description of the paper-trail and the procedures involved is given in a letter home from an emigrant, Juan Alfonso Velázquez, already settled in Michoacan, written in 1577 (Otte [1988]: 202, no. 223).

[11] Hook (1991; 1992–3a: 23–33; 1996: 135–52). See also my comments in the Introduction to the present volume, and the pertinent observations of Carlos Alvar in his chapter here.

[12] All parenthetical references are to the cited volumes of Bermúdez Plata (1940–80) and Boyd-Bowman (1964–8).

[13] Many details in this entry are curiously similar to those of the emigrant of the same name on 8 October 1512 (Bermúdez Plata 1940–80: I: 799). Indeed, these first three entries raise more questions than they provide answers.

[14] In this case, since Juan Tello and his wife Juana Muñoz were migrating with their children (as well as his brother), we may be fairly sure that Leonís was a minor. The records do not routinely include ages of emigrants.

[15] Iseo was one of three siblings travelling with their mother; her case is apparently not recorded by Boyd-Bowman.

[16] Unless, of course, the inspiration for this and other cases of 'Ginebra' in its various spellings was the story from Boccaccio's *Decameron*. Even in this case, however, the presumably pious intentions of those bestowing the name may well have been frustrated if its primary association for friends and neighbours of the various Ginebras turned out to be with Arthur's queen rather than the virtuous Italian lady. For the latter, see Boccaccio, *Decameron*, ed. Branca (1976: 155–65), Seconda giornata, novella 9.

[17] Since 'Belmana' does not appear to be the name of any settlement in Spain, one wonders whether this is a fully literary name, in the style of 'bellas manos'.

[18] This lady's surname, transcribed as 'Munuel' in the document (an otherwise unrecorded form), is indexed as 'Manuel', which is the normal Spanish form.

[19] Mentioned in a letter from Diego del Castillo in Veragua to Juan de la Peña in Madrid, dated 10 May 1580 (Otte [1988]: 277–8, no. 315).

[20] Otte [1988]: 125–6, no. 119.

[21] An example from outside the Arthurian legends is the case, among early emigrants to the New World, of Bernardino Gorvalán (Bermúdez Plata 1940–80: II: 795) and Francisco de Gorvalán, from Medina de Rioseco, and Catalina Gorvalana (Bermúdez Plata 1940–80: II: 3666), a resident of Madrigal, whose names recall those of the literary character Corbalán in the medieval Spanish Crusade narrative, the *Gran conquista de Ultramar*; but there is also a village of a similar name, Corbalán, in the province of Teruel. In some instances, then, a name of apparently literary inspiration may have a quite different explanation.

[22] A current website at *www.babynameguide.com/* contains a category 'Arthurian' which gives an alphabetical list of names of characters with their roles and relationships in the Arthurian legends (accessed 14 December 2012). See also my comment on the recent onomastic effects of *Game of Thrones* in the Introduction to this volume.

[23] Otte [1988]: 125–6, no. 119.

[24] The document is in the Archivo General de Indias in Seville, with the reference Lima, 567, Legajo 7, fols 397v–398r. An additional complication is that the Amerindian mother of the child is apparently described as 'Juana from Guatemala' in the document granting permission, addressed to the Audiencia de Lima and the Justices of Quito, but as 'Iseo' in the register. The case requires further investigation before firm conclusions can be reached.

[25] Quotations from the edition by Serés (2011). I am grateful to Rafael Ramos for providing me with this edition.

[26] Sahagún 1938: II, 277–8. Testimony concerning the nature and extent of readership of Arthurian material among the educated clergy of the XVIth century is, of course, also provided by allusions of this nature.

[27] Fray Bartolomé de Las Casas, ed. O'Gorman (1967: I, 447).

[28] Similar material is known in the Old Testament Pseudepigrapha, with chapter 5 of the *Testament of Reuben* in the *Testaments of the Twelve Patriarchs* relating the impregnation of human women by heavenly beings (though in this instance the primary blame is misogynistically placed on the women for enticing the latter in the first place), which results in the birth of the Giants (Charlesworth 1983–5: I, 782–5, at p. 784).

[29] *El Baladro del sabio Merlín según el texto de la edición de Burgos de 1498*, ed. Bohigas (1957–62): I, 33.

[30] Examples are given in Leonard (1949 [1992]), Torre Revello (1940) and Fernández del Castillo (1914 [1982]).

[31] See, for his residence in Panama, Otte ([1998]: 250–1, nos. 278–9), two letters written from Panama dated 9 May 1578, and both to the bookseller Diego de Torres in Valladolid.

[32] A digital facsimile of this edition is available at the University of Michigan library website with the URL *http://quod.lib.umich.edu/p/philamer/auj6883.0001.001* (consulted 20 November 2012).

[33] Huet (2006), consulted 20 November 2012 at *http://www.culturaspopulares.org/textos%20I-1/articulos/Huet.pdf*.

[34] Fansler (1916: 201–81) is also available at *http://filipiniana.net/publication/metrical-romances-in-the-philippines/12791881642731* (consulted 20 November 2012).

[35] Eugenio 1987: 33–9. The *Coronica de los nobles cauualleros Tablante de Ricamonte y de Jofre hijo del conde Donason* was printed at Toledo by Juan Varela de Salamanca in 1513 (Norton 1978: no. 1093); another edition of 1519 is recorded in the catalogue of the library of Ferdinand Columbus (Norton 1978: no. 1365) but no copy has been located in modern times. The other XVIth-century editions are Toledo 1528 (Catálogo Colectivo del Patrimonio Bibliográfico Español, CCPB000030166–3), Burgos: Herederos de Juan de Junta, 1558 (CCPB000030167–1) and Estella: Adrian de Anvers, 1564 (CCPB000030168-X). The chapbook *Historia* editions, of variously 24pp. and 32pp., include CCPB000081603–5 (Valladolid: Santarén, 1837), CCPB 000466409–4 (Valladolid: Santarén, 1848), CCPB000790732-X (Madrid: Marés, n.d.), CCPB000465257–6 (Madrid: Minuesa, 1879) and CCPB0010073658–2 (Madrid: Sucesores de Hernando, n.d.).

[36] Whitney (1879: p. 366), *s.n. Tablante de Ricamonte y Jofre Donason. Nuevamente reformada*. Valladolid, 1845, '24pp. sm. 4°.'

[37] The *Bernardo del Carpio* story in the Philippines is studied by Barbaza ([2005]: 247–62); and, together with other non-Arthurian *corrido* texts, in Ventura Castro et al. (1985, with a general account of the *corrido* genre, pp. 1–6).

[38] Sharrer 1978: 137–46. On other chapbooks by the same author, see Sharrer 1984b: 59–74.

[39] See Cantel (1970: 175–85), Diégues Júnior (1986: 27–177), and Fachine Borges (1996: 107–14). The absence of any Arthurian material from the survey by Cascudo (1953: 12–25) is a good measure of its lack of importance in this cultural phenomenon.

[40] On the theme of chivalry and the limitations of possible debt to specifically Arthurian material, see Ferreira 1993. The 'Genevra' of the chapbook *História de D. Genevra* is not, it must be noted (as Ferreira indeed points out, p. 46), the adulterous Arthurian queen but her antitype, the virtuous wife from Boccaccio's *Decameron* (II: 9); for this title, see Nunes Batista (1986: 369–468, at 424–5, no. 621). For more recent *cordel* Arthuriana, see Causo, 'Mistura de tradições: Cordel e Fantasia Arturiana', at: *http://terramagazine.terra.com.br/ficcaoespeculativa/blog/2008/11/01/mistura-de-tradicoes-cordel-e-fantasia-arturiana/* (2008; consulted 17 May 2014), and Luciano, 'Heróis da Távola Redonda em versos de Cordel', at: *http://www.vermelho.org.br/noticia/169388–11* ([2011]; consulted 17 May 2014).

[41] See Ferreira (1979: 41–6, 125–6). On the two chapbooks, see *Literatura popular em verso. Catálogo*, I (1961): p. 68, no. 199 (*Joana d'Arc*), and p. 191, no. 572 (*Romance do príncipe*).

[42] Thus, Jerusa Pires Ferreira initially classifies this group of chapbooks as 'Cavaleiresco maravilhoso com possível referência arturiana' (1979: 123), alluding there to Arthurian influence merely as a possibility; but even here two pages later (p. 125) the heading is less cautious: 'Cavaleiresco maravilhoso com referências arturianas'. Unless specifically Arthurian names or uniquely Arthurian narrative situations (with detailed textual parallels, whether structural or verbal) are involved, the general label 'chivalresque' is preferable for this *cordel* material.

[43] Modern Arthurian fiction in Spanish (a topic examined in the chapter by Juan Zarandona in this volume) has also achieved diffusion in remote rural areas of Latin America: see the comments of Barbara D. Miller on children's stories by Graciela Montes circulating in villages on the border between Chile and Argentina (Miller 2003: 213).

XII

THE CONTEMPORARY RETURN OF THE MATTER OF BRITAIN TO IBERIAN LETTERS (XIXTH–XXIST CENTURIES)

Juan Miguel Zarandona

Introduction

The New Arthurian Encyclopedia (1996), edited by Professor Norris J. Lacy, is no doubt the most important general reference book on Arthurian subject matters available. The *Encyclopedia* is well provided with specific entries devoted to different national relevant traditions. Consequently, scholars and those interested in Arthurian literature can read about medieval traditions such as Irish (244), Welsh (507–9), English (133–6), Dutch (122–3), French (160–2), German (182–8), Italian (245–7), Scandinavian (398–401), Czech (106–8), and Spanish and Portuguese (425–8; Sharrer 1996a: 425–8). The *Encyclopedia* is also provided with a second series of entries devoted to modern national Arthurian literary traditions, but the number of these is much smaller: only the English (136–44), French (162–6), German (188–94) and Dutch (123–4) ones are included, thereby giving the misleading impression that the other relevant medieval traditions do not seem to have enjoyed continuity or revival whatsoever.

I cannot claim to know what has happened in modern Scandinavia or Italy, but it is unfortunate that the *Encyclopedia* did not include modern Arthurian Spanish and Portuguese literature. In 1994 I had published an article examining a long metrical legend, *Los encantos de Merlín (Merlin's charms)* (1868), written by the popular Romantic Spanish poet José Zorrilla, who was inspired by one of Tennyson's *Idylls*, 'Merlin and Vivien'. From that moment onwards, I started compiling my own list, corpus or canon of modern Spanish and Portuguese Arthurian literature. And this interest, much rewarded with fruitful findings, finally resulted in a doctoral thesis (2001): *Alfred Tennyson y la literatura artúrica española de los siglos XIX y XX: traducción, manipulación e intertextualidad (Alfred Tennyson and Modern Arthurian Spanish Literature: Translation, Manipulation and Intertextuality)* (Zarandona 2003). The apparent non-existence of a modern Iberian tradition never made sense to me, but I can now affirm that, although not much noticed, it does exist and it is well provided with a good number of excellent writers and outstanding works, written in all the languages of Spain and Portugal. The aforementioned poem of 1868 by José Zorrilla and the works of a few other pioneers opened a gate closed in Spain since the publication of the Second Part of *Don Quixote* in 1615 and its fierce attacks on all Arthurian and chivalric romance. But, once those Romantic men of letters reopened it, with or without the help of Tennyson, the stream of Arthurian inspiration, although almost always the result of minority endeavours, has never ceased (Zarandona 2007).

The truth is that Spanish-speaking and Portuguese-speaking readerships of Arthurian literary works usually enjoy Arthurian legend and myth by means of translations, rather than original creative output in Spanish, other Hispanic languages or Portuguese. The number of translations available is just amazing, but this chapter will focus on original output only. Nevertheless, I will mention now two very representative examples: Arthurian poems by Tennyson translated into Spanish, and Arthurian librettos by Wagner translated into Catalan. As stated, the 1868 metrical legend by Zorrilla, very freely translated from or closely inspired by one of Tennyson's *Idylls*, was one of the main inspirations for the return of the Matter of Britain to Iberia. In addition, although they are very difficult to translate, Tennyson's Arthurian poems have also been translated on other occasions since then. And regarding Wagner, the impact of his highly artistically elaborated librettos was a determining factor in the surge of Catalan Modernism or *Modernisme*. Of course, the key role and influence of both masters, the English Tennyson and the German Wagner, in the revival and development of Arthurian subject matters in XIXth-century Europe is beyond doubt. However, a complete catalogue of the Iberian corpus or canon of Arthurian works in translation will have to wait.

For the purposes of clarity, I have classified the contemporary Iberian Arthurian original works in eight different sections, according to different criteria that will be stated afterwards: 'Pioneers', 'In the wake of Tennyson', 'In the wake of Wagner', 'In support of a Celtic Galicia', 'Neo-medieval revivals', 'New Tristans, with or without their Isoldes', 'Children's literature', and 'The Latin American collection'. Within each of these sections, all occurrences are presented in chronological order according to the year when they were published for the first time, which may or may not be the year corresponding to the edition I have used. If two works happen to have been published the same year, then they will appear alphabetically using their writers' family names.

López Soler, Juan Arolas, Zorrilla and Castelo Branco: The Pioneers

At the beginning of it all, a young Catalan, Ramón López Soler (1806–36), published a novel that has always been regarded as the first leading example of the Spanish Romantic historical novel. It appeared in 1830 and it was entitled: *Los bandos de Castilla o el Caballero del Cisne*. López Soler was also co-editor of the journal *El Europeo* (1823–4), a publication that played a fundamental role in the coming of Romanticism to the lands of Iberia. *Los bandos de Castilla* takes after Walter Scott's

(1771–1832) *Ivanhoe* (1820) very closely, but this is not its only source. It is also very well provided with Arthurian elements: Lancelot and many other Camelot characters are often mentioned; there are numerous allusions to Amadís and other knights from Spanish romances of chivalry; the Knight of the Swan or Lohengrin (Caballero del Cisne), a name taken from Spanish and European medieval sources, much before Wagner. And, above, all, a character named Merlin: astrologer, seer, Satanist, expert in sorcery and occult sciences, etc. And what is more important: it probably is the first fully Iberian Arthurian work that made possible the return of the Matter of Britain to Iberia after so many years.

Juan Arolas Bonet (1805–49) was a Catholic priest with a great talent for writing poetry and an artist of Romantic tastes. Among his many favourite subject matters – Classical, religious, or oriental ones – he cultivated medieval Romantic legends with a deep interest. He mostly wrote about the heroes or heroines of medieval Spain, from the Cid to King Alfonso and the beautiful Zaida. But, fortunately enough, he also published in *Diario Mercantil*, a newspaper, his poem *El manto encantado* as early as 1841. The poem consists of only 125 lines but they are enough to deal with Arturo, Ginebra, Lanzarote, Gauvén and Urganda la Desconocida, a character from *Amadís de Gaula*.

In 1868, the popular Romantic poet and playwright José Zorrilla (1817–93) published a book of legends entitled *Ecos de las montañas*. He was supposed to translate all the *Idylls of the King* by Tennyson, but he finally half-translated only one of them, 'Merlin and Vivien', as 'Los encantos de Merlín', and included it after a collection of legends related to the medieval history of Catalonia. His translated Arthurian poem can be defined as a long legend in metrical lines somewhere between a very free translation and an original work. New elements related to Spain are frequent. Bibiana (Vivien), for example, becomes a Spanish noble lady. Tennyson's original philosophical and melancholic mood disappears and Zorrilla substitutes new intentions of his own. It also represents the definite comeback of Arthurian subject matter to the literature of Spain after a very long absence (Zarandona 2004).

In Portugal, the XIXth-century classic fiction writer, Camilo Castelo Branco (1825–90) included, within the huge corpus of his works, two novels very closely inspired by Tristan and Isolde's unfortunate love story: *Memórias de Guilherme do Amaral* (1863) and *O Sangue. Romance* (1868).

In the Wake of Tennyson (1809–92)

Once Zorrilla had opened the gate and Tennyson started to enjoy a reception in Iberia, many followed and translated, imitated or benefited from the Victorian's talent, his Arthurian long and short poems included. As early as 1875 Lope Gisbert (1823–88) published a volume entitled *Idilios. Elena, Enid*. It included two outstanding verse translations of the idylls 'Elaine' and 'Enid'. Indeed he had already published 'Elena' a year before, 1874, and 'Enid', the same year, 1875, in *Revista Europea*, a Madrid journal. The unique and most difficult formal characteristics of Tennyson's style are surprisingly well translated into Spanish. Unfortunately, Gisbert translated only these two idylls, the aforementioned 'Elaine' and 'Enid'. He chose the good ladies rather than the evil ones, Vivien or Guinevere, the other first two idylls that were published in 1859 by Tennyson before enlarging his great *The Idylls of the King*.

Eight years later, in 1883, Vicente de Arana (1848–90) published *Poemas de Alfredo Tennyson. Enoch Arden. Gareth y Linette. Merlín y Bibiana. La Reina Ginebra. Dora. La Maya.* From then on, Tennyson was mainly known in Spain thanks to the prose translations made by Vicente de Arana, a Basque industrialist who also had a good taste in poetry. He even met Tennyson during one of his long stays in the United Kingdom. But he chose to translate only three idylls: 'Gareth y Linette', 'Merlín y Bibiana', and 'La reina Ginebra'. Arana added many more elements of his own and can be regarded as a very creative translator.

In the same year, 1883, José Ojea published *Célticos. Cuentos y leyendas de Galicia*, a volume that included a legend entitled 'Énide'. Ojea took part in the late XIXth-century Galician Celtic revival and also drew much of his inspiration from Tennyson, as this legend of his proves. Manuel Murguía, the writer of the Introduction, is regarded as the patriarch of modern letters in the Galician language and as the main elaborator of the myth of Galicia as a Celtic nation.

In Portugal, the master novelist José Maria Eça de Queirós (1845–1900) did not live to see the publication of one of his most popular books, *Cartas de Inglaterra e Crónicas de Londres*, in 1905. It collected the articles that he sent to the Brazilian newspaper *Gazeta de Notícias*, while working as the Portuguese consul in Bristol, and that were published between 1880 and 1882. The compiler also thought that 'A festa das crianças', published in 1885 for the first time, also belonged to this series, included it, and it has been part of the volume since then. The essay-short story describes a children's fancy dress party in Cornwall, somewhere near Tintagel, that Eça de Queirós attended. All the boys and girls were dressed up as Arthurian knights and ladies, but, due to their youth, could not behave as they were supposed to do, which is the origin of much fun; Tennyson, who is mentioned, is the clear source of inspiration. His short stories, 'Contos', were also published posthumously in 1902, but then the editor overlooked and did not include some of them, for example one entitled 'Sir Galahad', one of Tennyson's favourite subjects. This text was not published until 1966, when it could not be fully reconstructed. However, the poetic quality of its prose has been highly celebrated ever since.

In 1916, Barcelona and Spain saw the publication of a full volume of poems by Tennyson in translation: *Alfred Lord Tennyson. Las mejores poesías líricas*. It included an excellent verse translation of the early Arthurian poem 'Sir Galahad'. It was made by the first Iberian woman translator of Tennyson, Carmela Eulate Sanjurjo (1871–1961).

Benjamín Jarnés (1888–1949), disciple of José Ortega y Gasset and celebrated experimental novelist, produced a number of Arthurian texts in the early decades of XXth-century Spain, that second Golden Age of Spanish letters ('Edad de Plata'). The short 'Viviana y Merlín. Leyenda' (1929) was the first text by Jarnés dealing with the love story of Merlin and Vivien, a story he read in Arana's prose translation of this idyll by Tennyson, an idyll that captivated his spirit for many years. Then came *Tántalo. (Farsa)* (1935), a novel in which the characters are actors and actresses who are about to stage a play dealing with the story of Merlin and Vivien (a play within a novel). During the rehearsal process, they fully identify themselves with the Arthurian characters they represent. The third was 'Viviana y Merlín' (1936); indeed, this is a second or final version of the novel by Jarnés on Merlin and Vivien. A shorter version was published in 1930. The order of the names in the title, where Viviana is placed before Merlin, was devised on purpose. The writer turns the myth and traditional plot totally upside down. Viviana is seen as a character representing all positive values of life: energy, initiative, sensuality, true love etc. Merlin, on the contrary, symbolises decadence and uselessness. In the end, Viviana beats Merlin completely and takes him to Spain in search of happiness and a new beginning. And finally, 'En el mundo de Viviana y Merlín' (1936), a chapter included in his book *Cita de ensueños. Figuras del cinema* (1936). Viviana is again first. This essay is a critique of a movie based on *A Midsummer Night's Dream* by Shakespeare. This world of fairies and merry fantasies takes the writer immediately back to the world of Vivien and Merlin.

In 1978 Luis Alberto de Cuenca (1950–), the famous Spanish intellectual and writer, translated the popular and early Arthurian poem by Tennyson, 'The Lady of Shalott', for the first time into Spanish. Ten years later, in 1988, Ramón Sainero, an expert in Celtic Studies, published a volume entitled *Los grandes mitos celtas y su influencia en la literatura*. The manual included translations from all Celtic languages and traditions. Tennyson is chosen to represent the English Celtic heritage. In other words, we have three partial, word-for-word translations of the idylls 'The Coming of Arthur', 'The Passing of Arthur' and 'Guinevere'. The interest is not aesthetic, but fully functional: Celtic Studies erudition.

Some years later, in 2002, an anthology of poems in translation published by the University of Extremadura, *Antología poética (texto bilingüe)*, featured the second Spanish translation of the 'La Dama de Shalott', dated 2000, by Jorge Paolantonio (1947–). The same year, 2002, saw the great event of a new book totally devoted to Tennyson in translation: *Alfred Tennyson. La Dama de Shalott y otros poemas*. The translator of the whole volume, Antonio Rivero Taravillo (1963), included the translation of three early short Arthurian poems by Alfred Tennyson: 'La dama de Shalott', for the third time, 'Morte d'Arthur', 'Lanzarote y la Reina Ginebra'.

In the Wake of Wagner (1813–83)

A short story entitled 'El Santo Grial' was published in 1899. In it, a vision in a dream of the Holy Grail saves the empty and tedious life of an apathetic gentleman, familiar only with material pleasures. The impact of Wagner's Arthurian operas is evident. Its author, Emilia Pardo Bazán (1851–1921), the great Spanish woman writer from La Coruña, Galicia, was known to be a devotee of his music and plots. Consequently, she continued writing Arthurian texts for many years. For example, her novel *Dulce Dueño* (1911), a text which was very far from her former realist-naturalist style. This is a beautiful combination of symbolist, aestheticist, and Pre-Raphaelite elements. It is also an Arthurian work following Richard Wagner and his *Lohengrin*. Some chapters are impossible to decipher without taking this opera into account. A performance of it is also included in the plot. Doña Emilia also wrote thousands of newspaper and magazine articles during her long literary career. Most of them have been collected and republished recently (Sinovas 1999a, 1999b; Dorado 2005; Sotelo 2006). Especially those published between 1898 and 1916 in *La Nación* (Buenos Aires) and *La Ilustración Artística* (Barcelona) are full of references, allusions, comments, and full treatments of Wagner, his Arthurian operas, the medieval Matter of Britain and the Spanish chivalric tradition within the context of the general Arthurian one.

But the main focus of Wagnerism in the Iberian Peninsula was to be located in a different region. Immediately before and after the beginning of the new XXth century, all arts and avant-garde movements flourished in Barcelona, capital city of Catalonia. It was the so-called Catalan Modernism which included among its many sources a great cult of Wagner promoted in those years by the Associació Wagneriana (The Wagner Association), founded in 1901. This institution became the meeting point for Catalan modernist artists, for example Magí Morera i Galícia (1853–1927) who authored a poem entitled 'Lohengrin. Impressió' around 1900.

Much more prolific was the modernist poet Jeroni Zanné (1873–1934) whose examples of Arthurian poems include the following titles: 'L'Encís del Sant Divendres' (1905), a religious Arthurian poem full of Wagnerian and Pre-Raphaelite influences, in which Parsifal complains bitterly against Nature for its blooming beauty on Good Friday, the day our Lord Jesus Christ died, and in which Montsalvat and the Holy Grail are also mentioned; 'Espectral' (1906), devoted to Tristan and his night thoughts and visions; 'Tristany i Iselda' (1906), presenting the fatal love of Tristan and Isolda and their suffering; 'Eliana' (1906), inspired in the work of the Italian poet Gabriele d'Annunzio, in which two Arthurian characters are mentioned, Eliana and Morgana; 'A Richard Wagner' (1906), a composition clearly in honour of Richard Wagner, in which one important Arthurian motif, the Holy Grail, is present; 'El cavaller del temple' (1906), a poem enjoying a complex medieval, Wagnerian and Pre-Raphaelite atmosphere; 'Deliris de Tristany' (1909), a longer poem displaying an original combination of long and short lines, which, closely inspired by Wagner, presents the agonised nocturnal suffering of Tristan when remembering his love Isolde; and 'Visions d'hivern' (1912), also showing a very strong Wagnerian inspiration. The leading characters of all the three Arthurian operas by Wagner are present: Parsifal, Isolda and Lohengrin. Jeroni Zanné also published in 1900 a short story entitled 'Bianca Maria degli Angeli' full of Pre-Raphaelite and Arthurian resonances.

Another Catalan modernist poet whom it is essential to mention was Xavier Viura (1882–1948), who published first 'La vida nova' (1902), inspired, on the one hand, by the Italian medieval poet Dante Alighieri and his *Vita Nuova*, and, on the other hand, by Wagnerian and Pre-Raphaelite Arthurian motifs; and secondly, 'Percival Infant' (1904), devoted not to the great deeds of the hero's adult life but instead to a minor passage of his life, that is to say, his mother's unsuccessful struggle to keep him away from knighthood. Wagner also plays a leading role.

The third great figure of Catalan Modernism letters who was very fond of Arthurian subject matters was Alexandre de Riquer (1856–1920), a poet and artist, who in 1899 published *Crisantemes*, a beautifully illustrated prose poem that combines Classical (Arcadia), medieval, oriental and Arthurian motifs: Merlin and his end in the depths of a wood, for example. From 1906 is his sonnet 'La Bella Dama sens Mercé', devoted to Merlin and Vivien and the forest, which is indeed the main character. It is fully Pre-Raphaelite. Although Riquer benefited from the Catalan cult of Wagner, he learned Arthuriana mainly from Britain, a place he used to visit very frequently. In the third place, *El poema del bosch* (*The Poem of the Wood*) (1910) is the most important composition by Alexander de Riquer, which consists of eighteen books or cantos and thousands of lines. The poem fully reviews the wood as a literary motif from the Greek to modern writers. It is also a passionate defence of Nature against destructive civilisation. The Matter of Britain is present in the opening sonnet and in Books/ Cantos I and VII: 'Sonet'; 'Cant I. El bosch'; and 'Cant VIII. Escalibor'. The sonnet identifies the Holy Grail with Poetry, Love and the Renaissance of Catalonia and Catalan letters and culture in general. Canto I is full of Arthurian motifs and characters, closely associated with the Celtic wood: Merlin, Isolda, Tristany, Viviana, la Dama del Llach (The Lady of the Lake), Artús, Lancelot, Guinebra, Lionel, Bleciana, el Sant Graal etc. In Canto VIII, Arthur's sword Escalibor is made to symbolise the revival of Catalonia and the new Catalan modernist high ideals of Faith and Love. A waste land turns into a blooming countryside.

Among the main fruits of the endeavours of the Associació Wagneriana mentioned above, the translations of the Wagner opera librettos are an essential element. Between 1904 and 1907 most of his librettos were translated into Catalan by respected members of the association. The data for the Arthurian ones are the following: *Tristan y Isolda* (1904), translated by Joan Maragall (1860–1911) and Antoni Ribera (1873–1956); *Lohengrin* (1905), by Joseph Lleonart (1850–1951) and Antoni Ribera; *Lohengrin* (1905), by Xavier Viura (1882–1948) and Joaquim Pena (1873–1944); *Tristan y Isolda* (1906), by Jeroni Zanné (1873–1934) and Joaquim Pena; and *Parcival* (1907) by Jeroni Zanné and Joaquim Pena. In 1955, on the occasion of the Wagner Festivals that took place in Barcelona, Anna D'Ax (1902–88) (whose real name was Núria Sagnier) translated afresh the three Arthurian librettos by Wagner: *Lohengrin, Tristan i Isolde* and *Parsival*.

A curious phenomenon is the influence of Wagner's *Lohengrin* on the Spanish national lyrical genre, the *zarzuela* or Spanish light opera. In 1905 Miguel Echegaray (1848–1927), brother of the Spanish winner of the Nobel Prize for Literature José Echegaray, wrote *El cisne de Lohengrin*. Ruperto Chapí (1851–1909) composed the music. The comical plot centres around a village divided between those who want to stage Wagner's opera and those in favour of bullfighting. Another example was Salvador María Granés's (1840–1911) *Lorenzín, o, El camarero del cine* (1910), a full parody of the original opera.

Before the Catalan Amadeu Vives (1871–1932) left his region in 1897, and settled down in Madrid to become a successful musician and popular composer of *zarzuelas*, he had already started his artistic career in Barcelona. For example, in 1895 he finished an Arthurian opera entitled *Artús*, which was only staged for one day in the Barcelona Novedades theatre in 1897. Neither the scores nor the libretto have ever been published, nor has the opera been staged again nor recorded. The librettist was a wealthy local writer and journalist, Sebastià Trullol i Plana (1842–1946), who made use of Walter Scott's 'Lyulph's Tale', an Arthurian text within the text *The Bridal of Triermain* (1813), to construct the words of Vives's opera *Artús*. Fortunately, this libretto was not totally lost and could finally be published in 2011 thanks to a manuscript copy of it found in the Biblioteca de Catalunya, Barcelona (Trullol 2011: 255–79). However, once in Madrid, Amadeu Vives never lost interest in Wagner, operas and the Arthurian legend. For more than thirty years (1897–1932), he contributed articles to different periodicals where his allusions, comments, and treatment of Arthuriana subject matters were constant: Parsifal, Tristan, etc. These essays were finally compiled and published in two volumes entitled: *Julia (Ensayos literarios)* (1971) and *Sofía* (1973).[1]

In Portugal, the Decadentist poet António Patrício (1878–1930) was also a lover of Wagner, as two of his sonnets prove: 'Parsifal' and 'Jardins de Klingsor'. Both poems were published posthumously in 1942 in a book entitled *Poesías*, but were written years before, following scenes from the opera *Parsifal* very closely: the coming of Parsifal on Holy Friday and the sensual garden of the flower girls.

In 1932, the talented Spanish playwright Alejandro Casona (1903–65) published *Flor de leyendas*, his own retellings of many world myths and legends. The selection included a 'Lohengrin' and a 'Tristan e Iseo'. Both follow Wagner's librettos very closely.

A few years before D'Ax's translations and the Barcelona Wagner Festivals, another Catalan lover of Wagner, Daniel Mangrané (1910–85), produced and directed, in collaboration with Carlos Serrano de Osma (1916–84), a film entitled *Parsifal* in

1951, the fiftieth anniversary of the founding of the Associació Wagneriana. The screenplay of this cinematic version of the Wagner opera was written by Mangrané himself with the help of Francisco Naranjo, Ángel Zúñiga and Carlos Serrano de Osma. The whole text is structured by means of a flashback. A group of soldiers, surviving a Third World War, finds a book among the ruins of a monastery in which they can read the story of Parsifal. The music of Wagner and the mountain scenery of Montserrat (Montsalvat) play key roles in this production. In the wake of this success, Mercedes Rubio won the Barcelona Novel Prize 'Elisenda de Montcada' in 1956 with a novel entitled *Las siete muchachas del Liceo* (1956), where Wagner's Parsifal plays a leading role.

In the XXIst century Gustavo Martín Garzo (1948–) returned to Wagner and his operas when he published his novel *Los amores imprudentes* in 2004. The novel is set in a small village in the province of Burgos during the Second World War. Everything that happens there resembles the plot and motifs of Wagner's *Lohengrin*: the lake and the Knight of the Swan, Elsa and Lohengrin, the Holy Grail and Montsalvat, etc. The Nazi anthropologist Otto Rank and the Nazi obsession with the Holy Grail are also mentioned.

Specifically, this Nazi interest in Wagner and the Holy Grail, and the actual visit of Heinrich Himmler, founder of the SS, to the monastery of Montserrat (in the province of Barcelona) in 1940, in search of the Grail, have proved excellent subject matter for many XXIst-century Spanish thriller novelists. For example, José Calvo Poyato (1951–) and his *La orden negra* (2005), Montserrat Rico Góngora (1964) and her work published first in Catalan and then in Spanish, *L'abadia profanada* (2007) and *La abadía profanada* (2008); and Sergio Lechuga Quijada and his *Calix* (2009). They all share the same ingredient: a combination of facts and fancy; intrigue, suspense and dangers; esoteric clues and pseudo-history (medievalism); reinterpretations of the Scriptures; secret societies and orders; Franco's Spain and a Second World War background combined with the present; and many Arthurian elements.

María Lourdes Alonso, under her own name or using two different pseudonyms, Michelle Angela and Christabelle Columela, published two Wagnerian essays, *Las mujeres de Wagner* (2011) and *Wagner's Women* (2012), where she deals with two main Arthurian female characters, Isolde and Kundry. She is also the author of some other essays devoted to XIXth-century British and Spanish literature, Celticism, and the Matter of Britain: *La magia celta según Gustavo Adolfo Bécquer, Oscar Wilde y la literatura artúrica contemporánea* (1999), or *Las hadas de Bécquer y Wilde* (2011). Alonso has also published a number of Arthurian novels: *Camelot reconstruido* (2000), *El hada blanca. Novela artúrica e inmenso cuento de hadas para lectores maduros e iniciados* (2001), *Ector, el príncipe de negro. Los elfos de Camelot* (2004), *Gades Avallonia* (2006) and *Gades y Camelot* (2012). Alonso brings the world of Camelot to the old Roman city of Gades (present day Cadiz, Andalucia). So far, the Matter of Britain in Spain has been restricted to northern Spain, from Galicia to the Pyrenees.

In Support of a Celtic Galicia

From the end of the XIXth century a group of intellectuals and writers imagined a Celtic past for their homeland of Galicia, and were successful in persuading their countrymen that it was all true. Manuel Murguía (1833–1923) and his *Historia de Galicia* (1865–1911) were the first makers of this myth that took deep root not only in the popular imagination but in regional letters ever since, in something that has become a very successful literary tradition. Many of these Galician writers have also made great use of the Celtic Matter of Britain and the legends of Camelot.

For example, Ramón Cabanillas (1876–1956), known as the Poet of the Galician people, made use of two main sources to write his epic poetic trilogy, *A noite estrelecida. Sagas* (1926): Arthurian material (Tennyson) and Celtic Ossianism, which he fully identifies with Galicia, a Celtic nation as well. The first part or saga of the trilogy, 'A espada Escalibor', centres around the finding of the sword Escalibor in the isle of Sálvora (Galicia). The second part, 'O cabaleiro do Sant Grial', centres around the search for the Holy Grail by Arthur and his knights. Galahad finds it at Mount Cebreiro (Galicia). And the third, 'O soño do rei Arturo', sees the end of Arthur and his departure towards his resting place in Galicia.

Vicente Risco (1884–1963), a close follower of Manuel Murguía, can be regarded as another founding father of the idea of a Celtic nation named Galicia. Apart from many articles and essays on Galicia, the druids, and the Celtic peoples, he also wrote his own history of Galicia which was published in 1952. Risco published a large numbers of works both in Galician and in Spanish: fictional narratives, plays, essays and non-literary prose always combining the humanities and social sciences and Galicia. And, above all, Risco was an enthusiast about authors on the Holy Grail. In this regard his major and late work was the book *Mitología cristiana* (1963). Most of the book is devoted to the Grail from all points of view and traditions. It becomes fascinating when, for example, Risco starts theorizing on the so-called 'seven doctors of the Grail', namely, the sage Merlín, the Moor Flegetanis, the Armenian Kyot, Chrétien de Troyes, Wolfram von Eschenbach, Ana Catalina Emmerich and Richard Wagner. But his interest in the Holy Grail started long before this date. In 1935 he published a short text entitled 'A leenda do Santo Graal', and around 1920 he wrote one of his most curious texts: *Doutrina e ritual da moi nobre orde galega do Sancto Graal*, which was not published until 1998. The text has two parts: a first one devoted to the doctrine of a very noble Galician order of the Holy Grail, and a second one to its rituals. He added a collection of beautiful drawings depicting the symbols of the order: banner, costumes, shield, sword, the Holy Grail etc. Risco may have had the intention to found a real order with this name, but the plain truth is that it never existed. Years later, he returned to the subject matter with another two short articles: 'De Sigfrido a Parsifal' (1939) and 'El misterio del Santo Grial' (1942), just before his aforementioned major work.

Both Cabanillas and Risco opened a door through which many would pass after them, Álvaro Cunqueiro (1911–81), for example. He was a very prolific fiction writer and journalist, but the number of his Arthurian texts is just amazing. This Galician author was the most important modern Iberian writer of Arthuriana. He never stopped producing Arthurian texts both in Galician and Spanish during his whole life. Merlin was always his favourite. It all probably started in 1941 with an essay entitled 'Hazaña y viaje del Santo Grial', where he not only wrote about Chrétien de Troyes, Wolfram von Eschenbach, Corbenic, Logres, Tule, but also about the Iberian places associated with the Grail: Montsalvatge in the Pyrenees and Cebreiro in Galicia. Secondly, in 1953, he continued with 'Los países del señor Merlín', an imaginary journey where he displayed all his knowledge about the magician, whom he combines with many other mythical characters, and 'La flauta de Merlín'. In 1955, there appeared 'Carta de Irlanda', which is a study of the myths associating Celtic Galicia and Ireland, with allusions to Arthurian characters such as Vivien. Also in 1955, his major longer fiction work, *Merlín e familia e outras historias*, was published. After the end of Camelot and the Round Table, and the departure of Arthur, Merlin and Guinevere settle down in Miranda (Galicia) and start a peaceful new life. However, although retired, Merlin attracts a varied array of characters who come to his home looking for advice and help. Galician folk motifs, Arthurian traditions, fantasy beings and all kinds of mythical entities get together in Miranda under the benign figure of Merlin. In 1956, in an 'Epílogo' for a new edition of *El baladro del sabio Merlín (1498)*, he describes his lifetime fascination for Merlin and claims that the magician is for him just like a close friend. Also in 1956, 'El caballero, la muerte y el diablo y otras dos o tres historias'. Cunqueiro first wrote this short novel on the life of Felipe de Amancia in *c*.1940, and then he rewrote and published it in 1956. As Felipe became Merlin's aide in *Merlín e familia*, this is the story of the life of this new Arthurian character before and after meeting the wise old man. Another entry for 1956 was *As crónicas do Sochantre*, a novel set in Brittany, a land Cunqueiro had not visited yet, but had read a lot about. References to Arthur and the Matter of Britain/Brittany are abundant. One year later, in 1957, *Merlín y familia y otras historias* was a Spanish-language, enlarged version of *Merlin e familia*, that is to say, a new original rather than a very faithful self-translation. In 1958 there followed 'Merlín y Don Pedro el Cruel', in which he wrote a text summarising an old Castilian legend related to King Pedro I, and claiming that his death had been predicted by Merlin. The writer also analyses the reception of his bilingual *Merlín e familia / Merlín y familia*. In 1959, in 'Inventando Bretaña', Cunqueiro not only wrote about the Matter of Britain very frequently, but also about Brittany, the French region, as well. From Brittany he travels to the Arthurian subject matters very easily, as is the case here. In 1961, 'Las historias de Llwyn' features a pilgrim who lives in a ruined castle by the seashore and who tells the story of his meetings with Parsifal and Isolde. From 1962, 'La tumba de Arturo' is a newspaper essay reviewing the finding of Guinevere and Arthur's tomb in Glastonbury Abbey

(Somerset). Cunqueiro declares himself very offended by this claim: everybody knows that Arthur did not die, but that he is waiting in Avalon for his second coming as the Once and Future King. In 1963, 'San Criduec y su palma' associates St Criduec's legendary travel with the search for the Holy Grail. In 1964, in 'Los guardianes de la cruz' Cunqueiro makes connections among Don Quixote, Amadis of Gaul, Galahad and other Arthurian knights. Also in 1964, 'Peregrinos de Bretaña' was published: Brittany and Galicia got much closer by means of those pilgrims who travelled to Saint James's tomb in Santiago de Compostela (Galicia). In 1965, there appeared 'La flor de los caminos'. The Way of Saint James towards Santiago de Compostela crosses Mount Cebreiro, where the Holy Grail is kept. There you can see Galaz (Galahad) and Parsifal from time to time. In 1968, Cunqueiro published one short text on the Grail, 'O Graal' and its French medieval sources. In 1970, in 'Merlín en Carmarthen', Cunqueiro demonstrates the key roles that Arthur and Merlin still play in modern Britain. Legend and myth are more important than current politicians guess. In 1972, he published *Vida y fugas de Fanto Fantini della Gherardesca*. Fanto, the main character in the novel, is a nephew-grandson of Lanzarote. Capovilla, his old domestic servant, sings the *Song of Lancelot* and knows all Arthurian books by heart. Isolda is also mentioned frequently. From 1974 is *El año del cometa con la batalla de los cuatro reyes*, a novel full of Arthurian motifs. Paulos, the main character, is aided by the Lady of the Lake, travels to a decaying Camelot, where he visits Arthur and Guinevere, finds Isolde's shoe, dresses up as Lancelot, and gets the help of Kings Arthur and David, as well as Julius Caesar, when battling his enemies. Avalon is also mentioned. Published in 1977, 'Pasei a porta' is a poem about the kings of Britain; Isolde is mentioned. In 1979, 'Tristán García' tells of a young Galician boy, named Tristán, who finally finds out who Tristán was when reading about Tristán and Isolde's love story. From then on, he sets out in search of somebody named Isolde, which proves very difficult. In the end, he meets an old lady named Isolde, who has also spent her life waiting for a Tristan to find her. Love is impossible because of their age difference. In 1980, in 'Merlín misionero', Merlin becomes a theologian and tries to convert the Jewish people with his magic. Also in 1980 there was published 'Dona Flamenca', a poem in which Galahad, Guinevere and Lancelot are mentioned. And finally, in 1991, came the posthumous 'A xénese da novela occidental'. In this essay Cunqueiro claims that the story of the love of Tristan and Isolde is not Celtic in origin but Persian, and was taken into Europe by means of the Arab invasions. And also in 1991, in 'A maravillosa historia de Tristán e Isolda', he again displayed his erudition concerning the Arthurian legends.

The first heir of Cunqueiro can be said to be Xosé Luís Méndez Ferrín (1938–). New generations of Galician writers have kept their interest in the Arthurian traditions. With Méndez Ferrín, Arthurian characters become enigmatic, nightmarish, experimental, absurd, revolutionary and profoundly original, as his first Arthurian short story, 'Percival' (1958) proves. Some years later, in 1982, he returned to

Arthurian subject matter with his major work 'Amor de Artur'. It can be defined as a very challenging and sophisticated reinterpretation of the Arthurian tradition and the love triangle among Arthur, Guinevere and Lancelot. Méndez Ferrín breaks the triangle and, at first, he seems to turn it into a square by adding Liliana (Elaine), but the result is rather a circle where everybody shares his or her love with everybody else. In a few words, it is a mysterious, enigmatic, symbolic, oneiric, and an extremely lyrical text. Two years later, in 1985, his *Arnoia, Arnoia*, which can be defined as revolutionary political fiction full of intertextual references, many of them to the Matter of Britain, particularly Percival and the forest of Broceliande. Another two years later, *Bretaña, Esmeraldina*, another radical and politically inspired novel by Méndez Ferrín, who never fails to include Arthurian references in his texts, as is the case here: romances of chivalry and the Welsh *Mabinogion*. And finally, in 1997, comes 'Lanzarote ou o sabio consello'. A young man loves the wife of a Scottish prince, and a wise old man warns him against this love by telling him the story of Arthur, Guinevere and Lancelot. The Arthurian heroes are described not in ideal terms, but in very negative words.

In 1972, Gonzalo Torrente Ballester (1910–90) published another landmark in the history of contemporary Iberian Arthurian literature, his monumental novel *La saga/ fuga de J.B.* In an imaginary Galician town, Castroforte del Baralla, a group of citizens decides to found a New Round Table. Many years later, another group of locals gets to know what their ancestors did, and try again to found a New Round Table and become new Arthurs, Lancelots, Galahads, Merlins and Guineveres. Vicente Risco's dream of a Galician order of the Holy Grail seems to have come true, but both experiments fail absolutely. The novel is a great humorous parody of human weaknesses in general, and of Galicia and its collective myths in particular. The text is also an outstanding example of experimental post-structuralist literary style.

Five years later, in 1977, the Galician legends that Leandro Carré (1888–1976) had compiled and rewritten were published posthumously in a volume entitled *Las leyendas tradicionales gallegas*. Two of these legends dealt with the Matter of Britain and Galicia. The first one, 'El Santo Grial del Cebreiro', retells the traditional Galician legend locating the finding of the Holy Grail on Mount Cebreiro, next to the Way of Saint James, where it enters Galicia. The second one, 'Galaaz y el Santo Grial', has Galahad travelling to Galicia where, on Holy Friday, he finds the Holy Grail on Mount Cebreiro.

Another heir of Cunqueiro, Darío Xohán Cabana (1952–), started his career as an Arthurian writer in 1982 when he published 'Cebreiro en materia de Bretaña', a sonnet about the mythical Mount Cebreiro in Galicia, where the Holy Grail is. Arthur, Galahad, Lancelot and Percival are mentioned. One year later, in 1983, he changed poetry for fiction and published 'A invasión'. In a symbolic world of evil, and surrounded by a nightmarish and oppressive atmosphere, only some Arthurian knights can offer some hope: King Arthur, Galván (Gawain), Lancelot, Galahad and Percival.

In 1987, again back to poetry with 'Guenebra', a sonnet devoted to Queen Guinevere and her two loves, Arthur and Lancelot. In 1987, he published another poem, 'Galván en Demonte', a third Arthurian sonnet on the adventures of Gawain and other Arthurian knights in Galicia in search of the Holy Grail. The year 1989 finally saw the publication of his major Arthurian work, *Galván en Saor*. Galván, or Gawain, leaves Arthur's Court and travels to Saor (Galicia), where he meets Merlin, now a bus driver, and settles down for a while. The novel takes place in two different moments, namely, the present and medieval times. And the action jumps from one to the other without interruption. We may see Gawain riding a horse now, and driving a motorbike immediately afterwards. Galician folk stories and popular traditions are widely used. Later on, in 1992, Cabana published a romance of chivalry, *Cándido Branco e o Cabaleiro Negro*, very close to the Arthurian romances.

Antón Castro (1959–) is the author of a short story entitled *Vida infame de Tristán Fortesende* (1984). It can be considered as a continuation of Tristan's life. After living in Wales and Brittany, etc., he retires and dies in Galicia.

Carlos González Reigosa (1958–) can also be regarded as an heir of Cunqueiro studied in this section. In 1987 he published *Irmán Rei Artur*, a trilogy of Arthurian stories. 'A tentación de Lanzarote' was the first part of his Galician trilogy on King Arthur and his knights. González Reigosa presents himself as a passionate defender of the suitability of the Arthurian tradition for Galicia. Here we see a Lancelot tortured by doubts related to the viability of the ideas of the Round Table and the real intentions of King Arthur. 'Amor de Merlín' was the second part of this trilogy. For Reigosa, the traditional version of the Vivien–Merlin love affair does not make sense. He cannot believe that Vivien could beat Merlin. Indeed, Merlin here manipulates Vivien in order to get peace and retire from the world. 'A morte do rei Artur' is the third and last part of the trilogy. Reigosa follows Malory very closely now, but emphasises the inner feelings of his characters. In spite of their diverging destinies, Arthur, Lancelot and Guinevere continue loving each other.

In 1991, another respected Galician writer, Ricardo Carvalho Calero (1910–90), published 'Soneto', a sonnet mixing Galician folk traditions and myths, Arthurian motifs, and new Galician interpretations of the matter such as those by Méndez Ferrín. Don Quixote is also mentioned.

The last literary star of a Celtic Galicia is Xosé Ramón Loureiro Calvo (1965–), a bilingual novelist in Galician and Spanish who has recently published the following novels: *O corazón portugués* (2000), *As galeras de Normandía* (2005), *Las galeras de Normandía* (2007; a self-translation of the previous one), *León de Bretaña* (2009), *El lejano reino de la vía lactea* (2013) and *La asombrosa conquista de la isla ballena* (2013). Regarded as the heir of Cunqueiro and Torrente Ballester, he locates his novels in the so-called Land of Escandoi, or mythical North Galicia, the last possible Britain/Brittany. As Cunqueiro did, in all his fiction he makes Merlin appear as a character.

Neo-Medieval Revivals

The interest in the Middle Ages is a literary and cultural fascination that has never stopped producing works of art since the XIXth century. Let us start with another contribution by Emilia Pardo Bazán, her short novel entitled *La última fada*, dated 1916. This brilliant text fuses two Arthurian stories: the love stories of Tristan and Isolde, and of Merlin and Vivien. Pardo Bazán also added new very original developments of the traditional arguments. By putting the fairies on the verge of disappearing, the novel depicts a battle between decaying fantasy and plain realism. In addition, Isayo, the young protagonist and secret son of Tristan and Isolde, is made to travel to medieval Castile (Spain), and is promoted to the role of Christian champion against Moorish infidels.

José Echegaray (who was awarded the Nobel Prize for Literature in 1904, as stated above), the most popular, prolific and melodramatic playwright of his time, presented his most famous drama, *El gran Galeoto*, in 1881. The title takes after Canto V of Dante's first part of the *Divina Commedia* (*c*.1308–21), 'Inferno' [Hell]. Francesca, when narrating her illicit love for Paolo, remembers Galeotto, a friend of Lancelot who facilitated his adulterous love affair with Guinevere. This literary motif becomes a recurrent reference in Echegaray's work.

In 1929 the surrealist writer Agustín Espinosa García (1897–1939) published a personal vision of the Canary Island of Lanzarote (Lancelot), *Lancelot 28°–7°*, where he identifies knight and island.

Some years later, Francisco Villaespesa (1877–1936) published a tragedy entitled *El Rey Galaor* in 1930. He set it in an imaginary medieval scenery. The name Galaor, as well as Galaz, are Spanish adaptations of the name Galahad. Galaor also comes from *Amadís de Gaula*.

In Portugal, Afonso Lopes Vieira (1878–1946) established himself as an Arthurian writer from 1922 when he published his *Em demanda do Graal*. Indeed, it is a very miscellaneous book where he mainly collected previous articles, essays and lectures on Portugal, its history, culture, art and literature: the exploration of Africa (Vasco da Gama), the legend of Dom Pedro and Inês de Castro (Portugal's Tristan and Isolde), Camões, Gil Vicente, Eça de Queirós, Portuguese patriotism, the popularity of the Matter of Britain in Portugal during the Middle Ages, and more besides. He mentions and alludes to many Arthurian characters, motifs and episodes as something very Portuguese, but there is no full development or retelling of the matter, the Holy Grail especially. Why, then, did he use this title for the whole volume? The answer may be in the 'dedication', where he claims that his intention has been to save the soul of Portugal, i.e., his ideal and lyrical search of the Grail. Secondly, in 1923, he published his most famous book, *O Romance de Amadis*, a reconstruction of a possible lost primitive medieval version of *Amadís de Gaula* in Portuguese. He shortened the Castilian enlarged version by Garci Rodríguez de Montalvo (*c*.1450–*c*.1505), dated

1508, the only complete version today extant, and chose what he thought belonged to the hypothetical medieval Portuguese original. This nationalistic experiment was very successful. He even published a second version of it for children in 1940: *O Conto de Amadís de Portugal*. The very same year of 1940, he offered his readers a sequel to his first Arthurian volume: *Nova demanda do Graal*. Its structure and contents are very similar to his first Grail book. However, the prologue here states very clearly the reason why he chose this title: to serve Portugal and our ideals as if we were new knights in search of the Grail.

From the 1940s, the brilliant intellectual, researcher, art critic and experimental poet Juan Eduardo Cirlot (1916–73), famous for his *Diccionario de símbolos* (1958), started to publish his books of poems, and to express his fondness for the Matter of Britain and everything Celtic. The following poems can prove this claim: 'Tristán' (1945), 'Sir Tristán' (1946), 'Sir Galahaz' (1949), 'A San Juan de la Cruz' (1952), where he compares the saint to Tristán, or 'Richard Wagner' (1972). Brief allusions to other Arthurian and/or Celtic motifs and characters are frequent in other poems. But his major work, Celtic and Arthurian, is his huge cycle *Bronwyn* (1967–72), consisting of sixteen books: *Bronwyn I, II, III, IV, V, VI, VII, VIII, N, Z, X, Y, Con Bronwyn, Bronwyn Permutaciones, Bronwyn W* and *La Quête de Bronwyn*. Cirlot himself acknowledged the *Mabinogion*, Chrétien de Troyes, the *Vulgate* and Wagner. The search of the Holy Grail is clearly behind this search of Bronwyn, a Celtic female character of his imagination who has the very Grail as her heart.

In 1957, the Catalan writer Joan Perucho (1920–2003) published a contemporary novel of knighthood, *Llivre de cavalleries*. The author acknowledged that he got his inspiration from Mark Twain's *A Connecticut Yankee in King Arthur's Court* (1889). Consequently, the novel mixes medieval and contemporary times. However, it is more a novel of chivalry than a full Arthurian text in the tradition of classical Spanish romances of chivalry such as the famous *Amadís de Gaula* (1508). Years later, in 1981, he published a second contemporary novel of knighthood, *Les aventures del cavaller Kosmas*, again very close to the Arthurian world combined with science fiction motifs. Finally, in 1990, Perucho published a short essay displaying another Arthurian title, 'La fata Morgana', a text describing a natural phenomenon that usually takes place in Calabria (Italy) and which has been popularly named Fata Morgana. In 1996, a compilation of all his short texts from 1953 was published, *Fabulaciones*, where his readers could enjoy new adventures of Kosmas and other knights: 'La última Navidad del caballero Arístides Cardellach de la Harche', 'San Simeón el estilita y el caballero bizantino Kosmas', 'Las aventuras de Kosmas' or 'Un caballero erudito'. There is also one essay entitled 'El caballero inexistente', clearly indebted to Italo Calvino's (1923–85) neo-Arthurian Italian novel of the same title, *Il cavaliere inesistente* (1959).

Francisco Fortuny (1958–), a famous Spanish poet, published a book entitled *Fata Morgana o Los efectos de la causa* (1958). There is one poem of the same title, 'Fata Morgana', where the Arthurian motif is developed.

In 1965, a film entitled *Fata Morgana* was premiered in Spain. It got its Arthurian title, and Arthurian intertextuality, from a poem written by the French surrealist poet André Breton, as confessed by Vicente Aranda (1926–) and Gonzalo Suárez (1934–), who wrote the screenplay.

Carmelina Sánchez-Cutillas (1927–2009) published a book entitled *Matèria de Bretanya* (Matter of Britain) in 1976. The book title is also the title of its last chapter. The author writes about her own childhood and about the time when she started reading about Arthur and his world of knights and ladies.

The same year Felipe Mellizo (1932–2000) published *Arturo, rey* (1976), a collection of essays on international and Iberian Arthurian subject matters.

Mariano José Vázquez Alonso (1936–) published in 1982 a comprehensive rewriting of the Arthurian legends, *La leyenda del Grial* giving a complete account of them from the days of the Round Table to the Quest of the Holy Grail. He followed the examples of T. H. White, *The Once and Future King* (1958) and John Steinbeck, *The Acts of King Arthur* (1976), targeted a wide readership and devoted chapters to all the main knights: Perceval, Lancelot, Galahad, Gawain etc.

Jaume Fuster (1945–98) was a devoted admirer of J. R. R. Tolkien and his trilogy *The Lord of the Rings*. This is the reason why he followed Tolkien's example and wrote his own trilogy: *L'illa de les tres taronges* (1983), *L'anell de ferro* (1985) and *El jardi de les tres palmeres* (1993). Fuster's L'Home Savi (The Wise Man) takes after Gandalf the Grey, who also takes after Merlin, all of them belonging to the same kind of archetypal creations.

The Arthurian tales by Joseba Sarrionandia (1958–) are outstanding not only because they are very original reinterpretations of the Arthurian motifs, but also because they are written in the minority language of Basque. 'Ginebra erregina herbestean' ('Queen Guinevere in Exile') is the first one of these short stories (1983). After the end of Camelot, Arthur and Guinevere go into exile from their homeland and settle down in a rural area in the Basque Country. Lancelot leaves them, but his son Galahad settles down next to his king and queen. Guinevere misses Lancelot, and because of their similarity she seduces young and pure Galahad, which seems the end of the possibility of finding the Holy Grail. Arthur finds out and kills Galahad out of revenge. But hope can never be uprooted: Guinevere is pregnant and is carrying Galahad's son in her womb. 'Amorante ausarta' ('The Bold Lover') (1990) deals with the love story of Merlin and Vivien, now living in the rural core of the Basque Country. 'Eguziak ortza urdinean nabegatzen' ('The Sun is Sailing in the Firmament') (1996) centres around Percival and a fatal hunting of the Unicorn. The knight also falls in love with a Pre-Raphaelite-looking rural lady. And 'Ezpata hura arragoan' (1996) ('The Sword in the Crucible') presents old King Arthur in his Basque Country retirement talking to his servant Fool about the good old days for ever lost. It is very melancholic in mood.

Paloma Díaz-Mas (1954–), a well-known novelist, published her *El rapto de Santo Grial o El Caballero de la Verde Oliva* in 1984, where she takes advantage of many traditional Arthurian motifs in order to imagine and write about a whole new set of motifs of her own: new plots and characters. Nobody believes in the ideal any more; Arthur is just a sceptical old man; Lancelot and Perceval become fully useless for deeds of knighthood; women play the role of knights. The new star is young Pelinor, the new hero of Camelot. It is a parody of the Round Table and its ideals. Many ballads and popular traditions of Spain are also incorporated into the text. One year later, in 1985, Díaz-Mas published a second Arthurian text, another novel: *Tras las huellas de Artorius*. Here some academics centre their research on difficult anonymous medieval texts. References to the Matter of Britain and to the Breton *Lais* by Marie de France are frequent.

The same year of 1985, another Basque-language writer, Luigi Anselmi (1954–), published a poem entitled 'Beafeater'. It is based on a word play. In Basque, as in Spanish, *Guinevere* and *Gin* sound the same: *Ginebra*.

In 1985, Luis Alberto de Cuenca published, for the first time, a poetry book, *La caja de plata*, which included a poem entitled 'Urganda la desconocida'. In other words, a poem devoted to this popular character of *Amadís de Gaula*. Later on, in 1996, he compiled all the articles he had published in *ABC* from 1990 to 1995 and gave the book the title *Álbum de Lecturas*. This collection of essays included a good number of texts devoted to Arthuriana, specifically the following: 'Un diccionario de mitología céltica', 'La aventura caballeresca', 'Textos medievales de caballería', 'Arturo de Bretaña', 'Leonor de Aquitania', 'Tristán e Iseo', 'El Guillaume d'Angleterre de Chrétien de Troyes', and 'Hartmann von Aue'. Again, in 2014, he published a poem entitled 'Ensueño celta' in his book *Cuaderno de vacaciones*, devoted to the Celtic world, Arthur and Merlin included.

In 1993, Pablo Mañé Garzón (1921–2004) offered Iberian readers another general, popular account of the Arthurian legends, *El rey Arturo y los caballeros de la Tabla Redonda*, similar to those made by Steinbeck and White in English. Here the story starts with the very origin of Arthur and ends with the destruction of Camelot and the death of Arthur (the full cycle).

Four years later, Ángel Almazán de Gracia (1958–) published a very atypical text, half fiction, half compilation of legends, entitled: *Los códices templarios del río Lobos. Los custodios del Grial* (1997). The most original part of this proposal is the disclosure of sites associated with the Templars, the Cathars and the Holy Grail in the Spanish province of Soria.

Ana María Matute (1926–), a popular realist writer, surprised her readers in 1998 and 2000 when she published two fantasy romances of chivalry set in the Middle Ages: *Olvidado Rey Gudú* and *Aranmanoth*. Both are very close to Arthurian literature.

But what really surprised many readers was the publication in 2002 of an Arthurian novel by the popular fiction writer Manuel Vázquez Montalbán (1939–2003), famous for his detective stories and travel books. The novel was entitled *Erec y Enide* and was a bestseller for many weeks in Spain. Inspired by the medieval romance of the same title by Chrétien de Troyes, a set of present-day characters are made to match their medieval counterparts by Professor Emeritus Julio Matasanz, specialist in Arthurian medieval literature. Vázquez Montalbán confessed that it has been a project of his since since those times of his youth when he studied Medieval Literature under Professor Martín de Riquer in Barcelona, but he had never been able to finish it until then. It can be seen as a manifesto novel in favour of feelings, communication and love with the help of very old characters. Indeed, Vázquez Montalbán published some years before a long essay/chronicle entitled *Un polaco en la corte del rey Juan Carlos* (1996). From the very title, the intertextualities with Mark Twain's *A Connecticut Yankee in King Arthur's Court* are very clear.

But Vázquez Montalbán has not been the only Spanish popular novelist who has experimented with the Middle Ages and Arthuriana in recent years. Soledad Puértolas (1947–) published her *La rosa de plata* in 1999. Her acknowledgements are to Sir Thomas Malory and Chrétien de Troyes. Morgana is the protagonist, but Arthur, Guinevere and Lancelot also play leading roles. Rosa Montero (1951–) did the same with her *Historia del rey transparente* in 2005. The protagonist is another woman, Leola, a young country girl who dresses as a knight and starts a number of adventures. From time to time the characters take a rest and get together to listen to the Arthurian romances written by Robert Wace, Marie de France or Chrétien de Troyes, their XIIth-century contemporaries. Montero also mentions contemporary Arthurian author John Steinbeck as a source. Finally, César Vidal (1958–) published his own Arthurian novel in 2006, *Artorius*, set in Britannia during the Dark Ages, after the withdrawal of Rome and just before the coming of the Germanic tribes. It seeks to tell the story of the real Arthur, Lucius Artorius Castus, based on the documents still extant. This text adjusted perfectly to the latest trends in Arthurian fiction in English.

The first decade of the XXIst century also brought a craze for popular fiction and thrillers dealing with medieval Cathars and Templars. Among the many offerings, there have been some works also including Arthurian motifs, mainly the Grail. For example, José Luis Corral's (1953–) *El caballero del Templo* (2006); Antoni Dalmau's (1951–) *El testamento del último cátaro* (2006); and Esteban Martín (1956–) and Andreu Carranza's (1957–) *La clave Gaudí* (2007) and *La clau Gaudí* (2007), Spanish and Catalan versions of the same work. The same characteristics can be found in all these texts: mystery and intrigue, medieval history and contemporary research, an endless number of plots, secret codes and orders etc.

The vogue for stories of the Grail has also reached Spanish audiovisual industry in recent times with the following three examples. Juan Pablo Aragüés Millás (1982–) wrote the screenplay, directed, produced and saw his short film *Perceval* finally premiered in 2007. It deals with the wanderings of Perceval in search of the Grail in the sites related to the legend of the Holy Chalice in north Aragon, close to the Pyrenees, for example the monastery of San Juan de la Peña. The music is by the heavy metal group Saxon, whose leader, Byford Biff, also plays the role of King

Arthur. In 2011, a film version of the classical Spanish comic *Capitán Trueno* was presented for the first time ever. It was also turned into a story of the Holy Grail, entitled *El Capitán Trueno y el Santo Grial*, found in the Holy Land and taken to Spain for protection. The film was directed by Antonio Hernández (1953–), and the screenplay was written by Pau Vergara (1956–). And finally, from 2009 up to 2013 (the fifth season), a very successful Spanish television serial entitled *Águila Roja* has been shown in Spain and in many other countries. It is set in Golden Age XVIIth-century Spain and, although it presents a realistic approach, among the many intrigues, plots and subplots it has recently started to hold a search for the Grail, from its fortieth chapter. It is written by a team of scriptwriters led by Pilar Nadal.

Returning to comics, the Spanish national tradition displays two legendary heroes *El Guerrero del Antifaz* (*The Masked Fighter*), by Manuel Gago, and *El Capitán Trueno*, by Miguel Ambrosio (illustrations) and Víctor Mora (texts). The first series was published between 1944 and 1966, and the second between 1959 and 2005. Both Spanish heroes are much indebted to Harold Forter's *Prince Valiant* (1937–). Consequently, in spite of their nationalistic approach, they are full of Arthurian motifs and intertextualities. However, Manuel Gago published *El Aguilucho* (*The Eaglet*), a minor series, between 1959 and 1961, a comic which displays real Arthurian characters such as Merlin. Víctor Mora also tried a full Arthurian product in 1976, when he published, under the pseudonym of Vincent Mulberry, *Claudio y la Tabla Redonda*.

More recently, Francisco Pérez Navarro, as writer, and Martín Saurí, as illustrator, published their two-volume recounting of the Arthurian cycle: *Arturo 1. El único y futuro rey* (2010) and *Arturo 2. Excalibur* (2012). It can be termed the most comprehensive Spanish comic retelling ever of the Arthurian legend.

The end of the XXth century and the first years of the new century have seen a surge of poets finding their inspiration in Arthuriana. In 1996, David Pujante (1953–) published *Estación marítima*, a homage to Galicia, the land of Perceval, as the first poem states. In 2000, Carmen Borja (1957–) also included references to Perceval in her book *Libro de la Torre*. In 2004, Antonio Enrique (1953–) offered his readers a bilingual English–Spanish book entitled *Silver Shadow*. The sequence of poems resembles Arthur's diary and reproduces the king's deepest and strongest feelings about Guinevere and Lancelot's illicit love. In 2007, José Ramón Trujillo (1966–) published *Grial*. The book has three parts, each one devoted to Lanzarote, Gauvain and Perceval respectively. In 2010, Francesc Cornadó (1949–) published a bilingual Spanish-Catalan book *Falsos jardines / Falsos jardins*. There are many echoes from *Parsifal*. And finally, the Portuguese poet Ana Margarida Chora (1972–) collected all her best previous short poems and published them in a single volume entitled *Janela sobre o Tempo* (2010). The following poems are Arthurian: 'O Tor' (1995), 'Meditação de Erec sobre a morte da irmã' (1999), 'Última prece de Genevra' (1999), 'Assim como Briolanja' (82), related to *Amadís de Gaula*, 'O culto antigo dividiu' (97), and 'Glastonbury Revisited' (107). More recently, she has published *Diadema* (2014), which includes three Arthurian poems: 'Esmeralda sangrenta' (59), 'Tempo dos profetas' (69–70), and 'Morgan *Le Fay* de Frederick Sandys' (87–8).

Juan Eslava Galán (1948–) is one of the most popular and prolific Spanish writers who specialised in publishing bestsellers, mainly historical essays and novels. Among his hundreds of titles, there is a clear recurrent interest in dealing with the Templars and Christian relics, the Holy Grail included. Among the essays, the following must be included: *Los templarios y otros enigmas medievales* (1992), *La lápida templaria* (1996), *El fraude de la Sábana Santa y las reliquias de Cristo* (1997), *Los templarios y la mesa de Salomón* (2004), *España insólita y misteriosa* (2006), *La lápida templaria descifrada* (2008), and *Templarios, griales, vírgenes negras y otros mitos de la historia* (2011). His fictional contribution to this subject matter consists of *Los dientes del dragón* (2001) and of the following trilogy: *Trilogía templaria I. Los falsos peregrinos* (2001); *Trilogía templaria II. Las trompetas de Jérico* (2002); *Trilogía templaria III. La sangre de Dios* (2002), all of them published under the pseudonym Nicholas Wilcox.

Finally, another recent essay on the Holy Grail was published in 2010: *La copa sagrada* by Chema Ferrer Cuñat. And the Canarian poet Selena Millares published a poem entitled 'Lancelot' in 2013 in a bilingual edition of her poems, *Cuaderno de Sassari / Quaderni di Sassari*, including its translation into Italian as 'Lancilotto'.

New Tristans, with or without their Isoldes

Tristan and Isolde have symbolised tragic, fatal love and unfortunate lovers since the Middle Ages. Many writers have used their names and plot to add dramatic force to their own love stories. Contemporary Iberian Arthurian texts also present clear examples of this creative trend and intertextuality games. This literary device can already be located in the Romantic period, when the so-called Romantic historical novel was so much in vogue all around Spain, partly imitating the formula popularised by Walter Scott. One clear example was the text entitled *Tristán el ermitaño, ó un amor desgraciado*, published in Barcelona in 1839 by Miguel Pons y Guimerá. The unfortunate lovers, Alfonsina and José, suffer persecution from Tristán, a bloody villain at the service of evil Louis XII, a medieval king of France. The lovers put an end to their misery only when they are killed. Hoewer, they are buried together as Tristan and Isolde were.

Years later, in 1887, Vicente Blasco Ibáñez (1887–1928), the popular novelist, published 'Tristán sepulturero' in a volume entitled *Cuentos medievales*. Here the male lover honours the name of the unfortunate knight and the female lover the name of the unfortunate Laura, Petrarch's lady.

Another great novelist, Benito Pérez Galdós (1843–1920), published one of his most popular works, *Tristana*, in 1892, five years later. Tristana, the character, is a kind of unhappy female Tristan trapped between an old husband (King Mark) and a young lover (Tristan/Isolde): the tragic triangle. Years later, at the end of his literary career, he returned to the Arthurian realm of fantasy with a contemporary romance of knighthood, *El caballero encantado. Cuento real... inverosímil* (1909). Don Carlos de Tarsis, the knight, finds his counterpart in José Augusto del Becerro, a Merlinesque seer and magician. Merlin is quoted frequently by the characters.

The following century, in 1906, the also very popular Armando Palacio Valdés (1853–1938) offered his readers another novel, *Tristán o el pesimismo*, full of intertextualities. The writer chooses the name Tristan, a new Tristan, for the main character of his novel, which depicts another sad love story.

In 1926, José María Pemán (1897–1981) wrote a play entitled *Isoldina y Polión: Tragicomedia irrepresentable*. Set in the Middle Ages, Arthurian elements abound: there is a love triangle between Isoldina and her lover, Polión, and Isoldina's father (not her husband), the king. There is a page named Galaor, i.e., Galahad in the Hispanic tradition, and an old, Merlin-like sage named Critón.

Many years later, in 1969, *Tristana*, the classic Spanish film directed by the legendary Spanish director Luis Buñuel (1900–85), who also was co-author of the screenplay, with Julio Alejandro (1906–95), was premiered. It was based on the novel *Tristana* by Pérez Galdós mentioned already. Tristana here continues to be a kind of female Tristan.

Carlos Romeu (1948–) started a series of novels for teenagers whose protagonist is a new young Tristan who, with his cousins Violeta and Guillermo (a new triangle), lives many adventures in different countries: *Tristán en Egipto* (1998), *Tristán en Escocia* (2002), *Tristán en Yucatán* (2003) and *Tristán en París* (2004).

In 2014, Alma Idamons, under the pseudonym Anonymus Cinco, published the play or possible libretto *Fol Tantris. Ópera Magna*, closely inspired by different Tristan authors: Gottfried von Strassburg, Richard Wagner and Salvador Dalí. Tantris is indeed Tristan with its syllables in inverted order.

Children's Literature

Out of necessity, this is going to be a miscellaneous section. Whether or not writers of children's literature may have found their sources in Tennyson or in medieval legend or literature; whether or not they may share in the belief in a Celtic Galicia and strive to support it, among other questions, the overriding factor for inclusion here will be their readership: infants, children and young adults.

The trend to adapt classics for children started in Spain with the legendary *Colección Araluce*, founded in Barcelona in 1914 by Ramón Araluce (1865–1941). He used similar British collections as the right models. In this very same year, this publisher printed the following Arthurian adapted titles: *Los caballeros de la Tabla Redonda*, taken from *Le Mort D'Arthur* by Thomas Malory and the *Idylls of the King* by Alfred Tennyson, *Tristán e Isolda*, taken from Joseph Bédier, *Historias de Wagner*, and *Amadís de Gaula*. Manuel Vallvé adapted the first three works, and María Luz Morales (1889–1980) the fourth. There were many reprints of them all until the 1960s, when Araluce closed down.

In 1927, the same María Luz Morales was responsible for the publication of a volume entitled: *Historias de Tennyson contadas a los niños*. The publisher was again the popular Editorial Araluce and the book was a new abridged version for children of Tennyson's idylls previously translated by Vicente de Arana in the XIXth century. Morales included this time two of Arana's Arthurian idylls from Tennyson: 'Gareth y Lynette' and 'Merlín y Bibiana'.

In 1956, José Miguel Velloso offered Spanish children another Arthurian adaptation: *Los caballeros de la Tabla Redonda*. The prologue listed his sources: Wace, Chrétien de Troyes, Malory and Alfred Tennyson. The whole Arthurian cycle was summarised in this volume provided with beautiful illustrations. Portuguese children also enjoyed a very similar adaptation dated 1969: *Os cavaleiros da Távola Redonda*, which was made by Augusto da Costa Dias (1920–2004). Although Lancelot is the main protagonist, again, there is a complete account of the legends for children and for adults interested in this enjoyable presentation of the material.

The myth of a Celtic Galicia soon spread to the realm of children's literature in Galician. Manuel Lourenzo (1943–) can be regarded as another heir of Cunqueiro. He specialised in children's plays, a genre in which he has published three Arthurian titles: *Todos os fillos de Galaad* (1981), *Viva Lanzarote* (1982) and *A sensación de Camelot* (1991). In the first one Galahad is king of the Country of Tales, where the most curious individuals dwell – Galahad's children. Merlin is also a character. In the second, Lancelot takes refuge in rural Galicia. When he and Guinevere finally meet, she is not very happy to accompany him, as he cannot offer a kingdom any more. The third play performs a number of comic conflicts between some of the most popular Arthurian characters.

Xicu Monteserín's (1960–) short story, *Un ermitañu de nome Merlín* (1984), is very special, as it was written in a very minority northern Iberian language, Asturian. A group of children go on an excursion and camp in the open somewhere in the woods and mountains of Asturias. There they come across a hermit named Merlin. The hermit tells them the long story of his life.

In 1996, the Argentinian writer Graciela Montes (1947–) published a complete retelling of the Arthurian cycle for children in nine volumes. The general title was *Los caballeros de la Tabla Redonda*, and the titles for the nine volumes are the following: *Arturo, el dueño de la espada*, about the coming of Arthur and the sword in the stone; *El mago Merlín*, or the story and powers of Merlin and his battle against two dragons; *El misterio del Santo Grial*, about Perceval and his search for the Holy Grail and the Fisher King; *Lanzarote, el caballero enamorado*, about Lancelot, who is in love with

Guinevere and saves her from kidnappers; *Tristán e Isolda*, or the beautiful love story between Tristan and Isolda, including the battle of Tristan against a terrible monster to save Ireland; *El caballero del León*, or the story of Ivain and his combat against a terrible knight; *Perceval y el caballero Rojo*, i.e., how Perceval left his homeland in Wales and becomes a knight like the Red Knight; and *La hija del rey*, on Gineth, daughter of Arthur, who makes a mess of the whole court. It is almost impossible not to think of Chrétien de Troyes, Robert of Boron or the *Vulgate* and their cycles.

In 1998, Miguel Ángel Moleón Viana (1965–) published a major Arthurian work for children, his *El rey Arturo cabalga de nuevo, más o menos*, where a 250-year-old King Arthur leaves Avalon and experiences a new series of delicious and humorous adventures typically devised for young readers. Camelot, the Round Table, Merlin and Vivien and many other fanciful beings accompany him. Urganda, the character from *Amadís de Gaula*, also plays a role.

In 2001, three Galician-language writers, Carmen Domech (1963–), Jorge Rey (1957–) and Marilar Aleixandre (1947–), published a joint project, the play *El-Rei Artur e a Abominable Dama*. In spite of her ugliness, the Abominable Lady proves to be very helpful in Camelot. Three years later, in 2004, Marilar Aleixandre and another ten writers took part in another joint project, the collection of short stories for children on the *Camiño de Santiago* (Way of Saint James). The general title was *Postais do Camiño*. Helena Villar Janeiro's (1940–) title was 'Os ollos de Galahaz'. As a group of children are making the pilgrimage, they learn about King Arthur, Camelot, the Round Table and the Holy Grail. When they cross Mount Cebreiro they visit the sanctuary of the Grail and focus their attention on Galahad, the best knight.

At the end of the first decade of the XXIst century, Gemma Lienas (1951–) started publishing a whole series of adventure books for children. The name of the general series is *La tribu de Camelot* (2008–11), which makes a total number of eighteen volumes so far. Each entry to the series is published both in Catalan and Spanish. A group of six children, led by Carlota, and a cat, take Arthurian names (Morgana, Ginebra, Lancelot, Tristán, Viviana, Merlín and Celinda) and establish the tribe of Camelot. Now they are ready for the most exciting adventures. One child is a Muslim immigrant. The group leader is a girl. Everything is very politically correct. The books combine reading with games, beautiful illustrations, and magical tints and smells.

In 1983, Roser Capdevila (1939–) started her heavily illustrated short stories for children, both in Catalan and Spanish, *Les tres bessones / Las tres mellizas*. Herself the mother of girl triplets, her stories soon became a major success that have been translated into all major languages and published in more than 135 countries. Soon, in 1994, the series was adapted for television, and achieved the same international success. In the middle of the first decade of the XXIst century, an independent series started to be published under the general title of *The Great Library of the Triplets*. It made the triplets share adventures with great historical figures and literary characters. Issues number 14 (2006), devoted to Tristan and Isolde, and number 16 (2006) to

Merlin (2006), were published in both Catalan and Spanish. Here Roser Capdevila is only the author of the big, beautiful illustrations. The texts were written by Teresa Blanch. The stories are accompanied by many educational paratexts (historical background, activities, etc) and a DVD with the story in audiovisual format (cartoons).

The Latin American Collection

Spain and Portugal cannot be understood without Latin America, or Iberian America, and its peoples and cultures. The Matter of Britain has also been retold in Spanish and Portuguese in the Americas. Many texts are still there waiting to be located; this is a research field still very much open. (For the chapbook publications, the *literatura de cordel*, of north-eastern Brazil, see the chapter by David Hook in the present volume.) As examples, the following can be listed. In Argentina, Jorge Luis Borges (1899–1986) in his essay *Literaturas Germánicas Medievales* (1966), and María Esther Vázquez (1937–) studied Arthur, the Round Table, Layamon and his *Brut*. Also from Argentina, Graciela Montes, who has been studied before in this chapter, wrote a whole series of books on Arthurian legends for small children (1996). In Colombia, Germán Arciniegas (1900–99) produced another essay entitled *El estudiante de la mesa redonda* (1932), where a group of students debate the history of Latin America around their new Round Table. A second Colombian, Germán Espinosa (1938–), published a short story, 'La píxide', in 1977, on the Holy Grail according to Chrétien de Troyes, and a novel of chivalry, *Crónicas de un caballero andante* (1999). And also from Colombia, Giovanni Quessep (1939–) must be mentioned because of the poetry book *Muerte de Merlín* (1985). There is a poem with the same title 'Muerte de Merlín', his Arthurian contribution. In Mexico, Agustín Yañez (1904–80) published *Melibea, Isolda y Alda en tierras cálidas* (1945). The story of Tristan and Isolda is located in Mexico and given all kinds of local flavour. Another Mexican, Hugo Hiriart (1942–), has a novel entitled *Galaor* (1972), a name taken from *Amadís de Gaula*. Tristán is also a character in this text. A third Mexican is Luisa Josefina Hernández (1928–), author of *La memoria de Amadís* (1967), a long fictional work where the hard realities of living in a big city are lived as if they were heroic deeds of knighthood (Amadís and Don Quixote). In Brazil, João Guimarães Rosa (1908–67) was responsible for the great epic novel *Grande Sertão, veredas* (1956). The Portuguese medieval *A Demanda do Santo Graal* is one of its main sources of inspiration. Also from Brazil Diogo Texeira produced a whole version of the Arthurian cycle for children and young adults: *Os cavaleiros da Távola Redonda* (1967). The allusions to the Round Table or the Grail are very frequent. From Venezuela, Ángel Rosenblat (1902–84) was responsible for the most popular abridged and modernised version of *Amadís de Gaula* (1967) in the Hispanic world. The Puerto Rican poet José Antonio Dávila (1898–1941) published in 1957 *Motivos de Tristán. Poemas*. The references to Tristan and

Isolde's unfortunate love are frequent. From Nicaragua we have the great Rubén Darío (1867–1916), also a Wagner lover, who composed two sonnets published under the common heading of *Wagneriana*: 'Lohengrin' and 'Parsifal' (*c.*1895), and a third sonnet entitled 'El cisne' (1896). From Peru, Mario Vargas Llosa and his book of essays *Carta de batalla por Tirant lo Blanc* (1993), on the Valencian medieval classic text of knighthood. And finally, from Chile, José María Navasal (1916–99) produced *Los caballeros del Rey Arturo* (1954), a Malory adaptation for young adults, and Eitan Melnick wrote another popular thriller on Wagner, Barcelona and the Holy Grail, *La clave Wagner* (2009).

Conclusions

King Arthur and his world belong not only to contemporary Spanish and Portuguese literature, but have also given rise to a distinctive canon of contemporary Iberian Arthurian literature, which deserves beyond doubt to be included within the pages of any Arthurian *Encyclopedia*. It should not be neglected any more by Spanish, Portuguese or international Arthurian scholars. It may not compare in output, for example, with the modern tradition in English, but it certainly does compare in quality and interest.

Both Tennyson and Wagner, the so-called modern heirs of Malory, also exercised a great influence in the Spanish revival of Arthurian legends and myths.

This canon listed here is comprised of both well-known authors belonging to the great canon of Spanish literature and lesser-known voices. It includes men and women; XIXth-, XXth- and XXIst-century writers; poets, narrators and thinkers; Romantic, realist, modernist, avant-garde or post-structuralist talents. Arthur has also captivated the most varied spirits of modern and contemporary Spain and Portugal.

Like other international modern traditions, the canon of Spanish Arthurian literature has always welcomed and debated all types of ideas and ways of thinking – those haunting or obsessing a given writer or his or her society during a given period of time: feminism, Utopia, the role of legend and myth in modern societies, aestheticism, commitment, ecology, materialism, spiritual values, oppression and revolution, passion and eroticism, etc.

It is also very irreverent towards the codified versions of the legends. It displays revolutionary innovations and very high levels of original treatment and demythification.

There is a very strong tendency to transport and locate Arthurian characters and motifs in Iberia – a tendency to naturalise them and make them seem and sound less exotic, that is to say, more or fully Spanish or Portuguese. This is very clear within Galician writers – a region of Spain that has always striven to emphasise its supposed but factually non-existent Celtic origins.

In contemporary Iberia, Merlin is also one of the most popular Arthurian characters, his love story with Vivien/Nimue especially, which has given rise to all kinds of versions and interpretations.

Although it has not been studied in these pages, Arthurian literature translated into Iberian languages is much more abundant and popular than original Arthurian works in Spanish, Portuguese or other Hispanic languages.[2] Frequently, native productions are very intellectual and directed to a limited audience. And, consequently, they are rapidly out of print. This is why the corpus of original output is not enough to feed such an avid interest or need for myth and fantasy. Popular bestselling translations fill the gap with the help of audiovisual formats such as comic strips, cinema and television.

This comprehensive canon of mine comprises Portuguese and five of the languages of Spain: Spanish or Castilian, Catalan, Galician, Basque and Asturian. But the task is not finished. Even within its present limits, I am positive there must be some more Spanish and Portuguese Arthurian poems or short stories, etc. waiting to be found.

And after covering the whole of the Iberian Peninsula, the canon opened itself again to include the modern Arthurian production of Spanish America and Brazil. Here there exists a great need to locate more findings, which can be regarded as another very demanding field of research. A new interest in these neglected modern Arthurian traditions may constitute a perfect new direction in Arthurian Studies for this new XXIst century we have just started.

Notes

[1] Isaac Albéniz (1860–1909), the great Spanish musician, also tried hard to become a famous opera composer. Among his projects there was an Arthurian opera trilogy, of which he could finish only the first title, *Merlin*, between the years 1898–1902. As was the fate of Vives's *Artús*, Albéniz's opera was also almost lost for nearly a century. However, *Merlin* was finally recorded in 2000 and staged in the Madrid Teatro Real in 2003. *Artús* is still awaiting its return and revival. This chapter has included *Artús* because the libretto was written in Spanish by a Spanish author, Sebastià Trullol. However, *Merlin*'s libretto was made by an Englishman, the Victorian writer Francis Burdett Money-Coutts (1853–1923), and is in English. This opera does belong to Iberian Arthurian musical and performing arts, but not to its literary tradition. The story of Iberian artistic output also needs compilation.

[2] Many Translation Studies theorists have frequently claimed the outstanding role of translated text within the general context of a given national literary polysystem (Even-Zohar 1978: 117–27; 1990). It is not usual to discover that translated literature is much more popular than original output. Although the scope of this chapter does not include translation, it is impossible to deny the fact that, in Iberia, as far as Arthurian texts are involved, readers have more access to the material in translation than in original texts (Zarandona 2002: 113–39). Examples abound: the translations of contemporary popular fiction authors such as Barron, Zimmer Bradley, Cornwell, Crossley-Holland, Lawhead, Markale, Miles, Asimov or Stewart, among many others; or the modernisation and translation of medieval classics, also very popular, by Thomas Malory, Chrétien de Troyes, Marie de France, the *Mabinogion*, the *Vulgate* etc. Two very recent examples are Carlos Alvar's *Historia de Lanzarote del Lago* (2010b), a new edition of his former translations of the story of Lancelot from the *Vulgate*; and Victoria Cirlot's *Historia del caballero cobarde y otros relatos artúricos* (2011), an anthology of the main medieval Arthurian texts in translation.

Appendix of Primary Sources

Every entry is also provided with two abbreviated codes related to: (1) the language in which the work is written; (2) the genre into which it must be classified. In other words, the following abbreviations for languages: 'AS: Asturian', 'BA: Basque', 'CA: Catalan (including Valencian)', 'EN: English', 'GA: Galician', 'PO: Portuguese', and 'SP: Spanish'; and for genres: 'ab: autobiography', 'cn: children's novel', 'cpy: children's play', 'css: children's short story', 'e: essay', 'l: libretto', 'lp: long poem', 'n: novel', 'pl: prose legend', 'py: play', 'pp: prose poem', 'sc: screenplay', 'co: comic', 'sn: short novel', 'sp: short poem', and 'ss: short story'.

Almazán de Gracia, Ángel, 1997. *Los códigos templarios del río Lobos. Los custodios del Grial* (Soria: Sotabur). [SP/pl n]
Alonso, María Lourdes, 1999. *La magia celta según Gustavo Adolfo Bécquer, Oscar Wilde y la literatura artúrica contemporánea* (Seville: Padilla Libros). [SP/e]
Alonso, María Lourdes, 2000. *Camelot reconstruido* (Seville: Padilla Editores). [SP/n]
Alonso, María Lourdes, 2001. *El hada blanca. Novela artúrica e inmenso cuento de hadas para lectores maduros e iniciados* (Seville: Padilla Editores). [SP/n]
Alonso, María Lourdes, 2004. *Ector, el príncipe de negro. Los elfos de Camelot* (Seville: Edita Michelle Ángela). [SP/n]
Alonso, María Lourdes, 2006. *Gades Avallonia* (Seville: Padilla Libros). [SP/n]
Alonso, María Lourdes, 2011a. *Las hadas de Bécquer y Wilde* (Cadiz: Los ojos del silencio). [SP/e]
Alonso, María Lourdes, 2011b. *Las mujeres de Wagner* (Cadiz: Los ojos del silencio). [SP/e]
Alonso, María Lourdes, 2012a. *Wagner's Women. Symbolic Analysis of Three Female Wagnerian Characters: Isolde, Brünnilde and Kundry* (Cadiz: Los ojos del silencia). [EN/e]
Alonso, María Lourdes, 2012b. *Gades y Camelot* (Cadiz: Los ojos del silencio). [SP/n]
Anonymus Cinco, 2014. *Fol Trantis. Ópera Magna* (Seville: Autoeditora Aldamaly). [SP/py]
Anselmi, Luigi, 1985. 'Beafeater', in *Luka eta lurra. Euskal poesia 80ko hamarkadan*, ed. Jon Kortazar (Bilbao: Bilbao Bizkaia Kutxa–Labayru Ikastegia), p. 575. [BA/sp]
Arana, Vicente de, trans., 1883a. Alfred Tennyson, 'Gareth y Linette', in *Poemas de Alfredo Tennyson*, illustrated by José Riudavets (Barcelona: Verdaguer), pp. 75–161. [SP/pl]
Arana, Vicente de, trans., 1883b. Alfred Tennyson, 'Merlín y Bibiana', in *Poemas de Alfredo Tennyson*, illustrated by José Riudavets (Barcelona: Verdaguer), pp. 163–223. [SP/pl]
Arana, Vicente de, trans., 1883c. Alfred Tennyson, 'La reina Ginebra', in *Poemas de Alfredo Tennyson*, illustrated by José Riudavets (Barcelona: Verdaguer), pp. 225–67. [SP/pl]
Aranda, Vicente, and Gonzalo Suárez, 1965. *Fata Morgana* (Madrid: Films Internacionales). [SP/sc]
Arciniegas, Germán, 1959. *El estudiante de la mesa redonda* (Barcelona/Buenos Aires: Edhasa). [SP/e]
Arolas Bonet, Juan, 1982a. *Obras de Juan Arolas 1* (Madrid: Atlas). [SP/sp]
Arolas Bonet, Juan, 1982b. *Obras de Juan Arolas 2* (Madrid: Atlas). [SP/sp]
Arolas Bonet, Juan, 1982c. 'El manto encantado', in *Obras de Juan Arolas 2. Leyendas, baladas y poemas caballerescos* (Madrid: Atlas), pp. 163–331. [SP/sp]
Arolas Bonet, Juan, 1982d. *Obras de Juan Arolas 3* (Madrid: Atlas). [SP/sp]
Blasco Ibáñez, Vicente, 1996. 'Tristán sepulturero', in *Cuentos medievales* (Madrid: Libros Clan), pp. 115–37. [SP/ss]
Borges, Jorge Luis, 1978. *Literaturas germánicas medievales*, in collaboration with María Esther Vázquez (Madrid: Alianza Editorial). [SP/e]
Borja, Carmen, 2000. *Libro de la Torre* (Barcelona: Los Libros de la Frontera). [SP/sp]
Buñuel, Luis, and Julio Alejandro, 1969. *Tristana* (Madrid: Época Films/Talia Films). [SP/sc]

Cabana, Darío Xohán, 1982. 'Cebreiro en materia de Bretaña', in *Dorna. Expresión Poética Galega*, no. 7 (Santiago de Compostela: Universidade de Santiago de Compostela), p. 36. [GA/sp]

Cabana, Darío Xohán, 1983. 'A invasión', in *VII Concurso de Narrative Curta Rodríguez Figueiredo do Patrona to de Pedrón de Ouro* (Sada-A Coruña: Edicións do Castro), pp. 61–74. [GA/ss]

Cabana, Darío Xohán, 1987. 'Guenebra', in *Amor e tempo liso (Cancioneiro)* (Santiago de Compostela: Concello de Santiago), p. 38. [GA/sp]

Cabana, Darío Xohán, 1989a. 'Galván en Demonte', in *Patria do mar* (Vigo: Ir Indo Edicións), p. 81. [GA/sp]

Cabana, Darío Xohán, 1989b. *Galván en Saor* (Vigo: Xerais). [GA/n]

Cabana, Darío Xohán, 1992. *Cándido Branco e o Cabaleiro Negro* (Vigo: Xerais). [GA/n]

Cabanillas, Ramón, 1976a. 'A espada Escalibor', in *A noite estrelecida. Sagas* (Santiago de Compostela: Universidade de Santiago de Compostela), pp. 257–65. [GA/lp]

Cabanillas, Ramón, 1976b. 'O cabaleiro do Sant Grial', in *A noite estrelecida. Sagas* (Santiago de Compostela: Universidade de Santiago de Compostela), pp. 266–73. [GA/lp]

Cabanillas, Ramón, 1976c. 'O soño do rei Arturo', in *A noite estrelecida. Sagas* (Santiago de Compostela: Universidade de Santiago de Compostela), pp. 274–82. [GA/lp]

Calvo Poyato, José, 2005. *La orden negra* (Barcelona: Plaza y Janés). [SP/n]

Capdevila, Roser, Teresa Blanch et al., 2006a. *Tristany i Isolda*. La gran biblioteca de les tres bessones, 14 (Barcelona: Cromosoma – Televisió de Catalunya). [CA/css].

Capdevila, Roser, Teresa Blanch et al., 2006b. *Tristán e Isolda*. La gran biblioteca de las tres mellizas, 14. Trans. Margarida Trias (Barcelona: Cromosoma – Televisió de Catalunya). [SP/css]

Capdevila, Roser, Teresa Blanch et al., 2006c. *El mag Merlí*. La gran biblioteca de les tres bessones, 16 (Barcelona: Cromosoma – Televisió de Catalunya). [CA/css].

Capdevila, Roser, Teresa Blanch et al., 2006d. *Merlín el encantador*. La gran biblioteca de las tres mellizas, 16. Trans. Margarida Trias (Barcelona: Cromosoma – Televisió de Catalunya). [SP/css]

Carré, Leandro, 1999a. 'El Santo Grial del Cebreiro', in *Las leyendas tradicionales gallegas* (Madrid: Espasa Calpe), pp. 110–11. [SP/pl]

Carré, Leandro, 1999b. 'Galaaz y el Santo Grial', in *Las leyendas tradicionales gallegas* (Madrid: Espasa Calpe), pp. 282–6. [SP/pl]

Carvalho Calero, Ricardo, 1991. 'Soneto', in *Actas do Segundo Congreso de Estudios Galegos* (Vigo: Galaxia), pp. 393–4. [GA/sp]

Casona, Alejandro, 1985a. 'Lohengrin', in *Flor de Leyendas* (Madrid: Edaf), pp. 73–83. [SP/pl]

Casona, Alejandro, 1985b. 'Tristán e Iseo', in *Flor de Leyendas* (Madrid: Edaf), pp. 134–57. [SP/pl]

Castelo Branco, Camilo, 1989. *Memórias de Guilherme do Amaral* (Lisbon: Círculo de Leitores). [PO/n]

Castelo Branco Camilo, 1999. *O Sangue. Romance* (Coimbra: Quarteto). [PO/n]

Castro, Antón, 1984. *Vida infame de Tristán Fortesende* (Sada, A Coruña: Ediciós do Castro). [GA/ss]

Chora, Ana Margarida, 2010a. 'O Tor', in *Janela sobre o Tempo* (Lisbon: Centro de Estudos Bocageanos), p. 49. [PO/sp]

Chora, Ana Margarida, 2010b. 'Meditação de Erec sobre a norte da irmã', in *Janela sobre o Tempo* (Lisbon: Centro de Estudos Bocageanos), pp. 74–5. [PO/sp]

Chora, Ana Margarida, 2010c. 'Última prece de Genevra', in *Janela sobre o Tempo* (Lisbon: Centro de Estudos Bocageanos), p. 76. [PO/sp]

Chora, Ana Margarida, 2010d. 'Assim como Briolanja', in *Janela sobre o Tempo* (Lisbon: Centro de Estudos Bocageanos), p. 82. [PO/sp]

Chora, Ana Margarida, 2010e. 'O culto antigo dividiu', in *Janela sobre o Tempo* (Lisbon: Centro de Estudos Bocageanos), p. 97. [PO/sp]

Chora, Ana Margarida, 2010f. 'Glastonbury Revisited', in *Janela sobre o Tempo* (Lisbon: Centro de Estudos Bocageanos), p. 107. [PO/sp]

Chora, Ana Margarida, 2010g. *Janela sobre o Tempo* (Lisbon: Centro de Estudos Bocageanos). [PO/sp]

Chora, Ana Margarida, 2014. *Diadema* (Lisbon: Chiado Editora). [PO/sp]

Cirlot, Juan Eduardo, 2005a. 'Tristán', in *En la llama. Poesía (1943–1959)*, ed. Enrique Granell (Madrid: Siruela), pp. 82–3. [SP/sp]
Cirlot, Juan Eduardo, 2005b. 'Sir Tristán', in *En la llama. Poesía (1943–1959)*, ed. Enrique Granell (Madrid: Siruela), p. 188. [SP/sp]
Cirlot, Juan Eduardo, 2005c. 'Sir Galahaz', in *En la llama. Poesía (1943–1959)*, ed. Enrique Granell (Madrid: Siruela), p. 291. [SP/sp]
Cirlot, Juan Eduardo, 2005d. 'A San Juan de la Cruz', in *En la llama. Poesía (1943–1959)*, ed. Enrique Granell (Madrid: Siruela), p. 431. [SP/sp]
Cirlot, Juan Eduardo, 2005e. *En la llama. Poesía (1943–1959)*, ed. Enrique Granell (Madrid: Siruela). [SP/sp]
Cirlot, Juan Eduardo, 2008a. 'Richard Wagner', in *Del no mundo. Poesía (1961–1973)*, ed. Clara Janés (Madrid: Siruela), p. 870. [SP/sp]
Cirlot, Juan Eduardo, 2008b. *Del no mundo. Poesía (1961–1973)*, ed. Clara Janés (Madrid: Siruela). [SP/sp]
Cirlot, Juan Eduardo, 2001. *Bronwyn*, ed. Victoria Cirlot (Madrid: Siruela). [SP/lp]
Cornadó, Francesc, 2010. *Falsos jardines / Falsos jardins* (El Vendrell, Tarragona: March Editor). [SP CA/sp]
Corral, José Luis, 2006. *El caballero del Templo* (Barcelona: Planeta DeAgostini). [SP/n]
Cuenca, Luis Alberto de, 1996a. 'Arturo de Bretaña', in *Álbum de lecturas (1990–1995)* (Madrid: Huerga y Fierro Editores), pp. 127–8. [SP/e]
Cuenca, Luis Alberto de, 1996b. 'El Guillaume d'Angleterre de Chrétien de Troyes', in *Álbum de lecturas (1990–1995)* (Madrid: Huerga y Fierro Editores), pp. 135–7. [SP/e]
Cuenca, Luis Alberto de, 1996c. 'Hartmann von Aue', in *Álbum de lecturas (1990–1995)* (Madrid: Huerga y Fierro Editores), pp. 139–40. [SP/e]
Cuenca, Luis Alberto de, 1996d. 'La aventura caballeresca', in *Álbum de lecturas (1990–1995)* (Madrid: Huerga y Fierro Editores), pp. 121–2. [SP/e]
Cuenca, Luis Alberto de, 1996e. 'Leonor de Aquitania', in *Álbum de lecturas (1990–1995)* (Madrid: Huerga y Fierro Editores), pp. 129–31. [SP/e]
Cuenca, Luis Alberto de, 1996f. 'Textos medievales de caballería', in *Álbum de lecturas (1990–1995)* (Madrid: Huerga y Fierro Editores), pp. 125–6. [SP/e]
Cuenca, Luis Alberto de, 1996g. 'Tristán e Iseo', in *Álbum de lecturas (1990–1995)* (Madrid: Huerga y Fierro Editores), pp. 133–4. [SP/e]
Cuenca, Luis Alberto de, 1996h. 'Un diccionario de mitología céltica', in *Álbum de lecturas (1990–1995)* (Madrid: Huerga y Fierro Editores), pp. 27–8. [SP/e]
Cuenca, Luis Alberto de, 1996i. *Álbum de lecturas (1990–1995)* (Madrid: Huerga y Fierro Editores). [SP/e]
Cuenca, Luis Alberto de, 2003. 'Urganda la desconocida', in *La caja de plata* (Madrid: Fondo de Cultura Económica de Madrid), p. 81. [SP/sp]
Cuenca, Luis Alberto de, trans., 1978. Alfred Tennyson, 'La dama de Shalott', in *Museo* (Barcelona: Antoni Bosch), pp. 215–22. [SP/sp]
Cuenca, Luis Alberto de, 2014. 'Ensueño céltico', in *Cuaderno de vacaciones* (Madrid: Visor), pp. 23–4. [SP/sp]
Cunqueiro, Álvaro, 1941. 'Hazaña y viaje del Santo Grial', in *Escorial*, no. 13, 261–8. [SP/e]
Cunqueiro, Álvaro, 1956–57. 'Epílogo', in *El baladro del sabio Merlín (1498)*, ed. Justo García Morales (Madrid: Biblioteca Nacional-Colección Joyas Bibliográficas), pp. 195–9. [SP/e]
Cunqueiro, Álvaro, 1968. 'O Graal', in *Grial*, vol. IV, pp. 486–7. Under the pseudonym of Álvaro Labrada. [GA/e]
Cunqueiro, Álvaro, 1972. *Vida y fugas de Fanto Fantini della Gherardesca* (Barcelona: Destino). [SP/n]
Cunqueiro, Álvaro, 1974. *El año del cometa con la batalla de los cuatro reyes* (Barcelona: Destino). [SP/n]

Cunqueiro, Álvaro, 1983. 'Tristán García', in *Obra en galego completa. Semblanzas III* (Vigo: Galaxia), pp. 417–9. [GA/ss]
Cunqueiro, Álvaro, 1984a. 'El caballero, la muerte y el diablo y otras dos o tres historias', in *Flores del año mil y pico de ave* (Barcelona: Seix Barral), pp. 9–45. [SP/ss]
Cunqueiro, Álvaro, 1984b. *As crónicas do Sochantre* (Vigo: Galaxia). [GA/n]
Cunqueiro, Álvaro, 1986a. 'Carta de Irlanda', in *Viajes imaginarios y reales* (Barcelona: Tusquets). [SP/e]
Cunqueiro, Álvaro, 1986b. 'La flor de los caminos', in *Viajes imaginarios y reales* (Barcelona: Tusquets), pp. 5–57. [SP/e]
Cunqueiro, Álvaro, 1986c. 'Los países del señor Merlín', in *Viajes imaginarios y reales* (Barcelona: Tusquets), pp. 229–31. [SP/e]
Cunqueiro, Álvaro, 1986e. 'Merlín en Carmarthen', in *Viajes imaginarios y reales* (Barcelona: Tusquets), pp. 289–91. [SP/e]
Cunqueiro, Álvaro, 1986d. 'La flauta de Merlín', in *Viajes imaginarios y reales* (Barcelona: Tusquets), pp. 232–4. [SP/e]
Cunqueiro, Álvaro, 1986e. 'Merlín misionero', in *Viajes imaginarios y reales* (Barcelona: Tusquets), pp. 116–19. [SP/e]
Cunqueiro, Álvaro, 1986f. *Merlín y familia y otras historias* (Barcelona: Destino). [SP/n]
Cunqueiro, Álvaro, 1988a. 'Inventando Bretaña', in *Los otros caminos* (Barcelona: Tusquets), pp. 233–5. [SP/e]
Cunqueiro, Álvaro, 1988b. 'La tumba de Arturo', in *Los otros caminos* (Barcelona: Tusquets), pp. 167–8. [SP/e]
Cunqueiro, Álvaro, 1988c. 'Los guardianes de la cruz', in *Los otros caminos* (Barcelona: Tusquets), pp. 269–70. [SP/sp]
Cunqueiro, Álvaro, 1988d. 'Peregrinos de Bretaña', in *Los otros caminos* (Barcelona: Tusquets), pp. 271–2. [SP/e]
Cunqueiro, Álvaro, 1988e. 'San Criduec y su palma', in *Los otros caminos* (Barcelona: Tusquets), pp. 238–9. [SP/sp]
Cunqueiro, Álvaro, 1991a. 'A xénese da novela occidental', in *Obra en Galego Completa*, vol. IV / ensaios (Vigo: Galaxia), pp. 9–12. [GA/e]
Cunqueiro, Álvaro, 1991b. 'Dona Flamenca', in *Herba aquí ou acolá* (Vigo: Galaxia), p. 68. [GA/sp]
Cunqueiro, Álvaro, 1991c. 'Pasei a porta', in *Herba aquí ou acolá* (Vigo: Galaxia), pp. 69–70. [GA/sp]
Cunqueiro, Álvaro, 1991d. 'A maravillosa historia de Tristán e Isolda', in *Obra en Galego Completa*, vol. IV / ensaios (Vigo: Galaxia), pp. 125–7. [GA/e]
Cunqueiro, Álvaro, 1992a. 'Las historias de Llwyn', in *O reino da chuvia. Artigos esquencidos* (Lugo: Diputación Provincial), pp. 473–4. [Sp/e]
Cunqueiro, Álvaro, 1992b. 'Merlín y Don Pedro el Cruel', in *O reino da chuvia. Artigos esquencidos* (Lugo: Diputación Provincial), pp. 117–18. [SP/e]
Cunqueiro, Álvaro, 1996. *Merlín e familia e outras historias* (Vigo: Galaxia). [GA/e]
Dalmau, Antoni, 2006. *El testamento del último cátaro* (Madrid: Ediciones Temas de Hoy). [SP/n]
Darío, Rubén, 1967a. 'El cisne', in *Poesías completas* (Madrid: Aguilar), pp. 587–8. [SP/sp]
Darío, Rubén, 1967b. 'Lohengrin', in *Poesías completas* (Madrid: Aguilar), p. 963. [SP/sp]
Darío, Rubén, 1967c. 'Parsifal', in *Poesías completas* (Madrid: Aguilar), p. 964. [SP/sp]
Dávila, José Antonio, 1972. *Motivos de Tristán* (Río Piedras, Puerto Rico: Editorial Edil). [SP/sp]
D'Ax, Anna, trans., 1955a. Richard Wagner, *Lohengrin* (Barcelona: Gràfiques El Tinell). [CA/l]
D'Ax, Anna, trans., 1955b. Richard Wagner, *Parsival* (Barcelona: Gràfiques El Tinell). [CA/l]
D'Ax, Anna, trans., 1955c. Richard Wagner,*Tristan i Isolde* (Barcelona: Gràfiques El Tinell). [CA/l]
Dias, Augusto da Costa, 2004. *Os cavaleiros da Távola Redonda* (Porto: Público Comunicação Social). [PO/pl]
Díaz-Mas, Paloma, 1984. *El rapto de Santo Grial o El Caballero de la Verde Oliva* (Barcelona: Anagrama). [SP/n]

Díaz-Mas, Paloma, 1985. *Tras las huellas de Artorius* (Cáceres: Institución Cultural El Brocense). [SP/n]
Domech, Carmen, Jorge Rey and Marilar Aleixandre, 2001. *El-Rei Artur e a Abominable Dama* (Vigo: Ir Indo Edicións). [GA/cpy]
Eça de Queirós, José Maria, 1902. *Contos* (Porto: Livraria Chadron de Lello & Irmão). [PO/ss]
Eça de Queirós, José Maria, 2001. 'A festa das crianças', in *Cartas de Inglaterra e Crónicas de Londres* (Lisbon: Livros do Brasil), pp. 38–98. [PO/ss e]
Eça de Queirós, José Maria, 2003. 'Sir Galahad', in *Contos II* (Lisbon: Imprensa Nacional – Casa da Moeda), pp. 119–34. [PO/ss]
Echegaray, José, 1989. *El gran Galeoto* (Madrid: Cátedra). [SP/py]
Echegaray, Miguel, 1905. *El cisne de Lohengrin* (Madrid: Sociedad de Autores Españoles). [SP/l]
Enrique, Antonio, 2004. *Silver Shadow* (Granada: Dauro). [SP EN/lp]
Eslava Galán, Juan, 2004a. *Los templarios y otros enigmas medievales* (Barcelona: Planeta). [Sp/e]
Eslava Galán, Juan, 2004b. *El fraude de la Sábana Santa y las reliquias de Cristo* (Barcelona: Planeta). [Sp/e]
Eslava Galán, Juan, 2004c. *Los dientes del dragón* (Barcelona: Devir Contenidos). [Sp/n]
Eslava Galán, Juan, 2006. *España insólita y misteriosa. Un viaje por la España de la brujería, las leyendas y los tesoros ocultos* (Barcelona: Planeta). [Sp/e]
Eslava Galán, Juan, 2007. *Los templarios y la mesa de Salomón* (Barcelona: Planeta). [SP/e]
Eslava Galán, Juan, 2008a. *La lápida templaria descrifrada* (Barcelona: Planeta). [Sp/e]
Eslava Galán, Juan, 2008b. *La lápida templaria* (Barcelona: Planeta). [Sp/e]
Eslava Galán, Juan, 2010a. *Trilogía templaria I. Los falsos peregrinos* (Barcelona: Planeta). [Sp/n]
Eslava Galán, Juan, 2010b. *Trilogía templaria II. Las trompetas de Jérico* (Barcelona: Planeta). [Sp/n]
Eslava Galán, Juan, 2010c. *Trilogía templaria III. La sangre de Dios* (Barcelona: Planeta). [Sp/n]
Eslava Galán, Juan, 2011. *Templarios, griales, vírgenes negras y otros mitos de la historia* (Barcelona: Planeta). [Sp/e]
Espinosa, Germán, 1998. 'La píxide', in *Cuentos completos* (Bogotá: Arango Editores), pp. 349–56. [SP/ss]
Espinosa, Germán, 1999. *Crónicas de un caballero andante* (Bogotá: Ediciones Aurora). [SP/n]
Espinosa García, Agustín, 1929. *Lancelot 28°–7°* (Madrid: Ediciones ALFA).
Ferrer Cuñat, Chema, 2010. *La copa sagrada* (Valencia: Carena Editors). [SP/e]
Fortuny, Francisco, 1995. 'Fata Morgana', in *Fata Morgana o Los efectos de la causa* (Valencia: Pre-Textos), p. 13. [SP/sp]
Fuster, Jaume, 1983. *L'illa de les tres taronges* (Barcelona: Planeta). [CA/n]
Fuster, Jaume, 1985. *L'anell de ferro* (Barcelona: Planeta). [CA/n]
Fuster, Jaume, 1993. *El jardi de les tres palmeres* (Barcelona: Planeta). [CA/n]
Gisbert, Lope, trans., 1875a. Alfred Tennyson, 'Elena', in *Idilios. Elena, Enid* (Madrid: Medina y Navarro), pp. 3–88. [SP/lp]
Gisbert, Lope, trans., 1875b. Alfred Tennyson, 'Enid', in *Idilios. Elena, Enid* (Madrid: Medina y Navarro), pp. 91–190. [SP/lp]
Gago, Manuel, 1959–61. *El Aguilucho*, vols 1–68 (Valencia: Editorial Valenciana). [SP/co]
González Reigosa, Carlos, 1987a. 'A morte do rei Artur', in *Irmán Rei Artur* (Vigo: Xerais), pp. 97–126. [GA/ss]
González Reigosa, Carlos, 1987b. 'A tentación de Lanzarote', in *Irmán Rei Artur* (Vigo: Xerais), pp. 39–71. [GA/ss]
González Reigosa, Carlos, 1987c. 'Amor de Merlín', in *Irmán Rei Artur* (Vigo: Xerais), pp. 72–96. [GA/ss]
Granés, Salvador María, 1910. *Lorenzín, ó, El camarero del cine: parodía de la ópera Lohengrín* (Madrid: R. Velasco). [SP/l]
Guimarães Rosa, João, 1968. *Grande-Sertâo: Veredas* (Rio de Janeiro: J. Olympio). [PO/n]
Hernández, Luisa Josefina, 1967. *La memoria de Amadís* (Mexico City: Editorial Joaquín Mortiz). [SP/n]

Hiriart, Hugo, 1972. *Galaor* (Mexico City: Joaquín Mortiz/Nueva Narrativa Hispánica). [SP/n]
Jarnés, Benjamín, 1935. *Tántalo (Farsa)* (Madrid: Los Cuatro Vientos). [SP/n]
Jarnés, Benjamín, 1974. 'En el mundo de Viviana y Merlín', in *Cita de ensueños. Figuras del cinema* (Madrid: Ediciones del Centro), pp. 94–8. [SP/e]
Jarnés, Benjamín, 1994a. 'Viviana y Merlín. Leyenda', in *Viviana y Merlín* (Madrid: Cátedra-Letras Hispánicas), pp. 259–83. [SP/ss]
Jarnés, Benjamín, 1994b. *Viviana y Merlín,* ed. Rafael Conte (Madrid: Cátedra-Letras Hispánicas). [SP/n]
Lechuga Quijada, Sergio, 2009. *Calix* (Barcelona: Planeta). [SP/n]
Lienas, Gemma, 2009a. *La tribu de Camelot. Carlota y el misterio del canario robado* (Barcelona: Planeta). [SP/cn]
Lienas, Gemma, 2009b. *La tribu de Camelot. La Carlota i el misteri del botí pirata* (Barcelona: Estrella Polar). [CA/cn]
Lienas, Gemma, 2009c. *La tribu de Camelot. La Carlota i el misteri del canari robat* (Barcelona: Estrella Polar). [CA/cn]
Lienas, Gemma, 2009d. *La tribu de Camelot. La Carlota i el misteri del passadís secret* (Barcelona: Estrella Polar). [CA/cn]
Lienas, Gemma, 2010a. *La tribu de Camelot. Carlota y el misterio de la casa encantada* (Barcelona: Planeta). [SP/cn]
Lienas, Gemma, 2010b. *La tribu de Camelot. Carlota y el misterio de la catedral gótica* (Barcelona: Planeta). [SP/cn]
Lienas, Gemma, 2010c. *La tribu de Camelot. Carlota y el misterio de la varita mágica* (Barcelona: Planeta). [SP/cn]
Lienas, Gemma, 2010d. *La tribu de Camelot. Carlota y el misterio del pasadizo secreto* (Barcelona: Planeta). [SP/cn]
Lienas, Gemma, 2010e. *La tribu de Camelot. La Carlota i el misteri de la casa encantat* (Barcelona: Estrella Polar). [CA/cn]
Lienas, Gemma, 2010f. *La tribu de Camelot. La Carlota i el misteri de la catedral gótica* (Barcelona: Estrella Polar). [CA/cn]
Lienas, Gemma, 2010g. *La tribu de Camelot. La Carlota i el misteri de la vareta màgica* (Barcelona: Estrella Polar). [CA/cn]
Lienas, Gemma, 2010h. *La tribu de Camelot. La Carlota i el misteri del túnel del terror* (Barcelona: Estrella Polar). [CA/cn]
Lienas, Gemma, 2011a. *La tribu de Camelot. Carlota y el misterio de la extraña vampira* (Barcelona: Planeta). [SP/cn]
Lienas, Gemma, 2011b. *La tribu de Camelot. Carlota y el misterio de las ranas encantadas* (Barcelona: Planeta). [SP/cn]
Lienas, Gemma, 2011c. *La tribu de Camelot. Carlota y el misterio de los gatos hipnotizados* (Barcelona: Planeta). [SP/cn]
Lienas, Gemma, 2011d. *La tribu de Camelot. Carlota y el misterio de los mensajes anónimos* (Barcelona: Planeta). [SP/cn]
Lienas, Gemma, 2011e. *La tribu de Camelot. Carlota y el misterio del botín pirata* (Barcelona: Planeta). [SP/cn]
Lienas, Gemma, 2011f. *La tribu de Camelot. Carlota y el misterio del túnel del terror* (Barcelona: Planeta). [SP/cn]
Lienas, Gemma, 2011g. *La tribu de Camelot. La Carlota i el misteri de l'estranya vampira* (Barcelona: Estrella Polar). [CA/cn]
Lienas, Gemma, 2011h. *La tribu de Camelot. La Carlota i el misteri de les granotes encantades* (Barcelona: Estrella Polar). [CA/cn]
Lienas, Gemma, 2011i. *La tribu de Camelot. La Carlota i el misteri dels gats hipnotitzats* (Barcelona: Estrella Polar). [CA/cn]

Lienas, Gemma, 2011j. *La tribu de Camelot. La Carlota i el misteri dels missatges anònims* (Barcelona: Estrella Polar). [CA/cn]
Lleonart, Joseph, and Antoni Ribera, trans., 1905. Richard Wagner, *Lohengrin* (Palma: Imp. Bartolomé Rotger). [CA/l]
López Soler, Ramón, 1975. *Los bandos de Castilla. El caballero del Cisne* (Madrid: Tebas). [SP/n]
Loureiro Calvo, Ramón, 2000. *O corazón portugués* (Vigo: Galaxia). [GA/n]
Loureiro Calvo, Ramón, 2005. *As galeras de Normandía* (Vigo: Xerais). [GA/n]
Loureiro Calvo, Ramón, 2007. *Las galeras de Normandía* (Madrid: Edaf). [SP/n]
Loureiro Calvo, Ramón, 2009. *León de Bretaña* (Madrid: Edaf). [SP/n]
Loureiro Calvo, Ramón, 2013a. *El lejano reino de la vía láctea* (Madrid: Edaf). [SP/n]
Loureiro Calvo, Ramón, 2013b. *La asombrosa conquista de la isla ballena* (Orense: Eurisaces). [SP/n].
Lourenzo, Miguel, 1981. 'Todos os fillos de Galahad', in *Traxicomedia do vento de Tebas namorado dunha forca. Todos os fillos de Galaad* (Sada, A Coruña: Ediciós do Castro), pp. 101–38. [GA/cpy]
Lourenzo, Miguel, 1982. 'Viva Lanzarote', in *Teatro para nenos* (Sada, A Coruña: Ediciós do Castro), pp. 37–100. [GA/cpy]
Lourenzo, Miguel, 1991. 'A sensación de Camelot', in *Forno de teatro fantástico* (Sada, A Coruña: Ediciós do Castro), pp. 33–70. [GA/cpy]
Mangrané, Daniel, Francisco Naranjo, Ángel Zúñiga and Carlos Serrano de Osma, 1951. *Parsifal* (Barcelona: Daniel Mangrané). [SP/sc]
Mañé Garzón, Pablo, 2000. *El rey Arturo y los caballeros de la Tabla Redonda* (Barcelona: Ediciones 29). [SP/pl]
Maragall, Joan, and Antoni Ribera, trans., 1903. Richard Wagner, *Tristan y Isolda* (Barcelona: Edició Catalunya). [CA/l]
Martín Garzo, Gustavo, 2004. *Los amores imprudentes* (Barcelona: Areté). [SP/n]
Martín, Esteban, and Andreu Carranza, 2007a. *La clave Gaudí* (Barcelona: Plaza y Janés). [SP/n]
Martín, Esteban, and Andreu Carranza, 2007b. *La clau Gaudí* (Barcelona: Plaza y Janés). [CA/n]
Matute, Ana María, 1998. *Olvidado Rey Gudú* (Madrid: Espasa Calpe). [SP/n]
Matute, Ana María, 2000. *Aranmanoth* (Madrid: Espasa Calpe). [SP/n]
Mellizo, Felipe, 1997. *Arturo, rey* (Madrid: Huerga y Fierro, editores). [SP/e]
Melnick, Eitan, 2009. *La clave Wagner* (Madrid: Alagaida). [SP/n]
Méndez Ferrín, Xosé Luís, 1982. 'Amor de Artur', in *Amor de Artur (e novos contos con Tagen Ata ao lonxe)* (Vigo: Xerais), pp. 9–35. [GA/sn]
Méndez Ferrín, Xosé Luís, 1987. *Bretaña, Esmeraldina* (Vigo: Xerais). [GA/n]
Méndez Ferrín, Xosé Luís, 1993. 'Percival', in *Percival e outras historias* (Vigo: Xerais), pp. 15–25. [GA/ss]
Méndez Ferrín, Xosé Luís, 1997a. 'Lanzarote ou o sabio consello', in *Trabe de Ouro. Publicación Galega de Pensamento Crítico*, no. 31 (Santiago de Compostela: Grupo Soteblan), pp. 399–405. [GA/ss]
Méndez Ferrín, Xosé Luís, 1997b. *Arnoia, Arnoia* (Vigo: Xerais). [GA/n]
Millares, Selena, 2013. 'Lancelot / Lancilotto', in *Cuadernos de Sassari / Quaderni di Sassari*, trans. Domenico Antonio Cusato (Messina: Andrea Liporis Editore), pp. 114–15. [SP/sp]
Moleón Viana, Miguel Ángel, 2002. *El rey Arturo cabalga de nuevo, más o menos* (Madrid: SM). [SP/cn]
Montero, Rosa, 2005. *Historia del rey transparente* (Madrid: Alfaguara). [SP/n]
Montes, Graciela, 2001a. *Arturo, el dueño de la espada*, illustrated by Mikel Valverde (Madrid: SM). [SP/css]
Montes, Graciela, 2001b. *El caballero del León*, illustrated by Mikel Valverde (Madrid: SM). [SP/css]
Montes, Graciela, 2001c. *El mago Merlín*. illustrated by Mikel Valverde (Madrid: SM). [SP/css]
Montes, Graciela, 2001d. *El misterio del Santo Grial*, illustrated by Mikel Valverde (Madrid: SM). [SP/css]
Montes, Graciela, 2001e. *La hija del rey*, illustrated by Mikel Valverde (Madrid: SM). [SP/css]
Montes, Graciela, 2001f. *Lanzarote, el caballero enamorado*, illustrated by Mikel Valverde (Madrid: SM). [SP/css]

Montes, Graciela, 2001g. *Perceval y el caballero Rojo*, illustrated by Mikel Valverde (Madrid: SM). [SP/css]

Montes, Graciela, 2001h. *Tristán e Isolda*, illustrated by Mikel Valverde (Madrid: SM). [SP/css]

Monteserín, Xicu, 1984. *Un ermitaño de nome Merlín* (Oviedo: Academia de la Llingua Asturiana). [AS/ss]

Mora, Víctor, et al., 1976. *Claudio y la Tabla Redonda* (Barcelona: Bruguera). [SP/co]

Morales, María Luz, adap., 1914. Anónimo, *Amadís de Gaula* (Barcelona: Araluce). [SP/pl]

Morales, María Luz, adap., 1960a. Alfred Tennyson, 'Gareth y Lynette', in *Historias de Tennyson contadas a los niños* (Barcelona: Araluce), pp. 11–70. [SP/pl]

Morales, María Luz, trans., 1960b. Alfred Tennyson, 'Merlín y Bibiana', in *Historias de Tennyson contadas a los niños* (Barcelona: Araluce), pp. 109–22. [SP/pl]

Morera i Galicia, Magí, 'Lohengrin. Impressió', in *Antologia de la Poesía Modernista*, ed. Jordi Castellanos (Barcelona: Edicions 62), p. 187. [CA/sp]

Navasal, José María, adap., 1954. Thomas Malory, *Los caballeros del Rey Arturo* (Santiago de Chile: Zig-Zag). [SP/pl]

Ojea, José, 1883. 'Énide', in *Célticos. Cuentos y leyendas de Galicia*, introduction by Manuel Murguía (Orense: Imprenta de Antonio Otero), pp. 261–315. [SP/pl]

Palacio Valdés, Armando, 1971. *Tristán o el pesimismo* (Madrid: Narcea). [SP/n]

Paolantonio, Jorge, trans., 2002. Alfred Tennyson, 'La Dama de Shalott', in *Antología poética (texto bilingüe)* (Cáceres: Universidad de Extremadura), pp. 150–63. [SP/sp]

Pardo Bazán, Emilia, 1916. 'La última fada', in *La Novela Corta. Revista Semanal Literaria*, año I, no. 46 (Madrid: La Novela Corta), pp. 3–33. [SP/sn]

Pardo Bazán, Emilia, 1989. *Dulce Dueño*, ed. Marina Mayoral (Madrid: Castalia). [SP/n]

Pardo Bazán, Emilia, 1990. 'El Santo Grial', in *Cuentos Completos*, vol. IV, ed. Juan Paredes Núñez (La Coruña: Fundación Pedro Barrie de la Maza), pp. 422–4. [SP/ss]

Pardo Bazán, Emilia, 1999a. *La obra periodística completa en* La Nación *de Buenos Aires (1879–1921)*, I, ed. Juliana Sinovas Mate (A Coruña: Diputación Provincial). [SP/e]

Pardo Bazán, Emilia, 1999b. *La obra periodística completa en* La Nación *de Buenos Aires (1879–1921)*, II, ed. Juliana Sinovas Mate (A Coruña: Diputación Provincial). [SP/e]

Pardo Bazán, Emilia, 2005. *La vida contemporánea*, ed. Carlos Dorado (Madrid: Hemeroteca Municipal de Madrid). [SP/e]

Pardo Bazán, Emilia, 2006. *Un poco de crítica. Artículos en el* ABC *de Madrid (1918–1921)*, ed. Marisa Sotelo Vázquez (San Vicente de Raspeig, Alicante: Universidad de Alicante). [SP/e]

Patrício, António, 1980a. 'Parsifal', in *Poesía completa* (Lisbon: Assirio e Alvim), p. 152. [PO/sp]

Patrício, António, 1980b. 'Jardins de Klingsor', in *Poesía completa* (Lisbon: Assirio e Alvim), p. 153. [PO/sp]

Pemán, José María, 1950. 'Isoldina y Polión: Tragicomedia irrepresentable', in *Obras completas. Teatro*, tomo IV (Madrid: Escelicer), pp. 37–97. [SP/py]

Pérez Galdós, Benito, 1946. *El caballero encantado (cuento real... inverosímil)* (Buenos Aires: Losada). [SP/n]

Pérez Galdós, Benito, 1997. *Tristana* (Madrid: Alianza Editorial). [SP/n]

Pérez Navarro, Francisco, and Martín Saurí, 2010. *Arturo 1. El único y futuro rey* (Barcelona: Norma Editorial). [SP/co]

Pérez Navarro, Francisco, and Martín Saurí, 2012. *Arturo 2. Excalibur* (Barcelona: Norma Editorial). [SP/co]

Perucho, Joan, 1990a. 'La fata Morgana', in *El basilisc* (Barcelona: Destino, 1990), pp. 58–9. [CA/e]

Perucho, Joan, 1990b. *Les aventures del cavaller Kosmas* (Barcelona: Edicions 62). [CA/n]

Perucho, Joan, 1996a. *Llivre de cavalleries* (Barcelona: Edicions 62). [CA/n]

Perucho, Joan, 1996b. *Fabulaciones* (Madrid: Alianza Editorial). [SP/ss]

Perucho, Joan, 1996c. 'La última Navidad del caballero Arístides Cardellach de la Harche', in *Fabulaciones* (Madrid: Alianza Editorial), pp. 541–6. [SP/ss]

Perucho, Joan, 1996d. 'San Simeón el estilita y el caballero bizantino Kosmas', in *Fabulaciones* (Madrid: Alianza Editorial), pp. 562–6. [SP/ss]
Perucho, Joan, 1996e. 'Las aventuras de Kosmas', in *Fabulaciones* (Madrid: Alianza Editorial), pp. 653–6. [SP/ss]
Perucho, Joan, 1996f. 'Un caballero erudito', in *Fabulaciones* (Madrid: Alianza Editorial), pp. 688–91. [SP/ss]
Perucho, Joan, 1996g. 'El caballero inexistente', in *Fabulaciones* (Madrid: Alianza Editorial), pp. 699–702. [SP/ss]
Pons y Guimerá, Miguel, 1844. *Tristán el ermitaño, ó un amor desgraciado* (Barcelona: Imprenta de J. Roger). [SP/n]
Puértolas, Soledad, 1999. *La rosa de plata* (Barcelona: Planeta DeAgostini). [SP/n]
Pujante, David, 1996. *Estación marítima* (Madrid: Huerga y Fierro Editores). [SP/sp]
Quessep, Giovanni, 1985. *Muerte de Merlín* (Bogotá: Instituto Caro y Cuervo). [SP/sp]
Rico Góngora, Montserrat, 2007. *L'abadia profanada* (Barcelona: Columna Edicions). [CA/n]
Rico Góngora, Montserrat, 2008. *La abadía profanada* (Barcelona: Planeta). [SP/n]
Riquer, Alexandre de, 1899. *Crisantemes* (Barcelona: Verdaguer). [CA/pp]
Riquer, Alexandre de, 1906. 'La Bella Dama sens Mercé' in *Aplech de sonets. Les cullites. Un poema d'amor* (Barcelona: Verdaguer), p. 33. [CA/sp]
Riquer, Alexandre de, 1910a. 'Sonet', in *El poema del bosch* (Barcelona: Verdaguer), p. 11. [CA/lp]
Riquer, Alexandre de, 1910b. 'Cant I. El bosch', in *El poema del bosch* (Barcelona: Alvar Verdaguer), pp. 13–21. [CA/lp]
Riquer, Alexandre de, 1910c. 'Cant VIII. Escalibor', in *El poema del bosch* (Barcelona: Alvar Verdaguer), pp. 61–71. [CA/lp]
Risco, Vicente, 1935. 'A leenda do Graal', in *Nós*, no. 139–44: 176–82. [GA/e]
Risco, Vicente, 1939. 'De Sigfrido a Parsifal', in *Misión*, no. 55. [SP/e]
Risco, Vicente, 1942. 'El misterio del Santo Grial', in *Misión*, no. 128. [SP/e]
Risco, Vicente, 1963. *Mitología cristiana* (Madrid: Editora Nacional). [SP/e]
Risco, Vicente, 1998. *Doutrina e ritual da moi nobre orde galega do Sancto Graal* (Santiago de Compostela: Xunta de Galicia). [GA/e]
Rivero Taravillo, Antonio, trans., 2002a. Alfred Tennyson, 'La dama de Shalott', in *Alfred Tennyson. La Dama de Shalott y otros poemas* (Madrid: Editorial Pre-Textos), pp. 16–33. [SP/sp]
Rivero Taravillo, Antonio, trans., 2002b. Alfred Tennyson, 'Morte d'Arthur', in *Alfred Tennyson. La Dama de Shalott y otros poemas* (Madrid: Editorial Pre-Textos, 2002), pp. 64–83. [SP/sp]
Rivero Taravillo, Antonio, trans., 2002c. Alfred Tennyson, 'Lanzarote y la Reina Ginebra', in *Alfred Tennyson. La Dama de Shalott y otros poemas* (Madrid: Editorial Pre-Textos), pp. 90–3. [SP/sp]
Romeu Muller, Carlos, 1998. *Tristán en Egipto* (Madrid: Ediciones SM).
Romeu Muller, Carlos, 2002. *Tristán en Escocia* (Madrid: Ediciones SM). [SP/cn]
Romeu Muller, Carlos, 2003. *Tristán en Yucatán* (Madrid: Ediciones SM). [SP/cn]
Romeu Muller, Carlos, 2004. *Tristán en París* (Madrid: Ediciones SM). [SP/cn]
Rosenblat, Ángel, adap., 1979. Anónimo, *Amadís de Gaula* (Buenos Aires: Losada). [SP/n]
Rubio, Mercedes, 1957. *Las siete muchachas del Liceo* (Barcelona: Editorial Garbo). [SP/n]
Sainero, Ramón, trans., 1988a. Alfred Tennyson, 'La llegada de Arturo', in *Los grandes mitos celtas y su influencia en la literatura* (Barcelona: Edicomunicación), pp. 234–62. [SP/lp]
Sainero, Ramón, trans., 1988b. Alfred Tennyson, 'La muerte de Arturo', in *Los grandes mitos celtas y su influencia en la literatura* (Barcelona: Edicomunicación), pp. 263–78. [SP/lp]
Sainero, Ramón, trans., 1988c. Alfred Tennyson, 'Ginebra', in *Los grandes mitos celtas y su influencia en la literatura* (Barcelona: Edicomunicación), pp. 279–317. [SP/lp]
Sánchez-Cutillas, Carmelina, 1976. *Matèria de Bretanya* (Valencia: Eliseu Climent). [CA/ab]
Sanjurjo, Carmela Eulate, trans., 1916. Alfred Tennyson, 'Sir Galahad', in *Alfred Lord Tennyson. Las mejores poesías líricas* (Barcelona: Editorial Cervantes), pp. 21–2. [SP/sp]

Sarrionandia, Joseba, 1983. 'Ginebra erregina herbestean', in *Narrazioak* (Donostia: Elkar), pp. 25–36. [BA/ss]
Sarrionandia, Joseba, 1990. 'Amorante ausarta', in *Ifar aldeko orduak* (Donostia: Alkar), pp. 87–99. [BA/ss]
Sarrionandia, Joseba, 1996a. 'Eguziak ortza urdinean nabegatzen', in *Atabala eta euria* (Donostia: Elkar), pp. 7–17. [BA/ss]
Sarrionandia, Joseba, 1996b. 'Ezpata hura arragoan', in *Atabala eta euria* (Donostia: Elkar), pp. 71–80. [BA/ss]
Texeira, Diogo, 1962. *Os cavaleiros da Távola Redonda* (Rio de Janeiro: Récord). [PO/pl]
Torrente Ballester, Gonzalo, 1995. *La saga/fuga de J.B.* (Barcelona: Ediciones Destino). [SP/n]
Trujillo, José Ramón, 2007. *Grial* (Palma: Universitat de les Illes Balears). [SP/lp]
Trullol i Plana, Sebastià, 2011. 'Artús', in *Miscel·lània in memoriam Alfons Serra-Baldó (1909–1993) en el centenari del seu naixement*, reconstructed and transcribed by Juan Zarandona (Barcelona: Publicacions de l'Abadia de Montserrat–Editorial Barcino), pp. 255–79. [SP/l]
Vallvé, Manuel, adap., 1914a. Thomas Malory and Alfred Tennyson, *Los caballeros de la Tabla Redonda* (Barcelona: Araluce). [SP/pl]
Vallvé, Manuel, adap., 1914b. Joseph Bédier, *Tristán e Isolda* (Barcelona: Araluce). [SP/pl]
Vallvé, Manuel, adap., 1914c. Richard Wagner, *Historias de Wagner* (Barcelona: Araluce). [SP/pl]
Vargas Llosa, Mario, 2008. *Carta de batalla por Tirant lo Blanc* (Madrid: Santillana). [SP/e]
Vázquez Alonso, Mariano José, 2002. *La leyenda del Grial* (Madrid: Edaf). [SP/pl]
Vázquez Montalbán, Manuel, 1996. *Un polaco en la corte del rey Juan Carlos* (Madrid: Alfaguara). [SP/e]
Vázquez Montalbán, Manuel, 2002. *Erec y Enide* (Barcelona). [SP/n]
Velloso, José Miguel, 1956. *Los caballeros de la Tabla Redonda* (Madrid: Aguilar). [SP/pl]
Vidal, César, 2006. *Artorius* (Barcelona: Random House–Mondadori). [SP/n]
Vieira, Afonso Lopes, 1922. *Em demanda do Graal* (Lisbon: Imprenta Libanio da Silva). [PO/e]
Vieira, Afonso Lopes, 1923. *O romance de Amadís*, introduction by Carolina Michaëlis de Vasconcelos (Lisbon: Livraria Bertrand). [PO/n]
Vieira, Afonso Lopes, 1940a. *O conto de Amadis de Portugal* (Lisbon: Livraria Bertrand). [PO/ss]
Vieira, Afonso Lopes, 1940b. *Nova demanda do Graal* (Lisbon: Livraria Bertrand). [PO/e]
Villaespesa, Francisco, 1930. *El rey Galaor*, El Teatro Moderno, año 6, núm. 262 (Madrid: Prensa Moderna). [SP/py]
Villar Janeiro, Helena, 2004. 'Os ollos de Galahaz', in *Postais do Camiño* (Vigo: Galaxia), pp. 169–93. [GA/css]
Viura, Xavier, 1904a. 'La vida nova', in *Preludi. Poesies* (Barcelona: Vilà y Compª), p. 109. [CA/lp]
Viura, Xavier, 1904b. 'Percival Infant', in *Preludi. Poesies* (Barcelona: Vilà y Compª), p. 161. [CA/sp]
Viura, Xavier, and Joaquim Pena, trans., 1905. Richard Wagner, *Lohengrin* (Barcelona: Associació Wagneriana). [CA/l]
Vives, Amadeu, 1971. *Julia (Ensayos Literarios)* (Madrid: Espasa Calpe). [SP/e]
Vives, Amadeu, 1973. *Sofía* (Madrid: Espasa Calpe). [SP/e]
Yáñez, Agustín, 1946. *Melibea, Isolda y Alda en tierras cálidas* (Buenos Aires: Colección Austral/Espasa Calpe). [SP/ss]
Zanné, Jeroni, 1905. 'L'Encís del Sant Divendres', in *Assaigs estétics* (Barcelona: L'Avenç), pp. 51–3. [CA/sp]
Zanné, Jeroni, 1906a. 'Espectral', in *Imatges i melodies* (Barcelona: L'Avenç), p. 15. [CA/sp]
Zanné, Jeroni, 1906b. 'Tristany i Iselda', in *Imatges i melodies* (Barcelona: L'Avenç), p. 17. [CA/sp]
Zanné, Jeroni, 1906c. 'A Richard Wagner', in *Imatges i melodies* (Barcelona: L'Avenç), p. 42. [CA/sp]
Zanné, Jeroni, 1906d. 'El cavaller del temple', in *Imatges i melodies* (Barcelona: L'Avenç), p. 91. [CA/sp]
Zanné, Jeroni, 1906e. 'Eliana', in *Imatges i melodies* (Barcelona: L'Avenç), p. 102. [CA/sp]

Zanné, Jeroni, 1909. 'Deliris de Tristany', in *Ritmes* (Barcelona: Fidel Firó), pp. 87–8. [CA/sp]
Zanné, Jeroni, 1912a. 'Bianca Maria degli Angeli', in *Novel les i poemes* (Barcelona: L'Avenç), pp. 2–12. [CA/pp ss]
Zanné, Jeroni, 1912b. 'Visions d'hivern', in *Elegies australs* (Barcelona: Fidel Giró), pp. 27–33. [CA/sp]
Zanné, Jeroni, and Joaquim Pena, trans, 1906. Richard Wagner, *Tristan y Isolda* (Barcelona: Associació Wagneriana). [CA/l]
Zanné, Jeroni, and Joaquim Pena, trans., 1907. Richard Wagner, *Parcival* (Barcelona: Associació Wagneriana). [CA/l]
Zorrilla, José, 1894. 'Los encantos de Merlín', in *Ecos de las montañas*, illustrated by Gustave Doré (Barcelona: Montaner y Simón), pp. 389–444. [SP/lp]

BIBLIOGRAPHY

This Bibliography does not include the modern literary works discussed in Chapter XII, which are listed separately in the Appendix to that chapter. For all manuscripts cited in this book, see the Index of Manuscripts.

Abaurre, Maria Luiza Marques, 1990. 'Os cães do inferno a serviço de Deus', *Estudos Portugueses e Africanos*, 15: 77–91.

Adams, James N., 1982. *The Latin Sexual Vocabulary* (London: Duckworth).

Adroher, Miquel, 2005–6. 'La *Stòria del Sant Grasal*, version franciscaine de la *Queste del Saint Graal*', *BRABL*, 50: 77–119.

Aguilar Perdomo, María del Rosario (ed.), 2009. Francisco Enciso de Zárate, *Corónica del invencible cavallero Florambel de Lucea*, Los Libros de Rocinante, 26 (Alcalá de Henares: CEC). [Valladolid 1532]

Ailenii, Simona, 2009. 'O arquétipo da tradução portuguesa da *Estoire del Saint Graal* à luz de um testemunho recente', *RGF*, 10: 11–38; also in Maria do Rosário Ferreira, Ana Sofia Laranjinha and José Carlos Ribeiro Miranda (eds), *Seminário medieval (2007–2008)* (Porto: Estratégias Criativas), pp. 129–56, and at *Guarecer on-line*, 2009, pp. 11–38: *http://www.seminariomedieval.com/ineditos.html*.

Ailenii, Simona, 2009–10. 'A morte de Galaad e Perceval', *Destiempos. Caballerías*, 4/23: 232–56.

Ailenii, Simona, 2013a. 'Os primeiros testemunhos da tradução galego-portuguesa do romance arturiano' (unpublished doctoral thesis, Universidade do Porto).

Ailenii, Simona, 2013b. 'A tradução galego-portuguesa do romance arturiano nos séculos XIII e XIV', *e-Spania. Revue Interdisciplinaire d'Études Hispaniques Médiévales et Modernes*, 16 [consulted 25 July 2014: *http://espania.revues.org/22611*; DOI : 10.4000/e-spania.2211].

Ailenii, Simona, Ana Sofia Laranjinha, Isabel Correia and José Carlos Ribeiro Miranda (eds), 2013. *Estória do Santo Graal (Livro Português de José de Arimateia), edição do ms 643 do A. N. T. T.* (Porto: Estratégias Criativas).

Albert, Carmen, and María del Mar Fernández Vega, 2003. *Un inventario anónimo en Castilla la Nueva: 1494–1506* (Madrid: CSIC).

Alcoberro, Agustí (ed.), 1997. Carbonell, Pere Miquel, *Cròniques d'Espanya*, 2 vols, Els Nostres Clàssics, B-16 (Barcelona: Barcino).

Alemany Ferrer, Rafael, 1995. 'En torno al desenlace del *Tirant lo Blanc*', in *Estudios sobre el 'Tirant lo Blanc'*, ed. Juan Paredes Núñez, Enrique J. Nogueras Valdivieso and Lourdes Sánchez Rodrigo, Crítica Literaria, 192 (Granada: Universidad de Granada), pp. 11–26.

Alemany Ferrer, Rafael, 2005a. 'Artús i Espèrcius o el culte al meravellós en el *Tirant lo Blanc*', in *Actes del X Congrés Internacional de l'Associació Hispànica de Literatura Medieval*, ed. Rafael Alemany, Josep Lluís Martos and Josep Miquel Manzanaro (Alacant: Institut Interuniversitari de Filologia Valenciana), I: 241–53.

Alemany Ferrer, Rafael, 2005b. 'L'episodi tirantià d'Artús és necessàriament un entremés?', in *Actas del IX Congreso Internacional de la Asociación Hispánica de Literatura Medieval (A Coruña, 18–22 de septiembre de 2001)*, 3 vols, ed. Carmen Parrilla and Mercedes Pampín, Biblioteca Filológica, 13 (Noia: Editorial Toxosoutos; A Coruña: Universidade da Coruña), I, pp. 251–65.

Alfonso X el Sabio, 2009. *General* Estoria, ed. Pedro Sánchez-Prieto Borja. 10 vols (Madrid: Fundación Castro).

Allaire, Gloria, ed. and trans., 2002. *Italian Literature*, 2 vols, I: *Il Tristano Panciatichiano*; II: *Tristano Riccardiano* (Cambridge: D. S. Brewer, 2002–6), I.

Almeida, Ana Cristina, 1994. 'O sentimento de honra n'*A Demanda do Santo Graal*', *Máthesis*, 3: 199–212.

Almeida, Ana Cristina, 1995. 'O prólogo ao *Livro de José de Arimateia* e o pergaminho de Riba d'Âncora', *Máthesis*, 4: 149–58.

Almeida, Ana Cristina, 1996. 'O romance no século XIII. A propósito do maravilhoso no *Livro de José de Arimateia*', *Máthesis*, 5: 237–45.

Almeida, Ana Cristina, 2003, 'O maravilhoso no *Livro de José de Arimateia*' (unpublished doctoral thesis, Universidade de Coimbra).

Almeida, Isabel Adelaide, 1998. *Livros portugueses de cavalarias, do Renascimento ao Maneirismo* (Lisbon: Universidade de Lisboa).

Almeida, Miguel Eugênio, 2004. 'O emprego dos clíticos em *A Demanda do Santo Graal*', in *Actas do VIII Congresso Nacional de Linguística e Filologia. Em homenagem a Mário Barreto* (Rio de Janeiro: http://www.filologia.org.br/viiicnlf/anais/caderno10-12.html) [consulted 14 January 2013].

Alonso, Álvaro, 1999. 'Rodríguez del Padrón, Inés de Castro y la materia de Bretaña', in *Ines de Castro. Studi. Estudos. Estudios*, ed. Patrizia Botta (Ravenna: Longo Editore; Rome: Facoltà di Lettere dell'Università di Roma 'La Sapienza'; Lisbon: Instituto Camões), pp. 35–44.

Alonso, Dámaso, 1947. 'La leyenda de Tristán e Iseo y su influjo en España', in André Mary (ed.), *Tristán* (Barcelona: Janés), pp. 189–204; rpt in *Obras completas. Estudios y ensayos sobre literatura*, 3 vols (Madrid: Gredos, 1973–5), II, pp. 189–204.

Alonso Cortés, Narciso, 1933. 'Montalvo, el del *Amadís*', *RH*, 81: 434–42.

Alpalhão, Margarida Santos, 2003. 'Do mediador como instrumento de descifração', in *Da descifração em textos medievais. IV Colóquio da Secção Portuguesa da Associação Hispânica de Literatura Medieval*, ed. Ana Paiva Morais, Teresa Araújo and Rosário Santana Paixão (Lisbon: Colibri), pp. 275–87.

Alturo i Perucho, Jesús, 1997–8. 'Restes codicològiques en el més antic manuscrit del *Jaufré* amb algunes consideracions sobre aquesta novel·la provençal', *BRABL*, 46: 9–22.

Alturo i Perucho, Jesús, 1999. 'La aportación del estudio de los fragmentos y *membra disiecta* de códices a la historia del libro y de la cultura', in *Studia in codicum fragmenta* (Bellaterra, Barcelona: Universitat Autònoma de Barcelona), pp. 11–40.

Alvar, Carlos, 1977. *La poesía trovadoresca en España y Portugal*, Planeta Universidad, 11 (Madrid: Cupsa).

Alvar, Carlos, 1983. 'El *Lanzarote* en prosa: Reflexiones sobre el éxito y difusión de un tema literario', in *Serta Philológica F. Lázaro Carreter natalem diem sexagesimum celebranti dicata*, ed. Emilio Alarcos Llorach et al., 2 vols (Madrid: Cátedra), II, pp. 1–12.

Alvar, Carlos, 1984. 'Poesía y política en la corte alfonsí', *Cuadernos hispanoamericanos*, 410: 5–20.

Alvar, Carlos, 1991. *El rey Arturo y su mundo: Diccionario de mitología artúrica* (Madrid: Alianza Editorial).

Alvar, Carlos, 1993. 'Poesía gallegoportuguesa y Materia de Bretaña: algunas hipótesis', in *O Cantar dos trobadores: Actas do Congreso celebrado en Santiago de Compostela entre os días 26 e 29 de abril de 1993*, ed. Mercedes Brea, Colección de difusión cultural, 2 (Santiago de Compostela: Xunta de Galicia), pp. 31–51.

Alvar, Carlos 1996. 'Consideraciones a propósito de una cronología temprana del *Libro de Alexandre*', in A. Menéndez and V. Roncero (eds), *Nunca fue pena mayor. Estudios de literatura española en homenaje a Brian Dutton* (Cuenca: Universidad de Castilla-La Mancha), pp. 35–44.

Alvar, Carlos, 2001. '*Tristanes* italianos y *Tristanes* castellanos', *SMV*, 47: 57–75; rpt as Appendix in Alvar 2002; and in Alvar 2010a: 245–55.

Alvar, Carlos, 2002. 'Raíces medievales de los libros de caballerías', *Edad de Oro*, 21 (2002): 61–84.

Alvar, Carlos 2004. *Leyendas artúricas* (Madrid: Espasa).

Alvar, Carlos, 2008. 'La Materia de Bretaña', in *Amadís de Gaula 1508: Quinientos años de libros de caballerías*, ed. J. M. Lucía Megías (Madrid: Biblioteca Nacional de España and Sociedad Estatal de Conmemoraciones Culturales), pp. 19–46.

Alvar, Carlos, 2009. *El Quijote: letras, armas, vida* (Madrid: Sial).

Alvar, Carlos, 2010a. *De los caballeros del Temple al Santo Grial*, Trivium: Biblioteca de Textos y Ensayo, 22 (Madrid: Sial).

Alvar, Carlos, 2010b. *Historia de Lanzarote del Lago* (Madrid: Alianza Editorial).

Alvar, Carlos, 2013a. 'Antroponimia artúrica: Ayer y hoy', *Arba (Acta Romanica Basiliensia)*, 24: 21–51.

Alvar, Carlos, 2013b. 'Don Denís, Tristán y otras cuestiones entre materia de Francia y materia de Bretaña', *e-Spania* [consulted 20 December 2013: *http://e-spania.revues.org/22628*; DOI : 10.4000/e-spania.22628].

Alvar, Carlos, and Vicente Beltrán, 1985. *Antología de la poesía gallego-portuguesa* (Madrid: Alhambra).

Alvar, Carlos, and José Manuel Lucía Megías, 1999. 'Hacia el códice del *Tristán de Leonís* (cincuenta y nueve nuevos fragmentos de la Biblioteca Nacional de Madrid)', *RLM*, 11: 9–135.

Alvar, Carlos, and José Manuel Lucía Megías (eds), 2002. *Diccionario filológico de literatura medieval española* (Madrid: Castalia).

Alvar, Carlos, and José Manuel Lucía Megías, 2009. *Repertorio de traductores del siglo XV* (Madrid: Ollero y Ramos).

Álvarez Pellitero, Ana María (ed.), 1993. *Cancionero de Palacio. Ms. 2653 Biblioteca Universitaria de Salamanca* ([Valladolid]: Junta de Castilla y León, Consejería de Cultura y Turismo).

Amadís de Gaula: see Rodríguez de Montalvo, Garci.

Amadís de Grecia (Cuenca, Cristóbal Francés, 1530): *see* Silva, Feliciano de, *Amadís de Grecia*.

Amaral, Andreia, 2006. 'Os lais de Bretanha. Uma proposta de edição crítica', *RFLLL*, 23: 49–78.

Anales Toledanos I: Enrique Flórez (ed.), *España sagrada, XXIII* (Madrid: Antonio Marín, 1767), 381.

Annales Cambriae: Faral, Edmond, 1993 [1929]. *La légende arthurienne. Études et documents*, 3 vols (Paris: Honoré Champion), III, pp. 44–50.

Antonio, Nicolás, 1672. *Bibliotheca hispana*, 2 vols (Romae: ex Officina Nicolai Angeli Tinassii); 2nd edn, 2 vols, *Bibliotheca hispana Nova* (Matriti: apud Viduam et Heredes Joachimi de Ibarra typographi regii, 1683–8); facsimile edn, intro. by Mario Ruffini (Turin: Bottega d'Erasmo, 1963).

Aragão, Ludumula, 2002. *A produção dos sentidos como reprodução n' 'A Demanda do Santo Graal'* (Coimbra: Pé de Página Editores).

Aramon y Serra, Ramon, 1969. 'El *Tristany* català d'Andorra', in *Mélanges offerts à Rita Lejeune*, 2 vols (Gembloux: J. Duculot), I, 323–37; rpt in *Estudis de llengua i literatura* (Barcelona: Institut d'Estudis Catalans, 1997), pp. 413–29.

Arbor Aldea, Mariña, 2006. '"E era natural de Cornualha, filho de rei Mars...". Meraugis en *A Demanda do Santo Graal*', in *Los caminos del personaje en la narrativa medieval. Actas del Coloquio Internacional (Santiago de Compostela, 1–4 diciembre 2004)*, ed. Pilar Lorenzo Gradín (Florence: Edizioni del Galluzzo), pp. 117–30.

Arbor Aldea, Mariña, 2010. '*Lais de Bretanha* galego-portugueses e tradición manuscrita: as relacións entre *B* e *L*', in *Actes du XXVe Congrès International de Linguistique et de Philologie Romanes (3–8 septembre 2007, Innsbruck)*, ed. Maria Iliescu, Heidi Siller-Runggaldier and Paul Danler (Berlin: De Gruyter), VI, pp. 11–20.

Arderique (Valencia: Juan de Viñao, 1517): *see* Molloy Carpenter, D.

Arias Bonet, Juan Antonio, 1975. *Primera Partida: según el manuscrito add. 20.787 del British Museum* (Valladolid: Universidad de Valladolid).

Arnaut, Ana Paula, 2001. 'Donas e donzelas n'*A Demanda do Santo Graal*', *SBPS*, 5: 29–71.

Arnold, Ivor (ed.), 1938–40. *Le roman de Brut de Wace*, 2 vols (Paris: SATF).

Arretxe, Izaskun, and Roser Vich, 1993. 'La *Faula*, el *Llibre de Fortuna i Prudència* i les *Cobles de la divisió del regne de Mallorques*: tres variants d'un tema literari a la narrativa en vers del segle XIV', *Anuari de Filologia (C4)*, 16: 9–22.

Asperti, Stefano, 1986. 'Bacinetti e berroviere: problemi di lessico e datazione nel *Blandin de Cornoalha*', in *Studia in honorem prof. M. de Riquer*, 4 vols (Barcelona: Quaderns Crema), I, pp. 11–35.

Assis, Cicero Pedro de, 2011. *Rei Artur e os Cavaleiros da Távola Redonda* (São Paulo: Editora Nova Alexandria).

Aurell, Martin, 2007. *La légende du roi Arthur (550–1250)* (Paris: Perrin).

Aurell i Cardona, Jaume, 1996. *Els mercaders catalans al quatre-cents. Mutació de valors i procés d'aristocratització a Barcelona (1370–1470)*, Col·lecció Seminari: Sèrie Catalònia (Lleida: Pagès Editors).

Avalle-Arce, Juan Bautista, 1982. 'El nacimiento de Amadís', in *Essays on Narrative Fiction in the Iberian Peninsula in Honour of Frank Pierce*, ed. Robert B. Tate (Oxford: The Dolphin Book Company), pp. 15–25.

Avalle-Arce, Juan Bautista, 1984. 'Introducción', in Garci Rodríguez de Montalvo, *Amadís de Gaula*, I, Grandes clásicos universales (Barcelona: Círculo de Lectores), pp. 9–20.

Avalle-Arce Juan Bautista, 1990. *'Amadís de Gaula': El primitivo y el de Montalvo*, Lengua y estudios literarios (Mexico City: FCE).

Avalle-Arce, Juan Bautista (ed.), 1991. Garci Rodríguez de Montalvo, *Amadís de Gaula*, 2 vols, Austral, 119–20 (Madrid: Espasa Calpe).

Ayerbe-Chaux, Reinaldo 1986. 'Las *Islas Dotadas*: texto y miniaturas del manuscrito de París, clave para su interpretación', in John S. Miletich (ed.), *Hispanic Studies in Honor of Alan D. Deyermond. A North American Tribute* (Madison: The Hispanic Seminary of Medieval Studies), pp. 31–50.

Badia, Lola, 1989 [1993b]. 'De la *Faula* al *Tirant lo Blanc*, passant, sobretot, pel *Llibre de Fortuna e Prudència*', in *Quaderns Crema: deu anys. Miscel·lània* (Barcelona: Quaderns Crema), pp. 17–57; revised in *Tradició i modernitat als segles XIV i XV: estudis de cultura literària i lectures d'Ausiàs March* (València: Institut Universitari de Filologia Valenciana; Barcelona: Publicacions de l'Abadia de Montserrat, 1993), pp. 93–128.

Badia, Lola, 1991. 'Traduccions al català dels segles XIV–XV i innovació cultural i literària', *Estudi General = Llengua i Literatura de l'Edat Mitjana al Renaixement*, 11: 31–50.

Badia, Lola, 1993a. 'Literatura catalana i patronatge reial al segle XV: episodis d'un distanciament', *Pedralbes. Revista d'Història Moderna*, 13/2: 525–34.

Badia 1993b: see Badia 1989.

Badia, Lola, 1993c. 'El *Tirant* en la tardor medieval catalana', in *Actes 'Symposion Tirant'*: *Actes del 'Symposion Tirant lo Blanc'*, Assaig, 14 (Barcelona: Quaderns Crema), pp. 35–99.

Badia, Lola (ed.), 2003a. *Bernat Metge. Lo Somni* (1999; 3rd edn, Barcelona: Quaderns Crema).

Badia, Lola, 2003b. *Tres contes meravellosos del segle XIV*, Mínima Minor, 92 (Barcelona: Quaderns Crema).

Badia, Lola, and Jaume Torró, 2010. 'Curial entre Tristán y Orlando', in *Estudios sobre la Edad Media, el Renacimiento y la Temprana modernidad*, ed. Francisco Bautista Pérez and Jimena Gamba Corradine, Serie Mayor, 5 (San Millán de la Cogolla: SEMYR, and CiLengua), pp. 43–60.

Badia, Lola, and Jaume Torró (eds), 2011. *Curial e Güelfa*, Sèrie Gran, 26 (Barcelona: Quaderns Crema).

Baena, Juan Alfonso de, 1993. *Cancionero de Baena*, ed. B. Dutton and J. González Cuenca (Madrid: Visor).

Baist, Gottfried, 1897. 'Die spanische Literatur', in *Grundriss der romanischen Philologie*, ed. Gustav Gröber (Strassburg: Karl J. Trübner), II/2, pp. 430–40.

Baist, G[ottfried], 1907. 'Der portugiesische Josef von Arimathia', *ZrP*, 31: 605–7.

Baladro del sabio Merlín: see Bohigas, Pedro, 1957–62.

Baladro del sabio Merlín (Burgos: Juan de Burgos, 1498): see P. Bohigas (ed.), 1957–62. 2 vols (Madrid: Selecciones Bibliófilas).

Baladro del Sabio Merlín, 1535. *La demanda del Sancto Grial: Con los marauillosos fechos de Lançarote y de Galaz su hijo. El primero libro: el baladro del famossisimo profeta & nigromante Merlin con sus profeçías* (Seville: s. i.) [British Library G. 10241].

Baladro del sabio Merlín 1535 (Seville, 1535), ed. A. Bonilla y San Martín. *Libros de caballerías*, NBAE, 6 (Madrid: Bailly-Baillière, 1907), pp. 3–162.

Baldo, 1542 (Seville: Domenico De Robertis, 1542), ed. F. Gernert (Alcalá de Henares: CEC, 2002).

Ballesteros Beretta, Antonio, 1984. *Alfonso X el Sabio* (Barcelona: El Albir).

Baquero Moreno, Humberto, 1990. *Fernão Lopes. Crónica de D. João I, segundo o códice nº 352 do Arquivo Nacional da Torre do Tombo* (Barcelos: Livraria Civilização).

Barahona, Francisco, 1997. *Flor de caballerías*, ed. J. M. Lucía Megías (Alcalá de Henares: CEC).

Baranda, Nieves, 1990–1, 'En defensa del *Amadís* y otras fabulas. La carta anónima al caballero Pero Mexía', *JHP*, 15: 221–36.

Baranda, Nieves, 2002. '*Estoria del noble Vespasiano*', in *Diccionario filológico de literatura medieval española*, ed. C. Alvar and J. M. Lucía Megías (Madrid: Castalia), pp. 488–90.

Barbaza, Raniela, [2005]. 'Translation and the Korido: negotiating identity in Philippine metrical romances', in *Asian Translation Traditions*, ed. Eva Hung and Judy Wakabayashi (Manchester: St Jerome Publishing), pp. 247–62.

Barreto, Therezinha Maria Mello, 2005. 'Argumentadores discursivos na prosa medieval', in *Anais do V Encontro Internacional de Estudos Medievais (2 a 4 de Julho de 2003)*, ed. Célia Marques Telles and Risonette Batista de Souza (Salvador: Quarteto), pp. 237–41.

Barrick, Mac E., 1961–2. 'Bruto's Burned Boats', *Romance Notes*, 3: 49–52.

Barros, João de, 1945–6. *Ásia de João de Barros. Dos feitos que os portugueses fizeram no descobrimento e conquista dos mares e terras do Oriente*, ed. Hernani Cidade and Manuel Múrias, 4 vols, 6th edn (Lisbon: Divisão de Publicações e Biblioteca, Agência Geral das Colónias).

Barros, João de, 1953. *Crónica do Imperador Clarimundo* (Lisbon: Sá da Costa).

Barros, José d'Assunção, 2008. 'Os *Livros de Linhagens* na Idade Média portuguesa, um gênero híbrido', *Itinerários*, 27: 159–82.

Barton, Simon, 2004. *A History of Spain* (Basingstoke: Palgrave Macmillan).

Batista, Ana Cristina Pires dos Santos Trindade, 1996. 'O universo feminino na obra *A demanda do Santo Graal*' (unpublished doctoral thesis, Universidade Nova de Lisboa).

Baumgartner, Emmanuèle, 1975. *Le Tristan en prose. Essai d'interprétation d'un roman médiéval* (Geneva: Droz).

Baumgartner, Emmanuèle (†), 2006, translated by Sarah Singer. 'The Prose Tristan', in *Arthurian Literature in the Middle Ages*, IV: *The Arthur of the French. The Arthurian Legend in Medieval French and Occitan Literature*, ed. Glyn S. Burgess and Karen Pratt, ALMA, IV (Cardiff: UWP), pp. 325–41.

Bautista, Francisco, 2009. 'El motivo de los "Nueve de la Fama" en el *Victorial* y el poema de *Los Votos del Pavón*', *Atalaya. Revue d'études médiévales romanes*, 11: http://atalaya.revues.org/363 [consulted 6 February 2012].

Bautista, Francisco, 2010. 'Original, versiones e influencia del *Liber regum*: estudio textual y propuesta de *stemma*', *e-Spania. Revue Interdisciplinaire d'Études Hispaniques Médiévales et Modernes*, 9: http://e-spania.revues.org/19884 [consulted 21 September 2013].

Bautista, Francisco, 2013. 'Genealogías de la materia de Bretaña: del *Liber regum* navarro a Pedro de Barcelos (c. 1200–1350)', *e-Spania. Revue Interdisciplinaire d'Études Hispaniques Médiévales et Modernes*, 16: http://e-spania.revues.org/22632 [consulted 4 January 2014].

Beceiro Pita, Isabel, 1983. 'Los libros que pertenecieron a los condes de Benavente entre 1434 y 1530', *Hispania*, 154 : 237–81.

Beceiro Pita, Isabel, 1993. 'Modas estéticas y relaciones exteriores: la difusión de los mitos artúricos en la corona de Castilla (s. XIII – comienzos s. XVI)', *En la España Medieval*, 16: 135–67 (rpt in *Libros, lectores y bibliotecas en la España medieval*, Murcia: Nausícaä).

Beceiro Pita, Isabel, 2007. *Libros, lectores y bibliotecas en la España medieval*, Medievalia, 2 (Murcia: Nausícaä).

Beceiro Pita, Isabel, and Alfonso Franco Silva 1986. 'Cultura nobiliar y bibliotecas. Cinco ejemplos, de las postrimerías del siglo XIV a mediados del siglo XVI', *Historia, Instituciones, Documentos*, 12: 277–350.

Belenguer [Castromán], Iria, 2008. 'Aproximación codicológica al *Lanzarote del Lago* castellano: ms. 9611 de la Biblioteca Nacional de España', *RLM*, 20: 193–210.

Bell, Aubrey F. G., 1922, *Portuguese Literature* (Oxford: Clarendon Press).

Beltrán, Vicente, 1991. 'Tipos y temas trovadorescos. *Leonoreta / fin roseta*, la corte poética de Alfonso XI y el origen del *Amadís*', *CuN*, 51: 47–64.

Beltrán, Vicenç, 1996. 'Itinerario de los Tristanes', *Voz y Letra: Revista de Literatura*, 7/1: 17–44.

Beltrán Llavador, Rafael, 1983. *Tirant lo Blanc: evolució i revolta de la narració de cavalleries* (València: Institució Alfons el Magnànim, Diputació de València).

Beltrán Llavador, Rafael (ed.), 1994. Gutierre Díaz de Games, *El Victorial*, Clásicos Taurus, 25 (Madrid: Taurus).

Beltrán Llavador, Rafael (ed.), 1996. Gutierre Díaz de Games, *El Victorial. Estudio, edición crítica, anotación y glosario* (Salamanca: Universidad).

Beltrán Llavador, Rafael, 2006a. 'Los orígenes del grial en las leyendas artúricas: interpretaciones cristianas y visiones simbólicas', in *El santo cáliz. Entre la historia y el culto*, ed. Jaime Sancho Andreu (València: Generalitat Valenciana and Biblioteca Valenciana), pp. 87–136.

Beltrán Llavador, Rafael, 2006b. *'Tirant lo Blanc', de Joanot Martorell*, Col. Historia de la Literatura Universal, Obras, 6 (Madrid: Editorial Síntesis).

Beltrán Llavador, Rafael, 2007. 'Invenciones poéticas en *Tirant lo Blanch* y escritura emblemática en la cerámica de Alfonso el Magnánimo', in *De la literatura caballeresca al 'Quijote'*, ed. Juan Manuel Cacho Blecua, Colección Humanidades, 61 (Zaragoza: Prensas Universitarias de Zaragoza), pp. 59–94.

Beltrán Llavador, Rafael, 2010. 'Convergencias entre *El Victorial* y *Curial e Güelfa*: del *accessus* biográfico al contexto histórico de la París de 1405', *eHumanista*, 16: 442–59.

Beltrán, Rafael, and Isabel Vega, 2004. 'Dos mujeres ante el romance de don Tristán: del canto de la Emperatriz en el *Tirant lo Blanc* a la copla XLI del *Juego trovado* de Jerónimo del Pinar', *Tirant. Butlletí informatiu i bibliogràfic de la literatura de cavalleries*, 7, unpaginated: http://parnaseo.uv.es/Tirant/Butlleti.7/Nota.Beltran-Vega.Martorell-Pinar.htm.

Beneyto Pérez, Juan (ed.), 1947. *Glosa castellana al Regimiento de príncipes de Egidio Romano*, 3 vols, Biblioteca española de escritores políticos (Madrid: Instituto de Estudios Políticos).

Benhaim, Véronique, 2000. 'Les Thrésors d'*Amadis*', in *Les 'Amadis' en France au XVIe siècle*, Cahiers V.L. Saulnier, 17 (Paris: Édition Rue d'Ulm), pp. 157–81.

Bermúdez Plata, Cristóbal (ed.), 1940–80. *Catálogo de pasajeros a Indias durante los siglos XVI, XVII y XVIII*, vols I (1509–1534), II (1535–1538), III (1539–1559) (Seville: CSIC 'Instituto Gonzalo Fernández de Oviedo', 1940, 1942, 1946); IV (1560–1566), ed. Luis Romera Iruela and María del Carmen Galbís Díez (Madrid: Ministerio de Cultura, Dirección General de Bellas Artes, Archivos, y Bibliotecas, Subdirección General de Archivos; Seville: Archivo General de Indias, 1980).

Bernal, Fernando, 2003. *Floriseo*, ed. J. Guijarro Ceballos (Alcalá de Henares: CEC).

Berrini, Beatriz, 1981. '*A Demanda do Santo Graal* e suas ambiguidades', in *Livros de Portugal ontem e hoje* (São Paulo: Cortez Editora), pp. 51–76.

Bertolucci Pizzorusso, Valeria, 2003. 'Testi e immagini in codici attibuibili all'area pisano-genovese alla fine del Duecento', in *Pisa e il Mediterraneo. Uomini, merci, idee dagli Etruschi ai Medici (catalogo della Mostra)*, ed. M. Tangheroni (Milano: Schira), pp. 197–201.

Biddle, Martin, et al., 2000. *King Arthur's Round Table: An Archaeological Investigation* (Woodbridge: The Boydell Press).

BITAGAP [Bibliografía de textos antigos galegos e portugueses], 2013. ed. Arthur L.-F. Askins et al., in PHILOBIBLON (Berkeley: University of California): http://bancroft.berkeley.edu/philobiblon/citation_es.html.

Blanco, Antonio, 1998. *Esplandián Amadís 500 años* (Valladolid: Diputación Provincial de Valladolid).

Blay Manzanera, Vicenta, 1998. 'La convergencia de lo caballeresco y lo sentimental en los siglos XV y XVI', in R. Beltrán (ed.), *Literatura de caballerías y orígenes de la novela* (Valencia: Universidad), pp. 259–87.

Blecua, Alberto (ed.), 1992. Juan Ruiz, Arcipreste de Hita, *Libro de buen amor*, Letras hispánicas, 70 (Madrid: Cátedra).

Blecua, Alberto, 2001. 'Los problemas textuales del *Libro de buen amor*', in *Los orígenes del español y los grandes textos medievales: Mio Cid, Buen amor y Celestina*, ed. Manuel Criado de Val, Biblioteca de filología hispánica, 26 (Madrid: CSIC), pp. 171–90.

Blecua, Alberto, 2005. '*El molino de Amor* y *La mano de Amor*. ¿Dos obras nuevas de don Diego de Valera?', in *Dejar hablar a los textos. Homenaje a Francisco Márquez Villanueva*, ed. Pedro M. Piñero Ramírez (Seville: Universidad de Sevilla), I, pp. 153–72.

Boccaccio, Giovanni, 1976. *Decameron*, ed. Vittore Branca (Florence: Presso L'Accademia della Crusca), pp. 155–65 (Seconda giornata, novella 9).

Bofarull i Mascaró, Próspero (ed.), 1857. *Colección de documentos inéditos del Archivo General de la Corona de Aragón*, XIII (Barcelona: Imprenta del Archivo).

Bogdanow, Fanni, 1959. 'The *Suite du Merlin* and the Post-Vulgate *Roman du Graal*', in *Arthurian Literature in the Middle Ages: A Collaborative History*, ed. Roger Sherman Loomis (Oxford: Oxford University Press), pp. 325–38.

Bogdanow, Fanni, 1960a. 'Essai de classement des manuscrits de la *Suite du Merlin*', *Ro*, 81: 188–98.

Bogdanow, Fanni, 1960b. 'The Relationship of the Portuguese *Josep Abarimatia* to the Extant French MSS of the *Estoire del Saint Graal*', *ZrP*, 76: 343–75.

Bogdanow, Fanni, 1962. 'The Spanish *Baladro* and the *Conte du Brait*', *Ro*, 83: 383–99.

Bogdanow, Fanni (ed.), 1965. *La Folie Lancelot: A Hitherto Unidentified Portion of the* Suite du Merlin *Contained in MSS B.N.fr. 112 and 12599*, Beihefte zur *ZrP*, 109 (Tübingen: Max Niemeyer).

Bogdanow, Fanni, 1966. *The Romance of the Grail. A Study of the Structure and Genesis of a Thirteenth-Century Arthurian Prose Romance* (Manchester: Manchester University Press; New York: Barnes & Noble).

Bogdanow, Fanni, 1972. 'An attempt to classify the extant texts of the Spanish *Demanda del Sancto Grial*', in *Studies in Honor of Tatiana Fotitch*, ed. Josep M. Solà-Solé, Alessandro S. Crisafulli and Siegfried A. Schulz (Washington DC: The Catholic University of America Press and Consortium Press), pp. 213–26.

Bogdanow, Fanni, 1974–5. 'Old Portuguese *seer em car teudo* and the Priority of the Portuguese *Demanda do Santo Graal*', *RPh*, 28: 48–51.

Bogdanow, Fanni, 1975. 'The Relationship of the Portuguese and Spanish *Demandas* to the Extant French Manuscripts of the PostVulgate *Queste del saint Graal*', *BHS*, 52: 13–32.

Bogdanow, Fanni, 1976. 'Another Manuscript of a Fragment of the PostVulgate *Roman du Graal*', *Bulletin Bibliographique de la Société Internationale Arthurienne*, 28: 189–90.

Bogdanow, Fanni, 1980. 'Old Portuguese *o bem*: a note on the text of the Portuguese *Demanda do Sancto Graal*', in *Études offertes à Jules Horrent à l'occasion de son soixantième anniversaire*, ed. Jean-Marie d'Heur and Nicoletta Cherubini (Liège: GEDIT), pp. 27–32.

Bogdanow, Fanni, 1983. 'The Spanish *Demanda del Sancto Grial* and a Variant Version of the Vulgate *Queste del Saint Graal* (I): The Final Scene at Corbenic', *BF*, 28 (*Homenagem a Manuel Rodrigues Lapa, I*): 45–80.

Bogdanow, Fanni, 1985. 'A Hitherto Unkown Manuscript of the Post-Vulgate', *French Studies Bulletin*, 16: 4–6.

Bogdanow, Fanni, 1985–7. 'Textual criticism and the Portuguese *Demanda do Santo Graal*', in *Homenaje a Álvaro Galmés de Fuentes*, ed. Ana M. Cano González et al. (Madrid: Gredos; Oviedo: Universidad de Oviedo), II, pp. 301–12.

Bogdanow, Fanni, 1986–7 [1990]. 'The Spanish *Demanda del Sancto Grial* and a Variant Version of the Vulgate *Queste del Saint Graal*. Part II: A Hitherto Unnoticed Manuscript of the Variant Version of the Vulgate *Queste del Saint Graal* and Galaad's Final Adventures in the Spanish *Demanda*', *BF*, 31: 79–131.

Bogdanow, Fanni, 1991. 'A newly discovered manuscript of the Post-Vulgate *Queste del Saint Graal* and its place in the manuscript tradition of the Post-Vulgate', in *Studia in honorem prof. M. de Riquer*, 4 vols (Barcelona: Quaderns Crema), IV, pp. 347–70.
Bogdanow, Fanni (ed.), 1991–2001. *La version Post-Vulgate de la Queste del saint Graal et de la Mort Artu, Troisième partie du* Roman du Graal, Société des Anciens Textes Français, 5 vols (Paris: SATF, and Picard & Paillart).
Bogdanow, Fanni, 1999a. 'The Madrid *Tercero libro de don Lançarote* (Ms. 9611) and its Relationship to the *Post-Vulgate Roman du Graal* in the Light of a Hitherto Unknown French Source of One of the Incidents of the *Tercero libro*', *BHS*, 76: 441–52.
Bogdanow, Fanni, 1999b. 'L'importance des fragments de Bologne et d'Imola pour la reconstitution de la *Post-Vulgate*', in *Textos medievais portugueses e as suas fontes*, ed. Heitor Megale and Haquira Osakabe (São Paulo: Humanitas), pp. 17–55.
Bogdanow, Fanni, 2000. 'Un nouvel examen des rapports entre la *Queste Post-Vulgate* et la *Queste* incorporée dans la deuxième version du *Tristan en prose*', *Ro*, 118: 1–32.
Bogdanow, Fanni, 2003. 'The *Vulgate Cycle* and the *Post-Vulgate Roman du Graal*', in *A Companion to the Lancelot-Grail Cycle*, ed. Carol Dover (Cambridge: D. S. Brewer), pp. 33–51.
Bogdanow, Fanni, 2006. 'The Post-Vulgate *Roman du Graal*', in *The Arthur of the French: The Arthurian Legend in Medieval French and Occitan Literature*, ed. Glyn S. Burgess and Karen Pratt, ALMA, IV (Cardiff: UWP), pp. 342–52.
Bogdanow, Fanni, and Richard Trachsler, 2006. 'Rewriting prose romance: the Post-Vulgate *Roman du Graal* and related texts', in *The Arthur of the French: The Arthurian Legend in Medieval French and Occitan Literature*, ed. Glyn S. Burgess and Karen Pratt, ALMA, IV (Cardiff: UWP), 342–92.
Bognolo, Ana, 2003. 'Il *Progetto Mambrino*. Per un'esplorazione delle traduzioni e continuazioni italiane dei libros de caballerías', *Rivista di Filologia e Letterature Ispaniche*, 6: 190–202.
Bohigas Balaguer, P[ere/Pedro], 1920–2. 'Profecies catalanes dels segles xiv i xv: assaig bibliogràfic', *BBC*, 6: 24–49.
Bohigas, Pere [/Pedro], 1924. 'El *Lanzarote* español del manuscrito 9611 de la Biblioteca Nacional', *RFE*, 11: 282–97.
Bohigas, P[edro/Pere]. 1925a. *Los textos españoles y gallegoportugueses de la 'Demanda del Santo Grial'*, *RFE*, Anejo VII (Madrid: Junta para la Ampliación de Estudios - Centro de Estudios Históricos).
Bohigas, Pere, 1925b. 'Más sobre el *Lanzarote* español', *RFE*, 12: 60–2.
Bohigas, Pere, 1928–32 [1934]. 'Profecies de Merlí. Altres profecies contingudes en manuscrits catalans', *BBC*, 8: 253–79.
Bohigas, Pedro, 1929. Review of Northup (ed.), *El cuento de Tristan de Leonis* [ms. Vat. Lat. 6428], *RFE*, 16: 284–9.
Bohigas, P[edro]. 1933. Review of 'M. Rodrigues Lapa, *A 'Demanda do Santo Graal'. Prioridade do texto português*, Lisbon 1930', *RFE*, 20: 180–5.
Bohigas, Pedro, 1941. 'La *Visión de Alfonso X* y las *Profecías de Merlín*', *RFE*, 25: 383–98.
Bohigas, Pedro (ed.), 1957–62. *El 'Baladro del sabio Merlín' según el texto de la edición de Burgos de 1498*, Selecciones Bibliófilas, 2ª serie, 2, 14 and 15, 3 vols (Barcelona: Selecciones Bibliófilas).
Bohigas, Pere [/Pedro] 1961 [1982]. 'La Matière de Bretagne en Catalogne', *BBIAS*, 13: 81–98; Catalan translation, 'La matèria de Bretanya a Catalunya', in *Aportació a l'estudi de la literatura catalana* (Montserrat: Associació Internacional de Llengua i Literatura Catalanes, Fundació Congrés de Cultura Catalana, Publicacions de l'Abadia de Montserrat, 1982), pp. 277–94.
Bohigas Balaguer, Pere, 1962. 'Un nou fragment del *Lançalot* català', *Estudis Romànics* (=*Estudis de Literatura Catalana oferts a Jordi Rubió i Balaguer en el seu setanta-cinquè aniversari*, 2), 10: 179–87.
Bohigas 1982: *see* Bohigas 1961.
Bohigas, Pere, 1985. *Sobre manuscrits i biblioteques*, Textos i Estudis de Cultura Catalana, 10 (Barcelona: Publicacions de l'Abadia de Montserrat and Curial Edicions Catalanes), pp. 123–205.

Bohigas, Pere, and Jaume Vidal Alcover, eds, 1984. *Guillem de Torroella. La Faula*, Biblioteca Universitària Tarraco (Tarragona: Edicions Tàrraco).

Bonilla y San Martín, Adolfo (ed.), 1904. 'Fragmento de un *Tristán* castellano del siglo XIV', in *Anales de la literatura española (años 1900–1904)* (Madrid: Tello, 1904), pp. 25–8; rpt in *Libro del esforçado cauallero don Tristan de Leonis y de sus grandes fechos en armas (Valladolid, 1501)* (Madrid: Sociedad de Bibliófilos Madrileños, 1912), pp. 318–20.

Bonilla y San Martín, Adolfo (ed.), 1907a. *Libros de Caballerías*, I, NBAE, VI (Madrid: Bailly-Baillière).

Bonilla y San Martín, Adolfo (ed.), 1907b. *El Baladro del Sabio Merlín*, in *Libros de caballerías, I: Ciclo artúrico-Ciclo carolingio*, NBAE, VI (Madrid: Bailly-Baillière), pp. 3–162.

Bonilla y San Martín, Adolfo (ed.), 1907c. 'Libro del esforçado caballero don Tristan de Leonis y de sus grandes hechos en armas', in *Libros de caballerías, I: Ciclo artúrico-Ciclo carolingio*, NBAE, VI (Madrid: Bailly-Baillère), pp. 339–457. (Text based on 1528 edn).

Bonilla San Martín, Adolfo (ed.), 1907d. *La demanda del Sancto Grial, con los maravillosos fechos de Lanzarote y de Galaz, su hijo. Segunda parte de la Demanda del Sancto Grial*, in *Libros de caballerías, I: Ciclo artúrico-Ciclo carolingio*, NBAE, VI (Madrid: Bailly-Baillière), pp. 163–338.

Bonilla y San Martín, Adolfo (ed.), 1912. *Libro del esforçado cauallero don Tristan de Leonis y de sus grandes fechos en armas (Valladolid, 1501)*, Sociedad de Bibliófilos Madrileños, 6 (Madrid: Suárez and Sociedad de Bibliófilos Madrileños).

Bonilla y San Martín, Adolfo, 1913. *Las leyendas de Wagner en la literatura española, con un apéndice sobre el Santo Grial en el 'Lanzarote del Lago' castellano* (Madrid: Asociación Wagneriana de Madrid, Imprenta Clásica Española).

Borger, Julian, 'Blair's Boys', 2014. *Guardian Weekend*, 20 June: 18–27.

Bottini, Giuseppa, 1993. 'Simbolismo n'*A Demanda do Santo Graal*' (unpublished Master's dissertation, Universidade de São Paulo).

Box, J.B.H., 1976. 'The "Conte del Brait" and the Hispanic "Demanda del Sancto Grial"', *Medioevo Romanzo*, 3: 449–55.

Box, J. Benjamin Harvey, 1977. 'Medieval Hispanic romances of Joseph of Arimathea: a literary study' (unpublished doctoral thesis, University of London).

Box, J. B. H., and A. D. Deyermond, 1977. 'Mestre Baqua and the Grail Story', *RLC*, 51: 366–70.

Boyd-Bowman, Peter, 1964–8. *Indice geobiográfico de cuarenta mil pobladores españoles de America en el siglo XVI*, 2 vols, I (1493–1519) (Bogotá: Instituto Caro y Cuervo, 1964); II (1520–1539) (Mexico City: Editorial Jus, and Academia Mexicana de Genealogía y Heráldica, 1968).

Bozóky, Edina, 1974. 'La Bête Glatissant et le Graal: les transformations d'un thème allégorique dans quelques romans arthuriens', *Revue de l'Histoire des Religions*, 188: 128–48.

Braga, Theophilo, 1914. *Tristão o enamorado: Quadros de conjunto do romanceiro popular português* (Porto: Renacença Portuguesa).

Braga, Theophilo, and Carolina Michaëlis, 1897. 'Geschichte der portugiesischen Literatur', in *Grundriss der romanischen Philologie*, ed. Gustav Gröber (Strassburg: Karl J. Trübner), II/2, pp. 129–382.

Brandenberger, Tobias, 2008. 'A *Crónica do Imperador Clarimundo*: estratégias discursivas e distorsões exegéticas', *Iberoromania*, 59/1: 42–58.

Brasseur, Annette, 1989. *La chanson des Saisnes. Jehan Bodel*, 2 vols (Geneva: Droz).

Brea López, Mercedes, 1994. 'A voltas con Raimbaut de Vaqueiras e as orixes da lírica galego-portuguesa', in *Estudios galegos en homenaxe ó Prof. Giuseppe Tavani* (Santiago de Compostela: Xunta de Galicia), pp. 41–56.

Brea López, Mercedes (ed.), 1996. *Lírica profana galego-portuguesa. Corpus completo das cantigas medievais, con estudio biográfico, análise retórica e bibliografía específica*, 2 vols (Santiago de Compostela: Xunta de Galicia, Centro de Investigacións Lingüísticas e Literarias Ramón Piñeiro).

Brea, Mercedes, 1998. 'Andamos fazendo dança, cantando nossas bailadas', *Museo de Pontevedra*, 52: 387–407.

Bresc, Henri, 1987. 'Excalibur en Sicilie', *Medievalia*, 7: 7–21.
Brocardo, Maria Teresa (ed.), 1997. Gomes Eanes de Zurara, *Crónica do conde D. Pedro de Meneses*, Textos Universitários de Ciências Sociais e Humanas (Lisbon: Fundação Calouste Gulbenkian-Junta Nacional de Investigação Científica e Tecnológica).
Brocardo, Teresa, 2006. *Livro de Linhagens do Conde D. Pedro. Edição do fragmento manuscrito da Biblioteca da Ajuda (século XIV)* (Lisbon: Imprensa Nacional–Casa da Moeda).
Brugger, Ernst, 1906–10. 'L'Enserrement Merlin. Studien zur Merlinsage', *ZfSL*, 29: 56–140; 30: 169–239; 31: 239–81; 33: 145–94; 34: 99–150; 35: 1–55.
Brummer, Rudolf, 1962. 'Die Episode von König Artus im *Tirant lo Blanc*', *Estudis Romànics*, 10: 283–90.
Brummer, Rudolf, 1989. 'Algunes notes sobre una versió catalana gairebé oblidada de la *Queste del Saint Graal*', in *Miscel·lània Joan Fuster: estudis de llengua i literatura*, ed. Antoni Ferrando and Albert G. Hauf (Montserrat: Publicacions de l'Abadia de Montserrat, Departament de Filologia Catalana Universitat de València, Associació Internacional de Llengua i Literatura Catalanes), pp. 27–35.
Brunetti, Almir de Campos, 1974. *A lenda do graal no contexto heterodoxo do pensamento português* (Lisbon: Sociedade de Expansão Cultural).
Buescu, Maria Gabriela Carvalhão, 1968. *Demanda do Santo Graal. Introdução, seleção, notas e glossário* (Lisbon: Verbo).
Buescu, Maria Gabriela Carvalhão, 1991. *Perceval e Galaaz. Cavaleiros do Graal*, Biblioteca Breve, Série Literatura, 125 (Lisbon: Instituto de Cultura e Lingua Portuguesa, Ministério da Educação).
Buescu, Maria Gabriela Carvalhão, 1993. 'O interdito e a ocultação: dois topoi na *Demanda do Santo Graal*', in *Literatura Medieval. Actas do IV Congresso da Associação Hispânica de Literatura Medieval (Lisboa, 1–5 Outubro 1991)*, ed. Aires A. Nascimento and Cristina Almeida Ribeiro (Lisbon: Edições Cosmos), IV, pp. 57–64.
Buescu, Maria Gabriela Carvalhão, 2000. 'O *Livro de José de Arimateia*. História, lenda e religião', *Studia Lusitanica*, 3: 153–63.
Buescu, Maria Gabriela Carvalhão, 2002. 'Em demanda da Besta Ladrador: um emblema demoníaco e anti-cristão na *Demanda do Santo Graal*', in *Animalia. Presença e Representações*, ed. Miguel Alarcão, Luís Krus and Maria Adelaide Miranda (Lisbon: Colibri), pp. 113–21.
Burgess, Glyn S. and Karen Pratt (eds), 2006 *The Arthur of the French. The Arthurian Legend in Medieval French and Occitan Literature*, ALMA, IV (Cardiff: UWP, 2006).
Butinyà i Jiménez, Júlia, 1987–8. 'Sobre l'autoria del *Curial e Güelfa*', *BRABLB*, 41: 63–119.
Butinyà i Jiménez, Júlia, 1990. 'Una nova font del *Tirant lo Blanc*', *RFR*, 7: 191–6.
Cabarcas Antequera, Hernando, 1992. *Amadís de Gaula en las Indias. Estudios y notas para la impresión facsimilar de la edición de 1539 conservada en el Fondo Rufino José Cuervo de la Biblioteca Nacional de Colombia* (Santafé de Bogotá: Instituto Caro y Cuervo, 1992).
Cacho Blecua, Juan Manuel, 1979. *Amadís: heroísmo mítico cortesano*, Colecciones universitarias, 10 (Madrid: Cupsa-Universidad de Zaragoza).
Cacho Blecua, Juan Manuel, 1986. 'El entrelazamiento en el *Amadís* y en las *Sergas de Esplandián*', in *Studia in honorem prof. M. de Riquer*, 4 vols (Barcelona: Quaderns Crema), I, pp. 235–71.
Cacho Blecua, Juan Manuel (ed.), 1987–8. Garci Rodríguez de Montalvo, *Amadís de Gaula*, 2 vols, Letras hispánicas, 255–6 (Madrid: Cátedra).
Cacho Blecua, Juan Manuel, 1992. 'La cueva en los libros de caballerías: la experiencia de los límites', in P. Piñero Ramírez (ed.), '*Descensus ad inferos*': *La aventura de ultratumba de los héroes (de Homero a Goethe)* (Seville: Universidad de Sevilla), pp. 99–127.
Cacho Blecua, Juan Manuel, 1999. 'El género del *Cifar* (Cromberger, 1512)', in *La invención de la novela. Seminario Hispano-Francés organizado por la Casa de Velázquez, Madrid, noviembre 1992–junio 1993*, ed. Jean Canavaggio (Madrid: Casa de Velázquez), pp. 85–105.
Cacho Blecua, Juan Manuel, 2002. '*Los cuatro libros de Amadís de Gaula* y *Las sergas de Esplandián*: los textos de Garci Rodríguez de Montalvo', *Edad de Oro*, 21: 85–116.

Cacho Blecua, Juan Manuel, 2004–5. 'La configuración iconográfica de la literatura caballeresca: el *Tristán de Leonís* y el *Oliveros de Castilla* (Sevilla, Jacobo Cromberger)', *Letras. Libros de caballerías. El «Quijote». Investigación y Relaciones*, 50–1: 51–80.

Cacho Blecua, Juan Manuel, 2007. 'Los grabados del texto de las primeras ediciones del *Amadís de Gaula*: del *Tristán de Leonís* (Jacobo Cromberger, h. 1503–1507) a *La coronación de Juan de Mena* (Jacobo Cromberger, 1512)', *RILCE: Revista de Filología Hispánica [«Calamo currente»: homenaje a Juan Bautista de Avalle-Arce]*, 23/1: 61–88.

Cacho Blecua, Juan Manuel, 2010. 'Iconografía amadisiana: las imágenes de Jorge Coci', *eHumanista. Journal of Iberian Studies*, 16: 1–27.

Caetano, Priscila Miranda, Luana Batista Teodoro and Flavio Felicio Botton, 2012. 'Galaaz: Diálogos entre a Religiosidade Medieval e o Herói Messiânico', *Todas as Musas*, 3/2: 213–28.

Calado, Adelino de Almeida, 1991. *Estoria de Dom Nuno Alvarez Pereyra. Edição crítica da 'Corónica do Condestabre'* (Coimbra: Universidade de Coimbra).

Campos García Rojas, Axayácatl, 1997a. 'Florisdelfa: un episodio insular en *Tristán de Leonís* desde una interpretación de sus elementos geográficos y la magia', in *'Quien hubiese tal ventura': Medieval Hispanic Studies in Honour of Alan Deyermond*, ed. A. M. Beresford (London: Department of Hispanic Studies, Queen Mary and Westfield College), pp. 237–45.

Campos García Rojas, Axayácatl, 1997b. 'Las menciones de Egipto en *Tristán de Leonís*: vestigios de un posible origen oriental', *Anclajes. Revista del Instituto de Análisis Semiótico del Discurso*, 1/1: 59–80.

Campos García Rojas, Axayácatl, 2000. 'El simbolismo del juego de ajedrez en *Tristán de Leonís*', in *Proceedings of the Tenth Colloquium*, ed. A. Deyermond (London: Department of Hispanic Studies, Queen Mary and Westfield College), pp. 99–113.

Campos García Rojas, Axayácatl, 2001a. 'El rey o caballero perdido durante la caza: un motivo folclórico en narrativa y lírica', in *Lyra Mínima Oral (los géneros breves de la literatura tradicional). Actas del Congreso Internacional celebrado en la Universidad de Alcalá, 28–30 octubre 1998*, ed. C. Alvar et al. (Alcalá de Henares: Universidad de Alcalá), pp. 361–82.

Campos García Rojas, Axayácatl, 2001b. 'La Ínsula del Ploto en *Tristán de Leonís* y la construcción de un legado: el modelo ejemplar de los Reyes Católicos', in *Fechos antiguos que los cavalleros en armas passaron. Estudios sobre la ficción caballeresca*, ed. Julián Acebrón Ruiz (Lleida: Universitat de Lleida), pp. 75–96.

Campos García Rojas, Axayácatl, 2002a. 'El Mediterráneo como representación de un imperio: moros, corsarios y gigantes paganos en *Tristán el Joven*', in *Actas del II Congreso Internacional de Estudios Históricos: 'El Mediterráneo, un mar de piratas y corsarios' (Santa Pola, Alicante, del 23–27 de octubre, 2000)* (Santa Pola: Ayuntamiento de Santa Pola, Concejalía de Cultura), pp. 285–91.

Campos García Rojas, Axayácatl, 2002b. *Geografía y desarrollo del héroe en Tristán de Leonís y Tristán el Joven* (San Vicente del Raspeig: Publicaciones de la Universidad de Alicante).

Campos García Rojas, Axayácatl, 2003. 'El suicidio en los libros de caballerías castellanos', in *Propuestas teórico-metodológicas para el estudio de la literatura hispánica medieval*, ed. Lillian von der Walde Moheno, Publicaciones de Medievalia, 27 (Mexico City: Universidad Nacional Autónoma de México and Universidad Autónoma Metropolitana), pp. 385–413.

Campos García Rojas, Axayácatl, 2009–10. 'Heridas, veneno y búsqueda de salud: apuntes comparativos para la leyenda de *Tristán e Iseo*', in *Caballerías*, ed. L. Von der Walde Moheno and Mariel Reinoso, Colección de libros dossiers de la revista digital *Destiempos.com: Revista de curiosidad cultural*, 23, año 4: 257–78: *wwwdestiempos.com/n23/campos.htm*.

Canavaggio, Jean, 1992. 'Don Quijote baja a los abismos infernales: la cueva de Montesinos', in P. Piñero Ramírez (ed.), *'Descensus ad inferos': la aventura de ultratumba de los héroes (de Homero a Goethe)* (Seville: Universidad de Sevilla), pp. 155–74.

Cancioneiro B, 1982. *Cancioneiro da Biblioteca Nacional (Colocci-Brancutti) Cód. 10991* (Lisbon: Biblioteca Nacional and Imprensa Nacional – Casa da Moeda) [facsimile edition].

Cancionero de Baena: see Baena, Juan Alfonso de, *Cancionero de Baena*.
Cancionero General: see Castillo, Hernando del, *Cancionero General*.
Canettieri, Paolo, and Carlo Pulsoni, 1995. 'Contrafacta galego-portoghesi', in Juan Paredes Núñez (ed.), *Medievo y Literatura. Actas del V Congreso de la Asociación Hispánica de Literatura Medieval*, 4 vols (Granada: Universidad de Granada), I, pp. 479–97.
Cantalapiedra Jaén, Fernando, 1990. 'Evocaciones en torno a los nombres de Sosia y Tristán', *Celestinesca*, 14/1: 41–55.
Cantel, Raymond, 1970. 'La persistencia de los temas medievales de Europa en la literatura popular del nordeste brasileño', in Carlos H. Magis (ed.), *Actas del tercer Congreso internacional de Hispanistas, celebrado en Méxixo D.F. del 26 al 31 de agosto de 1968* (Mexico City: Colegio de México), pp. 175–85.
Capra, Daniela, 2003. 'Tristano e Isotta nelle letterature della Penisola Iberica', in *Tristano e Isotta. La fortuna di un mito europeo*, ed. Michael Dallapiazza (Trieste: Edicioni Parnaso), pp. 200–7.
Carbeurim, Cristina Helena, 2011. 'Bruxas e feiticeiras em novelas de cavalaria do ciclo arturiano: o reverso da figura feminina?', in *Anais do VII Encontro Internacional de Estudos Medievais*, ed. Silva Santos Bento and Ricardo da Costa (Cuiabá: EDUFMS / Associação Brasileira de Estudos Medievais), pp. 241–9.
Cardim, Luíz, 1923. 'Sobre o título II do *Nobiliário do Conde de Barcelos*', *A Águia*, 2 (3ª serie, XXII): 194–201; rpt in *Estudos de literatura e de linguística* (Porto: Facultade de Letras, 1929), pp. 91–110.
Cardoso, Wilton, 1977. *Da cantiga de seguir no cancioneiro peninsular da Idade Média* (Belo Horizonte: Universidade Federal de Minas Gerais).
Carrasco Tenorio, Milagros, 2010. 'Roboán y la materia de Bretaña', *Boletín Hispánico Helvético*, 15–16: 7–29.
Carré, Antònia, 2007. *Narrativa catalana medieval en vers (El 'Jaufré' i l'*Espill*' de Jaume Roig)*, col. Humanitats, 112 (Barcelona: Editorial UOC).
Carreto, Carlos da Fonseca Clamote, 2001. 'A figura do rei Artur na literatura genealógica. Intertextualidade e (des)construção da história', in *Figura. Actas do II Colóquio da Secção Portuguesa da Associação Hispânica de Literatura Medieval (Faro, 20 a 31 de Outubro de 1998)*, ed. António Branco (Faro: Universidade do Algarve), pp. 171–94.
Carter, Henry Hare (ed.), 1967. *The Portuguese Book of Joseph of Arimathea*, UNCSRLL, 71 (Chapel Hill: The University of North Carolina Press).
Carvajal, Micael de, 1932. *Tragedia Josephina*, ed. Joseph E. Gillet (Princeton: Princeton University Press; and Paris: PUF).
Carvalho, Júlio, 1990. 'O Grau da *Demanda*', *Idioma. Revista do Departamento III. Instituto de Letras*, 10: 121–32.
Casas Rigall, Juan (ed.), 2007. *Libro de Alexandre* (Madrid: Castalia).
Cascudo, Luís da Câmara, 1953. *Cinco livros do povo. Introdução ao estudo da novelística no Brasil*, Coleção Documentos Brasileiros, ed. Octavio Tarquinio de Sousa, 72 (Rio de Janeiro: Livraria José Olympio Editôra).
Castillo, Hernando del, 2004. *Cancionero General*. 5 vols, ed. J. González Cuenca (Madrid: Castalia).
Castro, Álvaro de, 2001. *Libro segundo de don Clarián de Landanís*, ed. Javier Guijarro Ceballos (Alcalá de Henares: CEC).
Castro, Ivo, 1976–9. 'Quando foi copiado o *Livro de José de Arimateia*? (Datação do cód. 643 da Torre do Tombo)', *BF*, 25: 173–83.
Castro, Ivo, 1983. 'Sobre a data da introdução na Península Ibérica do ciclo arturiano da Post-Vulgata', *BF (Homenagem a Manuel Rodrigues Lapa*, I), 28: 81–98.
Castro, Ivo, 1984. '*Livro de José de Arimateia*. Estudo e edição do cod. ANTT 643' (unpublished doctoral thesis, Universidade Clássica de Lisboa).
Castro, Ivo, 1988a. 'Karl Pietsch e a sua edição dos Spanish Grail Fragments', in *Actas del I Congreso Internacional de Historia de la Lengua Española (Cáceres, 30 de marzo–4 de abril de 1987)*, ed. Manuel Ariza, Álvaro Salvador and Antonio Viudas (Madrid: Arco Libros), II, pp. 1123–9.

Castro, Ivo, 1988b. 'Remarques sur la tradition manuscrite de l'*Estoire del Saint Graal*', in *Homenagem a Joseph M. Piel por ocasião do seu 85.º aniversário*, ed. Dieter Kremer (Tübingen: Max Niemeyer, Instituto de Cultura e Língua Portuguesa and Consello da Cultura Galega), pp. 195–206.

Castro, Ivo, 1991. *Curso de história da língua portuguesa* (Lisbon: Universidade Aberta).

Castro, Ivo, 1993a. '*Demanda do Santo Graal*', in *Dicionário da Literatura Medieval Galega e Portuguesa*, ed. Giulia Lanciani and Giuseppe Tavani (Lisbon: Caminho), pp. 203–6.

Castro, Ivo, 1993b. '*Livro de José de Arimateia*', in *Dicionário da Literatura Medieval Galega e Portuguesa*, ed. Giulia Lanciani and Giuseppe Tavani (Lisbon: Caminho), pp. 409–11.

Castro, Ivo, 1993c. 'Matéria de Bretanha', in *Dicionário da Literatura Medieval Galega e Portuguesa*, ed. Giulia Lanciani and Giuseppe Tavani (Lisbon: Caminho), pp. 445–50.

Castro, Ivo, 1998. 'O fragmento galego do *Livro de Tristan*', in Dieter Kremer (ed.), *Homenaxe a Ramón Lorenzo* (Vigo: Galaxia), I, pp. 135–49.

Castro, Ivo, 2000. 'Rodrigues Lapa e as origens do romance de cavalaria em Portugal', in *Filologia, Literatura e Linguística. Colóquio Internacional Curia 1997. Comemorações do Centenário do Nascimento do Professor Doutor Manuel Rodrigues Lapa* (Porto: Fundação Eng. António de Almeida), pp. 145–56.

Castro, Ivo, 2001. 'La Materia di Bretagna in Portogallo', in Luciana Stegagno Picchio (ed.), *Civiltà letteraria dei paesi di espressione portoghese. I: Il Portogallo. Dalle origini al Seicento* (Florence: Passigli), pp. 195–205.

Castro, Ivo, 2002a [2006]. 'Fallar e a tradição peninsular da *Demanda*', *Santa Barbara Portuguese Studies*, 6 (*A Special Issue devoted to the Middle Ages*): 262–71.

Castro, Ivo, 2002b. 'Sobre a edição do *Livro de José de Arimateia*', in *Matéria de Bretanha em Portugal, Actas do colóquio realizado em Lisboa nos dias 8 e 9 de Novembro de 2001*, ed. Leonor Curado Neves, Margarida Madureira and Teresa Amado (Lisbon: Colibri), pp. 59–68.

Castro, Ivo, 2003–6. 'A *Demanda do Santo Graal* e as suas edições', in *Miscelânea de Estudos in memoriam José G. Herculano de Carvalho. Revista Portuguesa de Filologia*, 25: 125–44.

Castro, Ivo, 2007. 'Josefes caminha sobre as águas', *eHumanista: Journal of Iberian Studies*, 8: 28–37: http://www.ehumanista.ucsb.edu/.

Castro, Ivo, 2008–9. 'Editando o *Livro de José de Arimateia*', *Filologia e Linguística Portuguesa*, 10–11: 345–64.

Castro García, Silvana, 2004. 'Os sete pecados capitais na *Demanda do Santo Graal*', in *XI Premio de Creación Literaria e Ensaio da Facultade de Filoloxía* (A Coruña: Universidade da Coruña), pp. 31–45.

Casula, Francesco C., 1977. *Carte reali diplomatiche di Giovanni I il Cacciatore, re d'Aragona, riguardanti l'Italia*, Publicazioni dell'Istituto di Storia Medioevale e Moderna dell'Università degli Studi di Cagliari, 23 / Archivio della Corona d'Aragona, Colección de Documentos Inéditos, 48 (Padua: CEDAM – Casa Editrice Dott. Antonio Milani).

Catalán Menéndez-Pidal, Diego, 1953. *Poema de Alfonso XI: fuentes, dialecto, estilo* (Madrid: Gredos).

Catalán Menéndez-Pidal, Diego, 1962. *De Alfonso X al Conde de Barcelos: cuatro estudios sobre el nacimiento de la historiografía romance en Castilla y Portugal*, Seminario Menéndez Pidal, 3 (Madrid: Gredos).

Catalán Menéndez-Pidal, Diego, 1970. 'Lanzarote y el ciervo de pie blanco', in *Por campos del romancero: estudios sobre la tradición oral moderna*, Biblioteca Románica Hispánica, 2: 142 (Madrid: Gredos), pp. 82–100.

Catalán, Diego, 1992. 'La expansión al occidente de la Península Ibérica del modelo historiográfico *Estoria de España*. Nuevas precisiones', in *La* Estoria de España *de Alfonso X, creación y evolución* (Madrid: Fundación Ramón Menéndez Pidal and Universidad Autónoma de Madrid), pp. 185–96.

Catalán, Diego, 1997. *De la silva textual al taller historiográfico alfonsí. Códices, crónicas, versiones y cuadernos de trabajo* (Madrid: Fundación Ramón Menéndez Pidal / Universidad Autónoma de Madrid).

Catalán, Diego, and María Soledad de Andrés (eds), 1971. *Edición crítica del texto español de la Crónica de 1344 que ordenó el Conde de Barcelos don Pedro Alfonso* (Madrid: Gredos and Seminario Menéndez Pidal).

Catalão, Pedro Miguel Nunes, 1992. 'O motivo da ilha mítica na literatura medieval portuguesa' (unpublished doctoral thesis, Universidade Nova de Lisboa).

Cátedra, Pedro. M. (ed.), 1986. *Història de Paris i Viana* (Girona: Diputació).

Cátedra, Pedro M., 1989. *La historiografía en verso en la época de los Reyes Católicos. Juan Barba y su «Consolatoria de Castilla»*, Acta Salmanticensia: Textos medievales, 13 (Salamanca: Universidad de Salamanca).

Cátedra, Pedro M., 1999. 'Lectura femenina en el claustro (España, siglos XIV–XVI)', in *Des femmes et des livres. France et Espagnes, XIVe–XVIIe siècle. Actes de la jounée d'étude organisée par l'École nationale des Chartes et l'École normale supérieure de Fontenay/Saint-Cloud (Paris, 30 avril 1998)*, ed. Dominique de Courcelles and Carmen Val Julián (Paris: École des Chartes), pp. 7–53.

Cátedra, Pedro M., 2002. *Nobleza y lectura en tiempos de Felipe II. La biblioteca de Don Alonso Osorio Marqués de Astorga*. (Valladolid: Junta de Castilla y León).

Cátedra, Pedro M., 2007. *El sueño caballeresco. De la caballería de papel al sueño real de don Quijote* (Madrid: Abada Editores).

Cátedra, Pedro M., and Jesús D. Rodríguez Velasco, 1999. 'El baladro del sabio Merlín y su contexto literario y editorial', in *El baladro del sabio Merlín con sus profecías* (Oviedo: Trea), pp. xxi–liii.

Cátedra, Pedro M., and Jesús D. Rodríguez Velasco, 2000. *Creación y difusión de 'El Baladro del sabio Merlín' (Burgos, 1498)* (Salamanca: SEMYR).

Causo, Roberto, 2008. 'Mistura de tradições: cordel e fantasia Arturiana', at: *http://terramagazine.terra.com.br/ficcaoespeculativa/blog/2008/11/01/mistura-de-tradicoes-cordel-e-fantasia-arturiana/* [consulted 17 May 2014].

Cervantes, Miguel de, 2004. *Don Quijote de la Mancha*, 2 vols, ed. Francisco Rico (Estella: Galaxia Gutenberg, Círculo de Lectores, and Centro para la Edición de los Clásicos Españoles).

Chambel, Pedro, 2000. *A Simbologia dos Animais n'"A Demanda do Santo Graal"* (Cascais: Patrimonia Historica).

Chambel, Pedro, 2002. 'Reflexões sobre "A Demanda Espiritual de Lancelote" n'*A Demanda do Santo Graal*', in *Matéria de Bretanha em Portugal. Actas do colóquio realizado em Lisboa nos dias 8 e 9 de Novembro de 2001*, ed. Leonor Curado Neves, Margarida Madureira and Teresa Amado (Lisbon: Colibri), pp. 267–76.

Chambel, Pedro, 2011. 'O Simbolismo das Cores no *Livro de José de Arimateia*', *Medievalista Online*, 10: *http://www2.fcsh.unl.pt/iem/medievalista/* [consulted 17 September 2012].

Charlesworth, James I. (ed.), 1983–5. *The Old Testament Pseudepigrapha*, 2 vols (London: Darton, Longman, & Todd, 1983; New York: Doubleday, 1985), I: *Apocalyptic Literature and Testaments*.

Chase, Carol J., 2003. 'The Gateway to the *Lancelot-Grail Cycle*: *L'Estoire del Saint Graal*', in *A Companion to the Lancelot-Grail Cycle*, ed. Carol Dover (Cambridge: D. S. Brewer), pp. 65–74.

Chevalier, Maxime, 1968. *Sur le public du roman de chevalerie* (Talence: Institut d'Études Ibériques et Ibéro-Américaines de l'Université de Bordeaux).

Chicote, Gloria B., 2001. 'Lanzarote en España: derroteros genéricos del caballero cortés', *RLM*, 13/1: 79–91.

Chora, Ana Margarida, 2004. *Lancelot. Do mito feérico ao herói redentor* (Lisbon: Colibri).

Chora, Ana Margarida, 2012. 'Os cavaleiros do Graal e o anti-heroísmo hagiográfico', *Medievalista Online*, 12: *http://www2.fcsh.unl.pt/iem/medievalista/* [consulted 2 May 2013].

Cigni, F[abrizio], 1992. 'Pour l'édition de la *Compilation* de Rustichello da Pisa: la version du ms. Paris, B.N. fr. 1463', *Neophilologus*, 76: 519–34.

Cigni, Fabrizio, ed. and trans., 1994. *Il romanzo arturiano di Rustichello da Pisa* (Pisa: Cassa di Risparmio).

Cigni, Fabrizio, 2012. 'Per un riesame della tradizione del *Tristan* in prosa, con nuove osservazioni sul ms. Paris, BNF, fr. 756–757', in Francesco Benozzo et al. (eds), *Culture, livelli di cultura e ambienti nel Medioevo occidentale. Atti del IX Convegno della Società Italiana di Filologia Romanza (S.I.F.R.), Bologna, 5–8 ottobre 2009* (Rome: Aracne Editrice), pp. 247–78.

Cingolani, Stefano M[aria], 1990–1. '"Nos en leyr tales libros trovemos placer e recreation." L'estudi sobre la difusió de la literatura d'entreteniment a Catalunya els segles XIV i XV', *Llengua & Literatura*, 4: 39–127.

Cingolani, Stefano M[aria], 1992–3a. 'Modelli storici, tradizioni culturali e identità letteraria nella Catalogna medievale', *Llengua & Literatura* 5: 479–94.

Cingolani, Stefano M[aria], 1992–3b. 'The *Sirventes-ensenhamen* of Guerau de Cabrera: A Proposal for a New Interpretation', *JHR*, 1: 191–201.

Cingolani, Stefano M[aria], 1994. 'Finzione della realtà e realtà della finzione. Considerazioni sui modelli culturali del *Curial e Güelfa*', in *Intel·lectuals i escriptors a la baixa Edat Mitjana*, ed. Lola Badia and Albert Soler, Textos i Estudis de Cultura Catalana, 36 (Barcelona: Curial Edicions Catalanes, and Publicacions de l'Abadia de Montserrat), pp. 129–59.

Cingolani, Stefano M[aria], 1995. 'Il *Blandin de Cornoalha* e la letteratura "popolare" fra Provenza e Catalogna', in *La narrativa in Provenza e Catalogna nel XIII e XIV secolo* (Pisa: Edizioni ETS), pp. 145–59.

Cingolani, Stefano M[aria], 1995–6. 'Clàssics i pseudo-clàssics al *Tirant lo Blanc*: reflexions a partir d'unes fonts de Joanot Martorell', *BRABL*, 45: 361–88.

Cintra, Geraldo de Ulhoa (ed.), 1946. *Crónica do Palmeirim de Inglaterra* (São Paulo: Anchieta).

Cintra, Luís Filipe Lindley, 1950a. 'O *Liber Regum* e outras fontes do *Livro de Linhagens* do Conde D. Pedro', *BF*, 11: 224–51.

Cintra, Luís Filipe Lindley, 1950b. 'Uma tradução galego-portuguesa desconhecida do *Liber Regum*', *BHi*, 52: 27–40.

Cintra, Luís Filipe Lindley (ed.), 1951a [1984–90]. *Crónica Geral de Espanha de 1344* (Lisbon: Imprensa Nacional – Casa da Moeda; rpt 1984–90).

Cintra, Luís Filipe Lindley, 1951b. 'Sobre uma tradução portuguesa da *General Estoria* de Afonso X', *BF*, 12: 184–91.

Cintra, Luís Filipe Lindley, 1956–7. 'D. Pedro, conde de Barcelos, Gomes Lourenço de Beja e a autoria da *Crónica Geral de Espanha de 1344*', *BF*, 16: 137–9.

Cirlot, Victoria, 1993. 'La ficción del original en los libros de caballerías', in *Actas del IV Congresso da Associação Hispânica de Literatura Medieval*, 4 vols (Lisbon: Cosmos), IV, pp. 367–73.

Cirlot, Victoria, 2011. *Historia del Caballero Cobarde y otros relatos artúricos* (Madrid: Siruela).

Cirongilio de Tracia 1545. (Seville, Jácome Cromberger, 1545): see Vargas, Bernardo de, *Cirongilio de Tracia*.

Claramunt, Salvador, 1996. 'El poder y la cultura', in *XV Congreso de Historia de la Corona de Aragón (Jaca, 20–25 de septiembre de 1993). El poder real en la Corona de Aragón (siglos XIV–XVI)*, 5 vols, Actas, 36 (Zaragoza: Diputación General de Aragón, Departamento de Educación y Cultura), I, pp. 335–87.

Clarián de Landanís I. 1518. (Toledo, Juan de Villaquirán, 1518): see Velázquez, Gabriel, *Clarián de Landanís*.

Clarián de Landanís II. 1522. (Toledo, Juan de Villaquirán, 1522): see Castro, Álvaro de, *Libro segundo de don Clarián de Landanís*.

Claribalte 1519. (Valencia: Juan Viñao, 1519): see Fernández de Oviedo, Gonzalo, *Claribalte*.

Cluzel, Irénée, 1954–6. 'A propos de l'*Ensenhamen* du troubadour catalan Guerau de Cabrera', *BRABLB*, 26: 87–93.

Conde de Lindquist, Josefa, 2006. 'Rethinking the Arthurian Legend Transmission in the Iberian Peninsula', *eHumanista: Journal of Iberian Studies*, 7: 72–85.

Contreras Martín, Antonio, 1995. 'El episodio de la carreta en el *Lanzarote del Lago* castellano (Ms. 9611BNMadrid)', in Juan Paredes Núñez (ed.), *Medievo y Literatura. Actas del V Congreso de la Asociación Hispánica de Literatura Medieval*, 4 vols (Granada: Universidad de Granada), II: 61–74.

Contreras Martín, Antonio, 1997. 'La traducción del *Lancelot propre* en la Castilla medieval', in *Actes del II Congrés Internacional sobre Traducció*, ed. M. Bacardí (Bellaterra: Universitat Autònoma de Barcelona and Departament de Traducció i d'Interpretació), pp. 465–93.

Contreras Martín, Antonio, 1999. 'La heráldica en la literatura artúrica castellana', in *Actes del VII Congrés de l'Associació Hispànica de Literatura Medieval*, ed. S. Fortuño Llorens and T. Martínez Romero, 2 vols (Castelló de la Plana: Publicacions de la Universitat Jaume I), II, pp. 71–84.

Contreras Martín, Antonio, 2000. 'Lanzarote del Lago, Arturo y Ginebra en la literatura artúrica castellana', in *Actas del VIII Congreso Internacional de la Asociación Hispánica de Literatura Medieval*, ed. M. Freixas and S. Iriso, 2 vols (Santander: Consejería de Cultura del Gobierno de Cantabria, Año Jubilar Lebaniego, AHLM), I, pp. 547–58.

Contreras Martín, Antonio, 2002a. 'La imagen de la caballería en el manuscrito 9611 de la Biblioteca Nacional de Madrid (*Lanzarote* castellano)' (unpublished doctoral thesis, Universidad de Barcelona, Departamento de Filología Románica).

Contreras Martín, Antonio, 2002b. 'El armamento personal en el *Lanzarote del Lago* (Ms. 9611BNMadrid)', *Tirant*, 5: 1–35.

Contreras Martín, Antonio, 2002c. 'La combinación y repetición de motivos en el *Lanzarote del Lago* (Ms. 9611 BNMadrid)', *RPM*, 9: 45–62.

Contreras Martín, Antonio, 2002d. '*Lancelot en prose*, *Lanzarote del Lago* hispánico y *Le Morte Darthur*: recepción del roman en España e Inglaterra', in *Estudios de Literatura Comparada. Actas del XIII Simposio de la Sociedad Española de Literatura General y Comparada (León, 25–28 de octubre de 2000)*, ed. José Enrique Martínez Fernández, María José Álvarez Maurín, María Luzdivina Cuesta Torre, Cristina Garrigós González and Juan Ramón Rodríguez de Lera (León: Secretariado de Publicaciones y Medios Audiovisuales, Universidad de León), pp. 503–18.

Contreras Martín, Antonio, 2002e. 'Aportación al estudio de *La Questa del Sant Grasal* catalana: las apariciones del Santo Grial', in *Actes del X Congrés Internacional de l'Associació Hispànica de Literatura Medieval*, ed. R. Alemany, J. Ll. Martos and M. Manzanaro, 3 vols (Alicante: Serveis de Publicacions de la Universitat d'Alacant), II, pp. 587–96.

Contreras Martín, Antonio, 2003. 'La investidura de armas: "pescozada" y "palmada" en el *Lanzarote del Lago*', *LC*, 32/1: 257–64.

Contreras Martín, Antonio, 2004. 'Las tres espadas maravillosas de *La Questa del Sant Grasal* catalana', *RPM*, 13: 11–26.

Contreras Martín, Antonio, 2005a. 'La geografía artúrica en el *Lanzarote del Lago* (Ms. 9611 BNMadrid), *RFR*, 22: 21–35.

Contreras Martín, Antonio, 2005b. 'La técnica del entrelazamiento y otros recursos narrativos en el *Lanzarote del Lago* (Ms. 9611 BNMadrid)', in *Del 'Libro de Alexandre' a la Gramática Castellana*, ed. M. Campos Souto (Lugo: Axac), pp. 9–26.

Contreras Martín, Antonio, 2005c. 'El arte de la novela en el *Lanzarote del Lago* castellano (Ms. 9611 BNMadrid)', in *Actas del IX Congreso Internacional da Asociación Hispánica de Literatura Medieval*, ed. Carmen Parrilla and Mercedes Pampín, 3 vols (Noia: Universidade da Coruña and Toxosoutos), II, pp. 123–33.

Contreras Martín, Antonio, 2005d. 'En torno a los folios finales del *Lanzarote del Lago* español (Ms. 9611 BNM)', in *Proceedings of the Thirteenth Colloquium*, ed. Jane Whetnall and Alan Deyermond, PMHRS, 51 (London: Department of Hispanic Studies, Queen Mary, University of London), pp. 111–18.

Contreras Martín, Antonio, 2005e. 'La configuración retórica de los sueños en *A Demanda do Santo Graal* gallegoportuguesa', in *Retórica. Actas do I Congresso Virtual do Departamento de Literaturas*

Românicas da Faculdade de Letras de Lisboa (28 de Março – 1 de Abril, 2005), ed. Ángela Correia and Cristina Sobral (Lisbon: CLEPUL-FCT), pp. 1–11.

Contreras Martín, Antonio, 2006a. 'El copista B del *Lanzarote del Lago* español (BNM MS 9611)', in *Manuscripts, Texts, and Transmission from Isidore to the Enlightenment. Papers from The Bristol Colloquium on Hispanic Texts and Manuscripts*, ed. David Hook (Bristol: H*i*PLAM), pp. 67–83.

Contreras Martín, Antonio, 2006b. 'Profecías y visiones en *A Demanda do Santo Graal* gallegoportuguesa', *Estudi General. Revista de la Facultat de Lletres de la Universitat de Girona*, 26: 23–4.

Contreras Martín, Antonio, 2007a. 'La heráldica en el *Lanzarote del Lago*', *HRJ*, 8/3: 211–16.

Contreras Martín, Antonio, 2007b. 'El juego del ajedrez en el *Lanzarote del Lago* (Ms. 9611 BNMadrid)', in *Actas del XI Congreso de la Asociación Hispánica de Literatura Medieval*, ed. A. López and L. Cuesta Torre, 2 vols (León: Secretariado de Publicaciones de la Universidad de León), I, pp. 431–7.

Contreras Martín, Antonio, 2007c. 'La imagen de Yvaín en la literatura artúrica castellana', *Revista de Erudición y Crítica*, 2: 68–72.

Contreras Martín, Antonio, 2007d. 'Las espadas de Galaz en *La Questa del Sant Grasal*', *RLM*, 19: 127–36.

Contreras Martín, Antonio, 2007e. 'Las mujeres en *A Demanda do Santo Graal* gallego-portuguesa: reflexiones sobre la reina Ginebra', in *Mulleres en Galicia e Galicia e os outros pobos da Península. Actas do VII Congreso Internacional de Estudos Galegos (Barcelona, 28 á 31 de maio de 2003)*, ed. Helena González Fernández and María Xesús Lama López (Sada: Ediciós do Castro; Barcelona: Universitat de Barcelona), pp. 85–93.

Contreras Martín, Antonio, 2009. 'Focalización y modalidad en el *Lanzarote del Lago* (Ms. 9611 BNE)', *Tirant*, 12: 71–107.

Contreras Martín, Antonio, 2010a. 'Compilador, copistas y composición en el *Lanzarote del Lago* (ms. 9611 BNE)', *Pecia (=Du scriptorium à l'atelier. Copistes et enlumineurs dans la conception du livre manuscrit au Moyen Âge)*, 13: 93–103.

Contreras Martín, Antonio, 2010b. 'Muerte y entierro de Tristán en el *Tristán de Leonís* (Valladolid, 1501)', in *Actas del XIII Congreso Internacional de la Asociación Hispánica de Literatura Medieval (Valladolid, 15–19 de septiembre de 2009). In memoriam Alan Deyermond*, ed. José Manuel Fradejas Rueda, Deborah Anne Dietrick, María Jesús Díez Garretas and Demetrio Martín Sanz, 2 vols (Valladolid: Universidad de Valladolid), I, pp. 553–62.

Contreras Martín, Antonio, 2012a. 'Sobre los rasgos lingüísticos occidentales del *Lanzarote del Lago* (Ms. 9611BNE): algunas consideraciones', *Verba. Anuario Galego de Filoloxía*, 39: 325–34.

Contreras Martín, Antonio, 2012b. 'La llamada de lo salvaje: reflexiones sobre la caza en la literatura artúrica castellana', in *Mundos medievales: espacios, sociedad y poder. Homenaje al profesor don José Ángel García de Cortázar*, ed. B. Arizaga Bolumburu, D. Mariño Veigas, C. Díaz Herrera, E. Peña Boscos, J. A. Solórzano Telechea, S. Guijarro González and J. Añíbarro Rodríguez, 2 vols (Santander: PubliCan and Ediciones de La Universidad de Cantabria), II, pp. 1177–88.

Contreras Martín, Antonio, 2012c. 'De encuentros especulares, sueños y visiones en *A demanda do Santo Graal* gallegoportuguesa: algunas consideraciones', *AEM*, 40: 925–35.

Contreras Martín, Antonio, 2012d. 'Sobre los rasgos lingüísticos occidentales del *Lanzarote del Lago* (ms. 9611 BNE): algunas consideraciones', *Verba. Anuario Galego de Filoloxía*, 39: 323–32.

Contreras Martín, Antonio, 2012e. '"Hic iacet": de sepulturas en *A demanda do Santo Graal* gallegoportuguesa y en la *Demanda del Santo Grial* castellana', in *Littératures ibèriques medievals comparades – Literaturas ibéricas medievales comparadas*, ed. Rafael Alemany Ferrer and Francisco Chico Rico (Alicante: Universitat d'Alacant and SELGYC), pp. 161–74.

Contreras Martín, Antonio 2013a. 'La *Historia Britanniae* de Geoffrey de Monmouth en tres versiones hispánicas', *Medievalia. Revista d'Estudis Medievals*, 16: 29–35.

Contreras Martín, Antonio 2013b. 'Algunas consideraciones sobre la construcción de la memoria en la literatura artúrica castellana: objetos y lugares', *RLM*, 25: 41–52.

Contreras Martín, Antonio 2013c. 'Tres textos artúricos hispánicos y sus contextos: lecturas de seis episodios', *Roda da Fortuna. Revista Eletrônica sobre Antiguidade e Medievo*, 2/2: 198–220.

Contreras Martín, Antonio, and Zulema Jiménez Mola, 1997. 'Las armas en el *Lanzarote del Lago* castellano (Ms. 9611 BNMadrid)', in *Actas del VI Congreso Internacional de la Asociación Hispánica de Literatura Medieval*, ed. C. Alvar and J. M. Lucía Megías, 2 vols (Alcalá de Henares: Servicio de Publicaciones de la Universidad de Alcalá de Henares), I, pp. 523–32.

Contreras Martín, Antonio, and Harvey L. Sharrer (eds), 2006. *Lanzarote del Lago*, Los Libros de Rocinante, 22 (Alcalá de Henares: CEC).

Cooper, Louis, 1960: *see Liber regum*.

Cooper, Louis, ed., 1979. *La Gran Conquista de Ultramar*. 4 vols (Bogotá: Instituto Caro y Cuervo).

Corbera, Esteban de, 2005. *Febo el Troyano*, ed. J. J. Martín Romero (Alcalá de Henares: CEC).

Corfis, Ivy A. (ed.), 1985. *The Text and Concordances of Vaticana MS 6428: Cuento de Tristan de Leonis* (Madison: Hispanic Seminary of Medieval Studies; microfiche edn); rpt in *Edition and Concordance of the Vatican Manuscript 6428 of the 'Cuento de Tristán de Leonís'*, ADMYTE 0 (1994); also at: http://chivalriccorpus.spanport.lss.wisc.edu/texts.html.

Corfis, Ivy A. (ed.), 2013. '*El Cuento de Tristan de Leonis*', *Tirant*, 16: 5–196.

Corominas, Joan: *see* Ruiz, Juan.

Corral Díaz, Esther, 1999. 'El motivo de la Besta Ladrador en la *Demanda do Santo Graal*', in *Actes del VII Congrès de l'Associació Hispánica de Literatura Medieval (Castelló de la Plana, 22–26 de setembre de 1997)*, ed. Santiago Fortuño Lloréns and Tomàs Martínez Romero, 3 vols (Castelló de la Plana: Universitat Jaume I), II, pp. 85–99.

Correia, Isabel Sofia Calvário, 2002. 'Os sonhos e a construção da ideologia da linhagem no *Livro de José de Arimateia*', in *Da decifração em textos medievais. IV Colóquio da Secção Portuguesa da Associação Hispânica de Literatura Medieval*, ed. Ana Paiva Morais, Teresa Araújo and Rosário Santana Paixão (Lisbon: Colibri), pp. 235–45.

Correia, Isabel Sofia Calvário, 2003. 'A construção da linhagem no *Livro de José de Arimateia*. Versão portuguesa da *Estoire del Saint Graal*' (unpublished doctoral thesis, Universidade de Lisboa).

Correia, Isabel Sofia Calvário, 2004. 'O Graal no *Livro de José de Arimateia*, versão portuguesa da *Estoire del Saint Graal*', *Espéculo. Revista de Estudios Literarios*, 26: http://www.ucm.es/info/especulo/numero26/graal.html [consulted 4 February 2013].

Correia, Isabel Sofia Calvário, 2005. 'O escudo e o cavaleiro branco do *Livro português de José de Arimateia* à *Demanda do Santo Graal*', in Ana Sofia Laranjinha and José Carlos Ribeiro Miranda (eds), *Modelo. Actas do V Colóquio da Secção Portuguesa da Associação Hispânica de Literatura Medieval* (Porto: Universidade do Porto), pp. 141–52.

Correia, Isabel Sofia Calvário, 2008. 'A Queda da Orgulhosa Guarda e a "Mescheance": um outro relato do *Lancelot en Prose*', *Guarecer on-line:* http://www.seminariomedieval.com/ineditos.htlm, 1–31.

Correia, Isabel Sofia Calvário, 2009. 'Do Amor no *Lançarote de Lago*', in J. Cañas Murillo, Francisco J. Grande Quejigo and J. Roso Díaz (eds), *Medievalismo en Extremadura. Estudios sobre Literatura y Cultura Hispánicas de la Edad Media* (Cáceres: Universidad de Extremadura), pp. 991–7.

Correia, Isabel Sofia Calvário, 2010a. *Do Lancelot ao Lançarote de Lago: tradição textual e difusão ibérica da versão do ms. 9611BNE* (doctoral thesis, Faculdade de Letras da Universidade do Porto).

Correia, Isabel Sofia Calvário, 2010b. 'O episódio da Carole Magique no *Lançalot* catalão e no *Lançarote* castelhano', in J. M. Fradejas Rueda, D. Dietrick Smithbauer, D. Martín Sanz and M. J. Díez Garretas (eds), *Actas del XIII Congreso Internacional de la Asociación Hispánica de Literatura Medieval. In memoriam Alan Deyermond*, 2 vols (Valladolid: Ayuntamiento de Valladolid and Universidad de Valladolid), I, pp. 573–82.

Correia, Isabel Sofia Calvário, 2010c. 'As Cores da (des)ordem: os Cavaleiros Vermelhos no *Lançarote de Lago*', in *Cores. Actas do VII Colóquio da Secção Portuguesa da Associação Hispânica de Literatura Medieval*, ed. I. de Barros Dias and C. F. Clamote Carreto (Lisbon: Universidade Aberta), pp. 157–63.

Correia, Isabel Sofia Calvário, 2010d. 'Em torno da circulação peninsular da matéria arturiana: o "Livro de Don Galás" e o "Lanzarote del Lago"', in Esther Corral Díaz (ed.), *In marsupiis peregrinorum. Circulación de textos e imágenes alrededor del Camino de Santiago en la Edad Media. Actas del Congreso Internacional, Santiago de Compostela, 24–28 marzo 2008* (Florence: Edizioni del Galluzzo), pp. 455–69.

Correia, Isabel Sofia Calvário, 2012a. 'O ciclo do Pseudo-Boron e o estatuto do *Lancelot* ibérico', in Lênia Márcia Mongelli (ed.), *De cavaleiros e cavalarias. Por terras de Europa e Américas* (São Paulo: Humanitas), pp. 271–83.

Correia, Isabel Sofia Calvário, 2012b. 'La corte, la clausura y la buena caballería: del *Lancelot en prose* al *Palmeirim de Inglaterra*', Online site: *http://www.academia.edu/* [consulted 12 May 2013] (unpublished paper given at the IV Congreso de la Sociedad de Estudios Medievales y Renacentistas, Universitat Autónoma de Barcelona, Bellaterra, 5–7 September 2012).

Correia, Isabel Sofia Calvário, 2013. 'Um outro manuscrito francês (Arsenal 3479–3480) e a tradição textual do *Lancelot* ibérico', *e-Spania. Revue Interdisciplinaire d'Études Hispaniques Médiévales et Modernes*, 16: *http://e-spania.revues.org/22641* [consulted 4 January 2014].

Correia, Isabel Sofia Calvário, and Jose Carlos Ribeiro Miranda, 2009–11. 'Os fragmentos A19 da BGUC e a tradição textual do *Lancelot*', *GUARECER on-line. Seminário Medieval*: *http://seminariomedieval.com/guarecer/sm0911/2%20Correia%20Miranda%20BGUC%20%28pp.%2013–48%29.pdf* [consulted 13 February 2014].

Correia, Maria Helena de Paiva, 2003. 'Artur e a serpente', in Maria Leonor Machado de Sousa (ed.), *Em Louvor da Linguagem. Homenagem a Maria Leonor Carvalhão Buescu* (Lisbon: Colibri), pp. 73–82.

Correia, Susana Marisa Fernandes Moreira, 2003. 'A aventura onírica no *Livro de José de Arimateia* (versão portuguesa da *Estoire del Graal*)' (unpublished doctoral thesis, Universidade de Lisboa).

Coutinho, Vitor Manuel da Assunção, 2000. 'A vingança e a traição na *Demanda do Santo Graal*' (unpublished doctoral thesis, Universidade Nova de Lisboa).

Couto, Diogo do, 1736. *Decadas da Asia, que tratam dos mares, que descobriram, armadas, que desbaratarão, exercitos, que vencerão, e das accoens heroicas, e façanhas bellicas, que obrarão os Portugueses nas conquistas do Oriente* (Lisboa Occidental: Na Officina de Domingos Gonsalves).

Crawford, J. P. Wickersham, 1925. 'El horóscopo del hijo del rey Alcaraz en el *Libro de Buen Amor*', *RFE*, 12: 184–90.

Crescini, Vincenzo, and V[enanzio] Todesco, 1913–14. 'La versione catalana dell'*Inchiesta del San Graal*', *Atti del Reale Istituto Veneto*, 73: 457–510.

Crescini, Vincenzo, and Venanzio Todesco (eds), 1917. *La versione catalana della 'Inchiesta del San Graal' secondo il codice dell'Ambrosiana di Milano I. 79 sup.*, Biblioteca Filològica, 10 (Barcelona: Institut d'Estudis Catalans).

Cropp, Glynnis M., 2002. 'Les vers sur les Neuf Preux', *Ro*, 120: 449–82.

Cuesta Torre, María Luzdivina, 1990. 'El Libro II de *Don Tristán de Leonís*: ideas sobre el amor y el matrimonio', *Estudios Humanísticos: Filología*, 12: 11–24.

Cuesta Torre, María Luzdivina, 1991. 'Los orígenes de la materia tristaniana: estado de la cuestión', *Estudios Humanísticos: Filología*, 13: 211–23.

Cuesta Torre, María Luzdivina, 1993a. *Estudio literario de 'Tristán de Leonís'* (doctoral thesis, microfiche edn, Universidad de León).

Cuesta Torre, [María] Luzdivina, 1993b. 'La transmisión textual de *Don Tristán de Leonís*', *RLM*, 5: 63–93.

Cuesta Torre, María Luzdivina, 1993c. 'Traducción o recreación: en torno a las versiones hispánicas del *Tristan en prose*', *Livius. Revista de Estudios de Traducción*, 3: 65–75.

Cuesta Torre, María Luzdivina, 1994a. *Aventuras amorosas y caballerescas en las novelas de Tristán* (León: Universidad de León, Secretariado de Publicaciones).

Cuesta Torre, María Luzdivina, 1994b. 'Más sobre los orígenes de la materia tristaniana', *Estudios Humanísticos: Filología*, 16: 27–47.

Cuesta Torre, María Luzdivina, 1996. 'Libro de caballerías y propaganda política: un trasunto novelesco de Carlos V', in José María Pozuelo Yvancos and Francisco Vicente Gómez (eds), *Mundos de ficción: Actas del VI Congreso Internacional de la Asociación Española de Semiótica, Investigaciones Semióticas VI*, 2 vols (Murcia: Universidad de Murcia), I, pp. 553–60.

Cuesta Torre, María Luzdivina, 1997a. 'Adaptación, refundición e imitación: de la materia artúrica a los libros de caballerías', *RPM*, 1: 35–70.

Cuesta Torre, María Luzdivina, 1997b. 'La estética del plagio en *El Quijote*', *Estudios Humanísticos: Filología*, 19: 107–23.

Cuesta Torre, María Luzdivina, 1997c. 'Tristán en la poesía medieval peninsular', *RLM*, 9: 121–43.

Cuesta Torre, María Luzdivina, 1997d. 'Unos folios recuperados de una edición perdida del *Tristán de Leonís*', in A. M. Beresford (ed.), *'Quien hubiese tal ventura': Medieval Hispanic Studies in Honour of Alan Deyermond* (London: Department of Hispanic Studies, Queen Mary and Westfield College), pp. 227–36.

Cuesta Torre, María Luzdivina (ed.), 1997e. *Tristán de Leonís y el rey don Tristán el Joven, su hijo* (Mexico City: UNAM).

Cuesta Torre, María Luzdivina, 1998a. 'Elementos míticos en el romance del *Conde Olinos*', in Túa Blesa (de.), *Mitos (Actas del VII Congreso Internacional de la Asociación Española de Semiótica celebrado en la Universidad de Zaragoza del 4 al 9 de noviembre de 1996)* (Zaragoza: AES and Anexos de *Tropelías*), pp. 123–9.

Cuesta Torre, María Luzdivina, 1998b. 'La teoría renacentista de la imitación y los libros de caballerías', in J. Matas, J. M. Trabado, María L. González and M. Paramio (eds), *Actas del Congreso Internacional sobre Humanismo y Renacimiento*, 2 vols (León: Universidad de León), II, pp. 297–304.

Cuesta Torre, María Luzdivina, 1998c. *Tristán de Leonís (Valladolid, Juan de Burgos, 1501): Guía de lectura*, Guías de lectura caballeresca, 3 (Alcalá de Henares: CEC).

Cuesta Torre, [María] Luzdivina, 1998d. 'Problemas para la edición de las traducciones medievales de la materia de Bretaña', in Carmen Parrilla, Begoña Campos, Mar Campos, Antonio Chas, Mercedes Pampín and Nieves Pena (eds), *Edición y anotación de textos. Actas del I Congreso de Jóvenes Filólogos (A Coruña, 25–28 de septiembre de 1996)* (A Coruña: Universidade da Coruña), I, pp. 193–205.

Cuesta Torre, María Luzdivina (ed.), 1999a. *Tristán de Leonís (Valladolid, Juan de Burgos, 1501)*, Los libros de Rocinante, 5 (Alcalá de Henares: CEC).

Cuesta Torre, María Luzdivina, 1999b. 'Personajes artúricos en la poesía de cancionero', in V. Beltrán, B. Campos, L. Cuesta and C. Tato (eds), *Estudios sobre poesía de Cancionero* (Noia, A Coruña: Toxosoutos), pp. 71–112.

Cuesta Torre, María Luzdivina, 1999c. *Tristán el Joven (Segunda parte de Tristán de Leonís, Sevilla, Domenico de Robertis, 1534): Guía de lectura*, Guías de lectura caballeresca, 35 (Alcalá de Henares: CEC).

Cuesta Torre, María Luzdivina, 2001. 'Las ínsulas del *Zifar* y el *Amadís* y otras islas de hadas y gigantes', in Julián Acebrón Ruiz (ed.), *Fechos antiguos que los cavalleros en armas passaron. Estudios sobre la ficción caballeresca*, Colección Ensayos Scriptura, 11 (Lleida: Edicions de la Universitat de Lleida), pp. 11–39.

Cuesta Torre, María Luzdivina, 2002a. '*El rey don Tristán de Leonís el Joven* [1534]', *Edad de Oro*, 21: 305–34.

Cuesta Torre, María Luzdivina, 2002b. 'La realidad histórica en la ficción de los libros de caballerías', in Eva Belén Carro Carvajal, Laura Puerto Morro and María Sánchez Pérez (eds), *Libros de caballerías (de Amadís al Quijote). Poética, lectura, representación e identidad (Actas del congreso internacional celebrado en Salamanca del 4 al 6 de junio de 2000)* (Salamanca: Universidad de Salamanca), pp. 87–109.

Cuesta Torre, María Luzdivina, 2002c. '*Tristán de Leonís*', in Carlos Alvar and José Manuel Lucía Megías (eds), *Diccionario filológico de literatura medieval española. Textos y transmisión* (Madrid: Castalia), pp. 972–8.

Cuesta Torre, María Luzdivina, 2007. 'Don Quijote y otros caballeros perseguidos por los malvados encantadores (el mago como antagonista en los libros de caballerías)', in Juan Manuel Cacho Blecua, Ana C. Bueno Serrano, Patricia Esteban Erlés and Karla Xiomara Luna Mariscal (eds), *De la literatura caballeresca al Quijote*, Serie Humanidades, 61 (Zaragoza: Prensas Universitarias), pp. 141–69.

Cuesta Torre, María Luzdivina, 2008a. 'Gloria y pecado de amar en la ficción artúrica castellana', in David Hook (ed.), *The Spain of the Catholic Monarchs: Papers from the Quincentenary Conference (Bristol, 2004)* (Bristol: HiPLAM), pp. 155–76.

Cuesta Torre, María Luzdivina, 2008b. '"Si avéis leído o leyerdes el libro de don Tristán y de Lançarote, donde se faze mención destos Brunes": Bravor, Galeote y el Caballero Anciano del *Tristán* castellano en el *Amadís* de Montalvo', in José Manuel Lucía Megías and María del Carmen Marín Pina (eds), *Amadís, 500 años después. Estudios en homenaje a Juan Manuel Cacho Blecua* (Alcalá de Henares: CEC), pp. 147–75.

Cuesta Torre, María Luzdivina, 2009a (enero-diciembre). 'El desastroso final de Aldaret: diferentes muertes para un traidor en las versiones italianas y castellanas del Tristán', *Letras*, 59–60 (*Studia Hispanica Medievalia* VIII, I: *Actas de las IX Jornadas Internacionales de Literatura Española Medieval, 2008 y de Homenaje al Quinto Centenario de Amadís de Gaula*): 165–75.

Cuesta Torre, María Luzdivina, 2009b. 'La lanza herbolada que mató a Tristán: la versión castellana medieval frente a sus correlatos franceses e italianos (cap. 80 del *Tristán de Leonís* de 1501)', in Jesús Cañas Murillo, Francisco Javier Grande Quejigo and José Roso Díaz (eds), *Medievalismo en Extremadura: estudios sobre literatura y cultura hispánicas en la Edad Media* (Cáceres: Universidad de Extremadura), pp. 499–514.

Cuesta Torre, María Luzdivina, 2009c. 'La venganza por la muerte de Tristán: la reconstrucción de un episodio del *Tristán* castellano medieval del ms. de Madrid a la luz de sus paralelos con versiones francesas e italianas y con el *Tristán el Joven* de 1534', in Antonio Chas Aguión and Cleofé Tato García (eds), *Siempre soy quien ser solía. Estudios de literatura española medieval en homenaje a Carmen Parrilla* (A Coruña: Universidade da Coruña, Servizo de Publicacións), pp. 83–105.

Cuesta Torre, María Luzdivina, 2010. 'Los funerales por Tristán: un episodio del *Tristán* castellano impreso en 1501 frente a sus paralelos franceses e italianos', in José Manuel Fradejas Rueda, Déborah Dietrick Smithbauer, Demetrio Martín Sanz and María Jesús Díez Garretas (eds), *Actas del XIII Congreso Internacional de la Asociación Hispánica de Literatura Medieval (Valladolid, 15 al 19 de septiembre de 2009). In memoriam Alan Deyermond*, 2 vols (Valladolid: Ayuntamiento, Universidad de Valladolid, and AHLM), I, pp. 599–16.

Cuesta Torre, María Luzdivina, 2014a. '"E así murieron los dos amados": ideología y originalidad del episodio de la muerte de los amantes en el *Tristán* español impreso, confrontado con las versiones francesas e italianas', *RLM*, 26, 141–61.

Cuesta Torre, María Luzdivina, 2014b. 'Magas y magia: de las adaptaciones artúricas castellanas a los libros de caballerías', in Eva Lara Aberola and Alberto Montaner (eds), *Señales, portentos y demonios: la magia en la literatura y cultura españolas del Renacimiento* (Salamanca: SEMYR), pp. 325–66.

Cuesta Torre, María Luzdivina. 2014c. 'Alterando sutilmente la tradición textual: elementos de religiosidad en el *Tristán de Leonís*', *Historias fingidas*, 2, 'Monografica', pp. 87–116. DOI 10.13136/22842667/18. ISSN 2284-2667. *http:/historiasfingidas.dlls.univr.it/index.php/hf/article/view/18/49*

Curial y Güelfa, 1982, ed. Giuseppe Sansone and Pere Gimferrer (Madrid: Alfaguara)

Curtis, Renée L., 1963–85. *Le Roman de Tristan en prose. Édition critique du début du Tristan en prose d'après le manuscrit Carpentras 404*, 3 vols, Arthurian Studies, 12–14 (I, Munich: Max Hueber, 1963; II, Leiden: Brill, 1976; both reprinted with III, Cambridge: D. S. Brewer, 1985).

Curtis, Renée L., 1988. 'A romance within a romance: the place of the *Roman du Vallet a la Cote Maltaillee* in the *Prose Tristan*', in Sally Burch North (ed.), *Studies in Medieval French Language and Literature Presented to Brian Woledge in Honour of his 80th Birthday*, Publications romanes et français, 180 (Geneva: Droz), pp. 17–35.

Da Costa, Avelino de Jesús, 1978. *Liber Fidei Sanctae Bracarensis Ecclesie*, 2 vols (Braga: Assembleia Distrital de Braga).

Da Cruz, Claudia Menezes, 2002. 'O simbolismo do Graal e a ideologia cisterciense na *Demanda do Santo Graal*' (unpublished doctoral thesis, Universidade de São Paulo).
Da Cunha, Teresa Maria Antunes Vieira, 1999a. 'Do medo ao êxtase: a simbólica do Além na *Demanda do Santo Graal*' (unpublished doctoral thesis, Universidade Nova de Lisboa).
Da Cunha, Teresa Maria Antunes Vieira, 1999b. 'As artes do demo na *Demanda do Santo Graal*', *Studia Lusitanica*, 2: 143–80.
Da Silva, Ademir Luiz, 2001–2. 'O ideal cavaleiresco de São Bernardo em *A Demanda do Santo Graal*', *Mirabilia*, 13: 27–57.
Da Silva, Elsa Maria Branco, 2002. '«Frui Deo» n'*A Demanda do Santo Graal*: expressões do inéfavel', in Leonor Curado Neves, Margarida Madureira and Teresa Amado (eds), *Matéria de Bretanha em Portugal. Actas do colóquio realizado em Lisboa nos dias 8 e 9 de Novembro de 2001* (Lisbon: Colibri), pp. 251–65.
Da Silva, José Pereira, 1998. 'A metodologia da crítica textual: análise de algumas edições críticas', *Revista Philologus*, 4: 97–111.
Da Silva, Juliana Sylvestre, 2004. 'A matéria de Bretanha e a historiografia medieval: da *Historia regum Britanniae* às primeiras crónicas peninsulares em língua romance' (unpublished doctoral thesis, Universidade Estadual de Campinas).
Da Silva, Rafaela Câmara Simões, 2009. 'Da Bíblia à Estória do Santo Graal. A linguagem divina e os sonhos dos eleitos' (unpublished doctoral thesis, Universidade do Porto).
Daniels, Marie Cort, 1992. *The Function of Humor in the Spanish Romances of Chivalry* (New York: Garland).
Darbord, Bernard, and César García de Lucas, 2007. 'Espacio, tiempo y movimiento en los textos artúricos del manuscrito 1877 de la Biblioteca universitaria de Salamanca', *Cahiers de Linguistique Hispanique Médiévale*, 30 (2007), pp. 197–213.
Darbord, Bernard, and César García de Lucas, 2008. 'Reflexiones sobre las variantes occidentales de la materia artúrica castellana', in Javier Elvira, Inés Fernández-Ordóñez, Javier García González and Ana Serradilla Castaño (eds), *Lenguas, reinos y dialectos en la Edad Media ibérica. La construcción de la identidad. Homenaje a Juan Ramón Lodares* (Frankfurt am Main: Verveurt; Madrid: Iberoamericana), pp. 149–65.
David, Pierre, 1945. 'Auguste Magne. *A Demanda do Santo Graal*', *Bulletin des Études Portugaises et de l'Institut Français au Portugal*, Nouvelle Série, 10.1: 235–9.
De Almeida, Manuel Lopes (ed.), 1977. *Rui de Pina. Chronica do Senhor Rey D. Affonso V* (Porto: Lello & Irmão).
De Ávila, Helena Lima, 2009. 'Sonho e fantasia: o imaginário medieval no *Scivias* en'*A Demanda do Santo Graal*' (unpublished doctoral thesis, Porto Alegre: Universidade Federal de Rio Grande do Sul).
De Brito, Sebastião Miranda Aviz Pereira, 1943. 'O *Livro de Joseph ad Aramatia*. O códice. A novela. O estilo. A linguagem' (unpublished doctoral thesis, Universidade de Lisboa).
De Caluwé, Jacques, 1978, 'Le *Roman de Blandin de Cornouailles et de Guillot Ardit de Miramar*: une parodie de roman arthurien?', *CuN*, 38: 55–66; rpt in *Mélanges de philologie romane offerts à Charles Camproux*, 2 vols (Montpellier: Université Paul Valéry, Centre d'Études Occitanes), I, pp. 263–7.
De Caluwé, Jacques, 1981. 'Quelques réflexions sur la pénétration de la matière arthurienne dans les littératures occitane et catalane médiévales', in Kenneth Varty (ed.), *An Arthurian Tapestry: Essays in Memory of Lewis Thorpe* (Glasgow: French Department of the University of Glasgow), pp. 354–67.
De Guimarães, Laurete Lima, 2011. 'A *Demanda do Santo Graal*. Notícias sobre uma nova edição', in *Anais do VII Encontro Internacional de Estudos Medievais*, ed. Silva Santos Bento and Ricardo da Costa (Cuiabá: EDUFMS and Associação Brasileira de Estudos Medievais), pp. 553–8.
De Medeiros, Maria Ana Sequeira, 2002. 'A simbologia do leão no *Livro de José de Arimateia*', in Leonor Curado Neves, Margarida Madureira and Teresa Amado (eds), *Matéria de Bretanha em Portugal. Actas do colóquio realizado em Lisboa nos dias 8 e 9 de Novembro de 2001* (Lisbon: Colibri), pp. 83–91.

De Medeiros, Maria Ana Sequeira, 2003. 'O Bestiário do *Livro de José de Arimateia*: o testemunho da tradição e a nova ndeologia' (unpublished doctoral thesis, Universidade de Lisboa).
De Moraes, Francisco, 1786. *Crónica de Palmeirim de Inglaterra* (Lisbon: Simão Thaddeo Ferreira).
De Moura e Silva, Leonor Isabel Duarte, 2004. 'Em demanda da Terra Prometida. Viagens e viajantes no *Livro de José de Arimateia*' (unpublished doctoral thesis, Universidade de Lisboa).
De Souza, Neila Matias, 2011. 'Modelando a cavalaria: uma análise da *Demanda do Santo Graal* (século XIII)' (unpublished doctoral thesis, Niteroi: Universidade Fluminense).
De Vasconcellos, Maria Elizabeth G., 1995. 'Aqueles lendários viajantes medievais. Por mares e florestas, em busca do Alem', in Lelia Rodrigues Roedel and Andréia C. L. Frazão da Silva (eds), *Anais da III Semana de Estudos Medievais* (Universidade Federal de Rio de Janeiro: Rio de Janeiro), pp. 5–12.
Défourneaux, Marcelin, 1949. *Les Français en Espagne aux XIe et XIIe siècle* (Paris: PUF).
Delcorno Branca, Daniela, 1980. 'Per la storia del "Roman de Tristan" in Italia', *CuN*, 40: 211–29.
Delcorno Branca, Daniela, 1998a. *Tristano e Lancillotto in Italia. Studi di letteratura arturiana*, Memoria del Tempo, 11 (Ravenna: Longo Editore).
Delcorno Branca, Daniela, 1998b. 'Il *Roman di Tristan*: storia italiana di un testo francese', in *Tristano e Lancillotto in Italia* (Ravenna: Longo Editore), pp. 49–76.
Delpech, François, 1993. *Histoire et légende: essai sur la genèse d'un thème épique aragonais* (Paris: Publications de la Sorbonne).
Delumeau, Jean, 1989. *El miedo en Occidente (siglos XIV–XVIII)* (Madrid: Taurus).
Demanda del sancto Grial, 1535. (Seville, 1535), ed. A. Bonilla y San Martín. *Libros de caballerías*, NBAE, 6 (Madrid: Bailly-Baillière, 1907), pp. 163–338.
Denis, Serge, 1934. 'Le voyage en France d'Alphonse V de Portugal', *BHi*, 36: 289–318.
Devoto, Daniel, 1975. 'Folklore et politique au Château Ténébreux', in Jean Jacquot and Elie Konigson (eds), *Les Fêtes de la Renaissance: fêtes et cérémonies au temps de Charles Quint* (Paris: Centre National de la Recherche Scientifique), II: 311–28.
Deyermond, Alan D., 1964 [1993]. 'El hombre salvaje en la ficción sentimental', *Filología* 10: 97–111; rpt in *Tradiciones y puntos de vista en la ficción sentimental*, Medievalia, 5 (Mexico City: UNAM, 1993), pp. 17–42.
Deyermond, Alan D., 1975. 'The Lost Genre of Medieval Spanish Literature', *HR*, 43: 231–59.
Deyermond, Alan, 1984. 'Problems of language, audience, and Arthurian source in a fifteenth-century Castilian sermon', in Antonio Torres-Alcalá et al. (eds), *Josep Maria Solà-Solé: homage, homenaje, homenatge (Miscelánea de estudios de amigos y discípulos)* (Barcelona: Puvill Libros), pp. 43–54.
Deyermond, Alan, 1986. 'Las relaciones genéricas de la ficción sentimental española', in *Symposium in honorem prof. M. de Riquer* (Barcelona: Universitat de Barcelona, and Quaderns Crema), pp. 75–92; rpt in *Tradiciones y puntos de vista en la ficción sentimental*, Medievalia, 5 (Mexico City: Universidad Nacional Autónoma de México, 1993), pp. 43–64.
Deyermond, Alan, 1997. 'Obras artúricas perdidas en la Castilla medieval', *Anclajes. Revista del Instituto de Análisis Semiótico del Discurso*, 1/1: 95–114.
D'Heur, Jean-Marie, 1972. 'Les lais arthuriens anonymes français et leur tradition galaico-portugaise', *BBIAS*, 24: 210.
D'Heur, Jean Marie, 1973–4. 'De Caradoc à Caralhote. Sur une pièce obscure de Martin Soares et son origine française présumée (Arturiana 1)', *MR*, 23–4: 251–64.
D'Heur, Jean-Marie, 1976. 'Gonçal'Eanes do Vinhal, ses "chansons de Cornouaille" et le respect de l'art poétique (Arturiana 2)', in Germán Colón and Robert Kopp (eds), *Mélanges de langues et de littératures romanes offerts à Carl Theodor Gossen* (Bern: Francke Verlag, and Liège: Marche Romane), pp. 185–94.
Di Stefano, Giuseppe, 1988. 'El *Romance de don Tristán*: edición "crítica" y comentarios', in *Studia Riquer: Studia in honorem prof. M. de Riquer*, 4 vols (Barcelona: Quaderns Crema), III, pp. 271–303.
Di Stefano, Giuseppe (ed.), 1993. *Romancero* (Madrid: Taurus).
Dias, Aida Fernanda (ed.), 1990–2003. *Cancioneiro Geral de Garcia de Resende*, 6 vols (Lisbon: Imprensa Nacional – Casa da Moeda).

Dias, Aida Fernanda, 1999. *El baladro del sabio Merlín con sus profecías*, 2 vols (Oviedo: Trea).
Dias, Aida Fernanda, 2003–6. 'A matéria de Bretanha em Portugal: relevância de um fragmento pergamináceo', in *Miscelânea de Estudos in memoriam José G. Herculano de Carvalho. Revista Portuguesa de Filologia*, 25/1: 145–222.
Dias, Isabel de Barros, 2002. 'Ética cavaleiresca e gigantismo. Particularidades da imagem de Hércules na *Crónica de 1344* como ponto de partida para uma reflexão sobre as "três matérias"', in Leonor Curado Neves, Margarida Madureira and Teresa Amado (eds), *Matéria de Bretanha em Portugal. Actas do colóquio realizado em Lisboa nos dias 8 e 9 de Novembro de 2001* (Lisbon: Colibri), pp. 205–14.
Dias, Isabel de Barros, 2007. 'Narrativas breves en gallego-portugués y en portugués en el marco de la producción medieval', in R. Huamán Mori (ed.), *De los orígenes de la narrativa corta en Occidente* (Lima: Ginebra Magnolia), pp. 267–95.
Dias, Isabel de Barros, 2009. 'Lais líricos e narrativos: separação total ou variações em campo comum?', in Jesús Cañas Murillo, Francisco Javier Grande Quejigo and José Roso Díaz (eds), *Medievalismo en Extremadura. Estudios sobre Literatura y Cultura Hispánicas de la Edad Media* (Cáceres: Universidad de Extremadura), pp. 295–304.
Díaz del Castillo, Bernal, 2011. *Historia verdadera de la conquista de la Nueva España*, ed. Guillermo Serés, Biblioteca Clásica de la Real Academia Española, 36 (Madrid: RAE, 2011).
Díaz de Games, Gutierre, 1996. *El Victorial*, ed. Rafael Beltrán (Salamanca: Universidad de Salamanca)
Díaz-Mas, Paloma (ed.), 1994. *Romancero* (Barcelona: Crítica).
Diccionario de autoridades: Real Academia Española, *Diccionario de la lengua castellana*, 3 vols (Madrid: RAE, 1726–37; facsimile rpt, Madrid: Gredos, 1984).
Diégues Júnior, Manuel, 1986. 'Ciclos temáticos na literatura de cordel (tentativa de classificação e de interpretação dos temas usados pelos poetas populares)', in Diégues Júnior, Manuel, et al., *Estudos. Literatura popular em verso*, Coleção reconquista do Brasil, 2ª série, 94 (Belo Horizonte: Editora Itatiaia Limitada; São Paulo: Editora da Universidade de São Paulo; and Rio de Janeiro: Fundação Casa de Rui Barbosa), pp. 27–177.
Díez Borque, José María, 2010. *Literatura (novela, poesía, teatro) en bibliotecas particulares del Siglo de Oro español (1600–1650)* (Frankfurt am Main: Verveurt; Madrid: Iberoamericana).
Díez de Revenga, Francisco Javier, 1985. 'Alfonso X y su condición de autor literario: la *General Estoria*', in Fernando Carmona and Francisco J. Flores (eds), *La lengua y la literatura en tiempos de Alfonso X. Actas del Congreso Internacional (Murcia, 5–10 de marzo de 1984)* (Murcia: Universidad de Murcia), pp. 159–67.
Díez Garretas, María Jesús, 1983. *La obra literaria de Fernando de la Torre* (Valladolid: Secretariado de Publicaciones de la Universidad de Valladolid).
Dionísio, João, 1997. 'A realidade sonhada nas cantigas trovadorescas en'*A Demanda do Santo Graal*', in José Jorge Letria (ed.), *Actas dos 3ᵒˢ Cursos Internacionais de Verão de Cascais (8 a 13 de Junho de 1996)*, 4 vols (Cascais: Cámara Municipal de Cascais), IV, pp. 19–33.
Dodds, Jerrilynn D., 1979. 'The Paintings in the Sala de Justicia of the Alhambra: Iconography and Iconology', *The Art Bulletin*, 61/2: 186–97.
Domingo del Campo, Francisca, 1984. *El lenguaje en el 'Amadís de Gaula'* (doctoral thesis, 117/84, Madrid: Universidad Complutense).
Domínguez Dono, Xesús, 1998. 'Algunas notas aproximativas a los *lais de Bretanha*: las dos "bailadas"', in José Luis Caramés Lage, Carmen Escobedo de Tapia and Jorge Luis Bueno Alonso (eds), *El discurso artístico Norte y Sur. Eurocentrismo y transculturalismo*, 2 vols (Oviedo: Universidad de Oviedo), I, pp. 383–400.
Don Juan Manuel, 1982. *Libro de la caza*, in *Obras completas*, ed. J. M. Blecua, 2 vols (Madrid: Gredos), I, pp. 515–56.
Donadello, Aulo (ed.), 1994. *Il libro di messer Tristano ('Tristano Veneto')* (Venice: Marsilio).
Dopico Blanco, Fernando, 2007. 'Historia xenealóxica dos Lago de Obaño e Barallobre nos séculos XV e XVI', *Cátedra. Revista eumesa de estudios*, 14: 185–220.

Dos Santos, Eugénia Neves, 2006. '*Beste Glatissante* et autres merveilles dans l'*Estoire del Saint Graal* et dans *A demanda do Santo Graal*', in Francis Gingras (ed.), *Une étrange constance: les motifs merveilleux dans la littérature d'expression française du Moyen Âge à nos jours* (Quebec: Presses de l'Université Laval), pp. 212–27.

Dos Santos, Eugénia Neves, 2010. 'Le "translateur" translaté: l'imaginaire et l'autorité d'un romancier médiéval à travers le cycle post-vulgate et son adaptation portugaise' (unpublished doctoral thesis, Université de Montréal).

Dos Santos, Eugénia Neves, 2011. '*Coita d'amor*: mémoire, désir et culpabilité dans la *Demanda do Santo Graal*', in Isabelle Arseneau and Francis Gingras (eds), *Cultures courtoises en mouvement* (Montreal: Les Presses Universitaires de Montréal), pp. 447–53.

Dubost, Francis, 1991. *Aspects fantastiques de la littérature narrative médiévale* (Geneva: Slatkine Reprints).

Duràn y Sanpere, A[gustí], 1917. 'Un fragment de *Tristany de Leonis* en català', *Estudis Romànics (Llengua i Literatura)*, 2 (Biblioteca Filològica de l'Institut de la Llengua Catalana, IX): 284–316.

Dutton, Brian, 1991. *Cancionero del siglo XV: c. 1360–1520*. 7 vols (Salamanca: Universidad de Salamanca).

Dutton, Brian, and Joaquín González Cuenca (eds), 1993. *Cancionero de Juan Alfonso de Baena*, Biblioteca filológica hispana, 13 (Madrid: Visor).

Dyggve, Holger Niels Petersen, 1938. *Moniot d'Arras et Moniot de Paris, trouvères du XIIIe siècle: édition des chansons et étude historique*, Mémoires de la Société Néo-Philologique de Helsinki – Helsingfors, XIII (Helsinki: Société Neo-Philologique).

Eisele, Gillian, 1980. 'A Reappraisal of the 1534 Sequel to *Don Tristán de Leonís*', *Tristania*, 5/2: 28–44.

Eisele, Gillian, 1981. 'A Comparison of Early Printed Tristan Texts in Sixteenth Century Spain', *ZrP*, 97: 370–82.

Eisenberg, Daniel, 1973. 'Who Read the Romances of Chivalry?', *KRQ*, 20: 209–33.

Eisenberg, Daniel, 1982. *Romances of Chivalry in the Spanish Golden Age*, Hispanic Monographs Series, Documentación cervantina, 3 (Newark, Del.: Juan de la Cuesta).

Eisenberg, Daniel, and María Carmen Marín Pina, 2000. *Bibliografía de los libros de caballerías castellanos*, Humanidades, 40 (Zaragoza: Prensas Universitarias de Zaragoza, 2000).

Elliott, Alison G., 1984. 'L'historiador com a artista: manipulació de la història a la crònica de Desclot', *Quaderns Crema*, 9: 27–52 (originally published in English, 'The Historian as Artist: Manipulation of History in the Chronicle of Desclot', *Viator*, 14 (1983): 195–209).

Entwistle, William J., 1922. 'Geoffrey of Monmouth and Spanish Literature', *Modern Language Review*, 17: 381–91.

Entwistle, William J., 1925. *The Arthurian Legend in the Literatures of the Spanish Peninsula* (London: J. M. Dent; New York: E. P. Dutton; rpt New York: Phaeton Press, 1975).

Entwistle, William J., 1942. *A lenda arturiana nas literaturas da Península Ibérica*, trans. António Alvaro Dória (Lisbon: Imprensa Nacional).

Escudero y Perosso, Francisco, 1894. *Tipografía Hispalense. Anales bibliográficos de la ciudad de Sevilla desde el establecimiento de la imprenta hasta fines del siglo XVIII* (Madrid: Sucesores de Rivadeneyra).

Espadaler, Anton M., 1986. 'El meravellós com a luxe i pedagogia', in Víctor Hurtado and Marcel·la Matheu (eds), *El món imaginari i el món meravellós a l'Edat Mitjana*, Curs, 15 (Barcelona: Fundació Caixa de Pensions), pp. 137–49.

Espadaler, Anton M., 1997. 'El Rei d'Aragó i la data del *Jaufré*', *CuN*, 57: 199–207.

Espadaler, Anton M., 1999. 'Un cançoner a la cort dels Comtes d'Urgell', in *Cançoner dels Comtes d'Urgell*, fascimile edn by A. Espadaler and Eloi Castelló (Lleida: Institut d'Estudis Ilerdencs), pp. 7–19.

Espadaler, Anton M., 1999–2000. 'El final del *Jaufré* i, novament, Cerverí de Girona', *BRABL*, 47: 321–34.

Espadaler, Anton M., 2001. 'La Catalogna dei re', in Piero Boitani, Mario Mancini and Alberto Vàrvaro (eds), *Lo spazio letterario del Medioevo*. 2: *Il Medioevo volgare*, 1: *La produzione del testo* (Rome: Salerno Editrice), II, pp. 873–933.

Espadaler, Anton M., 2002. 'Sobre la densitat cultural del *Jaufré*', in Lola Badia, Miriam Cabré and Sadurní Martí (eds), *Literatura i cultura a la Corona d'Aragó (segles XIII–XV). Actes del III Col·loqui 'Problemes i Mètodes de Literatura Catalana Antiga' (Universitat de Girona, 5–8 juliol de 2000)*, Textos i Estudis de Cultura Catalana, 85 (Barcelona: Curial Edicions Catalanes, and Publicacions de l'Abadia de Montserrat), pp. 335–53.

Espadaler, Anton M., 2014. 'La matèria de Bretanya en la poesia catalana medieval', in Immaculada Fàbregas, Araceli Alonso, and Christian Lagarde, eds, *Les Pays Catalans et la Bretagne au Moyen Age: autour de la 'matière de Bretagne' et de Saint Vincent Ferrier / Els Països Catalans i la Bretanya a l'Edat Mitjana: entorn de la 'matèria de Bretanya i sant Vicent Ferrer*, col. Cultura Catalana, 3 (Canet: Trabucaire Éditions).

Español, Francesca, 2001. *Els escenaris del rei. Art i monarquia a la Corona d'Aragó*, fotografies de Ramon Manent (Barcelona: Angle Editorial).

Espejo de Príncipes, 1580 (Alcalá de Henares: Juan Íñiguez de Lequerica, 1580): *see* Sierra, Pedro de la, *Espejo de príncipes y caballeros* (segunda parte).

Estoria de Merlín, La, 1924–5. [Biblioteca Universidad de Salamanca, MS 1877]. Ed. K. Pietsch, *Spanish Grail Fragments*. 2 vols (Chicago: University of Chicago Press).

Estorninho, Alice, António Domingues de Sousa Costa and Artur Moreira de Sá (eds), 1978. *Chartularium Universitatis Portugalensis (1288–1537)*, VIII (1471–81) (Lisbon: Instituto Nacional de Investigação Científica).

Eugenio, Damiana L., 1987. *Awit and Corrido: Philippine Metrical Romances* (Quezon City: University of the Philippines Press).

Even-Zohar, Itamar, 1978. 'The position of translated literature within the literary polysystem', in James Holmes et al. (eds), *Literature and Translation: Essays on the Theory and Practice of Literary Translation* (The Hague: Mouton), pp. 117–27.

Even-Zohar, Itamar, 1990. *Polysystem Studies* (Tel Aviv: The Porter Institute for Poetics and Semiotics).

Faccon, Manuela, 1996. 'Le *Cuento de Tristán de Leonís*: la transmission d'une légende dans l'Espagne du XIVème siècle', in D. Buschinger and W. Spiewok (eds), *Tristan et Iseut: Un thème éternel dans la culture mondiale. 30ème Congrès du Cercle de travail de la littérature allemande au Moyen Age* (Greifswald: Reineke Verlag), pp. 241–54.

Fachine Borges, Francisca Neuma, 1996. 'Literatura de cordel. De los orígenes europeos hacia la nacionalización brasileña', *Anuario brasileño de estudios hispánicos*, 6: 107–14.

Fallows, Noel, 2013. *The Twelve of England* (Wheaton: Freelance Academy Press).

Fansler, Dean S., 1916. 'Metrical romances in the Philippines', *Journal of American Folklore*, 29: 201–81.

Faral, Edmond, 1993 [1929]. *La légende arthurienne. Études et documents*, 3 vols (Paris: Honoré Champion).

Faria, Daniel, 2006a. 'Galaaz e a configuração com Cristo', *RFLLL*, série 2ª, 23: 29–37.

Faria, Daniel, 2006b. 'Ainda sobre a *Demanda do Santo Graal*', *RFLLL*, série 2ª, 23: 39–47 .

Faulhaber, Charles B., 1987. *Libros y Bibliotecas en la España Medieval: una bibliografía de fuentes impresas*, RBC, 47 (London, Grant & Cutler).

Febo el Troyano, 1576 (Barcelona: Pedro Malo, 1576): *see* Corbera, Esteban de, *Febo el Troyano*.

Félix Magno I–II, 1549 (Seville: Sebastián Trugillo, 1549; ed. Cl. Demattè, Alcalá de Henares: CEC, 2001).

Félix Magno III–IV, 1549 (Seville: Sebastián Trugillo, 1549; ed. Cl. Demattè, Alcalá de Henares: CEC, 2001).

Felixmarte de Hircania, 1556 (Valladolid: Francisco Fernández de Córdoba, 1556): *see* Ortega, Melchor de, *Felixmarte de Hircania*.

Fernández del Castillo, Francisco, 1914. *Libros y libreros en el siglo XVI* (facsimile rpt, Mexico City: Archivo General de la Nación and FCE, 1982).
Fernández de Oviedo, Gonzalo, 2001. *Claribalte*, ed. A. del Río Nogueras (Alcalá de Henares: CEC).
Fernández Flórez, José A. (ed.), 1994. *Colección diplomática del monasterio de Sahagún (857–1300)*, V (1200–1300), Colección de Fuentes y Estudios de Historia Leonesa, 46 (León: Centro de Estudios e Investigaciones 'San Isidoro', Caja España de Inversiones, Caja de Ahorros y Monte de Piedad, Archivo Histórico Diocesano, 1994).
Fernández-Ordóñez, Inés, 1992. *Las 'Estorias' de Alfonso el Sabio* (Madrid: Istmo).
Fernández-Ordóñez, Inés, 2006. 'La historiografía medieval como fuente de datos lingüísticos. Tradiciones consolidadas y rupturas necesarias', in J. J. de Bustos Tovar and J. L. Girón Alconchel (eds), *Actas del IV Congreso Internacional de Historia de la Lengua Española*, 2 vols (Madrid: Arco Libros), II, pp. 1779–807.
Ferrari, Anna, 1979. 'Formazione e struttura del Canzoniere portoghese della Biblioteca Nazionale di Lisbona (Cod. 10991: Colocci-Brancuti). Premesse codicologiche alla critica del testo (materiali e note problematiche)', *ACCP*, 14: 27–142.
Ferrari, Anna, 1984. 'Linguaggi lirici in contatto: *trobadors* e *trobadores*', *BF*, 29 (*Homenagem a Manuel Rodrigues Lapa*, II): 35–58.
Ferrari, Anna, 1993. 'Lai', in Giulia Lanciani and Giuseppe Tavani (eds), *Dicionário da literatura medieval galega e portuguesa* (Lisbon: Caminho), pp. 374–8.
F[errario] de Orduna, Lilia E., 1992. 'Paradigma y variación en la literatura caballeresca castellana', in Lilia E. F[errario] de Orduna (ed.), *Amadís de Gaula. Estudios sobre narrativa caballeresca castellana en la primera mitad del siglo XVI*, Problemata literaria, 6 (Kassel: Reichenberger), pp. 189–212.
Ferreira, Jerusa Pires, 1993. *Cavalaria em cordel: o passo das águas mortas* (1979; 2nd edn, São Paulo: Hucitec).
Ferreira, Maria de Fátima Leitão Camilo dos Prazeres Cabaço, 2004. 'Entre Eva e Maria. As imagens do feminino no *Livro de José de Arimateia*' (unpublished doctoral thesis, Universidade de Lisboa).
Ferreira, Maria do Rosário, 1998. 'Outros mundos, outras fronteiras. Ramiro, Tristão e a divisão da Terra de Espanha', in *IV Jornadas Luso-Espanholas de Histórica Medieval. As relações de fronteira no século de Alcañices (1250–1350)* (Porto: Universidade do Porto). *Revista da Faculdade de Letras*, série II, 15/2: 1567–78.
Ferreira, Maria do Rosário, 2002a. 'À sombra de Tristão: Do potencial estruturante da *Matéria de Bretanha* na mundivisão aristocrática do Portugal medieval', in Leonor Curado Neves, Margarida Madureira and Teresa Amado (eds), *Matéria de Bretanha em Portugal. Actas do colóquio realizado em Lisboa nos dias 8 e 9 de Novembro de 2001* (Lisbon: Colibri), pp. 159–75.
Ferreira, Maria do Rosário, 2002b. 'Entre linhagens e imagens: a escrita do Conde de Barcelos', in Francisco Bautista Pérez and Jimena Gamba Corradine (eds), *Estudios sobre la Edad Media, el Renacimiento y la Temprana Modernidad* (San Millán de la Cogolla: Cilengua / Instituto Biblioteca Hispánica), pp. 159–67.
Ferreira, Maria do Rosário, 2011. 'A estratégia genealógica de D. Pedro, Conde de Barcelos, e as refundições do *Livro de Linhagens*', *e-Spania. Revue Interdisciplinaire d'Études Hispaniques Médiévales et Modernes*, 11: http://e-spania.revues.org/20273#ftn7 [consulted 26 April 2013].
Ferreira, Maria do Rosário, 2013. 'Entre la terre et la guerre: Salomon, Tristan et les mythes d'alternance dans l'Espagne de la «Reconquête»', *e-Spania. Revue Interdisciplinaire d'Études Hispaniques Médiévales et Modernes*, 16: http://e-spania.revues.org/22657 [consulted 4 January 2014].
Ferrer Gimeno, María Rosario, 2011. 'Presencia del ciclo artúrico en las bibliotecas bajomedievales de la ciudad de Valencia (1416–1474)', *RLM*, 23 (2011): 137–52.
Ferrer Valls, Teresa, 1991. *La práctica escénica cortesana: de la época del Emperador a la de Felipe III*, Tamesis: A. Monografías, 143 (London: Tamesis Books and Boydell & Brewer).
Ferreti, Regina Micheli, 1994. 'Viagem em demanda do Santo Graal: o sonho do heroísmo e do amor' (unpublished doctoral thesis, Universidade Federal de Rio de Janeiro).

Filgueira Valverde, José (trans.), 1985. Alfonso X el Sabio, *Cantigas de Santa María* (Madrid: Castalia).
Finazzi-Agrò, Ettore, 1978. *A novelística portuguesa do século XVI* (Lisbon: Instituto de Cultura Portuguesa, M.E.C., Secretaria de Estado da Cultura).
Flood, John L., 2013. '*Amadís* in Frankfurt', in Barry Taylor, Geoffrey West and Jane Whetnall (eds), *Text, Manuscript, and Print in Medieval and Modern Iberia: Studies in Honour of David Hook*, Spanish Series, 155 (New York: Hispanic Seminary of Medieval Studies, 2013), pp. 311–27.
Flor de caballerías (Manuscrito, Granada, 1599): *see* Barahona, Francisco, *Flor de caballerías*.
Flores, Juan de, 2003. *Grisel y Mirabella*, ed. Maria G. Ciccarello (Rome: Di Blasi).
Flores, Juan de, 2008. *Grimalte y Gradisa*, ed. Carmen Parrilla (Alcalá de Henares: CEC).
Flórez, Enrique: *see Anales Toledanos I*.
Flori, Jean, 1998. *Chevaliers et chevalerie au Moyen Âge* (Paris: Hachette).
Florisel de Niquea III, 1546. (Seville: Juan Cromberger, 1546): *see* Silva, Feliciano de, *Florisel de Niquea* (tercera parte).
Floriseo, 1516. (Valencia: Diego de Gumiel, 1516): *see* Bernal, Fernando, *Floriseo*.
Fogelquist, James Donald, 1982. *El Amadís y el género de la Historia Fingida*, Studia humanitatis (Madrid: Porrúa Turanzas).
Fossier, Robert, 1998. *La Edad Media. El despertar de Europa 950–1250* (Barcelona: Editorial Crítica).
Foti, Vittoria, 1990. 'L'*Amadigi* de Bernardo Tasso e l'*Amadís* de García Rodríguez de Montalvo', *Schifanoia*, 7: 179–91.
Frappier, Jean (ed.), 1954. *La mort le roi Artur. Roman du XIIIème siècle*, Textes littéraires français, 58 (Lille: Droz).
Fratel, Undira Maria de Oliveira, 2005. 'A significação do silêncio n'*A Demanda do Santo Graal* à luz dos aspectos semântico-pragmáticos: dizer é não dizer', *Filologia e Linguística Portuguesa*, 7: 49–63.
Freire Nunes, Irene (ed.), 1995a. *A Demanda do Santo Graal* (Lisbon: Imprensa Nacional–Casa da Moeda).
Freire Nunes, Irene, 1995b. 'Arthur Ibérique', *Pris-Ma. Revue d'Études Médiévales*, 11/2: 221–30.
Freire Nunes, Irene, 1999a. *Le graal ibérique et ses rapports avec la littérature française* (Villeneuve d'Ascq: Presses Universitaires du Septentrion).
Freire Nunes, Irene, 1999b. 'A *Demanda do Santo Graal*', in Heitor Megale and Haquira Osakabe (eds), *Textos medievais portugueses e as suas fontes* (São Paulo: Humanitas), pp. 77–99.
Freire Nunes, Irene, 2001a. 'O tempo mítico na literatura arturiana', in Paulo Meneses (ed.), *Sobre o tempo. Actas do III Colóquio da Secção Portuguesa da Associação Hispánica de Literatura Medieval* (Ponta Delgada: Universidade dos Açores), pp. 273–92.
Freire Nunes, Irene, 2001b. '*A Demanda do Santo Graal*', in Francisco Lyon de Castro (ed.), *História da Literatura Portuguesa*, 7 vols (Lisbon: Alfa, 2001–3), II, pp. 343–62.
Freire Nunes, Irene, 2002. 'Merlim, o elo ausente', in Leonor Curado Neves, Margarida Madureira and Teresa Amado (eds), *Matéria de Bretanha em Portugal. Actas do colóquio realizado em Lisboa nos dias 8 e 9 de Novembro de 2001* (Lisbon: Colibri), pp. 29–58.
Freire Nunes, Irene (ed.), 2005. *A Demanda do Santo Graal*, 2nd edn (Lisbon: Imprensa Nacional–Casa da Moeda; 1st edn 1995); also in *Corpus informatizado del portugués medieval* (CIPM): http://cipm.fcsh.unl.pt/corpus/edicao.jsp?id=1283.
Freire Nunes, Irene (ed.), 2007. *Horto do Esposo*, in *Horto do Esposo*, ed. Helder Godinho (Lisbon: Colibri): pp. 1–400.
Frontón, Miguel Ángel, 1989. 'La difusión del *Oliveros de Castilla*: apuntes para la historia editorial de una historia caballeresca', *Dicenda. Cuadernos de Filología Hispánica*, 8: 37–51.
Fuente del Pilar, José Javier, 1988. *Baladro del Sabio Merlín* (Madrid: Miraguano, 1988).
Furtado, Antonio L., 2001a. 'O "José de Arimatéia" da tradição portuguesa', *Filologia e Linguística Portuguesa*, 4: 159–67.
Furtado, Antonio L., 2001b. 'Formação de uma alegoria na *Demanda do Santo Graal*', *Revista Palavra*, 7: 56–67.

Gaibrois de Ballesteros, Mercedes, 1922. *Sancho IV de Castilla*, 3 vols (Madrid: Tipografía de la *Revista de Archivos y Bibliotecas*).

Gallardo, Bartolomé José, 1863. *Ensayo de una Biblioteca Española de libros raros y curiosos*, ed. M. R. Zarco del Valle and J. Sancho Rayón, 4 vols (Madrid: Imprenta y Estereotipia de M. Rivadeneyra; facsimile rpt, Madrid: Gredos, 1968).

Gallé Cejudo, Rafael Jesús, 2005. 'La écfrasis de Iseo en el *Tristán* castellano', *Cuadernos de filología clásica. Estudios griegos e indoeuropeo*, 15: 155–74.

Galvão, António, 1944. *Tratado dos descobrimentos*, ed. Visconde de Lagoa and Elaine Sanceau, Biblioteca Histórica de Portugal e Brasil, Série Ultramarina, I (Porto: Livraria Civilização).

García de Enterría, María de la Cruz, 1984. 'Pliegos y romances de *Amadís*', in Enrique Rodríguez-Cepeda (ed.), *Actas del Congreso Romancero-Cancionero. UCLA (1984)*, Ensayos, 2 vols (Madrid: Porrúa-Turanzas), I, pp.121–35.

García de Lucas, César, 1997. 'La materia de Bretaña del manuscrito 1877 de la Biblioteca Universitaria de Salamanca' (unpublished doctoral thesis, Universidad de Alcalá de Henares).

García de Salazar, Lope, 2000. *Libro XI de la Historia de las bienandanzas e fortunas*, ed. Consuelo Villacorta (Bilbao: Universidad del País Vasco).

García Marsilla, Juan Vicente, 1996–7. 'El poder visible. Demanda y funciones del arte en la corte de Alfonso el Magnánimo', *Ars Longa*, 7–8: 33–47.

Garcia Marsilla, Juan Vicente, 2001. 'La cort d'Alfons el Magnànim i l'univers artístic de la primera meitat del quatre-cents', *Seu Vella. Anuari d'Història i Cultura*, 3: 13–54.

García Morales, Justo, 1956–60. *Baladro del Sabio Merlín*, Madrid: Joyas Bibliográficas.

García-Sabell Tormo, Teresa, 1993. 'Sobre a traducción de textos literarios franceses na Idade Media: o capítulo 6 de *Erec*', in Aires A. Nascimento and Cristina Almeida Ribeiro (eds), *Literatura Medieval. Actas do IV Congresso da Associação Hispânica de Literatura Medieval (Lisboa, 1–5 Outubro 1991)*, 4 vols (Lisbon: Edições Cosmos), IV, pp. 315–24.

García-Sabell Tormo, Teresa, and Santiago López Martínez-Morás, 2002. 'Motifs et formules dans le roman en prose: l'*Erec* et sa traduction galicienne-portugaise', in *VII Coloquio Asociación de profesores de Filología Francesa de la Universidad Española (Cádiz, 11–13 de febrero de 1998)*, 2 vols (Cadiz: Universidad de Cádiz, Servicio de Publicaciones), II, pp. 121–31.

Gardner, Edmund G., 1971. *The Arthurian Legend in Italian Literature* (London: Dent 1930; rpt New York: Octagon Books).

Gargano, Antonio (ed.), 1981. Juan de Flores, *Triunfo de Amor*, Collana di Testi e Studi Ispanici, I: Testi critici, 2 (Pisa: Giardini).

Gaunt, Simon, and Ruth Harvey, 2006. 'The Arthurian Tradition in Occitan Literature', in Glyn S. Burgess and Karen Pratt (eds), *The Arthur of the French: The Arthurian Tradition in Medieval French and Occitan Literature*, ALMA, IV (Cardiff: UWP), pp. 528–45.

Gavetas: see *Torre do Tombo*.

Gerli, E. Michael, 1983. 'Calisto's Hawk and the Images of a Medieval Tradition', *Ro*, 104: 83–101.

Gil-Albarellos, Susana, 1999. *'Amadís de Gaula' y el género caballeresco en España*, Literatura, 46 (Valladolid: Universidad de Valladolid).

Gil de Gates, María Cristina, 1989. '*Don Tristán el Joven* y el discurso novelístico marginal como síntoma de una época de transición' (unpublished doctoral thesis, Universidad Nacional de Buenos Aires).

Gil de Gates, María Cristina, 1995. 'El humor como marca de lo diferente: a propósito de Miliana en *Tristán el Joven*', in R. Penna et al. (eds), *Studia Hispanica Medievalia III. Actas de las IV Jornadas Internacionales de Literatura Española Medieval* (Buenos Aires: Universidad Católica Argentina), pp. 242–6.

Gil de Gates, María Cristina, 1997. 'El humor como privilegio y el humor como estigma en *Tristán el Joven*', *Anclajes. Revista del Instituto de Análisis Semiótico del Discurso*, 1/1: 21–40.

Gili Gaya, Samuel, 1947. 'Las *Sergas de Esplandián* como crítica de la caballería bretona', *Boletín de la Biblioteca Menéndez Pelayo*, 23: 105–11.

Gillard, Julia, 2014. 'Game of Thrones and seats of power', *The Guardian*, 8 April: 5.
Gillet, Joseph E. (ed.), 1932. Micael de Carvajal, *Tragedia Josephina* (Princeton: Princeton University Press; Paris: PUF).
Gilman, Stephen, 1978. *La España de Fernando de Rojas* (Madrid: Taurus).
Gimber, Arno, 1996a. 'Tristan und Isoldes Kinder zu einer Fortsetzung des Tristan-Romans in der spanischen Renaissanceliteratur', in A. Crépin and Wolfgang Spiewok (eds), *Tristan-Tristrant: Mélanges en l'honneur de Danielle Buschinger à l'occasion de son 60ème anniversaire*, Wodan, 66 (Greifswald: Reineke), pp. 183–93.
Gimber, Arno, 1996b. 'Les Banquets dans les différentes versions du *Tristan* espagnol', in *Banquets et Manières de Table au Moyen Âge*, *Sénéfiance*, 38 (Aix-en-Provence: Centre Universitaire d'Études et de Recherches Médiévales), pp. 425–32.
Gimber, Arno, 2004. 'La continuación castellana del *Tristán de Leonís* de 1534 y su traducción italiana de 1555', in *Letteratura cavalleresca tra Italia e Spagna (da 'Orlando' al 'Quijote')*, ed. Pedro M. Cátedra, Javier Gómez-Montero and Bernhard König (Salamanca: SEMYR), pp. 415–28.
Giménez, Helio 1973. *Artificios y motivos en los libros de caballerías* (Montevideo: Géminis).
Gimeno Blay, Francisco, 2007. 'Entre el autor y el lector: producir libros manuscritos en catalán (siglos XII–XIV)', *AEM*, 37/1: 305–66.
Gimeno Casalduero, Joaquín, 1971. 'La profecía medieval en la literatura castellana y su relación con las corrientes proféticas europeas', *NRFH*, 20: 64–89.
Gimeno Casalduero, Joaquín, 1975. *Estructura y diseño en la literatura castellana medieval* (Madrid: José Porrúa Turanzas).
Godinho, Helder, 1996. 'O desconhecimento da origem e a procura da identidade', *Revista da Faculdade de Ciências Sociais e Humanas*, 9: 223–31.
Godinho, Helder, 1997. 'A viagem ao passado', in Ettore Finazzi-Agrò (ed.), *Per via. Miscellanea di studi in onore di Giuseppe Tavani* (Rome: Bulzoni), pp. 101–16.
Gomes, Aleixo, 1978. *Estudos literarios: o tema da Besta Ladrador na 'Demanda do Santo Graal'* (Lisbon: Macário).
Gómez-Montero, Javier, 1992. *Literatura caballeresca en España e Italia (1483–1542). El 'Espejo de cavallerías' (Deconstrucción textual y creación literaria)*, Beihefte zur *Iberoromania*, 9 (Tübingen: Max Niemeyer Verlag).
Gómez Redondo, Fernando, 1988. 'Carta de Iseo y respuesta de Tristán', *Dicenda: Cuadernos de Filología Hispánica*, 7 (*Arcadia: estudios y textos dedicados a Francisco López Estrada*, ed. Ángel Gómez Moreno, Javier Huerta Calvo and Víctor Infantes): 327–56.
Gómez Redondo, Fernando, 1998–2007. *Historia de la prosa medieval castellana*, 4 vols, Crítica y estudios literarios (Madrid: Cátedra).
Gómez Redondo, Fernando, 2002. '*Crónica de Alfonso XI*', in Carlos Alvar and José Manuel Lucía Megías (eds), *Diccionario filológico de literatura medieval española* (Madrid: Castalia), pp. 278–84.
Gonçalves, Elsa, 1976. 'La *Tavola Colocciana. Autori portughesi*', *ACCP*, 10: 387–448.
Gonçalves, Francisco de Souza, 2011. '*Magis movent exempla quam verba* – As pecadoras, os cavaleiros e uma retórica de condenação do feminino em *A Demanda do Santo Graal*', *E-Scrita. Revista do Curso de Letras da UNIABEU*, 2/6: 144–57.
Gonçalves, Susana, 2001. 'Representações do espaço insular e do espaço onírico no *Livro de José de Arimateia*', *Românica. Revista de Literatura*, 10: 53–65.
Gonçalves, Susana, 2002. 'Estória do Rei Label – estudo de um episódio do *Livro de José de Arimateia*', in Leonor Curado Neves, Margarida Madureira and Teresa Amado (eds), *Matéria de Bretanha em Portugal. Actas do colóquio realizado em Lisboa nos dias 8 e 9 de Novembro de 2001* (Lisbon: Colibri), pp. 93–103.
Gonçalves, Susana, 2003. 'A Aventura Onírica no *Livro de José de Arimateia*. Versão Portuguesa da *Estoire del Saint Graal*' (unpublished doctoral thesis, Universidade de Lisboa).
González Cuenca, Joaquín (ed.), 2004. Hernando del Castillo, *Cancionero general*, 5 vols, Nueva biblioteca de erudición y crítica, 25 (Madrid: Castalia).

González Jiménez, Manuel, 2004. *Alfonso X el Sabio* (Barcelona: Ariel).
Gonzalo Sánchez-Molero, José Luis, 2005. *Regia Bibliotheca. El libro en la corte española de Carlos V* (Mérida: Editora Regional de Extremadura).
Goodman, Jennifer R., 1992. 'European Chivalry in the 1490s', *Comparative Civilizations Review*, 26: 43–72.
Gouiran, Gérard (ed.), 1987. *Le seigneur-troubadour d'Hautefort: l'oeuvre de Bertran de Born* (Aix-en-Provence: Université de Provence).
Gracia, Paloma, 1991. *Las señales del destino heroico*, Héroes y dioses, 4 (Barcelona: Montesinos).
Gracia, Paloma, 1992. 'Tradición heroica y eremítica en el origen de Esplandián', *RFE*, 72: 133–48.
Gracia, Paloma, 1993. 'Variaciones sobre un tema mítico: Edipo en la *Demanda do Santo Graal*', *CuN*, 53: 197–214.
Gracia, Paloma, 1995. 'Sobre la tradición de los autómatas en la Ínsola Firme. Materia antigua y materia artúrica en el *Amadís de Gaula*', *RLM*, 7: 119–35.
Gracia, Paloma, 1996. 'El ciclo de la *Post-Vulgata* artúrica y sus versiones hispánicas', *Voz y Letra*, 7/1: 5–15.
Gracia, Paloma, 1998. 'Editar la *Demanda del Sancto Grial* en el marco textual de la *Post-Vulgata Queste* y *Mort Artu*: algunas consideraciones previas y una propuesta de edición', in Carmen Parrilla, Begoña Campos, Mar Campos, Antonio Chas, Mercedes Pampín and Nieves Pena (eds), *Edición y anotación de textos. Actas del I Congreso de Jóvenes Filólogos (A Coruña, 25–28 de septiembre de 1996)*, 2 vols (A Coruña: Universidade da Coruña), I, pp. 315–21.
Gracia, Paloma, 1999. 'Sobre el espíritu del primer *Amadís de Gaula*', *RLM*, 11: 247–53.
Gracia, Paloma, 2002. 'El *Amadís de Gaula* entre la tradición y la modernidad: Briolanja en la Ínsola Firme', in María Sánchez, Eva B. Carro and Laura Puerto (eds), *Libros de caballerías (del 'Amadís' al 'Quijote'). Poética, lectura, representación e identidad* (Salamanca: Seminario de Estudios Medievales y Renacentistas), pp. 135–46.
Gracia, Paloma, 2007. 'Los *Merlines* castellanos a la luz de su modelo subyacente: la *Estoria de Merlín* del ms. 1877 de la Biblioteca Universitaria de Salamanca', in Juan Manuel Cacho Blecua (ed.), *De la literatura caballeresca al 'Quijote'* (Zaragoza: Prensas Universitarias de Zaragoza), pp. 233–48.
Gracia, Paloma, 2009. 'La restitución como objetivo y el problema de los leonesismos en los *Spanish Grail Fragments* editados por Karl Pietsch', in *Actas de las IX Jornadas Internacionales de Literatura Española Medieval y homenaje al quinto centenario de 'Amadís de Gaula'* (Buenos Aires: Pontificia Universidad Católica Argentina), *Letras. Revista de la Facultad de Filosofía y Letras de la Pontificia Universidad Católica Argentina Santa María de Buenos Aires*, 59–60/1 (Studia Hispanica Medievalia, VIII, 1): 189–97.
Gracia, Paloma, 2010a. 'El pasaje de la concepción de la Bestia Ladradora en el *Baladro del sabio Merlín* (1498 y 1535), testimonio de una *Demanda del santo Grial* primigenia', *eHumanista*, 16: 184–94.
Gracia, Paloma, 2010b. '*Baladro del sabio Merlín* (Sevilla, 1535): una edición en marcha', in Francisco Bautista Pérez and Jimena Gamba Corradine (eds), *Estudios sobre la Edad Media, el Renacimiento y la temprana modernidad* (San Millán de la Cogolla: Cilengua), pp. 607–12.
Gracia, Paloma, 2011. 'La *Estoria de Merlín* en los *Spanish Grail Fragments* de Karl Pietsch: el valor de la reescritura y la metodología de la edición de textos medievales derivados de traducciones', *BHS*, 88: 879–91.
Gracia, Paloma, 2012. 'Avatares ibéricos del ciclo artúrico de la *Post-Vulgate*: el título del *Baladro del sabio Merlín con sus profecías* (Burgos, 1498) y la colección profética derivada de la *Historia Regum Britanniae*', *ZrP*, 128: 507–21.
Gracia, Paloma, 2013a. 'Reescritura celestinesca de un episodio del *Baladro del sabio Merlín*: prostitución y libertad en el incunable publicado en Burgos, 1498', *RLM*, 25: 87–102.
Gracia, Paloma, 2013b. 'El "sueño de Merlín" y los episodios novedosos de los *Baladros* impresos en 1498 y 1535 respecto a la *Suite du Merlin Post-Vulgate* conservada', *e-Spania. Revue Interdisciplinaire*

d'*Études Hispaniques Médiévales et Modernes*, 16: http://e-spania.revues.org/22728 [consulted 4 January 2014].

Graf, Arturo, 1892–3. 'Artù nell'Etna', in *Miti, leggende e superstizioni del Medio Evo*, 2 vols (Torino: E. Loescher), II, pp. 303–25.

Grimbert, Joan Tasker, 2009. 'The "Matter of Britain" on the Continent and the Lay of Tristan and Iseult in France, Italy, and Spain', in Helen Fulton (ed.), *Companion to Arthurian Literature* (rpt 2012; Malden, MA, and Oxford: Wiley-Blackwell), pp. 145–59.

Gran Conquista de Ultramar, La, 1919. Ed. Louis Cooper. 4 vols (Bogotá: Instituto Caro y Cuervo).

Guadalajara, José, 1996, *Las profecías del Anticristo en la Edad Media* (Madrid: Gredos).

Guardiola, Conrado, 1988. 'La mención del *Amadís* en el *Regimiento de príncipes*, aclarada', in Vicente Beltrán (ed.), *Actas del I Congreso de la Asociación Hispánica de Literatura Medieval (Santiago de Compostela, 2 al 6 de diciembre de 1985)* (Barcelona: PPU), pp. 337–45.

Gudayol, A. M., 1990. 'Arturo, Morgana y la sierpe. Algunas anotaciones sobre las intervenciones en francés en *La Faula* de Guillem de Torroella', *Parole. Revista de Creación Literaria y de Filología*, 3: 93–8.

Guincho, Maria dos Anjos, 1996. '*A Demanda do Santo Graal* et la religiosité médiévale portugaise', in *Die Ritterorden im Mittelalters / Les Ordres Militaires au Moyen Âge. VII Jahrestagung der Reineke-Gesellschaft (Rhodos, 21.05—28.05.1995) / 7ème Congrès Annuel de la Société Reineke (Rhodos, 21.05–28.05.1995)* (Greifswald: Reineke), pp. 83–96.

Gutiérrez García, Santiago, 1998. 'A corte poética de Afonso III o Bolonhês e a materia de Bretaña', in Derek W. Flitter and Patricia Odber de Baubeta (eds), *Ondas do Mar de Vigo. Actas do Simposio Internacional sobre a Lírica Medieval Galego-Portuguesa* (Birmingham: University of Birmingham), pp. 108–23.

Gutiérrez García, Santiago, 1999. *Merlín y su historia* (Madrid: Alianza Editorial).

Gutiérrez García, Santiago, 2000–1. 'O Cabaleiro das Dúas Espadas e a recepción da materia de Bretaña na Península Ibérica', *Revista de Lenguas y Literaturas Catalana, Gallega y Vasca*, 7: 235–46.

Gutiérrez García, Santiago, 2001. '*O Marot haja mal-grado*: lais de Bretanha, ciclos en prosa e recepción da materia de Bretaña na Península Ibérica', *BGL*, 25: 35–49.

Gutiérrez García, Santiago, 2003a. *A fada Morgana* (Santiago de Compostela: Lea).

Gutiérrez García, Santiago, 2003b. 'Personajes históricos y literarios y casuística amorosa en la lírica provenzal', *RFR*, 20: 103–19.

Gutiérrez García, Santiago, 2007a. 'La poética compositiva de los *lais de Bretanha*: *Amor, des que m'á vos cheguei* y los lais anómalos de la *Post-Vulgata*', in *RPM*, 19: 93–113.

Gutiérrez García, Santiago, 2007b. 'La recepción hispánica de la materia de Bretaña y la cantiga *B*479 / *V*62 de Alfonso X', in Armando López Castro and María Luzdivina Cuesta Torre (eds), *Actas del XI Congreso Internacional de la Asociación Hispánica de Literatura Medieval (León, 20 a 24 de septiembre de 2005)*, 2 vols (León: Universidad de León), II: 661–71.

Gutierrez Garcia, Santiago, 2007–08. 'En torno al caballero encantador de Jaufré y sus posibles modelos no artúricos', *Estudios Románicos*, 16–17: 503–14.

Gutiérrez García, Santiago, 2013. 'Caballería y poder en la literatura artúrica hispánica de fines del siglo XV y principios del XVI', *e-Spania. Revue Interdisciplinaire d'Études Hispaniques Médiévales et Modernes*, 16: http://e-spania.revues.org/22738 [consulted 4 January 2013].

Gutiérrez García, Santiago, and Pilar Lorenzo Gradín, 2001. *A literatura artúrica en Galicia e Portugal na Idade Media*, Biblioteca de Divulgación, Serie Galicia, 25 (Santiago de Compostela: Universidade de Santiago de Compostela).

Gwara, Joseph J., 1997. 'Another Work by Juan de Flores: *La coronación de la señora Gracisla*', in J. J. Gwara and E. M. Gerli (eds), *Studies on the Spanish Sentimental Romance (1440–1550)* (London: Tamesis Books), pp. 75–110.

Haebler, Konrad, 1903–17. *Bibliografía ibérica del siglo XV*, 2 vols (The Hague: Nijhoff; Leipzig: Hiersemann; facsímile rpt, Madrid: Julio Ollero, 1992).

Haidu, Peter, 1968. *Aesthetic Distance in Chrétien de Troyes: Irony and Comedy in 'Cligès' and 'Perceval'* (Geneva: Droz).

Hall, J. B., 1974. '*Tablante de Ricamonte* and Other Castilian Versions of Arthurian Romances', *RLC*, 48: 177–89

Hall, J. B., 1982. 'La matière arthurienne espagnole. The Ethos of the French Post-Vulgate *Roman du Graal* and the Castilian *Baladro del sabio Merlín* and *Demanda del Sancto Grial*', *RLC*, 56: 423–36.

Hampe Martínez, Teodoro, 1986. 'Libros profanos y sagrados en la biblioteca del tesorero Antonio Dávalos (1582)', *Revista de Indias*, 46 (1986): 385–402; rpt in *Bibliotecas privadas en el mundo colonial. La difusión de libros e ideas en el virreinato del Perú (siglos XVI–XVII)*, Textos y Estudios Coloniales y de la Independencia, 1 (Frankfurt am Main: Verveurt; Madrid: Iberoamericana, 1996), pp. 118–25, 243–49.

Harney, Michael, 2003. 'The Spanish Lancelot-Grail heritage', in Carol Dover (ed.), *A Companion to the Lancelot-Grail Cycle* (Cambridge: D. S. Brewer), pp. 185–94.

Hauf i Valls, Albert-Guillem, 1990a. 'Artur a Constantinoble. Entorn a un curiós episodi del *Tirant lo Blanc*', *L'Aiguadolç*, 12–13: 13–31.

Hauf, Albert-Guillem, 1990b. 'Introducció a *Lo Crestià*', in *D'Eiximenis a sor Isabel de Villena. Aportació a l'estudi de la nostra cultura medieval*, Biblioteca Sanchis Guarner, 19 (Barcelona: Abadia de Montserrat, and Institut de Filologia Valenciana), pp. 59–123.

Hauf, Albert-Guillem, 2000. '"Artús, aycell qui atendon li bretó?" *La Faula*, seducció o reivindicació políticomoral?', *Bolletí de la Societat Arqueològica Lul·liana*, 56: 7–24.

Heijkant, Marie José, 1989. *La tradizione del 'Tristan' in prosa in Italia e proposte di studio sul 'Tristano Riccardiano'* (Nijmegen: Katholieke Universiteit te Nijmegen).

Heijkant, Marie-José (ed.), 1991. *Tristano Riccardiano*, testo critico di E.G.Parodi (Parma: Pratiche Editrice).

Heijkant, Marie-José (ed.), 1997. *La Tavola Ritonda*, testo critico di F. L. Polidori (Milan and Trento: Luni).

Heijkant, Marie-José, 2004. Review of 'Enrique Andrés Ros Domingo, *Arthurische Literatur der Romania: die iberoromanischen Fassungen des Tristanromans und ihre Beziehungen zu den französischen und italienischen Versionen*, Bern, Peter Lang, 2001', *Estudis Romànics*, 26: 384–9.

Herculano, Alexandre (ed.), 1856. *Livros de linhagens*, in *Portugaliae Monumenta Historica* (Lisbon: Imprensa Nacional – Casa da Moeda).

Hernández González, María Isabel, 1998. 'Suma de inventarios de bibliotecas del siglo XVI (1501–1560)', in Pedro M. Cátedra, María Luisa López Vidriero and María Isabel Hernández González (eds), *El libro antiguo español*, IV: *Coleccionismo y Bibliotecas (Siglos XV–XVIII)* (Salamanca: Universidad de Salamanca; Madrid: Patrimonio Nacional and Sociedad Española de Historia del Libro), pp. 375–446.

Hernández, María Isabel (ed.), 1999. *El baladro del sabio Merlín con sus profecías*, with preliminary studies by Ramón Rodríguez Álvarez, Pedro M. Cátedra and Jesús D. Rodríguez Velasco, 2 vols (Gijón: Trea).

Hillgarth, J. N., 1976–8. *The Spanish Kingdoms 1250–1516*, 2 vols (Oxford: Clarendon Press).

Hook, David, 1986. '*L'Estoire del Saint Graal*, fuente de un episodio de *La Estoria del Noble Vaspasiano*', in *Estudios en Homenaje a Don Claudio Sánchez Albornoz en sus 90 años*, Anejos *Cuadernos de Historia de España*, 4 vols (Buenos Aires: Universidad de Buenos Aires, Facultad de Filosofía y Letras, and Instituto de Historia de España, 1986), IV, pp. 491–503.

Hook, David, 1990–1. '*Domnus Artux*: Arthurian Nomenclature in 13th-c. Burgos', *RPh*, 44: 162–4.

Hook, David, 1991. *The Earliest Arthurian Names in Spain and Portugal*, Fontaine Notre Dame, I (St Albans: David Hook).

Hook, David, 1992. 'Some questions concerning the status of the Portuguese *Estoria do muy nobre Vespesiano emperador de Roma*', in Helder Macedo (ed.), *Studies in Portuguese Literature and History in Honour of Luis de Sousa Rebelo* (London: Tamesis), pp. 29–45.

Hook, David, 1992–3a. 'Further Early Arthurian Names from Spain', *LC*, 21/2: 23–33.
Hook, David, 1992–3b. '"Espladian" (Logroño, 1294) and the *Amadís* Question', *JHR*, 1: 273–4.
Hook, David 1993. 'Transilluminating Tristan', *Celestinesca*, 17/2 (otoño 1993): 53–84.
Hook, David, 1996. 'Esbozo de un catálogo cumulativo de los nombres artúricos peninsulares anteriores a 1300', *Atalaya. Revue Française d'Études Médiévales Hispaniques*, 7: 135–52.
Hook, David, 2000. *The Destruction of Jerusalem: Catalan and Castilian Texts*, KCLMS, XVI (London: King's College London Centre for Late Antique and Medieval Studies).
Hook, David, 2002. 'Fuentes para la reconstrucción de una comunidad: problemas y posibilidades de la documentación ayamontina del s. XVI. El caso del librero Alfonso Fernández', in Enrique R. Arroyo Berrones (ed.), *VI Jornadas de Historia de Ayamonte* (Ayamonte: Patronato Municipal de Cultura), pp. 101–23.
Hook, David, 2004. 'Arthurian ancestry: legend and lineage in a Portuguese antiquarian manuscript', in Margarida Calafate Ribeiro, Teresa Cristina Cerdeira, Juliet Perkins and Phillip Rothwell (eds), *A Primavera toda para ti. Homenagem a Helder Macedo. A Tribute to Helder Macedo* (Lisbon: Editorial Presença), pp. 62–7.
Huet, Charlotte, 2006. 'Brève étude comparée du devenir et de la circulation d'un texte populaire: l'histoire de Jaufré, son évolution en Espagne et France', *Culturas populares. Revista electrónica*, núm. 1 (2006), *http://www.culturaspopulares.org/textos%20I-1/articulos/Huet.pdf* [consulted 20 November 2012].
Hutchinson, Amélia P., 1984. 'European Relations of Portuguese Arthurian Literature' (unpublished doctoral thesis, University of Manchester) .
Hutchinson, Amélia P., 1988. 'As Relações Luso-Britânicas e o Desenvolvimento da Literatura Arturiana em Portugal', in Manuel Gomes da Torre (ed.), *Actas do Colóquio Comemorativo do VI Centenário do Tratado de Windsor* (Porto: Universidade do Porto), pp. 275–88.
Hutchinson, Amélia P., 1995. 'Nun'Alvares Pereira: a Portuguese hero in the Arthurian mould', in Thomas F. Earle and Nigel Griffin (eds), *Portuguese, Brazilian, and African Studies: Studies Presented to Clive Willis on His Retirement* (Warminster: Aris & Phillips), pp. 55–68.
Hutchinson, Amélia P., 2004. 'Reading between the lines: a vision of the Arthurian world reflected in Galician-Portuguese poetry', in Bonnie Wheeler (ed.), *Arthurian Studies in Honour of P. J. C. Field*, Arthurian Studies, 57 (Cambridge: D. S. Brewer), pp. 117–31.
Hutchinson, Amélia P., 2007. '"Os Doze de Inglaterra": a romance of Anglo-Portuguese relations in the latter Middle Ages?', in María Bullón-Fernández (ed.), *England and Iberia in the Middle Ages, 12th–15th Century: Cultural, Literary, and Political Exchanges* (New York: Palgrave Macmillan), pp. 167–87.
Infantes, Víctor, 1988–9. 'La prosa de ficción renacentista: entre los *géneros* literarios y el *género* editorial', *JHP*, 13: 115–24.
Infantes, Víctor, 1999. 'Aquí comiença la historia del libro llamado Amadís de Gaula', in *Los quatro libros del Uirtuoso cauallero Amadís de Gaula*, Singular (Madrid: Instituto de España), pp. 7–15.
Iragui, Sebastian, 1995. *Les Adaptations ibériques du 'Tristan en prose'* (Lille: Atelier National de Reproduction de Thèse de l'Université de Lille III). (Doctoral thesis, Université de Paris IV-Sorbonne; microfiche published 1996).
Iragui, Sebastian, 1996. 'The Southern Version of the *Prose Tristan*: The Italo-Iberian Translations and their French Source', *Tristania*, 17: 39–54.
Izquierdo, Josep, 2003. 'Traslladar la memòria, traduir el món: la prosa de Ramon Muntaner en el context cultural i literari romànic', *Quaderns de Filologia. Estudis Literaris*, 8: 189–244.
Jaufré: see Espadaler 2002; Gaunt and Harvey 2006: 534–41; Lee 2000, 2003; Remy 1959.
Jones, Kirkland C., 1974. 'The Relationship between the Versions of Arthur's Last Battle as they Appear in Malory and in the *Libro de las Generaciones*', *BBIAS*, 26: 197–205.
Juárez Blanquer, Aurora, and Antonio Rubio Flores, 1991. *Partida Segunda de Alfonso X el Sabio: manuscrito 12794 de la B. N.* (Granada: Imprendisur).

Junqueira, Renata Soares, 1996. 'O triste destino de Tristão na versão portuguesa d'*A Demanda do Santo Graal*', in M. H. R. Cunha, Lênia Márcia Mongelli, L. M. Vieira, Y. F. Franchetti, C. A. Iannone and M. V. Z. Gobbi (eds), *Atas do I Encontro Internacional de Estudos Medievais* (São Paulo: Humanitas), pp. 349–57.

Kassam, Ashifa, 2014. 'Swords and Superfans: Game of Thrones Invades Osuna', *The Guardian*, 3 November.

Kasten, Lloyd, 1970. 'The Utilization of the *Historia Regum Britanniae* by Alfonso X', *HR*, 38/5 (*Studies in Memory of Ramón Menéndez Pidal*): 97–114.

Keen, Maurice, 2005. *Chivalry* (New Haven: Yale University Press).

Kennedy, Edward D., 1970. 'Arthur's Rescue in Malory and the Spanish Tristan', *Notes and Queries*, N.S., 17: 6–10.

Kennedy, Elspeth (ed.), 1980. *Lancelot do Lac: The Non-Cyclic Old French Romance*, 2 vols (Oxford: Clarendon Press).

Kennedy, Elspeth, 1986. *Lancelot and the Grail: A Study of the Prose Lancelot* (Oxford: Clarendon Press).

Kennedy, Elspeth (†), 2006, ed., Michelle Szkilnik, Rupert T. Pickens, Karen Pratt and Andrea M. L. Williams, 2006. 'Lancelot with and without the Grail: *Landelot do Lac* and the Vulgate cycle', in *The Arthur of the French: The Arthurian Legend in Medieval French and Occitan Literature*, ed. Glyn S. Burgess and Karen Pratt, ALMA, IV (Cardiff: UWP), pp. 274–324.

Klob, Otto, 1900–1. 'Dois episódios da *Demanda do Santo Graal*', *RL*, 6: 332–46.

Klob, Otto, 1902. 'Beiträge zur Kenntnis der spanischen und portugiesischen Gral-Litteratur', *ZrP*, 26: 169–205.

Kurtz, Julia, 1986–7. 'The Multiple Endings of *Ferido está don Tristán*: Triumph of the Flesh or the Spirit', *Tristania*, 12/1–2: 25–43.

Lacy, Norris J. (ed.), 1996. *The New Arthurian Encyclopedia* (New York–London: Garland).

Lagares Díez, Xoán Carlos, 2000. *E por esto fez este cantar. Sobre as rúbricas explicativas dos cancioneiros profanos galego-portugueses* (Santiago de Compostela: Laiovento).

Lançarote, 1924–5. [Biblioteca Universidad de Salamanca, MS 1877], ed. K. Pietsch, *Spanish Grail Fragments*, 2 vols (Chicago: University of Chicago Press).

Lanciani, Giulia, and Giuseppe Tavani, 1995. *As cantigas de escarnio* (Vigo: Edicións Xerais).

Lang, H[enry] R., 1892. 'Textverbesserungen zur *Demanda do Santo Graal*', *ZRP*, 16: 217–22.

Lang, Henry R., 2010. *Cancioneiro d'el rei Dom Denis e estudos dispersos*, ed. L. M. Mongelli and Y. Frateschi Vieira (Niterói, Rio de Janeiro: UFF).

Lanzarote, 2006: *Lanzarote del Lago* [MS BNE 9611], ed. A. Contreras Martín and H. L. Sharrer (Alcalá de Henares: CEC).

Lapa, Manuel Rodrigues, 1929–30. 'A *Demanda do Santo Graal*. Prioridade do texto português' (Lisbon). *A Língua Portuguesa*, 1: 266–79, 305–16; rpt in *Miscelânea de língua e literatura portuguesa medieval*, Acta Universitatis Coimbrigensis (Coimbra: Universidade de Coimbra, 1982), pp. 303–40 [=1982a].

Lapa, Manuel Rodrigues, 1948. 'Augusto Magne, *A Demanda do Santo Graal*', *NRFH*, 2: 285–9; rpt in *Miscelânea de língua e literatura portuguesa medieval*, Acta Universitatis Coimbrigensis (Coimbra: Universidade de Coimbra, 1982), pp. 355–63 [= 1982c].

Lapa, Manuel Rodrigues, 1970a. *Cantigas d'escarnho e maldizer dos cancioneiros medievais galego-portugueses* (Vigo: Galaxia).

Lapa, Manuel Rodrigues, 1970b. 'A questão do *Amadis de Gaula* no contexto peninsular', *Grial*, 27: 14–28.

Lapa, Manuel Rodrigues, 1970c. *Lições de literatura portuguesa. Época medieval* (Coimbra: Coimbra Editora).

Lapa, Manuel Rodrigues, 1982a: see Lapa 1929–30.

Lapa, Manuel Rodrigues, 1982b. 'Em torno da "Demanda do Santo Graal". Reparos a uma crítica', in *Miscelânea de Língua e Literatura Portuguesa Medieval* (Coimbra: Universidade de Coimbra), pp. 341–53; rpt from *A Lingua Portuguesa*, 2 (1931): 286–96.

Lapa, Manuel Rodrigues, 1982c.: *see* Lapa 1948.
Lapesa, Rafael, 1956, 'El lenguaje del "Amadís" manuscrito', in Rodríguez-Moñino, Antonio, with studies by Rafael Lapesa and Agustín Millares Carlo, 'El primer manuscrito de *Amadís de Gaula* (noticia bibliográfica)', *BRAE*, 36: 199–225, at pp. 219–25.
Lapesa, Rafael, 1980. *Historia de la lengua española*, 8th edn (1st edn 1942; Madrid: Gredos).
Laranjinha, Ana Sofia, 1997. 'Um microcosmos textual? O episódio do Pentecostês do Graal na *Demanda portuguesa*', in Cristina Almeida Ribeiro and Margarida Madureira (eds), *O género do texto medieval. Actas do colóquio organizado pela Secção Portuguesa da Associação Hispânica de Literatura Medieval* (Lisbon: Cosmos), pp. 85–96.
Laranjinha, Ana Sofia, 2007–8. 'A fonte e os pecados de Artur: da *Suite du Merlin* à *Demanda do Santo Graal*', *GUARECER on-line. Seminário Medieval*: http://seminariomedieval.com/guarecer/sm0809/IsabelNET%20definitivo%20_23.3.2008_%5B1%5D.pdf [consulted 12 February 2014].
Laranjinha, Ana Sofia, 2009. 'Outro, o passado e a desordem: a *Besta Ladrador* e o paganismo na *Demanda do Santo Graal*', in Jesús Cañas Murillo, Francisco Javier Grande Quejigo and José Roso Díaz (eds), *Medievalismo en Extremadura. Estudios sobre Literatura y Cultura Hispánicas de la Edad Media* (Cáceres: Universidad de Extremadura), pp. 1077–84.
Laranjinha, Ana Sofia, 2010a. *Artur, Tristão e o Graal. A escrita romanesca no ciclo do Pseudo-Boron* (Porto: Estratégias Criativas).
Laranjinha, Ana Sofia, 2010b. 'A história de Erec entre a *Folie Lancelot* e a *Demanda do Santo Graal*: vítimas inocentes de cavaleiros virtuosos, ou uma visão pessimista da cavalaria', in José Manuel Fradejas Rueda, Deborah Anne Dietrick, María Jesús Díez Garretas and Demetrio Martín Sanz (eds), *Actas del XIII Congreso Internacional de la Asociación Hispánica de Literatura Medieval (Valladolid, 15 al 19 de septiembre de 2009). In memoriam Alan Deyermond*, 2 vols (Valladolid: Universidad de Valladolid, Ayuntamiento de Valladolid, and AHLM), II, pp. 1097–1106.
Laranjinha, Ana Sofia, 2011a. 'Linhagens arturianas na Península Ibérica: o tempo das origens', *e-Spania. Revue Interdisciplinaire d'Études Hispaniques Médiévales et Modernes*, 11: http://e-spania.revues.org/20317 [consulted 2 December 2012].
Laranjinha, Ana Sofia, 2011b. 'Le chevalier désobéissant dans la littérature arthurienne: modèle ou repoussoir?', *CEHM*, 34: 113–28.
Laranjinha, Ana Sofia, 2012. 'A matéria tristaniana do ciclo do Pseudo-Boron, da *Suite du Merlin* à *Demanda do Santo Graal*', in Lênia Márcia Mongelli (ed.), *De cavaleiros e cavalarias. Por terras de Europa e Américas* (São Paulo: Humanitas), pp. 101–9.
Laranjinha, Ana Sofia, 2013. 'O *Livro de Tristan* e o *Livro de Merlin* segundo Lope García de Salazar: vestígios do ciclo do Pseudo-Boron em terras castelhanas', *e-Spania. Revue Interdisciplinaire d'Études Hispaniques Médiévales et Modernes*, 16: http://e-spania.revues.org/22753 [consulted 4 January 2014].
Las Casas, Fray Bartolomé de, 1967. *Apologética historia sumaria*, ed. Edmundo O'Gorman, 2 vols, Serie de historiadores y cronistas de Indias, I (Mexico City: Universidad Nacional Autónoma de México, Instituto de Investigaciones Históricas, 1967).
Lawrance, Jeremy N. H., 1979. *Un tratado de Alonso de Cartagena sobre la educación y los estudios literarios*, Publicaciones del Seminario de Literatura Medieval y Humanística (Bellaterra: Universidad Autónoma de Barcelona).
Lawrance, Jeremy N. H., 1984. 'Nueva luz sobre la biblioteca del Conde de Haro: inventario de 1455', *El Crotalón*, I: 1073–111.
Lawrance, Jeremy N. H. 1985. 'The Spread of Lay Literacy in Late Medieval Castile', *BHS*, 62: 79–94.
Le Gentil, Pierre, 1966. 'Pour l'interprétation de l'*Amadís*', in *Mélanges à la mémoire de Jean Sarrailh*, 2 vols (Paris: Centre de Recherches de l'Institut d'Études Hispaniques), II: 47–54.
Le Goff, Jacques, 1996. 'Los gestos del Purgatorio', in *Lo maravilloso y lo cotidiano en el Occidente medieval* (Barcelona: Gedisa), pp. 44–51.

Leal, Larissa do Socorro Martins, 2012. 'Um estudo sobre a *Demanda do Santo Graal*: gênero, ciclos, características e personagens', *Anthesis. Revista de Letras e Educação da Amazônia Sul-Ocidental*, 1/2: 303–12.

Lee, Charmaine, 2000. 'L'elogio del re d'Aragona nel *Jaufré*', in Margarita Freixas, Silvia Iriso and Laura Fernández (eds), *Actas del VIII Congreso Internacional de la Asociación Hispánica de Literatura Medieval (Santander, 22–26 de septiembre de 1999)*, 2 vols (Santander: Consejería de Cultura del Gobierno de Cantabria, Año Jubilar Lebaniego, and AHLM), I, pp. 1051–60.

Lee, Charmaine, 2003. 'I frammenti del *Jaufre* nei canzonieri lirici', in Fernando Sánchez Miret (ed.), *Actas del XXIII Congreso Internacional de lingüística y filología románica (Salamanca, 2001)*, 6 vols (Tübingen: Max Niemeyer Verlag), IV, pp. 135–47.

Lee, Charmaine, 2006. 'Artù mediterraneo: la testimonianza del *Libro del Cavallero Zifar*', in Margherita Lecco (ed.), *Materiali arturiani nelle letterature di Provenza, Spagna, Italia*, Studi e Ricerche, 49 (Alessandria: Edizioni dell'Orso), pp. 97–113.

Lendo Fuentes, Rosalba, 2003. *El proceso de reescritura de la novela artúrica francesa: la 'Suite du Merlin'* (Mexico City: Universidad Nacional Autónoma de México).

Leomarte, 1932. *Sumas de historia troyana*, ed. Agapito Rey (Madrid: Centro de Estudios Históricos).

Leonard, Irving A., 1949 [1992]. *Books of the Brave: Being an Account of Books and Men in the Spanish Conquest and Settlement of the Sixteenth-century New World*, introduction by Rolena Adorno (1949; revised edn, Berkeley: University of California Press, 1992).

Leonardi, L., 1996. 'Un nuovo frammento del *Roman de Tristan in prosa*', in Domenico de Robertis and Franco Gavazzeni (eds), *Operosa Parva: per Gianni Antonini* (Verona: Valdonega), pp. 9–24.

Liber regum, 1960. Louis Cooper, *El Liber Regum. Estudio lingüístico* (Zaragoza: Institución Fernando el Católico, 1960).

Libro de Alexandre, 2007, ed. Juan Casas Rigall (Madrid: Castalia).

Libro de Josep Abarimatia, 1924–5. [Biblioteca Universidad de Salamanca, MS 1877], ed. Karl Pietsch, *Spanish Grail Fragments*. 2 vols (Chicago: University of Chicago Press).

Libro del Cauallero Zifar (El libro del Cauallero de Dios), 1929, ed. Charles Philip Wagner (Ann Arbor: University of Michigan Press).

Lida, María Rosa, 1945. 'Notas para el texto del *Alexandre* y para las fuentes del *Fernán González*', *Revista de Filología Hispánica*, 7: 47–51.

Lida de Malkiel, María Rosa, 1952–3. 'El desenlace del *Amadís* primitivo', *RPh*, 6: 283–9; rpt in *Estudios de literatura española y comparada* (Buenos Aires: Losada, 1984), pp. 185–94.

Lida de Malkiel, María Rosa, 1954. 'Juan Rodríguez del Padrón: influencia', *NRFH*, 8: 1–38; rpt in *Estudios sobre la literatura española del siglo xv* (Madrid: José Porrúa Turanzas, 1978), pp. 106–14.

Lida de Malkiel, María Rosa, 1959. 'Arthurian literature in Spain and Portugal', in Roger Sherman Loomis (ed.), *Arthurian Literature in the Middle Ages. A Collaborative History* (Oxford: Clarendon Press), 406–18.

Lida de Malkiel, María Rosa, 1962. *La originalidad artística de la 'Celestina'* (Buenos Aires: EUDEBA).

Lida de Malkiel, María Rosa, 1966: see Lida de Malkiel 1984.

Lida de Malkiel, María Rosa, 1984. 'La literatura artúrica en España y Portugal', in *Estudios de literatura española y comparada* (Buenos Aires: Eudeba, 1966; Buenos Aires: Losada, 1984), pp. 134–48. (Spanish trans. of Lida de Malkiel 1959).

Lisuarte de Grecia, 1525 (Seville, Jacobo y Juan Cromberger, 1525): see Silva, Feliciano de, *Lisuarte de Grecia* (Libro VII de *Amadís de Gaula*).

Literatura popular em verso, 1961. *Literatura popular em verso. Catálogo*, I, Coleção de Textos da Língua Portuguesa Moderna, 4 (Rio de Janeiro: Ministério da Educação e Cultura, Casa de Rui Barbosa).

Little, William Thomas, 2002. 'Notas preliminares para unos textos subversivos de Garci Rodríguez de Montalvo, ¿converso?', *Dicenda. Cuadernos de filología hispánica*, 20: 157–96.

Llompart, Gabriel, 1986. 'La silla de Alfábia y la materia de Bretaña en la Mallorca de la Baja Edad Media', *Archivo Español de Arte*, 59/236: 353–62.
Llull, Ramon: *see* Soler.
Longobardi, Monica, 1987a. 'Un frammento della *Queste* della PostVulgata nell'archivio di Stato di Bologna', *SMV*, 33: 5–24.
Longobardi, Monica, 1987b. 'Frammenti di codici in antico francese dalla Biblioteca Comunale di Imola', *CuN*, 47: 223–55.
Longobardi, Monica, 1992. 'Nuovi frammenti della *Post-Vulgate*: la *Suite*, la *Continuazione* della *Suite du Merlin*, la *Queste* e la *Mort Artu* (con l'intrusione del *Guiron*)', *SMV*, 38: 119–35.
Loomis, Roger Sherman (ed.), 1959a. *Arthurian Literature in the Middle Ages: A Collaborative History* (Oxford: Clarendon Press; reprints 1969, 1974).
Loomis, Roger Sherman, 1959b. 'Morgain la Fée in Oral Tradition', *Ro*, LXXX: 337–67.
Loomis, Roger Sherman, and Laura H. Loomis, 1938. *Arthurian Legends in Medieval Art* (London: Oxford University Press; New York: Modern Languages Association).
López de Ayala, Pero, 1987. *Rimado de Palacio*, ed. Germán Orduña (Madrid: Castalia).
López de Ayala, Pero, 1991. *Crónicas*, ed. José L. Martín (Barcelona: Planeta).
López de Gómara, Francisco, 1979. *La conquista de México*, ed. Jorge Gurría Lacroix (Caracas: Ayacucho).
López de Mendoza, Iñigo, Marqués de Santillana. 1988. *Obras completas*, ed. Angel Gómez Moreno and Maxim P. A. M. Kerkhof (Barcelona: Planeta).
López Estrada, Francisco, 1984. *Las poéticas castellanas de la Edad Media* (Madrid: Taurus).
López Martínez-Morás, Santiago, 1999. 'Apuntes sobre o *Livro de Tristán* galego', in Rosario Álvarez and Dolores Vilavedra (eds), *Cinguidos por unha arela común. Homenaxe ó profesor Xesús Alonso Montero*, 2 vols (Santiago de Compostela: Universidade de Santiago de Compostela), II, pp. 845–59.
López Sangil, José Luis, 2005. *A nobreza medieval galega. A familia Froilaz-Traba* (Noia: Toxosoutos).
Lorenzo Gradín, Pilar, 2005. 'A ignominia dunha carreta. Lanzarote e o coteife afonsí', in Ana Isabel Boullón Agrelo, Xosé Luís Couceiro and Francisco Fernández Rei (eds), *As tebras alumeadas. Estudos filolóxicos ofrecidos en homenaxe a Ramón Lorenzo* (Santiago de Compostela: Universidade de Santiago de Compostela), pp. 553–65.
Lorenzo Gradín, Pilar, 2008a. 'Lancelot comme toile de fond d'Alphonse X?', *CCM*, 51: 143–55.
Lorenzo Gradín, Pilar, 2008b. 'Los lais de Bretanha y las rúbricas explicativas en *B* y *V*', in Corrado Bologna and Marco Bernardi (eds), *Angelo Colocci e gli studi romanzi* (Vatican City: Biblioteca Apostolica Vaticana), pp. 405–29.
Lorenzo Gradín, Pilar, 2013. 'Los *lais de Bretanha*: de la compilación en prosa al cancionero', *e-Spania. Revue Interdisciplinaire d' Études Hispaniques Médiévales et Modernes* [consulted 20 December 2013]: *http://e-spania.revues.org/22767*; DOI : 10.4000/e-spania.22767.
Lorenzo Gradín, Pilar, and Eva María Díaz Martínez, 2004. 'El fragmento gallego del *Livro de Tristán*. Nuevas aportaciones sobre la *collatio*', *Ro*, 122: 371–96.
Lorenzo Gradín, Pilar, and José Antonio Souto Cabo (eds), 2001. *'Livro de Tristan' e 'Livro de Merlin'. Estudio, edición, notas e glosario* (Santiago de Compostela: Xunta de Galicia; Centro Ramón Piñeiro).
Lorenzo Vázquez, Ramón, 1975, *La traducción gallega de la Crónica General y de la Crónica de Castilla* (Orense: Instituto de Estudios orensanos 'Padre Feijoo').
Lorenzo Vázquez, Ramón, 1993. 'Crónica de 1404', in Giulia Lanciani and Giuseppe Tavani (eds), *Dicionário da Literatura Medieval Galega e Portuguesa* (Lisbon: Caminho).
Lorenzo Vázquez, Ramón, 2000. 'Prosa medieval', in *Galicia: Literatura*, XXX: *A Idade Media* (A Coruña: Hércules de Ediciones), pp. 364–429.
Lorenzo [Vázquez], Ramón, 2002. 'La interconexión de Castilla, Galicia y Portugal en la confección de las crónicas medievales y en la transmisión de textos literarios', *RFR*, 19: 93–123.
Lorenzo Vázquez, Ramón, in press. *Colección diplomática do mosteiro de Montederramo (séculos XII–XVI)* (Santiago de Compostela).

Löseth, Eilert, 1891. *Le roman en prose de Tristan, le roman de Palamède et la compilation de Rusticien de Pise. Analyse critique d'après les manuscrits de Paris*, Bibliothèque de l'École des Hautes Études, 82 (Paris: Bouillon; rpt New York: Burt Franklin, 1970; Geneva: Slatkine Reprints, 1974).

Lucía Megías, José Manuel, 1994. 'Notas sobre la recepción del «Lanzarote» español en el siglo XVI (Biblioteca Nacional de Madrid: ms. 9611)', *Verba Hispanica*, 4: 83–96.

Lucía Megías, José Manuel, 1996a. 'Testimonios del *Libro del cavallero Zifar*' in Francisco Rico (gen. ed.), *Edición facsímil del 'Libro del cavallero Zifar': ms. Esp. 36 de la Bibliothèque Nationale de France* (Barcelona: Moleiro), pp. 95–136.

Lucía Megías, José Manuel, 1996b. Review of 'María Luzdivina Cuesta Torre, *Aventuras amorosas y caballerescas en las novelas de Tristán*', León, 1994', *RLM*, 8: 244–51.

Lucía Megías, José Manuel, 1998a. 'Catálogo descriptivo de libros de caballerías hispánicos. X: *Tirante el Blanco* ante el género editorial caballeresco', *Tirant. Butlletí informatiu i bibliogràfic de la literatura de cavalleries*, 1: [http://parnaseo.uv.es/Tirant/Art.Lucia.html].

Lucía Megías, José Manuel, 1998b.'Nuevos fragmentos castellanos del códice medieval de *Tristán de Leonís*', *Incipit*, 18: 231–53.

Lucía Megías, José Manuel, 2000. *Imprenta y libros de caballerías* (Madrid: Ollero & Ramos).

Lucía Megías, José Manuel (ed.), 2001a. *Antología de libros de caballerías castellanos* (Alcalá de Henares: CEC).

Lucía Megías, José Manuel, 2001b [2002]. 'Imágenes del *Tristán de Leonís* castellano. I. Las miniaturas del códice medieval (BNM MS. 22.644)', in Germà Colón Domènech and Ricardo Pardo Camacho (eds), *De re militari*, *BSCC*, 77: 73–113.

Lucía Megías, José Manuel, 2001c. 'La senda portuguesa de los libros de caballerías castellanos: *Segunda parte de la Selva de cavalarias famosas*', in Leonardo Funes and José Moure (eds), *Studia in honorem Germán Orduna* (Alcalá de Henares: Universidad de Alcalá de Henares), pp. 393–413.

Lucía Megías, José Manuel, 2004. *De los libros de caballerías manuscritos al 'Quijote'* (Madrid: Sial).

Lucía Megías, José Manuel, 2005a. 'El *Tristán de Leonís* castellano: análisis de las miniaturas del códice BNM: ms. 22.644', *e-Humanista. Journal of Iberian Studies*, 5 (2005): 1–47. [*http:\www.spanport. ucsb.edu/projects/ehumanista/volumes/volume_05/Articles*].

Lucía Megías, José Manuel, 2005b. 'Libros de caballerías castellanos en la biblioteca del Cigarral del Carmen (Toledo)', *Tirant. Butlletí informatiu i bibliogràfic de la literatura de cavalleries*, 8. [http:// parnaseo.uv.es/Tirant/Butlleti.8/LibrosCaballeria.pdf].

Lucía Megías, José Manuel, 2005c. 'Literatura caballeresca catalana: de los testimonios a la interpretación (un ensayo de crítica ecdótica)', *Caplletra*, 39: 231–56.

Lucía Megías, José Manuel, 2007. *El libro y sus públicos* (Madrid: Ollero & Ramos).

Lucía Megías, José Manuel, 2008. 'Los fragmentos del *Tristán de Leonís* de la Biblioteca Nacional: los tesoros de las encuadernaciones', in J. M. Lucía Megías (ed.), *Amadís de Gaula (1508): quinientos años de libros de caballerías* (Madrid: Biblioteca Nacional de España – Sociedad Estatal de Conmemoraciones Culturales), pp. 47–50.

Lucía Megías, José Manuel, and Emilio José Sales Dasí, 2007. 'La otra realidad social en los libros de caballerías. III. El caballero "anciano"', in Armando López Castro and María Luzdivina Cuesta Torre (eds), *Actas del XI Congreso Internacional de la Asociación Hispánica de Literatura Medieval (León, 20–24 de septiembre de 2005)*, 2 vols (León: Universidad de León), II, pp. 783–95.

Luciano, Aderaldo, [2011]. 'Heróis da Távola Redonda em versos de Cordel', at: *http://www.vermelho. org.br/noticia/169388-11* [consulted 17 May 2014].

Macedo, José Rivair, 2003. 'O sangue nos romances arturianos', *Brathair*, 3/2: 35–43.

Machado, José Barbosa, 2007. 'A utilização do gerúndio na versão portuguesa medieval de *A Demanda do Santo Graal*', *Revista Portuguesa de Humanidades*, 11: 173–95.

Machado, Elsa Paxeco, and José Pedro Machado (eds), 1949–64. *Cancioneiro da Biblioteca Nacional, antigo Colocci-Brancuti: leitura, comentários e glossário*, 8 vols (Lisbon: Edição da Revista de Portugal).

MacKay, Angus, 1977. *Spain in the Middle Ages: From Frontier to Empire 1000–1500* (London: Macmillan).
Madureira, Margarida, 2002. 'Sangue Redentor: o *Orto do Esposo*, a *Queste del Saint Graal* e a tradição exemplar medieval', in Leonor Curado Neves, Margarida Madureira and Teresa Amado (eds), *Matéria de Bretanha em Portugal. Actas do colóquio realizado em Lisboa nos dias 8 e 9 de Novembro de 2001* (Lisbon: Colibri), pp. 241–9.
Madurell i Marimon, Josep Maria, 1974. *Manuscrits en català anteriors a la impremta (1321–1474). Contribució al seu estudi* (Barcelona: Associació Nacional de Bibliotecaris).
Magalhães, Hilda Gomes Dutra, and Izabel Cristina dos Santos Teixeira, 2006. 'O imaginário cristão nas novelas de cavalaria e nas cantigas de amor', *Mirabilia. Revista Electrônica de História Antiga e Medieval*, 6: 50–62.
Magne, Augusto, 1927. '*Demanda do Santo Graal*. Ms. Num. 2594 da Bibliotheca Nacional de Vienna d'Austria', *RLP*, 8/n° 45: 33–56; 10/n° 46: 17–34.
Magne, Augusto, 1928. '*Demanda do Santo Graal*. Ms. Num. 2594 da Bibliotheca Nacional de Vienna d'Austria', *RLP*, 10/n° 56: 81–114.
Magne, Augusto, 1929. '*Demanda do Santo Graal*. Ms. Num. 2594 da Bibliotheca Nacional de Vienna d'Austria', *RLP*, 10/n° 57: 81–116; 10/n° 59: 11–38; 10/n° 60: 61–78; 11/n° 61: 55–98.
Magne, Augusto (ed.), 1944. *A Demanda do Santo Graal*, 3 vols (Río de Janeiro: Imprensa Nacional, Instituto Nacional do Livro, Ministério da Educação e Saude).
Magne, Augusto, 1948. 'A Demanda do Santo Graal', *NRFH*, 2: 285–9.
Magne, Augusto, 1955–70. *A Demanda do Santo Graal. Reprodução fac-similar e transcrição crítica do códice 2594 da Biblioteca Nacional de Viena*, 2 vols (Río de Janeiro: Instituto Nacional do Livro, Ministério da Educação e Cultura).
Magne, Augusto, 1965. 'Amostra da segunda edição do glossário da *Demanda do Santo Graal*', in Leodegário A. de Azevedo Filho (ed.), *Miscelânea Filológica em honra à memória do professor Clóvis Monteiro* (Rio de Janeiro: Publicações da Editôra do Professor), pp. 25–45.
Magne, Augusto, 1967. *Glossário da Demanda do Santo Graal*. I: *A-D* (Rio de Janeiro: Instituto Nacional do Livro, Ministério da Educação e Cultura).
Maler, Bertil, 1956. *Orto do Esposo*, 2 vols (Rio de Janeiro: Ministério de Educação e Cultura – Instituto Nacional do Livro).
Maleval, Maria do Amparo Tavares, 2004. 'Representações diabolizadas da mulher em textos medievais', in Sérgio Nazar David (ed.), *As mulheres são o diabo* (Rio de Janeiro: EDUERJ), pp. 45–80.
Maleval, Maria do Amparo Tavares, 2012. 'Ainda sobre Nun'Álvares e o ideal da cavalaria', in Lênia Márcia Mongelli (ed.), *De cavaleiros e cavalarias. Por terras de Europa e Américas* (São Paulo: Humanitas), pp. 441–54.
Malory, Thomas. 1977. *Works*, ed. Eugène Vinaver, 2nd edn (Oxford: Oxford University Press).
Manuel, don Juan: *see* Don Juan Manuel.
Marcenaro, Simone, 2010. *L'equivocatio nella lirica galego-portoghese medievale* (Alessandria: Edizioni dell'Orso).
Marianella, Conchita H., 1979. *'Dueñas' and 'doncellas': A Study of the 'Doña Rodríguez' Episode in 'Don Quixote'* (Chapel Hill: University of North Carolina).
Marín Pina, María Carmen, 1990. 'El personaje y la retórica del nombre propio en los libros de caballerías españoles', *Tropelías: Revista de Teoría de la Literatura y Literatura Comparada*, 1: 165–75.
Marín Pina, María del Carmen, 1991. 'La mujer y los libros de caballerías. Notas para el estudio de la recepción del género caballeresco entre el público femenino', *RLM*, 3: 129–48.
Marín Pina, María Carmen, 1994. 'El tópico de la falsa traducción en los libros de caballerías', in María Isabel Toro Pascua (ed.), *Actas del III Congreso de la Asociación Hispánica de Literatura Medieval*, 2 vols (Salamanca: Universidad de Salamanca), I, pp. 541–9.
Marín Pina, María Carmen, 1995. 'La historia y los primeros libros de caballerías españoles', in Juan Paredes Núñez (ed.), *Medioevo y Literatura: Actas del V Congreso de la Asociación Hispánica de Literatura Medieval 1993*, 4 vols (Granada: Universidad de Granada), III, pp. 183–92.

Marín Pina, María Carmen, 1996. 'La ideología del poder y el espíritu de cruzada en la narrativa caballeresca del periodo fernandino', in Esteban Sarasa Sánchez (ed.), *Fernando II de Aragón, el rey Católico* (Zaragoza: Institución Fernando el Católico), pp. 87–105.

Marín Pina, María Carmen, 1998. 'Motivos y tópicos caballerescos', in Francisco Rico (ed.), Miguel de Cervantes, *Don Quijote de la Mancha: Volumen complementario* (Barcelona: Instituto Cervantes, and Crítica), pp. 857–902.

Marín Pina, María Carmen, 2004–5. 'La carta de Iseo y la tradición epistolar troyana en el *Tristán de Leonís* (Valladolid, 1501)', *Letras*, 50–1 (*Libros de caballerías. El «Quijote». Investigación y Relaciones*): 235–51.

Marín Pina, María Carmen, 2007a. 'La doncella andante en los libros de caballerías españoles: antecedentes y delimitación del tipo (I)', in A. López Castro and L. Cuesta Torre (eds), *Actas del XI Congreso Internacional de la Asociación Hispánica de Literatura Medieval (León, 20–24 de septiembre de 2005)*, 2 vols (León: Universidad de León. Secretariado de Publicaciones) II, pp. 817–25.

Marín Pina, María Carmen, 2007b. 'Palmerín de Inglaterra: una encrucijada intertextual', *Península. Revista de Estudos Ibéricos*, 4: 79–94.

Marín Pina, María Carmen, 2010. 'La doncella andante en los libros de caballerías españoles: la libertad imaginada (II)', *eHumanista*, 16: 221–39: http://www.ehumanista.ucsb.edu/volumes/volume_16/post/2%20articles/12%20ehumanista%2016.marin_pina.pdf.

Marín Sánchez, Ana María, 1999. *Istoria de las bienandanzas e fortunas de Lope García de Salazar (Ms. 9–10–2/2100 R.A.H.)*, en *Memorabilia*, 3 (1999): http://parnaseo.uv.es/Lemir/Textos/bienandanzas/Menu.htm.

Mariño Paz, Ramón, 1998. *Historia da lingua galega* (Santiago de Compostela: Sotelo Blanco).

Martin, George R. R., 1996. *A Game of Thrones* (London: HarperVoyager).

Martin, Georges, 1992. *Les juges de Castille. Mentalités et discours historique dans l'Espagne médiévale* (Paris: Klincksieck).

Martín Abad, Julián, 2002. *Post-Incunables ibéricos* (Madrid: Ollero & Ramos).

Martines, Vicent, 1993. 'La versió catalana de la *Queste de Saint Graal*: estudi i edició' (unpublished doctoral thesis, Departament de Filologia Catalana, Universitat de Alacant).

Martines, Vicent, 1994 . 'La versión catalana de *La Queste del Saint Graal* (16 de mayo de 1380)', in Luis Charlo Brea (ed.), *Reflexiones sobre la traducción: Actas sobre el primer encuentro interdisciplinar 'Teoría y Práctica de la Traducción'* (Cádiz: Universidad de Cádiz), pp. 379–89.

Martines, Vicent, 1995a. 'Del *Girart de Rosselló* a la *Questa del Sant Grasal*: "Durament ama Déu e Ternitaz lo caveler benuhirat"', in *Miscel·lània Germà Colón*, 7 vols, *Estudis de Llengua i Literatura Catalanes*, 28–34 (Barcelona: Publicacions de l'Abadia de Montserrat; Amsterdam: Associació Internacional de Llengua i Literatura Catalanes), III (*Estudis*, 30), pp. 23–36.

Martines, Vicent, 1995b. *Els cavallers literaris. Assaig sobre literatura cavalleresca catalana medieval* (Madrid: UNED, 1995).

Martines, Vicent, 1995c. 'La versió catalana de la *Queste del Saint Graal* i l'original francès', in Juan Paredes Núñez (ed.), *Actas del V Congreso de la Asociación Hispánica de Literatura Medieval*, 4 vols (Granada: Universidad de Granada), III, pp. 241–52.

Martines, Vicent, 2002. 'La recherche du saint Graal dans la littérature médiévale catalane: la version catalane de la *Queste del Saint Graal*', *Revue de Langues Romanes*, 106/2: 457–74.

Martínez de Toledo, Alfonso, 1998. *Arcipreste de Talavera o Corbacho*, ed. Michael Gerli, 5th edn (Madrid: Cátedra).

Martínez Ferrando, J. Ernesto, 1953–4. *Catálogo de la documentación de la Cancillería Regia de Pedro de Portugal (1464–1466)*, 2 vols, Catálogos de archivos y bibliotecas (Madrid: Dirección General de Archivos y Bibliotecas).

Martínez Pérez, Antonia, 1994. 'En torno a las transposiciones intertextuales de la tradición artúrica en la *Faula* de Guillem de Torroella', *RLM*, 6: 133–45.

Martins, Mário, 1952. 'O *Livro de José de Arimateia*, da Torre do Tombo', *Brotéria*, 55: 289–98; rpt in *Estudos de Literatura Medieval* (Braga: Livraria Cruz, 1956), 48–57.

Martins, Mário, 1956. *Estudos de Literatura Medieval* (Braga: Livraria Cruz).
Martins, Mário, 1962. 'A lenda de Caifás', *Brotéria*, 75: 530–4.
Martins, Mário, 1974. 'A morte do Rei Artur', *Itinerarium*, 20/84: 152–8.
Martins, Mário, 1975a. *Alegorias, símbolos e exemplos morais da literatura medieval portuguesa* (Lisbon: Brotéria).
Martins, Mário, 1975b. 'A Eucaristia no *Livro de José de Arimateia* e na *Demanda do Santo Graal*', *Itinerarium*, 21/87: 16–30.
Martins, Mário, 1975c. 'Emparedadas arturianas e vida reclusa em Portugal', *Itinerarium*, 21/90: 410–26.
Martins, Mário, 1977. 'Frases de orientação nos romances arturianos e em Fernão Lopes', *Itinerarium*, 23/95: 3–24.
Martins, Mário, 1979a. 'Tristão e Isolda, ontem e hoje,' *Itinerarium*, 25: 334–42.
Martins, Mário, 1979b. 'Os prantos de Palamedes no *Tristan* e na *Demanda do Santo Graal*', *Itinerarium*, 25/104: 223–32.
Martins, Mário, 1980. 'O Cromlech de Stonehenge no *Livro de José de Arimateia* e em *Merlim*', *Itinerarium*, 26/107: 217–22.
Martins, Mário, 1981. 'O ideal de Galaaz no *Livro de José de Arimateia*', *Estudos Medievais*, 1: 5–24.
Martins, Mário, 1982. *Vida e morte de Galaaz* (Lisbon: Brotéria).
Martins, Mario, 1983a. 'O pré-cervantismo em *Tristan de Leonis*', *BF*, 28 (*Homenagem a Manuel Rodrigues Lapa*, I): 33–44.
Martins, Mário, 1983b. 'Merlim numa Cantiga de Santa Maria', in *Estudos de Cultura Medieval* (Lisbon: Brotéria), III, pp. 45–9.
Martins, Mário, 1983c. 'Simbologia das vestes sacerdotais no *Livro de José de Arimateia*', *Didaskalia. Revista da Faculdade de Teologia de Lisboa*, 13/1–2: 303–9.
Martins, Mário, 1985. 'De Galaaz a um cavaleiro de Alcácer Ceguer', *Brotéria*, 119: 52–7.
Martins, Mário, 1988. *Nossa Senhora nos romances do Santo Graal e nas ladainhas medievais e quinhentistas* (Braga: Magnificat).
Martorell, Joanot (Martí Joan de Galba), 2005. *Tirant lo Blanch / Tirante el Blanco*, ed. A. Hauf and V. Escartí, 2 vols (València: Tirant lo Blanc).
Mattoso, José, 1980. *Livro de linhagens do Conde D. Pedro*, in *Portugaliae Monumenta Historica*, Nova Série, II/1 (Lisbon: Academia de Ciências de Lisboa).
Mattoso, José, 1981a. 'Os livros de linhagens portugueses e a literatura genealógica europeia da Idade Média', in *A Nobreza Medieval Portuguesa. A Família e o Poder* (Lisbon: Estampa), pp. 35–53.
Mattoso, José, 1981b. 'As fontes do *Nobiliário* do Conde D. Pedro', in *A Nobreza Medieval Portuguesa. A Família e o Poder* (Lisbon: Estampa), pp. 55–98.
Mattoso, José, 1983. *Narrativas dos Livros de Linhagens* (Lisbon: Imprensa Nacional–Casa da Moeda).
Mattoso, José, 1985a. *Portugal medieval. Novas interpretações* (Lisbon: Imprensa Nacional–Casa da Moeda).
Mattoso, José, 1985b. *Ricos-homens, infanções e cavaleiros. A nobreza medieval portuguesa nos séculos XI e XII* (Lisbon: Guimarães Editora).
Mattoso, José, 1988. *Identificação de um país. Estudio sobre as origens de Portugal (1096–1325)* (Lisbon: Editorial Estampa).
Mattoso, José, 1993. '*Livros de linhagens*', in Giulia Lanciani and Giuseppe Tavani (eds), *Dicionário da Literatura Medieval Galega e Portuguesa* (Lisbon: Caminho), pp. 420–1.
Mattoso, José, 2009a. 'Sobre as fontes do conde de Barcelos', in *Naquele tempo. Ensaios de História Medieval* (Lisbon: Círculo de Leitores), pp. 259–65.
Mattoso, José, 2009b. 'A transmissão textual dos livros de linhagens', in *Naquele tempo. Ensaios de História Medieval* (Lisbon: Círculo de Leitores), pp. 267–83.
Matulka, Barbara 1931. *The Novels of Juan de Flores and their European Diffusion. A Study in Comparative Literature* (New York: Institute of French Studies).
McGrady, Donald, 1986. 'The Hunter Loses his Falcon: Notes on a Motif from *Cligés* to *La Celestina* and Lope de Vega', *Ro*, 107: 145–82.

Megale, Heitor, 1986. 'In Search of the Narrative Structure of *A Demanda do Santo Graal*', *Arthurian Interpretations*, 1: 26–34.

Megale, Heitor, 1986–7. 'A *Demanda* portuguesa de Viena: confronto das edições Magne', *BF*, 31: 133–60 (French version: 'Le Texte portugais de la *Demanda do Santo Graal*: les éditions de 1944 et de 1955–1970', in *Medievalia Lovaniensia: Arturus Rex*, II: *Acta Conventus Lovaniensis, 1987*, ed. Willy van Hoecke, Gilbert Tournoy and Werner Verbeke, Series I / Studia, XVII (Leuven: Leuven University Press, 1987–91); II (1991), pp. 436–61.

Megale, Heitor, 1988. *A Demanda do Santo Graal: manuscrito do século XIII* (São Paulo: T. A. Queiroz, and Universidade de São Paulo).

Megale, Heitor, 1990. '*Demanda do Santo Graal*: do manuscrito ao texto modernizado', in *Anais. II Encontro de Edição e Crítica Genética. Eclosão do Manuscrito* (São Paulo: Universidade de São Paulo), pp. 23–9.

Megale, Heitor, 1992. *O jogo dos Anteparos. A Demanda do Santo Graal. A estrutura ideológica e a construção da narrativa* (São Paulo: T. A. Queiroz).

Megale, Heitor, 1993. *A Demanda do Santo Graal. Fragmentos* (São Paulo: Ateliê Editora).

Megale, Heitor, 1995a. 'As mudanças de mão no códice d'*A Demanda do Santo Graal*', in Cecília Almeida Salles and Philippe Willemart (eds), *Gênese e Memória: IV Encontro Internacional de Pesquisadores do manuscrito e de edições da Associação de Pesquisadores do Manuscrito Literário* (São Paulo: Annablume), pp. 215–21.

Megale, Heitor, 1995b. 'A Matéria de Bretanha: da França ao Ocidente da Península Ibérica', in Maria Miquelina Barra Rocha (eds), *Anais do Segundo Encontro de Estudos Românicos* (Belo Horizonte: Universidade Federal de Minas Gerais), pp. 11–23.

Megale, Heitor, 1996a. 'A questão da prioridade da tradução da Post-Vulgata arturiana na Península Ibérica à luz dos testemunhos franceses' (unpublished doctoral thesis, Universidade de São Paulo).

Megale, Heitor, 1996b. 'A *Post-Vulgata* arturiana na Península Ibérica: suas relações com os testemunhos-fonte agora divulgados', *Estudos Linguísticos e Literários*, Special Issue: 43–53.

Megale, Heitor, 1996c. 'A *Post-Vulgata* arturiana na Península Ibérica: qual foi sua primeira tradução?', *Confluência*, 11: 39–57.

Megale, Heitor, 1997. 'Textos arturianos portugueses e galegos', in Maria Helena Nery Garcez and Rodrigo Leal Rodríguez (eds), *O Mestre. Homenagem das literaturas de língua portuguesa ao professor António Soares Amora* (São Paulo: Universidade de São Paulo), pp. 239–49.

Megale, Heitor, 1999. 'Variação lexical no códice da *Demanda do Santo Graal*', *EL. Anais do Seminário do GEL*, 28: 176–81.

Megale, Heitor, 2001. *A Demanda do Santo Graal. Das origens ao códice português* (Cotia, São Paulo: Ateliê Editorial).

Megale, Heitor, 2002a. 'As Cinco *Cantigas* Bretãs Portuguesas', *SBPS*, 6: 116–33.

Megale, Heitor, 2002b. 'A presença de dois periodos do português arcaico em um mesmo códice do século XV: *A Demanda do Santo Graal*', in Gladis Massini-Cagliari (ed.), *Descrição do português: Linguistica Histórica e Historiografia Linguística* (Araraquara: Cultura Acadêmica), pp. 119–40.

Megale, Heitor, 2003. 'Manuel Rodrigues Lapa e a questão da prioridade da tradução portuguesa da *Post-Vulgata* arturiana na Península Ibérica', in Maria Valéria Zamboni, Maria Lucia Outeiro Fernandes and Renata Soarez Junqueira (eds), *Intelectuais portugueses e a cultura brasileira. Depoimentos e estudos* (São Paulo: Universidade do Estado de São Paulo), pp. 168–79.

Megale, Heitor, 2005. 'A *Demanda do Santo Graal*: tradição manuscrita e tradição impressa', *EL*, 34: 135–40.

Ménard, Philippe (gen. ed.), 1987–97. *Le Roman de Tristan en prose*, 9 vols, Textes littéraires français, 353, 387, 398, 408, 416, 437, 450, 462, 474 (Geneva: Droz).

Ménard, Philippe, 1997. 'La réception des romans de chevalerie à la fin du Moyen Âge et au xvie siècle', *BBIAS-Bulletin Bibliographique de la Societé Internationale Arthurienne*, 49: 234–73.

Ménard, Philippe (gen. ed.), 1997–2007. *Le Roman de Tristán en Prose. Version du manuscrit français 757 de la Bibliothèque nationale de Paris*, 5 vols (Paris: Honoré Champion).

Meneghetti, María Luisa, 1984. *Il pubblico dei trovatori. Ricezione e riuso dei testi lirici cortesi fino al XIV secolo* (Modena: Mucchi Editore).

Meneghetti, Maria Luisa, 1987. 'Palazzi sotterranei, amori proibiti', *Medioevo Romanzo*, 12: 443–56.

Menéndez Pidal, Ramón, 1968. *Romancero Hispánico*. 2nd edn, 2 vols (Madrid: Espasa Calpe).

Menéndez Pidal, Ramón (ed.), 1971. *Crestomatía del español medieval*, 2nd edn, 2 vols (Madrid: Gredos).

Menéndez y Pelayo, Marcelino, 1905–15. *Orígenes de la novela, I: Introducción: tratado histórico sobre la primitiva novela española*, NBAE, 1 (Madrid: Bailly-Baillière; rpt Madrid: Gredos, 2008, 2 vols).

Mérida Jiménez, Rafael M., 2001. *'Fuera de la orden de natura'. Magias, milagros y maravillas en el 'Amadís de Gaula'*, Estudios de literatura, 66 (Kassel: Reichenberger).

Mérida Jiménez, Rafael M., 2010. 'La "Materia de Bretaña" en las culturas hispánicas de la Edad Media y del Renacimiento: textos, ediciones y estudios', *RLM*, 22: 289–350.

Mettmann, Walter (ed.), 1986–9. *Alfonso X el Sabio. Cantigas de Santa María*, 3 vols (Madrid: Castalia).

Mettmann, Walter, 1987. 'Algunas observaciones sobre la génesis de la colección de las *Cantigas de Santa María* y sobre el problema del autor', in *Studies on the Cantigas de Santa Maria: Art, Music and Poetics. Proceedings of The International Symposium on the CSM of Alfonso X el Sabio (1221–1284)* (Madison: Madison University Press), pp. 355–66.

Micha, Alexandre, 1957. 'Fragment de la Suite-Huth du *Merlin*', *Ro*, 78: 37–45.

Micha, Alexandre, 1959. 'Miscellaneous French Romances in Verse', in Roger Sherman Loomis (ed.), *Arthurian Literature in the Middle Ages: A Collaborative History* (Oxford: Clarendon Press), pp. 358–92.

Micha, Alexandre (ed.), 1978–83. *Lancelot. Roman en prose du XIIIe siècle*, 9 vols, Textes littéraires français, 247, 249, 262, 278, 283, 286, 288, 307 and 315 (Paris and Geneva: Droz).

Micha. Alexandre, 1987. *Essais sur le cycle du Lancelot-Graal* (Geneva: Droz).

Michael, Ian, 1967. 'A Parallel between Chrétien's *Erec* and the *Libro de Alexandre*', *Modern Language Review*, 62: 620–8.

Michael, Ian, 1989. ''From her shall read the perfect ways of honour': Isabel of Castile and chivalric romance', in Alan Deyermond and Ian Macpherson (eds), *The Age of the Catholic Monarchs, 1474–1516: Literary Studies in Memory of Keith Whinnom* (Liverpool: Liverpool University Press), pp. 103–12.

Michaëlis [de Vasconcelos], Carolina, 1900–1. '*Lais de Bretanha*: capitulo inedito do *Cancioneiro da Ajuda*', *RL*, 6: 1–43.

Michaëlis de Vasconcelos, Carolina (ed.), 1904. *Cancioneiro da Ajuda*, 2 vols (Halle: Max Niemeyer; rpt. Tübingen: Max Niemeyer, 1979, and Lisbon: Imprensa Nacional–Casa da Moeda, 1990).

Michaëlis de Vasconcelos, Carolina, 1908. 'Contribuições para o futuro diccionário etimológico das línguas hispánicas', *RL*, 11: 1–62.

Michelli, Regina, 2001. 'O perfil masculino em *Demanda*, o poder do rei, o dever do cavaleiro, o saber do eremita', in Maria do Amparo Tavares Maleval (ed.), *Atas do III Encontro Internacional de Estudos Medievais da ABREM* (Rio de Janeiro: Ágora da Illa), pp. 448–54.

Michelli, Regina, 2002. 'O heroismo nas asas do sonho: o perfil masculino épico na ambiência cavaleiresca', in Grabiel Bianciotto and Claudio Galderisi (eds), *L'épopée romane. Actes du XVe Congrès International Rencesvals (Poitiers, 21–27 août 2000)* (Poitiers: Université de Poitiers), pp. 949–57.

Michels, Ralph J., 1935. 'Deux traces du *Chevalier de la Charrete* observées dans l'*Amadís de Gaula*', *BHi*, 37: 478–80.

Michon, Patricia, 1991. 'Le *Tristan* en prose galaïco-portugaise', *Ro*, 112: 259–68.

Michon, Patricia, 1994. 'Marc de Cornouailles au royaume de Logres dans les romans arthuriens de la péninsule ibérique', *Les Lettres Romanes*, 48: 163–73.

Michon, Patricia, 1996. *A la lumière du 'Merlin' espagnol* (Geneva: Droz).

Michon, Patricia, 1999. 'Le personnage du Morholt dans le «Baladro del Sabio Merlin»', in *À la lumière du Merlin espagnol* (Geneva: Droz), pp. 11–28.

Middleton, Robert, 2006. 'The Manuscripts', in Glyn S. Burgess and Karen Pratt (eds), *The Arthur of the French. The Arthurian Legend in Medieval French and Occitan Literature*, ALMA, IV (Cardiff: UWP, 2006), pp. 8–92.

Milá y Fontanals, Manuel, 1874. *De la poesía heroico-popular castellana* (Barcelona: Verdaguer); 2nd edn by Martín de Riquer and Joaquín Molas (Barcelona: CSIC, 1959).

Milá y Fontanals, Manuel, 1889. *De los trovadores en España, Obras completas de D. Manuel Milá y Fontanals*, 8 vols, II (Barcelona: Librería de Álvaro Verdaguer; rpt Barcelona: Instituo Miguel de Cervantes, 1966).

Millares Carlo, Agustín, 1956. 'Nota paleográfica sobre el manuscrito del "Amadís"', in Antonio Rodríguez-Moñino, with studies by Rafael Lapesa and Agustín Millares Carlo, 1956. 'El primer manuscrito de *Amadís de Gaula* (noticia bibliográfica)', *BRAE*, 36: 199–225, at pp. 217–18.

Miller, Barbara D., 2003. 'Merlin in Spanish Literature', in *Merlin: A Casebook*, ed. Peter H. Goodrich and Raymond H. Thompson (London: Routledge, 2003), pp. 193–213.

Miller, Barbara D., 2006. 'Hispanic Arthurian Literature', in *A History of Arthurian Scholarship*, ed. Norris J. Lacy (Cambridge: D. S. Brewer), pp. 179–89.

Miquel y Planas, Ramon (ed.), 1914. *Llegendes de l'altra vida*, Biblioteca Catalana (Barcelona: R. Miquel y Planas).

Miralles, Eulàlia (ed.), 2007. *Antoni Viladamor. Història General de Catalunya*, 2 vols, Textos i Documents, 40–1 (Barcelona: Fundació Noguera).

Miranda, José Carlos Ribeiro, 1993. 'Realeza e Cavalaria no *Livro de José de Arimateia*, Versão Portuguesa da *Estoire del Saint Graal*', in Aires A. Nascimento and Cristina Almeida Ribeiro (eds), *Literatura Medieval. Actas do IV Congresso da Associação Hispânica de Literatura Medieval (Lisboa, 1–5 Outubro 1991)*, 4 vols (Lisbon: Edições Cosmos), III, pp. 157–61.

Miranda, José Carlos Ribeiro, 1994. *Conto de Perom, o melhor cavaleiro do mundo: texto e comentário de uma narrativa do 'Livro de José de Arimateia', versão portuguesa da 'Estoire del Saint Graal'* (Porto: Casa do Livro; 2nd edn Porto: Granito, 1998).

Miranda, José Carlos Ribeiro, 1996. 'Como o rei Artur e os cavaleiros da sua corte demandaram o reino de Portugal', *Colóquio / Letras*, 142: 83–102.

Miranda, José Carlos Ribeiro, 1998a. *A Demanda do Santo Graal e o ciclo arturiano da Vulgata* (Porto: Granito Editores e Livreiros).

Miranda, José Carlos Ribeiro, 1998b. *Galaaz e a Ideologia da Linhagem* (Porto: Granito Editores e Livreiros).

Miranda, José Carlos Ribeiro, 2002. 'Elaim, o Branco, e o devir da linhagem santa', in Leonor Curado Neves, Margarida Madureira and Teresa Amado (eds), *Matéria de Bretanha em Portugal. Actas do colóquio realizado em Lisboa nos dias 8 e 9 de Novembro de 2001* (Lisbon: Colibri), pp. 215–26.

Miranda, José Carlos Ribeiro, 2004. 'A edição castelhana de 1535 da *Demanda del Sancto Grial*: o retorno de Excalibur às águas...', *Península. Revista de Estudos Ibéricos*, 1: 53–63.

Miranda, José Carlos Ribeiro, 2006. 'Eliezer e a cavalaria. Sobre a estrutura temática do romance arturiano em prosa', in Pilar Lorenzo Gradín (ed.), *Los caminos del personaje en la narrativa medieval. Actas del Coloquio Internacional (Santiago de Compostela, 1–4 diciembre 2004)* (Florence: Edizioni del Galluzzo), pp. 211–29.

Miranda, José Carlos Ribeiro, 2010. 'Do *Liber regum* em Portugal antes de 1340', *e-Spania, Revue Interdisciplinaire d'Études Hispaniques Médiévales et Modernes*, 9: http://e-spania.revues.org/19315 [consulted 2 February 2013].

Miranda, José Carlos Ribeiro, 2012. 'Do *Livre de Lancelot* aos Ciclos Arturianos', in Lênia Márcia Mongelli (ed.), *De cavaleiros e cavalarias. Por terras de Europa e Américas* (São Paulo: Humanitas), pp. 305–12.

Miranda, José Carlos Ribeiro, 2013. 'Lancelot e a recepção do romance arturiano em Portugal', *e-Spania. Revue Interdisciplinaire d'Études Hispaniques Médiévales et Modernes*, 16: http://e-spania.revues.org/22778 [consulted 4 January 2014].

Moisés, Massaud, 1951. 'O processo dialéctico-narrativo na *Demanda do Santo Graal*', *Investigações*, 26: 65–9.
Moisés, Massaud, 1955a. 'A *Demanda do Santo Graal*', *Revista de História*, 2/6: 275–81.
Moisés, Massaud, 1955b. 'À margem da *Demanda do Santo Graal*', *Revista de História*, 4/21–2: 319–22.
Moisés, Massaud, 1975. *A novela de cavalaria no Quinhentismo Português* (São Paulo: Universidade de São Paulo).
Moisés, Massaud, 1997. 'A concepção medieval da vida expressa na *Demanda do Santo Graal*', in Maria Helena Nery Garcez and Rodrigo Leal Rodríguez (eds), *O Mestre. Homenagem das literaturas de língua portuguesa ao professor António Soares Amora* (São Paulo: Universidade de São Paulo), pp. 427–39.
Molloy Carpenter, Dorothy (ed.), 2000. *Arderique* (Alcalá de Henares: CEC).
Molteni, Enrico, 1880. *Il canzoniere portoghese Colocci-Brancuti, pubblicato nelle parti che completano il codice vaticano 4803* (Halle: Max Niemeyer).
Mone, Frank Joseph, 1838. 'Zur Literatur der romanischen Völker', *Anzeiger für Kunde der deutschen Vorzeit*, 7: 545–51.
Mongelli, Lênia Márcia, 1988a. '*A Demanda do Santo Graal*, aventura e peregrinação' (unpublished doctoral thesis, Universidade de São Paulo).
Mongelli, Lênia Márcia, 1988b. 'An Unorthodox Reading of *A Demanda do Santo Graal*', *Arthurian Interpretations*, 3: 16–24.
Mongelli, Lênia Márcia, 1988c. 'A Besta Ladrador e a Apocalipse de São João: a educação pelo terror na *Demanda do Santo Graal*', in João Ribeiro (ed.), *Anais do I Congresso da Associação Brasileira de Literatura Comparada* (Porto Alegre: Universidade Federal de Minas Gerais / Associação Brasileira de Literatura Comparada), pp. 56–60.
Mongelli, Lênia Márcia, 1995a. *Por quem peregrinam os cavaleiros de Artur* (São Paulo: Ibis).
Mongelli, Lênia Márcia, 1995b. 'Ética cristã e androginia (em torno da *Demanda do Santo Graal*)', *Veritas*, 40: 577–82.
Mongelli, Lênia Márcia (ed.), 2012. *De cavaleiros e cavalarias. Por terras de Europa e Américas* (São Paulo: Humanitas), pp. 441–54.
Monmouth, Geoffrey of, see Faral 1993; Wright 1996.
Montaner Frutos, Alberto, 2008. 'Del *Amadís* primitivo al de Montalvo: cuestiones de emblemática', in José Manuel Lucía Megías and María del Carmen Marín Pina (eds), *Amadís de Gaula: quinientos años después. Estudios en homenaje a Juan Manuel Cacho Blecua* (Alcalá de Henares: CEC), pp. 541–64.
Montero Cartelle, Emilio, 1996. 'Eufemismo y disfemismo en gallego medieval', *Verba*, 23: 307–36.
Montero Cartelle, Enrique, 1991. *El latín erótico. Aspectos léxicos y literarios* (Seville: Universidad de Sevilla).
Montoliu, Manuel de, 1925. 'Sobre els elements èpics, principalment arturians, de la *Crònica* de Jaume I', in *Homenaje ofrecido a Menéndez Pidal: miscelánea de estudios lingüísticos, literarios e históricos*, 3 vols (Madrid: Librería y Casa Editorial Hernando), I, pp. 697–712.
Moralejo Alvarez, Serafín, 1985. 'Artes figurativas y artes literarias en la España medieval: románico, romance y *roman*', *Boletín de la Asociación Europea de Profesores de Español*, 17: 61–70; rpt in *Patrimonio artístico de Galicia y otros estudios. Homenaje al Prof. Dr. Serafín Moralejo Álvarez*, 3 vols (Santiago de Compostela, Xunta de Galicia, 2004), II, pp. 55–60.
Moreira, Thiers Martins, 1944. 'O significado literário da publicação de *A Demanda do Santo Graal*', *Verbum*, 1: 249–56.
Morley, S. Griswold, and Richard W. Tyler, 1961. *Los nombres de personajes en las comedias de Lope de Vega*, 2 vols (Valencia: Castalia; Los Ángeles: University of California Press).
Morros, Bienvenido, 1988. 'Los problemas ecdóticos del *Baladro del sabio Merlín*', in Vicente Beltrán (ed.), *Actas del I Congreso de la Asociación Hispánica de Literatura Medieval (Santiago de Compostela, 1985)* (Barcelona: PPU), pp. 457–71.

Morros, Bienvenido, 2004. 'Amadís y don Quijote', *Criticón*, 91: 41–65.
Moura, Leonor, 2002. 'A Representação do Feminino no *Livro do José de Arimateia*', in Leonor Curado Neves, Margarida Madureira and Teresa Amado (eds), *Matéria de Bretanha em Portugal. Actas do colóquio realizado em Lisboa nos dias 8 e 9 de Novembro de 2001* (Lisbon: Colibri), pp. 69–79.
Moure, José Luis, 1983. 'Sobre la autenticidad de las cartas de Benahatin en la *Crónica* de Pero López de Ayala: consideración filológica de un manuscrito inédito', *Incipit*, 3: 53–93.
Muir, Lynette, 1957. 'The Questing Beast, its Origins and Development', *Orpheus*, 4: 24–32.
Mundó, A. M., 1980. 'Les col·leccions de fragments de manuscrits a Catalunya', *Faventia*, 2/2: 115–23.
Muniz, Márcio Ricardo Coelho, 2004. 'Reiteração e desconstrução de um modelo: a imagem de Cristo n'*A Demanda do Santo Graal* e em *O Físico Prodigioso* de Jorge de Sena', *Via Atlântica*, 7: 99–109.
Nascimento, Aires Augusto, 1984. 'Hábitos tabeliónicos num manuscrito literário – O *Livro de José de Arimateia* – Lisboa, ANTT, Cod. 643', *BF*, 29 (*Homenagem a Manuel Rodrigues Lapa*, II): 119–27.
Nascimento, Aires Augusto, 2008. 'As voltas do «Livro de José de Arimateia»: em busca de um percurso, a propósito de um fragmento trecentista recuperado', *Península. Revista de Estudos Ibéricos*, 5: 129–40.
Nascimento, Aires Augusto, and João Palma-Ferreira (eds), 1998. *Jorge Ferreira de Vasconcelos. Memorial das proezas da Segunda Távola Redonda ao muito alto e muio poderoso Rei Dom Sebastião primeiro deste nome em Portugal, nosso Senhor* (Lisbon: Lello & Irmão).
Neri, Stefano, 2008. 'El *Progetto Mambrino*. Estado de la cuestión', in *Tus obras los rincones de la tierra descubren. Actas del VI Congreso Internacional de la Asociación de Cervantistas* (Alcalá de Henares: Asociación de Cervantistas and CEC), pp. 577–89.
Neto, Serafim da Silva, 1948. 'Textos antigos portuguêses', *BF* [Rio de Janeiro], 8: 233–48.
Neto, Serafim da Silva, 1956. *Textos medievais portuguêses e seus problemas* (Rio de Janeiro: Ministerio da Educação e Cultura / Casa de Rui Barbosa).
Neto, Sílvio de Almeida Toledo, 1997. 'Variação gráfica de algumas consoantes sibilantes do *Livro de José de Arimatéia* (Cod. ANTT 643)', *EL*, 27: 876–81.
Neto, Sílvio de Almeida Toledo, 1999a. '*Liuro de Josep ab Aramatia* and the Works of Robert de Boron', *Quondam et Futurus*, 3/3: 36–45.
Neto, Sílvio de Almeida Toledo, 1999b. 'Variação do morfema número-pessoal da 2ª pessoa do plural no *Livro de José de Arimatéia*', *EL*, 28: 194–9.
Neto, Sílvio de Almeida Toledo, 1999c. 'Aspectos da variação gráfica no português arcaico: as variantes consonantais no *Livro de José de Arimatéia* (Cód. ANTT. 643)', in Ângela Cecília de Souza Rodrigues (ed.), *I Seminário de Filologia e Língua Portuguesa* (São Paulo: Humanitas), pp. 55–63.
Neto, Sílvio de Almeida Toledo, 1999d. 'Breve notícia da matéria arturiana anterior às traduções ibéricas da *Post-Vulgata*', in Heitor Megale and Haquira Osakabe (eds), *Textos medievais portugueses e as súas fontes. Materia da Bretanha e cantigas com notação musical* (São Paulo: Humanitas), pp. 129–56.
Neto, Sílvio de Almeida Toledo, 2000. 'Dêiticos demonstrativos no *Livro de José de Arimatéia*', *EL*, 29: 387–92.
Neto, Sílvio de Almeida Toledo, 2001a. *O 'Livro de José de Arimatéia' (Lisboa, AN/TT. Livraria CÓD. 643): camadas linguísticas da tradução ibérica ao traslado quinhentista* (São Paulo: Universidade de São Paulo).
Neto, Sílvio de Almeida Toledo, 2001b. 'Representação gráfica das terminações nasais no *Livro de José de Arimateia*', *EL*, 30: 1–6.
Neto, Sílvio de Almeida Toledo, 2003. 'A distinção de punhos no *Livro de José de Arimateia*', *EL*, 32: 1–4.
Neto, Sílvio de Almeida Toledo, 2007. 'O *Livro de José de Arimateia*: breve comentário sobre questões atuais', *Veredas. Revista da Associação Internacional de Lusitanistas*, 8: 347–60.
Neto, Sílvio de Almeida Toledo, 2012. 'Os testemunhos portugueses do *Livro de José de Arimateia* e o seu lugar na tradição da *Estoire del Saint Graal*: colação de exemplos', in Lênia Márcia Mongelli

(ed.), *De cavaleiros e cavalarias. Por terras de Europa e Américas* (São Paulo: Humanitas), pp. 579–89; and http://editora.fflch.usp.br/sites/editora.fflch.usp.br/files/579-589.pdf.

Neves, Leonor Curado, 2001. 'Percepção e representação do tempo no *Livro de José de Arimateia*, versão portuguesa da *Estoire del Saint Graal*: o episódio da Nau de Salomão', in Paulo Meneses (ed.), *Sobre o Tempo. Secção Portuguesa da AHLM. Actas do III Colóquio* (Ponta Delgada: Universidade dos Açores), pp. 257–72.

Nitze, William A., 1936. 'The Beste Glatissant in Arthurian Romance', *ZrP*, 56: 409–18.

Nitze, William A., and T. Atkinson Jenkins (eds), 1932–7. *Le Haut Livre du Graal. Perlesvaus*, Modern Philology Monographs of the University of Chicago, 2 vols (Chicago: University of Chicago Press; rpt New York: Phaeton, 1972).

Northup, George Tyler, 1912. 'The Italian Origin of the Spanish Prose Tristram Versions', *RR*, 3: 194–222.

Northup, George Tyler, 1913–14. 'The Spanish Prose Tristram Source Question', *MP*, 11: 259–65.

Northup, George Tyler (ed.), 1928. *El Cuento de Tristán de Leonís Edited from the Unique Manuscript Vatican 6428* (Chicago: University of Chicago Press).

Norton, F. J., 1978. *A Descriptive Catalogue of Printing in Spain and Portugal, 1501–1520* (Cambridge: Cambridge University Press).

Nunes, Irene Freire, see Freire Nunes, Irene.

Nunes, José Joaquim, 1906. *Crestomatia arcaica: excertos da literatura portuguesa desde o que de mais antigo se conhece até ao século XVI* (Lisbon: Ferreira & Oliveira).

Nunes, José Joaquim, 1908. 'Textos Antigos Portugueses. Uma amostra do *Livro de Josep ab Arimatia*', *RL*, 11: 223–37.

Nunes, José Joaquim, 1932. *Florilégio da literatura portuguesa arcaica: Trechos coligidos em obras escritas desde o começo do século XIII até os primeiros anos do século XVI* (Lisbon: Imprensa Nacional).

Nunes Batista, Sebastião, 1986. 'Restituição da autoria de folhetos do Catálogo, tomo I, da *Literatura popular em verso*', in Manuel Diégues Júnior et al. (eds), *Estudos. Literatura popular em verso*, Coleção reconquista do Brasil, 2ª Série, 94 (Belo Horizonte: Editora Itatiaia Limitada; São Paulo: Editora da Universidade de São Paulo; and Rio de Janeiro: Fundação Casa de Rui Barbosa, 1986), pp. 369–468.

Obrador, Matheu, 1903. 'Fragment d'un Lançalot català, transcrit per Matheu Obrador', *Revista de Bibliografia Catalana*, 3: 21–5.

O'Callaghan, Joseph F., 1975. *A History of Medieval Spain* (Ithaca: Cornell University Press).

O'Connor, John J., 1970. '*Amadis de Gaule' and its Influence on Elizabethan Literature* (New Brunswick: Rutgers University).

Old Testament Pseudepigrapha: see Charlesworth, James T.

Olival, Fernanda, 2012, 'Honra, cavalarias e ordens (Portugal, séculos XVI–XVII): dos romances de cavalaria às práticas e das práticas aos textos', in Lênia Márcia Mongelli (ed.), *De cavaleiros e cavalarias. Por terras de Europa e Américas* (São Paulo: Humanitas), pp. 205–14.

Olivar, Alexandre, 1977. *Catàleg dels manuscrits de la Biblioteca del Monestir de Montserrat*, Scripta et Documenta, 25 (Barcelona: Abadia de Montserrat).

Olivar, Marçal, 1986. *Els tapissos francesos del rei En Pere el Cerimoniós*. Col. Opera Minora (Barcelona: Ed. Artur Ramon / Manuel Barbié).

Oliveira, António Resende de, 1993. 'A caminho da Galiza. Sobre as primeiras composições em galego-português', in *O Cantar dos trobadores* (Santiago de Compostela: Xunta de Galicia), pp. 249–61.

Oliveira, António Resende de, 1994. *Depois do espectáculo trovadoresco. A estrutura dos cancioneiros peninsulares e as recolhas dos séculos XIII e XIV* (Lisbon: Edições Colibri).

Oliveira, António Resende de, 2010. 'D. Afonso X, infante e trovador, II. A produção trovadoresca', *La Parola del Testo*, 14/1: 7–19.

Orazi, Veronica, 2006. 'Artù e Tristano nella letteratura spagnola (XV–XVI secolo)', in Margherita Lecco (ed.), *Materiali arturiani nelle letterature di Provenza, Spagna, Italia*, Studi e Ricerche, 49 (Alessandria: Edizioni dell'Orso), pp. 115–42.

Orduna, Germán (ed.), 1987. Pero López de Ayala, *Rimado de Palacio*, Clásicos Castalia, 156 (Madrid: Castalia).

Orduna, Germán, and Lília E. F. de Orduna, 1991. *Catálogo descriptivo de los impresos en español, del siglo XVI, en la Biblioteca 'Jorge M. Furt' (Los Talas, Luján, Pcia. de Bs. As. – Argentina)*, Publicaciones de Incipit, I (Buenos Aires: SECRIT, 1991).

Ors, Joan, 1986. 'De l'encalç del cèrvol blanc al creuer de la balena sollerica: la funció narrativa del motiu de l'animal guia', in *Studia in honorem prof. M. de Riquer*, 4 vols (Barcelona: Quaderns Crema), I, pp. 565–77.

Ortega, Melchor de, 1998. *Felixmarte de Hircania*, ed. María del Rosario Aguilar Pardomo (Alcalá de Henares: CEC).

Osakabe, Haquira, 1987. 'Nota sobre o amor na *Demanda do Santo Graal*', *Estudos Portugueses e Africanos*, 10: 69–75.

Osakabe, Haquira, 2003. 'Neither sublime nor gallant: the Portuguese *Demanda* and the new destiny of man', in Carol Dover (ed.), *A Companion to the Lancelot-Grail Cycle* (Cambridge: D. S. Brewer), pp. 195–203.

Otte, Enrique, [1988]. *Cartas privadas de emigrantes a Indias, 1540–1616* (Seville: V Centenario, Consejería de Cultura, Junta de Andalucía and Escuela de Estudios Hispano-Americanos de Sevilla).

Pacheco, Arseni, 1977. 'El *Blandín de Cornualha*', in Joseph Gulsoy and Josep M. Solà-Solé (eds), *Catalan Studies / Estudis sobre el català. Volume in Memory of Josephine de Boer / Volum en memòria de Josephine de Boer*, Lacetania, 4 (Barcelona: Hispam), pp. 149–61.

Pacheco, Arseni, 1982. 'Notes per a l'estudi de la narrativa catalana en vers dels segles XIV i XV', in Manuel Duran, Albert Porqueras-Mayo and Josep Roca-Pons (eds), *Actes del segon Col·loqui d'Estudis Catalans a Nord-Amèrica (Yale, 1979)*, Biblioteca Abat Oliba, 24 (Barcelona: Publicacions de l'Abadia de Montserrat), pp. 151–61.

Pacheco, Arseni, 1983, ed. *Blandín de Cornualla i altres narracions en vers dels segles XIV i XV*, Les Millors Obres de la Literatura Catalana, 96 (Barcelona: Edicions 62).

Pacheco, Elsa, and Machado, José Pedro, 1949–64. *Cancioneiro da Biblioteca Nacional* (Lisbon: Edição da Revista de Portugal), 8 vols.

Pacheco, Graça M. Lérias, 2002. 'O cavaleiro adormecido n'*A Demanda do Santo Graal*: o sonho no romance arturiano. Comparação com alguns trechos da historiografia medieval', in Leonor Curado Neves, Margarida Madureira and Teresa Amado (eds), *Matéria de Bretanha em Portugal. Actas do colóquio realizado em Lisboa nos dias 8 e 9 de Novembro de 2001* (Lisbon: Colibri), pp. 191–204.

Pagès, Amédée, 1936. *La poésie française en Catalogne du XIIIe siècle à la fin du XVe* (Toulouse: Privat, and Paris: Henri Didier).

Paixão, Rosário Santana, 2012. 'O imaginário do Graal: reflexões sobre a espressão literaria e artística do pensamento medieval entre o humano e o divino', in Juan Paredes Núñez (ed.), *De lo humano y lo divino en la literatura medieval: santos, ángeles y demonios* (Granada: Universidad de Granada), pp. 275–84.

Pallares, María Carmen, and Ermelindo Portela, 1983. 'Aristocracia y parentesco en Galicia en los siglos centrales de la Edad Media. El grupo de los Traba', *Hispania*, 53: 823–40.

Palma-Ferreira, João, Luís Carvalho Dias, and Fernando Filipe Portugal (eds), 1983. *Crónica do imperador Maximiliano: cód. 490, Col. Pombalina da Biblioteca Nacional* (Lisbon: Imprensa Nacional – Casa da Moeda).

Palmerín de Olivia, 1511. (Salamanca, [Juan de Porras?], 1511): *El libro del famoso e muy esforçado cavallero Palmerín de Olivia*, ed. G. Di Stefano (Pisa: Università, 1966).

Pardo de Guevara y Valdés, Eduardo, 2012. *De linajes, parentelas y grupos de poder. Aportaciones a la historia social de la nobleza bajomedieval gallega* (Madrid: CSIC).

Paredes Núñez, Juan, 1991. 'Comparatismo e interdisciplinariedad. En torno a los nobiliarios medievales portugueses', *RFR*, 6/1: 171–6.

Paredes Núñez, Juan, 1992. *La guerra de Granada en las cantigas de Alfonso X el Sabio* (Granada: Universidad de Granada).

Paredes Núñez, Juan, 1993. 'La Materia de Bretaña en la literatura peninsular (La literatura genealógica)', in Aires A. Nascimento and Cristina Almeida Ribeiro (eds), *Actas do IV Congresso da Associação Hispânica de Literatura Medieval (Lisboa, 1–5 Outubro 1991)*, 4 vols (Lisbon: Edições Cosmos), III, pp. 233–7.

Paredes Núñez, Juan, 1995. *Las narraciones de los 'Livros de linhagens'* (Granada: Universidad de Granada).

Paredes Núñez, Juan, 2001. *El cancionero profano de Alfonso X* (Rome: Japadre Editore).

Paredes Núñez, Juan, 2010. *El cancionero profano de Alfonso X el Sabio. Edición crítica, con introducción, notas y glosario* (Santiago de Compostela: Universidad).

P[aris], G[aston], 1887. Review of 'Karl von Reinhardstoettner, *Historia dos cavalleiros da Mesa Redonda e da demanda do Santo Graal*', *Ro*, 16: 582–6.

Paris, Gaston, and Jacob Ulrich (eds), 1886. *Merlin: roman en prose du XIIIe siècle publié avec la mise en prose du poème de Robert de Boron d'après le manuscrit appartenant à M. Alfred H. Huth*, 2 vols, Société des Anciens Textes Français (Paris: Firmin Didot).

Parrilla García, Carmen, 1988. 'La obra literaria de Juan de Flores', in Carmen Parrilla García (ed.), Juan de Flores, *Grimalte y Gradisa* (Santiago de Compostela: Universidad de Santiago), pp. xxxvi–xl.

Pastoureau, Michel, 1990. *Couleurs, images, symboles* (Paris: Le Léopard d'or).

Paton, Lucy Allen (ed.), 1927. *Les Prophécies de Merlin*, 2 vols (New York: D. C. Heath and Company; London: Oxford University Press).

Pauphilet, Albert, 1907. 'La *Queste du saint Graal* du ms. Bibl. Nat. Fr 343', *Ro*, 36: 591–609.

Paz, Demétrio Alves, 2004. 'Galaaz: a cristianização do herói do Graal' (unpublished doctoral thesis, Porto Alegre: Universidade Federal de Rio Grande do Sul).

Pedrazim, Ana Lucia, 2001. '*A Demanda do Santo Graal* e a busca do misterio' (unpublished doctoral thesis, Universidade de São Paulo).

Pedrosa, José Manuel, 2012. 'La reina Ginebra y su sobrino: la dama, el paje, la tormenta y el manto (metáforas líricas y motivos narrativos)', *RPM*, 26: 237–84.

Pelegrín, B., 1975. 'Flechazo y lanzada, Eros y Tánatos (Ensayo de aproximación al "Romance de don Tristán de Leonís y de la reina Iseo, que tanto amor se guardaron')", *Prohemio*, 6: 83–118.

Pellegrini, Silvio, 1928. 'I *lais* portoghesi del Codice Vaticano Lat. 7182', *AR*, 12: 303–17; rpt in *Studi su trove e trovatori della prima lirica ispano-portoghese* (Turin: Giuseppe Gambino, 1937; rpt Bari: Adriatica Editrice, 1959), pp. 184–99.

Pensado Tomé, J[osé] L. (ed.), 1962. *Fragmento de un 'Livro de Tristán' galaicoportugués*, Cuadernos de estudios gallegos, Anejo XIV (Santiago de Compostela: CSIC, Instituto P. Sarmiento de Estudios Gallegos).

Perdomo García, José, 1942. 'Las Canarias en la literatura caballeresca', *Revista de Historia Canaria*, 8: 218–33.

Pereira, Cláudia Sousa, 1993. 'Rei Lear: percurso de uma lenda', in Aires A. Nascimento and Cristina Almeida Ribeiro (eds), *Literatura Medieval. Actas do IV Congresso da Associação Hispânica de Literatura Medieval (Lisboa, 1–5 Outubro 1991)*, 4 vols (Lisbon: Edições Cosmos), II, 289–93.

Pereira, Cláudia Sousa, 2000. 'Um exemplário amoroso para D. Sebastião: o *Memorial das Proezas da Segunda Távola Redonda* de Jorge Ferreira de Vasconcelos' (unpublished doctoral thesis, Universidade de Évora).

Pereira, Paulo Alexandre, 2007. 'Uma Didáctica da Salvação: o *Exemplum* no *Horto do Esposo*', in Helder Godinho (ed.), *Horto do Esposo* (Lisbon: Colibrí), pp. liii–lxxvi.

Pereira, Rita de Cássia Mendes, 1996. 'O Herói e o Soberano. Modelo heróico e representação da soberania na *Demanda do Santo Graal*' (unpublished doctoral thesis, Universidade de São Paulo).

Pereira, Rita de Cássia Mendes, 2007. 'Artur, Galaaz e os cavaleiros do Graal: modelos monárquicos de soberania em Portugal nos séculos XII e XIII', *Brathair*, 7/2: 50–79.

Pérez, Elisa Cifuentes, 2002. 'El lai bretón como género literario: una breve aproximación', *Thélème. Revista Complutense de Estudios Franceses*, 17: 171–8.
Pérez López, José Luis, 1990. 'Otra noticia del *Amadís de Gaula* anterior a Montalvo: una referencia a Beltenebrós', *Dicenda. Cuadernos de filología hispánica*, 9: 207–8.
Pérez Pascual, Ignacio 1990. '*Crónica de 1404*' (unpublished doctoral thesis, 2 vols, Universidad de Salamanca).
Pérez Priego, Miguel Ángel (ed.), 2006. Pero Tafur, *Andanças e viajes*, en *Viajes medievales*, II (Madrid: Biblioteca Castro).
Pickford, Cedric E., 1959. *L'Évolution du roman arthurien en prose vers la fin du Moyen Âge d'après le manuscrit 112 du fonds français de la Bibliothèque Nationale* (Paris: Nizet).
Pickford, C[edric] E[dward]., 1961. 'La priorité de la version portugaise de la *Demanda do Santo Graal*', *BHi*, 63: 211–16.
Piel, Joseph Maria, 1945. 'Anotações críticas ao texto da *Demanda do Santo Graal*', *Biblos*, 21: 175–206.
Piel, Joseph Maria, and Irene Freire Nunes (eds), 1988. *A Demanda do Santo Graal*, completed by Irene Freire Nunes, prologue by Ivo Castro (Lisbon: Imprensa Nacional–Casa da Moeda; 2nd revised edn, 2005).
Pietsch, Karl, 1913–14. 'Concerning MS. 2-G-5 of the Palace Library at Madrid', *MPh*, 11: 1–18.
Pietsch, K. 1915–16. 'On the Language of the Spanish Grail Fragments', *MPh*, 13: 369–78, 625–46.
Pietsch, K. 1920–1. 'The Madrid Manuscript of the Spanish Grail Fragments', *MPh*, 18: 147–56, 591–6.
Pietsch, Karl, 1924–5. *Spanish Grail Fragments. El libro de Josep Abarimatia. La Estoria de Merlin. Lançarote*, Modern Philology Monographs of the University of Chicago, 2 vols (Chicago: University of Chicago Press; rpt Whitefish, Mont.: Kessinger Publishing, 2003).
Pietsch, Karl, 1925. 'Zur spanischen Grammatik aus einem Komentar zu den spanischen Gralfragmenten', in *Homenaje a Menéndez Pidal*, 3 vols (Madrid: Hernando), I, pp. 33–47.
Pimenta, Maria Helena de Almeida, 1996. '*A Demanda do Santo Graal*: o desejo e a visão ou a iluminação da palavra' (unpublished doctoral thesis, Universidade Nova de Lisboa).
Pina, Margarida Esperança, 1997. 'O percurso alimentar na viagem ao mundo maravilhoso. Considerações sobre a *Demanda do Santo Graal* e *Le conte du graal* de Chrétien de Troyes', in Ana Margarida Falcão, Maria Teresa Nascimento and Maria Luísa Leal (eds), *Literatura de viagem. Narrativa, história, mito* (Lisbon: Cosmos), pp. 517–24.
Piñero Ramírez, Pedro M., 2005. 'De lo que le aconteció a la reina doña Ginebra en el camino de Córdoba', in Pedro M. Piñero Ramírez (ed.), *Dejar hablar a los textos. Homenaje a Francisco Márquez Villanueva*, 2 vols (Sevilla: Universidad de Sevilla), II, pp. 967–83.
Pinheiro, Marília Futre, 1993. 'Do romance grego ao romance de cavalaria: As *Etiópicas* de Heliodoro e a *Demanda do Santo Graal*', in Aires A. Nascimento and Cristina Almeida Ribeiro (eds), *Literatura Medieval. Actas do IV Congresso da Associação Hispânica de Literatura Medieval (Lisboa, 1–5 Outubro 1991)*, 4 vols (Lisbon: Edições Cosmos), IV, pp. 147–54.
Pio, Carlos, 2004. 'O lugar do *Livro de José de Arimateia* na tradição de *Estoire del Saint Graal*' (unpublished doctoral thesis, Universidade de Lisboa).
Pio, Carlos, 2007. 'Da *Estoire del Saint Graal* ao *Livro de José de Arimateia*: as relações entre a edição de Paris de 1516 e o ms. português', in Armando López Castro and María Luzdivina Cuesta Torre (eds), *Actas del IX Congreso Internacional de la Asociación Hispánica de Literatura Medieval (León, 20–24 de septiembre de 2005)*, 2 vols (León: Universidad de León), II, pp. 953–8.
Pirot, François, 1972. *Recherches sur les connaissances littéraires des troubadours occitans et catalans des XIIe et XIIIe siècles: les 'sirventes-ensenhamens' de Guerau de Cabrera, Guiraut de Calanson et Bertrand de Paris*, Memorias de la Real Academia de Buenas Letras de Barcelona, 14 (Barcelona: Real Academia de Buenas Letras de Barcelona).
Pitta, Maria Helena Abrantes, 1992. *A Demanda do Santo Graal: obediência e transgressão na prática cavaleiresca* (Rio de Janeiro: Universidade Federal de Rio de Janeiro).
Place, Edwin B., 1954. 'El *Amadís* de Montalvo como manual de cortesanía en Francia', *RFE*, 38: 151–69.

Place, Edwin B., 1956. 'Fictional Evolution: The Old French Romances and the Primitive *Amadís* Reworked by Montalvo', *PMLA*, 71: 521–9.

Platir, 1533 (Valladolid, Nicolás Tierri, 1533), ed. María C. Marín Pina (Alcalá de Henares: CEC, 1997).

Poema de Alfonso XI: see Yáñez, Rodrigo

Polindo, 1526 (Toledo: [Miguel de Eguía?], 1526), ed. M. Calderón Calderón (Alcalá de Henares: CEC, 2003).

Ponceau, Jean-Paul (ed.), 1997. *L'estoire del saint Graal*, 2 vols (Paris: Honoré Champion).

Porta, Aida Amelia, 1992. '*Amadís de Gaula*: el "llamado" al lector', in Lilia E. F [errario] de Orduna (ed.), *Amadís de Gaula. Estudios sobre narrativa caballeresca castellana en la primera mitad del siglo XVI*, Problemata literaria, 6 (Kassel: Reichenberger), pp. 61–79.

Prado-Vilar, Francisco, 2010. '*Nostos*: Ulises, Compostela y la ineluctable modalidad de lo visible', in Manuel Castiñeiras (ed.), *Compostela y Europa. La historia de Diego Gelmírez* (Mila: Skira Editore).

Presotto, Marco (ed.), 1997. Juan de Dueñas, *La nao de Amor. Misa de Amor*, Agua y peña, 4 (Lucca: Marco Baroni).

Primaleón, 1512 (Salamanca: Juan de Porras, 1512), ed. María Carmen Marín Pina (Alcalá de Henares: CEC, 1998).

Pujol, Josep, 2002. *La memòria literària de Joanot Martortell: Models i escriptura en el 'Tirant lo Blanc'*, Textos i Estudis de Cultura Catalana, 87 (Barcelona: Curial Edicions Catalanes, and Publicacions de l'Abadia de Montserrat).

Pujol, Josep, 2006. 'Traducciones y cambio cultural entre los siglos XIII y XV', in Francisco Lafarga and Luis Pegenaute (eds), *Historia de la traducción en España*, Biblioteca de Traducción, 9 (Salamanca: Ambos Mundos), pp. 623–50.

Punzi, Arianna, 2005. *Tristano. Storia di un mito*, Biblioteca Medievale, Saggi, 18 (Rome: Carocci).

Raimundo, Dulce Helena Morgado, 1996. 'O cavaleiro n'*A Demanda do Santo Graal*' (unpublished Master's dissertation, Universidade de Coimbra).

Ramos, Rafael, 1994. 'Para la fecha del *Amadís de Gaula*: "Esta sancta guerra que contra los infieles començada tienen"', *BRAE*, 74: 503–21.

Ramos, Rafael, 1995. '*Tirant lo Blanc*, *Lancelot du Lac* y el *Llibre de l'orde de cavalleria*', *LC*, 23/2: 74–87.

Ramos, Rafael, 1997. '*Tirant lo Blanc* y el *Libro del caballero Zifar* a la zaga del *Amadís de Gaula*', in Andrew Beresford (ed.), '*Quién hubiese tal ventura': Medieval Hispanic Studies Presented to Alan Deyermond* (London: Queen Mary and Westfield College), pp. 207–25.

Ramos, Rafael, 1999. 'La transmisión textual del *Amadís de Gaula*', in Santiago Fortuño Llorens and Tomàs Martínez Romero (eds), *Actes del VII Congrés de l'Associació Hispànica de Literatura Medieval (Castelló de la Plana, 22–26 de setembre de 1997)*, 3 vols (Castelló de la Plana: Universitat Jaume I), III, pp. 199–212.

Ramos, Rafael, 2000. 'Castigos al *Amadís de Gaula*', in Margarita Freixas, Silvia Iriso y Laura Fernández (eds), *Actas del VIII Congreso de la Asociación Hispánica de Literatura Medieval (Santander, 22–26 de septiembre de 1999)*, 2 vols (Santander: Consejería de Cultura del Gobierno de Cantabria, Año Jubilar Lebaniego and AHLM), II, pp. 1511–22.

Ramos, Rafael, 2002. 'Problemas de la edición zaragozana del *Amadís de Gaula* (1508)', in Eva Belén Carro Carbajal, Laura Puerto Moro and María Sánchez Pérez (eds), *Libros de caballerías (De 'Amadís' al 'Quijote'). Poética, lectura, representación e identidad*, Actas, 1 (Salamanca: Seminario de Estudios Medievales y Renacentistas and Sociedad de Estudios Medievales y Renacentistas), pp. 319–42.

Ramos, Rafael, 2003. 'Lectura y lectores de relatos caballerescos en la Castilla medieval', *Ínsula*, 675: 24–7.

Ramos, Rafael, 2006. 'Libros y lectores en Sant Feliu de Guixols', in David Hook (ed.), *Manuscripts, Texts, and Transmission from Isidore to the Enlightenment* (Bristol: HiPLAM), pp. 85–115.

Redondo, Augustin, 1981. 'El proceso iniciático en el episodio de la cueva de Montesinos del *Quijote'*, *Iberoromania*, 13: 47–61.
Rego, A. da Silva: *see Torre do Tombo*.
Reinhardstöttner, Karl von, 1887. *A historia dos cavalleiros da Mesa Redonda e da demanda do Santo Graal: Handschrift nº 2594 der K. K. Hofbibliothek zu Wien* (Berlin: A. Haack).
Remy, Paul, 1959. '*Jaufré*', in Loomis (ed.),1959a, pp. 400–5.
Rey, Agapito (ed.), 1932: *see* Leomarte.
Rico, Francisco, 1997. 'Entre el códice y el libro (Notas sobre los paradigmas misceláneos y la literatura del siglo XIV)', *RPh*, 51/2: 151–69.
Rico, Francisco (gen. ed.), 2004. Miguel de Cervantes, *Don Quijote de la Mancha* (Barcelona: Centro para la Edición de los Clásicos Españoles and Círculo de Lectores).
Riquer [Permanyer], Isabel de, 1989. 'La literatura francesa en la Corona de Aragón en el reinado de Pedro el Ceremonioso (1336–1387)', in Francisco Lafarga (ed.), *Imágenes de Francia en las letras hispánicas*, Estudios de Literatura Española y Comparada, 4 (Barcelona: PPU), pp. 115–26.
Riquer, Isabel de, 1991. 'El viaje al otro mundo de un mallorquín', *Revista de Lengua y Literatura Catalana, Gallega y Vasca*, I: 25–36.
Riquer, Isabel de, 1994. 'Los libros de Violante de Bar', in María del Mar Graña Cid (ed.), *Las sabias mujeres: educación, saber y autoría (siglos III–XVII)*, Laya, 13 (Madrid: Asociación Cultural Al-Mudayna), pp. 161–73.
Riquer Isabel de, 1995. 'Jaufré Rudel y los *prechs d'amor*', in Juan Paredes Núñez (ed.), *Medioevo y literatura. Actas del V Congreso de la Asociación Hispánica de Literatura Medieval (Granada, 27 septiembre - 1 octubre 1993)*, 4 vols (Granada: Universidad de Granada), IV, pp. 151–64.
Riquer Isabel de, 1996. 'Presencia trovadoresca en la Corona de Aragón', *AEM*, 26: 933–66.
Riquer, Isabel de, 1997. 'La réception du Graal en Catalogne au Moyen Âge', in Marie-Madeleine Fragonard and Caridad Martínez (eds), *Transferts de thèmes, transferts de textes. Mythes, légendes et langues entre Catalogne et Languedoc / Transferèrencies de temes, transferències de textos: mites, llegendes i llengües entre Catalunya i Languedoc* (Barcelona: PPU), pp. 49–60.
Riquer, Isabel de, 2005. 'Lo " maravilloso" y lo cotidiano en *La faula* de Guillem de Torroella', *RFR*, 22: 175–182.
Riquer, Martín de, 1953. 'Sobre el romance *Ferido está don Tristán*', *RFE*, 37: 225–7.
Riquer, Martín de, 1955. 'La *Tragèdia de Lançalot*, texto artúrico del siglo XV', *Filologia Romanza*, 2: 113–39.
Riquer, Martín de, 1957. 'Fernando de Rojas y el primer acto de *La Celestina*', *RFE*, 41: 373–95.
Riquer, Martín de, 1964 [4th edn, 1984]. *Història de la literatura catalana. Part antiga*, 3 vols (Barcelona: Ariel).
Riquer, Martín de, 1965. *Vida caballeresca en la España del siglo XV* (Madrid: Real Academia Española).
Riquer, Martín de, 1967. *Caballeros andantes españoles*, Austral, 1397 (Madrid: Espasa Calpe; rpt Madrid: Gredos, 2008).
Riquer, Martín de (ed.), 1971. *Guillem de Berguedà. Estudio histórico, literario y lingüístico*, Scriptorium Populeti, 5 (Espluga de Francolí: Abadía de Poblet).
Riquer, Martín de, 1975 [2nd edn, 1983]. *Los trovadores. Historia literaria y textos*, Letras e Ideas, 3 vols (Barcelona: Ariel).
Riquer, Martín de, 1980. 'Las armas en el *Amadís de Gaula*', *BRAE*, 60: 331–427; rpt in *Estudios sobre el Amadís de Gaula* (Barcelona: Sirmio, 1987), pp. 55–187.
Riquer Martín de (ed.), 1984. *Mossèn Gras. Tragèdia de Lançalot. Amb el facsímil de l'incunable* (Barcelona: Quaderns Crema).
Riquer, Martín de, 1987. *Estudios sobre el Amadís de Gaula*, Biblioteca General, 3 (Barcelona: Sirmio).
Riquer, Martín de, 1990. *Aproximació al 'Tirant lo Blanc'*, Assaig, 8 (Barcelona: Quaderns Crema).
Riquer, Martín de, 1992. *'Tirant lo Blanch', novela de historia y de ficción*, Biblioteca General, 13 (Barcelona: Sirmio).
Riquer 2008: *see* Riquer 1967.

Riquer, Martín de, and Henning Krauss, 1965. 'Appendices: Les cas particuliers de la Catalogne et de l'Italie, I. El caso particular de Cataluña', *Grundiss der romanischen Literaturen des Mittelalters*, 10 vols to date (Heidelberg: Carl Winter-Universitätsverlag), IV, pp. 665–6.

Roach, William, and Robert H. Ivy (eds), 1971. *Continuations of the Old French Perceval of Chrétien de Troyes*, IV. *The Second Continuation* (Philadelphia: University of Pennsylvania Press).

Roberts, Kimberley S., 1956. *An Anthology of Old Portuguese* (Lisbon: Livraria Portugal).

Robinson, Cynthia, 2008. 'Arthur in the Alhambra? Narrative and Nasrid Courtly Self-Fashioning in the Hall of Justice Ceiling Paintings', *Medieval Encounters*, 14.2: 164–98.

Rodríguez de Montalvo, Garci, 1987. *Amadís de Gaula*, ed. Juan M. Cacho Blecua, 2 vols (Madrid: Cátedra).

Rodríguez de Montalvo, Garci, 2003. *Sergas de Esplandián*, ed. Carlos Sáinz de la Maza (Madrid: Castalia).

Rodríguez del Padrón, Juan, 1976. *Siervo libre de Amor*, ed. Antonio Prieto (Madrid: Castalia).

Rodríguez-Moñino, Antonio, 1956, with studies by Rafael Lapesa and Agustín Millares Carlo. 'El primer manuscrito de *Amadís de Gaula* (noticia bibliográfica)', *BRAE*, 36: 199–225, at pp. 199–216.

Rodríguez-Moñino, Antonio, 1997. *Nuevo diccionario bibliográfico de pliegos sueltos poéticos del siglo XVI*, rev. edn by A. L.-F. Askins and V. Infantes (Madrid: Castalia).

Rodríguez Velasco, Jesús D., 1991. '"Yo soy de la Gran Bretaña, no sé si la oísteis acá decir" (La tradición de Esplandián)', *Revista de literatura*, 53/105: 49–61.

Rodríguez Velasco, Jesús D., 2010. *Order and Chivalry: Knighthood and Citizenship in Late Medieval Castile*, The Middle Ages Series (Philadelphia: University of Pennsylvania Press).

Romancero. 1993, ed. Giuseppe Di Stefano (Madrid: Taurus).

Romero Portilla, Paz, 2002. 'Exiliados en Castilla en la segunda mitad del siglo XIV. Origen del partido portugués', in Carlos M. Reglero de la Fuente (ed.), *Poder y sociedad en la Baja Edad Media hispánica. Estudios en homenaje al profesor Luis Vicente Díaz Martín*, 2 vols (Valladolid: Universidad de Valladolid), I, pp. 519–40.

Ron Fernández, Xosé Xabier, 2005. 'Anotacións sobre a coordinación medieval galego-portuguesa dende a praxe tradutora: o caso da *Demanda do Santo Graal*', in Rosario Álvarez Blanco, Francisco Fernández Rei and Antón Santamarina (eds), *A lingua galega: historia e actualidade. Actas do I Congreso Internacional (16–20 de setembro de 1996, Santiago de Compostela)*, 4 vols (Santiago de Compostela: Instituto da Lingua Galega), III, pp. 251–76.

Roncaglia, Aurelio, 1958. 'Carestia', *CuN*, 18: 121–37.

Roques, Mario, 1978. *Les Romans de Chrétien de Troyes, édités d'après la copie de Guiot (Bibl. Nat. Fr. 794). III. Le Chevalier de la Charrette, Lancelot* (Paris: Honoré Champion).

Ros Domingo, Enrique Andrés, 1995. *Die spanischen Prosaversionen des Tristanromans* (doctoral thesis, Bern: Copy Quick).

Ros Domingo, Enrique Andrés, 2001. *Arthurische Literatur der Romania. Die iberoromanischen Fassungen des Tristanromans und ihre Beziehungen zu den französischen und italienischen Versionen* (Bern: Peter Lang).

Rossi, Luciano, 1979. *A literatura novelística na Idade Média portuguesa* (Lisbon: ICALP).

Rossi, Luciano, 1992. 'La chemise d'Iseut et l'amour tristanien', in Gérard Gouiran (ed.), *Contacts de langues, de civilisations et intertextualité. IIIème Congrès international de l'Association internationale d'études occitanes (Montpellier, 20–26 septembre 1990)*, 3 vols (Montpellier: Centre d'Études Occitanes Université de Montpellier), III, pp. 1121–37.

Roubaud-Bénichou, Sylvia 2000. *Le roman de chevalerie en Espagne. Entre Arthur et Don Quichotte* (Paris: Champion).

Roubaud, Sylvia, 2001. 'De la cour d'Arthur à la Bibliothèque de Charles Quint: la longue errance des chevaliers de roman', *Iberica*, 13: 239–50.

Roussineau, Gilles (ed.), 1996. *La Suite du Roman de Merlin*, Textes Littéraires Français, 472, 2 vols (Geneva: Droz).

Roussineau, Gilles, 1998. 'Remarques sur les relations entre la *Suite du Roman de Merlin* et sa Continuation et le *Tristan en prose*', in J. Claude Faucon, Alain Labbé and Danielle Quéruel (eds),

Miscellanea Mediaevalia. Mélanges offerts à Philippe Ménard, 2 vols (Paris: Honoré Champion), II, pp. 1149–62.

Rubió y Lluch, Antonio, 1908–21. *Documents per l'Història de la Cultura Catalana Mig-eval*, 2 vols (Barcelona: Institut d'Estudis Catalans); rpt as Antoni Rubió i Lluch, *Documents per a la història de la cultura catalana medieval*, 2 vols, introduction by Albert Balcells and A. Hauf, Memòries de la Secció Històrico-Arqueològica, 54 (Barcelona: Institut d'Estudis Catalans, 2000).

Rubió i Lluch, A[ntonio], and Matheu Obrador, 1903. 'Notícia de dos manuscrits d'un *Lançalot* català', *Revista de Bibliografia Catalana*, 3: 5–25.

Rubio Pacho, Carlos, 1996. 'Aproximación a los temas amoroso y caballeresco en el *Cuento de Tristán de Leonís*', in Lillian von der Walde, Concepción Company and Aurelio González (eds), *Caballeros, monjas y maestros en la Edad Media (Actas de las V Jornadas Medievales)* (Mexico City: Universidad Nacional Autónoma de México and Colegio de México), pp. 123–31.

Rubio Pacho, Carlos, 2000. 'El amor destructor de Iseo en el *Cuento de Tristán de Leonís*', in M. Freixas, S. Iriso and L. Fernández (eds), *Actas del VIII Congreso de la Asociación Hispánica de Literatura Medieval*, 2 vols (Santander: Consejería de Cultura del Gobierno de Cantabria, Año Jubilar Lebaniego and AHLM), II, pp. 1569–74.

Rubio Pacho, Carlos, 2001. 'Tradición e innovación en dos episodios del *Tristán* hispánico', in Julián Acebrón Ruiz (ed.), *Fechos antiguos que los cavalleros en armas passaron. Estudios de la ficción caballeresca*, Ensayos Scriptura 11 (Lleida: Edicions de la Universitat de Lleida), pp. 61–73.

Rubio Pacho, Carlos, 2002. 'La negativa presencia femenina en el *Cuento de Tristán de Leonís*', in A. González, L. von der Walde and C. Company (eds), *Visiones y crónicas medievales (Actas de las VII Jornadas Medievales)* (Mexico City: El Colegio de México, Univ. Nacional Autónoma de México and Univ. Autónoma Metropolitana), pp. 279–89.

Ruiz, Juan, 1973. *Libro de buen amor*, ed. Joan Corominas (Madrid: Gredos).

Ruiz, Juan, 1992: see Blecua, Alberto.

Ruiz-Domènec, José Enrique, 1993. *La novela y el espíritu de la caballería* (Barcelona: Mondadori).

Ruiz García, Elisa, 1998. 'Hacia una tipología del libro manuscrito castellano en el siglo XV', in *Calligraphica et Tipographia. Arithmetica et Numerica. Cronologia*, Rubrica: Palaeographica et diplomatica studia, 7 (Barcelona: Universitat, 1998), pp. 405–35.

Ruiz García, Elisa, 2004. *Los libros de Isabel la Católica. Arqueología de un patrominio escrito*, Serie maior, 6 (Madrid and Salamanca: Instituto de Historia del Libro y de la Lectura).

Rumble, Thomas C., 1969. 'The Tale of Tristram: Development by Analogy', in R. M. Lumiansky (ed.), *Malory's Originality: A Critical Study of Le Morte Darthur* (Baltimore: The Johns Hopkins University Press), pp. 122–44.

Rychner, Jean, 1968. 'Le sujet et la signification du *Chevalier de la charrette*', VR, 27: 50–76.

Sabaté, Glòria, and Lourdes Soriano Robles, 2000. 'Martorell i la Taula Rodona: la matèria de Bretanya al *Tirant lo Blanch*', in Margarita Freixas, Silvia Iriso and Laura Fernández (eds), *Actas del VIII Congreso Internacional de la Asociación Hispánica de Literatura Medieval (Santander, 22–26 de septiembre de 1999)*, 2 vols (Santander: Consejería de Cultura del Gobierno de Cantabria, Año Jubilar Lebaniego, and AHLM), II, pp. 1575–85.

Sahagún, Bernardino de. 1938. *Historia general de las cosas de Nueva España por el M. R. P. Fr. Bernardino de Sahagún*, 5 vols (Mexico City: Editorial Pedro Robredo).

Sainz de la Maza, Carlos (ed.), 2003. Garci Rodríguez de Montalvo, *Sergas de Esplandián*, Clásicos Castalia, 272 (Madrid: Castalia).

Sales Dasí, Emilio José, 1991, '*Tirant lo Blanc* i la mítica cavalleria medieval', in Antoni Ferrando and Albert G. Hauf (eds), *Miscel·lània Joan Fuster. Estudis de llengua i literatura*, 8 vols, Biblioteca Abat Oliba, 97 (Barcelona: Departament de Filologia Catalana Univ. València, Associació Internacional de Llengua i Literatura Catalanes, and Publicacions de l'Abadia de Monserrat), IV, pp. 97–117.

Sales Dasí, Emilio, 1995. '"Visión" literaria y sueño nacional en las *Sergas de Esplandián*', in Juan Paredes Núñez, (ed.), *Medioevo y literatura. Actas del V Congreso de la Asociación Hispánica de*

Literatura Medieval (Granada, 27 septiembre–1 octubre 1993), 4 vols (Granada: Universidad de Granada), IV, pp. 273–88.

Sales Dasí, Emilio J., 1996. 'Las *Sergas de Esplandián* y las continuaciones del *Amadís* (*Florisandos y Rogeles*)', *Voz y Letra*, 7/1: 131–56.

Sales Dasí, Emilio 1999a. 'Algunos aspectos de lo maravilloso en la tradición del *Amadís de Gaula*: serpientes, naos y otros prodigios', in Santiago Fortuño Llorens and Tomàs Martínez Romero (eds), *Actes del VII Congrés de l'Associació Hispànica de Literatura Medieval (Castelló de la Plana, 22–26 de setembre de 1997)*, 3 vols (Castellón de la Plana: Universitat Jaume I), III, pp. 345–60.

Sales Dasi, Emilio J., 1999b. '"Garci Rodríguez de Montalvo, regidor de la noble villa de Medina del Campo"', *RFE*, 79: 123–58.

Salvador Miguel, Nicasio, 2010. 'Garci Rodríguez de Montalvo, autor del *Amadís de Gaula*', in José Manuel Fradejas Rueda, Déborah Dietrick Smithbauer, Demetrio Martín Sanz and María Jesús Díez Garretas (eds), *Actas del XIII Congreso Internacional de la Asociación Hispánica de Literatura Medieval (Valladolid, 15 al 19 de septiembre de 2009). In memoriam Alan Deyermond*, 2 vols (Valladolid: Ayuntamento de Valladolid, Universidad de Valladolid, and AHLM), I, pp. 245–83.

Sánchez Ameijeiras, Rocío, 2003. 'Cistercienses y leyendas artúricas: el Caballero del León en Penamaior (Lugo)', in *El tímpano románico. Imágenes, estructuras y audiencias*, ed. Rocío Sánchez Ameijeiras and José Luis Senra Gabriel y Galán (Santiago de Compostela: Xunta de Galicia, Consellería de Cultura, Comunicación Social y Turismo), 295–321.

Sánchez Cantón, Francisco Javier, 1950. *Libros, tapices y cuadros que coleccionó Isabel la Católica* (Madrid: CSIC).

Sánchez-Prieto Borja, Pedro, 2009. *Alfonso X el Sabio. General Estoria*. Primera Parte, 2 vols (Madrid: Biblioteca Castro).

Santanach i Suñol, Joan, 2003. 'El *Còdex Miscel·lani* de l'Arxiu de les Set Claus (Andorra la Vella, Arxiu Històric Nacional)', *AEM*, 33/1: 417–62: *http://estudiosmedievales.revistas.csic.es/index.php/estudiosmedievales/article/view/206/210*.

Santanach i Suñol, Joan, 2010. 'Sobre la tradició catalana del *Tristany de Leonís* i un nou testimoni fragmentari', *Mot So Razo*, 9: 21–38.

Santanach i Suñol, Joan (ed.), in press. *Tristany de Leonís. Fragments conservats de la traducció catalana medieval* (Barcelona: Barcino).

Santiago, Iara Romeiro Silva, 1999. '*A Demanda do Santo Graal*: a duplicidade básica' (unpublished doctoral thesis, Araraquara: Universidade Estadual Paulista).

Santos, Ana Paula Vieira, 2001. 'O desejo e a ascese: a encruzilhada do Graal (análise da presença feminina n'*A Demanda do Santo Graal*' (unpublished doctoral thesis, Universidade de São Paulo).

Santos, Luiz Felipe Pereira de Mello Santos, 2007. 'A mulher como representação do Bem e do Mal n'*A Demanda do Santo Graal*' (unpublished doctoral thesis, Universidade do Estado de Rio de Janeiro).

San Pedro, Diego de, 1995. *Cárcel de Amor, con la continuación de Nicolás* Núñez, ed. Carmen Parrilla (Barcelona: Crítica).

Saraiva, António José, 1971. 'O autor da narrativa da batalha do Salado e a refundição do *Livro do Conde D. Pedro*', *BF*, 22 (1964–71 [1973]): 1–16.

Sarmati, Elisabetta, 1996. *La critiche ai libri di caballería nel Cinquecento spagnolo (con uno sguardo sul Seicento): un'analisi testuale*, Collana di Testi e Studi Ispanici, II: Saggi, 8 (Pisa: Giardini).

Schenkel, Luciana de Moraes, 2009. '*A Demanda do Santo Graal* e seus entrecruzamentos' (unpublished doctoral thesis, Porto Alegre: Universidade Federal de Rio Grande do Sul).

Schiff, M[ario], 1905. *La bibliothèque du marquis de Santillane* (Paris: Plon).

Schreiner, Elisabeth, 1981. 'Die *Matière de Bretagne* im *Libro del Cavallero Cifar*. Zur Rezeption der *Matière de Bretagne* in zwei Episoden des *Libro del Cavallero Cifar*', in Dieter Messner and Wolfgang Pöckl with Angela Birner (eds), *Romanisches Mittelalter Festschrift zum 60. Geburtstag von Rudolf Baehr* (Göppingen: Kümmerle), pp. 269–83.

Scudieri Ruggieri, Jole, 1966. 'Due note di letteratura spagnola del sec. XIV. 1) La cultura francese nel

Caballero Zifar e nell'*Amadís*; versioni spagnole del Tristano in prosa. 2) "De ribaldo"', *CuN*, 26/1: 233–52.
Scudieri Ruggieri, Jole, 1980. *Cavalleria e cortesia nella vita e nella cultura di Spagna* (Modena: Mucchi).
Segura, Joan, 1907–8. *Història d'Igualada*, 2 vols (Barcelona: Estampa d'Eugeni Subirana).
Seidenspinner-Núñez, Dayle, 1981–2. 'The Sense of an Ending: The Tristán Romance in Spain', *Tristania*, 7: 27–46.
Seidenspinner-Núñez, Dayle, 1987–8. 'Fathers and Sons: Notes on the Evolution of the Romance Hero', *Tristania*, 13: 19–34.
Serés, Guillermo (ed.), 2011. Bernal Díaz del Castillo, *Historia verdadera de la conquista de la Nueva España*, Biblioteca clásica de la Real Academia Española, 36 (Madrid and Barcelona: Real Academia Española, Galaxia Gutenberg and Círculo de Lectores).
Sergas de Esplandián: see Rodríguez de Montalvo, Garci.
Serra Desfilis, Amadeo, 2002. '*Ab recont de grans gestes*. Sobre les imatges de la història i de la llegenda en la pintura gòtica de la Corona d'Aragó', *Afers*, 41: 15–35.
Serrano y Sanz, M[anuel], 1919–21. '*Cronicón Villarense* (*Liber Regum*). Primeros años del siglo XIII. La obra histórica más antigua en idioma español', *BRAE*, 6 (1919): 192–220, and 8 (1921): 367–82.
Serrano y Sanz, M[anuel] (ed.), 1928. 'Fragmento de una versión galaico-portuguesa de *Lanzarote del Lago* (manuscrito del siglo XIV)', *BRAE*, 15: 307–14.
Sharrer, Harvey L., 1971. 'The Passing of King Arthur to the Island of Brasil in a Fifteenth-Century Spanish Version of the Post-Vulgate *Roman du Graal*', *Ro*, 92: 65–74.
Sharrer, Harvey L., 1977 [1978]. *A Critical Bibliography of Hispanic Arthurian Material. I, Texts: The Prose Romance Cycles*, RBC, 3 (London: Grant & Cutler Ltd).
Sharrer, Harvey L. 1978. 'Two Eighteenth-century Chapbook Romances of Chivalry by António da Silva, Mestre de gramática: *Lançarote do Lago* and *Dário Lobondo Alexandrino*', *HR*, 46/2: 137–46.
Sharrer, Harvey L. (ed.), 1979a. *The Legendary History of Britain in Lope García de Salazar's 'Libro de las bienandanzas e fortunas'*, Haney Foundation Series, XXIII (Philadelphia: University of Pennsylvania Press).
Sharrer, Harvey L., 1979b. 'Malory and the Spanish and Italian Tristan Text: The Search for the Missing Link', *Tristania*, 4/2: 36–43.
Sharrer, Harvey L., 1981. 'The Provenance and Date of the Spanish Prose *Lancelot*', *BBIAS*, 33: 311.
Sharrer, Harvey L., 1981–2. 'Letters in the Hispanic Prose Tristan Text: Iseut's Complaint and Tristan's Reply', *Tristania*, 7: 3–20.
Sharrer, Harvey L., 1984a. 'La fusión de las novelas artúrica y sentimental a fines de la Edad Media', *El Crotalón: Anuario de Filología Española*, 1: 147–57.
Sharrer, Harvey L. 1984b. 'Eighteenth-century Chapbook Adaptations of the *Historia de Flores y Blancaflor* by António da Silva, mestre de gramatica', *HR*, 52.1: 59–74.
Sharrer, Harvey L., 1986. 'Spanish and Portuguese Arthurian Literature', in Norris J. Lacy, Geoffrey Ashe, Sandra Ness Ihle, Marianne E. Kalinke and Raymond H. Thompson (eds), *The Arthurian Encyclopedia* (New York: Garland Publishing), pp. 516–21.
Sharrer, Harvey L., 1986–7. 'Notas sobre la materia artúrica hispánica (1979–1986)', *LC*, 15/2: 329–40.
Sharrer, Harvey L., 1988a. 'Juan de Burgos: impresor y refundidor de libros caballerescos', in María Luisa LópezVidriero and Pedro M. Cátedra (eds), *El libro antiguo español: Actas del Primer Coloquio Internacional (Madrid: 18 al 20 de diciembre de 1986)* (Salamanca: Ediciones de la Universidad de Salamanca; Madrid: Biblioteca Nacional and Sociedad Española de Historia del Libro), pp. 361–9.
Sharrer, Harvey L., 1988b. 'La materia de Bretaña en la poesía gallego-portuguesa', in Vicente Beltrán (ed.), *Actas del I Congreso de la Asociación Hispánica de Literatura Medieval (Santiago de Compostela, 2 al 6 de diciembre de 1985)* (Barcelona: PPU), pp. 561–9.
Sharrer, Harvey L., 1990–1. 'Briolanja as a Name in Early Fifteenth-century Portugal: Echo of a Reworked Portuguese *Amadís de Gaula*?', *LC*, 19/1: 112–18.
Sharrer, Harvey L., 1994. 'The Acclimatization of the Lancelot-Grail Cycle in Spain and Portugal', in

William W. Kibler (ed.), *The Lancelot-Graal Cycle: Text and Transformations* (Austin: University of Texas Press), pp. 175–90.

Sharrer, Harvey L., 1996a. 'Spanish and Portuguese Arthurian Literature', in Norris J. Lacy (ed.), *The New Arthurian Encyclopedia* (New York and London: Garland), pp. 425–8.

Sharrer, Harvey L., 1996b. 'Spain and Portugal', in Norris J. Lacy (ed.), *Medieval Arthurian Literature. A Guide to Recent Research*, Garland Reference Library of the Humanities (New York: Garland Publishing), pp. 401–49.

Sharrer, Harvey L., and Antonio Contreras Martín (eds), 2006. *Lanzarote del Lago* (Alcalá de Henares: CEC).

Shirt, David, 1973. 'Chrétien de Troyes and the cart', in Lewis Thorpe et al. (eds), *Studies in Medieval Literature and Languages in Memory of Frederick Whitehead* (Manchester: Manchester University Press; New York: Barnes & Noble).

Sholod, Barton, 1982. 'The Fortunes of *Amadís* among the Spanish Jewish exiles', in Josep Maria Solà-Solé, Samuel G. Armistead and Joseph H. Silverman (eds), *Hispania Judaica: Studies on the History, Language, and Literature of the Jews in the Hispanic World, II: Literature*, Biblioteca Universitaria Puvill, I: Estudios, 3 (Barcelona: Puvill), pp. 89–99.

Sierra, Pedro de la, 2003. *Espejo de príncipes y caballeros* (Segunda parte), ed. José Julio Martín Romero (Alcalá de Henares: CEC).

Silva, Feliciano de, 1999. *Florisel de Niquea* (Tercera parte), ed. J. Martín Lalanda (Alcalá de Henares: CEC).

Silva, Feliciano de, 2002. *Lisuarte de Grecia (Libro VII de Amadís de Gaula)*, ed. Emilio José Sales Dasí (Alcalá de Henares: CEC).

Silva, Feliciano de, 2004. *Amadís de Grecia*, ed. Ana Bueno and C. Laspuertas (Alcalá de Henares: CEC).

Silvério, Carla Alexandra Serapicos de Brito, 2002. 'As imagens do corpo e as representações da sociedade medieval n'*A Demanda do Santo Graal*', in Leonor Curado Neves, Margarida Madureira and Teresa Amado (eds), *Matéria de Bretanha em Portugal. Actas do colóquio realizado em Lisboa nos dias 8 e 9 de Novembro de 2001* (Lisbon: Colibri), pp. 227–40.

Simó, Meritxell, 2007. 'A propósito de la primera traducción francesa en prosa de la *Historia Regum Britanniae*', *RLM*, 19: 243–71.

Simó, Meritxell, 2008. 'Les primeres traduccions romàniques en prosa de la *Historia Regum Britanniae*', *Estudis Romànics*, 30: 39–53.

Simões, João Gaspar, 1967. 'A prosa narrativa da Idade Média. O ciclo carolíngio. O aparecimento do rei Artur na novelística peninsular', in *História do romance português* (Lisbon: Estúdios Cor), pp. 21–64.

Simões, João Gaspar, 1987. 'Os livros de cavalarias. Da *Demanda do Santo Graal* ao *Memorial das proezas da Segunda Távola Redonda*', in *Perspectiva histórica da ficção portuguesa. Das origens ao século XX* (Lisbon: Publicações Dom Quixote), pp. 31–76.

Simonin, Michel, 1984. 'La disgrâce d'*Amadís*', *Studi francesi*, 28: 1–35.

Siqueira, Ana Marcia Alves, 2005. 'A Crônica do sonho imperial português', *Politeia. História e Sociedade*, 5/1: 119–31.

Siqueira, Ana Marcia Alves, 2012. 'Configuração do Mal na *Demanda do Santo Graal*', in Lênia Márcia Mongelli (ed.), *De cavaleiros e cavalarias. Por terras de Europa e Américas* (São Paulo: Humanitas), pp. 87–100.

Soberanas, Amadeu-J., 1979. 'La version galaïco-portugaise de la *Suite du Merlin*. Transcription du fragment du XIVe siècle de la Bibliothèque de Catalogne, ms. 2434', *VR*, 38: 174–93.

Soldevila, Ferran, 1926. 'La llegenda arturiana en la nostra literatura', *Revista de Catalunya*, V: 593–602.

Soldevila, Ferran, 1957. 'Un poema joglaresc sobre l'engendrament de Jaume I', in Rafael de Balbín (ed.), *Estudios dedicados a Menéndez Pidal*, 7 vols (Madrid: CSIC, Patronato Marcelino Menéndez y Pelayo), VII: 71–80.

Soldevila, Ferran (ed.), 2007. *Les quatre grans Cròniques. I. Llibre dels feits del rei en Jaume*, revisió filològica de Jordi Bruguera, revisió històrica de M. Teresa Ferrer i Mallol, Memòries de la Secció Històrico-Arqueològica, LXXIII (Barcelona: Institut d'Estudis Catalans).

Soldevila, Ferran (ed.), 2008. *Les quatre grans Cròniques. II. Crònica de Bernat Desclot*, revisió filològica de Jordi Bruguera, revisió històrica de M. Teresa Ferrer i Mallol, Memòries de la Secció Històrico-Arqueològica, LXXX (Barcelona: Institut d'Estudis Catalans).

Soldevila, Ferran (ed.), 2011. *Les quatre grans Cròniques. III. Crònica de Ramon Muntaner*, revisió filològica de Jordi Bruguera, revisió històrica de M. Teresa Ferrer i Mallol, Memòries de la Secció Històrico-Arqueològica, LXXXVI (Barcelona: Institut d'Estudis Catalans).

Soler i Llopart, Albert, 1989. '"Mas cavaller qui d'açò fa lo contrari". Una lectura del tractat lul·lià sobre la cavalleria', *Estudios Lulianos*, 29/1: 1–23; 29/2: 101–24.

Soler, Albert, and Santanach, Joan (eds), 2009. Ramon Llull, *Romanç d'Evast e Blaquerna*, Nova Edició de les Obres de Ramon Llull, VIII (Palma de Mallorca: Patronat Ramon Llull).

Sommer, H. O[skar], 1907. 'The Queste of the Holy Grail, Forming the Third Part of the Trilogy Indicated in the *Suite du Merlin* Huth Ms', *Ro*, 36: 369–402, 543–90.

Sommer, H. O., 1908. 'Zur Kritik der altfr[anzösischen] Artus-Romane in Prosa: Robert und Helie de Borron', *ZrP*, 32: 323–7.

Sommer, H. Oskar (ed.), 1908–16. *The Vulgate Version of the Arthurian Romances, Edited from Manuscripts in the British Museum*, 8 vols, Publications of the Carnegie Institution, 74 (Washington: The Carnegie Institution; rpt New York: AMS, 1969). [Volumes cited: 1, *L'Estoire del Saint Graal* (1909); 2, *L'Estoire de Merlin* (1908); 3–5, *Le Livre de Lancelot du Lac* (1910–12); 7, *Le livre d'Artus* (1913).]

Sommer, H.O. (ed.), 1913. *Die Abenteuer Gawains, Ywains und Le Morholts mit den drei jungfrauen, aus der Trilogie (Demanda) des Pseudo-Robert de Borron*, Beihefte zur *ZrP*, 47 (Halle: Max Niemeyer).

Soriano Robles, Lourdes, 1999a. 'La edición del fragmento gallego-portugués del *Livro de Tristan*', in Carmen Parrilla et al. (eds), *Edición y anotación de textos Actas del Congreso de jóvenes filólogos (A Coruña, 25–28 de septiembre de 1996)*, 2 vols (A Coruña: Universidade da Coruña), II, pp. 667–76.

Soriano Robles, Lourdes, 1999b. 'Els fragments catalans del *Tristany de Leonís*', in Santiago Fortuño Llorens and Tomàs Martínez Romero (eds), *Actes del VIIe Congrés de L'Associació Hispànica de Literatura Medieval (Castelló de la Plana, 22–26 de setembre de 1997)*, 3 vols (Castelló de la Plana: Servei de Publicacions Universitat Jaume I), III, pp. 413–28.

Soriano Robles, Lourdes, 2000. 'Traducciones medievales en la Península Ibérica: el caso del *Tristan en prose*: una aproximación a su transmisión textual' (unpublished doctoral thesis, Universidad de Barcelona, Departament de Filologia Romànica).

Soriano Robles, Lourdes, 2001. '"E que le daria ponçoña con quel el muriese": los tres intentos de envenenamiento de Tristán a manos de su madrastra', *CuN*, 61: 319–33.

Soriano Robles, Lourdes, 2003a. '"E qui vol saber questa ystoria, leçia lo Libro de Miser Lanciloto": a vueltas con el final original del *Tristan en prosa* castellano', *Studi medio-latini e volgari*, 49: 203–17.

Soriano Robles, Lourdes, 2003b. 'Los *lais de Bretanha* gallego-portugueses y sus modelos franceses (*Tristan en prose* y *Suite du Merlin* de la Post-Vulgata artúrica)', in Jesús L. Serrano Reyes (ed.), *Cancioneros en Baena. Actas del II Congreso Internacional 'Cancionero de Baena'. In memoriam Manuel Alvar*, 2 vols (Baena: Ayuntamiento de Baena, Delegación de Cultura), II, pp. 27–46.

Soriano Robles, Lourdes, 2005. '"Tres cosas vos quiero dezir": una lectura del prólogo del *Tristán de Leonís y el rey don Tristán el Joven, su hijo* (Sevilla, 1534)', in Rafael Alemany, Josep Lluís Martos and Josep Miquel Manzanaro (eds), *Actes del X Congrés Internacional de l'Associació Hispànica de Literatura Medieval (Alacant, 16–20 setembre de 2003)*, 3 vols (Alicante: Institut Interuniversitari de Filologia Valenciana), III, pp. 1485–97.

Soriano Robles, Lourdes, 2006. *Livro de Tristan. Contribución al estudio de la filiación textual del fragmento gallego-portugués* (Rome: Edizione Nuova Cultura).

Soriano Robles, Lourdes, 2007. 'La *Historia de Inglaterra con el Fructo de los Tiempos* de Rodrigo de Cuero (1509)', in Armando López Castro and Luzdivina Cuesta Torre (eds), *Actas del XI Congreso Internacional de la Asociación Hispánica de Literatura Medieval (León, 20–24 de septiembre de 2005)*, 2 vols (León: Universidad de León), II, pp. 1055–68.

Soriano Robles, Lourdes, 2010. 'Sobre la tipologia material de la literatura artúrica peninsular: els textos catalans', in José Manuel Fradejas Rueda, Déborah Dietrick Smithbauer, Demetrio Martín Sanz and María Jesús Díez Garretas (eds), *Actas del XIII Congreso Internacional de la Asociación Hispánica de Literatura Medieval (Valladolid, 15 a 19 de septiembre de 2009). In Memoriam Alan Deyermond*, 2 vols (Valladolid: Ayuntamento de Valladolid, Universidad de Valladolid, and AHLM), II, pp. 1697–1712.

Soriano Robles, Lourdes, 2013. 'El *Lancelot en prose* en bibliotecas de la Península Ibérica: Ayer y hoy', *Medievalia. Revista d'Estudis Medievals*, 16: 265–83.

Souto Cabo, José António, 2012. *Os cavaleiros que fizeram as cantigas. Aproximação às origens socioculturais da lírica galego-portuguesa* (Nitéroi–Rio de Janeiro: Universidade Federal Fluminense).

Spaggiari, Barbara, 1999. 'La *Demanda do Santo Graal* en portugais dans ses rapports avec la tradition française', *Études Médiévales*, 1: 357–66.

Stegagno-Picchio, Luciana, 1966. 'Fortuna iberica di un topos letterario: la corte di Constantinopoli, dal *Cligès* al *Palmerín de Olivia*', in Giuseppe di Stefano and Mario Manici (eds), *Studi sul 'Palmerín de Olivia'*, III: *Saggi e ricerche* (Pisa: Università di Pisa), pp. 99–136.

Steiner, Roger J., 1966–7. '*Domaa/Demanda* and the Priority of the Portuguese *Demanda*', *MPh*, 64: 64–7.

Stones, Alison, 1977. 'The Earliest Illustrated Prose *Lancelot* Manuscript?', *Reading Medieval Studies*, 3: 3–44.

Suárez Pallasá, Aquilino, 1995. 'La importancia de la impresión de Roma de 1519 para el establecimiento del texto del *Amadís de Gaula*', *Incipit*, 15: 65–114.

Suárez Pallasá, Aquilino, 2006. 'La *Historia regum Britanniæ* de Geoffrey of Monmouth, fuente del *Amadís de Gaula* primitivo. Perspectiva onomástica de la cuestión', in Lilia E. Ferrario de Orduna (ed.), *Nuevos estudios sobre literatura caballeresca*, Estudios de literatura, 104 (Kassel: Reichenberger), pp. 11–69.

Suárez Pallasá, Aquilino, 2006–8. 'Onomástica geográfica antigua en el *Amadís de Gaula* de Garci Rodríguez de Montalvo', *Stylos*, 16: 97–220; 17: 125–228; 18: 75–192.

Subirats, Jean, 1982. *Jorge Ferreira de Vasconcelos. Visages de son oeuvre et de son temps* (Coimbra: Universidade de Coimbra).

Subirats, Jean, 1986. 'Les sortilèges du rêve chevaleresque. Propos sur Jorge Ferreira de Vasconcelos et son «Memorial» das proezas da Segunda Tavola Redonda', *Cultura, História e Filosofia*, 5: 219–37.

Surles, Robert L., 1984–5. 'Herido está don Tristán: Distance, Point of View and "Piggy-Back" Poetics', *Tristania*, 10/1–2: 53–65.

Tafur, Pero, 2006. *Andanças e viajes*, ed. Miguel Angel Pérez Priego, 2 vols (Madrid: Biblioteca Castro).

Tarré, José, 1943. 'Las profecías del sabio Merlín y sus imitaciones', *Analecta Sacra Tarraconensia*, 16: 135–71.

Tavani, Giuseppe, 1980a. 'Literatura i societat a Barcelona entre la fi del segle xiv i el començament del xv', in *Actes del Cinquè Col·loqui Internacional de Llengua i Literatura Catalanes (Andorra, 1–6 d'octubre 1979)* (Barcelona: Publicacions de l'Abadia de Montserrat), pp. 7–40 (rpt *Per una història de la cultura catalana medieval*, Biblioteca de Cultura Catalana, 83 (Barcelona: Curial Edicions Catalanes), 1996, pp. 83–131).

Tavani, Giuseppe, 1980b. 'La poesia lirica galego-portoghese', in *Grundriss der romanischen Literaturen des Mittelalters*, II/6 (Heidelberg: Carl Winter), pp. 5–165.

Tavani, Giuseppe, 1991. *A poesía lírica galego-portuguesa* (Vigo: Galaxia).

Tavani, Giuseppe, 1999. *Arte de trovar do Cancioneiro da Biblioteca Nacional de Lisboa*. Introdução, edição crítica e fac-símile (Lisbon: Edições Colibri).

Terra, Sandra Salviano, 2003. 'Uma leitura de "Genevras" no jogo paralelístico d'*A Demanda do Santo Graal*', in Ângela Vaz Leão and Vanda de Oliveira Bittencourt (eds), *Anais do IV Encontro Internacional de Estudos Medievais* (Belo Horizonte: Pontifícia Universidade Católica de Minas), pp. 742–6.

Thomas, Henry, 1952. *Las novelas de caballerías españolas y portuguesas. Despertar de la novela caballeresca en la Península Ibérica y expansión e influencia en el extranjero* (Madrid: CSIC).

Ticknor, George: *see* Whitney, James Lyman.

Toldrà, Maria, 1992–3. 'Notes sobre la suposada lectura "sebastianista" de *La faula*', *Llengua & Literatura*, 5: 471–6.

Torre do Tombo, 1960–70. *As Gavetas da Torre do Tombo*, ed. A. da Silva Rego (Lisbon: Centro de Estudos Históricos Ultramarinos, 1960–70), vols 1–8.

Torre Revello, José. 1940. *El libro, la imprenta y el periodismo en América durante la dominación española*, Publicaciones del Instituto de Investigaciones Históricas, LXXIV (Buenos Aires: Facultad de Filosofía y Letras, Universidad de Buenos Aires, 1940).

Torró i Torrent, Jaume: *see* Turró i Torrent, Jaume.

Toury, Marie-Noëlle, 2001. *Mort et fin'amor dans la poésie d'oc et d'oïl aux XIIe et XIIIe siècles* (Paris: Honoré Champion).

Trachsler, Richard, 1997. *Les romans arthuriens en vers après Chrétien de Troyes* (Paris and Rome: Memini).

Tristán de Leonís 1501 (Valladolid: Juan de Burgos, 1501), ed. Luzdivina Cuesta Torre (Alcalá de Henares: CEC).

Tristán de Leonís, 1999 [MS fragments, XIVth century]: Carlos Alvar and José Manuel Lucía Megías, 'Hacia el códice del *Tristán de Leonís* (cincuenta y nueve fragmentos en la BNM)', *RLM*, 11: pp. 9–135.

Triste deleytaçión, 1982: *Triste deleytaçion. An Anonymous Fifteenth Century Castilian Romance*, ed. E. Michael Gerli (Washington, DC: Georgetown University Press).

Trujillo, José Ramón, 2004. 'La versión castellana de la *Demanda del Santo Grial*: edición y estudio' (unpublished doctoral thesis, Universidad Autónoma de Madrid).

Trujillo, José Ramón, 2008. 'Magia y maravillas en la materia artúrica hispánica. Sueños, milagros y bestias en la *Demanda del Santo Grial*', in José Manuel Lucía Megías and María Carmen Marín Pina (eds), *Amadís de Gaula, quinientos años después. Estudios en homenaje a Juan Manuel Cacho Blecua* (Alcalá de Henares: CEC), pp. 789–818.

Trujillo, José Ramón, 2009. 'La edición de traducciones medievales en la Edad de Oro. Textos e impresos de la materia artúrica hispánica', *Edad de Oro*, 28: 401–48.

Trujillo, José Ramón, 2011. 'Los nietos de Arturo y los hijos de Amadís. El género editorial caballeresco en la Edad de Oro', *Edad de Oro*, 30: 415–41.

Trujillo, José Ramón, 2012. 'Manifestaciones de Dios y del Diablo en la *Demanda del Santo Grial*', in Juan Paredes (ed.), *De lo humano y lo divino en la literatura medieval: santos, ángeles y demonios* (Granada: Universidad de Granada), pp. 355–68.

Trujillo, José Ramón, 2013. 'Traducción, refundición y modificaciones estructurales en las versiones castellanas y portuguesa de *La Demanda del Santo Grial*', *e-Spania. Revue Interdisciplinaire d'Études Hispaniques Médiévales et Modernes*, 16: *http://e-spania.revues.org/22919* [consulted 4 January 2014].

Turró i Torrent, Jaume. 1963. 'Una cort a Barcelona per a la literatura del segle XV', *Revista de Catalunya*, 163: 97–123.

Ubieto Arteta, Antonio (ed.), 1989. *Corónicas navarras* (Zaragoza: Anubar).

Urbina, Eduardo, 1991. *El sin par Sancho Panza: parodia y creación*, Serie Cervantina, 1 (Barcelona: Anthropos).

Uría Varela, Jesús, 1997. *Tabú y eufemismo en latín* (Amsterdam: A. M. Hakkert).

Usero González, Rafael 1986. *Sir Lanzarote do Lago e a súa proxenie cedeiresa* (O Castro-Sada: Fundación Munic. Villabrille).

Valero Moreno, Juan Miguel, 2010a. 'El prólogo de *Amadís* (1508) y las *Estorias de Troya*. Transferencias', *Troianalexandrina*, 10: 9–33.

Valero Moreno, Juan Miguel, 2010b. 'La vida santa de los caballeros: camino de perfección, flor de santidad. Reflexiones en torno al manuscrito 1877 de la Biblioteca Universitaria de Salamanca', *RFR*, 27: 327–57.

Van Beysterveldt, Anthony, 1982. *Amadís-Esplandián-Calisto. Historia de un linaje adulterado*, Studia humanitatis (Madrid: Porrúa Turanzas).

Van Coolput-Storms, Colette-Anne, 1999. 'Souillure, indignitas et haïne de soi: l'impossible rechat dans la *Demanda do Santo Graal*', in Heitor Megale and Haquira Osakabe (eds), *Textos medievais portugueses e as súas fontes. Matéria da Bretanha e cantigas com notação musical* (São Paulo: Humanitas), pp. 57–75.

Van der Horst, C.H.M. (ed.), 1974. *Blandin de Cornouaille. Introduction. Édition diplomatique. Glossaire* (The Hague: Mouton).

Vaquero, Mercedes, 2003. *Cultura nobiliaria y biblioteca de Fernán Pérez de Guzmán* (Ciudad Real: Oretania).

Vargas, Bernardo de, 2004. *Cirongilio de Tracia*, ed. Javier Roberto González (Alcalá de Henares: CEC).

Vargas Díaz-Toledo, Aurelio (ed.), 2007a. 'Edición crítica y estudio del *Leomundo de Grécia*, de Tristão Gomes de Castro' (unpublished doctoral thesis, Universidad Complutense de Madrid).

Vargas Díaz-Toledo, Aurelio, 2007b. 'Un mundo de maravillas y encantamientos: los libros de caballerías portugueses', in Armando López Castro and Luzdivina Cuesta Torre (eds), *Actas del XI Congreso Internacional de la Asociación Hispánica de Literatura Medieval (León, 20–24 de septiembre de 2005)*, 2 vols (León: Universidad de León), II, pp. 1099–1108.

Vargas Díaz-Toledo, Aurelio, 2010. 'Los libros de caballerías portugueses', *Destiempos. Revista de Curiosidad Cultural*, 23: 217–31.

Vargas Díaz-Toledo, Aurelio, 2012a. *Os livros de cavalarias portugueses dos séculos XVI–XVIII* (Lisbon: Pearlbooks).

Vargas Díaz-Toledo, Aurelio, 2012b. 'A literatura cavaleiresca portuguesa: estado da questão', in Lênia Márcia Mongelli (eds), *De cavaleiros e cavalarias por terras de Europa e Américas* (São Paulo: Humanitas), pp. 145–56.

Vargas Díaz-Toledo, Aurelio, 2013. 'A Matéria Arturiana na literatura cavaleiresca portuguesa dos séculos XVI–XVII', *e-Spania. Revue Interdisciplinaire d'Études Hispaniques Médiévales et Modernes*, 16: http://e-spania.revues.org/22796 [consulted 4 January 2014].

Varnhagen, Francisco Adolfo, 1872. *Da literatura dos livros de cavalarias* (Vienna: Filho de C. Gerold).

Várvaro, Alberto, 2001. 'El *Tirant lo Blanch* en la narrativa europea del segle XV', *Estudis Romànics*, 24: 149–67.

Veiga, Augusto Botelho da Costa Veiga, 1942. 'Os nossos nobiliários medievais. Alguns elementos para a cronologia da sua elaboração', *ABA*, série II/15: 165–93.

Velázquez, Gabriel, 2004. *Clarián de Landanís*, ed. A. J. González Gonzalo (Alcalá de Henares: CEC).

Ventura, Leontina, 2006. *D. Afonso III* (Lisbon: Círculo de Leitores).

Ventura Castro, Jovita, et al. (eds), 1985. *Philippine Metrical Romances*, Anthology of ASEAN Literatures (Quezon City: ASEAN Committee on Culture and Information).

Vicent Santamaria, Sara, 2005. '"Parole qui n'est entendue / vaut autretant comme perdue": els problemes d'edició de *La Faula* de Guillem de Torroella', *Randa*, 55: 15–42.

Vicent Santamaria, Sara, 2007. '*La Faula* de Guillem de Torroella: ¿literatura o política?', *Res Publica. Revista de Filosofia Política*, 17: 341–56.

Vicent Santamaria, Sara, 2008. 'Noves aportacions sobre el rerefons polític de *La Faula* de Guillem de Torroella', in *II Jornades d'Estudis Locals a Sóller. En homenatge a Joan Estades i Ensenyat* (Sóller: Ajuntament de Sóller), pp. 255–75.

Vicent Santamaria, Sara (ed.), 2011. *Guillem de Torroella. La Faula*, Clásicos (València: Tirant lo Blanch).

Vicente, Maria Graça, 2011. 'A viagem de D. Afonso V a França', *Iacobvs. Revista de Estudios Jacobeos y Medievales*, 29–30: 117–35.

Vidal Alcover, Jaume, 1980. 'La fada Morgana en la tradició oral mallorquina', *Randa*, 11: 179–82.

Vieira, Elsa Mónica, 2009, 'Em demanda de Boorz pela Península Ibérica', in Jesús Cañas Murillo, Francisco Javier Grande Quejigo and José Roso Díaz (eds), *Medievalismo en Extremadura. Estudios sobre Literatura y Cultura Hispánicas de la Edad Media* (Cáceres: Universidad de Extremadura), pp. 1139–48.

Vieira, Yara Frateschi, 2012. 'Os *Lais de Bretanha*: voltando à questão da autoria', in Lênia Márcia Mongelli (ed.), *De cavaleiros e cavalarias por terras de Europa e Américas* (São Paulo: Humanitas), pp. 655–68.

Vilariño Martínez, Agustín, 2005. 'Estudio de las divergencias en torno a las traducciones ibéricas del cap. IX del *Erec en prose*', in Rosario Álvarez Blanco, Francisco Fernández Rei and Antón Santamarina (eds), *A lingua galega: historia e actualidade. Actas do I Congreso Internacional (16–20 de setembro de 1996, Santiago de Compostela)*, 4 vols (Santiago de Compostela: Instituto da Lingua Galega), III, pp. 329–47.

Vilela, Fernando. 2006. *Lampião & Lancelote* (São Paulo: CosacNaify, 2006).

Villacorta, Consuelo (ed.), 2000. Lope García de Salazar, *Libro XI de la Historia de las Bienandanzas e Fortunas* (Bilbao: Universidad del País Vasco).

Vinaver, Eugène, 1959. 'The Prose Tristan', in Roger Sherman Loomis (ed.), *Arthurian Literature in the Middle Ages: A Collaborative History* (Oxford: Clarendon Press, 1959, rpt 1974), pp. 339–47.

Víñez Sánchez, Antonia, 1994. 'Súplica y réplica: Don Enrique en la lírica gallego-portuguesa', in María Isabel Toro Pascua (ed.), *Actas del III Congreso Internacional de la Asociación Hispánica de Literatura Medieval*, 2 vols (Salamanca: Universidad de Salamanca), II, pp. 1161–70.

Víñez Sánchez, Antonia, 2004. *El trovador Gonçal'Eanes do Vinhal. Estudio histórico y edición, Verba*, Anexo 55 (Santiago de Compostela: Universidade de Santiago de Compostela).

Vivas, Juan, 2006. *La Quête du saint Graal et la mort d'Arthur*, trans. Vincent Serverat and Philippe Walter (Grenoble: ELLUG).

Wagner, Charles Philip, 1903. 'The Sources of *El cavallero Cifar*', *RH*, 10: 5–104.

Wagner, Charles Philip, 1929. *El libro del Cauallero Zifar (El libro del Cauallero de Dios)* (Ann Arbor: Univ. of Michigan).

Waley, Pamela, 1961. 'Juan de Flores y *Tristán de Leonís*', *Hispanófila*, 12: 1–14.

Waley, Pamela, 1972. 'Introduction', in Juan de Flores, *Grimalte y Gradissa*, ed. Pamela Waley (London: Tamesis Books), pp. xxv–xxvii.

Waley, Pamela (ed.), 1982. *Curial and Guelfa* (London: George Allen & Unwin).

Wechssler, Eduard, 1895. *Über die verschiedenen Redaktionen des Robert von Borron zugeschriebenen Graal-Lancelot-Cyklus* (Halle: Max Niemeyer).

Wechssler, Eduard, 1898. *Die Sage vom heiligen Gral in ihrer Entwicklung bis auf Richard Wagners Parsifal* (Halle: Max Niemeyer).

Weddige, Hilkert, 1975. *Die 'Historien vom Amadis auss Franckreich'. Dokumentarische Grundlegung zur Entstehung und Rezeption*, Beiträge zur Literatur des xv. bis xviii. Jahrhunderts, 2 (Wiesbaden: Franz Steiner).

West, George D., 1978. *An Index of Proper Names in French Arthurian Prose Romances* (Toronto: University of Toronto Press).

Whitney, James Lyman, 1879. *Catalogue of the Spanish Library and of the Portuguese Books Bequeathed by George Ticknor to the Boston Public Library. Together with the Collection of Spanish and Portuguese Literature in the General Library* (Boston: Printed by Order of the Trustees, 1879).

Wild, Gerhard, 1989. 'Säkularisierung und Dissoziation: *A Demanda do Santo Graal*', *ZrP*, 105: 322–36.

Williams, G[race] S., 1909. 'The *Amadis* Question', *RH*, 21: 1–167.

Williams, Mary, 1922–5. *Gerbert de Montreuil, La Continuation de Perceval*, 2 vols (Paris: Champion)

Wolf, Ferdinand, 1865. *Ein Beitrag zur Rechts-symbolik aus spanischen Quellen* (Vienna: Karl Gerold's Sohn).

Wolf, Ferdinand J., and Konrad Hofmann, 1856. *Primavera y flor de romances y refranes ó colección de los mas viejos y mas populares romances castellanos* (Berlin: A. Asher).

Wolfzettel, Friedrich, 1994. 'Artus en cage: quelques remarques sur le roman arthurien et l'histoire', in Keith Busby and Norris J. Lacy (eds), *Conjunctures: Medieval Studies in Honor of Douglas Kelly* (Amsterdam: Rodopi), pp. 575–88.

Wright, Neil (ed.), 1996. *The Historia Regum Britanniae of Geoffrey de Monmouth.* I, *Bern. Burgerbibliothek, MS. 568* (Cambridge: D. S. Brewer).

Yáñez, Rodrigo, 1956. *Poema de Alfonso XI.* Ed. Yo Ten Cate (Madrid: CSIC).

Yllera, Alicia, 1991. 'Gauvain / Gawain: Las múltiples transposiciones de un héroe', *RLM*, 3: 199–221.

Zarandona, Juan (ed.), 2002. *Cultura, literatura y traducción artúrica* (Soria: Diputación de Soria).

Zarandona, Juan, 2003. *Alfred Lord Tennyson y la literatura artúrica española de los siglos XIX y XX: traducción, manipulación e intertextualidad* (Zaragoza: Universidad de Zaragoza).

Zarandona, Juan, 2004. *Los* Ecos de las montañas *de José Zorrilla y sus fuentes de inspiración: de Tennyson a Doré* (Valladolid: Universidad de Valladolid).

Zarandona, Juan, 2007. *La recepción de Alfred Lord Tennyson en España. Traductores y traducciones artúricas* (Valladolid: Universidad de Valladolid).

Zierer, Adriana Maria de Souza, 2003. 'Artur como modelo régio nas fontes ibéricas (I): *A Demanda do Santo Graal*', *Brathair*, 3/2: 44–61.

Zierer, Adriana Maria de Souza, 2004. 'Artur nas fontes ibéricas medievais (II). *Libro de las generaciones* e *Nobiliário do Conde Dom Pedro*', *Brathair*, 4/2: 141–58.

Zierer, Adriana Maria de Souza, 2007. 'O Nobre e o Rei. A influência de Galaaz na elaboração da imagem de Nun'Alvares Pereira', *Brathair*, 7/2: 80–105.

Zierer, Adriana Maria de Souza, 2012a. 'Virtudes e vícios dos cavaleiros n'*A Demanda do Santo Graal*', in Lênia Márcia Mongelli (ed.), *De cavaleiros e cavalarias. Por terras de Europa e Américas* (São Paulo: Humanitas), pp. 37–47.

Zierer, Adriana Maria de Souza, 2012b. 'Entre Eva e Maria: a ambiguidade feminina n'*A Demanda do Santo Graal*', in Mârcia Manir Niguel Feitosa and Renata Ribeiro Lima (eds), *Anais XXIII. Congresso Internacional da Associação Brasileira de Professores de Literatura Portuguesa* (São Luis: Universidade Federal do Maranhão), pp. 20–41.

Zumthor, Paul, 2000 [1943]. *Merlin le Prophète* (Geneva: Slatkine Reprints).

Zurara, Gomes Eanes de, 1949. *Crónica dos feitos de Guiné*, ed. António J. Dias Dinis, *Vida e obras de Gomes Eanes de Zurara*, 2 vols (Lisbon: Divisão de Publicações e Biblioteca, Agência Geral das Colónias, 1949).

INDEX OF MANUSCRIPTS

Aberystwyth, NLW
  MS 446-E, 320, 363
Ajuda: Biblioteca do Palácio da Ajuda
  Cancioneiro da Ajuda, 102–3, 455, 489
  Livro de linhagens, 102–3, 455
Andorra la Vella, Arxiu Històric Nacional (Arxiu de les Set Claus)
  MS 1, 13, 40, 57, 314, 501
  MS 12, 49

Barcelona, Arxiu Històric de Barcelona
  MS B-109, 167
Barcelona, Biblioteca de Catalunya
  MS 271, 24, 32, 170, 250–1
  MS 2434, 22, 38, 83, 150, 273, 280, 503
  MS 8999/1, 13, 41
Berkeley, California, Bancroft Library, University of California
  MS UCB 115, 45, 368

Cambridge, Fitzwilliam Museum
  MS McClean 180, 44
Cambridge, University Library
  MS Add. 7071, 84, 272, 280–1
Campos, Mallorca, Arxiu Parroquial
  Catalan *Lançalot*, 12, 35, 289, 305–6
Cervera, Arxiu Històric Comarcal
  MS B-343, 2, 13, 30, 40, 47–8, 56, 64, 72, 172, 314, 317, 319, 321–2, 328–9, 331, 334, 338, 470
Coimbra, Biblioteca Geral da Universidade
  MS A19, 63, 464

El Escorial, Monasterio de San Lorenzo
  MS h-I-13, 367
  MS P-II-22, 171
  MS X-i-8, 152

Geneva, Bodmer
  MS 105, 272

Lisbon, Arquivo Nacional da Torre do Tombo
  MS 643, 22, 37, 63, 71–2, 121, 273, 275, 279, 446, 457, 492

Lisbon, Biblioteca Nacional
  MS Cod. 10991, 23, 96, 124, 126, 141, 200, 456, 472, 484, 494
London, British Library
  Ms Add. 38117 (Huth Manuscript), 69, 84, 271–2, 280–1
  MS Harley 4389, 363

Madrid, Archivo Histórico Nacional
  Cod. Leg. Carp. 1501B no. 7, 23, 41, 155
Madrid, Biblioteca Nacional de España
  MS 485, 171
  MS 1634, 46
  MS 8817, 105
  MS 9611, 16, 40, 71, 113, 142, 268, 289, 451, 453, 461–3, 480, 484
  MS 9750, 45, 56
  MS 10133, 170
  MS 11309, 45
  MS 12915 (see also MSS 20262, 22644), 42
  MS 20262$_{19}$, 19, 31, 41, 45, 191, 309, 317, 337 (see also MS 22644)
  MS 22021, 20, 43, 220, 222, 309, 311, 336, 346
  MS 22644$_{1-51}$, 19, 31, 41, 45, 191, 296, 309, 317, 330–1, 337 (see also MS 20262)
Madrid, Biblioteca Real (Biblioteca de Palacio)
  MS 2105, 44
  *olim*MS 2-G-5 (see also Salamanca, Biblioteca Universitaria, MS 1877), 17, 37–9, 273, 276, 284–6, 496
Madrid, Real Academia de la Historia
  MS 9–10–2/2100, 46, 486
Mataró, private library of Francesc Cruzate
  Catalan *Lancelot*, 12, 35, 55, 172, 290–1, 305–6
Milan, Biblioteca Ambrosiana
  MS I.79.Sup., 12, 36, 55, 172, 464
Modena, Biblioteca Estense
  ALPHA T.3.11 (olim 59), 363
Montserrat, Abadia
  MS 1042-VIII, 171

New York, Hispanic Society of America
  MS B2278 (Vindel MS), 151, 153

Oxford, Bodleian Library
  MS French d.16, 34.
  Rawlinson D874, 272

Paris, Bibliothèque Nationale de France
  MS fonds esp. 13, 14, 170
  MS fonds esp. 36, 44, 484
  MS f. fr. 112, 84, 87, 89, 100, 272–3, 280, 286, 452, 496
  MS f. fr. 116, 89
  MS f. fr. 337, 85
  MS f. fr. 340, 87, 272–3
  MS f. fr. 343, 12, 87, 89, 272–3, 495
  MS f. fr. 751, 16, 291, 306, 308
  MS f. fr. 760, 320–1, 363
  MS f. fr. 1463, 45, 320–1, 363, 459
  MS f. fr. 12599, 100, 272–3, 452
  MS f. fr. 17177, 15
Porto, Arquivo Distrital do Porto
  MS PT/ADPRT/NOT/CNSTS01/001/0012 (I/18/2–212), 2, 22, 37, 55, 63, 71–3, 75, 121, 278, 280
Puigcerdà, Arxiu Comarcal de la Cerdanya
  MS Fons Martí i Terrada, s/n, *Lancelot en prose*, 171
  Deulofeu i Fatjó Collection, s/n, 171

Rennes, Bibliothèque Municipale
  MS 255, 34, 279
  MS 2427, 75

Rome, Vatican City, Biblioteca Apostolica Vaticana
  MS Vat. Lat. 3217, 96–7, 113, 115, 475
  MS Vat. Lat. 6428, 19, 41, 55, 309, 332, 453, 463, 493
  MS Vat. Lat. 7182, 23, 55, 96, 113, 200, 495

Salamanca, Biblioteca Universitaria
  MS 1877, 17, 37–9, 47, 56, 67–8, 114, 255, 269, 273, 275–6, 278–9, 281, 283–5, 399, 467, 471, 474, 476, 480, 482, 507
  MS 2656, 103
Santander, Biblioteca Menéndez y Pelayo
  MS M62, 152
Siena, Archivio di Stato
  MS s/n, 114

Tours, Bibliothèque Municipale
  MS 942, 34
Turin, Biblioteca Nazionale Universitaria
  MS s/n, *Blandín de Cornualla*, 174, 449

Valencia, Arxiu de la Diputació de València
  MS fons de la Duquesa de Almodovar, e.4.1., caixa 15, 45
Venice, Biblioteca Marciana
  MS fr. XXIII (*olim* 234), 363
Vienna, Österreichische Nationalbibliothek
  MS 2542, 23, 100, 157, 315
  MS Lat. Ser. Vetus 2594, 22, 38, 55, 86–8, 114, 273, 283, 485, 498

GENERAL INDEX

Abbreviations
abp. archbishop
d. daughter
k. king
m. married
q. queen
s. son
w. wife

Abaurre, M.L.M. 446
abbey of Saint-Benoît, Vierzon 106–7
Aben Alhamar, k. of Granada 131
Abubacar, k. of Valencia 152
A Coruña 142, 413
Adams, James M. 150, 446
Adorno, Rolena 482
Adroher, Miquel 12, 36, 171, 446
Aeneas 103, 110, 129, 239,
   and Dido, canonical lovers 233, 242
Afonso I Henriques, k. of Portugal 59, 60, 110
Afonso III, k. of Portugal (m. Matilda, countess
   of Boulogne; 'o Bolonhés', Count of
   Boulogne) 21–3, 60–5, 119–21, 137, 142,
   159, 286, 290, 308, 477, 507
Afonso V, k. of Portugal 106, 114, 508
Afonso, prince 120, 370
'Agrajes' (Pedro de Ircio, named after character in
   Amadís) 386, 395, 397–8
Aguilar de la Frontera 139
Agustí, Antoni, abp. of Tarragona 50, 366
Ailenii, Simona 37–8, 41, 73, 75, 121, 155, 288,
   446
Ajuda, Palácio da 102–3
alba 99
Albéniz, Isaac 434
Albert, Carmen 255, 446
Alcácer do Sal 59
Alcazarquivir, battle of (1578) 111
Alcobaça, monastery of 115
Alcoberro, Agustí 183, 446
Alcover, Antoni M. 174
Aleixandre, Marilar 431, 439
Alejandro, Julio 429, 435
Alemany Ferrer, Rafael 25, 32, 182, 446, 462

Alexander the Great 183, 237, 241, 248, 252–3
alfaquí 127, 243
Alfons I (Alfonso I), k. of Aragon 118, 163, 187
Alfons II, k. of Aragon 187
Alfons III, k. of Aragon 30
Alfons V el Magnànim, k. of Aragon 13, 172,
   179–80, 258, 451, 474
Alfonso II, k. of Asturias 118
Alfonso VI, k. of León/Castile 118
Alfonso VII, k. of León/Castile 119–20, 187–8
Alfonso VIII, k. of Castile 15, 159, 188, 200,
   234–5
   m. Eleanor, d. of Henry II of England 15
Alfonso IX, k. of León 119, 189
Alfonso X, 'el Sabio', k. of Castile/León 7, 15,
   22, 24, 46, 61, 63, 69, 87, 102, 113, 122–3,
   125–31, 134–7, 139, 142, 151–2, 159–60,
   169–70, 194, 200–1, 236–7, 239–40, 243,
   248, 250–2, 268, 292, 327, 345, 357, 446,
   450, 453, 458, 469, 473, 476–7, 479–80,
   489, 495, 501
   'Ben sabia eu, mia senhor' 113, 201
   Cantigas de Santa Maria 22, 61, 127–8, 473,
   489
   'Don Gonçalo, pois queredes ir daqui pera
   Sevilha' 61, 135–7
   Estoria de Espanna 151–2, 236–7, 458
   General Estoria 15–6, 22, 46, 122, 152, 160,
   237–40, 268, 446, 460, 469, 501
      Galician translation *Xeral Estoria* 161
   Siete Partidas 132, 448, 479
   'Vi un coteife de mui gran granhon' 22, 63, 131,
   292
Alfonso XI, k. of Castile/León 24, 44, 240, 244,
   249, 251–2, 268, 366–7, 451, 458, 475,
   509
   Libro de la montería 44
alguazil 132
Alhambra, Granada, paintings in Sala de Justicia
   1, 31, 189–91, 247, 268, 308
Aljafería, Palace of, Zaragoza 167, 169, 172, 189,
   258
Aljubarrota, battle of (1385) 106, 113, 194, 210
Allaire, Gloria 322, 325, 447

allegory 29, 81, 96, 115, 143–4, 200, 220
allomorphemes 301
allosemantemes 301
Almazán de Gracia, Ángel 425, 435
Almeida, Ana Cristina 447
Almeida, Isabel Adelaide 447
Almeida, Miguel E. 447
Alonso, Álvaro 219, 447
Alonso, Dámaso 319, 447
Alonso, María Lourdes 416, 435
Alonso Cortés, Narciso 380, 447
Alpalhão, Margarida Santos 447
Alsace, Philip of 60, 159
Alturo i Perucho, Jesús 50, 447
Alvar, Carlos 2, 4, 8, 22, 31, 41–2, 120, 125, 129, 135–6, 142, 159, 172, 187, 191–2, 200, 232, 234, 262, 292, 296, 308–11, 314, 316, 319–20, 323–5, 327–30, 333, 337, 339–40, 352, 362–3, 384, 405, 434, 447–8, 450, 456, 463, 465, 475, 506
Álvares, Manuel, *corregidor* 37, 72–4, 110, 114, 279
Álvares, Sebastião 114
Álvarez de Villasandino, Alfonso 224–6, 249, 252, 268
Álvarez Pellitero, Ana María 292, 448
Alvim, Leonor de, w. of Condestabre of Portugal 106
Amadís, anonymous *comedia* 377
Amadís and Oriana, canonical lovers 184, 365
Amadís de Gaula 8, 25, 28, 33, 45, 50, 56–7, 64–5, 107–10, 112–13, 117, 184, 204, 207–16, 218, 220, 223, 253–5, 257, 259–60, 264, 268–9, 291, 297–8, 301, 303, 308, 322, 340–2, 348, 351–3, 357, 362, 364–81, 382–3, 386, 392, 395, 397–8, 401–2, 405, 410, 419, 422–3, 425, 427, 430–2, 439, 442–4, 447–51, 455–6, 465–6, 469, 472–4, 476–82, 489–93, 496–503, 505–8
Amadís de Grecia 215, 218, 448, 503
Amaral, Andreia 101, 448
Americas, export of books to 400–2
Americas, ban on fiction for 400–01
Amerindian individuals with Arthurian names 395–6
'Amor des que m'a vos cheguei' 23, 96, 99, 127, 477
'Amors, de vostre acointement' 98–9, 116
amplificatio 71, 84, 89, 99–100, 147, 165, 238, 300–1, 331, 335, 338, 344
Amposta 169
analepsis 301–2
Anales navarro-aragoneses 104, 234–5, 267

Anales toledanos primeros 15, 104, 122, 200, 234–5, 267, 448
Andalucia 6, 10, 119, 123, 131, 136, 139, 393, 416
Andorra 13, 40, 48–9
 Arxiu de les Set Claus 13, 40, 48–9, 57, 314, 518
 Arxiu Històric Nacional 13, 48
 Codex Miscel.lani 13, 57, 501
 Consell General de les Valls 48
 fragments of *Tristany* MS 56, 172, 222, 314, 316–17, 328–30, 333, 335–6, 338, 448, 501
 pariatge (1270) 48
Andrés, María Soledad de 104, 153–4, 161, 235–6, 459
'Angela, Michelle', pseudonym of María Lourdes Alonso 416
Angevins 59
Annales Cambriae 234, 448
'Anonymus Cinco', pseudonym of Alma Idamons 429, 435
Anselmi, Luigi 425, 435
Antología castellana de relatos medievales (MS Esc. h-I-13) 367
Antonio, Nicolás 18, 366, 448
apocryphal Gospels 80
Apostles, Twelve 80, 92, 95, 130
Aragão, Ludumula 448
Aragon, Carlos de, Príncipe de Viana 53–4
Aragon, Catherine of 5
Aramon y Serra, Ramon 30, 40, 48, 314, 448
Arana, Vicente de 411–12, 430, 435
Aranda, Vicente 424, 435
Arbor Aldea, Mariña 448
Arciniegas, Germán 432, 435
Arderique 215, 217, 269, 448, 491
Argonáutica da Cavalaria 111–12
Arias Bonet, Juan Antonio 132, 448
Arimathea, Joseph of (including *Libro* and *Livro de*) 2, 11, 17, 22, 33, 37, 46–7, 51, 55, 57–8, 60, 63–5, 67, 71–82, 85–7, 94–6, 110, 114, 121, 154, 215, 224–5, 236, 240, 254–6, 267–9, 273, 275–80, 284–5, 287–8, 301, 321, 373, 446–7, 449, 452, 454–5, 457–9, 463–4, 467–8, 472–3, 475, 482, 486–7, 490, 492–3, 496
Ariosto, Ludovico 214, 378
Arnaut, Ana Paula 448
Arnold, Ivor 108, 130, 160, 448
Arolas Bonet, Juan 409–10, 435
Arras, Moniot d' 60, 470
Arretxe, Izaskun 179, 448
art, Arthurian themes in 4, 21, 30, 123, 134–5, 159, 167, 169, 176, 188–91, 207, 253, 317
artes poeticae 124, 141, 301
Arthur, Prince. s. of Henry VII of England 5

Articulos e sancta fe de los cristianos, Los 47
Asperti, Stefano 174, 449
Assis, Cicero Pedro de 405, 449
Associació Wagneriana 413–4, 416
Assumption of the Virgin Mary 130–1
Athayde, João Martins de 404
Aurell, Martin 183, 449
Aurell i Cardona, Jaume 173, 185, 449
Austria, Ana de, attends performance of *Amadís* 377
Austria, Juana de 109
Austria, Margaret of, owns *Cavallero Zifar* 44
Austria, Maria of, owns *Perceforest* 255
Avalle-Arce, Juan Bautista 32, 208, 291, 367, 376, 379–80, 449, 456
Avis, dynasty of 110, 380
Ayamonte 10
Ayerbe-Chaux, Reinaldo 449

Badda, q., w. of k. Reccared 186
Badia, Lola 32, 171–2, 178–9, 181–2, 184, 294, 449, 460, 471
Baena, Juan Alfonso de 223–4, 226, 249, 252–3, 269, 380, 449
Baena, Cancionero de 24, 210, 223–7, 248–9, 268, 292, 449, 470, 504
bailada 98, 454, 469
Baist, Gottfried 66, 277, 284–5, 449
Baladro del sabio Merlín 18–19, 26–8, 31, 33, 39, 71, 84–5, 100, 105, 107, 114, 116, 155, 170, 215, 219, 227, 236, 250–4, 269–70, 273, 275–6, 280–2, 285, 288, 296, 341, 344, 347, 348, 350, 399, 407, 418, 437, 449, 452–4, 459, 469, 473–4, 476, 478, 490–1
Baldo 216, 450
ballads, Portuguese 23; for Spanish, see *romancero*
Ballesteros Beretta, Antonio 131, 136, 450
Baquero Moreno, Humberto 106, 450
Barahona, Francisco, *Flor de caballerías* 216, 450, 473
Baranda, Nieves 377, 450
Barba, Juan de 226, 340, 380, 459
Barbaza, Raniela 407, 450
Barlaam e Josaphat (also *Vida de Berlan*) 47
Barreto, Therezinha Maria Mello 450
Barrick, Mac E. 30, 450
Barros, João de 110, 366, 383, 405, 450
Barros, João de, *Crónica do imperador Clarimundo* 110, 450, 454
Barros, José d'Assunção 450
Barton, Simon 6, 450
Basque language 1, 6, 424–5, 434
Basurto, Fernando, *Florindo* 215

Batista, Ana Cristina Pires dos Santos Trinidade 450
Baumgartner, Emmanuèle 157, 160, 315–16, 363, 450
Bautista, Francisco 97, 105, 153, 253, 405, 449–50, 472, 476
Beaumont, Francis 378
Beceiro Pita, Isabel 33, 57–9, 122, 194, 254, 367, 380, 450
Belenguer Castromán, Iria 36, 451
Bell, Aubrey F.G. 87, 451
Beltrán, Vicente (Vicenç) 31, 116, 159, 314, 367, 448, 451, 465, 477, 491, 502
Beltrán Llavador, Rafael 30, 32, 172, 180, 241–2, 253, 363, 451, 469
Bembo, Pietro 378
Benedict XIII, pope 172, 332
Beneyto Pérez, Juan 379, 451
Benhaim, Véronique 378, 451
Berguedà, Guillem de 120, 162–3, 234, 498
Bermúdez Plata, Cristóbal 386–93, 396, 406, 451
Bernal, Fernando, *Floriseo* 215, 269, 451, 473
Bernardo del Carpio 403, 407
Bernart de Ventadorn 125–6
Bernat de So, *La Vesió* 167
Béroul 331
Berrini, Beatriz 451
Bertolucci Pizzorusso, Valeria 325, 451
BETA xiii, 38–43, 307
Bible, biblical references 16, 33, 80, 95, 103, 152–3, 237, 243, 253, 399
Bicket, Robert, *Lai du cor* 202
Biddle, Martin 10, 260, 451
Binche, royal pageant at (1549) 28
BITAGAP xiii, 37–8, 41, 50, 155, 451
BITECA xiii, 30, 35–7, 40–1, 307
Blanch, Teresa 432, 436
Blanche d'Anjou 168
Blanche of Castile 119
Blanco, Antonio 380, 451
Blandín de Cornualla 174–7, 179, 185, 449, 460, 467, 494, 507
Blasco Ibáñez, Vicente 428, 435
Blay Manzanera, Vicenta 219, 451
Blecua, Alberto 379–80, 452, 500
Blondel de Nesle 125
boats, uncrewed, motif of 81, 206–7, 262–4, 312
Boccaccio, Giovanni 10, 181, 218, 221, 406–7, 452
Bodel, Jean, *Chanson des Saisnes* 151, 454
Bofarull i Mascaró, Próspero 172, 452
Bogdanow, Fanni 16–17, 19, 23, 30–1, 37, 66–7, 69–71, 75, 79, 82, 84–9, 91, 93, 100, 113–14, 120, 272–4, 277, 279, 283, 286–8, 296, 452–3

Bognolo, Ana 378, 453
Bohigas Balaguer, Pedro (Pere) 7, 12, 16, 29–32, 35–36, 39–40, 67, 73, 89, 162–3, 166, 168, 170, 173, 178, 250–1, 283, 285–6, 288–91, 296, 305, 307, 314, 319, 330, 399, 407, 449, 453–4
Bonilla y San Martín, Adolfo 31, 40–2, 113, 191, 219, 251, 288, 309, 317–19, 328, 337, 344–5, 450, 454, 468
book censorship 252, 400–2
book ownership 13–14, 30, 33–4, 44, 51–4, 57, 73, 86–7, 169, 171–3, 185, 217, 253–6, 274–5, 287–8, 293, 317, 324–5, 332, 343, 348, 380, 401–2, 405, 407
booksellers, book trade 50–1, 401, 405, 407, 472
Borger, Julian 10, 454
Borges, Jorge Luis 432, 435
Borja, Carmen 427, 435
Born, Bertran de 163, 476
Bottini, Giuseppa 454
Box, J. B. H. 454
Boyd-Bowman, Peter 386–8, 390, 392–4, 405–6, 454
Bozóky, Edina 143, 454
Braga 102, 105
Braga, Theophilo 23, 87, 454
Bragança, Teotonio de, abp. of Evora 37, 73
Brandenberger, Tobias 110, 454
Brantôme, Pierre de 378
Brassavola, Antonio Muso, *Examen omnium simplicium medicamentorum* 257
Brasseur, Annette 151, 454
Brea López, Mercedes xiv, 98, 119, 160, 447, 454
Bresc, Henri 175, 455
Breton, André 424
Brittany, Geoffrey of 163
Brocardo, Maria Teresa 103, 366, 455
Brugger, Ernst 70, 455
Brummer, Rudolf 26, 29, 455
Brunetti, Almir de Campos 455
Brutus 15–16, 24, 46,103, 110, 129, 153, 165, 238–42, 247
Buescu, Maria Gabriela Carvalhão 38, 455
Buñuel, Luis 429, 435
Burgess, Glyn S. 244, 450, 453, 455, 474, 480, 490
Burgos, Juan de, printer 19–20, 39, 42, 84, 228, 269, 281, 309, 340–2, 344–5, 347–8, 350, 449, 465, 502, 506
Burgundy, Raymond, count of Galicia and Portugal 118, 188
Burgundy, library of the dukes of 44
Butinyà i Jiménez, Júlia 28, 32, 177, 455
Byzantine romance 111, 117, 205

caballero villano, status of 131
Cabana, Darío Xohán 420–1, 436
Cabanillas, Ramón 417–18, 436
Cabarcas Antequera, Hernando 405, 455
Cabra, *juglar* 11, 120, 163
Cábrega, Marqués de 38, 87
Cabrera, Guerau III de 11
Cabrera, Guerau IV de 11, 29, 120, 163, 293, 460, 496
Cacho Blecua, Juan Manuel 32, 113, 211, 212, 214, 265, 309, 340–1, 369, 372, 375–6, 380–1, 451, 455–6, 466, 476, 491, 499, 506
Caetano, Priscila Miranda 456
Calado, Adelino de Almeida 106, 456
California, fictional place-name in *Las sergas de Esplandian* 397
Calvo Poyato, José 416, 436
Camões, Luis de, *Os Lusíadas* 112, 422
Campos García Rojas, Axayácatl 314, 355–6, 358–60, 456
Campos, Mallorca 12, 35, 289, 305–6
Canals, Antoni, 'Carta de Sant Bernat a la seva germana (De modo bene vivendi)' 172
Canavaggio, Jean 266, 455–6
Cancioneiro B 96, 124, 126, 141, 456
Cancioneiro Colocci-Brancuti, see Colocci, Angelo
Cancionero de Baena, see Baena, Cancionero de
Cancionero de Barrantes 224, 269
Cancionero de Estúñiga 224
Cancionero de Herberay 224
Cancionero de Martínez de Burgos 224
Cancionero de obras de burlas 225
Cancionero de Palacio 224, 269, 292, 448
Cancionero de Pero Guillén 224
Cancionero de romances 229, 231, 233
Cancionero de San Román 224, 269
Cancionero de Toledo del Marqués de Santillana 380
Cancionero General 225, 231, 269, 457, 475
Cancionero llamado Flor de enamorados 231
Cancionero manuscrito de Pedro del Pozo 232
Cancionero musical de Palacio 231
Cancionero de romances 233
Canettieri, Paolo 124, 457
Cantalapiedra Jaén, Fernando 32, 457
Cantare della morte di Tristano 322
Cantare della Vendetta di Tristano 324
cantares de Cornoalha 22, 61, 124, 201
Cantel, Raymond 407, 457
cantigas de amigo 199
cantigas de amor 124–5, 199, 485
cantigas de escarnho/escarnio 131, 135, 139, 150, 199, 480

cantigas de Santa Maria 22, 61, 127–8, 243, 473, 487, 489
  see also Alfonso X, k. of Castile
cantigas de seguir 124, 457
Capdevila, Roser, Teresa Blanch 432, 436
Capra, Daniela 314, 457
Carbeurim, Cristina Helena 457
Carbonell, Pere Miquel, *Cròniques d'Espanya* 182–3, 446
Cardim, Luíz 30, 104, 457
Cardoso, Wilton 124, 457
Carlos III, k. of Navarre 199
Carranza, Andreu 426, 441
Carrasco Tenorio, Milagros 207, 457
Carré, Antònia 185, 457
Carré, Leandro 420, 436
Carreto, Carlos da Fonseca Clamote 457, 463
Carrión, Juan, illuminator 44
'Carta enviada por Hiseo la Brunda a Tristán de Leonís' 20, 43, 221–2, 311, 336, 346, 475
  see also 'Respuesta'
Carter, Henry Hare 31, 37, 73–4, 78–82, 86, 113–14, 159, 288, 457
cart(s), carter(s) 22, 63, 132–4, 160, 262, 295, 306
Cartagena, Alonso de 254, 355, 380, 481
Cartagena, Pedro de 380
Carvajal, Micael de, *Tragedia Josephina* 256–7, 457, 475
Carvalho, Júlio 457
Carvalho Calero, Ricardo 421, 436
Carvalho Dias, Luis 494
Casas Rigall, Juan 200, 457, 482
Caschifellone, Caffaro da, *Liber de liberatione civitatum Orientis* 258
Cascudo, Luís da Câmara 407, 457
Casona, Alejandro 415, 436
Castelo Branco, Camilo 409–10, 436
Castiglione, Baldassare 378
Castillo, Hernando del 225, 231, 269, 457, 475
Castro, Álvaro de, *Clarián de Landanís, II* 215, 457, 460
Castro, Antón 421, 436
Castro, Inês de 219, 422, 447
Castro, Ivo 23, 31, 37, 60–3, 65–7, 72–5, 86, 88–9, 105–6, 114, 121, 127, 148, 158–9, 277, 279, 286–8, 327, 457–8, 496
Castro García, Silvana 458
Casula, Francesco C. 10, 458
Catalán Menéndez-Pidal, Diego 7, 16, 31–2, 46, 104–5, 151, 153–5, 161, 235, 236, 458–9
Catalão, Pedro Miguel Nunes 459
Cátedra, Pedro M. 33, 36, 39, 51, 217, 274, 287, 341, 348, 351, 380, 459, 475, 478, 502
Causo, Roberto 405, 407, 459
'Cavalga doña Ginebra' 229, 232, 270

Caxton, William 202
Cervantes, Miguel de 8, 25, 116, 205, 231–2, 259–67, 293, 351–2, 358–9, 362, 371, 377, 404, 409, 419, 421, 432, 448, 451, 456, 459, 465–6, 484–6, 492, 497–8
Cerverí de Girona, *Maldit-Bendit* 164, 166
Chambel, Pedro 81, 95, 114, 459
chanson de geste 11
chanson de toile 99
chant courtois 119–20
chapbooks 402–5, 407
Charlemagne 90, 166, 187, 200, 228, 253
Charles I and V, Holy Roman Emperor and k. of Spain 5, 20, 28–9, 44, 255, 360–1
Charlesworth, James I. 406, 459
Charlo Brea, Luis 486
Chase, Carol J. 81–2, 459
Châtillon, Gautier de, *Alexandreis* 199–200, 237
Chevalier, Maxime 377, 459
Chevalier au lion, Le 21, 134, 189
Chevalier aus Deux Espées, Le 137–8, 160, 282
Chevalier de la charrette, Le 63, 132, 133, 140, 231, 499, 500
Chicago, Newberry Library 40, 281
Chicote, Gloria B. 31, 40, 292, 459
chivalry 6, 19, 24–5, 43, 50–1, 79, 90, 92–3, 105–12, 116–7, 134, 167, 173, 177, 179–82, 184, 203, 207, 213–19, 222, 254–5, 257, 259, 261–6, 291, 294, 306, 311, 323, 333, 351–3, 359–61, 372, 375–7, 397, 400, 403
  chivalric feasts and tournaments 106, 109, 112, 138, 167, 180, 241, 295, 299, 310, 312–13, 317, 320–1, 332, 334, 337, 344, 351, 353
  dramatic performance 26, 182, 266, 415
Chora, Ana Margarida 427, 436, 459
Christ, Christianity 76–7, 79–82, 91–2, 94–5, 114, 127–8, 143–4, 146, 159, 168, 172, 187, 189–91, 201, 204–5, 209, 213, 235, 237, 241, 246, 248, 257, 261, 277, 279, 323, 335, 350, 356, 360, 365, 372, 375–6, 383, 413, 422, 428
Christendom 6, 118, 375–6
Chronica de los muy notables caualleros Tablante de Ricamonte y de Jofre hijo del conde don Ason 333, 400, 402–3, 407
Cigni, Fabrizio 45, 160, 317, 331, 459–60
Cingolani, Stefano Maria 11, 13–14, 29–30, 33, 52, 120, 162–4, 168, 171, 174, 180, 185, 293, 324, 460
Cintra, Geraldo de Ulhoa 460
Cintra, Luís Filipe Lindley 102, 104, 460
Cirlot, Juan Eduardo 423, 437
Cirlot, Victoria 351, 434, 460
Cirongilio de Tracia 460, 507

Claramunt, Salvador 165, 168–9, 460
Clarián de Landanís 215, 265, 346, 376, 457, 460, 507
Claribalte 215, 460, 472
Cligès 26, 34, 478, 487, 505
Cluny, Order of 187–8, 191, 258
Cluzel, Irénée 29, 460
codex, common chivalric 43–6, 51
codex, courtly chivalric 44
Colocci, Angelo 115–16, 483
    Cancioneiro Colocci-Brancuti 125, 160, 456, 472, 484, 491
    Tavola Colocciana 96–7, 113, 115, 475
Colonna, Egidio *De regimine principum* 209
Columbus, Christopher (Colón, Cristobal) 3, 385, 394–5
Columbus, Ferdinand (Colón, Fernando) 42, 368, 407
'Columela, Christabelle', pseudonym of María Lourdes Alonso 416
conception 3, 14, 18, 20, 80, 91, 93, 124, 144, 146, 153, 165–6, 185, 278, 281, 295, 358, 399, 400
Conde de Lindquist, Josefa 59, 327, 460
Condesa Traidora, La, Castilian legend 398
Conquesta del Sant Grasal 30, 53–4
Constança, d. of k. Denis of Portugal, q. of Fernando IV of Castile 74, 203, 244
Constantinople 25–6, 111, 117, 181, 184, 212, 365, 376, 478, 505
Conte du Brait 288, 452, 454
Contes del Graal, Li 15, 82, 167
Contreras Martín, Antonio 8, 30, 40, 96, 160, 172, 183, 185, 289–308, 323, 351, 381, 461–3, 480, 503
Cooper, Louis 256, 463, 477, 482
Corbera, Esteban de, *Febo el Troyano* 216, 463, 471
Corfis, Ivy A. 31, 41, 309, 332–3, 338, 463
Cornadó, Francesc 427, 437
Corominas, Joan 223, 463, 500
Corps of Lovers, Portuguese 106
Corral, José Luis 426, 437
Corral, Pedro de, *Crónica sarracina* 367, 376
Corral Díaz, Esther 142, 463–4
Correas, Gonzalo, *Vocabulario de refranes* 257
Correia, Isabel Sofia Calvário 40, 57, 63, 73, 79, 110, 113, 290–1, 307, 446, 463–4
Correia, Maria Helena de Paiva 464
Correia, Susana Marisa Fernandes Moreira 464
corrido, metrical form in Brazil and Philippines 402–3, 407, 471
Coutinho, Gonçalo, *Crónica de D. Duardos* 112
Coutinho, Vitor Manuel da Assunção 464
Couto, Diogo do 384, 405, 464

Covarrubias, Sebastián de, *Tesoro de la lengua castellana* 257, 259
Crawford, J.P. Wickersham 28, 464
Crescini, Vincenzo 29, 36, 464
Creuze de Lesser, Auguste-François de 378
Cromberger, Jacobo and Juan, printers 42–3, 270, 309, 341–2, 455–6, 460, 473, 482
Crónica carolingia 253
Crónica de 1344 46, 69, 105, 236, 240, 268, 469
Crónica de 1404 16, 24, 31–2, 46, 69, 104–5, 151, 153–4, 236, 268, 274–5, 483, 496
Crónica de Castilla 104–5, 151, 483
Crónica de Castilla, Galician translation as *Crónica de Castela* 105
Crónica de D. Duardos see Coutinho, Gonçalo
Crónica de D. João I (Fernão Lopes) 106, 113, 450, 487
Crónica del rey don Pedro (Pero López de Ayala) 24, 246
Crónica do Condestabre 106
Crónica do imperador Beliandro 111–2
Crónica do imperador Maximiliano 108, 494
Crónica geral de 1344 24, 97, 101–3, 153, 236, 460
Crònica reyal 169
Crónica troyana 341, 344–6, 348, 367, 486
Crónica xeral 151
Crónicas navarras 15
Cronicón Villarense, see Liber regum 104, 153, 235, 502
Cropp, Glynnis M. 253, 405, 464
Croy, Charles de, library of 44
Crucifixion 143, 279
Crusades 59, 120, 181, 187, 214, 258, 317, 331, 376, 406
Cruzate, Francesc 12, 35, 290–1, 305–6
Cuenca, Luis Alberto de 412, 425, 437
Cuervo, Rufino José 405
Cuesta Torre, María Luzdivina 8, 19, 20, 30–1, 42–3, 116, 159, 183, 185, 205, 214–15, 224, 292, 296, 309–81, 461–2, 464–6, 477, 484, 486, 496, 504, 505–7
Cunqueiro, Álvaro 418–21, 430, 437–8
Curial e Güelfa 28, 45, 56, 179–82, 184, 294, 325, 369, 449, 451, 455, 460, 466, 508
Curtis, Renée L. 137–8, 145, 147, 157, 161, 315, 318, 320, 325, 373, 466

Da Costa, Avelino de Jesús 159, 466
Da Costa, João, notary 73
Da Cruz, Claudia Menezes 467
Da Cunha, Teresa Maria Antunes Vieira 467
Da Cunha, Tristão 382, 383
Da Silva, Ademir Luiz 467
Da Silva, António 404, 502

Da Silva, Elsa Maria Branco 467
Da Silva, José Pereira 467
Da Silva, Juliana Sylvestre 467
Da Silva, Rafaela Câmara Simões 467
Da Silva, Virgulino Ferreira ('Lampião') 405
Dalí, Salvador 429
Dalmau, Antoni 426, 438
Daniels, Marie Cort 352–3, 467
Darbord, Bernard 68, 467
Dares and Dictys 152, 237
Darío, Rubén 433, 438
David, Pierre 114, 467
Davila, José Antonio 432, 438
D'Ax, Anna 415, 438
De Almeida, Manuel Lopes 467
De Ávila, Helena Lima 467
De Brito, Sebastião Miranda Aviz Pereira 73, 467
De Caluwé, Jacques 164, 175, 183, 467
De Guimarães, Laurete Lima 467
De la Marche, Olivier, *Le Chevalier delibéré* 255
De Medeiros, Maria Ana Sequeira 95, 467–8
De Moraes, Francisco 109–10, 216, 468
De Moura e Silva, Leonor Isabel Duarte 468
De Souza, Neila Matias 468
De Vasconcellos, Maria Elizabeth G. 468
Défourneaux, Marcelin 191, 468
Dekker, Thomas 378
Delcorno Branca, Daniela 171, 185, 318–19, 320–1, 325, 468
Delpech, François 14, 468
Delumeau, Jean 132, 468
Demanda del santo Grial, La / Demanda do santo graal 11, 16, 18–19, 22–4, 28, 31, 33, 37–9, 51, 55, 57–8, 60, 63–5, 67, 79–80, 86–95, 105, 107, 113, 115–16, 121, 137, 147–8, 154, 215–16, 224, 227, 236, 250–1, 254–5, 257, 259, 269–71, 273–9, 281–8, 290, 297, 301, 333, 402, 422–3, 432, 444, 446–55, 457–9, 461–4, 467–82, 484–5, 487–92, 494–9, 501, 503, 505–9
Denain, Gauchier de, *Compendi historial* 170
Denis I, k of Portugal 68, 74, 97–8, 102, 116, 120, 125–6, 148, 200–1, 223, 448, 480
Denis, Serge 116, 468
Descartes, René 378
Desclot, Bernat 14, 165–6, 470, 504
Destruction de Jérusalem, La 2
Deulofeu i Fatjó Collection, Puigcerdà 171
Devil, devils 19, 26, 76, 94–5, 114, 127, 146, 149, 206, 261–2, 278, 282–3, 339, 359
Devoto, Daniel 29, 468
Deyermond, Alan D. 3, 17, 27, 30, 220, 379, 400, 449, 454, 456, 461–3, 465–6, 468, 481, 489, 497, 501, 505
D'Heur, Jean Marie 22, 113, 124, 140, 452, 468

Di Stefano, Giuseppe 31, 228–31, 233, 363, 468, 494, 499, 505
Dias, Aida Fernanda 22, 37, 60, 63, 65, 73–5, 114, 121, 278, 288, 468–9
Dias, Augusto da Costa 430, 438
Dias, Isabel de Barros 469
Díaz de Games, Gutierre, *El Victorial* 16, 30, 241–2, 247–8, 253, 269, 450–1, 469
Díaz del Castillo, Bernal 377, 396–8, 469, 502
Díaz Martínez, Eva María 41, 127, 157–8, 313, 483
Díaz-Mas, Paloma 292–3, 424–5, 438–9, 469
Diccionario de autoridades 371, 469
Diégues Júnior, Manuel 407, 469, 493
Díez Borque, José María 255, 469
Díez de Revenga, Francisco Javier 102, 469
Díez Garretas, María Jesús 292, 340, 380, 462–3, 466, 469, 481, 501, 505
Dinaanang Buhay ni Tablante di Ricamonte 402
Dionísio, João 469
Disputa del alma y el cuerpo (Revelación de un ermitaño) 250
Dodds, Jerrilynn D. 31, 189, 308, 469
Domech, Carmen 431, 439
Domènech, Jaume 169–70
    Compendi historial 169
    Genealogia dels reis d'Aragó 170
Domingo del Campo, Francisca 368, 469
Domínguez Dono, Xesús 469
Don Juan Manuel 192, 250–1, 268, 292, 469
Donadello, Aulo 469
Donne, John 378
Dopico Blanco, Fernando 197, 199, 469
Dos Santos, Eugénia Neves 470
'Doze de Inglaterra' 112, 479
dream episodes 2, 18, 27, 75–7, 79, 81, 92, 94–6, 114–5, 129, 184, 214, 282, 294, 352–4, 372, 413
Duarte I, k. of Portugal 86
Dubost, Francis 145, 470
Dueñas, Juan de 224, 226, 380, 497
Duràn i Sanpere, Agustí (Agustín Durán y Sanpere) 30, 41, 47–8, 314, 319, 470
Duràn, Eulàlia 41, 314
Dutton, Brian 225, 292, 380, 447, 449, 470
Dyggve, Holger Niels Petersen 60, 470

Eça de Queirós, José Maria 411, 422, 439
Echegaray, José 415, 422, 439
Echegaray, Miguel 415, 439
Edgar, k. of England 160
Edward I, k. of England 159, 317, 327, 331
Edward III, k. of England 258
Edwards, John 9–10
Eilhard 331

Eisele, Gillian 42, 355, 360, 470
Eisenberg, Daniel 352, 355, 376–7, 470
Eiximenis, Francesc, *Dotzè del Crestià* 185, 294, 478
Eleanor, d. of Henry II of England 15, 188, 234
Eleanor of Aquitaine 159
Eleanor of Castile, q. of Edward I of England 317, 327–8
Elliott, Alison G. 166, 470
'En Ávila por la A', anon. 226
enchanters 94–5, 108–9, 111, 128, 144, 148–9, 261, 351–2, 364, 371, 374, 418, 429
Enciso de Zárate, Francisco, *Florambel de Lucea* 216–7
England 15, 21, 46, 59–60, 108, 110–12, 124, 128, 159, 170–1, 188, 197, 217, 234–5, 242, 275, 317, 327–8, 331, 366, 372, 378, 479
Enrique II, k. of Castile 24, 240, 244, 246–7, 251, 254
Enrique III, k. of Castile 151–2, 246, 248, 292
Enrique IV, k. of Castile 33, 44, 210, 239, 350
Enrique, prince, 'El Senador' 136
Enrique, Antonio 427, 439
Entwistle, William J. 2, 4, 23, 29–30, 67, 72, 100, 104, 109, 113–14, 116, 119, 162, 171, 176, 207, 230–2, 236, 285, 290–1, 318–19, 327, 345, 363, 367, 470
Erec et Enide 174, 474
Escudero y Perosso, Francisco 309, 470
Eslava Galán, Juan 428, 439
Espadaler, Anton M. 162, 164–7, 169, 177–8, 184, 470–1, 479
Español, Francesca 167, 471
Espejo de príncipes 216, 218, 264, 471, 503
Espinosa, Germán 432, 439
Espinosa García, Agustín 422, 439
espoir des Bretons *see* expectation
Esquio, Fernand', 'Disse hum infante ante sa companha' 68, 97–8, 142–8, 200–1
Estevan da Guarda, 'Com'avêeo a Merlin de morrer' 69, 97–8, 148–50, 200–1
Estoire del Saint Graal 2, 27, 32, 37, 70, 74–5, 81, 86, 121, 144, 155, 240, 271–5, 278–9, 288, 446, 452, 458–9, 470, 478, 492, 496–7, 504
Estoria de dos amadores, see *Historia*
Estoria de Merlín (Salamanca, Biblioteca Universitaria, MS 1877) 17, 47, 269, 273, 276, 277–8, 281, 399, 471, 476, 496
Estoria del noble Vaspasiano, Castilian 2, 27, 240, 450, 478
Estoria do muy nobre Vespesiano, Portuguese 27, 240, 450, 478
Estorninho, Alice 380, 471
Estúñiga, Lope de 224, 226

ethnography, use of Arthurian material in 398–9
Eugenio, Damiana L. 403, 407, 471
euphemism, sexual 150
Eusebius 152
Even-Zohar, Itamar 434, 471
expectation of Arthur's return 130, 162–4, 175, 178, 183, 217, 266, 398

Faccon, Manuela 314, 471
Fachine Borges, Francisca Neuma 407, 471
Fallows, Noel 471
Fansler, Dean S. 403, 407, 471
Faral, Edmond 127, 130, 160, 234, 448, 471
Faria, Daniel 95, 471
Faria e Sousa, Manuel 366
Faulhaber, Charles 254, 471
Febo el Troyano 216, 463, 471
Febrer, Andreu 164
Félix Magno 216, 471
Felixmarte de Hircania 216, 471, 494
Fernández de Heredia, Juan, *Grant Coronica d'Espanya* 16, 169, 170
Fernández de Oviedo, Gonzalo, *Claribalte* 215, 371, 460, 472
Fernández de Velasco, Pedro, count of Haro 33, 254, 481
Fernández del Castillo, Francisco 401, 407, 472
Fernández Flórez, José A. 4, 472
Fernández-Ordóñez, Inés 68, 467, 472
Fernández Vega, María del Mar 255, 446
Fernando I, k. of Portugal 366
Fernando II, k. of León 119
Fernando III, k. of Castile/León 118–9, 136, 139, 152, 187, 235, 237, 250
Fernando IV, k. of Castile 74, 105, 203
Fernando V, 'the Catholic', k. of Castile 6, 211–2, 251–2
Ferrari, Anna 31, 97–8, 101, 125, 472
Ferrario de Orduna, Lilia E. 376, 405, 472, 505
Ferreira, Jerusa Pires 404, 407, 472
Ferreira, Jorge 9
Ferreira, Maria de Fátima Leitão Camilo dos Prazeres Cabaço 472
Ferreira, Maria do Rosário 116, 446, 472
Ferrer Cuñat, Chema 428, 439
Ferrer Gimeno, María Rosario 34, 324–5, 472
Ferrer Valls, Teresa 377, 472
Ferreti, Regina Micheli 472
Ferruz, Pedro 224–5, 268, 292
Filgueira Valverde, José 473
Finazzi-Agrò, Ettore 65, 109, 473, 475
Fiore, Joachim of 128, 243, 251–2
Flood, John 378, 473

Flor de caballerías 216, 450, 473
Florambel de Lucea, Corónica del invencible cavallero 217
Flores, duke 240
Flores, Francisco J. 469
Flores, Juan de 20, 27, 220, 222, 269, 344, 346, 349, 380, 473–4, 477, 487, 495, 508
  Grimalte y Gradissa 27, 220, 344, 346, 349, 473
  Grisel y Mirabella 220, 473
  La coronación de la señora Gracisla 477
Flores and Blancaflor, canonical lovers 176, 184, 191, 223, 502
Flores de filosofía 204
Flores de Grèce 378
Flórez, Enrique 234, 448, 473
Flori, Jean 131, 473
Floriant et Florete 176
Florindo 215
Florisel de Niquea 216, 269, 353, 473, 503
Floriseo 215, 451, 473
Fogelquist, James Donald 352, 371, 473
Foix, Joana de 52–3
Folie Lancelot 70, 99, 272–4, 452, 481
Folquet de Romans 125
Fortuny, Francisco 423, 439
Fossier, Robert 131, 473
Foti, Vittoria 378, 473
Franco, Francisco 276, 416
Franco Silva, Alfonso 254, 450
Frappier, Jean 473
Frare-de-goig i Sor-de-plaer 185
Fratel, Undira Maria de Oliveira 473
Freire Nunes, Irene 31, 38, 88–90, 92–5, 114–15, 119, 137, 146–7, 154, 288, 473, 496
Frías, Damasio de 371
Frontón, Miguel Angel 107, 473
Fuente del Pilar, José Javier 39, 473
Furtado, Antonio L. 473
Fuster, Jaume 424, 439

Gago, Manuel 427, 439
Gaibrois de Ballesteros, Mercedes 292, 474
Galician Celticism 417
Gallardo, Bartolomé José 309, 474
Gallé Cejudo, Rafael Jesús 345, 474
Galvão, António, *Tratado dos descubrimentos* 384–5, 474
Galvão, Duarte, Portuguese emissary to Abyssinia 383
Game of Thrones 4, 10
García, k. of Galicia 118
García de Campos, Diego 200, 267
García de Enterría, María de la Cruz 377, 474

García de Lucas, César 37–9, 67–8, 467, 474
García de Salazar, Lope 27, 46, 69, 205, 239–41, 340, 474, 481, 486, 502, 508
García Marsilla, Juan Vicente 180, 474
García Morales, Justo 39, 437, 474
García-Sabell Tormo, Teresa 474
Gardner, Edmund G. 345, 474
Gargano, Antonio 380, 474
Garter, Order of the 112, 258
Gaunt, John of: *see* John of Gaunt
Gaunt, Simon 163, 184, 199, 474, 479
Gelmírez, Diego, abp. of Santiago de Compostela 118–19, 497
Gerli, E. Michael 32, 474, 477, 486, 506
Gil-Albarellos, Susana 376, 474
Gil Vicente, *Tragicomedia de Amadís de Gaula* 377, 422
Gili Gaya, Samuel 32, 474
Gillard, Julia 4, 10, 475
Gillet, Joseph E. 257, 457, 475
Gilman, Stephen 345, 475
Gimber, Arno 20, 354, 355, 358, 475
Giménez, Helio 214, 475
Gimeno Blay, Francisco 36, 475
Gimeno Casalduero, Joaquín 32, 247, 475
Gironella, Guillem Ramón de, 'Gen m'apareill' 164
Gisbert, Lope 410–11, 439
Godinho, Helder 473, 475, 495
Goethe, Johann Wolfgang von 378
Gomes, Aleixo 475
Gómez-Montero, Javier 376, 475
Gómez Redondo, Fernando 31, 43, 63, 122, 131, 152, 209, 222, 239, 244, 247, 291, 311, 314, 332, 339, 367, 380, 475
Gonçal'Eanes do Vinhal 22, 61, 98, 123–5, 136–9, 200–1, 468, 508
  'Amigas, eu oí dizer' 136
  'Maestre, todolus vossos cantares' 22, 61, 124, 201
  'Sei eu, donas, que deitad'é d'aquí' 136
Gonçalves, Elsa 475
Gonçalves, Francisco de Souza 475
Gonçalves, Susana 81, 475
Gonçalves Pereira, Álvaro, prior of Crato 102
Gonçalves Pereira, Gonçalo, abp of Braga 102
González, Javier Roberto 507
González Cuenca, Joaquín 228–9, 292, 380, 449, 457, 470, 475
González Jiménez, Manuel 136, 476
González Reigosa, Carlos 421, 439
Gonzalo Sánchez-Molero, José Luis 255, 476
Goodman, Jennifer R. 376, 476
Gouiran, Gérard 163, 476, 499

Gracia, Paloma 7–8, 11, 18, 25, 27, 31–32, 38–40, 67, 84, 85, 92, 114–16, 271, 274, 277–8, 287–8, 351, 371, 380, 476–7
Gracia Dei, Pedro 371
Graf, Arturo 175, 477
Grail, as object and theme 1, 3, 14, 18, 29, 46–7, 76–80, 82, 90–2, 94–5, 100–1, 114, 116, 139, 154, 172, 180, 209, 224, 256–9, 263, 268, 271–3, 276, 278–9, 282, 284, 295, 307, 313, 351, 372, 402, 413–14, 416–28, 430–3
Gran conquista de Ultramar, La 57, 256, 367, 406, 463, 477
Granés, Salvador María 415, 439
Grant Coronica d'Espanya, see Fernández de Heredia, Juan.
Gras, Mosen, *Tragèdia de Lançalot* 12–13, 36, 179, 182, 269, 498
Grimbert, Joan Tasker 477
Guadalajara, José 227, 477
Guardiola, Conrado 209, 379, 477
Gudayol, A.M. 175, 477
Guillem de Varoic 181
Guimarães Rosa, João 432, 439
Guincho, Maria dos Anjos 477
Guiron le Courtois 100, 483
Gurrea y Aragón, Gaspar Galcerán de, Conde de Guimerà 171
Gutiérrez García, Santiago 4, 8, 23, 31, 37, 58, 61, 63, 99–100, 121, 123, 125–6, 131, 133, 137, 140, 149–50, 159, 163, 166, 200, 477
Guy de Warwick 181
Guzmán, Fernán Pérez de 211, 225–6, 254, 369, 507
Guzmán, Gaspar de, Conde de Olivares 171
Guzmán, Juan de 225
Gwara, Joseph J. 222, 311, 346, 477

Haebler, Konrad 36, 477
Haidu, Peter 120, 125, 478
Hall, J.B. 90, 332–3, 478
Hampe Martínez, Teodoro 401, 478
Harney, Michael 37, 478
Harvey, Ruth 163, 184, 199, 474, 479
Hauf i Valls, Albert-Guillem 26, 32, 182, 184–5, 455, 478, 487, 500
Haute escriture del Saint Graal 82
Heijkant, Marie José 31, 319, 321–3, 328, 478
Henry, Prince, 'the Navigator' 382–3
Henry II, k. of England 15, 159, 188, 234
Henry IV, k. of England 59
Henry VII, k. of England 5
Henry VIII, k. of England 5
Herculano, Alexandre 103, 478
Heredia, Ricardo 343, 405

'Herido está don Tristán' 20–1, 26, 345, 505
Hernández, Antonio 427
Hernández, Luisa Josefina 432, 439
Hernández González, María Isabel 31, 39, 288, 478
Higden, Ranoulf, *Polychronicon* 104
Hillgarth, J.N. 6, 478
Himmler, Heinrich 416
Hiriart, Hugo 432, 440
Histoire ancienne jusqu'à César (MS esp. 13, BNF) 14–16
Historia de dos amadores 19, 27, 84, 219, 282, 288
Historia de los nobles cavalleros Oliveros de Castilla y Artús de Algarbe 323, 341–2, 344–5, 347, 456, 473
Historia de los valientes caballeros Tablante de Ricamonte y Jofre Donason 403
Historia de proeliis 152
Historia del santo Grial 254, 276
Historia do principe Belidor Anfibio e da princeza chamada Corsina 111–12
Historia dos Cavaleiros da Mesa Redonda e da Demanda do Santo Graal 87
Historia notavel em que se trata da vida, e valereosas obras do animoso cavalleiro andante Lançarote do Lago (1764), chapbook 404
Hofmann, Konrad 87, 509
Hook, David 3–4, 10, 15, 27–8, 32, 58, 122, 162, 186, 192, 194, 199–200, 240, 243, 308, 379, 382, 405, 432, 462, 466, 473, 478–9, 497
Horto do Esposo 64, 115, 473, 485, 495
Houdenc, Raoul de 85, 203
    Meraugis de Portlesguez 85, 221
    Vengeance Reguidel 203
Huet, Charlotte 403, 407, 479
Hungary, Maria of 28, 44, 255
Hutchinson, Amélia P. 59, 112, 479
Huth MS 69, 84, 271–2, 280–1, 489, 495, 504

Idamons, Alma, *see* 'Anonymus Cinco'
Imperial, Francisco 224–5, 268, 292
Index librorum prohibitorum 252
indigenous persons with Arthurian names 384, 395–6
Infantes, Víctor 376, 379, 475, 479, 499
Iragui, Sebastian 31, 314, 318, 320–1, 325, 327, 330, 363, 479
Isabel I, 'the Catholic', q. of Castile 6, 28, 30, 33, 191, 208, 211–3, 228–9, 254–5, 274–5, 293, 350, 355, 489, 500–1
Isabel of Portugal 255
Isidore, St 151, 187, 237, 259, 380

GENERAL INDEX

Ivy, Robert H. 85, 499
Izquierdo, Josep 166, 479

Jarnés, Benjamín 412, 440
Jaufré 166–7, 169, 175, 179, 184, 189, 402, 447, 457, 470–1, 477, 479, 482, 498
Jaume I, k. of Aragon 14, 164–7, 169, 185, 491, 503–4
  Llibre dels fets 165, 504
  conception of 14, 166, 185
Jaume II, k. of Aragón 14, 30, 34, 52, 54, 163, 168–9, 179, 293
Jaume III, k. of Mallorca 178
Jaume IV, Infant of Mallorca 178
Jenkins, T. Atkinson 143, 493
Jerome, St, *Canones chronici* 152
Jews 76, 127–8, 143, 227, 503
Jiménez de Rada, Rodrigo, abp. of Toledo 200, 235–6
  De rebus Hispaniae 153, 235–6
  Catalan translation, *Crónica d'Espanya* 170
Jiménez Mola, Zulema 304, 463
Joan I, k. of Aragon 14, 30, 52, 54, 171–2, 179, 185
Joanne of Flanders 60, 159
João I, k. of Portugal 59, 106, 112–13, 450
João III, k. of Portugal 72–3, 109–10, 279, 384
John of Gaunt 59, 112
Jones, Kirkland C. 479
Jonson, Ben 378
Josephus 152
Juan I, k. of Castile 240, 246
Juan II, k. of Castile 33, 197, 210, 239, 248–9, 253, 269, 292
Juárez Blanquer, Aurora 132, 479
Julius Caesar 15–16, 160, 238, 241, 253, 419
Junqueira, Renata Soares 480, 488

Kassam, Ashifa 10, 480
Kasten, Lloyd 15, 238, 480
Keats, John 378
Keen, Maurice 196, 480
Kennedy, Edward D. 318, 339, 480
Kennedy, Elspeth 289–91, 295, 308, 480
Khaleesi, as personal name 4–5, 10
Klob, Otto 40, 66, 73–4, 87–8, 284, 480
Krauss, Henning 499
Kurtz, Julia 21, 363, 480

La Torre, Fernando de 226, 292, 340, 380, 469
Lacy, Norris J. 408, 480, 490, 502–3, 509
Lagares Díez, Xoán Carlos 96, 115, 480
Lai de Hélys 98, 116
Lai de Tyrolet 231
Lai du cort mantel 202

Lai du plour 98, 116
Lancaster, Philippa of 59
Lançalot 12, 14, 52–3, 268, 289–308, 453, 463, 493, 500
Lançalot del Lach 53
Lancelot du Lac 116, 171, 181, 184, 497, 504
Lancelot en prose 12, 14, 25, 28, 133–5, 140, 166, 171, 289–308, 316, 380, 461, 463–4, 505
Lancelot-Graal cycle 61–2, 69–70, 86–7, 91, 94, 489, 502
Lancelot propre 16, 30, 62–3, 70–1, 99, 110, 133, 135, 141, 149, 272, 461
Lanzarote del Lago 21, 51, 55, 63, 71, 113, 220, 268, 289–308, 351, 353, 450, 453–4, 461–3, 480, 484, 502–3
'Lanzarote y el ciervo de pie blanco' 20–1, 292, 458
'Lanzarote y el orgulloso' 20, 292–3
Lanciani, Giulia 131, 458, 472, 480, 483, 487
Lang, Henry R. 480
langue d'oïl 63, 120, 163–4, 168
Lapa, Manuel Rodrigues 23, 60, 63, 64, 65, 66, 67, 74, 86, 87, 113, 114, 132, 136, 148, 285, 286, 288, 367, 452, 453, 457, 458, 472, 480–1, 487, 488, 492
Lapesa, Rafael 67, 191, 368, 481, 490, 499
Laranjinha, Ana Sofia 57, 70, 73, 81, 91, 115, 145, 446, 463, 481
Larraya, Martín de 236
Las Casas, Fray Bartolomé de 399, 406, 481
Lawrance, Jeremy N. H. 33, 253–4, 380, 481
Le Gentil, Pierre 376, 481
Le Goff, Jacques 94, 481
Le opere magnanime de i due Tristani 311
Leal, Larissa do Socorro Martins 482
Lechuga Quijada, Sergio 416, 440
Lee, Charmaine 167, 175–6, 479, 482
Lendo Fuentes, Rosalba 31, 288, 482
Leomarte 239–40, 242, 268, 348, 482
Leonard, Irving A. 401–2, 407, 482
Leonardi, L. 315, 319, 482
Liber regum 24, 69, 104–5, 122, 153–4, 200, 234–8, 241, 267–8, 450, 460, 463, 482, 490, 502
libraries, noble, Italian 185
  see also book ownership
Libro de Alexandre 28, 199–200, 252, 268, 447, 457, 461, 482, 489
Libro de Josep Abarimatia 17, 47, 273, 275–6, 279, 284–5, 482, 496
  see also Livro de Josep Abaramatia
Libro de las bienandanzas e fortunas, see García de Salazar, Lope
Libro de las generaciones 16, 24, 31, 46, 104–5, 153–4, 236, 241, 479, 509

Libro de Merlín (also Estoria de Merlín) 17, 47, 57, 269, 273, 276–8, 281, 399, 471, 476, 496
Libro del Caballero Zifar (or *Cavallero Çifar*) 44–5, 56, 64, 204–8, 214–16, 223, 240, 268, 301, 336, 340, 362, 367, 376, 455, 465, 482, 484, 497, 501, 508
Lida de Malkiel, María Rosa 2, 4, 25, 27, 29, 32, 64, 67, 84, 119, 142, 162, 199, 219, 314, 344–6, 367, 369, 482
Lidamarte de Armenia 265
Lienas, Gemma 431, 440–1
Lisuarte de Grecia 215, 218, 264, 482, 503
literatura de cordel 402–5, 407
Little, William Thomas 380, 482
Livro de Josep Abaramatia 11, 22, 236, 268, 273, 275, 278–9, 284, 288, 467, 493
  see also *Libro de Josep Abarimatia*
Livro do Deão 102–3
Livro primeiro da primeira parte dos Triunfos de Sagramor 109–10
Livro velho 102–3
Lleonart, Joseph 414, 441
Llompart, Gabriel 162, 483
Llull, Ramon 28, 48, 167–8, 181, 504
  Evast e Blaquerna 167, 504
  Doctrina puerill 48
  Llibre de l'orde de cavalleria 167–8, 181
Longobardi, Monica 272, 483
Longuyon, Jacques de, *Voeux du paon* 252
Loomis, Roger Sherman ix, 189, 452, 482–3, 489, 498, 508
Loomis, Laura 483
Lopes, Fernão, *Crónica de D. João I* 106, 113, 450, 487
López de Ayala, Pero 24, 116, 209, 240, 246–7, 249, 251–2, 268, 292, 367, 379, 483, 492, 494
López de Gómara, Francisco 377, 398, 483
López de Mendoza, Iñigo, Marqués de Santillana 33, 41, 155, 252, 254, 380, 483
López Estrada, Francisco 252, 475, 483
López Martínez-Morás, Santiago 64, 313, 474, 483
López Sangil, José Luis 120, 483
López Soler, Ramón 409, 441
Lorenzo Gradín, Pilar 4, 8, 22–3, 31, 38, 41, 63–4, 83, 85, 118, 123, 125–7, 131, 137, 140, 147–8, 150, 156–8, 280, 288, 384, 448, 477, 483, 490
Lorenzo Vázquez, Ramón 21, 151, 154, 161, 483
Löseth, Eilert 13, 23, 98, 138, 145, 147, 157, 160, 222, 315–21, 324–5, 373, 484
Loureiro Calvo, Ramón 421, 441
Lourenzo, Miguel 430, 441

Lucía Megías, José Manuel 2, 8, 23, 29, 31, 33, 37–42, 44, 51, 109, 111, 115, 159, 170, 172, 185, 191, 255, 289, 296, 307, 309–10, 314, 316, 325, 330, 332–3, 337, 339–40, 351, 353, 354, 362, 400, 447–8, 450, 463, 465–6, 475, 484, 491, 506
Luciano, Alderado 405, 407, 484
Lucan, *Pharsalia* 237–8

Macedo, José Rivair 484
Machado, Elsa Paxeco 140, 484, 494
Machado, José Barbosa 140, 484, 494
Machado, José Pedro 484, 494
MacKay, Angus 6, 485
Madureira, Margarida 115, 458–9, 467, 469, 472–3, 475, 481, 485, 490, 492, 494, 503
Madurell i Marimon, Josep Maria 30, 168, 485
Magalhães, Hilda Gomes Dutra 485
Magne, Augusto 31, 38, 88, 288, 467, 480, 485, 488
Maler, Bertil 115, 485
Maleval, Maria do Amparo Tavares 485, 489
Malmesbury, William of, *Gesta regum Anglorum* 160
Malory, Thomas 104, 161, 202, 318, 339, 421, 426, 430, 433–4, 442, 444, 479–80, 485, 500, 502
Manessier, *III Continuation-Perceval* 60, 159
Mangrané, Daniel 415–16, 441
Mañé Garzón, Pablo 425, 441
Map, Walter, *De nugis curialium* 265
Maragall, Joan 414, 441
Marcenaro, Simone 141, 485
Mariana, Juan de 10
Marianella, Conchita H. 232, 485
Marín Pina, María Carmen 109, 310, 344–6, 351, 355, 360, 376–7, 466, 470, 485–6, 491, 497, 506
Marín Sánchez, Ana María 46, 340, 486
Mariño Paz, Ramón 307, 486
Martí I, l'Humà, k. of Aragón 52, 172, 179
Martín, Esteban 426, 441
Martin, George R. R. 4, 486
Martin, Georges 153, 486
Martín Abad, Julián 42, 486
Martín Garzo, Gustavo 416, 441
Martines, Vicent 29, 36, 486
Martínez de Medina, Diego 226
Martínez de Toledo, Alfonso, Arcipreste de Talavera 269, 292, 340, 486
Martínez Ferrando, J. Ernesto 380, 486
Martínez Pérez, Antonia 32, 486
Martins, Mário 23, 72–3, 81, 114, 359, 486–7
Martorell, Joanot, *Tirant lo Blanch* 25–6, 45, 51, 56, 117, 167, 179, 181–2, 184, 228, 269,

294, 376, 446, 449, 451, 455, 460, 478, 487, 497–8, 500, 507
Mary I, q. of England 5
Mattoso, José 102–3, 116, 122, 131, 136, 487
Matulka, Barbara 220, 467
Matute, Ana María 425, 441
McGrady, Donald 32, 488
Megale, Heitor 23, 38, 66, 86, 101, 114, 283, 286–8, 453, 473, 488, 492, 507
Mejía, Hernán 227
Meliadux 169, 171–2
Meliadux, k. 48, 321, 338, 352
Mellizo, Felipe 424, 441
Melnick, Eitan 433, 441
Membrilla, Martín de la 231
Mena, Juan de 242, 341–2, 456
Ménard, Philippe 98, 137, 145–6, 156–8, 161, 315, 318, 376, 488–9, 499
Méndez Ferrín, Xosé Luís 419–21, 441
Mendoza, Aldonza de, duchess of Arjona 33, 254
Meneghetti, María Luisa 120, 125, 288, 489
Menéndez Pidal, Ramón 228, 309, 480, 489, 491, 496, 503
Menéndez y Pelayo, Marcelino 66, 152, 284, 489
Mérida Jiménez, Rafael M. 29, 35–43, 159, 183, 314, 372, 489
Merlin 17–18, 30, 32–3, 38–9, 52, 54, 57, 70, 87, 114, 121, 129, 155, 205, 220–1, 240, 269, 271–6, 278, 280–1, 287–8, 399, 471, 476–7, 481, 483, 489, 490, 495–6, 504
  see also *Libro de Merlín, Suite du Merlin, Baladro*
mescheance 93, 463
Metge, Bernat 172, 179, 448–9
  Lo somni 172, 449
  Llibre de Fortuna e Prudència 179, 448–9
Mettmann, Walter 127–30, 489
Micha, Alexandre 114, 133–5, 141, 160, 289, 291, 295–6, 305–6, 373–4, 380, 489
Michael, Ian 9, 28, 489
Michäelis de Vasconcelos, Carolina 31, 60, 66, 73, 86–7, 96–8, 101, 284, 444, 454, 489
Michelli, Regina 489
Michels, Ralph J. 32, 489
Michon, Patricia 31, 147, 157–8, 288, 313, 327, 489–90
Middleton, Robert 34, 44, 490
Migir, Fray 225, 292
Milá y Fontanals, Manuel (Milà i Fontanals) 21, 66, 120, 284, 293, 490
Milán, Luis de, *El cortesano* 231
Millares, Selena 428, 441
Millares Carlo, Agustín 368, 481, 490, 499
Miller, Barbara D. 29, 407, 490
Milton, John 378

Miquel y Planas, Ramon 185, 490
Miragres de Santiago 64
Miralles, Eulàlia 186, 490
Miranda, José Carlos Ribeiro 30, 37, 40, 52, 57, 60, 63, 66, 70, 73, 79–80, 92, 95, 274, 290, 446, 463–4, 490–1
'miscellany' manuscripts 20, 47–9, 52, 71, 100, 170, 314
Modernism 409
Moisés, Massaud 491
Moleón Viana, Miguel Ángel 431, 441
Molina, María de, q. of Castile 203–4, 209, 244
Molino de Amor, El 369, 452
Molloy Carpenter, Dorothy 217, 448, 491
Molteni, Enrico 101, 491
Mone, Frank Joseph 87, 491
Money-Coutts, Francis Burdett 434
Mongelli, Lênia Márcia 464, 479–81, 485, 490–493, 503, 507–9
Moniot d'Arras 60, 470
Monmouth, Geoffrey of 14–16, 29–30, 46, 69, 85, 104, 122, 124, 127, 129–31, 149, 153–4, 160, 166, 170, 183, 202, 234–8, 240, 242–3, 252, 258, 462, 470, 505, 509
Montaigne, Michel de 378
Montaner Frutos, Alberto 380, 466, 491
Montero, Rosa 426, 441
Montero Cartelle, Emilio 160, 491
Montero Cartelle, Enrique 141, 150, 491
Montes, Graciela 407, 430, 432, 441–2
Monteserín, Xicu 430, 442
Montoliu, Manuel de 14, 165–6, 491
Montreuil, Gerbert de, *Roman de la Violette* 60
  IV Continuation-Perceval 143, 508
Mora, Víctor 427, 442
Moralejo Álvarez, Serafín 21, 123, 189, 491
Morales, María Luz 430, 442
Moraes, Francisco de, *Palmeirim de Inglaterra* 109–10, 112, 216, 468
Moreira, Thiers Martins 491
Morera i Galicia, Magí 413, 442
Morley, S. Griswold 267, 491
Morros, Bienvenido 39, 288, 377, 491, 492
Mort Artu 17–19, 22, 27–8, 32, 38–9, 53, 70, 86, 88, 90–1, 104, 129, 131, 169, 175, 177, 182, 217, 220–1, 233, 271–6, 279, 283, 286, 296, 301, 453, 476, 483
Mort le roi Artu 12–13, 5, 202, 271, 273, 373, 375, 473
Morte Arthur, anon. English poem 104, 161
Moura, Leonor 81, 492
Moure, José Luis 247, 484, 492
Muhammad V, k. of Granada 31, 190, 247, 308
Muir, Lynette 143, 492
Mundó, A. M. 50, 492

Muniz, Márcio Ricardo Coelho 492
Muntaner, Ramon, *Crònica* 14, 165–7, 183–4, 384, 479, 504

names, personal, of Arthurian origin 1, 3–5, 8, 14–15, 28, 33, 58–9, 122–3, 162, 191–8, 223, 380, 382–96, 405–6
Naranjo, Francisco 416, 441
Nascimento, Aires Augusto 37, 58, 73–4, 279–80, 288, 455, 474, 490, 492, 495–6
Navasal, José María 433, 442
Nebrija, Elio Antonio de, *Gramática de la lengua castellana* 230
Neri, Stefano 378, 492
Neto, Serafim da Silva 73, 492
Neto, Sílvio de Almeida Toledo 37, 492
Neves, Leonor Curado 81, 458–9, 467, 469, 472–3, 475, 485, 490, 492–4, 503
Nicolás, poet 225
Nitze, William A. 143, 160, 493
Norgales 77, 372
Northup, George Tyler 31, 41, 296, 309, 314, 316, 318–21, 330, 332–3, 335–6, 338, 453, 493
Norton, F. J. 347, 402, 407, 493
'Nunca fuera cavallero' 229, 231–2, 260, 270, 293
Nunes, José Joaquim 63, 66, 73, 87–8, 101, 493
Nunes Batista, Sebastião 407, 493
Núñez de Toledo, Catalina 33, 287

Obrador, Matheu 29, 35, 289, 493, 500
O'Callaghan, Joseph F. 6, 493
O'Connor, John J. 378, 493
O'Gorman, Edmundo 399, 406, 481
Ojea, José 411, 442
Old Testament Pseudepigrapha 406, 459, 493
Olival, Fernanda 111–12, 493
Olivante de Laura 265
Olivar, Alexandre 171, 493
Olivar, Marçal 162, 169, 493
Oliveira, António Resende de 119, 136, 142, 493
operatic adaptations of *Amadís de Gaula* 378–9
Orazi, Veronica 314, 493
Orduna, Germán 209, 379, 405, 483–4, 494
Orduna, Lília E. F. de, *see* Ferrario de Orduna, Lília
Ors, Joan 175, 494
Ortega, Melchor de, *Felixmarte de Hircania* 216, 471, 494
Ortiz, Petrus (copyist/compiler, Salamanca MS 1877) 17, 273, 277
Ortúñez de Calahorra, Diego, *Espejo de príncipes y cavalleros* 264
Osakabe, Haquira 453, 473, 492, 494, 507
Otte, Enrique 405–7, 494
Ovid 152, 172, 184, 218, 221–2, 237, 379

Pacheco, Arseni 174, 175, 494
Pacheco, Elsa: see Machado, Elsa Paxeco and José Pedro Machado
Pacheco, Graça M. Lérias 494
Pagès, Amédée 30, 494
Paixão, Rosário Santana 447, 463, 494
Palacio Valdés, Armando 429, 442
palavras cubertas 141, 160
Pallares, María Carmen 120, 494
Palma-Ferreira, João 108, 492, 494
Palmerín de Olivia 218, 357, 494, 505
Palmireno, Juan Lorenzo, *Vocabulario del humanista* 257
Paolantonio, Jorge 412, 442
paper, in book-trade 45, 50–2
Pardo Bazán, Emilia 413, 422, 442
Pardo de Guevara y Valdés, Eduardo 197, 494
Paredes Núñez, Juan 30, 126, 131, 136, 442, 446, 457, 461, 485–6, 494–5, 498, 500, 506
Paris, Gaston 17, 69–70, 87, 271, 278, 495
Paris and Helen, canonical lovers 126, 176
Paris and Viana, canonical lovers 184
Parodi, E. G. 319, 321, 478
Parrilla García, Carmen 346, 446, 461, 465–6, 473, 476, 495, 501, 504
Pastoureau, Michel 122, 495
Paton, Lucy Allen 128, 495
Patrício, António 415, 442
Pauphilet, Albert 87, 495
Paz, Demétrio Alves 495
Pedrazim, Ana Lucia 495
Pedro de Portugal, count of Barcelos, *Livro das linhagens*16, 23–4, 30–1, 46, 69, 97–8, 101–5, 148, 153, 236, 268, 450, 455, 457–60, 472, 478, 487, 495, 501
    Crónica geral de Espanha de 1344 103–4, 460
Pedro I, k. of Castile 24, 170, 190, 197, 210, 240, 244, 246–7, 251, 418, 438
Pedro I, k. of Aragon: see Pere I
Pedrosa, José Manuel 233, 495
Peire Cardenal 125–6
Pelayo 376
Pelegrín, B. 21, 495
Pellegrini, Silvio 31, 101, 123, 495
Pemán, José María 429, 442
Pena, Joaquim 414–15, 444–5
Pensado Tomé, José L. 31, 41, 64, 155, 313, 495
Perceforest 145, 185, 255
Perceval 60, 85, 114, 143–4, 159, 203, 263, 478, 499, 508
Perceval en prose 85
Perdomo García, José 355, 495
Pere, *infant* of Aragon, receives *Lansalot* from Jaume II (1321) 14, 168
Pere el Catòlic, k. of Aragon 165

GENERAL INDEX

Pere I el Gran, k. of Aragon 184
Pere III, k. of Aragon 12, 14, 30, 52–3
Pere IV el Ceremoniòs, k. of Aragon 165, 167–8, 171, 178–9, 493
Pereira, Cláudia Sousa 116, 495
Pereira, Nun'Alvares, condestabre of Portugal 106, 479, 485, 509
Pereira, Paulo Alexandre 115, 495
Pereira, Rita de Cássia Mendes 495
Perellós, Ramón de, *Viatge al Purgatori de Sant Patrici* 185, 202–3
Pérez, Elisa Cifuentes 496
Pérez Galdós, Benito 428–9, 442
Pérez López, José Luis 380, 496
Pérez Navarro, Francisco 427, 442
Pérez Pascual, Ignacio 151–2, 161, 496
Pérez Priego, Miguel Ángel 256, 496, 505
Perlesvaus 143–4, 493
Perucho, Joan 423, 442
Phaedra, as lover of Hippolytus 184
Philip II, k. of Spain 5, 28, 111, 255, 377
Philip the Fair 44
Philippa of Lancaster 59
Piccolomini, Eneas Silvio, *Historia de duobus amantibus* 218, 221
Pickford, Cedric E. 23, 66, 69–70, 148, 286, 496
Piel, Joseph Maria 31, 38, 88, 92–5, 114–15, 288, 458, 496
Pierozzi, Antonino, *Chronicon* 38, 83
Pietsch, Karl 17, 23, 37–9, 66–7, 121, 255, 276–8, 284–5, 287, 457, 471, 476, 480, 482, 496
Pimenta, Maria Helena de Almeida 496
Pimentel y Enríquez, Alonso, count of Benavente 33. 254, 450
Pina, Margarida Esperança 496
Pina, Rui de 107, 116, 467
Pinar, Jerónimo de 226, 228–30, 269, 451
Piñero Ramírez, Pedro M. 356, 452, 455–6, 496
Pinheiro, Marília Futre 496
Pio, Carlos 37, 66, 75, 496
Pirot, François 29, 496
Pitta, Maria Helena Abrantes 496
Place, Edwin B. 378, 380, 496–7
Planeta, see García de Campos, Diego
Platir 216–17, 497
Poema de Alfonso XI 24, 244, 249, 251–2, 458, 497, 509
  see also Yáñez, Rodrigo
Poema de mio Cid 199
Polindo 215, 265, 497
Ponceau, Jean-Paul 287–8, 497
Pons y Guimerá, Miguel 428, 443
Porta, Aida Amelia 375, 497
Portela, Ermelindo 120, 494
Portugal, Fernando Filipe 494

Post-Vulgate Cycle 7–8, 16–19, 21–2, 24–8, 30, 32, 57, 60–5, 69–71, 75, 79–80, 82, 85–91, 93–4, 97–101, 105, 107, 113, 116, 120–1, 137–9, 142, 144–50, 154, 157, 160, 204, 209, 220, 223, 236, 240–1, 255, 260, 271–88, 290, 296, 304, 306, 315, 452–3, 457, 470, 476–8, 483, 488, 492, 502, 504
  see also Pseudo-Robert de Boron
Prado-Vilar, Francisco 159–60, 189, 497
Pratt, Karen 244, 450, 453, 455, 474, 480, 490
Pre-Raphaelites 413–4, 424
Presotto, Marco 380, 497
Primaleón 215, 218, 497
Proceso de cartas de amores see Segura, Juan de
Profecies de Merlí 52, 170, 172, 453
prophecies of Merlin, tradition of 18, 24, 61, 85, 111, 128, 154, 170, 224, 227, 240–1, 243–52, 268, 282, 288, 495
proverbial reference to Holy Grail 257
Pseudo-Robert de Boron 7, 35, 37, 39–40, 46–7, 51, 55–6, 62–5, 69–70, 75, 82, 85, 87, 89, 91, 93–4, 100, 121, 131, 137, 144, 146, 148, 150, 155, 160, 315, 464, 481, 504
  see also Post-Vulgate Cycle
Puértolas, Soledad 426, 443
Pujante, David 427, 443
Pujol, Josep 166, 171, 180–2, 185, 497
Pulsoni, Carlo 124, 457
Punzi, Arianna 316, 319, 324, 497
Pyramus and Thisbe, canonical lovers 176, 184

Quercy, Mathieu de, 'Tant suy marritz que no.m puesc alegrar' 167
Quessep, Giovanni 432, 443
Queste del Saint Graal 12, 16–19, 22, 28–30, 32, 36, 38–9, 53, 55, 70, 80, 86, 88–9, 91, 93, 98, 113, 131, 137, 146–8, 155, 168–9, 171–2, 185, 233, 271–4, 276, 279, 283, 285–6, 315, 446, 452–3, 455, 476, 483, 485–6, 495, 504, 508
Quetzalcoatl, myth of, compared to King Arthur by Sahagún 398

Raimundo, Dulce Helena Morgado 497
Rainaldo e Lesengrino 185
Ramos, Rafael 8, 25, 32, 181, 308, 324, 325, 364–81 397–8, 406, 497
Raoul de Soissons 125–6
readers, readership 44, 50–2, 96, 106, 108, 111, 167, 169, 173, 185, 200, 207, 212, 262–5, 324–5, 346–8, 350–1, 375–7, 397, 404–5, 409, 429
recreantisse 174, 260
redemption 81, 92
Redondo, Augustín 265–6, 498

Rego, A. da Silva 405, 498, 506
Reinhardstöttner, Karl von 73, 87–8, 495, 498
Remy, Paul 479, 498
repartimientos 139, 194
repentance 84, 92, 129, 213, 312, 349–50
'Respuesta de Tristán' 20, 43, 221–2, 311, 336, 346, 475
  see also 'Carta'
return of Arthur, *see* expectation
rewriting 18, 20, 25, 63–4, 71, 134, 150, 182, 244, 271, 273, 281–2, 347, 350, 362, 424, 453
Rexach, G, Catalan copist/translator? 12, 36, 171
Rey, Agapito 239, 498
Rey, Jorge 431, 439
Rey de Artieda, Andrés, *Amadís* 377
Ribera, Antoni 414, 441
Ribera, Suero de 226, 292
Ribot d'Aixirivall, Miquel, notary, copyist of *Codex miscel.lani* 13, 49, 57
Richard d'Irlande, Richard of Ireland, *Les Prophécies de Merlin* 62, 128, 243–4, 246, 252, 495
Rico, Francisco 71, 377, 459, 484, 486, 498
Rico Góngora, Montserrat 416, 443
Riquer, Alexandre de 414, 443
Riquer, Isabel 29, 30, 32, 162–4, 171, 176, 185, 291, 498
Riquer, Martín de 26, 28, 30, 32, 36, 120, 162–3, 166–8, 171, 175–6, 180–5, 293, 366, 368, 380, 426, 448, 452, 455, 468, 490, 494, 498–9
Risco, Vicente 417–18, 420, 443
Rivero Taravillo, Antonio 412, 443
Roach, William 85, 499
Roberts, Kimberley S. 73, 88, 499
Robinson, Cynthia 31, 499
Rodríguez de Montalvo, Garci 25, 107, 109–10, 112, 207–8, 211–13, 215–16, 220, 269, 297, 308, 322, 340, 368–71, 375–6 379, 397, 422, 447–9, 455, 466, 473, 482, 491, 496, 499–502, 505
Rodríguez del Padrón, Juan, *Siervo libre de amor* 20, 27, 84, 218–22, 269, 376, 447, 482, 499
Rodríguez-Moñino, Antonio 229, 231, 368, 481, 490, 499
Rodríguez Velasco, Jesús D. 33, 39, 274, 348, 367, 375, 459, 478, 499
Roig, Jaume, *Spill* 185, 457
Rojas, Fernando de, *Celestina* 26–7, 210, 242–3, 267, 269, 345, 358, 385, 452, 475, 482, 488, 498
Román, Comendador 226
Roman de Thèbes 152, 237
Roman du Graal 46, 69, 121, 220, 271, 296, 315, 452–3, 478, 502

Roman van Lancelot 231
romancero, romances 20, 31, 22–9, 231–3, 267, 269, 292, 356, 377, 425, 458, 468–9, 474, 489, 499, 508
Romero Portilla, Paz 113, 499
Romeu Muller, Carlos 429, 443
Ron Fernández, Xosé Xabier 499
Roncaglia, Aurelio 120, 125, 499
rondalles, Mallorcan 174
  'La fada Morgana' 174
  'Na Joana i la fada Mariana' 174
Ronsard, Pierre de 378
Roques, Mario 133, 499
Ros Domimgo, Enrique Andrés 30–1, 41, 314, 318–19, 321, 325, 327–8, 330, 335, 347, 355–6, 360, 478, 499
Rosenblat, Ángel 432, 443
Rossi, Luciano 64, 74, 87, 113, 120, 125, 499
Rotger, Matheu 289
Rothstein, antiquarian bookseller 405
Roubaud-Bénichou, Sylvia 353, 499
Roussineau, Gilles 31, 83, 99, 116, 137–9, 144–5, 149–50, 157, 160, 280, 296, 499–500
Rubio, Mercedes 416, 443
Rubio Flores, Antonio 132, 479
Rubió i Lluch, Antonio (Rubió y Lluch, Antonio) 7, 29, 35, 168–9, 171, 184, 289, 291, 293, 299, 307, 500
Rubio Pacho, Carlos 328, 333, 335, 338, 500
Ruiz, Juan, Arcipreste de Hita, *Libro de buen amor* 28, 223, 227, 268, 340, 362, 367, 379, 451–2, 464, 500
Ruiz-Domènec, José Enrique 306, 500
Ruiz García, Elisa 30, 33, 43, 45, 57, 255, 287, 293, 500
Rumble, Thomas C. 318, 500
Rupescissa, Johannes de 47, 249, 251–2
Rustichello da Pisa, *Compilation* 45, 71, 317–24, 327, 331, 349, 363, 459
Rychner, Jean 160, 500

Sabaté, Glòria 182–3, 500
Sahagún 4, 192–3, 196, 267, 472
Sahagún, Fray Bernardino de 398, 406, 500
Sainero, Ramón 412, 443
Sáinz de la Maza, Carlos 370, 499, 500
Sales Dasí, Emilio José 181, 264, 376, 380, 484, 500–1, 503
Salvá, Vicente 405
Salvador Miguel, Nicasio 501
San Pedro, Diego de 27, 43, 220–1, 269, 501
Sánches, João (or Juan Sánchez) 74, 78, 87, 121, 159, 280
Sánchez Ameijeiras, Rocío 21, 134, 189, 501
Sánchez Calavera, Fernán 226

Sánchez Cantón, Francisco Javier 191, 501
Sánchez-Cutillas, Carmelina 424, 443
Sánchez-Prieto Borja, Pedro 160, 446, 501
Sancho II, k. of Portugal 60–1, 120, 136–7, 142
Sancho IV, k. of Castile 23, 192, 203, 208, 250, 285, 292, 328, 474
Sancho, s. of Alfonso VI 118
Sanjurjo, Carmela Eulate 412, 443
Santanach i Suñol, Joan 13, 30, 40–1, 48–9, 57, 168, 172, 314, 324–5, 329–30, 333, 336, 363, 501, 504
Santiago, Iara Romeiro Silva 501
Santiago de Compostela 4, 105, 118, 123, 142, 188, 193, 267, 419
Santiago, pilgrimage route to 21, 59–60, 66, 118–19, 135, 187–8, 191, 194, 327, 419, 431, 464
Santiago, Order of 60, 121
Santillana, Marqués de 33, 41, 155, 252, 254, 380, 483
Santos, Ana Paula Vieira 501
Santos, Luiz Felipe Pereira de Mello 501
San Pedro, Diego de 27, 43, 220, 269, 501
Saraiva, António José 116, 501
Sarmati, Elisabetta 255, 377, 501
Sarrionandia, Joseba 424, 444
Saurí, Martín 427, 442
Schenkel, Luciana de Moraes 501
Schiff, Mario 254, 501
Schreiner, Elisabeth 207, 501
Scotland 40, 51, 127–8, 220, 243, 281, 310, 337, 344, 372
Scott, Sir Walter 378, 409, 415, 428
Scudieri Ruggieri, Jole 319, 330, 501–2
Segura, Joan 173, 502
Segura, Juan de, *Processo de cartas de amores* 218
Seidenspinner-Núñez, Dayle 20, 311, 346, 355–6, 502
Serés, Guillermo 377, 406, 469, 502
Sergas de Esplandián 208, 211–12, 297, 369, 373, 375–6, 397, 402, 455, 474, 499, 500
sermon 3, 204–5, 400, 468
Serra Desfilis, Amadeo 165, 502
Serrano de Osma, Carlos 415–16, 441
Serrano y Sanz, Manuel 31, 41, 104, 155, 313, 502
Sharrer, Harvey L. 3, 9, 16, 20, 22, 27–30, 35–43, 46, 58, 62–3, 84, 99, 113, 116, 125, 128, 142, 159–60, 172, 185, 200, 219, 222, 240–1, 255, 288–92, 294, 296, 307, 309, 311, 318–9, 332, 344–6, 351, 380–1, 404, 407–8, 463, 480, 502–3
Shirt, David 160, 503
Sholod, Barton 380, 503
'Si os valga', anon. 227

Sidney, Philip 378
Sierra, Pedro de la, *Espejo de príncipes* 216, 471, 503
Siete Infantes de Lara 403
Silva, Delarme Monteiro, *Joana d'Arca, heroína de França* 404
Silva, Feliciano de, *Lisuarte de Grecia* 112, 215–16, 218, 264, 448, 473, 482, 503
 Amadís de Grecia 215, 218, 448, 503
 Florisel de Niquea 216, 353, 473, 503
Silva y de Toledo, Juan de, *Policisne de Boecia* 216
Silvério, Carla Aexandra Serapicos de Brito 503
Simó, Meritxell 14, 16, 503
Simões, João Gaspar 503
Simonin, Michel 378, 503
Siqueira, Ana Marcia Alves 93, 503
Sir Orfeo 265
Sleeping Beauty, motif of 175
Soares, Martin, *also* Soarez 22, 61–2, 68–9, 98, 139–42, 150, 200–3, 292, 468
 'Hunha donzela jaz aqui' 22, 61–2, 139–41, 200–3, 292, 468
 'Joan Fernandes' 201, 203
Soberanas, Amadeu-J. 31, 38, 50, 64, 82–4, 150, 280–1, 504–5
Soldevila, Ferran 165–6, 184, 503–4
Soler i Llopart, Albert 28, 167–8, 460, 504
Sommer, H. Oskar 12, 17, 30, 39, 66, 70, 86–7, 104, 144, 149, 205, 272, 277, 288–9, 291, 295–6, 305–6, 373, 504
Soriano Robles, Lourdes 3, 5, 8, 29, 31, 41, 100, 157, 162–86, 189, 203, 289, 293, 313–15, 318–21, 323–5, 327, 330, 357, 363, 384, 405, 500, 504–5
Southey, Robert 378
Souto Cabo, José António 31, 38, 41, 64, 83, 85, 119–20, 147–8, 150, 156, 158, 280, 288, 313, 483, 505
Spaggiari, Barbara 505
Spenser, Edmund 378
Splandiano, Il secondo libro delle prodezze di 378
Stegagno-Picchio, Luciana 111, 117, 458, 505
Steinbeck John 424
Steiner, Roger J. 67, 286, 505
Stones, Alison 75, 505
Stòria del Sant Grasal 12, 29–30, 35–6, 53, 55, 268, 446
Strassburg, Gottfried von 429
Suárez, Gonzalo 424, 435
Suárez Pallasá, Aquilino 371, 380, 505
Subirats, Jean 109, 505
Suite du Merlin 18, 22, 26–7, 30, 32, 38–9, 55, 61, 69–71, 82–5, 93–4, 99–100, 116, 137–9, 144–5, 149–50, 155, 160, 219, 240, 271–4,

276, 279–81, 288, 296, 303, 452, 476, 481–3, 489, 499, 503–4
Surles, Robert L. 363, 505

Tablante de Ricamonte, see *Chronica de [...] Tablante de Ricamonte*
Tafur, Pero 256, 496, 505
Tapia, Juan de 226, 340
Tarré, José 32, 227, 244, 505
Tasso, Bernardo, *Amadigi* 378, 401, 473
Tasso, Torquato 378
Tavani, Giuseppe 119, 124, 131, 160, 173, 454, 458, 472, 475, 480, 483, 487, 505
Tavola Ritonda 322–4, 328, 349–50, 363, 478
Teixeira, Izabel Cristina dos Santos 485
Tennyson, Alfred 408–12, 417, 429–30, 433, 435, 437, 439, 442–4, 509
Tercera parte de la Silva de varios romances 231
Terra, Sandra Salviano 506
Testament of Reuben 406
Testaments of the Twelve Patriarchs 406
Texeira, Diogo 432, 444
Thomas, Henry 66, 505
Ticknor, George 403, 508
Tilbury, Gervaise of, *Otia imperialia* 175–6
Timoneda, Juan de, *Rosa de amores* 233
Tirant lo Blanch 25–6, 45, 51, 56, 117, 167, 179, 181, 184, 228, 269, 294, 376, 433, 444, 446, 449, 451, 455, 460, 478, 484, 487, 497–8, 500, 507
Todesco, Venanzio 29, 36, 464
Toldrà, Maria 178–9, 506
Tolkien, J. R. R. 424
Torquemada, Antonio de 371
Torre do Tombo xiii, 22, 37, 55, 63, 71–3, 103, 121, 273, 275, 279, 288, 383, 405, 450, 457, 474, 486, 497, 506
Torre Revello, José 402, 407, 506
Torrente Ballester, Gonzalo 420–1, 444
Torró, Jaume, see Turró i Torrent
Torroella, Guillem de, *La Faula* 26, 32, 174–9, 181, 448–9, 453, 477–8, 486, 498, 506–7
Toury, Marie-Noëlle 125, 506
Traba, Counts of 68, 118–20, 189, 494
Trachsler, Richard 137, 453, 506
Tractatus de Purgatorio Sancti Patricii 202
Tratado dos descobrimentos, see Galvão, António
'Tres hijuelos había el rey' 20, 229–32
Trésors de l'Amadis 378
Tressan, Comte de 378
Tristán, Códice de 309–11, 313, 316–7, 322–5, 328–40, 343–4, 348–50, 357, 448, 484, 506
Tristán de Leonís, Cuento de 19, 41, 55, 219, 222, 269, 296, 309–10, 316, 322, 324, 328–36, 338, 346, 358, 453, 463, 471, 493, 500

Tristán de Leonís 19–21, 27, 35, 40–3, 55–6, 105, 107, 116, 194, 215, 219, 222, 255, 269–70, 296–8, 301, 308–11, 313, 317, 321–4, 327–45, 347–4, 356–8, 448, 453–4, 456, 462–6, 470–1, 475, 484, 486–7, 493, 495, 500, 504, 506, 508
Tristán de Leonís el joven 20, 43, 215, 310–11, 316–17, 322–3, 330, 341, 353–8, 360, 362, 456, 465–6, 474, 504
Tristan en prose 13, 19–21, 23, 25, 28, 30–1, 40, 48, 62, 69–71, 86, 88–9, 98–101, 113, 116, 127, 137–9, 144–8, 155–8, 160, 165–6, 168, 171–2, 181, 185, 233, 271–4, 296, 304, 306, 315–25, 327, 330, 335, 339, 349–50, 375–6, 450, 453, 464, 466, 479, 488–9, 499, 504
Tristano Panciatichiano 322–3, 325, 349, 363, 447
Tristano Riccardiano 319, 321, 325, 336, 363, 447, 478
Tristano Veneto 317, 322, 324, 349, 363, 469
Tristany 13, 30, 35, 47–9, 54, 56, 222, 314, 325, 328–9, 448, 470, 501, 504
Triste deleytaçión 221, 506
Troyes, Chrétien de 12, 14–15, 28, 34, 60, 63, 85, 131–5, 140, 159–60, 165, 167, 174, 189, 203, 231, 308, 417–18, 423, 425–6, 430–2, 434, 437, 478, 489, 496, 499, 500, 503, 506
Trujillo, José Ramón 39, 62, 63, 90, 107, 116, 506
Truijllo, José Ramón, *Grial* 427, 444
Trullol i Plana, Sebastià 415, 434, 444
Turmeda, Anselm, *Cobles de la divisió del regne de Mallorques* 179
Turró i Torrent, Jaume 179, 181, 184, 294, 449, 506
Twain, Mark 423
Tyler, Richard W. 267, 491

Ubieto Arteta, Antonio 234, 506
Ulrich, Jacob 17, 271, 278, 495
Urbina, Eduardo 352, 506
Uría Varela, Jesús 141, 150, 506
Urraca, q. of León/Castile 118–9
Urriés, Hugo de 226
Usero González, Rafael 197, 506

Valcárcel, Pedro de 225
Valdés, Alfonso de 371
Valdés, Juan de 357
Valero Moreno, Juan Miguel 287, 380, 507
Vallés, Pedro, *Libro de refranes* 257
Vallvé, Manuel 430, 444
Van Beysterveldt, Anthony 375, 380, 507
Van Coolput-Storms, Colette-Anne 93, 507
Van der Horst, Cornelis Henricus Maria 174, 507
Vaquero, Mercedes 254, 507
Vargas, Bernardo de 460, 507

Vargas Díaz-Toledo, Aurelio 65, 107–8, 110–12, 507
Vargas Llosa, Mario 433, 444
Varnhagen, Francisco Adolfo 73–4, 87, 507
Várvaro, Alberto 180, 471, 507
Vasconcelos, Jorge Ferreira de, *Memorial das proezas da Segunda Távola Redonda* 109–10, 492, 495, 505
Vázquez, Francisco, *Primaleón* 215, 218, 497
Vázquez Alonso, Mariano José 424, 444
Vázquez Montalbán, Manuel 425–6, 444
Vega, Isabel 363, 451
Veiga, Augusto Botelho da Costa 116, 507
Velázquez de Castillo, Gabriel, *Clarián de Landanís, I* 215, 265, 346, 460, 507
Velloso, José Miguel 430, 444
Vélez de Guevara, Luis, *El diablo cojuelo* 41
Vengeance Nostre Seigneur 2, 240
Ventadorn, Bernart de 125–6
Ventura, Leontina 119, 507
Ventura Castro, Jovita 407, 507
Vergara, Pau 427
Vicent Santamaria, Sara 175–8, 185, 507
Vicente, Maria Graça 106, 508
Vich, Roser 179, 448
Vida de Berlan e del infante Josafa (MS BUSalamanca 1877) 47
Vida de Sant Macario e de Sergio e Alchino (MS BUSalamanca 1877) 47
Vidal, César 426, 444
Vidal Alcover, Jaume 174, 178, 454, 508
Vidas de los sanctos padres (MS BUSalamanca 1877) 47
Vieira, Afonso Lopes 422, 444
Vieira, Elsa Mónica 508
Vieira, Yara Frateschi 508
Vilariño Martínez, Agustín 508
Vilela, Fernando 404, 508
Viladamor, Antoni, *Història general de Catalunya* 186, 490
Villacorta, Consuelo 46, 240, 474, 508
Villaespesa, Francisco 422, 444
Villar Janeiro, Helena 431, 444
Villena, Enrique de, *Doze trabajos de Ercules* 347
Vinaver, Eugène v, 202, 315, 485, 508
Víñez Sánchez Antonia, 123, 136, 139, 508
Visión de Filiberto 250
Vita di Santa Margherita (BUSalamanca MS 1877), 36
Vita, miracoli e morte di S. Bernardo (BUSalamanca MS 1877) 36
Viura, Xavier 414, 444
Vivas, Joam (Juan Bivas) 22, 23, 60, 65, 74, 113, 121, 236, 276, 279, 285, 288, 508
Vives, Amadeu 415, 434, 444

Votos del pavón, Los 252
Vulgate Cycle 12, 16–17, 19, 22, 25, 28, 34–5, 52–3, 62–3, 69, 70, 75, 80, 82, 85–6, 88–9, 91–3, 99, 104, 113, 120–1, 129, 131, 133, 135, 140–2, 144–5, 149, 155, 157–8, 165–6, 169, 171–2, 181–2, 185, 202, 205, 209, 214, 240, 255–6, 260, 271–3, 278, 283, 285, 289–90, 302, 304, 306, 315, 349, 423, 431, 434, 452–3, 480, 504

Wace, Robert, *Roman de Brut* 15–16, 24, 31, 46, 69, 104, 108, 129–31, 153–4, 159, 202, 235–6, 238, 241–2, 275, 426, 430, 448
Wagner, Charles Philip 205, 207, 215, 482, 508
Wagner, Richard 409–10, 413–17, 423, 429–30, 433, 435, 437–8, 441, 444–5, 454, 508
Wales 203, 244, 320, 421, 431
Waley, Pamela 27, 185, 220, 344, 346, 508
Wechssler, Eduard 70, 73, 88, 508
Weddige, Hilkert 378, 508
West, George D. 135, 508
White, T. H. 424
Whitney, James Lyman 407, 508
Wild, Gerhard 508
William of Tyre, *Historia rerum in partibus transmarinis gestarum* 256, 258
Williams, Andrea M.L. 480
Williams, Grace S. 32, 380, 508
Williams, Mary 143, 508
Winchester 5, 372
Wolf, Ferdinand J. 87, 508–9
Wolfzettel, Friedrich 26, 509
Wright, Neil 108, 509
Wroth, Lady Mary 378

Xabregas, tournament at (1522) 109

Yáñez, Agustín 432, 444
Yáñez, Rodrigo 244, 246, 249, 252, 268, 509
Yllera, Alicia 233, 509

Zanné, Jeroni 413–15, 444–5
Zaragoza 167, 172, 189, 207–8, 231–2, 258, 269, 297, 368
Zarandona, Juan Miguel 3, 7–9, 404, 407, 408–45, 509
zarzuela 415
Zibaldone da Canal 321, 363
Zierer, Adriana Maria de Souza 92, 509
Zorrilla, José 408–10, 445, 509
Zumthor, Paul 128, 149, 509
Zúñiga, Ángel 416, 441
Zurara, Gomes Eanes de 366, 382, 405, 455, 509
Zurita, Jerónimo de 50